Motorcycles

Fundamentals, Service, and Repair

by

Bruce A. Johns
David D. Edmundson
Robert Scharff

Publisher
THE GOODHEART-WILLCOX COMPANY, INC.
Tinley Park, Illinois

Library of Congress Catalog Card Number 98-23297
International Standard Book Number 1-56637-479-0

1 2 3 4 5 6 7 8 9 10 99 02 01 00 99 98

Important Safety Notice

Proper service and repair is important to the safe, reliable operation of motorcycles, ATVs, and scooters. Procedures recommended and described in this book are effective methods of performing service operations. Some require the use of tools specially designed for this purpose and should be used as recommended. Note that this book also contains various safety procedures and cautions, which should be carefully followed to minimize the risk of personal injury or the possibility that improper service methods may damage the engine or render the vehicle unsafe. It is also important to understand that these notices and cautions are not exhaustive. Those performing a given service procedure or using a particular tool must first satisfy themselves that neither their safety nor engine or vehicle safety will be jeopardized by the service method selected.

This book contains the most complete and accurate information that could be obtained from various authoritative sources at the time of publication. Goodheart-Willcox cannot assume any responsibility for any changes, errors, or omissions.

Library of Congress Cataloging in Publication Data

Johns, Bruce A.
Motorcycles: fundamentals, service, and repair by
Bruce A. Johns, David D. Edmunson, Robert Scharff.
p. cm.
Includes index.

ISBN 1-56637-4-479-0
1. Motorcycles--Maintenance and repair. I. Edmunson, David D.
II. Scharff, Robert. III. Title.
TL444.J63 1999
629.28'775—dc21 98-23297
CIP

Introduction

The third edition of **Motorcycles Fundamentals, Service, and Repair,** like the first two editions, is designed to help prepare you to work on motorcycles. Because of the similarity of their engineering, this edition also covers the service of all terrain vehicles (ATVs) and scooters. It is written in general terms that apply to all motorcycle, ATV, and scooter makes and models. The text and illustrations summarize the most important aspects relating to the operation, construction, design, testing, maintenance, and repair of these vehicle systems and components.

Motorcycles have changed greatly in recent years. Today's motorcycles use electronic ignition systems, power drives, fuel injection, and many other innovations. **Motorcycles** covers anti-lock brake systems (ABS), emission control systems, cruise controls, and conventional design features as well as the latest engineering advances. All technical terms are defined as soon as they are mentioned. A glossary is also provided at the end of the text. This assures that you can easily understand the many terms essential to motorcycle technicians. Each chapter opens with several objectives that tell you what will be learned. Each chapter also prepares you for the chapters that follow. Knowledge builds systematically as you progress through the text.

Motorcycles' easy to understand language and large number of illustrations make the content easy to comprehend and remember. Illustrations are generously used to supplement the text. Since many service and repair operations can be dangerous, all safety rules are denoted by icons. **Motorcycles** can be used by the novice technician to learn the basics or by the experienced technician as a reference.

A Workbook for **Motorcycles** is also available. It acts as a convenient study guide and directly correlates to this text.

Bruce A. Johns
David D. Edmundson
Robert Scharff

Table of Contents

CHAPTER 3

TOOLS, MEASURING INSTRUMENTS, AND SHOP EQUIPMENT 49

CHAPTER 4

FASTENERS, GASKETS, AND DIAGNOSTIC PROCEDURES 77

CHAPTER 5

BASIC ELECTRICAL AND ELECTRONIC THEORY 101

CHAPTER 6

ENGINES 121

CHAPTER 7

CHAPTER 8

CHAPTER 9

CHAPTER 10

CHAPTER 11

COOLING SYSTEMS 245

CHAPTER 12

EXHAUST SYSTEMS AND EMISSIONS CONTROL 257

CHAPTER 13

POWER TRANSMISSION SYSTEMS 273

CHAPTER 14

WHEELS AND TIRES 305

CHAPTER 15

BRAKES 327

CHAPTER 16

CHAPTER 17

CHAPTER 18

CHAPTER 19

TWO-STROKE ENGINE OVERHAUL 409

CHAPTER 20

FOUR-STROKE ENGINE OVERHAUL 431

CHAPTER 21

POWER TRANSMISSION OVERHAUL . . . 463

CHAPTER 22

TUNE-UP AND GENERAL SERVICE 485

CHAPTER 23

Introduction to Motorcycles, ATVs, and Scooters

After studying this chapter, you will be able to:

- Understand the role of the professional technician in servicing motorcycles.
- Describe the basic functions of ATVs.
- Name the eight styles or types of motorcycles.
- Explain the various motorcycle systems.
- Identify the important parts of a motorcycle.
- List common motorcycle design differences.

The growing interest in motorcycles, ATVs, and powered scooters has created a growing need for technicians who can service these vehicles. This chapter will introduce, illustrate, and explain the parts of motorcycle, ATV, and scooter systems. As a result, you will be better prepared for the other chapters in this textbook. The major emphasis of each chapter in the text will be on motorcycles, however, the other two vehicles will be covered where needed.

The Role of Qualified Service Technicians

In the past, almost every motorcycle owner was his/her own technician. But now, there are very few riders who can fix their own bikes. The vast majority of these owners have their vehicles serviced by dealers or independent technicians who specialize in motorcycle, ATV, and scooter repair. In addition, today's bikes are more sophisticated, requiring well-trained and qualified technicians to service them properly. As the motorcycle industry continues to grow, the demand for trained people will increase.

There are thousands of on- and off-road bikes, **Figure 1-1A,** in use. All-terrain vehicles (ATVs) are fast becoming the workhorses for outdoor sports, agriculture, and home maintenance, **Figure 1-1B,** while scooters are the backbone of the quick delivery businesses in cities.

What is the role of the service technician in the motorcycle industry? The basic goals and qualifications of professional service technicians are:

- The service technician performs adjustments and repairs on customers' vehicles. He or she must have excellent mechanical skills and a thorough working knowledge of all product systems. This knowledge includes theories of operation, the interrelationships of systems, and diagnostic skills to quickly identify and locate a problem. Qualified technicians constantly update their knowledge by studying technical bulletins, manuals, and by attending seminars and training courses given by the manufacturers.
- A professional service technician is well-organized and thorough. This technician does not lose time because tools are lost, broken, disorganized, or misplaced. Work is done with care and service manuals are referenced frequently.
- The professional technician relies on reason, research, and experience to diagnose and troubleshoot problems. Time is not wasted on random attempts to

A

B

Figure 1-1. A—Typical off-road motorcycle. B—All-terrain vehicle (ATV).

solve problems. A qualified technician thinks a problem through, then uses logical troubleshooting procedures.

- The technician looks and acts like a professional and does nothing to discredit the industry. He or she wears a service uniform and is clean and neat. Above all, the professional technician strives to maintain high work and ethical standards in order to ensure customers are receiving professional service. The technician understands the importance of each job and keeps the customer's safety, as well as the shop's reputation and profitability a primary goal at all times.

A professional attitude wins customer confidence and trust. Today's service technician must perform service work required on a customer's vehicle in a professional manner with these duties in mind:

- Service each customer's bike according to repair order instructions.
- Perform all service and adjustments in accordance with service manual procedures.
- Advise the service manager or customer of additional work that is required or recommended.
- Attend training courses and seminars regularly.
- Maintain a neat and orderly appearance and work area.
- Maintain awareness of the latest technical bulletins and service procedures.

Complete information on shop operations, opportunities for advancement, and personnel and duties involved are in **Chapter 23.**

Styles and Designs of Motorcycles, ATVs, and Scooters

Before an overview of the systems that make these vehicles run, you will first study basic styles and designs of motorcycles, ATVs, and scooters. There are eight styles or types of motorcycles that may come into your shop for service or repair:

- **Cruiser.** The "classic" street motorcycle, these machines usually offer swept back handlebars, laid-back seating positions, and often a stepped seat for two people.
- **Touring.** These models are designed for long-range touring. Their standard features often include AM/FM cassette/CD stereo, CB and intercom systems, cruise control, and luggage compartments. Some touring bikes have enough power to pull a small camper or trailer.
- **Sport.** Has the looks of a closed track racing motorcycle. This motorcycle has power and handling characteristics similar to a racing bike. However, it does not have the comfort features of the touring bike. Sometimes referred to as a "superbike." Modified versions of these motorcycles are used in high-speed track racing.
- **Sport Touring.** Lighter and has greater performance than touring bikes. Sport touring motorcycles offer comforts such as good wind protection and luggage carrying capacity.
- **Standard.** A bike with clean, uncluttered design, and few, if any, special features. The design allows the owner to customize the bike to his or her tastes.
- **Dual-Purpose.** Designed for most types of terrain, these bikes combine street and off-road capabilities. Although equipped with strong frames, they are light and easy to handle.
- **Dirt-Off-Road.** Light, powerful and rugged, these bikes are capable of handling extremely rugged terrain. While they pass government standards for noise restrictions on public lands, they are not street legal and most states require the rider to possess a special off-road license.

- **Motocross/Enduro.** Similar to off-road motorcycles, but for closed-course use only. These are light, fast, motorcycles designed for the competitive sport of motocross. They are not legal for street or off-road use.

All motorcycles, no matter how modified, can be classified in one of these categories.

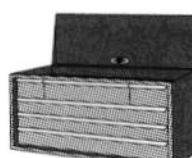

Note: In some places, this text will refer to all motorcycles, ATVs, and scooters, using the term "bike."

ATVs are available in various transmission speeds, engine types, and drives.

Scooters are available with two- and four-stroke engines, automatic transmissions, and can travel over 100 miles (160 km) on just 1 gallon (3.8 L) of gasoline, **Figure 1-2.** They are by far the most economical vehicles on the road.

Note: Recommend to your customers that all ATV riders, regardless of age, take an approved training course. Information on the availability of these courses can be obtained from the ATV Safety Institute, 2 Jenner St., Suite 150, Irvine, CA 92718.

While these vehicles look different, their operation is quite similar. These vehicles all have a number of systems (related group of parts or components) that work together to provide a safe, dependable means of transportation and/or sport. Each of these systems performs a particular function. For example, the brake system of all three

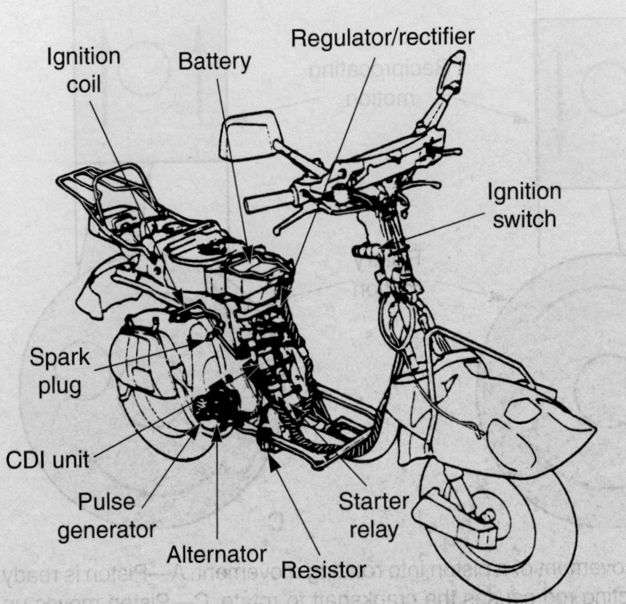

Figure 1-2. Typical scooters are available with two-stroke or four-stroke engines.

designs must stop the bike quickly, yet safely. The fuel system must supply the correct ratio of fuel to air for efficient engine operation. The ignition system must ignite the fuel mixture in the engine to start combustion and provide a source of energy for the vehicle.

Motorcycle, ATV, and scooter systems may be divided as follows:

- Engine.
- Fuel system.
- Charging system.
- Ignition system.
- Cooling system.
- Lubrication system.
- Exhaust system and emission control.
- Power transmission system.
- Wheels and tires.
- Brakes.
- Chassis.
- Accessory systems.

Engine

A motorcycle, ATV, or scooter engine is a group of assembled parts designed to change the heat energy of burning fuel into useful mechanical energy. The engine provides the power that turns the rear drive wheel(s). It indirectly generates the electricity needed for the lights, horn, and other devices.

Engine Parts

A ***simple engine*** is made up of a cylinder, piston, connecting rod, crankshaft, and crankcase. **Figure 1-3** illustrates these engine components. The piston reciprocates (slides up and down) in the cylinder. The connecting rod and crankshaft change this reciprocating movement into rotating movement. See **Figure 1-4.**

For the engine to operate, air, fuel, compression (pressure inside the engine), and combustion (burning air-fuel mixture) are needed. An engine must:

- Produce a vacuum which draws air and fuel into the cylinders.
- Compress the air-fuel mixture to produce efficient combustion.
- Ignite the air-fuel mixture under pressure.
- Use the resulting combustion pressure to do work.
- Remove the combustion waste products.

When these requirements are provided in proper proportions and sequence, the engine will run.

For an engine to form a vacuum and compress the mixture, the cylinder must be sealed. This is accomplished by the cylinder head, piston, and piston rings, **Figure 1-5.** They produce a relatively leakproof enclosure and form

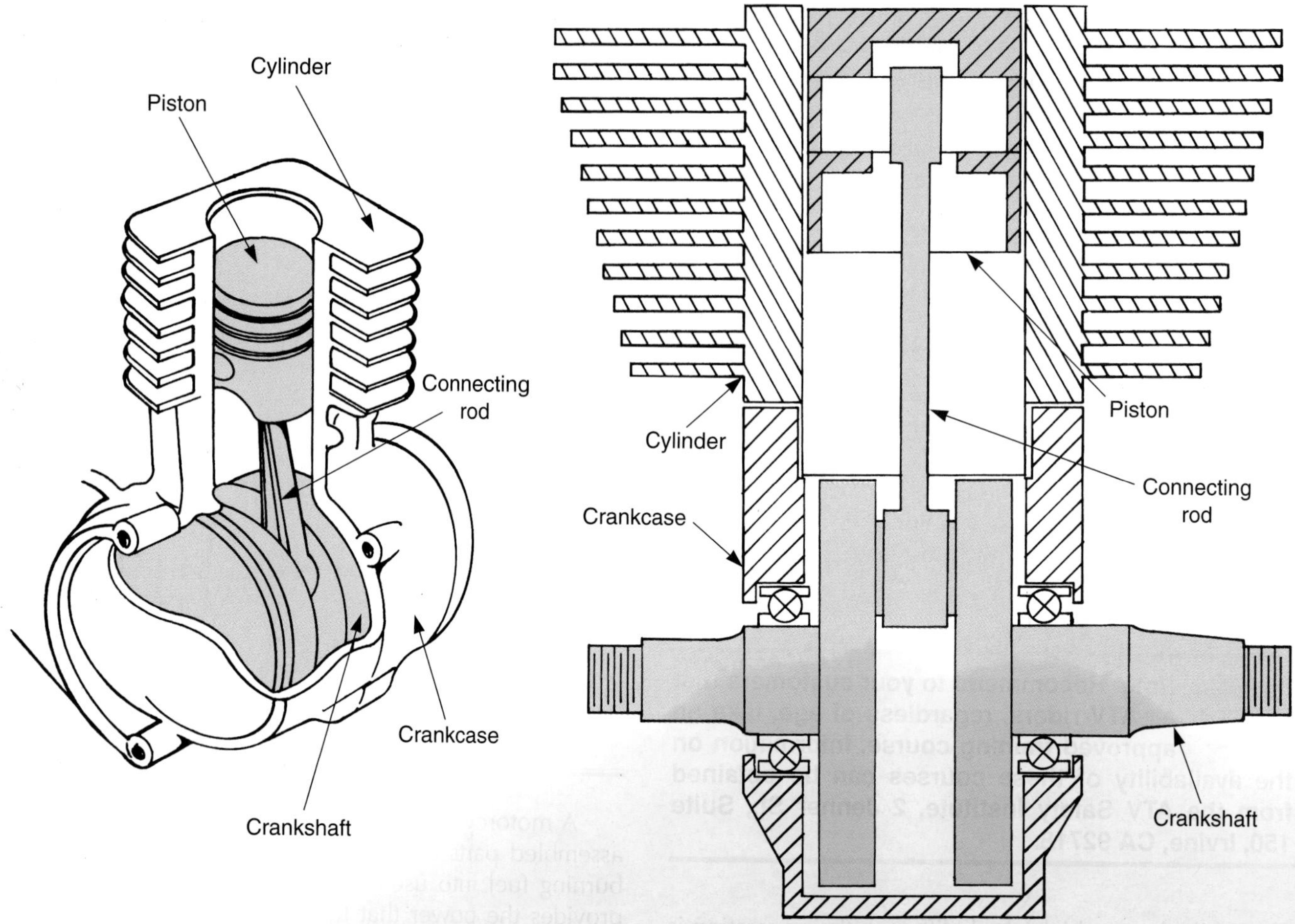

Figure 1-3. A piston, connecting rod, crankshaft, cylinder, and crankcase are some of the major components of a simple engine.

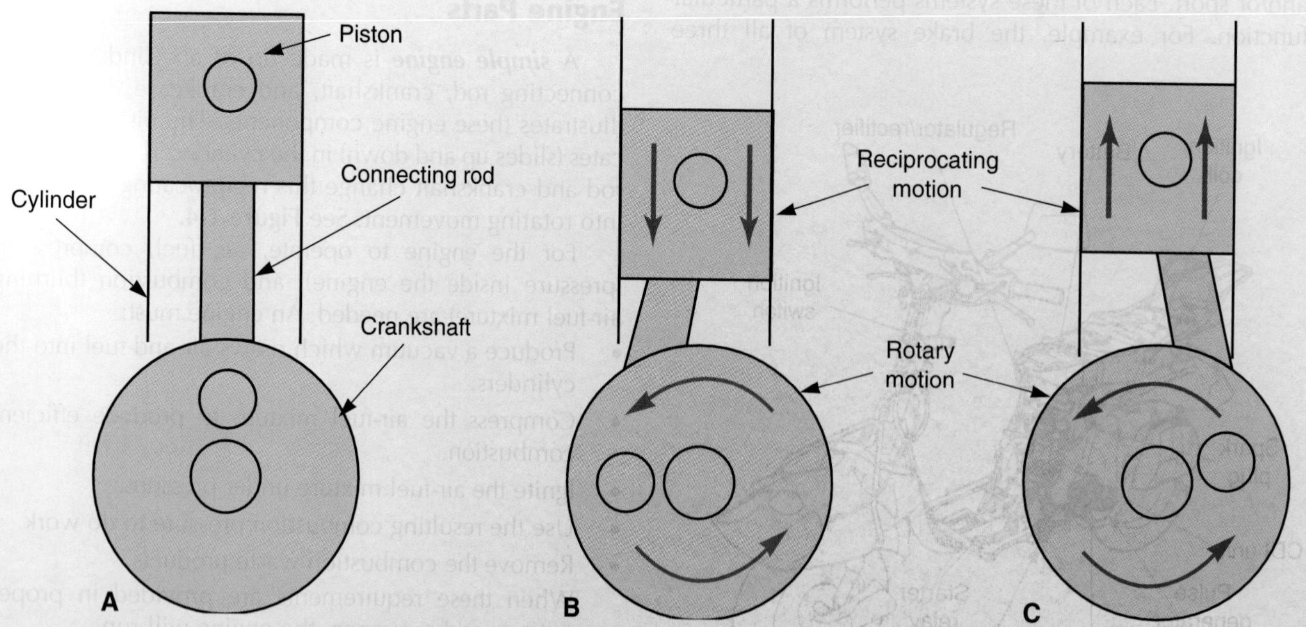

Figure 1-4. Connecting rod and crankshaft change the reciprocating movement of a piston into rotating movement. A—Piston is ready to move down the cylinder. B—As the piston moves down, the connecting rod causes the crankshaft to rotate. C—Piston moves up the cylinder as the crankshaft continues to rotate.

the combustion chamber (area in the engine where the air-fuel mixture is burned). Then, when the piston moves down, a vacuum or low pressure area is developed in the cylinder. When the piston moves up, the mixture is squeezed under pressure.

To allow the air-fuel mixture into the cylinder, an intake valve and port (passage) are required. A smaller exhaust valve and port allow the burned gases to exit the engine cylinder. Fundamental valve and port action is illustrated in **Figure 1-6.** This type of engine is termed a four-stroke cycle engine.

Four-Stroke Cycle Engine

A ***four-stroke cycle engine*** requires four up-and-down piston movements or strokes to complete one full cycle. Look at **Figure 1-7.** The sequence of events in a four-stroke cycle engine as follows:

- The first downward piston movement while the intake valve is open is the intake stroke. When this occurs, the air-fuel mixture is pulled into the cylinder.

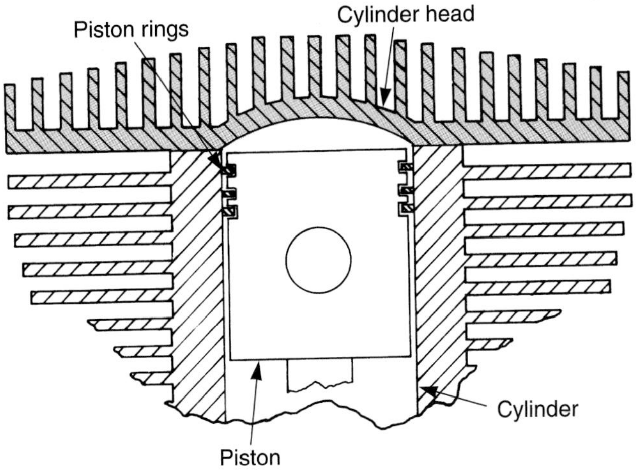

Figure 1-5. Each cylinder is sealed by a piston, piston rings, and cylinder head.

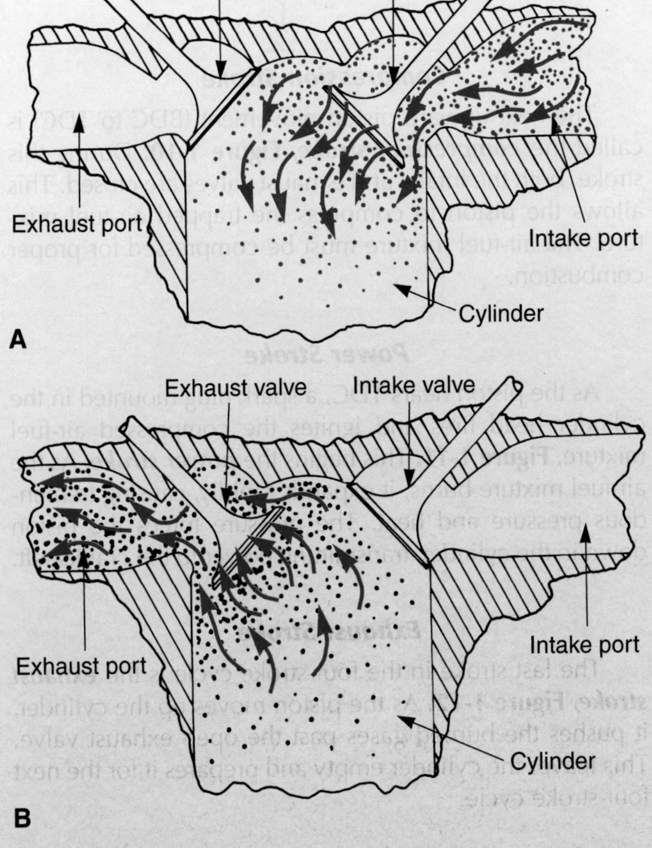

Figure 1-6. A—When the intake valve is open, air-fuel mixture can flow through the intake port into the cylinder. B—Burned gases leave the cylinder by flowing past the open exhaust valve into the exhaust port.

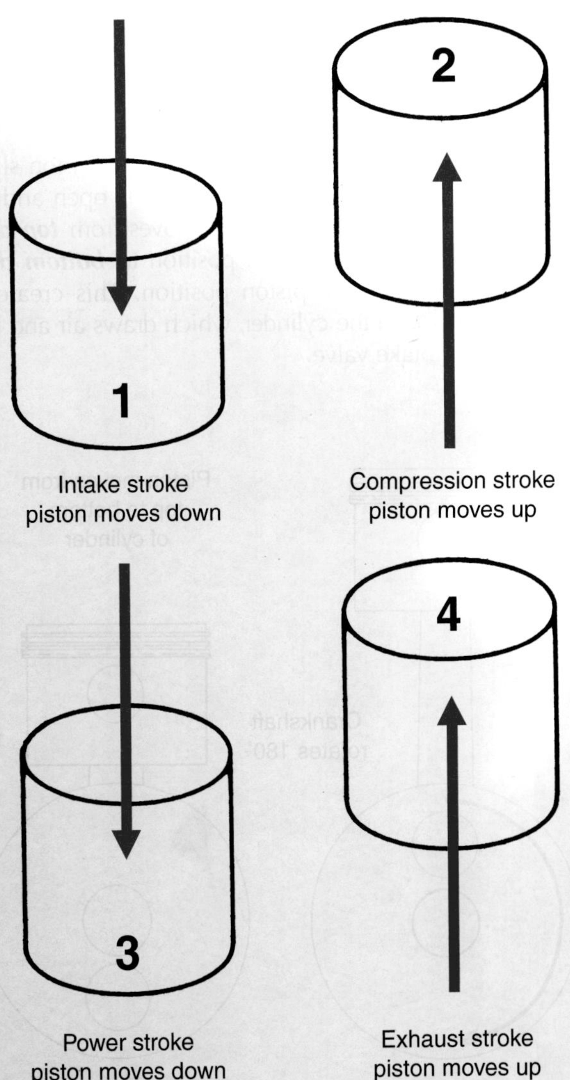

Figure 1-7. The sequence in a four-stroke engine is intake, compression, power, and exhaust.

- The compression stroke is the first upward piston movement, which pressurizes the air-fuel mixture.
- The second downward piston movement is the power stroke, caused by the heat, expansion, and pressure of combustion.
- The exhaust stroke is the second upward piston movement, which occurs while the exhaust valve is open. Burned gases are pushed from the engine.

Each stroke will rotate the crankshaft one-half revolution (180°). This is shown in **Figure 1-8.** To complete one full cycle, the crankshaft must make two complete revolutions (720°).

Four-Stroke Cycle Engine Operation

To fully understand the operation of a four-stroke cycle engine, you must be able to visualize valve operation in relation to piston movement. By studying what each engine part is doing during the four engine strokes, you will better understand engine operation.

Intake Stroke

During the ***intake stroke,*** **Figure 1-9,** the piston slides down the cylinder while the intake valve is open and the exhaust valve is closed. The piston moves from ***top dead center (TDC)*** or highest piston position to ***bottom dead center (BDC)*** or lowest piston position. This creates a vacuum (suction) in the cylinder, which draws air and fuel past the open intake valve.

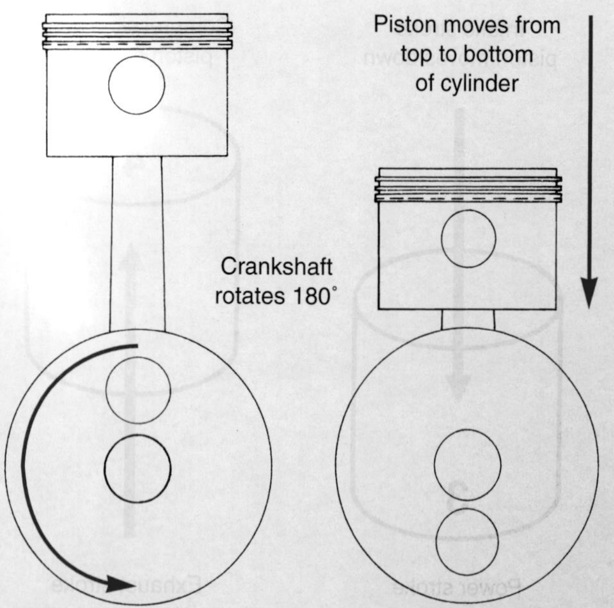

Figure 1-8. Each stroke moves the crankshaft one-half revolution.

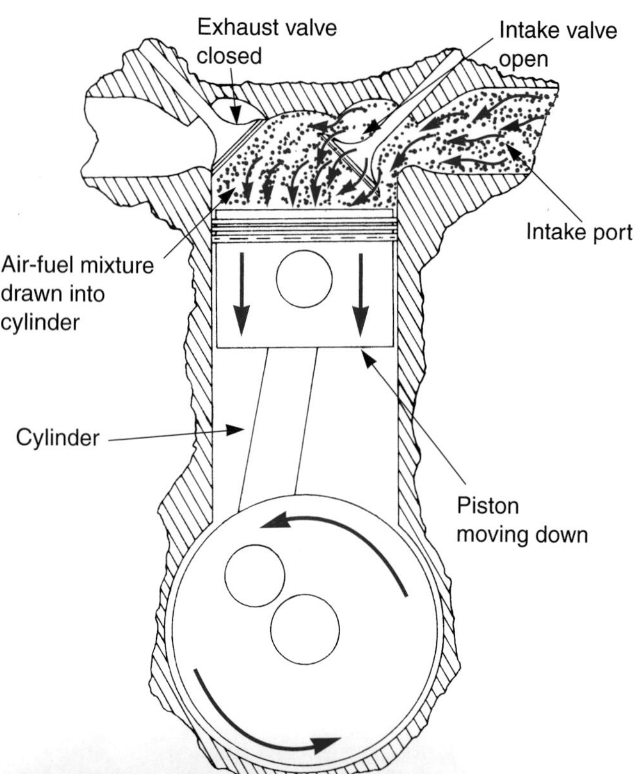

Figure 1-9. During the intake stroke, air and fuel are drawn into the cylinder through the intake port. Piston is moving down in the cylinder.

Compression Stroke

The next upward piston movement (BDC to TDC) is called the ***compression stroke,*** **Figure 1-10.** During this stroke, both the intake and exhaust valves are closed. This allows the piston to compress the trapped air-fuel mixture. The air-fuel mixture must be compressed for proper combustion.

Power Stroke

As the piston nears TDC, a spark plug mounted in the cylinder head fires and ignites the compressed air-fuel mixture, **Figure 1-11.** This begins the ***power stroke.*** As the air-fuel mixture burns, it expands rapidly, causing tremendous pressure and heat. The pressure forces the piston down in the cylinder, transmitting power to the crankshaft.

Exhaust Stroke

The last stroke in the four-stroke cycle is the ***exhaust stroke,*** **Figure 1-12.** As the piston moves up the cylinder, it pushes the burned gases past the open exhaust valve. This leaves the cylinder empty and prepares it for the next four-stroke cycle.

Valve Overlap

You learned earlier the intake valve is open while the piston moves down on the intake stroke. To better fill the

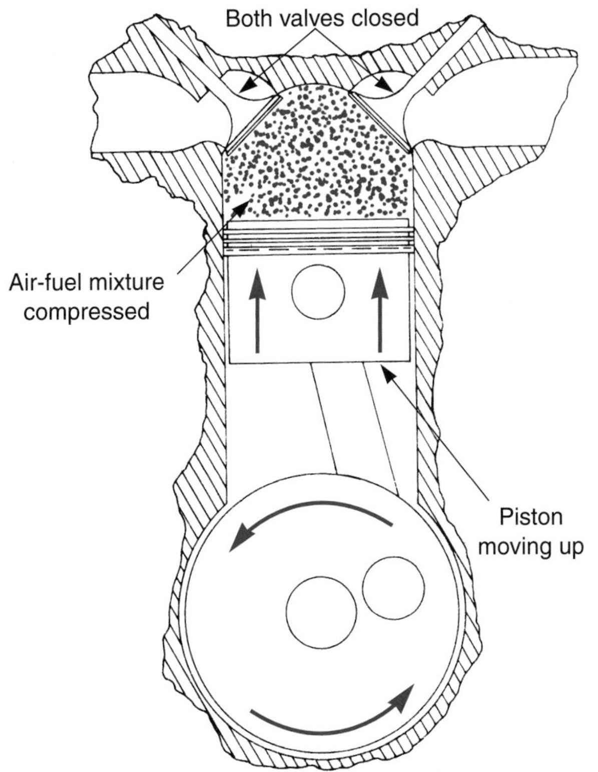

Figure 1-10. During the compression stroke, the air-fuel mixture is compressed as the piston moves up the cylinder.

cylinder, the intake valve actually opens before the piston begins its downward movement at the end of the exhaust stroke. Also, the exhaust valve remains partially open during the start of the intake stroke.

This period of time when both valves are open is called ***valve overlap.*** Valve overlap helps to draw fresh air and fuel into the cylinder, and aids in expelling the spent charge (burned gases). See **Figure 1-13.**

Intake Valve Closing

Once the intake charge is in the cylinder, it will continue to move. The fresh charge will flow until its inertia is overcome by pressure in the cylinder. This occurs after the piston starts to move up the cylinder on its compression stroke. For this reason, the intake valve remains open during the beginning of the compression stroke to allow the cylinder to completely fill.

Exhaust Valve Opening

At the end of the power stroke, cylinder pressure has decreased to the point that it is no longer useful for making power. By opening the exhaust valve at the end of the power stroke, the remaining pressure is used to start the movement of burnt gases out the exhaust port. This aids in clearing the cylinder. As the piston nears the end of the exhaust stroke, the point of valve overlap is again reached, **Figure 1-14.**

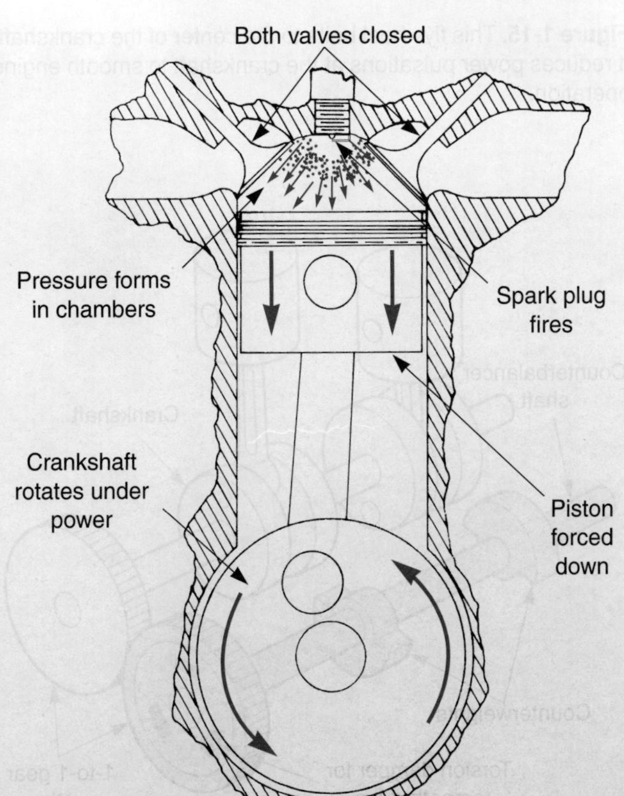

Figure 1-11. In the power stroke, the spark plug ignites the compressed air-fuel mixture. Combustion pressure and heat drives piston down in cylinder.

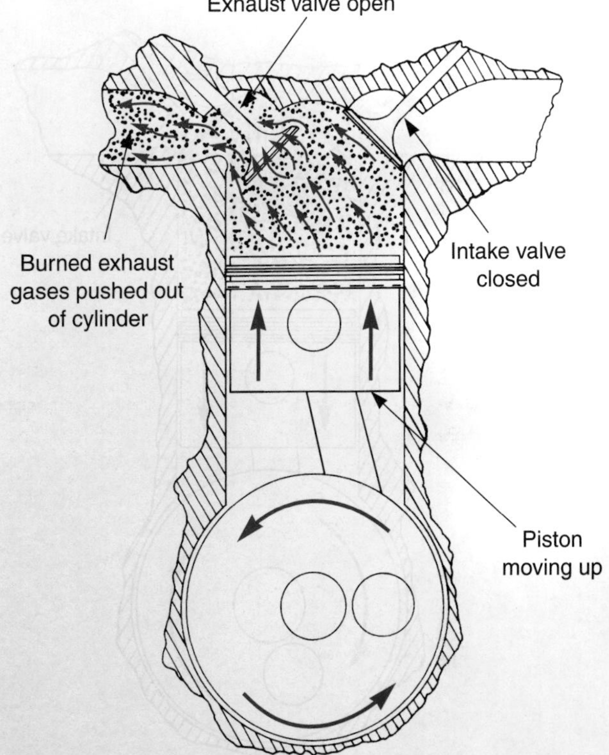

Figure 1-12. As the piston moves up during the exhaust stroke, it forces burned gases past the open exhaust valve and through the open port.

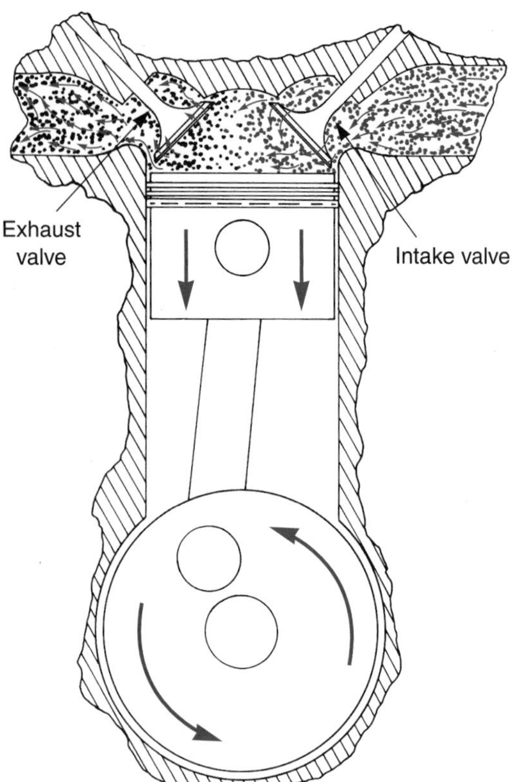

Figure 1-13. The exhaust valve closes after the intake stroke begins. As air-fuel mixture enters the cylinder, it helps push the last of the burned gases out the open port. Valve overlap is the time when both intake and exhaust valves are open.

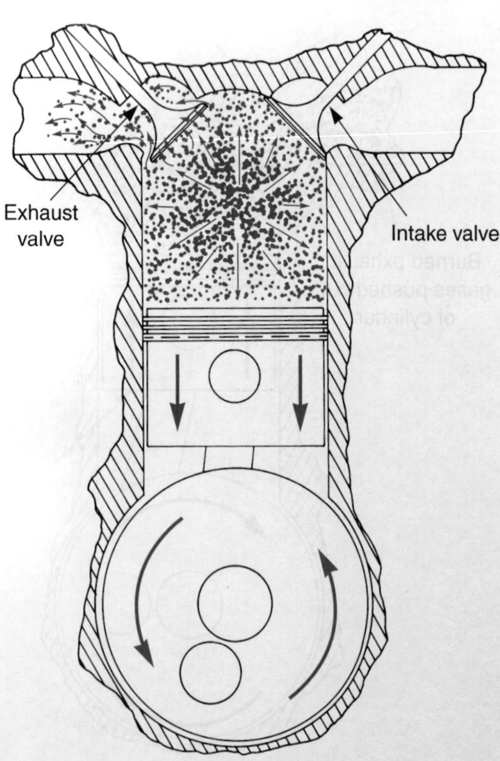

Figure 1-14. Exhaust valve opens before the end of the power stroke. This allows combustion pressure to start the movement of gases into the exhaust port before the exhaust stroke begins.

Flywheel

A ***flywheel*** is a large, round, disc-shaped weight attached to the crankshaft, **Figure 1-15.** It helps to keep the engine spinning during the non-power producing strokes. Since there is only one power stroke for every two crankshaft revolutions, the flywheel inertia will also aid in smoothing abrupt crankshaft movement during the power stroke. Some engines may also use a chain or gear-driven counterbalancer. It is designed to reduce vibration. See **Figure 1-16.**

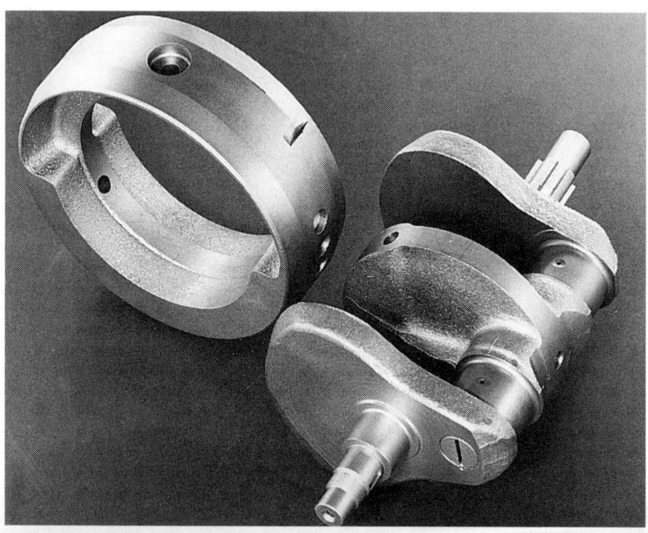

Figure 1-15. This flywheel bolts to the center of the crankshaft. It reduces power pulsations at the crankshaft to smooth engine operation.

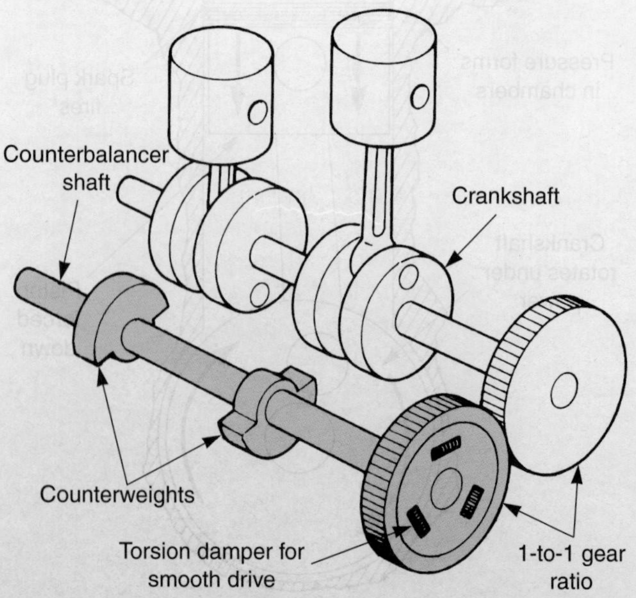

Figure 1-16. A crankshaft-driven counterbalancer helps reduce engine vibration. Sometimes, a chain drive may be used. (American Suzuki Motor Corporation)

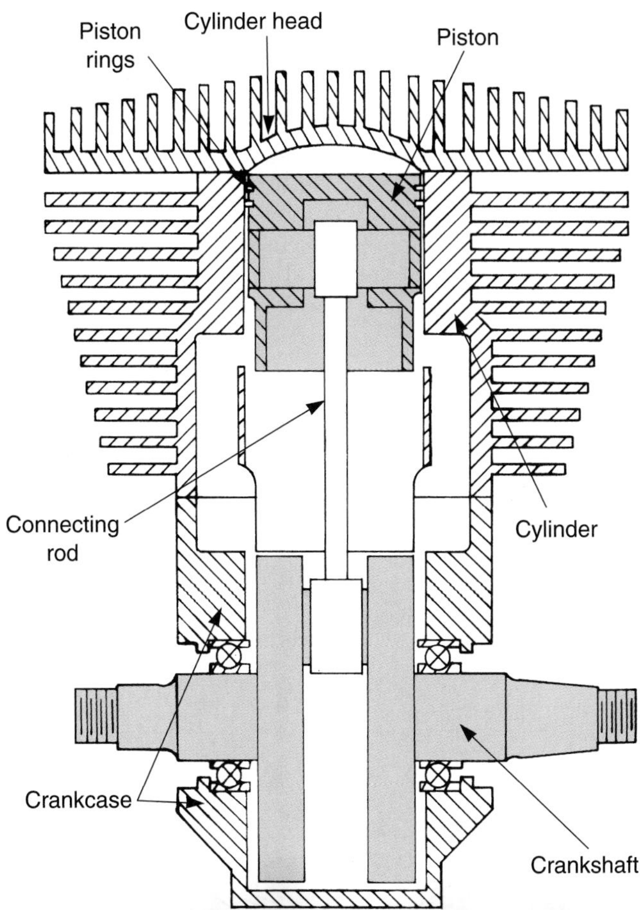

Figure 1-17. A two-stroke cycle engine has many of the same components used in a four-stroke cycle engine.

Two-Stroke Cycle Engine

A ***two-stroke cycle engine*** produces power once during each crankshaft revolution. It has a power stroke twice as often as a four-stroke cycle engine. Most of the fundamental parts are the same (crankcase, crankshaft, connecting rod, piston, rings, cylinder, and cylinder head). See **Figure 1-17.** The primary difference is in the method of controlling air-fuel mixture flow into and out of the engine.

In a two-stroke cycle engine, the same events take place as in a four-stroke cycle engine. However, the two-stroke cycle events are controlled and overlap differently. The differences between two- and four-stroke cycle engines are:

- Two-stroke cycle engines have a power stroke every crankshaft revolution.
- Two-stroke cycle engines do not use valves.
- Two-stroke cycle engines pass their air-fuel mixture into the crankcase before reaching the combustion chamber.
- Intake and exhaust timing is controlled by the piston, not by the valve mechanism.

Two-Stroke Cycle Engine Operation

Since two-stroke engines produce power once every revolution, several events must happen at the same time, **Figure 1-18.** A few two-stroke characteristics should be explained before two-stroke cycle operation can be fully understood:

- Flow through the engine is controlled by the piston covering and uncovering ports (openings) in the cylinder wall.
- Air-fuel mixture enters the crankcase below the piston and then is transferred from the crankcase to the area above the piston.
- Burned air-fuel mixture is exhausted during the power stroke.

Cylinder Ports

Three openings, **Figure 1-19,** are used in a two-stroke cycle engine cylinder:

- The intake port lets the air-fuel mixture flow into the crankcase.
- The transfer port connects the crankcase to the upper cylinder.
- The exhaust port allows burned gases to leave the engine cylinder.

Starting with the piston at TDC, the air-fuel mixture is compressed in the combustion chamber and ready for

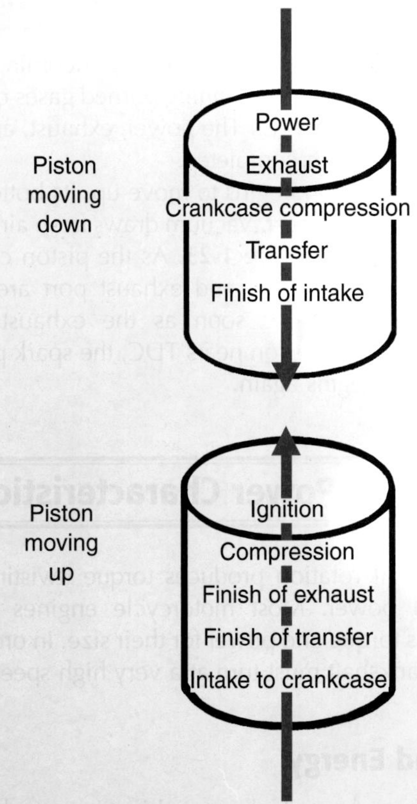

Figure 1-18. The series of events that take place during each up and down piston movement in a two-stroke engine.

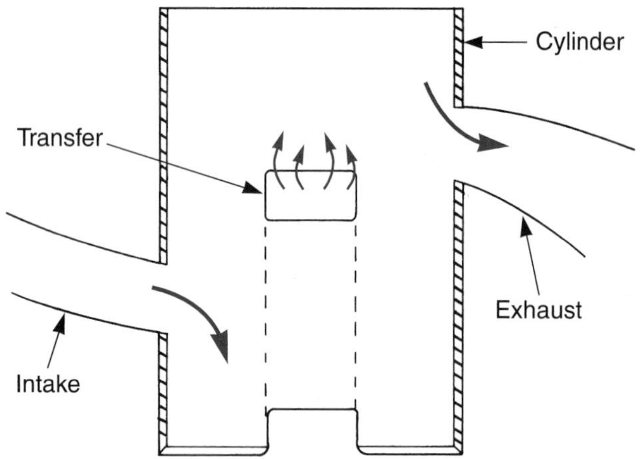

Figure 1-19. The intake and transfer ports direct air-fuel mixture through a two-stroke cycle engine. The exhaust port directs burned gases out the engine.

ignition. At the same time, the crankcase is filled with uncompressed air and fuel. When ignition occurs, the resulting combustion drives the piston downward to produce power, **Figure 1-20.**

Moving the Fuel Charge

As the piston moves down, it uncovers the ***exhaust port,*** allowing burned air-fuel mixture to leave the cylinder. At the same time, downward piston movement compresses the fresh air-fuel charge in the crankcase, **Figure 1-21.**

As the piston continues downward, the ***transfer port*** is uncovered. This allows air and fuel from the crankcase to pass upward into the cylinder. The incoming air-fuel mixture helps push any remaining burned gases out of the exhaust port, **Figure 1-22.** The power, exhaust, and transfer events have been completed.

When the piston begins to move up, its bottom edge uncovers the ***intake port.*** Vacuum draws fresh air and fuel into the crankcase, **Figure 1-23.** As the piston continues upward, the transfer port and exhaust port are closed. Compression begins as soon as the exhaust port is blocked. When the piston nears TDC, the spark plug fires and the cycle begins again.

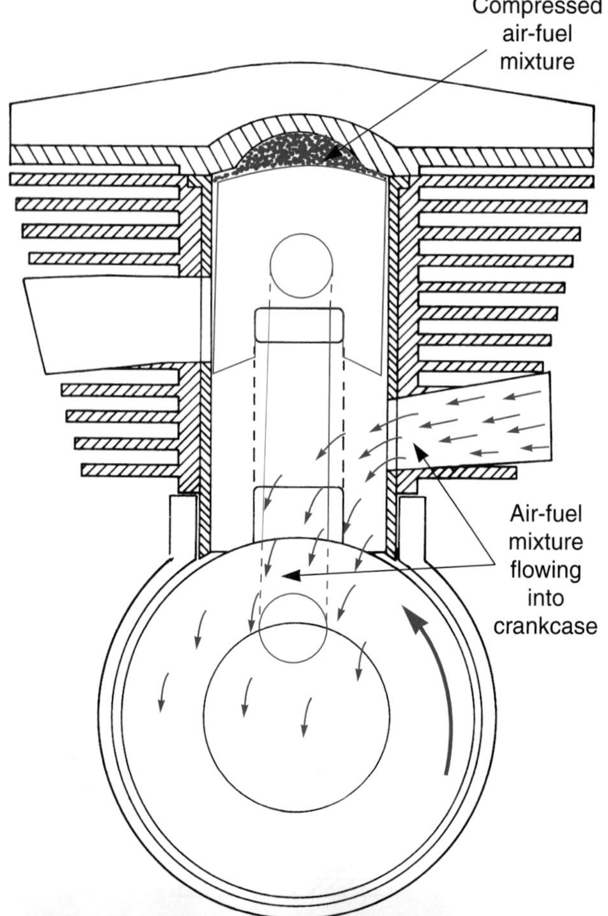

Figure 1-20. When the piston is at top dead center, the air-fuel mixture above the piston is compressed. Compression prepares the air-fuel mixture for ignition. During compression, a new air-fuel charge is entering the crankcase through the intake port.

Engine Power Characteristics

Crankshaft rotation produces torque (twisting force) and useful power. Most motorcycle engines produce tremendous torque and power for their size. In order to do this, the crankshaft must turn at a very high speed.

Work and Energy

Work is performed when an object is moved. Work is measured in foot-pounds (ft.-lbs.) or joules (J). Work is done when weights are lifted, springs compressed, or shafts are rotated. ***Energy*** is the ability to perform work. A gallon of gasoline, for example, has a specific amount of heat energy stored in it. When the gasoline is burned to release energy, work can be done.

Torque and Power

Torque is a turning or twisting motion, as when you pull on a wrench handle. Torque is measured in foot-pounds (ft.-lbs.) or Newton-meters (N•m). See **Figure 1-24.** Torque is different from work. Motion is not needed to produce torque, while work requires motion. ***Power*** is a measurement of the amount of work being completed. It is stated in horsepower (hp) or kilowatts (kw). The term power refers to rate instead of force.

Horsepower

Most engines are rated in the amount of horsepower they are capable of producing. One ***horsepower*** is the rating for the amount of work needed to lift 33,000 pounds (14 850 kg) a distance of one foot (.30 m) in one minute. Horsepower equals work divided by time.

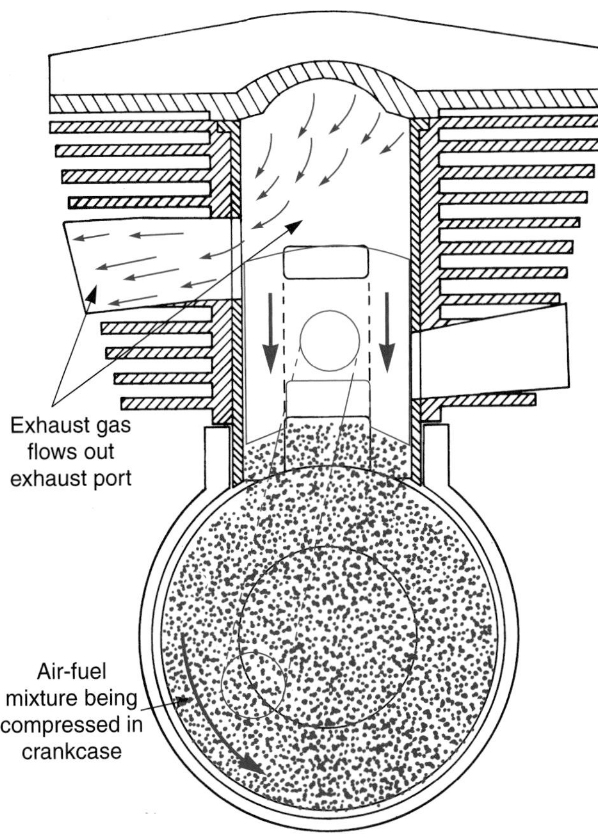

Figure 1-21. After combustion, the piston moves down, exposing the exhaust port. This allows exhaust gases to flow out the cylinder. The piston downward movement covers the intake port. Fresh air and fuel is compressed in crankcase.

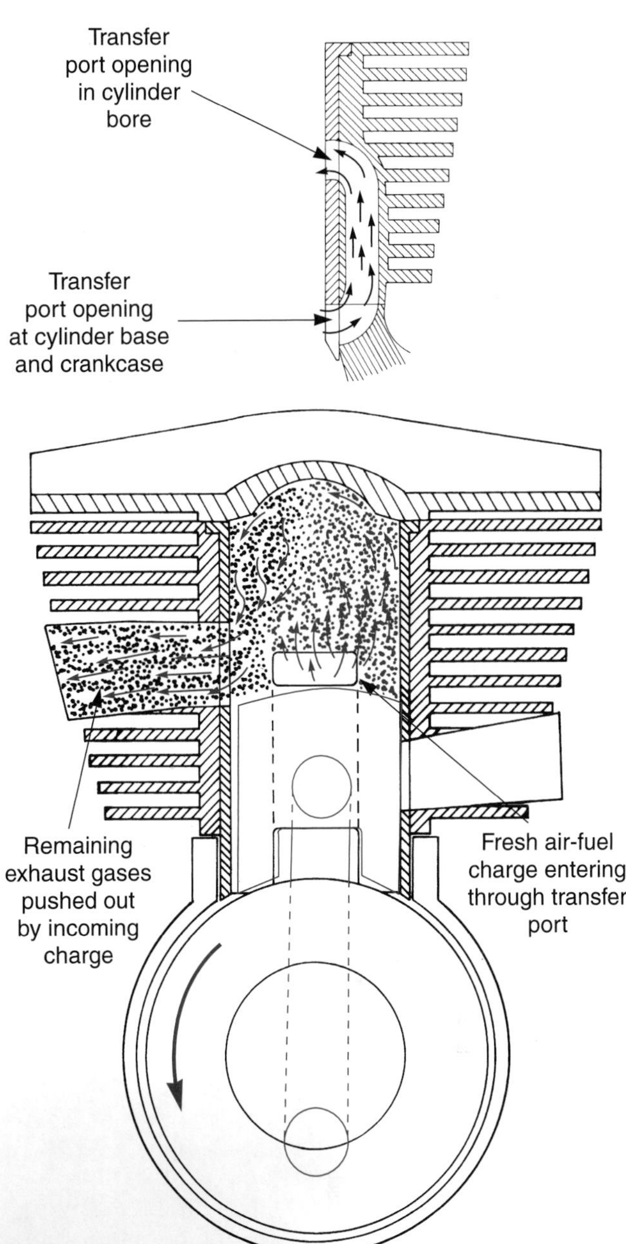

Figure 1-22. The transfer port is opened as the piston moves down. This allows air-fuel mixture to flow from the crankcase into the cylinder area above the piston. Since the exhaust port is open, the new charge helps to move the last part of the exhaust gases out the cylinder.

Fuel System

The ***fuel system*** must store fuel, mix the air and fuel together in the proper proportions for delivery, and supply this mixture to the engine. The fuel system on a motorcycle consists of the fuel tank, fuel shutoff valve, fuel filter, fuel lines, carburetor or injectors, and air cleaner. A typical carburetor fuel system is shown in **Figure 1-25.**

Carburetor

The ***carburetor,*** **Figure 1-26,** is the most complex part of the fuel system. It must supply the engine with an air-fuel mixture of about 15:1 (15 parts air to 1 part fuel by weight).

However, at certain throttle settings, the carburetor varies this ratio, **Figure 1-27.** Under starting conditions, for example, a rich (high fuel content) air-fuel mixture of 3:1 (3 parts air, 1 part fuel) is needed. While cruising, this ratio can be leaner (more air, less fuel) or around 16:1 (16 parts air, 1 part fuel).

Carburetor Operation

A carburetor relies on pressure differences for operation. It uses the venturi principle to draw fuel into the airstream, **Figure 1-28.** A ***venturi*** is a restriction formed in the carburetor throat. As air passes through the venturi, it causes an increase in air velocity (speed) and vacuum.

Figure 1-29 shows a simple carburetor that uses the venturi principle. Notice that outside atmospheric pressure is greater than venturi pressure, causing fuel to be drawn from the carburetor fuel reservoir into the airstream. The fuel is atomized (broken into small droplets) as it enters the airstream.

The ***throttle twist grip,*** connected to the carburetor butterfly or throttle slide, controls airflow through the carburetor throat, **Figure 1-30.** As the throttle is opened,

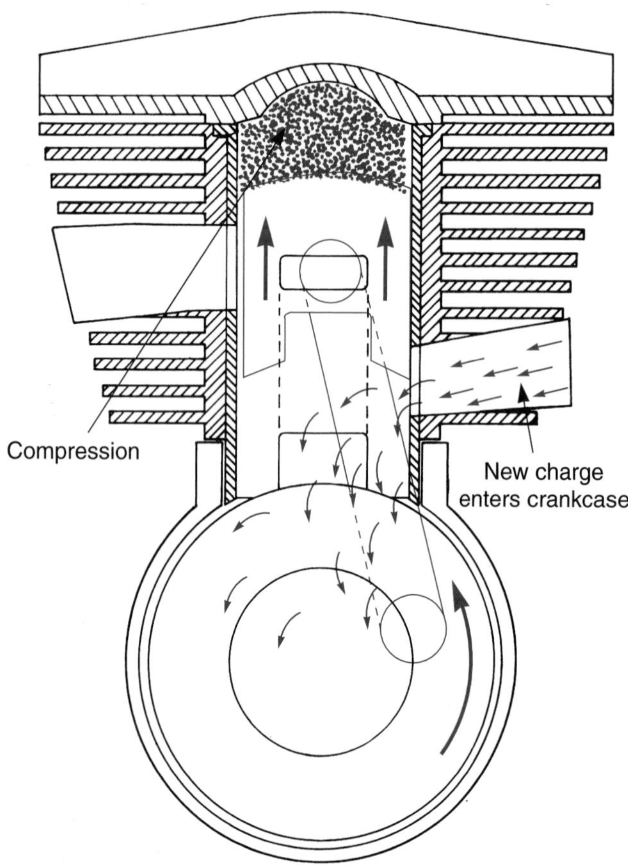

Figure 1-23. As the piston moves back up, the air-fuel charge that was just transferred is compressed. At the same time, the piston movement exposes the intake port, allowing a new charge of air and fuel to enter the crankcase.

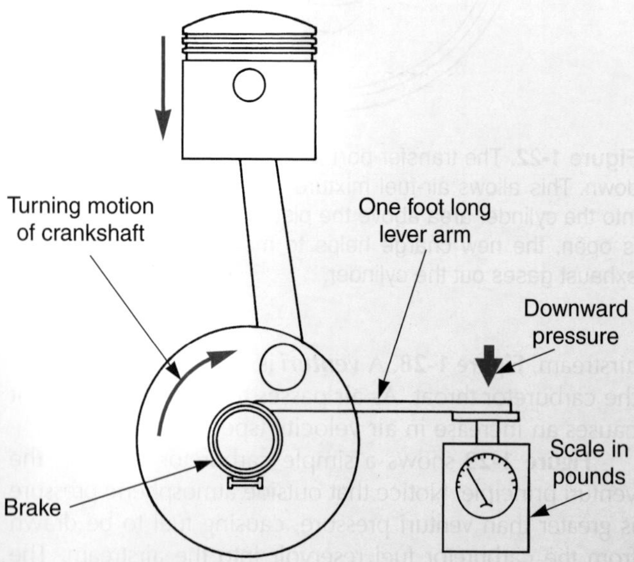

Figure 1-24. Torque can be measured by attaching a brake and a one-foot long lever arm to the crankshaft. As the brake is tightened, the lever pushes down on a scale. If the scale reads 50 pounds, 50 ft.-lbs. of torque is being produced.

more air passes through the carburetor, causing more fuel to be drawn into the airstream. This results in increased engine speed and power. An ***air cleaner*** is provided in the fuel system to keep airborne dirt from being carried into the carburetor and engine. The basic action of an air cleaner is shown in **Figure 1-31.**

Electronic Fuel Injection

Electronic fuel injection (EFI) is a fairly recent development in motorcycle fuel systems. Exhaust emissions regulations for motorcycles are not quite as stringent as those imposed on the automotive industry. However, many carbureted motorcycles suffer from the effects of lean air-fuel mixtures used to meet emission standards. Lean air-fuel mixtures burn cleaner than rich mixtures, however, they tend to reduce engine power and smoothness, and contribute to certain forms of exhaust emissions.

Electronic fuel injection eliminates the performance problems caused by lean carburetor settings by delivering a precise amount of fuel to each cylinder. Fuel injection is capable of more precisely controlling the amount of fuel entering each cylinder. It uses an electrically controlled fuel injector mounted in each intake port. See **Figure 1-32.** The brain for this system is the ***electronic control module (ECM),*** which decides how long to open the injectors based on information received from several monitoring devices.

The EFI fuel system is somewhat different from the fuel system in a carbureted engine, **Figure 1-33.** It uses an electric fuel pump, fuel filter, pressure regulator, high pressure fuel lines, electrically activated fuel injectors, and a fuel tank. The function of fuel injectors is to spray the proper amount of fuel into the intake port. The injector is a sealed unit which acts as an electrically controlled fuel valve. When a signal is received from the ECM, the injector opens, discharging fuel into the intake port. The air-fuel ratio is determined by the length of time the injector remains open, which is controlled by the ECM. The ECM keeps the air-fuel ratio as close to 14.7:1 as possible.

A typical EFI ***electronic fuel injection control system*** is made up of sensors, actuators, and related wiring that is tied to the ECM. The ECM is the actual metal box that houses the microprocessor and its related components.

All ***sensors*** perform the same basic function. They detect a mechanical condition (movement or position), chemical state, or temperature condition. Most sensors then modify a base voltage sent to them into an electrical signal that can be used by the computer to make decisions. Some sensors generate their own electrical signal. The ECM makes decisions based on information it receives from each sensor, **Figure 1-34.**

Each sensor used in a particular system has a specific job, for example, monitor throttle position, engine coolant temperature, intake manifold pressure, barometric pressure, etc. These sensors provide information to help the computer form a complete picture of vehicle operation.

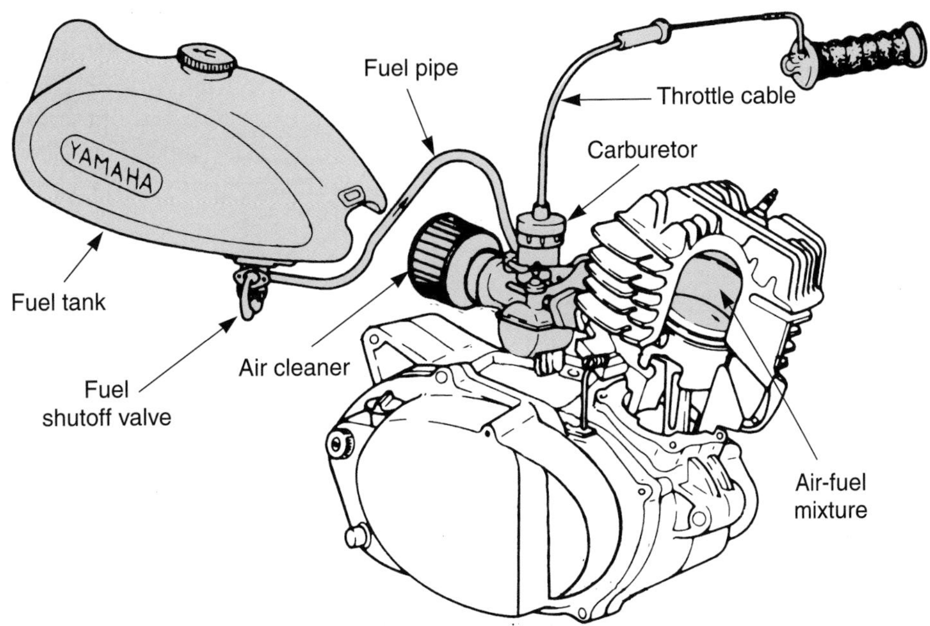

Figure 1-25. Parts of a typical motorcycle fuel system. These parts regulate the flow of air and fuel into the engine. (Yamaha Motor Corporation, U.S.A.)

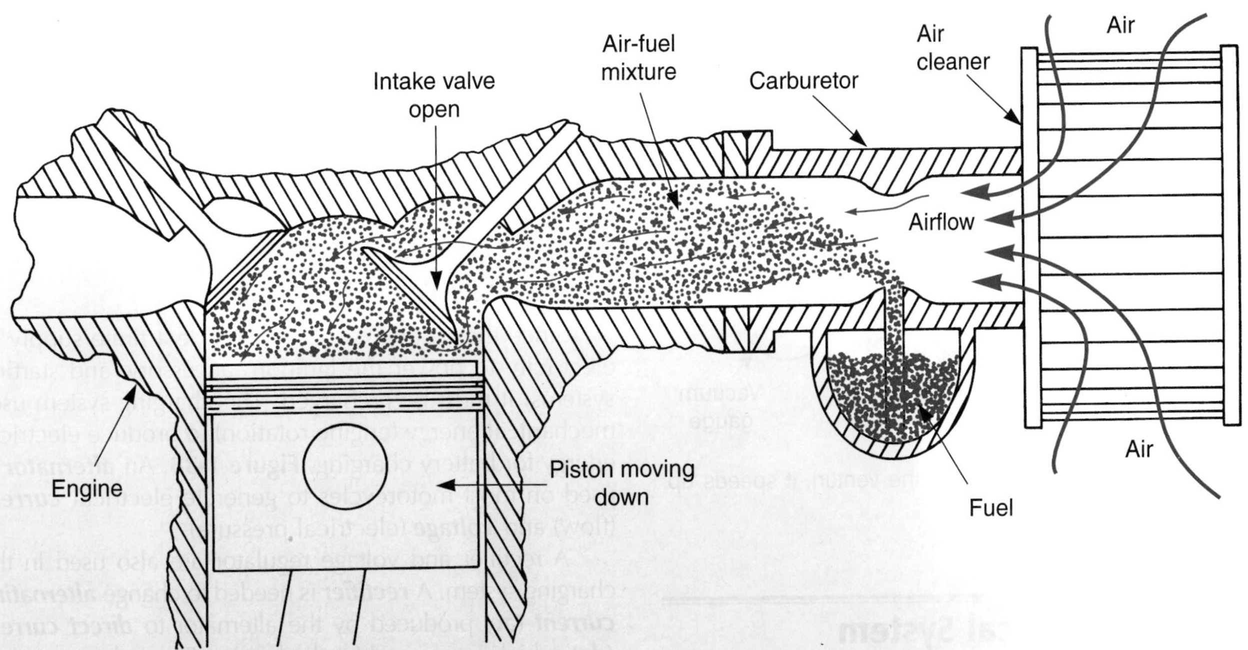

Figure 1-26. A carburetor is a device that mixes air and fuel together. The piston downward movement draws the air-fuel mixture into the cylinder.

The computer has complete control over fuel delivery to the engine.

Comparison of Carburetion and Fuel Injection

The carbureted fuel system mixes air and fuel using engine vacuum. It provides a predetermined air-fuel mixture to the engine. The EFI system monitors engine conditions and provides precise fuel delivery based on engine requirements.

As a result, an electronic fuel injection system has the advantage of being able to make precise adjustments in the amount of fuel delivered to the engine. An EFI system automatically compensates for varying conditions (altitude, humidity, worn parts, load, valve adjustment, etc.) that could affect the engine's performance.

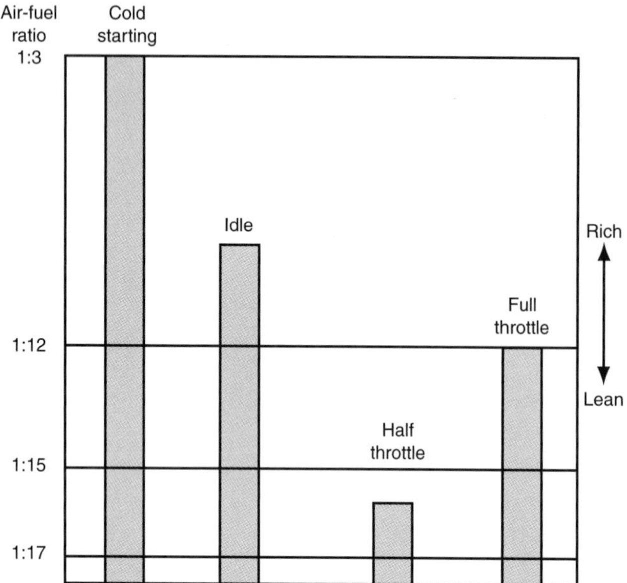

Figure 1-27. A carburetor must provide different air-fuel ratios, depending upon the throttle opening and engine load.

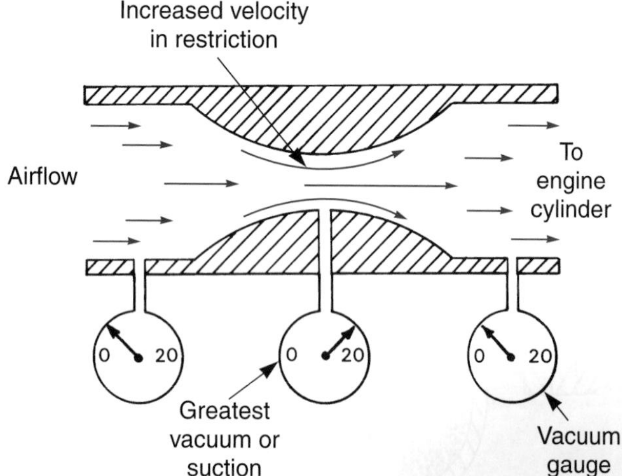

Figure 1-28. As air passes through the venturi, it speeds up, creating a vacuum.

Electrical System

The ***electrical system*** supplies electrical power to all the various components on the motorcycle. Electrical power is used to fire the spark plugs, turn the starting motor, and illuminate the lights. The electrical system is composed of three subsystems:

- Starting system.
- Charging system.
- Ignition system.

Many motorcycles use a ***battery*** to store and supply electricity for initial starting, ignition, and lighting. **Figure 1-35** shows the layout of a typical battery powered electrical system.

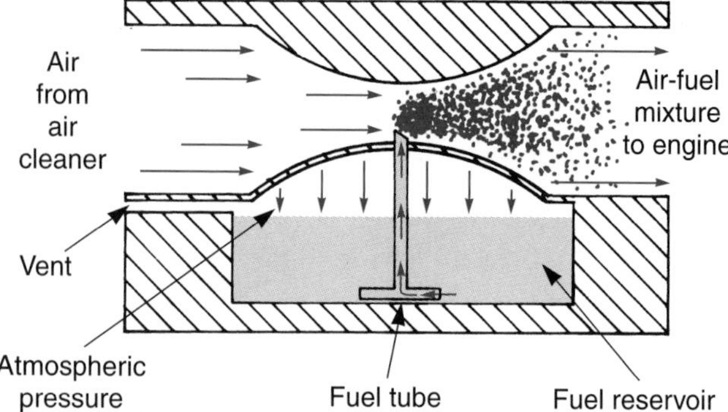

Figure 1-29. Atmospheric pressure pushes down on fuel in the carburetor reservoir. When vacuum is produced by airflow through the venturi, fuel is pushed through the fuel tube into the airstream.

Starting System

The ***starting system*** is used on many motorcycles to provide engine cranking and initial starting, **Figure 1-36.** It eliminates the need to kick start the engine using a foot pedal. The starting system consists of the battery, start switch, solenoid (relay), and starter motor, **Figure 1-37.**

When the start switch is pushed, a small amount of current flows to the relay. The current activates the relay, which causes contact points in the relay to close. The battery-to-starter circuit is completed and high current flows to the starter motor. As soon as the engine is running, the start switch is released to de-energize the starter.

Charging System

Since the battery can only provide a finite supply of electricity to power the ignition, accessory, and starting systems, it must be recharged. The charging system uses mechanical energy (engine rotation) to produce electrical energy for battery charging, **Figure 1-38.** An ***alternator*** is used on most motorcycles to generate electrical ***current*** (flow) and ***voltage*** (electrical pressure).

A rectifier and voltage regulator are also used in the charging system. A ***rectifier*** is needed to change ***alternating current (ac)*** produced by the alternator to ***direct current (dc),*** which is required for the battery. Since alternator output is directly related to engine speed, a ***voltage regulator*** is used to prevent battery overcharging. The regulator matches the charge rate to the needs of the battery and other electrical components.

Ignition System

The ***ignition system*** ignites the air-fuel mixture in the combustion chamber by means of an electrical arc at the spark plug.

Most motorcycle ignition systems are powered by the battery. The ignition system must step up (increase) battery voltage (about 12 volts) to as high as 45,000 volts. High

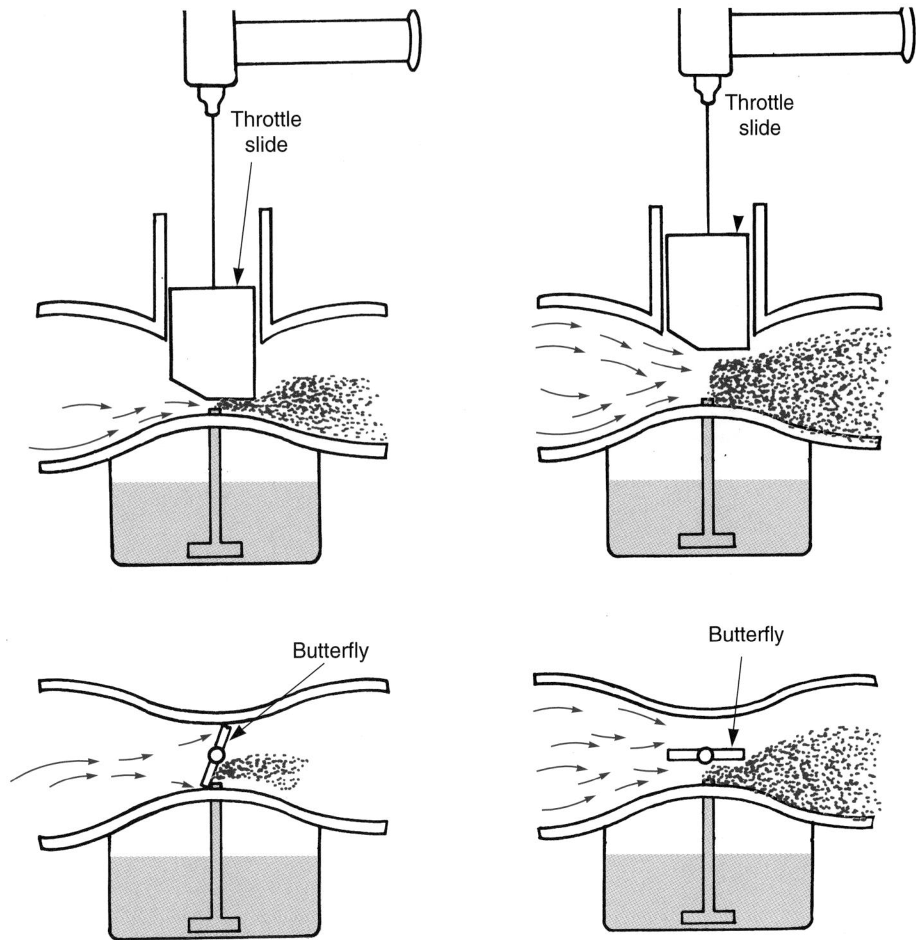

Figure 1-30. The throttle twist grip controls air and fuel flow through the carburetor by changing the slide or butterfly position.

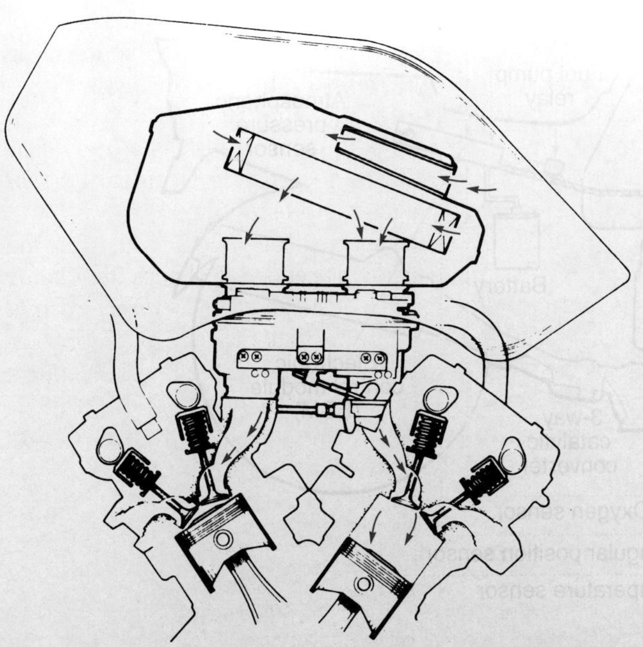

Figure 1-31. Outside air enters the air cleaner, passes through the air filter and carburetors, and flows into the engine. The air filter removes airborne dirt, protecting the engine from abrasive wear and damage. (Yamaha Motor Corporation U.S.A.)

voltage is needed to fire the spark plug. An ***ignition coil*** is actually a step-up transformer that provides this high voltage. An ignition coil is shown in **Figure 1-39.**

The ignition system must also provide a spark at the proper time during compression. A switching device driven by the crankshaft or camshaft is used to trigger the coil at the proper time, **Figure 1-40.** Contact points or a magnetic triggering device are used. Provisions are made for ignition timing adjustment to compensate for part wear.

Some dual purpose and off-road bikes use a ***magneto*** or energy transfer ignition system. In this system, the ignition is powered directly by the alternator. **Figure 1-41** illustrates a typical magneto ignition system.

Cooling System

Both two- and four-stroke engines use either ***air cooling*** or ***liquid cooling.*** In the combustion process, a great amount of heat is produced. Some of this heat is used for power production (piston movement). The remainder must be transferred away from the engine to prevent engine damage.

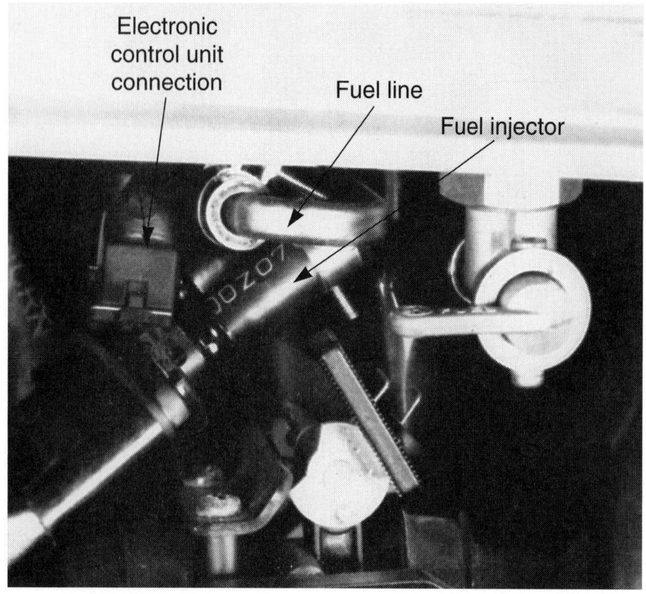

Figure 1-32. An electronic fuel injection system delivers fuel under pressure directly into the engine's intake port. A fuel injector is an electronic solenoid-operated valve. When the electronic control module (ECM) sends a pulse to the solenoid, the injector opens and sprays fuel toward the intake valve.

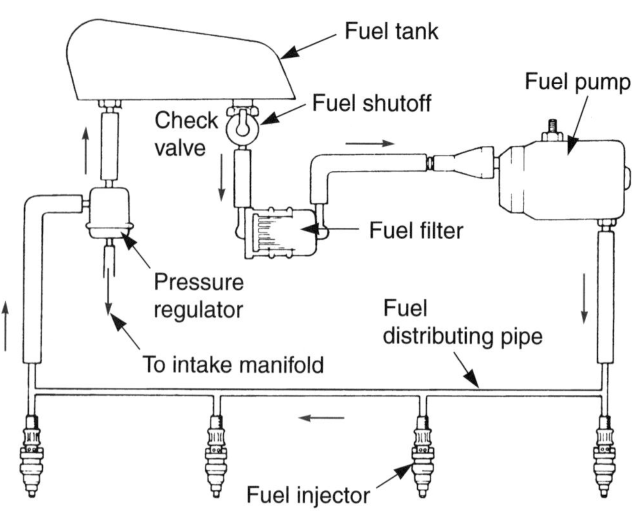

Figure 1-33. A fuel pump and pressure regulator maintain constant fuel pressure above intake manifold vacuum. (Kawasaki Motors Corporation, U.S.A.)

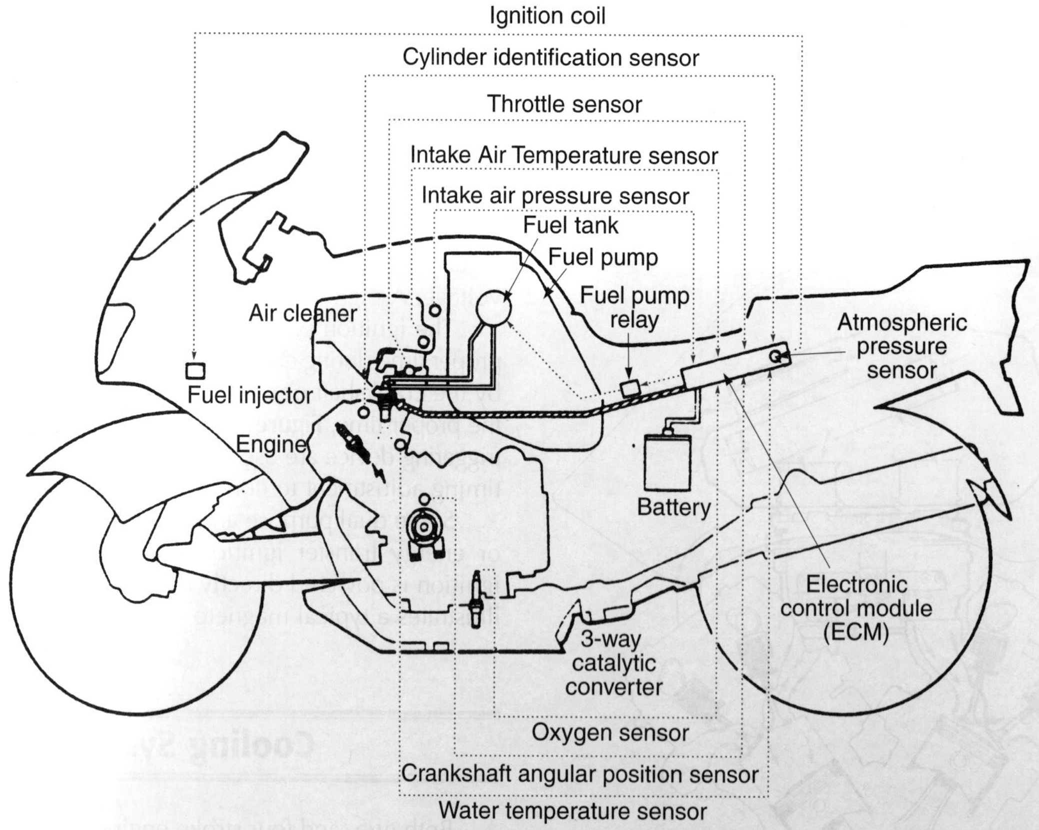

Figure 1-34. In electronically controlled fuel systems, sensors track everything from atmospheric pressure to engine rpm to crankshaft position. The system's ECM is located under the seat. (Honda Motor Co., Ltd.)

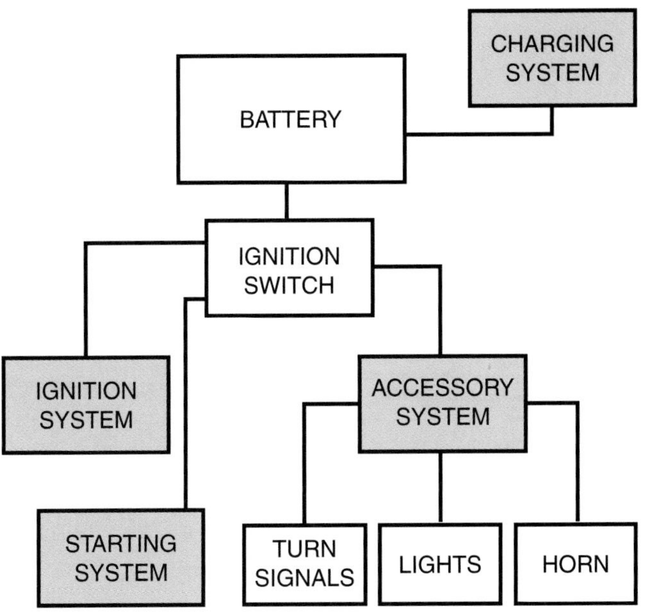

Figure 1-35. The components of a battery-powered electrical system. A battery supplies electrical power for ignition, starting, and accessory systems during engine start-up. The charging system recharges the battery and supplies electricity while the engine is running.

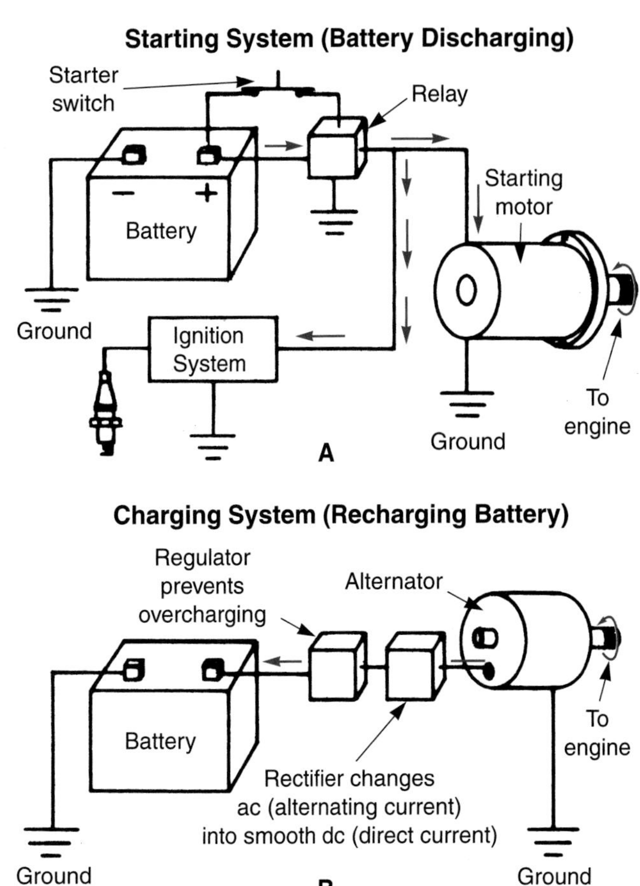

Figure 1-37. A—Current flows out of the battery and into the starting motor and ignition system. The motor spins the engine for starting. B—Once the engine has started, the charging system supplies current to the battery for recharging.

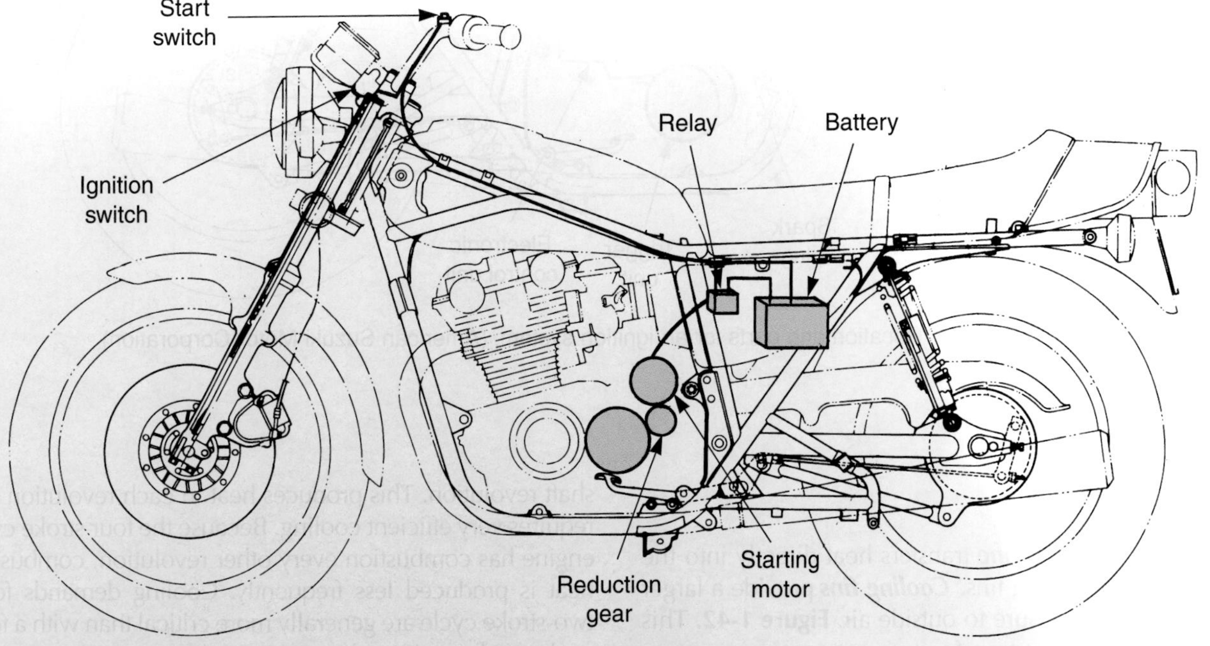

Figure 1-36. Note the general location and parts of the starting system. An electric motor spins the engine when activated by a start switch, relay, and battery. (American Suzuki Motor Corporation)

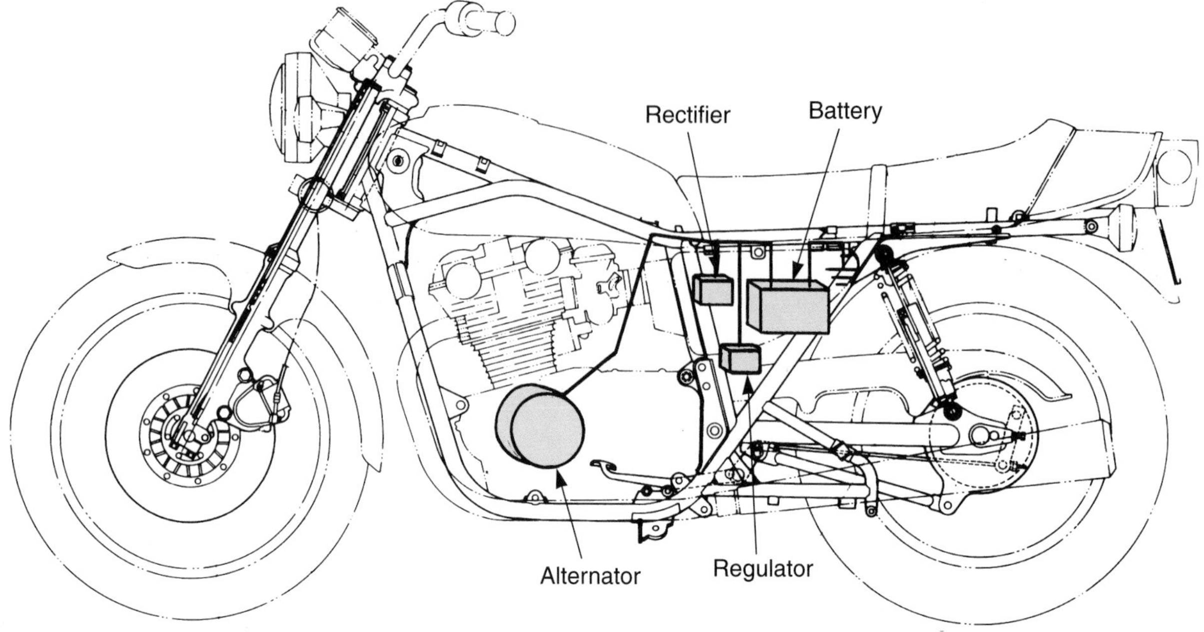

Figure 1-38. The alternator is spun by the engine and produces current that flows back into the battery and the electrical system. (American Suzuki Motor Corporation)

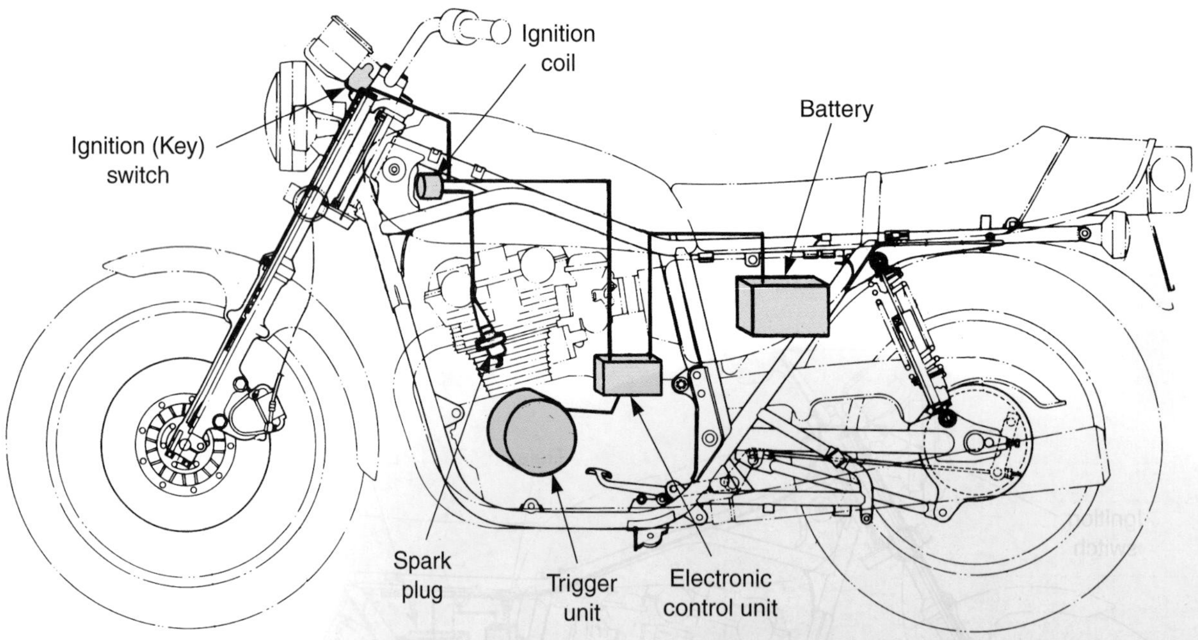

Figure 1-39. General location and parts for an ignition system. (American Suzuki Motor Corporation)

Air Cooling

The ***air-cooled engine*** transfers heat directly into the air by means of cooling fins. ***Cooling fins*** provide a larger surface area for exposure to outside air, **Figure 1-42.** This allows for greater heat transfer.

In the two-stroke cycle engine described earlier in this chapter, combustion takes place once during each crankshaft revolution. This produces heat in each revolution and requires very efficient cooling. Because the four-stroke cycle engine has combustion every other revolution, combustion heat is produced less frequently. Cooling demands for a two-stroke cycle are generally more critical than with a four-stroke cycle engine.

A two-stroke cycle engine cooling system must be capable of dissipating a large amount of heat. Fins may be

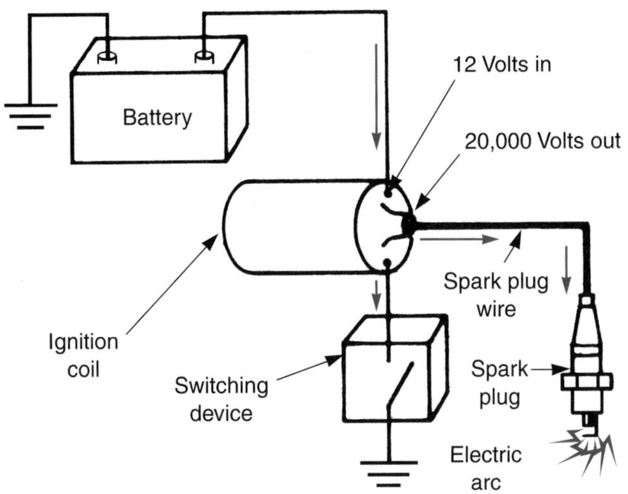

Figure 1-40. A crankshaft-driven switching device (magnetic trigger wheel and electronic control module or breaker points) operates an ignition coil. The coil increases battery voltage (12 volts) to over 20,000 volts. High voltage is required to make a spark jump the gap at the spark plug.

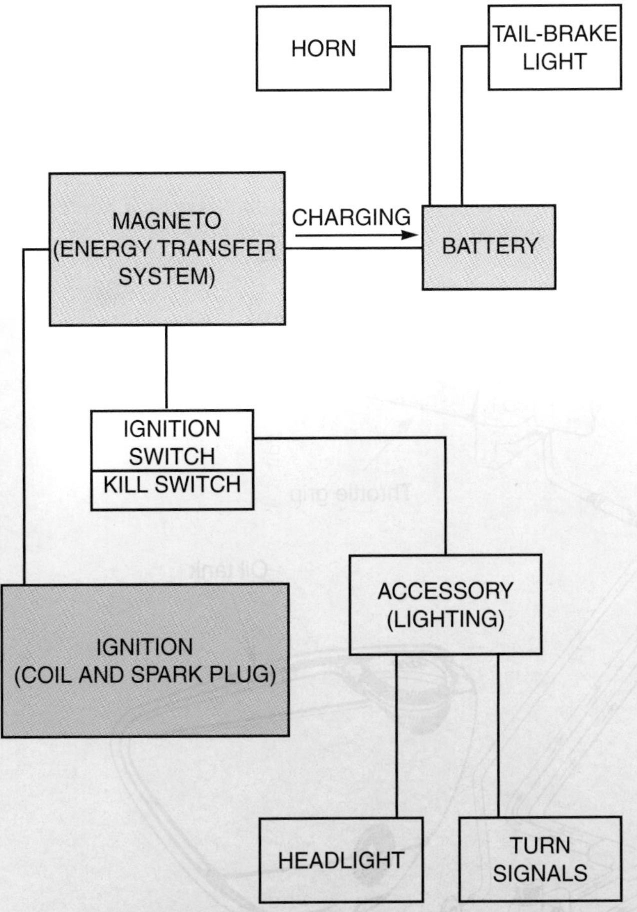

Figure 1-41. Magneto ignition systems are used on many small, dual-purpose motorcycles. If accessories are required, a battery is used along with the magneto. A lighting circuit in magneto provides battery recharging.

present on cylinders, cylinder heads, and crankcases. They must be kept clean and not heavily coated with paint for proper heat transfer.

Liquid Cooling

The ***liquid-cooled engine*** transfers engine heat into ***coolant*** (water and antifreeze solution). The coolant circulates through cavities in the cylinder, head, and crankcase. The hot liquid coolant is then piped to a ***radiator*** which efficiently transfers heat to the outside air. Operation of the liquid-cooling system is illustrated in **Figure 1-43.**

The major advantage of a liquid cooling system is that it maintains a more consistent engine operating temperature than an air-cooled system. An air-cooled engine's operating temperature can rise and fall with changes in outside air temperature. Because of the liquid-cooled engine's

Figure 1-42. An air-cooled engine has cooling fins built into its design. (Yamaha Motor Corporation, U.S.A.)

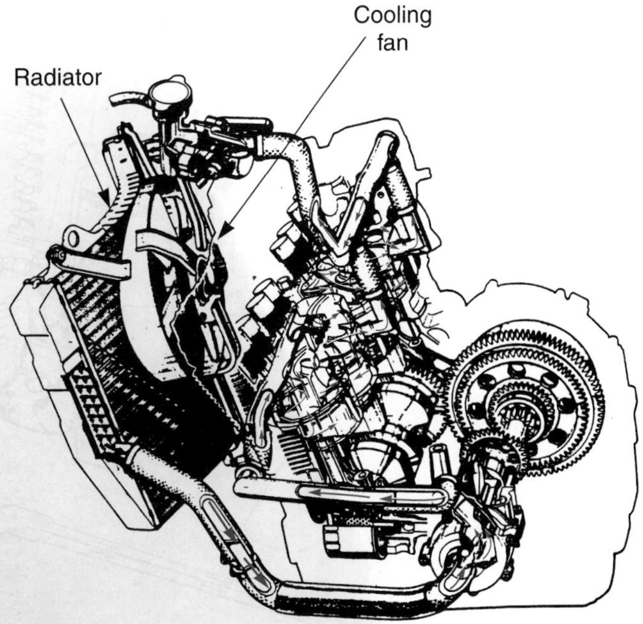

Figure 1-43. Typical coolant flow through a liquid-cooled engine. (American Suzuki Motor Corporation)

controlled operating temperature, more precise clearances between moving parts can be utilized. This results in quieter operation, improved efficiency, and longer engine life. However, a liquid-cooled engine costs more to manufacture, purchase, and maintain than an air-cooled engine.

Lubrication Systems

The ***lubrication system*** is designed to reduce the friction caused by engine operation. Lubrication is accomplished by circulating oil to high friction points in the engine. The engine lubricating oil not only helps to reduce friction (lubricates), it also cleans, cools, and seals.

Two methods are used to provide lubrication in two-stroke engines; premixed fuel and oil, and oil injection, **Figure 1-44.** Lubrication differs greatly between two- and four-stroke engines. Rather than burning the oil during combustion, the four-stroke cycle engine circulates the same oil throughout the parts of a four-stroke cycle engine, **Figure 1-45.**

There are three common types of four-stroke cycle lubrication systems: dry sump, wet sump, and common sump. The word ***sump*** refers to the lowest portion of the crankcase cavity. It is the area where oil collects in the bottom of the engine.

Exhaust System

The ***exhaust system*** is a vital key to the motorcycle's operation and performance. It has three functions:

- Routes burned exhaust gases to the rear of the motorcycle.
- Enhances the engine's power curve.

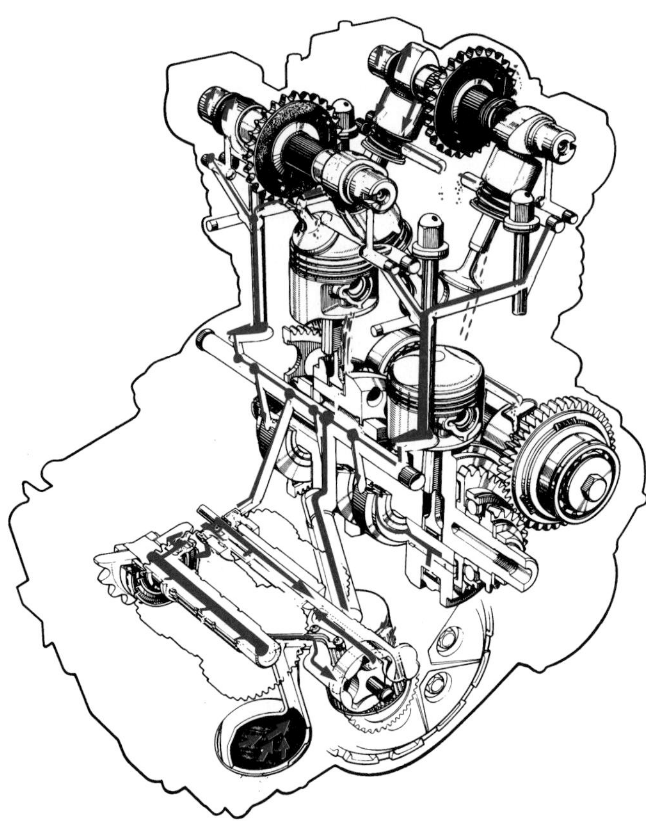

Figure 1-45. Oil flow through a four-stroke engine with a sump. (American Suzuki Motor Corporation)

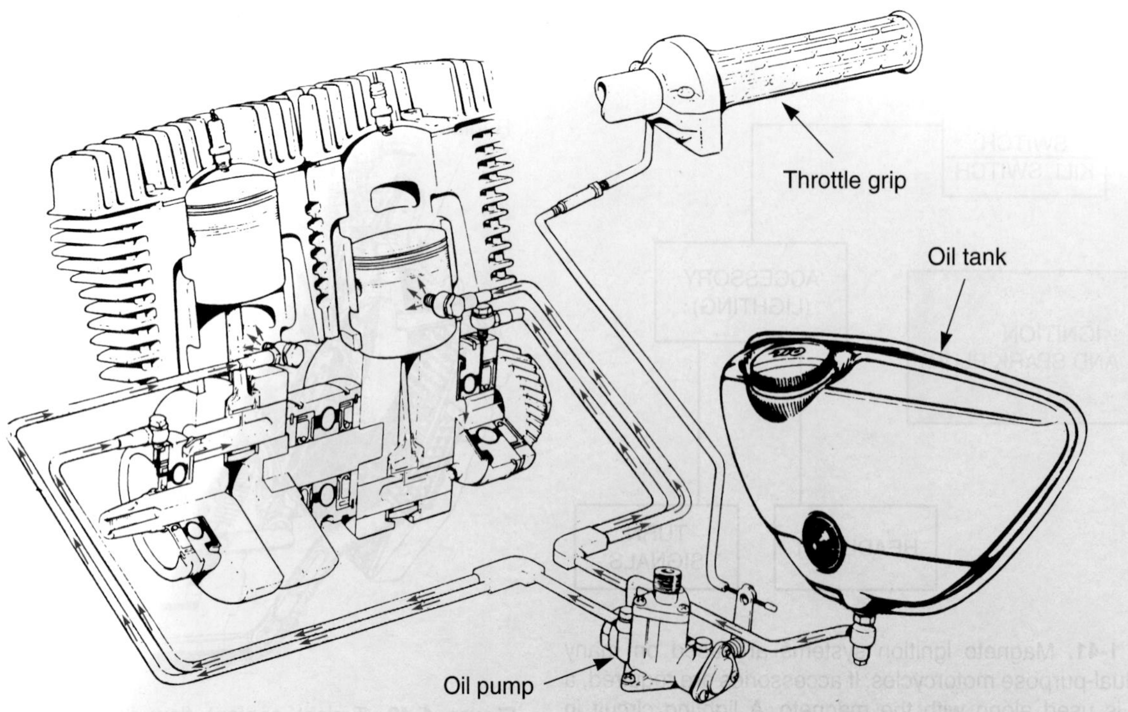

Figure 1-44. Oil flow through a two-stroke engine. (American Suzuki Motor Corporation)

- Reduces engine exhaust noise.

Exhaust systems are normally made of steel, covered with a layer of chrome plating or heat-resistant paint. Some newer exhaust pipes are made of stainless steel to lessen corrosion problems. A heat shield may be placed over the outer side of the exhaust system. The heat shield protects the rider from being burned on the hot exhaust pipe or muffler.

There are numerous exhaust system designs. Designs vary with the number of engine cylinders, engine type (two-stroke or four-stroke cycle), and application.

For example, a street bike normally has the exhaust system located close to the ground, **Figure 1-46.** This keeps exhaust heat away from the rider and helps lower the bike's weight and center of gravity. An off-road motorcycle, however, frequently has the exhaust system mounted higher. This provides more ground clearance for riding in rough terrain.

Power Transmission

The ***power transmission*** in a motorcycle sends power from the engine crankshaft to the rear wheel. A series of gears, chains, and/or shafts are used, **Figure 1-47.** The motorcycle must be able to make the best use of available power and torque. To do this, the power transmission allows the engine to operate in its most efficient power range at all times. A series of gears in the transmission provides a wide variance in rear wheel speed while the engine operates within a relatively narrow speed range.

Gear Action

A combination of gears will accomplish a reduction in speed and a multiplication of torque. Consider the effect of a ten-tooth gear driving a thirty-tooth gear, **Figure 1-48.** The ten-tooth gear will make three revolutions for each revolution of the thirty-tooth gear. With this setup, the large gear will turn at one-third the speed of the small gear.

If the ten-tooth gear is driving the thirty-tooth gear with 1 ft-lb (1.35 N•m) of torque, **Figure 1-49,** the thirty-tooth gear will deliver 3 ft.-lbs. (4.05 N•m) of torque or three times as much torque as the ten-tooth gear. This gear setup is considered to have a three-to-one (3:1) gear reduction ratio.

Primary Drive

A typical motorcycle power transmission uses a ***primary drive*** to deliver engine power from the crankshaft to the transmission. A clutch is provided in the primary drive to engage and disengage power to and from the transmission. A primary drive serves two main functions:

- It provides a convenient mounting place for the clutch.
- It provides initial gear reduction, allowing the transmission to be more compact.

Primary Drive Reduction

A primary drive will have a reduction ratio of approximately three-to-one (3:1). The need for a primary drive is easily understood using an example. Assume that a typi-

Figure 1-46. The location of the exhaust pipe(s) on a street motorcycle can vary with the bike's design. (Yamaha Motor Corporation U.S.A.)

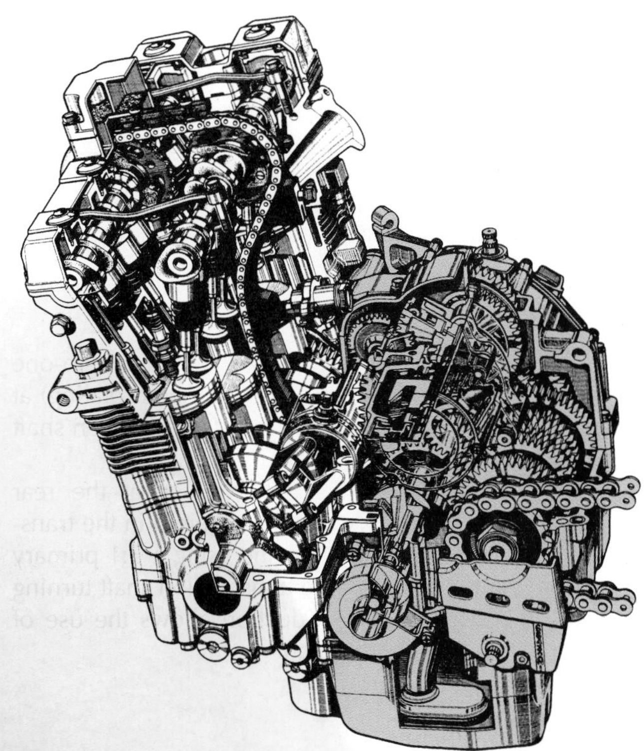

Figure 1-47. Primary drive and transmission transfer power from the engine crankshaft to the final drive system. (American Suzuki Motor Corporation)

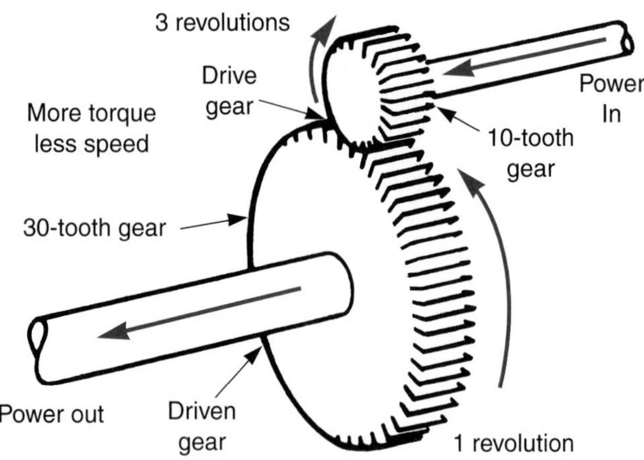

Figure 1-48. When a small gear drives a large gear, speed is reduced (large gear rotates slower) and torque is multiplied (large gear has more turning power).

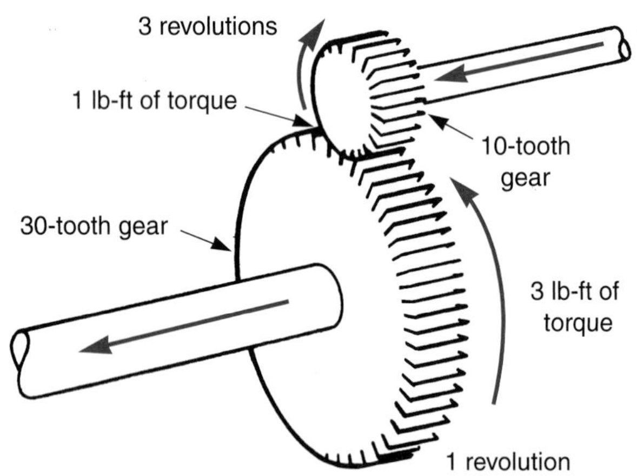

Figure 1-49. If a ten-tooth gear applies 1 ft.-lb. of torque to a thirty-tooth gear, the thirty-tooth gear will apply 3 ft.-lbs. of torque to its shaft. The small gear will turn three times to make the large gear turn once. This is a 3:1 gear ratio or reduction.

cal engine is driving a transmission with a one-to-one (1:1) ratio. If the engine is turning (crankshaft rotating) at 3000 revolutions per minute (rpm), the transmission shaft will also turn at 3000 rpm.

In order to reduce this rpm for use at the rear wheel(s), very large gears would be required in the transmission. However, this same engine using a 3:1 primary reduction would now have the transmission shaft turning at 1000 rpm. This primary reduction allows the use of smaller gears in the transmission.

Clutch

A ***clutch*** provides a means of connecting and disconnecting the primary drive and the transmission. As shown in **Figure 1-50,** the clutch is located between the primary drive chain or gears and the transmission.

Anytime the engine is running, the primary drive spins. However, with the clutch disengaged, power does not flow into the transmission and to the rear wheel(s). This allows the motorcycle to stand still with the engine running. When the clutch is engaged, the motorcycle is propelled forward.

The clutch uses spring-loaded plates (round discs) inside a clutch basket (housing), **Figure 1-51.** If the springs are pressing the clutch plates together, friction causes power to be transferred through the clutch. If the clutch lever on the handle bar is pulled, a cable operated lever acts against spring pressure to release friction inside the clutch. This uncouples the engine and transmission. **Figure 1-52** shows a typical adjustable clutch lever found on a handlebar.

Transmission

A ***transmission,*** or *gearbox* as it was once called, is a set of shafts and gears which connect the primary drive to the final drive mechanism to the rear wheel(s). Motorcycles and ATVs commonly have anywhere from 4-10 different speeds or ratios. This is accomplished by engaging and disengaging gears of different sizes (varied number of teeth), as shown in **Figure 1-53.**

Recent power transmission design uses an automatic primary drive and clutch with the transmission. ATVs are available, as mentioned earlier, with two- and four-wheel drive transmissions.

Final Drive

The ***final drive*** connects the transmission to the rear wheel(s). It is the last element in the motorcycle's power transmission system. The three designs commonly used are shaft drive, chain drive, and belt drive. These are shown in **Figure 1-54** while a typical ATV chain final drive is shown in **Figure 1-55.** The final drive will generally have a reduction ratio of approximately 3:1. A change in overall ratio can be made quickly by changing chain sprocket sizes.

Chassis

The motorcycle ***chassis*** includes everything but the engine, fuel system, and electrical systems, although these systems are assembled on the chassis, **Figure 1-56.** The frame and suspension form the chassis.

Frame

The motorcycle ***frame*** provides a means of rigidly mounting the engine, suspension, and accessories. Many different frame designs are used.

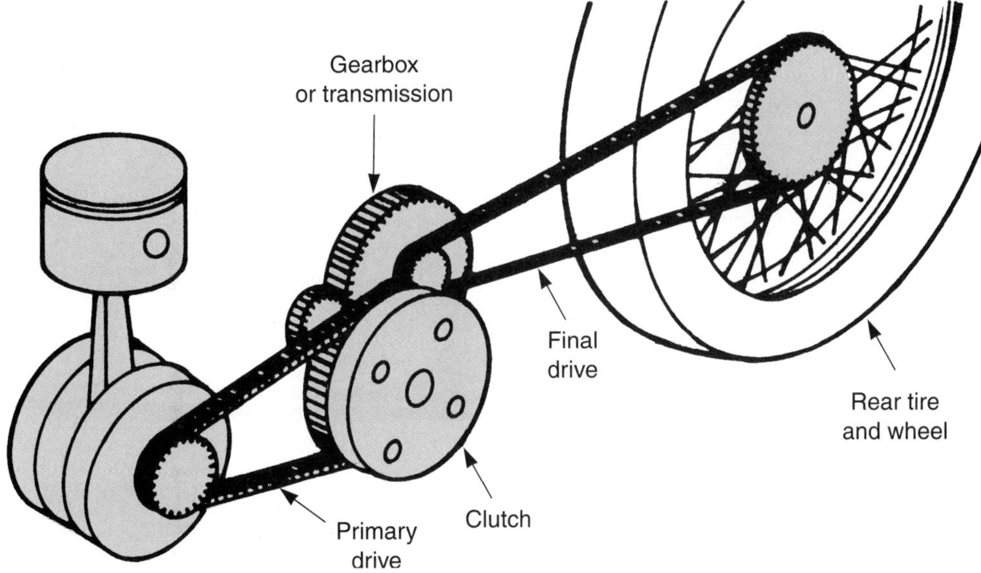

Figure 1-50. The primary drive transfers power from the engine to the clutch. The clutch can couple or uncouple the engine from the transmission. The transmission provides various gear ratios while the final drive transfers power from the transmission to the rear wheel.

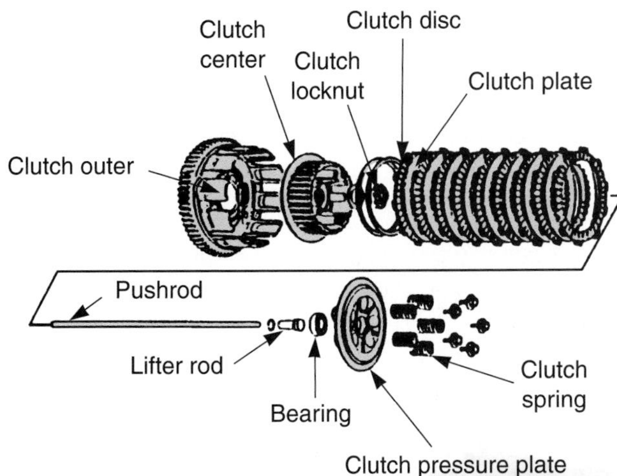

Figure 1-51. A typical clutch plate assembly. (Honda Motor Co., Ltd.)

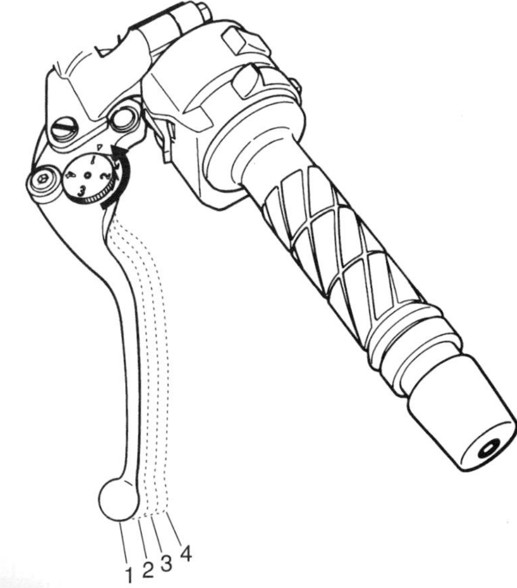

Figure 1-52. An adjustable clutch lever. (Yamaha Motor Corporation, U.S.A.)

Regardless of why a certain frame design is used (low manufacturing cost, lightweight, strength), it must be understood that the frame's job is not easy. The frame must:

- Support for the rider, passenger, and all components.
- Be rigid enough to assure accurate wheel alignment during acceleration, deceleration, and cornering.
- Be strong enough to resist flexing under adverse conditions (rough surfaces, hard cornering).
- Provide rigidity between front and rear suspension mounting points.
- Provide rigid mounting of the engine for accurate alignment of drive train components.
- Be light enough to provide good performance.

Suspension

The ***suspension system*** uses springs and hydraulic dampers to smooth the ride of a motorcycle. Modern motorcycle suspension systems can be classified into two general categories:

- Suspensions designed for highway or road use.
- Suspensions designed for off-road use.

In both designs, it is the suspension's job to keep the wheels on the ground over bumps. At the same time, the

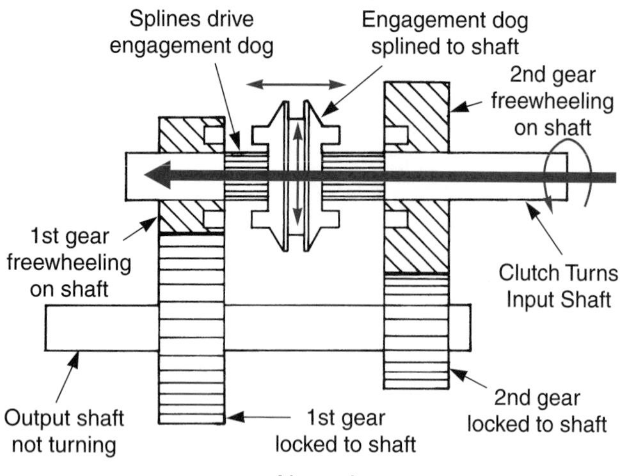

Neutral

A—When gearbox is in neutral, input shaft and engagement dog turn. Since 1st and 2nd gears on input shaft are not locked to shaft, they do not turn or drive output shaft.

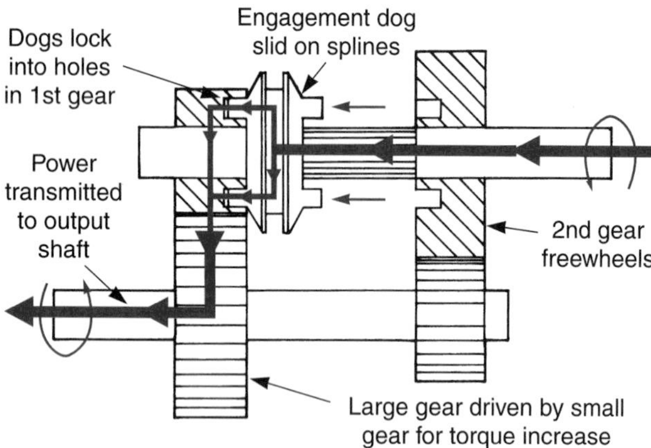

First gear

B—First gear is engaged by sliding engagement dog to left. Projections (dogs) index or fit into holes in side of 1st gear. Since engagement dog is splined to input shaft, 1st gear now turns with shaft and drives output shaft.

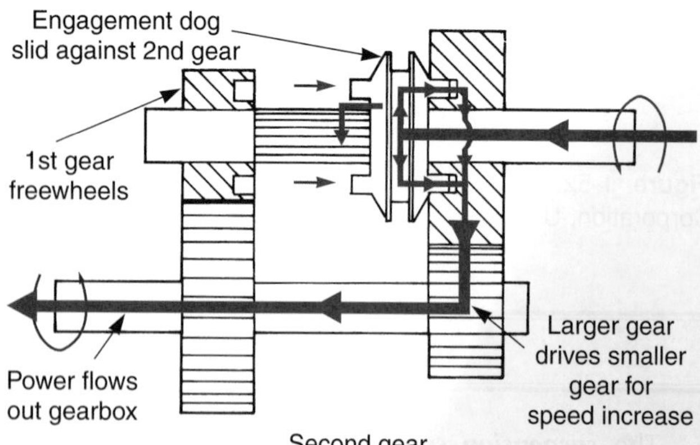

Second gear

C—Second gear is engaged by sliding engagement dog to right. When dogs are indexed into holes in side of 2nd gear, 2nd gear turns with input shaft and drives output shaft.

Figure 1-53. Gear position and power flow in neutral, first, and second gears.

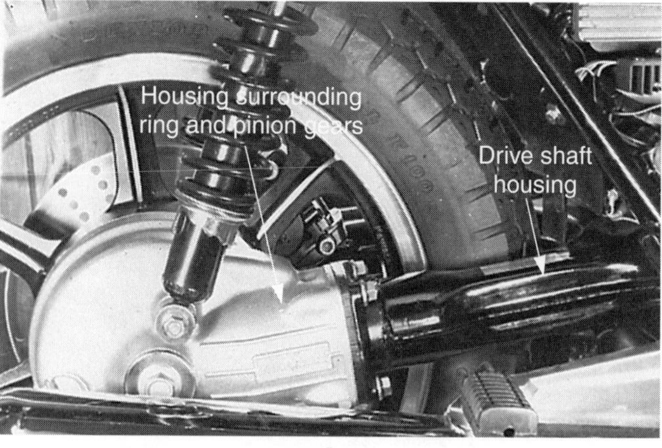

A

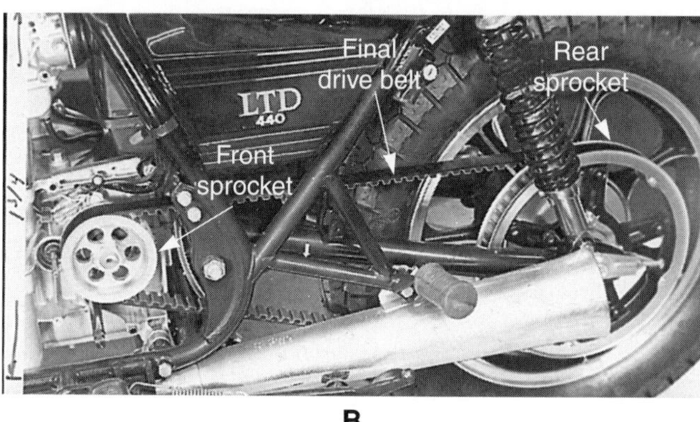

B

Figure 1-54. Two motorcycle final drive designs. A—Shaft drive. B—Belt drive.

Figure 1-55. A typical chain final drive as used on an ATV. (Yamaha Motor Corporation, U.S.A.)

suspension must absorb the jolts of rough roads before they are transmitted to the frame and rider.

Suspension Operation

Suspension operation involves compression and extension. As the wheels roll over a bump, the suspension compresses against a spring, **Figure 1-57.** After the wheel

Figure 1-56. A typical aluminum frame. (Yamaha Motor Corporation, U.S.A.)

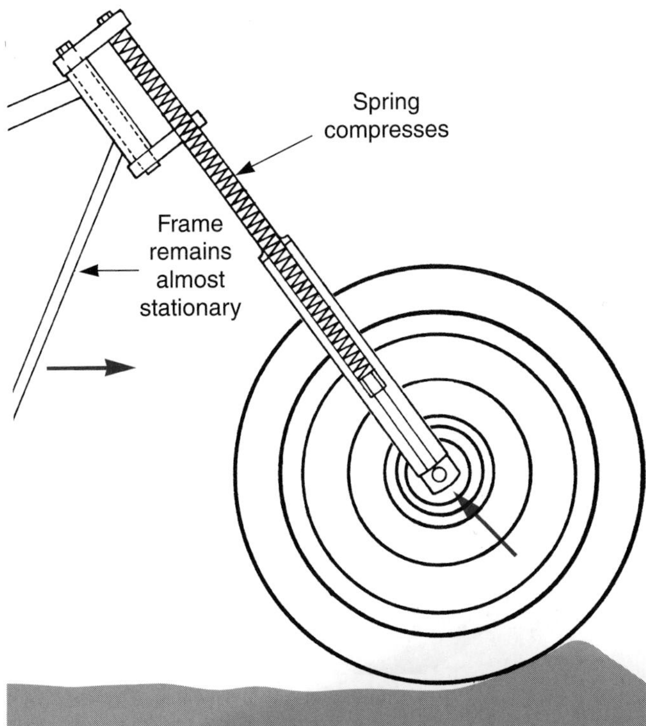

Figure 1-57. Force applied to the front suspension by a bump, which is absorbed by the fork springs.

leaves the bump, the spring tends to rapidly extend the suspension. Unchecked, this will result in uncontrolled bounce effect. To avoid this condition, ***dampers*** are provided inside the suspension components. These dampers are designed to help control the up and down movement of the suspension, **Figure 1-58.**

The most common types of motorcycle suspension are composed of ***telescoping forks*** (tubes) on the front and a ***swing arm*** with shock absorbers on the rear, **Figure 1-59.**

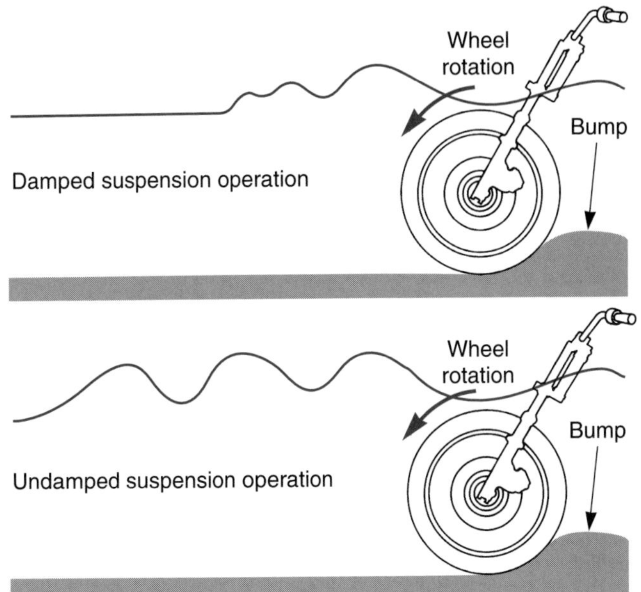

Figure 1-58. Without suspension damping, a motorcycle would be very uncomfortable to ride and hard to control over bumps. Suspension dampers are designed to eliminate uncontrolled recoil or bouncing.

Wheels and Tires

Wheels provide a mounting place for inflatable rubber tires. The wheel/tire assemblies support the motorcycle and provide traction for cornering, braking, and delivery of engine power to the ground.

During the last few years, new wheel designs have emerged. In the past, the traditional spoke wheel was widely used. As motorcycles became heavier and more powerful, the need for a stronger wheel arose. To fill this need, manufacturers designed a one-piece cast alloy wheel. This design offers a very rigid, maintenance-free wheel, **Figure 1-60.**

The spoke wheel still has its place. It is less expensive to manufacture and, in some applications (off-road, for example), its ability to flex is needed. The spoke wheel consists of a hub, spokes, and rim. See **Figure 1-61.** This assembly provides a place to mount the tire, tube, and brake.

Tires provide traction for moving the motorcycle, absorbing bumps, and to assist the brakes in stopping. Today's tires are made of many different rubber compounds and tread designs, either tube or tubeless. The service technician installs tires ranging from knobby designs for off-road, dirt riding motorcycles, to street tires, to heavy-duty tires for ATVs, **Figure 1-62.**

Brakes

Brakes provide a controllable means of stopping the motorcycle. Common brake designs are *disc* and *drum*

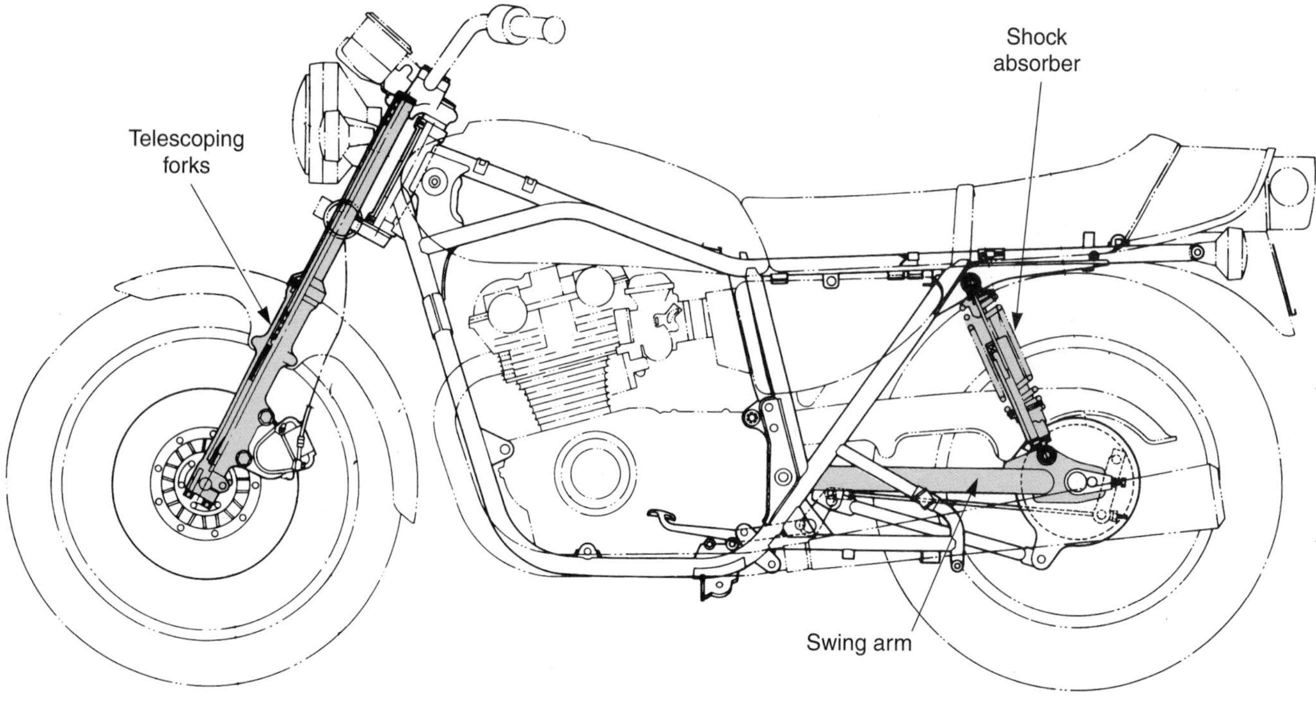

Figure 1-59. Telescoping forks are used for front suspensions on most motorcycles. Shock absorbers and a swing arm are commonly used for rear suspensions. (American Suzuki Motor Corporation)

Figure 1-60. A cast alloy wheel requires little maintenance, is very strong, and good looking.

Figure 1-61. Some wheels uses spokes with nipples to attach the hub and rim.

types. **Figure 1-63A** shows a drum brake assembly while **Figure 1-63B** illustrates disc brakes. Proper wheel, tire, and brake design is necessary for a safe, good-handling motorcycle. These as well as newer systems such as the linked braking system (LBS) and anti-lock brakes system (ABS) are covered in **Chapter 15.**

Accessory System

The ***accessory system*** includes all electrical components and wiring other than charging, starting, and ignition systems mentioned earlier in the chapter. Lights, horn, turn signals, and warning lights are some of the components in the accessory system. **Figure 1-64** shows the layout of a typical accessory system. These systems are all powered by the battery or alternator. ***Fuses*** are added to prevent damage in case of component or wiring failure.

Summary

The growing interest in motorcycles, ATVs, and powered scooters has created a growing need for technicians who can service these vehicles. In the past, almost every motorcycle owner was his/her own technician. But now, there are very few riders who can fix their own bike. As the motorcycle industry continues to grow, the demand for trained people will continue to grow. There are eight styles or types of motorcycles that may come into your shop for service or repair.

Figure 1-62. Heavy-duty tire design used by ATV's. (Yamaha Motor Corporation, U.S.A.)

A motorcycle, ATV, or scooter engine is a group of assembled parts designed to change the heat energy of burning fuel into useful mechanical energy. For the engine to operate, air, fuel, compression, and combustion are needed. Motorcycles use either a two-stroke, or four-stroke engine. The cylinders of a two-stroke engine produce power at each cycle while four-stroke engines produce power every other cycle.

The fuel system on a motorcycle consists of the fuel tank, fuel shutoff valve, fuel filter, fuel lines, carburetor or injectors, and air cleaner. The carbureted fuel system mixes air and fuel using engine vacuum. It provides a predetermined air-fuel mixture to the engine. The electronic fuel injection system monitors engine conditions and provides precise fuel delivery based on engine requirements.

The electrical system supplies electrical power to all the various components on the motorcycle. The electrical system is composed of three subsystems; starting system, charging system, and ignition system. Many motorcycles use a battery to store and supply electricity for initial starting, ignition, and lighting.

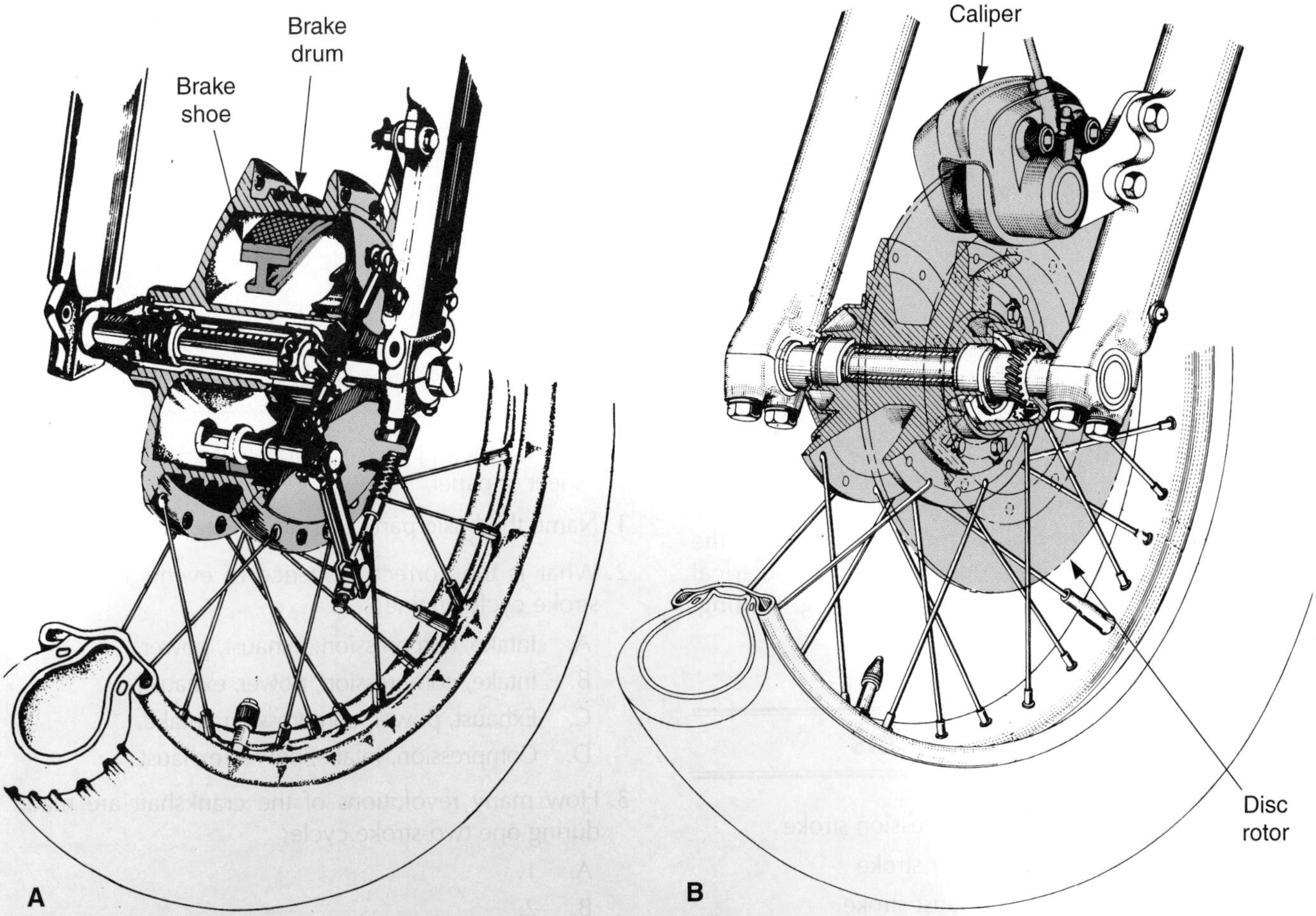

Figure 1-63. Two common brake designs. A—A drum brakes uses shoes that are pressed against a revolving brake drum. B—Disc brakes use brake pads that contact a spinning disc. (Kawasaki Motors Corporation U.S.A.)

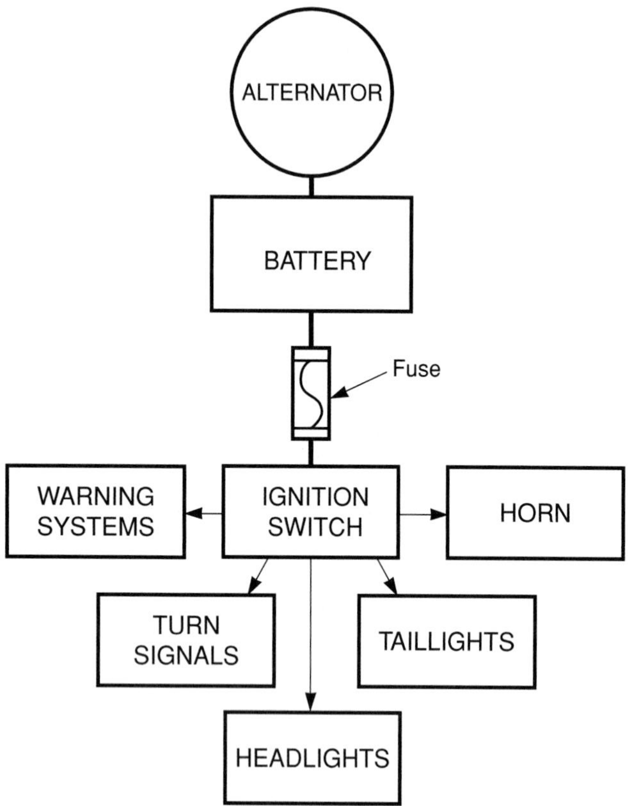

Figure 1-64. Typical accessory breakdown. Depending on the bike, there may be additional systems.

The power transmission in a motorcycle sends power from the engine crankshaft to the rear wheel(s). A series of gears, chains, and/or shafts are used. A series of gears in the transmission provides a wide variance in rear wheel speed while the engine operates within a relatively narrow speed range.

The motorcycle frame provides a means of rigidly mounting the engine, suspension, and accessories. Many different frame designs are used. The suspension system uses springs and hydraulic dampers to smooth the ride of a motorcycle. The wheel/tire assemblies support the motorcycle and provide traction for cornering, braking, and delivery of engine power to the ground. Brakes provide a controllable means of stopping the motorcycle. The accessory system includes all electrical components and wiring other than charging, starting, and ignition systems.

Know These Terms

Simple engine
Four-stroke cycle engine
Intake stroke
Top dead center (TDC)
Bottom dead center (BDC)
Compression stroke
Power stroke
Exhaust stroke
Valve overlap
Flywheel
Two-stroke cycle engine
Exhaust port
Transfer port
Intake port
Work
Energy
Torque
Power
Horsepower
Fuel system
Carburetor
Venturi
Throttle twist grip
Air cleaner
Electronic fuel injection (EFI)
Electronic control module (ECM)
Electronic control system
Sensors
Electrical system
Battery
Starting system
Alternator
Current
Voltage
Rectifier
Alternating current (ac)
Direct current (dc)
Voltage regulator
Ignition system
Ignition coil
Magneto
Air cooling
Liquid cooling
Air-cooled engine
Cooling fins
Liquid-cooled engine
Coolant
Radiator
Lubrication system
Sump
Exhaust system
Power transmission
Primary drive
Clutch
Transmission
Final drive
Chassis
Frame
Suspension system
Dampers
Telescoping forks
Swing arm
Wheels
Tires
Brakes
Accessory system
Fuses

Review Questions—Chapter 1

Do not write in this text. Place your answers on a separate sheet of paper.

1. Name the basic parts of a simple engine.
2. What is the correct sequence of events for a four-stroke cycle engine?
   A. Intake, compression, exhaust, power.
   B. Intake, compression, power, exhaust.
   C. Exhaust, power, compression, intake.
   D. Compression, intake, power, exhaust.
3. How many revolutions of the crankshaft are made during one two-stroke cycle?
   A. 1.
   B. 2.
   C. 4.
   D. 8.

4. List two major differences between two-stroke and four-stroke cycle engines.
5. The _____ opens and closes the transfer port in a two-stroke cycle engine.
   A. valve
   B. crankshaft
   C. flywheel
   D. piston
6. Torque is a _____ force.
   A. pushing
   B. pulling
   C. twisting
   D. compression
7. The purpose of a carburetor venturi is:
   A. to increase air velocity in the carburetor throat.
   B. to decrease air pressure in the carburetor throat.
   C. to allow atmospheric pressure to push fuel into the carburetor throat.
   D. All of the above.
8. Which of the following is *not* monitored by the electronic fuel injection ECM?
   A. Throttle position.
   B. Air temperature.
   C. Engine rpm.
   D. Fuel pressure.
9. What is an electronic fuel injector?
10. List four functions of engine oil.
11. A _____ engages and disengages power to the transmission.
   A. clutch
   B. brake
   C. rectifier
   D. flywheel
12. A flywheel _____ the crankshaft inertia.
   A. increases
   B. decreases
   C. maintains
   D. stops
13. A _____ allows a motorcycle engine to make the best use of available power and torque.
   A. clutch
   B. power transmission
   C. belt drive
   D. gear sprocket
14. A primary drive connects the _____ to the _____.
15. List the two types of motorcycle brakes.

Suggested Activities

1. Make a chart comparing the differences between two-stroke and four-stroke cycle engines.
2. Select three two-stroke and three four-stroke motorcycle engines of the same displacement. Make a chart comparing the following features of the six engines. Use magazine articles, advertising brochures, owner and shop manuals to find the information.
   A. Exact displacement.
   B. Number of cylinders.
   C. Bore size.
   D. Stroke.
   E. Maximum horsepower at rpm.
   F. Maximum torque at rpm.
3. Research and find the most common direction of rotation for vertical, twin four-stroke engines. Then, identify an engine which rotates in the opposite direction and determine why.
4. Inspect any type of motorcycle and list the following information on a sheet of paper.
   A. Number of carburetors used.
   B. Type of air filter.
   C. Location of electrical system fuses.
   D. Type of ignition system.
   E. Type of wheels.
   F. Type of front and rear brakes.
   G. Type of tires.
   H. Frame type.
   I. Type of final drive.
   J. Type of transmission.

Safety in the shop is important. Maintaining good cleaniness is only one part of keeping a motorcycle shop safe. (J.D. Gerhart)

Shop Safety and Environmental Protection

After studying this chapter, you will be able to:

- Explain the use of safety notices in this text and service manuals.
- Explain the importance of shop safety in a repair shop.
- Describe the personal safety precautions that a technician must follow.
- Outline the general shop housekeeping procedures that must be maintained.
- Describe the three basic types of fires.
- Describe the proper use of the different types of fire extinguishers.
- Know your rights under the Right-to-Know laws.

To produce a safe working environment, a safety conscious attitude must be developed. Safety in the shop is a matter of simple common sense. Taking safety for granted can result in a serious accident or injury. An accident can not only injure the technician or damage the motorcycle, but can also affect the environment. This chapter discusses shop safety and procedures to be used to protect yourself, the customer's bike, and the environment.

Safety Notices

When using this text, as well as most service manuals, the words warning, caution, and note have a specific meaning. Warnings, cautions, and notes that are in this book are set apart for emphasis, **Figure 2-1.**

A ***warning*** emphasizes areas or improper procedures where personal injury or even death could result. Mechanical damage to the motorcycle may also occur.

Cautions are given to prevent the technician from making an error that could damage the motorcycle or one of its systems. Failure to heed a caution could cause permanent mechanical damage; however, personal injury is unlikely.

A ***note*** gives added information that will help to complete a particular procedure or make a task easier. Disregarding a note may cause inconvenience, but would not cause damage or personal injury.

Most manuals contain safety symbols that provide additional warning for the need to use caution. Personal safety is the number one consideration when working with motorcycles, ATVs, and scooters. Safety is not a matter of do's or don'ts, it is a matter of understanding the job and using common sense.

Caution: Do not use a piece of wire, metal or other conductor in place of a fuse.

Figure 2-1. This is a typical caution you will see in this text. Warnings and notes will have a similar style.

Personal Safety

Work like a professional. While learning to become a motorcycle technician, it is easy to become excited about your work. However, avoid working too fast as you could overlook a repair procedure or safety rule and cause an accident.

While motorcycles, ATVs, and scooters do not appear to present the danger to personal safety as other larger motor vehicles, they are more than capable of injuring or killing you if you do not exercise caution in handling, working on, and riding them.

There are a multitude of hazards present in all shops, any one alone or a combination of two or more can cause property damage, serious injury, or death. For example, a small oil spill may not seem like a hazard. However, this oil, combined with sparks from a nearby welding operation, could start a dangerous fire.

Proper Dress

Dress like a technician. Remove all rings, bracelets, necklaces, watches, other jewelry and ties. They can become caught in chain drives or short a circuit. Wear short sleeved shirts or roll up long sleeves. Wear long pants, as shorts will not protect your legs from sparks, metal splinters, or other debris. If your job position requires you to wear a tie, tuck it inside your shirt.

Proper footwear is the most important part of your uniform. Wear only comfortable shoes or boots, preferably steel-toed with oil resistant soles. This will protect your feet from parts or tools accidentally dropped as well as slipping on an oil- or water-covered floor. The shoe or boot should have enough support to allow you to stand for the entire day on concrete floors, which are common to most shops. Open-toed shoes, sandals, and athletic shoes are not considered appropriate footwear.

You should maintain your appearance as this promotes professionalism as well as good hygiene. Always wear a clean, pressed uniform and keep yourself neat and clean. If you wear your hair long, tie it back or secure it under a hat for safety. Wash your hands regularly and keep your fingernails clean. This not only gives a good appearance, it also allows any small cuts, nicks, and abrasions on your hands a chance to heal with less risk of infection.

Protective Equipment

To prevent the absorption of solvent and other chemicals into your skin while cleaning parts, wear a pair of protective gloves. Also wear thick insulated gloves when working with heated parts.

Wear safety glasses, goggles, or a face shield during all operations involving drilling, grinding, welding, using a cold chisel, or any time you feel unsure about the safety of your eyes, **Figure 2-2.** Protective eyewear should also be worn any time compressed air is used to clean a part. Hearing protection, such as earplugs, should be worn whenever you are exposed to loud noise. While damage may not occur right away, hearing loss can occur gradually over years of exposure.

While most work on a motorcycle will probably be performed on a bench, there may be some cases where you will be required to work sitting or on your knees. A quality creeper seat or a good pair of protective knee pads should be used, depending on the position you will be working.

Shop Hazards

Keep the shop clean and organized as it promotes professionalism as well as safety. Return all tools and equipment to their proper storage areas. Never lay tools or parts on the floor as they can become lost or damaged. All surfaces should be kept clean, dry, and uncluttered. Keep workbenches clean and neat. Throw away any defective parts that are not recyclable as scrap. Keep all recyclable scrap in a secure, designated area.

Any oil, coolant, or grease on the floor can cause slips that could result in serious injuries. To clean up oil, be sure to use a commercial oil absorbent. Keep all water off the floor. Remember, water is an excellent conductor of electricity. Aisles and walkways should be kept clean and wide enough for safe clearance. Do not park bikes in the walkways.

Having a stack of clean shop rags on hand is important when performing engine work. However, oil and solvent soaked rags can become a fire hazard. To prevent spontaneous combustion from a pile of soiled rags, store them in a lid-sealed metal container until they can be washed or discarded.

Ventilate your work area when needed. Turn on the shop ventilation fan or open the shop doors any time fumes are present in the shop. Never run an engine in the shop until provisions are made for exhaust gas removal.

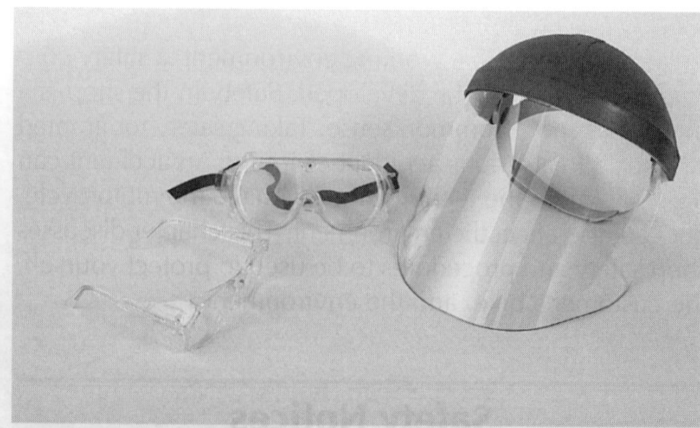

Figure 2-2. Always wear safety glasses or goggles whenever you are in the shop. Other types of eye protection are available for specific jobs. (Jack Klasey)

Space heaters, along with exhaust gas, are sources of carbon monoxide (CO), an odorless, colorless, potentially lethal gas. Heaters should be periodically inspected to make sure they are adequately vented and do not become blocked. Proper ventilation is very important in areas where volatile solvents and chemicals are used.

Smoking is a serious fire hazard in a motorcycle shop considering the proximity of fuel, cleaning solvents, charging batteries, and other flammable materials. Do not smoke in the shop. Store gasoline and other flammable materials in approved containers with a lid. Keep sources of heat away from the engine's fuel system.

Work Properly

Lift heavy parts with your legs, not with your back. There are many motorcycle assemblies that are very heavy. When lifting, bend at the knees while keeping your back as straight as possible, **Figure 2-3.** Get help whenever you are lifting something heavy. When mounting an engine or motorcycle on a stand or lift, get help and be certain the assembly is secure. A small hydraulic jack and a block of wood can be used to raise the chassis. Block the front and rear wheels if they are to remain on the ground. If the transmission is not going to be worked on and the drive chain or drive belt is connected to the rear wheel, shift the transmission into first gear.

Do not open more than one tool chest drawer at one time as it might flip over. Serious injury could result because some cabinet tool chests, fully loaded, can weight more than 1000 lbs (450 kg). Be sure to close each drawer before opening the next.

Use the right tool for the job. A good technician will know when, where, and why a particular tool will work better than another. Even though more than one tool may be used to loosen a bolt, usually one will do a better job. Never carry sharp tools or parts in your pockets as they can easily puncture your skin.

Discard and replace broken tools. Also wipe tools clean and dry after each use. A greasy or oily tool is not only unprofessional, but dangerous. It is very easy for your hand to slide off a dirty wrench, cutting or even breaking a finger or hand. Always follow manufacturer operating instructions for special tools and equipment. Always keep equipment guards or shields in place.

Use welding equipment only in designated areas. If welding or brazing on the bike is required, remove the fuel tank and rear shocks to a safe distance, at least 50 feet (15.24 m) away. Welding on a gas tank requires special safety precautions and must be performed by someone skilled in the process. Do not attempt to weld or braze a leaking gas tank without the proper precautions and training.

Wipe up gasoline spills right away. Do not spread oil absorbent on gasoline because the absorbent will become flammable. Gasoline contaminated oil absorbent is also considered a hazardous waste. Do not use water to dilute the fuel as it will simply spread it over a wider area. Check to be sure that all drain covers are snugly in place. Open drains can cause toe, ankle, and leg injuries.

Disconnect the negative battery cable when working on or near the electrical, clutch, or starter systems and before disconnecting any wires. On most batteries, the negative terminal will be marked with a minus (–) sign and the positive terminal with a plus (+) sign. If it becomes necessary to remove a battery, be careful not to spill battery electrolyte. Always protect your eyes, skin, and clothing. If electrolyte gets into your eyes, flush your eyes thoroughly with clean water and get prompt medical attention.

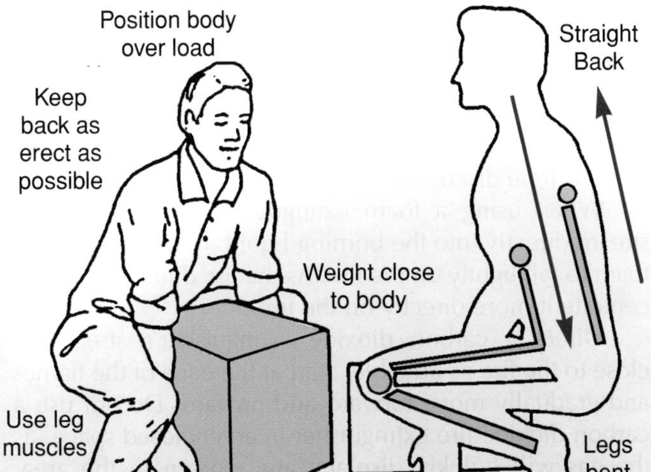

Figure 2-3. Use proper form when picking up any weight, no matter how light it may seem. Get help when lifting heavy or bulky items.

Vehicle Safety Rules

When moving a motorcycle about the shop, do so with great care. Do not operate the vehicle; push it about the shop. Operate it under power only when necessary. When moving the bike, do not sit in the seat. Stand on one side and move the bike while holding the handlebars with both hands. If the motorcycle is to be parked on its sidestand, check the stand to make sure it is secure and not damaged.

When working on any motorcycle, check all equipment for proper operation. Make sure the brakes, forks, wheels, handlebars, seats, and other accessories are in good shape and working properly. This check is for your safety as well as the safety of the rider. Inform the bike's owner of any problems you find.

Whenever you are working on a motorcycle, make sure that it is securely mounted in the stand, lift, or supported by its sidestand. If a motorcycle, ATV, or scooter begins to fall, do not attempt to catch the bike. Get out of the way and allow it to drop.

When you are test riding a bike, follow the rules of the road (if you are on the road) and wear all protective equipment as needed or required by law. Obey the local speed limits and do not ride recklessly.

Fire Prevention

Gasoline, oil, and other chemicals present in most motorcycle shops are highly flammable. Care must be taken when handling or storing fuel and other combustibles such as cleaning fluids and paints. The following three conditions must be present at the same place and time in order for combustion to occur:

- Oxygen must be present.
- There must be a supply of burnable material, or fuel, available.
- Temperature must be above the fuel's flash point.

There are three basic types of fires that can occur in the typical motorcycle shop. Each has its own characteristics and subsequently, a different type of extinguishing medium must be used for each. Most shops now have multipurpose ABC dry chemical ***fire extinguishers*** that are capable of fighting all three types of fires.

- ***Class A***—A fire where the combustible material consists of paper, wood, cloth, or trash. Extinguishing this type of fire involves using lots of water, a solution containing a high percentage of water and/or foam, or a multipurpose dry chemical extinguisher.
- ***Class B***—The combustible material is a liquid such as gasoline, oil, grease, or solvents. This is the most common type of fire that can occur in the shop. Extinguish this fire with smothering from either foam, carbon dioxide, or dry chemical. Using water on this type of fire will only cause it to spread.
- ***Class C***—In this case, the burning material consists of live electrical equipment—motors, switches, generators, or wiring. To extinguish this type of fire, use a nonconductive smothering agent such as carbon dioxide or dry chemical. Do not use foam or water as they are both electrically conductive.

General Fire Safety Rules

Become familiar with the location and operation of all fire fighting equipment in the shop area. Make sure that any fire extinguisher that has been used is recharged immediately, **Figure 2-4.** Here are some fire safety rules that should be followed in any motorcycle shop.

- Never create flames or sparks near fuel or any other flammable liquid.
- Store volatile liquids in properly labeled containers and keep them stored safely in an isolated area.
- Keep batteries away from sparks or flame to avoid possible explosions.

Figure 2-4. Various types of fire extinguishers may be found in the motorcycle shop. The most common extinguishers are Class B and multipurpose. (Photo courtesy of Lab Safety Supply, Inc. Janesville, WI)

An important fact to remember is that you can only hope to contain a small fire at best with a fire extinguisher. If the fire extinguisher cannot contain the fire after a short period of time, the fire begins to spread, or creates great quantities of smoke, get out of the shop immediately and call the fire department.

Using a Fire Extinguisher

Here are some suggestions for the proper use and handling of different types of fire extinguishers. More extensive on-site training can be scheduled by contacting your local fire department. Since most shops have foam, carbon dioxide, or dry chemical fire extinguishers, only these will be discussed.

When using a foam extinguisher, do not aim the stream directly into the burning liquid. Instead, allow the foam to fall lightly on the fire. As the fire diminishes, concentrate it more directly on the fire.

Direct a carbon dioxide extinguisher's stream as close to the fire as possible. Start at the edge of the flames and gradually move forward and upward. Do not use a carbon dioxide fire extinguisher in an enclosed space, as the gas will quickly displace any oxygen in the area, possibly causing asphyxiation.

The use of a dry chemical extinguisher depends on the type of fire. In most cases, direct the stream at the base of the flames. With a Class A fire, continue to direct the dry chemical stream at any remaining burning materials.

Environmental Protection

Oil, gasoline, solvents, and other chemicals must be handled and stored properly or they can cause damage to the environment. In the past, much damage was caused by the careless handling and disposal of these products. There are less obvious sources of pollution, such as scrap parts, paper and cardboard, plastics, and gases such as hydrocarbons from a poorly running engine. All can cause environmental damage.

Motorcycle shops are generators of waste materials. While they do not produce the waste of most automotive shops, preventing the careless disposal of wastes should be a priority in any shop. Remember, anyone can be a polluter.

A good policy to take to protect the environment is recover, repair, and recycle. Be sure to recover any hazardous materials, such as used oil and contaminated fuel. Repair any bike that is not operating at peak performance. A poor running engine wastes fuel, increases wear, and increases exhaust pollutants. Recycle all used chemicals and parts that can be rebuilt or have value as scrap.

Hazardous Materials

Hazardous materials and wastes of most concern to the motorcycle technician are organic solvents, flammable, corrosive, and/or toxic materials, and wastes that contain heavy metals, including lead. Some common materials include:

- Used engine oil.
- Contaminated fuel.
- Antifreeze.
- Used gear oil
- Solvents.
- Coolants used in grinders and cutters.

The areas of most concern to the motorcycle technician will be used chemicals and any cleaning solutions, **Figure 2-5.** Most shops generate a large quantity of used oil, fuel, and antifreeze, which must be stored properly for pickup. Cabinets and dip tanks that use caustic chemicals produce high alkaline solutions and contain heavy metals. Small parts washers generally use solvents that are classified as hazardous materials. Testing for hazardous wastes can be done by any qualified laboratory that performs tests on drinking water.

It should be noted that no material is considered hazardous waste until the shop is finished using it and is ready for disposal. When the shop is ready to dispose of hazardous waste, it must be handled accordingly. For instance, a caustic cleaning solution with a heavy concentration of lead is not considered hazardous waste until it is ready to be replaced.

Right-to-Know Laws

Every employee of a motorcycle shop is protected by ***right-to-know laws.*** Right-to-know laws were first outlined in 1983 in the Occupational Safety and Health Administration (OSHA) Hazard Communication Standard. This publication was originally created for chemical companies and manufacturers who require their employees to handle potentially hazardous materials in the workplace.

The law is intended to ensure that employees are provided with a safe working place in regard to hazardous materials. There are three major areas of employer responsibility:

- *Employee Training and Education.* Under this legislation, all employees must know about their rights, as well as the type of hazardous chemicals in their workplace, the labeling of these chemicals, and the information about each chemical as posted on ***Material Safety Data Sheets (MSDS).*** MSDS sheets give product composition and precautionary information for any product that could present a health or safety hazard, and are prepared by the material's supplier. It is important that all employees understand the proper use, major characteristics, protective equipment needed, and accident or spill procedures associated with all major chemical groups. New employees should receive this training as part of their orientation, and they should be updated annually.
- *Labels and/or Information about Potentially Hazardous Chemicals.* All hazardous materials should be properly labeled to show what health, fire, or reactivity hazard they may have and to indicate what type of protective equipment to use when handling each chemical. The material's manufacturer must also provide all warnings and precautionary information for the user to read before application.
- *Record Keeping.* A company must keep records of the hazardous materials in the work area, proof of training programs, and records of accidents and/or spill incidents. The company must also keep a list of employee requests for Material Safety Data Sheets, as well as a Right-to-Know procedure manual containing company policies.

Note: When handling any hazardous material, be sure to wear the safety equipment listed in the MSDS and follow all recommended procedures correctly.

Handling Hazardous Waste

There are equipment and services available to help motorcycle shops cope with hazardous waste disposal. There are now parts cleaners that use non-evaporative, recyclable cleaning solvent. There are also machines that will now recycle antifreeze (and other material considered hazardous), as well as companies that pick up used

Hazardous Material Reference Chart

	Hazard Statement	Special Content Information	Handling Instructions Special Equipment: Safety Eyewear	Handling Instructions Special Equipment: Respiratory	Handling Instructions Special Equipment: Skin	Exposure Symptoms
Degreasers & Corrosives	Flammable / Extremely Flammable	Includes: Caustics Carb Cleaner Battery Acid	**Required**	Recommended	Gloves & Impervious Clothing Recommended	• Headache • Dizziness • Confusion • Unconsciousness • Staggering
Lubricating Fluids	Low Flammability	Includes: Engine Oil Trans Oil HD Grease	Recommended		Gloves Recommended to Prevent Contact	• Skin Irritation
Hydraulic/ Cooling Fluids	Low Flammability	Includes: Brake ATF Antifreeze	Recommended		Gloves Recommended to Prevent Contact	• Skin Irritation
Solvents/ Removers/ Cleaners	Flammable / Extremely Flammable		**Required**	Recommended	Gloves & Impervious Clothing Recommended	• Headache • Dizziness • Confusion • Unconsciousness • Staggering
Compressed Gases	Flammable	Includes: Acetylene Oxygen	**Required**		Gloves & Special Clothing Recommended	• Headache • Dizziness • Confusion • Unconsciousness • Staggering
Adhesives/ Epoxies	Flammable		Recommended	Recommended	Gloves **Required**	• Headache • Dizziness • Confusion • Unconsciousness • **Respiratory Irritation** • Staggering
Fuels	Extremely Flammable	Includes: Gasolines	**Required**	Recommended	Gloves Recommended to Prevent Contact	• Headache • Dizziness • Confusion • Unconsciousness • Staggering
Paint Products	Flammable / Extremely Flammable	Enamels May Contain **Lead**	Recommended	Recommended	Gloves Recommended to Prevent Contact	• Dizziness • Confusion • Unconsciousness • Staggering

Figure 2-5. Chart listing various hazardous materials common to most motorcycle shops.

Hazardous Material Reference Chart

First Aid Procedures							
Eye Contact	**Skin Contact**	**Inhalation**	**Swallowing**	**Spill Clean-Up**	**Fire Fighting Procedures**	**Storage & Transfer of Liquids**	**Disposal**
Flush with Water for 15 Minutes Consult a Doctor if Irritation Continues	Wash with Water If Severe—See a Doctor			For Flammables:	Extinguisher: Class "B" Foam— Carbon Dioxide—	Transfer & Mixing: Small Amounts Only	Consult Your Shop Manager for Instructions
	Wash Affected Area with Clean Water & Soap			Remove Ignition Sources	Chemical Powder—	Always Use Static Lines	
	Wash Affected Area with Clean Water & Soap	Move to Fresh Air	**Do Not** Induce Vomiting	Avoid Breathing Fumes	Wear Full Protective Equipment Including Air Supplied Respirator		Follow Local, State, & Federal Regulations
	Wash with Water If Severe—See a Doctor	Restore Breathing		Use: Inert Absorbent Non-Sparking Tools to Remove		Storage: Store All Flammables Below 120°F in Building and/or Metal Cabinet Designed for Flammables	**Do Not** Incinerate in Closed Containers
		Keep Warm & Quiet	Consult a Doctor Immediately		Fog Nozzles Recommended (If Water Is Used)		
	Wash Affected Area with Clean Water	Consult a Doctor					
	Wash Affected Area with Clean Water & Soap						
	Wash Affected Area with Clean Water & Soap						

oil and recycle it. Some space heaters are designed to burn used engine oil. There are recycling companies that will pick up the hazardous material at a shop and dispose of it in accordance with environmental regulations. It is important that any recycling equipment or recycling company is EPA approved.

Note: These shop safety rules are only a guideline. You must constantly think about safety to maintain a good safety record in your shop. Other safety precautions are given throughout this book when a procedure calls for it.

Summary

Most manufacturer's engine service manuals contain safety symbols that signal a need for the use of caution or safety. Always pay attention to these symbols. Always wear safety glasses, goggles, or a safety face shield whenever the job requires it. Long hair should be tied up or kept under a hat to ensure it does not become caught. Avoid wearing loose clothing, ties, or jewelry that can become caught in moving machinery. Proper footwear such as steel-toed work shoes or boots are recommended, as they can protect against flying sparks, heavy falling objects, and even battery acid.

Always use any extra safety devices or protective equipment provided for special jobs such as welding or grinding. Report all accidents right away so proper first aid or medical assistance can be given. Always be aware of and follow machine safety rules. Lift heavy objects by bending at the knees in order not to strain the back muscles.

When lifting an engine from a vehicle, be sure that the lift or crane has the capability to do the job. Push bikes in and out of the shop, only ride a bike when necessary. Clean up any spilled oil, grease, or other fluids from the floor area. Store any oily rags in self-closing metal safety containers.

There are three types of fires that can occur in the motorcycle shop. Use the right type of fire extinguisher for the fire. Motorcycle shops generate large quantities of hazardous waste. This waste must be dealt with in accordance with environmental regulations. There are many companies that will pick up the hazardous material and recycle or dispose of it properly.

Know These Terms

Warning
Cautions
Note
Fire extinguishers
Class A
Class B
Class C
Right-to-Know laws
Material Safety Data Sheets (MSDS)

Review Questions—Chapter 2

Do not write in this text. Place your answers on a separate sheet of paper.

1. Which of the following is *not* acceptable shop attire?
   A. Steel toe shoes.
   B. Long pants.
   C. Rings.
   D. Short sleeve uniform shirt.
2. It is *not* dangerous to wear ______ when working in the shop.
   A. steel toe boots
   B. watches
   C. bracelets
   D. cut-off shorts
3. *True or False?* Gasoline is acceptable as a parts cleaning solvent.
4. Soiled rags should be ______.
   A. piled in a corner
   B. stored in a lid-sealed metal container
   C. stored in a plastic bucket
   D. burned
5. *True or False?* Oil absorbent can be used to clean a gasoline spill.
6. Name the three conditions that must be present for a fire to take place.
7. List the three fire extinguishers found in most shops.
8. Which of the following materials is *not* a hazardous waste?
   A. Used gear oil.
   B. Contaminated fuel.
   C. Solvents.
   D. Distilled water.
9. Every employee of a motorcycle shop is protected by ________ when handling dangerous chemicals.
   A. Right-to-Know laws
   B. Record keeping
   C. OSHA
   D. hazardous waste disposal
10. Every chemical in the shop must have a(n) ________.

Suggested Activities

1. Tour the shop and note the location of all safety equipment, including fire extinguishers, first aid kits, eye wash stations, fire alarms, and emergency exits.
2. Research all available materials and use this information to begin a safety notebook.
3. Contact your local fire department for information on scheduling training on the use of fire extinguishers.

3

Tools, Measuring Instruments, and Shop Equipment

After studying this chapter, you will be able to:

- Identify the most common hand tools and equipment used by a motorcycle technician.
- List the safety rules for hand tools and equipment.
- Select the correct tool for the job.
- Describe the advantages and disadvantages of various tools.
- Compare conventional and metric measuring systems.
- Identify common measuring tools.
- Select the appropriate measuring tool for the job.
- Use precision measuring tools.
- Properly maintain precision measuring tools.
- List the most common motorcycle parts cleaning techniques.
- Compare the advantages and disadvantages of different cleaning methods.
- Select the correct cleaning method for the job.
- Describe safety rules that apply to various cleaning techniques.
- List safety rules for machining, cutting, drilling, welding, and other special operations.

As a motorcycle technician, you must be familiar with the tools of the trade. Many jobs involve checking sizes, clearances, and alignments. A careless or inaccurate measurement can be costly in terms of money, customer relations, and technician reputation. To properly maintain and repair motorcycles, ATVs, and scooters, an investment must be made in reliable tools. This chapter will help you become familiar with the proper use and selection of tools and equipment. It will prepare you for the chapters covering the repair of specific motorcycle systems and components.

Tools and Equipment

In most cases, you should invest in good quality tools that are backed by a lifetime warranty. Then, if a tool is broken or damaged, the manufacturer's warranty will replace the tool at no cost. There are many different brands of tools available for varying quality and cost. It is not economical to invest in inferior tools. While you may save some money initially, an inferior tool is more likely to break sooner than a quality tool. When an inferior tool breaks, you will have to buy a new tool versus trading it for a replacement. The tools and equipment needed for the maintenance, service, and repair of motorcycles can be divided into these categories:

- Common hand tools.
- Electrical testing and service tools.
- Measuring tools.
- Engine service and repair tools.
- Special service tools.
- Fuel system service tools.
- Wheel, suspension, and frame service tools.
- Cleaning tools.

- Power hand tools.
- General shop equipment.
- Machining equipment.

Tool Boxes

When beginning to assemble your tool collection, one of the first purchases should be a good ***tool box.*** A tool box stores and protects your tools when not in use. Major tool manufacturers offer tool sets ranging from starter sets to master technician sets, **Figure 3-1.** There are three main parts to a typical tool box. These include:

- Large roll-around cabinet.
- Upper tool box that sits on the roll-around cabinet.
- Small carrying or tote tray, usually placed in the upper box.

The lower ***roll-around cabinet*** holds the bulky, heavy tools. Large power tools are normally kept in this part of the box. Extra storage compartments can be hung from the sides of the roll-around cabinet.

The ***upper chest*** is normally filled with commonly used tools. Being near eye level, tools can be easily seen and reached without bending. This saves time and increases production. The small ***carrying tray*** is for holding commonly used tools. For example, if you frequently perform suspension repairs, all wheel, suspension, and frame service tools can be kept in the tray.

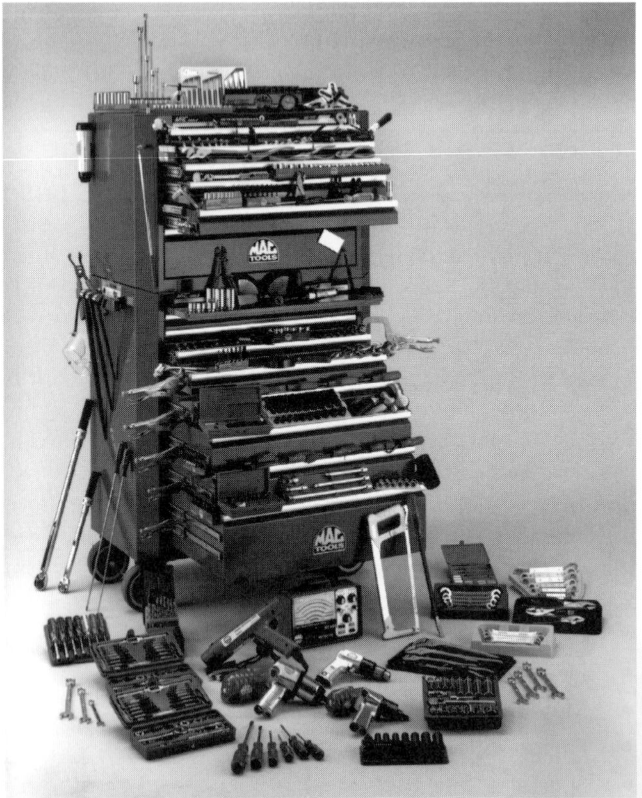

Figure 3-1. A technician's starter set contains a variety of wrenches, sockets, screwdrivers, and miscellaneous hand tools. (Mac Tools)

In tool box organization, related tools are normally kept in the same tool box drawer. Various types of hammers may be stored in one drawer, screwdrivers in another. Small or delicate tools should not be kept with large heavy tools as they could be damaged.

Tool holders (small clip racks, cloth or plastic pouches, or socket trays) help organize small tools. They are often used to protect tools and to keep them organized by size. Holders allow a full set of tools to be taken to the job. Tool box organization tells a lot about your attitude toward work. A sloppy technician usually does sloppy work.

When choosing a tool box, do not buy one that simply holds the tools you currently own. Purchase a box that is large enough to accommodate some growth in your tool inventory. However, do not purchase a box that is too large. Often, tool dealers may take old tool boxes in exchange toward the purchase of a larger box, so it does not pay to buy an extremely large tool box until you need the storage space.

Hand Tools

Common ***hand tools*** are used everyday by the motorcycle technician. Some of the tools normally found in these sets are wrenches, ratchets, sockets, pliers, screwdrivers, and hammers.

Many times, different tools can be used to accomplish the same task. It is important for you to know when to select one tool over another. As each tool is discussed, pay close attention to the advantages and disadvantages.

Caution: Tools, fasteners, and motorcycle, ATV, and scooter parts are classified as either United States Customary (USC) or metric (SI). Metric tools and fasteners are not interchangeable with those designated for United States Customary use. Using incorrect tools and fasteners may cause severe damage to components.

Wrenches

Various types of wrenches are utilized by motorcycle technicians. Wrenches may be broken down into five categories: box-end wrenches, open-end wrenches, combination wrenches, flare-nut wrenches, and adjustable wrenches, **Figure 3-2.** ***Box-end wrenches*** are closed on both ends. ***Open-end wrenches*** have a full opening at both ends. ***Combination wrenches*** are open on one end and have a box-end or flare-nut on the other.

Box-end, open-end, and combination wrenches are usually available with various offsets and head angles. Metric and U.S. customary sizes are necessary. On standard fasteners, use a box-end wrench whenever possible. It gives better support and reduces the possibility of fastener damage.

Flared tubing nuts (nuts on fuel lines and brake lines) require the use of a ***flare-nut wrench.*** This type of wrench is similar to a box-end wrench, but has a slot in the end. The slot allows it to be slipped over tubing and onto the flare nut, **Figure 3-2.**

An ***adjustable end wrench*** is an open-end wrench that has one movable jaw to accommodate a range of sizes. This wrench is useful in applications where the proper wrench is not available. In motorcycle repair, an adjustable wrench is a fill-in tool and is the least desirable of all wrenches. Its movable jaw provides the least amount of support and can easily slip and round off the head of a fastener.

Always use the proper size wrench. When loosening or tightening fasteners, always pull rather than push the wrench. When a wrench is pulled rather than pushed, you are less likely to be injured if the wrench slips. Whenever possible, use a box-end rather than an open-end wrench. A box-end grips the fastener head on all sides. Never hammer on wrenches to increase loosening or tightening torque. Always replace a damaged wrench immediately. Do not use a pipe or another wrench as an extension to increase leverage or use shims on a wrench as damage to the tool and fastener may result.

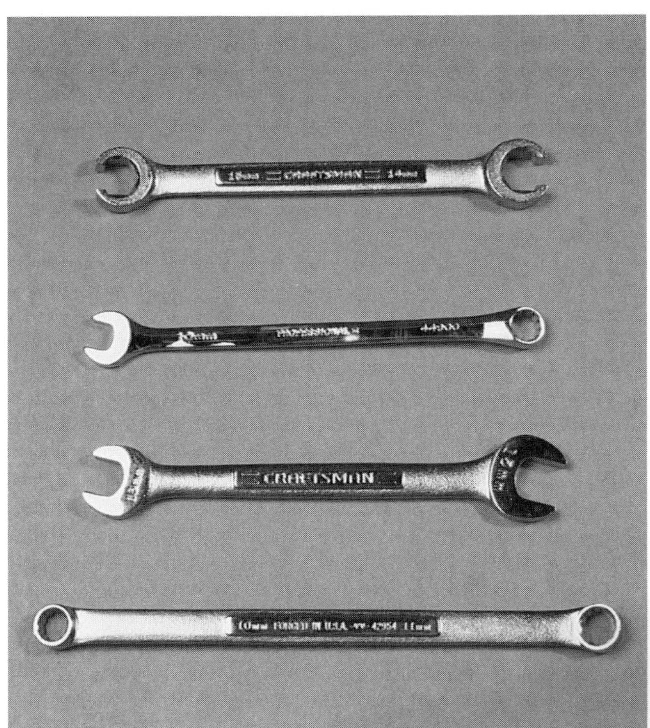

Figure 3-2. Note the differences between flare-nut, combination, open-end, and box-end wrenches. Flare-nut wrenches are used on brake lines and other tube fittings.

Screwdrivers

Two categories of screwdrivers are commonly used for motorcycle repair: ***straight tip*** and ***Phillips tip*** (cross point), **Figure 3-3.** Many different sizes are available for both straight and Phillips screwdrivers. To prevent damage to the head of the fastener, the correct screwdriver tip size must be used. Proper and improper examples are given in **Figure 3-4.** The most common Phillips bit sizes used on motorcycles are numbers 2 and 3.

Phillips head screws can sometimes be very difficult to loosen. An ***impact driver,*** **Figure 3-5,** provides the high torque and inward bit pressure sometimes needed to loosen Phillips and other fasteners without damage.

Warning: Always wear eye protection when using an impact driver. Bits of fastener can fly into your face.

To prevent injury and screwhead or screwdriver damage, you should:

- Always use the proper size screwdriver for the application.
- Avoid using screwdrivers as pry bars or chisels.
- Never use a screwdriver so that the screwdriver tip could stab you if it slipped.
- Do not hammer on screwdrivers.
- Never use screwdrivers with worn tips. Damage to the fastener or injury may result.

Sockets and Socket Drivers

Sockets and socket drivers provide a fast, versatile means of loosening and tightening fasteners. A ***socket*** resembles a box-end wrench that has a square opening designed to fit on a handle. The socket fits over the fastener head with the other end of the socket fitting onto the driver

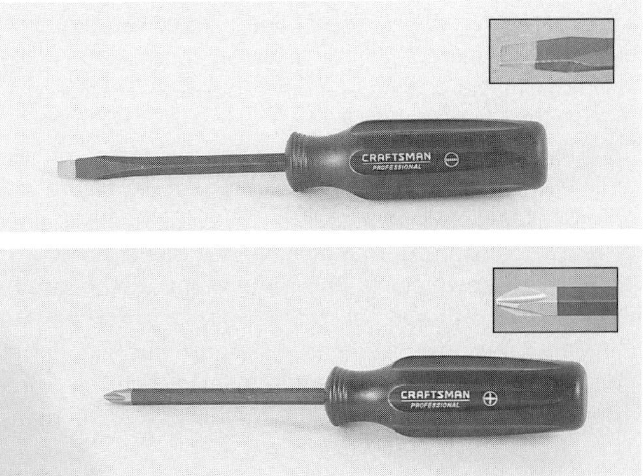

Figure 3-3. Two general types of screwdrivers. A—Straight tip. B—Phillips tip.

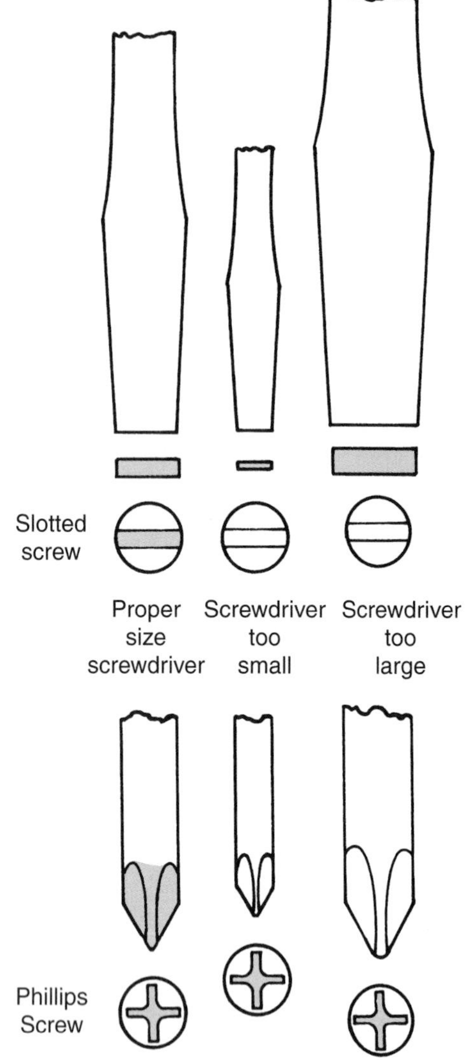

Figure 3-4. Use the correct size screwdriver to avoid damage to fastener or screwdriver.

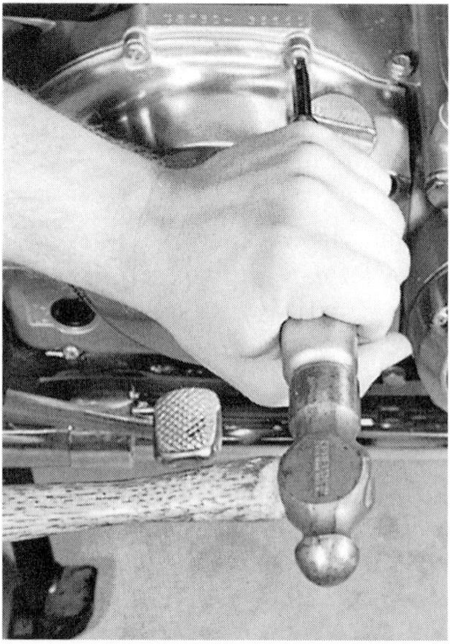

Figure 3-5. An impact driver provides necessary inward pressure and torque to loosen stubborn fasteners without damaging them. When driver is hit with a hammer, driver rotates with tremendous force.

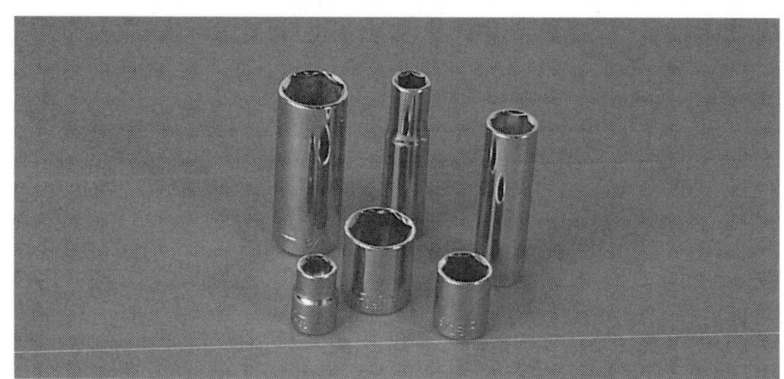

Figure 3-6. Typical sockets used in motorcycle repair.

handle. There are four common variations of sockets: standard sockets, deep sockets, 6-point sockets, and 12-point sockets. Sockets are available in metric and USC sizes.

A ***standard socket*** is short and is the most frequently used socket. **Figure 3-6** shows examples of sockets. A ***deep socket*** is longer than a standard socket. It is needed to reach over a long stud bolt.

The terms ***6-point*** and ***12-point*** refer to the number of fastener driving edges or corners in the socket, **Figure 3-7.** A 6-point socket is preferable to a 12-point socket since there is less chance of rounding off the fastener head.

Drive size refers to the dimensions of the square driving head on a ratchet, breaker bar, or speed handle. Different drive sizes are needed because of space limitations and varying torque requirements. There are three drive sizes commonly used by motorcycle technicians: 1/4″, 3/8″, and 1/2″ drive.

A 3/8″ drive is the most frequently used size. A 1/4″ drive is used for very small fasteners. A 1/2″ drive is strong enough to handle larger jobs that require high turning force.

Figure 3-7. Motorcycles use fasteners that must be removed with 6- and 12-point sockets. Damage is less likely to a fastener head when a 6-point socket is used because it contacts more area on flats of fasteners.

Socket Drives

Socket drivers include ratchets, breaker bars, and speed handles. A ***ratchet*** is the most commonly used type of socket driver. A ratchet allows quick selection of turning direction for either loosening or tightening, **Figure 3-8.**

A breaker bar resembles a ratchet, except that it does not use a ratchet mechanism, **Figure 3-8.** ***Breaker bars*** are

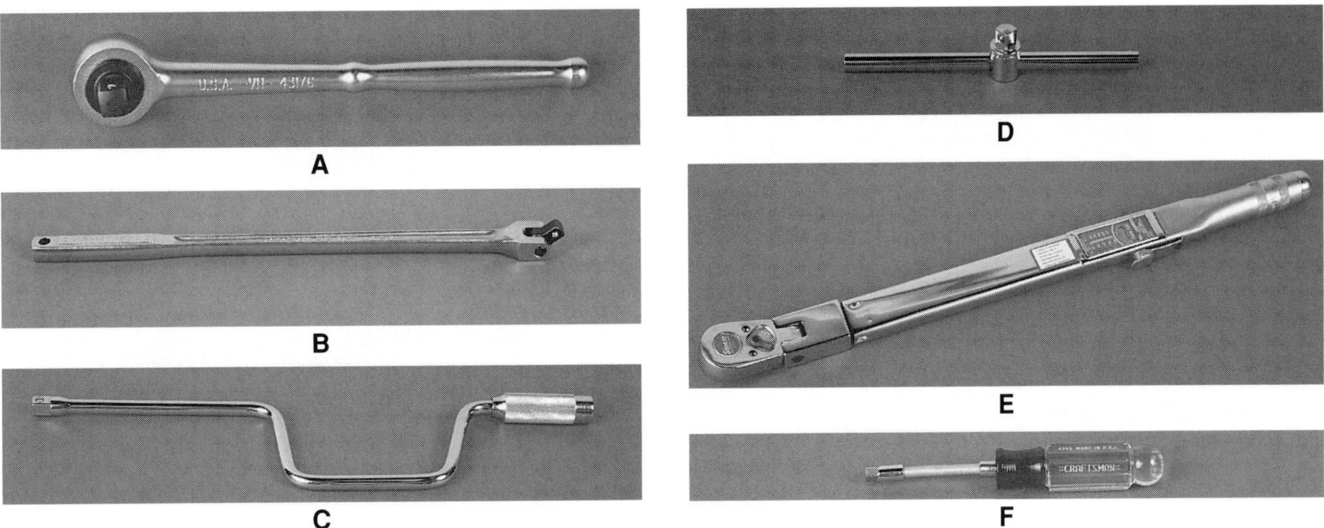

Figure 3-8. Various types of socket drivers. A—Ratchet. B—Breaker bar. C—Speed handle. D—T-handle. E—Torque wrench. F—Hand driver.

designed to break loose extremely tight fasteners which may overload and damage a ratchet. A ***speed handle*** is used for rapid turning of loose fasteners, **Figure 3-8.** It is not designed to apply final tightening or initial loosening torque. ***Torque wrenches*** allow you to tighten fasteners to a specific torque in order to meet manufacturer's specifications. A ***T-handle*** is used when space for a ratchet is limited while the ***hand driver*** is used for low torque applications.

Universals and Extensions

Universals and extensions increase the driving capabilities of sockets and handles. A ***universal,*** also called a *swivel joint,* allows the ratchet to drive the socket at an angle. An ***extension*** increases the distance between the ratchet and the socket, **Figures 3-9** and **3-10.** Both are needed to drive fasteners in hard-to-reach locations. Universals and extensions are available in several drive sizes and designs to meet varying demands.

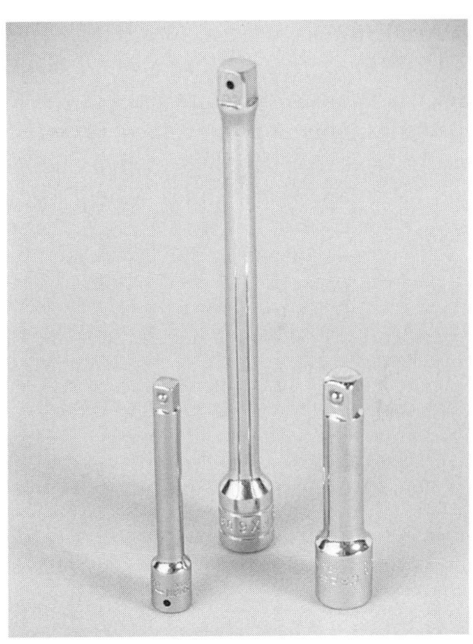

Figure 3-9. Extensions are available in lengths from one inch to over one foot.

Proper Use of Sockets and Socket Drivers

There are several rules to remember when working with sockets and socket drivers. These include using the proper size socket and ratchet or breaker bar for the application. When loosening or tightening fasteners with a ratchet or breaker bar, always pull rather than push on the tool. When space permits, use a socket rather than an open-end wrench. Keep the ratchet as close as possible to the socket. Use extensions and deep sockets only when necessary.

When using extensions, support the ratchet or breaker bar head to prevent applying side load pressure on the socket and fastener. Never hammer on ratchets or breaker bars to increase loosening or tightening torque. Never use a pipe as an extension to improve leverage on a ratchet or breaker bar. Do not use hand sockets with air impact tools. Always replace damaged sockets, ratchets, and breaker bars.

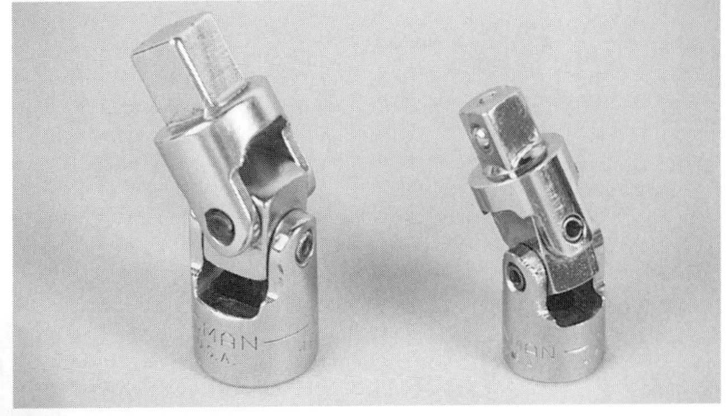

Figure 3-10. A universal joint is helpful when trying to reach partially hidden fasteners.

Pliers

Pliers fall into an often misused tool category. Pliers should never be used as a substitute for the proper wrench, socket, or screwdriver. Pliers should only be used for gripping or holding. If pliers are used to grasp the head of a bolt, for example, the bolt head can be rounded off or damaged.

Common types of pliers, **Figure 3-11,** for motorcycle repair are:

- Standard or slip joint pliers.
- Adjustable pliers or channel locks.
- Locking pliers or vise grips.
- Side cutters or diagonals.
- Needle nose pliers.
- Snap ring pliers.
- Metal cutters or snips.

Allen Wrenches

Allen wrenches are used to loosen and tighten hex socket head screws. This is illustrated in **Figure 3-12.** Allen wrenches come in metric and USC sizes. They are also available as Allen sockets. ***Allen sockets*** fit on a ratchet or breaker bar for high torque applications. Remember to follow these rules when using Allen wrenches:

- Always select the correct size Allen wrench for the job.
- Always replace worn Allen wrenches.
- Never use an air impact wrench on Allen sockets.

Hammers

Several different types of ***hammers*** are used by the motorcycle technician. The major difference in hammers is the size and the material used to make the head. Hammer types commonly found in a motorcycle shop are the ball peen, brass, plastic, dead blow, rawhide, and rubber hammer. These types of hammers are shown in **Figure 3-13.**

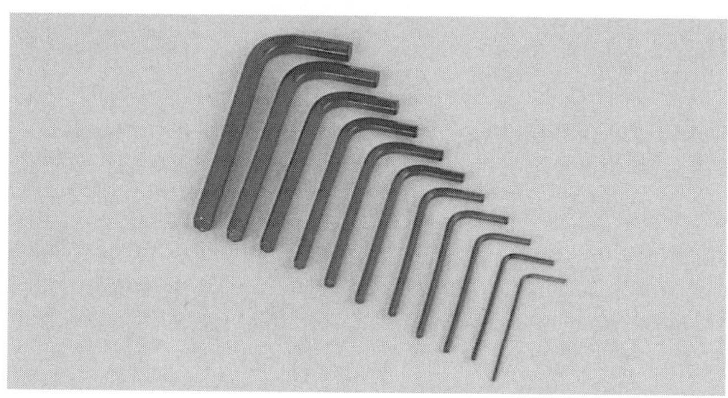

Figure 3-12. Allen wrenches (keys) and Allen sockets are needed to remove some fasteners.

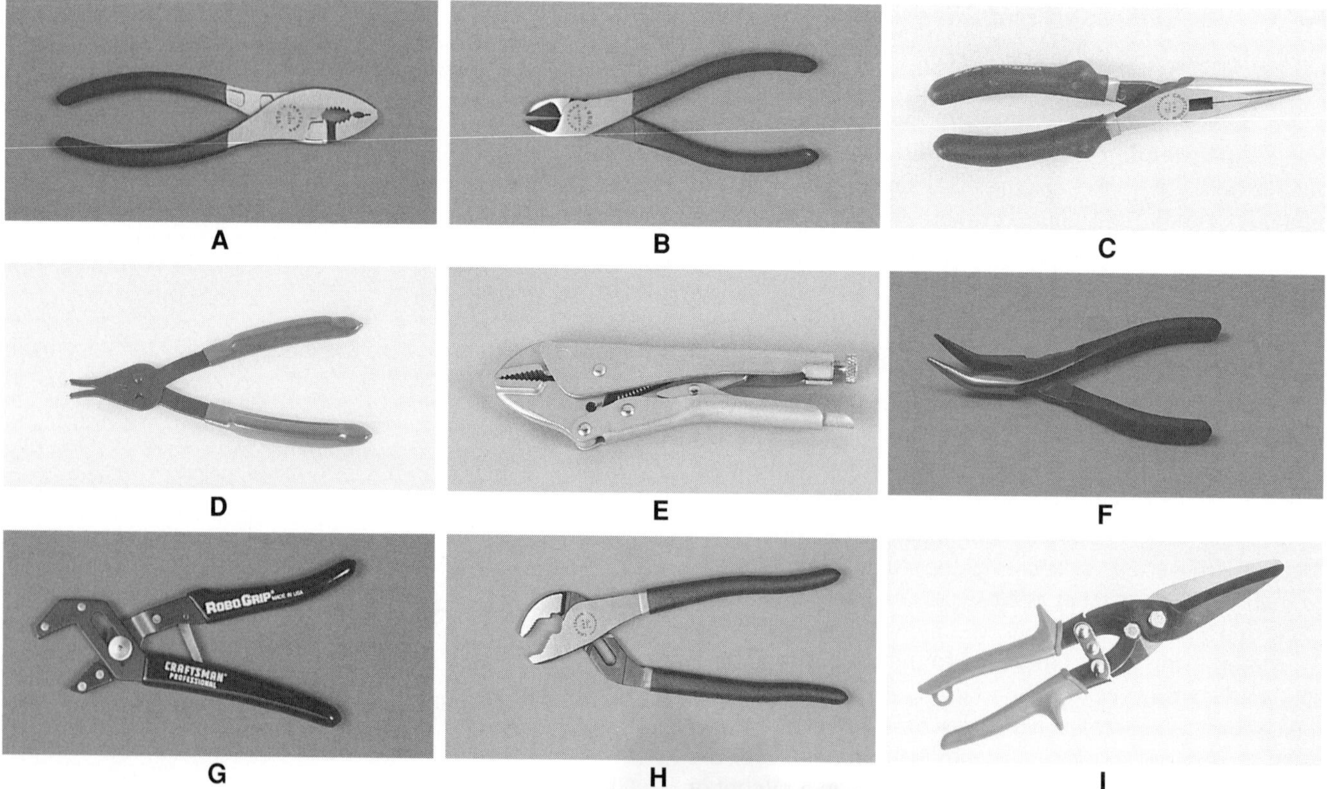

Figure 3-11. Pliers are used to grip, hold, or pull on non-threaded components such as: removing cotter pins, pulling out chain master-link clips, or when pulling wire. A—Slip joint pliers. B—Diagonal, side cutting pliers. C—Needle nose. D—Snap ring pliers. E—Vise grip pliers. F—Bent needle nose pliers. G—Spring-loaded rib joint pliers. H—Rib joint pliers. I—Metal snips.

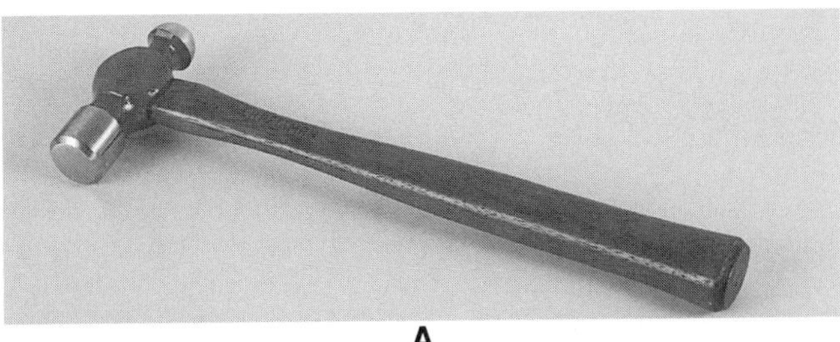

A

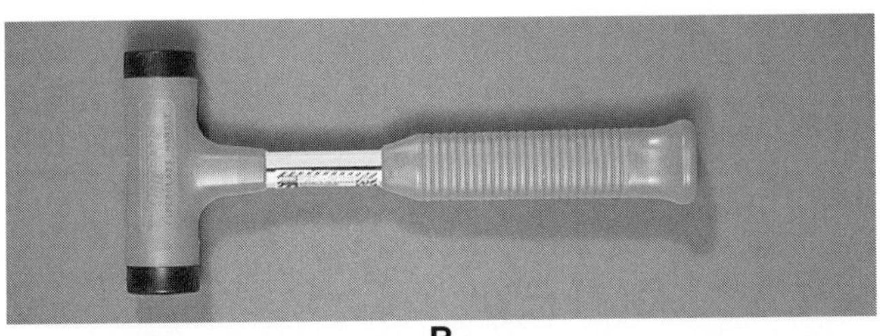

B

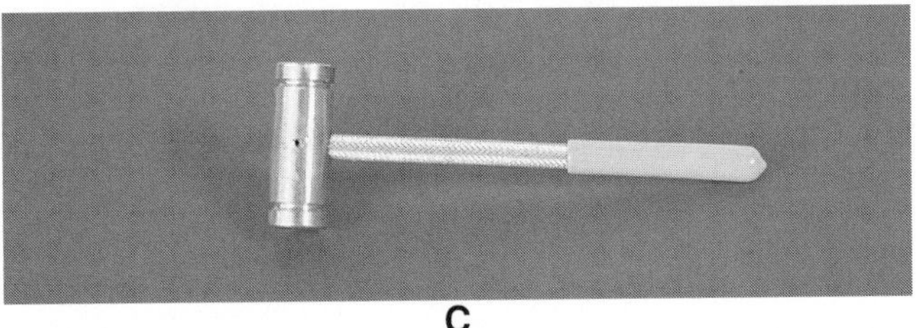

C

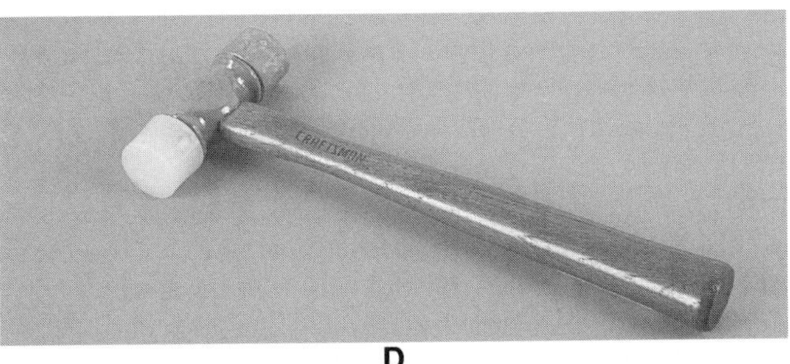

D

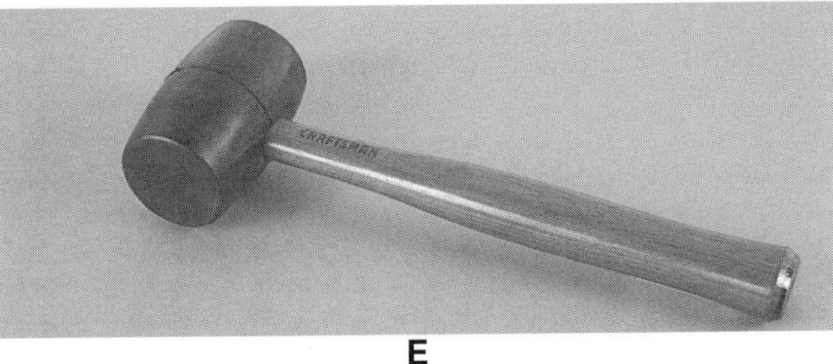

E

Figure 3-13. Various hammers are needed for striking tasks on motorcycles. A—Ball peen hammer. B—Dead blow hammer. C—Brass hammer. D—Plastic hammer. E—Rubber mallet.

Hammer heads are made of soft and hard materials. The heads are available in different weights for specific applications. A hammer head should be softer than the material (part) being struck. For instance, a plastic hammer should be used to strike soft aluminum. Some common examples for utilizing each type of hammer are:

- Ball peen and dead blow hammers—general purpose hammering and striking.
- Brass hammer—used for light blows on metal parts that can be easily damaged.
- Plastic and rawhide hammers—tapping an axle into place or breaking case covers loose.
- Rubber hammer—assistance in assembling or disassembling easily dented parts.

Proper Hammer Use

To use a hammer safely without part or tool damage, you should never use a hammer handle as a pry bar. Never use a damaged hammer (cracked handle, loose head, etc.). Never use a hammer with an oily handle or when oil or grease is on your hands. Always wear safety glasses when hammering.

Files

Files are designed to remove small amounts of metal for smoothing or shaping parts, **Figure 3-14.** Files are classified as single cut, double cut, fine, and coarse. These are easily identified by the file tooth pattern. Files come in a variety of shapes and sizes. **Figure 3-15** shows various file cuts and shapes.

File teeth cut only on the forward stroke. Large file teeth are for soft materials. Small file teeth are for hard materials. A ***file card*** is used to clean the file, **Figure 3-16.** When filing, you should follow these rules to increase file life and working efficiency. Never use a file without a securely attached handle. Always cut away from yourself. Apply light pressure on the forward stroke; do not drag the file over the work on the backstroke. Always wear safety glasses when filing. Do not use worn files; replace them.

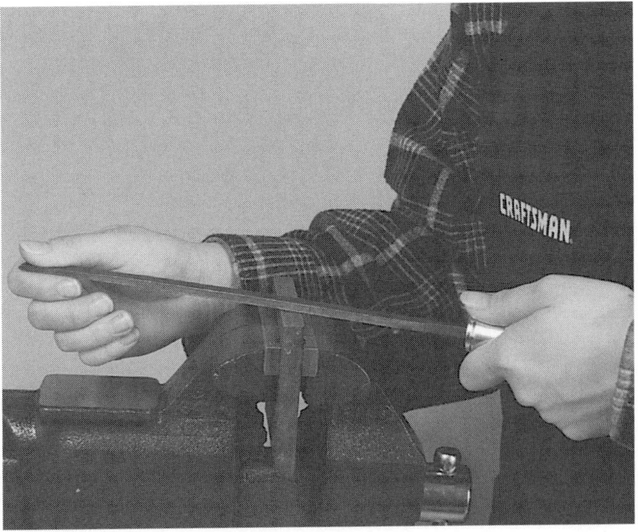

Figure 3-14. Grasp the file as shown. By pushing it across the workpiece, metal can be removed for smoothing or shaping. Files are designed to cut on the forward stroke only. Filing on the backstroke will dull the file quickly.

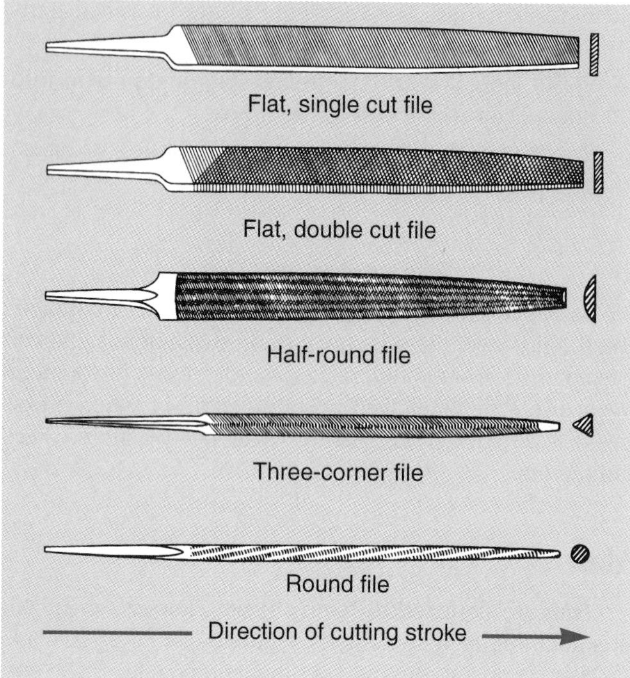

Figure 3-15. Study various file shapes and cuts. Also note the cutting direction. (L.S. Starrett)

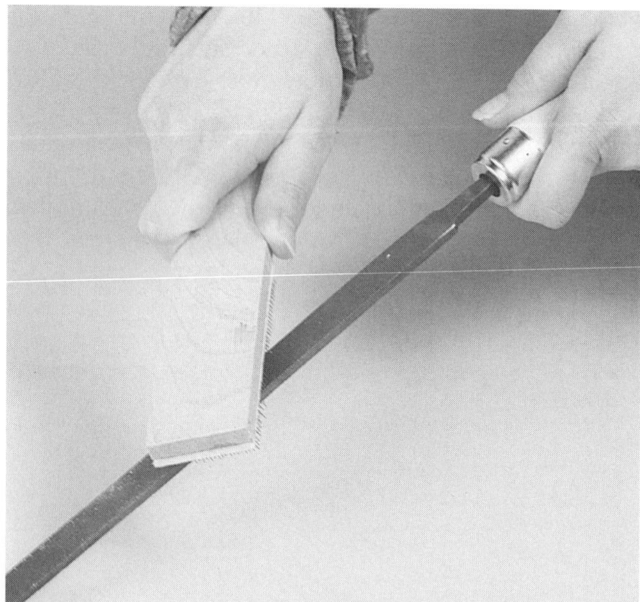

Figure 3-16. Rub a file card across the file to remove metal from clogged teeth.

Punches, Chisels, and Pry Bars

Some common punches and chisels are shown in **Figure 3-17.** A ***center punch*** is frequently used to mark parts for reassembly or for indenting parts before drilling. A ***drift punch*** is used to drive shafts and bolts out of parts. ***Alignment punches*** can be inserted in the holes of mating parts to align them before starting bolts. A ***chisel*** is sometimes used to cut damaged fasteners. ***Pry bars*** will exert high leverage for lifting or moving heavy or large parts.

Punches, chisels, and pry bars can be very dangerous if misused. To utilize these tools safely, never use punches or chisels with mushroomed ends. Repair the tool by grinding or filing a chamfer on the end. Always wear safety glasses when using punches, chisels, and pry bars. Hold punches, chisels, and pry bars in such a way that you will not injure yourself if the tool slips. Never use punches or chisels to loosen undamaged fasteners.

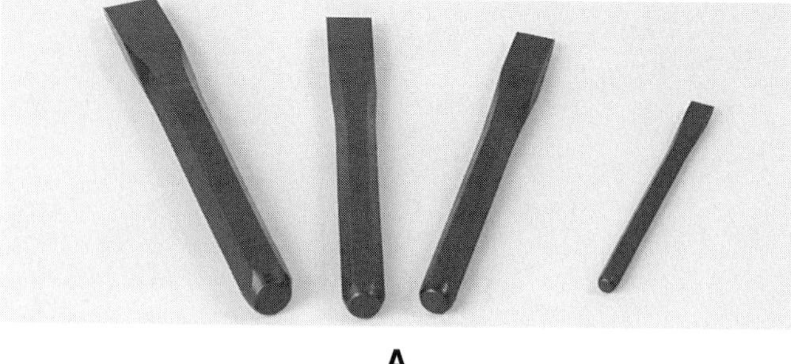

A

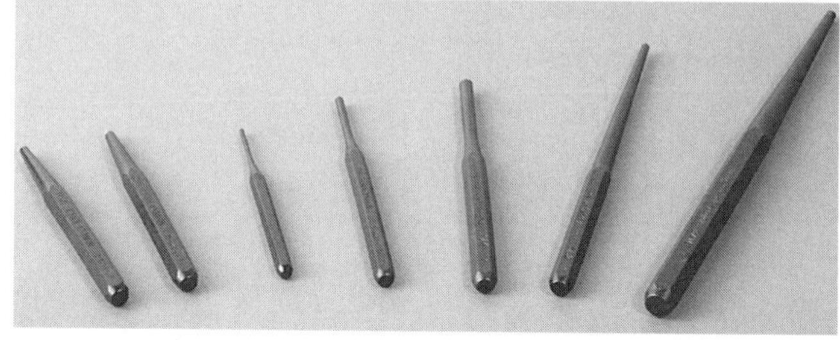

B

Figure 3-17. A—You should own a variety of chisels. B—Punches are available in a variety of shapes and lengths. Both chisels and punches are best purchased as a set.

Hacksaw

A ***hacksaw*** is used for cutting metal parts, **Figure 3-18.** Hacksaw blades are available in various pitches (number of teeth per inch). ***Coarse blades*** are for cutting soft metals such as aluminum. ***Fine blades*** are for cutting thin tubing or hard materials. Hacksaw teeth only cut in one direction. The teeth cut on the push stroke. Install the hacksaw blade in the frame with the teeth pointing from the handle.

To prolong hacksaw blade life and avoid injury, you should:

- Always cut away from yourself and only apply light pressure on the cutting stroke.
- Be sure the blade is tight.
- Never use a damaged blade (cracked, kinked, missing teeth).
- Always wear safety glasses when using a hacksaw.
- Use full strokes to get maximum life from the blade.
- Release downward pressure on the backstroke.

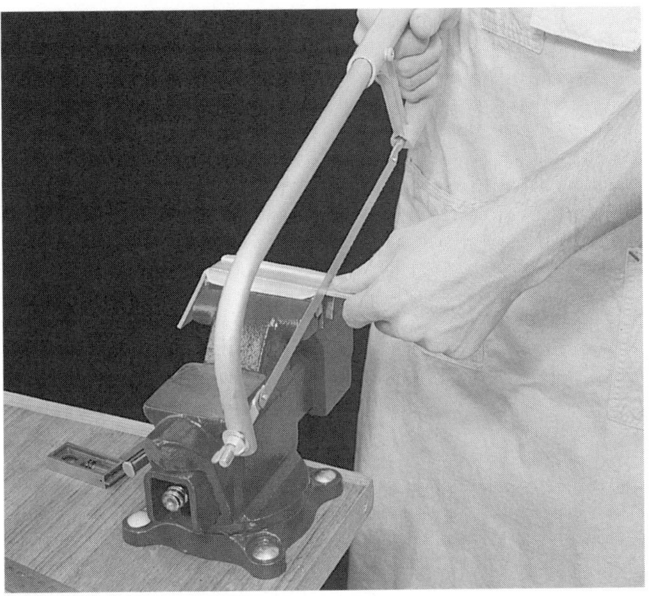

Figure 3-18. Hacksaws, like files, are designed to cut only on the forward stroke. Replacement blades are available with 12, 16, 18, 20, 24, and 32 teeth per inch.

Engine Service and Repair Tools

Engine service and repair tools include a variety of tools often used on several engine models. They are needed for motorcycle engine testing, tear down, and assembly. Some of these tools may be provided in factory service tool sets, **Figure 3-19.**

Special Service Tools

Special service tools are also provided in factory service tool sets, **Figure 3-20.** Some of these tools are designed to do one specific job on one specific type of motorcycle. In some cases, there is no other tool that will work. Other special service tools may be more universal in their use and application. Factory service manuals often refer to factory service tools by part number in their directions for disassembly, assembly, or service procedures.

Wheel, Suspension, and Frame Service Tools

Wheel, suspension, and frame tools are specialized tools frequently used by the motorcycle technician. See

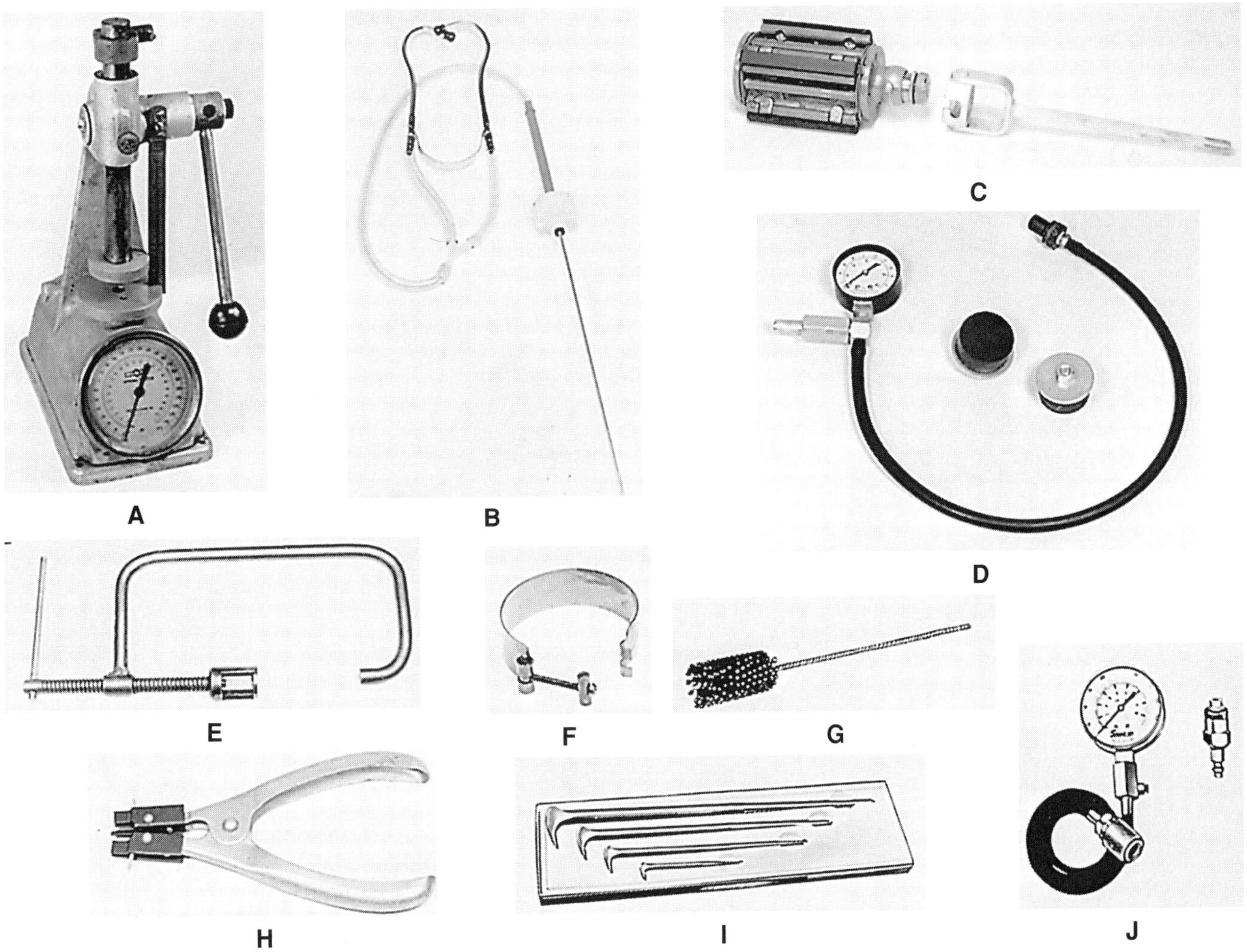

A B C D E F G H I J

Figure 3-19. Engine service and repair tools. A—Valve spring tester. B—Stethoscope. C—Cylinder hone. D—Crankcase leak tester. E—Valve spring compressor. F—Ring compressor. G—Cylinder deglazer. H—Ring expander. I—Pry bars. J—Compression tester.

Figure 3-21. They are usually not brand oriented, but are useful in servicing all motorcycles. While there are other tools that can be used in place of some of these, their design can make a job easier or safer.

Cleaning Tools

Cleaning tools are needed for proper removal of old gaskets, baked on oil or grease, and carbon. Several

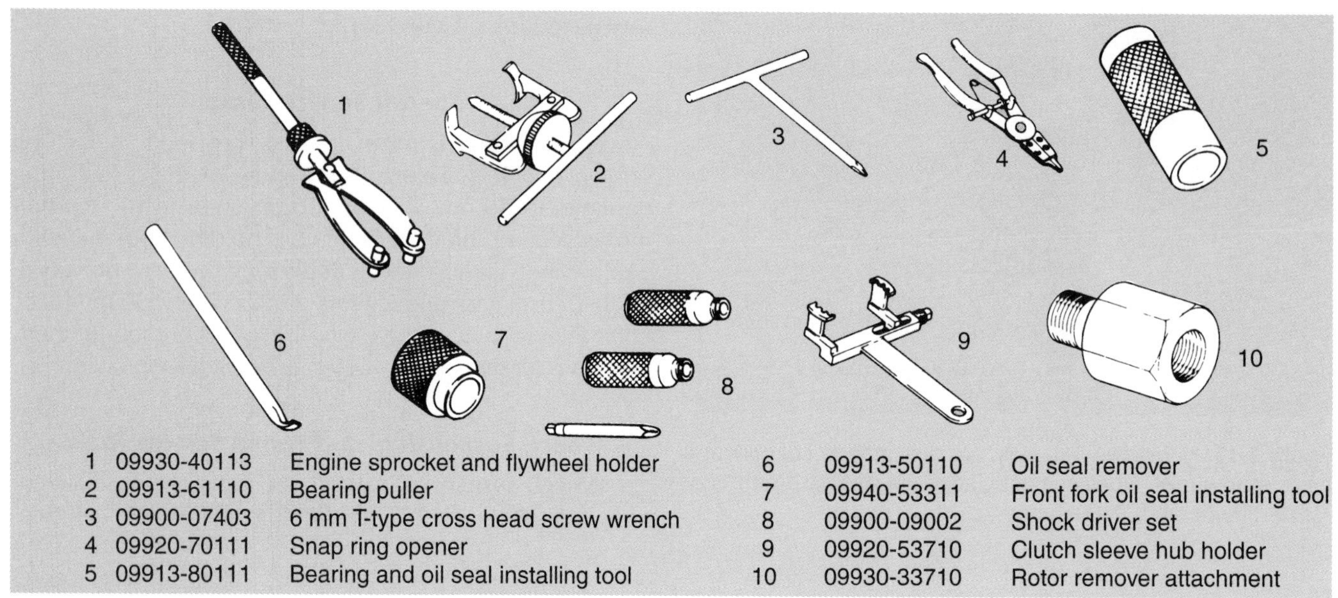

Figure 3-20. Manufacturer's special service tools (factory shop tools) are necessary for some motorcycle repairs. Tools are usually assigned a special part number. (American Suzuki Motor Corporation)

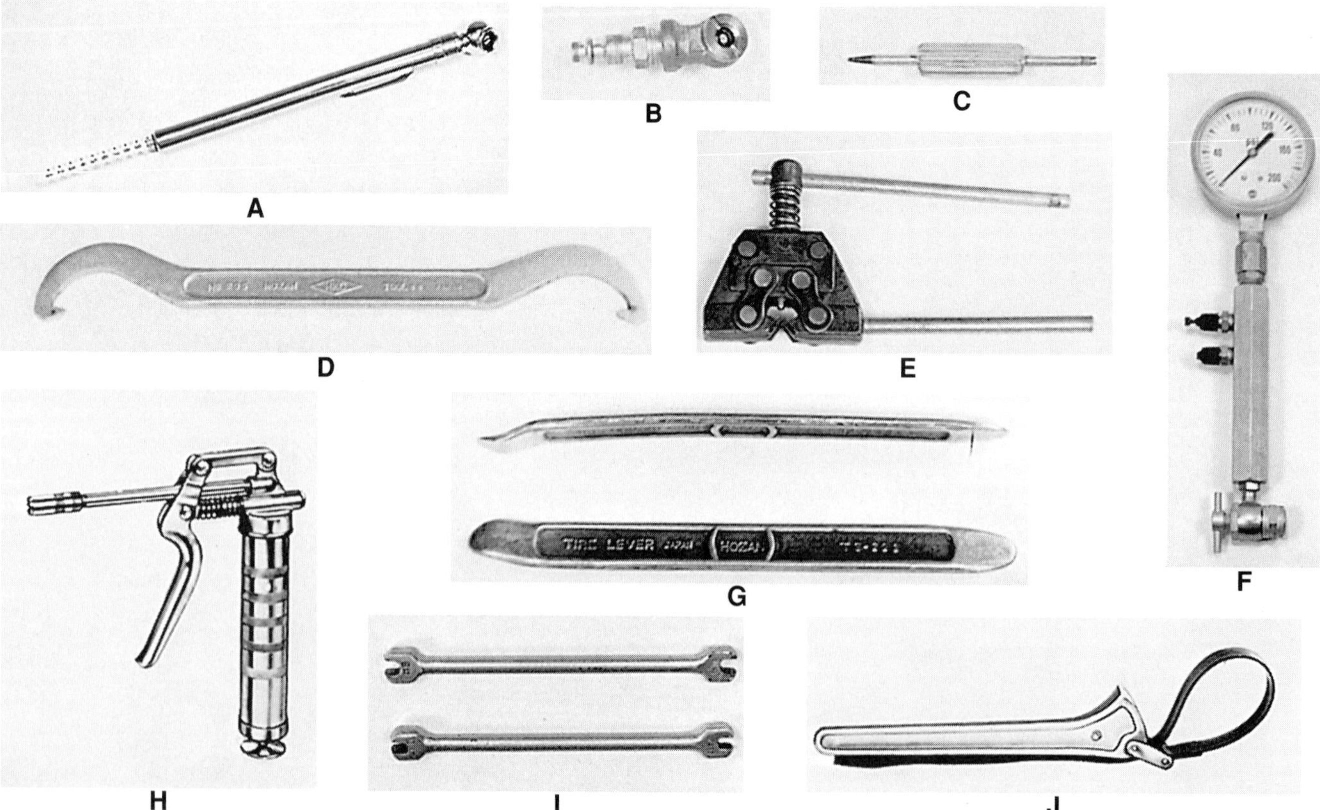

Figure 3-21. Wheel suspension, and frame service tools: A—Tire pressure gauge. B—Tire chuck. C—Core tool. D—Hook spanner wrench. E—Chain breaker. F—Fork/shock pressure gauge. G—Tire irons. H—Grease gun. I—Spoke wrenches. J—Strap wrench.

general types of cleaning tools are shown in **Figure 3-22.** Choose the cleaning tool that is the most appropriate for the task.

Power Hand Tools

Power hand tools can be driven by either air pressure or electricity. A few power hand tools are shown in **Figure 3-23.** ***Air wrenches*** increase work speed or are helpful during the removal of stubborn fasteners, **Figure 3-24.**

Great care must be exercised when using air tools. They can easily overtorque and break fasteners, warp cases, strip threads, and permanently damage components. Special heavy-duty impact sockets are designed for use with air impacts. Impact sockets are usually flat black in color. Do not use a hand socket with air tools.

Caution: Never start a bolt or nut with an impact. The fastener could cross-thread, causing fastener or part damage. Always start a nut or bolt by hand before using an impact.

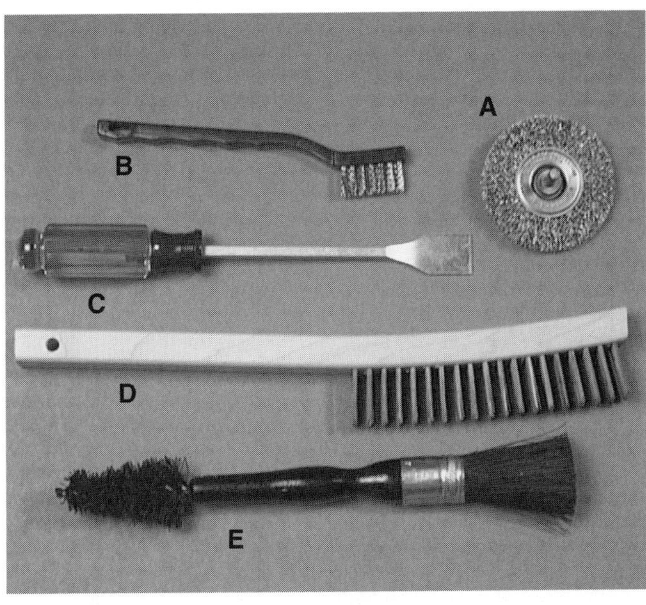

Figure 3-22. Cleaning tools: A—Rotary wire brush. B—Small wire brush. C—Gasket scraper. D—Large wire brush. E—Solvent brush.

Proper Care and Use of Tools

Hand tools are only as good as the technician using them and the care they receive. It is important to keep your tools well organized, clean, and lubricated as necessary.

Any motorcycle, ATV, or scooter repair job can be broken down into separate operations—one of them being tool care. A professional technician will wipe tools clean and put them away at the completion of each operation. Proper care and organization of tools saves time, extends their life, and reduces the possibility of loss.

General Shop Equipment

General shop equipment is normally provided by the motorcycle repair facility. However, some technicians purchase some of the less expensive equipment themselves. Before deciding to purchase a piece of equipment that is provided by the shop, be sure to determine if you will use the tool enough to justify its expense.

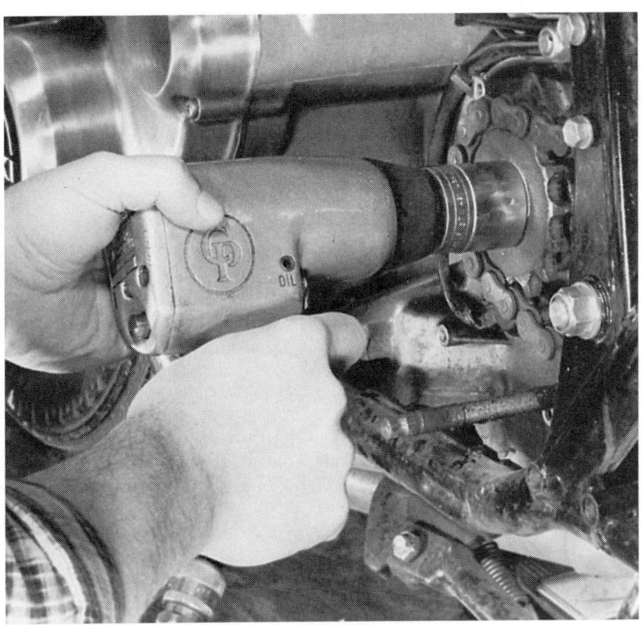

Figure 3-24. Large, stubborn fasteners, like countershaft sprocket nuts, can be easily loosened with a 1/2″ drive air impact wrench.

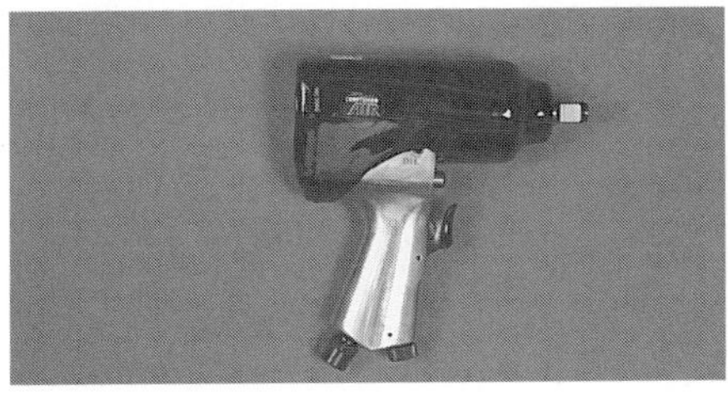

A

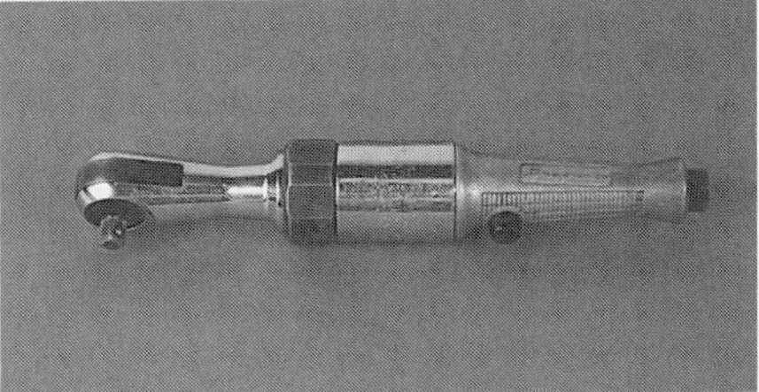

B

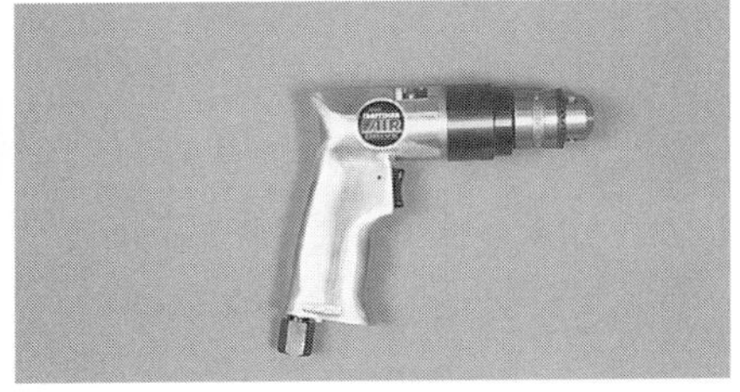

C

Figure 3-23. A—Air impact with 1/2″ drive. B—Air ratchet with 3/8″ drive. Both can be used to speed up disassembly, but they should not be used for assembly. C—Air drill. All are handy power hand tools.

Electrical Test Equipment

Electrical test equipment is used to diagnose and test the electrical systems of a motorcycle. **Figure 3-25** shows a variety of electrical testing and service tools. Learn to identify each type. Details on how to use electrical test equipment can be found in **Chapter 5.**

Measurement

Just about every aspect of motorcycle repair involves some type of measurement. A tune-up, engine overhaul, or even a simple chain adjustment requires measurement.

There are two measuring systems: US Conventional (USC) and metric (SI). You are probably more familiar with the conventional or USC measuring system. It uses values such as foot (ft.), pound (lb.), and pounds per square inch (psi). The system used on most imported motorcycles is the metric system. This system uses values such as centimeter (cm), kilogram (kg), and kilopascal (kPa).

The conventional system uses random number indexes. For example, it states that there are 12 inches in a foot and 3 feet in a yard. The average size for parts of the human body set the standards for the conventional measuring system. The metric system is a more consistent measuring system that uses scientific multiples of 10 to index all measurements. For example, 1000 millimeters equals 100 centimeters equals 10 decameters equals 1 meter. Each of these numbers is equal and divisible by ten. This makes measurements with the metric system simpler and more consistent than with the USC system.

Conversion charts located in the Appendix are valuable for all conversions. A ***decimal conversion chart*** can also be found in the Appendix and is commonly used to interchange and find equal values for fractions, decimals, and millimeters. Fractions are only accurate to about 1/64 of an inch. For smaller measurements, either decimals or millimeters should be used. A decimal conversion chart may be needed to change a ruler measurement (fraction) into a decimal specification.

Yardstick (Meterstick)

A steel ***yardstick*** or ***meterstick*** can be used as a straightedge to check part alignment and for measurements not requiring extreme accuracy. Many have conventional and metric scales. One very common use for a steel yardstick is to verify chain adjustment, **Figure 3-26.**

Six-inch Scale

Several types of ***six-inch scales*** or rulers are available. Frequently termed a *pocket scale,* the most useful type has

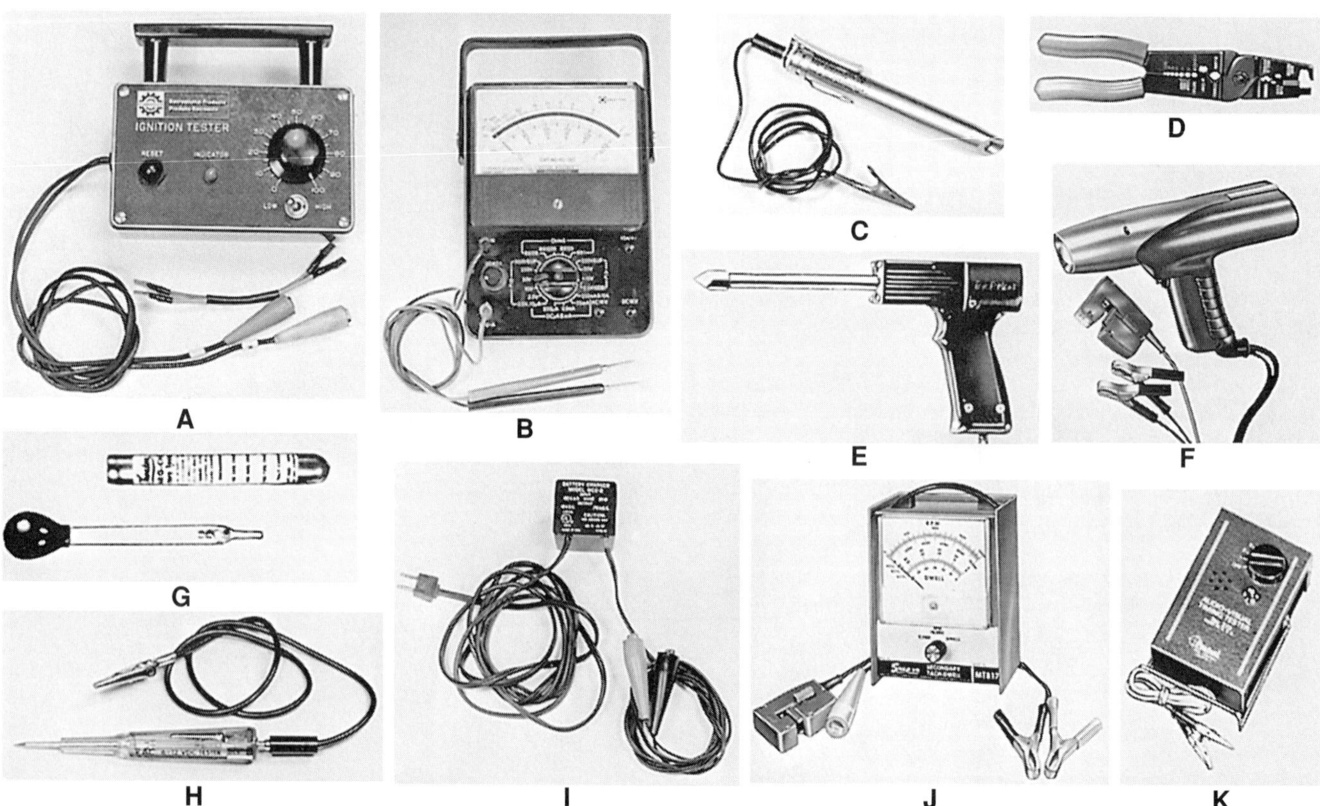

Figure 3-25. Electrical testing and service tools: A—Ignition tester. B—VOM (volt-ohm-milliammeter). C—Continuity light. D—Wire crimp tool. E—Soldering iron. F—Timing light. G—Battery hydrometer. H—Low voltage test light. I—Battery charger. J—Dwell meter. K—Timing tester.

both conventional and metric scales, **Figure 3-27.** A pocket or six-inch scale is a very handy tool which can help the technician perform hundreds of different rough measurements on small parts.

Combination Square

A ***combination square*** has a sliding square (a frame with a 90° angle edge) mounted on a steel ruler. It is needed when the ruler must be held perfectly square (straight) against the part being measured.

Outside Micrometer

The ***outside micrometer*** is one of the most important and frequently used precision measuring tools. It is used for the accurate measurement of numerous part dimensions. Most outside micrometers are accurate to within .001″ (.01 mm). Some micrometers can read up to .0001″ (.001mm).

Reading a Micrometer

Before reading a micrometer, you must first become familiar with the parts and scales of the micrometer. **Figure 3-28** illustrates the fundamental parts of a typical micrometer. Note the two scales used to make readings, the sleeve scale and the thimble scale.

The ***sleeve scale*** on a conventional micrometer is marked off in increments of .025″. Each tenth of an inch (.100″) has a numeral. The ***thimble scale*** is marked off in

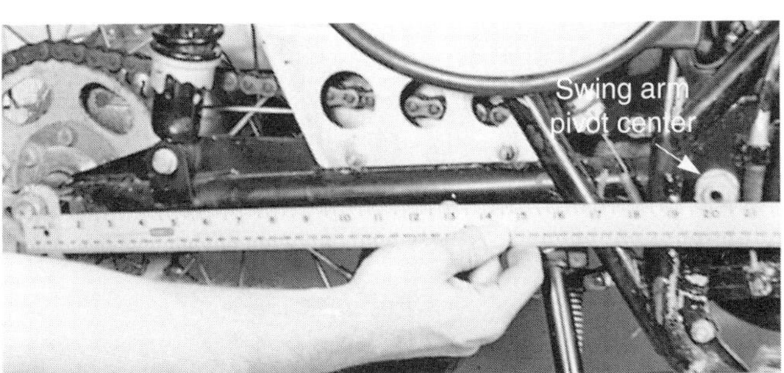

Figure 3-26. Chain and wheel alignment can be verified with a steel yardstick. Measure the distance between the axle center and swingarm pivot center on both sides of the motorcycle. Both measurements will be the same if the wheel is straight in the frame.

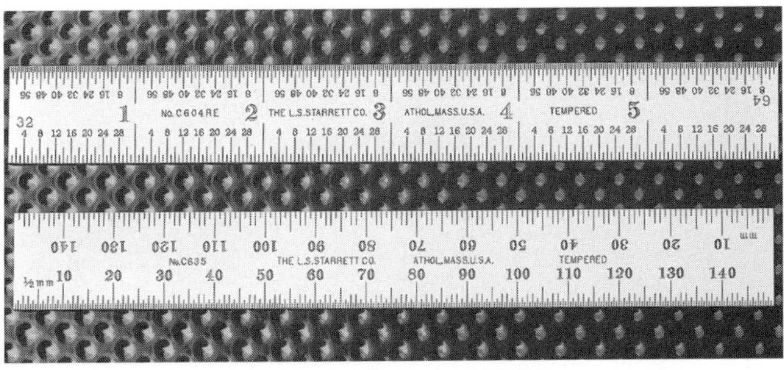

Figure 3-27. This six-inch pocket scale has both conventional and metric scales. (L.S. Starrett)

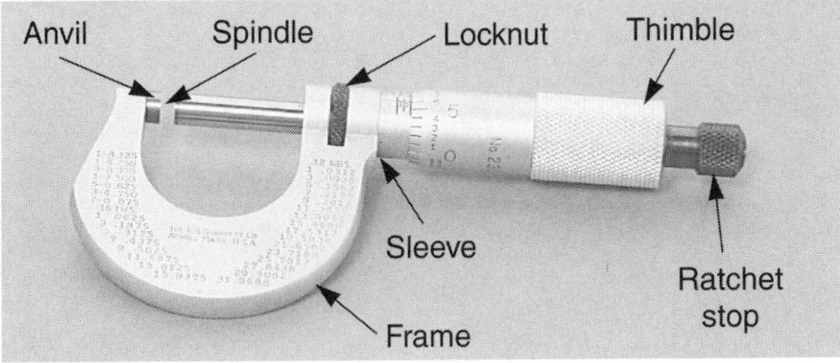

Figure 3-28. Note the parts of this outside micrometer.

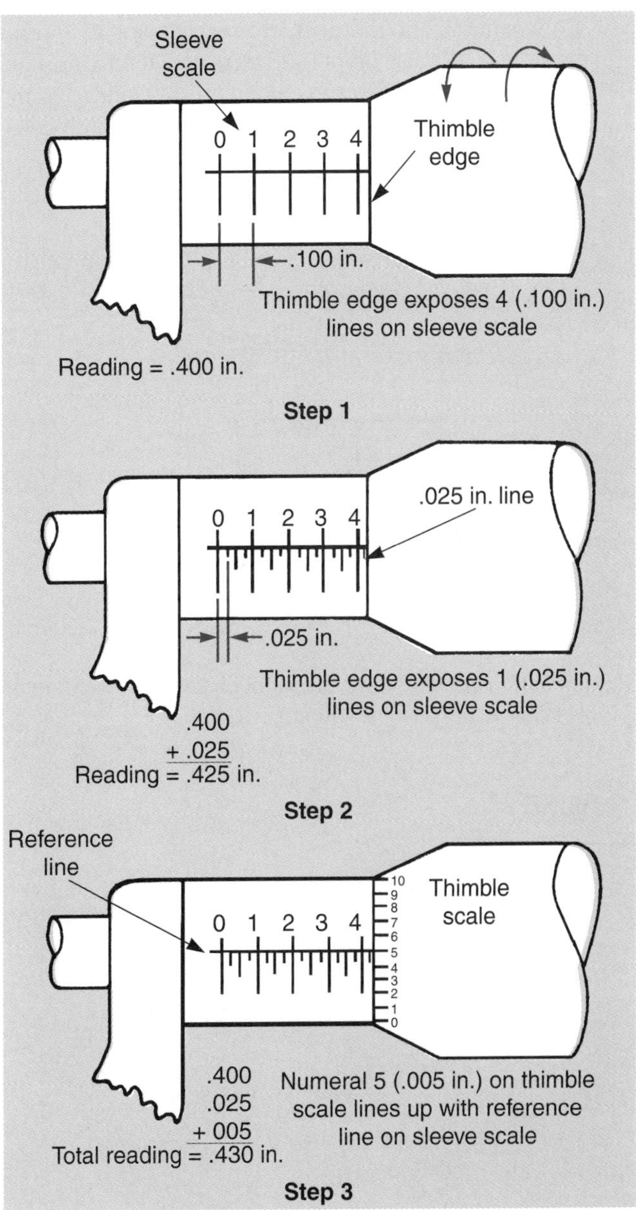

Figure 3-29. The addition of Steps 1, 2, and 3 will give the micrometer reading. First, take the sleeve reading; then the thimble edge reading and finally, read the thimble and add all three readings.

.001″ increments. Each full turn of the thimble moves the micrometer spindle .025″. The edge of the thimble is used to indicate which sleeve marking to read. A horizontal reference line on the sleeve scale indicates which thimble number to read.

Adding the sleeve and thimble scales give the final micrometer reading. **Figure 3-29** shows the procedure for reading a micrometer. Read the largest sleeve number visible (each one equals .100″). Count the visible sleeve marks past this number (each equals .025″). Then, count the number of thimble marks past the sleeve reference line (each equals .001″). If not perfectly aligned, round off your numbers. Finally, add the readings in Steps 1, 2, and 3. A metric micrometer is read the same way as a conventional micrometer, except the scale divisions are different, **Figure 3-30.**

Conventional and metric micrometers come in various ranges, 0-1″, 1-2″, and up or 0-25 mm, 25-50 mm, and up. The micrometer size (2″ for example) must be added to the micrometer reading (.236″ for example) to determine the total measurement (2.236″).

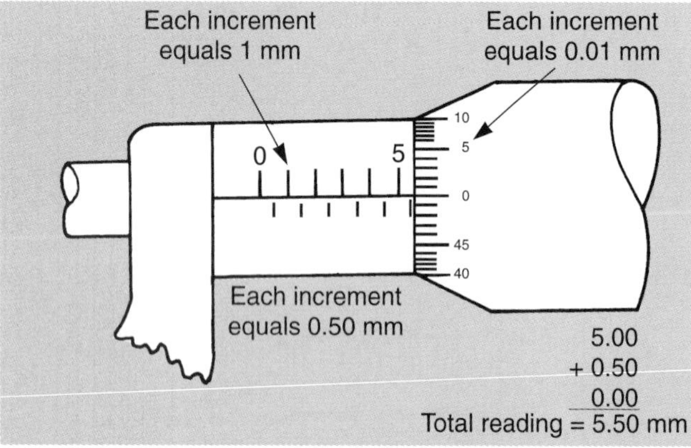

Figure 3-30. Note the scale divisions of a metric micrometer. They are given in millimeters (mm).

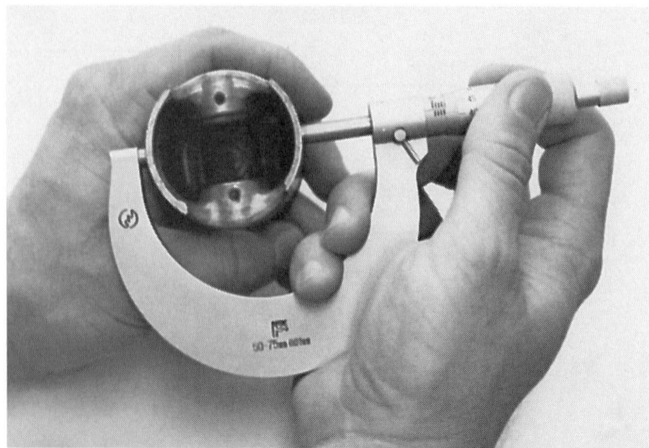

Figure 3-31. Practice is required before you can make consistently accurate measurements. Hold the tool as shown and gently screw the thimble into the part.

How to Use Outside Micrometers

Accurate measurements require proper handling of the micrometer as well as the ability to correctly read the scales. It takes practice to get the feel for consistent readings. Overtightening the micrometer or a loose fit on the part can cause inaccurate readings. The part being measured must fit snugly between the micrometer anvil and spindle. **Figure 3-31** shows how to hold and adjust a micrometer. Grasp the frame in your palm and rotate the thimble with your thumb and fingers.

Note: Some micrometers are equipped with a ratchet friction device to help obtain accurate and consistent readings.

Inside Micrometer

The ***inside micrometer*** works just like an outside micrometer. However, an anvil is not used. An inside micrometer will measure internal diameters and distances between surfaces. A typical example of inside micrometer use is shown in **Figure 3-32.**

Depth Micrometer

A ***depth micrometer*** is used to measure the depth of a hole or recess in a part, **Figure 3-33.** Depth micrometers are available in inch-graduated and metric models. The depth micrometer scale is read like other micrometers; however, it is adjusted in reverse.

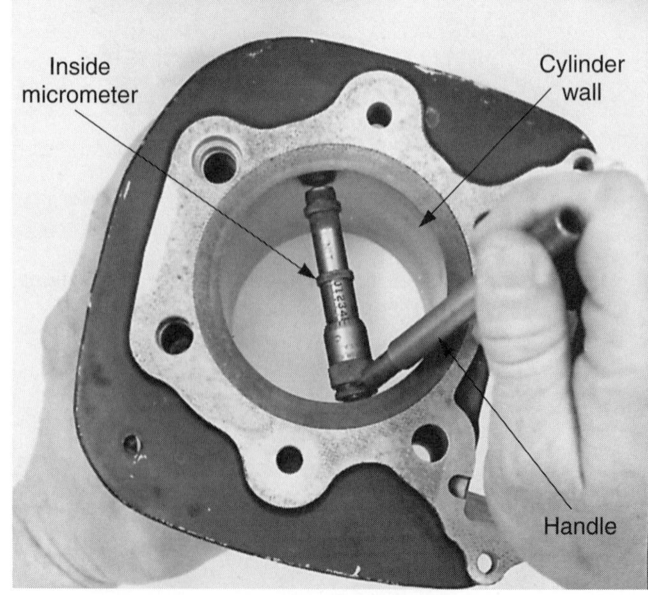

Figure 3-32. An inside micrometer is useful for accurately measuring cylinder bore inside diameter (ID). A reading larger than specifications would indicate cylinder wear.

Dial Caliper

A ***dial caliper*** is used to make inside, outside, and depth measurements, **Figure 3-34.** Dial calipers are available with either metric or conventional scales. The large dial face is very easy to read. Common uses of a dial caliper in motorcycle servicing are:

- Measuring carburetor float height.
- Checking transmission spacing.
- Measuring shim dimensions.
- Checking crankshafts during rebuilding.
- Other measurements requiring a tolerance of not less than .002″ (.05 mm).

Another type of caliper is the ***vernier caliper.*** This type of caliper is harder to read. For this reason, most technicians elect to use a dial caliper. Calipers are used for quick measurements requiring reasonable accuracy. They come in various shapes and sizes, **Figure 3-35.**

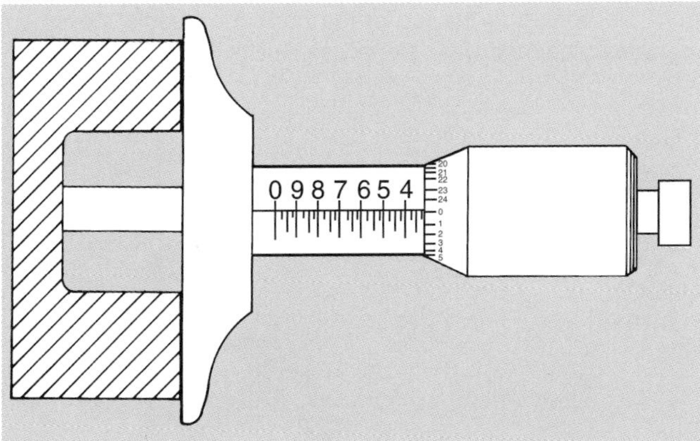

Figure 3-33. This is a typical application for a depth micrometer.

Figure 3-34. A dial caliper is capable of making inside, outside, and depth measurements.

Telescoping Gauge

A ***telescoping gauge*** is a spring-loaded, T-shaped instrument used to measure inside diameters or distances, **Figure 3-36.** A telescoping gauge by itself is of little use. As shown in **Figure 3-37,** it must be used with an outside micrometer. A telescoping gauge, like any precision measuring instrument, requires the proper feel and adjustment for accurate measurements.

Dial Indicator

A ***dial indicator,*** **Figure 3-38,** is used for a variety of measurements. In the dial indicator, a vertical rod actuates a circular scale pointer which measures movement. Each scale graduation normally represents thousandths of an inch or hundredths of a millimeter. Common uses of a dial indicator are:

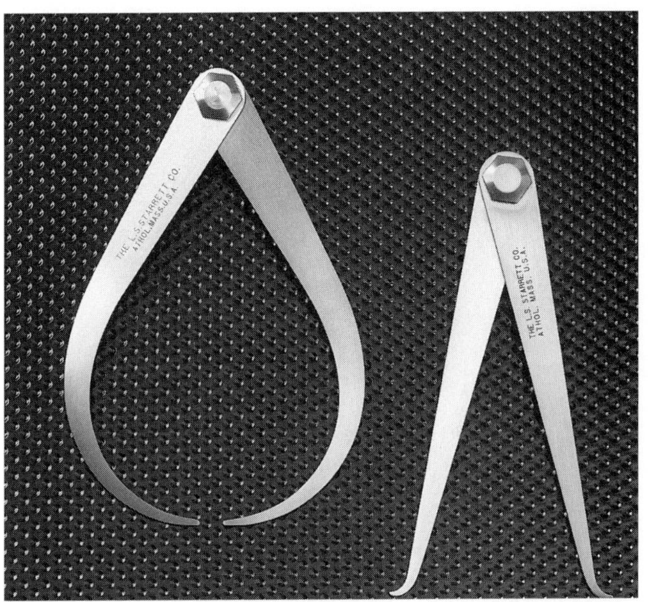

Figure 3-35. Calipers come in all sizes. They can be somewhat difficult to read.

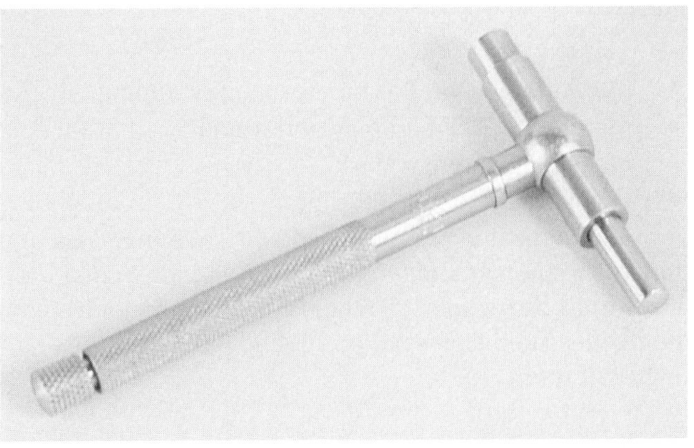

Figure 3-36. Telescoping gauges are used only for duplicating inside diameters. They will fit into a small hole easily and still allow adjustment.

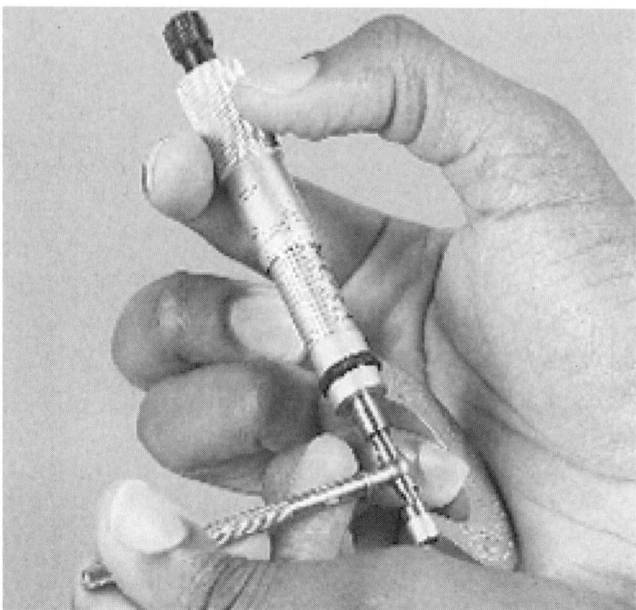

Figure 3-37. Once a dimension has been duplicated by the telescoping gauge, it is measured with an outside micrometer.

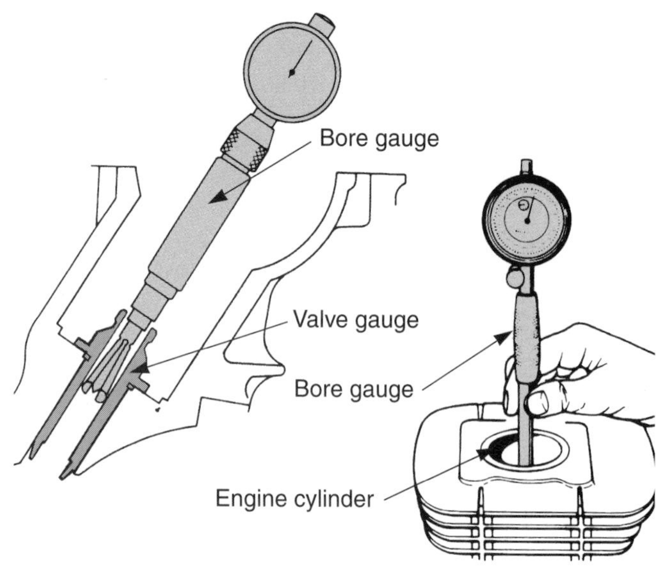

Figure 3-39. A dial bore gauge is used for quick, accurate measurements of a tapered bore. When the gauge is slowly moved from the bottom to the top of the bore, the needle movement indicates taper and wear. (American Suzuki Motor Corporation)

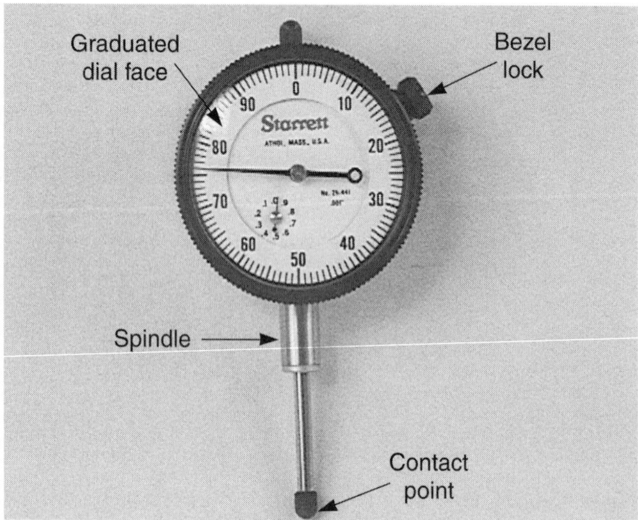

Figure 3-38. Dial indicator. Movement of the indicator rod is transferred to the indicator pointer.

- Measuring piston position for ignition timing.
- Measuring shaft end play and runout.
- Measuring gear backlash.
- Crankshaft and wheel truing.

Dial indicators are designed with face markings and ranges to suit many different measuring jobs. A dial indicator must be set up or mounted parallel to the movement being measured. If it is not positioned properly, false readings will result.

Dial Bore Gauge

A ***dial bore gauge*** is a combination dial indicator and telescoping gauge. This is illustrated in **Figure 3-39.** A dial bore gauge gives immediate measurement of an inside diameter. It is frequently used, for example, when measuring engine cylinder bore out-of-roundness and taper. Dial bore gauges are read in the same way as a dial indicator.

Figure 3-40. A flat feeler gauge is frequently used to check contact point gap.

Feeler Gauge (Wire Gauge)

A ***feeler gauge*** is used to measure small clearances between parts, **Figure 3-40.** It consists of a set of precision metal blades of wires or different thickness. Feeler gauges usually come in sets ranging in size from around .001–.025″ (.025–.635 mm). Each blade size is often marked with both metric and conventional sizes.

A ***flat feeler gauge,*** also called a strip or blade feeler gauge, will accurately measure flat, parallel surfaces. It is used to check contact points, **Figure 3-40. Figure 3-41** shows how it helps when inspecting for cylinder head warpage. A ***wire gauge*** is similar to a flat feeler gauge but it has short wires of a precise diameter, **Figure 3-42.** A wire gauge is used to measure the clearance between irregular surfaces, such as spark plug electrodes.

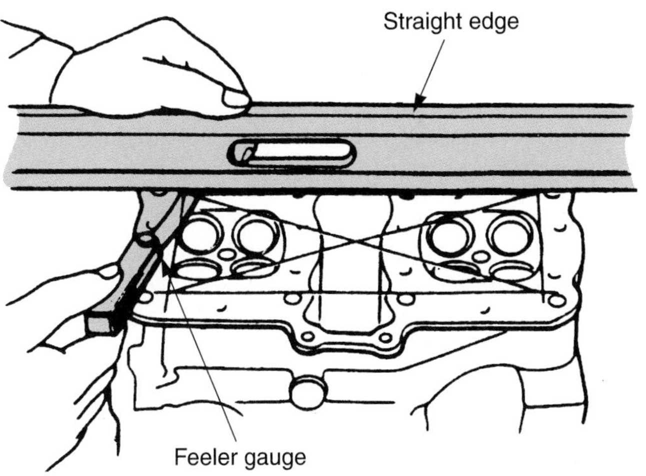

Figure 3-41. A flat feeler gauge and straight edge being used to check a cylinder head for warpage. (Honda Motor Co., Ltd.)

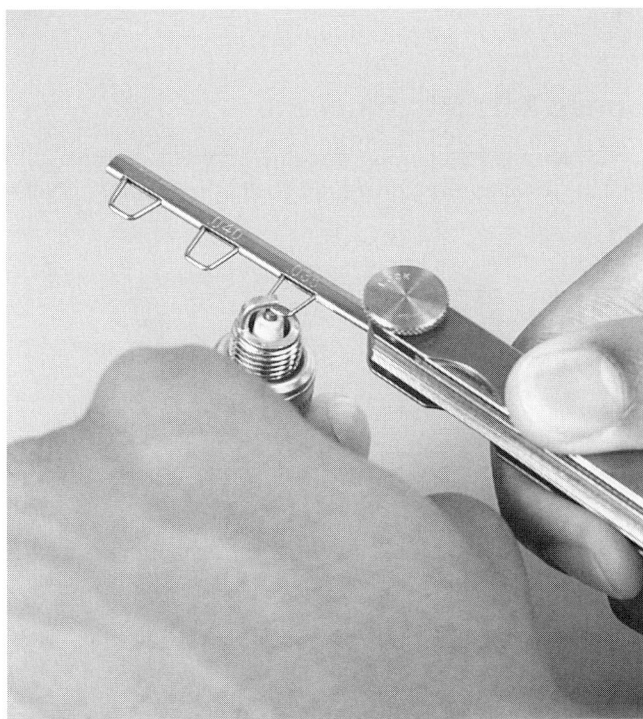

Figure 3-42. A gap gauge will measure spark plug gap. The gap is adjusted by bending the plug's ground electrode.

Plastigage

Plastigage is a disposable measuring device made of thin strips of a clay-like substance. It is used to measure assembled clearances between plain bearings (rod bearings, main bearings, cam bearings, etc.). An example of how Plastigage is used to check bearing clearance is given in **Figure 3-43.**

Pressure and Vacuum Measurements

Pressure and vacuum measurements frequently help the technician make accurate adjustments. They also aid in the diagnosis of many motorcycle problems. Typical applications for pressure and vacuum measurements are:

- Engine compression testing (check general engine condition).
- Two-stroke cycle crankcase leak testing (check seals and gaskets).
- Engine intake port vacuum measurement (carburetor adjustments and engine condition).
- Fluid pressure testing (checking fuel and oil pressure).
- Air pressure measurements (tire inflation).

Compression Gauge

A ***compression gauge*** measures the air pressure developed during the compression stroke in an engine's combustion chambers, **Figure 3-44.** This measurement quickly determines the condition of piston rings, cylinder walls, gaskets, and valves. The compression gauge reading should be within factory specifications. If a low reading results, an engine problem exists.

A compression gauge is installed or held in the spark plug hole. The engine is then turned over while the throttle is held wide open. Continue cranking the engine until the

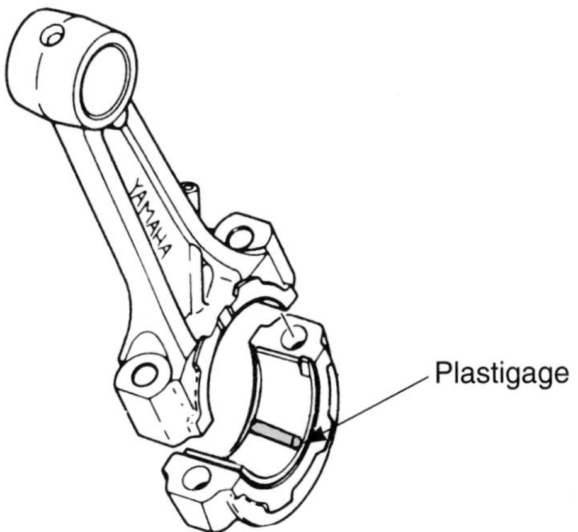

Figure 3-43. A strip of Plastigage is placed on a bearing. Then, the parts (connecting rod in this case) are assembled and torqued to specifications. After disassembly, the width of the smashed Plastigage is compared to a paper packaging scale. The Plastigage width indicates bearing clearance. (Yamaha Motor Corporation U.S.A.)

pressure stops climbing. The gauge will read engine compression stroke pressure. A compression gauge may be used on either a two- or four-stroke cycle engine.

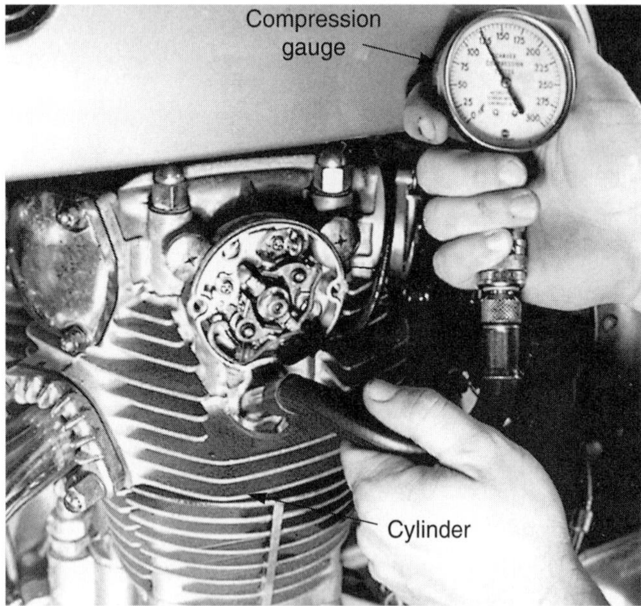

Figure 3-44. A compression gauge indicates engine condition by measuring the cylinder pressure on its compression stroke. If the pressure reading is lower than specifications, engine rings, valves, or another component may be leaking. A high pressure reading indicates carbon buildup in the combustion chamber.

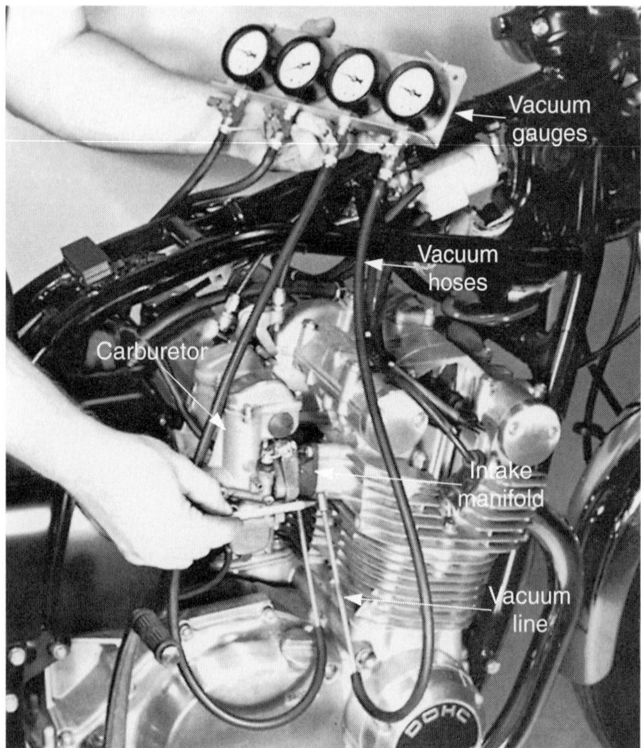

Figure 3-45. Vacuum gauges connected to the intake ports are used for making accurate throttle synchronization adjustments. They will also indicate vacuum leaks that could upset engine operation.

A ***wet compression test*** is used to determine exactly which parts inside a motorcycle engine might be causing low compression. Perform a regular compression test first. If the compression is lower than specifications, place about a teaspoon of motor oil in the low cylinder(s) and repeat the test.

If the compression gauge reading goes up, the rings or cylinder(s) are worn and leaking. If the gauge reading stays the same, then the valves or head gasket are probably at fault. The oil will temporarily seal any leakage past the piston rings.

Two-Stroke Cycle Leak Tester

A two-stroke cycle leak test checks for leakage in the engine's bottom and top end. A pressure source and vacuum is provided by a small pump and is monitored by a gauge. The procedure for this test is explained in the chapter on two-cycle engine overhaul.

Vacuum Gauge

A ***vacuum gauge*** is used to measure intake manifold vacuum (suction), **Figure 3-45.** The most common uses for this gauge are carburetor adjustment and to test for a vacuum leak at the carburetor or intake manifold. Vacuum readings lower than specifications point to a leak.

Fluid Pressure Gauge

A ***fluid pressure gauge*** can be used to measure fuel pressure or engine oil pressure. Sometimes, a vacuum gauge will also serve as a pressure gauge, **Figure 3-46.** It can be connected to the pump output to measure pump pressure.

Spring Rate Measurement

A ***spring tester*** is used to measure valve spring and clutch spring tension (pressure). Look at **Figure 3-47.** When

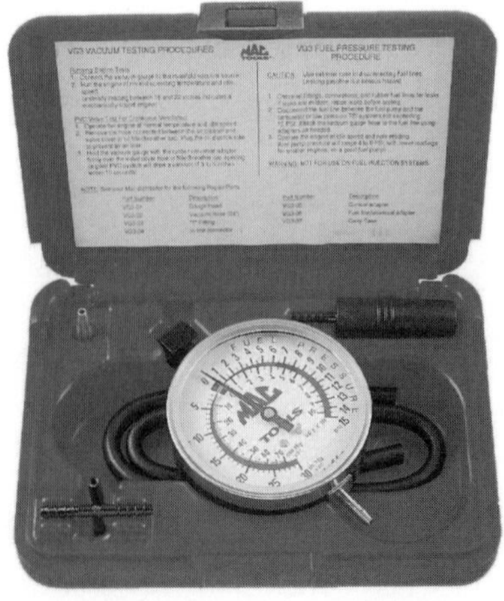

Figure 3-46. A fluid pressure gauge is useful for testing motorcycle fuel systems that have a fuel pump. (Mac Tools)

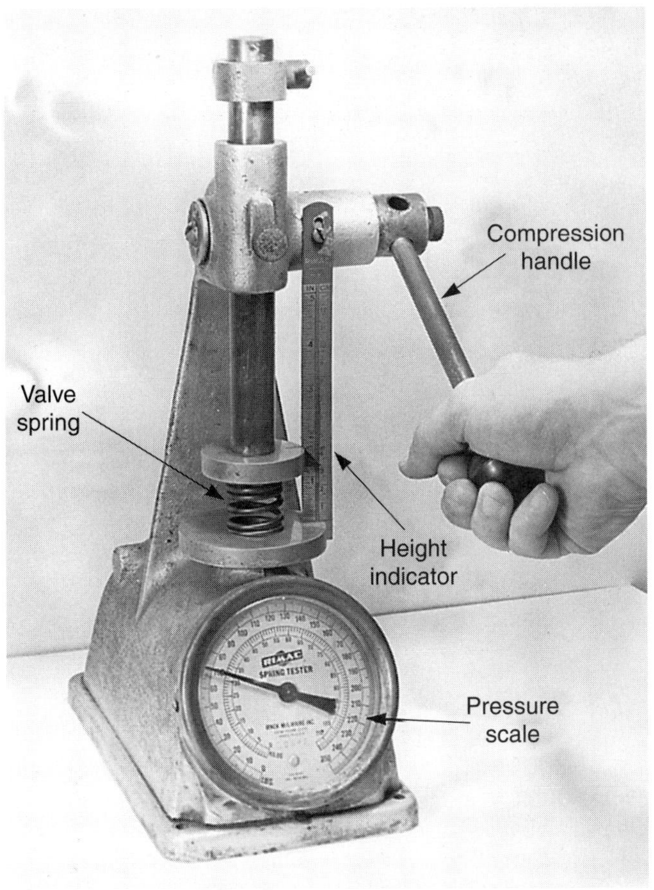

Figure 3-47. A spring tester accurately measures spring pressure at a given height. The pressure reading is compared to factory specifications to determine spring condition.

spring pressure is below specifications at a certain compressed height, the spring has weakened. Springs which do not meet specifications should be replaced.

Fluid Volume Measurement

Fluid volume measurement is necessary to accurately measure oil for forks, shock absorbers, gearboxes, primary chaincases, and fuel premixing. A ***graduated cylinder*** or measuring cup can be used for accurate fluid volume measurement. **Figure 3-48** shows a graduated cylinder. Graduated cylinders can be used to check and test fuel quality.

Care of Precision Measuring Tools

When selecting measuring tools that will be used for a period of years, it pays to buy top quality tools. The initial cost will obviously be higher. However, considering the importance of accuracy, the longer life span of superior tools easily justifies the extra cost.

After each use, wipe the tool with a lightly oiled, lint-free cloth. Never dip a precision measuring tool in solvent. Do not use an air hose to clean precision measuring tools. It is advisable to keep your measuring tools in protective cases. Also, keep them in an area that will not be subjected to excessive moisture.

When using a measuring tool, place it in a clean area where it will not fall or be struck by other tools. Never pry, hammer, or force precision tools. Remember, they are precision tools—keep them that way.

Check for Accuracy

It is good practice to occasionally check precision tools for accuracy. They may be checked against a tool of known accuracy or by using special gauges. If the tool is found out of specification, send it to be recalibrated.

If a tool is accidentally dropped or struck by some object, immediately check it for accuracy. Adjustments for wear or very minor damage are provided on many measuring tools. Follow the manufacturer's instructions.

Temperature

Many specifications for measurements will state room temperature, an exact temperature, or engine at normal running temperature. Remember that all metals expand and contract in direct proportion to their temperature. This makes it imperative that temperature specifications be followed when making precision measurements and settings. Measuring tools can be affected by extremes of heat and cold. If your tools must be used when the part to be measured is very cold or very hot, check them for accuracy before using.

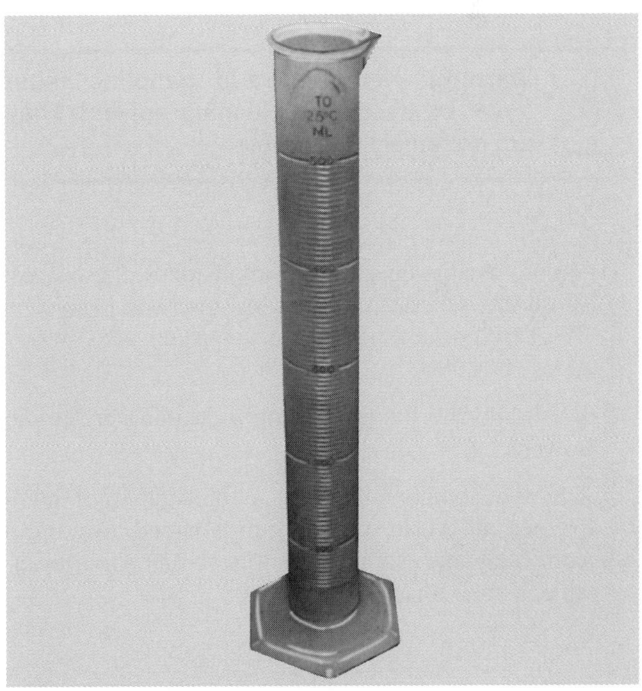

Figure 3-48. A graduated cylinder will measure liquid volumes in cubic centimeters or milliliters. Each line equals 5 cm^3 or 5 ml. Fluid level is matched to markings on the cylinder to determine the amount of fluid.

Parts Cleaning

It is general practice to always inspect and clean motorcycle parts during disassembly and before reassembly. Properly cleaned parts will make visual inspection easier. Also, clean parts will fit together easier and with less chance of failure due to dirt contamination.

Methods of Cleaning

Various types of deposits (carbon, varnish, sludge, dirt, grease, oil, rust, corrosion, and gum) are found in and on motorcycle parts. These deposits require several different cleaning techniques for removal. The common methods for cleaning motorcycle parts are:

- Degreasing solvents.
- Decarbonizing solvents.
- Wire wheel.
- Scraper.
- Dry blasting.

Degreasing Solvents

Degreasing solvents are normally used for the removal of oil, sludge, or grease. They will not remove carbon deposits, corrosion, rust, and hard varnish. A degreasing tank is shown in **Figure 3-49.** Commercially prepared degreasing solvents are usually petroleum based (made from crude oil), but are chemically structured *not* to ignite and burn easily.

Warning: Kerosene and gasoline must never be used as a cleaning solvent. They are extremely flammable.

To use degreasing solvents, simply follow these steps:

1. Rinse and soak the parts for a few moments in solvent. This is especially helpful on very dirty parts (heavy grease or sludge).
2. Wash and rub the parts using a cleaning brush and solvent.
3. Dry the components using a blowgun and compressed air. Make sure the gun is aimed away from your body and others. If compressed air is not available, a shop towel will work.

Warning: When using compressed air, wear safety glasses and use an approved blow gun.

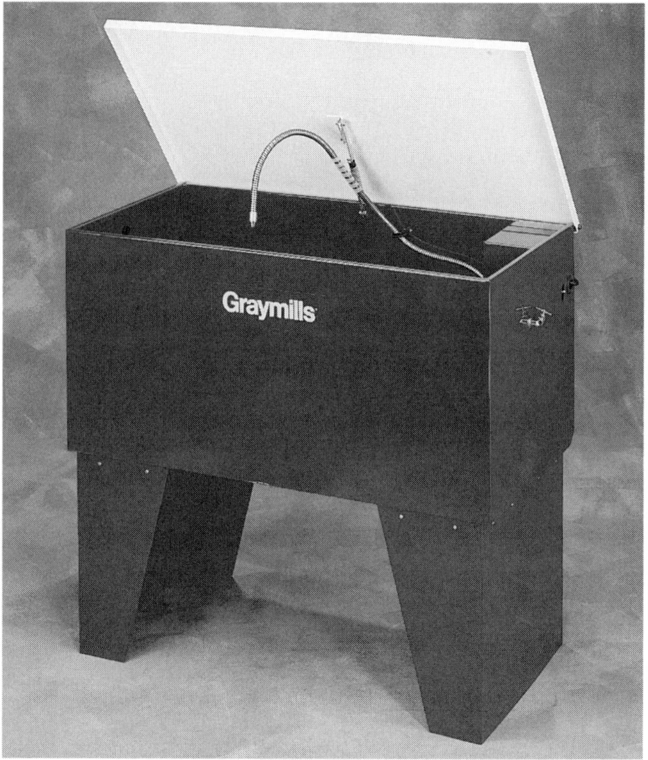

Figure 3-49. A parts cleaning tank makes degreasing and cleaning a safe, simple task. Solvent is pumped from a drum or tank through a flexible spout and then drains back through a filter. (Graymills Corp.)

Decarbonizing Solvents

Decarbonizing solvents, sometimes called ***cold soak cleaners,*** are specially formulated petroleum distillates that can loosen carbon, gum, and varnish buildup on metal parts, **Figure 3-50.** Decarbonizing solvents are needed to remove stubborn or hard deposits, or those not easily removed with a scraper and degreasing solvents. To use decarbonizing solvent, soak the parts for about 15-30 minutes. Then, wash the parts in water to rinse off the solvent. Due to the caustic nature of the solvent, many cold soak cleaners are now closed loop (contained) systems, which keep the cleaner and water from leaking into the ground.

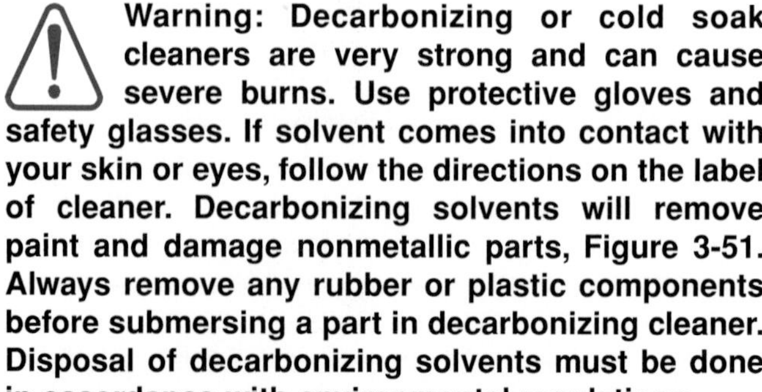

Warning: Decarbonizing or cold soak cleaners are very strong and can cause severe burns. Use protective gloves and safety glasses. If solvent comes into contact with your skin or eyes, follow the directions on the label of cleaner. Decarbonizing solvents will remove paint and damage nonmetallic parts, Figure 3-51. Always remove any rubber or plastic components before submersing a part in decarbonizing cleaner. Disposal of decarbonizing solvents must be done in accordance with environmental regulations.

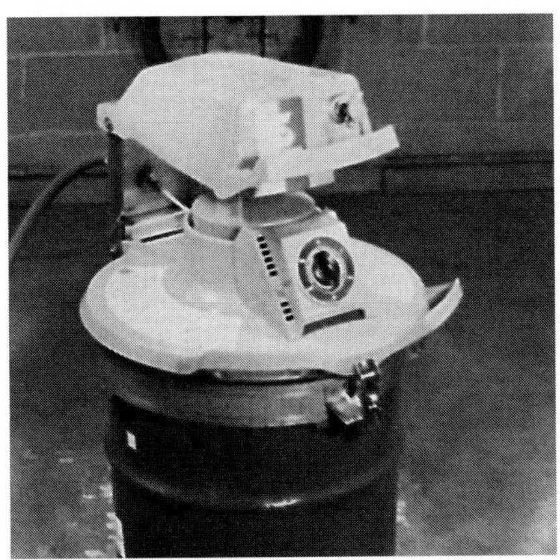

Figure 3-50. Cold soak solvent is normally used for decarbonizing and carburetor cleaning. This cold soak cleaning tank uses an air-driven agitator.

Wire Wheel (Wire Brush)

Deposits which are not removed by solvents (hard, thick carbon, rust, etc.) can usually be cleaned with a ***wire wheel,* Figure 3-52.** Since parts, especially soft aluminum parts, can be damaged by a wire wheel, use care and do not apply too much pressure.

Warning: When using a wire wheel, always wear safety glasses.

Common mistakes when using a wire wheel are:

- Damage to soft metal or aluminum parts (pistons, combustion chambers). Aluminum is easily scored by the wire wheel's rubbing action.
- Allowing parts to catch in the wheel. Parts not held tightly may be thrown and damaged or could cause injury.
- Removal of metal plating by use of unnecessary brush pressure. Use only enough pressure to remove deposits.
- Tool rest or safety shield not properly positioned—injury to face or eyes from flying debris.

Scraper

A ***scraper*** is used to remove gaskets, carbon, sludge, and sealing compounds from parts, **Figure 3-53.** When using a scraper, be careful not to slice into the metal or damage the part being cleaned. Even the slightest nick on a sealing surface can cause a leak. This is very critical on soft brass, copper, and aluminum parts.

Warning: When using a hand scraper, move it away from your body and always wear safety glasses.

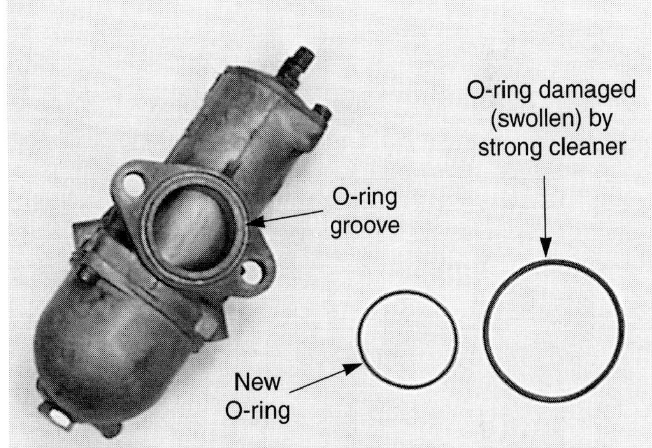

Figure 3-51. Cold soak decarbonizing solvent will ruin rubber, plastic, and fiber parts. Notice how much the O-ring on the right expanded after exposure to cold soak cleaning.

Figure 3-52. A wire wheel is often used to clean carbon off valve heads. Always use safety glasses when operating a wire wheel.

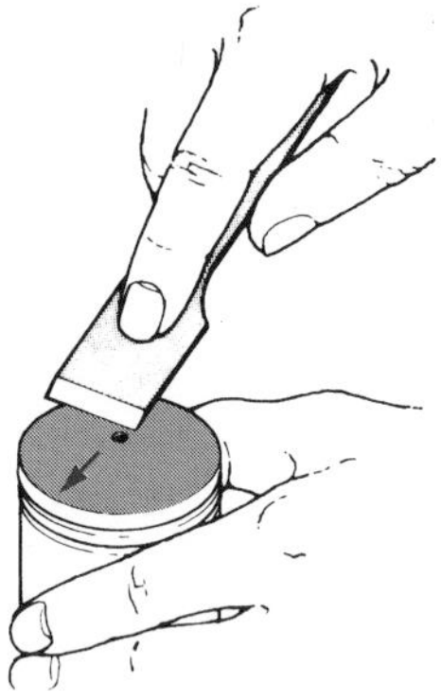

Figure 3-53. When removing carbon from a piston crown, use a dull scraper and be careful not to gouge the soft aluminum. A sharp scraper is acceptable on harder metals. (American Suzuki Motor Corporation)

Dry-Blasting

Dry-blast cleaning is the process of bombarding metal parts with shot (particles) to remove hard deposits. This method is quite different from sandblasting. Sandblasting is usually not acceptable for cleaning motorcycle parts because the sand will etch away the surface of the part being cleaned. **Figure 3-54** shows a typical dry-blast cleaner. A dry-blast or shot cleaner is useful for:

- Removing hard carbon.
- Removing rust and corrosion.
- Cosmetic cleaning of engine cases, cylinders, and cylinder heads.
- Surface preparation before painting.

A dry-blast cleaner is especially handy for cleaning hard to reach areas. It will clean in areas such as cylinder head cavities, cylinder ports, and between cylinder and case fins. Dry-blasting medium can be glass or metal beads. Biodegradable medium, such as crushed walnut shells, are gaining in popularity.

Obviously, the dry-blast cleaner is a great help to the technician. However, failure to remove all blasting grit can cause immediate damage to freshly assembled components. Proper preparation of parts before blasting and thorough cleaning after blasting eliminates this problem.

To prepare parts for dry-blasting:

1. Remove all oil with solvent and thoroughly dry parts (includes threaded holes). Oil or grease will clog a dry-blaster.
2. Remove all ball, roller, and needle bearings.
3. Remove all seals.
4. Mask (tape over) and protect any areas which may be damaged by dry-blast cleaning.

To remove grit after dry-blast cleaning:

1. Blow compressed air on the part for initial grit removal. Wear safety glasses.
2. Use solvent and a parts cleaning brush to remove grit.

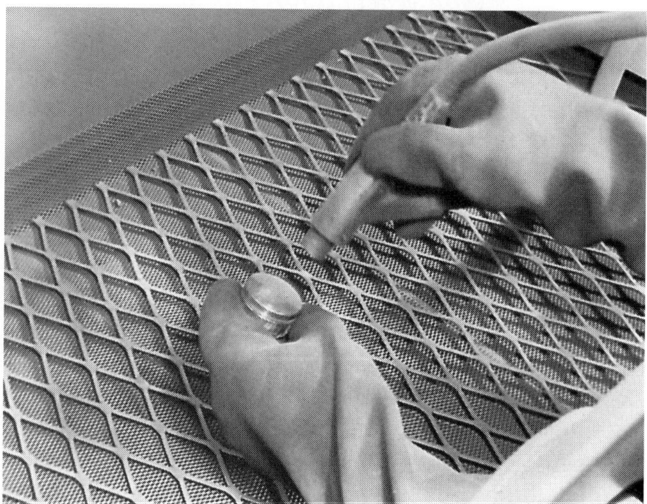

Figure 3-54. Dry-blast cleaning is handy for removing hard deposits without eroding or damaging component. It is also useful for cleaning hard-to-reach areas.

3. Rinse parts in clean solvent and blow dry.
4. Use an aerosol cleaner and compressed air to remove grit from all threaded holes.
5. Clean threads using a thread chaser and blow out holes.

Caution: Do not use a tap to clean blasting material from threaded holes. The tap may jam into the bead blast substance, damaging the part or tap.

Special Operations

As a motorcycle technician, you will sometimes run into situations when special machining, cutting, welding, or other fabrication type operations must be performed. Adding accessory components, repairing damaged parts, and other unusual jobs require special skills not covered in most service manuals.

Most of this equipment is not found in a motorcycle shop because it is very expensive. However, a machine or performance shop may have some or all of this equipment. Major machining operations in a motorcycle shop may require the use of a boring bar, lathe, or vertical mill.

Warning: All operations using power tools require safety glasses, protective clothing (no loose clothing or jewelry), correct operating procedures, and a safety conscious attitude. Make sure you have been fully trained before operating any type of machining equipment. They can be very dangerous if used improperly.

Boring Bar

A ***boring bar*** is commonly used to machine worn engine cylinders to a larger diameter, **Figure 3-55.** The cylinder is held in position by a clamp. A cutting bit mounted on a rotating shaft machines (cuts) the cylinder bore. The amount of material removed is determined by the position of the cutting bit. A special micrometer is used to set the cutting bit for the desired cut.

Boring bar operating procedures vary from one brand to another. Important steps to remember with any boring bar are:

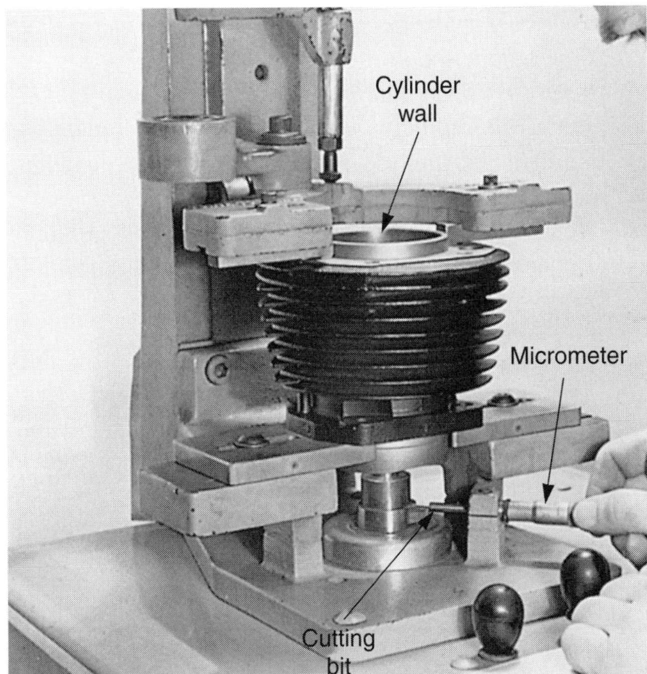

Figure 3-55. Accurate positioning of a boring bar cutting bit is done with a built-in micrometer. The cutter feeds up through the cylinder to true the wall surface and allow for oversize piston.

1. Double-check for accurate centering.
2. Make a .001″ (.025 mm) cut to verify centering.
3. Do not take excessively large cuts (see bar instructions).
4. Always use a sharp cutter.

Lathe and Vertical Mill

A ***lathe*** and ***vertical mill*** are expensive pieces of machine equipment. They are commonly found in specialized or high performance motorcycle machine shops. See **Figures 3-56** and **3-57.** With these two tools, an experienced machinist can do many custom motorcycle machining operations, including fabrication of specialized parts.

Drill Press and Drills

In motorcycle service, it is sometimes necessary to drill a hole. Drilling a hole is also required during bracket or frame fabrication, thread repairs, and many other instances where holes must be made in parts. A ***drill press*** or portable hand drill, **Figure 3-58** can be used with a variety of drill bits.

When using a drill, remember:

1. Always use a center punch to start the drill bit.
2. Drill a pilot hole if a large drill bit is to be used.
3. Make sure the drill bit is tight in the drill chuck, **Figure 3-59.**
4. Use cutting fluid (oil) on thick or hard metal.
5. Do not spin the drill bit too fast or press too hard. Overheating will quickly soften and ruin the bit.

Drilling usually causes a burr (rough edge) on both sides of the hole. A burr should be removed with a deburring tool or countersink.

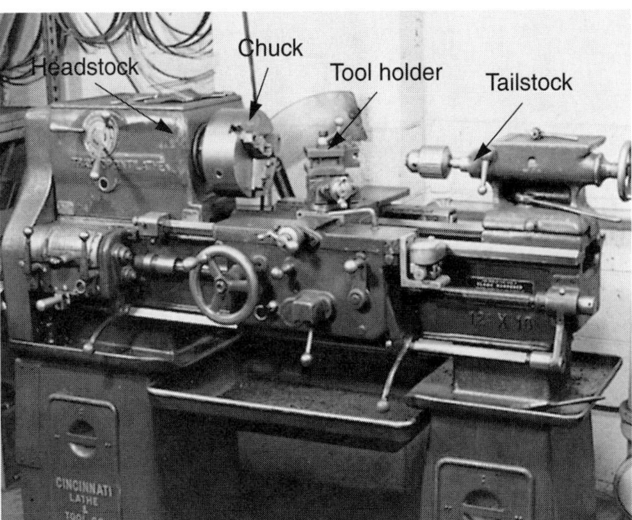

Figure 3-56. A lathe is a machine tool used to accurately shape and size cylindrical components. (Harrison)

Figure 3-57. A vertical mill uses a rotating cutter to accurately remove metal. (Bridgeport)

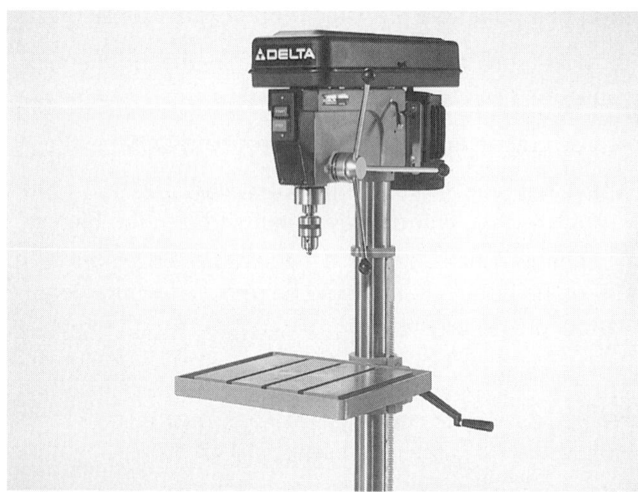

Figure 3-58. A drill press is used to accurately drill holes in parts. (Delta)

Resurfacing Parts

Resurfacing may be needed on a warped cylinder, cylinder head, or on damaged gasket surfaces. Minor resurfacing can usually be done on a ***flat plate*** covered with a piece of cutting paper, **Figure 3-60.** The part is rubbed on the cutting paper in a circular motion to remove high spots on the part. Badly nicked parts may also require draw filing.

Severely warped parts must be resurfaced by a machine shop. You would not be able to remove material accurately enough with a flat plate and cutting paper or by draw filing.

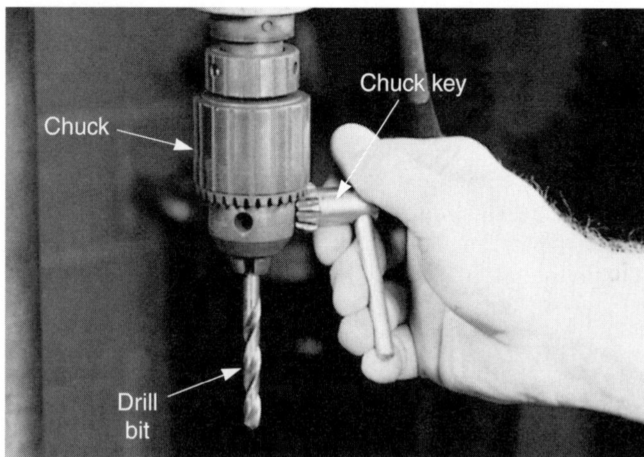

Figure 3-59. A chuck holds and turns the drill bit. Use a chuck key to firmly tighten the drill bit in the chuck. Never leave the key in the chuck.

Grinders

Most shops have a ***bench grinder,*** **Figure 3-61.** It is primarily used for rough metal removal. When one of the grinding wheels is replaced with a wire wheel, it can be used for parts cleaning. Some shops may also have a ***rotary grinder,*** which is a handy tool for tight places, **Figure 3-62.** Avoid grinding aluminum or brass with abrasive stones. These soft materials will clog the stone.

Warning: Improper use of a grinder can result in serious injury. Always wear eye protection and position the tool rest close to the stone.

Some other grinder rules to remember are:

- When grinding small parts, hold them with locking pliers. This can help prevent serious hand injuries.
- Use light pressure to avoid uneven stone wear, overheating, and catching.
- Use water to keep parts cool during the grinding operation.
- Do not grind near combustible materials.

Hydraulic Press

A ***hydraulic press*** will produce tons of force for the assembly or disassembly of pressed components, **Figure 3-63.** In engine rebuilding, the hydraulic press is commonly used to force crankshaft pins on assembled crankshafts. A special fixture is needed to support the crankshaft and prevent damage while driving.

Warning: Respect the force generated by a hydraulic press. Always wear eye protection and stand to one side during pressing operations.

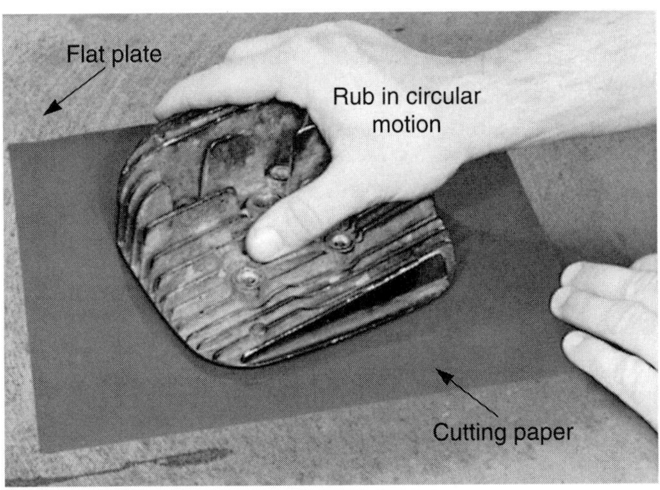

Figure 3-60. A slightly warped or damaged gasket surface may be repaired on a flat plate using cutting paper. Rub the part in a slow circular pattern. Solvent on both sides of the cutting paper aids in both cutting and holding the paper in place.

Figure 3-61. A bench grinder is a useful shop tool. (Delta)

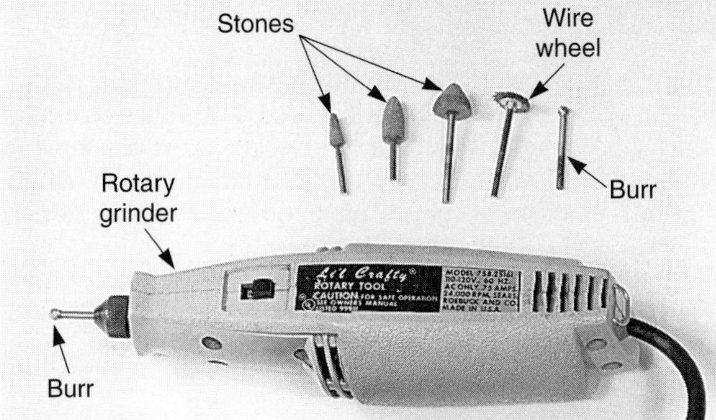

Figure 3-62. A rotary grinder is used for light grinding, shaping, and polishing.

Welding

Welding uses extreme heat to melt and fuse metal parts together. High temperatures and a filler rod permanently connect the two parts. Welding is utilized in the repair of broken parts and fabrication of new parts. A gas flame or electric arc can be used to produce sufficient heat for welding.

Common types of welding in motorcycle repair are oxyacetylene (gas) welding, oxyacetylene brazing, electric arc welding, and shielded gas arc (TIG and MIG) welding.

Oxyacetylene Welding

Oxyacetylene welding burns a mixture of oxygen and acetylene (flammable gas) to produce metal fusion, **Figure 3-64.** A filler rod is used to help fill the gap between the two parts. Oxyacetylene welding equipment is also used to heat and loosen seized parts.

Brazing

Brazing is another form of oxyacetylene gas welding. It differs, however, from gas welding. Brazing uses less heat and a different filler rod (easier melting filler rod) than traditional oxyacetylene welding.

Gas welding causes a large area on the parts to be heated. As a result, it is not advisable to use gas welding for frame repair or when part warpage is critical. Oxyacetylene is very useful for exhaust system fabrication and repair, or heating metal parts for bending.

Electric Arc Welding

There are two types of electric arc welding common to motorcycle repair. These are ac (alternating current) or electric arc welding and heliarc welding. ***Electric arc welding*** uses a large electric current and electric arc to produce extreme heat. A steel filler rod, called an ***electrode,*** is melted into the joint. **Figure 3-65** illustrates arc welding. Arc welding is frequently used for motorcycle frame repairs or when repairing other steel parts. Heat is concentrated in a small area which reduces part warpage.

Shielded Gas Welding

There are two types of ***shielded gas welding***: tungsten inert-gas (TIG) and metal inert-gas (MIG). The welding takes place inside an inert gas (helium, argon, nitrogen) shield. This gas shield is used to protect the weld pool from contamination.

These two welding techniques are designed primarily for repairing aluminum, copper, and other nonferrous (contains no iron) metals. They can also be used to weld ferrous (contains iron) metals.

The ***metal inert-gas (MIG)*** process is becoming the preferred method of the motorcycle industry.

Safety rules for welding include:

- Never look directly at the arc unless wearing a suitable helmet or face shield.
- Do not permit bystanders, unless they are wearing protective gear.
- Wear goggles when chipping or wire brushing.
- Wear protective clothing and gloves.
- Make certain that electric arc, MIG, and TIG welding machines are properly grounded.

Welding and brazing require training, practice, and proper safety precautions. If at all possible, sign up for a welding course. Specialized training in welding will help you become a better motorcycle technician.

Summary

To properly maintain and repair motorcycles, ATVs, and scooters, an investment must be made in reliable tools. In most cases, you should invest in good quality tools that are backed by a lifetime warranty. Then, if a tool is broken or damaged, the manufacturer's warranty will replace the tool at no cost.

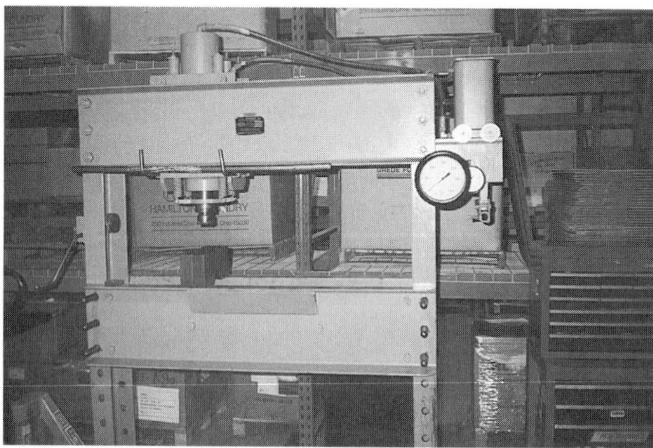

Figure 3-63. A hydraulic press will produce powerful driving force. It is used to push pins out of crankshafts. Wear eye protection and double-check that safety pins are holding the table in place before pressing.

Figure 3-65. An electric arc welder forces a very high current through cables, electrode, and workpiece. Since the electrode is held away from the workpiece, an electric arc jumps the gap between the electrode and the part. The arc produces tremendous heat which melts both the electrode and metal part. (Miller)

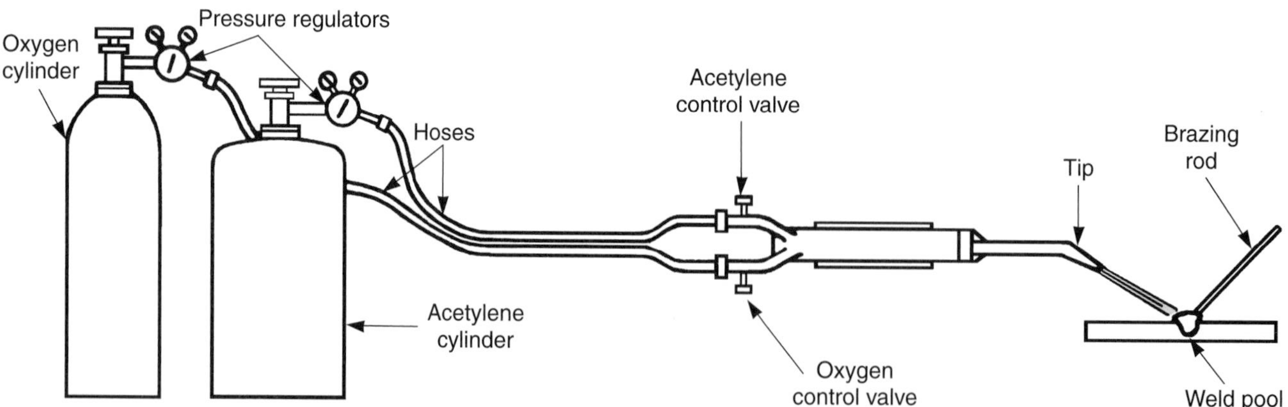

Figure 3-64. Oxyacetylene torch burns a mixture of oxygen and acetylene to produce an intensely hot flame for welding, heating, and cutting.

When beginning to assemble your tool collection, one of the first purchases should be a good tool box. When choosing a tool box, do not buy one that simply holds the tools you currently own. Purchase a box that is large enough to accommodate some growth in your tool inventory.

Wrenches may be broken down into five categories: box-end wrenches, open-end wrenches, combination wrenches, flare-nut wrenches, and adjustable wrenches. Two categories of screwdrivers are commonly used for motorcycle repair, straight tip and Phillips tip (cross point). Sockets and socket drivers provide a fast, versatile means of loosening and tightening fasteners. Socket drivers include ratchets, breaker bars, and speed handles. Universals and extensions increase the driving capabilities of sockets and handles.

Pliers should never be used as a substitute for the proper wrench, socket, or screwdriver. Allen wrenches come in metric and USC sizes. They are also available as Allen sockets. Hammer types commonly found in a motorcycle shop are the ball peen, brass, plastic, dead blow, rawhide, and rubber hammer. Files are designed to remove small amounts of metal for smoothing or shaping parts. Punches, chisels, and pry bars can be very dangerous if misused. Engine service and repair tools include a variety of tools often used on several engine models. They are needed for motorcycle engine testing, tear down, and assembly.

Power hand tools can be driven by either air pressure or electricity. Special heavy-duty impact sockets are designed for use with air impacts. Impact sockets are usually flat black in color. Do not use a hand socket with air tools. General shop equipment is normally provided by the motorcycle repair facility. However, some technicians purchase some of the less expensive equipment themselves.

Just about every aspect of motorcycle repair involves some type of measurement. A steel yardstick or meterstick can be used as a straightedge to check part alignment and for measurements not requiring extreme accuracy. The outside micrometer is used for the accurate measurement of numerous part dimensions. A depth micrometer is used to measure the depth of a hole or recess in a part. A telescoping gauge is a spring-loaded, T-shaped instrument used to measure inside diameters or distances. Dial indicators are designed with face markings and ranges to suit many different measuring jobs.

It is general practice to always inspect and clean motorcycle parts during disassembly and before reassembly. Degreasing solvents are normally used for the removal of oil, sludge, or grease. Decarbonizing solvents are specially formulated petroleum distillates that can loosen carbon, gum, and varnish buildup on metal parts. A scraper is used to remove gaskets, carbon, sludge, and sealing compounds from parts. Dry-blast cleaning is the process of bombarding metal parts with shot (particles) to remove hard deposits.

As a motorcycle technician, you will sometimes run into situations when special machining, cutting, welding, or other fabrication type operations must be performed. Common types of welding in motorcycle repair are oxyacetylene (gas) welding, oxyacetylene brazing, electric arc welding, and shielded gas arc (TIG and MIG) welding.

Know These Terms

Tool box
Roll-around cabinet
Upper chest
Carrying tray
Tool holders
Hand tools
Box-end wrenches
Open-end wrenches
Combination wrenches
Flare-nut wrench
Adjustable end wrench
Straight tip
Phillips tip
Impact driver
Socket
Standard socket
Deep socket
6-point
12-point
Drive size
Socket drivers
Ratchet
Breaker bars
Speed handle
Torque wrenches
T-handle
Hand driver
Universal
Extension
Pliers
Allen wrenches
Allen sockets
Hammers
Files
File card
Center punch
Drift punch
Alignment punches
Chisel
Pry bars
Hacksaw
Coarse blades
Fine blades
Special service tools
Cleaning tools
Air wrenches
General shop equipment
Decimal conversion chart
Yardstick
Meterstick
Six-inch scales
Combination square
Outside micrometer
Sleeve scale
Thimble scale
Inside micrometer
Depth micrometer
Dial caliper
Vernier caliper
Telescoping gauge
Dial indicator
Dial bore gauge
Feeler gauge
Flat feeler gauge
Wire gauge
Plastigage
Compression gauge
Wet compression test
Vacuum gauge
Fluid pressure gauge
Spring tester
Graduated cylinder
Degreasing solvents
Decarbonizing solvents
Cold soak cleaners
Wire wheel
Scraper
Dry-blast cleaning

Boring bar
Lathe
Vertical mill
Drill press
Flat plate
Bench grinder
Rotary grinder
Hydraulic press
Welding
Oxyacetylene welding
Brazing
Electric arc welding
Electrode
Shielded gas welding
Metal inert-gas (MIG)

Review Questions—Chapter 3

Do not write in this text. Place your answers on a separate sheet of paper.

1. List the five categories of wrenches used by the motorcycle technician.
2. Which of the following wrenches provides the best support and is least likely to damage the head of a fastener?
   A. Open-end wrench.
   B. Spanner wrench.
   C. Box-end wrench.
   D. Adjustable wrench.
3. Straight tip and _____ tip are the two most common types of screwdrivers used by the motorcycle technician.
4. Sockets and wrenches come in conventional and _____ sizes.
5. What are the three common ratchet drive sizes used for motorcycle repair?
6. A tool that resembles a ratchet but does *not* use a ratchet mechanism is called a _____.
7. Which of the following is *not* one of the common variations of sockets used in motorcycle repair?
   A. 12-point.
   B. 8-point.
   C. Deep.
   D. Standard (short).
8. The purpose of an _____ is to move the ratchet away from the socket.
9. Pliers are useful for _____ or _____.
10. *True* or *False?* Allen wrenches are available in metric and conventional sizes.
11. List four types of hammers commonly found in a motorcycle shop.
12. A measurement system which uses multiples of ten is called the _____ system.
13. The sleeve scale on a conventional (English) outside micrometer is marked off in increments of _____.
14. What type of micrometer has a scale that reads in reverse?
15. What measuring tool must be used in conjunction with a telescoping gauge?
    A. Inside micrometer.
    B. Outside micrometer.
    C. Dial indicator.
    D. Meterstick.
16. List the four common uses for a dial indicator.
17. What two measurement tools are combined into a dial bore gauge?
18. What is the common conventional and metric range of a feeler gauge set?
19. A ______ is commonly used to check and indicate internal engine condition. A ______ will help isolate the engine problem.
20. The most common use of a vacuum gauge is for ______ or _____.

Suggested Activities

1. Select appropriate engine parts and make practice measurements. Use each of the following precision measuring tools:
   A. Outside micrometer.
   B. Telescoping gauge.
   C. Dial caliper.
   D. Depth micrometer.
   E. Dial bore gauge.
   F. Plastigage.
2. A caliper makes inside, outside, and depth measurements. Compare caliper measurements to outside micrometer, telescoping gauge, and depth micrometer measurements on various parts.
3. Perform dry and wet compression tests on a motorcycle engine. Describe the results.

4

Fasteners, Gaskets, and Diagnostic Procedures

After studying this chapter, you will be able to:

- List the different types of fasteners.
- Determine which fastener is appropriate for a specific job.
- Torque fasteners to specifications when needed.
- Repair damaged or broken fasteners.
- Repair damaged threads.
- Remove broken fasteners.
- Describe gaskets, sealants, and seals.
- Describe the different types of service manuals.
- Find and use the service manual index and contents section.
- Explain the different kinds of information and illustrations found in a service manual.
- Summarize the other kinds of publications found in a motorcycle shop.
- Describe the correct diagnostic procedures.

Fasteners, gaskets, seals, and sealants are constantly used by the motorcycle technician. It is almost impossible to connect any two parts of a motorcycle without them. These various components are subjected to heavy loads, high frequency vibration, heat, and severe stress. As a result, fastener and gasket design, material, and torque settings have assumed a position of major importance. The final part of the chapter discusses service literature and troubleshooting techniques.

Fasteners

Fasteners include any type of holding device. Hundreds are used in the construction of a motorcycle. Some of the most common ones are shown in **Figure 4-1.** The materials and designs of fasteners used on a motorcycle are not arrived at by chance or accident. Fastener design determines the type of tool required for installation or removal. Fastener material is carefully selected to decrease the possibility of physical failure.

Bolt and Screw Terminology

Bolts and ***screws*** may be identified by type, length, major and minor diameters, pitch, length of thread, class of fit, material, tensile strength, and wrench size needed. They are measured by the ***United States Customary (USC)*** or the ***metric (SI)*** measuring systems. However, the points of measure differ, **Figure 4-2.** Most imported bikes use metric fasteners.

For example, the ***thread pitch*** of USC bolts is determined by the number of threads in 1″ of threaded bolt length. The pitch is expressed in number of threads per inch. The thread pitch in the metric system is determined by the distance in millimeters between two adjacent threads. To check the thread pitch of a bolt or stud, a ***thread pitch gauge*** is used, **Figure 4-3.** Gauges are available in both customary and metric dimensions.

Figure 4-1. Some of the types of fasteners used on motorcycles.

Caution: Metric bolts, nuts, and screws are not interchangeable with United States Customary fasteners. The use of incorrect tools and fasteners will cause damage to components.

There are some identifying measurements that are the same for both USC and SI bolts. In both, the bolt length is the distance measured from the bottom of the head to the bolt tip. The bolt's ***major diameter*** is measured from the top or crest of the threads on one side to the crest on the other. The ***minor diameter*** is determined by measuring from the bottom of the threads on one side to the bottom of the other. If you removed the threads, the diameter of the portion left would be the minor diameter. The metric bolt diameter and length are in millimeters, while USC are in fractions of an inch.

The bolt's ***grade,*** or tensile strength, is the amount of stress or stretch it is able to withstand. The bolt material and diameter determine its tensile strength. In the US Customary system, a bolt's tensile strength is identified by the number of radial lines (grade marks) on the bolt head. More lines mean higher tensile strength, **Figure 4-4.** In the metric system, bolt or stud tensile strength can be identified by a property class number on the bolt head, **Figure 4-5.** The higher the number, the greater the tensile strength.

Warning: When replacing a fastener, make sure to use one with the same measurements and strength as the old one. Incorrect or mismatched fasteners can result in damage to the vehicle and possible personal injury.

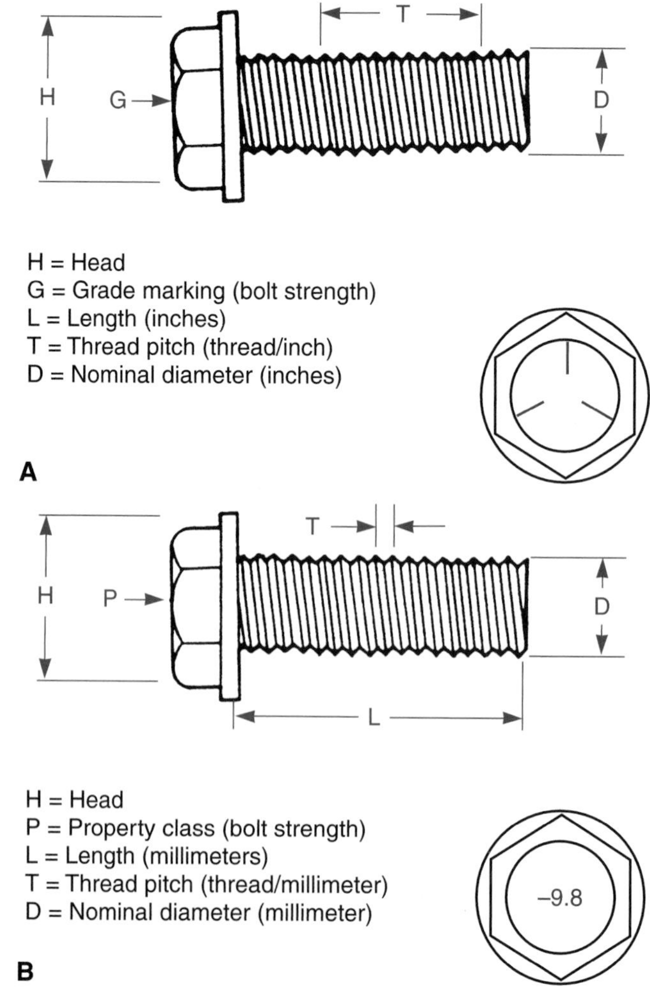

Figure 4-2. A—USC bolt. B—Metric bolt terminology.

Bolts and nuts also come in right- and left-hand threads. With common ***right-hand threads,*** the fastener must be turned *clockwise* to tighten. With the less common ***left-hand threads,*** turn the fastener in a *counter-clockwise* direction to tighten. The letter *L* may be stamped on fasteners with left-hand threads.

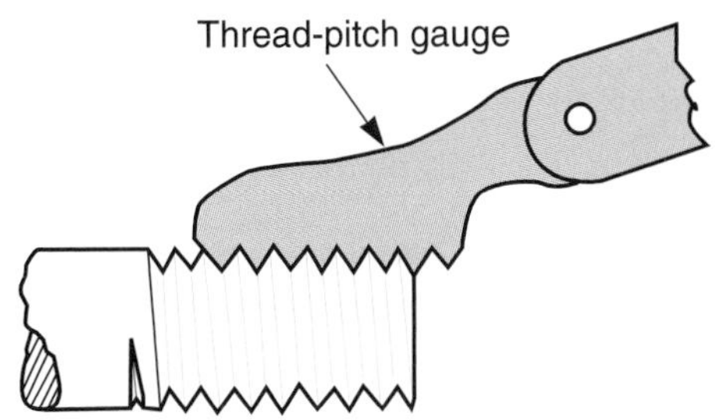

Figure 4-3. Using a thread-pitch gauge to determine the number of threads per inch or mm.

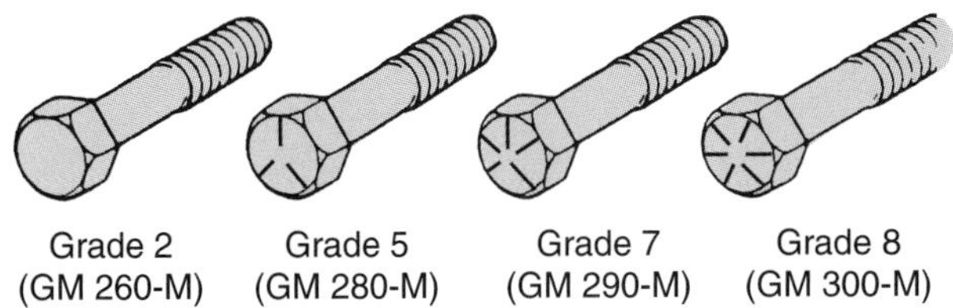

Figure 4-4. USC bolt identification marks correspond with bolt strength. Increasing numbers represent increasing strength.

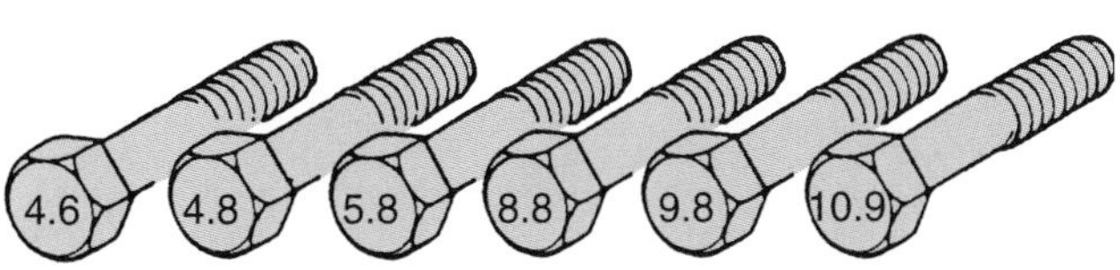

Figure 4-5. Metric bolt identification marks correspond with bolt strength. Increasing numbers represent increasing strength.

Nuts

Nuts are manufactured in a variety of sizes and styles, **Figure 4-6.** Nuts designed for motorcycle use are generally hexagonal in shape (six-sided) and are used on bolts and studs. The diameter and thread pitch must be the same. To join a nut and bolt or stud, the bolt diameter and the nut hole diameter must be the same. It is just as important that the threads on both be properly matched.

Nuts are also graded to match the strength of their respective bolts, **Figure 4-7.** For example, a grade 8 nut must be used with a grade 8 bolt. If a grade 5 nut is used instead, a grade 5 connection would result. The grade 5 nut cannot carry the load of the grade 8 bolt. Look for the nut markings, which are usually located on one side. Grade 8 and other critical applications require the use of fully hardened flat washers. Soft wrought washers can cause a loss of clamp load.

Studs

A ***stud*** is a metal rod threaded on both ends. The stud is turned into a threaded hole in a part. The part to be

U.S. Customary System	Metric System
Hex nut grade 5 — 3 dots	Hex nut property class 9 — Arabic 9
Hex nut grade 8 — 6 dots	Hex nut property class 10 — Arabic 10
Increasing dots represent increasing strength	Can also have finish or paint dab on hex flat. Increasing numbers represent increasing strength

Figure 4-7. Nut grade markings.

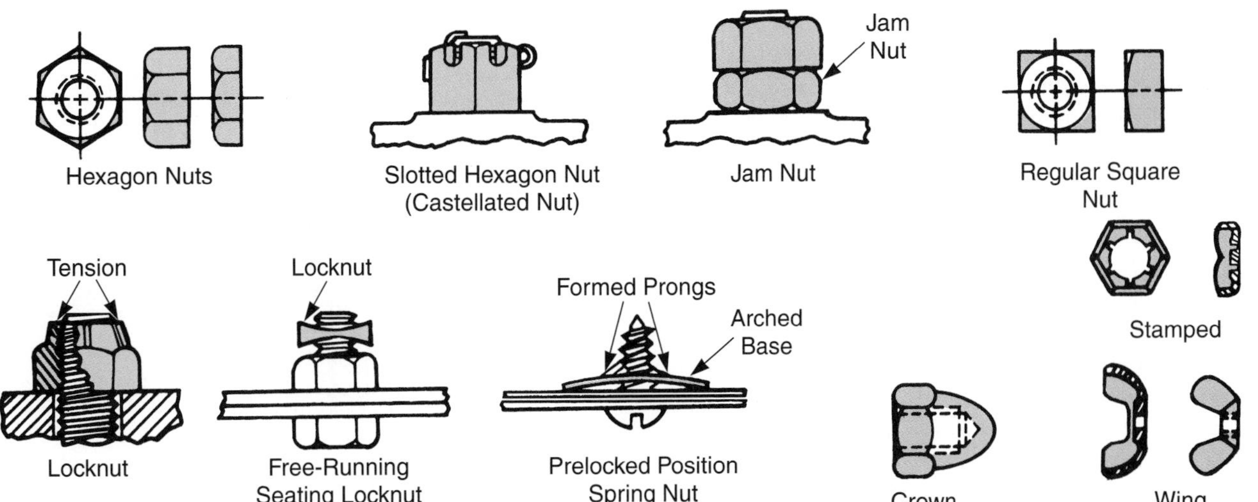

Figure 4-6. Various nuts that may be used on motorcycles.

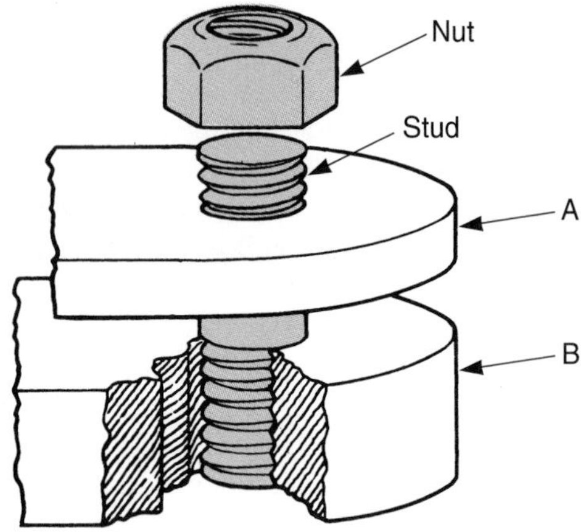

Figure 4-8. One use of a stud. The stud is threaded into part B. Part A is slipped over the stud and the nut is then placed on the stud and tightened.

secured is slipped over the stud. A washer is placed over the stud and a nut is installed to secure the part. Studs are available in many lengths and diameters. Some have a coarse thread on one end and a fine thread on the other. Others have the same thread on both ends, **Figure 4-8.** In some cases, this thread may run the full length of the stud.

Machine Screws

Machine screws are used without nuts. They are passed through one part and threaded into another. When the screw is tightened, the two parts are held in firm contact. As shown in **Figure 4-9,** there are many different types of machine screws and screw heads. Most are driven with some type of screwdriver.

Sheet Metal Screws

Sheet metal screws are used to fasten thin metal parts together and for attaching various items to sheet metal, **Figure 4-10.** They are much faster and less expensive than bolts. To use a sheet metal screw, punch a hole in the sheet metal. The hole should be slightly smaller than the screw's minor diameter. A punched hole is better than a drilled hole because the punched hole tends to close as the screw is tightened. This provides added gripping power.

Self-Locking Bolts and Nuts

Some nuts are designed to be self-locking. This is accomplished in various ways, but all share the same principle. They create friction or interference between the bolt or stud threads and the nut.

In **Figure 4-11A,** the nut utilizes a collar or insert of soft metal, fiber, or plastic. As the bolt threads pass through the nut, they must force their way through the collar. This forces the collar material tightly into the threads, locking the nut in place.

In **Figure 4-11B,** the nut's upper section is slotted and the segments are forced together. When the bolt passes through the nut, it spreads the segments apart, producing a locking action. **Figure 4-11C** shows a single slot in the side of the nut. The slot may be forced open or closed during manufacture, distorting the upper thread. This will create a jamming effect when the bolt pulls the nut threads back into alignment.

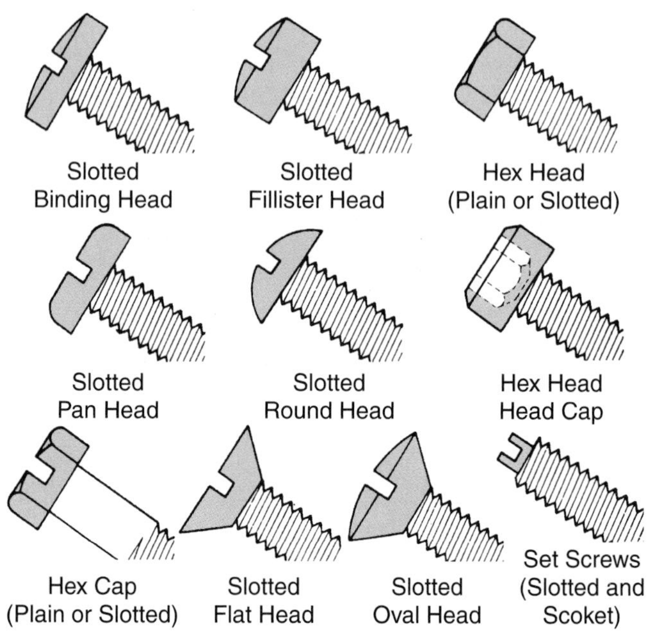

Figure 4-9. Machine screw head types.

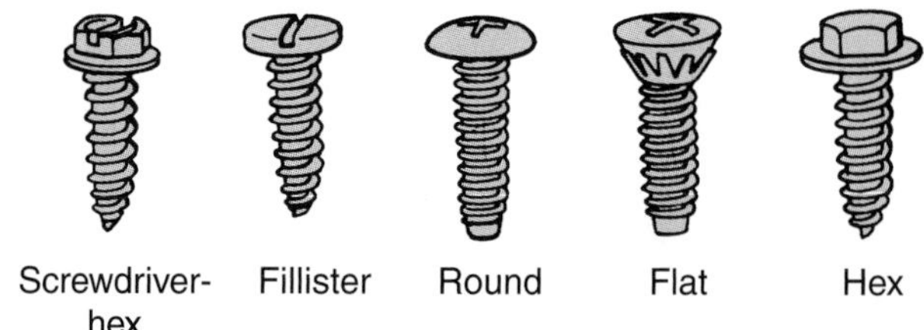

Figure 4-10. Types of self-tapping screws.

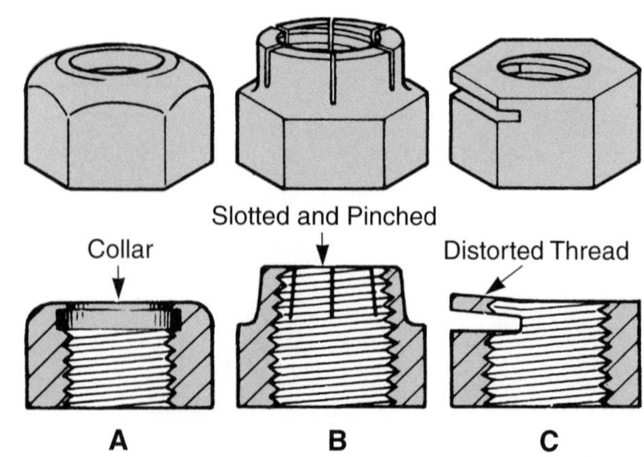

Figure 4-11. Self-locking nuts. A—Soft collar type. B—Top section slotted and pinched together. C—Slot to distort the upper thread area.

Some bolts have heads designed to spring when tightened to produce a self-locking effect. Occasionally, the threaded end of a bolt will be split and the halves slightly bent outward. When threaded into a hole, the halves are forced together. This creates friction between the threads.

Self-locking fasteners offer greater holding strength and better vibration resistance. Some prevailing torque fasteners can be reused if in good condition. Others form an initial locking condition when the nut is first installed. The insert forms closely to the bolt thread pattern, reducing any tendency to loosen. When the nut is removed, the locking efficiency is greatly reduced. When replacing self-locking fasteners, use only new fasteners of the same type and install them to prevailing torque.

Washers

Washers are used under bolt heads and nuts. Various types of washers are shown in **Figure 4-12.** Flat washers are simple discs with a hole to fit a bolt or screw. Lockwashers are either split or designed with internal or external teeth to prevent a fastener from working loose. When using lock washers with die cast or aluminum parts, a steel flat washer is frequently installed under the lock washer to prevent part damage.

Torquing Fasteners

The materials used to construct a motorcycle can be subjected to uneven torque stress if the fasteners used to hold the subassemblies are not correctly installed. Improper bolt tightening can result in breakage, leaks, premature bearing and seal failure, cylinder head warpage, and suspension failure from loose or missing fasteners.

When tightening bolts, be sure to torque them using a torque wrench to the specifications in the service manual. This type of wrench measures the amount of turning force being applied to a fastener. Conventional torque wrench scales usually read in foot-pounds (ft.-lbs.) or in Newton-meters (N•m).

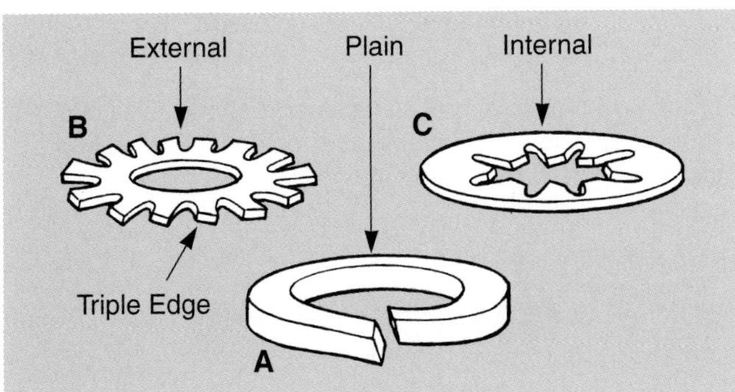

Figure 4-12. Washer types. A—Split lock washer. B—External lock washer. C—Internal lock washer.

Note: To convert foot-pounds to inch-pounds, multiply the foot-pounds by 12. To convert inch-pounds to foot-pounds, divide inch-pounds by 12. To convert foot-pounds to Newton-meters, multiply by 1.356.

Using a Torque Wrench

Torque wrenches are available in different sizes, ranges, and calibrations. A torque wrench such as the one shown in **Figure 4-13** is suitable for most motorcycle applications. The procedure for using a torque wrench is as follows:

1. Make sure that the fastener threads are clean and dry. Threads should be dry unless otherwise specified in the service manual.
2. When reading a torque wrench, look straight down at the scale. Viewing from an angle can give a false reading.
3. Only pull on the torque wrench handle. Do not allow the flex bar on beam torque wrenches to touch anything.
4. Place a steady pull on the torque wrench. Do not use short, jerky motions or inaccurate readings can result.
5. Torque specification charts give average bolt tightening values, **Figure 4-14.** This chart should be used only when factory specifications are not available.
6. Tighten all bolts and nuts in at least four steps: one-half recommended torque, three-fourth torque, full torque, and to full torque a second time.
7. A bolt tightening sequence, or pattern, may be required to ensure the part is fastened evenly. Tightening follows a crisscross pattern from one side to the other. The service manual illustrates the proper sequence when a torque pattern is critical.

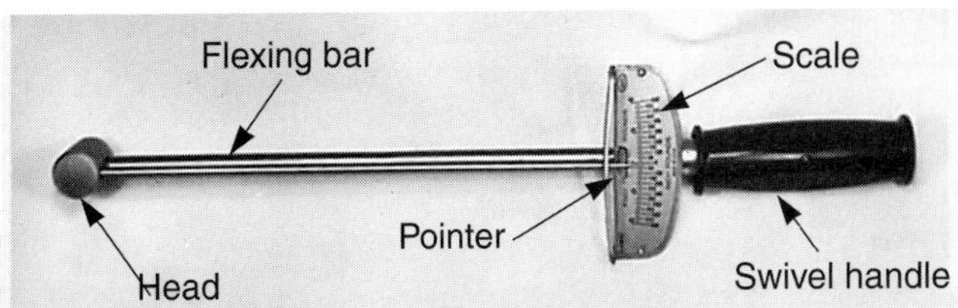

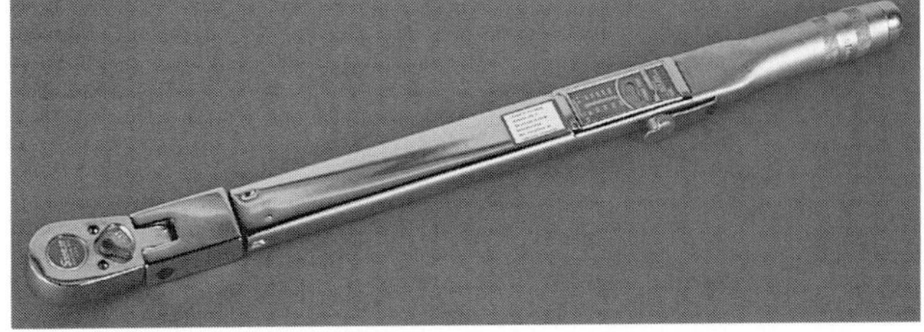

Figure 4-13. A torque wrench should be used to accurately tighten fasteners (head bolts, rod bolts, etc.).

Fastener Size	N•m	ft.-lb.
5 mm bolt and nut	4.5-6	3-4
6 mm bolt and nut	8-12	6-9
8 mm bolt and nut	18-25	13-18
10 mm bolt and nut	30-40	22-29
12 mm bolt and nut	50-60	36-43
5 mm screw	3.5-5	2-4
6 mm screw and 6 mm bolt with 8 mm head	7-11	5-8
6 mm flange bolt and nut	10-14	7-10
8 mm flange bolt and nut	24-30	17-22
10 mm flange bolt and nut	35-45	25-33

Figure 4-14. Torque specification chart.

8. Retorque fasteners when required. Some engine components may need to be retightened after operation and heating. Expansion and contraction, due to temperature changes, can cause fasteners to loosen.
9. Replace bolts when recommended by the motorcycle maker. Many manuals suggest that old bolts be thrown away and new ones installed.

If a bolt is stretched to its yield point, it takes a permanent set and will never return to its normal strength. For this reason, torque values are calculated with a margin 25% below the yield point. There are some fasteners, however, that are torqued intentionally just barely into a yield condition. This type of fastener, known as a ***torque-to-yield (TTY)*** bolt will produce 100% of its intended strength, compared to 75% when torqued to normal values. However, these fasteners should not be reused unless otherwise specified by the manufacturer. Used TTY bolts will have a champagne-bottle shape, referred to as a necked-out bolt. Service manuals usually state if TTY bolts are used.

Thread Repairs

Thread repairs are sometimes needed when threads have been stripped, broken out, or smashed, or when fasteners have been broken off inside a hole, **Figure 4-15.** There are a number of thread repairs that can be done quickly and inexpensively.

Minor thread repairs can be made without complete thread replacement. When a thread has minor damage, such as flattening or misalignment from cross threading, it may not be necessary to totally replace the thread. Two useful tools for minor thread repairs are a thread file and thread chaser.

A ***thread file*** is used for external (bolt and stud) thread repairs. It is simply rubbed parallel to the damaged threads to clean out the grooves. A ***thread chaser,*** **Figure 4-16,** is used much like a tap which cuts internal threads. It is installed into a threaded hole to cut away partially flattened threads. Major thread repair must be performed when fasteners are broken off or threads are badly stripped.

Removing Broken Fasteners

Overtightening, corrosion, or extreme side loads can cause a bolt, screw, or stud to break off. If the fastener is broken above the thread surface, locking pliers may be used to unscrew the fastener. When a bolt is broken off flush or below the surface, it may be necessary to drill out the broken fastener and use a screw extractor, **Figure 4-17.**

Note: In some cases, a left-hand drill bit can be used to remove a broken bolt. Carefully center punch and drill the broken fastener as if you were going to use a screw extractor. Often, a bolt that was broken by side load pressure will begin to turn and eventually remove itself from the hole. Be sure to check the hole threads for damage before installing a new fastener.

Accurate center punching and drilling is extremely important. Drilling the hole all the way through the fastener helps to relieve pressure and aids bolt removal. Be careful not to drill through the part as it could be damaged beyond repair.

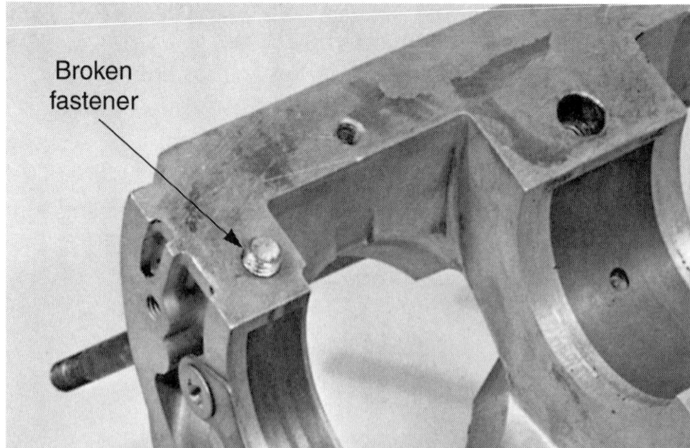

Figure 4-15. A typical broken fastener is shown. This one is in a hole which holds the crankcase together. The broken bolt must be removed to salvage the case.

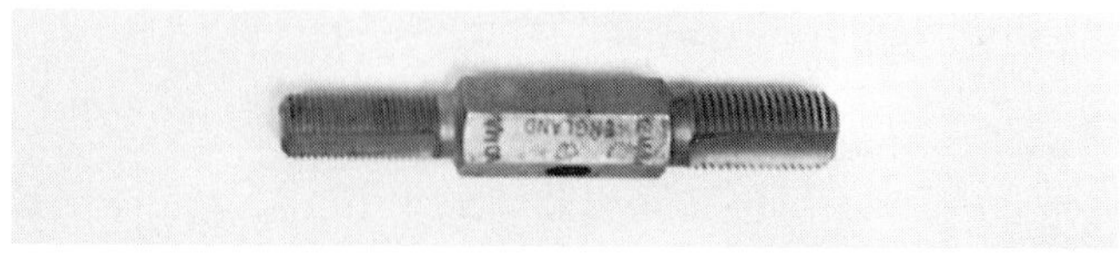

Figure 4-16. A thread chaser will repair lightly damaged inside threads. Avoid the use of a tap in place of a thread chaser.

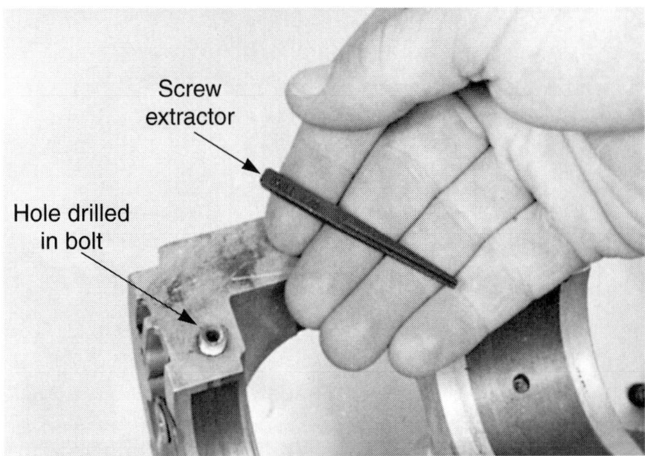

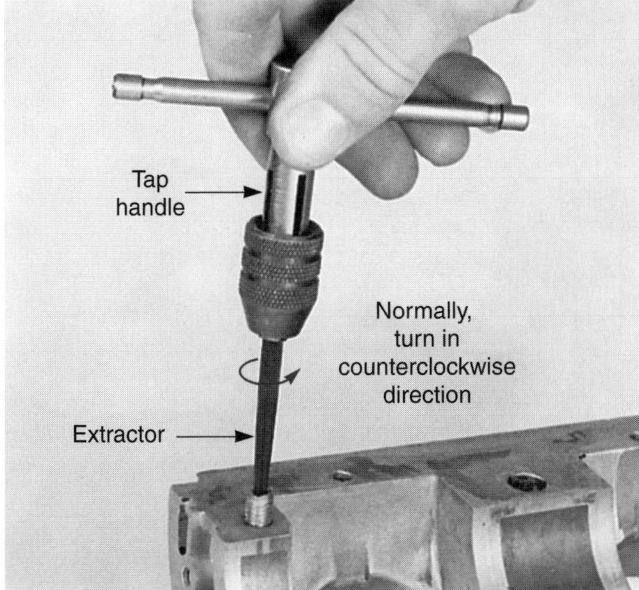

Figure 4-17. This fastener is broken off flush with the part's surface. It is easily removed by carefully drilling a hole in the center of the fastener and using an extractor. The extractor will unscrew the broken bolt section.

Thread Repair Inserts

Sometimes, it is not possible to remove a broken fastener without thread damage. When this happens, a thread repair insert can be installed, **Figure 4-18.** A ***thread repair insert*** is a dependable and economical way to restore a severely stripped thread. Several types of thread repair inserts are available. Installation of a thread repair insert involves:

- Drilling out the threaded hole.
- Tapping the hole for the thread insert.
- Installing the insert.

Note: Follow the instructions for the particular type of insert you are using as procedures can vary.

Figure 4-18. Thread repair sequence. 1—Drill damaged hole to smooth surface and remove any broken fastener. 2—Tap the hole, taking care to clean the tap as you work down. 3—Install thread insert. (Helicoil)

Cutting New Threads

Cutting new threads requires the use of a tap for internal threads or a die for external threads. Tap and die sets, **Figure 4-19,** are available in metric and US Customary sizes. Dies are not frequently used in motorcycle repair since they cut external threads. External threads are found on bolts and studs which can be replaced easily. ***Taps*** are often used for threading a new hole in parts being fabricated (brackets, accessory mounting) or preparing a hole for a thread repair insert.

To use a tap, it is necessary to drill a hole. Drilling (machining a hole) is also required during bracket fabrication, thread repairs, and many other instances where holes must be made in parts. As illustrated in Chapter 3, a drill press or portable electric drill can be used with a variety of drill bits.

Drilling usually causes a burr (rough edge) on both sides of the hole. A burr should be removed with a deburring tool or countersink. **Figure 4-20** shows how a rough drilled hole can be cleaned and smoothed.

Tapping a New Hole

The following procedure should be followed when tapping a new hole:

1. Drill a hole equal to the size needed for the tap. A tap-drill chart will give the right size bit to use for a specific size tap.
2. Lubricate the tap and hole with thread cutting fluid.
3. Start the tap squarely, **Figure 4-21.**
4. Back up (unscrew) the tap every one-half turn. This will clean cuttings out of the tap and prevent breakage, **Figure 4-22.**

When using taps, keep these three simple rules in mind:

- Never force a tap handle or the tool may break. Back off the handle as described to clean out metal shavings.
- Keep the tap well oiled to ease cutting.
- Always use the right size tap in a correctly sized and drilled hole.

Caution: Be extremely careful not to break a tap or screw extractor. They are case hardened and cannot be easily drilled out of a hole. You will compound your problems if you break one of these tools.

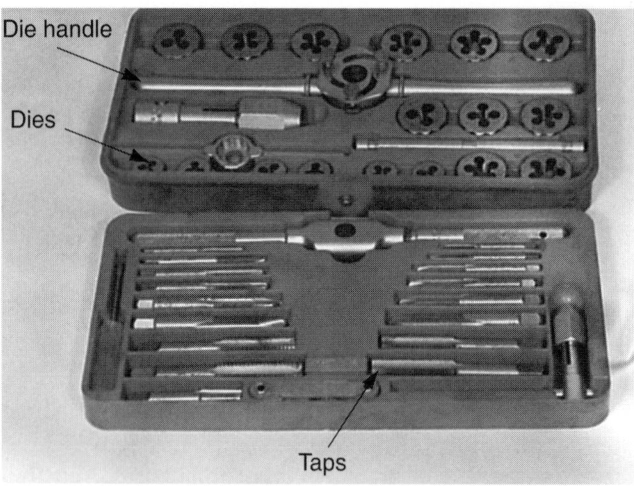

Figure 4-19. Tap and die sets are available in customary and metric sizes. Both are needed for motorcycle repair.

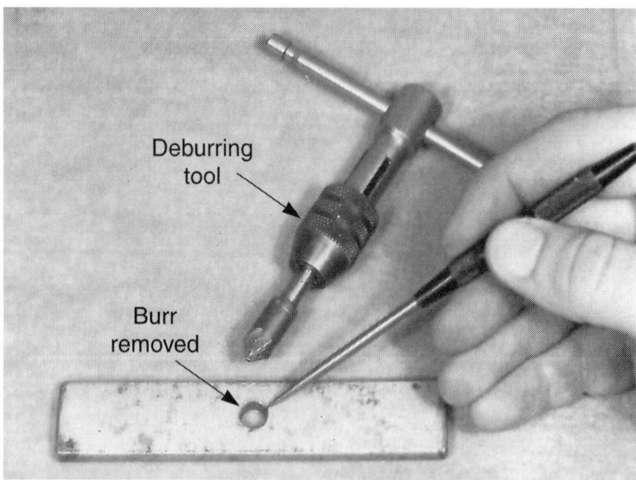

Figure 4-20. A deburring tool is used to remove burr from drilled holes. Inserting and rotating the tool will cut off any sharp edges.

Removing Damaged Nuts

Occasionally, nuts will be difficult to remove due to rust, dirt, and corrosion. When this happens, there are several methods that may be used to assist removal: heat, nut-splitter, chisel, or hacksaw. See **Figure 4-23.**

Penetrating Oil

Regardless of the removal method, it is a good idea to apply penetrating oil (special light oil used to free rusty and dirty parts) to the area. Applying heat will also help, if it is not injurious to the part. Use caution not to overheat the parts as they can warp, melt, or lose temper. Heat also ruins finishes, especially paint and plastics. If in doubt as to the effects, do not apply heat.

Warning: Never use a torch near a gas tank, battery, or other flammable material.

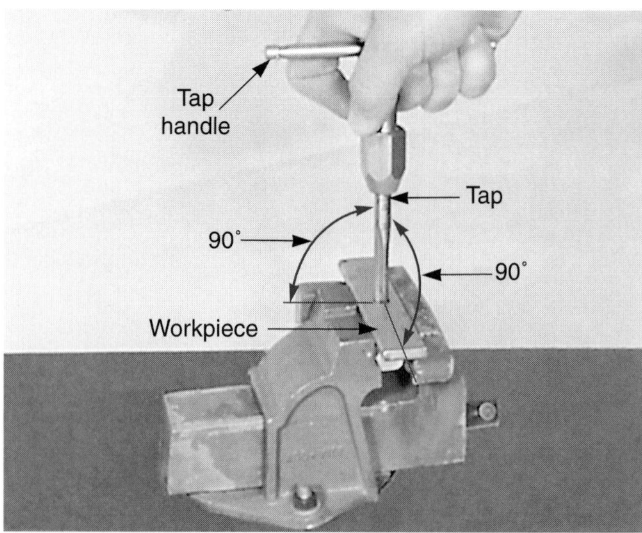

Figure 4-21. For a straight and accurately tapped hole, the tap must be started squarely. It is very easy to start it at an angle, ruining the threads and possibly breaking the tap.

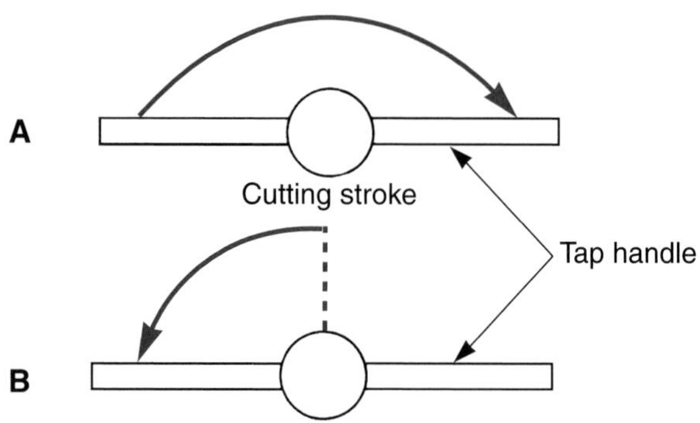

Figure 4-22. After the tap is started, it must be back cleaned throughout the threading process. A—Advance tap one-half turn at a time. B—After each half-turn of cutting, back clean the tap by turning it counterclockwise one-quarter turn. Always use cutting oil to ensure clean cutting and to lengthen tap life.

Nonthreaded Fasteners

Numerous types of nonthreaded fasteners are utilized in the assembly of a motorcycle, ATV, or scooter. It is essential to learn the most common types.

Cotter Pins

Cotter pins are used both with slotted and castle nuts as well as on clevis pins and linkage ends. Use as thick a cotter pin as possible. Cut off the surplus length and bend the ends as shown in **Figure 4-24.** If necessary, they may be bent around the sides of the nut. Make certain that the bent ends will not interfere with some part. Never reuse a cotter pin.

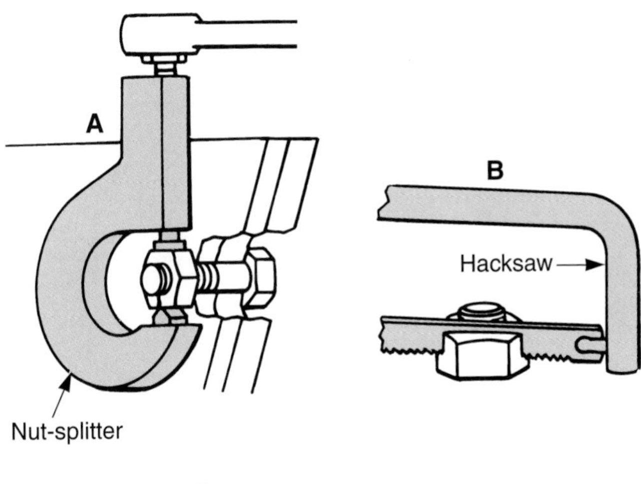

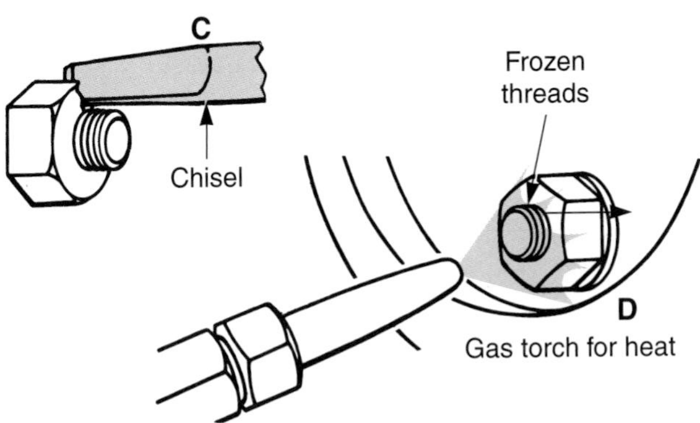

Figure 4-23. Four common methods of removing stubborn nuts. A—Nut-splitter. B—Hacksaw. C—Chisel. D—Propane or gas torch.

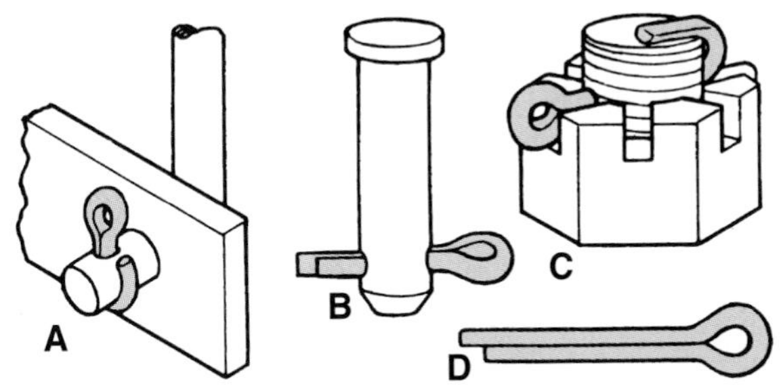

Figure 4-24. Uses of cotter pin. A—Linkage. B—Clevis pin. C—Slotted hex nut. D—Cotter pin.

Keys, Splines, and Pins

Keys, splines, and ***pins*** are used to attach gears, sprockets, and pulleys to shafts so they rotate as a unit. When a key or pin is used, the unit being attached to the shaft is fixed for no end-to-end movement. Splines will allow, when desired, longitudinal movement while still causing the parts to rotate together. In some cases, pins are used to fix shafts in housings to prevent end movement and rotation, **Figure 4-25.**

Locking Plates and Safety Wire

Locking plates are made of thin sheet metal. The plate is arranged so that two or more screws pass through it. The metal edge or tab is then bent up snugly against the bolt. Various patterns are used. Occasionally screws will be locked with ***safety wire*** (soft, ductile wire). The wire is passed from screw to screw in such a manner as to exert a clockwise pull, **Figure 4-26.** Never reuse safety wire and always dispose of locking plates with fatigued tabs.

Snap Rings

Snap rings are used to position shafts, bearings, gears, and other similar parts. There are both internal and external snap rings of numerous sizes and shapes, **Figure 4-27.**

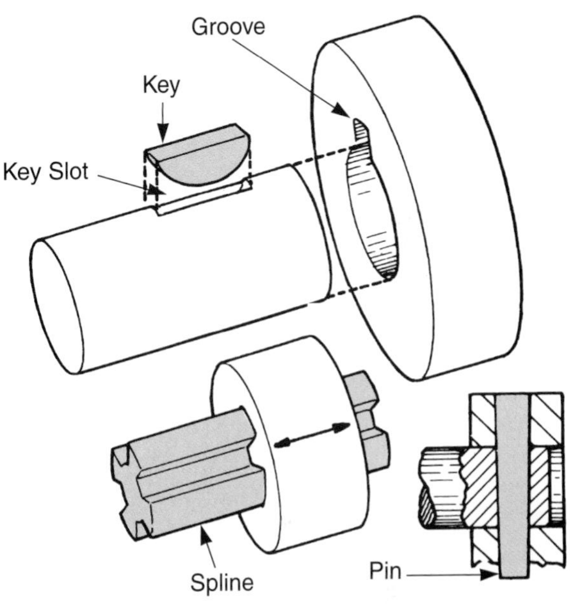

Figure 4-25. Key spline and pin. The spline allows end movement. The pin fixes the shaft to the housing, allowing no movement. The key is commonly referred to as a Woodruff key or a half-moon key.

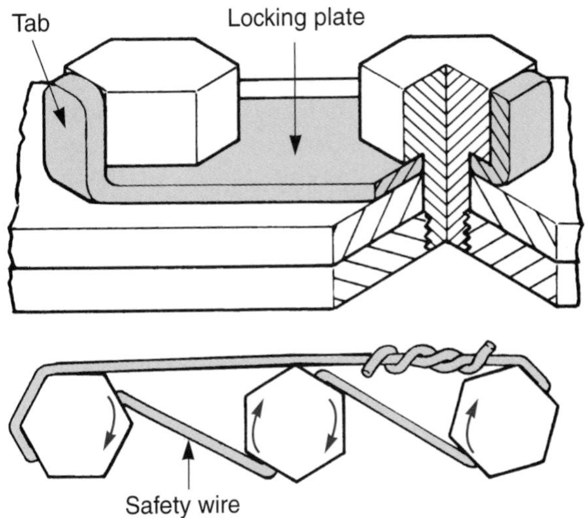

Figure 4-26. Locking plate and safety wire. Tabs must be bent firmly against the bolt flat to prevent rotation.

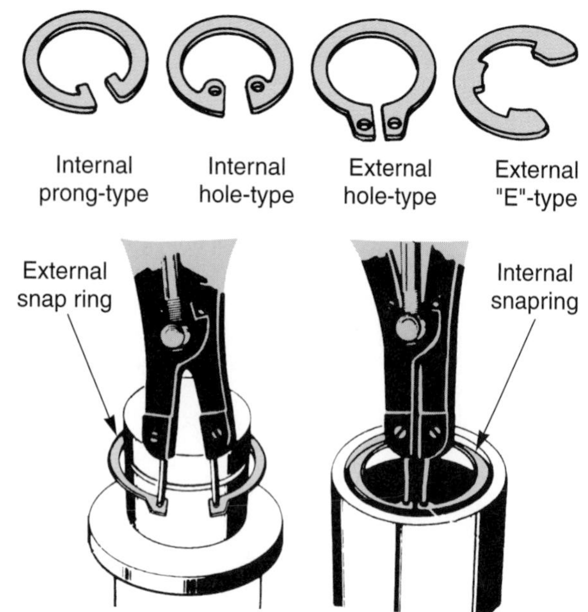

Figure 4-27. Snap ring types. External snap ring fits into a groove on the shaft. Internal snap ring fits into groove inside hole.

The snap ring is made of spring steel. Depending on the type, it must be expanded or contracted to be removed or installed. Special snap ring pliers are used. Be careful when installing or removing snap rings as overexpansion or contraction will distort and ruin them. If a snap ring is sprung out of shape, throw it away. Never attempt to pound one back into shape. Never compress or expand snap rings any more than necessary. Above all, do not pry one end free of the groove and slide it along the shaft. This may ruin the ring.

Setscrews

Setscrews are used to both lock and position pulleys and other parts to shafts. The setscrew is hardened and is available with different tips and drive heads, **Figure 4-28.**

Keep in mind that setscrews are poor driving devices because they often slip on the shaft. When used in conjunction with a Woodruff key, they merely position the unit. As a rule, do not install any unit without a Woodruff key. When a setscrew is used, the shaft will usually have a flat spot to take the screw tip. Make certain this spot is aligned before tightening the screw.

Rivets

Rivets are made of various metals, including brass, aluminum, and soft steel. They are used in several applications on a motorcycle. They are installed cold so there is no contraction that would allow side movement between parts. **Figure 4-29** shows several types of rivets.

When using rivets, there are several important considerations. The two parts to be joined must be held tightly together before and during riveting. The rivet should fit the hole snugly. The rivet material must be in keeping with the job to be done. The rivet must be the correct type (flat head, oval). The rivet should be set with a tool (rivet set) designed for the purpose. **Figure 4-30** illustrates the setting of solid and tubular rivets.

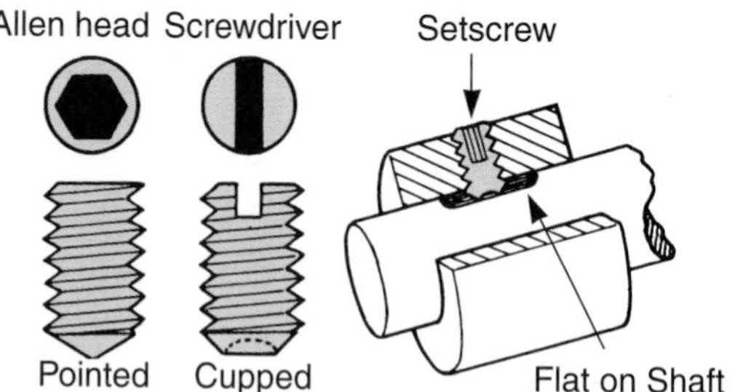

Figure 4-28. Typical setscrews. Setscrews are hardened and should be installed very tightly.

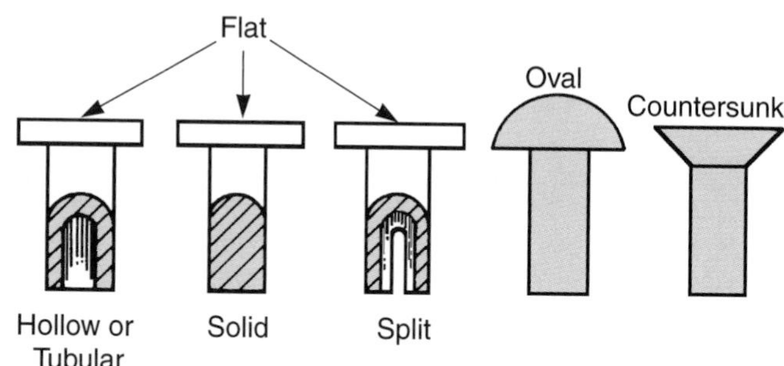

Figure 4-29. Several types of rivets.

Pop Rivets

When one side of the work to be riveted is inaccessible, ***pop rivets*** may be used. They can be set from the outside and make blind rivets practical. **Figure 4-31** illustrates the use of one form of pop rivet.

The pop rivet is inserted through the parts to be joined and a hand-operated setting tool is placed over the anvil pin. When the handles are closed, the anvil pin is pulled outward. As the anvil is drawn outward, the rivet head is forced against the work and the hollow stem is set. The setting process draws the two parts tightly together. Further pressure on the tool handles causes the pin to snap off just ahead of the anvil. The anvil remains in the set area.

Gaskets and Seals

Gaskets and ***seals*** are used throughout the motorcycle. They confine fuel, oil, water, and other fluids, in addition to air and vacuum to specific areas. They keep dust, dirt, water, and other foreign materials out of various parts. They play an important part in the proper function and service life of all components. If they are serviced improperly, mechanical failure can result.

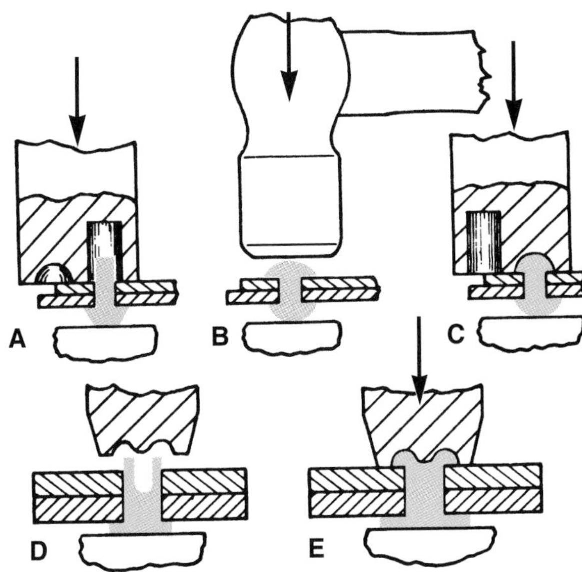

Figure 4-30. Setting rivets. A—Pieces brought together and rivet seated. B—Rivet bulged. C—Rivet crowned and set. D—Set used for tubular rivet. E—Set forced down, crowning rivet as shown.

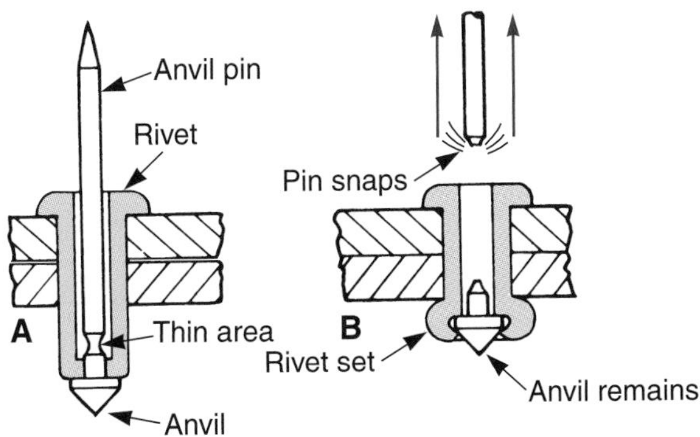

Figure 4-31. Installing a pop rivet. A—Pop rivet in place. B—Rivet tool has pulled the anvil pin outward, pulling the parts together, setting the rivet, and snapping the pin off.

Gaskets

A gasket is a flexible piece of material, or in some cases, a soft sealant placed between two or more parts. When the parts are drawn together, any irregularities (warped spots, scratches, dents) will be filled by the gasket material to produce a leakproof joint.

Gaskets can be made of fiber materials, rubber, neoprene (synthetic rubber), treated paper, cork, or thin metal (steel, copper, or aluminum). Chemical gasket materials are also available. The gasket material selected by the motorcycle's manufacturer will depend on the specific application, temperature, type of fluid to be confined, smoothness of mating parts, fastener tension, pressure of confined fluid, material used in the construction of mating parts, and part clearance relationship. All of these affect the choice of gasket material and design. Therefore, when replacing a gasket, always follow the manufacturer's recommendations in the service manual.

Gasket Installation Tips

When removing and installing a replacement gasket, keep the following in mind:

1. Inspect for leaks before engine disassembly. If the two parts are leaking, the part surface should be inspected closely for problems.
2. Avoid part damage during disassembly. Be careful not to nick, gouge, or dent mating surfaces while removing parts. The slightest unevenness could cause leakage.
3. Clean off old engine gasket carefully. All the old gasket material must be scraped or wire brushed from the parts. Use care especially on aluminum and other soft metals. These soft metals are easily damaged. Use a dull scraper and wire brush lightly as described later in this chapter.

Note: Some engine parts (valve covers for example) are plastic. They can be damaged easily during removal and cleaning.

4. Wash and dry parts thoroughly. After gasket removal, wash parts in solvent. Blow dry with compressed air. Then wipe mating surfaces with a clean shop rag.
5. Check new gasket shape. Compare the new gasket to the shape of the mating surface. Lay the new gasket into place. All holes and sealing surfaces must match perfectly.
6. Use sealer if needed. Sealer is normally used where two different gaskets come together. It will prevent leakage where gaskets overlap. Check a service manual for details. Use sparingly. Too much sealer could clog internal passages in the assembly.
7. Hand start all fasteners before tightening. After fitting the gasket and parts in place, install all bolts by hand. This will ensure proper part alignment and fastener threading.
8. Tighten in steps. When more than one bolt is used to hold a part, tighten each bolt a little at a time. Tighten each bolt to about one-half of its torque specification. Then, tighten the bolts to three-fourth, torque and then to full torque. Then retorque each fastener again.
9. Use a tightening pattern. Either a crisscross or factory recommended torque pattern should be used when tightening parts having multiple fasteners. This will assure even gasket compression and sealing.
10. Do not overtighten fasteners. It is very easy to tighten the bolts enough to dent sheet metal parts and smash or break gaskets. Apply only the specified torque.

Note: If it is necessary to make a gasket, and you do not have a suitable old gasket to use as a guide, apply engine oil to the part's gasket surface. Then place the part on the new gasket material and press the part slightly. The oil will leave an accurate outline on the gasket material that can be cut around.

Sealers

A ***sealer*** is frequently applied on a surface to help prevent leakage, and to hold a gasket in place during assembly. There are numerous kinds of sealers. They have different properties and are designed for different uses. Always read the manufacturer's label and a service manual before selecting a sealer.

Hardening sealers are used on permanent assemblies such as fittings and threads, and for filling uneven surfaces. They are usually resistant to most chemicals and heat. ***Nonhardening sealers*** are used for semipermanent assemblies: cover plates, flanges, threads, hose connections, and other applications. They are also resistant to most chemicals and moderate heat.

Form-in-Place Gaskets

Form-in-place gasket refers to a sealer that is used instead of a conventional fiber or rubber gasket. Two common types of form-in-place gaskets are RTV (room temperature vulcanizing) sealer and anaerobic sealer.

RTV or *silicone sealer* cures (dries) from moisture in the air. It is used to form a gasket on thin, flexible flanges and is applied in a continuous bead approximately 1/8″ (3 mm) to 3/16″ (1.6 mm) in diameter. All mounting holes must be circles. Uncured RTV may be removed with a rag.

Components should be torqued in place while the RTV is still wet to the touch (within about 10 minutes). Locating dowels are used to prevent the sealing bead from being smeared. If the continuous bead of silicone is broken, a leak may result.

Anaerobic sealer cures in the absence of air and is designed for tightly fitting, thick parts. It is used between two smooth, true surfaces, *not* on thin, flexible flanges. Use a 1/16–3/32″ (1.5-2 mm) diameter bead on the part's gasket surface. Be certain that the sealer surrounds each mounting hole.

When selecting a form-in-place gasket, refer to a manufacturer's service manual. Scrape or wire brush gasket surfaces to remove all loose material. Check that all gasket rails are flat. Using a shop rag and solvent, wipe off oil and grease. The sealing surfaces must be clean and dry before using a form-in-place gasket.

Seals

Seals prevent leakage between a stationary part and a moving part. A seal allows the shaft to spin or slide inside the nonmoving part without fluid leakage, **Figure 4-32.** Seals are normally made of synthetic rubber molded onto a metal body.

Servicing Seals

There are several procedures to remember when working with seals.

1. Inspect the seal for leakage before disassembly. If a seal is leaking, there may be other problems beside a defective seal. Look for a scored shaft, misaligned seal housing, or damaged parts. Leakage requires close inspection after disassembly.

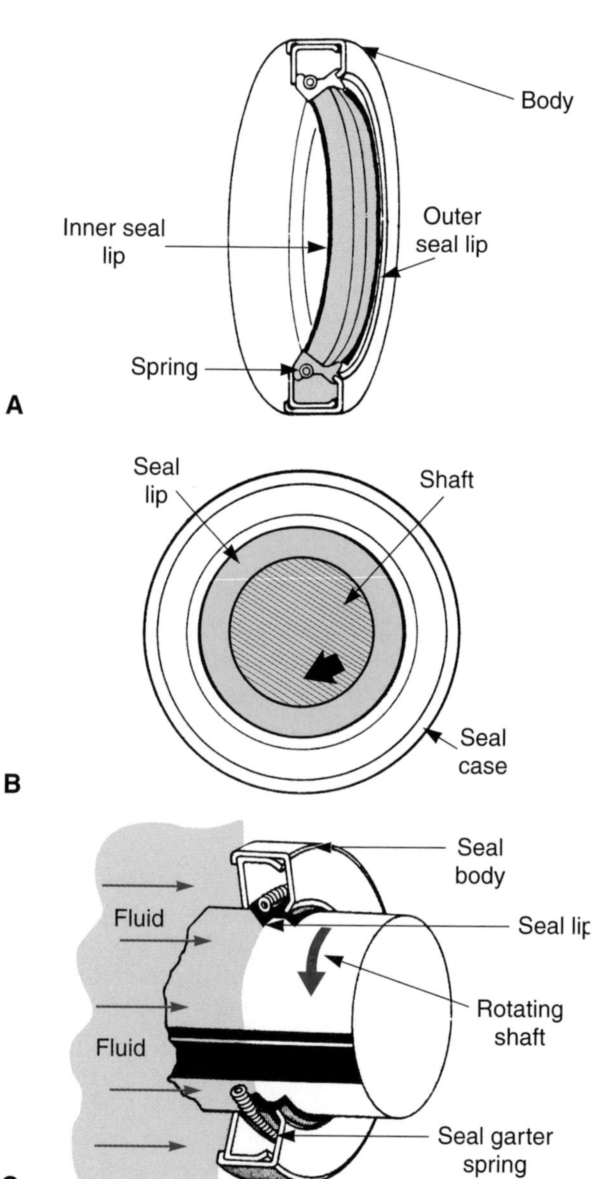

Figure 4-32. Seals prevent leakage between a rotating shaft and a stationary housing. A—Parts of a seal. B—Seal on a shaft. The shaft should be concentric with the seal. C—Seal action.

2. Remove the old seal carefully. Pry out the old seal without scratching the seal housing. Sometimes, a special puller is required for seal removal.
3. Inspect the shaft for wear and burrs. Look at the shaft closely where it contacts the seal. It should be smooth and flat. File off any burrs that could cut the new seal. A badly worn shaft will require polishing, a shaft sleeve repair kit, or replacement.
4. Compare the old seal to the new seal by holding them next to each other. Both the inside diameter (ID) and outside diameter (OD) must be the same. To double-check the inside diameter, slip the seal over the shaft. It should fit snugly.
5. Install the new seal correctly. Lubricate the inner lip of the seal with system fluid.
6. Install the seal with the sealing lip facing inside the part. If installed backwards, an oil leak will result. Use a seal driver to install the seal, do not tap directly on a seal. Check that the seal is squarely and fully seated in its bore.

O-Ring Seals

An ***O-ring seal*** is a stationary seal that fits into a groove between two parts, **Figure 4-33.** When the parts are assembled, the synthetic rubber seal is partially compressed and forms a leakproof joint. Sealants are not used on O-ring seals. Always check O-rings for cuts, nicks, and swelling. When in doubt about seal condition or installation, check in a service manual.

Adhesives

Adhesives (special glues) are also widely used on most late-model motorcycles. They hold body moldings, plastic and rubber parts, and body emblems. Some adhesives are designed to stay soft and pliable while others dry hard. Some take hours to dry, while others dry in seconds. Observe all directions and safety precautions when using adhesives.

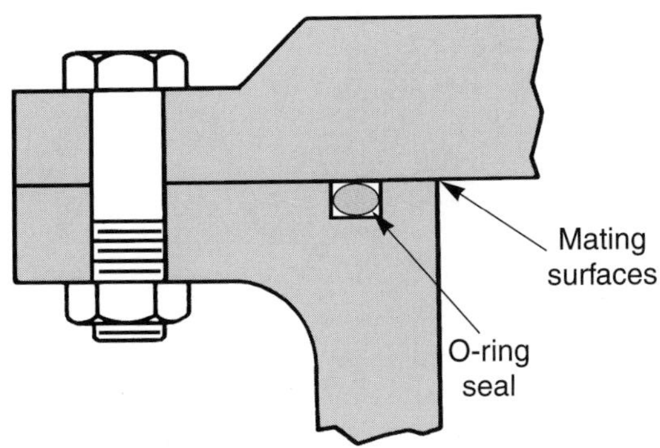

Figure 4-33. An O-ring seal is usually a stationary seal between parts.

Using Service Manuals

One of the most important tools of motorcycle technicians is the ***service manual.*** It has step-by-step procedures, specifications, diagrams, part illustrations, and other data for each motorcycle model. Every motorcycle shop will normally have a set of service manuals. They help the technician with difficult repairs.

Service manuals are written in very concise, technical language. They are designed to be used by well-trained technicians. After completing your studies in this text, you should be well prepared to understand service manuals.

Service Manual Types

There are various types of service manuals including manufacturer, general repair, and specialty manuals. It is important for you to understand their differences.

Manufacturer's service manuals are published by the various motorcycle makers. Also called *factory manuals,* each book covers motorcycles produced by that company, generally for a one year period. Other manufacturers produce a manual for a given model(s) and update with service bulletins or new editions as needed. In addition to bound books such as shown in **Figure 4-34,** some manufacturers provide their service manual information in microfiche form or on CD-ROM for use with a computer. No matter the form, it is vital for you to know what service literature the shop has and how to use it.

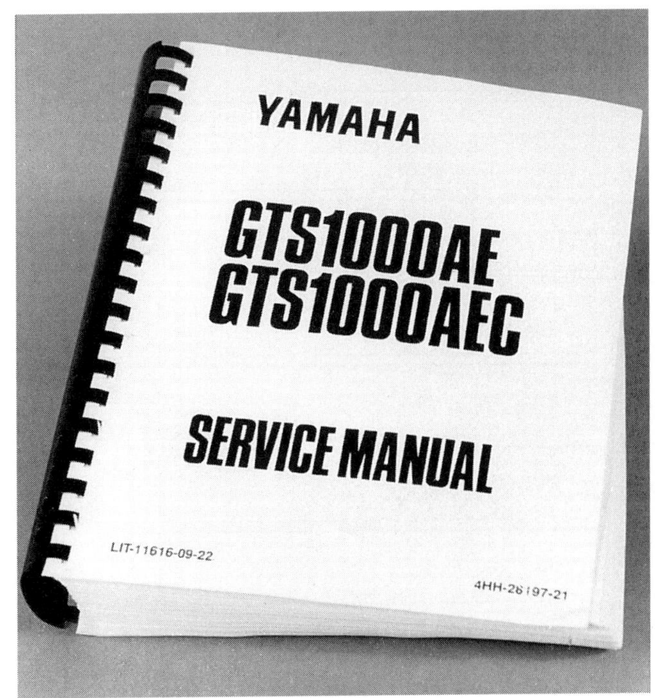

Figure 4-34. Manufacturer's service manuals are an absolute necessity when servicing a specific motorcycle, ATV, or scooter.

General repair manuals and ***specialty repair manuals*** are published by independent companies rather than the manufacturer. They may be general in nature or very specific covering one engine design over a period of years. Use these only if manufacturers manuals are not available.

Service Manual Sections

As shown in **Figure 4-35,** a typical manufacturer's service manual is divided into sections such as general information, periodic inspections and adjustments, engine overhaul, cooling system, carburetor or fuel injection, chassis, electrical, and appendices. The general information section, for example, usually contains such data as where to find the ***vehicle identification number (VIN)*** and engine serial number, recommendation for replacement parts, gasket, oil and seal, and special tools needed for various repairs and service tasks. It also gives the motorcycle, ATV, or scooter specifications.

Illustrated symbols are designed as thumb tabs to indicate the chapter's number and content. The tabs in some manuals are arranged so the tabs line up with thumb index tabs on the front or back cover. The technician can quickly find the first page of each section without looking through the table of contents. The symbols or section number printed at the top corner of each page can also be used as a quick reference system. Often, the beginning of a section contains an overview diagram of the components that will be covered in that section, **Figure 4-36.**

The repair sections of a service manual covers such information on the various motorcycle systems as:

- Disassembly/assembly procedures and tools.
- Inspection.
- Testing/troubleshooting.
- Repair.
- Adjustments.

Each chapter usually provides an exploded diagram before each section for ease in identifying correct disassembly and assembly procedures, **Figure 4-37.** Read each procedure completely while looking at the actual components before starting the repair or replacement. Make sure that you thoroughly understand exactly what has to be done and then follow the procedure to the letter, step-by-step.

Specifications such as bolt-tightening sequence or electrical circuit diagrams are in the service manual. Illustrated symbols are also used to identify the specifications appearing in the text. The note, caution, and warning indication system used in this text is also employed in most service manuals. It must be understood that these warnings cannot cover all conceivable ways in which accidents can happen.

Various types of illustrations and diagrams are used to supplement the written information in a service manual. Many diagrams use illustrated symbols to indicate the lubricant grade and location of the lubrication points.

Abbreviations are letters that stand for words and are often used in service manuals. Sometimes, abbreviations are explained as soon as they are used. They may also be explained at the front or rear of the manual in a chart. Since abbreviations vary from one service manual to another, this textbook only uses universally accepted abbreviations. It does not use those that only apply to one specific motorcycle manufacturer.

Index

Section	Tab
General Information	Gen Info 1
Periodic Inspections and Adjustments	Insp Adj 2
Engine	Eng 3
Carburetion	Carb 4
Drive Train	Driv 5
Chassis	Chas 6
Electrical	Elec 7
Appendices	Appx 8

Figure 4-35. Typical index breakdown into service sections. (Yamaha Motor Corporation U.S.A.)

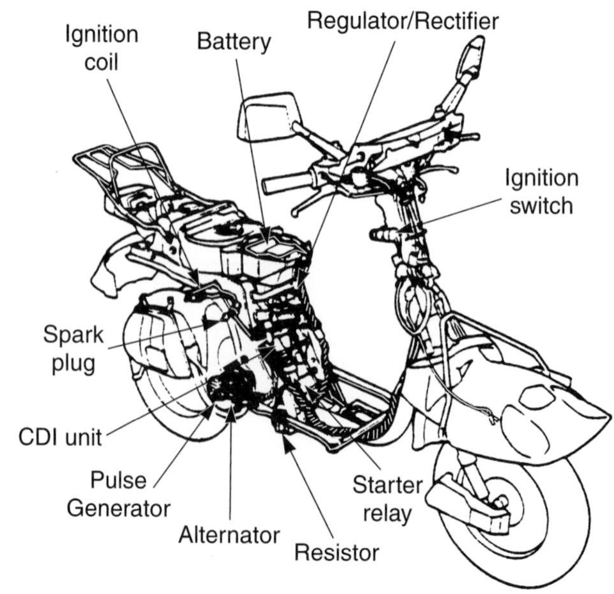

Figure 4-36. Overview of the electrical equipment found on a scooter. (Honda Motor Co., Ltd.)

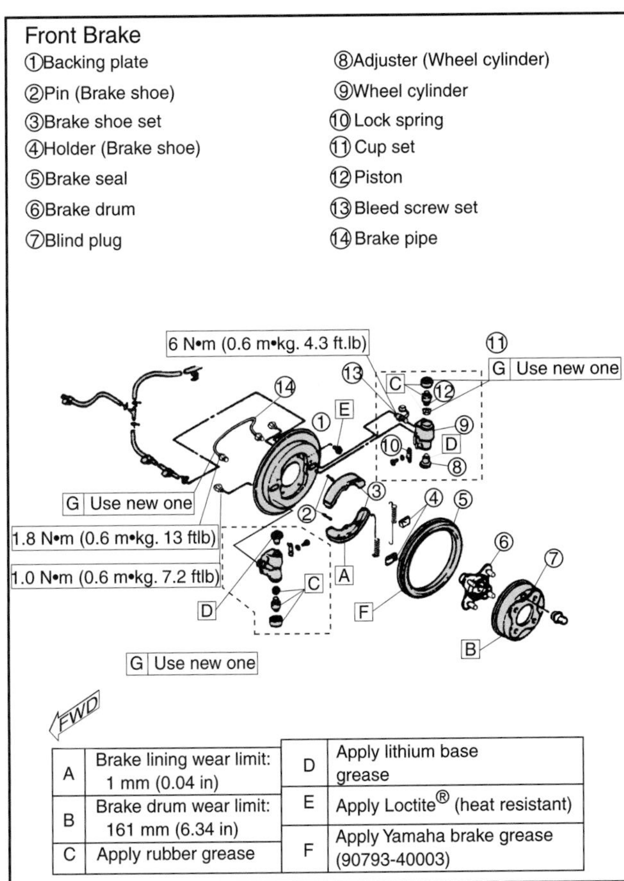

Figure 4-37. Exploded diagram and lubrication chart for the front brake of an ATV. (Yamaha Motor Corporation U.S.A.)

Troubleshooting and flow charts can also be found in a service manual that give the steps (inspections, tests, measurements, and repairs) for servicing and correcting problems on a bike, **Figure 4-38.** If the source of the problem is hard to find, a troubleshooting chart should be used. It will guide you to the most common causes for specific problems.

Using a Service Manual

To use a manufacturer's service manual or general repair manual, follow these steps:

1. Locate the right service manual. Some manuals come in sets or volumes that cover different repair areas. Others cover all subjects and motorcycle makes. If you are working on engines, find the manual that gives the most information for your type of engine.
2. Turn to the table of contents or the index. This will help you quickly find the needed information. Do not thumb through a manual looking for a subject.
3. Use the page listings given at the beginning of each repair section. Most manuals have small content tables at the beginning of each section, **Figure 4-39.** This will help you find a topic quickly. Also use thumbnail tabs, if the manual has them.
4. The word front, unless otherwise noted, refers to the front of the motorcycle. The front of any component is the end closest to the front of the motorcycle. The left- and right-hand sides refer to the position of the parts as viewed by a rider sitting on the seat and facing forward. For example, the throttle control is on the right-hand side.
5. Read the procedures carefully. A service manual will give highly detailed instructions. You must not overlook any step or the repair may fail.
6. Study the manual illustrations closely. The pictures in a service manual contain essential information. They cover special tools, procedures, torque values, and other data essential to the repair.

Technical Bulletins

Technical bulletins help the technician stay up-to-date with recent technical changes, repair problems, and other service-related information. No more than a few pages long, they are mailed to the shop manager who passes them to the technicians. Technical bulletins are published by motorcycle manufacturers and equipment suppliers.

Owner's Manuals

An ***owner's manual*** is a small booklet given to the purchaser of a new motorcycle. It contains information on starting the engine, maintaining the motorcycle, and operating vehicle accessories. New motorcycle owners should be encouraged to read their owner's manuals.

Diagnostic Procedures

In the remaining chapters of this text, the various systems of motorcycles, ATVs, and scooters and how they operate are covered. The chapters will also discuss various problems that may arise in these systems. The only way to solve them is by a systematic analysis of a problem. Whether the problem is mechanical, electrical, or performance related, a systematic approach must be used to find the problem quickly. The most common running problems are performance-related. A common customer complaint might be, "My motorcycle doesn't run right, it needs a tune-up." The first assumption by the customer is that a tune-up will solve all the motorcycle's problems. The second assumption is that the technician will be able to diagnose those problems quickly and efficiently.

The importance of developing and using a systematic approach to diagnosing or troubleshooting a problem cannot be overemphasized. Knowing how to successfully diagnose and troubleshoot separates a true motorcycle service technician from the parts changer. The most

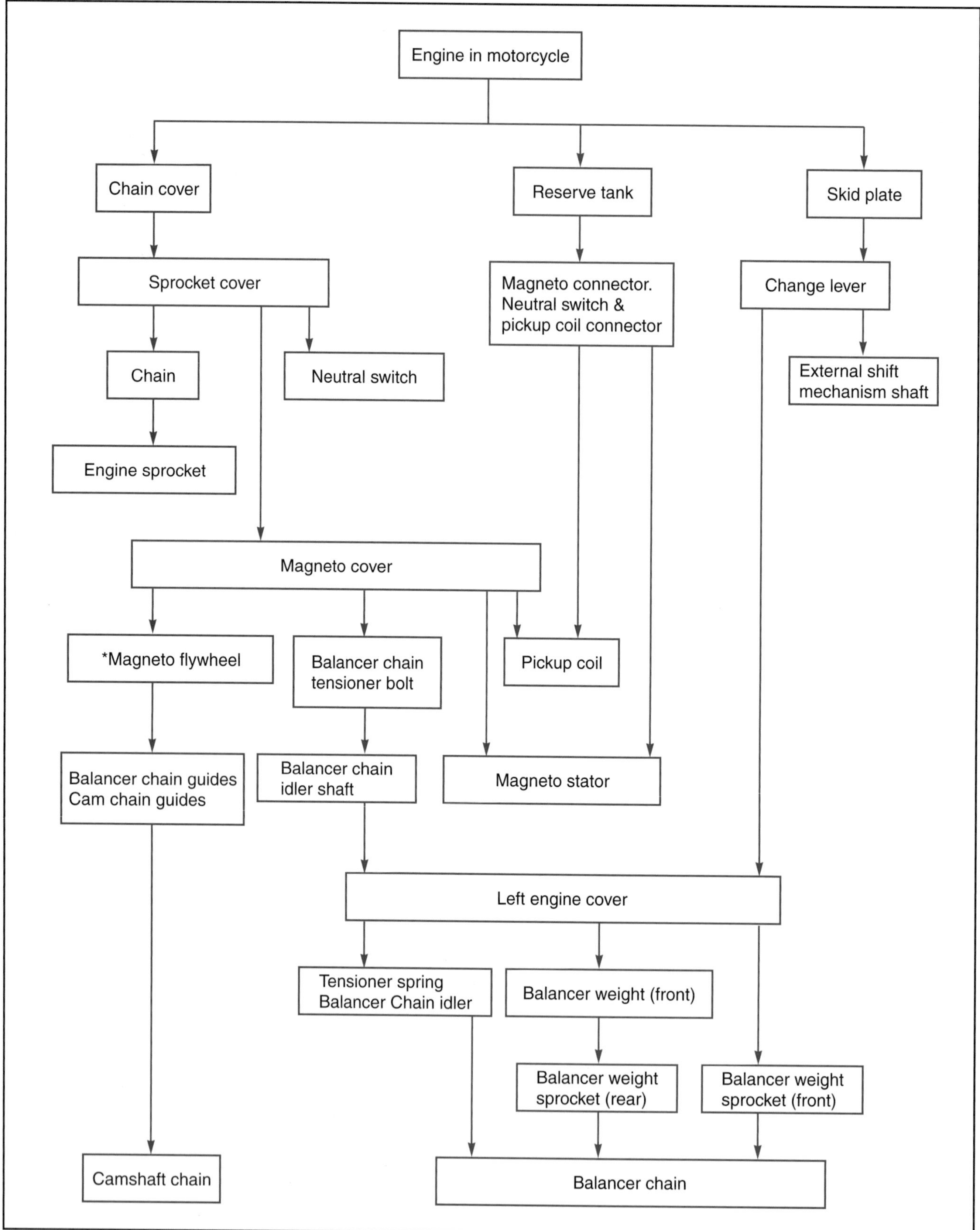

Figure 4-38. Flow charts are often used in service manuals to illustrate such tasks as parts removal or troubleshooting. (American Suzuki Motor Corporation)

2. Maintenance			
Fuel line	2-2	Drive chain	2-21
Fuel strainer screen	2-2	Drive chain slider, chain guide	
Throttle operation	2-3	Guide slider and rollers	2-24
Oil pump and oil line (2-stroke		Drive belt	2-24
separate oil supply motorcycle	2-4	Belt case air cleaner	2-25
Carburetor choke	2-5	Final drive oil level	2-25
Air cleaner	2-6	Battery	2-26
Air cleaner case drain tube		Brake fluid	2-27
(off-road motorcycles		Brake shoe wear	2-28
and ATVs)	2-7	Brake pad wear	2-28
Crankcase breather	2-7	Brake system	2-29
Spark plug	2-8	Brake light switches	2-30
Valve clearance	2-9	Headlight aim	2-31
Engine oil	2-11	Clutch system	2-31
Engine oil filter screen	2-14	Side stand	2-33
Decarbonizing		Suspension	2-34
(2-stroke engine)	2-15	Spark arrester (USA only)	2-35
Carburetor synchronization	2-16	Nuts, bolts, fasteners	2-36
Carburetor Idle speed	2-17	Wheels/tires	2-36
Radiator coolant	2-17	Steering head bearings	2-38
Cooling system	2-18	Wheel alignment (four trax)	2-39
Secondary air supply system	2-19		
Evaporative emission			
control system	2-19		
Transmission oil			
(2-stroke engine)	2-20		

Figure 4-39. The beginning of each section of the service manual usually has a summary of the information contained in that section. (Honda Motor Co., Ltd.)

important factor in developing a system is to think. Many technicians dive headfirst into a problem before thinking about what they are doing. This is the difference between an ordinary mechanic and a technician.

Several steps must be considered when developing a system for diagnostic testing. All steps are important and must always be performed. Failure to perform a part of the system usually causes improper diagnoses and comebacks.

Verifying the Problem

The first important step in diagnosing a problem is finding whether the problem exists. This is not as obvious as it sounds. A repair order may simply state tune-up, although the unit's condition suggests more work is needed. Nothing on the repair order gives an indication of what the customer wants, or if there is an actual problem or complaint. If the repair order has few or no instructions, or no customer input, try to obtain more information. This will reduce the chance of the repair job becoming a customer complaint, resulting in lost income. Verifying the problem is a mandatory step when diagnosing a problem.

The technician (or service writer in a larger motorcycle shop) must ask the customer questions about the unit's performance, the details of the problem, when and who performed the last service, and when the problem was noticed. A good service writer or technician asks these questions politely, showing the customer the service department is interested in doing the job right the first time, and that customer interest is the main concern.

To ask the right questions, the service writer or technician should use a ***customer interview checklist,*** **Figure 4-40.** The customer knows the details of the problem. The more information about when the problem occurs, the easier it will be to isolate the problem. This checklist is also a valuable diagnostic tool for the service technician. If the checklist is attached to the repair order, review the details of the complaint to make the diagnosis easier and faster.

If the problem is performance-related, it is extremely important to perform a test ride before the customer leaves the shop. A performance problem is hard enough to find with good information, but almost impossible to find with bad information. Most important is that the service writer or technician and the customer must agree about what condition is to be fixed. If you cannot duplicate the problem in the shop, do not simply install a part you think is the most likely cause. You are better off simply turning the bike back over to the customer than replacing a part that may or may not fix the problem. You or the service writer must be able to duplicate the problem either during the customer interview or in the shop.

Warning: Safety is the most important factor before and during the test ride. Even though the customer may have ridden his/her motorcycle several miles to the shop, it cannot be assumed the unit is mechanically safe and sound. Therefore, you or the service writer must check the unit carefully before the test ride. Bad tires, loose nuts and bolts, etc., must be found before the unit is ridden. The safety of all potential riders is the foremost consideration. Remember that a well-performed test ride is more than just a quick spin around the block. A diagnostic test ride involves close attention to the customer's riding habits and clues from the motorcycle.

Analyzing the Problem

It may seem that a lot of time is spent filling in paperwork instead of performing actual repair procedures, but actually, the majority of the diagnosis has been completed. When working on a problem, good questions and paperwork are the best tools you can use.

When you know what the problem is, when it occurs, and what the operating conditions of the bike are, you are ready to narrow the possible causes down to a single system. For instance, a rough idle condition can be caused by an electrical problem, a fuel system problem, or an engine mechanical problem. Quickly determining which system is at fault is the key to an efficient diagnosis. The type of problem will often give clues about where to look first.

The next step is to determine which system is at fault. The analysis chart shown in **Figure 4-41** will help in

A. Owner ______ Date ______ Mileage ______

Primary I.D.# ______ Model/Year ______

Machine is used for: ___ Commuting ___ Touring ___ Sport Riding ___ Racing ___ Other

B. What type of problem is it?

1. ___ Misfire
2. ___ Hesitation
3. ___ Bog or starvation
4. ___ Lack of power
5. ___ Surging (Steady throttle)
6. ___ Other

C. When does it happen?

1. ___ Acceleration
2. ___ Deceleration
3. ___ Steady throttle (RPM) ______
4. ___ Starting off
5. ___ When stopped
6. ___ Sporatically
7. ___ Heavy load (RPM) ___
8. ___ All of the time

D. What kind of conditions?

1. ___ When cold (eng)
2. ___ When hot (eng)
3. ___ Any temp (eng)
4. ___ In neutral
5. ___ In one gear
6. ___ In any gear
7. ___ Wet (rain)

A. Date last service performed? ______

B. Who performed last service? ______

C. What type of service was performed? ______

______

______

D. When did problem start? ______

Note: Check Owner's Manual service record for prior service information.

Figure 4-40. Typical customer interview checklist. (Yamaha Motor Corporation U.S.A.)

finding which system is most likely at fault. Keep in mind there are cases where the chart will not always be correct, but if used, you will save time in the long run. In other words, using a troubleshooting chart gives you a starting point that will usually lead to the cause of the problem more quickly than testing each system individually.

Types of Problems

The word "symptom" refers to the description of a problem. It is used in troubleshooting to describe an abnormal or out of the ordinary condition. One example, if a motorcycle does not accelerate well, the symptom is lack of power on acceleration. Troubleshooting problems fall into three categories:

- Permanent failures.
- Intermittent failures.
- Failures caused by improper service.

Permanent failures are often the easiest to find. They occur frequently or are constant. A defective starter motor that will not turn the engine is a good example of a permanent failure. Intermittent failures do not occur all the time. Intermittent problems are the hardest to diagnose because you must first duplicate the failure before beginning diagnosis. For example, the customer complains the motorcycle runs for a while and then blows a fuse. If you cannot get it to blow a fuse, the problem may be hard to find. With an intermittent condition like this, it is more difficult to pinpoint the cause because everything may pass your tests.

A failure caused by improper service can be either permanent or intermittent. For example, if a wire was chafed during the installation of a component, this could lead to an intermittent short circuit.

How to Troubleshoot

To troubleshoot properly, you must first think about the problem(s). Ask these questions:

- What is the symptom (noise, performance problem, color of smoke)?
- What system is involved (ignition, fuel, engine)?
- Is there a possibility of more than one system being involved (starting, lighting, charging)?

	Symptom					
	A. Running Condition	**Misfire**	**Hesitation**	**Surging**	**Bog/Starve**	**Lack of Power**
Problem Occurs When Engine Is At Any Temp.	Acceleration	E - F	E F	E F	F - M	M E
	Deceleration	F Back- M fire	N/A	F	N/A	N/A
	Steady Speed	E - F	N/A	E F - M	M F - E	F M - E
	Starting Off	F E	E - F	F - E	F - E	F M - E
	Idle When Stopped	E - F	N/A	Fluctuation F - M	No Idle F - M	N/A
	Heavy Load	E - F	F E - M	E F	M - F	F - M

	B. Running Condition	**Misfire**	**Hesitation**	**Surging**	**Bog/Starve**	**Lack of Power**
Problem Occurs When Engine Is Cold	Acceleration	F - E	F - E	F - E	F - M	F
	Deceleration	Backfire F - M	N/A	F	N/A	N/A
	Steady Speed	F - E	N/A	F	F - M	F - M
	Starting Off	F - E	F - E	F - E	E F - M	F - M
	Idle When Stopped	F - E	N/A	Fluctuation F - M	E F - M	N/A
	Heavy Load	F - E	F - E	F E - M	F - M	F

	C. Running Condition	**Misfire**	**Hesitation**	**Surging**	**Bog/Starve**	**Lack of Power**
Problem Occurs When Engine Is Hot	Acceleration	E - F	E - F	F E - M	M E	M E - F
	Deceleration	Backfire M - F	N/A	F	N/A	N/A
	Steady Speed	E - M	N/A	E M - F	F - M	M - E
	Starting Off	E - F	F E - M	E F - M	E F - M	M - E
	Idle When Stopped	E - M	N/A	Fluctua- F tion E - M	M E - F	N/A
	Heavy Load	F E	F E - M	F E - M	M E -	M E -

E = Electrical System F = Fuel System M = Mechanical System

Figure 4-41. Typical system analysis chart. The vertical columns list the types of conditions under which problems occur. The horizontal columns list the symptoms. Where the symptom and condition columns intersect, there are two letters. They represent the two systems most likely at fault. They are listed in order of priority. The first letter is the most common system at fault with symptoms and conditions of this type. The second letter is the next most common system at fault. If two letters appear, one over the other, the problem could be in either system. Chart A is for problems that occur at any engine temperature. Chart B is for problems occurring when the engine is cold. Chart C is for problems occurring when the engine is hot.

- Where is the most logical place to begin diagnosis?

Troubleshooting should begin with the easiest and most obvious checks. Progression to more difficult checks are done step-by-step.

One of the most common troubleshooting mistakes is to overlook the easiest or most obvious possible causes of a failure. More than one technician has serviced a carburetor when the actual problem was an empty fuel tank. When making these systematic checks, it is necessary to be 100% sure in verifying system or component condition.

Troubleshooting Steps

Troubleshooting should be broken down into seven steps:

1. Collect information pertinent to the problem (talk to the customer and test ride if possible).
2. Visual inspection, including symptom identification and system overlapping.
3. Systematic elimination of potential problems.
4. Isolating the cause of the problem.
5. Reverifying the diagnosis.
6. Repairing the malfunction.
7. Repair verification (test ride or tests).

An unofficial, but important eighth step is to document what was wrong with the bike and what you did to correct the problem. Good record keeping is as important as performing the repair properly. To make a troubleshooting job easier, it is important to gather as much information as possible.

Try to find out:

- All information possible about the bike's symptoms.
- When the problem first occurred.
- Service history.
- Has anyone else tried to fix the motorcycle? If so, what was done?

Study and make use of all the information you have collected. If a motorcycle develops a problem while being ridden (no one has worked on it for quite some time), this indicates a normal failure.

If a motorcycle has just been serviced and now it suddenly quits or performs poorly, this indicates improper service procedures. You, as the technician, must decide where to begin troubleshooting based on this type of information. Your proficiency as a troubleshooter will increase with experience if you remember a few simple guidelines:

- Think the problem through.
- Do not overlook the obvious.
- Do not assume there is only one problem.
- Do not take shortcuts.

Troubleshooting problems can be tough for an inexperienced technician. You need not be apprehensive about troubleshooting if you have the right attitude. Remember, the more troubleshooting you do, the more comfortable you will be about tackling troubleshooting problems. Developing confidence in your troubleshooting ability is a result of learning from experience. Finding the solution to a troubleshooting problem is very gratifying, and the more difficult the problem, the better you feel when it is solved.

Service Tips

Here are some service tips that you should keep in mind when servicing motorcycles, ATVs, and scooters:

- Special tools are designed to remove or replace a specific part or assembly without damage. The use of improper procedures or not using the specified special tools, may damage the parts.
- Clean the outside of a part or assembly before removing it from the motorcycle or opening its cover for service. Dirt accumulated on the outside could fall into the engine, chassis, or brake system and cause damage later.
- Clean the outside of a part or assembly before measuring them for wear. Parts should be washed in solvent and dried with compressed air. Beware of parts containing O-rings or oil seals since these are adversely affected by most cleaning solvents.
- Control cables must not be bent or distorted. This will lead to stiff operation and premature cable failure.
- Loosening a part with multiple fastener sizes should be done from the outside-in, in a crisscross pattern, loosening the small fasteners first. Loosening the big fasteners first may place excessive stress on the smaller fasteners.
- Complex assemblies, such as transmission parts, should be stored in the proper assembly order and held securely with wire. This will simplify reassembly at a later date.
- The reassembly position of critical parts should be noted before the parts are disassembled. This will allow those dimensions (depth, distance, or position) to be correctly duplicated upon reassembly.
- Non-reusable parts are always replaced whenever something is disassembled. These include the gaskets, metal sealing washers, O-rings, oil seals, snap rings, and cotter pins.
- Ball bearings are removed using tools which apply force against one or both (inner and outer) bearing races. If the force is applied against only one race (either inner or outer), the bearing will be damaged during removal and must be replaced. If the force is applied against both races equally, the bearing will not be damaged during removal.
- Ball bearings are cleaned in solvent, then dried with compressed air. Air dry the bearing while holding both races to prevent it from spinning. If the bearing is allowed to spin, the high speed generated by the air jet can overspeed the bearing and cause permanent damage.

- Ball bearings are checked (after cleaning) by slowly rotating the inner race while holding the outer race stationary. If any radial play or roughness is felt, it must be replaced. The bearing should have no axial play; if it has noticeable axial play, it must be replaced.
- Ball bearings are always installed with the manufacturer's name and size code facing out. (Facing out means the name and sizing code should be visible from the side the bearing is installed from.) This is true for open, single-sealed and double-sealed bearings. Apply the proper grease to open and single-sealed bearings before reassembly.
- Snap rings are always installed with the chamfered (rolled) edge facing away from the thrust of the mating part. Installed incorrectly, pressure against the rolled or chamfered edge could compress the snap ring, possibility dislodging it. Never reuse snap rings since they are often used to control end play and become worn with normal use. Wear is especially critical on snap rings which retain spinning parts such as gears. After installing a snap ring, always rotate it in its groove to be sure it is fully-seated.
- Bolt or screw lengths can vary for an assembly, cover, or case. These different lengths must be installed into the correct locations. If you become confused, place the bolts into their holes and compare the exposed lengths; each should be exposed by the same amount.
- Torquing multiple sized fasteners should be done as follows: tighten all to hand-tight, then torque big fasteners before little fasteners. Torque pattern should be crisscross from the inside-out. To minimize distortion, critical fasteners should be torqued in 2-3 increments. Unless specified otherwise, bolts and fasteners are installed clean and dry; do not use oil on the threads.
- Oil seals are always installed with grease packed into the seal cavity and the manufacturer's name facing the outside (dry side). When installing seals, the shaft over which the seal fits should be smooth and free of burrs.
- Old gasket material or sealant must be removed before reassembly. If the gasket surface is damaged slightly, it may be possible to smooth that area with an oil stone.
- Rubber hoses (fuel, vacuum, or coolant) should be installed so the end is bottomed onto its fitting. This allows adequate area for the hose clip to grip the hose, **Figure 4-42.**

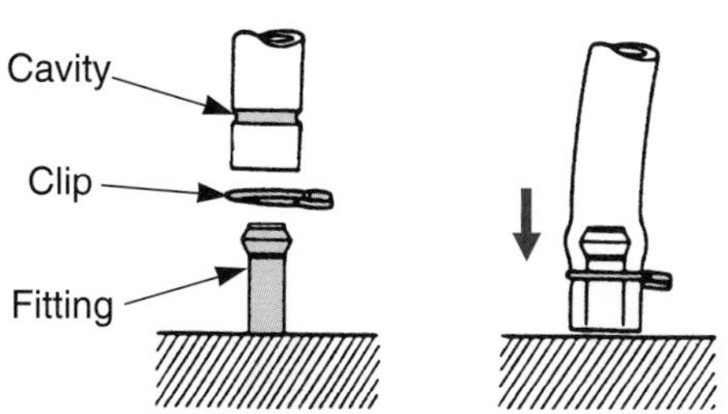

Figure 4-42. Installing a hose clip. (Honda Motor Co., Ltd.)

- Rubber or plastic dust/dirt boots should be replaced securely in their exact positions.

Summary

Fasteners, gaskets, seals, and sealants are constantly used by the motorcycle technician. It is almost impossible to connect any two parts of a motorcycle without them. Fasteners include any type of holding device. Hundreds are used in the construction of a motorcycle.

Bolts and screws may be identified by type, length, major and minor diameters, pitch, length of thread, class of fit, material, tensile strength, and wrench size needed. Nuts are manufactured in a variety of sizes and styles. Nuts are also graded to match the strength of their respective bolts. A stud is a metal rod threaded on both ends. Machine screws are used without nuts. They are passed through one part and threaded into another. Washers are used under bolt heads and nuts.

Torque wrenches are available in different sizes, ranges, and calibrations. When reading a torque wrench, look straight down at the scale. Viewing from an angle can give a false reading. Only pull on the torque wrench handle. Do not allow the flex bar on beam torque wrenches to touch anything. Place a steady pull on the torque wrench. Do not use short, jerky motions or inaccurate readings can result. Thread repairs are sometimes needed when threads have been stripped, broken out, or smashed, or when fasteners have been broken off inside a hole.

Numerous types of nonthreaded fasteners are utilized in the assembly of a motorcycle, ATV, or scooter. Cotter pins are used both with slotted and castle nuts as well as on clevis pins and linkage ends. Keys, splines, and pins are used to attach gears, sprockets, and pulleys to shafts so they rotate as a unit. Locking plates are made of thin sheet metal. Snap rings are used to position shafts, bearings, gears, and other similar parts. Setscrews are used to both lock and position pulleys and other parts to shafts. Rivets are made of various metals, including brass, aluminum, and soft steel.

Gaskets and seals are used throughout the motorcycle. A gasket is a flexible piece of material, or in some cases, a soft sealant placed between two or more parts. Gaskets can be made of fiber materials, rubber, neoprene, treated paper, cork, or thin metal. Sealer is frequently applied on a surface to help prevent leakage, and to hold a gasket in place during assembly. Seals prevent leakage between a stationary part and a moving part. A seal allows the shaft to spin or slide inside the nonmoving part without fluid leakage. An O-ring seal is a stationary seal that fits into a groove between two parts. Adhesives are also widely used on most late model motorcycles.

One of the most important tools of motorcycle technicians is the service manual. It has step-by-step procedures, specifications, diagrams, part illustrations, and other data for each motorcycle model. Technical bulletins help the technician stay up-to-date with recent technical changes, repair problems, and other service related information. The importance of developing and using a systematic approach to diagnosing or troubleshooting a problem cannot be overemphasized.

Know These Terms

Fasteners	Pins
Bolts	Locking plates
Screws	Safety wire
United States Customary (USC)	Snap rings
Metric (SI)	Setscrews
Thread pitch	Rivets
Thread pitch gauge	Pop rivets
Major diameter	Gaskets
Minor diameter	Seals
Grade	Sealer
Right-hand threads	Hardening sealers
Left-hand threads	Nonhardening sealers
Nuts	Shellac
Stud	Form-in-place gasket
Machine screws	RTV
Sheet metal screws	Anaerobic sealer
Self-locking fasteners	Seals
Washers	O-ring seal
Torque wrenches	Adhesives
Torque-to-yield (TTY)	Service manual
Thread repairs	Manufacturer's service manuals
Thread file	General repair manuals
Thread chaser	Specialty repair manuals
Thread repair insert	Vehicle identification number (VIN)
Taps	Abbreviations
Cotter pins	Technical bulletins
Keys	Owner's manual
Splines	Customer interview checklist

Review Questions—Chapter 4

Do not write in this text. Place your answers on a separate sheet of paper.

1. Define the term *fastener.*
2. Customary bolt heads are marked with ________ marks to indicate bolt strength. Metric bolts use a ______ system to indicate bolt strength.
3. A ______ is a metal rod threaded on both ends.
   A. tap
   B. die
   C. stud
   D. machine screw
4. A ______ is a safety device commonly used with a slotted nut.
5. What is a *bolt tightening sequence?*
6. Bolts that are intentionally torqued barely into a yield condition are referred to as ______.
   A. self-locking
   B. side torquing
   C. machine
   D. torque-to-yield
7. Which of the following is *not* used for thread repair?
   A. Tap.
   B. Die.
   C. Chaser.
   D. Chisel.
8. Name the three types of lock washers.
9. A ______ is used to position shafts, bearings, gears, and other parts.
   A. locking plate
   B. snap ring
   C. cotter pin
   D. rivet
10. Torquing should be in three initial steps. Fasteners drawn up to ______ of recommended torque then to ______ and finally to ______ torque.
11. A ______ is used for removing fasteners broken off below the surface.
12. Write the six basic steps for using a service manual.
13. ______ are letters that stand for words used in the service manual.
    A. Abbreviations
    B. Specifications
    C. Diagrams
    D. None of the above.
14. ______ help the technician stay up-to-date with recent technical changes.
    A. Service manuals
    B. Owner's manuals
    C. Technical bulletins
    D. Specifications

15. List in order the seven steps involved in troubleshooting a problem.

Suggested Activities

1. Take a sheet of paper. Wad it into a ball. Pull it back out and lay it on the table. If you were to try to press it out flat, where would you place your hands (fastener) first? In what direction (sequence) would you move them? Try it. How does this compare to tightening sequence?
2. Using a regular wrench, turn up several 3/8″ screws to what you would guess to be 15 ft.-lbs (20.34 N•m) of torque. Take a torque wrench and break them loose. Watch the scale carefully to determine the torque required to start them. Even though this will be different than true torque, how even were they? Was it close to 15 ft.-lbs. (20.34 N•m)?
3. Place two 1/4″ bolts (one with six radial lines on head and other with none) of equal length in a vise. Keep them about two inches apart and with the same amount of material in the jaws. Tighten the vise and using a suitable torque wrench, turn each bolt until it breaks. Watch the scale carefully to determine torque at the moment of failure. Was the reading the same? If not, why?
4. Thoroughly clean the parts of an engine. Make a visual inspection of all parts and list any parts which need replacement.
5. Obtain a small block of aluminum and a thread repair insert. Drill and tap the block for the insert. Follow the directions given by the insert manufacturer. Install the thread repair insert in the hole.
7. For practice in external thread repair, damage the threads of a 12-15 mm bolt. Use a thread file to repair the damage.
8. Recondition the gasket surface of a cylinder head for a single cylinder engine. Use cutting paper on a flat plate.

Motorcycles use electronics in almost every system.
(Yamaha Motor Corporation, U.S.A.)

Basic Electrical and Electronic Theory

After studying this chapter, you will be able to:

- Explain the principles of electricity.
- Describe the action of electric circuits.
- Compare voltage, current, and resistance.
- Describe the principles of magnetism and magnetic fields.
- Identify electrical and electronic components.
- Explain different kinds of motorcycle wiring.
- Connect a voltmeter, ohmmeter, and ammeter to a circuit.
- Perform fundamental electrical tests.
- Make electrical repairs.

Almost every system in a modern motorcycle, ATV, or scooter uses some type of electrical or electronic component. Fortunately, the electronic systems on modern vehicles are relatively trouble free. However, when problems occur, you must be familiar with electrical/electronic theory, system design, system operation, and proper use of test equipment. This knowledge will enable you to quickly and accurately diagnose and repair electrical problems. This chapter contains the safety precautions and basic knowledge required for servicing electrical and electronic systems.

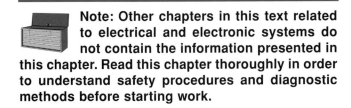

Note: Other chapters in this text related to electrical and electronic systems do not contain the information presented in this chapter. Read this chapter thoroughly in order to understand safety procedures and diagnostic methods before starting work.

Electrical Theory

What is electricity? The answer to this question may seem complex. However, after learning the basic principles, electricity is easy to understand. Part of the problem is that electricity itself cannot be seen. Only the results can be seen in the form of physical activity such as light, heat, and movement. When headlights are turned on, you can see the light bulb glow and feel its warmth. However, you cannot see what causes the bulb to function.

In order to service and troubleshoot electrical systems, an understanding of what electricity is, where it comes from, and how it is used is needed. This portion of the chapter discusses some basic ideas related to electricity and its role in motorcycle, ATV, and scooter systems.

Electricity

All matter is said to be electrical in nature. One of the oldest and most accepted theories is that electricity is comprised of moving electrons. ***Electrons*** are tiny particles of negatively charged matter that freely move about in an orbit around a nucleus made of neutrons and positively charged protons, **Figure 5-1.** Electricity flows when these electrons freely move outward from their orbits. Some materials allow free flow while others do not.

Electricity is the movement of electrons from one place to another. This is why electricity is said to flow. This flow is similar to the flow of water. However, to create the flow, there must be a source of energy. This source must be strong enough to force electrons out of their shells. Several kinds of energy are strong enough to force electrons out of their shells and cause electrical flow. Some of these energy sources are:

- Heat
- Friction
- Light
- Pressure
- Chemical reaction
- Magnetism

In a motorcycle, ATV, or scooter, electricity is produced by the last two sources of energy: chemical reaction and magnetism.

Electron Flow

In studying electron flow or ***current flow,*** there are actually two theories concerning the direction of electron flow, **Figure 5-2.** The ***conventional theory*** states that electrons flow from positive to negative. After the discovery of the electron and the structure of matter, the ***electron theory*** was developed. This theory states that current flows from negative to positive.

For a time, everyone was satisfied with the conventional theory concept. The electron theory began to gain in popularity when semiconductors were developed. Both theories are used; so long as there is flow, it makes little difference which theory is used. Today, most electrical schematics are drawn with arrows to show the flow of electricity.

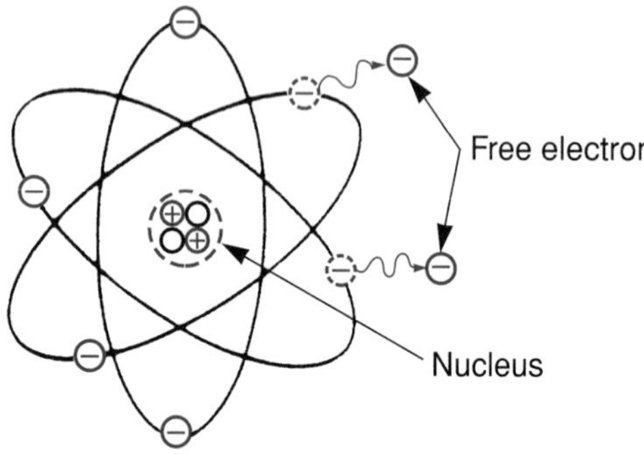

Figure 5-1. Electrons orbit about a nucleus comprised of positively charged protons and neutrons.

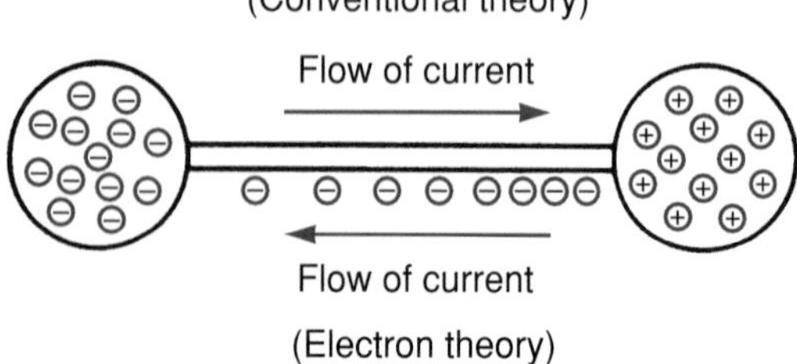

Figure 5-2. The two theories of electrical flow, the conventional theory states that current flows from positive to negative. The electron theory states that electrons flow from negative to positive.

Electric Current

Motorcycle and similar vehicle electrical systems use two types of electric current: direct current and alternating current. It is important to understand the differences between the two. The majority of motorcycle, ATV, and scooter systems use direct current.

Direct Current

In most motorcycles, the battery supplies ***direct current (dc)*** to power the electrical system. According to electron flow theory, direct current flows from the battery's negative terminal, through the circuit and returns to the battery's positive terminal. This is illustrated in **Figure 5-3.**

Direct current produces a square or analog waveform, which represents the presence of voltage. In most cases, direct current flows one way, **Figure 5-4.**

Alternating Current

Another type of electric current found in the motorcycle electrical system is ***alternating current (ac).*** A ***sine wave,*** **Figure 5-5,** represents the change in voltage and polarity (direction of current flow) which is associated with

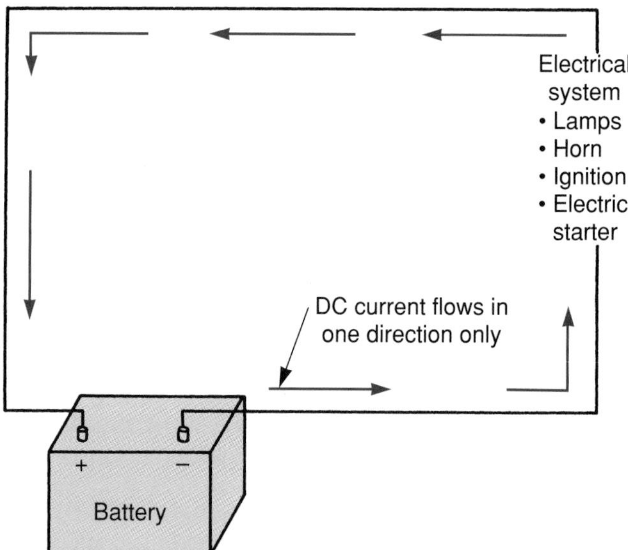

Figure 5-3. A battery supplies direct current to the electrical system. Current flows from the negative (–) battery terminal, through the circuit and returns to the positive (+) terminal.

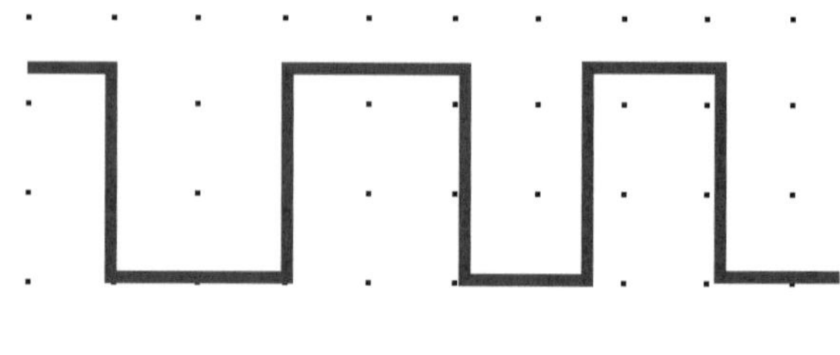

Figure 5-4. Direct current produces a square wave, which shows positive voltage only.

alternating current. Alternating current is produced by the alternator and some sensors. Current flows one way and then the other. Ac can be converted to dc by ***rectification.***

Electrical Circuits

A simple circuit consists of:

- A power source which supplies electricity for the circuit.
- Conductors that carry current between the power source and load.
- A load that uses the electricity.

As shown in **Figure 5-6,** the ***power source*** feeds electricity to the conductors and load. The ***conductors,*** such as wires and frames, carry the electricity to the loads and back to the source. Materials such as plastic, rubber, and ceramics are used as ***insulators*** to prevent short circuits. Components which change electricity into another form of energy (heat, light, movement) create a ***load*** in the circuit. The load or electrical parts change the electricity into another form of energy such as light, heat, or movement. The three types of electrical circuits used on motorcycles, ATVs, and scooters are the series circuit, parallel circuit, and series-parallel circuit.

The ***series circuit*** has all of the components connected one after the other with a single path for current flow. **Figure 5-7A** shows this type of circuit. If one bulb burns out (opens), all the other bulbs stop functioning.

A ***parallel circuit*** has a separate leg (path) for each component, **Figure 5-7B.** If one bulb in a parallel circuit burns out, the other bulbs still glow. They each have their own path for current flow. A ***series-parallel circuit*** contains both a series circuit and a parallel circuit, **Figure 5-7C.**

All circuits on a motorcycle are considered ***one-wire circuits*** since the vehicle frame or body is used as a return wire to the power source. An insulated wire connects the battery positive terminal to the load. Current goes from the battery's negative terminal through the frame and metal parts to the positive terminal. The term ***frame ground*** refers to the path current takes when it returns to the battery's positive terminal. A typical circuit with its symbols is shown in **Figure 5-8.**

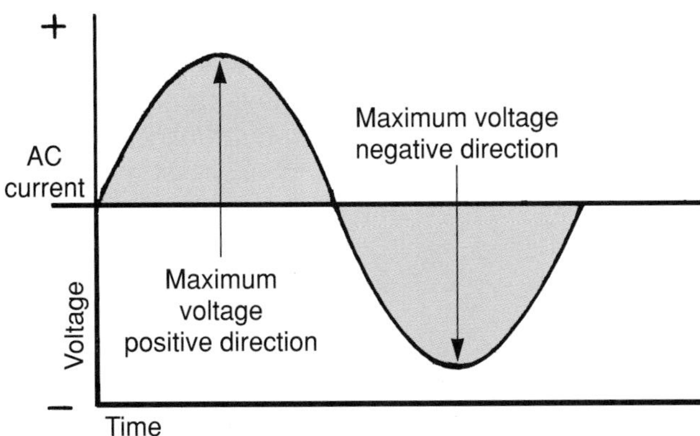

Figure 5-5. A sine wave is a graphic description of alternating current. Peaks on both positive and negative sides show maximum current flow in both directions.

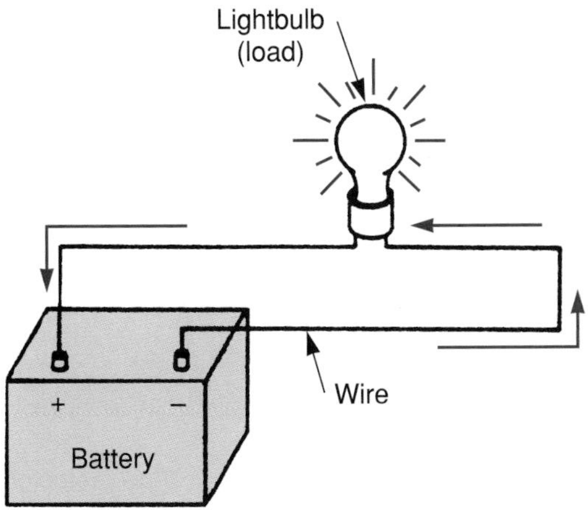

Figure 5-6. A simple electrical circuit consists of a power source (battery), a load (lightbulb), and conductors (wire) which connect the load to the power source.

Polarity

Polarity refers to the two sides of the electrical system, positive and negative. Motorcycle electrical components must be connected with the correct polarity. For example, a battery has a positive (+) and a negative (–) post.

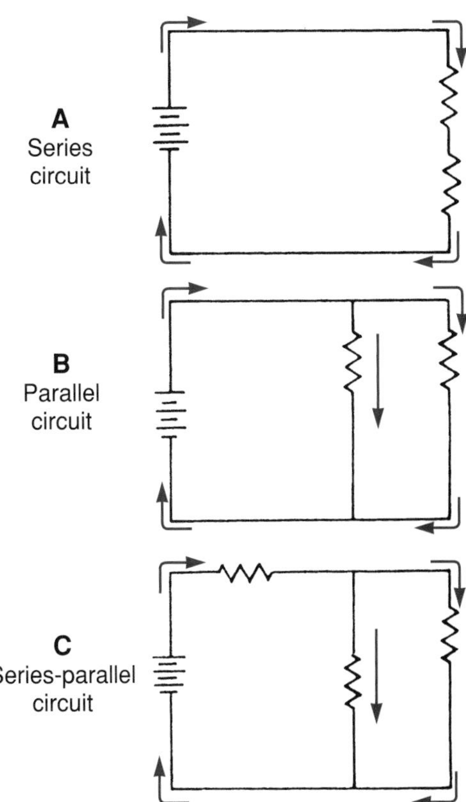

Figure 5-7. The three types of electrical circuits used in motorcycles: A—Series circuit has only one electrical path. B—Parallel circuit has more than one path providing voltage to each load. C—Series-parallel combines these two circuits.

The positive side of the battery is referred to as the *hot side,* and the negative as the *ground side.* The positive side of a circuit would include any point between the load (bulb) and battery positive. The negative side would be between the load and battery negative. Some systems may be positively grounded.

Units of Electricity

Electricity is affected by three factors:

- Amperage
- Voltage
- Resistance

Each factor has a direct influence on the others. ***Amperage*** is the number of free electrons flowing in a conductor. Amperage, or current, is measured with an ammeter in units called amperes or amps. The symbol for amps is A or I.

Voltage is the pressure that forces free electrons to flow in a conductor. Voltage is also known as *electromotive force.* Voltage is measured in units called volts using a voltmeter. The symbol for voltage is V and is sometimes represented by the symbol E, for electromotive force or EMF.

Resistance is the opposition to current flow. Resistance is measured with an ohmmeter in units called ohms. The symbol for ohms is the Greek letter omega (Ω). The letter R is also used to represent resistance.

A common analogy used to illustrate the three units of electricity is a water (hydraulic) circuit, **Figure 5-9.** Water pressure is comparable to voltage. Since water flow is the same as electrical current, resistance to water flow is like resistance to electrical current.

Ohm's Law

The relationship between voltage, current, and resistance in an electrical circuit is predictable and is governed by two basic laws. The first one, Ohm's law, can express mathematically, the relationship between current, voltage, and resistance.

Ohm's law states that current in an electrical circuit is directly proportional to voltage and inversely proportional to resistance. Therefore, an unknown electrical quantity can be found if the other two quantities are known. Ohm's law is stated in **Figure 5-10.**

Using the pyramid formula allows quick calculations and the formula can be easily remembered, **Figure 5-10.** For example, if a 6 Ω resistor is connected to a 12-volt battery, the current flowing through the resistor can be calculated by using Ohm's law:

Current = Voltage ÷ Resistance = 12 ÷ 6 = 2 A

When testing and troubleshooting an electrical circuit, ***voltage drop*** is usually measured. Voltage must be present for amperage to flow through a resistor (load).

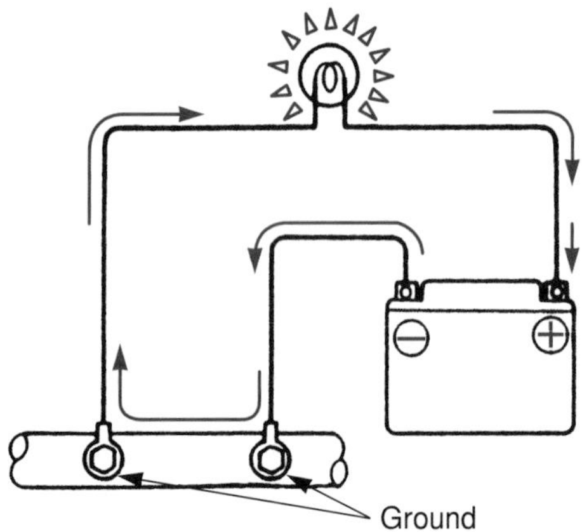

Figure 5-8. On most bikes, the vehicle frame or body is used as a ground path. (Honda Motor Co., Ltd.)

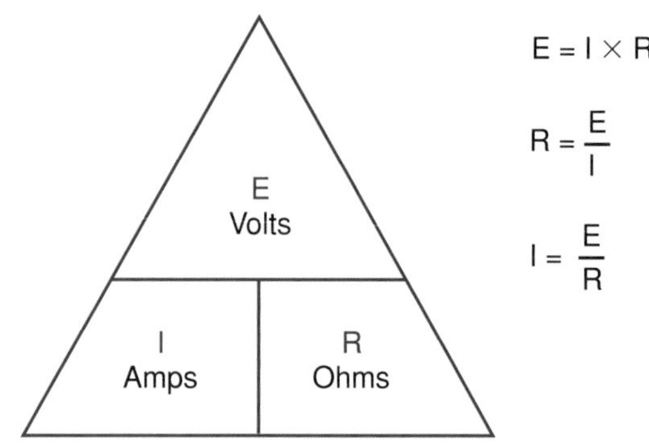

Figure 5-10. Pyramid formula for Ohm's law problems.

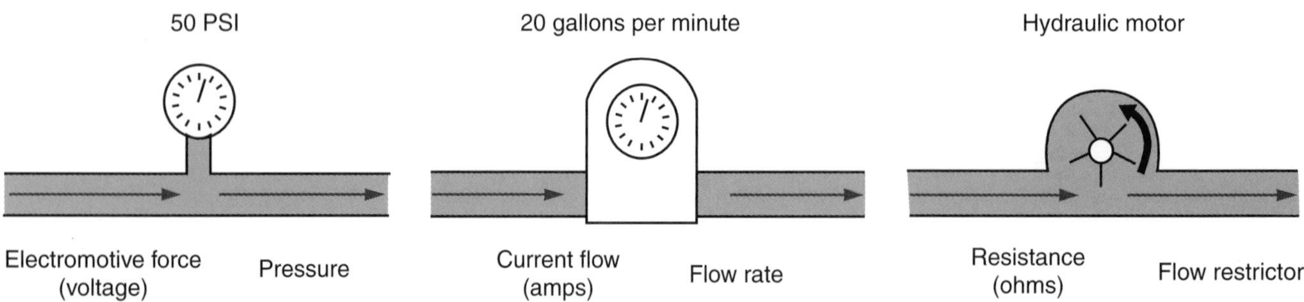

Figure 5-9. A water or hydraulic system is sometimes used to explain electricity. Pressure can be compared to voltage and flow past a point can be compared to electrical current. A hydraulic motor or turbine can be compared to an electrical component that creates resistance.

Voltage is dropped across each resistor that amperage flowed through. To determine the voltage drop across any resistor, simply use Ohm's law. In this case, use only the amperage and resistance at that particular resistor. Voltage drop at any resistor is shown as:

Voltage drop = Resistance (at any one resistor) × Amperage ($E = R \times I$)

Watt's Law

The second law relating to electricity is known as ***Watt's law*** or the power formula. This law states that in an electrical circuit, current is directly proportional to power and inversely proportional to voltage.

All motorcycle electrical devices consume electrical power at a given rate. This rate of power consumption is expressed in watts (W), and its symbol is P. As in Ohm's law, the symbol for current is I and is measured in amps. The symbol E is for the pressure in volts. Watt's law provides the equation for determining power consumption. As with Ohm's law, given any two of these factors, the third can be calculated, **Figure 5-11.**

To put Watt's law to work, pretend you are installing a front headlamp on a motorcycle. The wattage of the bulb is 50 watts, and the maximum available voltage is 13.8 volts. You want to know what size fuse to put in the circuit.

50 watts ÷ 13.8 volts = 3.62 amps

In this case, you would use the next highest available fuse, which would be 4 amps. How much wattage would be used if a 12 volt horn drew 4 amps?

12 volts × 4 amps = 48 watts

As with Ohm's law, given any two of the electrical factors, you can calculate the third.

Electrical Terms and Components

There are several electrical terms and components that motorcycle technicians must know. A switch allows an electric circuit to be turned on or off manually. When the switch is closed (on), the circuit is complete and will operate. When the switch is open (off), the circuit is disconnected (open) and does not function, **Figure 5-12.**

A ***short circuit*** or short is caused when an exposed wire or connector touches ground, causing excess current flow. A grounded circuit is created when a wire causes a circuit to operate with its controlling switch open.

Circuit Protection

If a short to ground exists between the battery and load, unlimited current flow can cause an electrical fire. A ***fuse*** protects a circuit against damage caused by a short circuit. The link in the fuse will melt and burn in half to stop excess current and further circuit damage, **Figure 5-13.** A ***fuse box*** usually contains all the fuses for the various circuits.

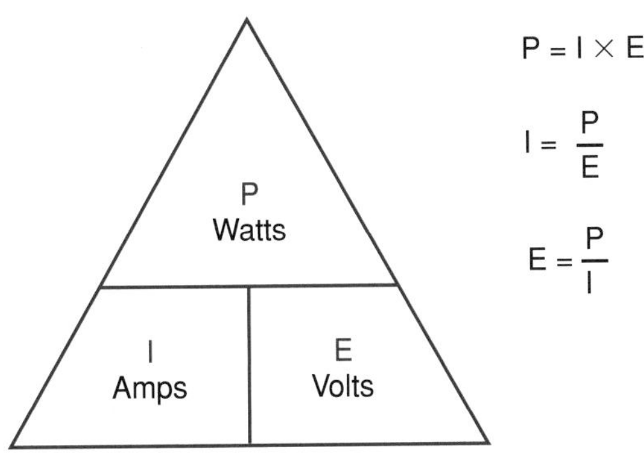

Figure 5-11. Pyramid formula showing Watt's law, which is used to solve power problems.

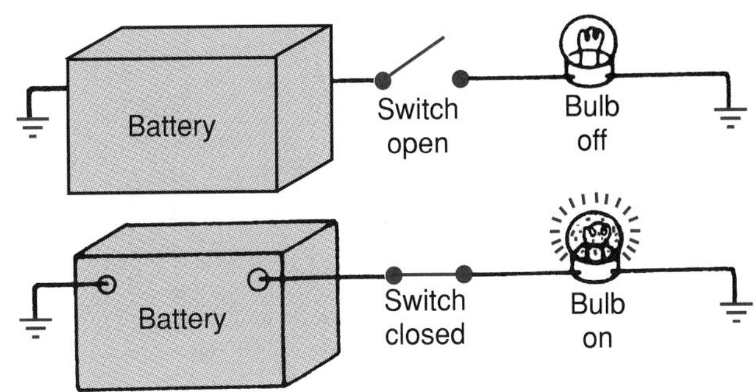

Figure 5-12. A switch provides a means of breaking the path for current in a circuit.

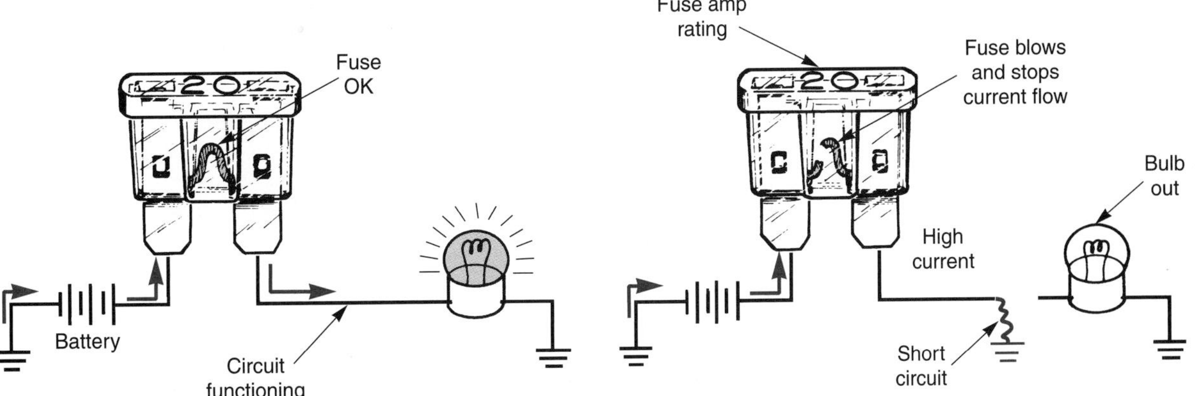

Figure 5-13. Note how a fuse will burn and open the circuit if a short causes too much current.

A ***circuit breaker*** performs the same function as a fuse. It disconnects the power source from the circuit when current becomes too high. However, a circuit breaker will automatically reset itself when current returns to normal levels, **Figure 5-14.**

Relays and Solenoids

A ***relay*** is an electric switch that allows a small amount of current to control high current. As shown in **Figure 5-15,** it consists of a control circuit and a power circuit. When the control circuit switch is open, no current flows to the coil and the windings are de-energized. When the switch is closed, the coil is energized, making the soft iron core into an electromagnet and drawing the armature down. This closes the power circuit contacts, connecting power to the load circuit.

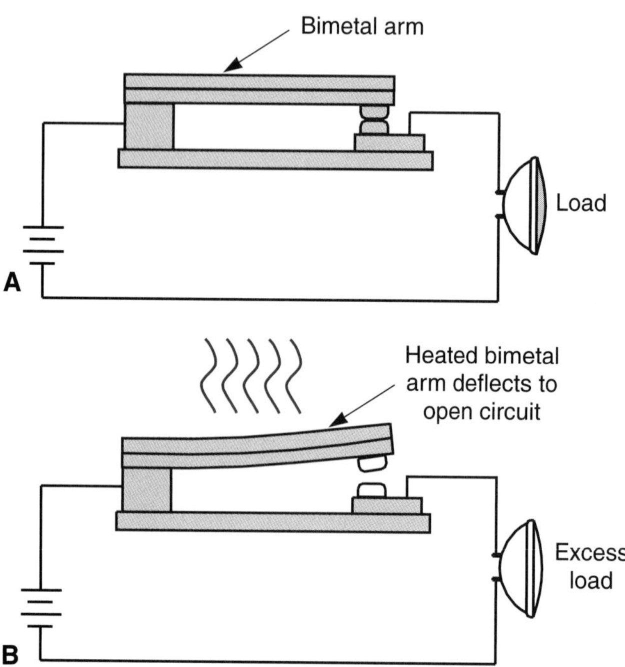

Figure 5-14. A—A circuit breaker performs the same function as a fuse. B—High current heats a bimetal strip, causing it to deform and open a set of points, stopping current flow in the circuit. When current drops to a normal level, the breaker cools and closes the points.

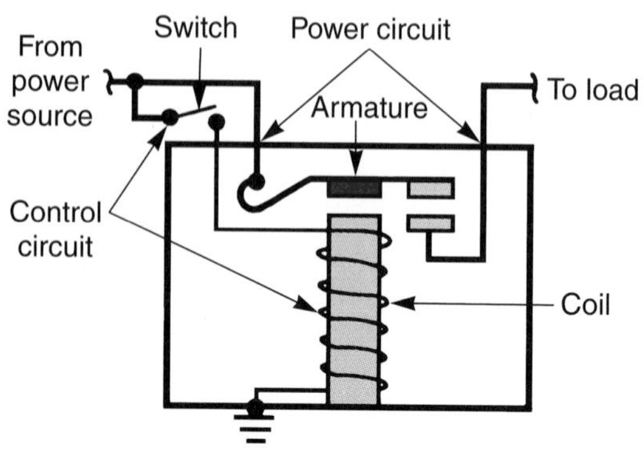

Figure 5-15. Typical relay construction.

A ***solenoid*** is another electromagnetic device. As shown in **Figure 5-16,** it is constructed with one or two coil windings wound around an iron tube. The iron tube acts as a bushing for a movable iron core. When electrical current is passed through the coil windings, it creates electromagnetic force that can be used to pull or push the iron core. When the core is connected to a lever or other mechanical device, the solenoid can put this mechanical movement to practical use.

Motorcycle Electronics

Many electronic devices are now present on newer motorcycles. Electronic ignition systems, electronic fuel injection, computerized engine systems, anti-lock brakes, and other advanced systems require technicians skilled in electricity and electronics. Electronics has become a special technology beyond electricity. Diodes, transistors, thyristors, thermistors, and other solid-state devices are all considered to be electronic devices rather than electrical devices.

Some electrical components use mechanical contacts. These contact points can wear, burn, or pit, and are relatively slow. In electronic systems, the components are solid state, do not have moving parts, and are extremely fast.

Solid state components use ***semiconductors,*** special substances capable of acting as both a conductor and an insulator. This characteristic enables semiconductor electronic devices to control current without mechanical points.

Diode

A ***diode*** is an electronic check valve that allows current to flow in only one direction, **Figure 5-17.** When

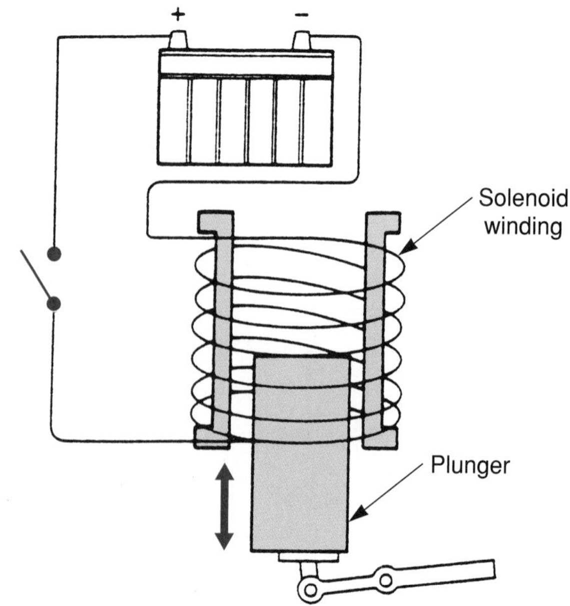

Figure 5-16. Solenoid construction details. A solenoid is a coil wrapped around a soft iron core.

current enters in the right direction, called ***forward bias,*** a diode acts a conductor and allows current flow. When current is flowing, there is a slight voltage drop across the diode. When current enters from the opposite direction, called ***reverse bias,*** the diode changes into an insulator and stops current from passing through the circuit.

Zener Diode

The ***Zener diode*** allows current to flow in one direction similar to the diode. When a certain reverse voltage is applied, current abruptly flows in the reverse direction. When the voltage is reduced below the reverse voltage, current flow in the reverse direction stops, **Figure 5-18.** Zener diodes on motorcycles, ATVs, and scooters are found in voltage regulators and a few other systems.

Thyristor (SCR)

Thyristors have three terminals, an anode (+), cathode (–), and gate. The current flowing from the anode to cathode is said to be in the positive direction. Like diodes, thyristors do not allow current flow in the opposite direction. Thyristors allow current to flow from anode to cathode only when the thyristor is turned on, **Figure 5-19.**

Transistor

A ***transistor*** performs the same function as a relay; it acts as a remote control switch or current amplifier. However, it is much more efficient than a relay. A transistor can switch on and off more than 200 times a second and does this without using moving parts. A transistor has three terminals; emitter (E), collector (C), and base (B), **Figure 5-20.** There are two types of transistors: PNP (Positive, Negative, Positive) and NPN (Negative, Positive, Negative).

Thermistor

The resistance value of most metals, including copper, increases as the temperature rises. In contrast, the resistance of a thermistor decreases as the temperature rises. When heat is applied to a substance, the activity of its molecules increases and prohibits the flow of free electrons. This increases the resistance. For thermistors, the number of free electrons increases as heat is applied. In this case, the activity of the molecules no longer obstructs the flow of electrons and the resistance decreases.

Other Electronic Devices

A ***condenser*** or ***capacitor*** is a device used to absorb unwanted electrical pulses (voltage fluctuations) in a circuit. They are used in various types of electrical and electronic circuits.

A capacitor is often connected into the supply wires going to a bike's radio. The capacitor absorbs any electrical noise (voltage pulses from the alternator or ignition system) which can be heard as a buzzing noise in the radio speakers. An ***integrated circuit (IC),*** contains miniaturized diodes, transistors, resistors, and capacitors in a wafer-like chip (small plastic housing with metal terminals). Integrated circuits are used in very complex electronic circuits.

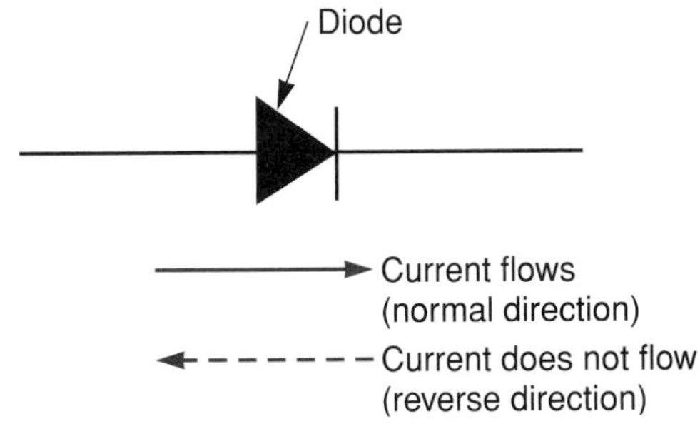

Figure 5-17. Current flow through a diode. Current will not flow in the opposite direction.

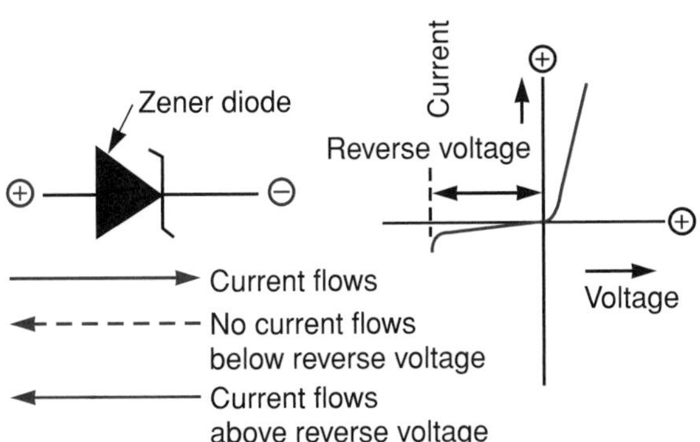

Figure 5-18. Operation of a Zener diode.

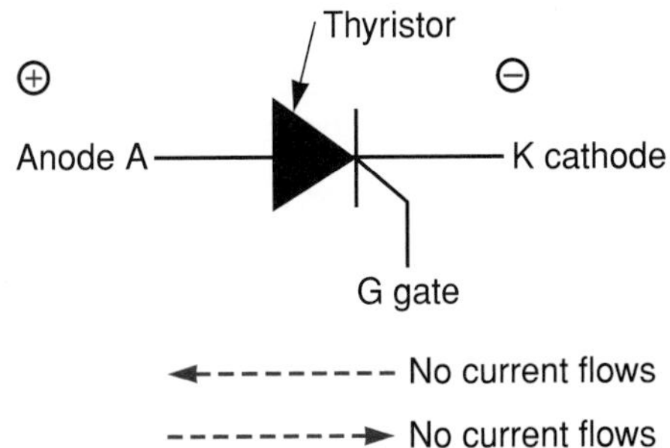

Figure 5-19. Operation of thyristor.

PNP type
NPN type
E C E C
B B
E: Emitter
C: Collector
B: Base

Figure 5-20. Transistor symbols.

Sources of Electricity

There are two primary ways to provide electrical power for use in motorcycle electrical systems. These are chemical (battery) and magnetism (alternators and dc generators).

Battery

A ***battery*** stores electricity and provides a steady supply of dc current for use in the electrical system. The battery will supply power for a considerable period of time, providing it is in good condition. As current is drawn from the battery, it becomes discharged. For this reason, a battery-supported electrical system must provide a means to recharge the battery.

Battery Operation

A motorcycle battery is made up of several two volt cells connected in series. This is illustrated in **Figure 5-21.** A 6-volt battery has three cells and a 12-volt battery has six cells. Each ***cell*** is made up of negative plates of sponge lead and positive plates of lead peroxide.

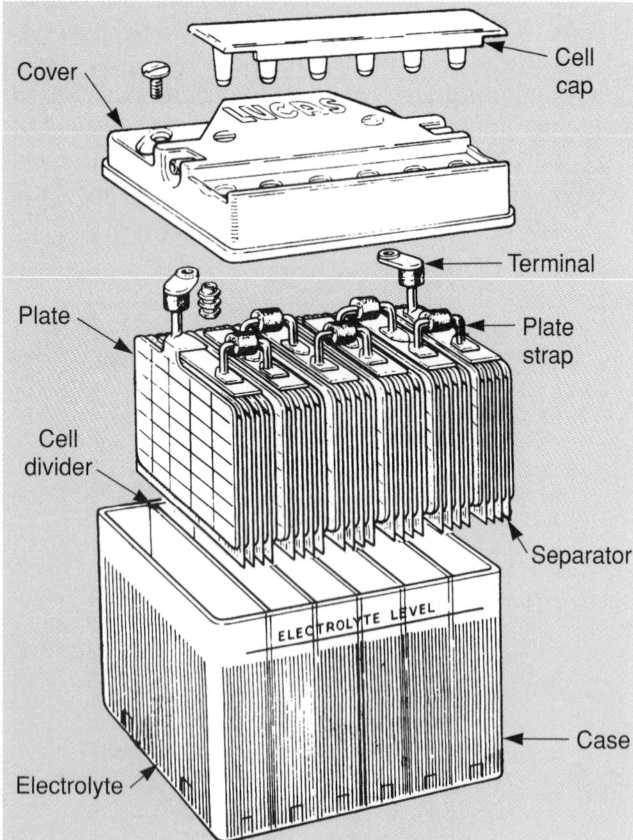

Figure 5-21. The parts of a battery. A cell is made up of negative (sponge lead) plates, positive (lead peroxide) plates, and separators (insulators). Most batteries have six cells. Each cell fits into a different compartment in a plastic battery case. (Triumph Motorcycles, Ltd.)

An ***electrolyte*** solution of dilute sulfuric acid (water and acid) is also contained in each cell. A chemical reaction occurs between the plates and the electrolyte that releases electricity. The battery becomes discharged as current is used. The charging system reverses this chemical reaction by supplying direct current to the battery, **Figure 5-22.** Full details on motorcycle, ATV, and scooter battery operations as well as care can be found in Chapter 8.

Magnetism

Magnetism is a very important factor when considering any motorcycle, ATV, or scooter electrical system. It is the force that controls the operation of such components as the flywheel magneto, alternator or generator, ignition coils, starter motor, and most mechanical relays.

A single bar magnet has a north and south pole. Illustrated in **Figure 5-23,** invisible force lines called ***magnetic lines of force,*** extend out of each pole of the magnet. Like poles (N and N or S and S) repel each other. Unlike poles (N and S) attract each other.

Magnetic lines of force can be used to produce movement or electricity. The attraction or repulsion of magnetic fields will cause motion, as in electric motors. If a wire cuts through a magnetic field, current will be induced in the wire. This is called ***induction,*** and it is used in generators and alternators.

When current flows through a wire, a ***magnetic field*** is formed, **Figure 5-24.** If a wire is wrapped around a soft iron core, a stronger magnetic field will result when current flows through the wire. The windings around the iron core make an ***electromagnet,*** **Figure 5-25.** The electromagnet, like a permanent magnet, can produce movement in fer-

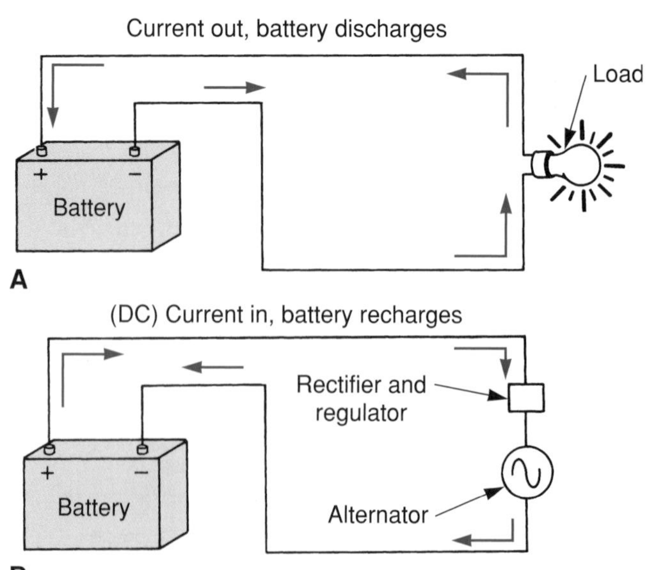

Figure 5-22. A—A battery discharges as it supplies electricity to the circuit load. B—An alternator is used to replenish the battery as needed. In a properly functioning charging system, electricity is supplied as it is used, keeping the battery charged at all times.

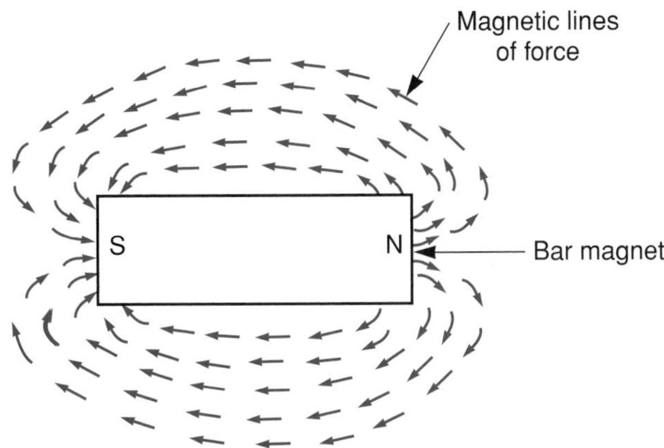

Figure 5-23. A magnet has invisible lines of force extending from the north pole to the south pole.

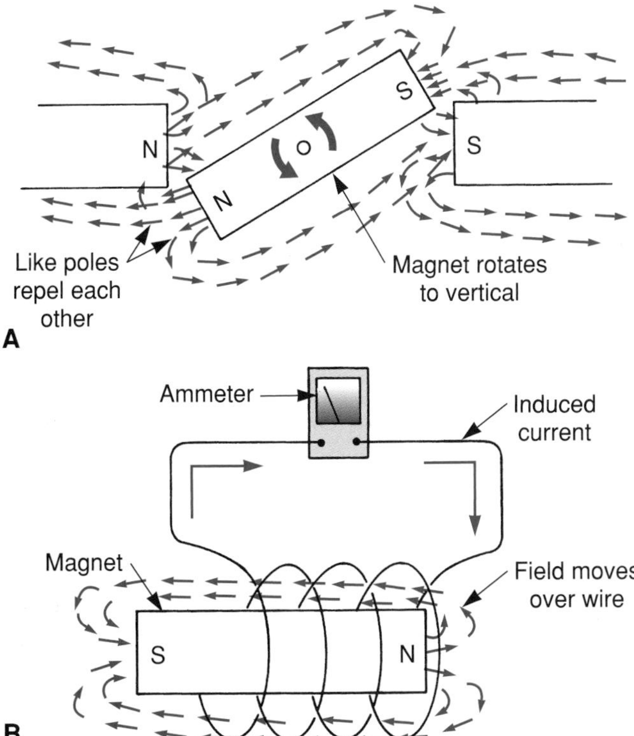

Figure 5-24. A magnetic field can be used to produce movement or current flow. A—Like magnetic fields would cause the center magnet to rotate into a vertical position. B—When a magnetic field is moved over the wire, current is induced in the wire.

rous metal objects. Ac alternators, dc generators, starting motors, ignition systems, and their use are described in Chapters 8 and 9.

Motorcycle Wiring

Motorcycles, ATVs, and scooters use various types and sizes of wiring in their many electrical systems. Wiring is used to transmit power as well as signals used to monitor and control electrical system operation. It is important to learn the different types, how they are used, and how to repair them.

Wire Types

Primary wire, **Figure 5-26,** is small and carries battery or alternator voltage. Primary wire has plastic insulation to prevent shorting. The insulation is usually color coded (different wires are marked with different colors) for easy troubleshooting. This lets you trace wires that are partially hidden.

Groups of primary wires are often enclosed in a wiring harness. A ***wiring harness*** is a plastic or tape covering that helps protect and organize the wires. **Figure 5-27** shows the proper method of handling a harness.

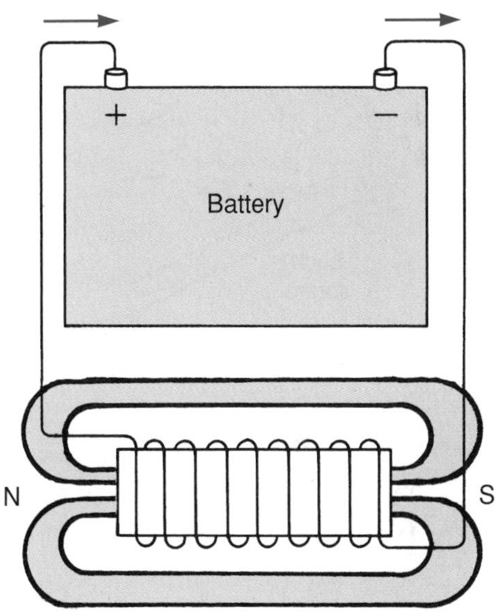

Figure 5-25. When a wire is wrapped around a soft iron core, current flowing through the wire will cause a magnetic field to form, creating an electromagnet.

Code	
B	Black
Br	Brown
G	Green
Gy	Gray
L	Blue
Lb	Light Blue
Lg	Light Green
O	Orange
R	Red
W	White
Y	Yellow

Figure 5-26. Primary wires are color coded with different colors.

Wire size is determined by the diameter of the wire's metal conductor. The diameter is stated in ***gage size,*** which is a number system. The larger the gage number, the smaller the wire conductor diameter, **Figure 5-28.** When replacing a section of wire, always use wire of equal or greater size. If a smaller wire is used, the circuit could malfunction due to high resistance. Undersize wire could heat up and melt its protective insulation, resulting in an electrical fire.

Secondary wire is used only in a motorcycle's ignition system. It has extra thick insulation for carrying high voltage from the ignition coil to the spark plugs, **Figure 5-29.** The conductor, however, is designed for very small currents.

Battery cable is extremely large gage wire capable of carrying high current from the battery to the starting motor. Usually, a starting motor draws more current than all the other electrical components combined. For this reason, very large conductors are required. ***Ground wires*** or ***ground straps*** connect electrical components to the motorcycle chassis or ground. Since they connect circuits or parts to ground, insulation is not needed. Wiring repairs and care are covered later in this chapter.

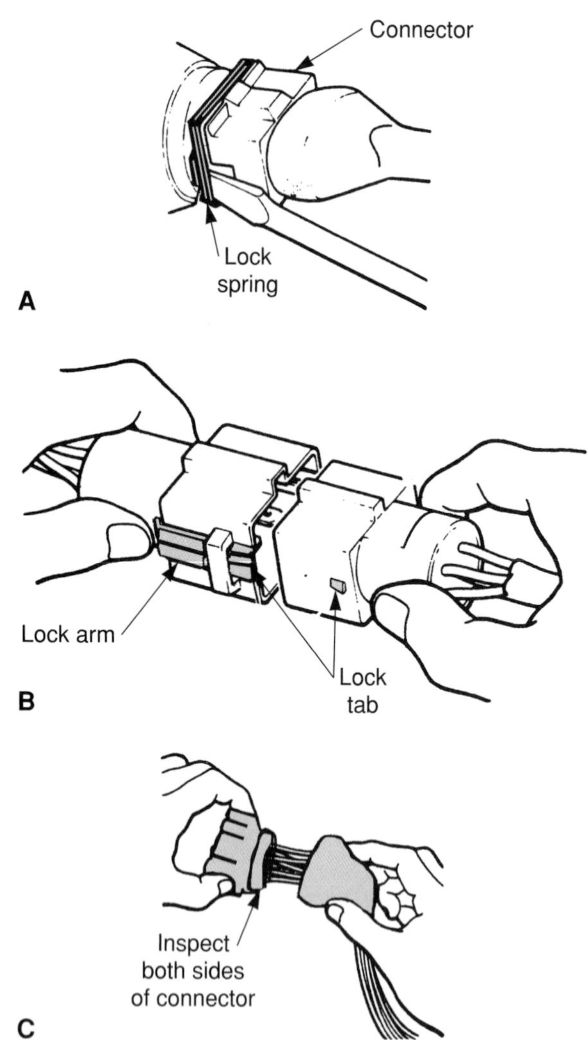

Figure 5-27. Always handle wiring harness connectors properly. A—This connector has a metal lock spring that keeps the connector from pulling apart. It must be released before disconnecting the connector. B—This connector has plastic arms that lock around tabs. The arms must be squeezed to free the connector. C—When inspecting a connector, check the terminals for corrosion and moisture on both sides of the connector. (Honda Motor Co., Ltd.)

Electrical Schematics and Symbols

To become good at diagnosing and repairing motorcycle electrical systems, you must first learn how to read electrical schematics (diagrams) and understand electrical symbols.

Schematics

A road map shows how various cities are connected by roads and highways. Similarly, a ***wiring diagram*** or ***schematic*** shows how electrical components are connected by wires. It serves as an electrical map that can help in diagnosing electrical problems.

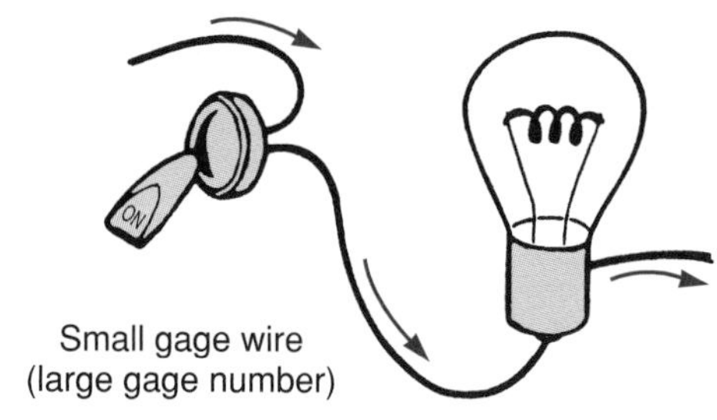

Figure 5-28. Wire gage size is matched to current draw. Small gage will only handle small current. Larger gage is needed for high current draws, starting motor for instance.

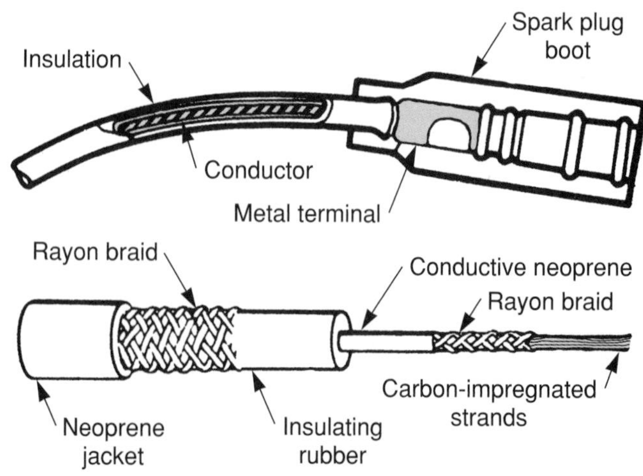

Figure 5-29. Secondary ignition wire has thick insulation to carry high voltage. Most secondary wires have carbon-impregnated strands that provide internal resistance to reduce radio noise. (Champion Spark Plugs Co.)

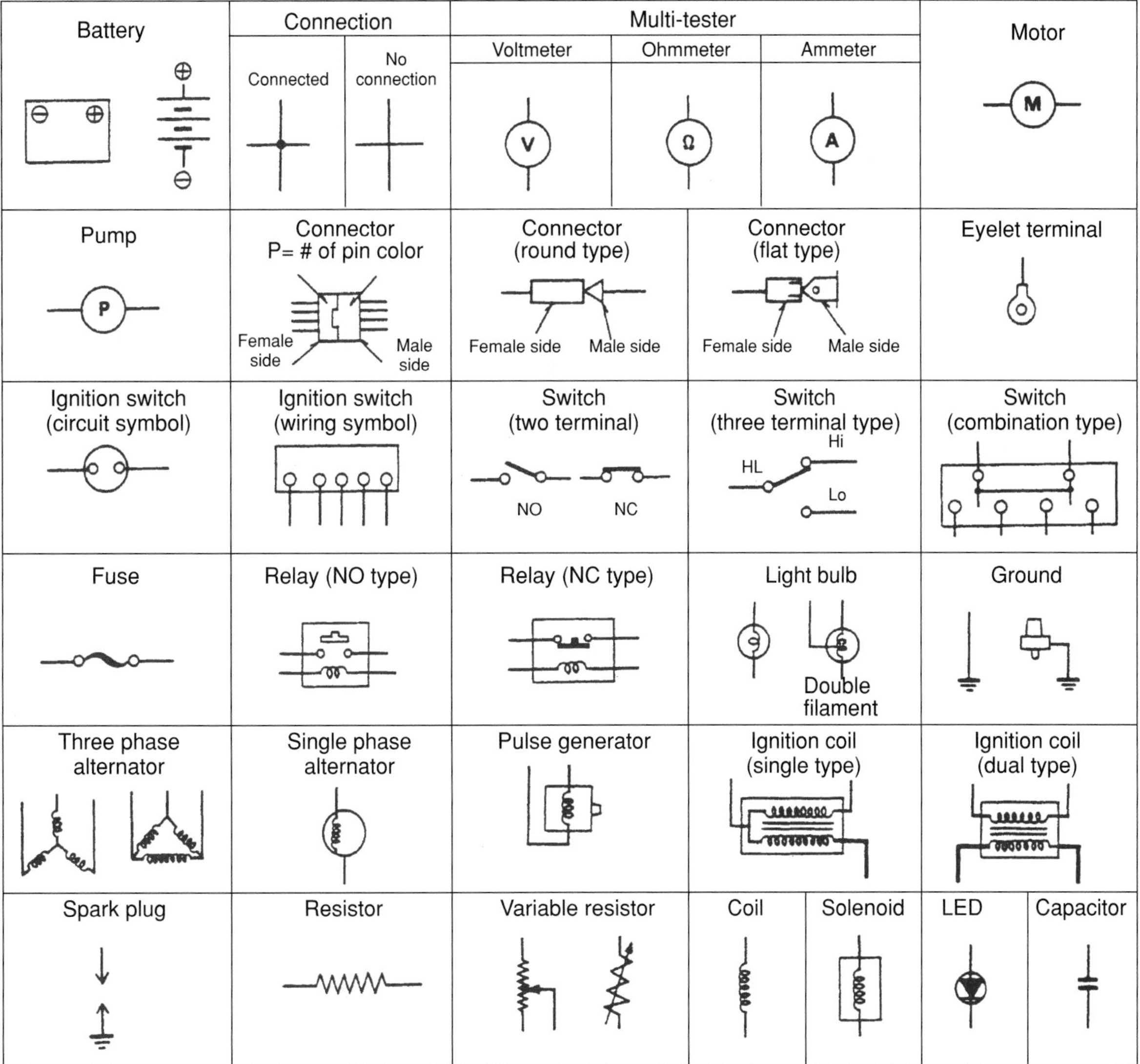

Figure 5-30. The most common types of device symbols used in motorcycle, ATV, and scooter schematics. Abbreviations used in switch devices are as follows: NO (normally open) and NC (normally closed). (Honda Motor Co., Ltd.)

When using wiring schematics, it is necessary to be able to identify the various symbols displayed on them. **Figure 5-30** gives some of the symbols commonly used in an electrical schematic. Many wiring schematics clearly name the components and wire colors. Not all schematics and diagrams are drawn the same, so you must learn to interpret the symbols used.

Some service manuals break-down electrical schematics into individual electrical component systems, **Figure 5-31.** Further information on reading schematics will be found in Chapters 9 and 17.

Electrical Systems Maintenance and Testing

Motorcycle electrical system maintenance and testing is not difficult. Most service manuals give adequate instructions for diagnosis and repair. Because there are so many different electrical systems, you should refer to wiring schematics in the service manual when testing an electrical system.

Basic Electrical Test Equipment

Various electrical tests and testing devices are used by a motorcycle technician. To be prepared for many later chapters, you should have an understanding of these tools and how to use them.

A ***jumper wire*** is handy for testing switches, relays, solenoids, wires, and other components, **Figure 5-32.** Typical jumper wires have inline fuses or circuit breakers to prevent a dangerous short circuit. The jumper can be substituted for the component. If the circuit begins to function with the jumper in place, the component being bypassed is defective.

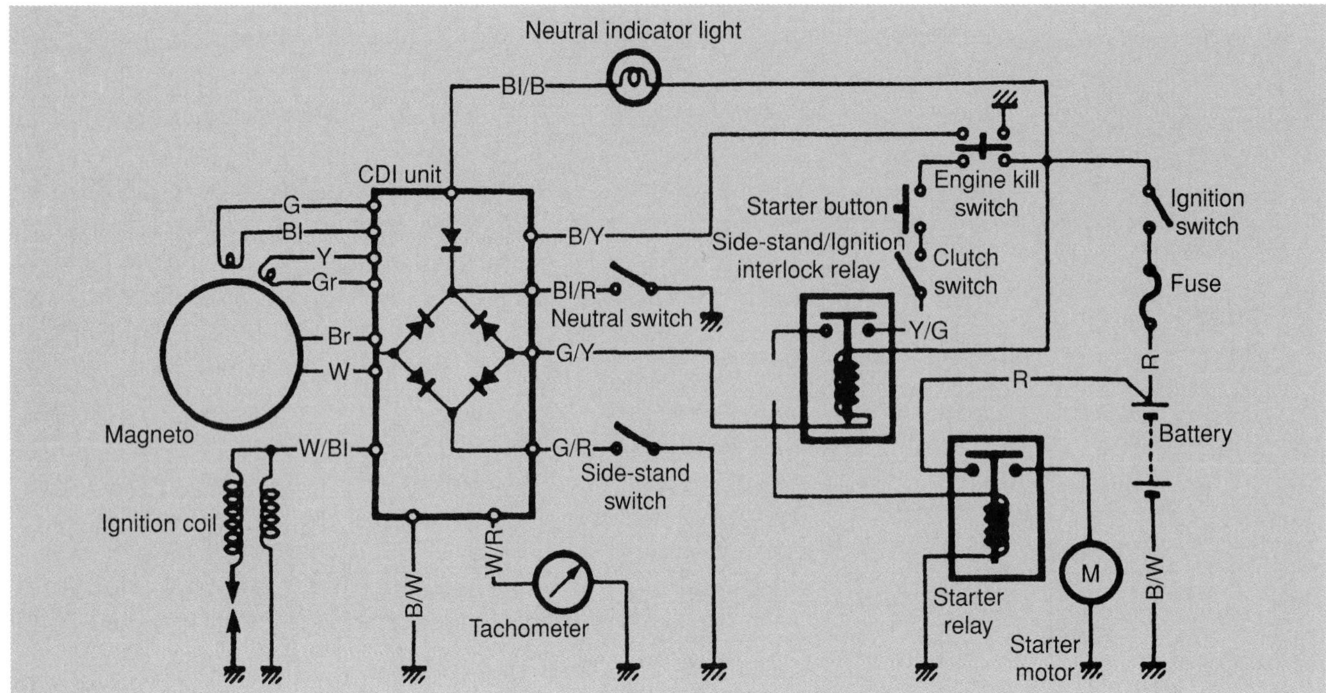

Figure 5-31. An electrical starter system schematic diagram. (American Suzuki Motor Corporation)

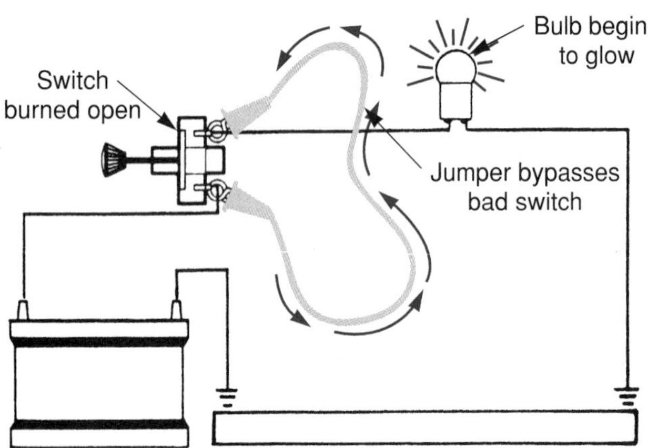

Figure 5-32. Jumper wire will let you bypass voltage around or to a component. For example, if you think a switch is defective, jumper around the switch. If the circuit begins to function, the switch is defective.

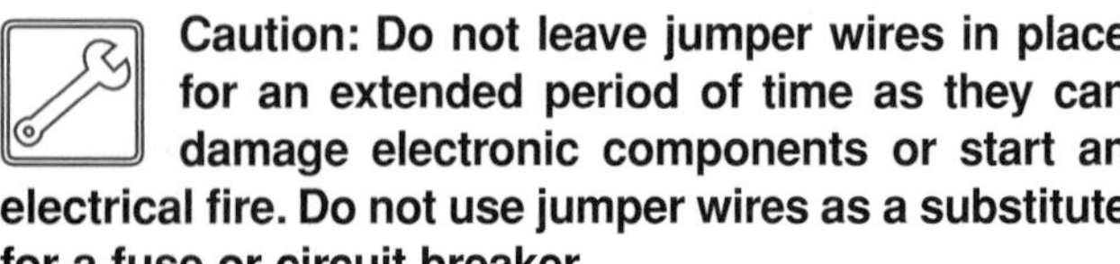

Caution: Do not leave jumper wires in place for an extended period of time as they can damage electronic components or start an electrical fire. Do not use jumper wires as a substitute for a fuse or circuit breaker.

A ***test light*** is used to check a circuit for power or voltage. It has an alligator clip that connects to ground, **Figure 5-33.** The pointed tip is then touched to the circuit to check for power. If there is voltage, the light will glow. If it does not glow, there is an open or break between the power source and the test point.

A ***self-powered test light*** contains batteries and is used to check for circuit continuity (verify whether the circuit is complete). To use this test light, the normal source of power (motorcycle battery or feed wire) must be disconnected. If the light glows, the circuit or part has continuity (low ohms). If it does not glow, there is an open or break (high ohms) between the two test points.

Voltmeter, Ammeter, and Ohmmeter

A ***voltmeter*** is used to measure the amount of voltage (volts) in a circuit, **Figure 5-34.** It is normally connected to the circuit in *parallel.* The voltmeter reading can be compared to specifications to determine whether an electrical problem exists.

An ***ammeter*** measures the amount of current (amps) in a circuit, **Figure 5-35.** Ammeters must be connected in *series* with the circuit. All of the current in the circuit must pass through the ammeter. A modern *inductive* or *clip-on ammeter* is simply slipped over the outside of the wire insulation. It uses the magnetic field around the outside of the wire to determine the amount of current in the wire. An inductive ammeter is very fast and easy to use

An ***ohmmeter*** will measure the amount of resistance (ohms) in a circuit or component. To prevent damage, an ohmmeter must never be connected to a source of voltage. The wire or part being tested must be disconnected

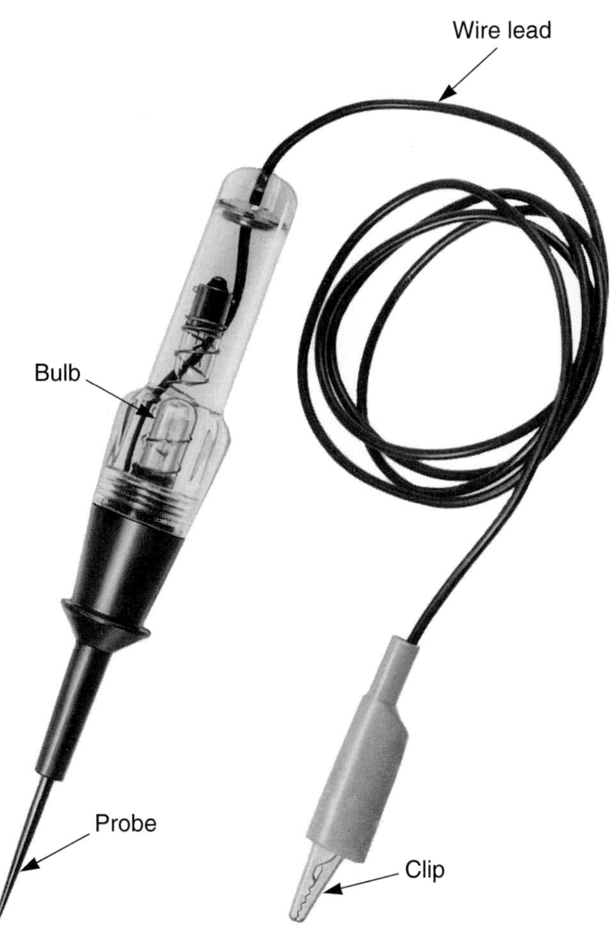

Figure 5-33. A test light can be used to quickly check for power in a circuit. Connect alligator clip to a good ground and touch the tip to circuit. The light will glow if there is power in the circuit. (Sonco Manufacturing Co.)

from the motorcycle's battery. As in **Figure 5-36,** the ohmmeter is connected in *parallel* with the wire or component being tested. Then, the ohmmeter reading can be compared to specifications.

A ***multimeter*** is an ohmmeter, ammeter, and voltmeter combined in one test unit. The multimeter's scale may be either analog or digital, **Figure 5-37.** With either type, by turning the control knob to the appropriate setting, almost any electrical measurement can be made. The multimeter must be connected to the circuit as descried for each individual meter.

Caution: Make sure your meter controls are set to the correct function (volts, amps, or ohms) and range (measuring value) before connecting the meter to a circuit. If set incorrectly, meter or circuit damage could occur. Any multimeter used should have a minimum impedance of 10 meg ohms.

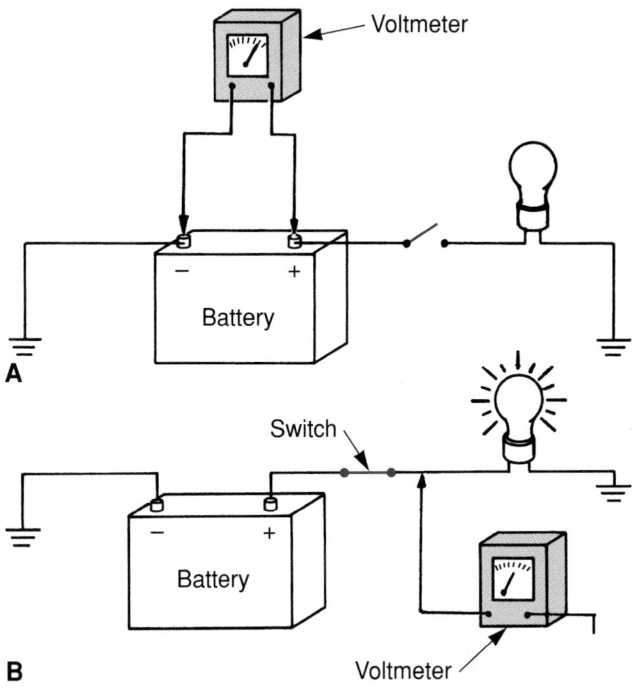

Figure 5-34. A voltmeter is connected in parallel. A—Common voltmeter connection to measure battery voltage. Low battery voltage would indicate a battery or charging system problem. B—A voltmeter will also check voltage in any part of the circuit. A low voltage reading, in this example, might indicate high resistance in the switch or other connection.

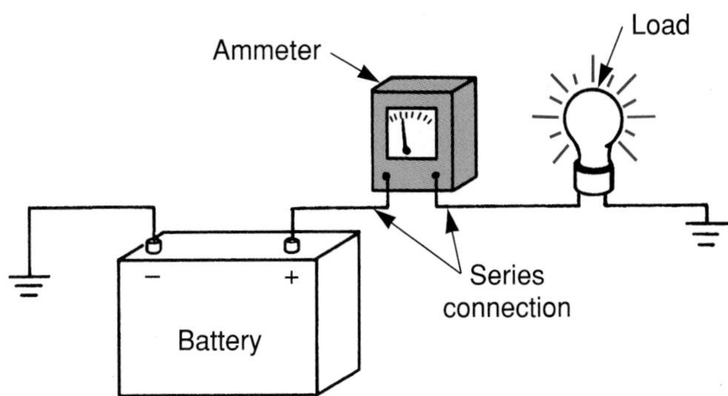

Figure 5-35. Ammeter must always be connected in series. This connection would allow circuit current to flow directly through the meter. In this example, the ammeter would read the current draw of the lightbulb.

Basic Electrical Diagnostic Methods

Like any other motorcycle, ATV, or scooter system, the process of electrical troubleshooting is a matter of identifying the type of problem and locating it in the circuit. If a good step-by-step troubleshooting approach is used, locating a problem is an easy process. Using a methodical approach to troubleshooting is the key to quick and accurate solutions. Listed below are four troubleshooting steps that apply to all electrical repair situations.

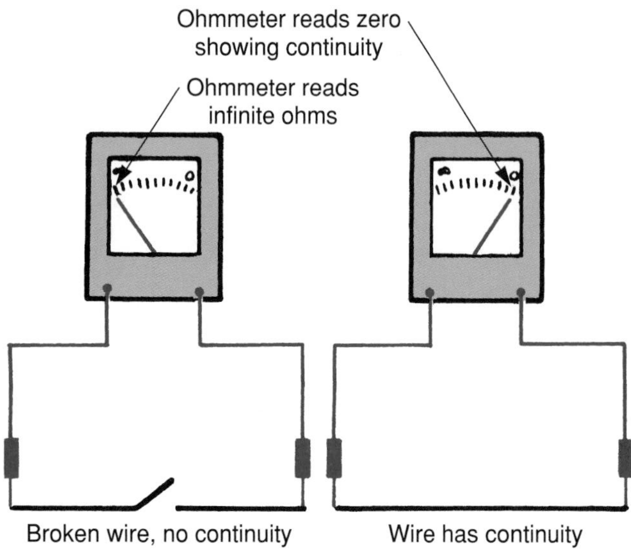

A–Checking wire continuity

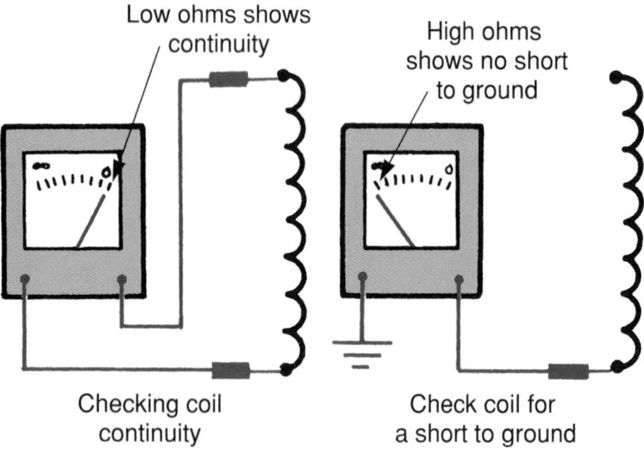

B–Checking coil

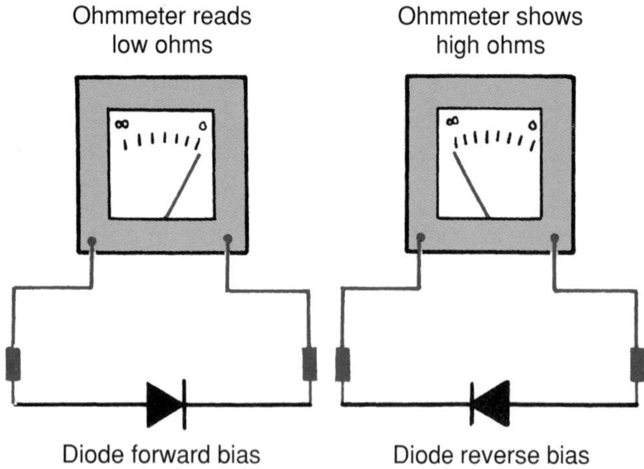

C–Checking diode

Figure 5-36. An ohmmeter must never be connected to a source of electricity or it may be damaged. A—A wire should have almost no resistance. B—Coil windings should have low resistance and not shorted to ground. C—A diode should have low resistance in one direction and high in the other direction.

1. Verify the problem. After hearing the customer complaint, operate the motorcycle to verify the problem and to identify the affected circuit. It is important to do this with the customer present so both parties agree what the problem is, and whether the problem is normal or abnormal.
2. Eliminate the obvious. Always check the condition of the battery and the fuses first. Use the appropriate test instruments to verify their condition. Visually check the motorcycle for damage. Broken, pinched or frayed wires, loose connectors, burn marks, and inoperative switches may lead directly to the problem. The visual inspection's primary purpose is to eliminate obvious causes of the problem.
3. Reference materials are crucial to effective troubleshooting. Refer to the schematic or wiring diagram for the problem circuit. Identifying all the components and wires in the circuit and understanding how current flows in the circuit are necessary before troubleshooting begins.
4. Use a systematic approach. Haphazard and unsystematic checks are a waste of time and probably will

Figure 5-37. A multimeter will make accurate measurements of voltage, current, and resistance. This is a digital multimeter. (OTC Division of SPX Corporation)

not reveal the problem's root cause. An accurate method of troubleshooting is the "divide and conquer" approach. The idea of this approach is that by dividing a circuit in half, troubleshooting time can be reduced. This approach is made possible by the fact that most modern motorcycle, ATV, and scooter electrical circuits are built around a central component.

Using Test Equipment in Troubleshooting

The following tests are representative examples of common meter measurements used to check electrical components. These tests can be done on virtually any motorcycle. However, the points or locations of meter connections may vary. For this reason, refer to the proper service manual for correct meter connections and output specifications.

Caution: When performing electrical tests, be careful not to touch hot wires on ground (metal parts of motorcycle connected to frame). Serious wiring and part damage could result.

Voltage Measurement

Measuring voltage is a fundamental method of checking components. The measurement is conducted for the following reasons:

- To see if voltage exists in the circuit.
- To measure the actual voltage value to determine if an electrical component is receiving or generating sufficient voltage.

Select a range that is one scale higher than the desired voltage value. Apply the red probe to the positive (+) end and the black probe to the negative (–) end of the circuit. Remember that voltmeters are always connected in parallel, not in series.

Using Voltmeters to Diagnose Circuit Failures

First study the circuit diagram in **Figure 5-38.** If the lightbulbs B and C do not work, and A is ok, the malfunction is between the grounds at B and C and switch A. If the lightbulb A does not work also, the problem is between the grounds at A, B, C, and the ignition switch.

1. With the ignition switch on, if lightbulbs B and C do not work, check for voltage at point 1.
2. If no voltage is measured at point 1, check the voltage at point 2 in the case of a false connection at connector A. If the voltage exists at point 2 and not at point 1, there is a problem in the connection at connector A. If voltage registers at both points 1 and 2, switch A should be checked.
3. If there is no voltage at points 1 and 2, check the voltage at points 3 and 4 in a similar manner. If there is no voltage at points 3 and 4, check the wiring between the ignition switch and the battery. If there is voltage at points 3 and 4, check for a broken wire or a short circuit in the wire harness. Exchange the wire harness with a new one if necessary. If there is voltage at point 4 and not at point 3, then check connector B for a loose connection.

Sometimes it is easier to diagnose a component by measuring from its input terminals directly. As shown in **Figure 5-39,** the (+) probe goes to the positive terminal and (–) probe goes to the ground wire of the component. If no voltage is measured, there are two possible causes:

- No voltage at the positive input terminal. Check for voltage between the input terminal leading to the power source and ground.
- A loose ground wire. Check for continuity between the terminal to ground.

Voltage measurement is frequently used to check a system that is not working correctly. For instance, if a lightbulb blows out frequently, it needs to be checked with a voltmeter to see if excessive voltage is present. In this case, you would measure the lightbulb terminal voltage to see if it is within the specified range.

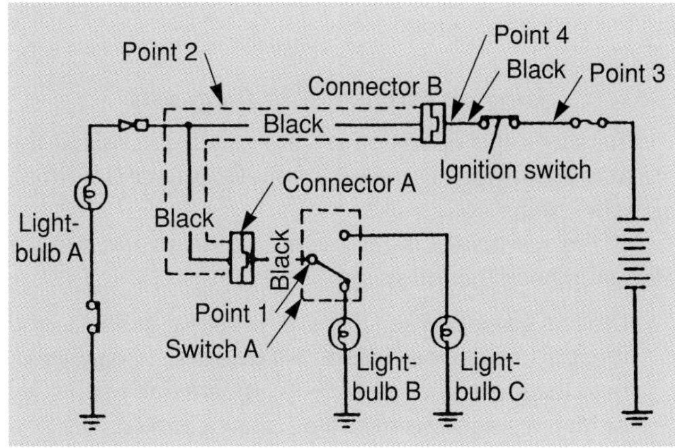

Figure 5-38. Electrical problem can occur almost anywhere in a circuit. (Honda Motor Co., Ltd.).

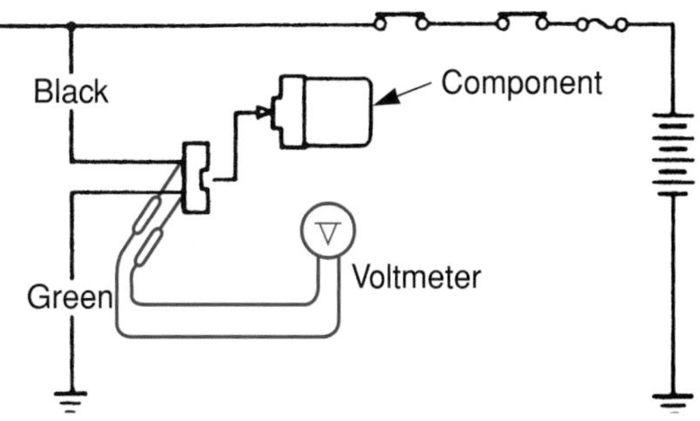

Figure 5-39. Checking a component by measuring from its input terminals. (Honda Motor Co., Ltd.)

Measuring Resistance

Along with voltage, resistance is another parameter for diagnosing circuits and their components. Resistance is measured to see if components are working properly. For example, the resistance value of an ignition coil indicates if it is normal or malfunctioning. Resistance is also used to check for a broken wire. A continuity check indicates if a wire is intact or broken.

Note: Proper ohmmeter calibration is necessary to obtain correct measurements. Touch the two probes and adjust the ohmmeter so that it registers 0 Ω.

Since the polarity of the terminals is not important, either probe may be applied to the terminal. However, since diodes allow current to flow in one direction only, polarity is important. Unlike measuring voltage, it is necessary to disconnect the component from the circuit. If resistance is measured with the entire circuit connected, the ohmmeter will read a smaller value than the correct value. Similarly, if a circuit has branches, the connector leading to the specific branch needs to be disconnected in order to read correctly, **Figure 5-40.**

When the ohmmeter is connected in series, resistance values are large. The resistance is measured by moving the probe to a ground.

Using an Ohmmeter in Diagnosis

To check the operation of an exciter coil, place the probes as shown in **Figure 5-41.** If the resistance is normal, then the exciter coil, is ok.

If the resistance is far off the value in the service manual, check the following:

1. Broken ground wire. Place a probe at point 1 and measure resistance, **Figure 5-42.** If 0 Ω is measured, then the green wire is properly grounded. If infinity (∞) or high resistance is measured, then a broken wire or a corroded or loose connection at the ground terminal is suspect.

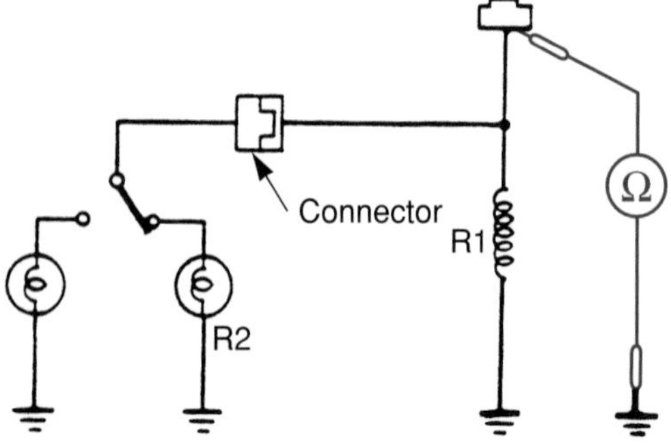

Figure 5-40. Checking resistance in a branch circuit. (Honda Motor Co., Ltd.)

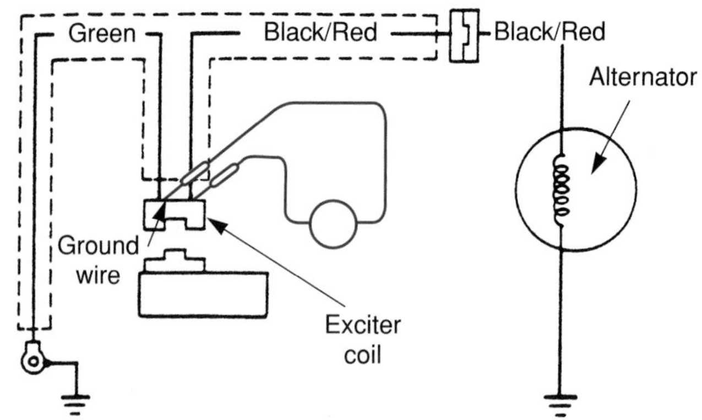

Figure 5-41. Checking the operation of an exciter coil. (Honda Motor Co., Ltd.).

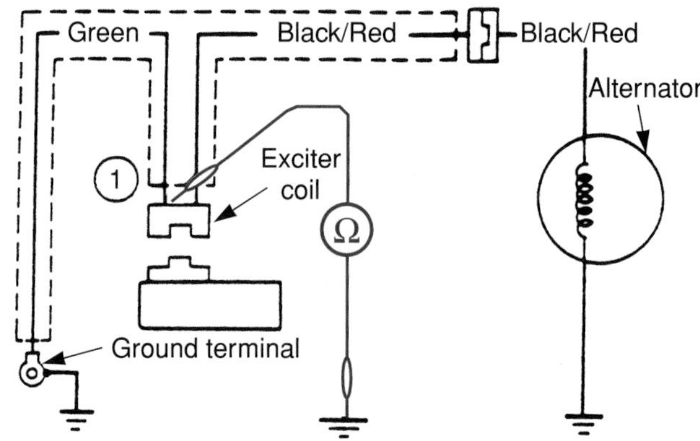

Figure 5-42. Checking for a broken ground wire. (Honda Motor Co., Ltd.)

2. Faulty exciter coil. Disconnect the alternator connector and measure the resistance to ground. Compare the resistance values at points 1 measured and 2, **Figure 5-43.** If the two values are not the same, suspect a broken black/red wire or a loose alternator connector. If both resistance values are the same, but not in the correct range, the exciter coil or alternator coil may be faulty.

3. Shorted wire or wire harness, **Figure 5-44.** To see if the green or black/red wire is shorted, check the continuity between different colored wires. If you have continuity between other wires, replace the wire harness.

Note: When measuring voltage and resistance of wire terminals using testers; insert the probes from behind the connector. For waterproof plug-in connectors, insert the probes from the front to avoid compromising the wire terminal.

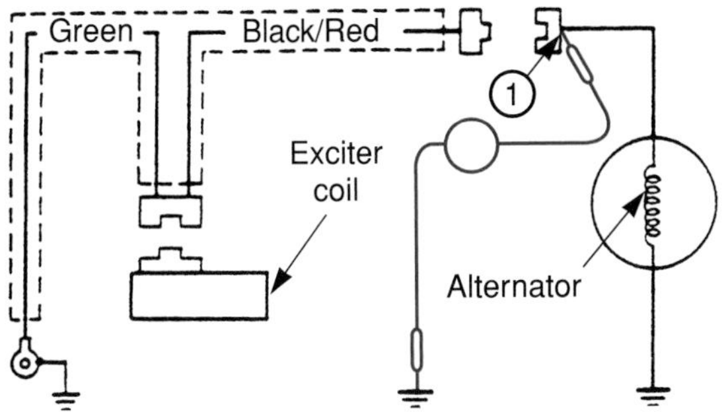

Figure 5-43. Checking for faulty exciter coil. (Honda Motor Co., Ltd.)

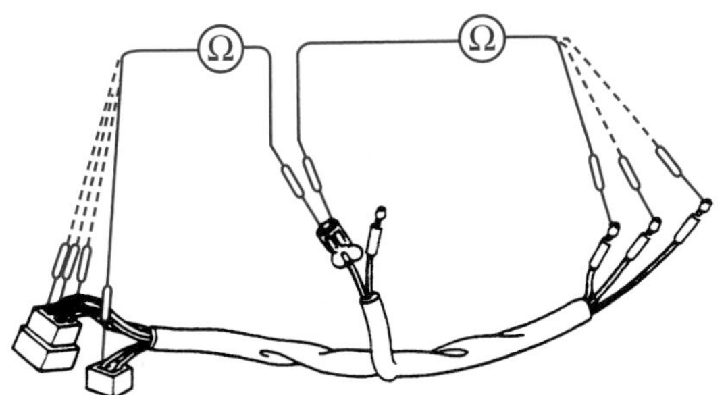

Figure 5-44. Checking for a shorted wire or wire harness. (Honda Motor Co., Ltd.)

Measuring Current

Current is not normally checked during motorcycle service procedures. Though it is used for testing components, such as the starting and charging system, current measurements are not used for checking continuity within circuits.

When it is necessary to check current, remember that the ammeter is always connected in series and it measures the current flowing through the circuit. Make sure the current flow does not exceed the maximum range selected.

Electrical System Repairs

Most electrical system components must be replaced if they are found to be defective. However, it is common to repair or replace broken or damaged wires and connectors. Numerous methods can be used to repair motorcycle wiring.Never simply twist wires together. Use a soldered or crimped connection.

Soldering

A ***soldering gun*** or iron can be used to permanently fasten wires to terminals or to other wires. The soldering gun or iron produces enough heat to melt solder. The soldering gun is touched to the wire and other component to preheat them. The solder is touched to the joint and melts. When cooled, the solder makes a solid connection between the electrical components. ***Rosin core solder*** should be used on all electrical repairs. It is usually purchased in a roll form for easy use and handling. Acid core solder will cause corrosion of wires and terminals and should not be used.

Crimp Terminals

Crimp connectors and terminals can be used to quickly repair wiring, **Figure 5-45.** ***Terminals*** allow a wire to be connected to an electrical component. ***Connectors*** allow a wire to be connected to another wire. ***Crimping pliers*** are used to compress the connector or terminal around the wire. When installing a crimp-on connector, **Figure 5-46,** keep the following in mind:

1. Strip 1/4" of insulation from the end of the wire.
2. Select the proper connector, for the wire size and application. Remember to always place the insulator over the wire before crimping the connector, and be sure it is facing the proper direction.
3. Crimp the front portion of the crimp area over the bare wire, then crimp the rear section over the wire insulation.

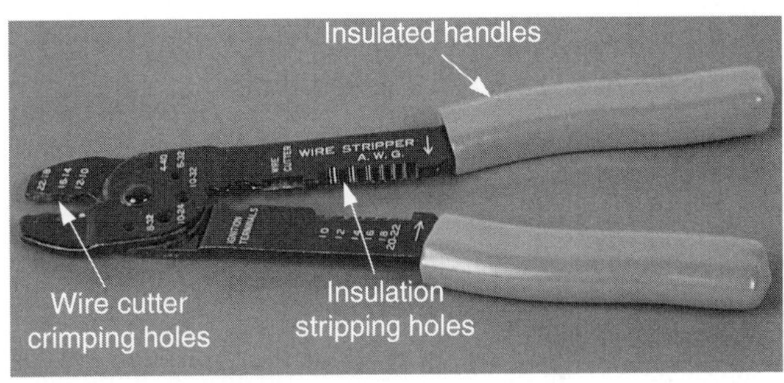

Figure 5-45. Solderless crimping tool. Crimp connectors are available to suit most applications. Always use a crimping tool to install crimp connectors.

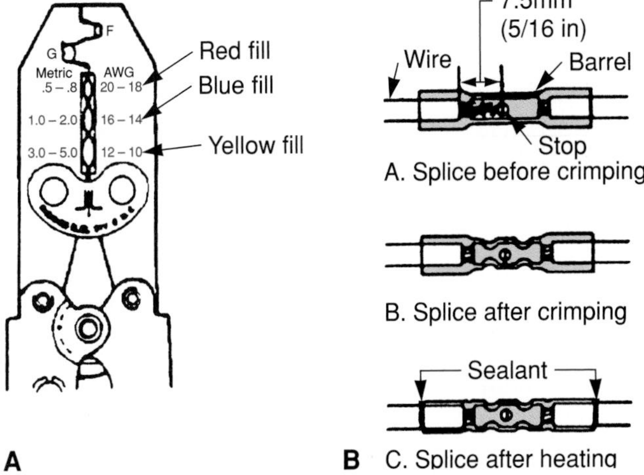

Figure 5-46. Installing crimp connectors and terminals. A—Use the right size crimping jaw to form the connector around the wire. B—Crimp the terminal in and heat the ends to seal the connection if a self sealing connector was used. Tug on the wire lightly to check the connection.

Heat-Shrink Tubing

Heat-shrink tubing is the fastest, most efficient, and professional way to insulate most connections. In order for heat-shrink tubing to work correctly, it is important to select the correct diameter tube for the wire being repaired. Heat-shrink tubing is sold in specific diameters to match the various wire gages.

To insulate a simple connection made between two wires that are not in a vulnerable location, such as near components, around a corner of a bracket or frame, or subject to movement or stretching, simply cut the heat-shrink tubing to approximately twice the length of the connection. Then, slip it into place, and use a heat gun to apply heat evenly over its entire length until it has shrunk uniformly into place.

Caution: Do not use too much direct heat or the wire could be damaged. Also do not apply heat near solid state electronic or fuel system components.

If the connection being made is vulnerable to sharp edges, movement or rubbing by cables or other wires, you should double the insulation. This may be done by using a second, shorter piece of heat-shrink tubing underneath the outside covering. Be careful to apply one or two wraps of plastic tape tightly around the connection before the heat-shrink tubing is applied. If many wires, such as a section of the wiring harness, are being spliced together, neatly wrap the entire connection with electrical tape or cover it with large diameter heat-shrink tubing. If the wire came from a harness, be sure to tuck it back in.

Electrical Service Precautions

There are a number of important precautions that must be followed when servicing electrical systems.

1. Do not reverse battery connections. This will burn out the diodes in the electrical system.
2. Always check the battery condition before condemning other parts of the electrical system. A fully charged battery is required for accurate electrical system tests.
3. Electrical parts should never be struck sharply or allowed to fall on a hard surface. Such a shock can damage the part.
4. Be careful about the placement of welding cables. Keep the electrical path as short as possible by placing the ground clamp near the point of welding. Do not place welding cables close to electronic displays or computers.
5. Take care when handling electrical and electronic displays and gauges. Never press on the gauge face as it could be damaged.
6. To prevent damage to electrical and electronic parts, do not disconnect the battery leads or any other electrical connections while the ignition switch is on or with the engine running.
7. Because of high current, never keep the starter switch pushed when the starter motor will not turn over, or the current may burn out the motor windings.
8. Do not use a meter illumination bulb rated higher than the voltage or wattage specified in the wiring diagram, as the meter or gauge panel could be warped by the excessive heat.
9. Take care not to short leads that are directly connected to the battery positive (+) terminal to chassis ground.
10. An electrical problem may involve one or more items. Never replace a defective part without determining what caused the failure. If the failure was brought on by another cause, correct the root cause, or the new part will eventually fail.
11. Make sure all connectors in the circuit are clean and tight, and examine wires for signs of burning, fraying, etc. Poor wires and bad connectors will affect electrical system operation.
12. Be careful not to damage connectors and terminals when removing electrical and electronic components. Some may require special tools for removal.

Summary

Almost every system in a modern motorcycle, ATV, and scooter uses some type of electrical or electronic component. Electricity itself cannot be seen except in the form of physical activity such as light, heat, and movement. One of the oldest and most accepted theories is that electricity is comprised of moving electrons. Matter is made up of negatively charged electrons that freely move about in an orbit around a nucleus made of neutrons and positively charged protons. There are two theories regarding electron flow: the conventional theory and electron theory. Motorcycles use direct and alternating current.

A simple circuit consists of a power source which supplies electricity for the circuit; conductors that carry current between the power source and load; and a load that uses the electricity. The three types of electrical circuits used on motorcycles, ATVs, and scooters are the series circuit, parallel circuit, and series-parallel circuit. Electricity is affected by amperage or current, voltage, or electromotive force, and resistance. The two laws that show the relationship of electricity are Ohm's law and Watt's law.

Many electronic devices such as electronic ignition systems, electronic fuel injection, computerized engine systems, and anti-lock brakes are now present on newer motorcycles. Diodes, transistors, thyristors, thermistors, and other solid-state devices are all considered to be electronic devices rather than electrical devices.

There are two primary ways to provide electrical power for use in motorcycle electrical systems. These are chemical (battery) and magnetism (alternators and dc generators). A battery stores electricity and provides a steady supply of dc current for use in the electrical system. A motorcycle battery is made up of several two volt cells connected in series. Each cell is made up of negative plates of sponge lead and positive plates of lead peroxide immersed in electrolyte. Magnetism is the force that controls the operation of such components as the flywheel magneto, alternator or generator, ignition coils, starter motor, and most mechanical relays.

Motorcycles use primary wiring, which is the small gage wire that carries direct current, and secondary wiring, which is used for ignition voltage only. A wiring diagram or schematic shows how electrical components are connected by wires. It serves as an electrical map that can help in diagnosing electrical problems. Electrical test equipment includes jumper wires, test lights, and multimeters. Wiring is repaired either by soldering or crimp terminals and insulated by heat-shrink tubing.

Know These Terms

Electrons
Current flow
Conventional theory
Electron theory
Direct current (dc)
Alternating current (ac)
Sine wave
Rectification
Power source
Conductors
Insulators
Load
Series circuit
Parallel circuit
Series-parallel circuit
One-wire circuits
Frame ground
Polarity
Amperage
Voltage
Resistance
Ohm's law
Voltage drop
Watt's law
Short circuit
Fuse
Fuse box
Circuit breaker
Relay
Solenoid
Semiconductor
Diode
Forward bias
Reverse bias
Zener diode
Thyristors
Transistor
Condenser
Capacitor
Integrated circuit (IC)
Battery
Cell
Electrolyte
Magnetism
Magnetic lines of force
Induction
Magnetic field
Electromagnet
Primary wire
Wiring harness
Wire size
Gage size
Secondary wire
Battery cable
Ground wires
Ground straps
Wiring diagram
Schematic
Jumper wire
Test light
Self-powered test light
Voltmeter
Ammeter
Ohmmeter
Multimeter
Soldering gun
Rosin core solder
Terminals
Connectors
Crimping pliers
Heat-shrink tubing

Review Questions—Chapter 5

Do not write in this text. Place your answers on a separate sheet of paper.

1. What is *electricity*?
2. All matter is said to be _____ in nature.
3. Explain the difference between a conductor and an insulator.
4. Which of the following is *not* part of a simple circuit?
   A. Electric motor.
   B. Load.
   C. Power source.
   D. Conductors.
5. Name the two types of electric current.
6. A _____ circuit has more than one load connected in a single electrical path.
7. A _____ circuit has more than one electrical path or leg.
8. What is a *one-wire circuit*?
9. Using Ohm's law, find the resistance in a circuit with 12 volts and 3 amps.
10. A _____ can be used to produce electricity.
    A. fuse
    B. magnetic field
    C. transistor
    D. None of the above.
11. Define the term *short circuit.*
12. Explain the functions of fuses and circuit breakers.
13. A _____ is an electrical, not electronic, device that allows a small current to control a larger current.
14. Explain the difference between an electric component and an electronic component.

15. Which of the following *are* electronic components.
    A. Diode.
    B. Transistor.
    C. Circuit breaker.
    D. All of the above.
16. An _____ is a solid state device that uses a very small current to control a very large current.
17. ______ is used to carry ignition voltage and has thick insulation.
18. Why are wires color coded?
19. Which of the following should *not* be used for electrical repairs?
    A. Acid core solder.
    B. Rosin core solder.
    C. Crimp connectors.
    D. Soldering gun.
20. Explain the purpose of wiring diagrams.

Suggested Activities

1. Using sketches and principles you have learned about electricity, prepare a presentation showing how electricity can be created through magnetism.
2. Using the wiring schematic from a current motorcycle, ATV, or scooter, trace the following circuits:
    A. Electric starter circuit.
    B. Main lighting circuit.
    C. Turn signal circuit.
    D. Horn circuit.
3. Practice using a voltmeter, ammeter, ohmmeter, or multimeter at various places in the electrical system of a motorcycle. Make a record of your tests and the results. Be sure to follow proper procedures.

6 Engines

After studying this chapter, you will be able to:

- Know the types of engines that are used in motorcycles, ATVs, and scooters.
- Explain the operating principles of a four-stroke engine.
- List the functions of major four-stroke engine parts.
- Describe the construction and design aspects of four-stroke engine components.
- Explain the different classifications of four-stroke engines.
- Explain two-stroke engine operation.
- Describe intake, exhaust, and transfer timing in regard to engine performance.
- Explain how a two-stroke engine crankcase is sealed.
- Explain reed and rotary valve operating principles.
- List design variations in two-stroke engine parts.
- Describe construction differences in two-stroke engines.

As stated in Chapter 1, motorcycle, ATV, and scooter engines are either four-stroke or two-stroke. Both two- and four-stroke engines are found in motorcycles and ATVs, while scooters use two-stroke engines almost exclusively. The first portion of this chapter explains the most common approaches used in the design and construction of modern four-stroke motorcycle engines.

Four-Stroke Engines

Most motorcycles use ***four-stroke engines,*** such as the one shown in **Figure 6-1.** Valve trains, cylinders, piston rings, crankshafts, and other important engine parts are discussed. This information will be very helpful in later text chapters when you are learning to diagnose, service, and repair engines. **Figure 6-2** illustrates the fundamental parts of a four-stroke engine.

Figure 6-1. Modern four-stroke motorcycle engine. Motorcycle engines come in a variety of sizes and configurations. (Yamaha Motor Corporation U.S.A.)

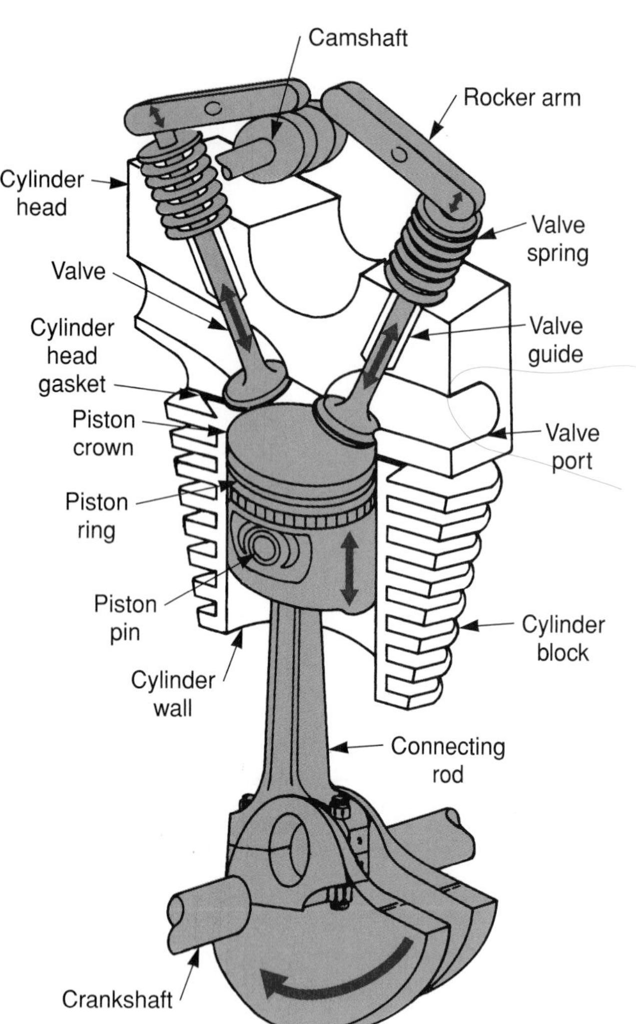

Figure 6-2. Parts of a basic four-stroke engine.

Valve Train

A four-stroke engine requires two crankshaft revolutions for each power stroke. To do this, the ***camshaft***, which controls the flow of air, fuel, and exhaust, must rotate at one-half crankshaft speed. The current valve train designs on four-stroke engines is divided into three types: a conventional chain drive, a belt drive, and a gear drive. Engine valves must be opened and closed precisely.

A ***chain drive*** is the most commonly used mechanism in current valve train design. Its simple construction allows for lower manufacturing cost. The automatic cam chain tensioner provides spring support by pressing the chain in the direction of tension and locking against any counter-pressure as shown in **Figure 6-3.** This provides the automatic elimination of chain slack. Because chain elongation eventually results in increased noise, adjustment is required from time to time. At some point, the chain, along with the tensioner, if used, must be replaced.

The ***belt drive*** is used on engines requiring less noise, such as on touring bikes. Valves driven by gears have minimal friction loss and maintains accurate timing even at high engine speeds. Belt drives require maintenance, that usually consists of belt replacement.

Camshaft Arrangement

Three common valve trains are used to operate the valves in four-stroke motorcycle engines. In one of these designs, the camshaft or camshafts are located in the crankcase. In the other designs, either single or double camshafts are positioned in the top of the cylinder head. The current camshaft arrangement in a four-stroke engine can be divided into two types: single overhead camshaft and dual overhead camshaft.

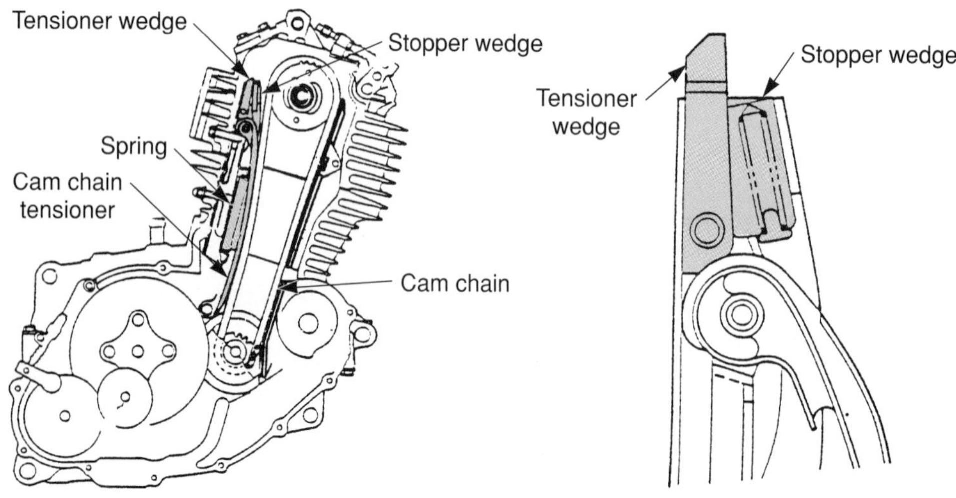

Figure 6-3. Typical automatic cam chain tensioner. (Honda Motor Co., Ltd.)

Single Overhead Camshaft (SOHC)

The ***single overhead camshaft (SOHC)*** design follows the basic design of four-stroke engines; operating intake and exhaust valves through rocker arms with one camshaft. The camshaft is located in the middle of the cylinder head and directly operates cam followers, which are similar to rocker arms. The cam followers push on and open the valves. The overhead camshaft design reduces reciprocating weight (weight of parts moving up and down) in the valve train by eliminating the need for lifters and push rods.

Dual Overhead Camshaft (DOHC)

The ***dual overhead camshaft (DOHC)*** configuration can be one of two designs. One type presses the valve bucket directly. A shim is provided in the bucket for valve clearance adjustment. The valve clearance is adjusted by replacing the shim. The shim is usually located between the bucket and cam lobe as illustrated in **Figure 6-4.** Some types have a small shim inserted between the underside of the bucket and the valve stem, reducing the actuating mechanism's weight.

The other type lifts the valve through the use of rocker arms. The rocker arms allow easier adjustment of valve clearance. The DOHC has a further advantage when used in four-valves per cylinder engines. Four-valves per cylinder provide for a larger valve area, enabling a greater intake volume, higher intake velocity, increased turbulence, and more efficient combustion. Valve weight is also less, consequently reducing the likelihood of valve float associated with high engine speeds. Furthermore, with a four-valve engine, the spark plug can be placed at the center of the combustion chamber, allowing good flame balance during combustion.

Compared to the DOHC, the SOHC engine is less expensive to manufacture and is easier to maintain due to a reduced number of parts. However, valve float (condition where the valve cannot accurately follow the camshaft) can occur at high speed, causing the valve to contact the piston, resulting in severe engine damage.

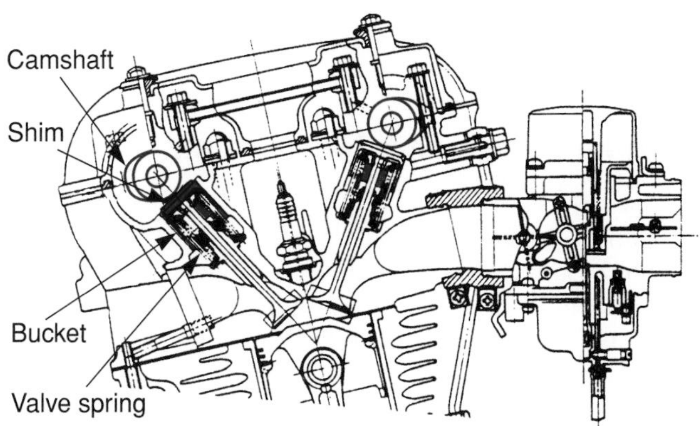

Figure 6-4. Example of DOHC with a bucket type design. (Honda Motor Co., Ltd.)

To decrease valve mass and reduce the possibility of engine damage during high engine speeds, four-stroke engines requiring high power use a DOHC design in which the valves are operated directly with two separate camshafts for intake and exhaust valves.

Closing the Valves

Valve springs are used to push the engine valves closed. When the cam lobe acts on the valve train, the valve is forced open, compressing the spring. Then, when the lobe rotates away from the follower or bucket, the valve spring tension forces the valve closed, **Figure 6-5.**

Sufficient spring tension is needed to ensure valve closure at high engine speeds. If the spring is too weak, valve float could occur. ***Valve float*** results when the spring fails to close the valve completely at high engine speeds. Engine miss, power loss, and possibly valve and piston damage can result.

Camshaft Design

Camshaft ***lobe*** (shape) design determines when, how quickly, how long, and how far a valve opens. Lobe profiles vary from engine to engine, as shown in **Figure 6-6.** Increased camshaft ***lift*** (distance valve opens) and ***duration*** (length of time valve stays open) will raise the engine's power range (rpm at which maximum power is developed). However, increased cam lift and duration will normally reduce engine power at low to medium speeds and will increase roughness at idle. Stock cam profiles usually provide the best compromise between power, efficiency, and smoothness.

Pistons, Crankshafts, and Cylinders

The ***piston*** and ***crankshaft*** assemblies are often termed the engine's reciprocating assembly. The piston and rod reciprocate or move up and down in the cylinder. The crankshaft changes the piston's linear (straight line) motion into more usable rotary (spinning) motion.

It is very useful to understand how these parts vary from one engine to another. Though their purpose may remain the same, part construction and design characteristics can differ considerably. For instance, cam design, as well as compression ratio and displacement, are factors that determine the amount of horsepower and torque that a four-stroke engine can produce. Engine configuration and layout are important factors in cooling, lubricating, and vehicle handling.

Single Cylinder Engine

A ***single cylinder engine*** is the simplest of all four-stroke engines and is usually found in small, lightweight

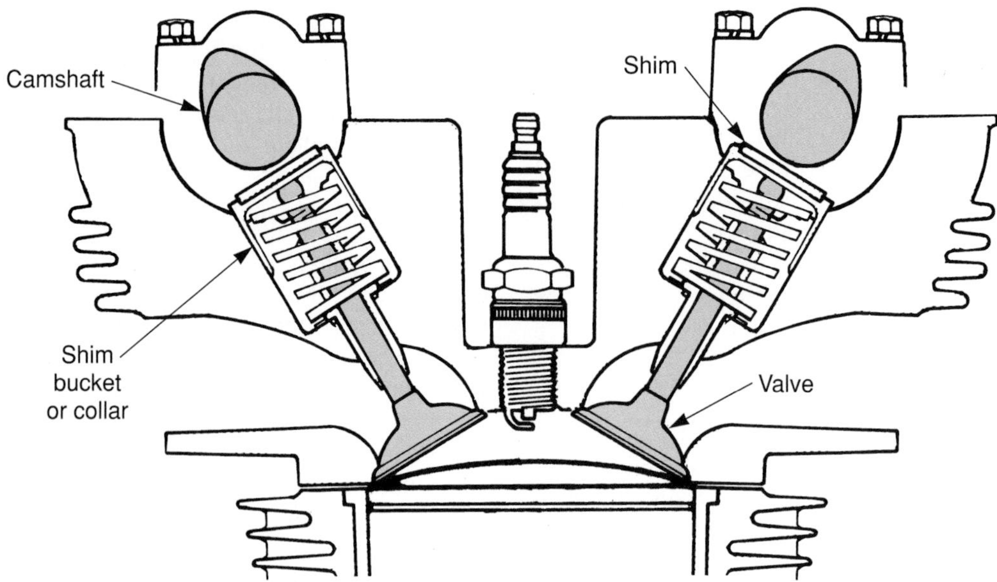

Figure 6-5. Reciprocating weight is further reduced in dual overhead cam (DOHC) engines by moving the camshafts closer to the valves. (Kawasaki Motors Corporation U.S.A.)

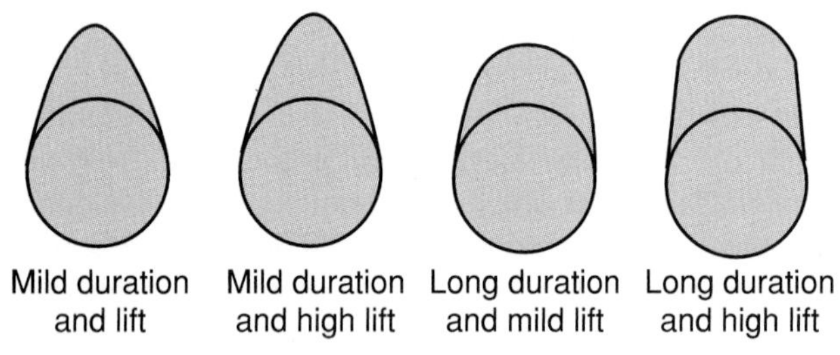

Figure 6-6. Numerous camshaft lobe profiles are used to vary valve lift and duration.

motorcycles, **Figure 6-7.** It consists of one piston, one cylinder, a crankshaft, intake and exhaust valves, a camshaft, and may use either pushrods or rocker arms. The crankshaft assembly is supported by bearings resting in the crankcase.

Twin Cylinder Engine

Twin cylinder engines are manufactured in four configurations: inline, vertical, opposed, and V-twin. An ***inline twin cylinder engine*** may have two pistons moving up and down together, termed a 360° crankshaft. In some cases, the pistons may slide up and down alternately, called a 180° crankshaft. The crankshaft is supported by main bearings in two or three places.

The ***vertical-twin cylinder engine*** can use either a 180° or 360° layout. If both pistons move together, it is a 360° layout. If one piston is up while the other is down, it is a 180° layout, **Figure 6-8.** This engine is small and compact. In the ***opposed-twin cylinder engine,*** the cylinders lay horizontally at right angles to the motorcycle frame, **Figure 6-9.** They lay in the same direction as the rider's foot pegs. With an opposed-twin, the pistons move to TDC (top dead center) and to BDC (bottom dead center) together. Because this design permits the engine to be mounted lower in the frame, a bike with opposed-twin cylinders has good handling characteristics because of weight distribution.

In a ***V-twin cylinder engine*** configuration, the cylinders are at an angle to each other. The cylinders form the letter "V" when viewed from the end of the crankshaft, **Figure 6-10.** Crankshafts for most V-twins have a common journal for both connecting rods. There are two methods of mounting the rods on the journal. In one design, the connecting rods are side-by-side as in **Figure 6-11A.** In another design, the connecting rods are ***siamesed*** (overlapped), **Figure 6-11B.**

Multi-Cylinder Engines

Multi-cylinder engines consist of either three, four, or six cylinders. Opposed and inline engines commonly use three, four, or six cylinders. V-configurations normally have two, four, or six cylinders. See **Figure 6-12.**

Cylinder Design and Construction

Cylinders are subject to considerable combustion heat and pressure. They are made of a one-piece aluminum casting with a pressed-in iron liner (sleeve). You may still find a few four-stroke motorcycle engines that use a one-piece cast iron cylinder block. Both designs are shown in **Figure 6-13.**

Due to normal wear, the cylinder bore will become tapered and out-of-round. A worn cylinder can cause blow-by, engine smoking, oil consumption, and spark plug fouling, which reduces engine efficiency.

The cylinder is normally designed so that it can be bored out (bore diameter increased by machining) to accept an oversized piston. This eliminates the need to replace the cylinder when it becomes worn. It also allows the technician to restore engine efficiency for minimum cost.

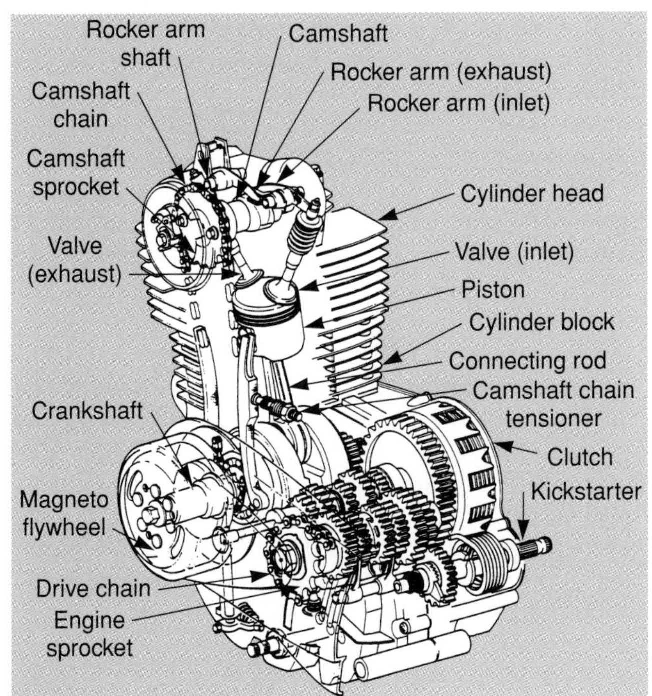

Figure 6-7. Single-cylinder four-stroke engine. (Kawasaki Motors Corporation U.S.A.)

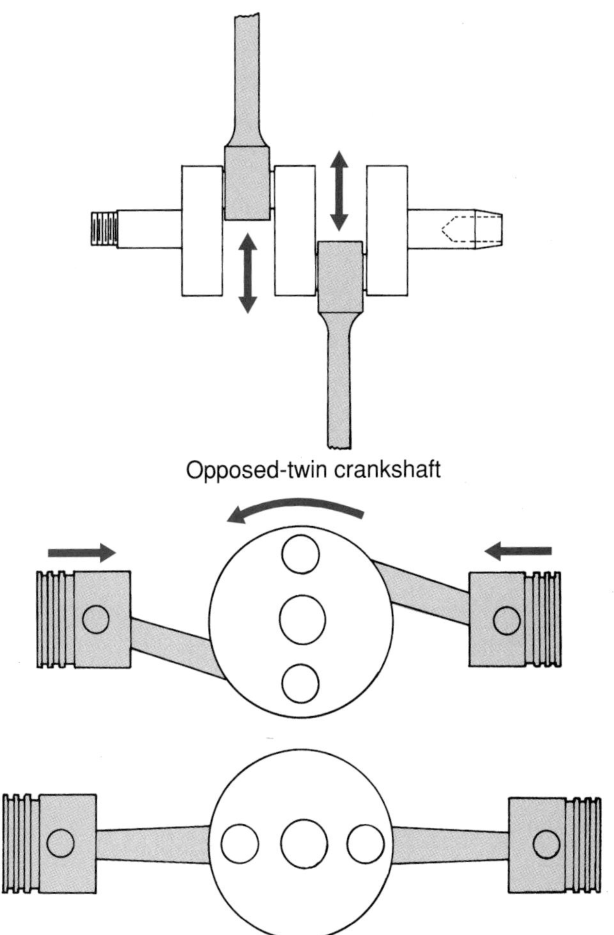

Figure 6-9. Opposed-twin engine pistons move from TDC to BDC together.

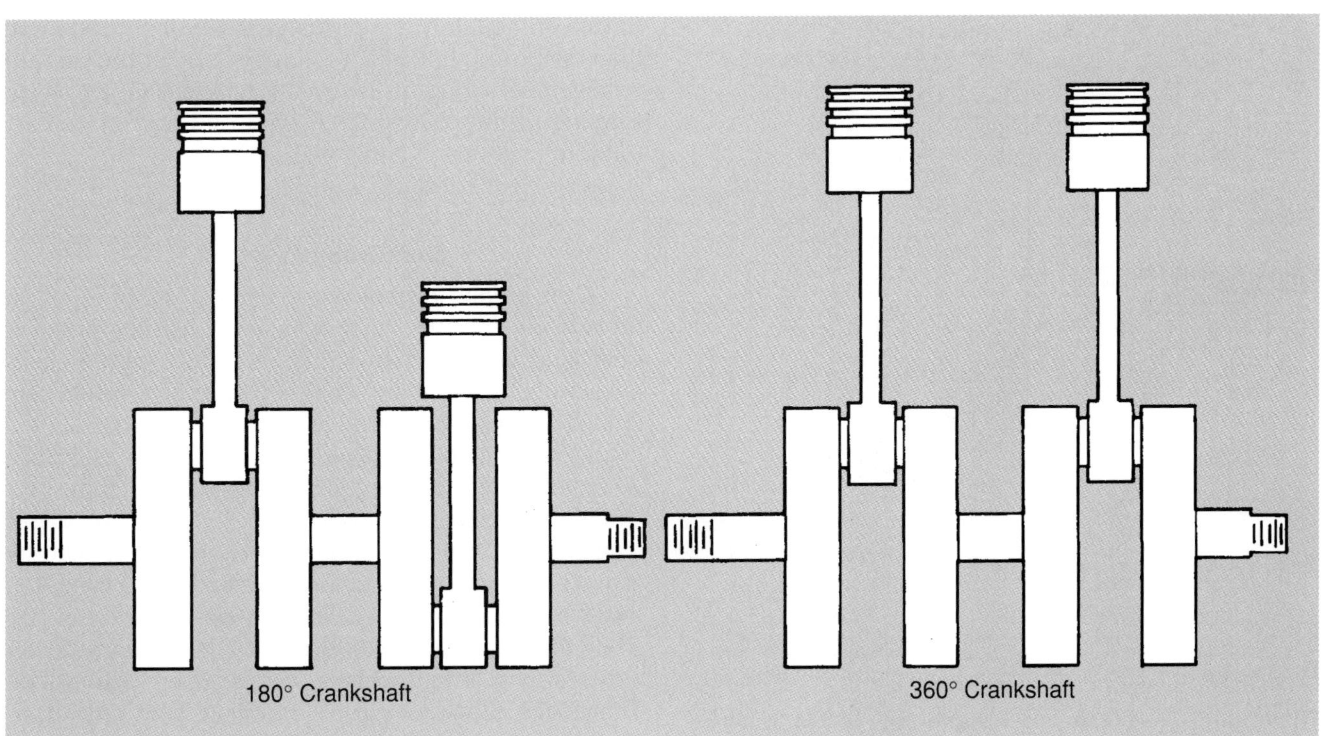

Figure 6-8. Pistons in an inline twin cylinder engine may move up and down together (360° crankshaft) or alternately (180° crankshaft).

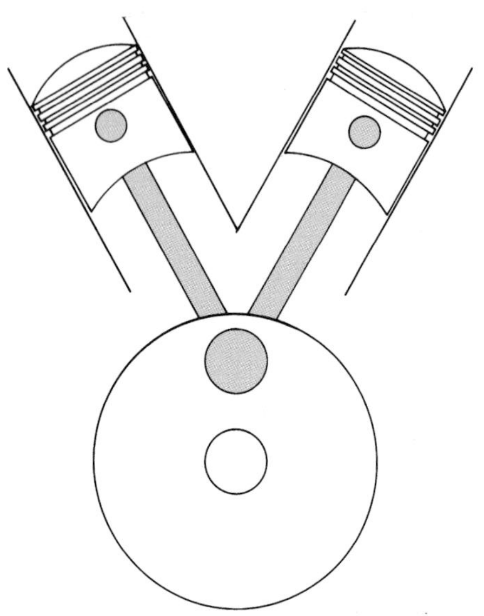

Figure 6-10. V-twin engine cylinders are at an angle to each other.

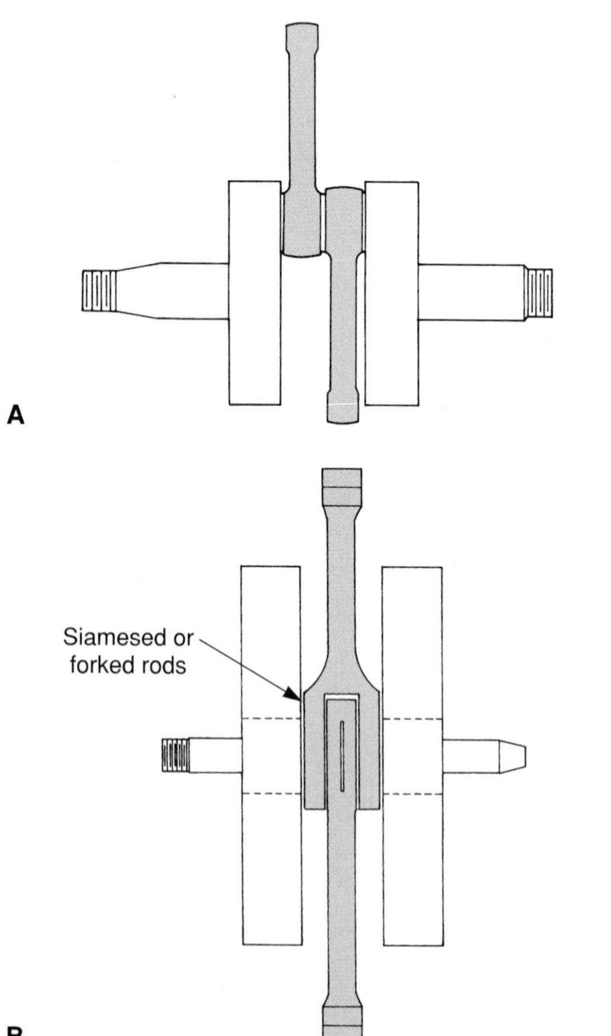

Figure 6-11. A—V-twin side-by-side rod with a common crankpin. B— Study construction of a V-twin using forked or siamesed rods.

Piston Construction and Design

Four-stroke motorcycle pistons are either cast (molten metal poured into mold) or forged (metal molded by pressure). The most common piston construction method uses high silicon content cast aluminum. The ***cast piston*** is less expensive to produce, lighter in weight, and expands less than the forged piston.

The major advantage of the ***forged piston*** is superior strength and higher rpm capabilities. Due to the increased expansion characteristics, the forged piston requires more cylinder-to-piston clearance. It is best suited to high performance applications.

A typical four-stroke motorcycle piston consists of the crown, pin hole, land, groove, skirt, pin boss, C-clip grooves, and oil holes. This is illustrated in **Figure 6-14.**

Piston Crown

The ***piston crown*** or top is directly exposed to the extreme heat and pressure caused by combustion. The crown must have the ability to transfer extreme pressure and heat to other piston parts. Otherwise, the piston crown could overheat and burn (hole pushed through partially melted piston top). **Figure 6-15** shows how the piston moves up to trap and compress the fuel mixture in the combustion chamber.

Piston Taper

Piston taper is required because the piston material mass is greater at the top (crown) than at the bottom (skirt). The crown is also exposed to higher temperatures, consequently, the piston crown will expand more than the piston skirt area. To compensate for this uneven enlargement, a piston is usually tapered, **Figure 6-16.** Cooling of the piston is achieved by constant contact (oil film) with the cylinder wall.

Cam Ground Pistons

Cam ground pistons are machined out-of-round to provide dependable, quiet operation when the piston is both cold and hot. Cam grinding reduces piston clearance when the piston is cold. This prevents ***piston slap*** (knocking sound produced as a cold piston rocks in the cylinder). Cam grinding also assures proper clearance when the piston reaches full operating temperature.

A cam ground piston, when cold, will look oval shaped when viewed from the top, **Figure 6-17.** The larger diameter is in a plane perpendicular to the piston pin. As the piston heats, the larger diameter will stay about the same size while the smaller diameter expands. The piston becomes almost round at full operating temperature, **Figure 6-18.** This design allows for quieter operation. It also maintains clearance for a lubricating film between the cylinder and piston skirt at all times.

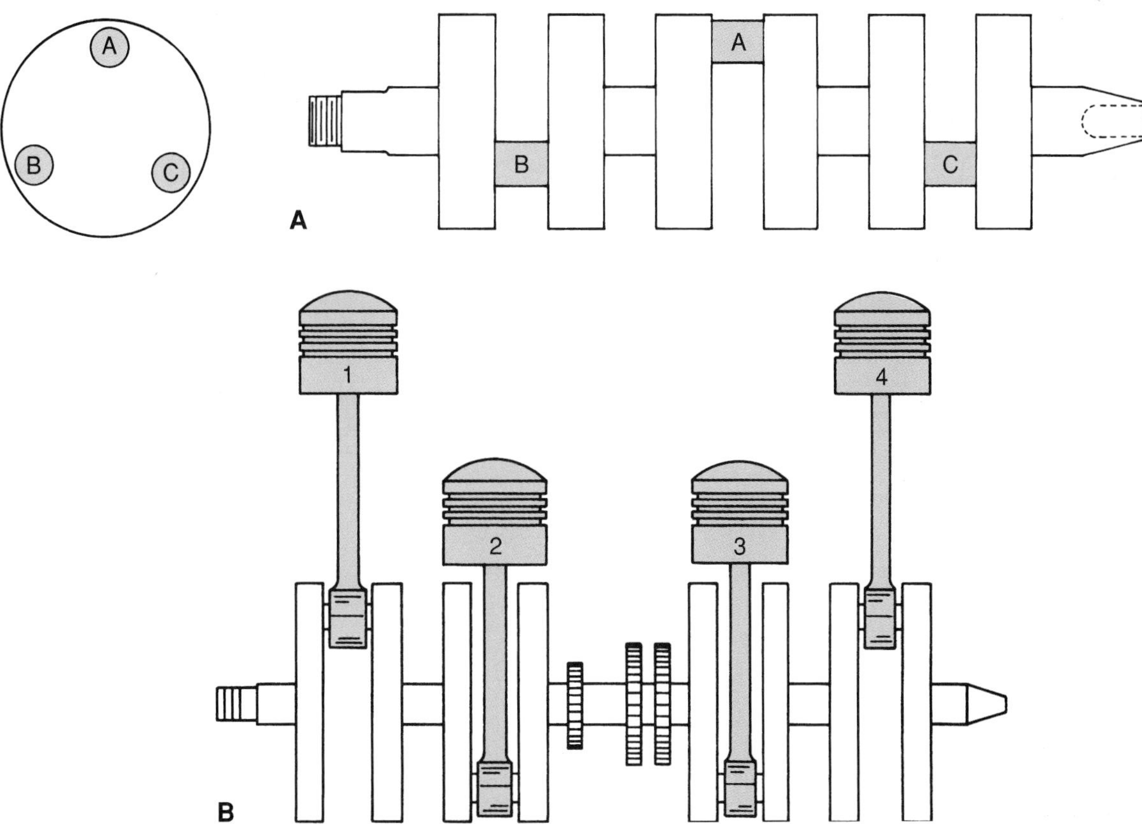

Figure 6-12. A—This three cylinder crankshaft has its rod journals (A, B, C) spaced 120° apart. B—Inline four-cylinder crankshaft. Pistons 1-4 and 2-3 move up and down together.

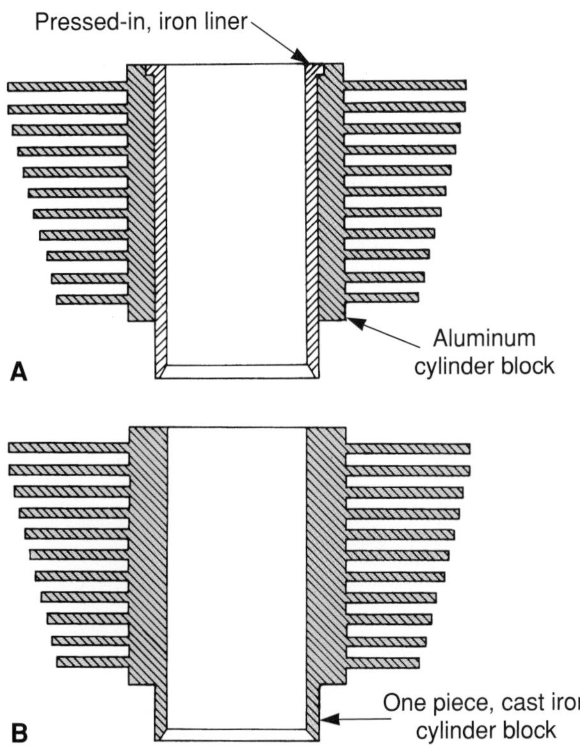

Figure 6-13. A—Most common cylinder designs use a cast aluminum cylinder block with a pressed-in iron liner (sleeve). B—One piece, cast iron cylinder blocks are also used, but not frequently.

Combustion Chamber Design

A ***combustion chamber*** is the area where combustion occurs in the cylinder. It is the area between the cylinder head and the top of the piston at top dead center. A combustion chamber is normally designed to work with a specific piston crown and valve port shape. Both the cylinder head and the piston must work together to produce efficient combustion. As the cylinder head is subject to considerable combustion heat and pressure, it must have both strength and cooling capability. Air-cooled engines are provided with cooling fins, and a liquid-cooled engine with a water jacket. Complete details on engine cooling is given in Chapter 10.

The ***hemispherical combustion chamber*** is a traditional design used in many four-stroke motorcycles, **Figure 6-19.** It provides a very smooth dome shaped chamber. This design increases combustion efficiency.

In search of more performance, lower exhaust emissions, and better fuel economy, most manufacturers have changed to three- and four-valve chamber designs. For instance, **Figure 6-20** illustrates the ***side squish combustion chamber*** which is a hemispherical design that employs two intake valves and two exhaust valves. The squish area is formed around the outside edges of the combustion chamber. Flat-top or low-dome pistons are used to reduce the height of the combustion chamber.

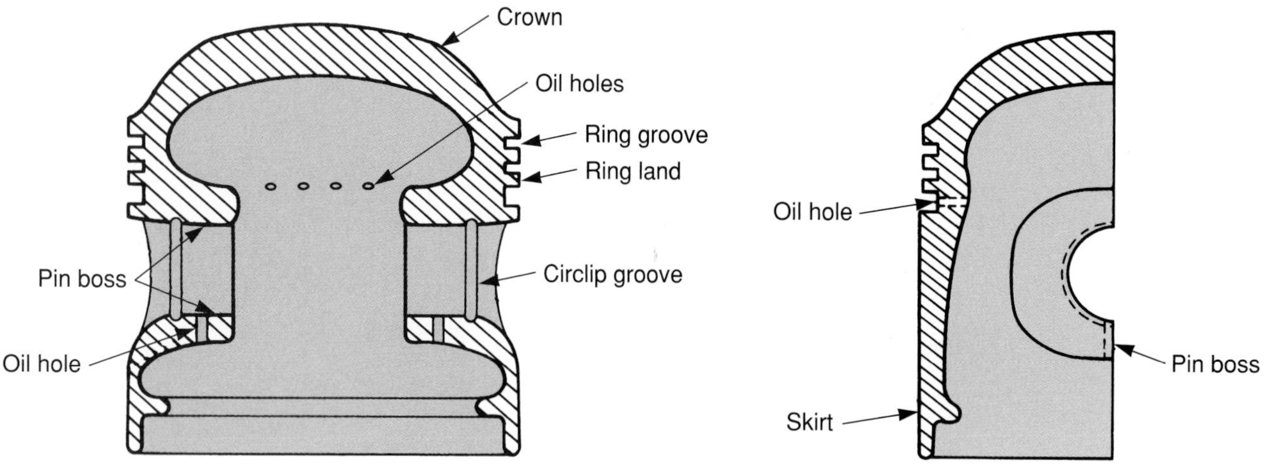

Figure 6-14. A typical four-stroke motorcycle piston. Note the thickness of the crown in relation to the rest of the piston.

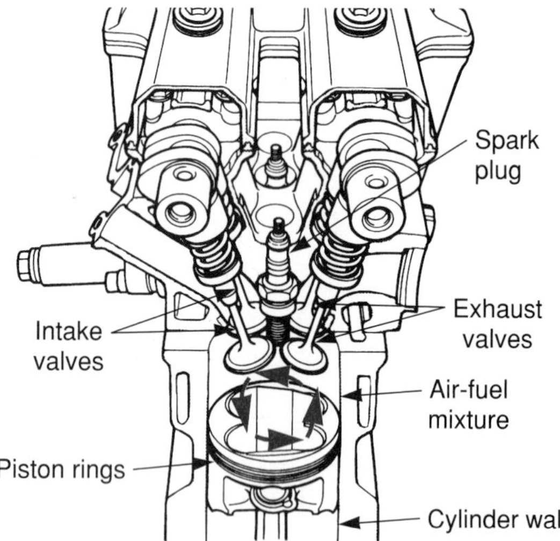

Figure 6-15. The piston moves up to compress the air-fuel mixture for combustion. The top of the piston is exposed to the burning air-fuel mixture. (Honda Motor Co., Ltd.)

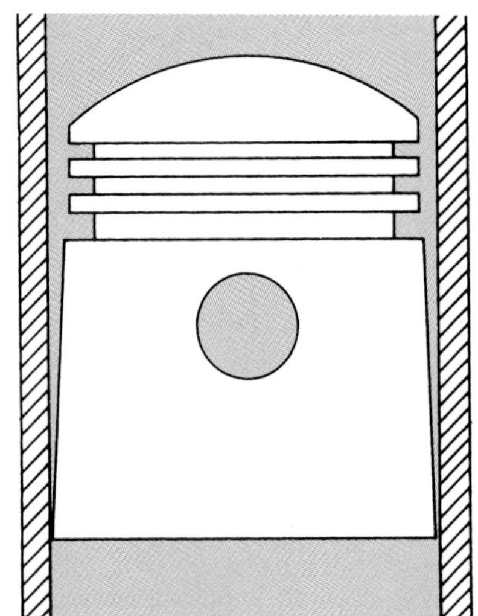

Figure 6-16. Pistons are tapered to compensate for greater heat and expansion at the crown.

The ***semispherical combustion chamber*** shown in **Figure 6-21** utilizes three intake valves and two exhaust valves. The additional intake valve provides greater air-fuel flow by increasing the overall valve area. The combustion area is around the outer edge of the chamber.

The extra valves increase the engine's breathing efficiency and permits higher rpm and power levels. The additional valves can also improve efficiency by increasing turbulence in the combustion chamber.

Piston Ring Grooves

Ring grooves are machined below the piston crown to accept the piston rings. These grooves are spaced to provide adequate strength to support the rings. These supporting areas between the grooves are called ***ring lands.*** Four-stroke pistons usually have three ring grooves. The two upper ring grooves are for the ***compression rings.*** The lower groove holds the ***oil control ring.***

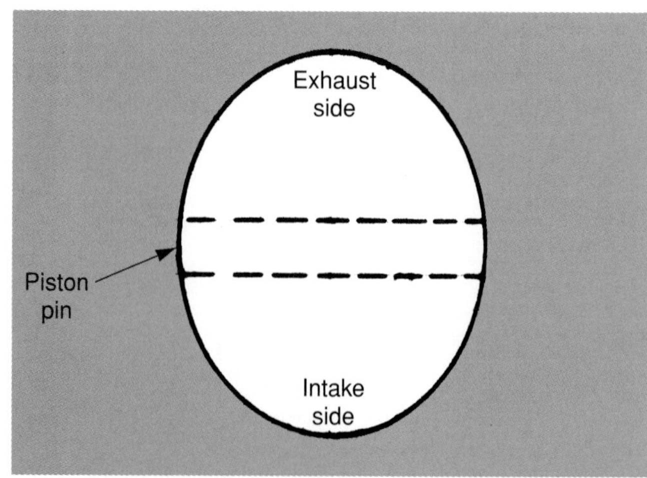

Figure 6-17. A piston is usually oval shaped to help control the amount and direction of piston expansion. As heat expands the piston, it becomes almost round.

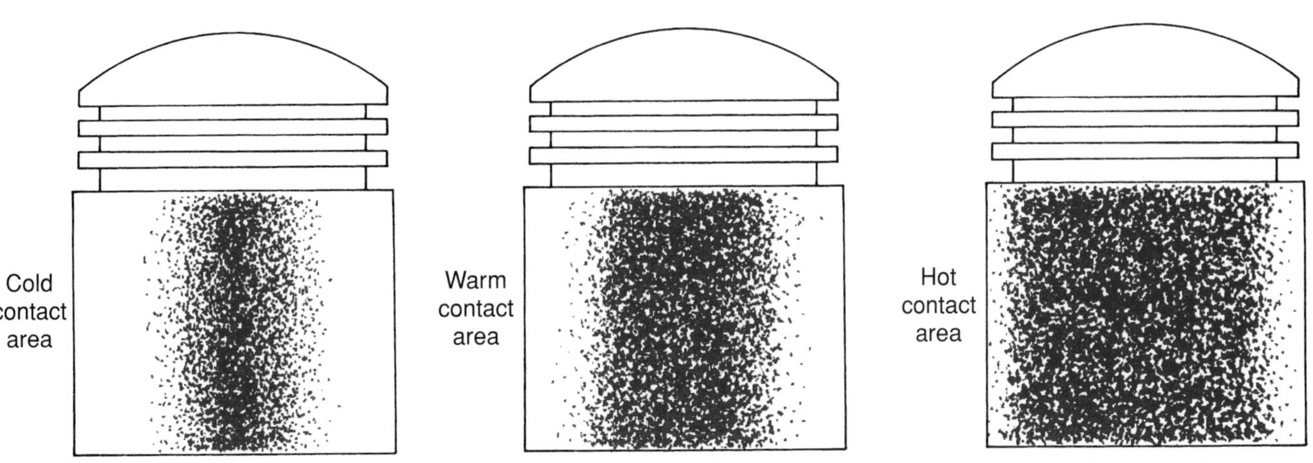

Figure 6-18. The piston skirt contact area changes with engine temperature.

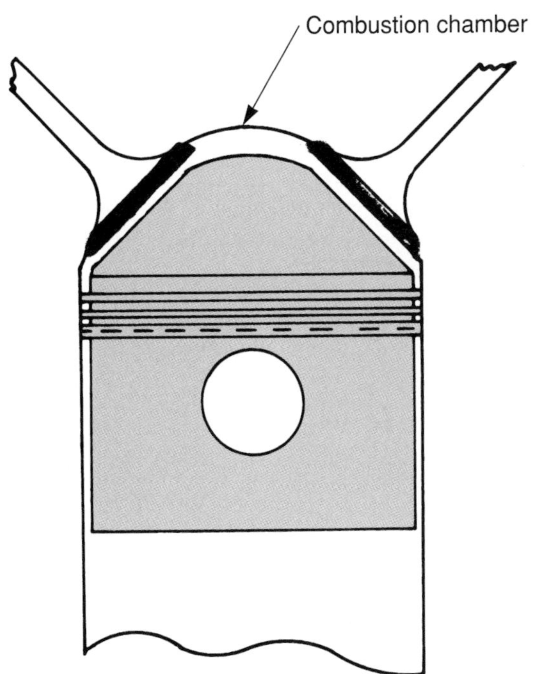

Figure 6-19. A domed piston is normally used with a hemispherical combustion chamber.

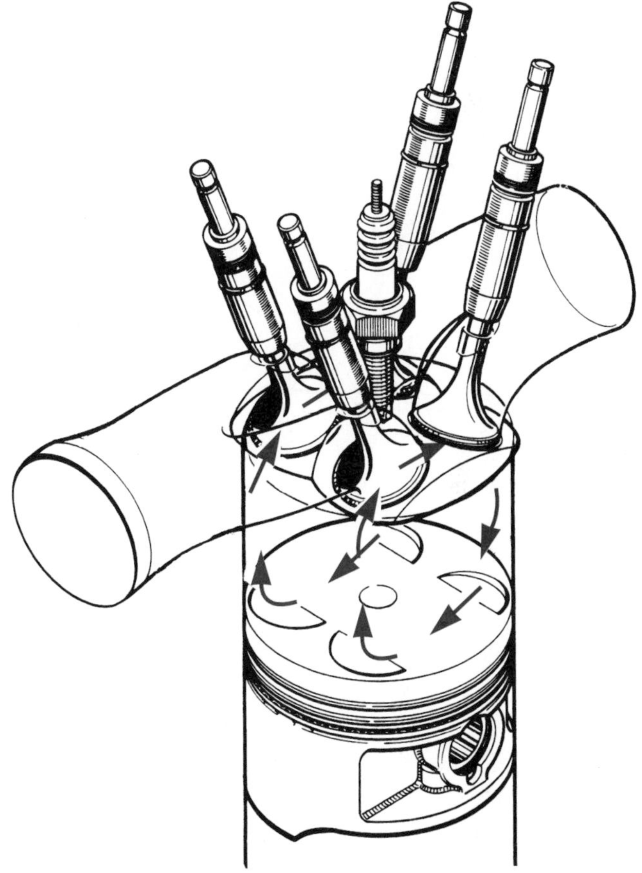

Figure 6-20. This is an example of a high performance cylinder head which has a four-valve combustion chamber. (American Suzuki Motor Corporation)

Piston Rings (Four-stroke)

The ***piston rings*** seal the space between the piston and the cylinder wall. They keep combustion pressure from entering the crankcase. The rings also keep oil from entering the combustion chamber.

Piston rings are usually made of cast iron. In order to prolong ring and cylinder life, the top compression ring often has hard chrome plating on the sealing surface (edge which contacts cylinder wall). Good piston ring performance is essential to efficient and dependable engine operation.

Each ring is designed to do a specific task. The *top piston ring* seals most of the combustion pressure. It must also withstand more heat and receives less lubrication than the other two rings. The *middle piston ring* also acts as a compression ring, but it is shaped to help remove excess oil from the cylinder wall. This dual function ring is sometimes called a ***scraper ring.*** The *bottom piston ring,* termed the ***oil control ring,*** has the primary function of removing oil from the cylinder wall each time the piston moves downward. This prevents an excessive amount of oil from reaching the scraper ring, compression ring, and combustion chamber.

Piston Ring Shape

Figure 6-22 shows a cross-section of a typical three ring set. The top compression ring is normally rectangular with the inside top edge chamfered. This chamfer causes combustion pressure to force the ring against the cylinder wall as illustrated in **Figure 6-23.** This helps the ring seal pressure inside the combustion chamber.

The scraper ring is also rectangular shaped, but the bottom outside edge is usually stepped. This stepped area provides a scraping action that controls oiling. The oil control ring has two scraping surfaces and oil passage slots located in the back of the ring, **Figure 6-24.** This allows oil, wiped from the cylinder wall, to return to the crankcase. On some pistons, a three-piece oil ring is used. The three-piece ring consists of an expander ring which is located between two thin steel rings, **Figure 6-25.**

Four Cycle Engine Bearings

The purpose of a ***bearing*** is to reduce friction while allowing movement between parts. The three types of bearings commonly used in the four-stroke engine are ball bearings, roller bearings, and plain bearings. Refer to **Figure 6-26.**

Ball bearings provide the greatest reduction of friction. However, ball bearings cannot withstand heavy loading as well as ***roller bearings.*** Both ball bearings and roller bearings can survive with minimal lubrication, however, a total lack of lubrication will destroy them.

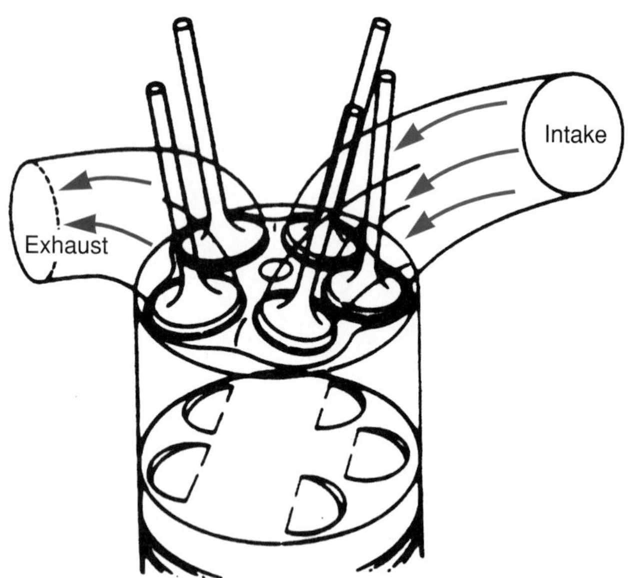

Figure 6-21. Semispherical combustion chamber which features three intake valves and two exhaust valves. (Yamaha Motor Corporation U.S.A.)

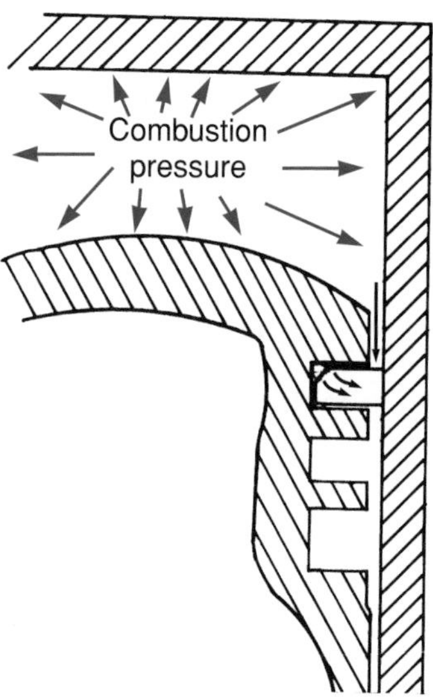

Figure 6-23. Combustion pressure is used to force the ring against the cylinder wall, aiding the sealing action.

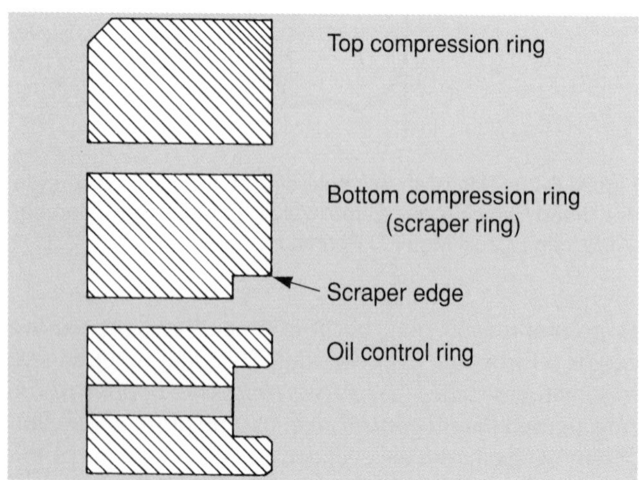

Figure 6-22. This shows the cross-section of a typical three-ring set.

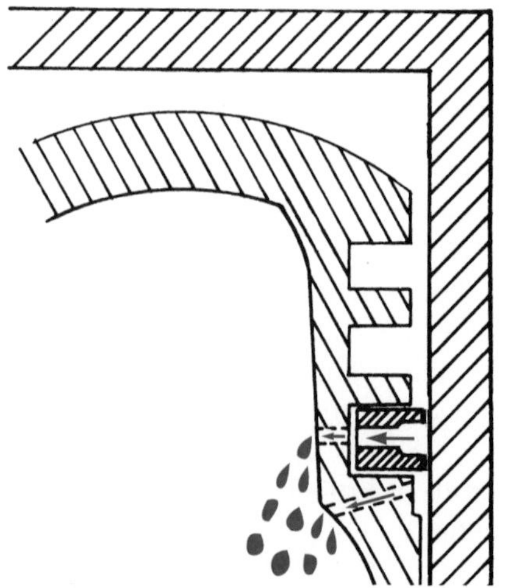

Figure 6-24. Oil scraped from the cylinder wall passes through small holes in the piston and returned to the sump.

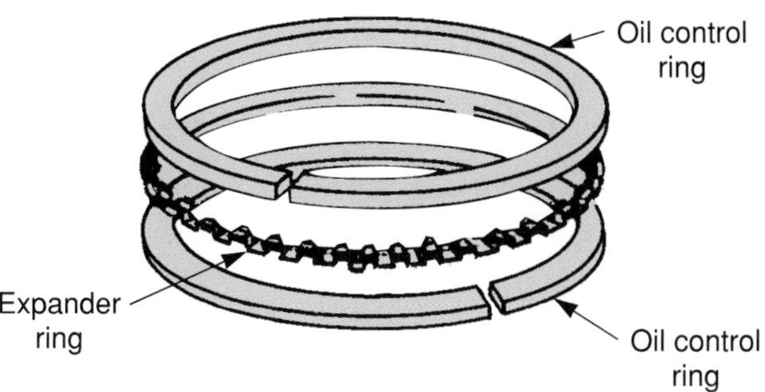

Figure 6-25. A three-piece oil ring uses two thin steel rings with an expander ring.

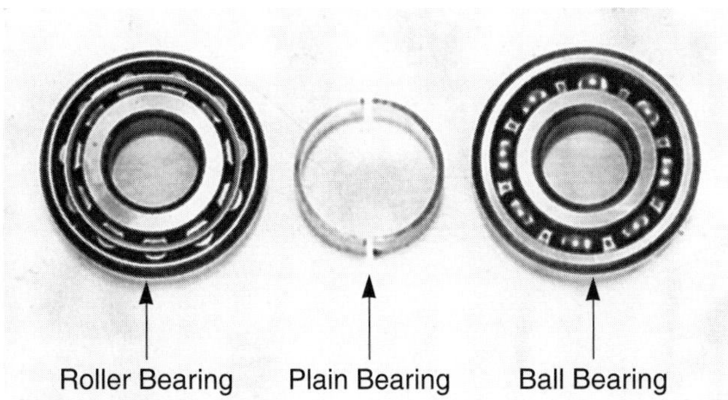

Figure 6-26. Roller, plain, and ball bearings are used in four-stroke engines.

A ***plain bearing,*** also termed a *friction bearing,* is capable of withstanding heavy loading, but it requires a lubricating oil film. Due to its larger surface area and sliding action, the plain bearing usually does not reduce friction as efficiently as ball or roller bearings. Engine design determines where each type of bearing should be utilized.

Engine Case

The ***engine case*** houses the engine crankshaft, bearings, gearbox, and related components. The cylinder block bolts to the case. In a few designs, the gearbox is located inside a separate case. Engine cases may be split horizontally or vertically.

Non-Unit Construction

Non-unit construction consists of a separate engine and gearbox assembly. The gearbox can be removed from the engine as a single unit. This arrangement can be found on a few large bikes. The engine and transmission are bolted solidly to the motorcycle frame, which provides proper engine-to-gearbox support, **Figure 6-27.**

Unit Construction

Unit construction utilizes a single case or crankcase casting that contains the engine, primary drive, and transmission, **Figure 6-28.** A single case ensures proper alignment, decreases the possibility of oil leakage, and makes for a compact, light assembly. Unit construction has been a very common and popular design for many years.

Vertical and Horizontal Split Crankcases

Most single cylinder four-stroke motorcycle engine crankcases are ***vertically split,*** **Figure 6-29.** However, motorcycle engines with two or more cylinders are normally ***horizontally split.***

In converting reciprocating energy into rotating energy, the engine crankshaft is subjected to extreme vertical loading. The crankcases must provide a mounting place for the crankshaft main bearings and withstand these vertical loads. Since the vertical split case provides a solid, one-piece mounting for the main bearings, it can easily support the crankshaft and yet remain lightweight.

Because horizontally split cases part at the crankshaft centerline, both the crankcase casting and the fasteners must be of very heavy construction. This is illustrated in **Figure 6-30.**

Advantages of horizontal split cases are:

- Easier disassembly.
- Less possibility of oil leakage.
- Easier transmission servicing.
- Lower production cost in multi-cylinder configurations.

Two-Stroke Engine

In this portion of the chapter, we will discuss ***two-stroke engines.*** It is very important for you to understand how engine design affects engine performance and driveability.

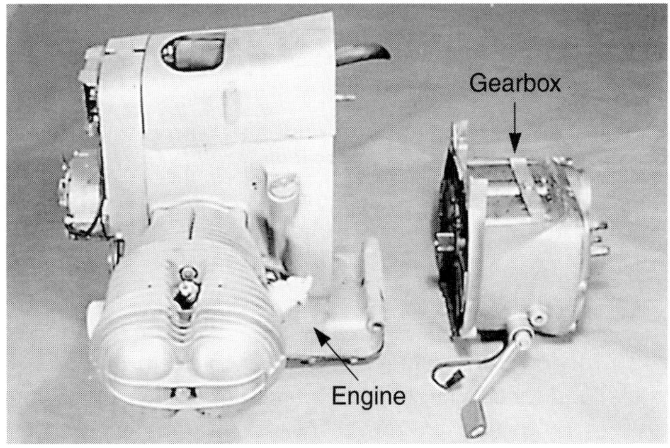

Figure 6-27. A non-unit engine uses a separate transmission case that can be removed from the engine while still assembled.

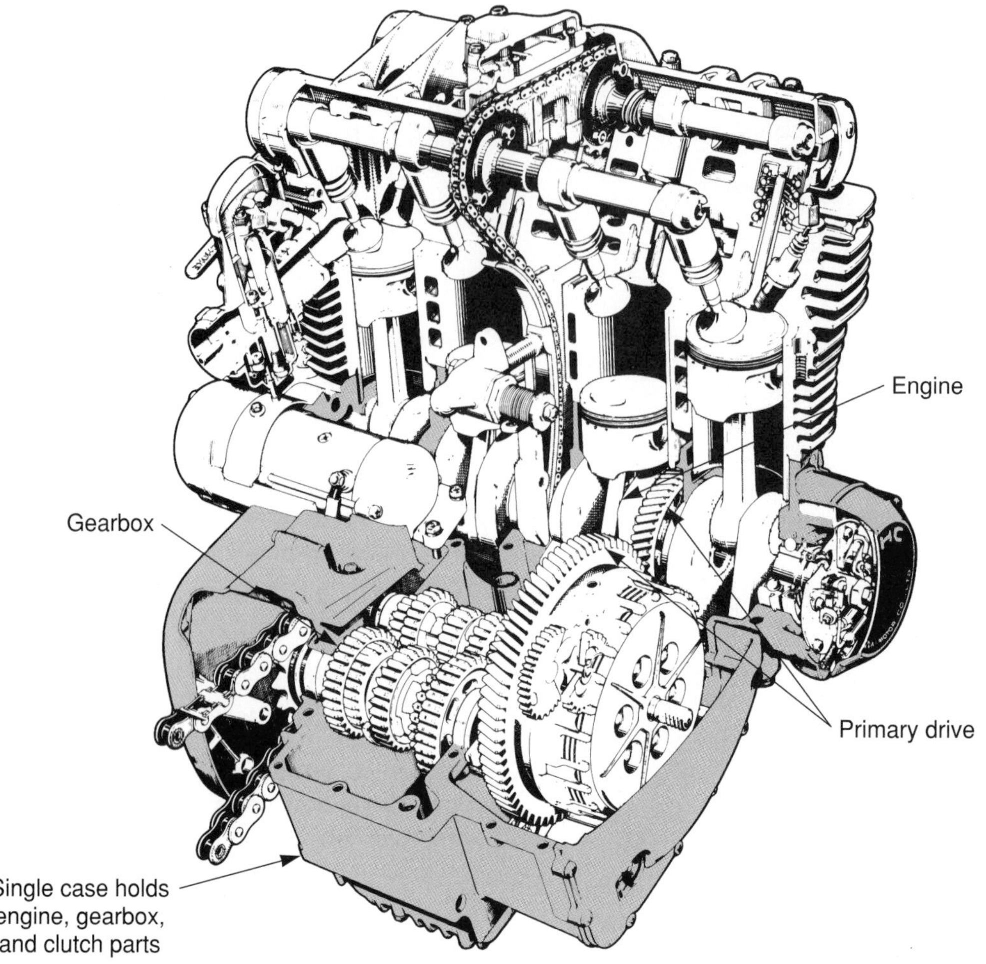

Figure 6-28. Unit-construction engines use the same case to house the engine, primary drive, and transmission. (American Suzuki Motor Corporation)

This knowledge will prepare you to correctly diagnose, service, and repair motorcycles.

The simple two-stroke engine discussed in Chapter 1 used the piston to regulate intake, transfer, and exhaust timing. More refined engine designs use other methods to control the air-fuel mixture movement through the engine.

Intake Timing

Intake timing refers to the opening and closing of the intake port in relation to the crankshaft and piston position. The three methods used to control intake timing are the piston port, reed valve, and rotary valve.

Piston Port

A ***piston port*** engine uses the piston skirt length and intake port location to control intake timing. It is one of the simplest and least expensive two-stroke engine designs. Cylinder port placement and piston skirt length determine how early the intake port opens and how late it closes, **Figure 6-31.** More air and fuel can enter the crankcase if the intake port is left open for a longer period of time.

Mild and Radical Timing

The power characteristics of the two-stroke engine are greatly affected by intake timing. ***Mild timing*** (intake port open for a moderate period of time) will provide good low and midrange power. ***Radical timing*** (intake port open for a long period of time) will give more top end (high rpm) power but will sacrifice some midrange and low end power.

High performance two-stroke engines require radical timing. Radical intake timing allows a larger amount of air-fuel mixture to enter the crankcase. However, if the port is open too long, crankcase compression will overcome the inertia of the incoming intake charge. This will force some of the air-fuel mixture out the intake port and carburetor or throttle body before the intake port is closed.

Due to the intake timing being symmetrical in relation to piston position over the port before and after TDC, there are limitations to piston port design. **Figure 6-32** shows that an intake port which opens at 80° before TDC will always close at 80° after TDC. This is undesirable because different intake timing is sometimes required.

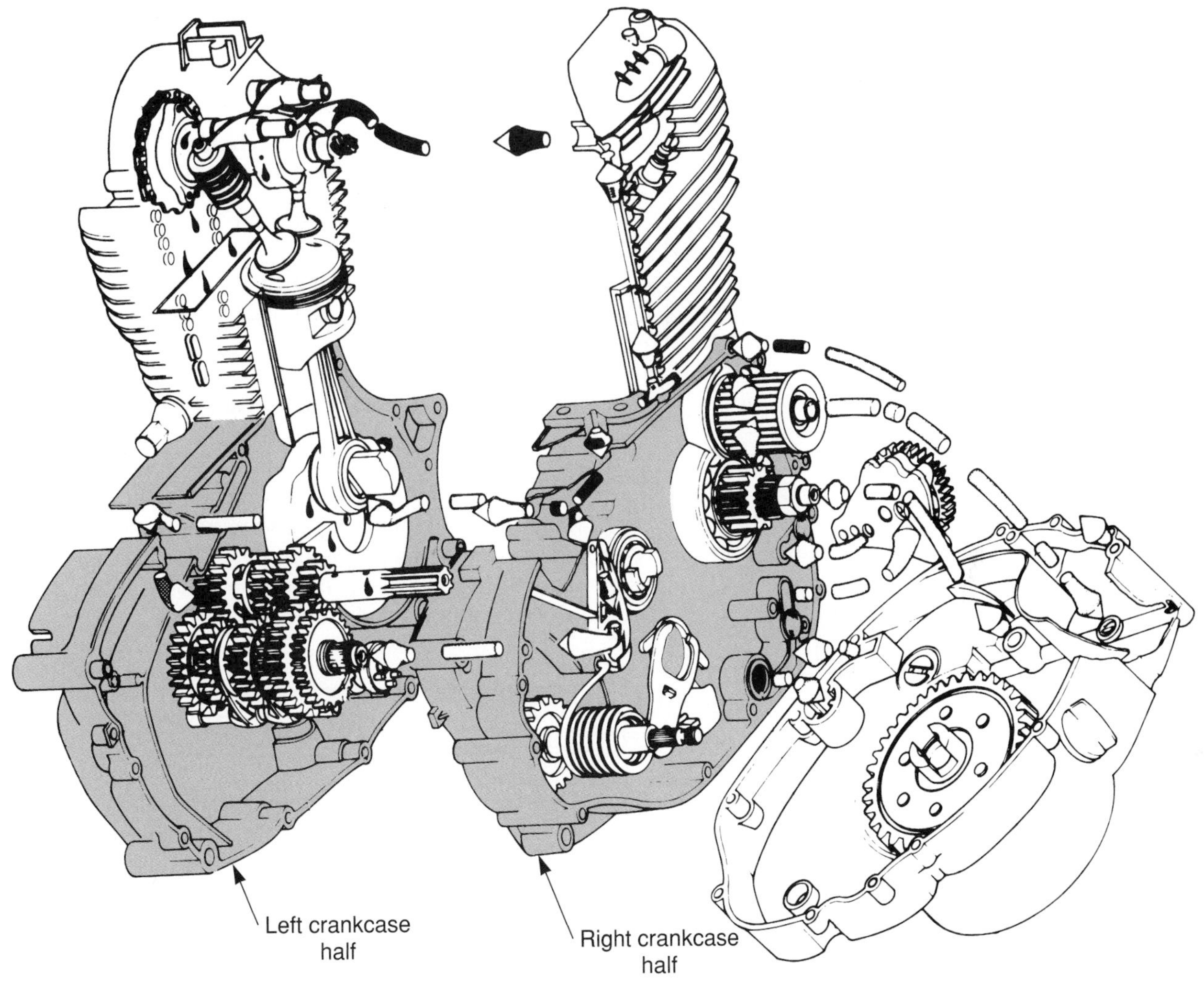

Left crankcase half

Right crankcase half

Figure 6-29. A typical four-stroke, single cylinder engine normally has a vertically split crankcase. (Kawasaki Motors Corporation U.S.A.)

Figure 6-30. Horizontally split crankcases must be heavily constructed to provide adequate support for the crankshaft and transmission shafts.

Reed Valve

The ***reed valve*** design eliminates standoff (backward flow of intake charge) when used with the piston port design. Reed valve operation is dependent on crankcase pressure and vacuum.

The reed valve may be used in conjunction with a piston controlled intake port to allow radical, non-symmetrical timing without the disadvantage of excessive standoff or backflow. **Figure 6-33** shows reed placement in the intake port. This design provides non-symmetrical intake timing because:

- The reed petals are opened by crankcase vacuum.
- The reed petals are closed by crankcase pressure.

Reed Valve Operation

As crankcase vacuum develops, the reed petals are lifted from the cage, **Figure 6-34A.** This allows the air-fuel mixture to flow into the crankcase. Air-fuel mixture will continue to flow as long as there is enough vacuum to

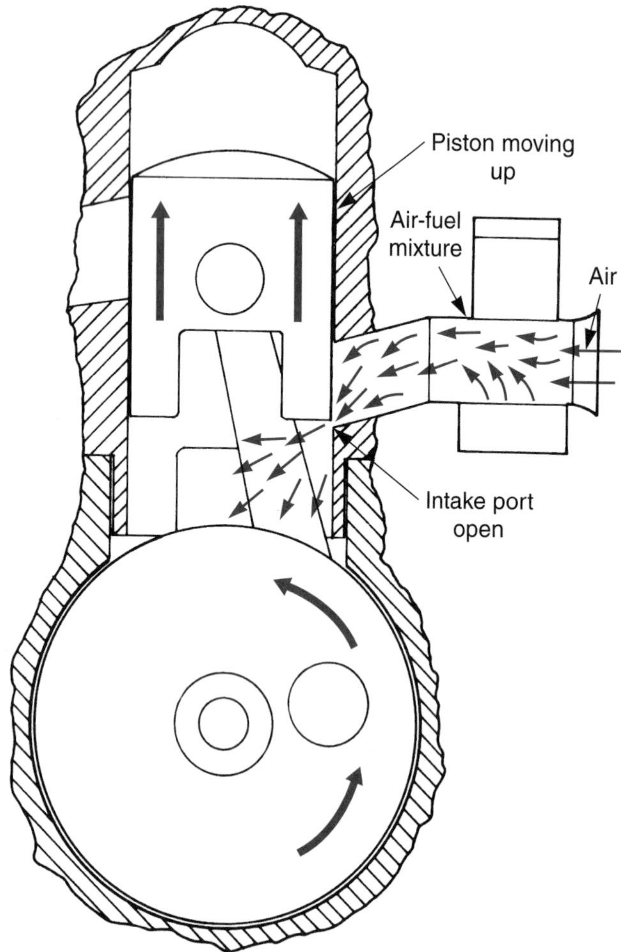

Figure 6-31. As the piston slides up the cylinder in a two-stroke engine, the intake port is opened and air-fuel mixture passes into the crankcase.

hold the reed petals open. As the crankcase begins to pressurize, **Figure 6-34B,** the reed petals are forced closed. This prevents the backflow of air-fuel mixture out the intake port.

Rotary Valve

A ***rotary valve*** is a thin metal disc which opens and closes the engine's intake port, **Figure 6-35.** This method of intake timing has the most flexibility. The intake port on the side of the engine case is covered and uncovered by the spinning action of the disc. The rotary valve controls the flow of the fuel charge into the crankcase.

A rotary valve is positioned between the carburetor and the crankcase and is keyed or splined to the engine crankshaft. As the crankshaft and disc rotate, air-fuel mixture enters the engine as the cutaway portion of the disc opens the port. When the uncut disc section moves in front of the port, the port is closed.

Since the disc can be changed quickly, intake timing can be easily altered. **Figure 6-36** shows two different disc configurations. Intake opening and closing can also be altered independently. Intake timing can be changed by using a disc with a larger or smaller cutout. In this way, the engine's power characteristics can be changed quickly and easily.

Transfer and Exhaust Timing

The piston controls ***transfer*** and ***exhaust timing*** in two-stroke engines. It is important that intake, transfer, and exhaust timing work together. An engine designed with mild intake timing will usually have mild transfer and mild exhaust timing. The same is true of radical timing.

Transfer and exhaust timing is determined by port height. This is illustrated in **Figure 6-37.** A raised or heightened port will open earlier and close later.

Recent engine designs allow for adjustable exhaust timing through the use of centrifugal linkage, **Figure 6-38.** The purpose of this design is to permit good torque in the middle rpm range and good horsepower at high rpm. As engine speed increases, the power valve is rotated, raising the exhaust port height.

Crankcase Sealing

A two-stroke engine must produce sufficient vacuum and pressure in the crankcase. ***Crankcase vacuum*** is used to draw the air-fuel mixture from the carburetor to the crankcase. ***Crankcase pressure*** is used to transfer air-fuel mixture from the crankcase to the upper cylinder. In order to produce vacuum and pressure, the crankcase must be sealed.

A two-stroke engine is sealed at the:

- Intake port (gasket or rubber flange between the carburetor and cylinder and an O-ring between the rotary valve cover and crankcase).
- Crankcase split line (gasket or chemical sealant).
- Crankshaft seals (lip seal between the crankshaft and crankcase).
- Cylinder base (gasket between the cylinder and crankcase).
- Cylinder head (head gasket, spark plug gasket).

Leakage at any of these points will affect engine operation, **Figure 6-39.** To produce the proper amount of vacuum and pressure, the piston, rings, and cylinder must be in good condition.

Crankshaft Configurations

In regard to cylinder and crankshaft configurations, common two-stroke engine designs include single cylinder, twin-cylinder, and multi-cylinder engines.

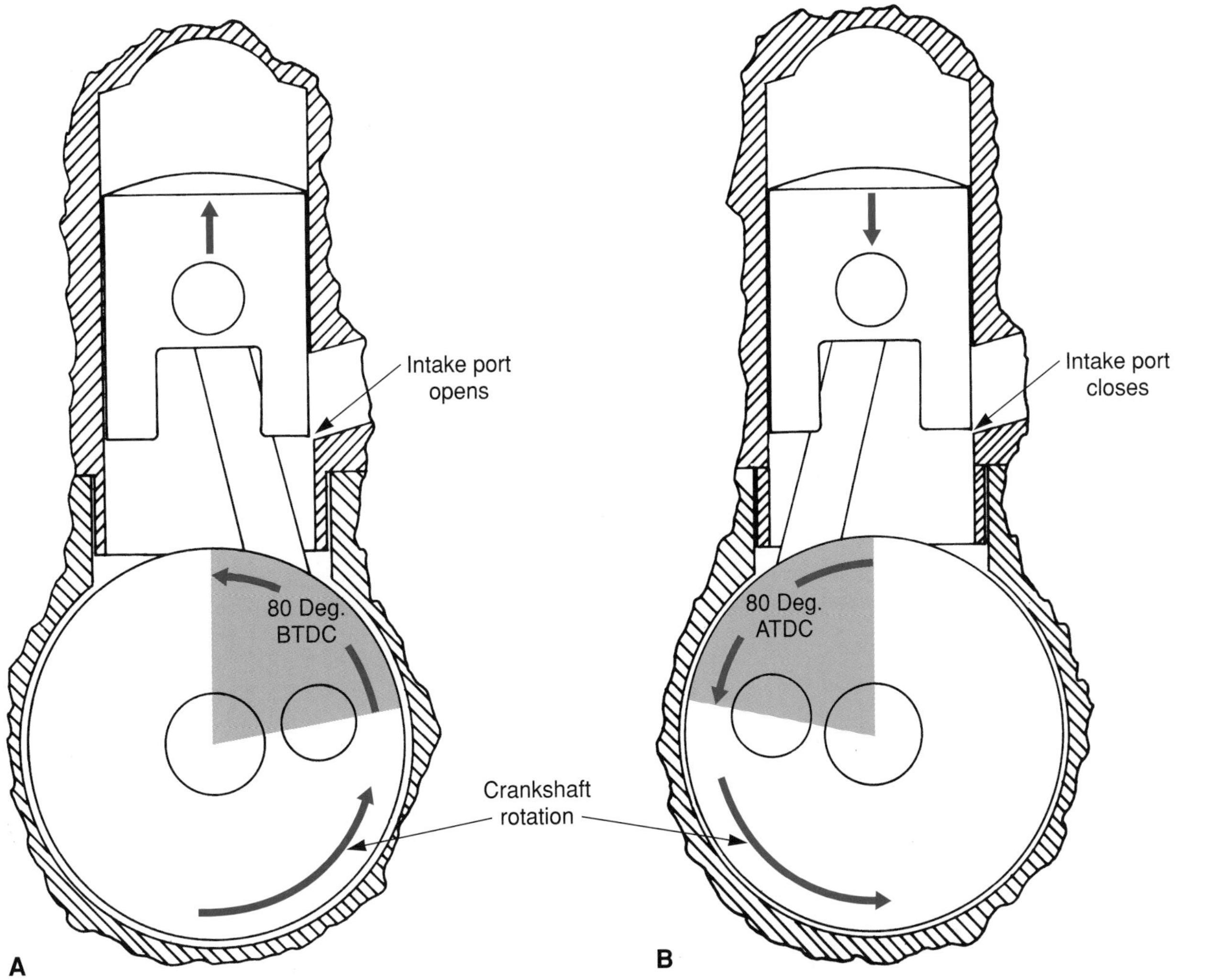

Figure 6-32. The piston skirt opens and closes the port at a precise angle before and after TDC. A—Piston skirt opens the intake port at 80° before TDC. B—The engine closes the intake port at 80° after TDC.

Single Cylinder Crankshaft

Two-stroke, single cylinder crankshafts are normally made of several components pressed together. They are often termed ***built-up crankshafts.*** One make of single cylinder crankshaft is shown in **Figure 6-40.** It consists of:

- Flywheels (provide inertia and hold crankpin).
- Crankpin (fits into flywheels and supports rod).
- Roller bearings and cage (reduces friction between rod and crankpin).
- Connecting rod (fastens crankpin to piston pin).
- Axle shaft (supports crank assembly in case and main bearings).
- Thrust washers (limit rod side or thrust movement).

Twin-Cylinder Crankshaft

A twin-cylinder, two-stroke crankshaft is simply two single cylinder crankshafts constructed side-by-side, **Figure 6-41.** A centered pin connects the two inner

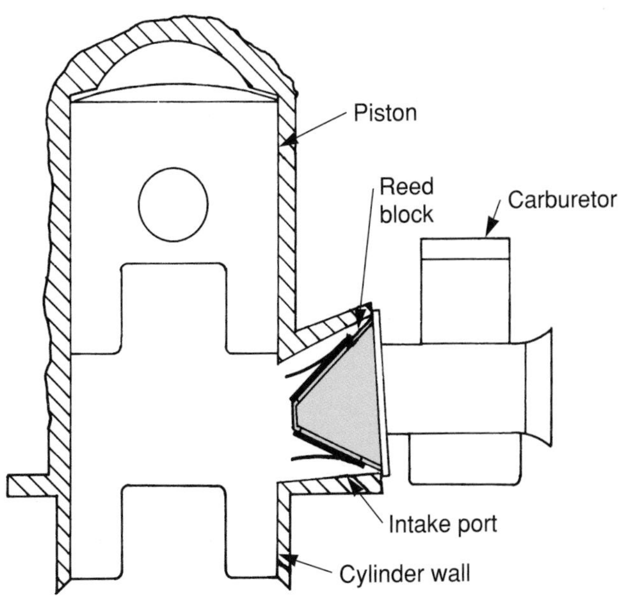

Figure 6-33. Reed petals move to operate valve. Reed assembly is mounted in the intake port between the carburetor or throttle body and the cylinder wall.

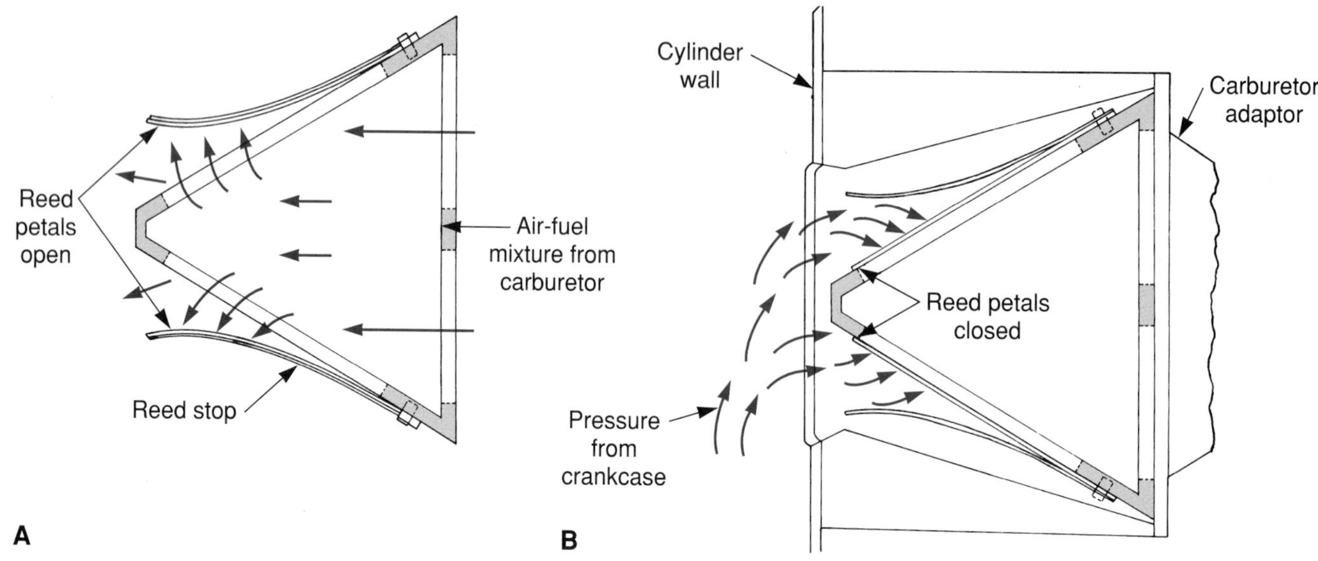

Figure 6-34. A—As vacuum builds in the crankcase, the reed petals are pushed away from the block. Air-fuel mixture flows into crankcase. Reed stops prevent over-flex and possible breakage. B—As pressure builds in the crankcase, the reed petals are forced shut.

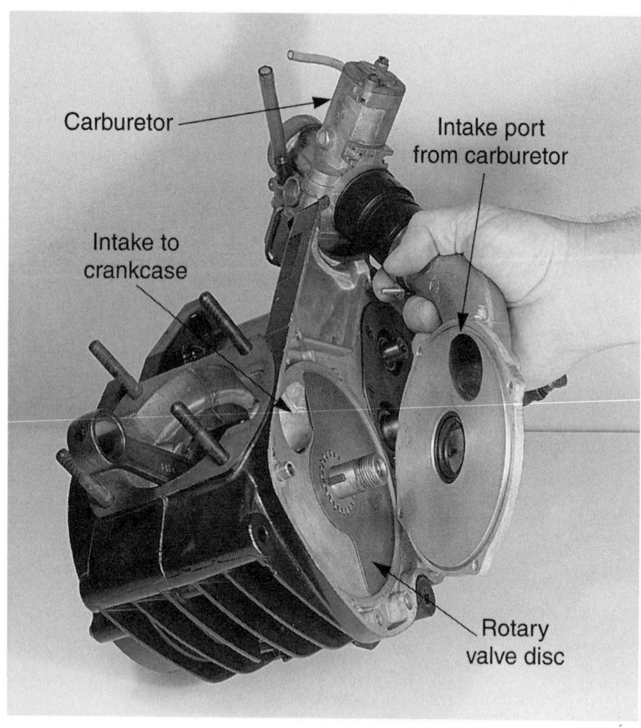

Figure 6-35. Rotary valves are used to control two-stroke intake timing.

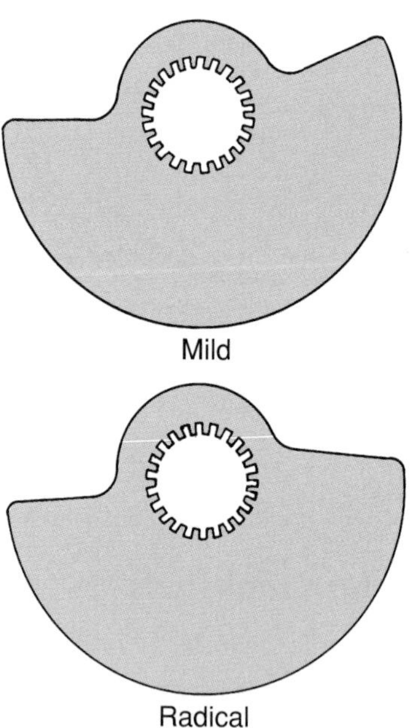

Figure 6-36. Mild rotary valve opens intake port later and closes it earlier than radical rotary valve.

flywheel halves together and is supported by a main bearing with seals on each side. The journals are located 180° from each other.

Multi-Cylinder Crankshaft

Multi-cylinder, two-stroke crankshafts consist of three or four sets of flywheel assemblies connected together. Main bearings and seals separate each flywheel assembly and crankcase cavity. **Figure 6-42** shows a multi-cylinder crankshaft. Three cylinder engine crankshafts have the journals positioned 120° apart. Four cylinder engine crankshafts have the journals positioned 180° apart.

Piston and Ring Design

Two-stroke pistons differ in a number of ways from four-stroke pistons. A two-stroke piston often has:

- Transfer cutouts below the piston pin boss.

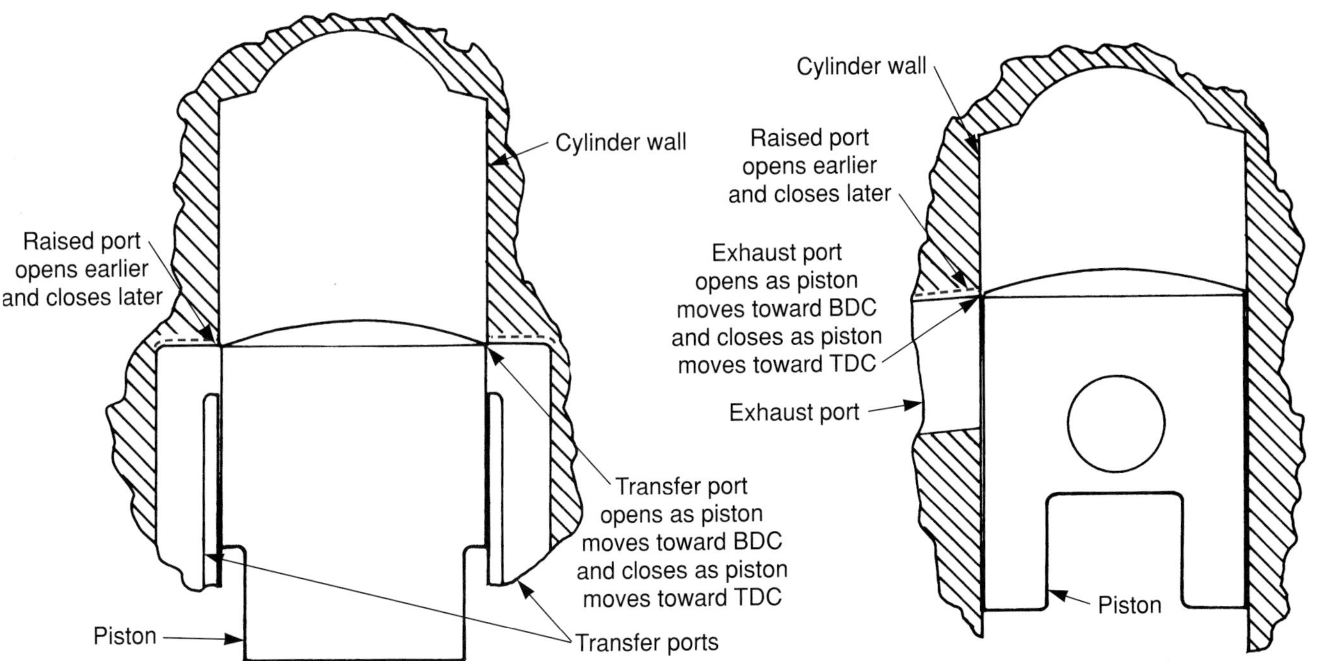

Figure 6-37. Transfer and exhaust timing is determined by port height. As the roof of the port is raised, the port is opened earlier and closed later.

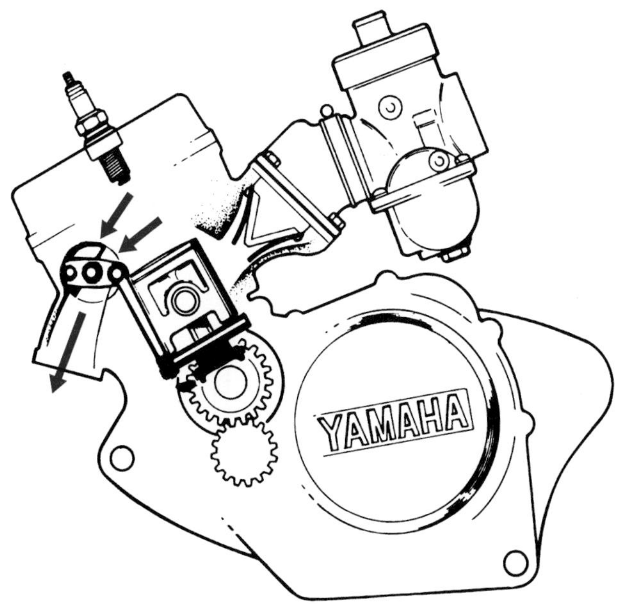

Figure 6-38. Valve raises the exhaust port as engine speed increases. (Yamaha Motor Corporation U.S.A.)

- Locating pins in the ring grooves.
- Variations in intake skirt design.
- No oil control ring.
- Needle bearings between the piston pin and rod small end.

Transfer Cutouts

With a two-stroke engine, the skirt area below the piston pin boss is cut out to allow free air-fuel mixture flow into the transfer ports. This is termed a ***transfer cutout.*** When the piston is at BDC, the transfer cutout matches the transfer opening in the cylinder wall and crankcase, **Figure 6-43.** As a result, fuel mixture can rapidly flow into the cylinder.

Ring Locating Pins

In a two-stroke engine, the piston rings must move past the port openings in the cylinder. To prevent ring breakage, it is necessary to locate the ring end gaps away from the port openings. This prevents the ring ends from protruding into and catching on the port edge. The ring could easily break on the port opening. Locating pins are positioned so that ring end gaps do not rotate in the cylinder and pass over the port, **Figure 6-44.**

Intake Skirt

Two-stroke piston skirts are not always shaped the same. Often, the intake and exhaust side of the piston will have different lengths. Intake skirts may be shortened, cutaway, or drilled to work properly with intake timing control. Common designs are shown in **Figure 6-45.**

Piston Expansion

To help control expansion and piston fit, two-stroke pistons are cam ground (machined out-of-round) and tapered (machined to smaller diameter at top). Since the two-stroke engine has a power stroke every revolution,

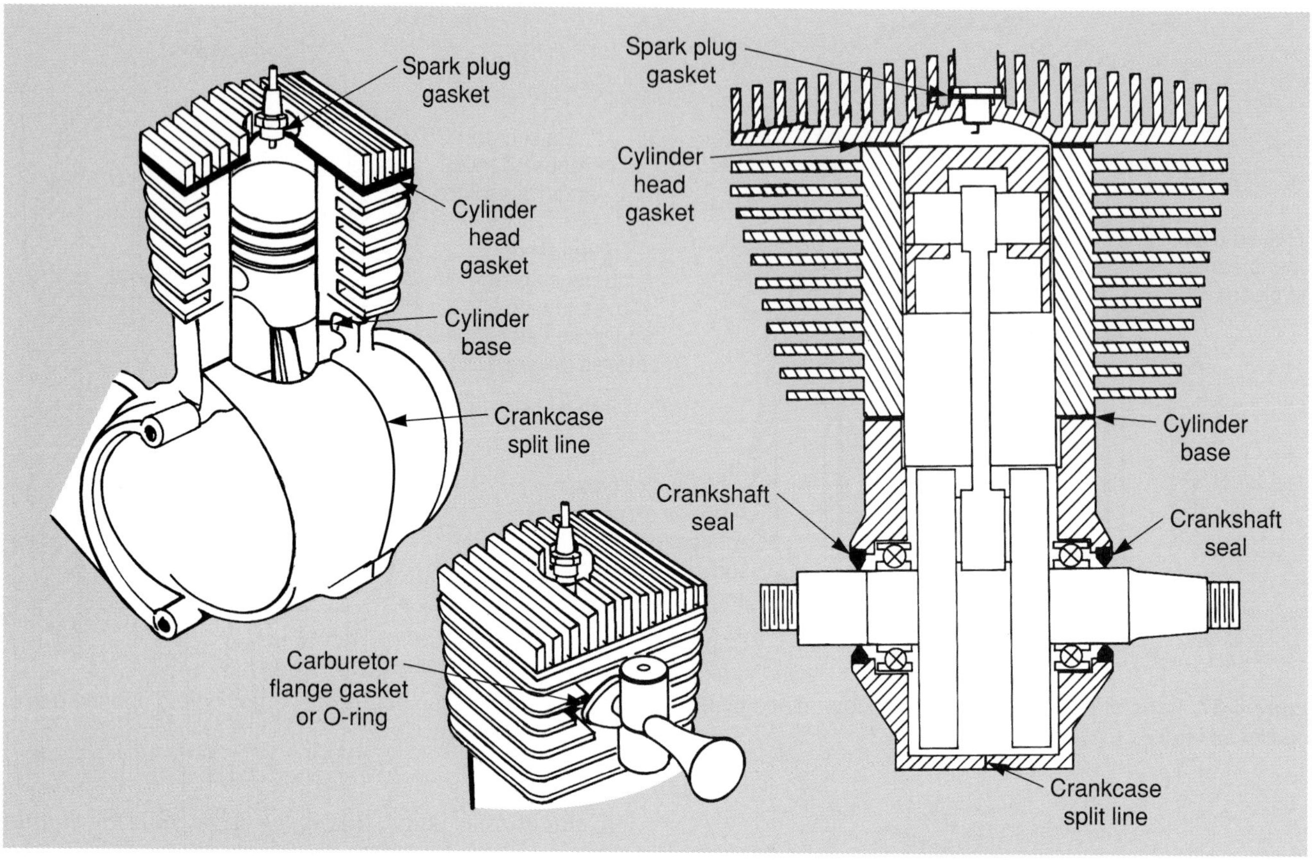

Spark plug gasket
Cylinder head gasket
Cylinder base
Crankcase split line
Carburetor flange gasket or O-ring
Spark plug gasket
Cylinder head gasket
Cylinder base
Crankshaft seal
Crankshaft seal
Crankcase split line

Figure 6-39. Leakage at any of these points will cause poor engine operation.

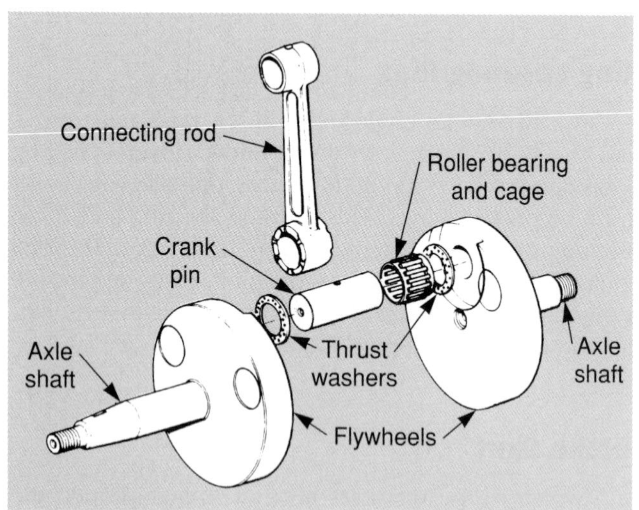

Figure 6-40. An assembled crankshaft is made of several components. The crankpin is pressed into one flywheel. Thrust washers, roller bearing, and connecting rod are installed on the crankpin. Then the other flywheel is pressed on. (Kawasaki Motors Corporation U.S.A.)

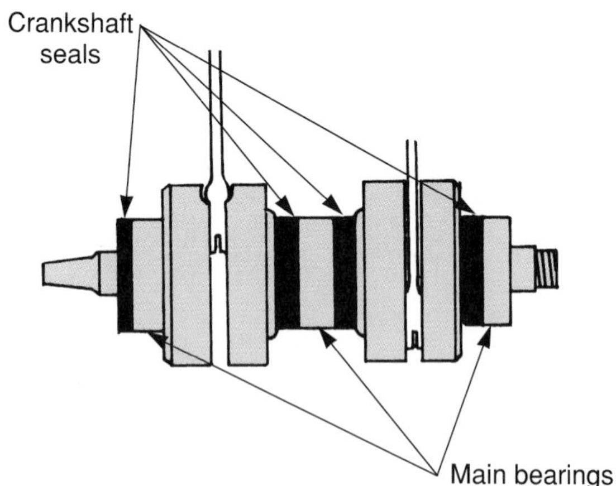

Figure 6-41. Note the construction of a typical twin-cylinder, two-stroke crankshaft.

the piston is subjected to much more heat than a four-stroke piston. Piston expansion can be a problem in a two-stroke engine.

Piston Rings

Two-stroke engines are designed to use either one or two piston rings. No oil control ring is needed because lubrication is provided by the air-fuel mixture. For this reason, the rings are only required to seal compression, vacuum, and combustion pressures. Shown in **Figure 6-46,** the three ring designs used in two-stroke engines are rectangular rings, dyke rings or L-rings, and keystone rings.

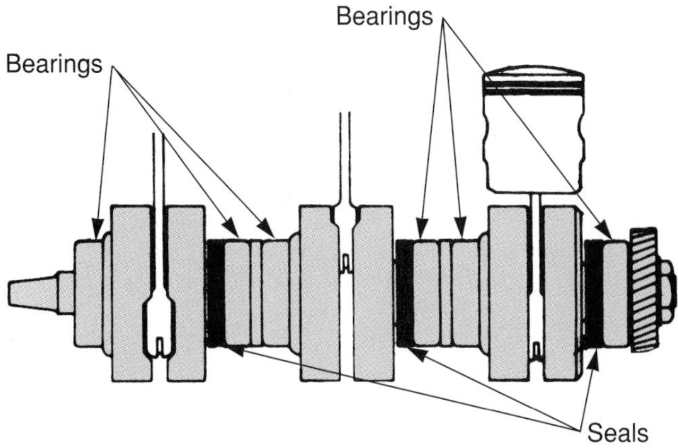

Figure 6-42. With a three-cylinder crankshaft, the main bearings and seals separate each flywheel assembly. (American Suzuki Motor Corporation)

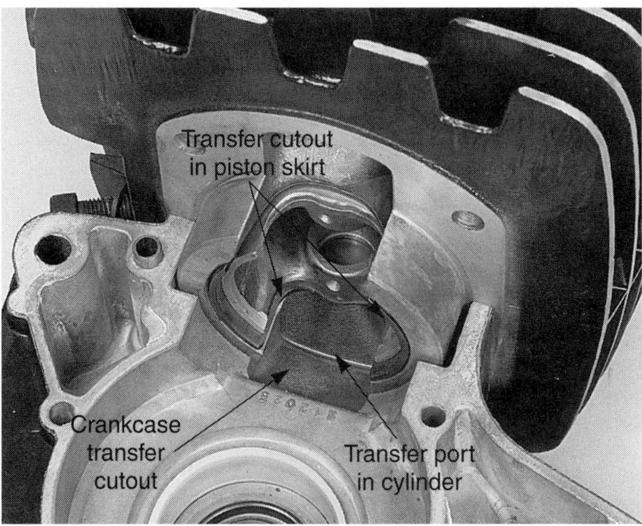

Figure 6-43. Transfer cutouts in the piston and crankcase match the transfer port in the cylinder.

A two-stroke ***rectangular ring*** is similar in design to a four-stroke compression ring. The major difference is that the two-stroke ring is locked in place by a pin in the piston ring groove. Also, rectangular rings may sometimes have a slight taper on their face.

The ***dyke ring,*** also termed an L-ring, is designed to use combustion pressure to aid in sealing. Shown in **Figure 6-47,** the L-shape allows combustion pressure to force the ring out against the cylinder wall. Because combustion pressure directly helps ring sealing, ***blow-by*** (movement of pressure and gas between the ring and cylinder wall) is held to a minimum.

Keystone rings also use combustion pressure to aid ring sealing. In this design, combustion pressure is trapped between the ring taper and ring groove, **Figure 6-48.** Combustion pressure pushes the ring out against the cylinder wall. This action is especially desirable at high engine speeds when ring tension may not be strong enough to hold the ring outward.

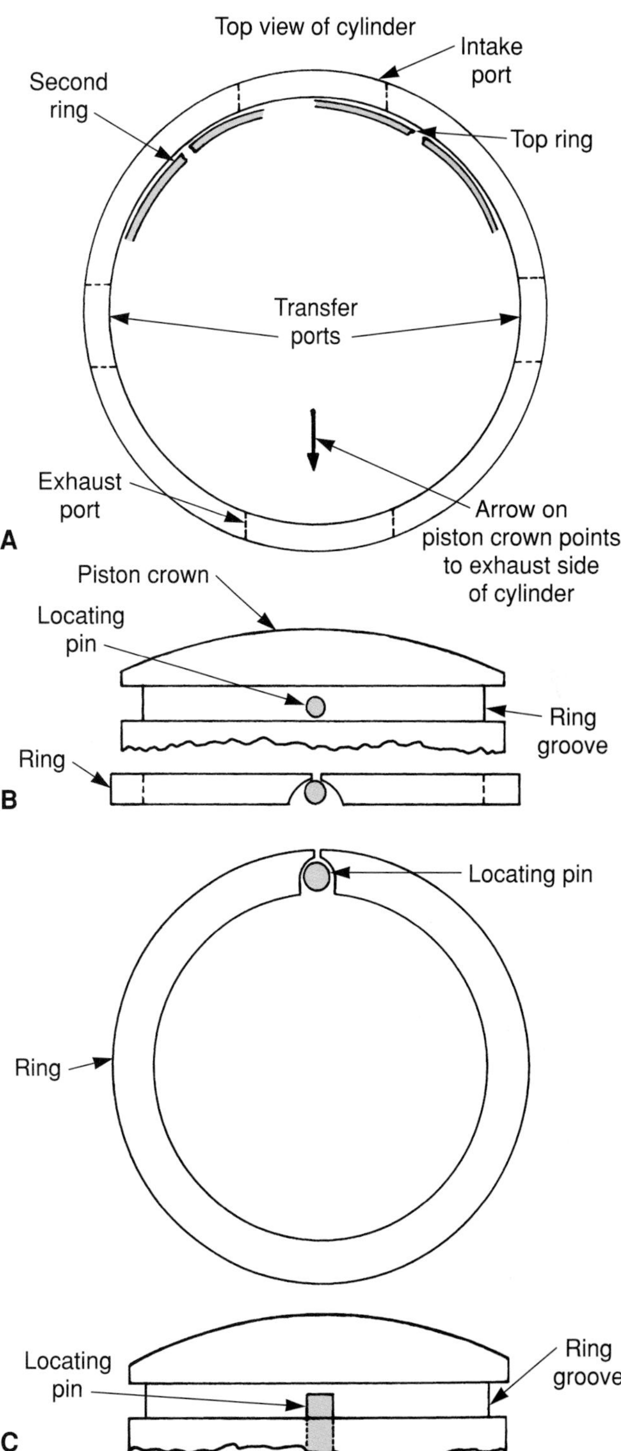

Figure 6-44. Piston rings in a two-stroke engine are normally located by pins. This prevents the rings from rotating. If rings turned on the piston, ring ends could get caught in the port windows. A—Proper location of ring end gaps. B—Horizontal locating pin. C—Vertical locating pin.

Cylinder Construction

Four methods of construction are used for two-stroke engines Each design has advantages and disadvantages:

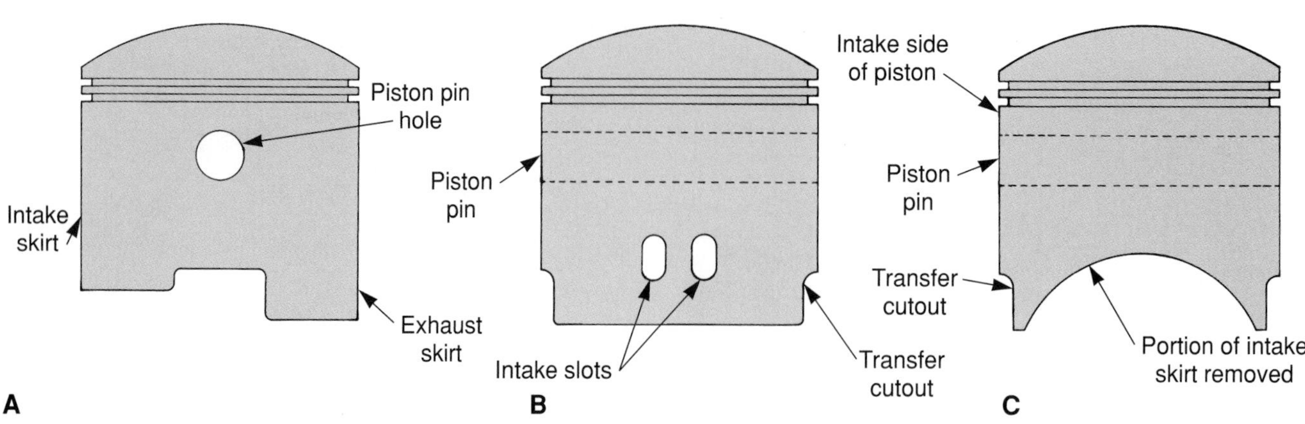

Figure 6-45. Common piston skirt designs. A— Engines with piston controlled intake use pistons with intake skirts shorter than exhaust skirts. B—Slots or holes in the intake skirt (used with reed valve). C—Intake skirt with radius (used with reed valve).

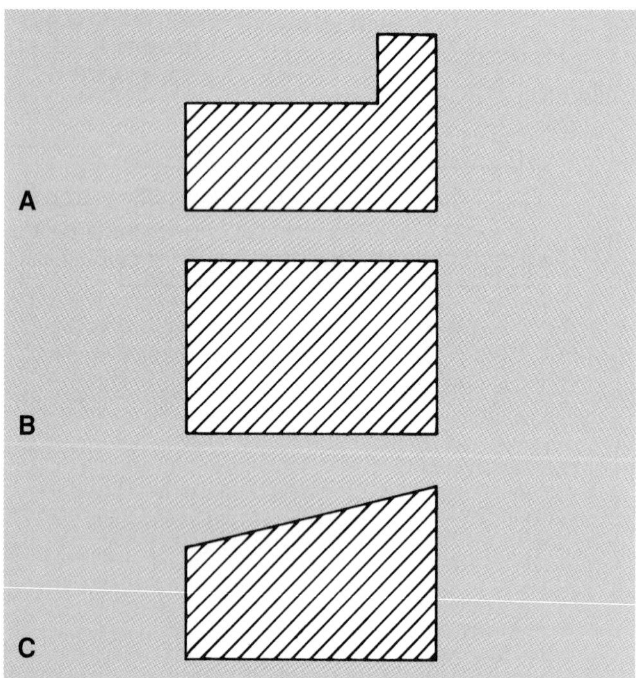

Figure 6-46. Three common ring shapes used in two-stroke engines. A—Dyke or L-shaped. B—Rectangular. C—Keystone.

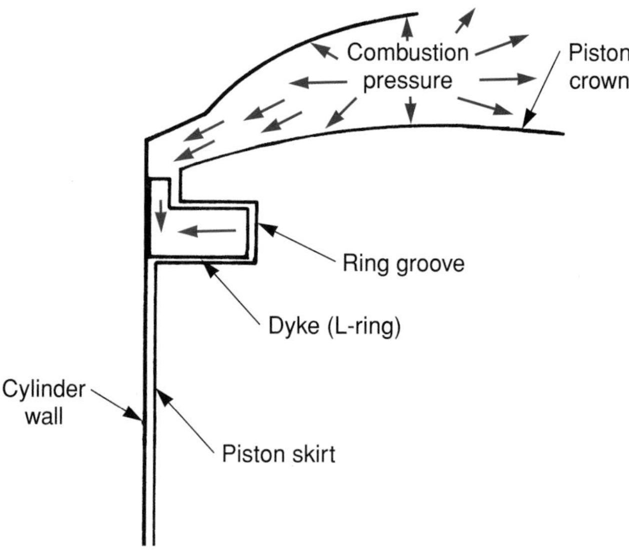

Figure 6-47. Combustion pressure forces a dyke (L-ring) against the cylinder wall to increase sealing ability.

- Pressed-in sleeve.
- Cast-in sleeve.
- Coated bore.
- Cast iron cylinder.

Pressed-In Sleeve

The ***pressed-in sleeve*** for a two-cycle engine is normally a cast iron liner machined to fit tightly into an aluminum cylinder block, **Figure 6-49.** An interference fit (sleeve is slightly larger than the cylinder hole) is used to lock the sleeve in place.

The major disadvantage of the pressed-in sleeve design is its manufacturing cost. The major advantage is the sleeve can be resized (bored) when worn. It can also be replaced

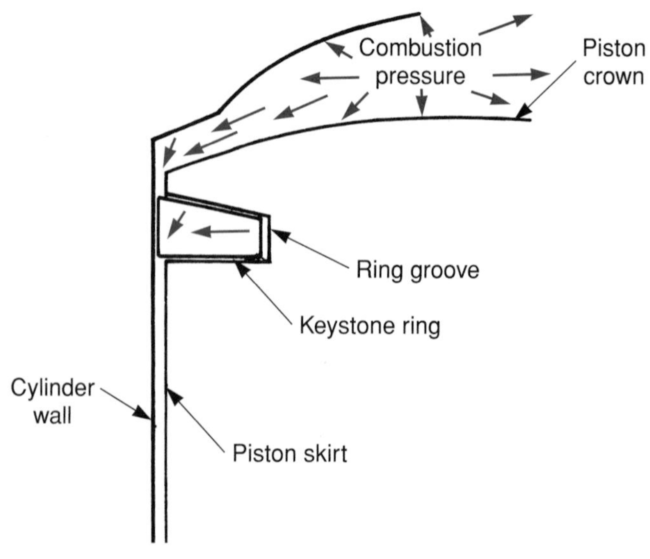

Figure 6-48. Combustion pressure forces the keystone ring against the cylinder wall to increase piston sealing.

(resleeved) when the cylinder cannot be bored oversize. This prevents the need for cylinder block replacement.

Cast-In Sleeve

A ***cast-in-sleeve*** uses an iron liner cast into the cylinder block. This design is inexpensive to produce. When it can no longer be bored, however, the cylinder block must be replaced. **Figure 6-50** shows the cast-in sleeve design.

Coated Bore

The ***coated bore*** cylinder does not use any type of inserted liner. Instead, a thin coating of chromium or iron is applied to provide a hard cylinder wall surface, as shown in **Figure 6-51.** This type of cylinder is expensive to produce and cannot be bored. However, superior heat dissipation, lightweight, and relatively long cylinder life is provided by a coated bore design.

Cast Iron Cylinder

Some small bore two-stroke engines still use a solid ***cast iron cylinder*** assembly, **Figure 6-52.** In this design, the bore is machined into a one-piece cylinder block. A cast iron cylinder is heavy and dissipates heat poorly. However, it is inexpensive and very dependable.

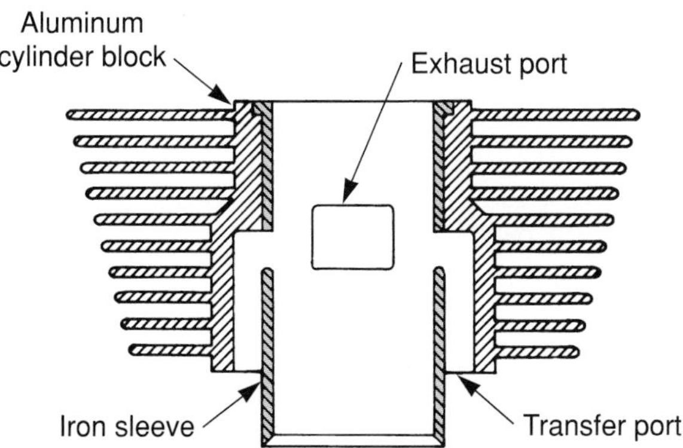

Figure 6-49. Pressed-in sleeve method of cylinder construction uses an iron sleeve pressed into an aluminum cylinder block.

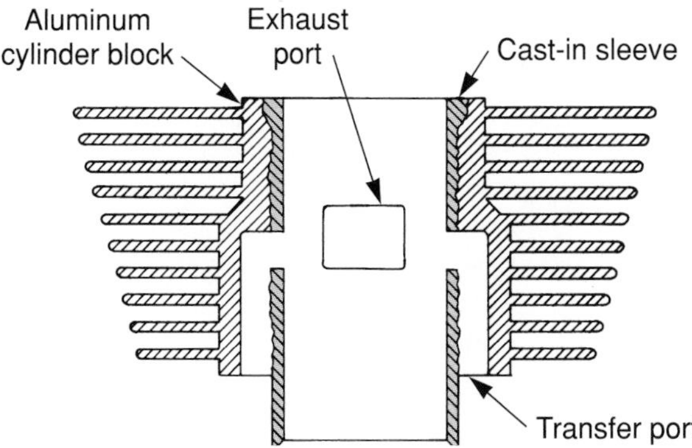

Figure 6-50. Cast-in sleeve method of cylinder construction normally begins with an iron sleeve. The aluminum cylinder block is then cast around the sleeve, making a one piece unit. Aluminum is lighter and dissipates heat better than iron.

Cylinder Ports

We already know that the primary function of two-stroke engine ***cylinder ports*** is to route the air-fuel mixture through the engine. They also allow exhaust gases to leave the engine cylinder. Since the piston and rings control port opening and closing, the port shape is important.

Piston rings pass the exhaust and transfer ***port windows*** twice during each engine revolution. Since the rings press out against the cylinder wall, they have a tendency to expand into the port. If the port windows are not shaped properly, the rings can bulge into, catch, and break on the port edge, or wear out prematurely. A number of port designs used to help eliminate this ring failure problem are the elliptical port, bridged port, and multiple ports.

Elliptical Port Shape

Elliptical port shape allows a relatively large port opening without the danger of ring catching. **Figure 6-53** shows the advantage of the elliptical port over the rectangular port. The curved sides of the elliptical port prevent the rings from catching on a horizontal or parallel edge. This port shape is most commonly seen in large exhaust ports.

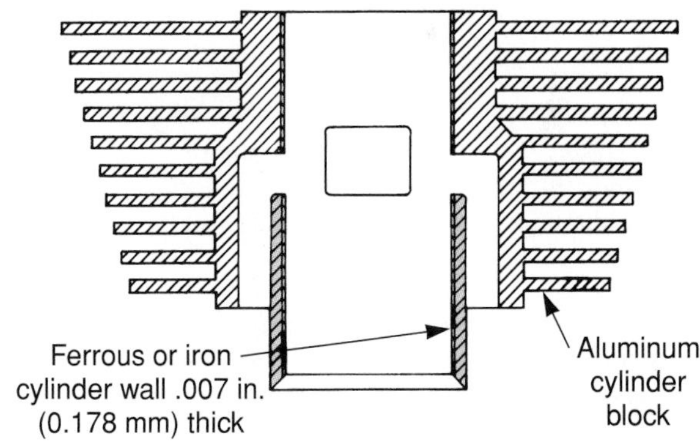

Figure 6-51. A—Cylinder construction uses iron that is electrically bonded to the aluminum cylinder block.

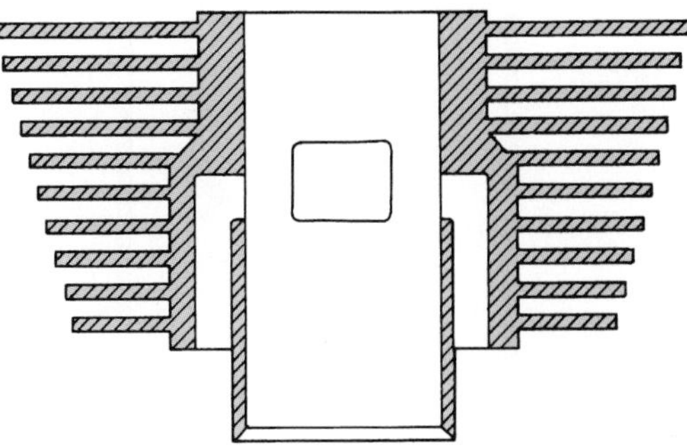

Figure 6-52. This is a cross-section of an all cast iron cylinder block and cylinder bore.

Bridged Port

The ***bridged port*** design uses a vertical bridge (rib) across the middle of the port opening. As illustrated in **Figure 6-54,** this supports the ring as it passes over the port window. It prevents the rings from bulging into the port. A bridge allows the use of a large rectangular port without the danger of ring breakage. Bridges are normally used on exhaust ports and piston controlled intake ports. This intake port design also prevents the piston skirt from swinging into and catching on the bottom of the port.

Multiple Ports

Multiple ports are mainly used as transfer ports, **Figure 6-55.** Multiple ports are a number of small ports placed around the cylinder. This allows a large total port area, even though the individual ports are small. A distinct advantage is that the incoming air-fuel charge can be better directed to help move exhaust gases out of the combustion chamber. Also, ring catching and breakage is avoided.

Many different combinations of port shapes are used. Regardless of shape, the ports must provide efficient crankcase filling as well as ***scavenging*** (cleaning) the cylinder. Port edges are chamfered (beveled) to keep the rings and piston from scuffing on the port. This must be done in all two-stroke cylinders.

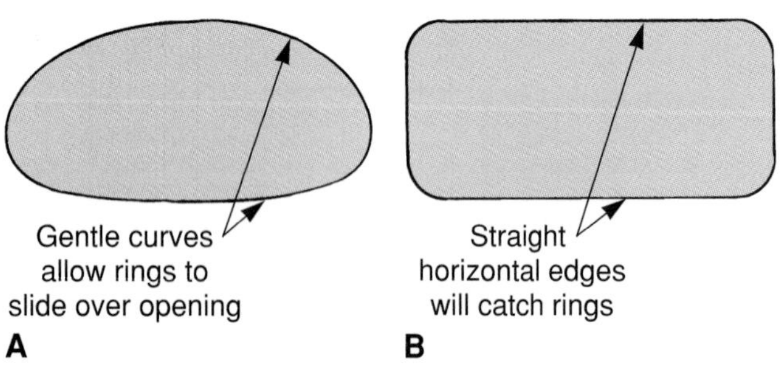

Figure 6-53. Port shapes used in two-stroke engines. A—Elliptical port shapes permits a larger port window to be used. B—Rectangular port shapes can catch rings on their horizontal edges.

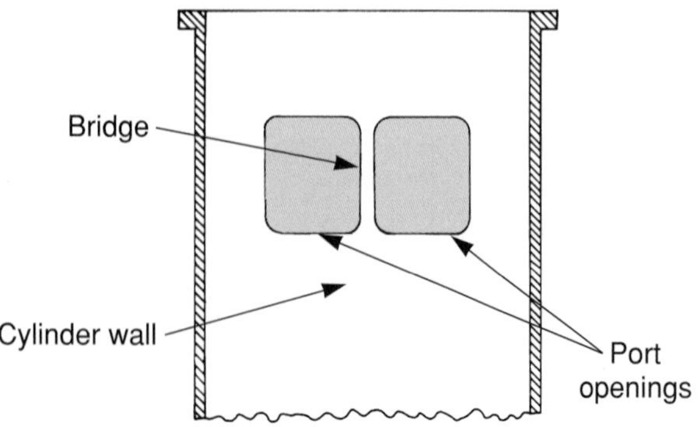

Figure 6-54. Using a bridge in the middle of a large rectangular port prevents rings from catching on the horizontal port edges.

Vertical and Horizontal Split Crankcases

Most single cylinder two-stroke engines have vertically split crankcases. This is the least expensive design to produce. **Figure 6-56** shows a typical single cylinder vertically split two-stroke engine.

Twin and multiple cylinder two-stroke engines are normally split horizontally, **Figure 6-57.** Since each cylinder must have its own sealed crankcase, it would be impractical to use the vertical split design.

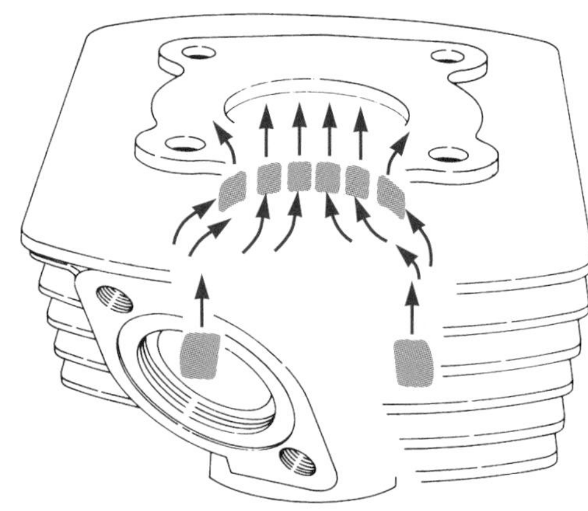

Figure 6-55. This example of multiple transfer ports uses six small port windows.

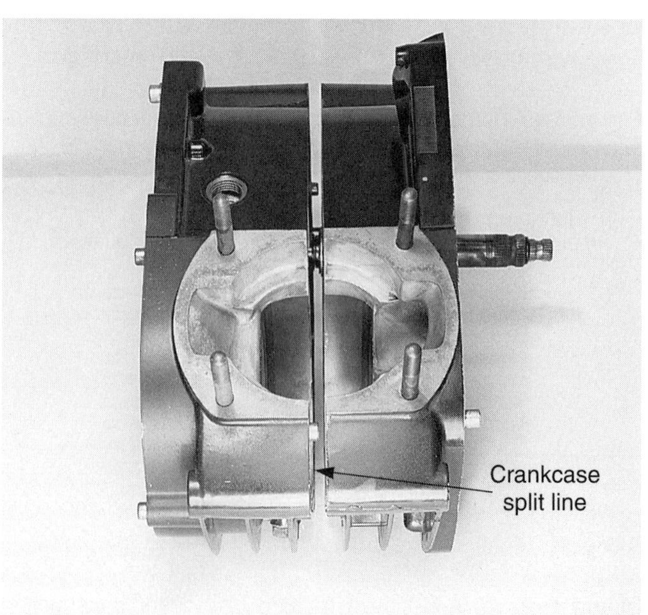

Figure 6-56. Single cylinder cases are normally split or divided vertically in the middle.

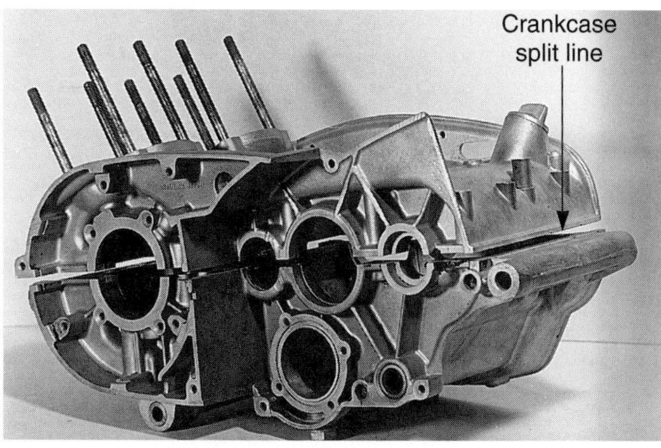

Figure 6-57. Horizontally split crankcases, such as this twin, are divided horizontally through the middle of the crankshaft and transmission shaft.

Summary

Motorcycle, ATV, and scooter engines are either four-stroke or two-stroke. A four-stroke engine requires two crankshaft revolutions for each power stroke. The camshaft, which controls the flow of air, fuel, and exhaust, must rotate at one-half crankshaft speed. Three common valve trains are used to operate the valves in four-stroke motorcycle engines. The current camshaft arrangement in a four-stroke engine can be divided into single overhead camshaft and dual overhead camshaft types. Camshaft lobe shape determines its lift and duration.

The piston and crankshaft assemblies are often termed the engine's reciprocating assembly. The piston and rod reciprocate or move up and down in the cylinder. The crankshaft changes the piston's linear motion into more usable rotary motion.

A single cylinder engine is the simplest of all four-stroke engines. Twin cylinder engines are manufactured in four configurations: inline, vertical, opposed, and V-twin. Multi-cylinder engines consist of either three, four, or six cylinders. Four-stroke motorcycle pistons are either cast or forged. The combustion chamber is the area where combustion occurs in the cylinder. Pistons contain three rings which seal the space between the piston and the cylinder wall. A bearing is to reduce friction while allowing movement between parts. The engine case houses the engine crankshaft, bearings, gearbox, and related components.

Two-stroke engines use the piston to regulate intake, transfer, and exhaust timing. The three methods used to control intake timing are the piston port, reed valve, and rotary valve. A piston port engine uses piston skirt length and intake port location to control intake timing. Mild timing will provide good low and midrange power while radical timing will give more top end power. A two-stroke engine must produce sufficient vacuum and pressure in the crankcase.

Two-stroke, single cylinder crankshafts are normally made of several components pressed together. A twin-cylinder, two-stroke crankshaft is simply two single cylinder crankshafts constructed side-by-side. Multi-cylinder, two-stroke crankshafts consist of three or four sets of flywheel assemblies connected together. The three ring designs used in two-stroke engines are rectangular rings, dyke rings or L-rings, and keystone rings.

Know These Terms

Four-stroke engines
Camshaft
Chain drive
Belt drive
Single overhead camshaft (SOHC)
Dual overhead camshaft (DOHC)
Valve springs
Valve float
Lobe
Lift
Duration
Piston
Crankshaft
Single cylinder engine
Twin cylinder engines
Inline twin cylinder engine
Vertical-twin cylinder engine
Opposed-twin cylinder engine
V-twin cylinder engine
Siamesed
Multi-cylinder engines
Cast piston
Forged piston
Piston crown
Piston taper
Cam ground pistons
Piston slap
Combustion chamber
Hemispherical combustion chamber
Side squish combustion chamber
Semispherical combustion chamber
Ring grooves
Ring lands
Compression rings
Oil control ring
Piston rings
Scraper ring
Oil control ring
Bearing
Ball bearings
Roller bearings
Plain bearing
Engine case
Non-unit construction
Unit construction
Vertically split
Horizontally split
Two-stroke engines
Intake timing
Piston port
Mild timing
Radical timing
Reed valve
Rotary valve
Transfer
Exhaust timing
Crankcase vacuum
Crankcase pressure
Built-up crankshafts
Transfer cutout
Rectangular ring
Dyke ring
Blow-by

Keystone rings
Pressed-in sleeve
Cast-in-sleeve
Coated bore
Cast iron cylinder
Cylinder ports
Port windows
Elliptical port shape
Bridged port
Multiple ports
Scavenging

Review Questions—Chapter 6

Do not write in this text. Place your answers on a separate sheet of paper.

1. List the three types of valve train operating mechanisms.
2. The camshaft ______ determines when, how long, how quickly and how far a valve opens.
   A. lobe
   B. bearing
   C. gear
   D. All of the above.
3. What are the two ways that connecting rods are attached to the crankshaft in a V-twin engine?
4. List the two types of piston construction and an advantage of each.
5. The _______ is exposed to the direct heat and pressure of combustion.
   A. piston pin
   B. lower ring grove
   C. piston crown
   D. upper ring groove
6. Name the three piston ring types.
7. Which piston ring serves a dual function?
   A. Top piston ring.
   B. Middle piston ring.
   C. Bottom piston ring.
   D. All of the above.
8. Name three methods used to control the intake timing of two-stroke engines.
9. A two-stroke engine which opens and closes its intake port at the same piston position before and after TDC has _____ port timing.
   A. rotary
   B. unsymmetrical
   C. symmetrical
   D. reed
10. A ______ helps to prevent standoff.
11. What makes a reed valve operate?
    A. Crankcase vacuum.
    B. Crankcase pressure.
    C. A camshaft and pushrod system.
    D. Both A & B.
12. A ______ keyed to the crankshaft may be used to open and close the intake port.
13. Name three differences between two and four-stroke pistons.
14. What are the three common port designs?
15. Twin and multicylinder, two-stroke engines use _____ split crankcases.
    A. opposed
    B. horizontally
    C. laterally
    D. vertically

Suggested Activities

1. Compare the valve train mechanisms of three different four-stroke engines.
2. Using a repair manual:
   A. Find two V-twin motorcycles which use different crankshaft configurations.
   B. Find two V-twins which use the same type of crankshaft configuration.
3. List as many different ring shapes as you can find for four-stroke engines. Use magazine articles, service manuals, and reference books.
4 Check manuals and determine the most popular type of two-stroke piston ring (rectangular, dyke, keystone). Also, determine whether one or two rings are used in most two-stroke engines.
5. Pick a popular two-stroke motorcycle engine and use the shop manual to determine:
   A. Exhaust port configuration (shape).
   B. Transfer port configuration (shape and number of ports).
   C. Intake configuration (piston port, rotary valve, reed valve).
   D. Type of cylinder construction (coated bore, cast-in sleeve).

7
Fuel Systems

After studying this chapter, you will be able to:

- Identify the parts of a fuel system.
- Explain the operating principles for each component of a fuel system.
- Describe carburetor circuits.
- List fundamental carburetor service and repair procedures.
- Explain the basic principles of electronic fuel injection.

As mentioned in Chapter 1, fuel systems can be classified into two types: carburetors and electronic fuel injection (EFI) systems. There are differences in the configuration and construction of fuel systems, but the functions are the same, to maintain an adequate supply of fuel to the engine. This chapter discusses the components of carbureted and fuel injection systems as used on motorcycles, ATVs, and scooters.

Fuel System Parts

Before discussing the operation of the carburetor and EFI systems, it is important for you to become familiar with the other major components of the fuel system, **Figure 7-1.** The function of these fuel delivery parts is the same for both systems. A typical motorcycle fuel system is made up of the components discussed in the following paragraphs.

Fuel Tank

The ***fuel tank*** holds the fuel supply for the motorcycle, ATV, or scooter. It is usually in the center of the bike, above the engine just behind the handle bars. Fuel tanks can be made of steel, aluminum, plastic, or fiberglass.

The tank is sealed by a gas cap. The gas cap may be vented or nonvented. Fuel tank venting is needed to prevent a vacuum as fuel flows from the tank and relieves pressure as the fuel's temperature rises. Nonvented systems use a separate vent hose.

Fuel Petcock

A ***fuel petcock*** is an on/off valve attached to the bottom of the fuel tank. This provides a means of stopping fuel flow in the system when the engine is not running. Fuel petcocks are vacuum, electronic, or manually operated.

The manually operated fuel petcock shown in **Figure 7-2A** has a three-position selector valve, providing standard, reserve, and off. In the standard position, fuel enters from approximately 1″ (25.4 mm) above the bottom of the tank. The reserve position allows the remaining fuel from the bottom of the tank to enter the line.

The vacuum operated fuel petcock shown in **Figure 7-2B** is operated by intake manifold or crankcase vacuum. When the engine is not operating and the control lever is in the on or reserve (RES) position, a vacuum-operated petcock automatically prevents fuel from flowing. A third position, called prime (PRI), is provided to allow rapid filling of an empty float bowl. The prime position is used when initially starting an engine.

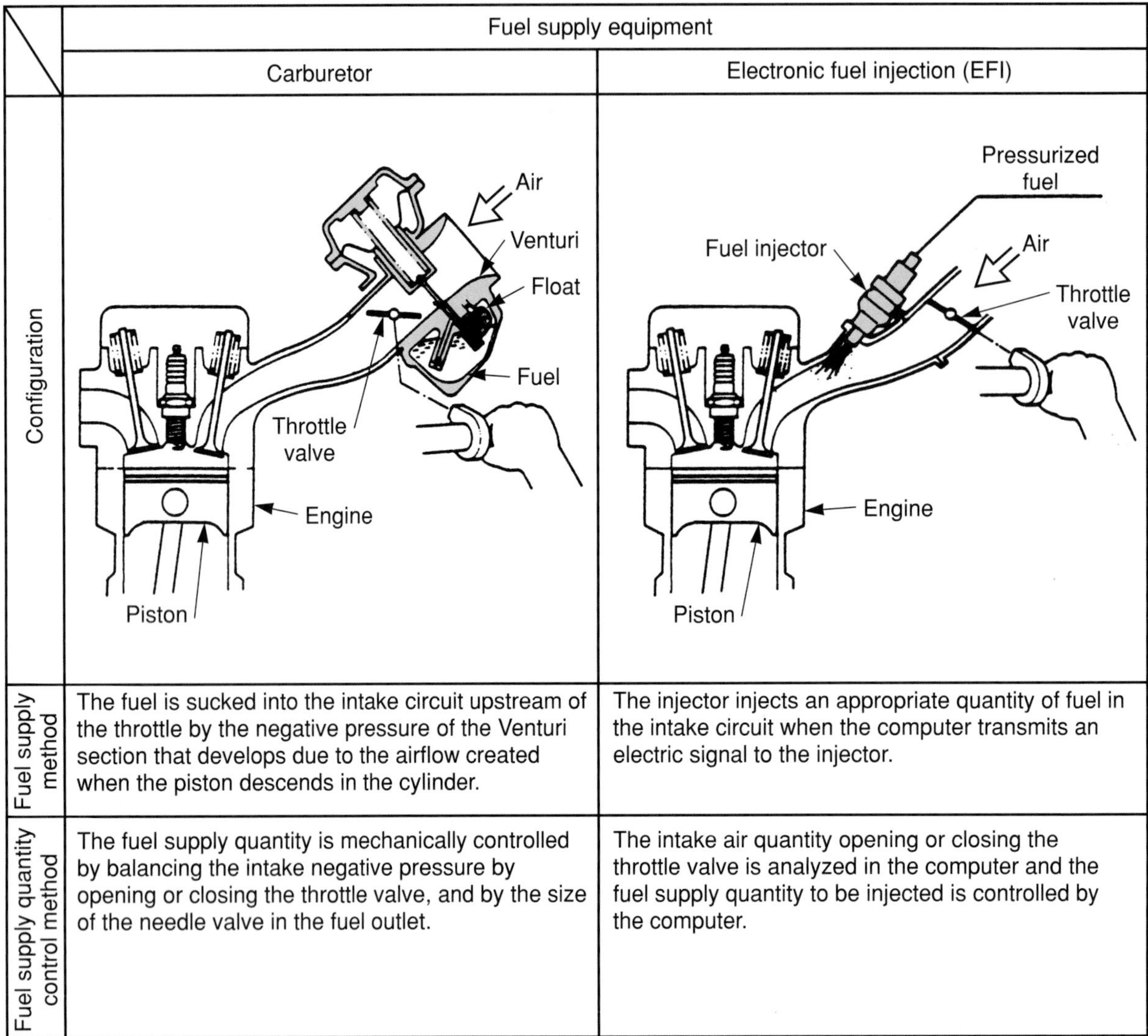

	Fuel supply equipment	
	Carburetor	Electronic fuel injection (EFI)
Configuration		
Fuel supply method	The fuel is sucked into the intake circuit upstream of the throttle by the negative pressure of the Venturi section that develops due to the airflow created when the piston descends in the cylinder.	The injector injects an appropriate quantity of fuel in the intake circuit when the computer transmits an electric signal to the injector.
Fuel supply quantity control method	The fuel supply quantity is mechanically controlled by balancing the intake negative pressure by opening or closing the throttle valve, and by the size of the needle valve in the fuel outlet.	The intake air quantity opening or closing the throttle valve is analyzed in the computer and the fuel supply quantity to be injected is controlled by the computer.

Figure 7-1. Types of fuel delivery systems. (Yamaha Motor Corporation U.S.A.)

The electronic petcock operates in same manner as the vacuum petcock. The difference is that a solenoid controls the vacuum in the petcock. When the fuel tank runs low, the ECM sends voltage to the solenoid, which in turn switches the petcock to the reserve position. Many petcocks incorporate a sediment bowl, **Figure 7-3.** The ***sediment bowl*** separates water and larger foreign materials (dirt, rust, scale) from the fuel before it enters the line.

Fuel Line

The ***fuel line*** is a neoprene or plastic tube that carries fuel from the petcock to the carburetor or fuel injector. It must be strong and flexible to withstand engine vibration. It should be routed to avoid contact with moving parts or extreme heat. Small clamps are normally used to hold the fuel line on its fittings.

Fuel Pump

A ***fuel pump*** is required on motorcycles having the fuel tank located too low for gravity flow to feed fuel to the carburetor. The fuel pump on carbureted bikes supplies fuel at pressures typically from 4-8 psi (28-55 kPa). **Figure 7-4** shows a typical fuel pump. On some bikes, it is necessary to use an electric fuel pump. Fuel injection fuel pumps can generate pressures from 45-50 psi (310-350 kPa).

Fuel Filter

A ***fuel filter*** is used to remove foreign matter from the gasoline before entry into the carburetor or fuel injector. Fuel filters can be classified as a petcock filter,

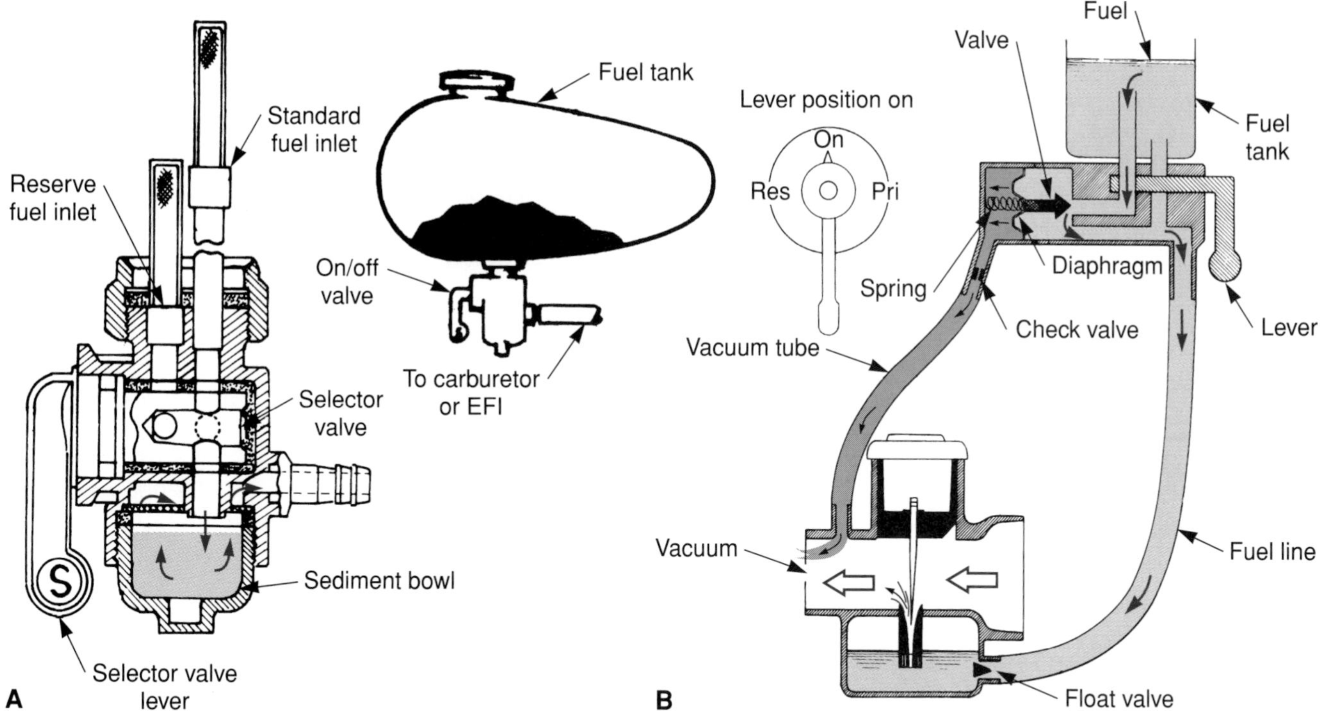

Figure 7-2. Major differences between a manual and vacuum fuel petcock. A—Manual petcock. B—Vacuum petcock.

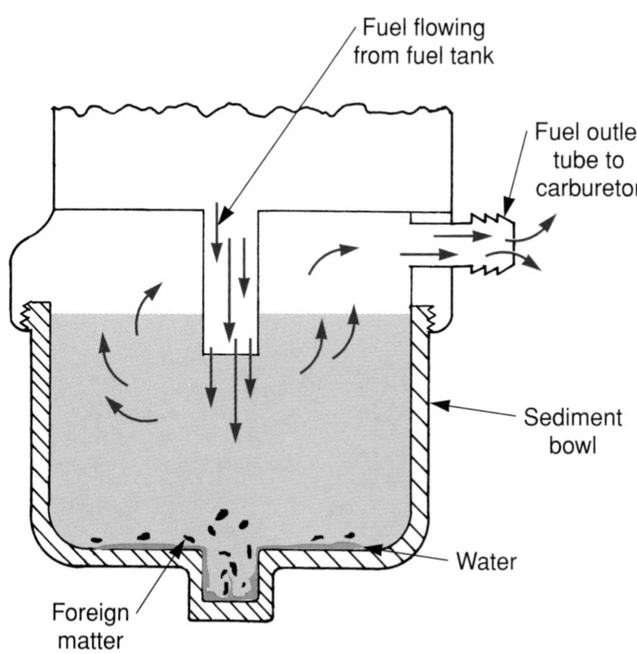

Figure 7-3. Heavy particles (dirt, rust, scale) and water settle in the bottom of the fuel petcock sediment bowl. Clean fuel flows through the sediment bowl before it reaches the outlet tube and fuel line.

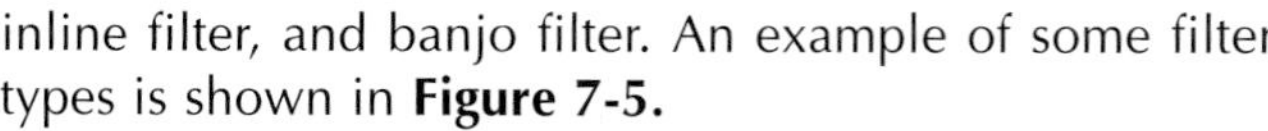
inline filter, and banjo filter. An example of some filter types is shown in **Figure 7-5**.

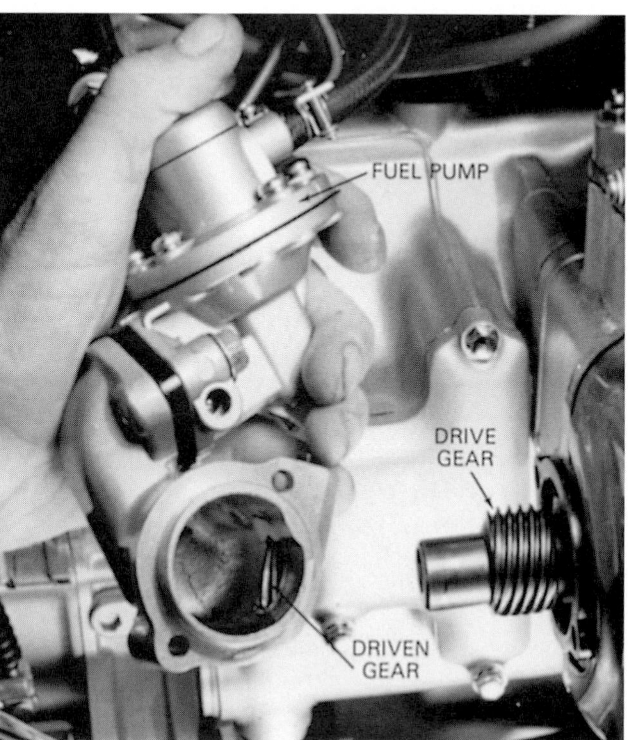

Figure 7-4. This fuel pump is driven by the engine's camshaft.

Air Filter and Intake Manifold

The ***air filter*** prevents airborne dirt and foreign material from entering the engine. Three types of filtering materials are used: paper, oiled foam, and oiled gauze.

Air filters and their mountings vary by application. In some applications, the air filter is attached directly to the engine. In most cases, however, the filter is enclosed in an ***air box*** connected to the engine by a rubber boot. This is illustrated in **Figure 7-6.** The air box provides a volume of still air for intake into the engine.

The ***intake manifold*** directs the air-fuel mixture to the engine. Intake manifolds are made of aluminum, steel, or neoprene. Two intake manifold types are shown in **Figure 7-7.**

Throttle Twist Grip

The ***throttle twist grip*** is attached to the right handlebar and changes the grip's rotating movement to a push-pull movement of the throttle cable. This is accomplished with a drum inside the twist grip mechanism, **Figure 7-8.**

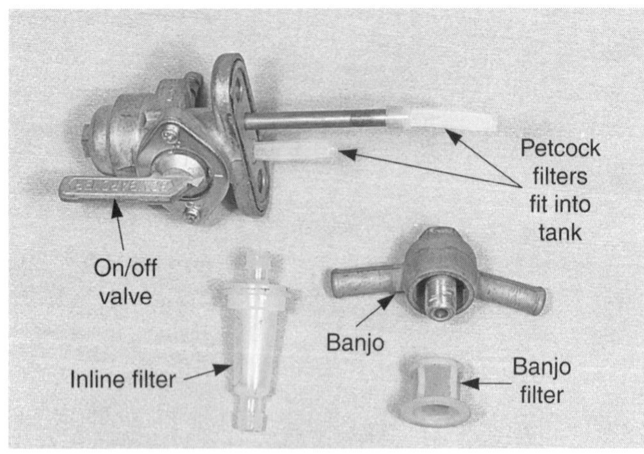

Figure 7-5. These fuel filters use fine nylon mesh to trap contaminants.

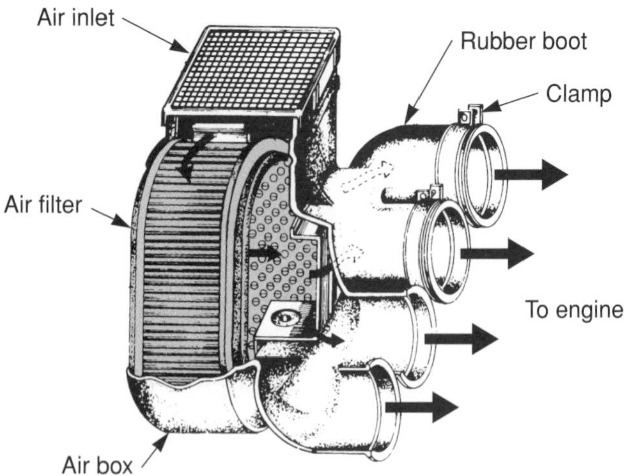

Figure 7-6. An air filter is usually mounted inside an air box. This allows one filter element to filter air for the engine, no matter which type of fuel system is used. The air box also helps protect the filter from water and rapid contamination. (Kawasaki Motors Corporation U.S.A.)

The twist grip rotation pulls on the throttle cable. In turn, the cable pulls on the carburetor or EFI throttle plate to increase engine speed and power. When the throttle twist grip is released, the carburetor or EFI throttle plate closes.

Some twist grips use two cables. In one type, both cables move in the same direction. In the other type, the cables move in opposite directions. In throttle grips with cables that move in opposite directions, positive throttle closing is assured at the carburetor or throttle plate.

Throttle Cable

The ***throttle cable*** connects to the twist grip at one end and to the carburetor or throttle plate linkage at the other end. As the twist grip is rotated, the cable changes the throttle plate angle. A means of adjusting cable free play is always provided. **Figure 7-9** shows a typical throttle cable mechanism.

Gasoline

Gasoline is a compound of the elements carbon and hydrogen and is distilled from crude oil. The amount and type of additives varies between grades as well as the desired ***octane rating,*** which is a measure of the gasoline's ability to resist knocking. The following additives are blended into the distilled gasoline at the refinery:

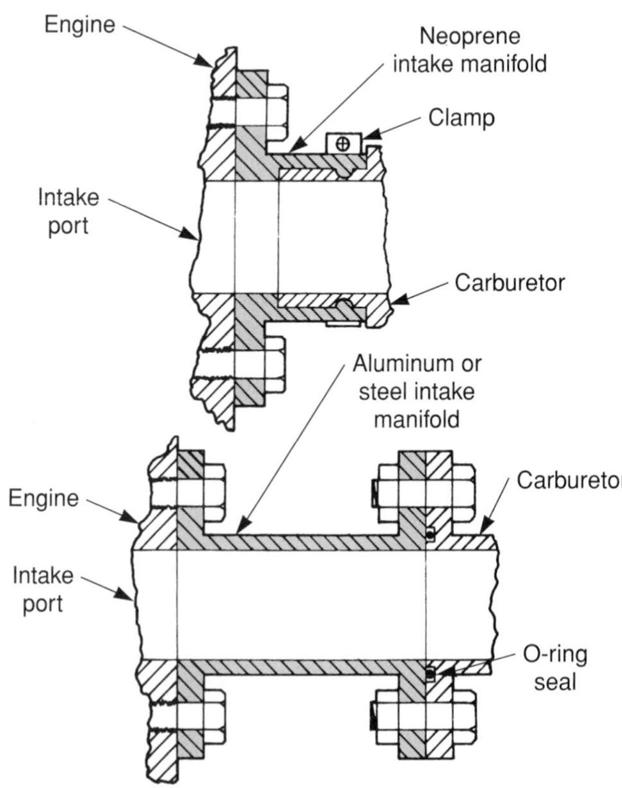

Figure 7-7. The intake manifold carries the air-fuel mixture to the engine. The carburetor or EFI throttle plate is bolted or clamped to intake manifold.

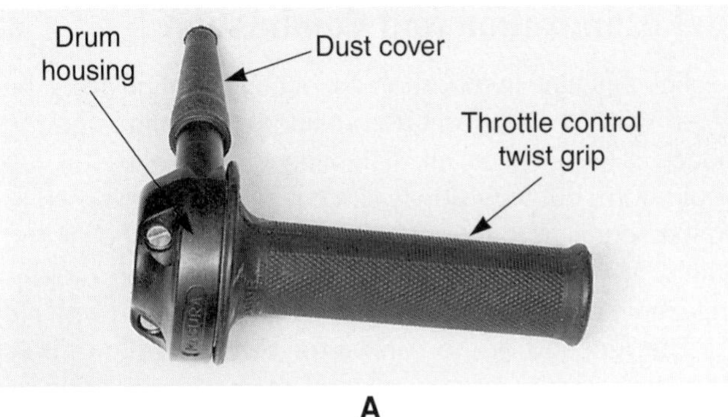

A

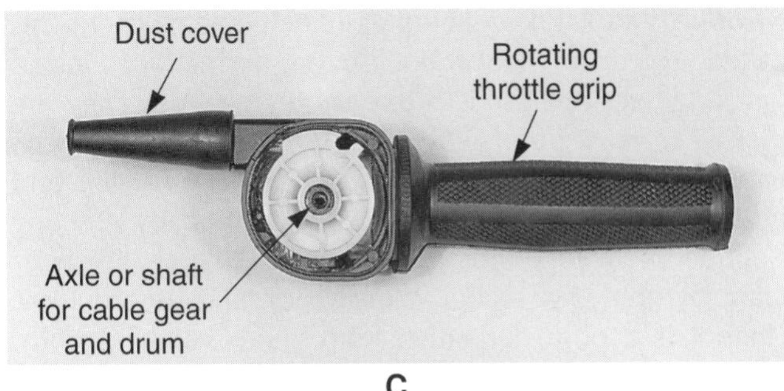

C

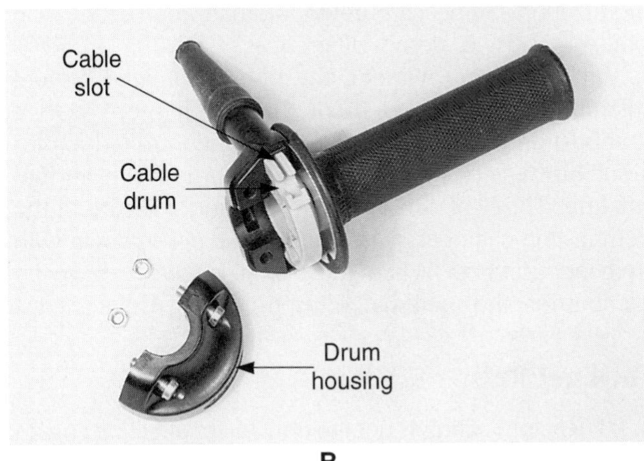

B

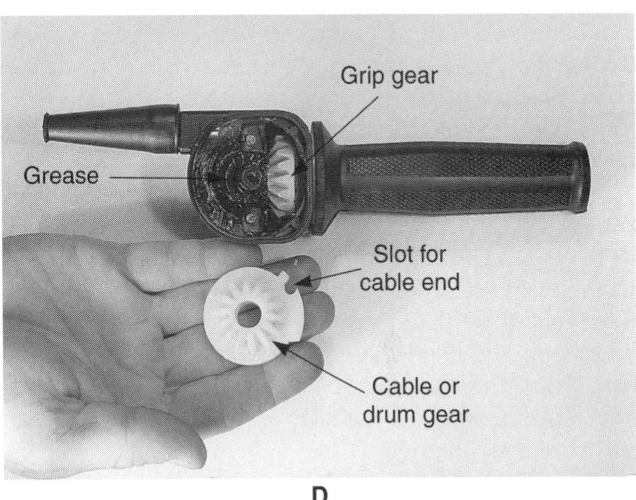

D

Figure 7-8. Two variations of drum throttle twist grip. A—Assembled throttle twist grip fastens to the right handlebar. B—This drum twist grip turns in the same direction as the throttle twist grip. C—Another variation of drum twist grip. D—Since the drum does not turn in the same direction as the throttle twist grip, a gear is used to transfer movement to the drum.

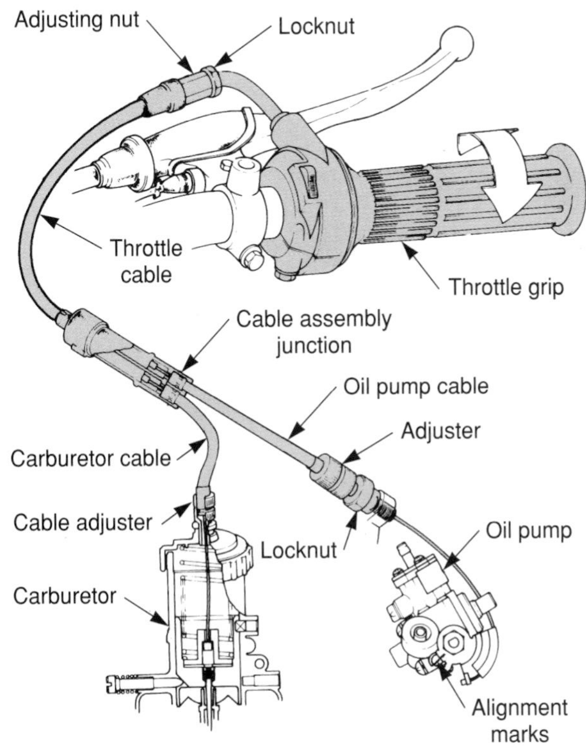

Figure 7-9. This throttle cable has free-play adjusters at the twist grip, carburetor, and oil pump. (Kawasaki Motors Corporation U.S.A.)

- Alcohols, such as denatured ethanol, as an octane enhancer, product extender, and to reduce carbon monoxide emissions.
- Anti-icers to prevent fuel system freeze-up in cold weather.
- Antioxidants to minimize gum formation in stored gasoline.
- Corrosion inhibitors to reduce fuel system corrosion.
- Detergents and fluidizer oils to remove or eliminate intake valve and fuel system deposits.
- Lead replacement additives to minimize exhaust valve recession.
- Metal deactivators to minimize the effect of metal-based components that may be present in refined gasoline on the fuel system.

To burn in the engine, gasoline must be ***vaporized,*** that is, changed from a liquid to a vapor. Gasoline blends are modified to increase or decrease the vaporization rate. In addition, the final gasoline blend depends to some extent on where the original crude oil came from. Crude oil varies between oil fields, and differences in sulfur content, viscosity, and volatility cannot be totally eliminated in the refining process. Since gasoline is such a complex, variable product, it can have an effect on an engine's performance.

In some parts of the country where ozone levels are excessively high, reformulated gasoline called ***oxygenated***

gasoline is sold. Oxygenated gasoline contains chemicals called *oxygenates* that reduce ozone formation. One of four additives are used to oxygenate gasoline. They are ***methyl tertiary butyl ether (MTBE), ethyl tertiary butyl ether (ETBE), tertiary amyl methyl ether (TAME),*** and ***ethanol.*** MTBE and ETBE are manufactured by reacting isobutylene with either methanol or ethanol. TAME is manufactured by reacting methanol and isoamylene. Ethanol is a pure derivative from grains, such as corn. Depending on the additive used, gasoline can have as much as 15% oxygenate by volume. Most motorcycle manufacturers allow between 10-15% oxygenate. Oxygenates have a tendency to chemically enlean the mixture, since there is more oxygen content in the fuel. Most major motorcycle manufacturers approve the use of oxygenated gasoline in their products.

Gasoline is primarily formulated to meet the needs of cars, trucks, and vans. For this reason, motorcycle manufacturers have to design their fuel systems around a fuel intentionally designed for automotive use. As a general rule, motorcycles, ATVs, and scooters should not be affected by the chemical composition or oxygenate content of most available gasoline, provided it is relatively free of excess dirt and water.

Most gasoline-related fuel system problems will be seasonal-related or caused by extended storage. You should also remember at all times that gasoline can become contaminated with dirt and water at any point along the distribution route from refinery to fuel tank. Carburetors are able to handle small amounts of water and dirt, but fuel injection systems are much more likely to be affected by impurities.

Note: Engine performance is directly related to the quality of the gasoline consumed. Therefore, it is important to be sure the fuel within the motorcycle, scooter, or ATV being serviced has not deteriorated. Valuable troubleshooting time may be saved by replacing fuel if its quality is in doubt. Detonation (or pinging) on acceleration is an indication that the fuel is either not of good quality or is too low in octane rating for the application. Fuel more than six to eight weeks old can cause minor performance problem, and fuel more than three months old may cause serious performance problems.

Carburetors

This section of the chapter explains carburetor operating and service principles. It is important for you to understand carburetors when studying tune-up, engine repair, and various other topics.

Fuel Atomization and Combustion

For efficient combustion to occur, gasoline must be mixed with air. In an open container of gasoline, the top surface is exposed to air. If ignited, the gasoline on top would burn, but very slowly since it is partially exposed to air. If an equal amount of fuel was sprayed into the air and ignited, it would burn much more violently and rapidly, since more of the gasoline is exposed to and mixed with air.

The function of the carburetor is to provide a finely ***atomized*** mixture of air and fuel to the engine. Engine efficiency is closely related to proper fuel metering and atomization. Some carburetors atomize fuel better than others because of design differences.

In an engine cylinder, the finely atomized air-fuel mixture is compressed to provide even more violent combustion. Combustion is not an uncontrolled explosion, but a very rapid, controlled burn of the air-fuel mixture. The heat causes expansion and pressure in the combustion chamber, which pushes the piston down with tremendous force. When the piston is forced down by combustion, the crankshaft spins, producing useful energy.

Air-Fuel Ratio

Fuel atomization is not the only factor affecting engine performance and economy. The amount or proportion of air and fuel taken into the engine, termed ***air-fuel ratio,*** also affects performance and economy.

An air-fuel ratio of 15:1 (15 parts air, 1 part fuel) is considered acceptable. However, at different engine speeds and loads, the carburetor must vary this ratio. As more fuel is mixed with air, the air-fuel ratio becomes rich. As less fuel is mixed with the air, the air-fuel ratio becomes lean. The air-fuel ratio may be as rich as 3:1 for cold starting and as lean as 17:1 for cruising speeds.

Venturi Principle

Carburetors rely on the ***venturi principle*** to draw fuel into the airstream. Look at **Figure 7-10.** A ***venturi*** is a restriction in the carburetor throat that causes an increase in velocity and a decrease in pressure (vacuum increase) as air passes through. Many carburetors have venturi that cannot be altered and are called ***fixed venturi carburetors.*** Carburetors that can alter the venturi diameter by throttle valve movement are known as ***variable venturi carburetors.***

A carburetor relies on this pressure difference to draw fuel into the airstream. **Figure 7-11** shows a simple carburetor using the venturi principle. Atmospheric pressure is greater than venturi pressure, causing fuel to be drawn into the airstream. The fuel is atomized into a fine mist as it enters the airstream.

Positive Carburetor Linkages

Positive carburetor linkages are used to operate throttles and chokes on some motorcycles. The purpose of a positive linkage is to open and close one or more throttles or chokes. Positive carburetor linkages use two cables. One cable pulls the throttle open and the other pulls it closed. The throttle cables are connected to opposite sides of a bell crank attached to a shaft. The shaft is connected to throttle slides or butterflies by arms and connecting links. When the bell crank is turned by the throttle cable, the shaft, arms, linkage, and slides or butterflies are moved in unison. **Figure 7-12** and **7-13** show positive carburetor linkages.

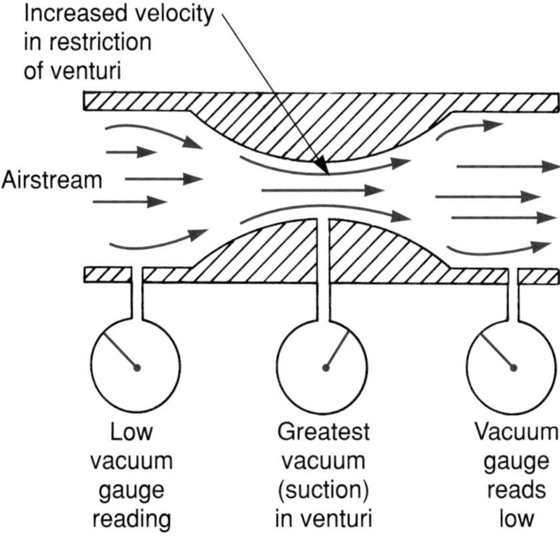

Figure 7-10. As air passes through the venturi, air speeds up, causing a vacuum (suction).

Common Carburetor Types

Modern motorcycle, ATV, and scooter engines commonly use one of three types of carburetors:

- Slide carburetors.
- Vacuum carburetors.
- Butterfly carburetors.

The major difference in these carburetor designs is in the venturi restriction. Slide and vacuum carburetors are considered variable venturi carburetors. The butterfly carburetor normally has a fixed venturi. There are other carburetor designs, but these three are used as original equipment. Each of these carburetor types can be found on four-stroke motorcycles and ATVs. Most two-stroke engines use slide carburetors.

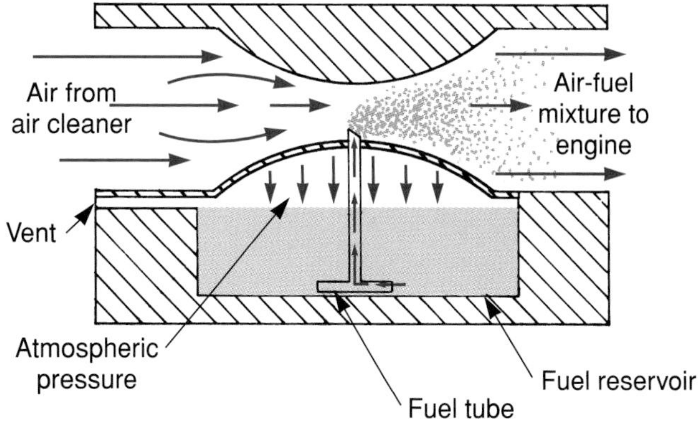

Figure 7-11. Atmospheric pressure pushes down on fuel in fuel reservoir. When vacuum is produced by venturi airflow, fuel is pushed through fuel tube and into airstream.

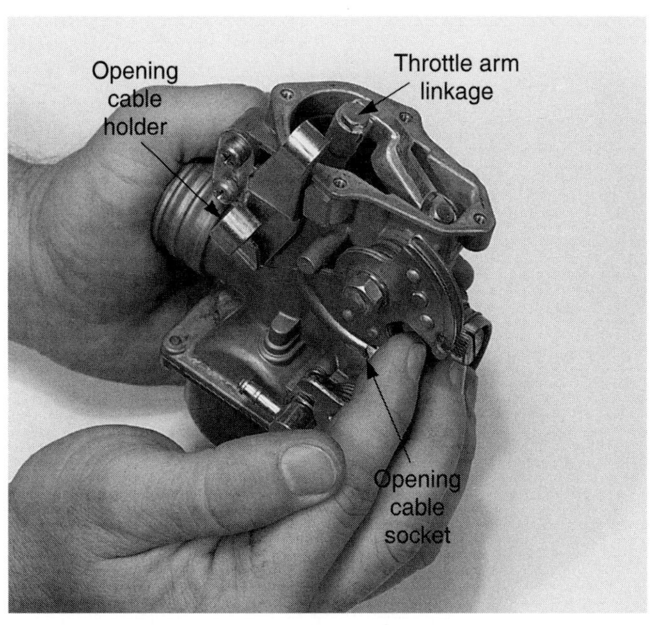

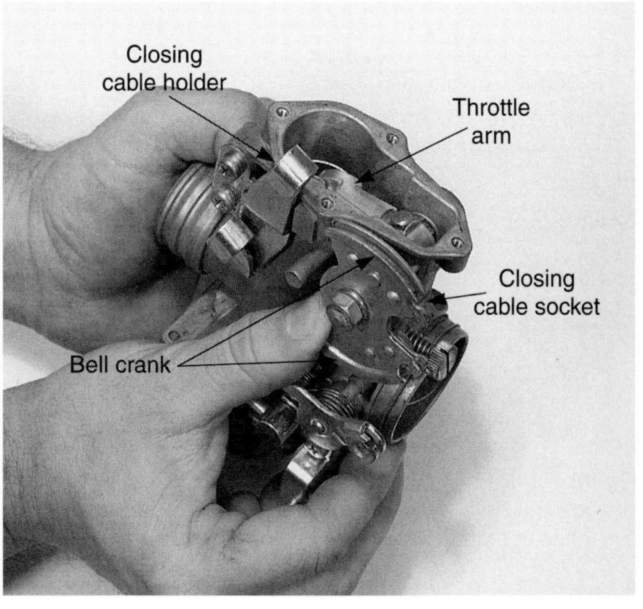

Figure 7-12. This single carburetor uses a positive throttle linkage. A—Throttle is open. B—Throttle is closed.

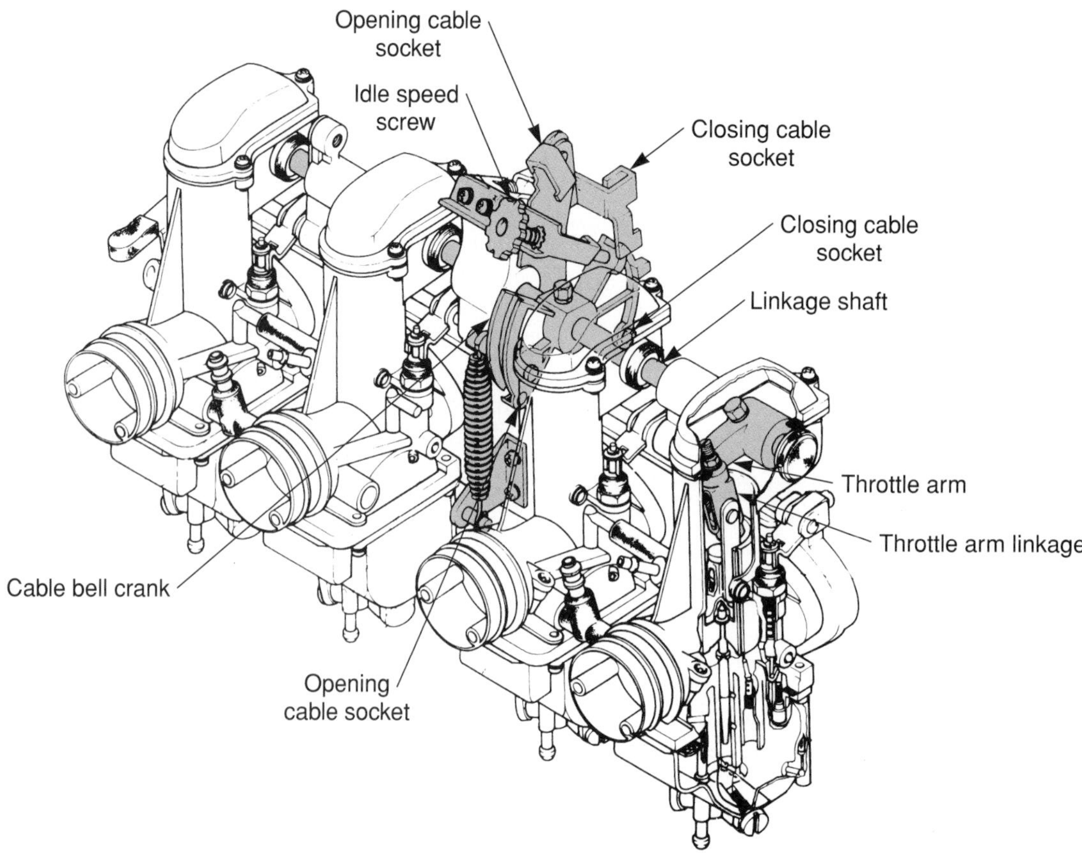

Figure 7-13. Positive carburetor linkages use one cable to open throttles and another to close them. (Kawasaki Motors Corporation U.S.A.)

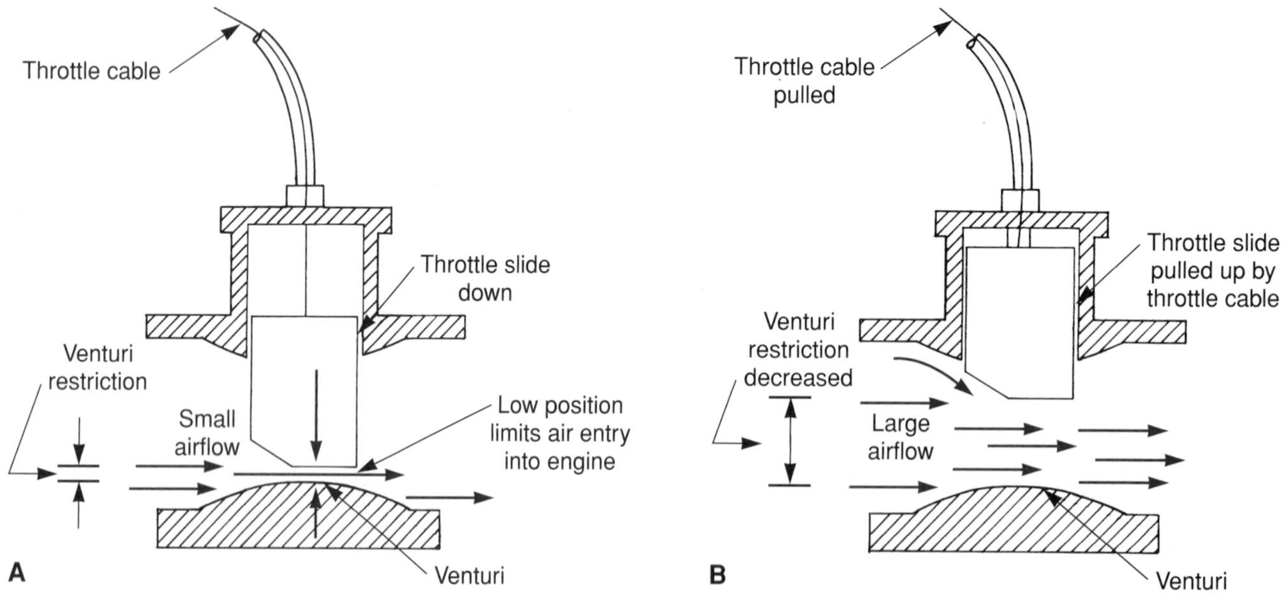

Figure 7-14. As the throttle slide is raised or lowered, the size of the venturi restriction is changed. A—The throttle slide is in a very low position, allowing a small amount of air to pass through the venturi. B—The slide is raised and causes much less restriction in the venturi. This allows more air to flow for added power.

Slide Carburetors

The ***slide carburetor*** uses a round slide piston to alter the venturi restriction. **Figure 7-14** shows how the slide changes venturi size. The slide is connected to the twist grip by the throttle cable. To provide the proper air-fuel mixture at all throttle openings, several fuel metering systems, also called *circuits,* are used. These include:

- Float circuit.
- Pilot circuit.
- Slide cutaway system.
- Needle circuit.
- Main fuel circuit.
- Slow circuit.
- Accelerator pump circuit.
- Starter circuit.

The fuel supply system varies with the degree of throttle opening and regulates fuel accordingly.

Float Circuit

The ***float circuit*** maintains a constant level of fuel in the float bowl. This extra supply of fuel is needed for each metering circuit. The float system is made up of:

- Float needle and seat or float valve to control fuel entry.
- Float bowl which stores fuel.
- Float assembly that operates the needle valve.
- Float pivot pin to allow float to swing up or down.
- Overflow tube that routes excess fuel from the bowl.
- Float bowl vent that releases pressure and vacuum.
- Float primer button to feed fuel for easy starting.

Figure 7-15 shows a typical float system. When the fuel petcock is turned on, the fuel flows past the opened ***needle*** and ***seat.*** Fuel pours into the ***float bowl,*** **Figure 7-16A.** As the fuel level rises in the float bowl, the float assembly pushes the needle against the seat which stops fuel flow into the bowl. See **Figure 7-16B.**

As fuel is used, the level in the bowl drops, causing the float to drop. This opens the needle and seat. This float assembly action keeps a constant level of fuel in the float bowl. An ***overflow tube*** is provided to prevent engine flooding in the event the float needle does not seat properly or sticks open.

The ***float bowl vent*** is needed to prevent a build-up of vacuum or pressure in the carburetor bowl. Vacuum build-up could keep the fuel from entering the airstream. A pressure build-up will keep fuel from flowing into the bowl.

Pilot Circuit

The ***pilot circuit*** or *idle circuit* meters air and fuel at and slightly above idle. It operates from idle to approximately one-eighth throttle opening. The pilot system consists of a jet, adjustment screw, and air and fuel passageways in the carburetor body.

The purpose of the ***pilot jet*** is to meter the proper amount of fuel to a chamber where it is mixed with air.

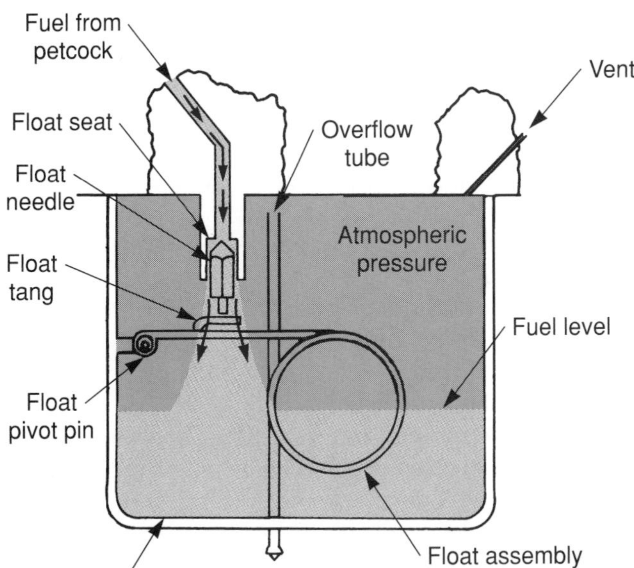

Figure 7-15. Although the float system is simple, it performs an important function by controlling the fuel level in the carburetor.

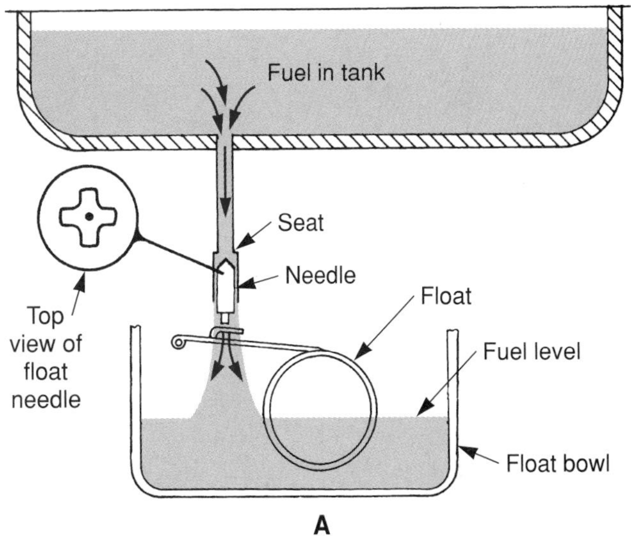

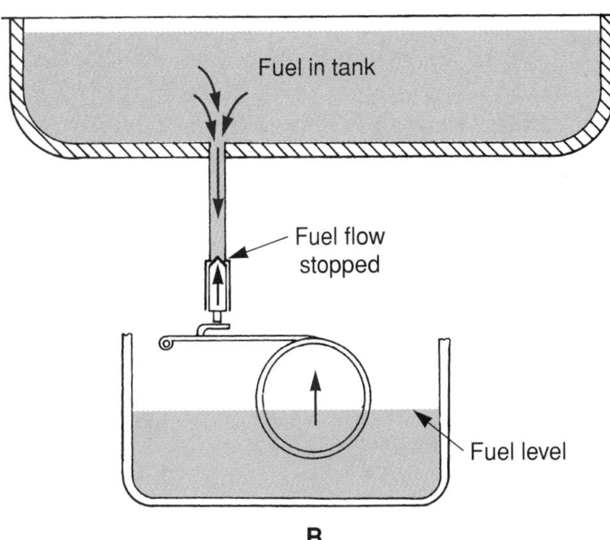

Figure 7-16. A—When the fuel level in the float bowl is low, the float is lowered. This allows the float needle to drop away from its seat and fuel refills the bowl. B—As the fuel level rises, the float rises, pushing the float needle against its seat and stopping fuel flow from the tank.

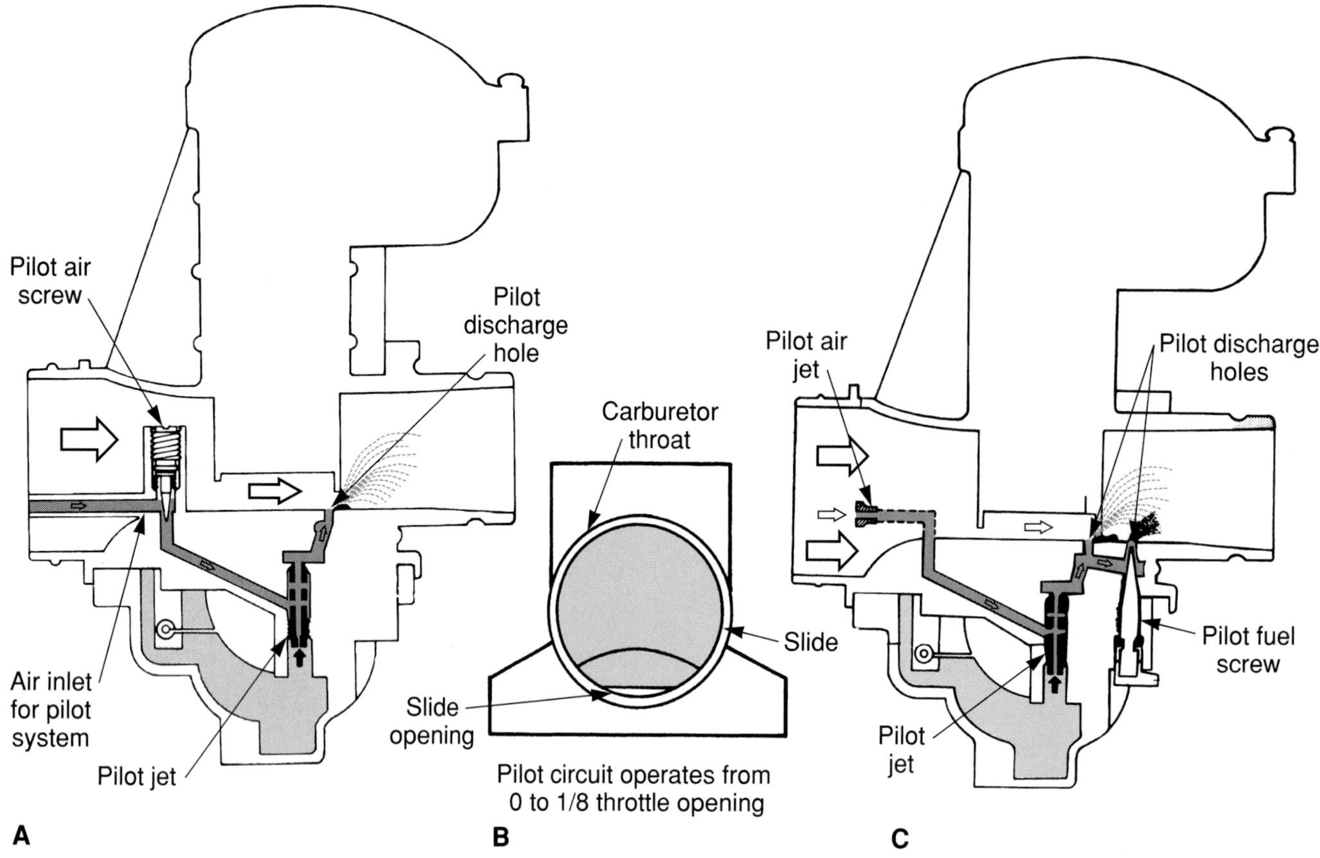

Figure 7-17. A—In air screw pilot systems, fuel is metered by pilot jet. Fine adjustment of the air-fuel ratio is done with the pilot air screw. Pilot air screw controls the amount of air mixed with fuel. B—Slide opening. C—In fuel screw pilot systems, fuel is metered by pilot jet while air is metered by pilot air jet. Pilot fuel screw adjusts the amount of air-fuel mixture discharged into the airstream in the carburetor's throat. (Kawasaki Motors Corporation U.S.A.)

The ***pilot adjustment screw*** controls the amount of air or fuel introduced, or bled, into the chamber. Once the air and fuel are mixed, the solution is fed to the carburetor throat through one or two discharge holes located in the venturi. **Figure 7-17** shows the two types of pilot circuits.

Slide Cutaway System (Off-Idle Circuit)

The ***slide cutaway system,*** also called the *off-idle circuit,* determines the air-fuel mixture from one-eighth to one-quarter throttle. The fuel for this circuit comes from the pilot and needle circuits. The air-fuel mixture is controlled by the cutaway on the throttle slide.

The front half (air cleaner side) of the slide bottom is cut at an angle. The height of this cutaway portion determines the amount of air that is mixed with fuel in the circuit. **Figure 7-18** shows the slide cutaway system in operation.

Needle Circuit

The ***needle circuit,*** also referred to as the *midrange circuit,* controls the air-fuel mixture from one-quarter to three-quarter throttle opening. The two types of needle systems are the primary and bleeder. The ***primary needle system*** consists of:

- Jet to surround and work with the needle.
- Needle to regulate fuel flow by enlarging or reducing the opening in the jet.
- Diffuser to premix air and fuel.
- Air jet to regulate airflow into the diffuser.

The amount of fuel flowing through this circuit is determined by the clearance between the jet and the needle. The needle is tapered, allowing greater clearance at larger throttle openings, **Figure 7-19.** As the needle is lifted out of its jet, fuel flow is increased. The amount of airflow is simply controlled by the throttle slide position.

Primary needle system operation is shown in **Figure 7-20.** The air jet provides for premixing in the diffuser before the air and fuel reaches the carburetor throat outlet. This permits better atomization.

The ***bleeder needle circuit*** uses the same components as the primary needle circuit. The differences between the two circuits is the primary needle circuit only meters fuel, not air. The bleeder needle circuit meters an air-fuel mixture or froth.

Since air and fuel are premixed in the jet rather than the diffuser, the bleeder needle circuit can provide better fuel atomization. See **Figure 7-21.** This is accomplished

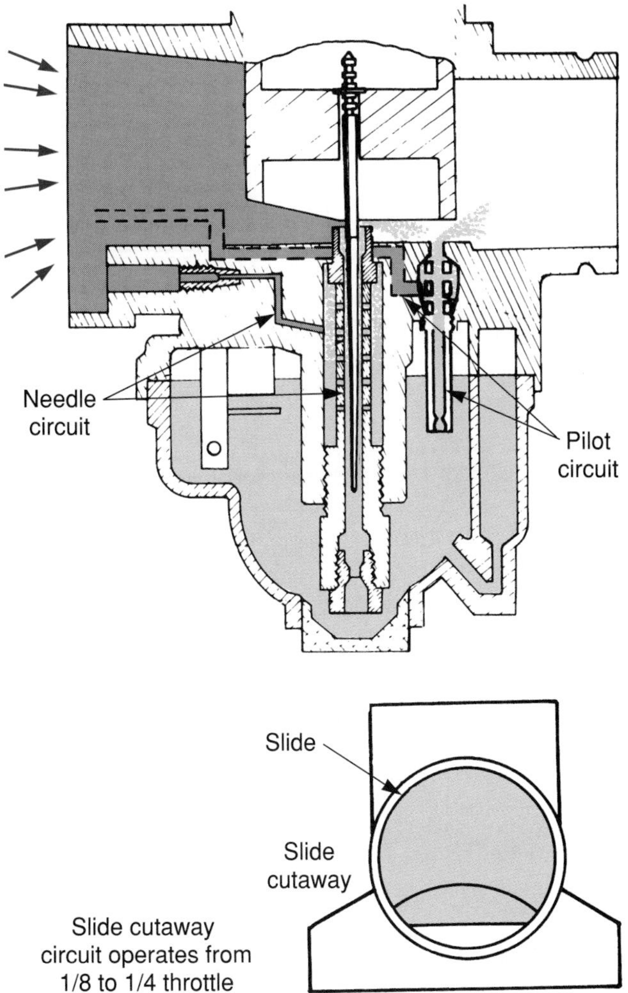

Figure 7-18. A higher slide cutaway allows more air to pass, giving a leaner air-fuel ratio. A lower cutaway allows less air to pass, giving a richer air-fuel ratio. Fuel for the slide cutaway system is drawn from the pilot and needle systems. (Kawasaki Motors Corporation U.S.A.)

by directing air into the body of the needle jet. Air and fuel are premixed before being metered by the needle.

Fuel passes through the main jet before it is metered by the needle circuit. However, since the main jet will allow more fuel to pass than the needle circuit can use, the main jet does not affect needle circuit operation.

Main Fuel Circuit

The ***main fuel circuit,*** also called the *high speed circuit,* controls the air-fuel mixture from three-quarter to wide open throttle. This circuit uses a single main jet to meter fuel flow, **Figure 7-22.** Fuel for the main circuit is metered by the main jet. Fuel then passes through the diffuser to reach the venturi. Even though fuel passes through the needle circuit, it does not alter the operation of the main circuit. Because clearance between the needle and jet at this throttle opening allows more fuel to pass than the main jet can supply, the main jet alone controls fuel metering. The air jet provides premixing of air

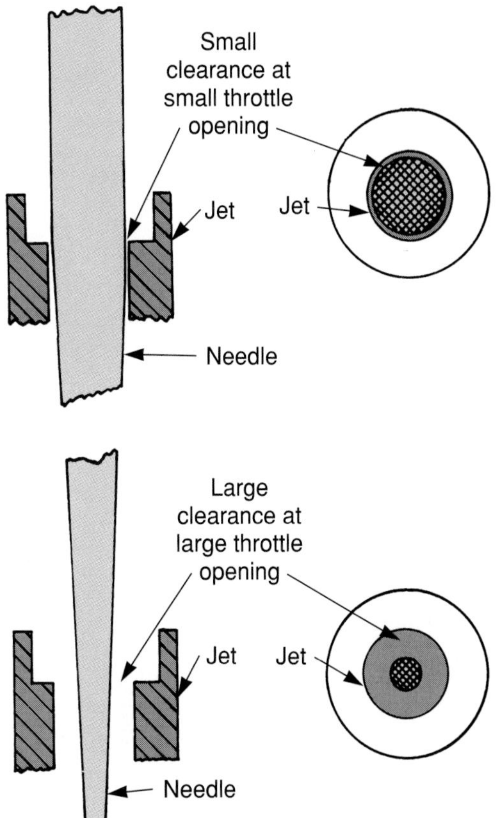

Figure 7-19. As the throttle is opened, the tapered jet needle is lifted, creating more clearance between the needle and jet. This allows more fuel to flow into the engine.

and fuel in the diffuser for the main and needle circuits. Although operation of the four fuel metering circuits (pilot, slide cutaway, needle, main) is controlled by throttle opening, there is some overlap between each circuit.

Accelerator Pump Circuit

Some carburetors are equipped with an accelerator pump. The ***accelerator pump circuit*** discharges a metered amount of fuel into the carburetor throat as the throttle is opened. When the throttle is opened suddenly, vacuum drops in the venturi, causing a momentary reduction of fuel flow through the needle and main jets, resulting in fuel starvation. This lean condition could cause the engine to hesitate or stumble momentarily.

The purpose of the accelerator pump is to prevent any hesitation by providing extra fuel during sudden throttle opening. **Figure 7-23A** shows a typical accelerator pump circuit. As the throttle valve is opened, the pump's diaphragm is depressed by the push rod, **Figure 7-23B.** When the inlet check valve is shut, the fuel pressure in the pump chamber increases. The outlet check valve opens and fuel is supplied to the main bore via the pump hole. As the throttle valve is closed, the accelerator pump's diaphragm is returned by spring action, **Figure 7-23C.** The inlet check valve is opened and fuel from the float chamber enters the pump chamber. The outlet check valve

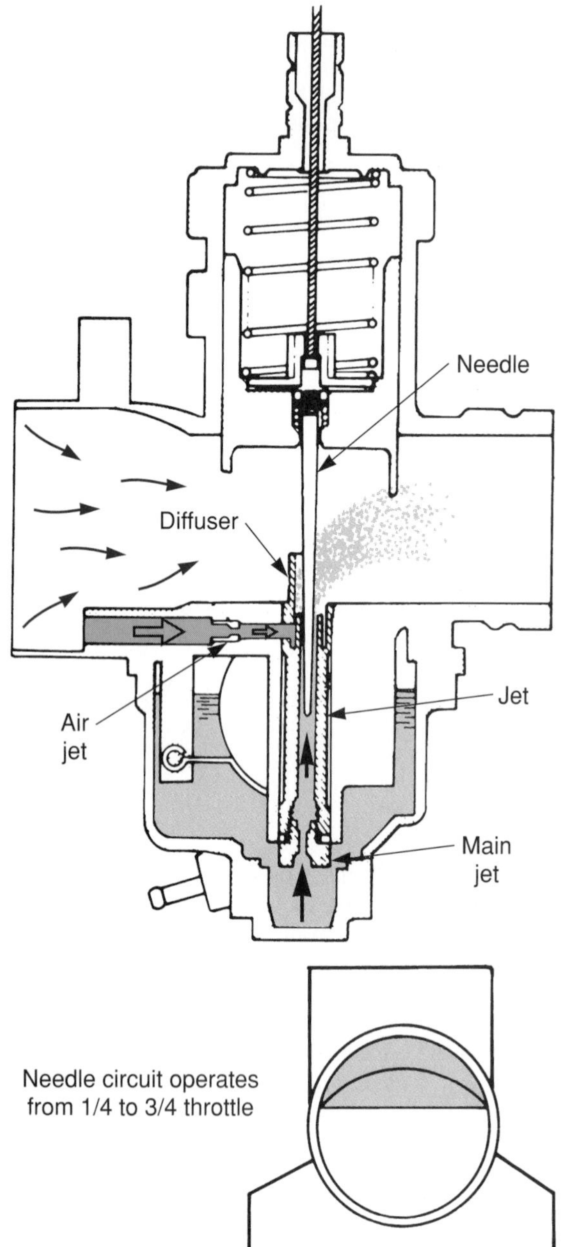

Figure 7-20. Venturi vacuum draws fuel for the needle circuit through the main jet and into the needle jet. Clearance between the jet and needle meters fuel flow into the venturi. Air jet mixes some air with fuel in the diffuser before reaching the venturi. This assists in fuel atomization and combustion. (Kawasaki Motors Corporation U.S.A.)

is closed at this point to prevent air from passing through the pump hole.

Air Cut-Off Valve

When the throttle lever is turned in the close direction and engine braking is applied, the fuel mixture becomes lean. An ignited air-fuel mixture is discharged into the exhaust pipe, resulting in a condition called *afterburn.* To prevent afterburn, the ***air cut-off valve*** shuts off airflow to the slow jet to temporarily enrich the air-fuel mixture, **Figure 7-24.**

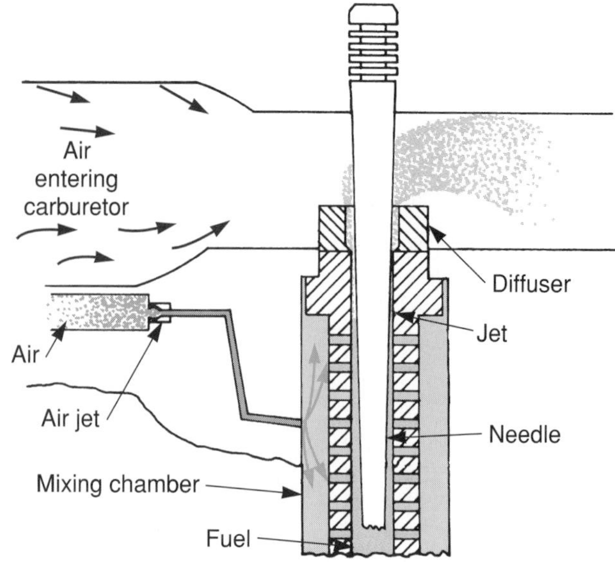

Figure 7-21. In bleeder needle circuit, perforations in the needle jet walls allow fuel to mix with air from the air jet. The resulting air-fuel mixture is then metered by needle and jet.

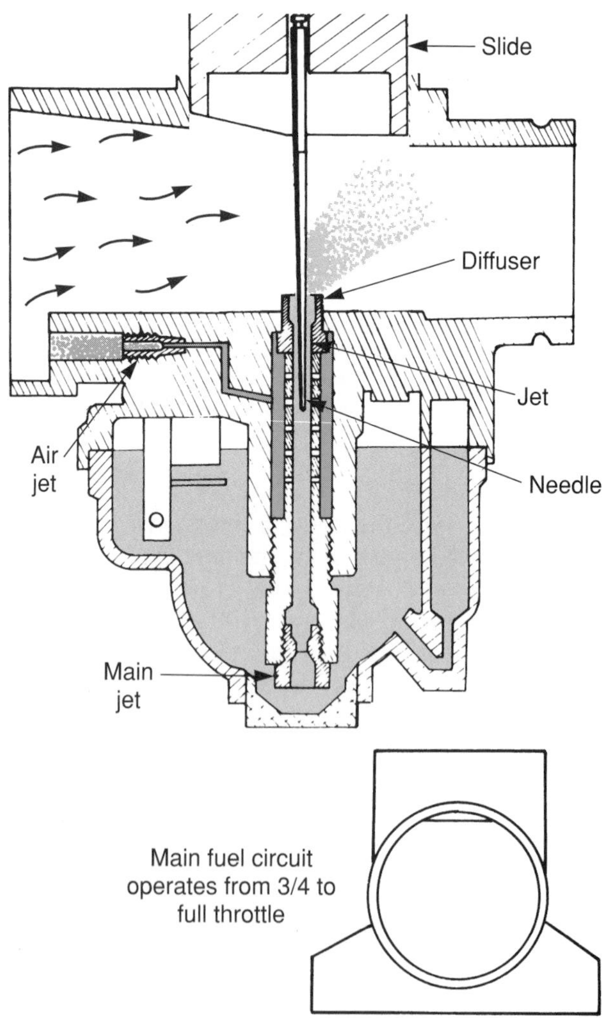

Figure 7-22. Main jet controls the air-fuel ratio in the main fuel circuit. Size of the jet meters maximum fuel flow. The main jet meters fuel only. (Kawasaki Motors Corporation U.S.A.)

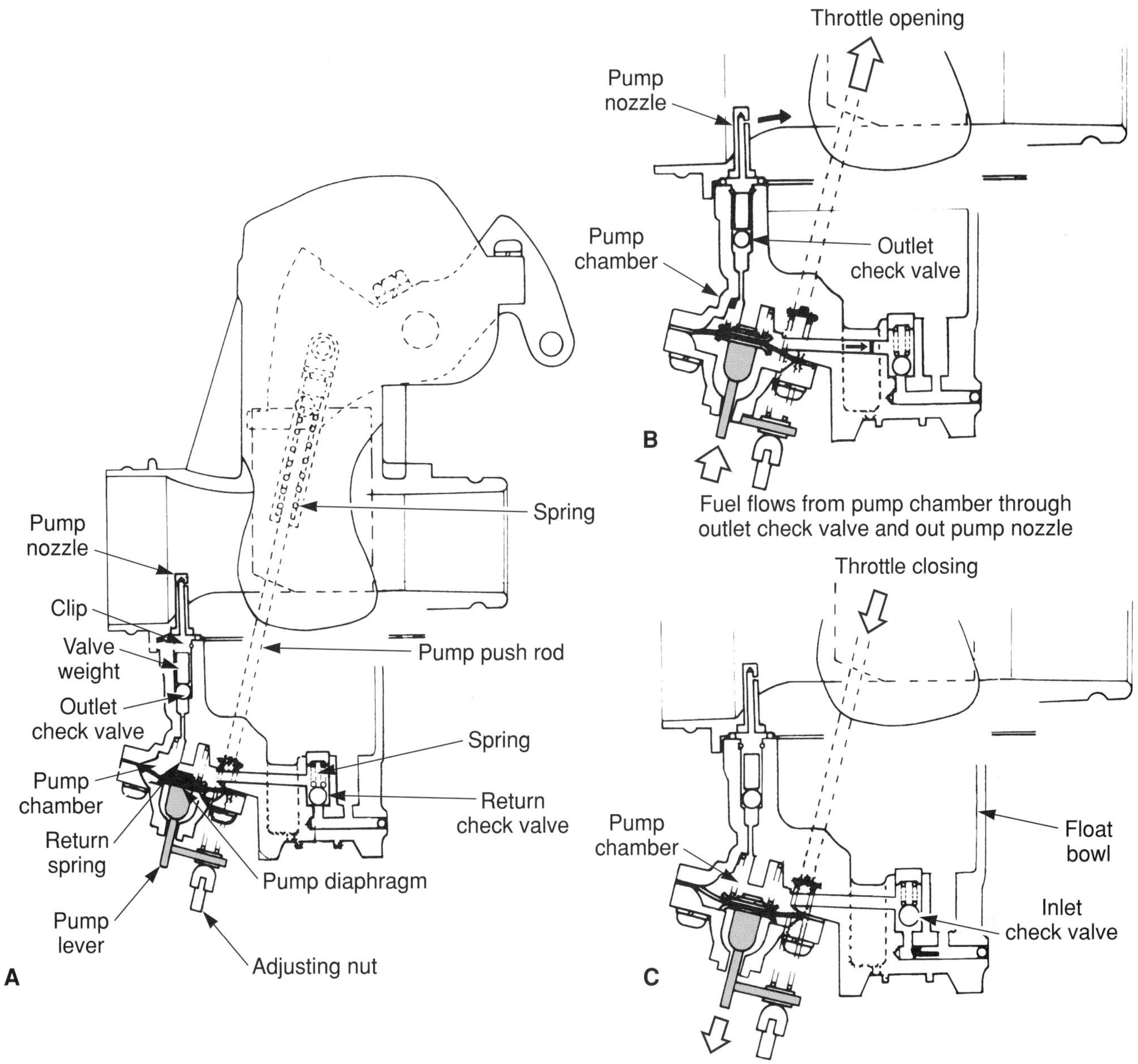

Figure 7-23. In this accelerator pump system, throttle opening lifts the pump push rod, raising the pump diaphragm in its chamber. This forces fuel in the pump chamber past the outlet check valve and out the pump nozzle. As the throttle is closed, the diaphragm lowers, drawing more fuel into the pump chamber. (Kawasaki Motors Corporation U.S.A.)

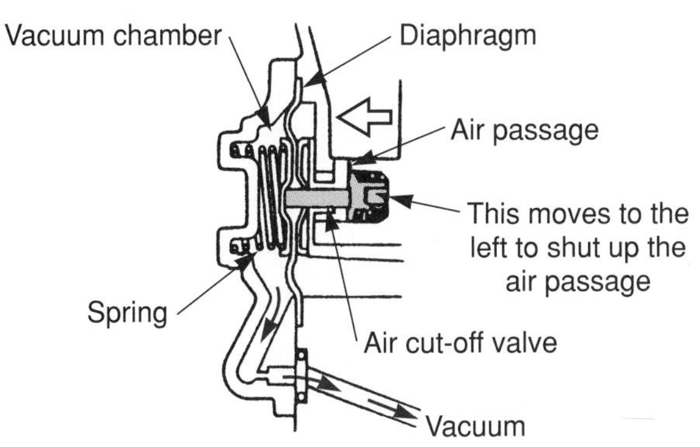

Figure 7-24. Operation of an air cut-off valve. (Honda Motor Co., Ltd.)

With the throttle valve or pump lever closed, and vacuum in the main bore increased, the air cut-off valve moves the diaphragm to shut the air passage. With the vacuum in the main bore decreased, the spring moves the diaphragm backward and opens the air passage.

Starter Circuit

The ***starter circuit*** provides an enriched mixture for cold engine operation. There are three methods used to provide a rich air-fuel mixture for cold start-up:

- Choke system.
- Tickler (primer) system.
- Enrichment system.

Choke System

The ***choke system*** restricts the amount of air entering the carburetor. Shown in **Figure 7-25,** it is a butterfly valve fitted in front of the venturi. A closed choke increases venturi vacuum and causes more fuel to flow into the engine. At the same time, less air is allowed to enter the carburetor throat. This provides an extremely rich air-fuel mixture for cold start-up.

Tickler System

The ***tickler system*** provides a rich mixture by temporarily raising the float level. This is accomplished by depressing a spring-loaded rod, which contacts the top of the float assembly. Because less vacuum is required to draw fuel into the venturi, it creates a rich air-fuel mixture. **Figure 7-26** shows the operation of the tickler system.

Enrichment System

The ***enrichment system*** is an air-fuel metering circuit separate from other carburetor circuits. Fuel for this circuit is drawn from the float bowl through an enrichment or starter jet. **Figure 7-27** shows the enrichment circuit air and fuel passageways. Air for the enrichment circuit is drawn into a drill-way at the mouth of the carburetor. This drill-way bypasses the carburetor throat and venturi.

The enrichment circuit or ***bystarter system*** as it is sometimes called, is controlled manually by cable or linkage that operates a plunger. When the plunger is down, the enrichment circuit is blocked and does not operate. Air and fuel cannot flow through the circuit, **Figure 7-28A,** and a normal air-fuel mixture is maintained.

When the plunger is raised, a rich air-fuel mixture is discharged from the enrichment port. This port is located directly behind the throttle slide, **Figure 7-28B.** An enrichment circuit works best with the carburetor slide closed (at idle). High vacuum behind the closed slide can then easily draw extra air and fuel throughout the enrichment circuit.

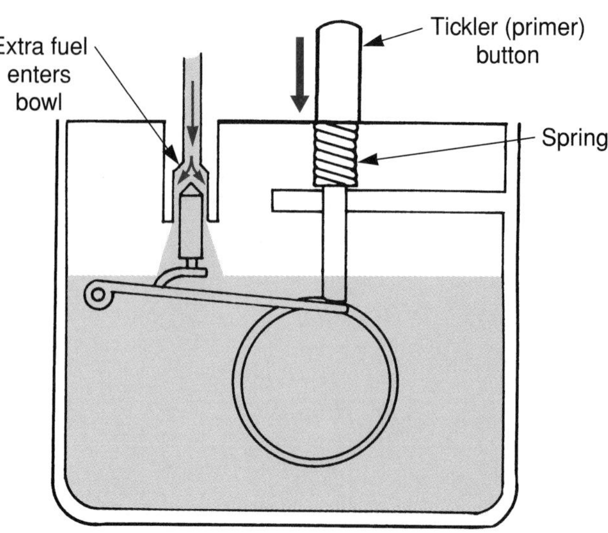

Figure 7-26. In the tickler system, the tickler button is pushed down, lowering the float and allowing extra fuel to flow into the bowl. This temporarily raises the fuel level. A rich air-fuel ratio results since less vacuum is required to pull fuel into the venturi.

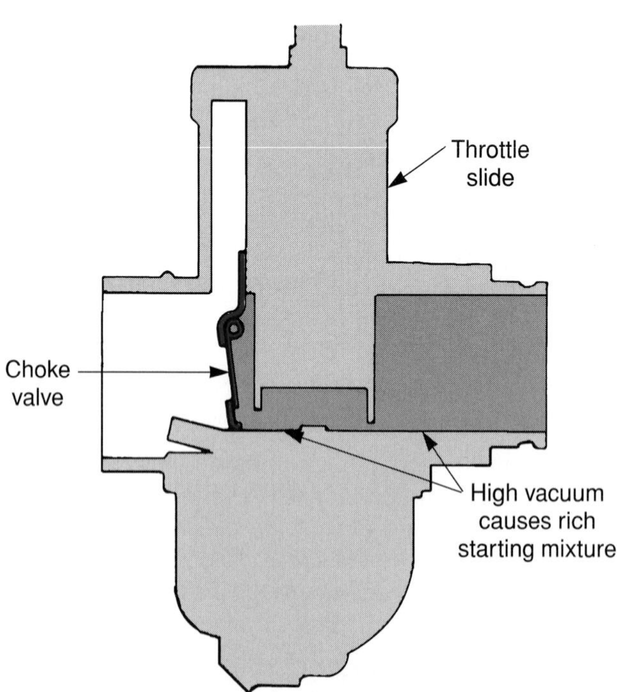

Figure 7-25. Choke plate is lowered into the carburetor throat for cold starting. A spring-loaded relief valve allows a small amount of air into the venturi. Blocking airflow in this manner increases venturi vacuum. Once the engine is started, the choke must be opened to prevent flooding. (Kawasaki Motors Corporation U.S.A.)

PTC Systems

The auto-enrichment or bystarter circuit has a ***PTC device*** in the system for increasing the fuel volume. It is comprised of a heating element, thermo-wax, a liquid medium, piston, and bystarter valve, **Figure 7-29.**

When the engine is stopped and there is no production of current from the alternator, the starter valve is maintained in the raised position by a spring. In this position, the fuel increase circuit is fully open. When the engine starts, fuel is supplied through the increase circuit. At the same time, the alternator sends current to the PTC for heating. The increase in heat causes the thermowax to expand. This movement is transmitted through the liquid medium to the piston, set collar, and set spring, depressing the starter valve. As the valve is lowered, the needle starts to shut off the fuel increase circuit. After a few minutes, the circuit closes fully, ending fuel compensation.

Vacuum Controlled Carburetor

Engine vacuum changes with throttle position and engine load. As the throttle is opened, vacuum decreases. When the throttle is closed, vacuum increases. Vacuum also changes as engine load changes. More load decreases

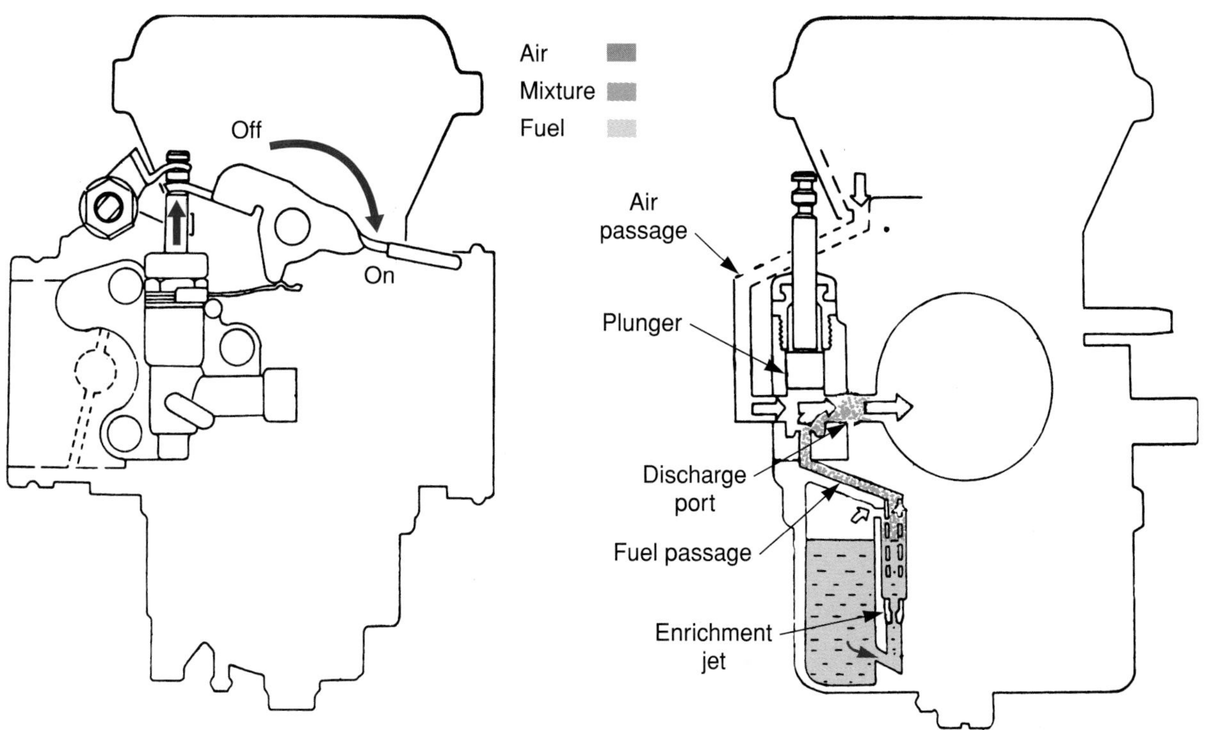

Figure 7-27. The enrichment circuit acts as a separate carburetor within a carburetor, but is only used for cold start and warm-up. When the lever is pushed down, a rich air-fuel mixture enters the engine. The plunger is lifted out of the passage so extra fuel can enter the bore. (Yamaha Motor Corporation U.S.A.)

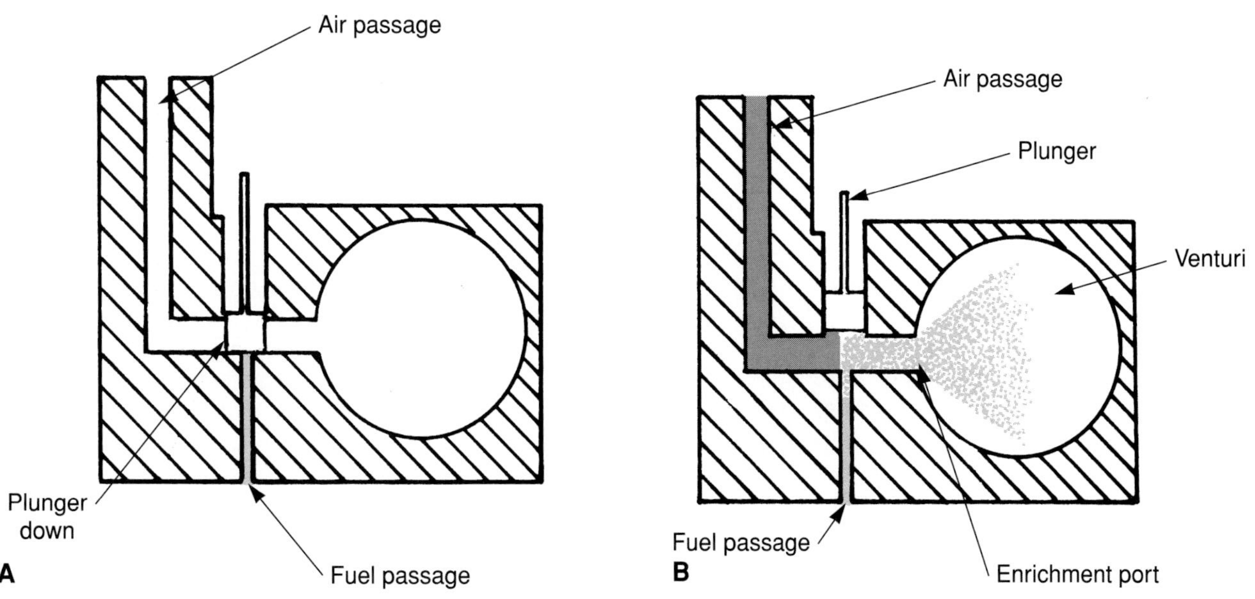

Figure 7-28. A—When the plunger is down, the air and fuel passages are blocked. Extra air and fuel does not enter the carburetor barrel. B—When the plunger is up, high vacuum behind the throttle slide pulls air and fuel through the passages and out the enrichment port.

vacuum and less load increases vacuum. For instance, as you begin to climb a hill, intake manifold vacuum will decrease (more load, less vacuum). As you crest the top of the hill and begin to go down the other side, there is less load on the engine, increasing vacuum.

If the throttle is snapped open, the air velocity in the venturi decreases. This reduces vacuum in the venturi and the engine becomes fuel-starved. As a result, the engine will hesitate or possibly stall because of an over-lean mixture. The vacuum controlled carburetor eliminates this problem.

A ***vacuum carburetor,*** also called a *CV* or *constant velocity* or *venturi carburetor,* uses both a slide valve and butterfly valve to control airflow through the venturi.

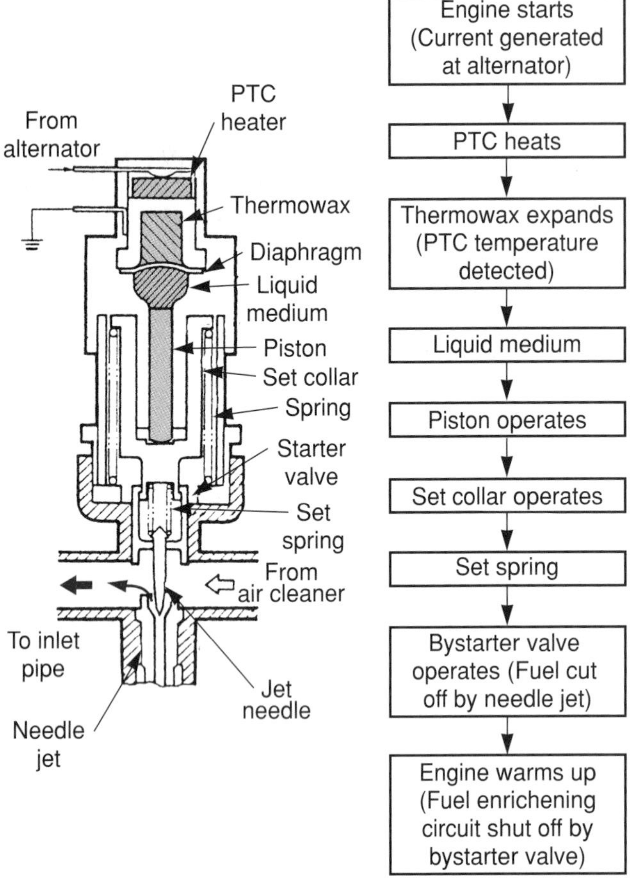

Figure 7-29. Operation of an auto-enrichment or bystarter circuit. (Honda Motor Co., Ltd.)

Intake manifold vacuum, produced by the engine, operates the carburetor. Movement of the twist grip changes butterfly position. The slide is not connected to the throttle cable, but is controlled by changes in vacuum. Vacuum acting on a piston or diaphragm causes the slide to raise or lower.

The fuel metering circuits are similar to those of the slide carburetor. The major differences are:

- The vacuum carburetor uses a butterfly throttle valve.
- Air flow through the venturi is controlled by a vacuum operated slide piston.
- The pilot adjustment screw controls fuel rather than air.
- A pilot bypass circuit controls off-idle air-fuel mixture.
- A primary and secondary main fuel circuit is used on some vacuum carburetors.

Butterfly Throttle

A vacuum carburetor uses a conventional butterfly throttle plate. This alone, however, does not control engine speed. The butterfly plate is the primary means of controlling air flow through the carburetor.

Vacuum Piston

The ***vacuum piston*** controls venturi restriction. Its position is determined by venturi vacuum. Venturi vacuum

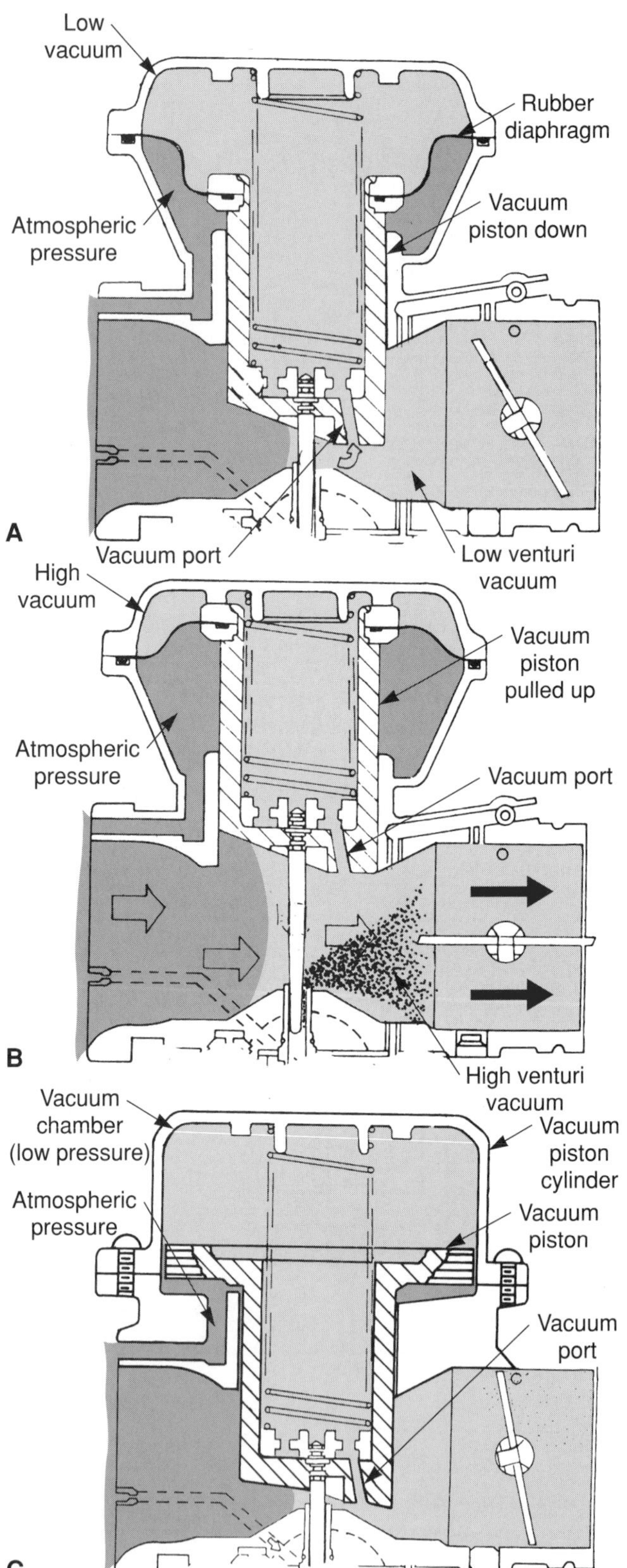

Figure 7-30. Diaphragm and cylinder vacuum pistons. With diaphragm vacuum pistons, the lower side of the diaphragm is exposed to atmospheric pressure. A—Vacuum port at the base of the vacuum piston admits venturi vacuum into the chamber above the diaphragm. B—As venturi vacuum increases, atmospheric pressure raises the diaphragm and piston. C—In cylinder vacuum piston, the diaphragm is replaced by a vacuum cylinder and large diameter piston. (Yamaha Motor Corporation U.S.A.)

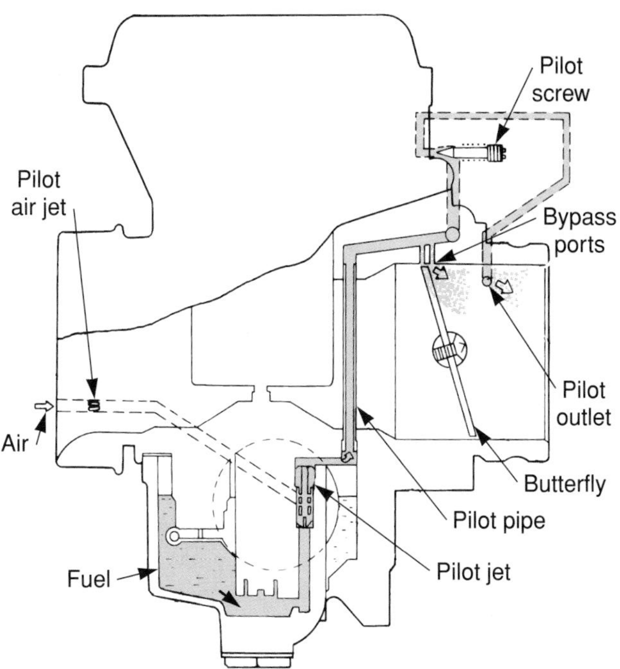

Figure 7-31. At idle, the butterfly is almost completely closed. Fuel is discharged only from the pilot outlet. As the throttle is opened, the butterfly rotates, exposing the bypass ports and allowing them to discharge fuel. Pilot and bypass ports continue to discharge fuel as the throttle is opened. (American Suzuki Motor Corporation)

causes a pressure difference between the top and bottom of the piston assembly. The vacuum piston is not mechanically connected to the butterfly. As venturi vacuum increases, the piston slides up.

There are two common types of vacuum pistons. One type uses a large diameter piston and cylinder. The other has a diaphragm attached to the top of the vacuum piston. **Figure 7-30** shows these two designs and how they operate.

Pilot Bypass Circuit

The vacuum piston in a vacuum carburetor does not use a cutaway. Instead, a ***pilot bypass circuit*** controls the off-idle air-fuel mixture. The fuel for this circuit is metered through the pilot jet and is controlled by the throttle plate position.

When the throttle plate is closed, the air-fuel mixture is controlled by the idle mixture screw (pilot adjustment screw). As the throttle is opened, the bypass port is exposed to vacuum and fuel begins to flow. This is shown in **Figure 7-31.**

On most CV carburetors, the needle and main fuel circuits function in the same manner as in the slide carburetor. However, some CV carburetors use primary and secondary main fuel circuits, **Figure 7-32.** This type of carburetor does not provide for needle adjustment (grooves at the top of the needle). During the transition from pilot bypass to needle circuit operation, air-fuel ratio is controlled by the primary main jet.

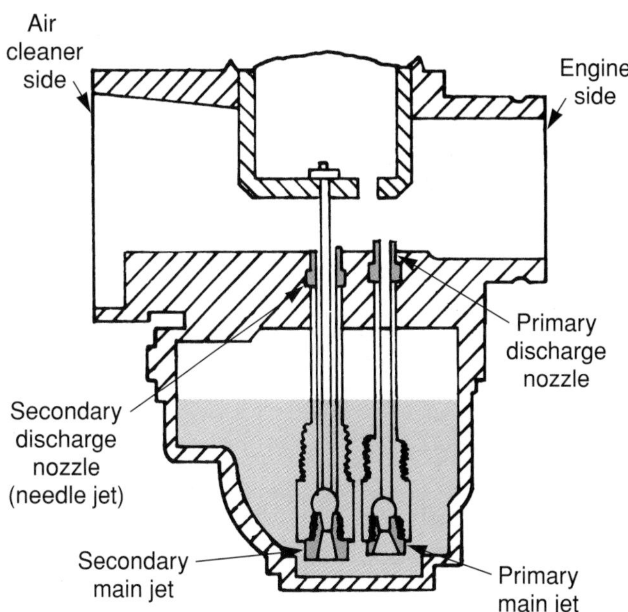

Figure 7-32. Some CV carburetors use primary and secondary main fuel circuits.

As the throttle is opened from idle, vacuum increases and fuel is drawn through the primary main jet, **Figure 7-33A.** As the throttle continues to open and vacuum increases, fuel is also drawn through the secondary circuit, **Figure 7-33B.**

Butterfly Controlled Carburetor

The ***butterfly controlled carburetor*** uses a butterfly valve (throttle plate) to control airflow through the venturi. The throttle cable is connected directly to the plate by a lever on the outside of the carburetor. **Figure 7-34** shows how the butterfly carburetor controls the airflow. When the butterfly is closed, airflow is limited, stopping venturi action. When opened, air and fuel flow increase for additional power. A butterfly carburetor is illustrated in **Figure 7-35.** A float system similar to those used in slide and CV carburetors, supplies fuel to the metering circuits. A butterfly carburetor uses three systems or circuits to meter fuel:

- Pilot circuit.
- Main circuit.
- Accelerator pump circuit.

Pilot Circuit

The purpose of the pilot circuit is to meter fuel from idle to intermediate throttle opening. Fuel from the main jet flows into the pilot jet where it is metered and mixed with air. A passageway in the carburetor transfers the air-fuel mixture to the idle and bypass discharge ports, **Figure 7-36.**

In the pilot circuit, fuel is drawn through the main jet to the pilot jet. The pilot jet meters and mixes fuel with air in the pilot bleeder tube. The resulting air-fuel mixture passes through a drilled passage in the carburetor body.

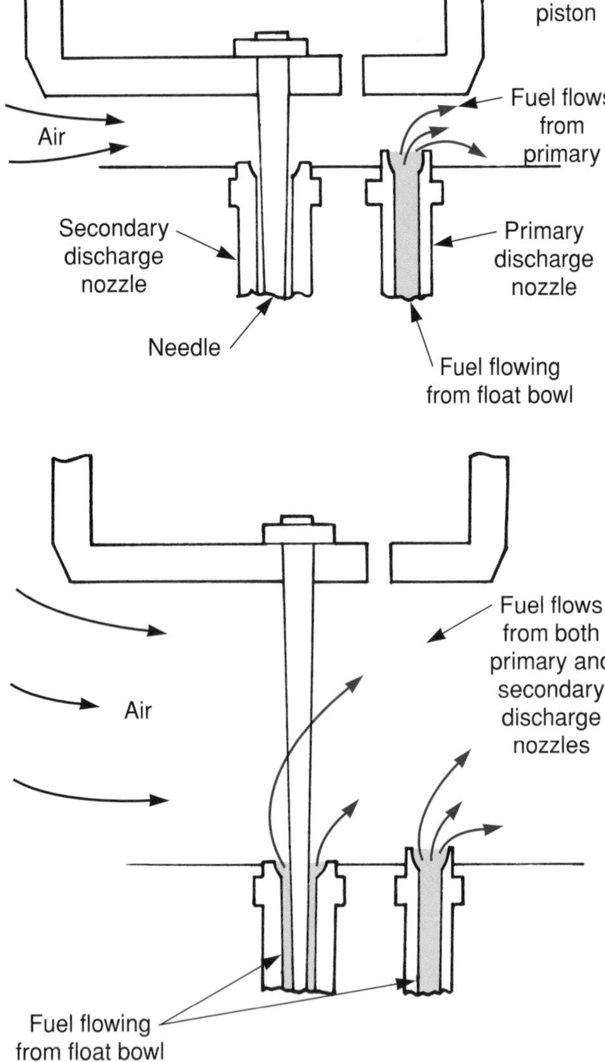

Figure 7-33. A—The higher profile of the primary discharge nozzle and its position relative to vacuum piston causes the primary circuit to be affected by manifold vacuum. It begins discharging fuel before the secondary circuit. B—As the throttle is opened farther and vacuum increases, fuel is discharged from both the primary and secondary circuits.

The fuel then enters the bypass chamber and pilot discharge port. A tapered needle (pilot mixture screw) partially blocks fuel flow through the pilot discharge port. As the pilot mixture screw is turned in or out, less or more fuel is allowed to pass into the airstream in the carburetor throat. This provides air-fuel ratio adjustment at idle.

As the throttle is opened, the bypass discharge ports are exposed to venturi vacuum and more fuel is discharged into the airstream. Pilot jet size determines the air-fuel ratio in the bypass stage.

Main Circuit

The purpose of the main circuit is to meter fuel from intermediate to full throttle. Fuel flows from the float bowl

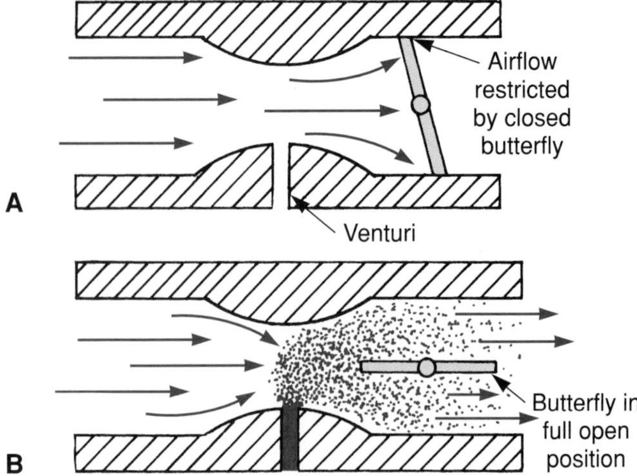

Figure 7-34. Another way to control airflow through venturi is through a butterfly throttle valve. A—Butterfly closed to restrict airflow and engine speed. B—Butterfly open to allow more air to enter the engine.

through the main jet into a bleeder tube. The bleeder tube mixes the fuel with air from the main jet.

As the throttle plate is opened, engine speed increases. Vacuum also increases in the venturi. When vacuum increases to a certain point, the air-fuel mixture begins to discharge through the main fuel nozzle, **Figure 7-37.** The air-fuel ratio for the main system is controlled by main jet size.

Accelerator Pump Circuit

The accelerator pump system provides mixture enrichment during rapid throttle opening. This compensates for sudden decreases in vacuum and resulting lean mixtures caused by quick throttle opening. This circuit does not rely on vacuum for fuel delivery. Instead, it uses a diaphragm pump connected to the butterfly to force fuel into the venturi, **Figure 7-38.** Acceleration circuit adjustment is accomplished by changing the pump's stroke. The butterfly carburetor uses a choke plate to provide high vacuum for cold start enrichment.

Carburetor Adjustment

To maintain the proper air-fuel mixture during the service life of the motorcycle, certain carburetor adjustments must be made. These common carburetor adjustments include:

- Idle mixture.
- Idle speed.
- Multicarburetor synchronization.
- Float level.
- Cable adjustment.

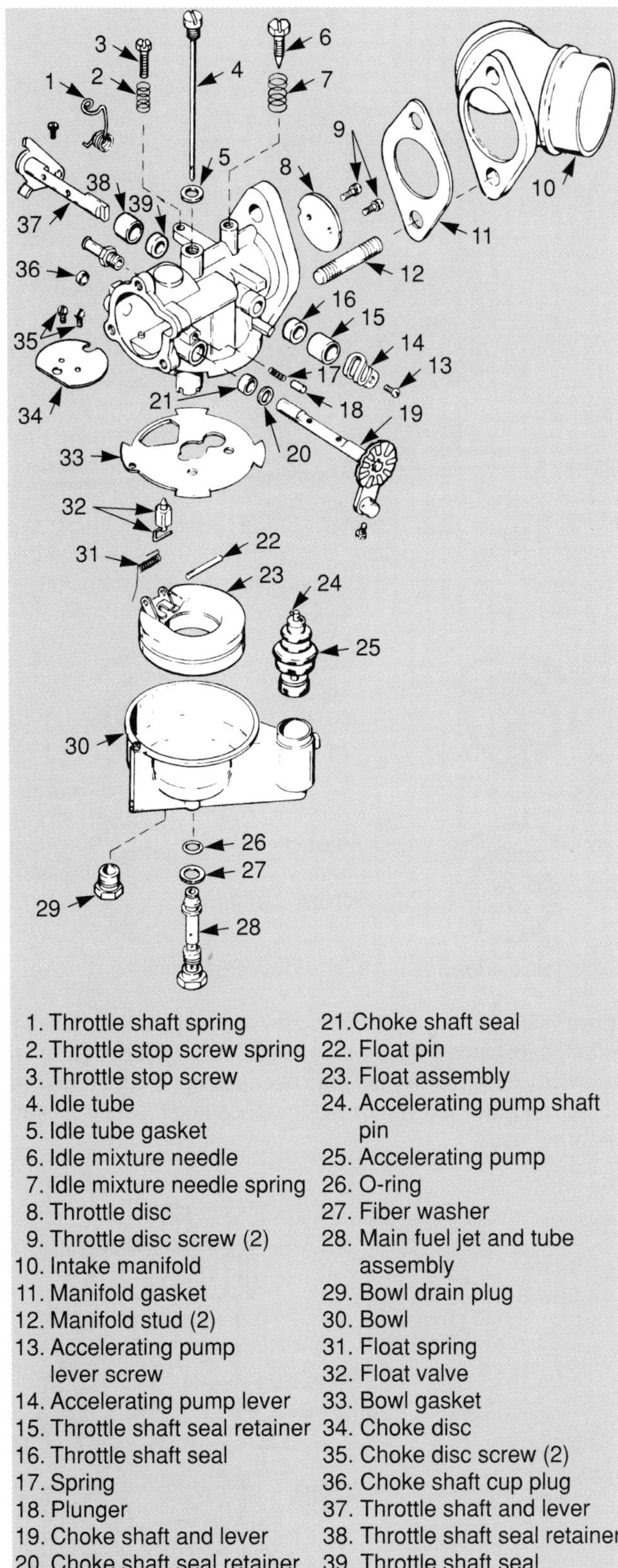

Figure 7-35. This butterfly carburetor is a compact and dependable design. (Harley-Davidson Motor Co., Inc.)

Idle Mixture

Depending on the carburetor type, ***idle mixture*** is determined by either pilot jet size or an idle mixture screw setting. Under normal conditions, it is not necessary to

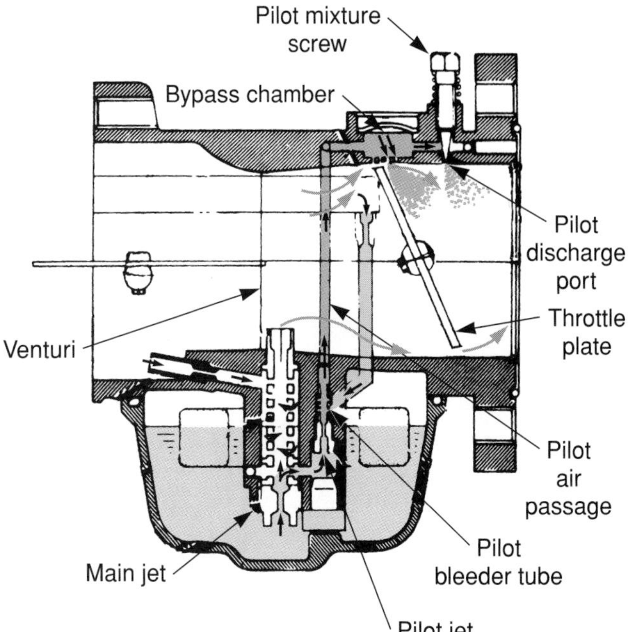

Figure 7-36. Pilot bypass consists of a small fuel chamber which is connected to the carburetor throat by a series of tiny holes. It is actually part of the pilot circuit. As the throttle plate opens from idle, successive bypass discharge holes are exposed to vacuum and more fuel flows into the carburetor throat. (Harley-Davidson Motor Co., Inc.)

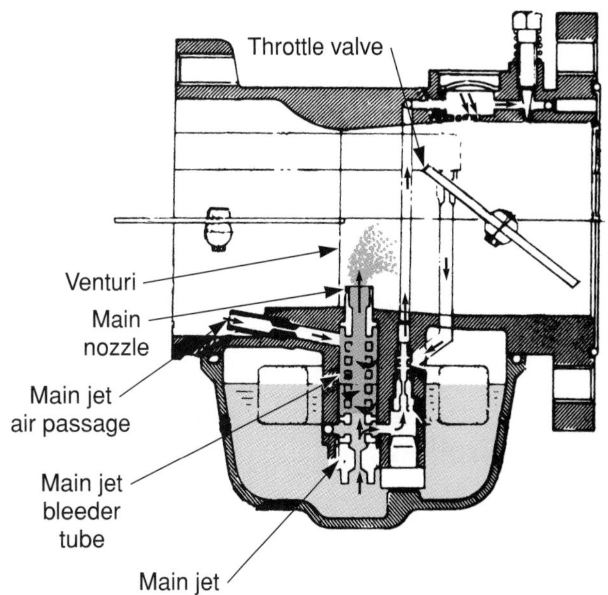

Figure 7-37. The main fuel circuit operates when vacuum in the venturi is high enough to draw fuel through the main nozzle (intermediate to full throttle). (Harley-Davidson Motor Co., Inc.)

change the pilot jet size. However, the air screw (slide carburetor) or fuel screw (CV carburetor) may require occasional adjustment to improve idle smoothness.

Normally, turning a ***pilot air screw*** clockwise (in) richens the idle mixture and turning it counter-clockwise (out) leans the idle mixture. Turning a ***pilot fuel screw*** in

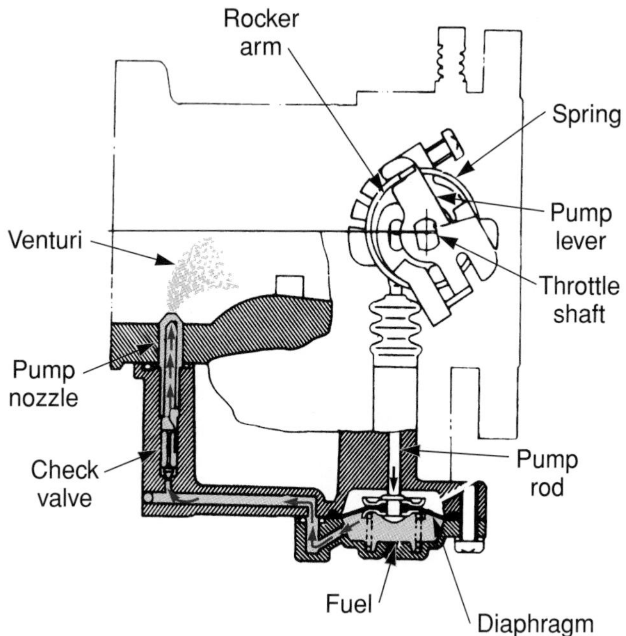

Figure 7-38. Accelerator pump supplies extra fuel to prevent a lean condition when the throttle is snapped open. A lever attached to the throttle shaft moves a diaphragm pump as the throttle is opened. The diaphragm pushes fuel through a drillway and check valve to pump nozzle where fuel is squirted into the carburetor throat. (Harley-Davidson Motor Co., Inc.)

leans the idle mixture and turning it out richens the idle mixture. **Figure 7-39** shows these adjustments.

Idle Speed

Engine ***idle speed*** is adjusted by means of a ***throttle stop screw.*** See **Figure 7-40.** This screw prevents the butterfly or throttle slide from closing completely. Engines with two or more cylinders may use a single stop screw which adjusts the throttle linkage position on all the carburetors.

Synchronization

For maximum performance and smooth engine operation, all cylinders of an engine must contribute equally. If one carburetor has a larger throttle opening than another (twin or multicylinder engine), the cylinder with the larger opening is forced to work harder. This can cause a rough running engine and possible overheating. Because cables can stretch and linkages wear, it is necessary to periodically check and synchronize throttle openings on any engine using two or more carburetors.

Carburetor synchronization is checked using vacuum gauges. Visual inspection may also be used to verify synchronization, however, vacuum gauges are more accurate. Adjustment is accomplished by a cable adjuster or by linkage adjustment, **Figure 7-41.** Carburetor synchronization procedures are covered later in this chapter.

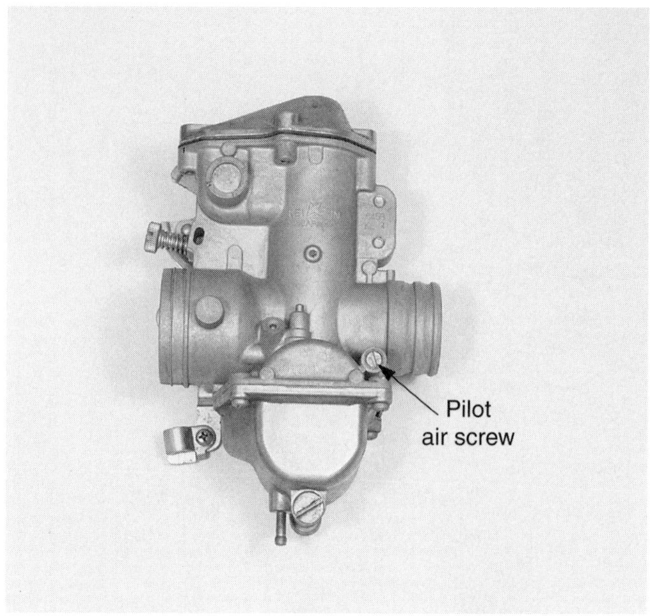

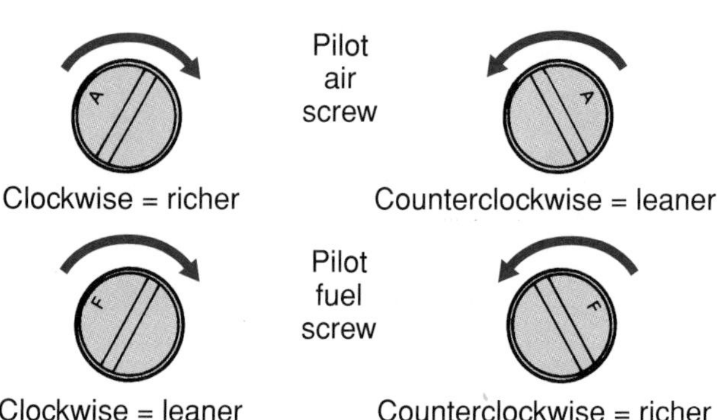

Figure 7-39. Turning a pilot air screw in (clockwise) richens the air-fuel ratio, since less air is admitted. Turning it out (counterclockwise) leans the air-fuel ratio because more air is admitted. Pilot air and fuel screws turned in opposite directions achieve the same result.

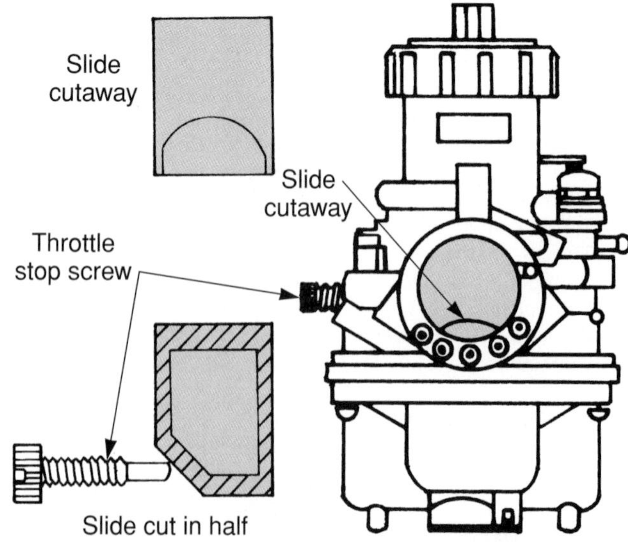

Figure 7-40. A throttle stop screw is used to adjust the idle speed by preventing the slide or butterfly from closing completely. Stop screw may act directly on the slide or on throttle linkage.

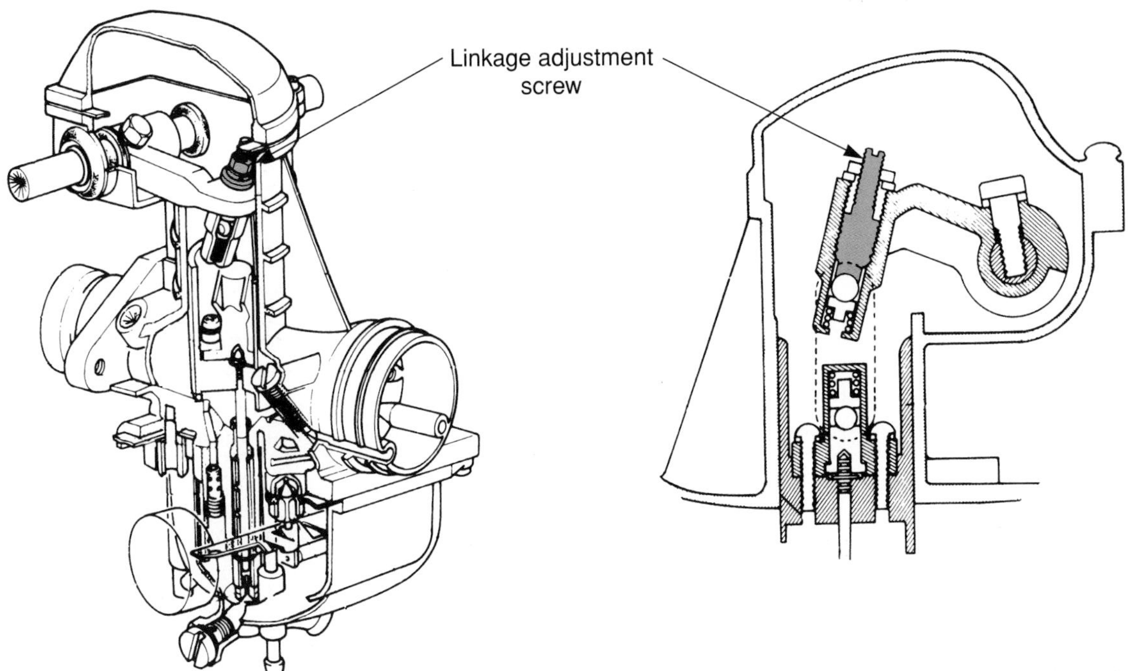

Figure 7-41. This is one type of linkage adjustment screw setup used to synchronize multiple carburetors. (Kawasaki Motors Corporation U.S.A.)

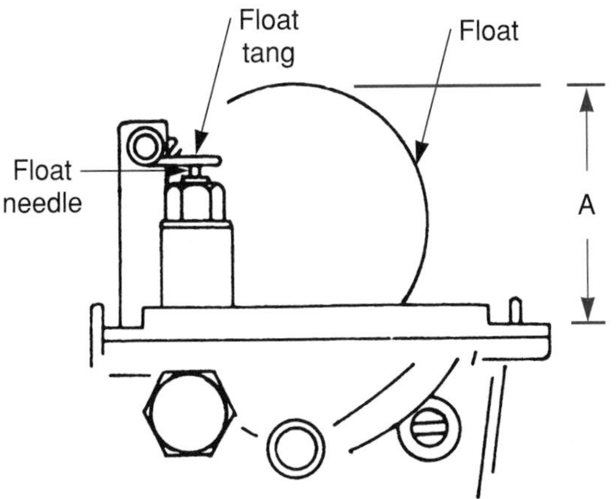

Figure 7-42. Typically, to check float level, measure distance A with the float tang just touching the tip of the float needle. The float level is high if the measurement is less than specified in the manual. The float level is low if the measurement is larger than specified. (Yamaha Motor Corporation U.S.A.)

Float Level

Float level refers to the level of fuel maintained in the float bowl. The correct level must be maintained for the carburetor to work properly. An improper adjusted carburetor float can affect engine operation at any speed.

Changes in float level will affect the air-fuel mixture. If the float level is too low, more vacuum is required to draw fuel into the venturi, producing a leaner mixture. As the float level is raised, less vacuum is required, producing a richer mixture.

Manufacturer's specifications should be followed for float level settings. The float level can be checked in several ways. The most common method measures the distance from the carburetor base to the bottom of the float assembly with the float needle closed. This is illustrated in **Figure 7-42.** The float level is adjusted by bending the tang on the float assembly.

Throttle Cable Adjustment

Proper throttle cable free play and synchronization is necessary for the safe and smooth operation of the motorcycle, ATV, or scooter. Cable free play is adjusted at the top of the carburetor, throttle linkage, or by inline cable adjuster, **Figure 7-43.** Free play is extremely important, as a throttle with little or no free play can cause the engine to race when the handlebars are turned. The handlebar movement can strain and pull on the cable, causing the throttle to open. Manufacturer's specifications must be followed for throttle cable free play adjustment.

Changing Carburetor Jets

A carburetor jet change will alter the air-fuel ratio in one or more carburetor circuits. Usually, jet changes are performed to compensate for changes in altitude or modifications to the engine.

At sea level, air is more dense than at higher altitudes. This requires larger jets so that more fuel will be mixed with the concentrated air. To achieve the proper air-fuel ratio at higher altitudes, smaller jets must be used. The air is thinner and requires less fuel.

Due to the many different designs of slide and CV carburetors, methods of changing jets in individual circuits vary. For accurate information, refer to your service manual before making any jet changes.

On many late-model road bikes, provisions for making jet changes in the idle and midrange circuits may be eliminated due to emissions regulations. It is common, however, for dirt and other off-road bikes to require jet changes.

A jet change may be required with modifications to the air intake system, exhaust system, engine, or at altitudes 1000 ft (304.8 M) or more above sea level. Use the adjustment table given in **Figure 7-44** and the service manual as a guide to changing the jets in each carburetor circuit.

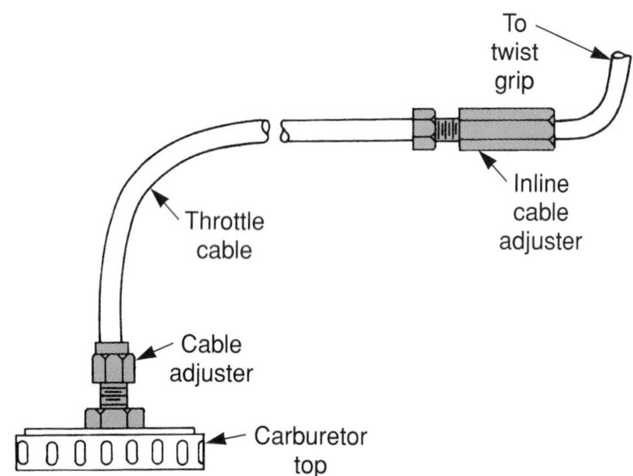

Figure 7-43. Carburetor top cable adjuster and inline cable adjuster are two ways of adjusting throttle cable free play. Shortening the outer cable housing increases cable free play.

Caution: Emissions regulations prohibit modifications that increase noise and pollution output levels on late-model motorcycles.

Carburetor Rebuilding

Motorcycle carburetors require rebuilding because of a buildup of varnish and other deposits. This is usually the result of improper storage. Occasionally carburetors need to be rebuilt as a result of normal wear. Improper air cleaner maintenance or removal of the air cleaner can accelerate wear. Carburetor rebuilding should also be done during an engine overhaul.

Carburetor Removal

Carburetors may be mounted to the engine in a number of ways. They may be mounted independently or together as a unit. A sleeve, spigot, or flange is used to attach the carburetor(s) to the engine. Refer to the proper service manual for correct carburetor removal procedures.

Carburetor Disassembly

Carburetors have a number of small parts that are easy to lose. Carburetor parts should always be placed in a shallow pan or container to prevent loss. Make sure

Throttle Opening	Carburetor Circuit	Jetting Adjustment Procedure
Idle	Pilot circuit (CV and slide type carburetor)	1. Adjust air or fuel screw. 2. Install larger or smaller pilot jet (only if proper mixture cannot be attained by air or fuel screw adjustment.)
Off-idle	Slide cutaway circuit (slide type carburetor) Primary fuel circuit (CV carburetor) Bypass circuit (CV)	1. Replace slide with one having higher or lower slide cutaway. 1. Install larger or smaller primary jet 1. No adjustment available
Midrange	Needle circuit (CV and slide type carburetors)	1. Adjust jet needle position by raising or lowering needle clip. 2. Install larger or smaller needle jet (only if proper mixture cannot be attained by needle clip adjustment).
Full-throttle	Primary fuel circuit (CV carburetor) Main fuel circuit (CV and slide type carburetors)	1. Install larger or smaller primary jet 1. Install larger or smaller main jet.

Figure 7-44. Jet adjustment chart. Use this chart along with, not to replace, the jet information in the service manual.

you disassemble the carburetor using the proper tools to prevent damage to the carburetor body and other parts.

It is also important to note how the parts fit together, in particular the needle clip and float. When more than one carburetor is disassembled, keep the parts for each carburetor separate. If deposits (rust, dirt, water) are found in the float bowl, the fuel system may be contaminated. Replace all fuel filters and drain and flush the fuel system.

Note: To minimize the possibility of mixing parts of multiple carburetors, rebuild each one separately. Finish each rebuild before beginning the next carburetor.

Make sure each carburetor is completely disassembled prior to cleaning, **Figure 7-45.** This allows the solvent cleaner to reach all areas of the carburetor. It also prevents the accidental destruction of nylon, rubber, or fiber carburetor parts.

Carburetor Cleaning

Two types of carburetor cleaning solvents are available. One is the aerosol type, which is used for external or light cleaning. This type is not adequate for carburetor rebuilding. The other type is a ***cold soak cleaner,*** which is ideal for thorough carburetor cleaning. All metal carburetor parts are put in a basket and submerged in the cleaner.

Cold soak cleaner is very strong. It is important that no rubber, nylon, or fiber carburetor parts be put in cold soak cleaner. Metal parts should not be left in cold soak cleaner longer than 30 minutes. Safety glasses and rubber gloves are worn to prevent burns. When parts are removed from the cleaner, they should be thoroughly rinsed in warm water and dried with compressed air.

Warning: If carburetor cleaner splashes into your eyes, seek medical attention. If it touches your skin, follow the directions given on the container.

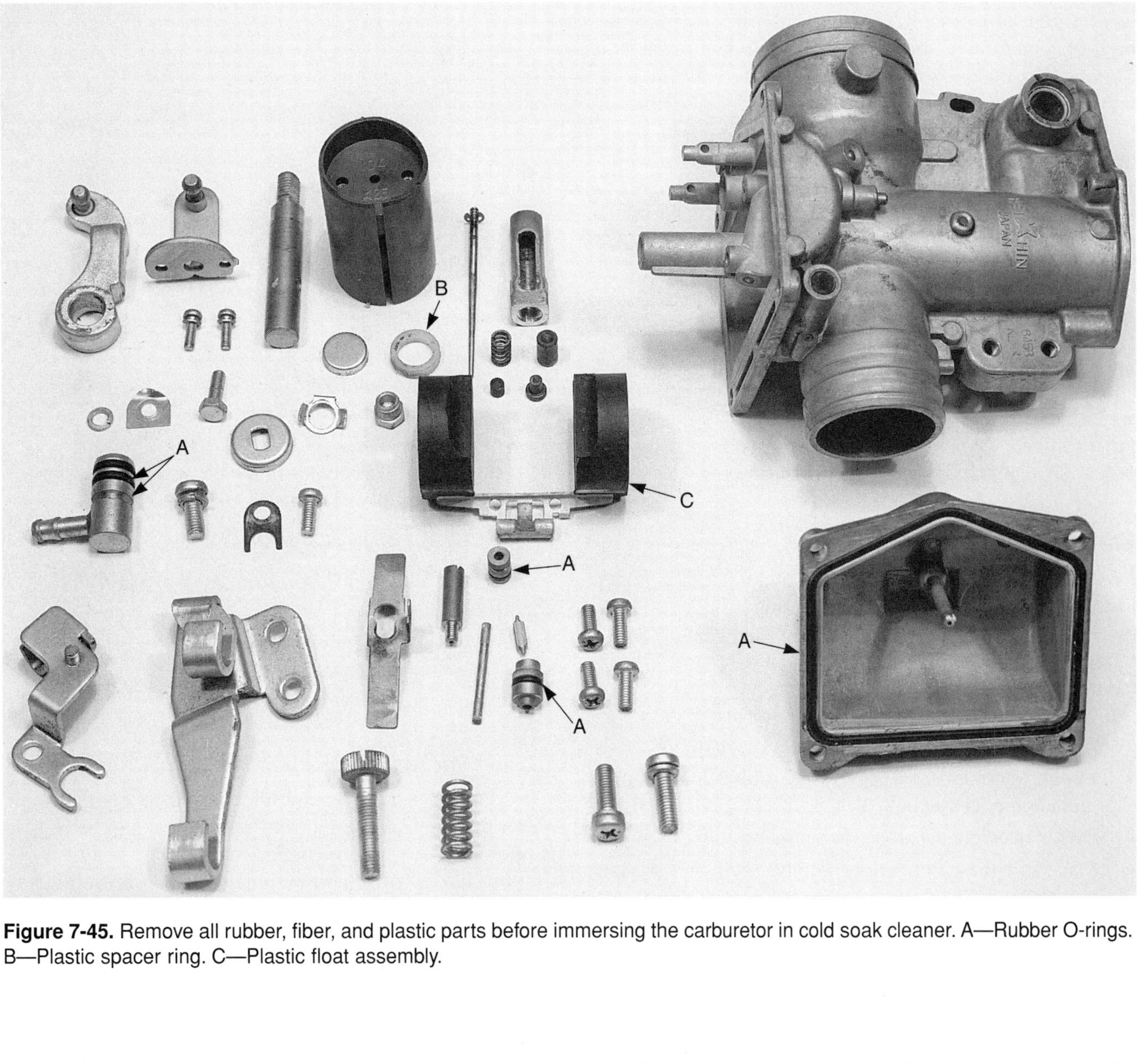

Figure 7-45. Remove all rubber, fiber, and plastic parts before immersing the carburetor in cold soak cleaner. A—Rubber O-rings. B—Plastic spacer ring. C—Plastic float assembly.

Parts Inspection and Replacement

Once the carburetor body and parts are clean and dry, place them on a clean shop towel for inspection. The lack of a thorough inspection can result in a poor rebuild. A proper carburetor inspection includes:

- Checking jet orifices for obstructions.
- Inspecting the float needle and seat for wear.
- Checking the float assembly for holes, cracks, and proper seal.
- Checking the carburetor body for varnish and corrosion.
- Inspecting all threads for damage.
- Checking the mounting flange and float bowl seating surfaces for straightness.
- Checking the rubber tip on the enrichment plunger for damage.
- Checking the carburetor slide for wear, damage, and freedom of movement through the length of the slide bore.

Carburetor Reassembly

Carburetor reassembly is relatively simple, but must be done carefully. It is important to use new gaskets and O-rings and make sure all jets and screws are properly tightened. Make sure the pilot adjustment and throttle stop screws are installed in the proper holes and the needle clip is seated properly and in the correct groove.

Most service manuals provide an exploded view of the complete carburetor. This helps ensure the carburetor is reassembled correctly. A typical exploded view of a carburetor is shown in **Figure 7-46.**

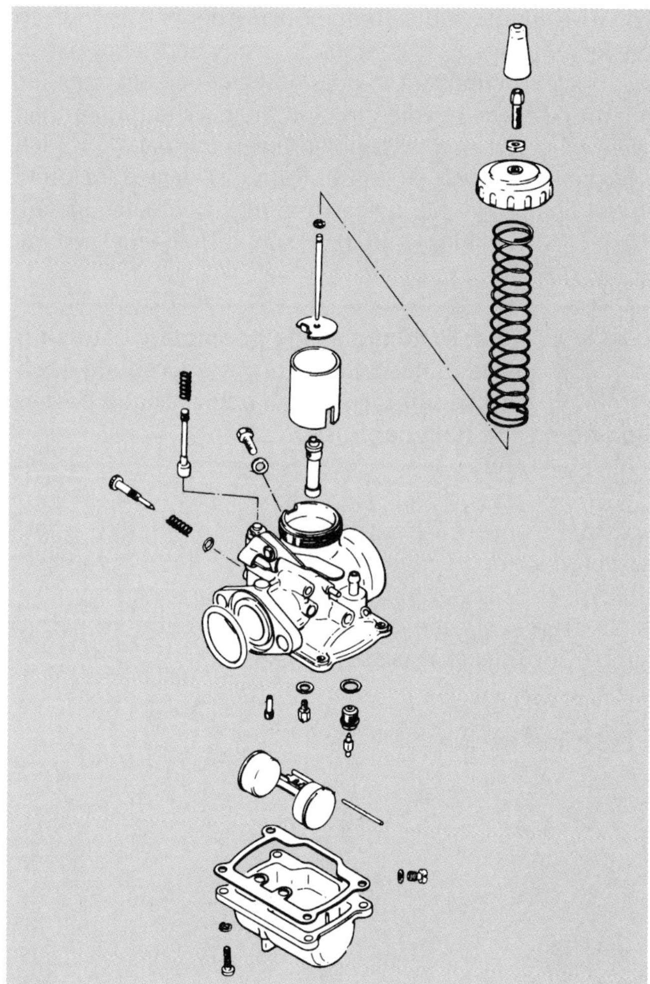

Figure 7-46. A carburetor exploded view can be helpful during reassembly. It shows the relative position of each part. (American Suzuki Motor Corporation)

Initial Settings

During reassembly, the float level should be checked and adjusted if necessary. The pilot adjustment screw should be set and multiple carburetor linkages visually synchronized. The shop manual gives specifications and procedures for initial settings and adjustments.

Carburetor Installation

To get the full benefit from a carburetor rebuild, proper installation is necessary. Mistakes during installation may result in air leaks, carburetor or manifold damage, and other problems. An air or vacuum leak can cause a lean mixture, rough idle, and engine damage.

To avoid problems during carburetor installation:

- Always use new carburetor mounting gaskets.
- Check condition of O-rings and rubber flanges and replace if necessary.
- Do not overtighten carburetor mounting bolts or clamps.
- Make sure the carburetors are fully seated and straight in their mounting flanges.
- Check throttle cable routing and freedom of operation.
- Check and service air cleaner and air box.
- Adjust cable free play.
- Visually synchronize throttles on non-linkage carburetors.
- Check, clean, or replace fuel filter and petcock screen.

Final Carburetor Adjustment

The last carburetor adjustments are made with the engine operating. These include:

- Throttle synchronization using vacuum gauges.
- Final pilot screw adjustment.
- Idle speed adjustment.

Using Vacuum Gauges for Final Synchronization

Using a vacuum gauge allows you to compare the performance of two or more carburetors while the engine is operating. A vacuum gauge is connected between the throttle slide or plate and the intake valve on each cylinder. Look at **Figure 7-47.** One gauge is required for each cylinder. Small changes in throttle openings will change the vacuum gauge reading, **Figure 7-48.**

Proper throttle synchronization is achieved when all the vacuum gauges read the same. If all readings are not the same, the linkage must be adjusted. Proper vacuum readings and procedures for linkage adjustment are outlined by the motorcycle manufacturer. Since linkage designs and vacuum specifications vary, refer to the service manual.

If one gauge reads lower than the others, its carburetor slide is open more than the others. You would need to lower the slide in that carburetor by adjusting its linkage. If one gauge reads high, its carburetor's slide is closed more than the others and must be opened. **Figure 7-49** shows these two conditions. If two or more carburetors read the same, leave them alone and adjust the others.

Note: Idle speed should be reset after carburetor synchronization.

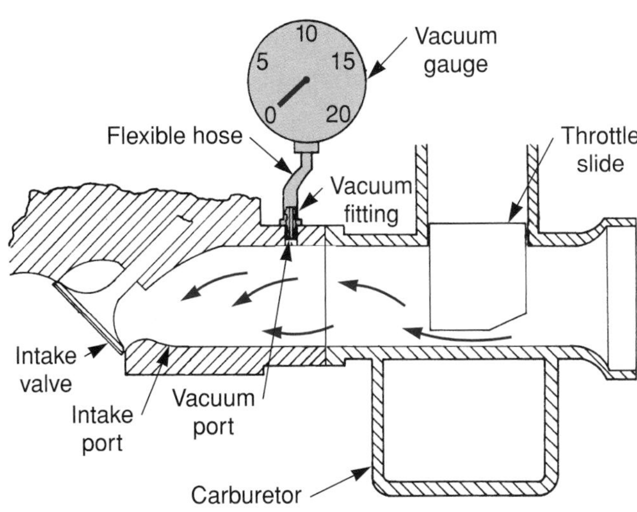

Figure 7-47. A vacuum gauge is connected to the intake tract between the throttle slide or butterfly and intake valve. A vacuum port will be located in the carburetor body or intake port.

Final Pilot Adjustment

Some manufacturers recommend a specific pilot screw setting. For example, you may have to loosen the pilot screw three-quarter to one turn. During this adjustment, the engine does not have to be operating. See **Figure 7-50.**

In other cases, an initial pilot setting is given and final adjustment is done with the engine running at operating temperature. To adjust with the engine running, turn the pilot screw in until the engine rpm begins to drop. Then, turn the pilot screw back out until the engine rpm begins to drop. The desired adjustment is halfway between the two rpm points, **Figure 7-50.**

Final Idle Speed Adjustment

Manufacturer's specifications should be followed for idle speed adjustment. Any twin or multicylinder engine which has individual throttle stop screws requires accurate adjustment of each stop screw. This is needed to ensure a smooth idle. Twin or multicylinder engines that use positive linkage to operate the throttles will have a single idle adjustment screw.

Carburetor Rebuilding Summary

Use the following summary when rebuilding a motorcycle carburetor. It will help you do a complete and professional job.

1. Clean and degrease the motorcycle.
2. Remove the fuel tank (if necessary).
3. Drain fuel from the carburetor(s).
4. Disconnect throttle cables.
5. Disconnect choke cables or linkages (if needed).
6. Remove air filters or air box (if necessary).

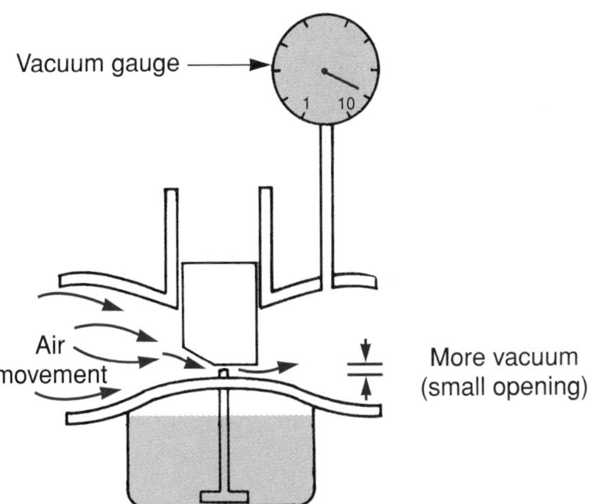

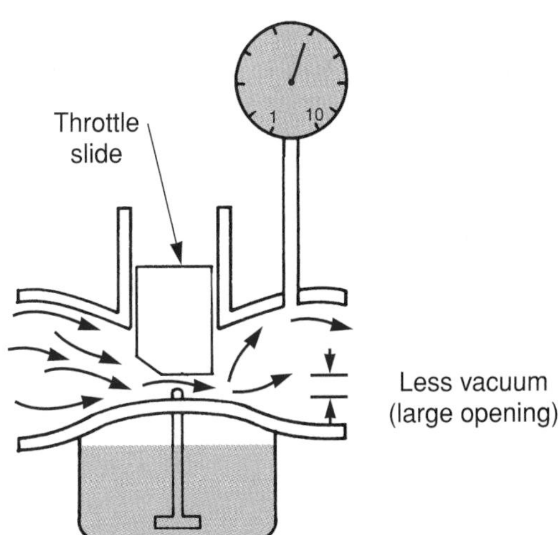

Figure 7-48. Small changes in slide position (exaggerated in this illustration) will affect engine vacuum. Very slight changes in throttle slide position can be detected using a vacuum gauge.

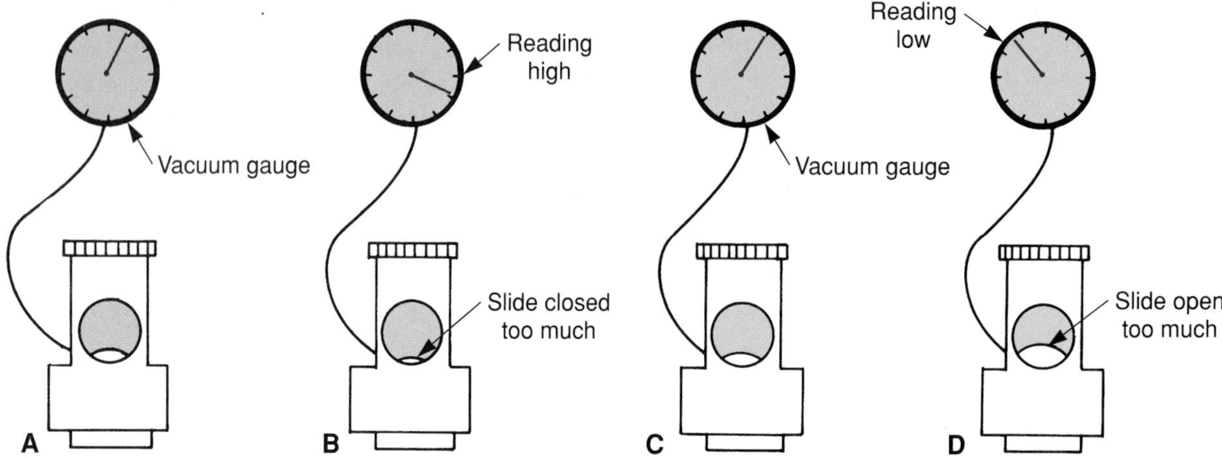

Figure 7-49. In this example, vacuum readings on carburetors B and D show that adjustment is necessary. Throttle slide on carburetor B should be raised to lower vacuum. Throttle slide on carburetor D should be lowered to raise vacuum.

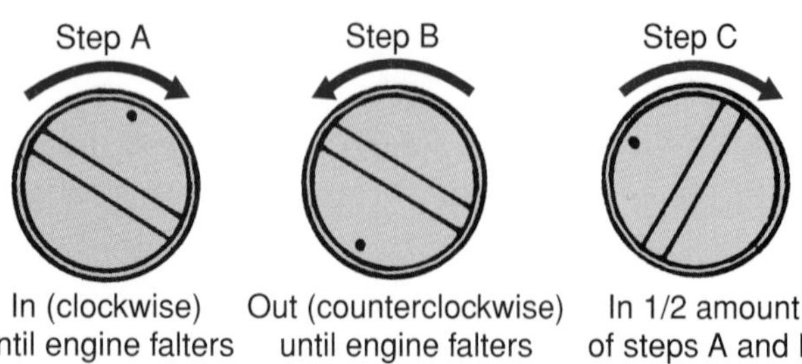

Figure 7-50. This is one way of adjusting pilot screws. The engine must be fully warmed and running for proper adjustment. Note the location of the pilot screw on this particular carburetor.

7. Loosen mounting hardware and remove carburetor.
8. Check condition of rubber mounting sleeves or insulator blocks.
9. Tape or plug off intake port.
10. Disassemble carburetor throttle linkage (if applicable).
11. Remove carburetors from mounting block (if applicable).
12. Remove float bowls.
13. Check and record float level measurements.
14. Disassemble carburetors completely and record needle settings.
15. Remove all plastic, fiber, and rubber parts.
16. Soak metal parts in cold soak cleaner (30 minutes maximum).
17. Wash parts in warm water and air dry thoroughly.
18. Organize all parts on a clean shop towel.
19. Inspect parts for wear, damage, and cleanliness.
20. Reassemble carburetors using new parts, gaskets, and O-rings where necessary.
21. Adjust needle position and float level to specifications.
22. Remount carburetors on mounting block (if applicable).
23. Visually synchronize throttle linkage (multicylinder engines).
24. Set pilot adjustment screws (initial setting).
25. Set idle speed stop screws to lowest setting.
26. Remount carburetors on engine.
27. Install air cleaners or air box.
28. Connect throttle and choke cables.
29. Adjust cable free play.
30. Visually synchronize throttles (multicable designs).
31. Inspect fuel tank for rust, varnish, and foreign material.

32. Clean fuel tank (if needed).
33. Clean fuel petcock filter.
34. Install fuel tank.
35. Connect all fuel lines and vacuum lines (vacuum operated petcock).
36. Turn on fuel petcock and check for leaks.
37. Install vacuum gauges (twin or multicylinder engines).
38. Start engine, warm-up, and set idle speed.
39. Adjust pilot mixture.
40. Synchronize carburetors using vacuum gauges.
41. Reset idle speed.
42. Remove vacuum gauges.
43. Road test.

Electronic Fuel Injection

The ability of a carburetors to adjust the air-fuel ratio depends upon the metering and balance between the intake air quantity and the size of the jet at the fuel outlet. Various auxiliary devices are needed to cope with the problems caused by varying engine operating conditions and air intake quantity. It is obvious the carburetor is limited as to the amount it can control the supply of fuel to deliver an optimum air-fuel ratio.

These problems can be overcome by using ***electronic fuel injection (EFI)*** systems with an on-board computer or electronic control module. The quantity of fuel injected is controlled based on information from various sensors which detect engine operating and external conditions to ensure an optimum supply of fuel at all times. This data is also used to control ignition timing. Using electronic control results in improved engine performance and reduced fuel consumption.

Function of EFI Components

Figure 7-51 shows the location of major components in an electronic fuel injection system. The sensors monitor engine functions including barometric pressure, throttle position, coolant temperature, intake manifold pressure, intake air temperature, crankshaft position, and camshaft position. All this information is needed by the electronic control module (ECM) to provide the engine's fuel and spark needs precisely. A typical fuel control system is illustrated in **Figure 7-52.**

Electronic Control Module (ECM)

The control operations performed by the ***electronic control module (ECM)*** may be broadly classified into three parts:

- Fuel injection control.
- Ignition system control.
- Self diagnostics.

All the sensor input signals to the ECM, **Figure 7-53,** pass through an ***input interface circuit*** before entering the ***central processing unit (CPU).*** The CPU (a microprocessor) checks the signal, processes it, and outputs the necessary control commands. The ***output interface circuit*** controls the various actuators. The electronic control module is typically located beneath the seat, close to the battery. To protect the ECM from water, it is covered by a plastic case and rubber cover.

ECM Internal Functions

Bikes equipped with an ECM ignition system have the igniter built into the ECM. A spark occurs at the spark plug when the ECM shuts off current to the ignition coil. Some ECM systems provide theft prevention. The main switch outputs a specific pulse signal when it is turned from the *off* position. The ECM checks for the correct signal before starting the control operations for injection and ignition. The engine will not start if the ECM receives the wrong signal or the main switch is bypassed.

Most ECMs have several fuel cut-off functions that operate with the side stand switch, clutch switch, and neutral switch. Depending on the position of one or more of these switches, engine operation may be stopped. Some motorcycles are equipped with a ***fall detection switch,*** which stops engine operation if the motorcycle overturns or is tilted too far. If the motorcycle is tilted by more than 45° from vertical, a signal from the fall detection switch allows the ECM to stop the engine.

Another major function built into the ECM is the ability to diagnose internal problems. If a fault is detected in the system, the ECM controls the fuel injection, ignition, and other portions of the electronic control system using default operating routines. Simultaneously, a warning light in the instrument cluster comes on and informs the rider of a fault in the system.

EFI Intake Air System

The amount of air entering the engine changes every moment, depending on engine speed, load, and the rider's throttle operations. In order for the ECM to accurately meter the amount of fuel to inject, the volume of air coming in the engine must be accurately measured. To perform this task, one or more engine speed sensors, intake air pressure sensor, and throttle position sensor provide input to the engine control system. The EFI intake system resembles the air intake of a carbureted engine, with the exception of the airflow meter, **Figure 7-54,** and/or atmospheric pressure sensor.

Speed Density and Throttle Opening

Some ECMs measure the amount of incoming air by monitoring sensors and then computing the amount of air

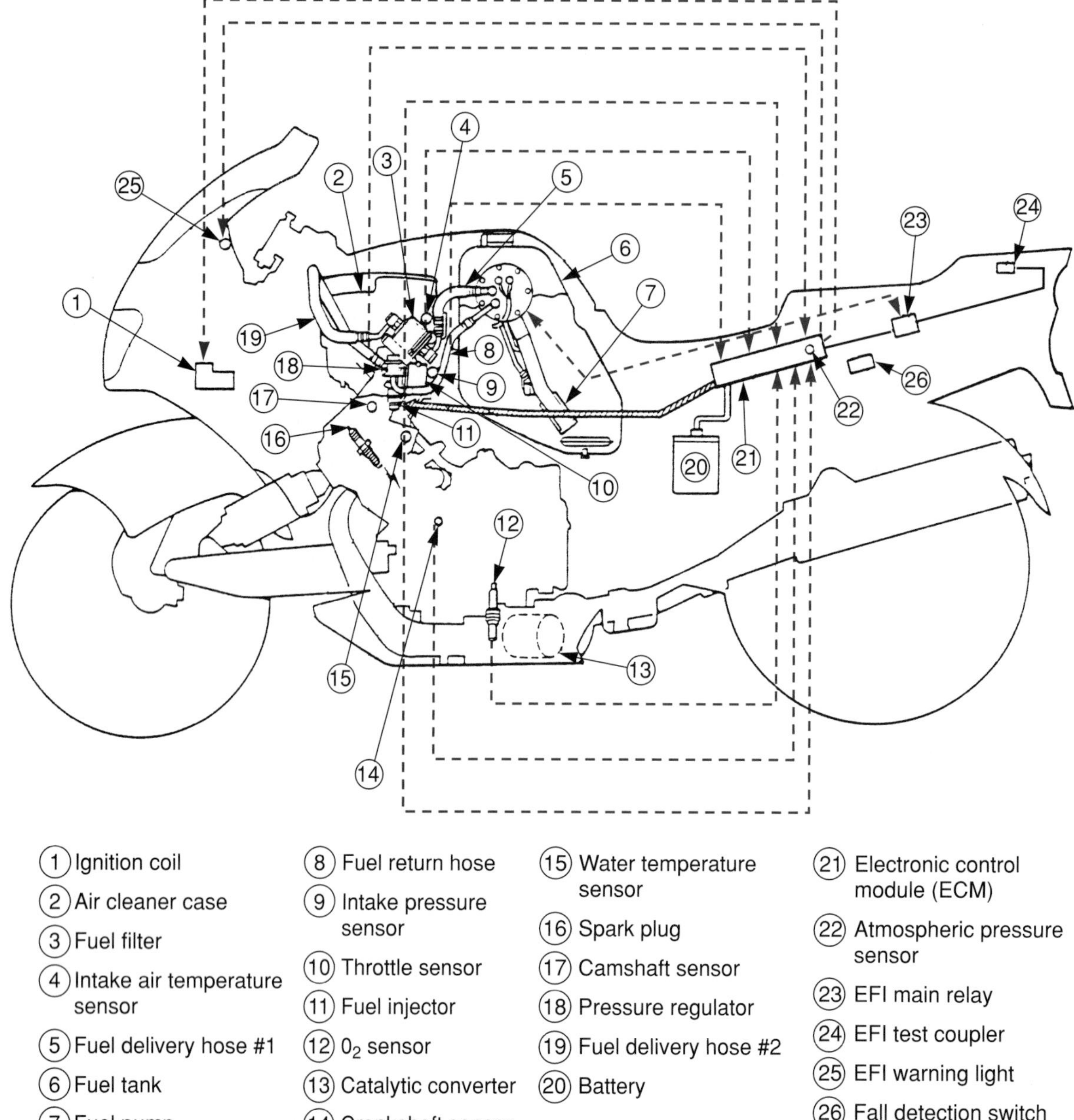

Figure 7-51. Components and their layout in an electronic fuel injection (EFI) system. (Yamaha Motor Corporation U.S.A.)

entering the engine. This system is referred to as speed density. A portion of the speed density system on bikes is dependent on throttle position for the majority of the air calculation decisions.

In a speed density/throttle opening system, the ECM monitors input from the bike's various sensors (engine speed, throttle position, coolant temperature, oxygen sensor) and "calculates" the amount of air entering the engine. While this system may appear to be crude, it works quite well.

Airflow Meter

The function of a typical ***airflow meter*** is to monitor the amount of air entering the engine. This mixture adjustment is done electronically through the use of a potentiometer. The potentiometer varies the circuit resistance and current flow to the ECM as the air flap changes position. Air flap movement is translated into an electrical signal which indicates the amount of air entering the engine. A fixed bypass passage supplies the engine with air at idle speeds.

Because the airflow meter is a mechanical device, it has been replaced in most systems with an air or atmospheric pressure sensor (described later in this chapter). Sometimes, this sensor is mounted in the airflow meter housing. This arrangement supplies complete air sensing.

The throttle valve or valves are connected to the twist grip. They regulate the amount of air being drawn into the engine. The electronic fuel injection throttle valve serves the same function as the slide or butterfly in the constant velocity and butterfly carburetors. The throttle valves are fitted on the throttle body. The air box and air cleaner are similar to those found on a carbureted engine. However,

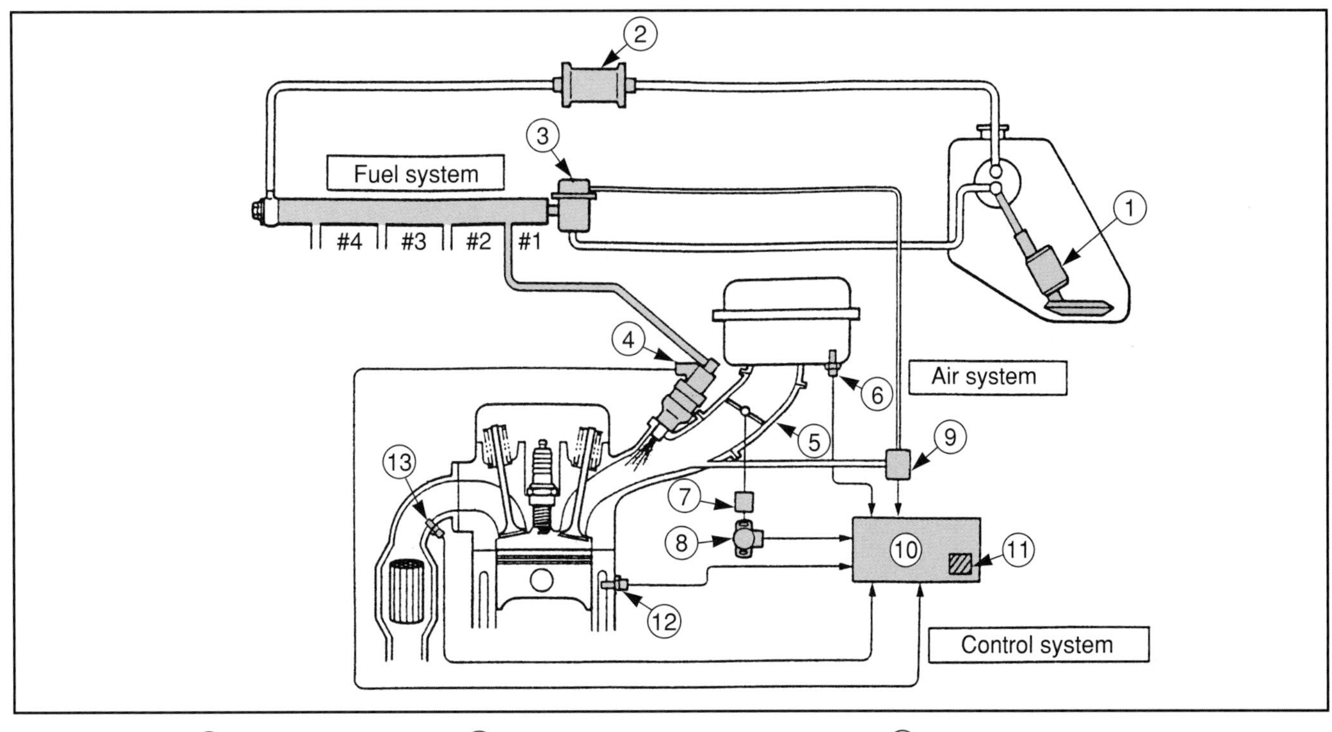

Figure 7-52. Typical fuel injection control and delivery system. (Yamaha Motor Corporation U.S.A.)

the air box in the fuel injected engine also helps to stabilize air flap movement.

Fuel Injector

The function of the ***fuel injector*** is to spray the proper amount of fuel into the intake port. It injects fuel when it receives an injection command from the ECM. In the initial position, the core is pressed down by the spring, **Figure 7-55.** The needle is integrated with the core on the lower side, which blocks the fuel path. If current flows through the coil, the core is pulled up. The flange section formed between the core and needle moves until it touches the spacer. Because of this construction, the distance moved by the needle and the fuel passage section area is constant.

The difference in the fuel pressure and the intake port pressure is maintained at a constant value by the pressure regulator. Therefore, the injected fuel quantity is directly proportional to the time the current is passed.

One injector is usually installed in the intake port of each cylinder. The injector injects the optimum quantity of fuel at optimum timing to suit the intake timing of each cylinder. This enables the injector to be arranged close to the intake port and to improve engine response. Most motorcycles use one injector per cylinder. For cold starts, most motorcycles use a cold start valve, which provides additional fuel for start-up.

Throttle Body

To control the amount of air that enters the engine, a ***throttle body*** is positioned at the intake opening. The throttle body is located in the place formerly occupied by the carburetor. The throttle body performs the same task as the throttle plate in a carburetor. It allows the rider to control the engine's air intake, **Figure 7-56.** Depending on the engine's design, multiple throttle bodies may be used. Multiple throttle bodies must be synchronized, similar to bikes with multiple carburetors.

EFI Pressure Regulator

The EFI fuel system consists of an electric fuel pump, fuel filter, pressure regulator, high pressure lines, electrically activated fuel injectors, and a conventional fuel tank. The fuel is supplied by the electric fuel pump at approximately 50 psi (350 kPa). The ***pressure regulator*** regulates the fuel pressure to the injector(s), **Figure 7-57.** It maintains a constant pressure difference with the intake

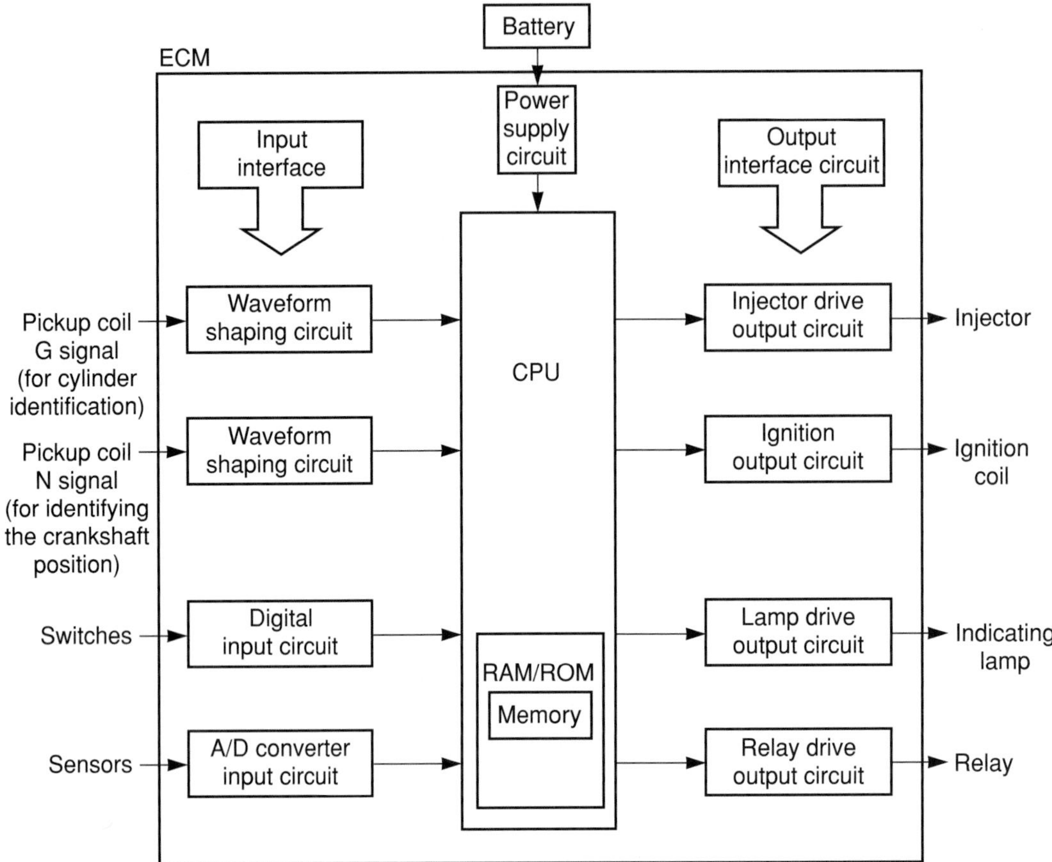

Figure 7-53. The main components in the ECM unit may be broadly divided into four blocks. These are the power supply circuit that supplies power to the ECM, the CPU (central processing unit) that controls and processes all systems, input/output interface circuits that send and receive various signals.

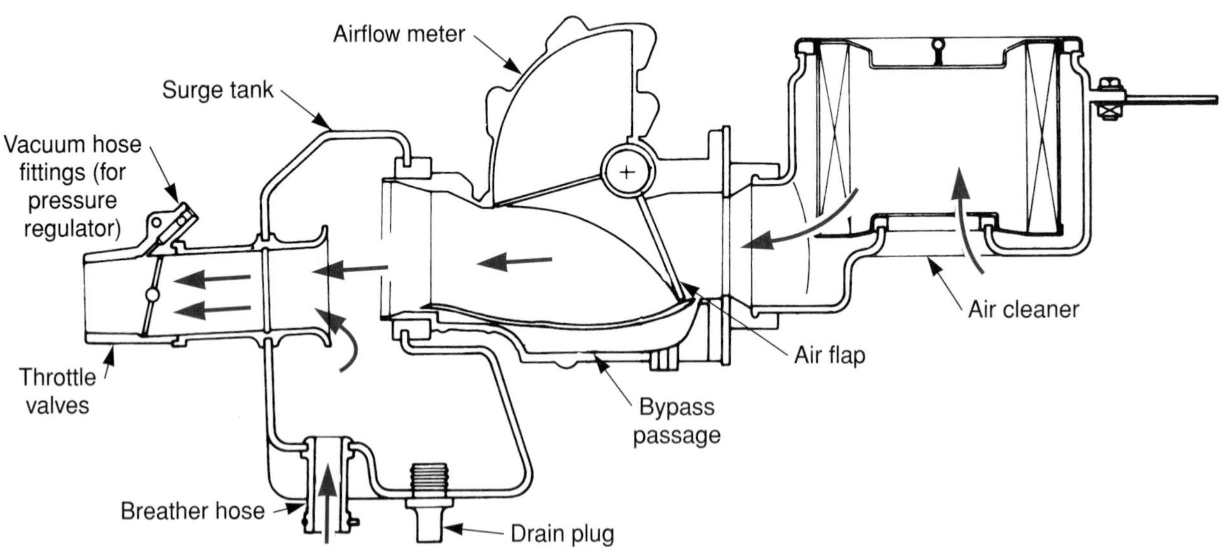

Figure 7-54. This EFI air intake system is similar to one used with a carbureted engine. (Kawasaki Motors Corporation U.S.A.)

port. Therefore, when the fuel path of the injector opens on a signal from the ECM, a quantity of fuel proportional to the opening time is injected into the intake port.

Pressurized fuel exerts pressure on the diaphragm while intake vacuum is transmitted to the spring chamber through the pipe. If the fuel pressure exceeds the regulator's vacuum pressure and spring force, the valve inside the regulator opens. Excess fuel is returned to the fuel tank through the fuel outlet and return hose.

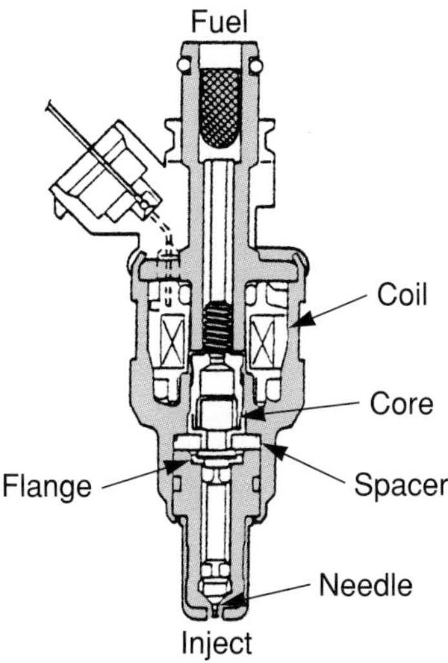

Figure 7-55. Typical fuel injector. (Yamaha Motor Corporation U.S.A.)

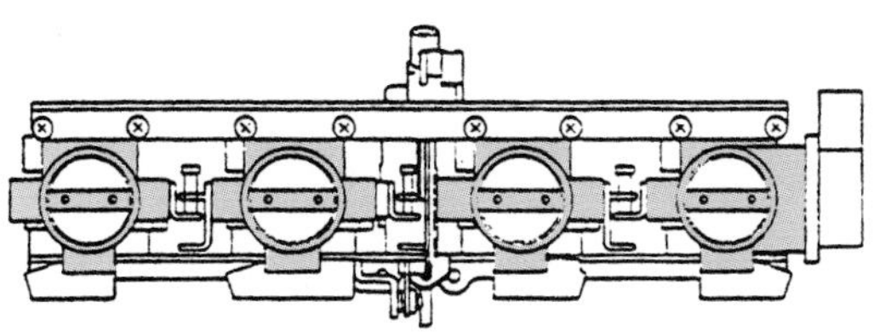

Figure 7-56. Fuel injected bikes use throttle bodies, which take the physical place of the carburetor at the entrance to the intake manifold. (Yamaha Motor Corporation U.S.A.)

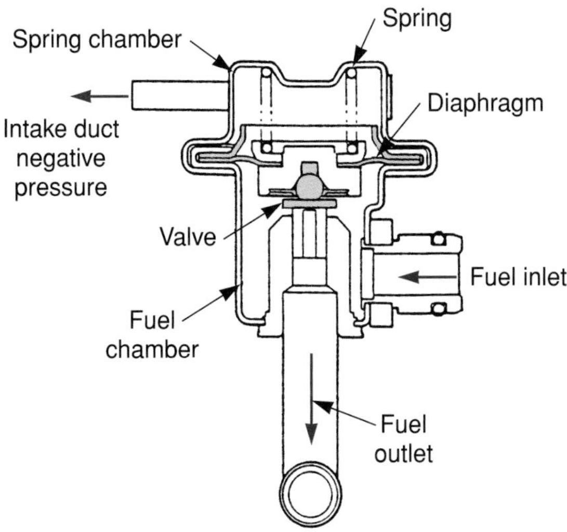

Figure 7-57. Typical pressure regulator. (Yamaha Motor Corporation U.S.A.)

Sensor System

The typical EFI electronic control system is made up of sensors, actuators, and related wiring. The length of time the injectors are open is determined by processing information from all the sensors. In some engine integrated control systems, there may be other sensors in use than the ones listed here. Consult the service manual for a listing of all sensors on each bike.

Intake Pressure Sensor

The ***intake pressure sensor*** converts the intake pressure to electrical signals. The sensor unit installed in the vacuum chamber converts the pressure to electric signals, **Figure 7-58.** These signals are amplified, adjusted, and compensated by circuits consisting of hybrid ICs. Electric signals that are proportional to the pressure are generated and sent to the ECM.

Atmospheric Pressure Sensor

The ***atmospheric pressure sensor*** is used to compensate for air density changes. Air density changes with air temperature and altitudes. Cool air is denser than warm air and as the altitude increases, air becomes less dense. Since cooler, denser air has more oxygen, it requires more fuel to maintain the proper air-fuel ratio at any load or throttle opening. This sensor may be built into the ECM or it may be located, as mentioned earlier, in an airflow meter.

Coolant Temperature Sensor

The ***coolant temperature sensor*** converts the engine's liquid coolant temperature to electrical resistance. The coolant temperature signal is used by the ECM to set fuel injection pulse width based on engine temperature. Since a warm engine needs less fuel, the ECM will reduce the time the injector(s) are open when the engine is warm.

Intake Temperature Sensor

Intake temperature sensors convert the temperature of the air entering the engine to electrical resistance. This thermistor is a semiconductor element that has high resistance at low temperature and low resistance at high temperature. The change in resistance value due to the change in temperature is read by the ECM.

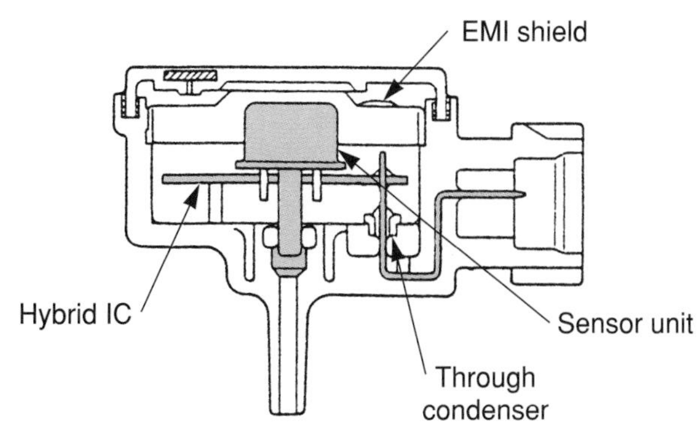

Figure 7-58. Typical parts of an intake pressure sensor. (Yamaha Motor Corporation U.S.A.)

Throttle Position Sensor

The ***throttle position sensor*** converts the physical angles of the throttle valve to electrical signals. The sensor converts the angles to proportional voltages by the relationship between a sliding contact that moves with the throttle shaft across a fixed resistor. In actual operation, a constant voltage (5v) is supplied at either end of the resistor from the ECM. Therefore, the partial voltage will be substituted at the electrical level of the sliding contact.

Oxygen (O_2) Sensor

Oxygen (O_2) sensors converts the concentration of oxygen in the exhaust gas to electrical signals. For the detection of oxygen concentration, the principle of oxygen's conductivity with zirconium is used. Platinum electrodes are installed on both sides of a zirconium test-tube shaped element. Air is introduced in the zirconium arrangement in such a manner that exhaust gas surrounds this test tube shaped element, resulting in the creation of a kind of oxygen concentrated battery. Voltage is generated because of the difference in oxygen concentrations in the exhaust gas and the atmosphere, **Figure 7-59.** This voltage is read by the ECM.

Camshaft and Crankshaft Sensors

Motorcycle engines use a ***camshaft sensor, crankshaft sensor,*** or both. One electromagnetic pickup is installed in the cylinder head cover for cylinder identification and one pickup in the crankcase for detecting the crankshaft rotation angle. There is a hole set in the cam lobe and in the crankweb. When the engine rotates, the gap in the pickup coil changes. When it passes by the pickup coil, the magnetic flux changes, generating voltage in the coil. The crankshaft position is detected by the changes in voltage.

Engine Control System Operation

The fuel injection period, injection timing, ignition timing and duration through the coil, as already described, are controlled by the ECM. The ECM first calculates the intake air quantity from the signals received from the intake pressure sensor, throttle position sensor, camshaft sensor, and other sensors. It then decides the base injection timing. See **Figure 7-60.** Then it adds the value calculated from the acceleration conditions and sensor signals, and decides final injection timing.

Simultaneously, it estimates the crankshaft angle and sends a command to the injector when the proper injection time is reached. Also, it calculates ignition timing and current passage time, based on the signals received from the various sensors and controls the current passage through the ignition coil.

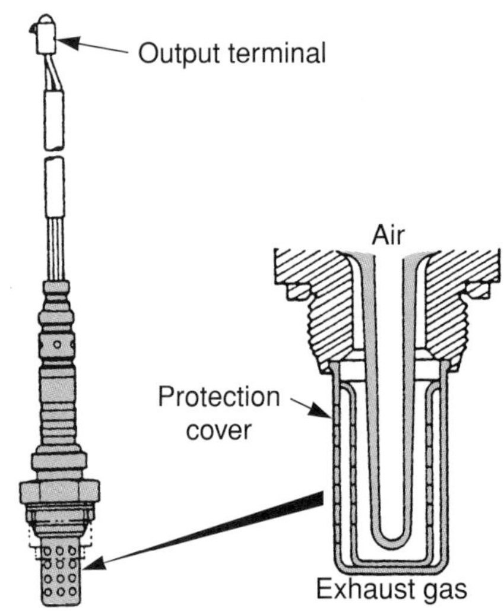

Figure 7-59. Typical oxygen (O_2) sensor. (Yamaha Motor Corporation U.S.A.)

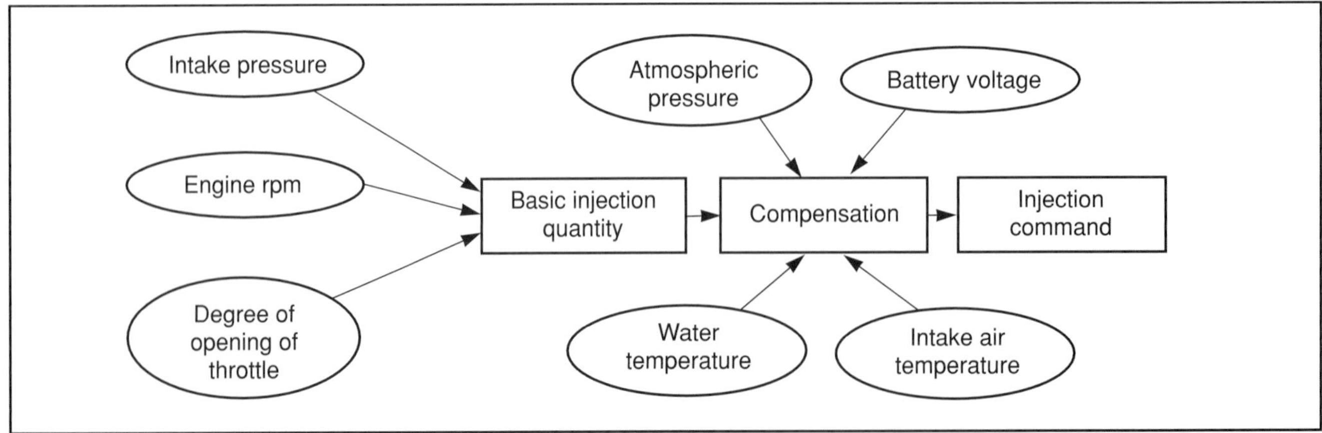

Figure 7-60. The operation of an engine integrated control system.

To operate the engine at optimum conditions, it is necessary to supply fuel at the optimum air-fuel ratio in relation to the intake air quantity, which changes from moment to moment, and to ignite the mixture at the correct time. To supply fuel at the optimum ratio, the intake air quantity must be accurately metered.

However, even if the intake air quantity is the same, the fuel quantity required during acceleration or deceleration varies depending on engine operating or weather conditions. Most ECMs can compensate for these conditions using the various sensors already mentioned. Compensation data is added to the base injection duration and the final injection duration is decided according to the engine operating conditions.

In addition to the fuel injection (synchronous injection) during normal running, the system also increases the fuel quantity by asynchronous injection, regardless of crankshaft rotation during situations such as sudden throttle opening. When conditions require that fuel is no longer needed, the system shuts down fuel delivery.

The typical engine integrated control system incorporates a highly efficient exhaust emission control system. It decreases substances such as carbon monoxide (CO), hydrocarbons (HC), and oxides of nitrogen (NO_x) from the exhaust gas by total control of air-fuel ratio, in association with the EFI system, the O_2 sensors and the ***three-way catalytic conversion system.***

Optimum combustion is realized by matching the air-fuel ratio with the engine's operating condition, using the EFI system. Also, maximum performance of the three-way catalytic converter is attained. With the aim of cleaning up the exhaust gas at high efficiency, an O_2 sensor is installed in the exhaust chamber. This sensor detects the residual oxygen in the exhaust gas.

Based on the data from the O_2 sensor, the ECM makes corrections to the base air-fuel ratio and attempts to maintain this ratio as close to the ***stoichiometric,*** or theoretically correct air-fuel ratio, of 14.7:1 as possible. The air feedback control system shown in **Figure 7-61** controls exhaust emissions while having no adverse effect on engine performance.

ECM Self-Diagnostics

As stated earlier, one of the ECM's major functions is to provide self-diagnostics to the EFI system. Fault codes that help to diagnose problems in the EFI system can be checked by using either the EFI warning light or by using a pocket voltage tester or diagnostic tester.

Using the EFI Warning Light

After setting the ECM in diagnosis mode as instructed in the service manual, the EFI warning light, in most systems, will blink according to two patterns.

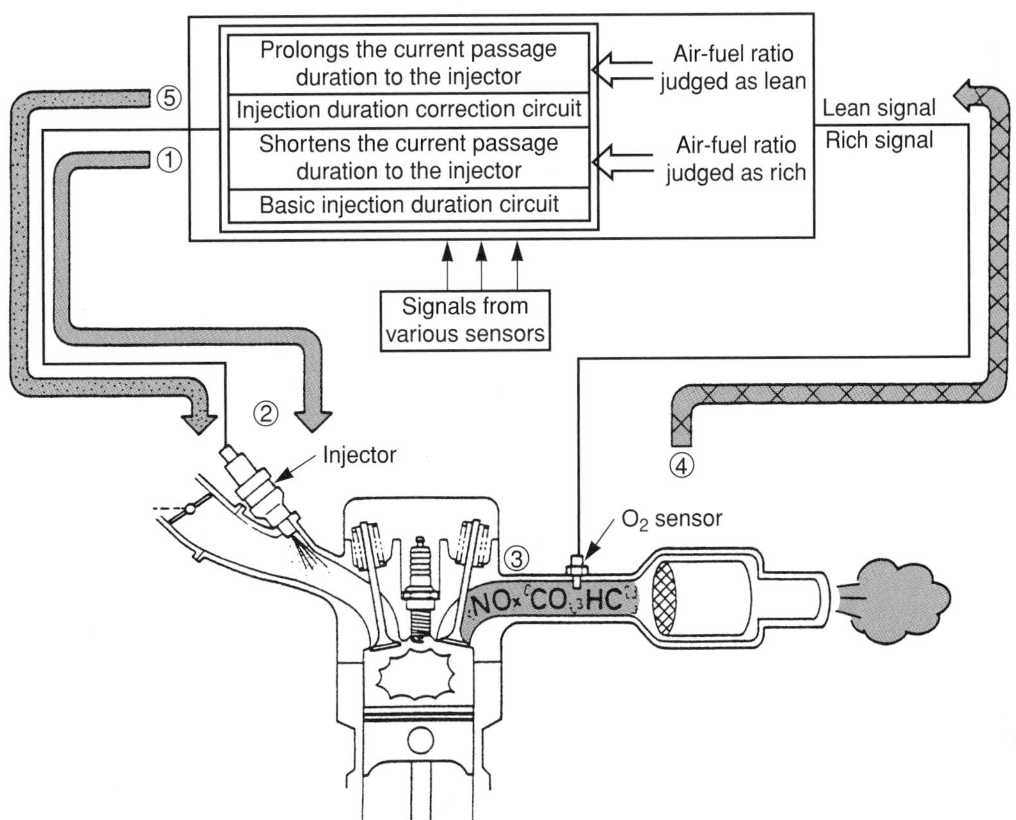

Figure 7-61. The operation of an air feedback control system. (Yamaha Motor Corporation U.S.A.)

1. If there is no fault in the system currently, the warning light will blink every .5-1 second. This is the normal code and nothing is wrong with the EFI system.

2. If the EFI warning light blinks irregularly, it is sending a fault code, which can be interpreted as follows. If the EFI warning light comes on for 1 second, this indicates the value 10. If the EFI warning light comes on for .5 seconds, the value 1 is indicated. The sum of 10 and 1 is the number of the fault code.

An example of how to read these fault indications is given in **Figure 7-62.**

Checking the Fault Code with a Voltmeter

To check for a fault code with a voltmeter, set it on the volt scale and connect the probes as described in the service manual, **Figure 7-63.** The fault code value can be read by observing the deflection of the voltmeter pointer. The fault code can be read by measuring the number of seconds the pointer stops on the 12-volt position:

- The pointer of the pocket voltage tester stops on the 12v position for 1 second, indicates the value 10.
- The pointer of the pocket voltage tester stops on the 12v position for .5 second, indicates the value 1.
- The sum of the values 10 and 1 gives the value of the fault code.

A typical example is shown in **Figure 7-64.**

The possibility of a fault in the system can be judged by using the fault code table in the service manual. See **Figure 7-65.** Read the fault code corresponding to the displayed value obtained by using the EFI warning light, voltmeter, or diagnostic tester. Using the test procedures given in the fault code table, find the cause, and repair it correctly.

The ECM is not field serviceable and must be replaced if defective. Due to the complexity of the system, problem solving often requires specific tests. These tests must be performed in the proper sequence with guidance from a factory service manual or troubleshooting guide.

Caution: Do not attempt to test the parts of an EFI system without following the specific procedures in a shop manual. The electronic system components can be damaged if tested improperly.

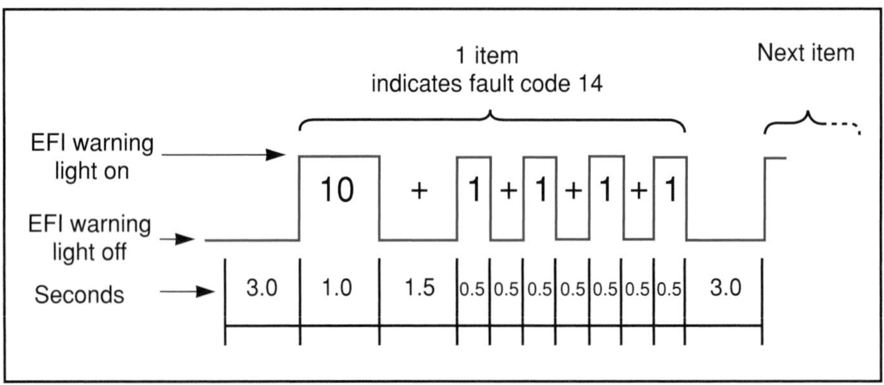

Figure 7-62. Reading a fault code as it appears on a warning light. (Yamaha Motor Corporation U.S.A.)

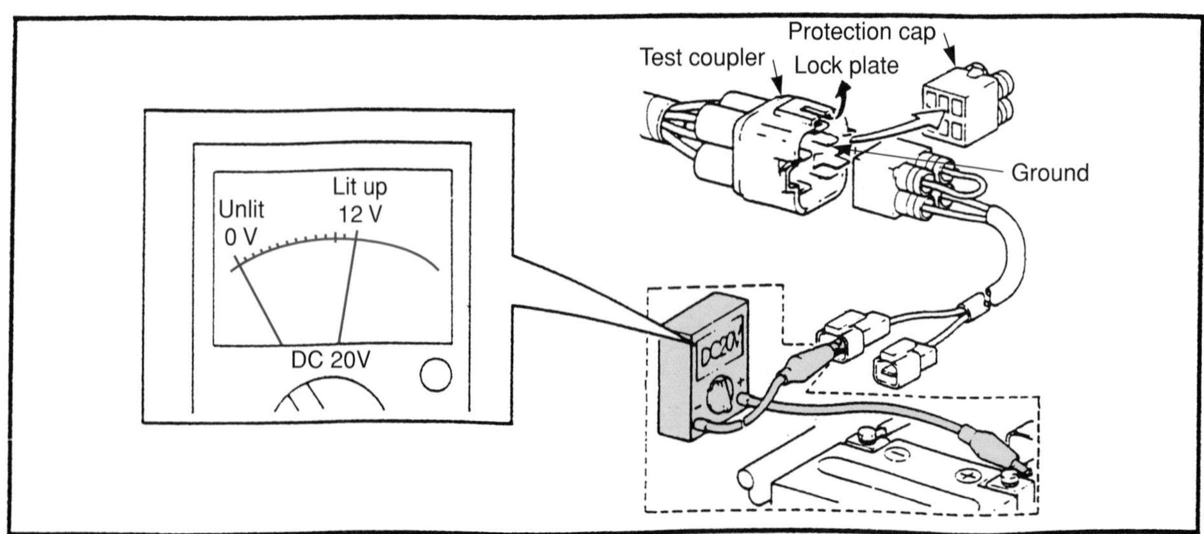

Figure 7-63. Voltmeter connections for voltmeter check. (Yamaha Motor Corporation U.S.A.)

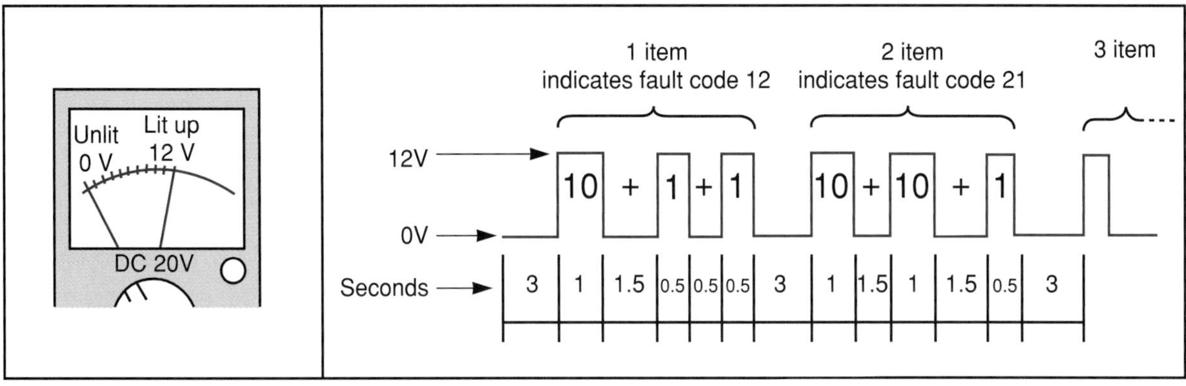

Figure 7-64. Checking for fault codes by pocket voltmeter tester. (Yamaha Motor Corporation U.S.A.)

Fault Code	Phenomenon	Check Description
11	The input of camshaft sensor signal (G signal) is not correct.	• Mounting of camshaft sensor • Connection of camshaft sensor, engine harness, main harness, and ECM coupler • Check the sensor unit • Continuity of engine harness and main harness
12	The input of crankshaft sensor signal (N signal) is not correct.	• Mounting of crankshaft sensor • Connection of camshaft sensor, engine harness, main harness, and ECM coupler • Check the sensor unit • Continuity of engine harness and main harness
13	Discontinuity or shorting of the pressure sensor detected.	• Connection of intake pressure sensor, engine harness, main harness, and ECM coupler • Check sensor unit • Continuity of engine harness and main harness
14	The intake pressure sensor hose is disconnected, atmospheric pressure is acting all the time, or the hose is clogged	• Disconnect, holes, biting, or bend in the intake pressure sensor hose.
15	Discontinuity or shorting of the throttle sensor is detected.	• Mounting of throttle sensor • Connection of throttle sensor, engine harness, main harness, and ECM coupler. • Check the sensor • Continuity of engine harness and main harness.
16	Fixed throttle sensor output.	• Mounting of throttle sensor. • Check the sensor

Figure 7-65. Typical fault code found in a service manual. (Yamaha Motor Corporation U.S.A.)

Summary

Fuel systems can be classified into two types: carburetors and electronic fuel injection (EFI) systems. The function of the fuel delivery parts are the same for both systems. The fuel tank holds the fuel supply for the motorcycle, ATV, or scooter. A fuel petcock is an on/off valve that provides a means of stopping fuel flow in the system when the engine is not running. The fuel line is a neoprene or plastic tube that carries fuel from the petcock to the carburetor or fuel injector. A fuel pump is required on some motorcycles. A fuel filter is used to remove foreign matter from the gasoline. The intake manifold directs the air-fuel mixture to the engine.

Gasoline is a compound of the elements carbon and hydrogen and is distilled from crude oil. Additives are blended into the distilled gasoline at the refinery. Gasoline blends are modified to increase or decrease the vaporization rate. In some parts of the country where ozone levels are excessively high, reformulated gasoline called oxygenated gasoline is sold. Oxygenated gasoline contains chemicals called oxygenates that reduce ozone formation. Gasoline is primarily formulated to meet the needs of cars, trucks, and vans. Often, motorcycle manufacturers have to design their fuel systems around a fuel intentionally designed for automotive use.

Carburetors rely on the venturi principle to draw fuel into the airstream. Many carburetors have venturi that cannot be altered and are called fixed venturi carburetors. Carburetors that can alter the venturi diameter by throttle valve movement are known as variable venturi carburetors. Modern motorcycle, ATV, and scooter engines commonly use one of three types of carburetors: slide carburetors, vacuum carburetors, and butterfly carburetors. The major difference in these carburetor designs is in the venturi restriction.

The slide carburetor uses a round slide piston to alter the venturi restriction. The float circuit maintains a constant level of fuel in the float bowl. The pilot circuit or idle circuit meters air and fuel at and slightly above idle. The slide cutaway system determines the air-fuel mixture from one-eighth to one-quarter throttle. The needle circuit controls the air-fuel mixture from one-quarter to three-quarter throttle opening. The main fuel circuit controls the air-fuel mixture from three-quarter to wide open throttle. The accelerator pump circuit discharges a metered amount of fuel into the carburetor throat as the throttle is opened. The starter circuit provides an enriched mixture for cold engine operation. The choke system restricts the amount of air entering the carburetor.

A vacuum carburetor, also called a CV or constant velocity or venturi carburetor, uses both a slide valve and butterfly valve to control airflow through the venturi. The butterfly plate is the primary means of controlling airflow through the carburetor. A vacuum piston controls venturi restriction. A butterfly carburetor uses three systems or circuits to meter fuel: pilot circuit; main circuit; accelerator pump circuit. To maintain the proper air-fuel mixture during the service life of the motorcycle, certain carburetor adjustments must be made. Usually, motorcycle carburetors require rebuilding because of a buildup of varnish and other deposits. Occasionally, carburetors need to be rebuilt as a result of normal wear.

Electronic fuel injection (EFI) systems use an on-board computer or electronic control module. The injection quantity is controlled based on information from various sensors which detect engine operating and external conditions to ensure an optimum supply of fuel at all times. The control operations performed by the electronic control module (ECM) may be broadly classified into three parts: fuel injection control; ignition system control; and self diagnostics. ECMs have additional built-in features, such as theft prevention, and several fuel cut-off functions that operate with the side stand switch, clutch switch, and neutral switch

One of the ECM's major functions is to provide self-diagnostics to the EFI system. Fault codes that help to diagnose problems in the EFI system can be checked by using either the EFI warning light or by using a pocket voltage tester or diagnostic tester.

Know These Terms

Fuel tank	Air filter
Fuel petcock	Air box
Sediment bowl	Intake manifold
Fuel line	Throttle twist grip
Fuel pump	Throttle cable
Fuel filter	Gasoline
Octane rating	Positive carburetor linkages
Vaporized	Slide carburetor
Oxygenated gasoline	Float circuit
Methyl tertiary butyl ether (MTBE)	Needle
Ethyl tertiary butyl ether (ETBE)	Seat
Tertiary amyl methyl ether (TAME)	Float bowl
Ethanol	Overflow tube
Atomized	Float bowl vent
Air-fuel ratio	Pilot circuit
Venturi principle	Pilot jet
Venturi	Pilot adjustment screw
Fixed venturi carburetors	Slide cutaway system
Variable venturi carburetors	Needle circuit
Primary needle system	Cold soak cleaner
Bleeder needle circuit	Electronic fuel injection (EFI)

Main fuel circuit	Electronic control module (ECM)
Accelerator pump circuit	Input interface circuit
Air cut-off valve	Central processing unit (CPU)
Starter circuit	Output interface circuit
Choke system	Fall detection switch
Tickler system	Airflow meter
Enrichment system	Fuel injector
Bystarter system	Throttle body
PTC device	Pressure regulator
Vacuum carburetor	Intake pressure sensor
Vacuum piston	Atmospheric pressure sensor
Pilot bypass circuit	Coolant temperature sensor
Butterfly controlled carburetor	Intake temperature sensors
Idle mixture	Throttle position sensor
Pilot air screw	Oxygen (O_2) sensors
Pilot fuel screw	Camshaft sensor
Idle speed	Crankshaft sensor
Throttle stop screw	Three-way catalytic conversion system
Float level	Stoichiometric

Review Questions—Chapter 7

Do not write in this text. Place your answers on a separate sheet of paper.

1. A fuel tank must be ______ to prevent a buildup of vacuum or pressure.
2. When is a fuel pump needed on a motorcycle?
3. What is a typical carburetor's air-fuel ratio at cruising speeds?
   A. 14.7:1.
   B. 3:1.
   C. 17:1.
   D. 7:1.
4. List the eight systems or circuits of a slide carburetor.
5. The ______ circuit controls air-fuel mixture from one-quarter to three-quarter throttle.
   A. pilot circuit
   B. off-idle circuit
   C. main circuit
   D. needle circuit
6. Which of the slide carburetor circuits controls the air-fuel mixture at wide open throttle?
7. Turn a carburetor pilot fuel screw ______ to richen the mixture and ______ to lean the mixture.
8. What must be done if rust or water is present in the carburetor?
   A. Carburetor rebuild.
   B. Fuel filter replacement.
   C. Drain and flush the fuel system.
   D. All of the above.
9. List three precautions when using a cold soak cleaner.
10. When one vacuum gauge reads too high during synchronization, this indicates that the carburetor slide is too ______.
11. Which of the following is *not* monitored by the electronic fuel injection ECM?
    A. Airflow.
    B. Air temperature.
    C. Fuel pressure.
    D. Engine rpm.
12. List the three parts of a motorcycle's electronic control system.
13. What is the function of the coolant temperature sensor in an EFI system?
14. Oxygen sensors use the principle of oxygen's conductivity with ____.
    A. zirconium
    B. titanium
    C. gold
    D. None of the above.
15. How does the ECM's self-diagnostic system function?

Suggested Activities

1. Disassemble a slide carburetor and a vacuum carburetor. Make a list of the differences between the two.
2. List which make motorcycle uses each of the following types of carburetors:
   A. Slide type.
   B. CV with vacuum piston.
   C. CV with vacuum diaphragm.
   D. Butterfly .
3. Complete a carburetor overhaul using the Carburetor Rebuilding Summary and a shop manual. Synchronize a set of carburetors using specific service manual instructions.
4. Locate all the sensors, ECM, and output devices on an electronic fuel injected bike.
5. Activate and use the self-diagnostic system in an ECM equipped bike.

Modern motorcycles use multiple valves for each cylinder. (Yamaha Motor Corporation U.S.A.)

8 Battery and Charging Systems

After studying this chapter, you will be able to:

- Describe the two types of batteries used in motorcycles.
- Understand the care of batteries.
- Name the components in an ac charging system.
- Explain half- and full-wave rectification.
- Describe the operation of permanent magnet and electromagnet alternator.
- Make necessary alternator service tests.
- Explain the differences between a mechanical and electronic valve regulator.

In Chapter 5, the fundamentals of electricity and electronics as applied to motorcycles, scooters, and ATVs was discussed. There are ways to generate and provide power for use in motorcycle electrical systems. In this chapter, the use of electricity to provide the source of starting and operating power will be covered.

Batteries

The ***battery*** stores electricity and is the primary source of power for the dc accessory circuits on a motorcycle, **Figure 8-1.** As such, its main function is to provide a source of reserve energy. The need for this reserve is most obvious in the case of the electric starter. Other less demanding circuits, such as the turn signals, also rely on the battery for proper operation. While these circuits could be powered directly by the charging system, their effectiveness would be too dependent on varying charging system output. The purpose of the battery is to provide initial starting power and to back up the charging system so the accessory circuits do not operate poorly at low rpm or stop functioning when the engine is shut off.

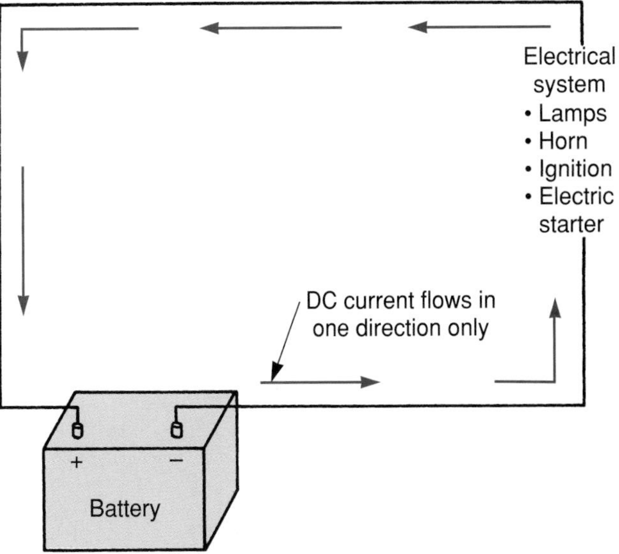

Figure 8-1. A battery supplies direct current to the electrical system. Current flows from the negative (–) battery terminal, through the circuit and back to positive (+) terminal.

Battery Safety Precautions

Batteries contain ***electrolyte,*** which is a mixture of water (H_2O) and ***sulfuric acid*** (H_2SO_4). For this reason, numerous warnings will be given throughout the text. The principle hazards in servicing batteries occur under charging conditions or when handling electrolyte. The following is a list of rules that must be observed when handling or charging batteries.

- All electrolyte spills should be immediately neutralized with baking soda and cleaned.
- When working with electrolyte, protective goggles or face shield and plastic gloves should be worn. Additional protective clothing may be required if many batteries are handled.
- When adding water or electrolyte, nonmetallic containers and/or funnels must be used.
- Electrolyte must not be stored in excessively warm locations or in direct sunlight. Make sure electrolyte containers are clearly marked.
- In cases where electrolyte contacts the skin or eyes, flush immediately with water for a minimum of five minutes. Get medical attention at once. If electrolyte splashes onto clothing, remove clothing as needed to avoid skin contact and rinse all affected areas immediately.
- Hydrogen gas is produced during charging as a part of normal battery operation. These gases can explode violently if flames or sparks are brought near the battery. Manufacturers' recommendations should be closely followed to restrict the charging rate to reduce the formation of hydrogen gas.
- When charging or using a battery in an enclosed area, always make sure there is adequate ventilation.
- Do not smoke around charging batteries.
- Exercise care to prevent tools or other metallic objects from falling across the battery terminals.
- Loosen the cell caps, but leave them in place when charging a battery.
- Check the vent tube for obstructions and proper routing. Gases trapped inside the battery can explode.
- Fill batteries only at a battery station to prevent contamination.

Battery Operation

There are two types of batteries used in motorcycles, scooters, and ATVs: the conventional battery and the maintenance-free (MF) battery. Conventional batteries have been in use for many years. Maintenance-free batteries have been used in mobile applications since the 1970s and have seen increased use in recent years.

Conventional Battery

A motorcycle battery is made up of several two volt cells connected in series. This is illustrated in the ***conventional battery,*** **Figure 8-2.** A 6-volt battery has three cells and a 12-volt battery has six cells. Each ***cell*** is made up of negative plates of sponge lead and positive plates of lead peroxide.

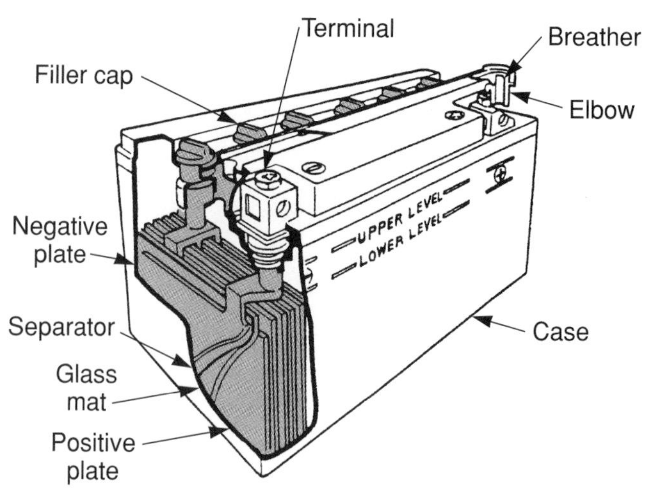

Figure 8-2. The components of a typical conventional battery. (Honda Motor Co., Ltd.)

The conventional battery conducts electricity when the electrolyte's chemical action takes place between the two plates, which are made of lead peroxide (PbO_2) and sponge lead (Pb). When the battery is discharged, the sulfate ion (SO_4) in the sulfuric acid combines with the lead in the plate materials, forming lead sulfate ($PbSO_4$). See **Figure 8-3A.** By passing electric current back into the battery, the plates revert to lead peroxide and lead, **Figure 8-3B.**

Since the ***specific gravity*** of electrolyte (relative weight of sulfuric acid as compared with an equal volume of water) can vary, a battery's state of charge is determined by measuring the electrolyte's specific gravity.

Because the motorcycle battery is constantly subjected to charging and discharging cycles, the water in the electrolyte is boiled off. When the water reaches the point where the plates become exposed, a white crystalline (lead sulfate) deposit forms. This process is called ***sulfation.*** This white crystalline lead sulfate is difficult to revert back to lead peroxide and lead, unlike the lead sulfate produced by discharging. This can cause damage to the battery, reducing its useful life. This can occur not only when the electrolyte level is low but also when the battery remains discharged for long periods. Remember that electrolyte levels go down when water in the battery evaporates. When refilling the battery, always add distilled water, not electrolyte.

Warning: Electrolyte is considered a hazardous substance. If electrolyte gets on your skin, flush with water. If electrolyte gets in your eyes, flush with water for at least 15 minutes. If swallowed, drink large quantities of water or milk and follow with milk of magnesia or vegetable oil. Do not induce vomiting. In both cases call a physician or poison control center for advice.

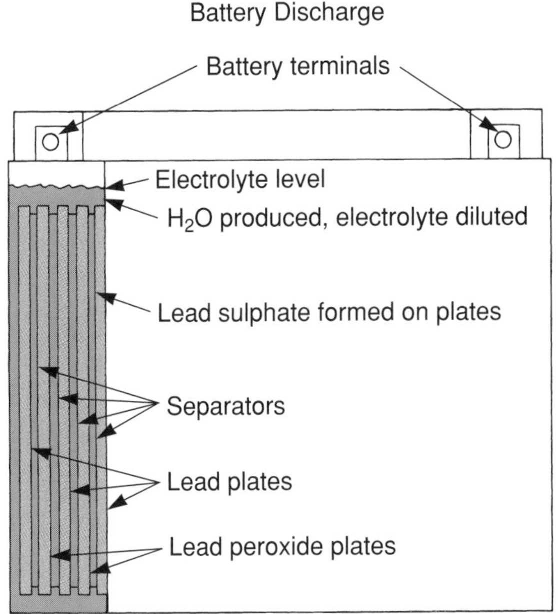

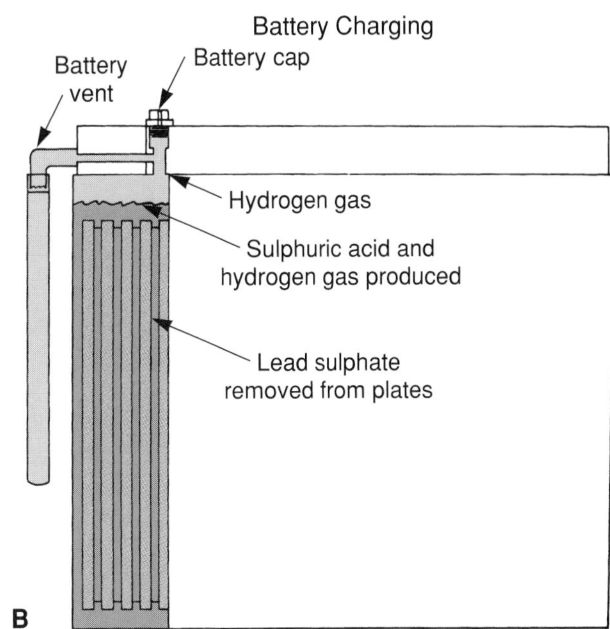

Figure 8-3. A—Lead sulfate and water are byproducts of a chemical reaction that takes place as a battery discharges. Lead sulfate is deposited on the plates and water dilutes the electrolyte. B—As a battery is charged, lead sulfate is removed from the plates, and sulfuric acid and hydrogen gas are produced. Hydrogen gas is very explosive and must be vented.

Some batteries have built-in sensors, or a sensor packaged with the battery. The primary function of the sensor is similar to a fuel gauge. When the electrolyte level drops below the required amount necessary for safe operation, the sensor causes a warning light to flash, alerting the owner that it is time to refill the battery with distilled water.

Caution: Original equipment sensor plugs vary in length, size, and diameter. Because of this, original equipment sensors are not recommended for use in aftermarket batteries. A plug that is too long could create a short in the battery and cause damage to the electrical system. If the plug is too short, it may cause the warning light to flash too soon.

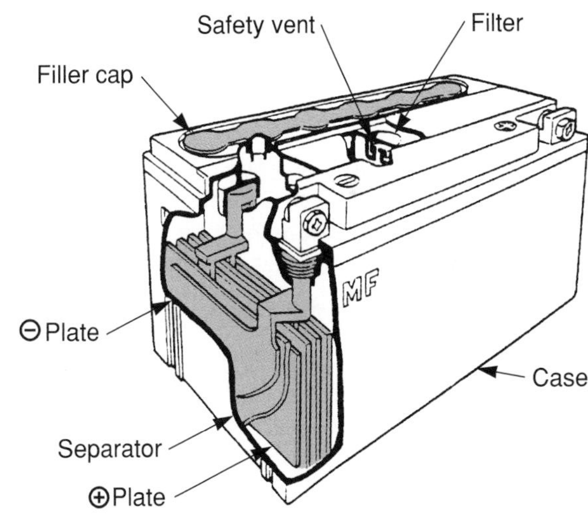

Figure 8-4. Typical maintenance-free battery.

Maintenance-Free Battery

The ***maintenance-free (MF) battery*** requires no electrolyte level inspection or periodic refilling. Similar in design to the conventional battery, the maintenance-free battery produces hydrogen and oxygen gas. However, the plates do not convert to lead completely, **Figure 8-4.** This state of lead is called *sponge lead.* When the battery is overcharged, the positive plates produce oxygen gas. The oxygen reacts with the hydrogen released from the negative plates and produces water. Therefore, water does not need to be added to maintenance-free batteries. This process, often called *gas recombination technology,* requires the battery to be permanently sealed, making it virtually spill proof.

Maintenance-free batteries have safety valves designed to open when excessive gas is produced. The safety valves close and seal the battery when internal pressure returns to normal. A ceramic filter is placed over the safety valves to prevent any combustion of the gases produced.

Battery Service

The battery is the heart of the electrical system and should be checked and serviced as indicated in the service manual. The majority of electrical system problems can be attributed to neglect of this vital component.

Battery service typically consists of:

1. Removing the battery from the bike.
2. Cleaning the battery.

3. Visual inspection.
4. Topping off conventional battery cells with distilled water.
5. Checking electrolyte specific gravity (when possible).
6. Charging the battery (if needed).
7. Preparing a new battery for service.
8. Installing the battery.

Removing the Battery

In the interest of safety, the first step is to remove the battery from the motorcycle, **Figure 8-5.** With the battery on a workbench, service procedures will be easier to perform. To remove the battery from the bike, first turn off the ignition switch. Then remove the terminal cover and disconnect the negative *(–)* battery cable, followed by the positive *(+)* cable.

Warning: Disconnecting the positive cable first could result in an accidental short between the two terminals or the positive terminal and ground if the tool used to disconnect the terminal contacts the frame. The spark could damage the battery, electrical components, or cause an explosion.

For conventional batteries, always disconnect the vent or breather tube. See **Figure 8-6.** Remember that some electrolyte may remain in the tube. Slide the battery out of its compartment and remove it from the motorcycle's frame.

Cleaning the Battery

After the battery has been removed from the motorcycle, check it for corrosion and dirt. The top of the battery in particular should be kept clean. Acid film and dirt will permit current to flow between the terminals, causing the battery to slowly discharge. ***Sulfate deposits*** are the whitish-gray material that clings to the plates and battery case. ***Sediment*** is contaminant or actual plate material that has settled to the bottom of the battery case. Sediment build-up can be caused by excessive vibration (from improper mounting) or from normal deterioration. If excessive sulfation or sediment is present, it will short circuit the battery. The battery, its box, and surrounding areas should be kept free of corrosion and oil.

For best results, first rinse the battery with clean water. Do not allow water to enter the cells. Then carefully wash the case, both terminals, and the battery box with a solution of baking soda and water. Keep the filler plugs sealed tight so none of the cleaning solution enters the cells. If cleaning solution enters a cell, it will neutralize the electrolyte and damage the battery. Brush the solution on with a stiff bristle parts cleaning brush. See **Figure 8-7.** Using strong spray from a hose, clean all the residue from the battery.

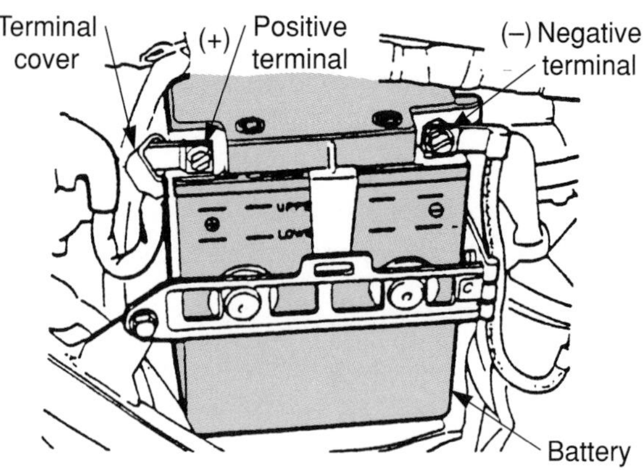

Figure 8-5. Typical battery mounting on a motorcycle. (Honda Motor Co., Ltd.)

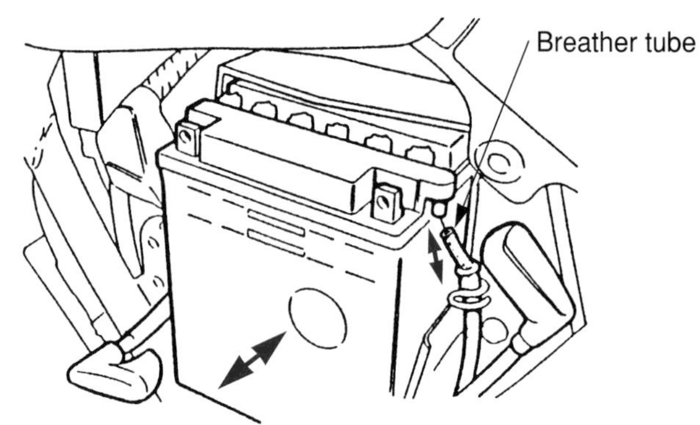

Figure 8-6. Removing the vent or breather tube from the battery. (Honda Motor Co., Ltd.)

Figure 8-7. Cleaning the terminals with a brush.

Once the battery has been cleaned, inspect the case for obvious damage such as cracks, leaks, discoloration, warping, or a raised top, which may indicate the battery has been overheated or overcharged. Also, inspect the battery terminals, screws, and cables for broken or loose connections.

Filling the Battery

To check the electrolyte level on batteries with transparent cases, the electrolyte level should be maintained between the two marks on the battery case. On other batteries, remove the battery caps and observe the level in the individual battery cells. If the electrolyte level is low, top off with distilled water to bring it up to the proper level. See **Figure 8-8.** Do not add acid, only water.

Do not use tap water or rainwater since it may contain impurities that could reduce battery life. It is not necessary, as mentioned earlier in the chapter, to add distilled water to maintenance-free batteries. After the fluid level has been corrected, reinstall the battery caps.

Caution: Be careful not to spill battery electrolyte on painted or polished surfaces. The liquid is highly corrosive and will damage the finish. If spilled, wash it off immediately with soapy water and thoroughly rinse with clean water.

While inspecting the electrolyte, check for sediment on the bottom of cells; if it touches the plates, shorting will occur. Inspect plates for sulfation or mossing. A white deposit may be sulfation, caused by excessive discharging or low electrolyte level. Mossing looks like little red lines and results from overcharging, overheating, or freezing. The battery shown in **Figure 8-9** is sulfated beyond recovery.

Battery Testing

There are two types of battery tests: unloaded and load. An ***unloaded test*** is made on a battery without discharging current. If a more precise reading is needed, the load test is used. Both tests give an accurate indication of the battery's state of charge. Battery design sometimes dictates which test is used.

Figure 8-8. Topping off the cells with distilled water.

Unloaded Test

Check the battery's state of charge by using either a voltmeter or hydrometer. With a voltmeter, voltage readings appear instantly to show the state of charge. Remember to hook the positive lead to the positive terminal, and the negative lead to the negative terminal, **Figure 8-10.**

When using a hydrometer, hold the barrel vertically and take the reading with your eyes level with the level of electrolyte in the barrel. Disregard the slight curvature of the liquid where it contacts the barrel sides and float stem.

Take an electrolyte specific gravity reading from each cell. If the readings are 1.260 or higher and are within

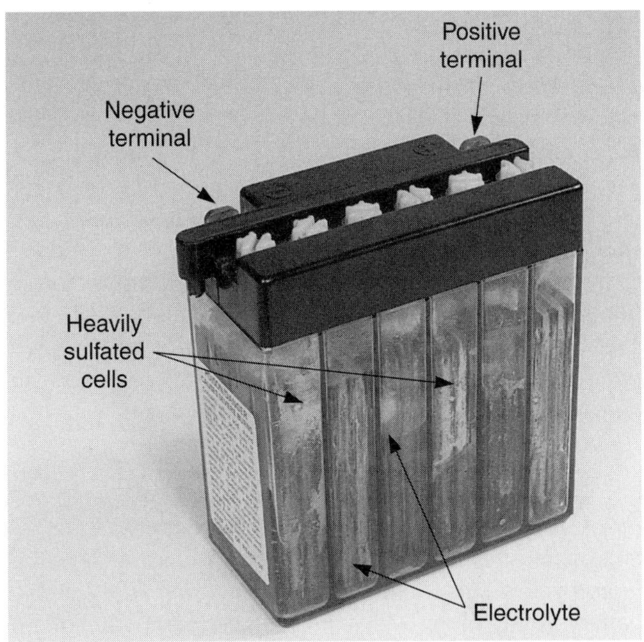

Figure 8-9. A badly sulfated battery beyond recovery.

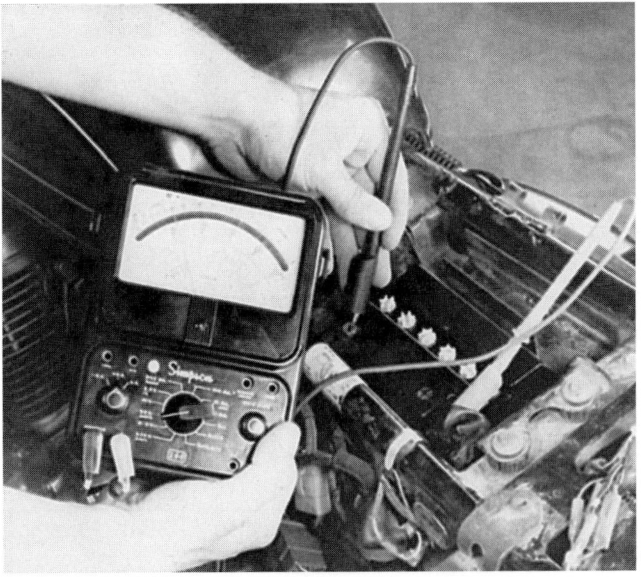

Figure 8-10. Checking the battery state of charge with a voltmeter.

.050 of each other for all cells, the battery is sufficiently charged. If the specific gravity readings are less that 1.260 or vary greatly between cells, recharge the battery and retest. The chart in **Figure 8-11** gives the state of charge in relation to readings by syringe hydrometer, **Figure 8-12**, digital voltmeter, and five-ball hydrometer.

Never take a hydrometer reading immediately after adding water to the cell or subjecting the battery to prolonged loads, such as heavy starter motor cranking. The best way of mixing water and electrolyte in a recently serviced cell is to charge the battery for a short period of time.

A battery's specific gravity changes with temperature. Ideally, readings should be taken at 77°F (24°C). A few degrees off this temperature will have little effect. Use the following conversion factor when conditions are extremely hot or cold:

- Add .001 to the specific gravity reading for every 3° above 77°F (1.8° above 24°C), or
- Subtract .001 from the specific gravity reading for every 3° below 77°F (1.8° below 24°C).

Cell voltage can be found by adding 0.84 to the specific gravity.

Test maintenance-free batteries with a voltmeter or multimeter. If the stabilized open circuit voltage is below 12.4 volts, the battery needs charging. For a stabilized open circuit reading, first allow the battery to remain in an open circuit condition for at least four hours.

Load Testing

A ***load test*** is used to check the battery's state of charge. This test is done by turning on a load, such as the motorcycle's lights, and taking a voltage reading at the battery. Many motorcycles are designed so the headlight and taillight come on when the ignition key is turned to run. Some motorcycles with an ac headlight, such as enduro models, turn on the taillight and stoplight. When connecting the meter, remember to connect positive to positive, negative to negative.

State of Charge	Syringe Hydrometer	Digital Voltmeter	Five-Ball Hydrometer
100% Charged Battery w/Sulfate Stop Additive	1.280	12.80V	5 Balls Floating
100% Charged	1.265	12.60V	4 Balls Floating
75% Charged	1.210	12.40V	3 Balls Floating
50% Charged	1.160	12.10V	2 Balls Floating
25% Charged	1.120	11.90V	1 Balls Floating
0% Charged	less than 1.100	less than 11.80V	0 Balls Floating

Figure 8-11. Battery state of charge and typical indications as measured by various test devices.

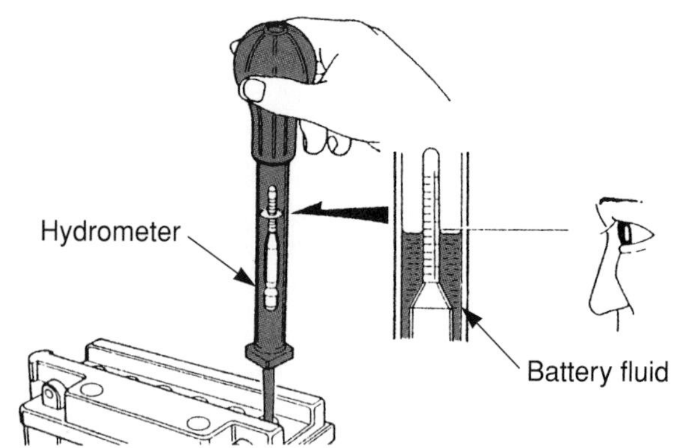

Figure 8-12. Checking the state of charge (specific gravity) with a syringe type hydrometer. (Honda Motor Co., Ltd.)

The battery in a 12-volt system with a light load should have at least 11.5 volts dc; a 6-volt system should have at least 5.75 volts. If the voltage drops below these levels, the battery needs to be charged. Check the service manual for the exact acceptable voltage; in some batteries the minimum is as low as 10.5 volts. If a battery voltage drops below manual specifications, the battery should be charged or replaced as needed.

Battery Ratings

There are two battery rating systems that motorcycle technicians should be familiar with. They are the capacity, or ampere-hour (AH) rating, and cold cranking amps (CCA), or cold start rating. The ***ampere-hour rating*** measures the battery's ability to discharge current for an extended period of time. The larger the plate area, the greater the ampere-hour rating.

Because the electrolyte chemical reaction is affected by temperature, a battery will have a lower ampere-hour rating in cold temperatures. Most small motorcycle engine batteries are rated at 10 hours, which means the battery has to last for that period of time at a given discharge rate. The discharge rate is no higher than the time it takes the cell voltage to drop to 1.75 volts. A 14 ampere-hour battery, for example, discharges at a rate of 1.4 ampere-hours for 10 hours. At this point, cell voltage drops to 1.75 volts for a 12-volt battery, or 5.25 volts for a 6-volt battery.

Cold cranking amps or cold start rating indicates how well a battery can be expected to perform in low temperatures. This rating is also based on plate area as well as thickness. The rating is determined by discharging the battery at a high rate while measuring the discharge with a voltmeter. The test continues until each cell has been discharged to 1 volt. As engine displacement increases, so does the cranking current. Since starting systems differ by model and manufacturer, it is best to check the service manual for original equipment replacement. If a special application demands higher cranking power, select a battery that fits the bike and its power requirements.

Charging the Battery

When you charge a conventional lead-acid battery, electrolysis breaks the water down into its components, hydrogen and oxygen. Be sure to loosen the filler plugs while charging the battery, **Figure 8-13.** Do not fully remove the battery filler plugs as acid could splash over the top of the battery while charging.

Caution: To prevent damage to maintenance-free batteries, never remove the sealing caps. Also, do not recharge a battery in the motorcycle's frame; the mist emitted from the battery during the charging process will corrode all surrounding surfaces.

The recharging procedure is as follows:

1. Connect the positive *(+)* charger lead to the positive battery terminal and the negative *(–)* charger lead to the negative battery terminal. See **Figure 8-14.**

Caution: Do not exceed the recommended charging amperage rate or charging time on the label attached to the battery.

2. Set the charger to the correct voltage. If the charger output is variable, it is best to select a low setting. Charge the battery at a rate of 10% of the amp hour rating. For example, a 10 amp hour battery would be charged at a rate of 1 amp.
3. Turn the charger on.
4. After the battery has been charged for the specified amount of time, turn the charger off, unplug it, and disconnect the charger and ammeter leads. Following this procedure reduces the chance of sparks.
5. Connect a voltmeter across the battery negative and positive terminals and measure the battery voltage. A fully charged battery should read 13-13.2 volts. If the voltage is 12.3 or less, the battery is undercharged.
6. If the battery remains stable for 1 hour at the specified voltage, the battery is considered charged and the specific gravity should be within the specified limits.
7. Clean the battery terminals and case. Coat the terminals with a thin layer of dielectric grease to retard corrosion and battery decomposition.

Never overcharge a battery. A battery is said to be overcharged when excess current is supplied to the battery. When the battery is overcharged, volatile gas is emitted from the plates, and electrolyte temperature rises. This temperature rise causes rapid water loss from the battery. This water loss and temperature rise will shorten the battery's life. If left unchecked, water loss and high temperature will permanently damage the battery.

Activating a New Conventional Battery

When filling a new conventional battery with electrolyte, first remove the filler plugs. Fill the battery with electrolyte that has an approximate specific gravity of 1.265. Fill to the level as indicated on the battery. The electrolyte should have a temperature between 60-86°F (16-30°C) before filling. Leave the battery standing for a minimum of thirty minutes to let the electrolyte "soak-in". The acid level may drop during the standing time. Fill with any remaining electrolyte or water to the upper level before starting the charge.

Place the battery on charge for 3-5 hours at approximately the current equivalent to 10% of its rated capacity. The battery can take a quick charge at a higher current up to 30% of capacity. However, a quick charge may only be taken by the battery plate surface areas, while the lower

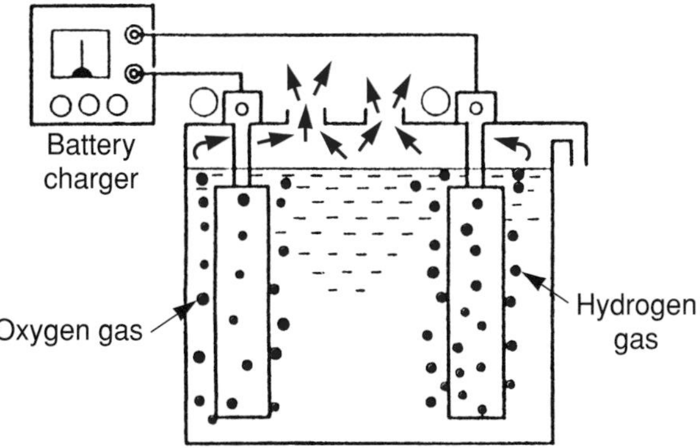

Figure 8-13. To prevent gas pressure buildup in the battery, remove the battery caps. (Honda Motor Co., Ltd.)

Figure 8-14. Leave the battery charger off and unplugged until charger leads are connected. Observe the proper polarity when connecting the battery charger leads to the battery terminals.

current will charge the battery uniformly. If the electrolyte level falls after charging, fill with distilled water to the upper level. After the water is added, continue charging 1-2 hours to mix water with the acid. After charging, replace the filling plugs, wash off any spilled acid with water, and dry the battery case. Make sure the battery terminals are completely clean of any acid.

Activating a Maintenance-Free Battery

Like conventional batteries, maintenance-free batteries are shipped dry charged from the manufacturer or supplier. Electrolyte must be added before the battery can be put into service. The filling procedure for a maintenance-free battery is as follows:

1. Remove the aluminum tape sealing the battery electrolyte filler holes, **Figure 8-15A.**
2. Hold the electrolyte container with its nozzles upright, and use wire cutters to cut off the ends of the nozzles at the designated locations (between the ends and the packing), **Figure 8-15B.**
3. Insert the electrolyte container nozzles into the battery's six electrolyte filler holes, holding the container firmly so that it does not fall, **Figure 8-15C.** Take precaution not to allow any fluid to spill.
4. Use wire cutters to cut the protruding part on the bottom of each container. Leave the container in this position for about 20 minutes.
5. To confirm electrolyte flow, make sure bubbles are coming up from all six filler holes. If no air bubbles are coming up from the filler holes, tap the bottom of the bottle two or three times. Do not remove the container or tilt the battery.
6. After confirming that the electrolyte has entered the battery completely, remove the electrolyte containers from the battery. Wait for approximately 10 minutes.
7. Insert the caps into the filler holes, pressing in firmly so the top of the caps do not protrude above the surface of the top cover, **Figure 8-15D.** The fill procedure is now complete.

Warning: Never remove the cap strip nor add any water or electrolyte to maintenance-free batteries.

Battery Installation

When installing a battery in a bike, be sure to route the breather or vent tube properly. Pay attention to the following:

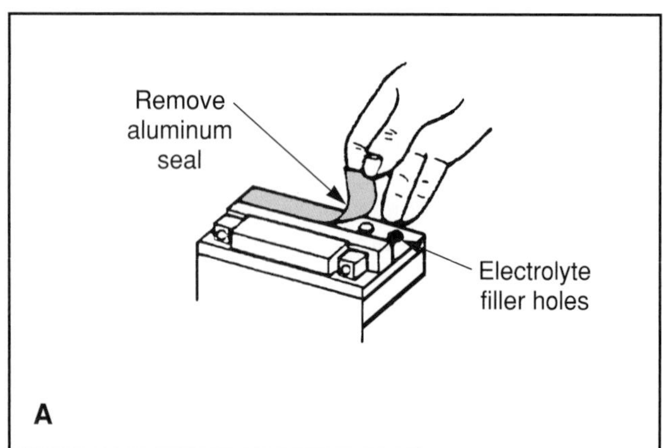

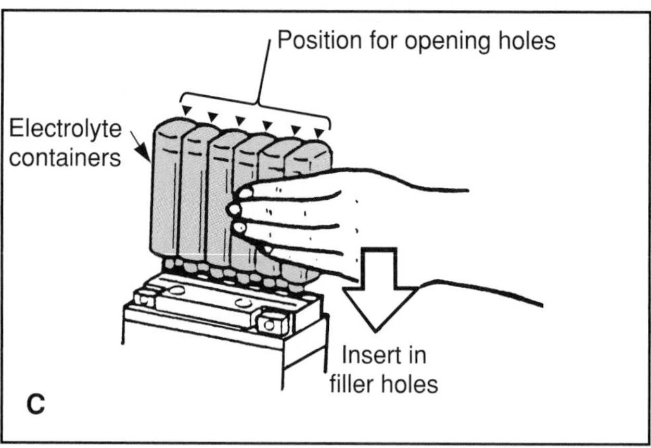

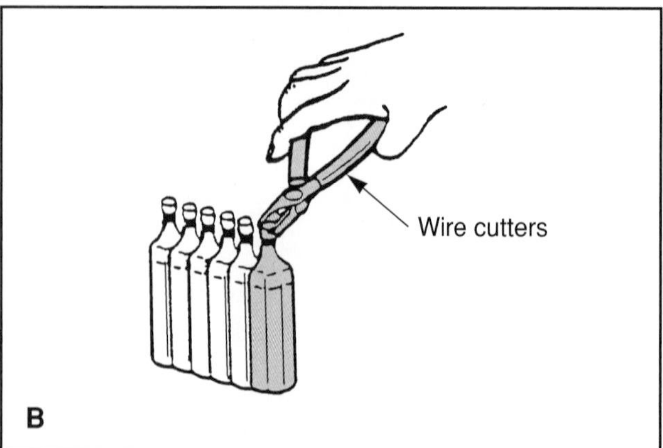

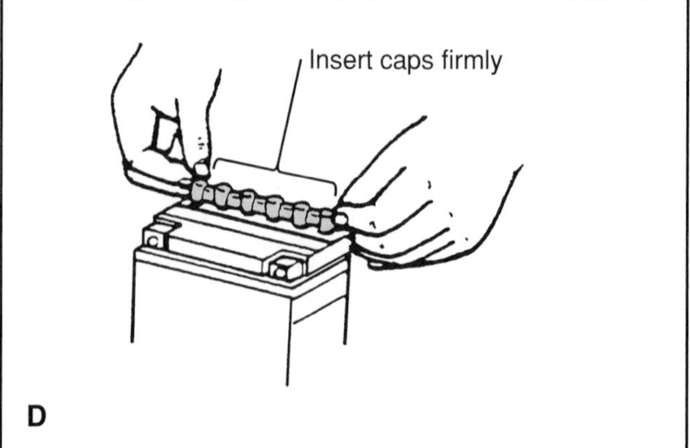

Figure 8-15. Steps in activating a maintenance-free battery. A—Remove seal from the cells. B—Cut the caps on the electrolyte container(s). C—Carefully position the electrolyte containers over the battery cells and allow to drain. D—After filling, install the battery cell caps. (American Suzuki Motor Corporation)

- Connect the vent tube securely.
- Follow all caution labels and route the tube accordingly.
- Avoid bending or pinching the vent tube. Make sure the breather tube has not been bent or pinched by surrounding components. Failure to replace a bent or kinked breather tube may lead to pressure buildup that can cause the battery to explode.

When replacing the battery, proceed as follows:

1. Place the battery into the frame. Make sure the battery fits properly in the frame.
2. Secure the battery with the battery holder. Improper installation may cause vibrations which can damage the battery case.
3. To prevent shorting, always connect the positive cable first. Attach the negative lead, making sure it has a good connection to the frame (ground). Remove paint from the frame, if necessary, to achieve a good ground.
4. After connecting the electrical cables, apply a light coating of dielectric grease or silicone spray to the battery's electrical terminals to retard corrosion and decomposition.

Note: When replacing an old battery with a new one, be sure to turn it in at a recycling center. The lead plates and plastic can be recycled. Never place an old battery in with shop refuse since it is illegal to place any hazardous materials in a landfill.

Troubleshooting Battery Problems

There are five major reasons why batteries fail:

- Normal battery deterioration.
- Poor physical condition.
- Prolonged under or overcharging.
- Undercapacity application.
- Lack of proper maintenance.

Normal battery cycling (charging and discharging) along with exposure to extreme heat and cold results in a gradual deterioration of the battery plates.

Poor Physical Condition

The physical condition of a battery is an obvious and very important factor in its operation. Causes of poor physical condition are:

- Improper battery mounting.
- Plugged vent tube.
- Overcharging.
- Leaking filler caps.
- Foreign materials placed near the battery.
- Improper mounting.

Prolonged Undercharging or Overcharging

Although batteries are constantly discharged and recharged with electricity, the exchange is usually well balanced. Conditions that can alter this balance are:

- Long periods of disuse.
- Installation of electrical accessories that draw excess current.
- A malfunctioning charging system.
- A short or ground.
- A change in the designed resistance of an electrical circuit.

Undercapacity Applications

A battery is selected for a specific job after careful consideration of the current requirements needed. While it is not often a problem, a particular battery may be too small for the application. A common complaint might be that the "battery goes dead every 500 miles." If a bike has this complaint after a recent battery replacement, check the amp-hour rating of the battery. Larger street motorcycles with electric starters and many accessories require batteries with high amp-hour ratings. Dual-purpose motorcycles require very little current, and can use very small batteries. If a low amp-hour rated battery or additional electrical accessories are installed on a motorcycle that was not designed for them, problems will occur.

If the amp-hour rating is correct, check the charging system output. Will it charge the battery under normal operating conditions? If not, disconnect the additional electrical accessories and retest the charging system output.

Lack of Proper Maintenance

Lack of maintenance is one of the greatest contributors to battery failure. Allowing dirt and residue to buildup on the battery surface, corroded terminals, and failure to check and add water will result in reduced battery life. Proper battery maintenance should be stressed to the customer.

Alternators

Some motorcycles do not have batteries in their electrical systems. These models power electrical components with electricity mechanically generated by an alternator, which is controlled by a regulator, **Figure 8-16.** For components using transistors which require dc current, a small rectifier (CD power unit) is used to convert alternator (ac) current to battery (dc) current.

To provide stable current without using a battery, an alternator that supplies high current at low engine rpm is used. If the alternator continues supplying current as engine rpm increases, the excessive current may burn out lightbulbs and damage computer components. To prevent this, the regulator maintains alternator output voltage in

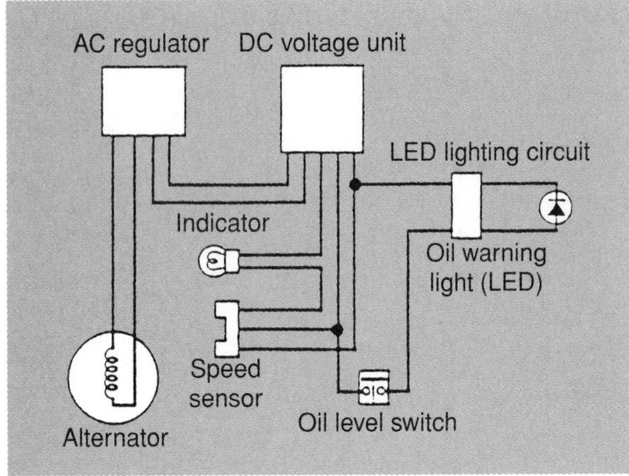

Figure 8-16. Typical ac alternator circuit. (Honda Motor Co., Ltd.)

the specified range. Some ac regulators have a protection circuit built into the alternator circuit to prevent abrupt voltage increases during cold engine starts.

The current generated from the alternator flows at voltage levels lower than the regulated value. As engine rpm increases, the regulator detects the voltage rise and directs current to the thyristor, switching the alternator's output to ground. When the alternator voltage goes over the specified voltage, the regulator shuts off the excess voltage, maintaining a constant voltage output.

Although some electrical components receive ac current, most systems require dc current to operate. Therefore, a compact and lightweight dc voltage unit regulates the ac current to these systems, **Figure 8-17.** There are systems and components designed for models that use ac systems, such as turn signals, that have front and rear signals that flash alternately.

Alternator Operation

An ***alternator*** is capable of changing mechanical energy (rotating motion) into electrical energy. A motorcycle alternator, **Figure 8-18,** is usually mounted on and driven by the engine crankshaft.

Refer to **Figure 8-19** as the operation of a simple alternator is explained. As the north pole approaches the coil, current begins to flow in the wire, *A.* As the north pole centers itself on the coil, current flow is at a maximum, *B.* As the north pole moves away from the coil, current begins to drop off, *C.* At the 90° position, current has stopped flowing completely, *D.* As the south pole begins to approach the coil, current starts flowing in the opposite direction, *E.* Movement of the south pole to the center position again causes maximum current flow, *F.* Movement away from the coil causes current to drop off, *G.* As you can see, each 180° movement of the magnet causes the current to reverse direction, *H.*

Three factors will affect the amount of current induced in our simple alternator:

- The strength of the magnetic field.
- Number of coil windings.

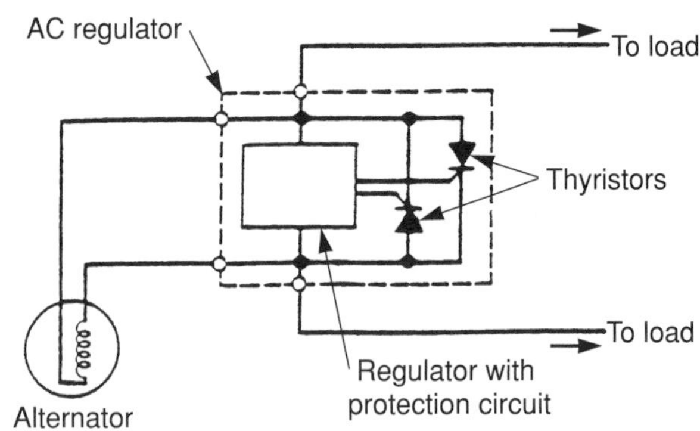

Figure 8-17. Location and schematic of dc voltage unit in an alternator circuit. (Honda Motor Co., Ltd.)

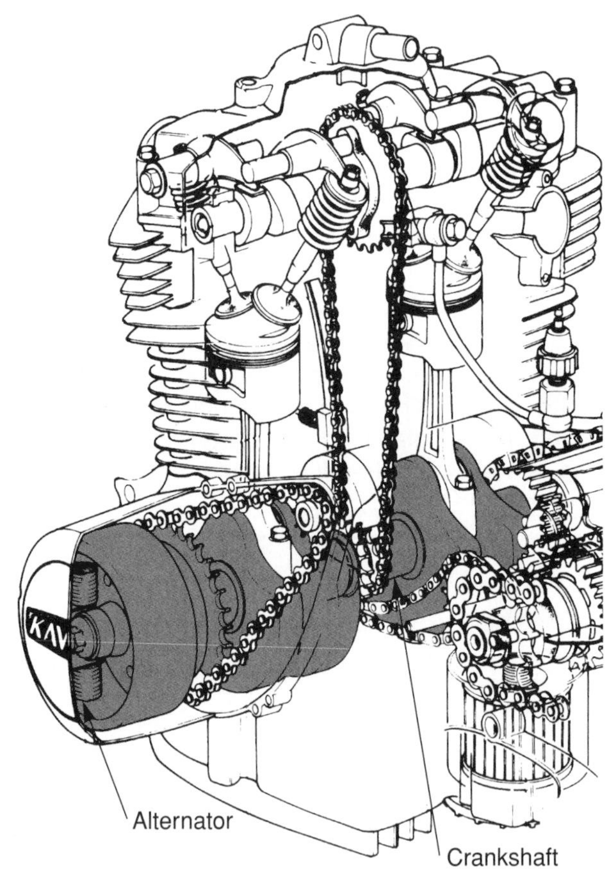

Figure 8-18. An alternator is mounted on end of the crankshaft. Mechanical energy is converted to electrical energy as the crankshaft spins the alternator. (Kawasaki Motors Corporation U.S.A.)

- Speed of the rotating magnet.

The alternator consists of a rotor and stator. The ***rotor*** consists of a crankshaft driven flywheel with a series of magnets attached. The ***stator*** consists of wire coils wound around a series of soft iron poles. When the engine starts, the rotor rotates with the crankshaft.

When the coil core passes through the magnetic field, current is generated. This is called electromagnetic induction, and systems such as the ignition system generate power using this principle. In addition, the rotor acts as a

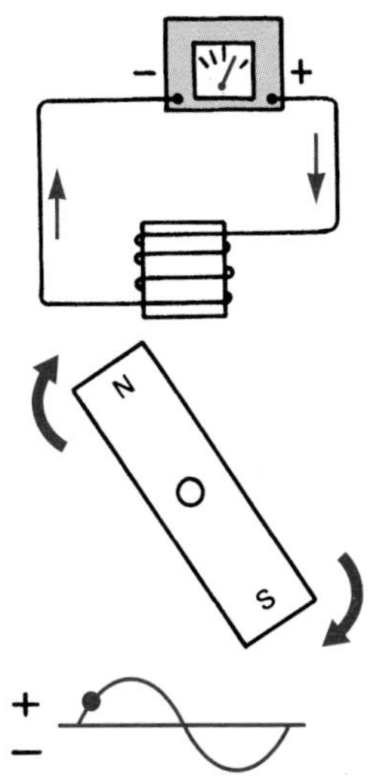

A—As N pole approaches coil, positive current flow begins.

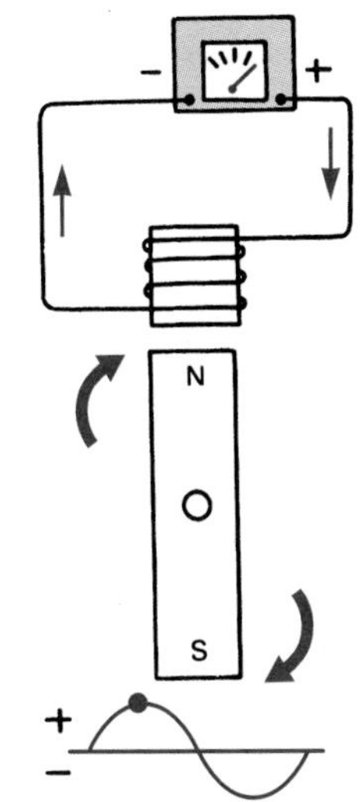

B—Positive current flow is at maximum as N pole passes coil.

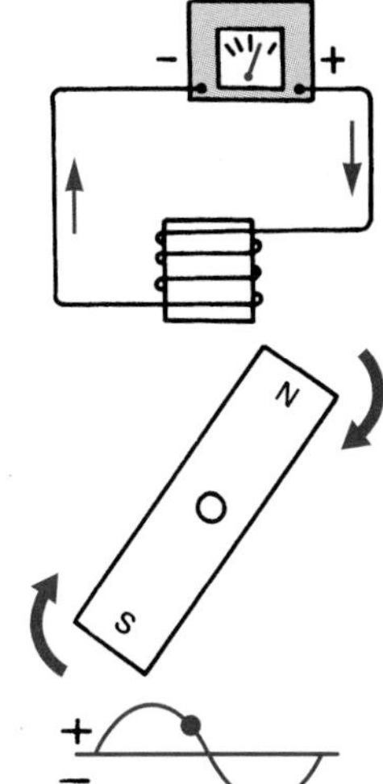

C—As N pole moves away from coil, positive current flow drops off.

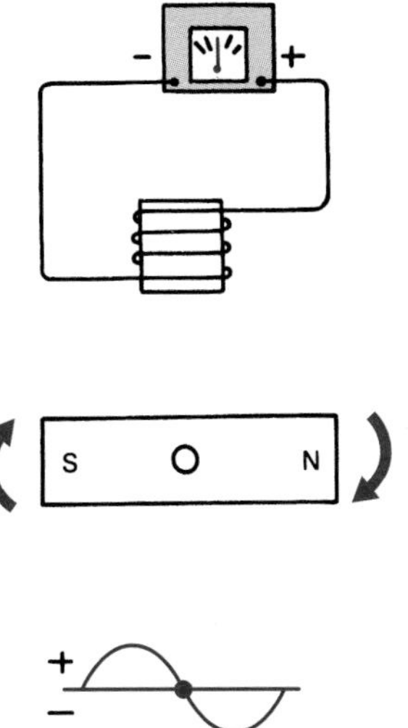

D—When N and S poles are 90° from coil, current flow stops.

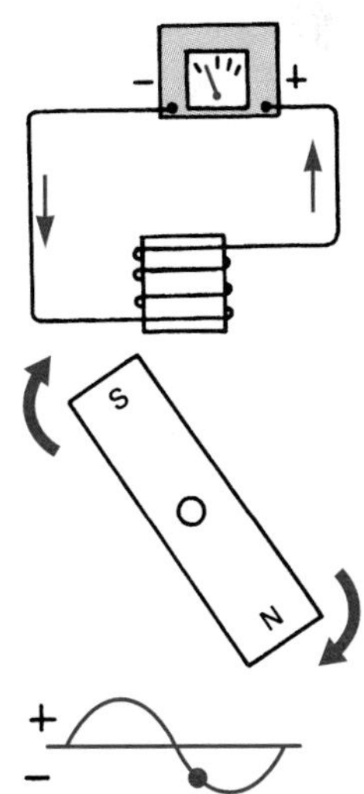

E—As S pole approaches coil, negative current flow begins.

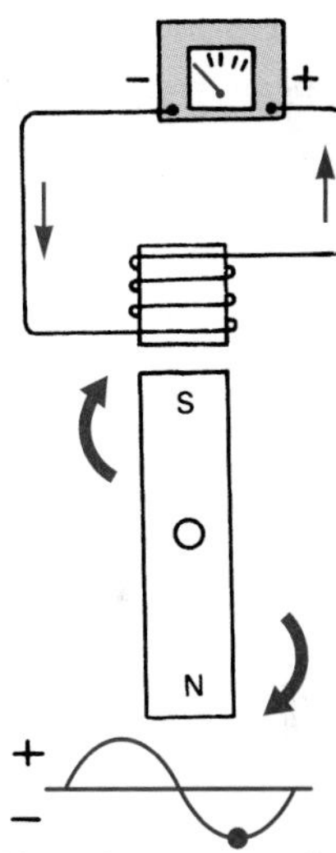

F—Negative current flow is at maximum as S pole passes coil.

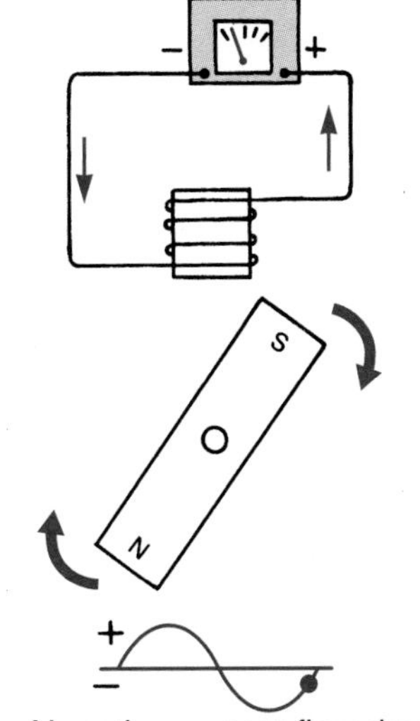

G—Negative current flow drops off as S pole moves away from coil.

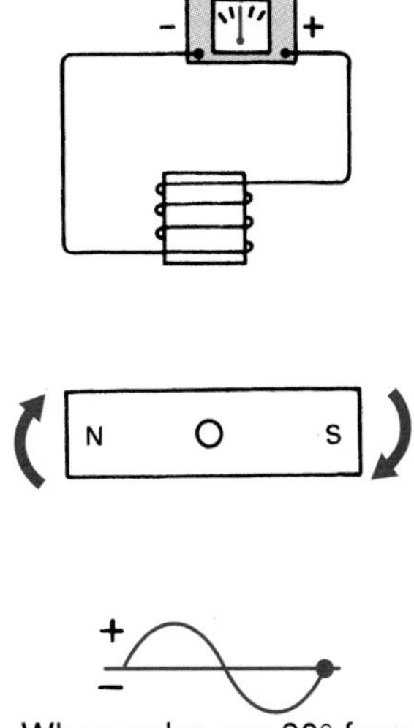

H—When poles are 90° from coil, current flow stops again.

Figure 8-19. Action of a voltmeter and sine wave as magnet rotates.

flywheel on the crankshaft, smoothing out engine pulsations at low engine rpm.

Ac Charging Systems

Ac charging systems are classified into three categories according to the alternator types:

- Permanent magnet alternator.
- Electromagnet alternator.
- Magneto.

Permanent Magnet Alternator

The ***permanent magnet alternator*** is the most common type of alternator with the stator placed inside the rotor. The permanent magnet is assembled on the inner walls of the rotor. See **Figure 8-20.**

The stator consists of several coils producing power for the charging, ignition, and lighting systems. Multiple coils and magnets are used to increase alternator output. In many systems, full output is not used most of the time. Sometimes, extra coils are wired into the alternator circuit to increase output when the lights are switched on. This is called a *dual-rate alternator,* **Figure 8-21.**

Most permanent magnet alternators are single-phase. Since this type uses only one charging coil, the output voltage is a single-phase ac wave. The output frequency varies depending on the number of magnets on the rotor. The alternator in **Figure 8-22** has two pairs of magnets, and its output has two cycles for each rotor revolution. The single-phase output alternator has low output and is best suited for small displacement engines and small electrical loads.

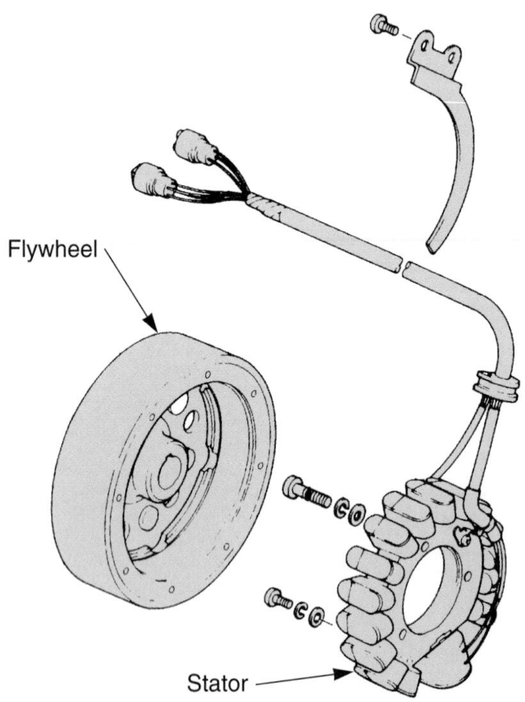

Figure 8-20. Permanent magnet alternator consists of a stator and rotor. The stator has coils and rotor contains magnets. (Yamaha Motor Corporation U.S.A.)

Electromagnet Alternator

An ***electromagnet alternator*** has a field coil which produces magnetism by induction, **Figure 8-23.** This design uses electric current, instead of permanent magnets, to produce magnetism. Either stationary or rotating field coils may be used. In the stationary coil alternator, the magnetic field produced by the field coil makes the rotor magnetic. The rotor's rotation induces current in the stator windings, **Figure 8-24.** This type of alternator is exposed to the outside air for cooling. The rotor speed is multiplied by gears or chains connected to the crankshaft. This type is primarily used for power on large displacement motorcycles.

Rotating field coil alternators supply current that energizes the alternator field. See **Figure 8-25.** In this type, the field coil is placed inside the rotor. Current flows

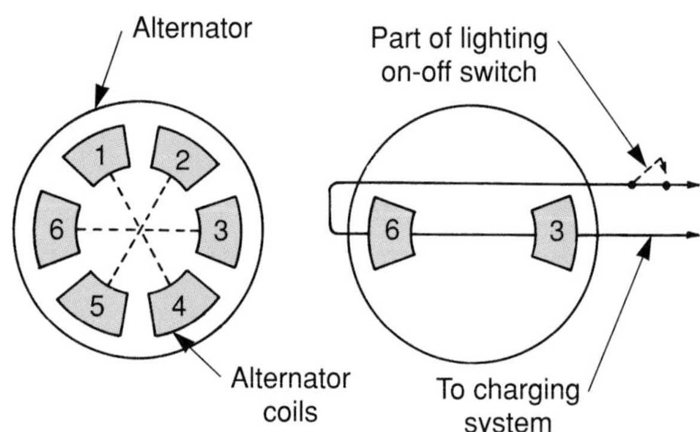

Figure 8-21. In this dual-rate alternator, coils 1, 2, 4, and 5 operate all the time, but coils 3 and 6 are only operated when the lights are switched on.

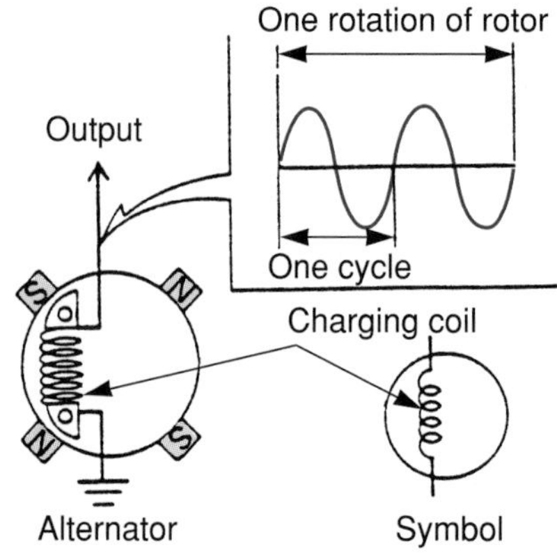

Figure 8-22. Waveform output from one revolution of the alternator rotor. (Honda Motor Co., Ltd.)

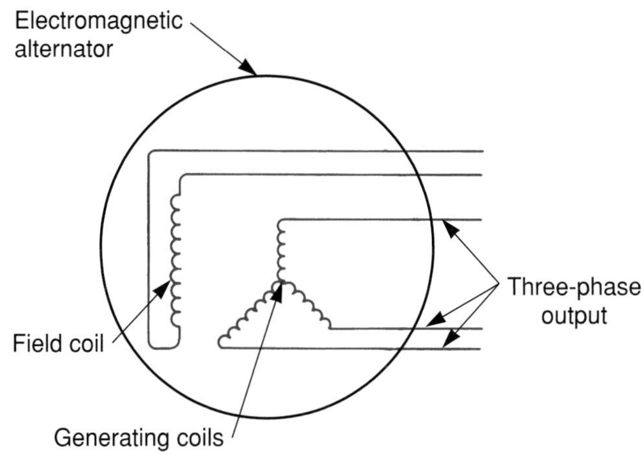

Figure 8-23. In an electromagnet alternator, magnetism is produced by induction in the field coil.

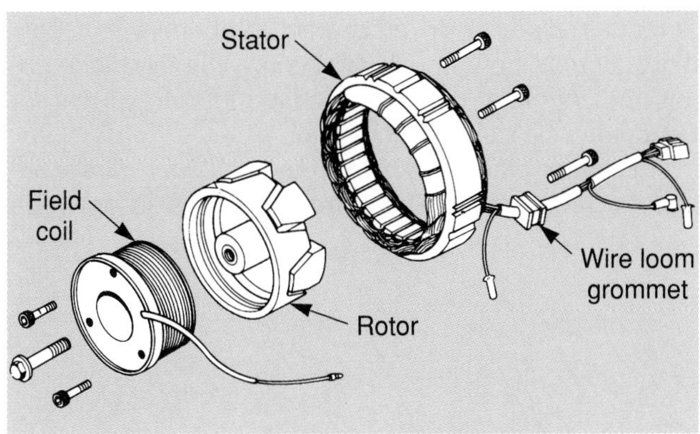

Figure 8-24. In this stationary field coil alternator, a magnetic field is produced by the field coil, which makes the rotor magnetic. Then, the rotor's rotation induces current in the stator windings. (Kawasaki Motors Corporation U.S.A.)

through the brushes to the field coil and electromagnetically induces the rotor. This generator has strong magnetic force, large output, and is small and lightweight.

The advantage of the electromagnetic alternator is that it can be designed precisely to match the battery's demands. A disadvantage is that battery voltage is required for initial alternator output. A motorcycle with a fully dead battery cannot be pushed or kickstarted since there is no voltage for the ignition system.

Electromagnet alternators are three-phase and capable of high output, **Figure 8-26.** Electromagnet alternators are ideal for touring bikes because their high output provides enough current for a large number of electrical accessories.

Flywheel Magneto

A ***flywheel magneto*** ignition system, frequently used on dirt bikes, functions in the same manner as a permanent magnet alternator. A true magneto is a self-contained ignition system. It is used to deliver high voltage to the spark plug. Because of the design of a flywheel magneto, it is also a convenient place to add extra coils for battery charging or direct ac lighting, **Figure 8-27.** A charging/magneto system is combined into one assembly.

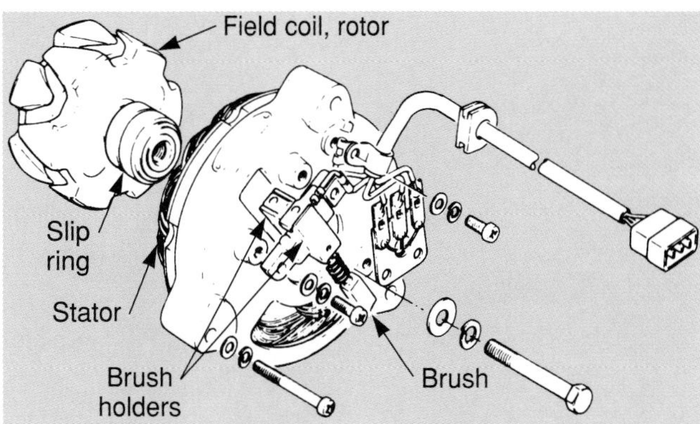

Figure 8-25. With a rotating field coil, current passes through brushes and slip rings to energize the alternator. (American Suzuki Motor Corporation)

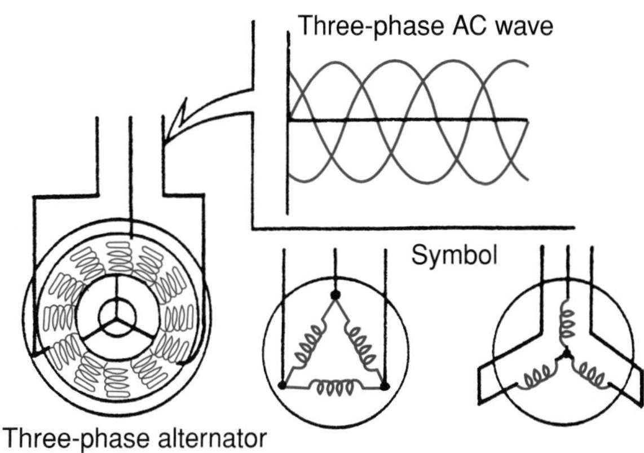

Figure 8-26. Output of a three-phase alternator. (Honda Motor Co., Ltd.)

Dc Generator

A ***dc generator*** works on the same principle as the alternator. Magnetism is used to induce current in the generator windings (armature). However, a generator differs from the simple alternator in three ways:

- Electromagnets, instead of permanent magnets, are used to produce the magnetic field.
- The coils (armature) rotate within the magnetic field.
- Coil polarity is switched every 180°, causing current to flow through the coil in the same direction at all times.

Since current always flows in the same direction through the coil, generator output is direct current (dc). **Figure 8-28** shows how a simple generator operates. Dc generators are rarely found in use on late-model motorcycles. However, some small dual-purpose dirt bikes use a dc generator for battery charging and electric starting.

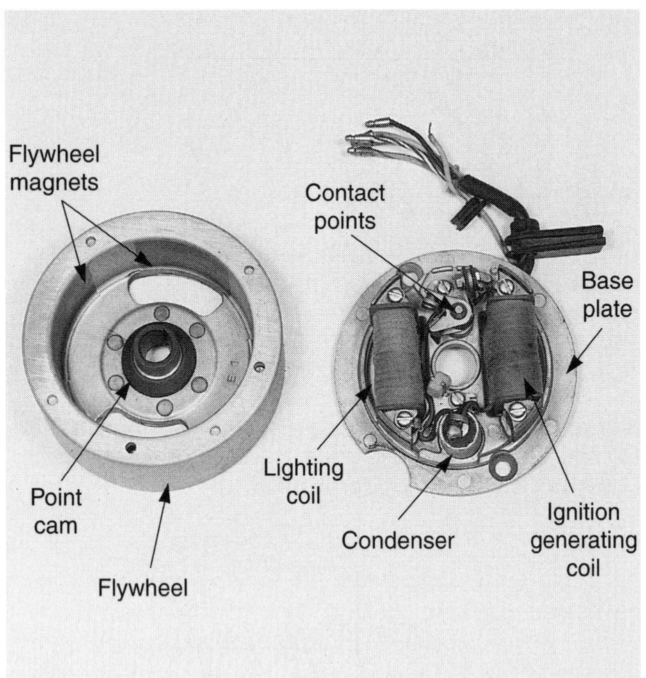

Figure 8-27. A flywheel magneto may have extra coils for charging and lighting purposes. This magneto uses an extra coil for lighting.

Charging System Rectification and Regulation

The alternator is capable of producing more low speed output than a dc generator. It will also recharge the battery at low engine rpm. The alternator produces ac current, which must be converted into dc for use by some systems and to charge the battery. In addition, alternators and dc generators must have a means of regulating the charge rate.

Rectifiers

An alternator-equipped charging system must include a rectifier to convert alternating current to direct current. A ***rectifier*** is normally a diode circuit connected to the alternator output terminal to change ac current into dc current. A ***diode*** is an electronic component that only allows current flow in one direction. With the diode circuit, the alternator output is rectified into dc current for the motorcycle's electrical system.

Selenium plates, thyristors, and/or ***Zener diodes*** are used for rectification. The current will flow in only one

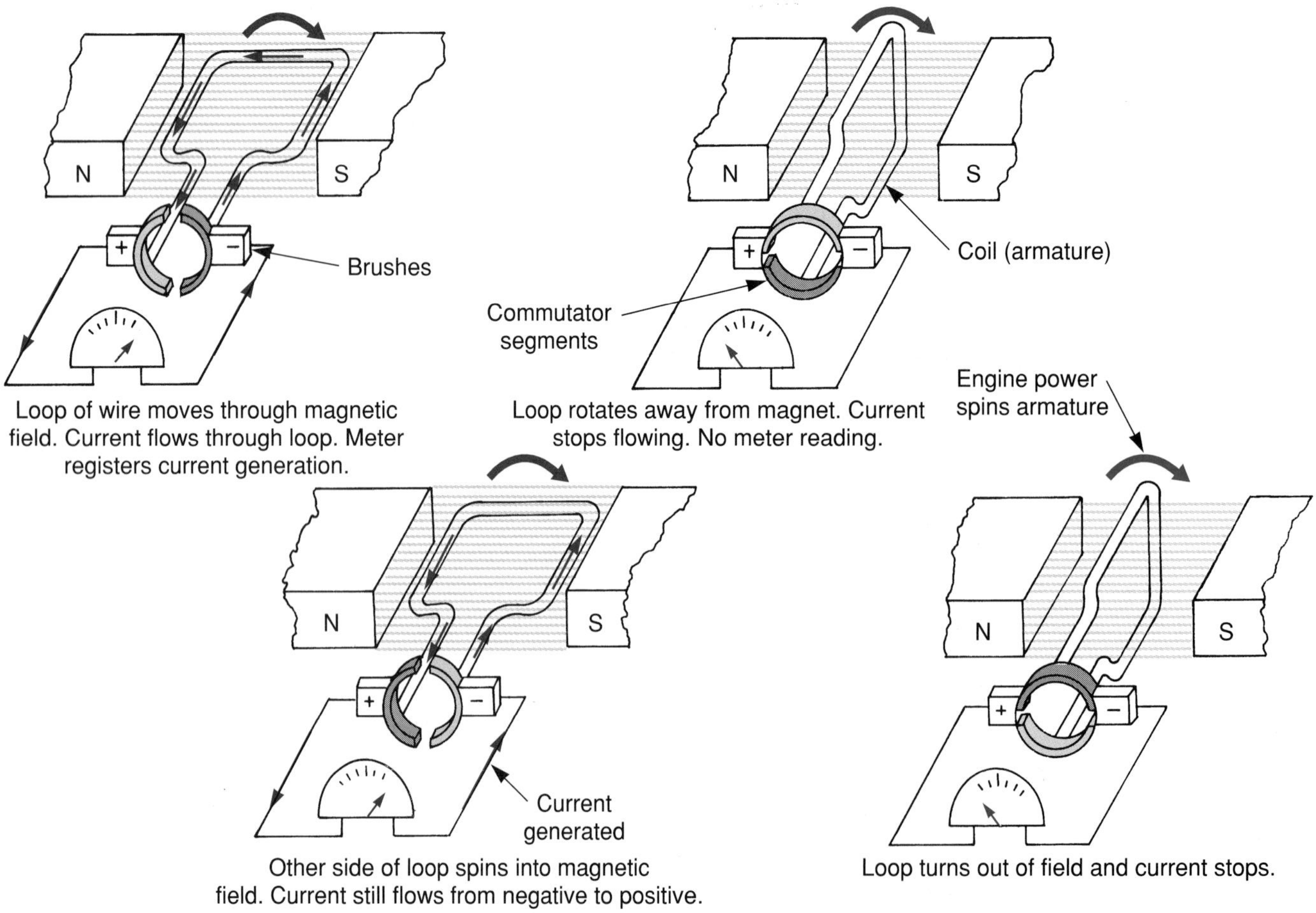

N
S
Brushes
Loop of wire moves through magnetic field. Current flows through loop. Meter registers current generation.

N
S
Coil (armature)
Commutator segments
Loop rotates away from magnet. Current stops flowing. No meter reading.

N
S
Current generated
Other side of loop spins into magnetic field. Current still flows from negative to positive.

Engine power spins armature
N
S
Loop turns out of field and current stops.

Figure 8-28. Generators use a segmented commutator and brushes to switch coil (armature) polarity every 180°. This forces current to flow in the same direction, producing direct current.

direction through a selenium plate. A Zener diode will allow current to flow in one direction, but will not permit flow in the opposite direction if the voltage is below a certain point. Once circuit voltage reaches or exceeds this point, the Zener diode allows current flow in the opposite direction.

There are two types of rectifiers: half-wave and full-wave. ***Half-wave rectifiers*** change ac current into dc current in magneto charging systems used on many small motorcycles. A half-wave rectifier only allows half of the alternator output to reach the battery. This is illustrated in **Figure 8-29.**

Full-wave rectifiers are used to provide full alternator output conversion to dc for battery charging. Bridged diodes redirect the negative portion of the ac sine wave. See **Figure 8-30.** Some older motorcycles used selenium plates. Full-wave rectifiers are used on medium displacement engines. Compared to the half-wave rectifier, the full-wave rectifier is more efficient in using the alternator output for charging the battery.

The ***three-phase full-wave rectifier*** is used in medium and large displacement engines. The rectifier is connected directly to the three-phase alternator, **Figure 8-31A.** Rectified three-phase ac is more stable than single-phase ac. See **Figure 8-31B.**

Voltage Regulators

Since dc generators produce direct current (dc), a rectifier is not needed in the charging system. However, a regulator is needed to control the charging voltage and current. A ***voltage regulator*** controls the voltage and current output of an alternator or generator. Either contact points or an electronic circuit is used in the regulator. They sense charging system output and either shut off or increase the amount of current exciting the alternator or generator.

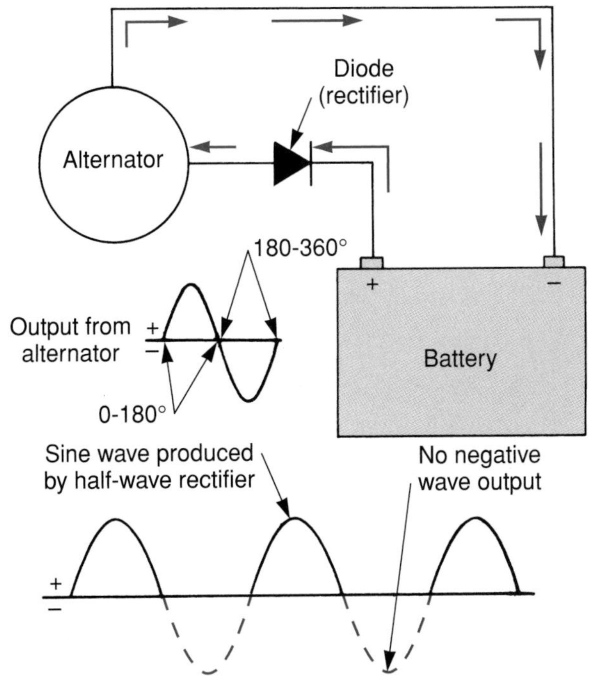

Figure 8-29. A half-wave rectifier allows only the positive half (0° to 180°) of current to pass. The negative half (180° to 360°) is not used.

Voltage regulators are classified in two categories: mechanical regulators and electronic regulators (solid state). All three types of alternators normally use a regulator, however, a magneto system may also use the battery as a form of regulator. Some regulators also disconnect the field coils from the battery when the generator's output voltage is lower than the battery's voltage.

Mechanical Regulator

A ***mechanical regulator*** is a device which uses one or more electromagnets and contact point sets to vary current flow through the alternator field coil to match the battery's needs. The schematic in **Figure 8-32** shows the placement of a mechanical regulator in a typical three-phase full-wave rectifier charging system.

One of the most common mechanical regulators is shown in **Figure 8-33.** When low voltage is applied to the regulator, the battery current flows directly to the field coil as the voltage is too low to energize the regulator field coil. The springs hold the point arm up. This causes the alternator to generate maximum output.

With normal alternator voltage, the battery voltage is high enough to partially energize the regulator relay. The coil's magnetic field pulls downward on the point arm. Current must then flow through the resistor, which reduces the current to the alternator field coil.

When alternator voltage is high, the battery voltage is high enough to fully energize the regulator relay. This action pulls the point arm down and the current flows to ground. No current flows to the alternator field coil and there is no alternator output.

Electronic Regulator

Electronic regulators are used in both electromagnetic and permanent magnet charging systems. An ***electronic regulator*** is a solid state device which controls charging system output, **Figure 8-34.** An electronic regulator is a sealed unit that contains one or more Zener diodes.

When an electronic regulator is used in an electromagnetic charging system, it serves the same function as a mechanical regulator. It matches alternator output to the battery's needs by controlling alternator field voltage.

When an electronic regulator is used in a permanent magnet charging system, it limits the voltage delivered to the battery. Since the faster a permanent magnet alternator spins, the more voltage it produces, the regulator absorbs the excess voltage to prevent battery overcharging.

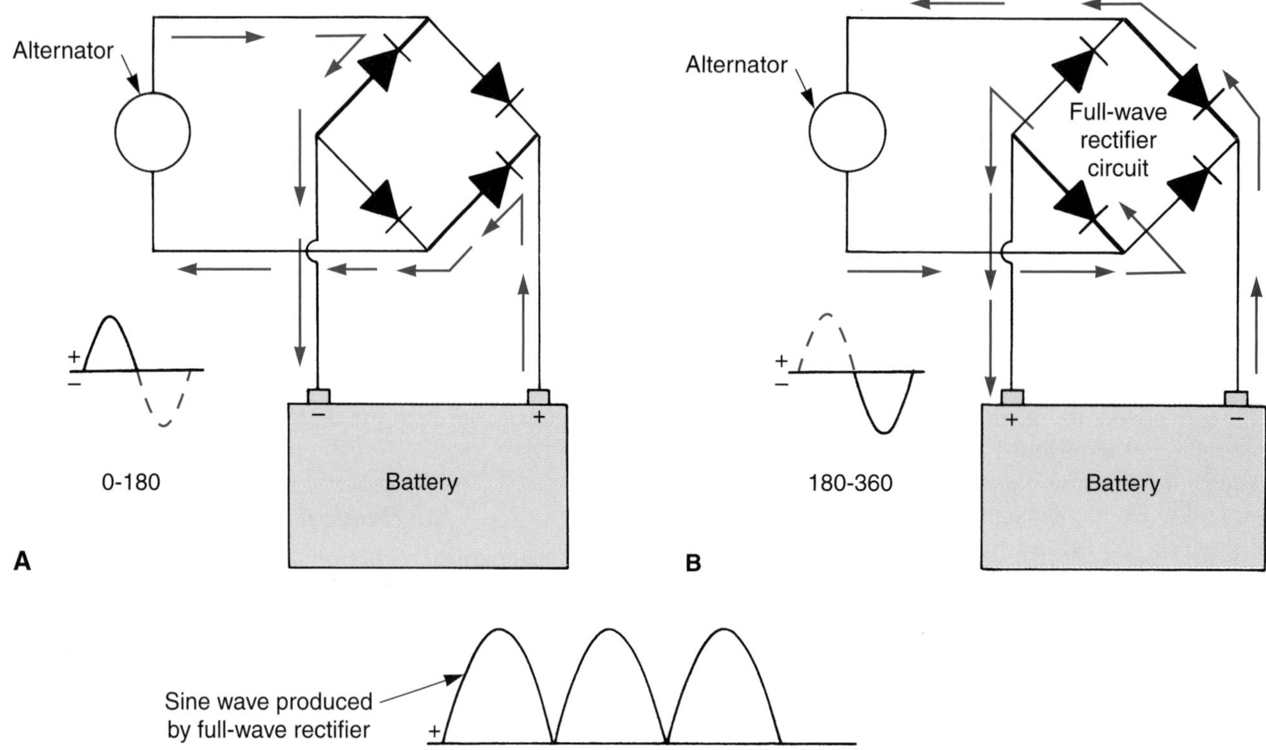

Figure 8-30. A—A full-wave rectifier commonly has four diodes wired in a bridge. It uses both positive (0-180°) and negative (180-360°) alternator pulses for battery charging. B—During the 180-360° phase, diodes redirect current through the battery in the proper direction.

Charging System Service

Before inspecting and servicing the charging system, observe the following precautions to prevent damage to charging system components.

- Disconnect the battery ground cable before removing leads from the system.
- Do not reconnect the battery ground cable until all wiring connections have been made.
- Avoid contact with the alternator output terminal. This terminal has voltage present at all times when the battery cables are connected.
- When installing a battery, be careful to observe the correct polarity. Reversing the cables will destroy the diodes.
- Observe proper polarity when connecting a booster battery.
- Always disconnect the battery ground cable before charging the battery.
- Never start or run the engine with the battery disconnected.
- Do not short across any connection.
- Never attempt to polarize an alternator.
- Never start the engine with the alternator disconnected from the rectifier/voltage regulator unless instructed by the service manual.

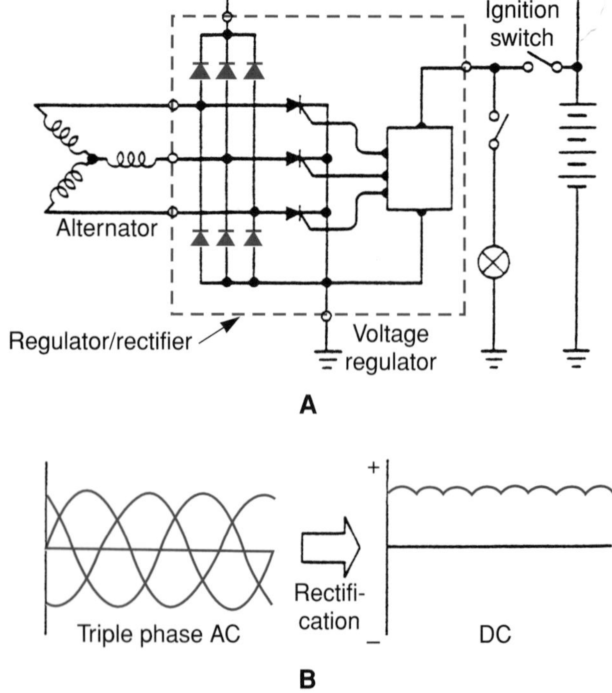

Figure 8-31. A—Three-phase alternator regulator/rectifier circuit. B—Output of a three-phase rectification circuit. (Honda Motor Co., Ltd.)

Whenever a charging system defect is suspected, make sure the battery is fully charged before beginning any testing. Clean and test the battery as described earlier in this chapter. If the battery is in good condition, test the charging system.

Parasitic Draw Test

Prior to performing voltage and current output tests, it is necessary to perform a leak or ***parasitic draw test.*** This test is used to determine if one or more components is shorted, grounded, or operating unnecessarily, causing the battery to drain.

1. Turn off the ignition switch and disconnect the ground cable from the battery.
2. Connect the positive test lead to the ammeter high amperage terminal.

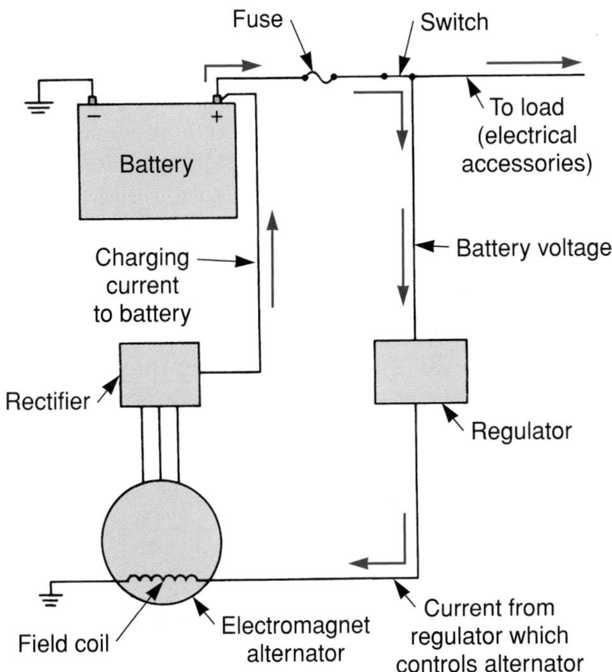

Figure 8-32. Schematic showing regulator placement in a three-phase charging system.

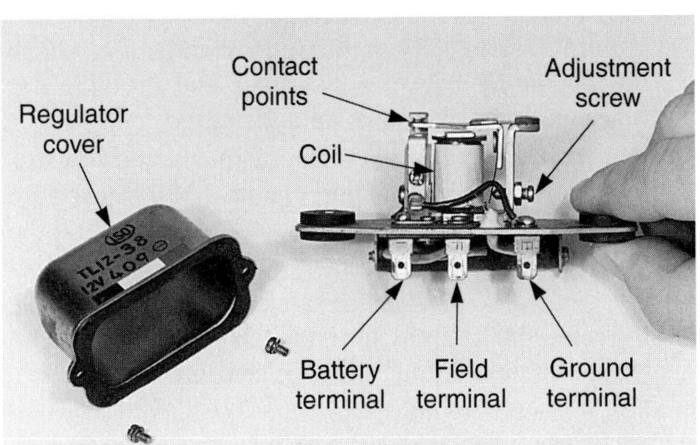

Figure 8-33. Parts of a mechanical (point) charging system regulator.

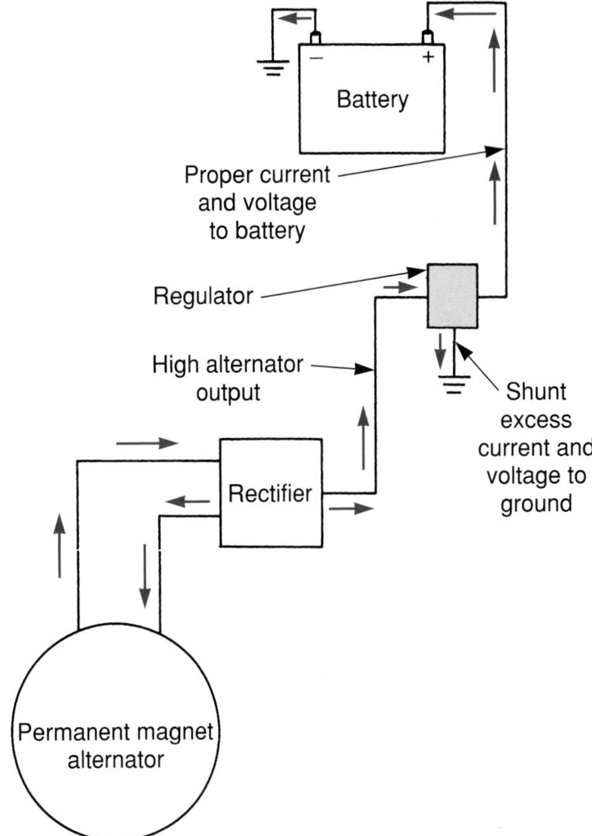

Figure 8-34. In a charging system that uses a permanent magnet alternator, the electronic regulator shunts excess voltage and current to ground to prevent battery overcharging.

3. Connect the ammeter between the negative terminal and the ground cable, **Figure 8-35.**
4. With the ignition switch off, measure the leakage current. If current leakage exceeds the standard value given in the service manual (usually less than .1 mA), a draw is present. Localize the draw to a particular circuit by disconnecting fuses one by one and measuring the current.

Caution: Be careful not to operate any high amperage circuits while performing this test. Damage to the meter may result.

Voltage Output Test

In the ***voltage output test,*** the output of the entire charging system (alternator, rectifier, voltage regulator, and wiring) is tested. Start the engine and run at about 2000 rpm. Then as shown in **Figure 8-36A,** battery voltage is measured to check battery condition.

The second step in checking voltage output, **Figure 8-36B,** is a no-load test to check the voltage regulator and alternator. The voltage should increase over battery voltage, but not beyond service manual specifications.

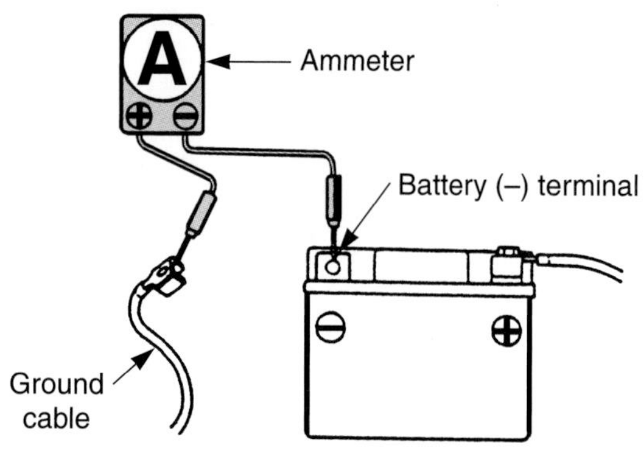

Figure 8-35. Ammeter connection for a parasitic leak test. (Honda Motor Co., Ltd.)

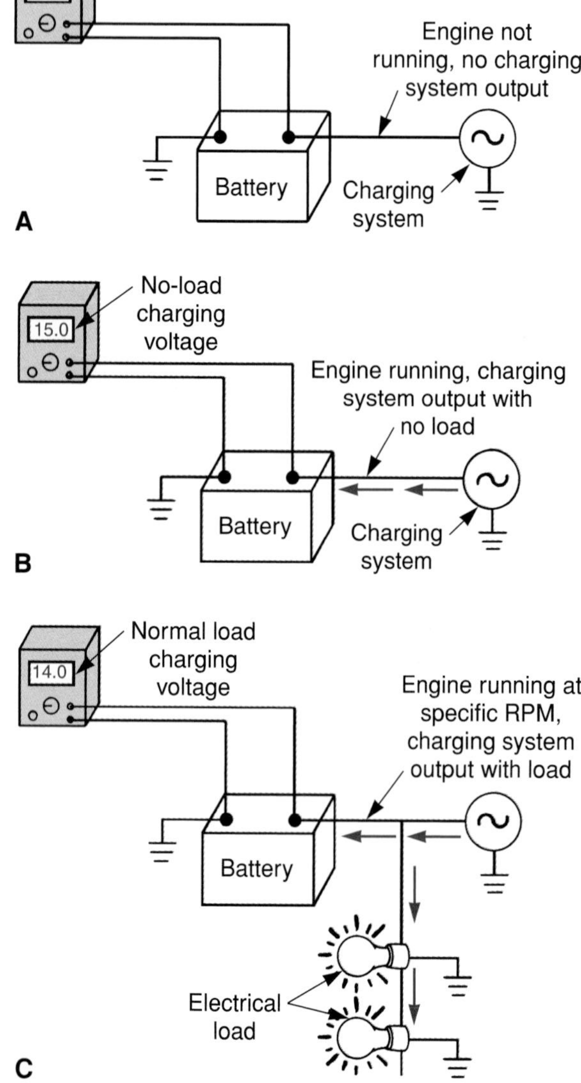

Figure 8-36. A charging system output test involves taking a battery voltage reading, no-load voltage reading, and voltage reading with normal load. Refer to a service manual and test equipment instructions for details.

Turn on the headlight high beams and taillights, **Figure 8-36C.** The voltage will drop, but should be above battery voltage. If the voltage is higher than in step one, the charging system is supplying sufficient current to charge the battery.

Current Output Test

During a ***current output test,*** a high capacity ammeter is used to measure charging system current (amperage). This tests the performance of every component in the charging system. See **Figure 8-37.** The current flow at a stated rpm must agree with service manual specifications. If the output is not within these specifications, individual system components must be checked to find the source of the problem.

Stator Continuity Test

In the ***stator continuity test,*** the condition of the alternator's stator windings will be checked. In the first part of the test, **Figure 8-38A,** measure the stator coil resistance and continuity. In the second part, **Figure 8-38B,** test for shorted or grounded stator coils. Compare test results to service manual specifications.

Note: Be sure the battery is fully charged before performing the voltage and current output tests. The amount of current flow may change abruptly if the battery is not sufficiently charged.

Charging Coil Test

It is not necessary to remove the alternator from the engine to perform a ***charging coil test.*** Disconnect the alternator connector and check the continuity between coil wires as follows:

- For single-phase coils whose ends are grounded, measure the resistance between the output line and ground, **Figure 8-39A.** If the value is not correct, check the continuity between the stator and ground, and between the alternator cover and ground.
- For coils with two output lines, measure the resistance between the two lines, **Figure 8-39B.** Make sure there is no continuity between engine ground and the output lines.
- For single-phase, combined charging/lighting coils, measure the resistance at the charging output line and at lighting output line. See **Figure 8-39C.**
- For three-phase coils, measure resistance between each output line, and check that there is no continuity between each output line and ground, **Figure 8-39D.**

If the resistance values are much higher than the

specified value, replace the stator. If measurements are only slightly off the specified value, the stator may not need to be replaced. Check other areas and decide if replacement is required. Since the regulator/rectifier is an electrical component that uses semiconductor devices, the component itself is not serviced. Instead, the connector on the regulator/rectifier is checked.

Charging System Troubleshooting

When checking the charging system, always question the customer to determine how his/her riding habits may be affecting battery condition. High rpm riding may overcharge the battery while low rpm riding with frequent brake/brake light usage may result in discharging the battery. On combined lighting/charging coil systems where the battery is overcharging, check the following areas.

- Headlight bulb rating (wattage too low).
- Broken output wire.
- Faulty headlight resistor (open headlight circuit).
- Faulty lighting switch connection.
- Broken regulator/rectifier ground wire or faulty connection.

Note: No check is necessary for independent lighting and charging systems.

Other causes of battery overcharging could be:

- A broken regulator/rectifier ground wire or faulty connection.
- Loose connection at the regulator/rectifier connection.
- No continuity between the field coil wire and ground.

If there are no problems in the above areas, replace the regulator/rectifier with a new one.

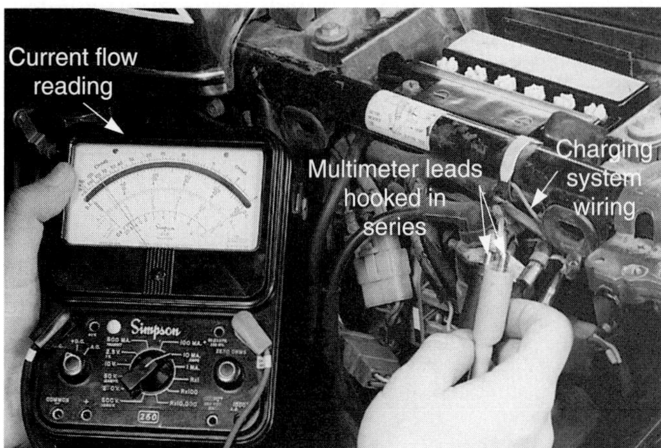

Figure 8-37. A charging system current output test involves connecting an ammeter in series with the charging system.

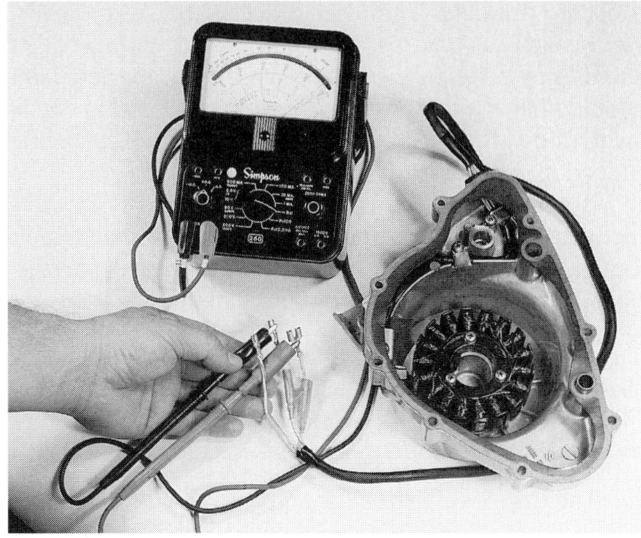

A

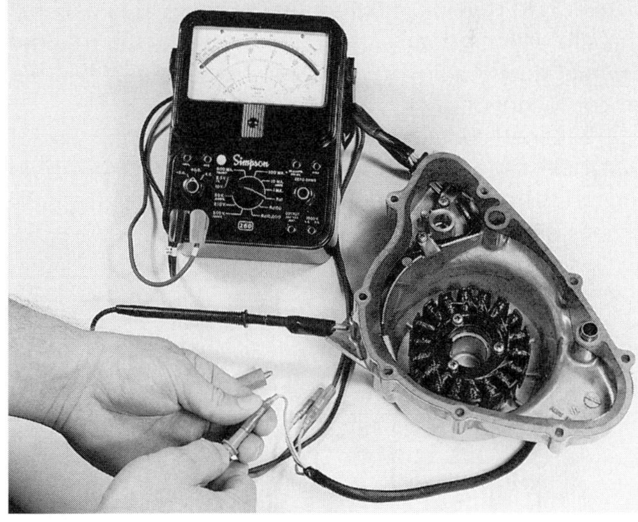

B

Figure 8-38. An ohmmeter is commonly used to check stator coils. A—Checking coil resistance. There is only .6 ohms resistance. B—Checking for grounded coils. Infinite resistance is shown, indicating the coils are not grounded. This stator is in good condition.

Electric Starting Motor

Motorcycle ***electric starting motors*** use direct current from the battery for starting. They are similar in construction to a dc generator. A dc motor uses electrical energy to magnetically force the armature to turn, which creates mechanical energy. **Figure 8-40** illustrates dc motor operation.

When the starter switch is closed, battery voltage appears at the relay switch. If the ground line's neutral or clutch switch is closed, current flows through the relay and the starter motor operates. To check switch continuity, a battery test light is connected across the switch leads, **Figure 8-41.** When the switch is closed, the test light should glow. When the switch is opened, the test light should not glow. An ohmmeter can also be used to check switch operation. Other electric starting troubleshooting procedures are given in Chapter 9.

A gear or chain drive and a simple clutch are normally used to engage and disengage the starter motor. **Figure 8-42** illustrates a starter and starter drive mechanism. **Figure 8-43** shows the starting motor and gears on an actual motorcycle.

Summary

There are ways to generate and provide power for use in motorcycle electrical systems. The battery stores electricity and is the primary source of power for the dc accessory circuits on a motorcycle. The purpose of the battery is to provide initial starting power and to back up the charging system so the accessory circuits do not operate poorly at low rpm or stop functioning when the motor is shut off.

Batteries contain electrolyte, which is a mixture of water (H_2O) and sulfuric acid (H_2SO_4). The principle hazards in servicing batteries occur under charging conditions or when handling electrolyte. There are two types of batteries used in motorcycles, scooters, and ATVs: the conventional battery and the maintenance-free (MF) battery. Battery service typically consists of removing the battery from the bike, cleaning the battery; visual inspection; topping off conventional battery cells with distilled water; checking electrolyte specific gravity (when possible); charging the battery (if needed); preparing a new battery for service; installing the battery.

There are two types of battery tests: unloaded and load. An unloaded test is made on a battery without discharging current. If a more precise reading is needed, the load test is used. There are two battery rating systems that motorcycle technicians should be familiar with. They are the capacity, or ampere-hour (AH) rating, and cold cranking amps (CCA), or cold start rating. There are five major reasons why batteries fail, including normal battery deterioration; poor physical condition; prolonged under or overcharging; undercapacity application; and lack of proper maintenance.

An alternator is capable of changing mechanical energy (rotating motion) into electrical energy. The alternator consists of a rotor and stator. The rotor consists of a crankshaft driven flywheel with a series of magnets attached. The stator consists of wire coils wound around a series of soft iron poles. When the engine starts, the rotor rotates with the crankshaft. Ac charging systems are classified into three categories according to the alternator types: permanent magnet alternator; electromagnet alternator; and magneto. A dc generator works on the same principle as the alternator. Magnetism is used to induce current in the generator windings (armature). However, a generator differs from the simple alternator in three ways: electromagnets, instead of permanent magnets, are used to produce the magnetic field; the coils (armature) rotate within the magnetic field; and coil polarity is switched every 180°, causing current to flow through the coil in the same direction at all times. There are several tests that can be performed to check the battery and charging system.

When checking the charging system, always question the customer to determine how his/her riding habits may be affecting battery condition. High rpm riding may overcharge the battery while low rpm riding with frequent brake/brake light usage may result in discharging the battery. Motorcycle electric starting motors use direct current from the battery for starting. They are similar in construction to a dc generator. A dc motor uses electrical energy to magnetically force the armature to turn, which creates mechanical energy.

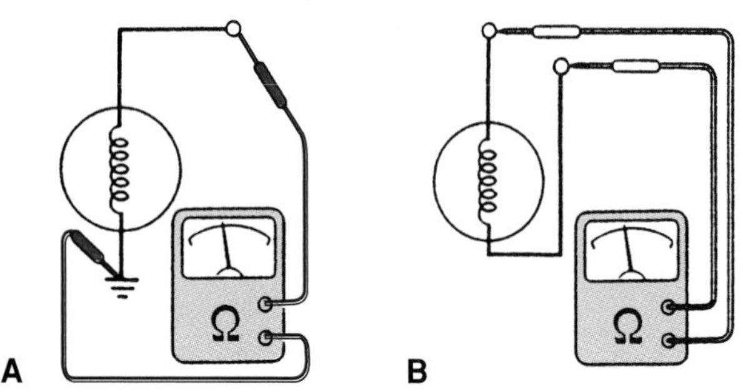

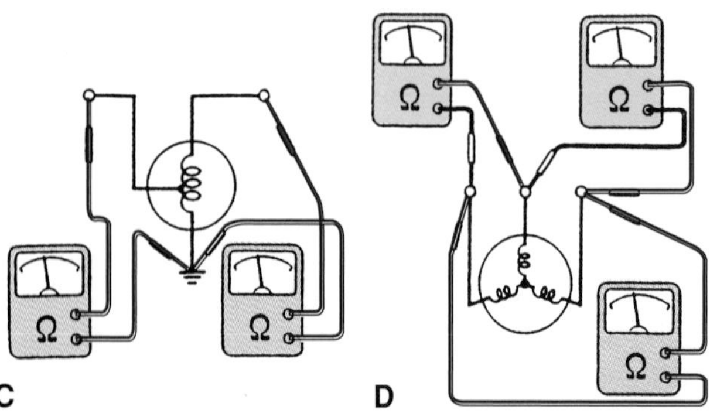

Figure 8-39. Checking a regulator/rectifier connector. A—Single-phase coil with grounded ends. B—Single-phase coil with two lines. C—Single phase combined charging/lighting coil. D—Three-phase coil. (Honda Motor Co., Ltd.)

Know These Terms

Battery
Electrolyte
Sulfuric acid
Conventional battery
Flywheel magneto
Dc generator
Rectifier
Diode

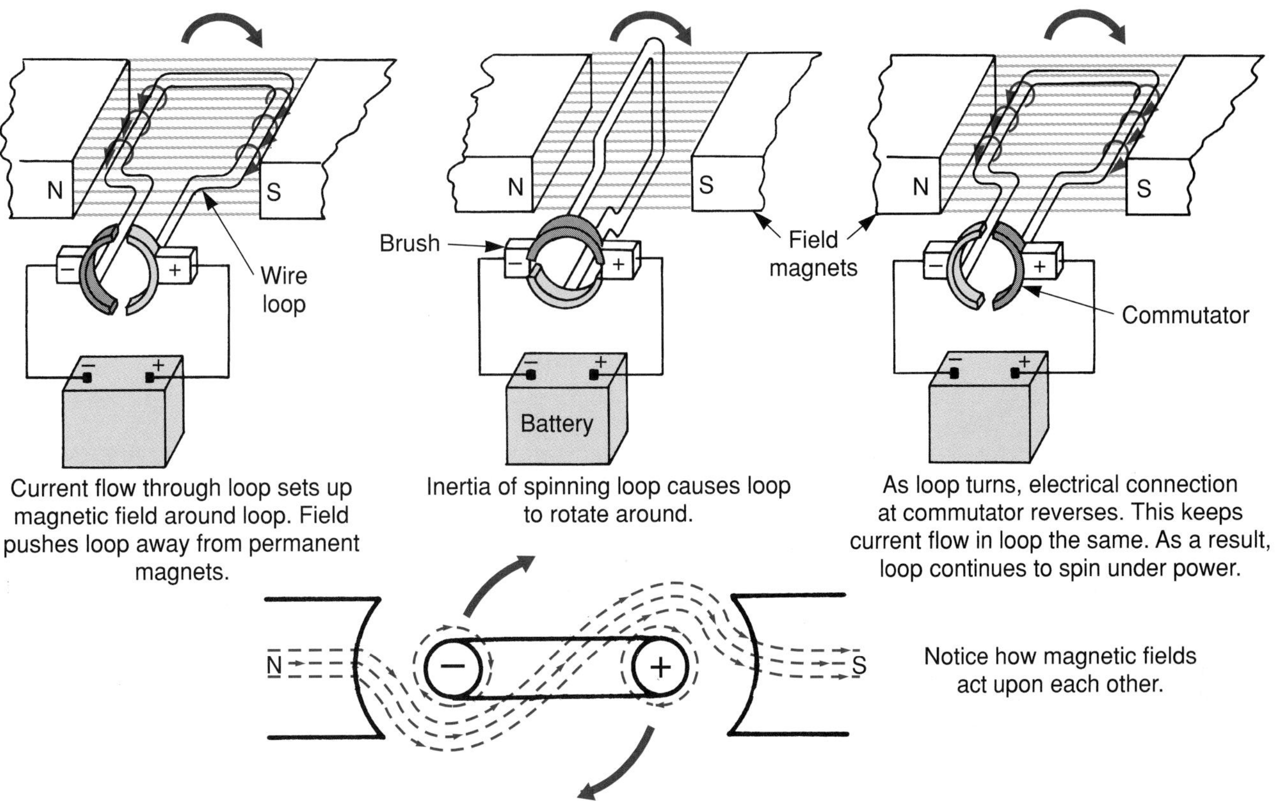
N
S
Wire
loop
Current flow through loop sets up magnetic field around loop. Field pushes loop away from permanent magnets.
Brush
Battery
Inertia of spinning loop causes loop to rotate around.
Field
magnets
Commutator
As loop turns, electrical connection at commutator reverses. This keeps current flow in loop the same. As a result, loop continues to spin under power.
Notice how magnetic fields act upon each other.

Figure 8-40. In many ways a dc motor is similar to a dc generator. Instead of spinning the wire loop to induce current, the motor is connected to a source of electricity. This makes the loop spin inside a stationary magnetic field.

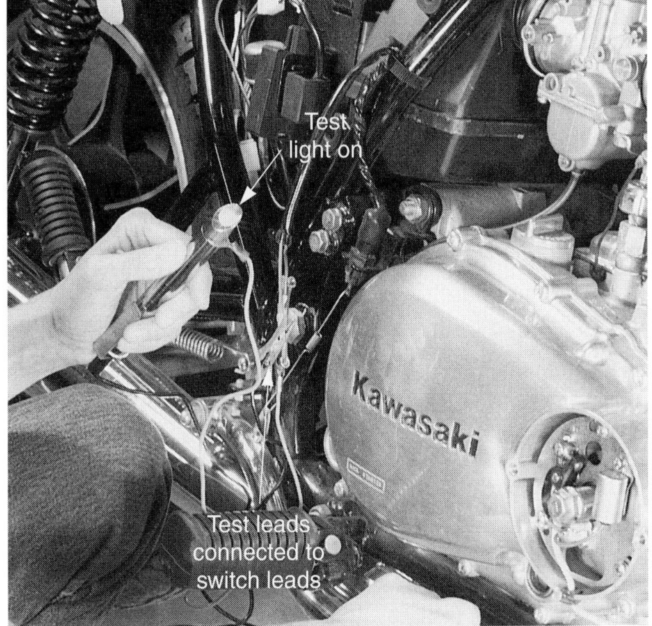
Test
light on
Kawasaki
Test leads
connected to
switch leads

Figure 8-41. A test light can be used to check switch continuity.

Cell
Specific gravity
Sulfation
Selenium plates
Thyristors
Zener diodes
Maintenance-free (MF) battery
Sulfate deposits
Sediment
Unloaded test
Load test
Ampere-hour rating
Cold cranking amps
Alternator
Rotor
Stator
Ac charging systems
Permanent magnet alternator
Electromagnet alternator
Half-wave rectifiers
Full-wave rectifiers
Three-phase full-wave rectifier
Voltage regulator
Mechanical regulator
Electronic regulator
Parasitic draw test
Voltage output test
Current output test
Stator continuity test
Charging coil test
Electric starting motors

Review Questions—Chapter 8

Do not write in this text. Place your answers on a separate sheet of paper.

1. Name the two types of batteries presently used for motorcycles.

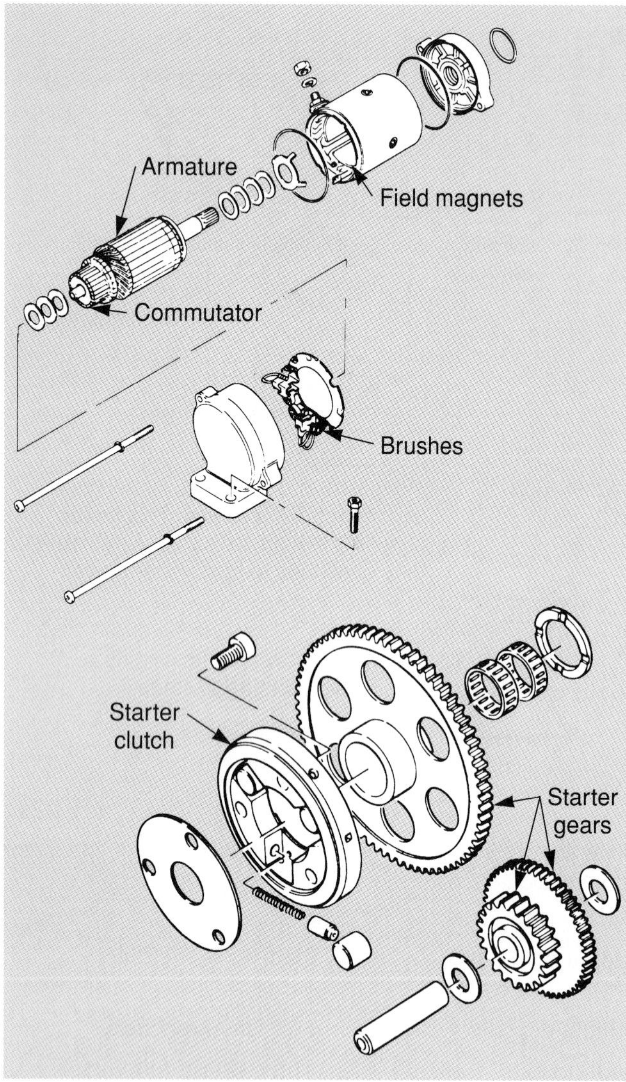

Figure 8-42. Parts of a starter mechanism. Gears and a simple clutch are normally used to engage and disengage the starter. (American Suzuki Motor Corporation)

Figure 8-43. Starter gears provide gear reduction, which increases the starter motor's turning force.

2. Describe the two types of plates found in a typical motorcycle battery.
3. A six volt battery has _____ cells; a _____ volt battery has six cells.
    A. 2,6
    B. 12,12
    C. 3,12
    D. 3,6
4. Which side of the battery should be disconnected first?
5. What is the first step in battery servicing?
6. What is the maximum quick charge rate for conventional battery charging?
    A. 10 amps at 2 hours.
    B. 6 amps at 1 hour.
    C. 10% of the amp hour rating.
    D. 6 amps at 5-10 hours.
7. Define the term *specific gravity* as it relates to electrolyte.
8. The specific gravity of a fully charged battery is:
    A. 1.460 to 1.480.
    B. 1.200 to 1.210.
    C. 1.260 to 1.280.
    D. 1.000 to 1.200.
9. Each _____ degrees of movement of an alternator magnet causes current to reverse direction.
10. List the three types of ac charging systems.
11. All electromagnetic alternators produce ______ current.
    A. direct
    B. single-phase
    C. dual-phase
    D. three-phase
12. An electromagnet alternator requires ______ to operate.
    A. battery voltage
    B. high resistance
    C. no control of charging current
    D. All of the above.
13. What is the purpose of a rectifier in an ac charging system?
14. Half-wave rectifiers provides:
    A. full alternator output.
    B. half of the alternator output.
    C. Half control of charging current.
    D. full control of charging current.
15. Where are full-wave rectifiers used?

16. What is the purpose of voltage regulators?
17. Why are two circuits necessary for the electric starter system?
18. An ammeter is connected in _____, and a voltmeter is connected in _____.
    A. parallel, series
    B. series, series
    C. parallel, parallel
    D. series, parallel
19. All of the following are causes of battery overcharging, *except:*
    A. broken regulator ground wire.
    B. continuity between the field coil wire and ground.
    C. broken voltage feedback line.
    D. loose connection at the regulator.
20. Name two types of voltage regulators used in motorcycle charging systems.

Suggested Activities

1. Select five motorcycles. Using a service manual, determine the following:
    A. What type of alternator is used.
    B. What type of rectifier is used.
    C. What type of regulator is used.
2. Completely test a three-phase solid state rectifier using an ohmmeter. Refer to the service manual and record your results.
3. Use a battery hydrometer to determine the condition of a motorcycle battery. If the battery needs charging, recheck it with the hydrometer after charging. Summarize your findings.

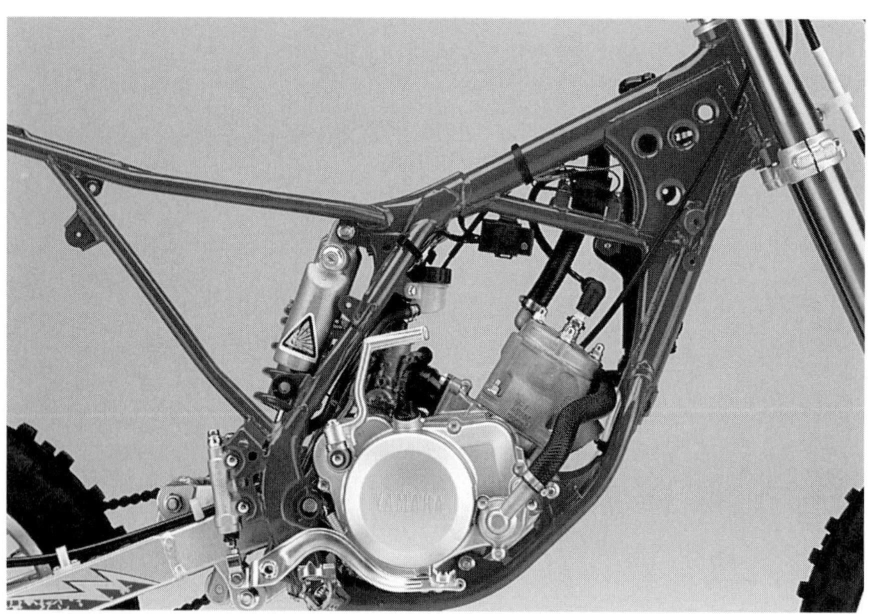

Find as many components of this motorcycle's ignition system as you can.
(Yamaha Motor Corporation U.S.A.)

Ignition Systems

After studying this chapter, you will be able to:

- Describe the operating principles of an ignition system.
- Explain the function of each major part of an ignition system.
- Define vacuum and centrifugal advance.
- Compare contact point, magneto, and electronic ignition systems.
- Describe the operation of ignition systems.

The efficient operation of a motorcycle engine requires a well maintained ignition system. Even when all other systems are in perfect working condition, a malfunctioning or improperly adjusted ignition system can cause poor engine performance or even a mechanical breakdown. This chapter discusses the operation and design of common motorcycle ignition systems. Before you can learn to perform diagnostic, service, and repair operations, you must have a complete understanding of how modern ignition systems operate.

Ignition Systems

An ***ignition system*** is used to start the controlled combustion of an air-fuel mixture in the engine. It must produce a spark during the end of the compression stroke, at just the exact moment. Most motorcycle ignition systems are powered by the battery. The ignition system must step up battery voltage (approximately 12 volts) to 40,000 volts or more. This high voltage is needed to fire the spark plug. An ignition coil, **Figure 9-1,** is used to provide this voltage increase.

A switching device driven by the crankshaft or camshaft is used to trigger the ignition coil at the proper time. See **Figure 9-2.** Some early ignition systems have contact points while many late-model systems use a magnetic-electronic switching device. Dual-purpose and off-road motorcycles use the magneto or energy transfer system. In this system, the ignition is powered by the alternator. **Figure 9-3** illustrates a typical magneto ignition system.

Normal engine operation requires the ignition system to produce an intense spark at the spark plug gap. It must overcome its own internal resistance as well as resistance caused by compression in the combustion chamber. Additional resistance to spark plug operation can be caused by:

- Extremely rich or lean air-fuel mixtures.
- Deposits on the spark plug (oil blow-by, low speed riding habits, contaminated air and fuel).
- Increased engine load.
- Excessive plug gap.

When the ignition system is functioning properly, it supplies enough voltage at the spark plug to overcome system and combustion chamber resistance. Because of lean air-fuel mixtures, which are harder to ignite, the job of the ignition system has become even more difficult. Lean mixtures improve certain exhaust emission levels.

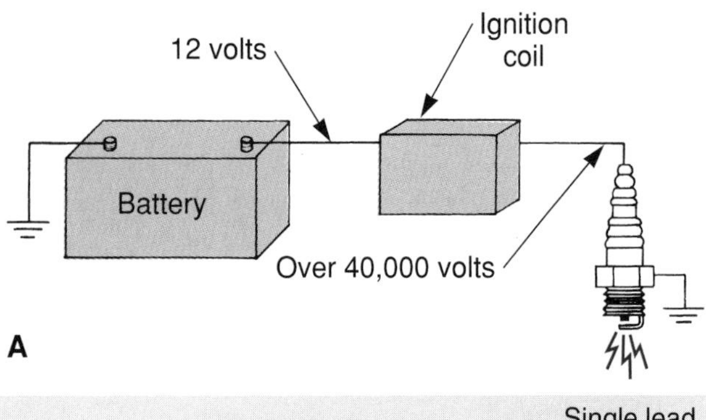

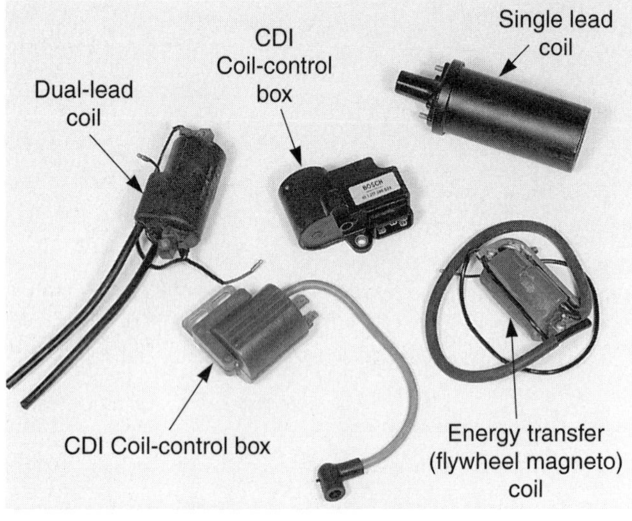

Figure 9-1. An ignition coil steps up battery voltage from 12 volts to over 40,000 volts to fire the spark plugs. A—Coil action. B—Different types of coils.

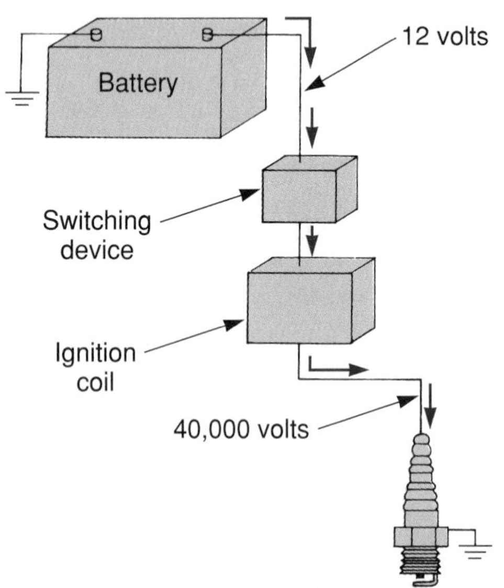

Figure 9-2. Contact points or a magnetic trigger and control module are used to operate the ignition coil and fire the spark plugs.

Proper combustion requires a strong electric arc at the spark plug. ***Spark intensity*** refers to the amount of voltage and spark duration at the spark plug. A satisfactory spark provides sufficient voltage for a sufficient period of time to ignite the air-fuel mixture. Ignition system performance depends upon several components within the system. If any of these components are marginal, spark intensity and engine performance may deteriorate.

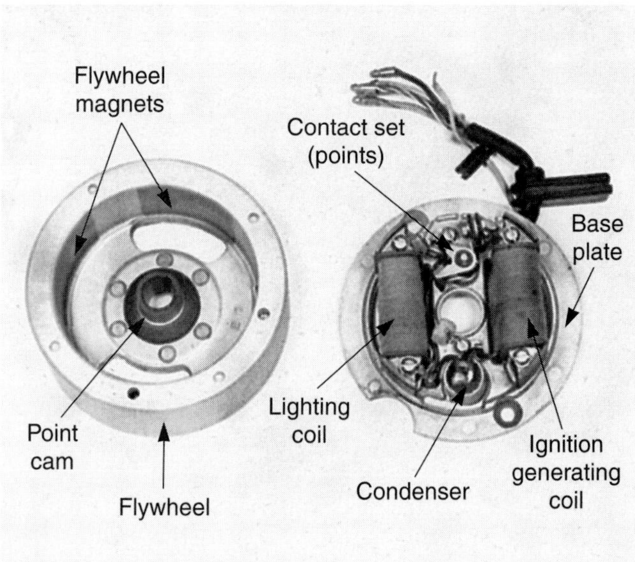

Figure 9-3. A magneto ignition system is used on many small, dual-purpose motorcycles. If any accessories are required, a battery is used along with the magneto. A lighting circuit in the magneto provides for battery recharging.

Ignition Primary Circuit

A battery and coil ***ignition primary circuit*** is made up of:

- Battery.
- Ignition switch.
- Interconnecting circuit wiring.
- Triggering device or circuit.
- Condenser (on some systems).
- Ignition coil primary windings.

All of the components using low voltage (battery voltage) are included in the ignition primary circuit. The battery provides power to the primary circuit when the ignition switch is turned on, **Figure 9-4.**

Ignition Triggering

In all ignition systems, the spark is triggered by a switching device. This switch may be a set of contact points or a magnetic-electronic device, **Figure 9-5.** This switching device determines the frequency of spark, depending on where it is located. These switching devices may be located:

- On the end of the crankshaft (frequency of operation–360°).
- On the end of a camshaft (frequency of operation–720°).

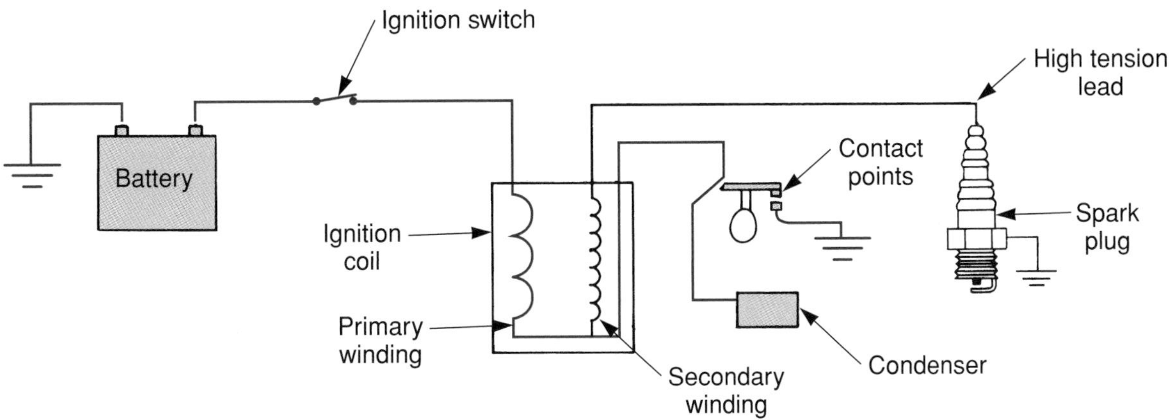

Figure 9-4. This schematic represents a simple battery and coil ignition system. Wires and components in the primary circuit are colored.

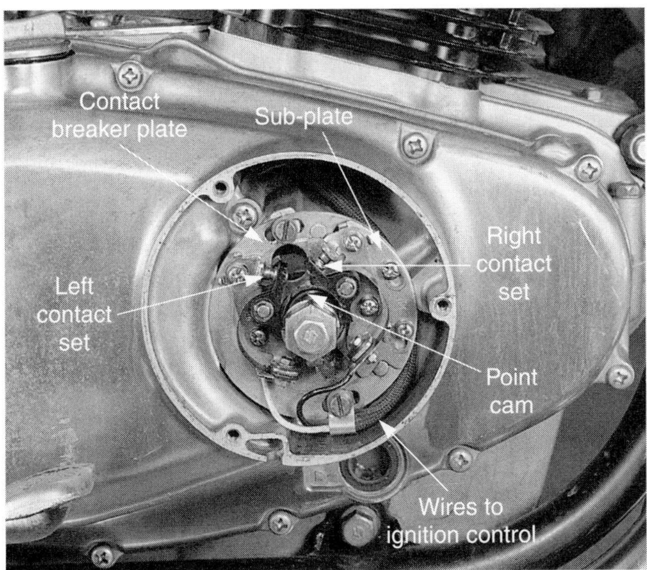

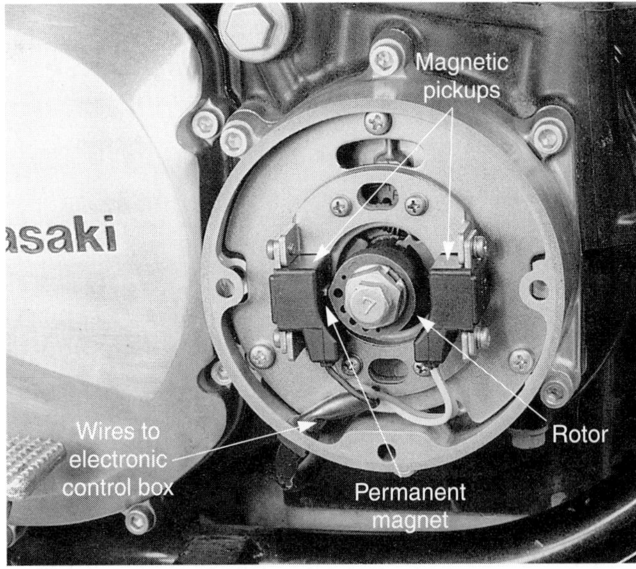

Figure 9-5. Two common methods of triggering the ignition coil. A—Contact points trigger the coil directly by opening and closing. B—A magnetic trigger operates a control module. This control module then interrupts current flow to the ignition coil, causing the coil to fire.

- On a crankshaft driven idler (frequency of operation–360° or 720°, depending on idler ratio).

A means of adjusting ignition timing is usually provided. The triggering device can be rotated in relation to the crankshaft, camshaft, or idler.

Ignition Coil

The ***ignition coil*** is the heart of the ignition system. It is a simple stepup transformer. The ignition coil relies on induction to step up battery voltage (12 volts) to approximately 40,000-65,000 volts. An extremely high voltage is needed to make electricity jump the gap at the spark plug.

The ignition coil is made up of a primary winding and a secondary winding, as shown in **Figure 9-6.** The ***primary winding*** consists of hundreds of turns of coarse wire wound around the secondary windings. The ***secondary winding*** is made up of thousands of turns of fine wire wound around an iron core.

When current (battery voltage) flows through the coil primary windings, a magnetic field is built up. When current flow through the primary windings is abruptly stopped, the magnetic field rapidly collapses. This collapse causes high voltage to be induced in the secondary windings, **Figure 9-7.** This dramatic stepup in voltage results from the difference in the number of turns of wire between the primary and secondary. High voltage flows to the spark plug where it produces an electric arc to start combustion.

Ignition Secondary Circuit

A battery and coil ***ignition secondary circuit*** is made up of:

- Ignition coil secondary windings.
- Spark plug wire (high tension lead).

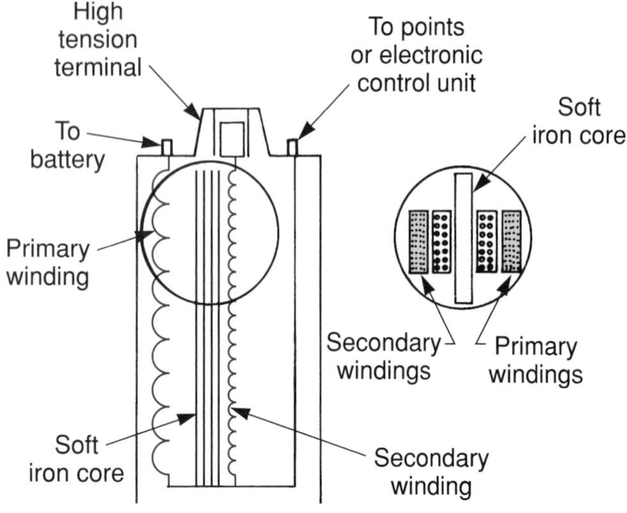

Figure 9-6. An ignition coil consists of primary and secondary windings wrapped around a soft iron core. Hundreds of turns of coarse wire are used for the primary windings. Thousands of turns of fine wire are used for the secondary windings.

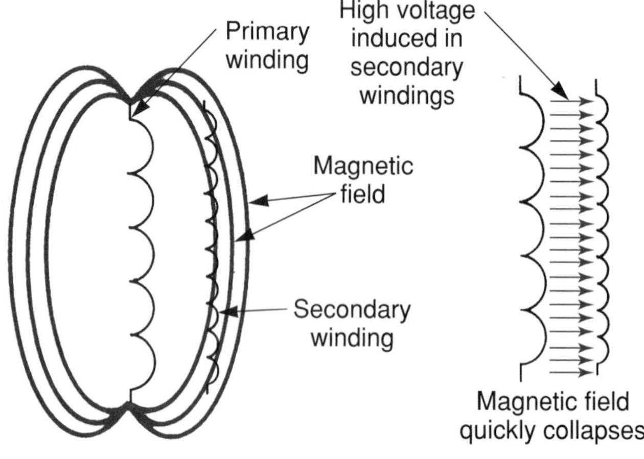

Figure 9-7. Current flow through the coil's primary windings causes a magnetic field to build-up. As the contact points or electronic circuit breaks current, the magnetic field collapses. This induces current in the secondary windings.

- Spark plug terminal.
- Spark plug.

The ignition secondary includes all the components that operate on high coil output voltage. See **Figure 9-8.** When the ignition coil voltage is stepped up, the spark plug wire (high tension wire) carries this voltage to the spark plug.

Ignition Timing

Since combustion is a controlled burning process rather than a rapid explosion, combustion must begin at the proper time. It must begin near the end of the compression stroke, before TDC. Since combustion takes time for completion, ignition must occur so that maximum cylinder heat and pressure develops immediately after TDC.

In **Figure 9-9A,** a spark occurs with the piston traveling up on the compression stroke. Then, in **Figure 9-9B,** combustion has finally formed maximum heat and pressure to force the piston down in the cylinder for the power stroke.

As engine speed increases, ignition timing must be advanced (occur earlier) because the piston will be moving faster. As shown in **Figure 9-10,** there would be less time for the air-fuel mixture to burn. This increase in ignition spark lead or advance can be accomplished by:

- Centrifugal advance.
- Electronic advance.

Centrifugal Advance Unit

A ***centrifugal advance unit*** causes the spark to occur sooner as engine rpm increases. This improves engine efficiency and power. A centrifugal advance mechanism uses spring-loaded weights attached to the point cam or rotor, **Figure 9-11.** As engine speed increases, the weights are thrown outward by centrifugal force.

With contact point ignition systems, movement of the weights rotates the point cam, allowing the points to open earlier. With an electronic ignition, the movement of the weights act on the rotor (trigger wheel) to make the spark plug fire sooner. This gives the air-fuel mixture more time to burn at higher rpm.

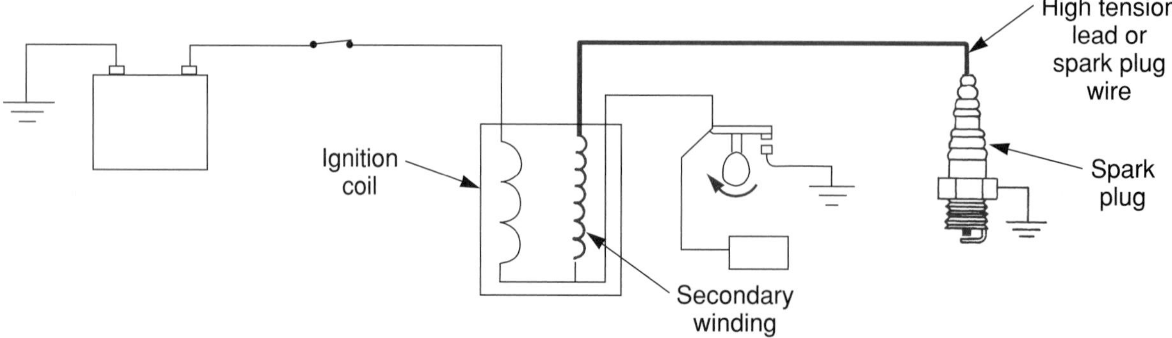

Figure 9-8. Schematic shows all wiring and components of the secondary circuit in color.

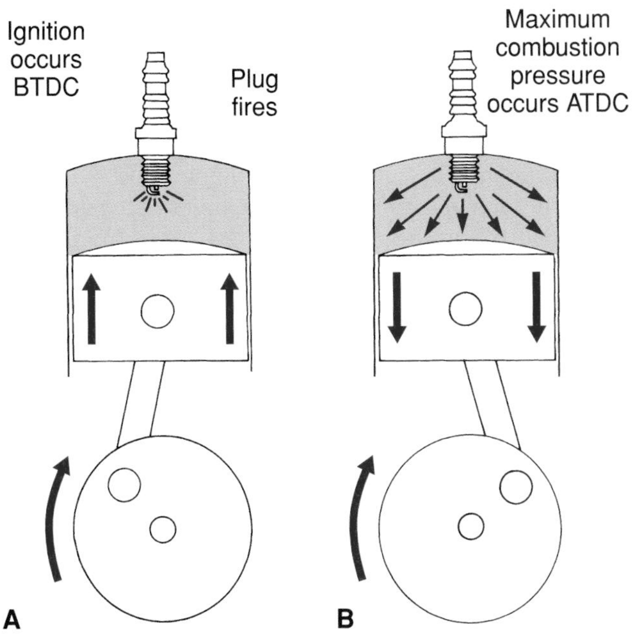

Figure 9-9. Combustion must begin before TDC so that maximum heat and pressure develops just after TDC.

Engine Speed	Crankshaft Degrees Required to Allow for Combustion Time Lapse
3000 rpm	25°
6000 rpm	35°

Figure 9-10. Chart shows how ignition timing is affected by engine speed.

Electronic Advance

Electronic advance of ignition timing is found in magneto supported and some transistorized ignition systems. Ignition timing advances as rpm increases due to the physical properties of magnetism and induction. Solid state devices may be used to modify the advance curve.

Electronic advance systems require no mechanical advance (or retard) and have no mechanical parts to wear. The overall design eliminates periodic adjustments and maintenance. Operation of an electronic advance system is covered later in this chapter.

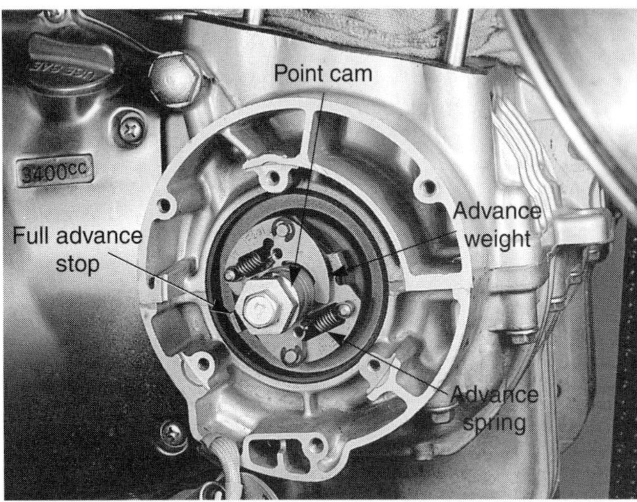

Figure 9-11. A centrifugal advance makes use of centrifugal force to advance ignition timing as engine rpm increases. Spring tension determines the amount of ignition advance as compared to engine speed. The stops limit maximum advance.

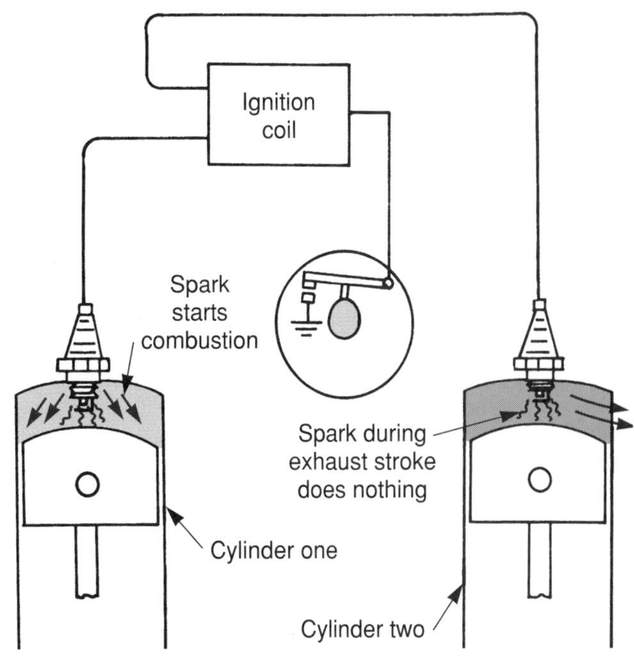

Figure 9-12. In this example, one contact breaker and ignition coil fires the spark plugs in both cylinders of a two-cylinder engine. One cylinder is on its compression stroke, the other is on its exhaust stroke.

Frequency of Spark

Frequency of spark refers to the number of times a spark plug fires during one cycle of operation for any given cylinder. For example, in some engines, the spark plug fires once in every cycle while in others, the spark plug fires twice. Ignition system design determines frequency of spark.

A four-stroke cycle engine requires an ignition spark in each cylinder for every 720° of crankshaft rotation. The spark must occur during the compression stroke. Some twin and multi-cylinder engines use a single ignition system that fires two cylinders. As shown in **Figure 9-12,** both spark plugs fire at the same time. One of the spark plugs initiates combustion and the other has no effect on engine operation. This spark may be referred to as an exhaust spark. It fires during the exhaust stroke, **Figure 9-13.** Other engines may use a separate ignition system for each cylinder. Notice that in **Figure 9-14,** each cylinder has its own breaker mechanism and ignition coil.

All two-stroke cycle engines require a separate ignition system for each cylinder. This is necessary because each spark plug must fire once for every cycle of operation (360°).

Spark Plug

The ***spark plug*** provides a spark gap in the engine's combustion chamber. This gap is between the spark plug's ground and center electrodes. The center electrode is attached to the spark plug wire, **Figure 9-15.** High voltage jumps between the two electrodes. The resulting spark ignites the air-fuel mixture in the combustion chamber. To do this effectively and at the proper time, the correct spark plug must be used, and must be kept clean and adjusted.

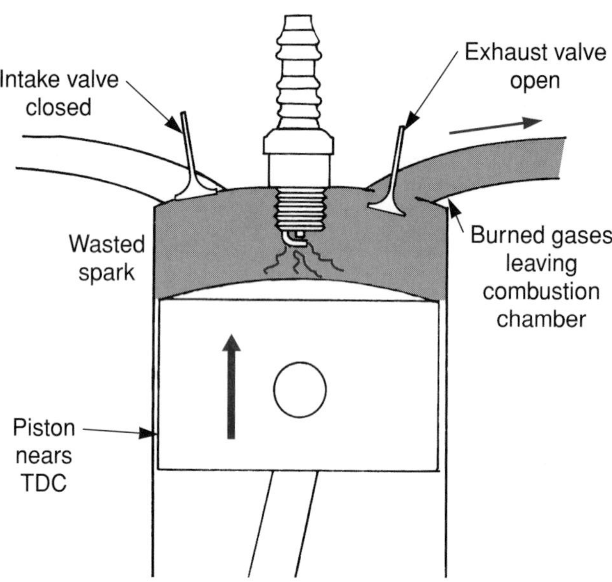

Figure 9-13. When cylinder one is on its compression stroke, cylinder two is on its exhaust stroke. Since both spark plugs fire at the same time, one makes power and two has a waste spark at the end of the exhaust stroke. When two is on its compression stroke, one has a waste spark.

As the spark plug is constantly exposed to the engine combustion gas, it is necessary to dissipate heat in order to keep the spark plug cool. The capacity of dissipating the heat is called the ***heating value*** or the ***heat range.***

Since spark plug requirements change with ignition and carburetion adjustments and riding conditions, the plugs must be removed to determine which particular heat range should be used. When a plug of the correct heat range is used, the electrodes will stay hot enough to keep from damaging the engine and itself. This temperature is about 750°F-1450°F (384°-773°C), and can be judged by noting the condition and color of the ceramic insulator around the center electrode. If the ceramic is

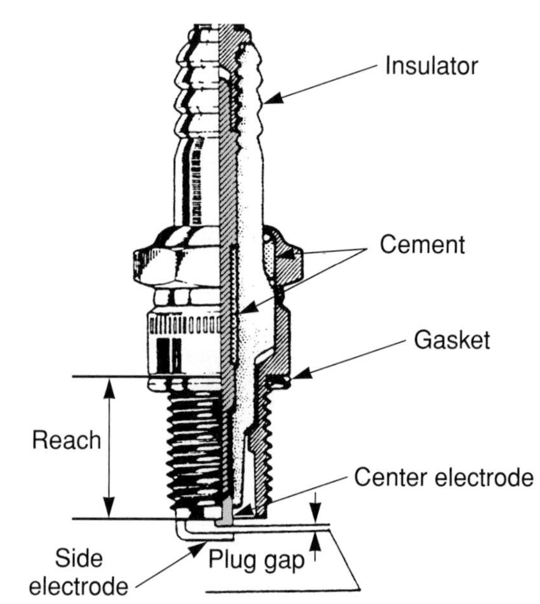

Figure 9-15. Spark plug construction. (Kawasaki Motors Corporation U.S.A.)

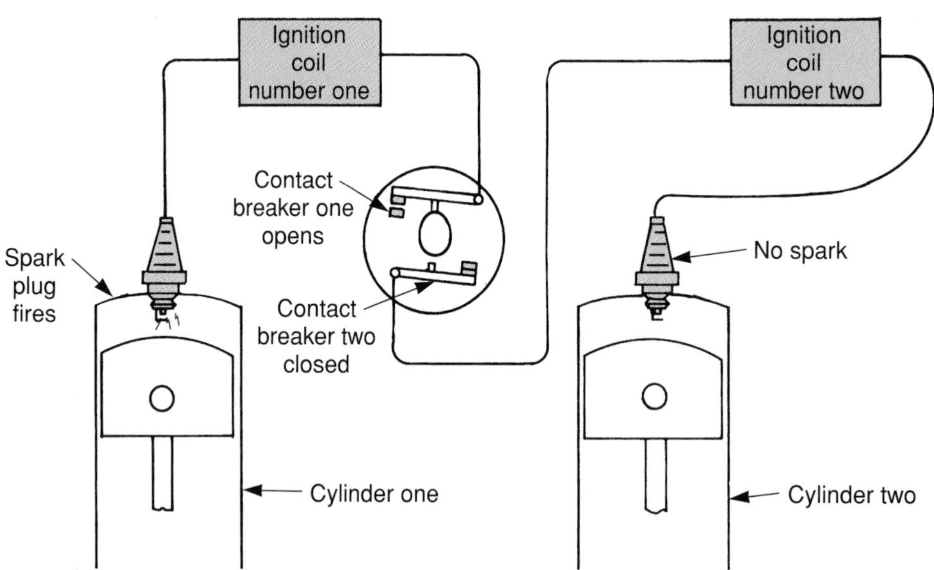

Figure 9-14. Each cylinder has its own ignition coil and contact breaker which operates independently. Each plug fires on the compression stroke to start combustion.

clean and a light brown color, the plug is operating at the right temperature.

Spark plugs with higher operating temperatures are used for racing. Such a plug is designed for better cooling efficiency so that it will not overheat and is often referred to as a colder plug, **Figure 9-16.** If a spark plug with too high a heat range is used, the combustion chamber will stay too cool to burn off residual carbon. The carbon will collect on the electrodes and the ceramic insulator. Since carbon is an electrical conductor, it can short the center electrode to ground by either coating the ceramic insulator or bridging across the gap.

Carbon build-up on the plug can also cause other problems. It can heat and cause preignition and knocking, which may eventually burn a hole in the top of the piston. Other common causes of spark plug fouling are shown in **Figure 9-17.**

Optional spark plugs are often listed in the service manual. Replace the plug with the optional one whenever the heat value of the original plug is not suitable for riding conditions. If a spark plug is replaced with a type other than the plug specified in the manual, make certain the replacement plug has the same thread pitch and reach (length of threaded portion) and the same insulator type (regular or projected type) as the standard plug, **Figure 9-18.**

- If the plug reach is too short, carbon will build up on the plug hole threads in the cylinder head, causing overheating and making it very difficult to insert the correct spark plug later.

Warning: The spark plug's heat range functions like a thermostat. Using the wrong type of spark plug can make the engine run too hot (resulting in engine damage) or too cold (with poor performance, misfiring, and stalling). The standard plug has been selected to match the normal usage of this motorcycle in combined street and highway riding. Unusual riding conditions may require a different spark plug heat range. For racing, install a colder plug.

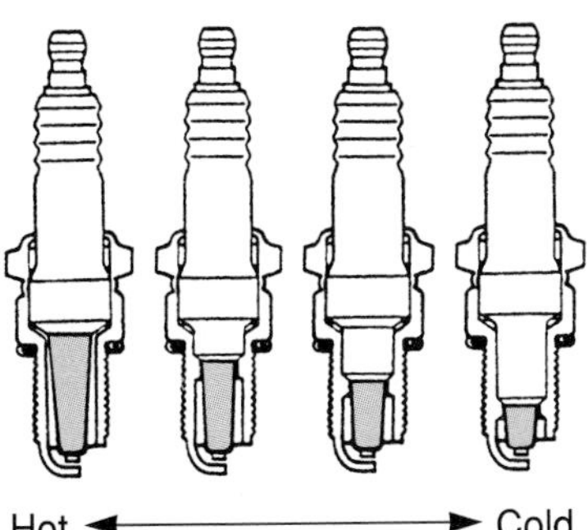

Figure 9-16. A spark plug's heating value, or heat range, are based on heat dissipation. (Honda Motor Co., Ltd.)

- If the reach is too long, carbon will build up on the exposed spark plug threads, causing overheating, preignition, and possibly burning a hole in the piston top. In addition, it may be impossible to remove the plug without damaging the cylinder head.

The spark plug gasket is an important factor in conducting the heat from the plug to the cylinder head. Unless plugs are properly tightened and gasket tension is correct, heat flow may be interrupted. A loose plug may be ruined by excessive heat if the bike is driven hard when cold. If hot plugs are driven hard when not properly tightened, they function improperly. Always torque the spark plug in its seat as directed in the service manual.

Spark Plug Wires

Motorcycles, scooters, and ATVs use thick insulated wire, referred to as ***spark plug wires,*** to transfer the high secondary voltage to the plugs, **Figure 9-19.** There are two types of spark plug wires used in ignition systems, resistor and non-resistor. Resistor wires are used on street bikes while non-resistor wires are for off-road use only.

Due to the high voltages they are required to carry and the exposure to the environment, spark plug wires are usually the cause of many ignition system problems. Spark plug wires should be replaced as part of routine maintenance, especially on bikes used in rough terrain or in harsh conditions. Spark plug wires on street bikes should be replaced, but not as frequently as on off-road bikes.

Types of Ignition Systems

Motorcycles use three types of ignition systems: battery and coil, electronic, and flywheel magneto. There are also variations to all these systems. It is important that you understand the similarities and differences of each type.

Battery and Coil Ignition

The ***battery and coil ignition system*** has been used for many years and is still in use. This is a relatively inexpensive and dependable system. A battery and coil ignition system is made up of two circuits: primary (low voltage) circuit and secondary (high voltage) circuit. A battery and coil ignition system can be triggered either by contact points or a magnetic-transistor triggering device.

The ***contact points*** make and break the primary circuit to fire the coil, **Figure 9-20.** When the contacts are closed, voltage flows through the coil primary windings, causing a magnetic field to build in the ignition coil. When the contacts open, current flow is stopped, collapsing the coil's magnetic field. The field cuts across the secondary windings to produce high voltage for spark plug operation.

A ***condenser*** is provided to minimize contact point arcing. It absorbs extra current flow to prevent point sparking and burning. Condenser operation can be broken

Normal Appearance
A spark plug in a sound engine operating at the proper temperature will have deposits that range from tan to gray in color. If LPG is used, the deposits will be brown. Under normal conditions, the electrode should wear slightly, but there should be no evidence of burning.

Carbon Fouling
Carbon fouling (dry, black, sooty carbon deposits) can be caused by plugs that are too cold for the engine, an over-rich fuel mixture, a clogged air cleaner, a faulty choke, or sticking valves. Installing a hotter plug will temporarily solve this problem.

Oil Fouling
Oil fouling (wet, black deposits) is caused by excessive oil in the combustion chamber. Worn rings, valve guides, valve seals, and cylinder walls can cause oil fouling. Switching to a hotter spark plug may temporarily relieve the symptoms, but will not correct the problem.

Ash Fouling
Ash fouling is caused by the buildup of heavy combustion deposits. These deposits are formed by burning oil and/or fuel additives. Although ash fouling is not conductive, excessive deposits can cause a spark plug to misfire.

Splashed Fouling
Splashed fouling can occur after a long-delayed tune-up. When a new plug is installed in an engine with excessive piston and combustion chamber deposits, the plug will restore regular firing impulses and raise the combustion temperature. When this occurs, accumulated engine deposits may flake off and stick to the hot plug insulator.

Gap Bridging
Gap bridging (combustion deposit bridging the center and ground electrodes) is caused by a sudden burst of high speed operation following excessive idling. It can also be caused by improper fuel additives, obstructed exhaust ports (two-cycle engines), and excessive carbon in the cylinder.

High Speed Glazing
High speed glazing (hard, shiny, electrically conductive deposits) can be caused by a sudden increase in plug temperature during hard acceleration or loading. High speed glazing can cause the engine to misfire at high speeds. If high speed glazing recurs, a cooler plug should be used.

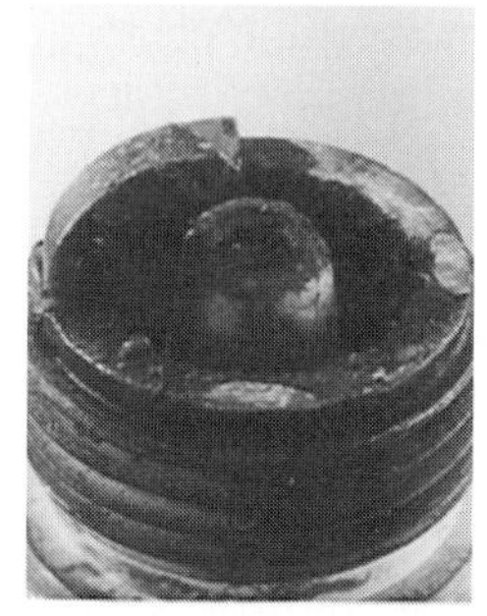

Preignition
Preignition (fuel charge ignited by a glowing combustion chamber deposit or a hot valve edge before the spark plug fires) can cause extensive plug damage. When plugs show evidence of preignition, check the heat range of the plugs, the condition of the plug wires, and the condition of the cooling system.

Detonation
Detonation can cause the insulator nose of a spark plug to fracture and chip away. The explosions that occur during heavy detonation produce extreme pressure in the cylinder. Detonation can be caused by low octane fuel, advanced ignition timing, or an excessively lean fuel mixture.

Overheating
Overheating (dull, white insulator and eroded electrodes) can occur when a spark plug is too hot for the engine. Advanced ignition timing, cooling system problems, detonation, sticking valves, and excessive high-speed operation can also cause spark plug overheating.

Mechanical Damage
Mechanical damage can be caused by a foreign object in the combustion chamber. It can also occur if the piston hits the firing tip of a spark plug with improper reach. When working on an engine, keep spark plug hole(s) and carburetor throat covered to prevent foreign objects from entering the combustion chamber.

Worn Out
Extended use will cause the spark plug's center electrode to erode. When the electrode is too worn to be filed flat, the plug must be replaced. Typical symptoms of worn spark plugs include excessive fuel consumption and poor engine performance.

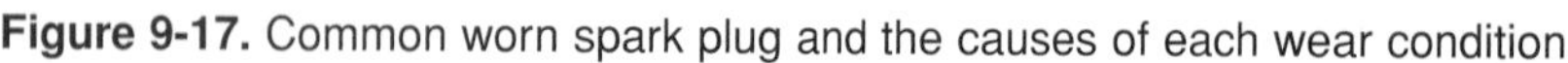

Figure 9-17. Common worn spark plug and the causes of each wear condition.

down into two phases: initial breaking of the contact points and self-induced voltage surge.

As the contact initially opens, the condenser absorbs excess current that would otherwise try to jump across the open contacts. As a result of the magnetic field's rapid collapse and build-up of secondary voltage, high voltage is induced in the primary windings. This high voltage also tries to arc across the contacts. When arcing occurs, contact surfaces are eroded and coil collapse is slowed, reducing secondary voltage.

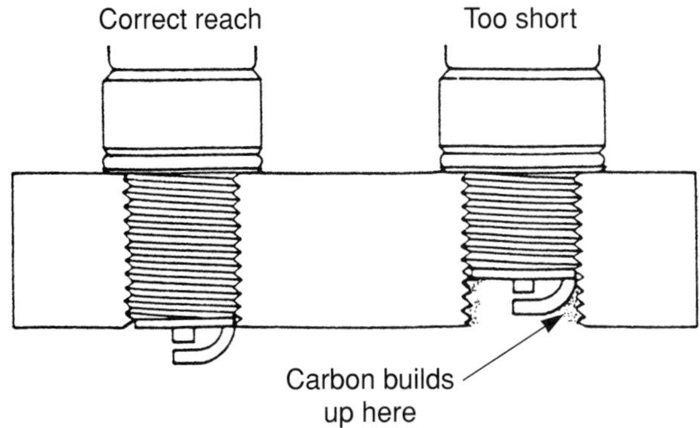

Figure 9-18. The effects of correct and incorrect reach. A—Correct reach allows the spark plug tip to just enter the combustion chamber. B—If the reach is too short, poor combustion and carbon buildup will result. (Kawasaki Motors Corporation U.S.A.)

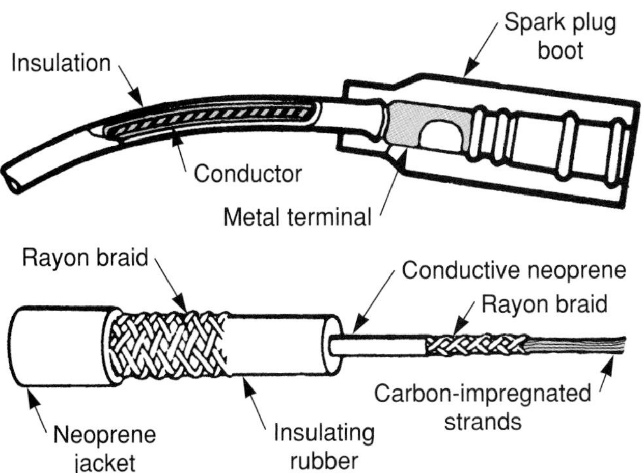

Figure 9-19. Cutaway of secondary wires used in ignition systems.

When the contacts close again, the condenser discharges and helps in rapid coil build-up. The condenser feeds stored electricity back into the system. Condenser operation is shown in **Figure 9-21.**

Electronic (Transistorized) Ignition

An ***electronic ignition*** or *transistorized ignition* is a battery and coil ignition system which uses a magnetic triggering device and solid state control module. The magnetic triggering device and control module replace the contact points and operate the ignition primary circuit. The magnetic device (magnet and pickup coil unit) generates a small pulse of electrical current. This electrical pulse is used to trigger the control module and ignition. **Figure 9-22** shows both contact point and transistorized ignition systems. Besides the parts mentioned at the beginning of the chapter, a typical transistorized ignition system consists of:

- Rotor (trigger wheel).
- Magnetic pickup (impulse generator).
- Control module (electronic switching device).

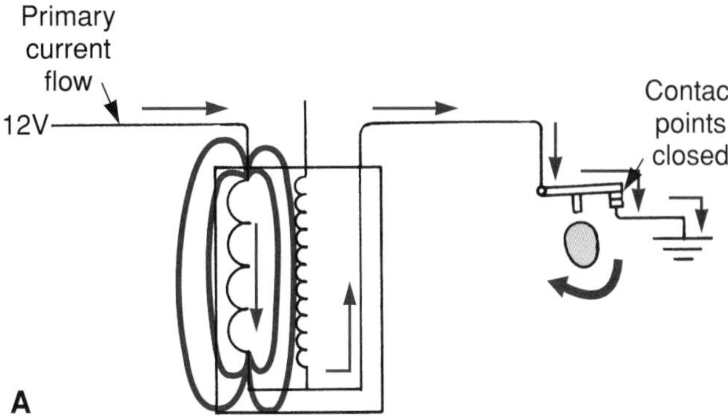

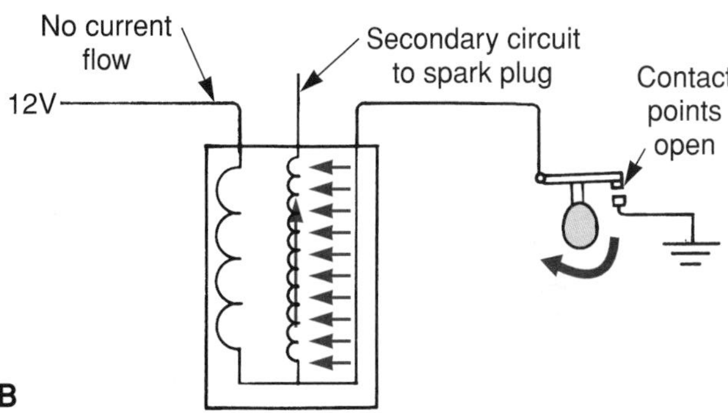

Figure 9-20. Ignition coil and primary circuit operation. A—Points closed. B—Points open.

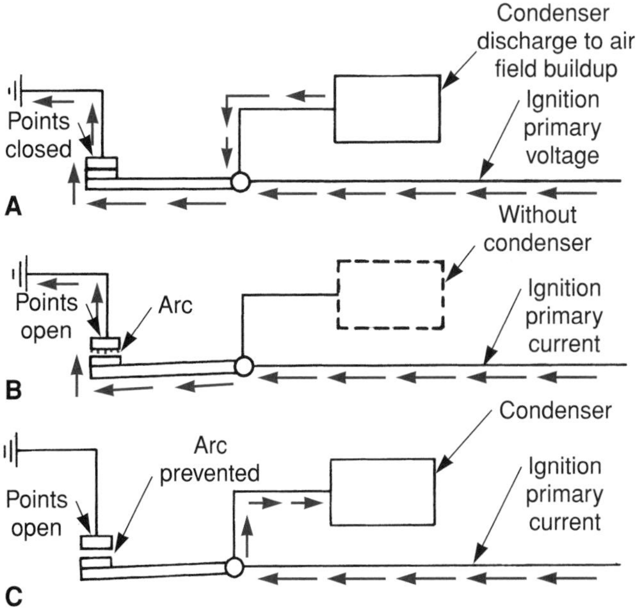

Figure 9-21. Condenser action. A—Contact points are closed and primary circuit is completed to ground. The charged condenser feeds current into the circuit. B—Without the condenser, an arc would occur as the points open, which would burn the contacts. C—The condenser absorbs and stores excess current to prevent point arcing and burning.

These parts take the place of the contact points and condenser. A transistor ignition system is shown in **Figure 9-23.**

Transistorized Ignition Operation

Power from the battery goes through the ignition switch to a solid state control module, **Figure 9-24.** An electric impulse from the rotor and magnet signals the control module to switch battery current on and off to the ignition coil primary windings. When current to the coil primary windings is switched off, the spark plug fires.

The rotor and magnetic pickup resemble a contact breaker plate and point cam, and are mounted similarly on the end of crankshaft or camshaft. The pickup assembly consists of a small permanent magnet and coil. The rotor (trigger wheel) is used to cut the pickup coil's magnetic field. This induces a tiny electrical current in the pickup coil windings. **Figure 9-25** shows how current is induced in a pickup coil. The control module uses this current pulse to operate the ignition coil. This type of rotor and pickup assembly is called a ***Darlington generator.***

Another type of magnetic trigger uses a ***Hall-effect integrated circuit*** (IC) to generate signal voltage. This type of system is called a Hall-effect transistorized ignition. A Hall-effect IC diverts electric current when it is exposed to a magnetic field, **Figure 9-26.** The diverted current is used to signal the control module.

The Hall-effect IC and a permanent magnet are separated by a rotating disc with a hole cut in it, **Figure 9-27.** The disc prevents the magnetic field from reaching the Hall-effect IC until the hole, Hall-effect IC, and magnet are aligned. At this point, current is diverted in the Hall-effect IC and sent to the control module. The control module then triggers ignition, **Figure 9-28.**

All motorcycle transistorized ignition systems work in basically the same way, however, there are variations in appearance and operation. We have covered two common methods of providing a signal voltage to the control module. Other ignition system variations include the different ways of controlling ignition advance and dwell. Ignition advance may be a centrifugal advance or electronic advance. Dwell may be controlled by the type of signal from the pickup or electronically by the circuit in the control module.

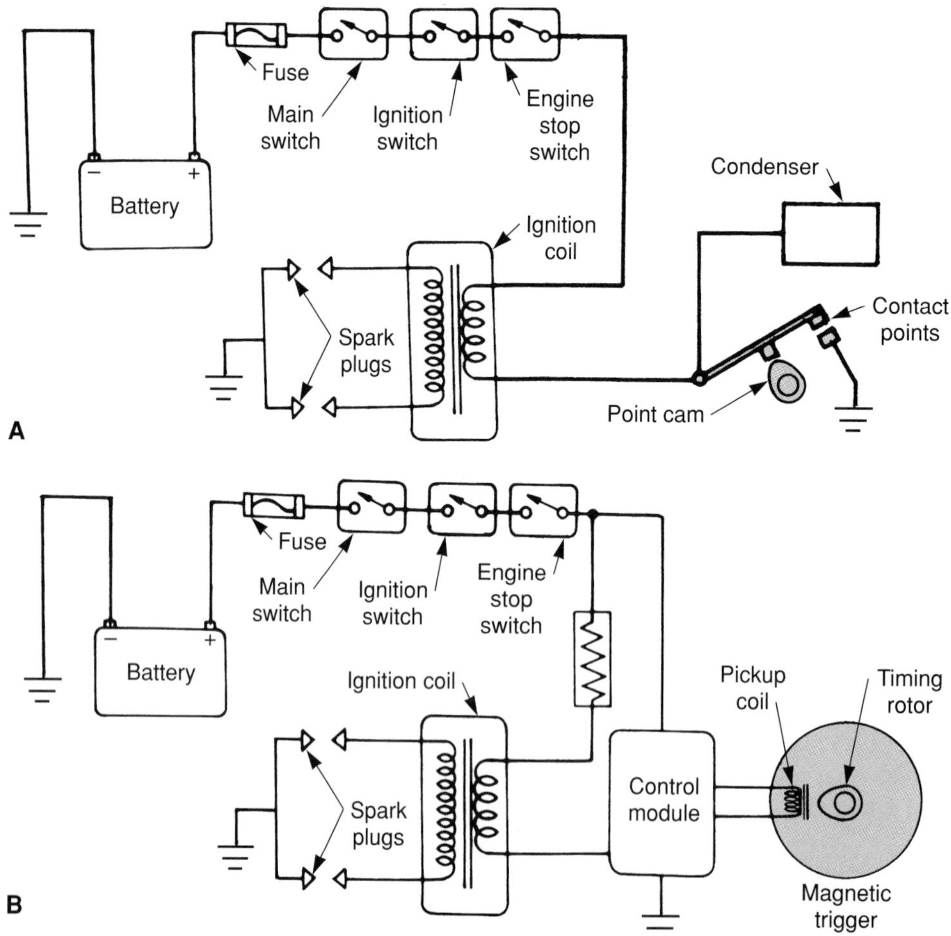

Figure 9-22. Compare contact point and transistor ignitions. A—Contact point ignition. B—In transistorized ignition, a magnetic triggering device (pickup coil and timing rotor) generates a small electrical pulse. The control module uses this pulse to switch primary current through the ignition coil on and off. (Kawasaki Motors Corporation U.S.A.)

Figure 9-23. These components make up a typical transistorized ignition system. Note the control module location in the upper left. Fins help dissipate heat from the electronic circuits.

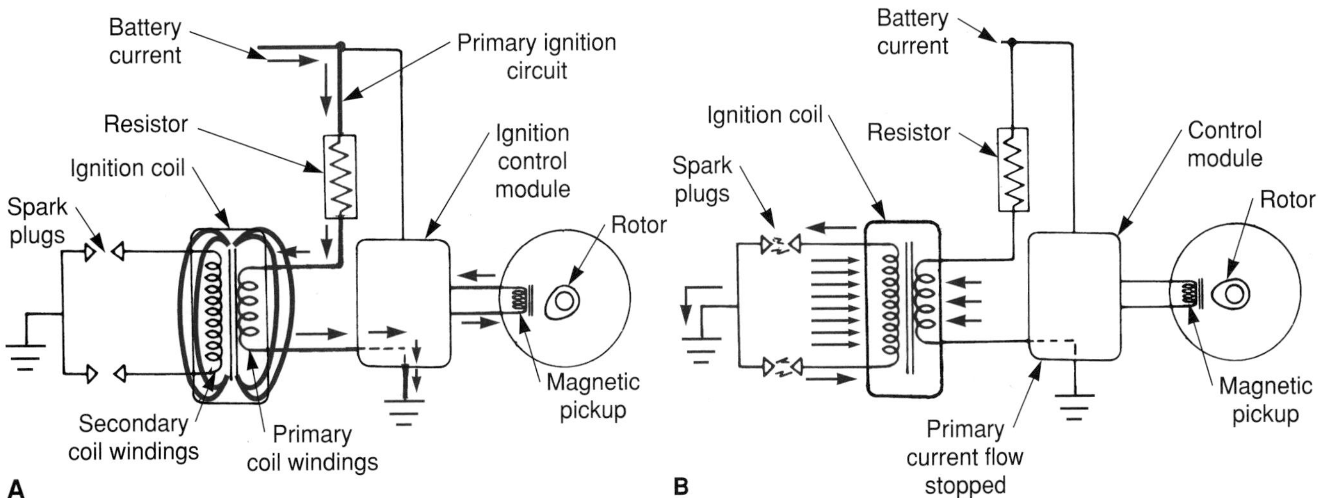

Figure 9-24. A—With the rotor away from the magnetic pickup, current flows through the coil primary windings and control module, building a magnetic field in the coil. B—As the rotor moves past the pickup, a pulse from the pickup coil causes the control module to open the primary circuit. The magnetic field in the primary coil windings collapse and induces current in the secondary windings, causing the spark plugs to fire. (Kawasaki Motors Corporation U.S.A.)

Flywheel Magneto Ignition System

The ***flywheel magneto ignition system*** uses alternating current rather than battery current to power the ignition system. Shown in **Figure 9-29,** a typical flywheel magneto ignition system is made up of:

- Flywheel.
- Ignition generating coil.
- Contact points.
- Condenser.
- Ignition coil.

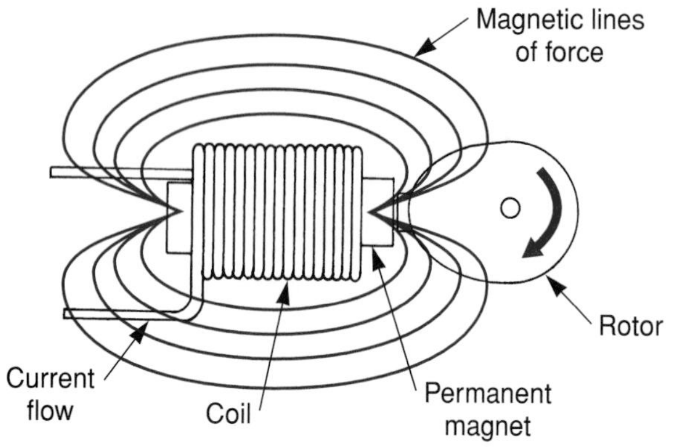

Figure 9-25. Current is induced in the magnetic pickup coil windings when the rotor cuts the coil's magnetic lines of force.

The current that powers this ignition system is produced by the flywheel magnets. The magnets induce current in the ignition generating coil. This is illustrated in **Figure 9-30.** Two types of flywheel magneto ignition systems are used on motorcycles. One type produces a high secondary voltage as a result of the magnetic field collapse. The other uses a rapid build-up (surge) of the magnetic field to induce high secondary voltage.

Field Collapse Magneto Ignition System

A ***field collapse magneto ignition system*** works much like a battery and coil ignition system. The major difference is that alternating current is used instead of direct current, **Figure 9-31.** Alternating current is produced in the ignition

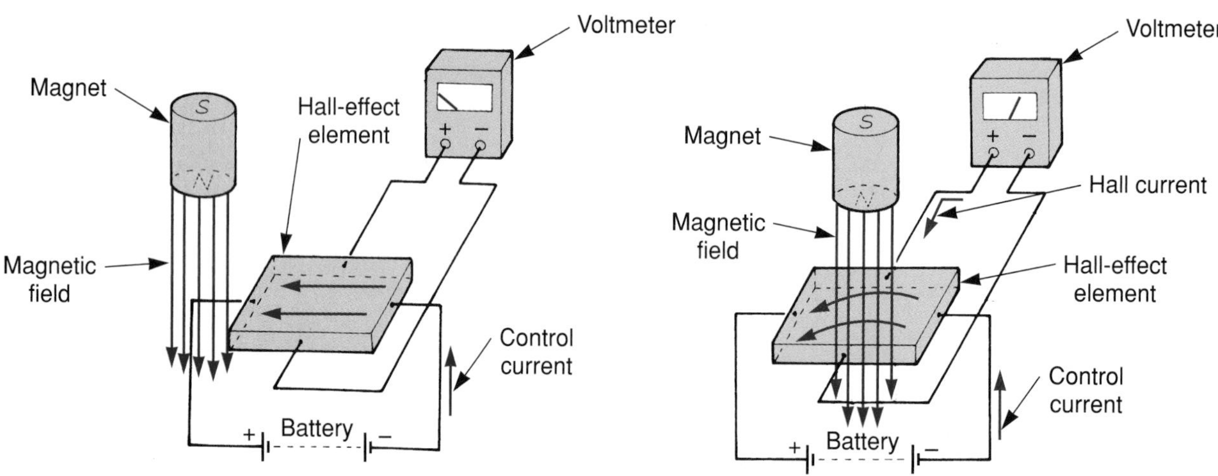

Figure 9-26. Hall-effect IC operation. A—Current from battery flows lengthwise through the Hall-effect element. B—When the Hall-effect element is exposed to a magnetic field, some current is diverted into a separate circuit. Current then flows crosswise through the element. This Hall-effect current is used to signal the control module. (Kawasaki Motors Corporation U.S.A.)

Figure 9-27. This six-cylinder engine uses three pickup (trigger) assemblies, each consisting of a permanent magnet and Hall-effect IC. Timing holes in the steel disc allow the magnetic field from the permanent magnet to reach the Hall-effect IC, triggering ignition.

generating coil. This current causes a magnetic field to form around the ignition coil primary windings. When the contact points open, the field is abruptly collapsed and high voltage is induced in the secondary windings. This fires the spark plug.

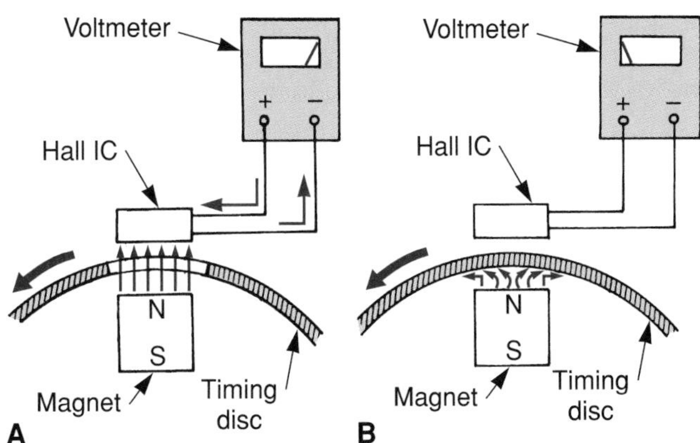

Figure 9-28. A—When the hole in the timing rotor lines up with the Hall-effect IC and magnet, Hall current is generated. B—Solid part of the timing disc prevents the magnetic field from reaching the Hall-effect IC and no current is produced. (Kawasaki Motors Corporation U.S.A.)

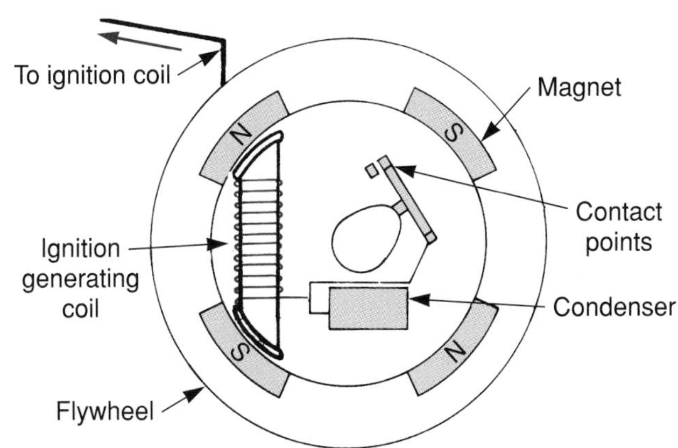

Figure 9-29. A flywheel magneto is a simple and compact ignition system.

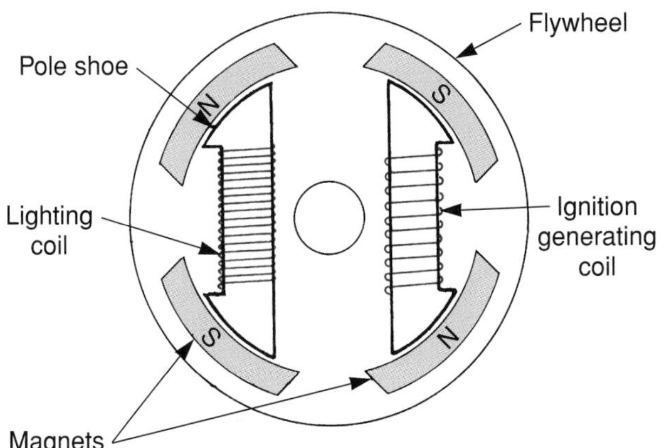

Figure 9-30. In a flywheel magneto, current is induced in the windings of the ignition generating coil as the flywheel magnets spin past the pole shoes.

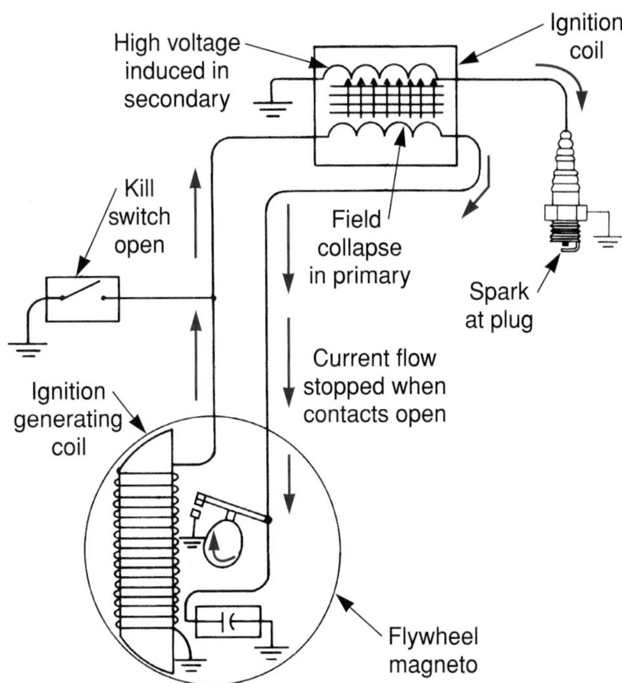

Figure 9-31. In a field collapse magneto, current produced in the generating coil flows through the primary coil windings, contacts, and condenser until the contacts open. When the contacts open, current flow stops and the magnetic field collapses. This induces current in the ignition coil secondary windings.

Field Build-up Magneto Ignition System

The ***field build-up magneto ignition system*** makes use of rapid magnetic field build-up to induce high voltage in the secondary windings, **Figure 9-32.** The same components are used for this system as in the field collapse magneto. The major difference is in the way the contacts are wired into the circuit.

In this system, closed contacts prevent primary current flow in the ignition coil. When the contacts open, current surges into the primary windings. This causes a rapid magnetic field build-up that induces high voltage in the ignition coil secondary windings. The contacts are timed to open just as maximum current is produced in the generating coil.

Digitally Controlled Transistorized Ignition System

The ***digitally controlled transistorized ignition system*** controls ignition timing using an electronic control module (ECM) inside the spark unit which calculates the ideal timing at all engine speeds. The ECM also has a fail-safe mechanism which cuts off power to the ignition coil(s) in case timing becomes abnormal.

The system consists of a pulse generator rotor, one or two pulse generators, the spark control unit, ignition coil(s), and spark plug(s). The ***pulse generator rotor*** has projections called ***reluctors*** that rotate past the pulse generator(s), producing electronic pulses that are sent to the spark control unit. The engine rpm and crankshaft position of each cylinder are detected by the relative position of the pulse generator's rotors. The control unit is non-serviceable and consists of a power distributor, signal receiver, computer, and distributor.

The ignition system operates as follows, **Figure 9-33.** When the key is turned on, the power distributor sends battery voltage to the ignition control. The signal receiver receives the electronic pulse from the pulse generator(s) and then converts the pulse signals to a digital signal. The digital signal is sent to the ECM, which has a memory and an arithmetic unit. The ECM memory stores the desired timing characteristics for rpm and crankshaft position. The arithmetic unit relays the rpm and crankshaft position to ECM memory. The memory then determines when to turn the transistor on and off to achieve the correct spark plug firing time. When the transistor is turned on, the ignition coil's primary windings are saturated. Memory then turns the transistor off when it is time to fire the spark plug.

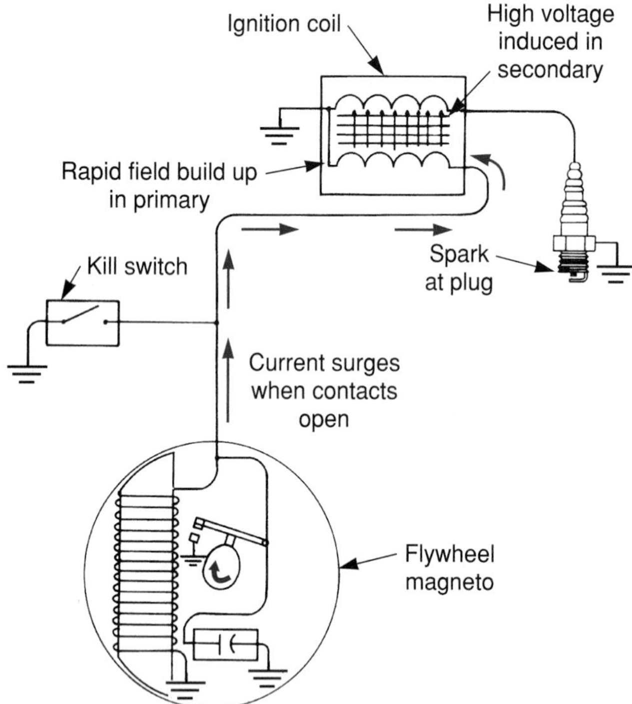

Figure 9-32. In a field build-up magneto, current flow surges into the primary coil windings when the contact points open. This surge of current occurs so quickly that current is induced in the secondary coil windings as the magnetic field is building up.

Capacitor Discharge Ignition (CDI)

A ***capacitor discharge ignition (CDI),*** is another form of electronic ignition system. It uses solid state components to control coil operation. Two advantages of CDI are:

- Low maintenance requirements (no moving parts to wear out).
- Extremely high secondary voltage is available.

Due to the CDI ignition system's high primary voltage (approximately 300-400 volts), contact points cannot be used. This high primary voltage would quickly burn and ruin mechanical points. Instead of contact points, electronic triggering and switching devices are used in the CDI ignition. A capacitor stores primary voltage, and a control module (switch) releases this voltage to the ignition coil. Coil induction in a CDI system works the same as the field build-up magneto. They both use a primary voltage surge.

Magneto Supported CDI

One of the most common systems in use today is the ***magneto supported CDI.*** This type is shown in **Figure 9-34.** Along with some of the other parts mentioned earlier in this chapter, the magneto supported CDI consists of:

- Flywheel.
- Base plate.
- Charging coil (excitor coil).
- Trigger coil.

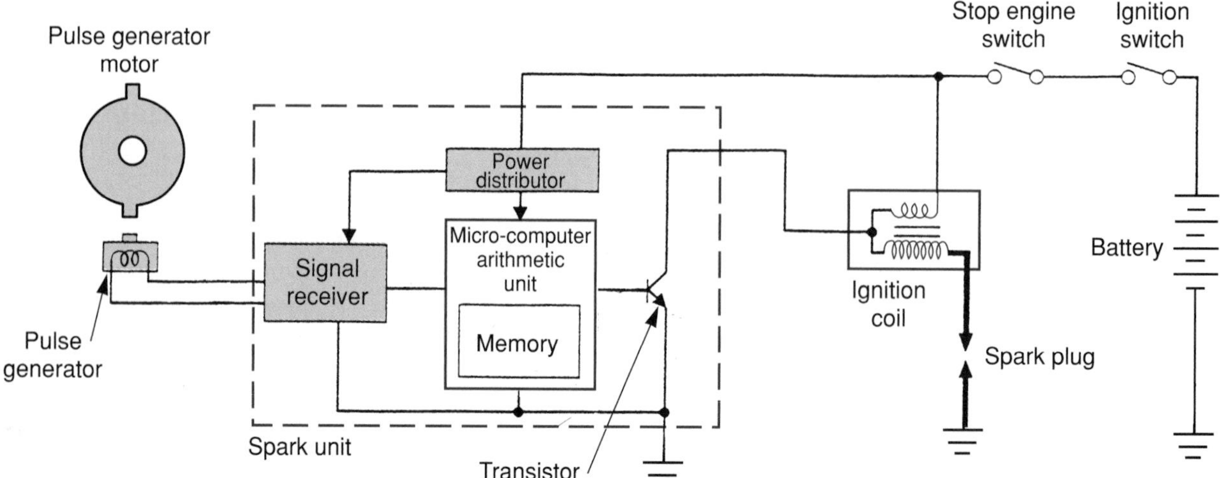

Figure 9-33. Typical digital controlled transistorized ignition system. (Honda Motor Co., Ltd.)

Figure 9-34. Magneto supported CDI systems are commonly used on off-road, two-stroke cycle motorcycles.

- Control module.
- Accessory coils (lighting or battery charging).

Most of these components replace the contact points, condenser, and electronic pickups used in other ignition systems.

Magneto Supported CDI Operation

The magneto supported CDI is similar in appearance to a conventional flywheel magneto. Energy (ac current) to power the system is generated by the flywheel magnet and charging coil. This current is fed into a control module which converts ac to dc. The electric charge is stored in a capacitor in the control module, **Figure 9-35.**

The rapid discharge of the capacitor into the primary windings of the ignition coil induces extremely high voltage in the secondary coil windings. This causes the spark plug to fire, **Figure 9-36.**

Discharge of the capacitor is controlled by a thyristor or ***silicone controlled rectifier (SCR)*** in the control module. Look at **Figure 9-37.** A thyristor is a solid state electronic device that can control or switch high voltages.

In a CDI system, the thyristor is used to hold back the voltage in the charged capacitor. The thyristor releases the capacitor charge when signaled by a low voltage impulse of approximately 5-10 volts. This low voltage impulse is produced and timed by the trigger coil and flywheel magnets, **Figure 9-38.**

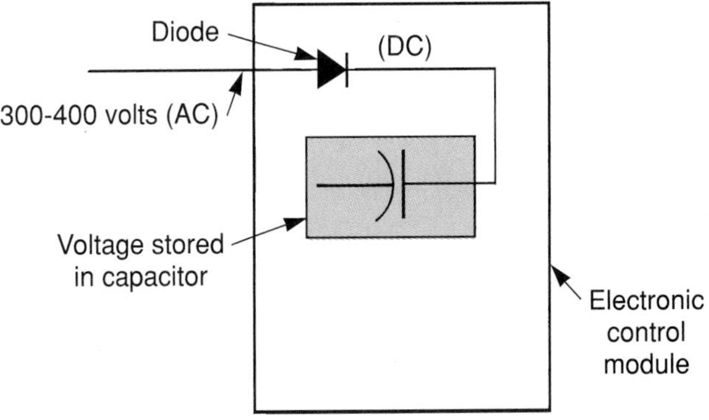

Figure 9-35. High voltage from the ignition generating coil is fed to the control module. It is converted to dc by a diode and stored in a capacitor.

Electronic Advance

Since the CDI has non moving parts, ignition advance must be done electronically. The ***CDI electronic advance*** is usually controlled by the properties of magnetism and induction between the trigger coil and flywheel magnets. Electronic advance is caused by the change in trigger coil voltage rise time as engine speed increases. See **Figure 9-39.**

The thyristor is designed to be activated at a predetermined voltage. For example, if a certain system requires 7 volts to switch the thyristor, it will release the charge

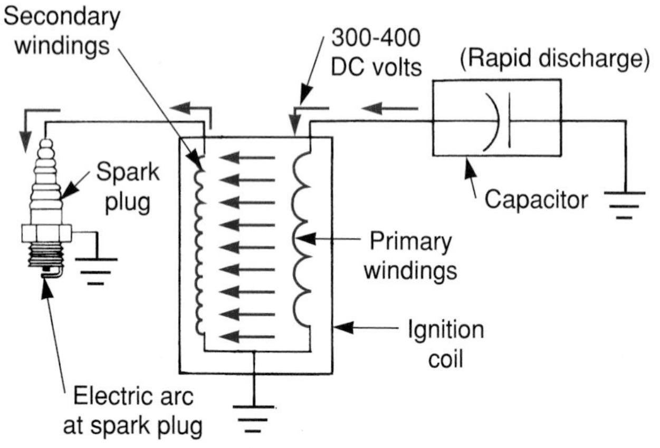

Figure 9-36. Rapid discharge of the CDI capacitor into the primary coil windings causes an abrupt magnetic field build-up. This induces high voltage in the secondary windings. A hot spark shoots across the gap at the spark plug.

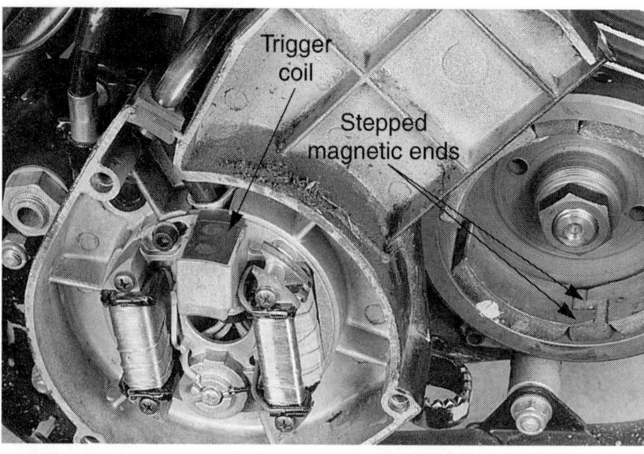

Figure 9-38. Trigger coil sends a low voltage impulse to the control module when the stepped magnet ends pass the trigger. Magnet ends are stepped in only one place on flywheel. The trigger coil and housing sit next to rotating magnets.

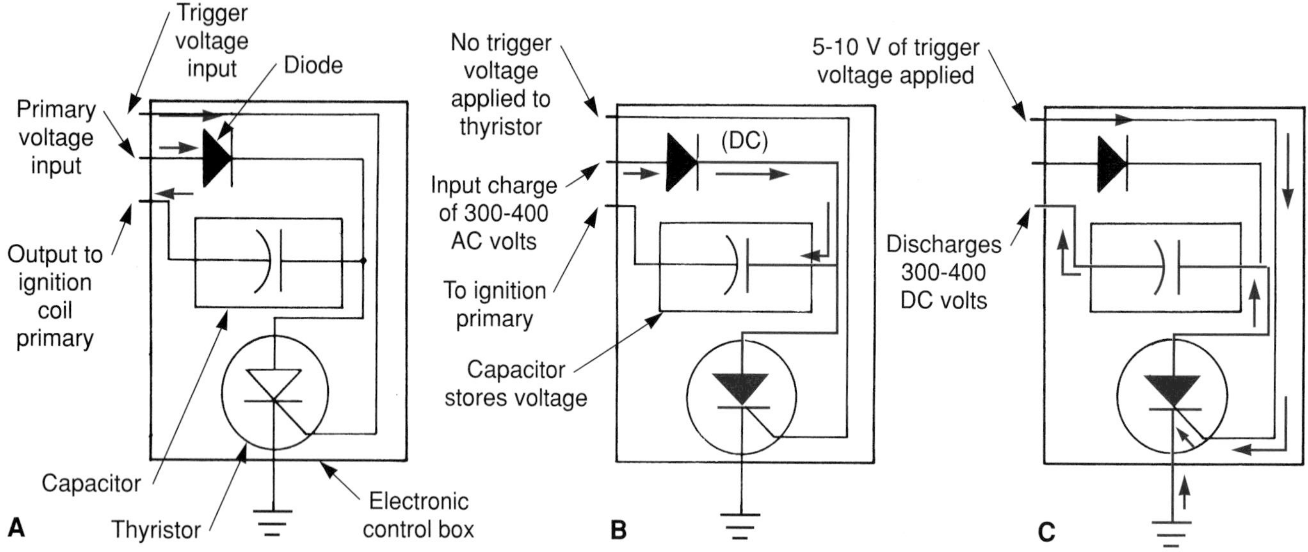

Figure 9-37. A—The components of a CDI control module are a diode, capacitor, and thyristor. B—The capacitor is charged by rectified current from the charging coil. Release of voltage from the capacitor is controlled by a thyristor. C—When low voltage from the trigger coil is applied to the thyristor, the capacitor is connected to ground, causing it to discharge into the ignition coil's primary windings.

from the capacitor as soon as 7 volts is reached. Look at **Figure 9-40.** Applying this to the electronic advance, it is obvious that:

- As engine speed increases, trigger coil voltage increases.
- As trigger coil voltage increases, voltage rise time also increases.
- Trigger voltage is always generated in the same number of crankshaft degrees.
- As engine speed increases, thyristor release voltage is reached earlier. This causes an advance of the ignition timing. **Figure 9-41** illustrates the factors that cause electronic ignition advance in a CDI ignition.

This type of electronic advance has some limitations. Most systems only produce a maximum of about 6° of advance. Once maximum advance is reached, higher engine speed does not produce more advance.

Due to the limited advance in a CDI ignition, solid state devices may be used in the control module to change the advance curve. The curve may be advanced beyond 6° electronically. In other systems, the curve is designed to retard slightly at peak engine rpm to aid combustion. The battery CDI may be found on some high performance two-stroke engine motorcycles.

DC/CDI Ignition System

The ***DC/CDI ignition system*** is like the standard CDI system except the battery is used as the power source, **Figure 9-42.** The DC/CDI control unit includes a DC/DC

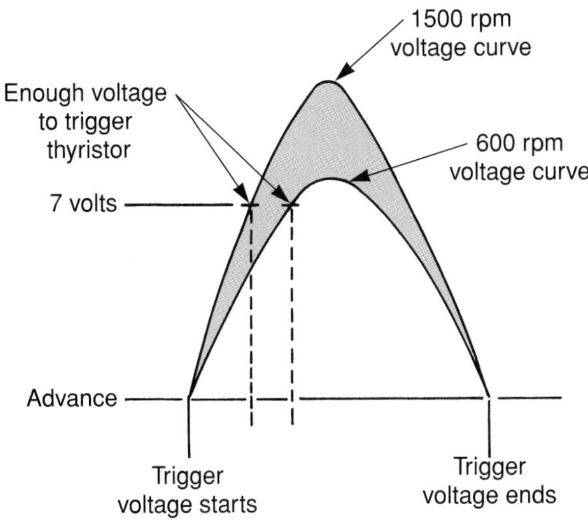

Figure 9-39. A controlling factor in electronic advance is trigger coil voltage rise time. As engine speed increases, the voltage curve becomes steeper. This principle is used to change ignition timing.

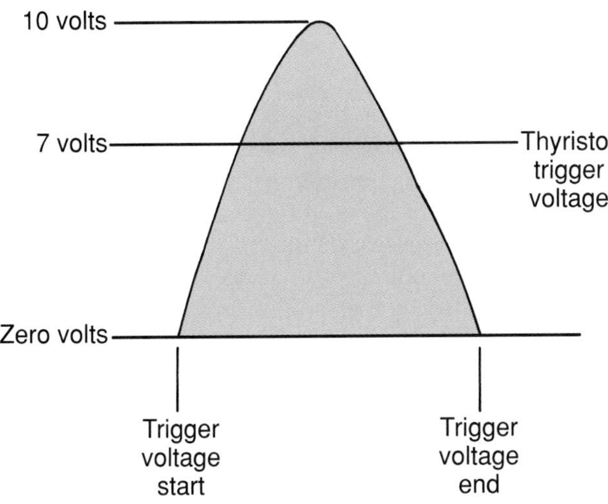

Figure 9-40. A thyristor will allow the capacitor to discharge when trigger voltage reaches a certain value (7 volts in this example). Higher voltage produced by the trigger coil has no effect.

converter. The converter amplifies the battery voltage to about 220 volts, which is then stored in a capacitor. Except for the DC/DC converter, the DC/CDI control unit is identical to the CDI unit. Compared to a conventional CDI system, the DC/CDI provides greater spark energy at low rpm since the power source is stable battery energy.

Ignition Problems

A faulty ignition system is often related to poor connections. Check all connections before proceeding with any troubleshooting procedures. Some of the more common ignition system problems and possible causes are as follows:

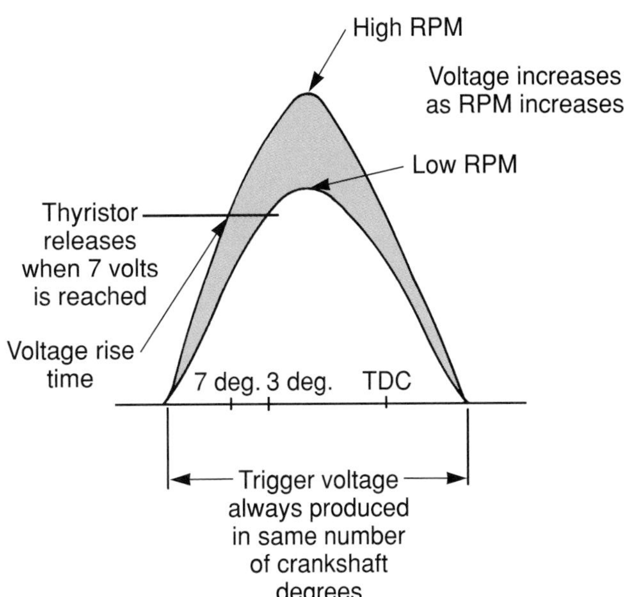

Figure 9-41. Since trigger voltage is produced over the same number of crankshaft degrees, regardless of engine speed, a steeper voltage curve causes automatic advance. This happens because trigger voltage (7 volts) is reached more quickly.

Engine Does Not Start, Starting Difficulty

- No spark.
- Spark weak.
- Spark plug dirty, broken, or misadjusted.
- Spark plug cap or high tension wiring problem.
- Spark plug cap not in good contact.
- CDI unit defective.
- Faulty pick-up coil.
- Ignition coil defective.
- Ignition coil resistor open.
- Ignition or engine stop switch shorted.
- Wiring shorted or open.
- Compression low.
- Spark plug loose.

Poor Running at Low Speed

- Spark weak.
- Spark plug dirty, broken, or misadjusted.
- Spark plug cap or high tension wiring problem.
- Spark plug cap not in good contact.
- Spark plug incorrect.
- CDI unit defective.
- Faulty pick-up coil.
- Ignition coil defective.
- Ignition coil resistor open.
- Ignition timing incorrect.

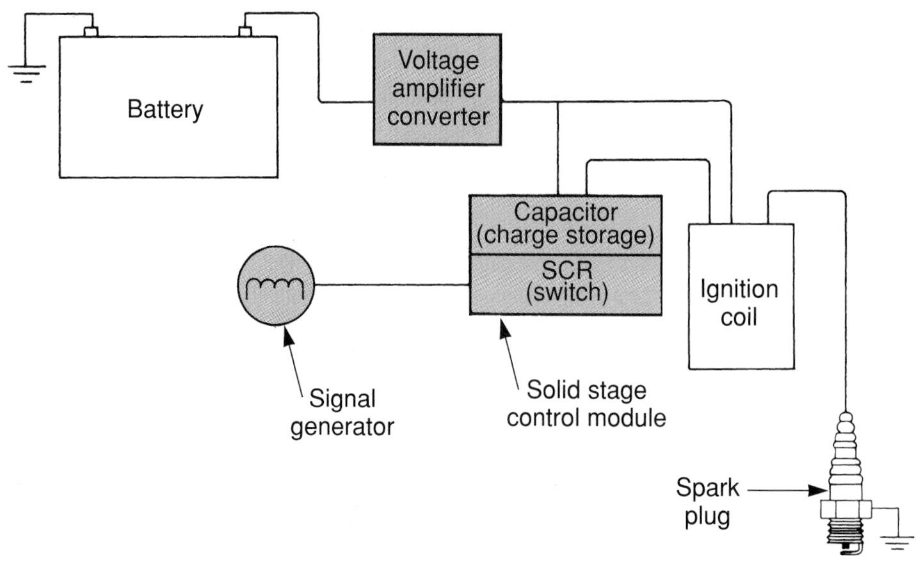

Figure 9-42. Battery supported CDI uses a voltage amplifier-converter to increase battery voltage for use in the primary ignition circuit. Signal generator and control module work in same manner as in magneto supported CDI. Generator triggers control module and control module triggers capacitor and ignition coil.

Poor Running or No Power at High Speed

Firing Incorrect

- Spark plug dirty, broken, or misadjusted.
- Spark plug cap or high tension wiring problem.
- Spark plug cap not in good contact.
- Spark plug incorrect.
- Spark plug loose.
- CDI unit defective.
- Faulty pick-up coil.
- Ignition coil defective.
- Ignition coil resistor open.
- Timing not advancing.

Knocking or Abnormal Engine Noise

- Spark plug incorrect.
- Overheating.
- Spark plug dirty, damaged, or misadjusted.
- Spark plug incorrect.

Ignition system timing adjustments and other servicing procedures are discussed in detail in Chapter 22.

Summary

The efficient operation of a motorcycle engine requires a well maintained ignition system. An ignition system is used to start the controlled combustion of an air-fuel mixture in the engine. The ignition system must step up battery voltage to 20,000 volts or more. When the ignition system is functioning properly, it supplies enough voltage at the spark plug to overcome system and combustion chamber resistance. Because of lean air-fuel mixtures, which are harder to ignite, the job of the ignition system has become even more difficult.

All of the components using low voltage (battery voltage) are included in the ignition primary circuit. In all ignition systems, the spark is triggered by a switching device. This switch may be a set of contact points or a magnetic-electronic device. The triggering device can be rotated in relation to the crankshaft, camshaft, or idler.

The ignition coil is the heart of the ignition system. It is a simple step-up transformer. The ignition coil relies on induction to step up battery voltage. The ignition coil is made up of a primary winding and a secondary winding. The primary winding consists of hundreds of turns of coarse wire wound around the secondary windings. The secondary winding has thousands of turns of fine wire wound around an iron core. The ignition secondary includes all the components that operate on high coil output voltage. When the ignition coil voltage is stepped up, the spark plug wire (high tension wire) carries this voltage to the spark plug. The spark plug provides a spark gap in the engine's combustion chamber.

Motorcycles use three types of ignition systems: battery and coil, electronic, and flywheel magneto. The battery and coil ignition system has been used for many years and is still in use. An electronic ignition or transistorized ignition is a battery and coil ignition system which uses a magnetic triggering device and solid state control module. The flywheel magneto ignition system uses alternating current rather than battery current to power the ignition system. A field collapse magneto ignition system works much like a battery and coil ignition system except that alternating current is used instead of direct current. The field build-up magneto ignition system makes use of rapid magnetic field buildup to induce high voltage in the secondary windings. The digitally controlled transistorized ignition system controls ignition timing using an ECM inside the spark unit that calculates the ideal timing at all engine speeds. A capacitor discharge ignition (CDI), is another form of electronic ignition system that uses solid state components to control coil operation.

Know These Terms

Ignition system	Condenser
Spark intensity	Electronic ignition
Ignition primary circuit	Darlington generator
Ignition coil	Hall-effect integrated circuit
Primary winding	Flywheel magneto ignition system
Secondary winding	Field collapse magneto ignition system
Ignition secondary circuit	Field build-up magneto ignition system
Centrifugal advance unit	Digitally controlled transistorized ignition system
Electronic advance	Pulse generator
Frequency of spark	
Spark plug	Reluctors
Heating valve	Capacitor discharge ignition (CDI)
Heat range	Magneto supported CDI
Spark plug wires	Silicone controlled rectifier (SCR)
Battery and coil ignition system	CDI electronic advance
Contact points	DC/CDI ignition system

Review Questions—Chapter 9

Do not write in this text. Place your answers on a separate sheet of paper.

1. The purpose of the ignition system is to ______ .
   A. charge the accessory system
   B. start controlled combustion
   C. cause detonation
   D. None of the above.
2. As engine speed increases, ignition must occur earlier because ______ .
   A. electricity does not travel as fast
   B. ignition does not occur earlier
   C. there is less time for the air-fuel mixture to burn
   D. the mixture will usually be richer
3. A two-stroke cycle engine requires ignition every _____ degrees of crankshaft rotation.
4. What is another name for a *step-up transformer?*
5. An ignition coil fires the spark plug when the contacts _____.
6. High voltage is induced in the secondary windings of an ignition coil because:
   A. the primary and secondary winding ratio is approximately 1:1.
   B. current flow through the primary coil windings continues when the spark plug fires.
   C. there are hundreds of windings of coarse wire in the secondary circuit.
   D. there are thousands of windings of fine wire in the secondary circuit.
7. A battery and coil ignition system may be triggered by ______ or a _____ triggering device.
8. The main purpose of a condenser is to minimize ______.
   A. contact point arcing
   B. detonation
   C. preignition
   D. timing advance
9. What is another name for a magnetically triggered ignition system?
10. What is a major advantage of a transistorized ignition system compared to a contact point ignition?
11. List the two means of controlling transistorized ignition system advance.
12. Name the two variations of a CDI system.
13. During CDI operation, the rapid _____ of the capacitor into the _____ windings of the ignition coil causes a _____ which induces high voltage in the coil secondary.
14. In a CDI system, a ______ discharges capacitor voltage.
    A. thyristor
    B. silicon control rectifier (SCR)
    C. condenser
    D. Both A & B.
15. What controls electronic ignition advance in a CDI system?

Suggested Activities

1. Select a motorcycle with a battery and coil ignition system. Using the wiring schematic, trace the complete primary and secondary ignition circuits, and label all the components. Do this on both a contact point and a transistorized ignition system.
2. Select a motorcycle with a flywheel magneto. Using the wiring schematic, trace the complete primary and secondary circuits, and label all components. Determine whether the system uses field collapse or field build-up to induce high voltage.
3. Select a motorcycle with a battery supported CDI, and one with a magneto supported CDI. Using the ignition wiring schematic, trace current flow through these systems, and label all the components.
4. On a workbench, connect an ignition coil to a battery and to a spark plug. Make and break the primary while observing coil action.

A motorcycle's carburetors are often under the fuel tank or seat on most motorcycles. (Yamaha Motor Corporation U.S.A.)

10
Lubrication Systems

After studying this chapter, you will be able to:

- List the types and characteristics of motor oil.
- Compare two-stroke and four-stroke engine lubrication systems.
- Describe gearbox systems.
- Identify the major parts of motorcycle lubrication systems.
- Perform service operations on motorcycle lubrication systems.

The importance of an engine lubrication system and quality lubricants cannot be overemphasized. Without proper lubrication, the moving parts inside an engine can get hot enough to melt. Moving parts can score or even lock together in a matter of minutes. This chapter introduces modern motorcycle lubrication systems. Both two-stroke and four-stroke engine lubrication systems will be covered. This chapter also explains oil classifications, ratings, and operating characteristics.

Friction

Friction is the resistance to movement between two touching parts. A ***lubricant*** is used to reduce this friction and resulting part wear. A motorcycle ***lubrication system*** is designed to provide an adequate supply of lubricant (oil) to points of high friction. Oil must be pumped or sprayed onto moving engine and gearbox parts. This reduces friction and prevents rapid part wear and damage.

Oil

Lubricating ***oil*** has four functions:

- Lubricates (reduces friction between moving parts).
- Cleans (carries contaminates to filter).
- Cools (helps to dissipate heat).
- Seals (prevents leakage past rings and seals).

Lubricating Action

The internal combustion engine consists of many moving parts that rub against each other. As a result, a certain amount of friction and heat is always present in an engine. It is the oil's job to reduce this friction. The oil provides a thin film between all moving parts to reduce heat and prevent metal-to-metal contact. **Figure 10-1** illustrates dry friction and friction after lubrication.

Cleaning Action

While the oil is lubricating parts, it is also cleaning the engine. Combustion and normal wear of engine parts produce tiny metallic particles, carbon particles, and other contaminants. The oil must keep these particles and contaminants in suspension (floating). Then, contaminants

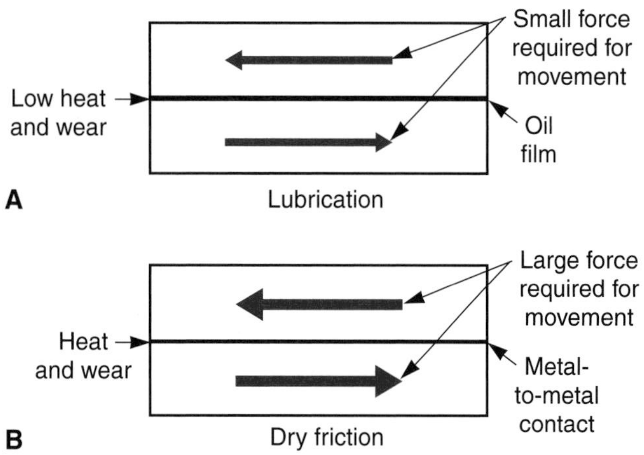

Figure 10-1. A—Surfaces are separated by an oil film. This prevents metal-to-metal contact and reduces friction. B— When unlubricated surfaces are in contact, any movement can cause friction, heat, galling, and wear.

can be trapped in the oil filter and removed from the engine by changing the oil and filter. Oil also helps prevent rust and corrosion. The oil must also be able to neutralize acids and dissolve varnish formed during the combustion process.

Cooling Action

In addition to lubricating and cleaning, oil helps to cool the engine. Oil absorbs and transfers heat to a cooler part of the engine. Shown in **Figure 10-2,** heat is dissipated into the oil and then into the air through crankcase cooling fins or an oil cooler.

Sealing Action

Another function of oil is to help the piston rings seal compression and combustion pressure. The thin oil film between the piston rings and cylinder wall is essential for proper ring sealing. See **Figure 10-3.** Oil between a piston ring and ring groove also aids in preventing pressure leakage.

Oil Types

There is a large selection of lubricating oils suitable for use in motorcycle engines. Specialized oils have been developed to meet specific needs. A list of the types of motorcycle oils includes:

- Four-stroke engine oil (petroleum based, derived from crude oil).
- Two-stroke engine oil (petroleum based, derived from crude oil).
- Synthetic four-stroke engine oil (manufactured chemically).
- Synthetic two-stroke engine oil (manufactured chemically).

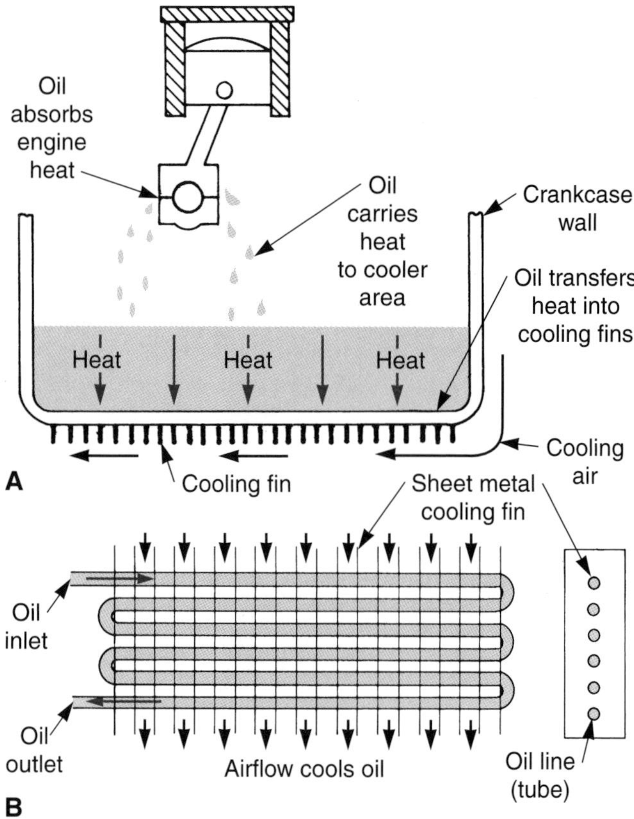

Figure 10-2. A—Oil is cooled by fins on the crankcase. B—Oil flows through a finned oil cooler to reduce oil temperature. Both methods transfer engine heat into the surrounding air.

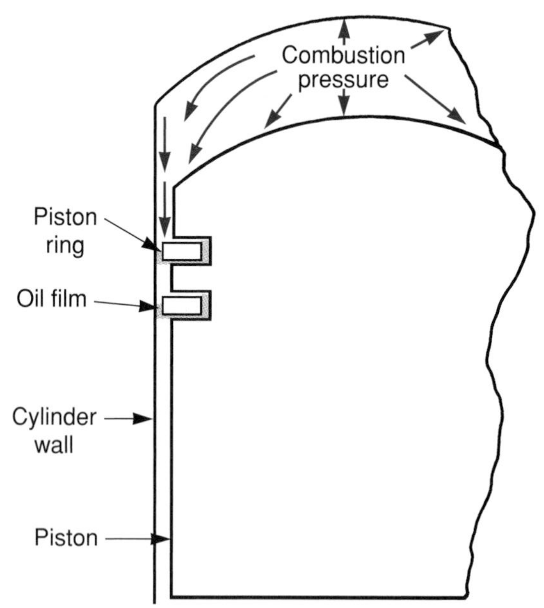

Figure 10-3. A thin film of oil is required between piston rings and the cylinder wall to seal combustion pressure. Without this sealing action, combustion pressure would blow past the rings, reducing power and efficiency.

- Gear oil (petroleum based).
- Two-stroke racing castor oil (vegetable oil).

Additives

Additives are carefully selected and used in the manufacture of oils to improve their operating qualities. Some desirable characteristics that result from the proper use of oil additives are:

- High film strength.
- Control of viscosity (thickness) at different temperatures.
- Resistance to oxidation.
- Resistance to foaming.
- Ability to keep contaminants in suspension.
- Ability to burn cleanly (two-stroke engine).

Film Strength

Film strength is the ability of an oil to remain between two lubricated parts, preventing metal-to-metal contact. Since extremely heavy loads are exerted on bearing surfaces, film strength is very important. Film strength is closely related to viscosity. Additives that help to increase film strength are used in quality oils.

Viscosity and Temperature

Viscosity refers to the thickness of an oil and is determined by the rate of oil flow under controlled conditions. Generally, high viscosity oils have high film strength.

Temperature plays an important role in changing oil viscosity. As oil heats up in an engine, it gets thinner and flows more freely. As oil is chilled (cold weather), it thickens and resists flow. Ideally, oil should flow as if it were thin and lubricate as if it were thick. Discussed later, the proper combination of additives during the production of oil can provide this desirable characteristic.

Oxidation

As oil is used, it combines with oxygen and picks up contaminants such as rust, combustion byproducts, condensed water, and acids. This action is referred to as ***oxidation.*** Oxidation increases drastically with higher temperatures and results in the formation of sludge and varnish. Since air-cooled motorcycle engines run very hot, oil oxidation can be a serious problem.

Although effective oxidation inhibitors are used in motorcycle oils, extreme temperatures still pose a problem. The only effective remedy for oil oxidation is regular oil and filter changes.

Foaming

As oil sprays around the inside of an engine crankcase, the oil comes into contact with fast moving parts (crankshaft, connecting rods, piston). Air is also present in the crankcase and can be mixed with the oil. This can cause the oil to become saturated with air bubbles, a condition called ***foaming.*** Foaming is undesirable because the oil's ability to lubricate and cool is greatly reduced and oxidation is accelerated. Additives that help control foaming are normally added to motorcycle oils.

Detergents

As mentioned, by-products of incomplete combustion and oil breakdown at high temperatures produce varnish and sludge. ***Detergent*** additives prevent the build-up of these deposits in an engine. Detergent additives keep unwanted products such as metal particles suspended in the oil so they can be caught in the filter and removed during an oil change. An oil which has these cleaning qualities is called a *detergent oil.* Detergent oil is normally recommended by motorcycle manufacturers. One reason oil becomes dirty quickly is because the detergents are doing their job.

Two-Stroke Oil Additives

Two-stroke lubricating oil is burned during combustion. The oil is mixed with gasoline and lubricates internal parts as the fuel is used to power the engine. Special additives are present in two-stroke oils to accommodate these conditions. Two-stroke oils must provide sufficient lubrication in a diluted state. They must also burn cleanly to prevent spark plug fouling, excessive carbon buildup, and air pollution.

API and SAE Oil Classifications

As internal combustion engines became more sophisticated, the operating requirements of engine oil have had to increase tremendously. Petroleum engineers and researchers have constantly worked to improve lubricating oils. As a result, a system was needed to test, standardize, and classify lubricating oils.

The ***American Petroleum Institute (API)*** and ***Society of Automotive Engineers (SAE)*** are the organizations responsible for the testing and classification of oils. They have classified oil in terms of intended use and viscosity.

Oil Use Classification

A double letter code is used to classify oils for specific uses. All oils for use in gasoline engines have a code beginning with the letter *S,* which means they are suitable for spark ignition engines.

The current highest quality oil is rated *SJ* and is recommended for all four-stroke motorcycle engines. Oil rated *SH* may also be used in four-stroke motorcycle engines. Engine oils that have a code beginning with *C* are designed for use in compression ignition engines, which are diesel engines. These oils are not suitable for use in some motorcycle engines.

In addition to these ratings, engine oils also carry an energy-conserving designation that means that they have less fluid friction while still meeting the viscosity requirements. Oils labeled *EC-I* offer at least a 1% reduction in fuel consumption, while oils labeled *EC-II* reduce energy consumption by 1.5%.

Viscosity Rating System

A ***viscosity rating system*** or numbering system identifies the thickness of oil; the higher the number, the thicker the oil. For instance, a 40 weight oil is thicker and will pour slower than a 30 weight oil. Look at **Figure 10-4.** The viscosity rating is normally printed on the bottle in large numbers.

As mentioned, engine oil tends to thicken when a motorcycle sits in cold weather. This could make the engine hard to kick over and start. After starting, when the engine heats to full operating temperature, the oil thins, losing some of its film strength.

To solve this problem, a ***multi-weight oil,*** also called multi-grade or multi-viscosity oil, was developed, **Figure 10-5.** It operates with the characteristics of a light oil (10 or 20 weight) when cold to allow easy starting. Then, when heated to operating temperature, it serves as thick oil (30 or 40 weight) to provide adequate film strength and protection. Multi-grade oil has the advantages of both high and low viscosity oils. Always follow manufacturer specifications for oil viscosity. They are listed in the owner's manual and the service manual.

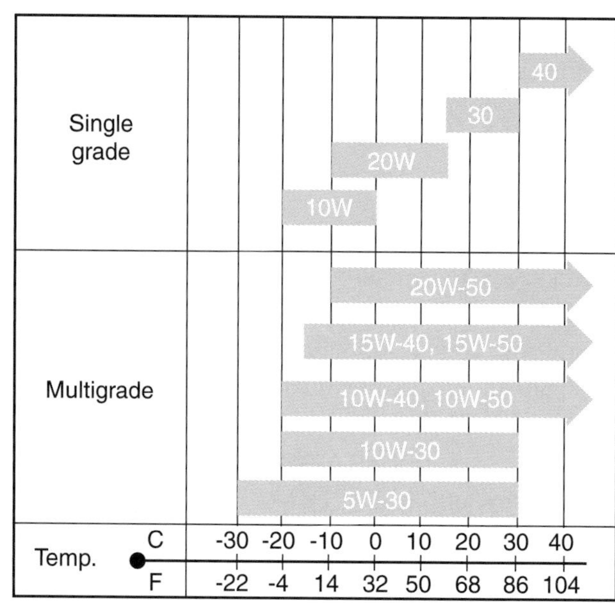

Figure 10-5. Recommended oil grades for various temperatures.

Two-Stroke Engine Lubrication

In the two-stroke engine, lubricating oil passes through the engine with the air-fuel mixture. It uses the internal crankcase area as a suction chamber. Two systems have been adopted in order to provide lubrication to the cylinder, piston rings, connecting rod, and crankshaft bearings. Each system relies on oil ingested together with the gasoline. Oil is combined with the gasoline before it reaches the carburetor in a premixed system. In separate oil or oil injection systems, engine lubricating oil is introduced downstream of the carburetor.

Figure 10-4. The oil viscosity rating and API service classification is printed on the front or back of the bottle.

Premix Lubrication

Premixed lubrication (engine oil mixed with gasoline) is the most widely used system on competition models. The combined air-fuel-oil mixture is introduced directly through the intake with the assistance of the carburetor, **Figure 10-6.** As this mixture is drawn into the crankcase, lubrication of the crankshaft, connecting rod bearings, piston rings, and cylinder walls is achieved. The fuel-oil ratio may vary from 16:1 (16 parts fuel, one part oil) to 48:1 (48 parts fuel to one part oil). With new synthetic and concentrated oils, the fuel-oil ratio could be as high as 100:1. The table in **Figure 10-7** indicates the amount of oil (ounces) required to achieve the desired premix ratio at the indicated volume of gasoline.

Caution: Use of a fuel-oil premix ratio other than the one recommended by the vehicle manufacturer may affect engine performance and might lead to premature engine wear or damage.

Oil Injection Lubrication

Virtually all street motorcycle, ATV, and scooter two-stroke engines use a pump-operated system to lubricate engine components. Oil in this type of system is drawn from a separate oil tank by a small pump that introduces

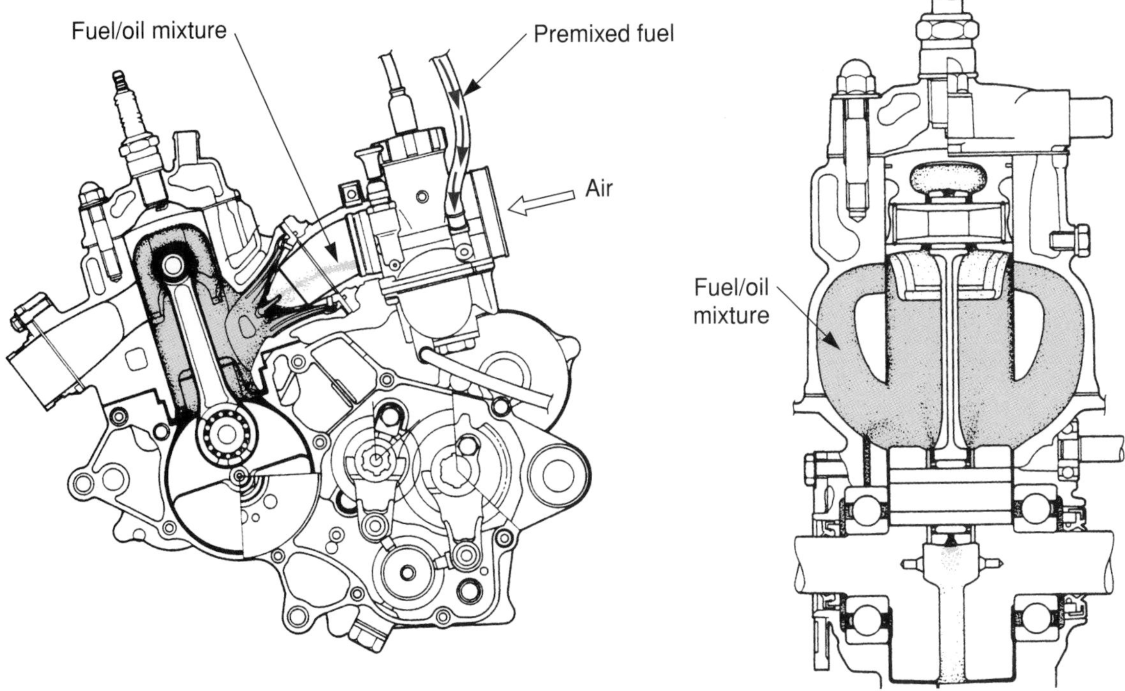

Figure 10-6. Premix lubrication system. (Honda Motor Co., Ltd.)

Gas-to-Oil Ratio (Two-Stroke Engines)									
Gasoline	16:1	20:1	24:1	28:1	32:1	36:1	40:1	44:1	48:1
1	8.0	6.4	5.3	4.6	4.0	3.5	3.2	2.9	2.7
2	16.0	12.8	10.7	9.1	8.0	7.1	6.4	5.8	5.3
3	24.0	19.2	16.0	13.7	12.0	10.7	9.6	8.7	8.0
4	32.0	25.6	21.3	18.2	16.0	14.2	12.8	11.6	10.7
5	40.0	32.0	26.7	22.9	20.0	17.8	16.0	14.5	13.3

Figure 10-7. Fuel-to-oil ratio chart for two-stroke engines. This chart should not be used in place of a similar chart in the bike's owner's or service manual.

the oil directly into the air-fuel inlet tract beyond the carburetor, **Figure 10-8.**

The pump forces oil into the engine depending upon both the throttle setting and engine rpm (speed), **Figure 10-9.** In this system, oil is stored in a separate reservoir (oil injection tank) and gasoline is stored in the fuel tank. The oil injection system automatically meters the correct amount of oil into the gasoline entering the engine. Since oil is continually drawn into the engine when it is running, refilling the oil tank and periodic level checks is required each time the fuel tank is filled.

Manifold Injection

Oil fed directly to the intake port is referred to as ***manifold injection,*** **Figure 10-10.** The same type of lubrication is provided as with the premix system. Oil is mixed with the air and fuel before entering the crankcase. The advantage of manifold injection is that it is not necessary to hand mix oil and gasoline each time the fuel tank is filled.

Direct Bearing Injection

Direct bearing injection provides undiluted oil directly to the engine main and connecting rod bearings. Oil used to lubricate the main bearings is thrown off and fed to the connecting rod by an oil slinger, **Figure 10-11.** Direct bearing injection provides superior lubrication and protection of bearings than manifold injection, giving longer engine life. Some engines use both direct bearing and manifold injection lubrication. A typical injection system provides a 100:1 fuel-oil ratio at idle and a 20:1 fuel-oil ratio at full throttle. A typical premix system provides a 20:1 fuel-oil ratio at all engine speeds.

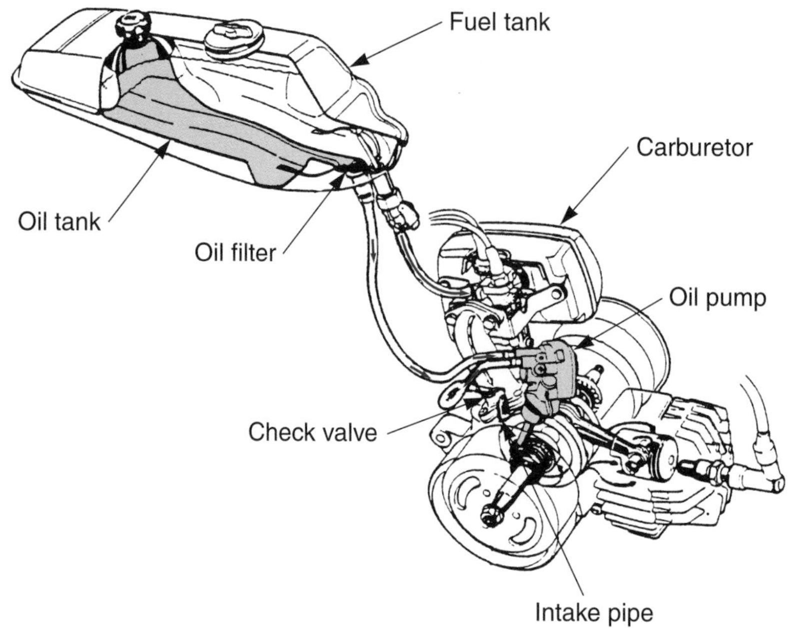

Figure 10-8. Oil injection lubrication system. (Honda Motor Co., Ltd.)

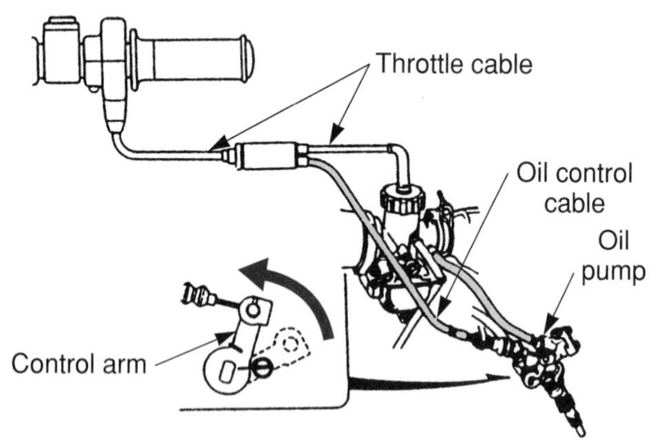

Figure 10-9. Oil pressure controls. (Honda Motor Co., Ltd.)

Oil Injection System Maintenance

Because oil consumption is controlled by engine speed and load, an oil injection system usually uses less oil than the premix system. Since proper lubrication is extremely important to engine life, you should check a two-stroke oil injection system periodically.

Oil Injection Pump Adjustment

The two-stroke oil injection pump is a metering device which controls oil flow to the engine. Its output is controlled by engine speed and throttle position.

The throttle cable is connected to the oil injection pump and carburetor by a cable assembly, **Figure 10-12.** Due to normal wear and stretch, cable adjustment is a critical maintenance procedure. Cable adjustment consists of aligning a reference mark on the oil injection pump lever with a stationary mark, usually on the housing, at a certain throttle position. Another method of adjustment requires measuring linkage free play at the pump with the throttle full open.

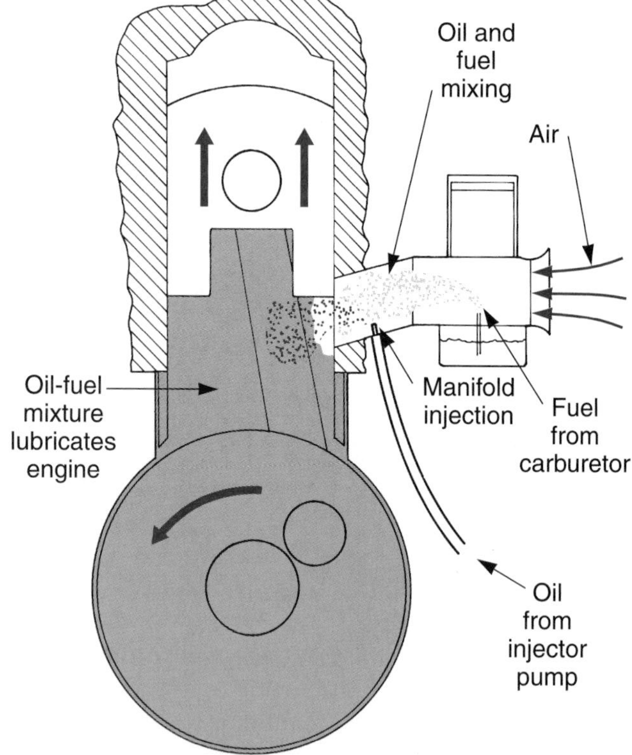

Figure 10-10. In two-stroke manifold injection systems, oil is discharged into the intake manifold. It then mixes with the incoming air-fuel mixture.

Oil injection pump cable adjustment is accomplished by turning an adjuster which varies the length of the outer oil pump cable housing. Oil pump adjustment is very important and is detailed in the service manual.

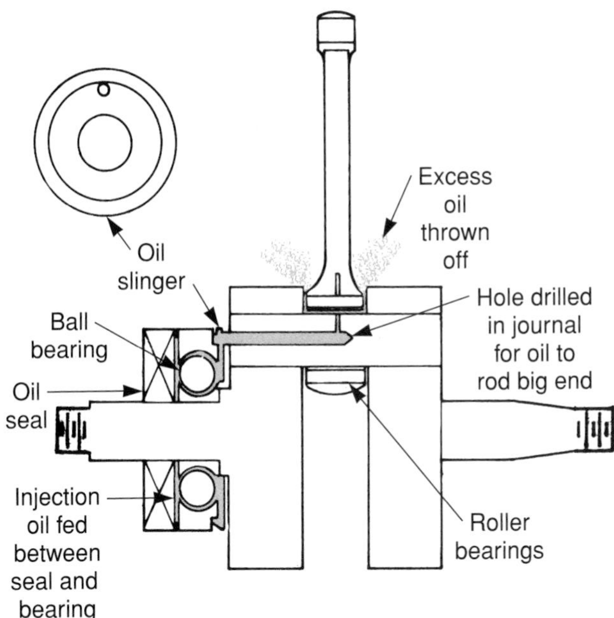

Figure 10-11. In a direct bearing injection system, oil is fed directly to the crankshaft main bearing. As oil is thrown out of the main bearing, it is trapped by the oil slinger. The slinger feeds oil into the hollow journal. This provides lubrication for connecting rod bearing.

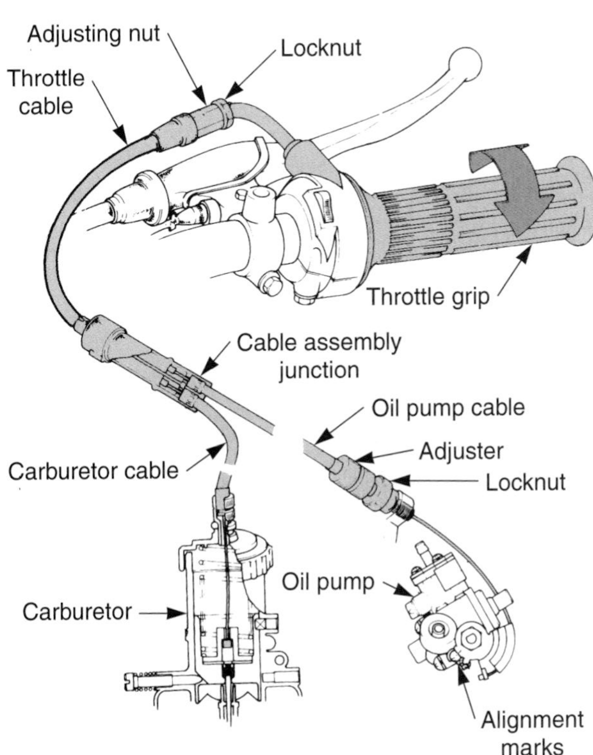

Figure 10-12. Turning the throttle grip opens the carburetor throat and increases oil pump output. As engine speed increases, oil injection output is also increased to maintain a correct fuel-oil mixture. (Kawasaki Motors Corporation U.S.A.)

Bleeding

Bleeding is required whenever air enters the feed line or oil injection pump. Air in the system can cause *cavitation* (air bubbles displace oil). Any air in the system will interrupt the flow of oil and may cause serious damage to the engine. Air can enter the oil supply line in a number of ways:

- Loose oil line.
- Empty oil tank.
- Hole in oil line.
- Disconnecting oil line and not bleeding pump.
- Plugged oil tank vent.

Most oil injection pumps have a bleed screw in the pump body (housing), **Figure 10-13.** Loosening the bleed screw allows gravity flow of oil to force the air out of the supply line and pump. Some oil injection pumps do not have a bleed screw. In this case, the oil line must be loosened at the pump to purge (remove) the air.

Oil Tank Vent

For oil to flow to the pump, the oil tank must be vented. Two methods are used to vent the oil tank. One uses a small vent hole in the tank cap. The other uses a vent line attached to the top of the oil tank. A clogged oil tank vent (dirt filled cap vent, kinked vent line) can allow a vacuum to build in the oil tank. The vacuum could then stop the flow of oil out of the tank and cause serious engine damage.

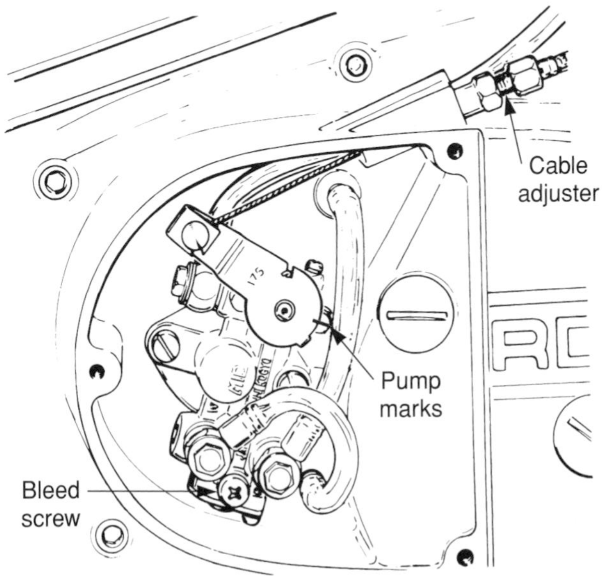

Figure 10-13. The bleed screw allows air to be removed from the pump and supply line. A two-stroke cable adjuster must be turned until the marks on the oil pump arm and body line up. The service manual should explain proper throttle position for oil injection pump adjustment. (Bombardier Ltd., Owner of the trademark CAN-AM)

Check Valves and Oil Feed Lines

Check valves are sometimes used in oil feed lines to allow flow in only one direction (toward the engine), **Figure 10-14.** If dirt becomes caught in the check valve, oil can flow in both directions within the feed line. This might allow oil to cycle back and forth in the line without entering the engine. Severe engine damage could result due to oil starvation. A sticking check valve can cause unwanted oil flow by gravity into the engine when it is not running. A check valve should only pass oil when pressure unseats the ball.

Oil Injection Filters

Oil injection systems are provided with either an inline or an in-tank oil filter. Both of these types should be checked or cleaned periodically, or when an oil supply problem exists.

Oil Injection Pump Output

Some manufacturers give specifications for checking injection pump output. If an oil supply problem is suspected, pump output should be measured. Oil injection pump testing consists of running the engine on premix and measuring the injection pump output at a given rpm for a specified time. If not within factory specifications, repairs are needed.

Primary Drive and Gearbox Lubrication

Since the two-stroke crankcase must be sealed, another means of lubrication is necessary for the primary drive and gearbox. An oil bath is commonly used for primary drive and gearbox lubrication in two-stroke engines, **Figure 10-15.** Special motorcycle gear oils are recommended. The amount and type of oil for the primary drive and gearbox is specified in the motorcycle's service manual.

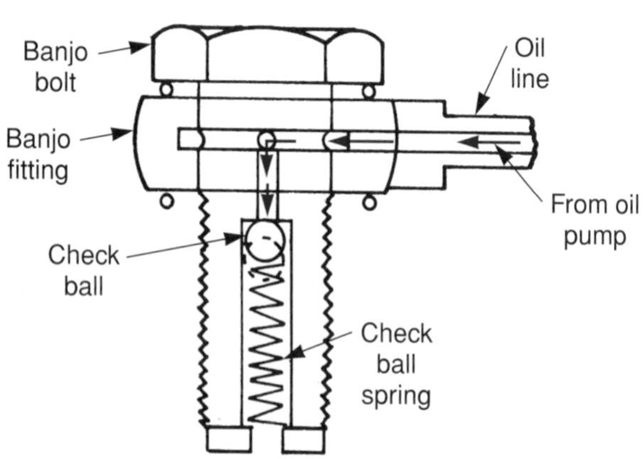

Figure 10-14. A check valve allows oil to flow in one direction only. In this example, the check valve is part of a banjo bolt fitting that attaches an oil line to the engine.

Four-Stroke Engine Lubrication

As mentioned in Chapter 1, four-stroke lubrication differs greatly from two-stroke engine lubrication. Rather than burning the oil during combustion, the four-stroke engine reuses its lubricating oil. An ***oil pump*** constantly circulates the same oil throughout the parts of a four-stroke engine. Refer to **Figure 10-16.**

There are three common types of four-stroke lubrication systems: dry sump, wet sump, and common sump. The word ***sump*** refers to the lowest portion of the crankcase cavity. It is the area where oil collects in the bottom of the engine.

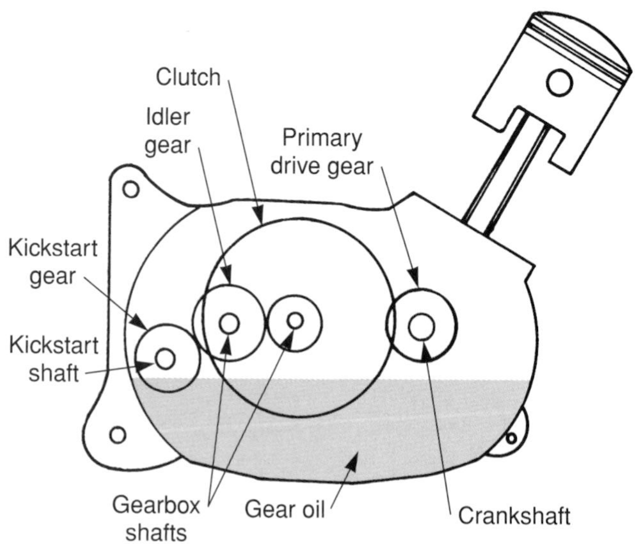

Figure 10-15. Primary drive oil bath lubrication. Lubrication is provided by gear movement through the oil. Oil is splashed around the case to lubricate, cool, and protect parts.

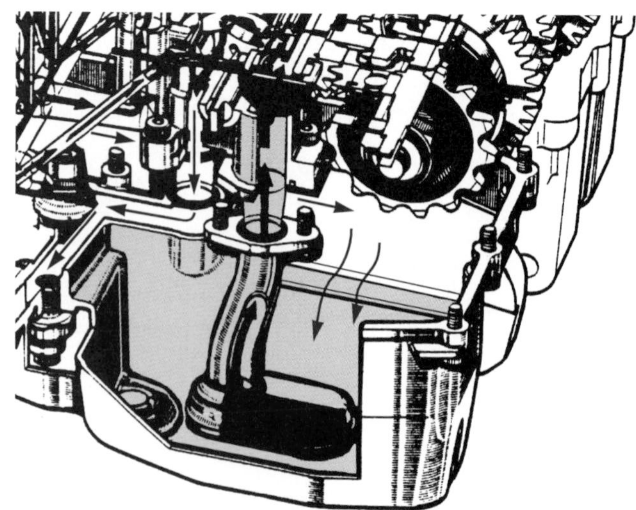

Figure 10-16. Oil pump provides oil flow through the engine. (American Suzuki Motor Corporation)

Dry Sump Lubrication

A typical ***dry sump lubrication*** system consists of:

- Oil tank.
- Oil feed line.
- Oil pump (two-sided pump with oil pressure feed and oil return).
- Oil return line.

Oil is gravity fed to the pressure side of the oil pump from a remote oil tank. Then, the pump forces oil under pressure through passages in the engine. This lubricates moving engine parts, which would otherwise be damaged by friction. Oil that is thrown off pressure fed parts lubricates other engine components by splash or vapor. Oil then drains into the sump where the return side of the oil pump transfers the oil back to the tank.

Since the dry sump design eliminates the need for space to contain the oil within the crankcase, the engine can be positioned lower than would otherwise be possible. This design often incorporates routing and oil storage configurations that aid in lowering oil temperature.

Wet Sump Lubrication

Wet sump lubrication differs from dry sump in two ways:

- Oil is stored in the sump.
- The oil pump does not have a return side.

The wet sump oil pump supplies oil under pressure in the same manner as the dry sump lubrication system. It pressure feeds oil to all high friction areas in the engine. The oil pump, however, draws oil from the sump rather than a remote tank. Oil that is pressure fed and thrown off drains back, by gravity, to the sump where it is again picked up and circulated by the oil pump.

Older wet sump engines may use only a strainer screen to filter the oil. Others use a combination of a strainer screen and a centrifugal filter, or a more conventional pleated paper filter. Since there are less components involved and no external oil lines, the wet sump system is simpler and less prone to leakage than the dry sump lubrication system.

A ***spray system*** is often utilized in either wet or dry sump designs as well as in some two-stroke engine designs, **Figure 10-17.** Oil is sprayed through jets directly

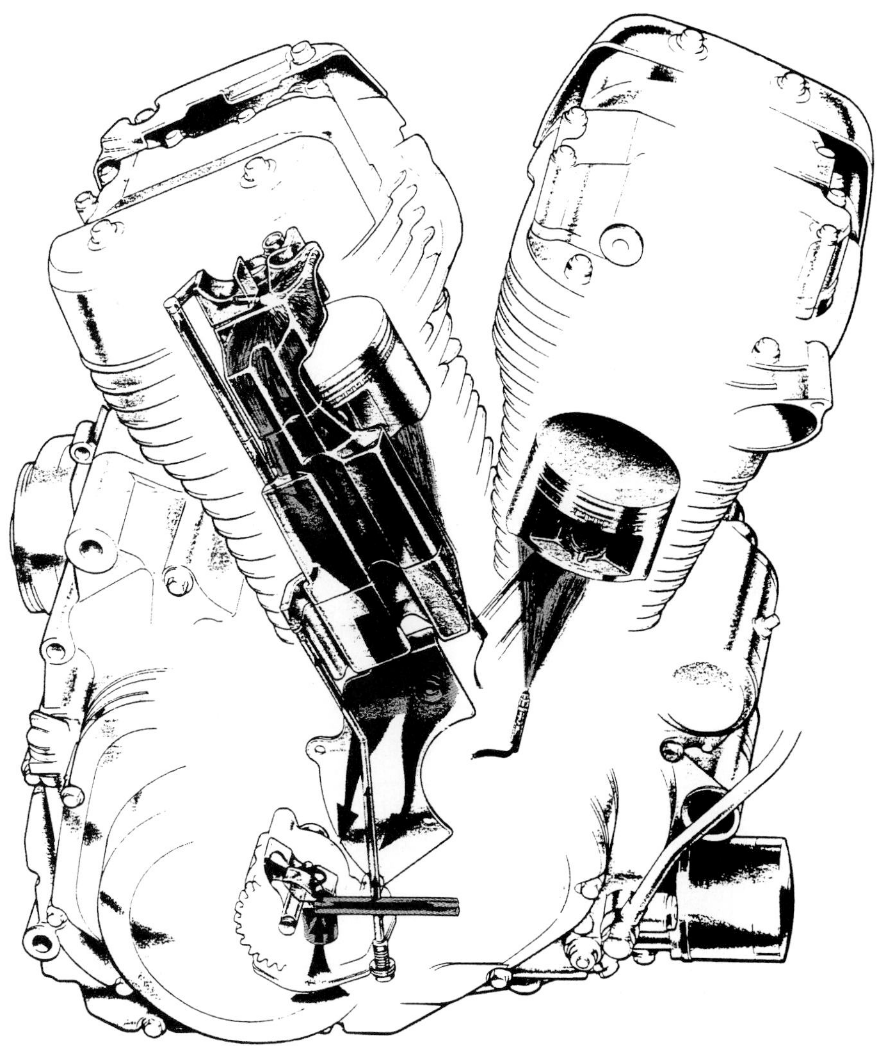

Figure 10-17. Components of a typical spray lubrication system. (Honda Motor Co., Ltd.)

into internal components such as the connecting rod, to help ensure lubrication and cooling.

Some systems include oil pressure relief valves to help ensure lubrication even if the filter is clogged or the oil temperature is so low that it will not flow through the filter. Oil filters and/or strainer screens are positioned within the lubrication system to trap contaminants before the oil is routed back into the lubricant pathways.

Common Sump Lubrication

Common sump lubrication is a design which uses engine oil to lubricate the gearbox and primary drive. This is only used on four-stroke motorcycle engines. A schematic for a typical common sump system is shown in **Figure 10-18.** As you can see, oil is pumped to both the engine and transmission. The common sump system is normally used with a wet sump lubrication system. However, some dry sump oiling systems also use a common sump.

Motorcycles that do not have a common sump design use sealed gearboxes that have their own oil supply. Transmission oil simply splashes around and lubricates the gears. Most dry sump systems use this method of gearbox lubrication.

Oil Pump Types

Four-stroke motorcycle engines use three oil pump designs: gear, plunger, and rotor. It is important that you fully understand the operation of each type.

Gear Oil Pumps

A ***gear oil pump*** consists of a housing, drive gear, and driven gear. Refer to **Figure 10-19.** The gear teeth rotate so oil is picked up at one side of the oil pump and oil is forced to the other side. Gear oil pumps produce moderate volume and pressure.

Plunger Oil Pumps

Virtually all non-premix lubricated two-stroke engines are equipped with a ***plunger oil pump.*** As shown in **Figure 10-20,** it consists of a pump gear, valve, drive shaft, plunger, spring control arm, and cam drive gear. Some plunger pumps are driven by the crankshaft via the oil pump gear shaft, and others are directly driven by the crankshaft.

The oil pump cam is depressed under the spring. Turning the cam causes the plunger to reciprocate so that the pumping movement is repeated. The amount of lubricant is controlled proportionally with the cam rotation. The pump is designed to control the amount of lubricant discharged per crankshaft rotation by varying the plunger stroke through the operation of the cam interlocked with the carburetor throttle. The combined function of these two mechanisms allows the proper flow of lubricant depending on load conditions and engine rpm. The plunger pump is capable of high pressure, but produces low volume.

Rotor Oil Pumps

A ***rotor oil pump,*** also called a *trochoid oil pump,* consists of a pump drive shaft, housing, inner rotor, and outer rotor, **Figure 10-21A.** It is the most common oil pump design used on four-stroke engines. Generally, the rotor oil pump is capable of high volume and high pressure.

The drive shaft is attached to the inner rotor and is free to spin in the housing. The drive shaft and inner rotor are offset in the housing. The outer rotor is free to turn in the housing and is driven by the inner rotor.

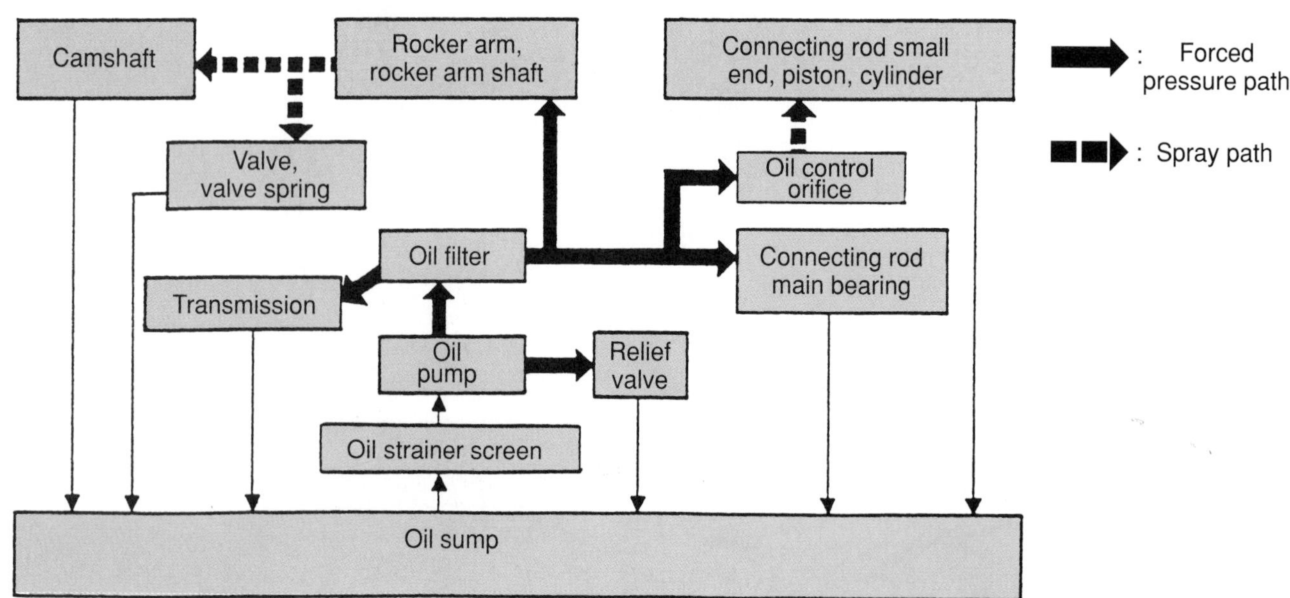

Figure 10-18. Flow schematic for a wet sump lubrication system. (Honda Motor Co., Ltd.)

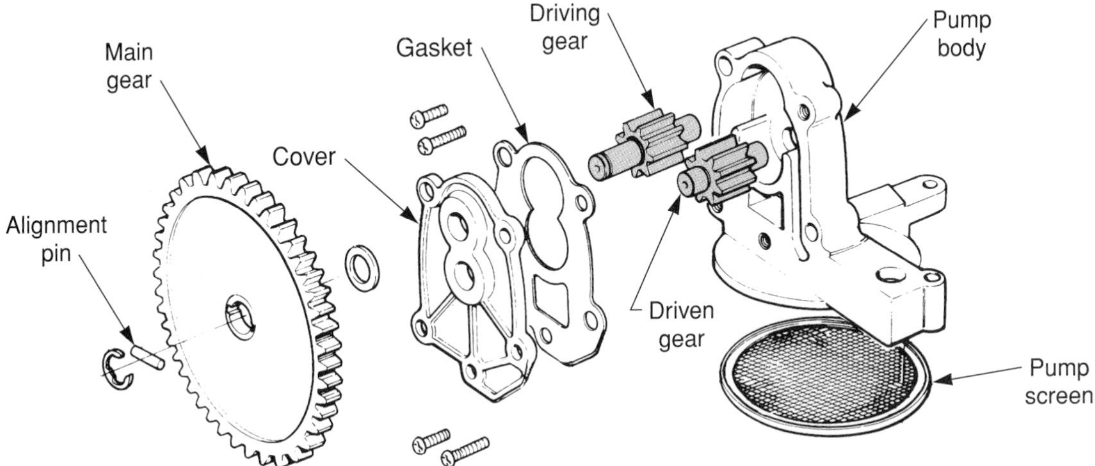

Figure 10-19. Gear oil pump is a common design. The gear teeth trap oil and produce oil pressure for the engine lubrication system. (Kawasaki Motors Corporation U.S.A.)

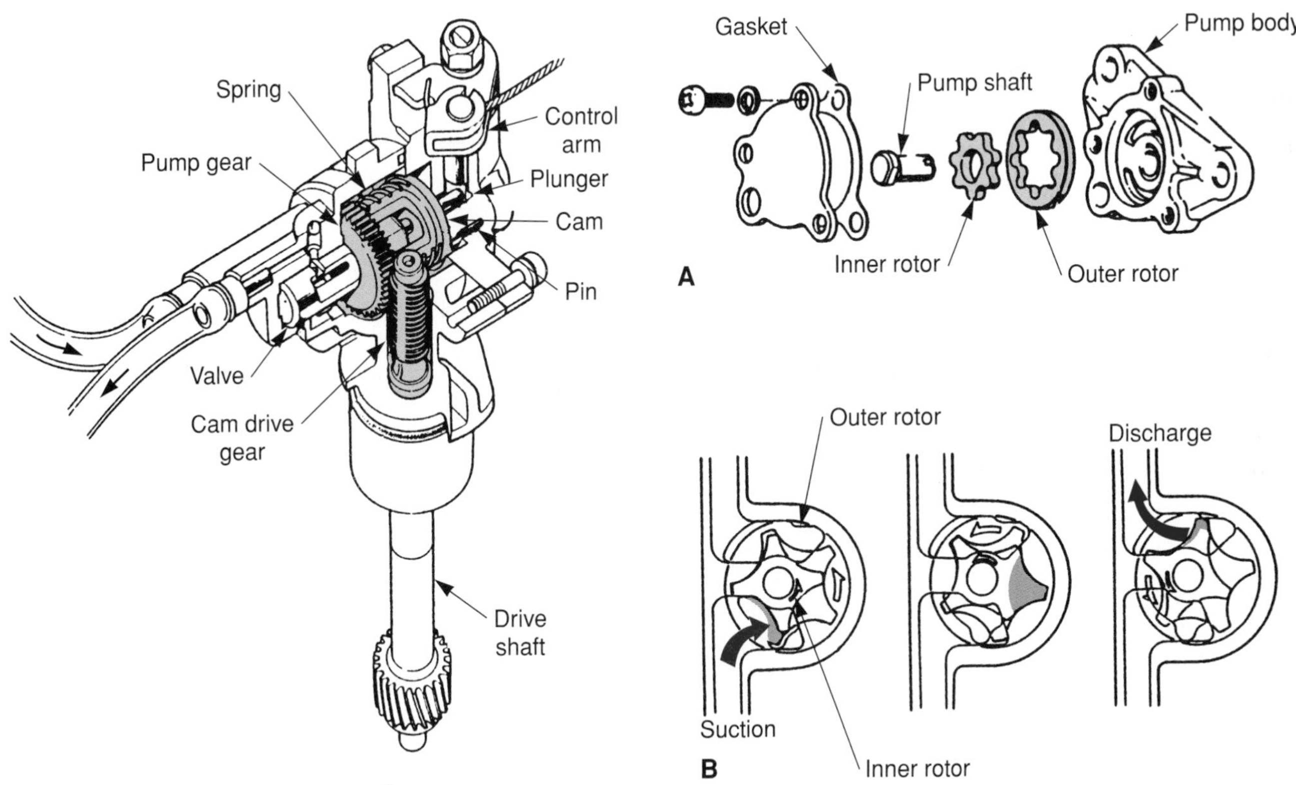

Figure 10-20. Cutaway of a plunger oil pump. (Honda Motor Co., Ltd.)

Figure 10-21. A—Components of a rotor oil pump. B—Operation of rotor oil pump. (Honda Motor Co., Ltd.)

The relationship of the inner rotor impellers and the outer rotor depressions constantly change as the pump turns. As the inner rotor "walks" around the inside of the outer rotor, oil is constantly being picked up from the inlet side, transferred, and pumped through the outlet side, **Figure 10-21B.** Oil is squeezed between the two (inner and outer) rotors to produce pressure. Some models have a double rotor pump that collects oil directly from both the cooler and the sump.

Check Valves

A ***check valve*** is a device which allows oil flow in only one direction. Spring-loaded balls or pistons provide this control. **Figure 10-22** shows both types of check valves. In the four-stroke motorcycle engine, check valves perform three functions:

- In the plunger pump, check valves are necessary to prevent oil from cycling back and forth in the pump.

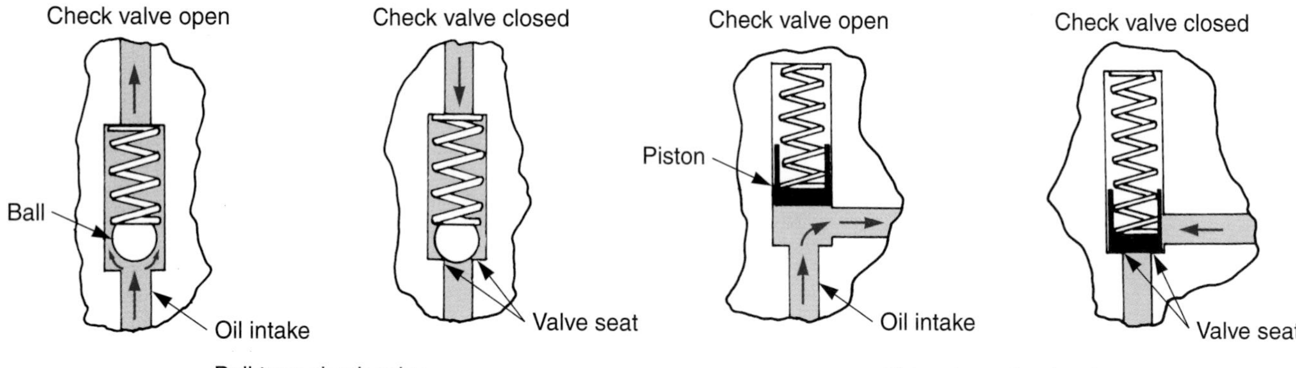

Figure 10-22. Check valves control the direction of oil flow. Oil pressure at the intake side forces the ball or piston away from the seat. This allows oil to flow through the valve. When there is no pressure at the intake side, the ball or piston is returned to its seat by spring pressure. This prevents oil from flowing in the opposite direction.

- In the dry sump system, check valves prevent oil from draining from the tank into the sump.
- A check valve on the output side of the oil pump prevents oil from draining out of the engine oil passages and back through the pump.

Check valves are relatively trouble free. Malfunctions may occur if foreign material is present in the valve. The check valve could stick open or closed.

Relief Valves

A ***relief valve*** is a device used to control maximum oil pressure. If oil pressure becomes too high, the spring-loaded relief valve opens, allowing excess oil to bleed off into the sump. Since oil pressure increases with engine speed, a relief valve is needed to maintain constant oil pressure. **Figure 10-23** illustrates the operation of a typical oil pressure relief valve.

A relief valve is similar in appearance to a check valve. The spring in the relief valve, however, is much stiffer. Since spring tension directly controls oil pressure, it is vital to the life of the engine. A weak spring or stuck piston can reduce oil pressure and cause serious engine damage.

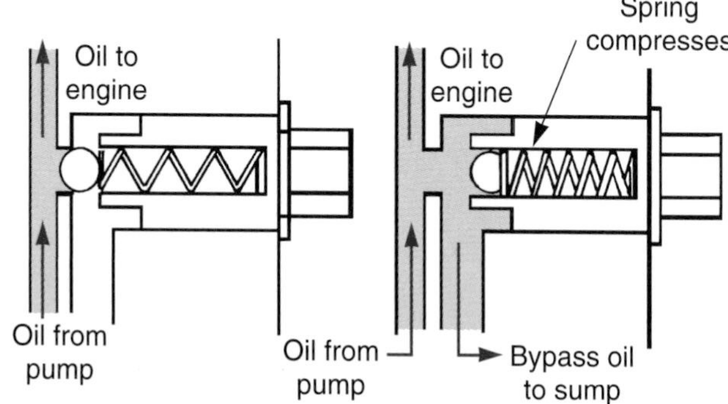

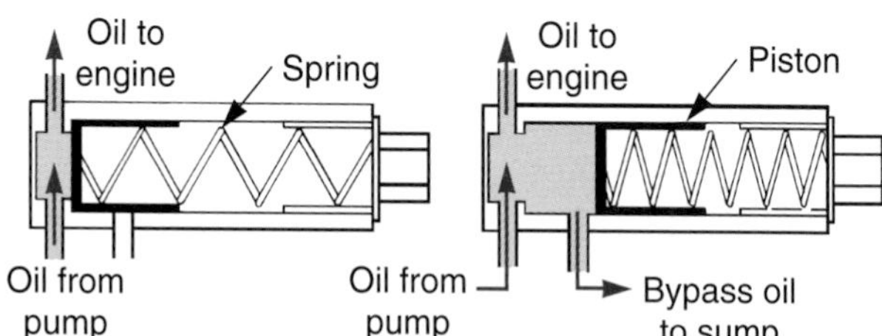

Figure 10-23. Action of oil pressure relief valves. Both ball and piston types use same principles. The operation is similar to a check valve, however, a relief valve is used to permit flow when the filter is clogged or to release excess pressure.

Oil Filters

The function of an ***oil filter*** is to remove foreign material from the oil and prevent its recirculation through the engine. Two common filter designs are used: centrifugal and element.

Centrifugal Oil Filters

One method of oil filtration is the ***centrifugal oil filter*** or *slinger*. One is shown in **Figure 10-24.** It uses centrifugal force to remove foreign material from the oil. As the slinger spins, foreign particles that are heavier than oil are thrown to the outside and held there. Oil slingers are attached to the engine crankshaft so they turn at relatively high speeds.

Oil Filter Elements

A very efficient method used to filter engine oil is the pleated paper ***oil filter element,*** **Figure 10-25.** Oil is circulated through the filtering material (element) where foreign particles are trapped before they can reach the engine.

Element filters are more efficient and easier to service than centrifugal filters. If an oil filter element becomes clogged and hinders oil flow, a bypass valve is normally provided, **Figure 10-26.** It lets oil flow around the clogged filter element and to the engine parts.

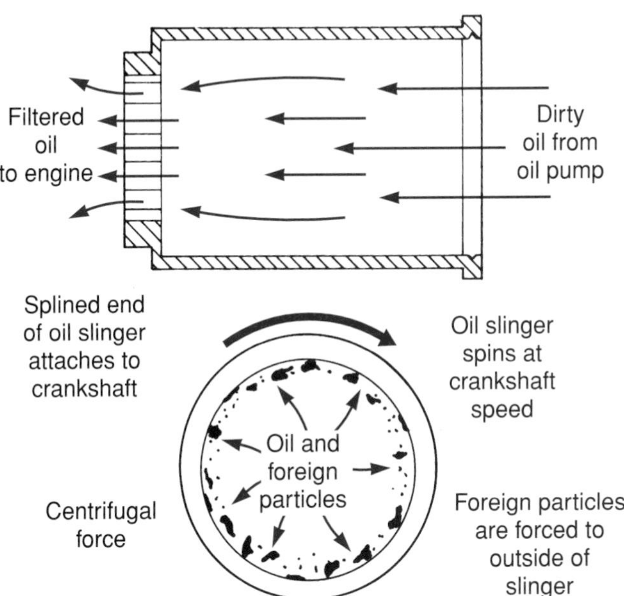

Figure 10-24. Spinning action forces oil contaminants to fly outward and into a filter. The particles remain trapped due to centrifugal force.

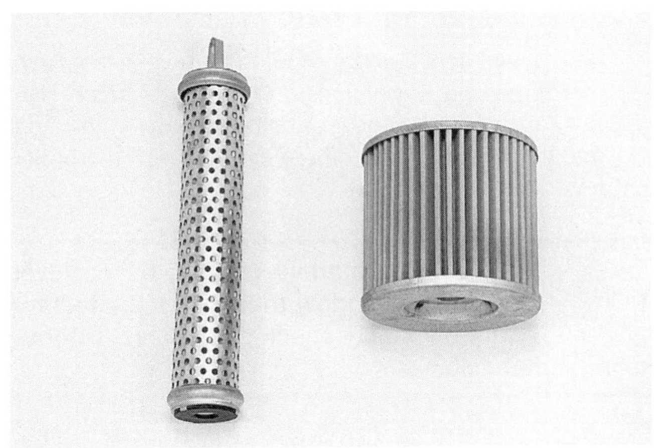

Figure 10-25. Pleated paper oil filters are easy to change and provide good filtration. Pleats increase element surface area and filter life.

Oil Cooler

An ***oil cooler*** is a most efficient means of cooling engine oil. It can reduce oil temperatures up to 30°. For this reason, some larger four-stroke engines use an oil cooler. Most look like a small radiator mounted near the front of the engine, **Figure 10-27.** Heat is removed from the oil as air flows through the cooler core. Normal maximum engine oil temperature is considered to be 250°F (121°C). Hot oil combined with oxygen oxidizes and forms carbon and varnish. The higher the temperature, the faster these deposits build. An oil cooler helps keep the oil at its normal operating temperature.

Inspect the oil cooler occasionally for bent or collapsed fins. Straighten any bent or collapsed fins with a suitable,

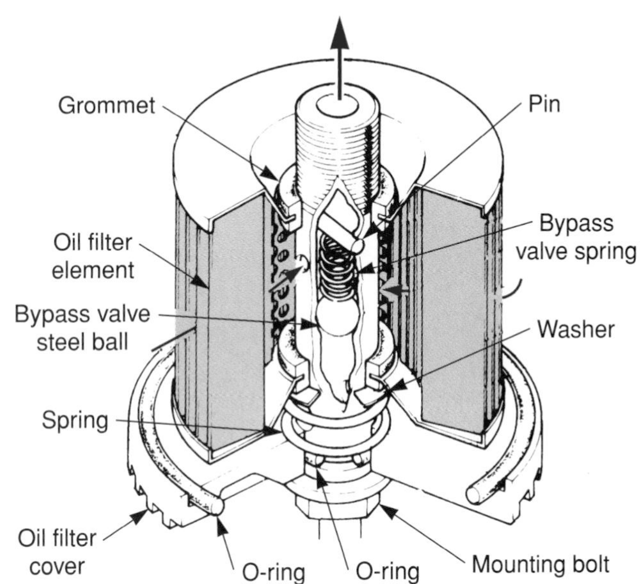

Figure 10-26. An oil filter bypass valve allows oil to flow even if filter is clogged. (Kawasaki Motors Corporation U.S.A.)

small blade screwdriver if necessary, **Figure 10-28.** Check the air passages for clogging or restriction. Blow dirt out from between the core fins with compressed air or wash off with water.

Caution: Be careful not to puncture or damage oil passages.

Lubrication System Maintenance

Proper service and maintenance of the lubrication system is very important. Basic lubrication system maintenance includes:

- Checking oil levels.
- Inspecting for leaks.
- Changing oil and filters at proper intervals.
- Periodic checking of oil pressure.

Checking Oil Levels

As the oil is gradually consumed, it is necessary to periodically check the oil level and replenish the oil volume to its proper level. If the oil level is too high, overall engine performance and clutch actuation may be affected. Too little oil may cause engine overheating as well as premature wear of various parts. If a different grade of oil or low quality oil is mixed when adding oil, its lubricating function deteriorates. Check the oil level only after starting

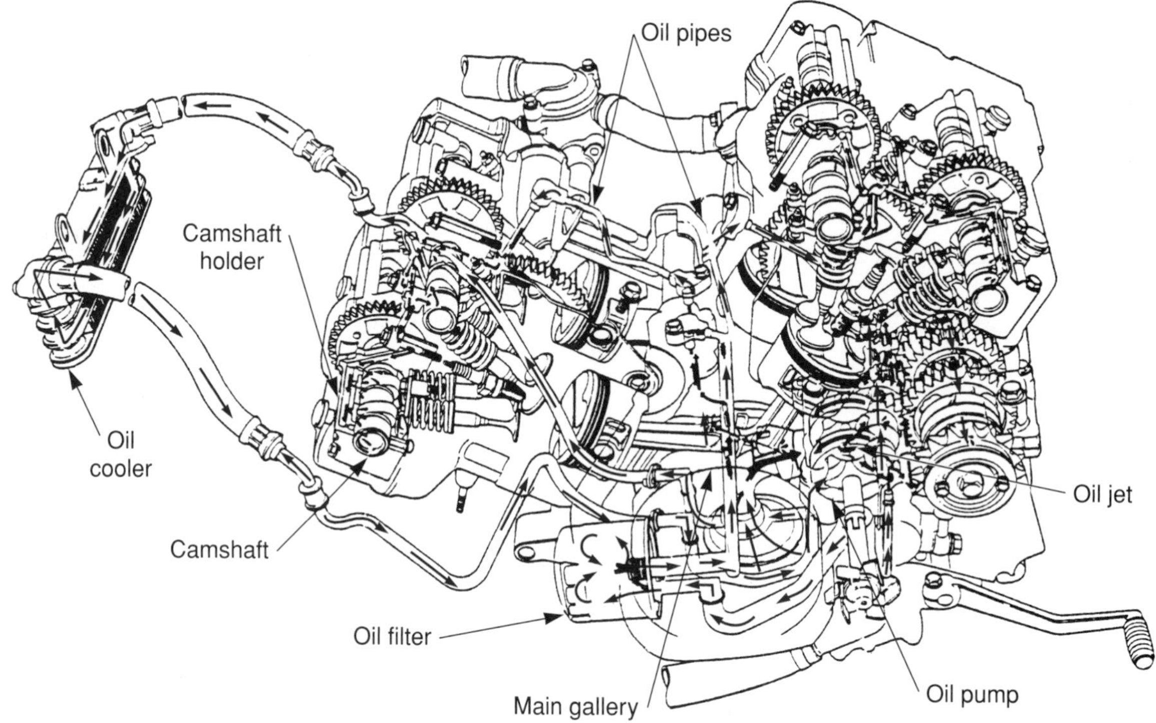

Figure 10-27. Location of the air oil cooler in a four-stroke engine lubrication system. (Honda Motor Co., Ltd.)

Figure 10-28. Straightening fins of an air oil cooler. The same method can be used to straighten radiator fins. (Honda Motor Co., Ltd.)

the engine and allowing the oil to circulate through the engine thoroughly. It is especially important to run the engine before checking the oil level on a dry sump engine, due to the comparatively large volume of oil.

To check the oil level in a typical four-stroke engine, either wet or dry sump, proceed as follows:

1. The motorcycle should be supported perfectly upright on a level surface. Then start the engine and let it idle for a few minutes.
2. Stop the engine, remove the oil level gauge/dipstick and wipe the oil from the engine with a clean cloth.
3. Insert the level gauge/dipstick into the oil filler tube 2-3 minutes after stopping the engine. The engine contains a sufficient amount of oil if the level is between the upper and lower lines on the gauge, **Figure 10-29.** If the oil level is near or below the lower line, add the amount of engine oil needed to reach the upper line.

Note: Some models contain an oil level inspection window that allows the technician to visually check the oil level without using a dipstick.

Leak Inspection

Inspect to see that there is no oil leaking from any part of the engine, oil pipes, oil hoses, etc. Locating engine oil leaks may appear to be an easy task. However, finding the actual point of a leak can be very difficult. Oil leaks are difficult to trace, because air passing over the engine causes the oil to spread and often accumulate far from the actual leak point. This can lead to inaccurate diagnosis of the leak point and needless replacement of undamaged gaskets and seals.

One of the easiest and most accurate ways to locate the source of an engine oil leak is to use the powder check method. First, thoroughly degrease the engine and then apply a light coat of spray trace powder around the suspected area. Start the engine and watch for the powder to darken by leaking oil. The which from oil darkens first is the leak area. If any oil leaks are detected, perform the proper procedure as directed in the service manual to correct the problem.

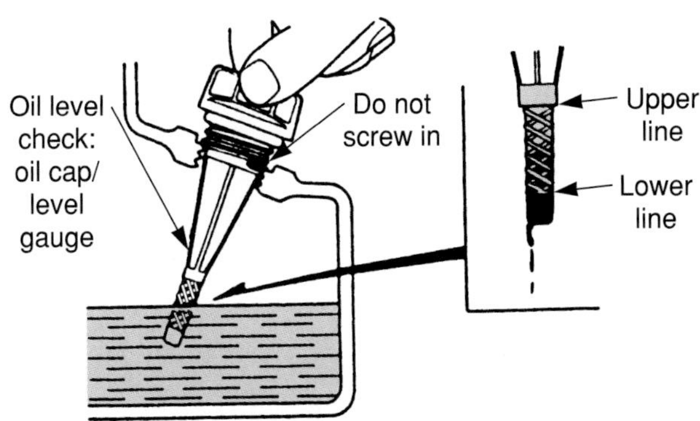

Figure 10-29. Checking oil level with an oil cap/level gauge. (Honda Motor Co., Ltd.)

Changing Oil and Filter

In four-stroke engines, sludge can build up and weaken the oil, due in part to the gases and residual gasoline which blow past the piston rings. To alleviate this contamination problem, change the oil and filter periodically.

Because many newly machined surfaces are moving against one another for the first time in new motorcycle engines, a noticeable amount of powdered metal circulates with the oil during this early stage of use. Therefore, it is extremely important to change the engine oil and to replace the oil filter or clean the oil strainer screen at the first maintenance interval (after 600 miles or 960 kilometers) in order to prolong engine life.

When changing the oil and filter, the engine should be at operating temperature. Oil drains plugs are located on the crankcase bottom, **Figure 10-30.** The hot oil will also carry out any foreign material and contaminants not trapped by the filter, **Figure 10-31.** When inspecting the oil filter, check to see if there is any dirt or debris on the oil filter screen which might hinder the flow of oil. Remove and clean the screen in solvent if any deposits are found on the screen, **Figure 10-32.** Refer to the service manual for oil filter screen removal, cleaning, and installation procedures. Refill the crankcase with clean engine oil, **Figure 10-33.**

The service manual outlines proper procedures for oil and filter service. Oil and filter change intervals should be considered maximum. Contaminated oil can increase engine part wear tremendously. When refilling the engine with motor oil, make sure you use the manufacturer recommended type and amount of oil.

Oil Pressure Check

To check oil pressure in a typical motorcycle, proceed as follows:

1. Check the oil level and fill if needed.
2. Remove the oil pressure inspection plug.
3. Install the oil pressure gauge, **Figure 10-34.**
4. If needed, connect a tachometer to the engine.

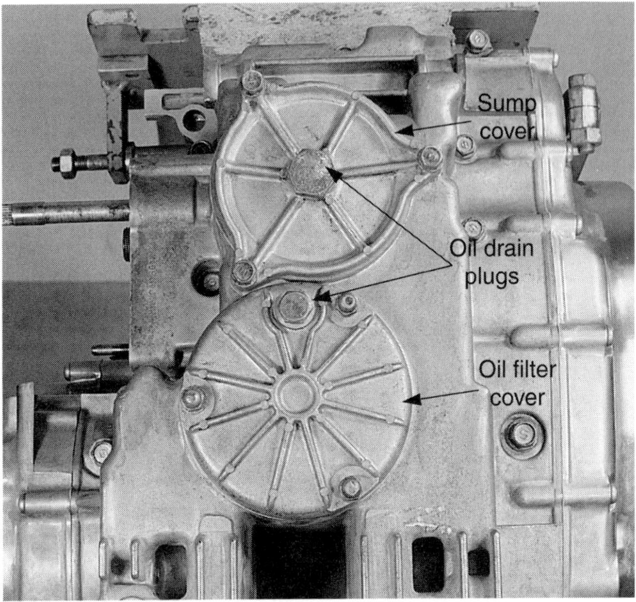

Figure 10-30. Note the shape and location of the oil drain plugs and filter on the bottom of this particular engine.

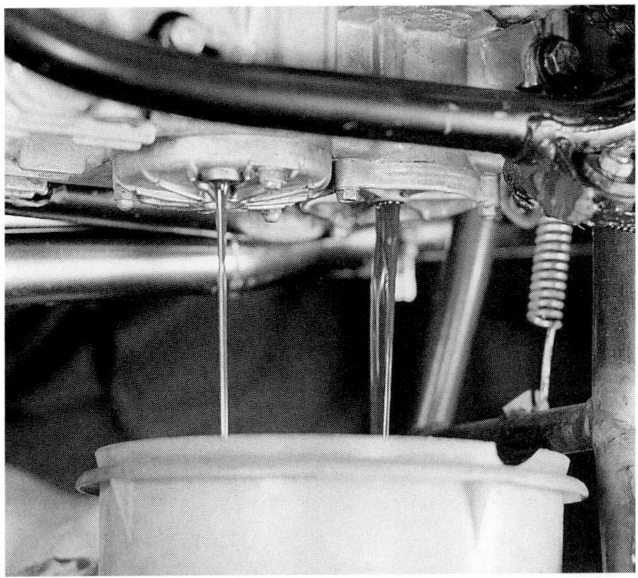

Figure 10-31. Drain oil after warming the engine to operating temperature. This will help suspend and drain deposits.

5. Warm-up the engine to operating temperature.
6. Follow the service manual directions for testing oil pressure.

If the oil pressure is lower or higher than the specifications given in the service manual, the following causes may be considered.

- Low oil pressure is usually the result of a clogged oil filter, oil leakage from the oil passage way, damaged oil seal, a defective oil pump or a combination of these situations.
- High oil pressure is usually caused by an engine oil which is too heavy (high viscosity), a clogged oil

passage, improper installation of the oil filter or a combination of these situations.

Correct any problems following the instructions in the service manual.

Troubleshooting Lubrication Systems

The following are some of the most common lubrication problems that a technician might encounter when troubleshooting either a two-stroke or a four-stroke lubrication system.

Two-Stroke Engines with Oil Injection System

The most common problems and their causes with this type of lubrication system are:

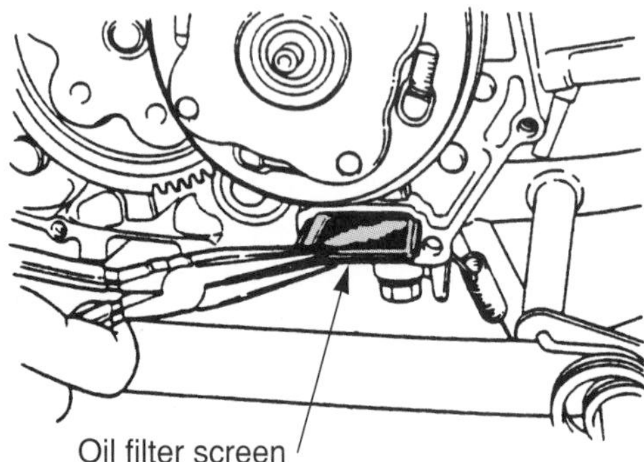

Figure 10-32. Checking oil filter screen. (Honda Motor Co., Ltd.)

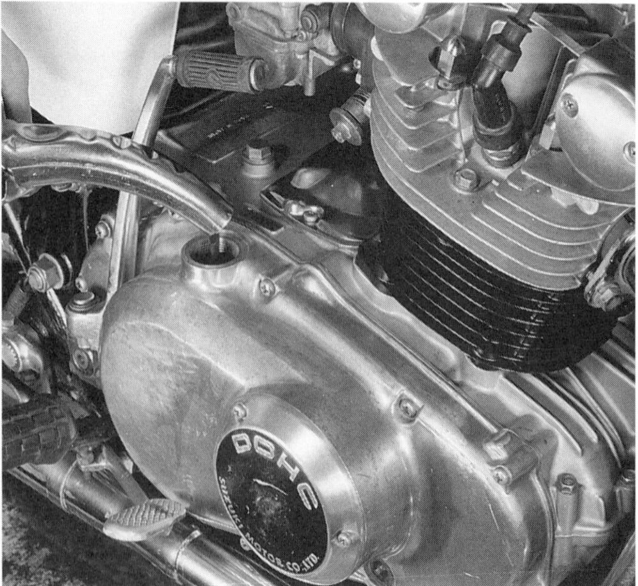

Figure 10-33. When changing engine oil, be sure to reinstall all drain plugs after the old oil has drained. Refill with the proper quantity of oil. Refer to the owner's manual or service manual for oil viscosity, service ratings, and quantity.

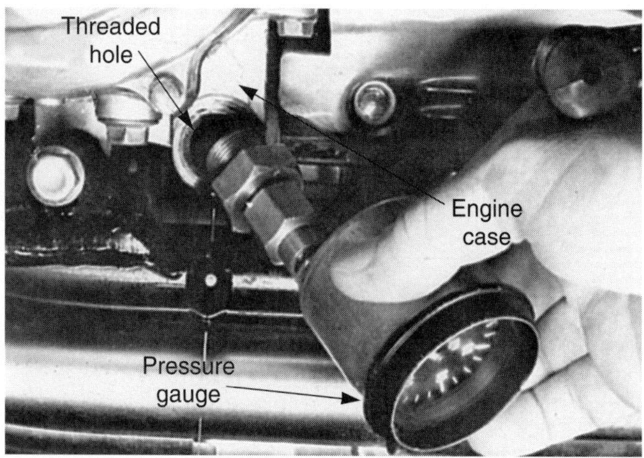

Figure 10-34. An oil pressure gauge will help to determine condition of lubrication system.

Excessive Smoke and/or Carbon on the Spark Plugs

- Faulty oil pump (too much oil flow).
- Low quality engine oil.

Overheating or Seized Piston

- No oil in tank or clogged oil line.
- Air in oil lines.
- Faulty oil pump (too little oil flow).
- Oil not flowing out of the tank.
- Clogged oil tank cap breather hole.
- Clogged oil strainer.

Two-Stroke Engines Using Premixed Oil

The problems and their causes with this type of lubrication system are:

Excessive Smoke and/or Carbon on Spark Plug

- Improper jetting for altitude, air temperature and/or external conditions.
- Improperly mixed fuel-oil; too much oil in fuel.
- Fuel-oil mixture too old; gasoline has evaporated/gone bad.

Overheating or Seized Piston

- Improper jetting for altitude, air temperature and external conditions.
- Fuel-oil mixture too old; oxidized oil/degraded lubrication.
- Premix oil too old; oxidized/degraded lubrication.
- Poor quality premix oil.
- Improperly mixed fuel-oil; too little oil in fuel.

Four-Stroke Engines

In a typical four-stroke engine lubricating system, the more common problems and their causes are:

Oil Level Low

- External oil leaks.
- Worn or incorrect piston ring installation.
- Worn valve guide or seal.
- Oil pump worn or damaged (dry sump engine).

Low or No Oil Pressure

- Clogged oil orifice(s).
- Incorrect oil being used.
- Defective oil pump.
- Leaking oil seal.

Oil Contamination (White Appearance)

- Coolant mixing with oil (liquid-cooled engine).
- Faulty water pump mechanical seal.
- Faulty head gasket.
- Water leak in crankcase.

Summary

Without proper lubrication, the moving parts inside an engine can get hot enough to melt. Moving parts can score or even lock together in a matter of minutes. Friction is the resistance to movement between two touching parts. A motorcycle lubrication system is designed to provide an adequate supply of lubricant (oil) to points of high friction. Oil must be pumped or sprayed onto moving engine and gearbox parts. The oil provides a thin film between all moving parts to reduce heat and prevent metal-to-metal contact.

There is a large selection of lubricating oils suitable for use in motorcycle engines. Additives are carefully selected and used in the manufacture of oils to improve their operating qualities. Film strength is the ability of an oil to remain between two lubricated parts. Viscosity refers to the thickness of an oil and is determined by the rate of oil flow under controlled conditions. Oxidation occurs as a result of the oil combining with oxygen and picking up contaminants. Air is also present in the crankcase, which contributes to a condition called foaming. Detergent additives prevent the build-up of these deposits in an engine. The American Petroleum Institute (API) and Society of Automotive Engineers (SAE) are the organizations responsible for the testing and classification of oils. They have classified oil in terms of intended use and viscosity.

In the two-stroke engine, lubricating oil passes through the engine with the air-fuel mixture. Oil is combined with the gasoline before it reaches the carburetor in a premixed system. In separate oil or oil injection systems, engine lubrication oil is introduced downstream of the carburetor.

Premixed lubrication is the most widely used system on two-stroke competition models. The combined air-fuel-oil mixture is introduced directly through the intake with the assistance of the carburetor. Oil fed directly to the intake port is referred to as manifold injection. Direct bearing injection provides undiluted oil directly to the engine main and connecting rod bearings.

Four-stroke lubrication differs greatly from two-stroke engine lubrication. Rather than burning the oil during combustion, the four-stroke engine reuses its lubricating oil. An oil pump constantly circulates the same oil throughout the parts of a four-stroke engine. There are three common types of four-stroke lubrication systems: dry sump, wet sump, and common sump. Four-stroke motorcycle engines use three oil pump designs: gear, plunger, and rotor.

The function of an oil filter is to remove foreign material from the oil and prevent its recirculation through the engine. Two common filter designs are used: centrifugal and element. An oil cooler is a most efficient means of cooling engine oil. It can reduce oil temperatures up to 30°. When changing the oil and filter, the engine should be at operating temperature. The service manual outlines proper procedures for oil and filter service. When refilling the engine with motor oil, make sure you use the manufacturer recommended type and amount of oil.

Know These Terms

Friction
Lubricant
Lubrication system
Oil
Film strength
Viscosity
Oxidation
Foaming
Detergent
American Petroleum Institute (API)
Society of Automotive Engineers (SAE)
Viscosity rating system
Multi-weight oil
Premixed lubrication
Manifold injection
Direct bearing injection
Bleeding
Oil pump
Sump
Dry sump lubrication
Wet sump lubrication
Spray system
Common sump lubrication
Gear oil pump
Plunger oil pump
Rotor oil pump
Check valve
Relief valve
Oil filter
Oil filter element
Oil cooler

Review Questions—Chapter 10

Do not write in this text. Place your answers on a separate sheet of paper.

1. The main purpose of a lubricant is to help reduce ______.
   A. friction
   B. compression
   C. combustion
   D. exhaust noise
2. List the four functions of oil.
3. List three characteristics which result from the proper use of additives during the production of lubricating oils.
4. Define the term *viscosity.*
5. A multi-weight oil has all the following characteristics *except:*
   A. low film strength when warm.
   B. high film strength when warm.
   C. detergents to suspend particles.
   D. low film strength when cold.
6. As oil temperature rises, oxidation tends to _____.
   A. decrease
   B. increase
   C. be eliminated
   D. increase, then diminish as temperature decreases
7. A detergent oil holds unwanted products in suspension so they may be caught in the _____ and removed during an oil change.
8. What does the *S* in SH and SJ mean?
   A. Standard.
   B. Slippery.
   C. Super.
   D. Spark.
9. Direct bearing injection provides better lubrication than:
   A. indirect injection.
   B. exhaust injection.
   C. manifold injection.
   D. cylinder injection.
10. ______ are sometimes used in oil injection system feed lines.
    A. Cap vents
    B. Filter screens
    C. Check valves
    D. None of the above.
11. List three types of four-stroke engine lubrication system designs.
12. Three types of four-stroke oil pumps are _____, _____, and _____.
13. A rotor type oil pump provides oil at _____ pressure and _____ volume.
14. A relief valve is similar to a check valve *except:*
    A. relief valves have a much weaker spring.
    B. both check valves and relief valves use spring-loaded balls.
    C. both check valves and relief valves use spring-loaded pistons.
    D. relief valves have a much stiffer spring.
15. The following are causes of low oil pressure *except:*
    A. clogged oil filter.
    B. damaged oil seal.
    C. clogged oil passage.
    D. defective oil pump.

Suggested Activities

1. List the different types of lubrication systems used for two-stroke motorcycle engines. Determine the advantages and disadvantages of each.
2. Make drawings and trace the flow of oil through a wet sump, dry sump, and common sump four-stroke engine.
3. Select five brands of two- and four-stroke motor oil and list the following:
   A. SAE viscosity rating.
   B. API use classification.
   C. base oil (petroleum, synthetic, vegetable).
   D. cost.
4. Choose three different motorcycles and list the oils you would use to lubricate the engine, gearbox, and primary drive. Base your answers on what you learned from Activity Number 3 and a service manual.

11 Cooling Systems

After studying this chapter, you will be able to:

- Explain the differences between air- and liquid-cooled systems.
- Identify the components of air- and liquid-cooled systems.
- Understand the use of coolant in liquid-cooled systems.
- Describe the functions of a radiator cap and of a thermostat in a liquid-cooled system.
- Know the servicing and troubleshooting procedures for both types of engine cooling systems.

In the combustion process, a great amount of heat is produced. Some of this heat is used for power production (piston movement). The remainder must be transferred away from the engine to prevent damage. Because of the importance of the cooling system, the technician must know how each type functions and when problems arise, be able to service them. Motorcycle engines use one of two methods of cooling.

Air-Cooled Engines

Air-cooled engines can be found on most designs of motorcycles, ATVs, and scooters. They can be used on both two- and four-stroke engines. The big advantage of the air-cooled system is lower production cost, since a separate cooling system is not required. However, since the finned cylinder relies on forced air to cool properly, forward motion is necessary when the engine is running. Prolonged idling can cause an overheating problem and possible engine damage.

As shown in **Figure 11-1,** cylinders are finned to increase the outside surface area of the engine. A large surface area is needed to transfer enough heat away from the engine and into the air. In the two-stroke engine, combustion takes place once during each crankshaft revolution.

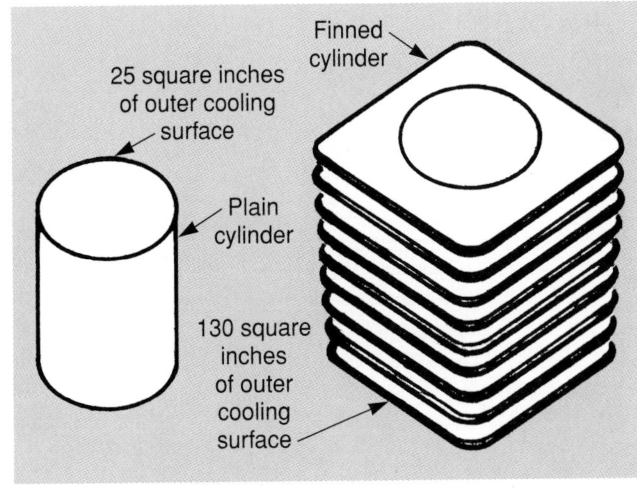

Figure 11-1. Notice how cooling fins increase the outside surface area of the cylinder. A large surface area is needed to transfer enough heat away from the cylinder and into the air.

This produces heat each revolution and requires very efficient cooling. Because the four-stroke engine has combustion on every other revolution, heat is produced less frequently. Cooling demands for a two-stroke engine are generally more critical than for a four-stroke engine.

A two-stroke engine's cooling system must be capable of dissipating large amounts of heat. This is shown by comparing two- and four-stroke air-cooled cylinders, **Figure 11-2.** Notice the difference in cooling fin area. The heat dissipating surface is much larger on the two-stroke cylinder.

Fins of all shapes and sizes are made of aluminum alloy or cast iron. Aluminum fins dissipate heat more efficiently and are used more frequently, while iron fins have less distortion. In some designs, fins may also be present on the crankcase.

Liquid-Cooled Engines

A ***liquid-cooled engine*** can maintain optimal engine operating temperature while preventing overheating and overcooling, two of the most prevalent problems with air-cooled engines. Two- and four-stroke liquid-cooled systems are very similar. Both engines benefit from liquid cooling in a number of ways.

The major advantage of a liquid-cooled engine is that it maintains a more consistent operating temperature than an air-cooled engine. An air-cooled engine's operating temperature can rise and fall with changes in outside air temperature. Because of the controlled operating temperature of the liquid-cooled engine, more precise clearances between moving parts can be utilized. This results in quiet operation, improved efficiency, and longer engine life. Liquid cooling is ideal for small and medium displacement two-stroke racing engines because it reduces the power loss caused by overheating. However, a liquid-cooled engine costs more to manufacture, purchase, and maintain than an air-cooled engine.

Liquid-Cooled System Components

In both two- and four-stroke engine cooling systems, **Figure 11-3,** a heat absorbing liquid (coolant) is moved by means of a water pump. Combustion heat is absorbed by the coolant in the course of its passage through the water hoses, water jackets, and cylinder head. The coolant then passes through the thermostat and upper radiator hose, into the radiator. The hot coolant is cooled by air passing through the radiator and then returned to the water pump through the lower radiator hose.

Coolant

Plain water is no longer recommended for cooling system use. Ethylene glycol-based coolant (antifreeze) has many advantages over water. It dissipates heat more readily, has a higher boiling temperature, and has rust inhibitors as well as water pump lubricants. Therefore, engine coolant should be used at all times even if the average temperature in the area never goes below the freezing point.

Engine ***coolant*** is normally a 50-50 mixture of ethylene glycol (or equivalent) and water. Distilled water is recommended over tap water because it does not contain minerals and other chemicals that could cause corrosion in the cooling system. The effectiveness of coolant decreases with the accumulation of rust or if there is a

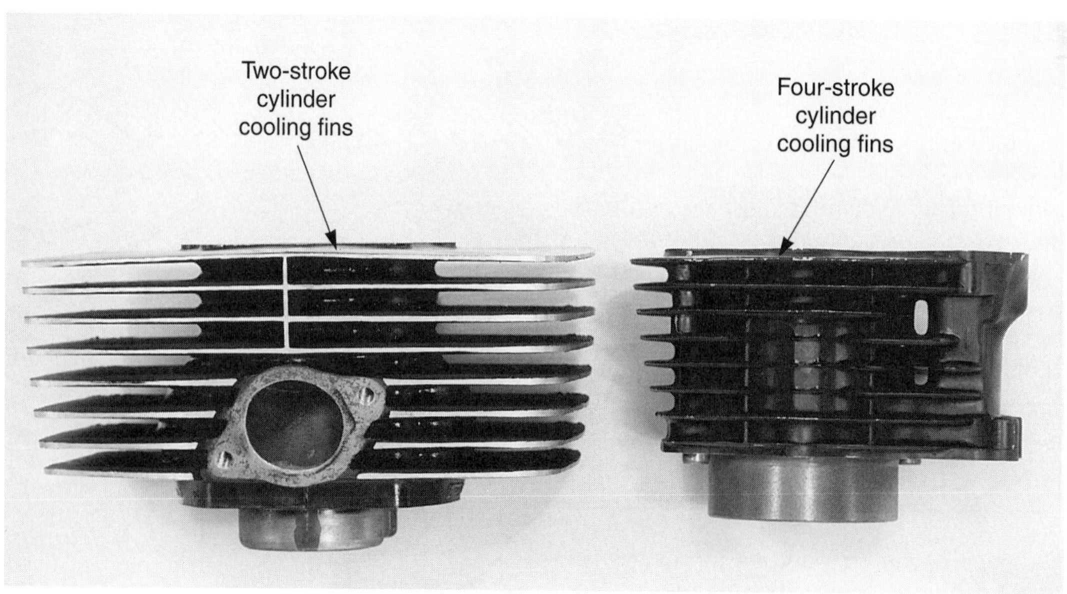

Figure 11-2. A two-stroke engine requires much more cooling fin area than an equal displacement four-stroke engine.

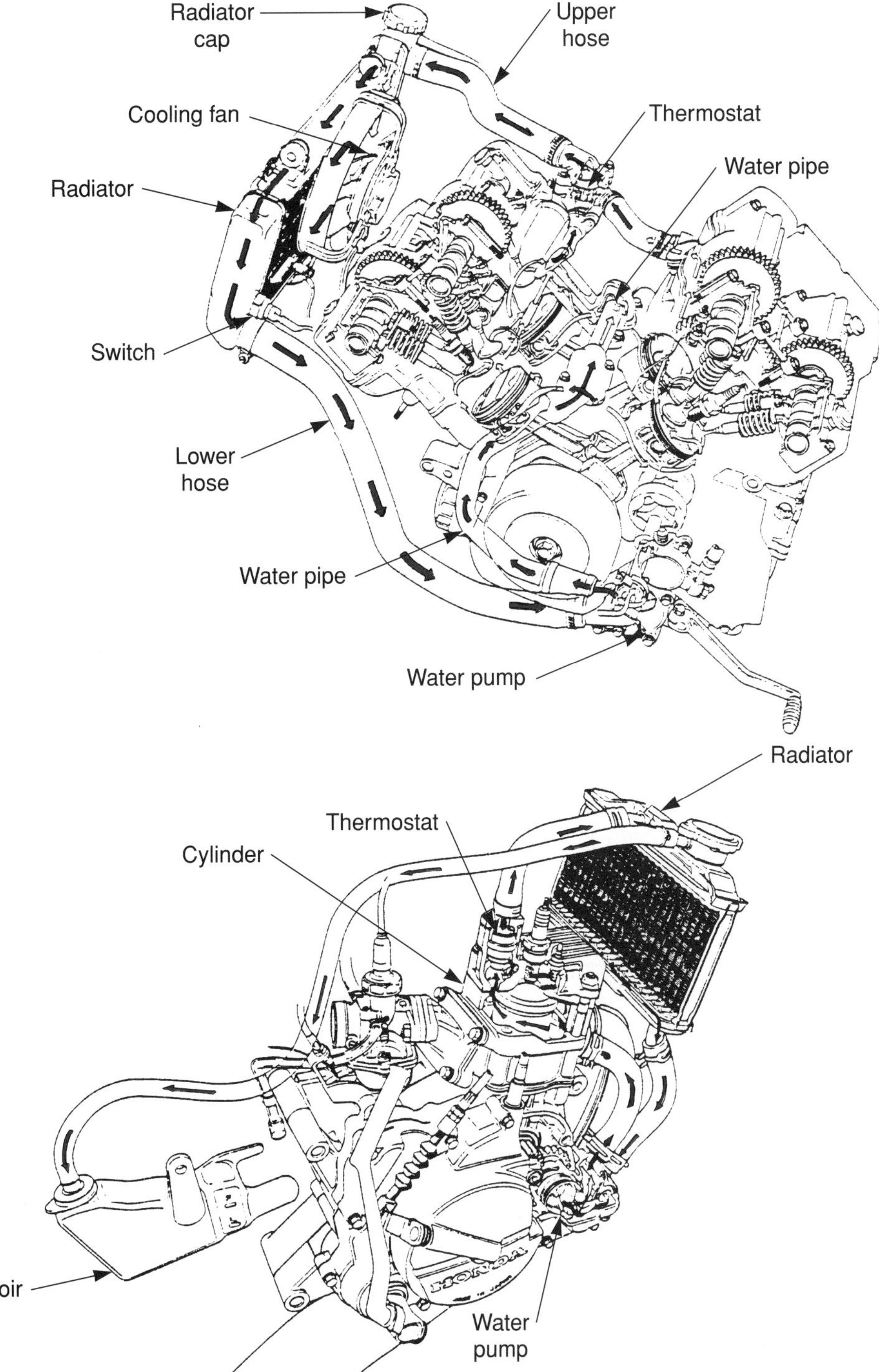

Figure 11-3. A—Four-stroke engine cooling flow pattern and components. B—Two-stroke engine cooling flow pattern and components. (Honda Motor Co., Ltd.)

change in the mixing proportion during usage. Therefore, for best performance, change the coolant regularly as specified in the maintenance schedule.

An antifreeze/water mixture should be limited to 60% antifreeze. Mixing beyond this would reduce its efficiency. If the antifreeze ratio is below 50%, rust inhibiting performance is greatly reduced. Be sure to mix it between 50-60%, even in areas where the atmospheric temperature does not drop below the freezing point.

Warning: Radiator coolant is toxic. Keep it away from eyes, mouth, skin, and clothes. If any coolant gets in your eyes, rinse with water. If any coolant is swallowed, drink water, induce vomiting, and in either case, consult a physician immediately. If any coolant gets on your skin or clothes, wash thoroughly with plenty of soap and water.

Radiator

The ***radiator*** is basically a heat exchanger, transferring heat from the engine to the air passing through it. The radiator itself is a series of tubes and fins that expose heat from the coolant to as much surface area as possible, maximizing the possibility of heat transfer to the passing air. Factors influencing the efficiency of the radiator are the basic design of the radiator; the area and thickness of the radiator core exposed to the cooling air; the amount of coolant going through the radiator; and the ambient air temperature.

Most motorcycle radiators are made of aluminum, **Figure 11-4.** It is important that air is permitted to pass so that heat is dissipated from the coolant to the radiator fins and into the atmosphere. Crushed or twisted fins will not permit heat to be dissipated because of the air's inability to pass through them, resulting in lowered cooling capacity. If one-third or more of the fins are crushed or twisted, the fins should be repaired. Most radiators feature petcocks or drain bolts that allow a technician to drain coolant from the system.

Recovery Tank

Many of today's motorcycle cooling systems have a ***recovery tank,*** which serves to temporarily store the cooling system's reserve volume. This aids to control the level in the cooling system. The recovery tank is connected to the radiator by means of a siphon tube.

Recovery tanks have markings indicating where coolant levels should be when the motorcycle is running and when it is not, **Figure 11-5.** To check coolant levels on a motorcycle without a recovery tank, remove the radiator cap (when the engine is cold) and see if the coolant is up to where it should be. If there are no markings, coolant should be covering the radiator core. If the coolant level is low after repeated filling, there is probably a leak in the cooling system.

Radiator Cap

In addition to liquid coolant, proper pressure is essential in a modern cooling system. Cooling systems are pressurized to allow the engine to run hotter without overheating. Every pound of pressure applied to the coolant raises the boiling point about 3°F (1.8°C). For example, the boiling temperature of ethylene glycol antifreeze coolant at sea level is around 220°F (104°C). However, add 15 psi (103.4 kPa) of pressure, and the boiling point jumps to about 265°F (125°C).

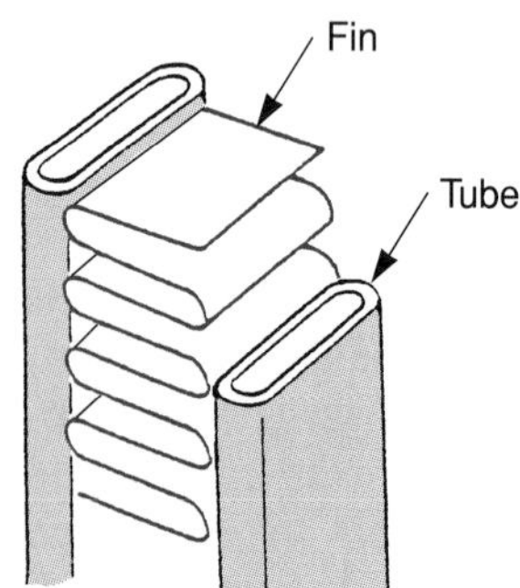

Figure 11-4. Typical radiator core construction. (Honda Motor Co., Ltd.)

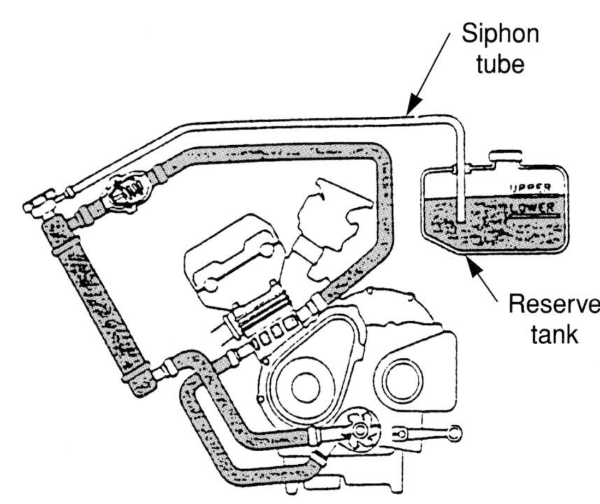

Figure 11-5. Location of coolant recovery tank in cooling system. (Honda Motor Co., Ltd.)

At one time the ***radiator cap*** was designed simply to keep the coolant from escaping from the radiator. Today, it still serves that purpose, but also does much more. Radiator caps are equipped with pressure springs and atmospheric vents. The cap increases pressure in the radiator, which raises the coolant's boiling point to a predetermined point, usually 12-14 psi (82.8-96.6 kPa).

As the coolant temperature increases, the difference in temperature between the coolant and atmosphere becomes greater. Coolant loss by vapor is prevented by the pressurized system, while the cooling effect is enhanced. The radiator cap is equipped with pressure and vent valves that maintain the pressure in the cooling system at a constant level, **Figure 11-6A.**

If the pressure exceeds the prescribed limit, the pressure valve opens and the cooling system is regulated by releasing coolant, whose volume has expanded due to the increase in temperature. The pressure at which the valve begins to open is called the *radiator valve opening pressure.* When the coolant temperature and pressure decreases after engine shutdown (with the coolant volume contracted), the vent valve is opened by atmospheric pressure and coolant from the recovery tank flows back into the cooling system, **Figure 11-6B.**

Warning: Wait until the engine is cool before slowly removing the radiator cap. Removing the cap while the engine is hot may cause pressurized coolant to escape, which can cause serious scalding.

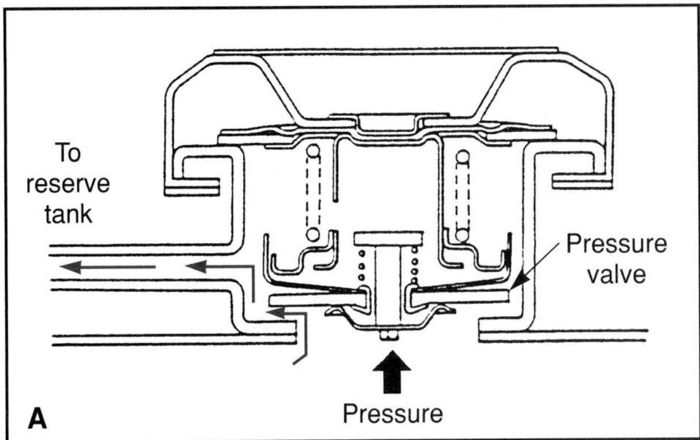

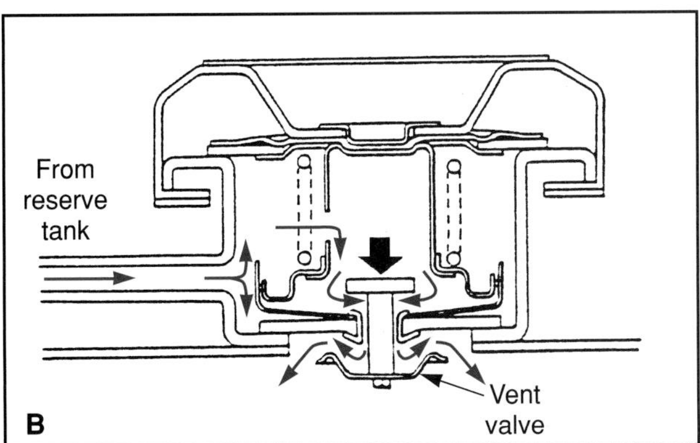

Figure 11-6. Operation of typical radiator cap. A—Pressure opens the valve, allowing coolant to flow to the recovery tank. B—When the engine cools, atmospheric pressure forces coolant back into the engine. (Honda Motor Co., Ltd.)

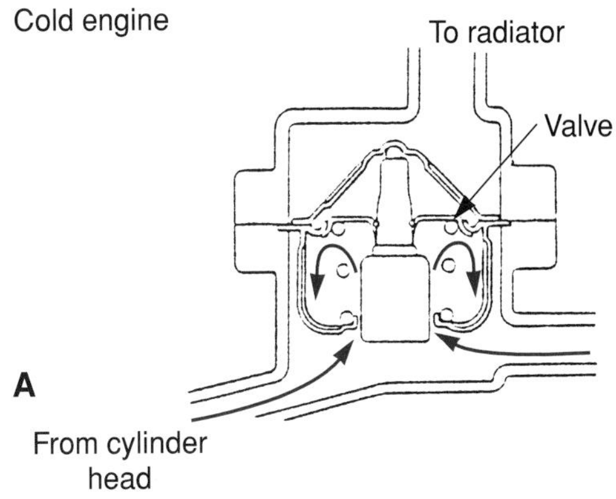

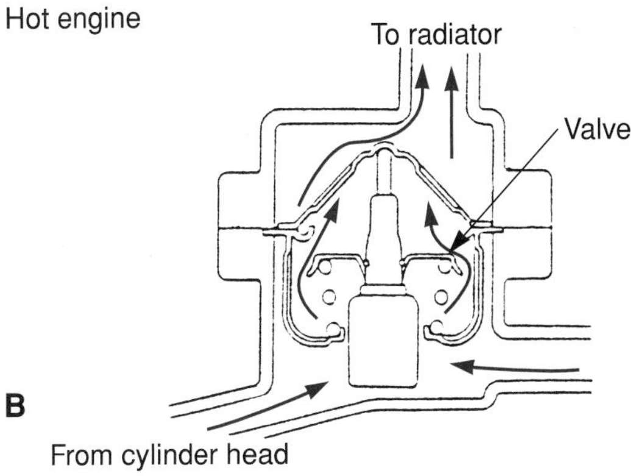

Figure 11-7. Operation of typical thermostat. A—Closed when the engine is cold. B—Opens when the engine reaches operating temperature. (Honda Motor Co., Ltd.)

Thermostat

A liquid-cooled engine's operating temperature is controlled by a ***thermostat.*** A thermostat is a temperature sensitive valve which controls coolant flow in the engine as temperature changes. Thermostat construction is shown in **Figure 11-7.**

When the engine is cold, the thermostat is closed. This prevents coolant flow through the radiator. As the engine warms up, the thermostat gradually opens, allowing the coolant to flow through the radiator and maintain a constant temperature.

Even if atmospheric temperature varies, the thermostat controls the engine temperature at a constant level. If the thermostat remains open, it will allow the coolant to circulate even at low temperatures. This prevents optimum engine operating temperature and leads to overcooling. If the thermostat remains closed, it contributes to overheating, since it prevents coolant circulation and prevents the radiator from dissipating heat if engine temperatures become excessive.

Water (Coolant) Pump

The heart of the cooling system is the ***water pump.*** It prompts the circulation of coolant in the system. It also feeds coolant uniformly to the engine's water jackets so that effective cooling is maintained

Most motorcycle water pumps are of the centrifugal design, with a rotating paddle wheel impeller to move the coolant. The shaft is mounted in the water pump housing and rotates on bearings. The pump contains a seal that keeps coolant from passing by the pump shaft. When the impeller turns, centrifugal force draws the coolant through the water pump inlet and discharges it into the engine's water jacket. See **Figure 11-8.**

Note: Although technically it is a coolant pump, the common name is water pump.

Cooling Fan

As mentioned earlier, cooling system efficiency is based on the amount of heat that can be removed from the engine and transferred to the air. Without air, the system would not be very efficient. At normal driving speeds, the ram air through the radiator is sufficient to maintain proper cooling. At low speeds and idle, the system needs additional moving air. This air is delivered by a fan.

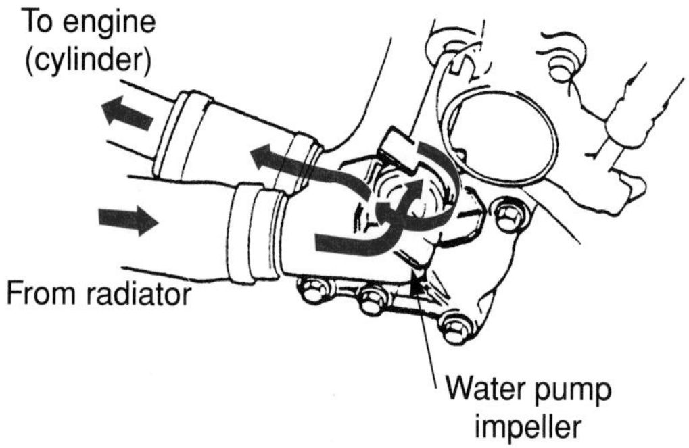

Figure 11-8. Typical impeller water pump operation. (Honda Motor Co., Ltd.)

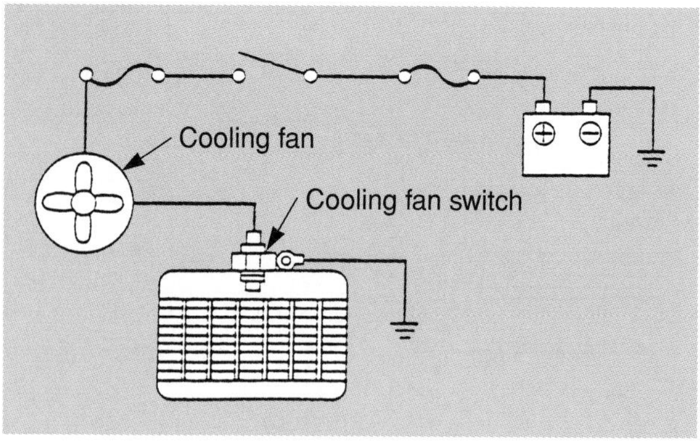

Figure 11-9. Schematic of a cooling fan electrical circuit. (Honda Motor Co., Ltd.)

A ***cooling fan*** maintains system performance under severe conditions. It forces air to flow through the radiator and around the engine to dissipate heat, whether the bike is moving or standing still. The fan switch on typical bikes will automatically start or shut down the cooling fan depending on the temperature of the coolant, **Figure 11-9.** Fan motor switch resistance is normally too high to conduct current when coolant temperature is low. As the temperature rises, switch resistance is reduced enough to conduct current, causing the cooling fan to run.

Warning: The fan motor may continue to run, even when the ignition switch is turned off. Keep your hands free of the fan. This is often part of normal cooling fan operation.

Hoses and Clamps

The primary function of a cooling system hose is to carry coolant between the different system components. Most hoses are made of butyl or neoprene rubber. All cooling system hoses are basically installed the same way. The hose is clamped onto inlet-outlet nipples on the radiator, water pump, and heater. **Figure 11-10** illustrates the four most common types of hose clamps.

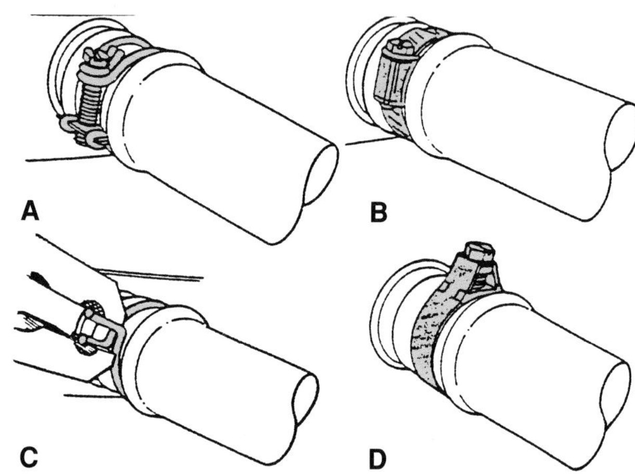

Figure 11-10. Common types of coolant hose clamps. A—Twin wire. B—Worm-drive. C—Spring. D—Screw tower.

Servicing and Troubleshooting Air-Cooled Systems

The air-cooled system is very simple to maintain and very little can go wrong if the following is done:

- Keep the engine properly tuned. Incorrect timing or lean carburetor settings can cause the engine to produce excess heat.
- Keep the engine free of any obstructions. Remove any dirt or mud that may coat the fins. This acts as an insulation to airflow and keeps engine heat in.
- Try not to overload the motorcycle. This can cause the engine to work harder which produces more heat.

Servicing Liquid-Cooling Systems

The liquid-cooling system must be inspected and serviced as a system. Replacing or cleaning one damaged part while leaving others that are damaged, dirty, or clogged will not increase system efficiency. Service the entire system to ensure good results.

Service involves both visual inspection of parts and connections and pressure testing to detect the presence of internal or external leaks. Before servicing a specific liquid-cooling system, consult the vehicle's service manual. The following is a basic servicing procedure for most motorcycle and ATV liquid-cooling systems.

Coolant Check

A ***hydrometer*** is used to determine the coolant's freezing point by checking its specific gravity. To make the test, operate the engine with the radiator cap loose until the engine reaches normal operating temperature. Then remove the cap and proceed as follows:

1. Measure the coolant temperature by drawing a sample; then returning the sample to the radiator. Repeat this step several times until the thermometer reading is stable.
2. Holding the hydrometer in a straight, vertical position, squeeze the bulb and pull enough coolant into the glass tube to raise the hydrometer float, **Figure 11-11.** Make sure the float does not touch the sides of the large tube.
3. Note the top letter touched by the coolant on the float scale; then return this sample to the radiator or recovery tank.
4. Compare the reading on the hydrometer thermometer to a temperature chart. Find the letter noted in the previous step, along with the thermometer reading taken in Step 1. The number found at this location is the degree of freezing protection provided.
5. After adding coolant, let the engine run for five minutes to allow the coolant to mix before rechecking the freezing point.

If the freezing point is not adequate, drain off some of the solution and replace it with pure, undiluted antifreeze until the desired temperature safe point is reached.

Always check the coolant level with the motorcycle in a vertical position on a flat, level surface. If equipped, check the coolant level at the recovery tank after the engine has been warmed up. Check to see if the coolant level in the recovery tank is somewhere between the upper and lower lines. If the level is somewhere between the upper and lower lines or below the lower line, add a 50-50 mixture of antifreeze and water to the upper line, **Figure 11-12.**

Replace coolant at the time intervals recommended in the service manual. Drain the coolant when the engine is cold. After draining, add a 50-50 coolant/water mixture and start the engine. With the radiator cap off, continue to add coolant and water until the level stabilizes at the top of the radiator, or the recovery tank. Start the engine and run until the thermostat opens. Then top off the recovery tank or radiator and replace the cap.

If the recovery tank becomes completely empty, there is a possibility of air getting into the cooling system. Be sure to remove all air from the cooling system:

1. Shift the transmission into neutral.
2. Start the engine and run it at idle for two to three minutes.
3. Snap the throttle 3-4 times to bleed air from the system.
4. Stop the engine and add coolant up to the filler neck.
5. Check the coolant level of the recovery tank and fill to the upper level if low.

Flushing the Cooling System

If the cooling system shows evidence of rust, scale, or lime in the coolant, it must be completely flushed. To do this, drain the coolant and replace the drain plug or close the petcock. Add a flushing compound, fill the system with water, and replace the radiator cap. Run the engine for approximately 10 minutes and then drain the system. Repeat this procedure a couple of times until the water is free of contaminants. Then follow the procedure for replacing coolant.

Testing the Radiator Cap

Install the proper adapter and radiator pressure cap to the tester. Pump the tester until the cap's relief valve releases pressure, **Figure 11-13.** The cap should hold pressure in its range as indicated on the tester gauge dial for one minute; if it does not, replace it. Remove the cap from the tester and visually inspect the condition of the cap's pressure valve and upper and lower sealing gaskets. If the gaskets are hard, brittle, or deteriorated, the cap will not hold pressure. It should be replaced with a new cap in the same pressure range.

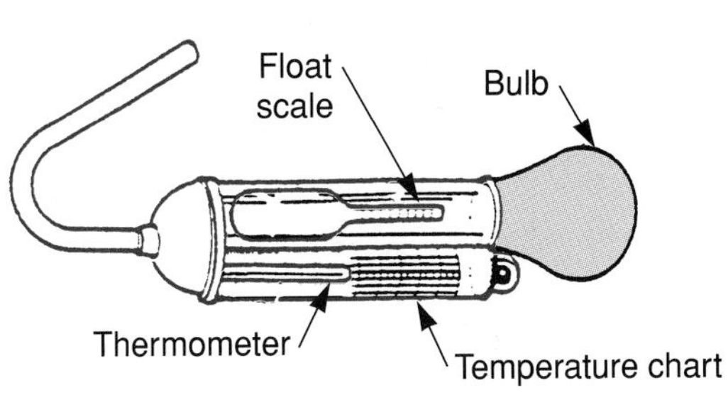

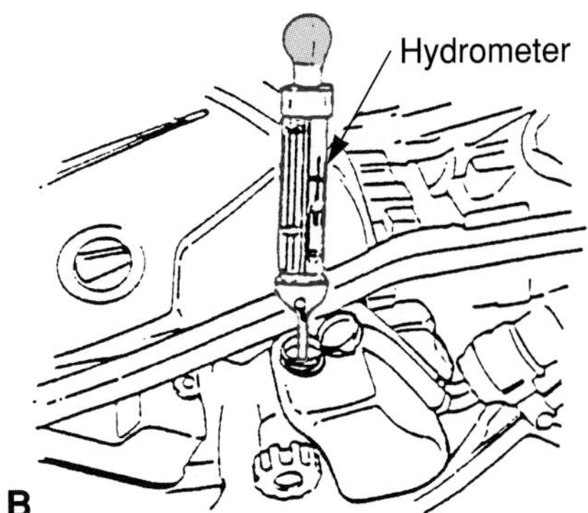

Figure 11-11. A—A typical coolant hydrometer. B—Using the hydrometer to check the coolant temperature range. (Honda Motor Co., Ltd.)

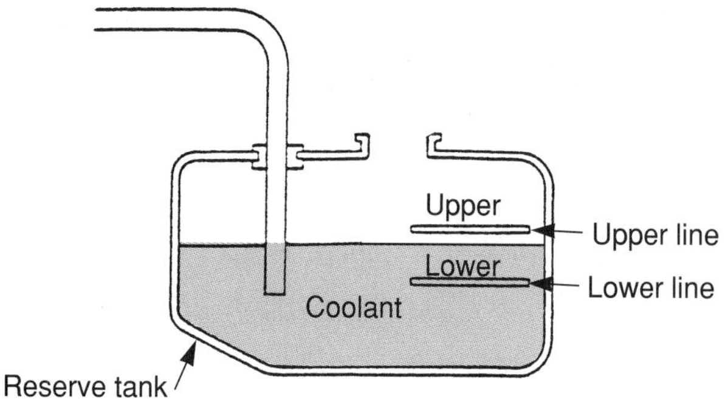

Figure 11-12. When adding coolant, be sure to fill to the upper line. (Honda Motor Co., Ltd.)

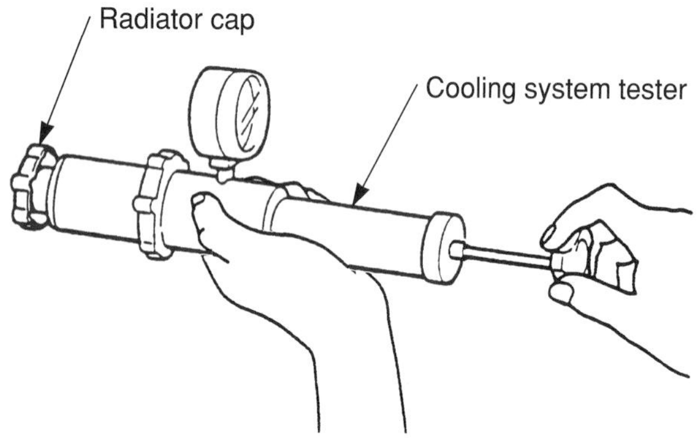

Figure 11-13. Using a radiator pressure tester to check the operation of a radiator cap. (Honda Motor Co., Ltd.)

Testing the Thermostat

There are several ways to test the opening temperature of a thermostat. First, do not remove the thermostat from the engine. Remove the radiator pressure cap from a cold or cool radiator and insert a thermometer. Start the engine and let it warm up. Watch the thermometer and the surface of the coolant. When the coolant begins to flow, this indicates the thermostat has started to open. The reading on the thermometer indicates the thermostat's opening temperature. If the engine is cold and coolant circulates, this indicates the thermostat is stuck open and must be replaced.

To verify a defective thermostat, remove it from the engine after the coolant has been drained. Suspend the thermostat submerged in a small container of water so it does not touch the bottom. Place a thermometer so that it does not touch the container and only measures water temperature and heat the water, **Figure 11-14.** When the thermostat valve begins to open, read the thermometer. This is the thermostat's opening temperature. If the valve does not open or stays open after the thermostat is removed from the water, the thermostat is defective and must be replaced. Several types of commercial testers are available. When using such a tester, be sure to follow the manufacturer's instructions.

Water Pump Service

The majority of water pump failures are attributed to leaks of some sort. The seals may simply wear out due to abrasives in the cooling system, or cracks due to thermal shock, such as adding cold water to an overheated engine. Most systems have a small "telltale" or weep hole directly below the water pump, **Figure 11-15.** When the pump seat fails, coolant will begin to seep out of the weep hole. If coolant leaks from this hole, the mechanical seal is defective and must be replaced. If, however, the mechanical seal is the built-in type, the water pump must be replaced as an assembly. The general procedure for removing a defective water pump and replacing it with a new one is as follows:

1. Drain the engine oil and coolant. Remove the water pump mounting bolts. Disconnect the water hoses and bypass tube, then remove the water pump. See **Figure 11-16.**
2. Remove the bolts and separate the pump cover from the body. Replace the water pump with a new one. Install a new O-ring into the groove in the pump cover, then install the cover on the pump. See **Figure 11-17.**

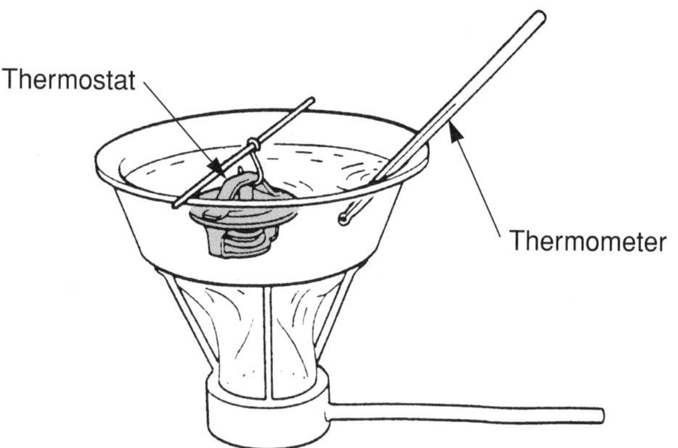

Figure 11-14. Common method of testing a thermostat. (Honda Motor Co., Ltd.)

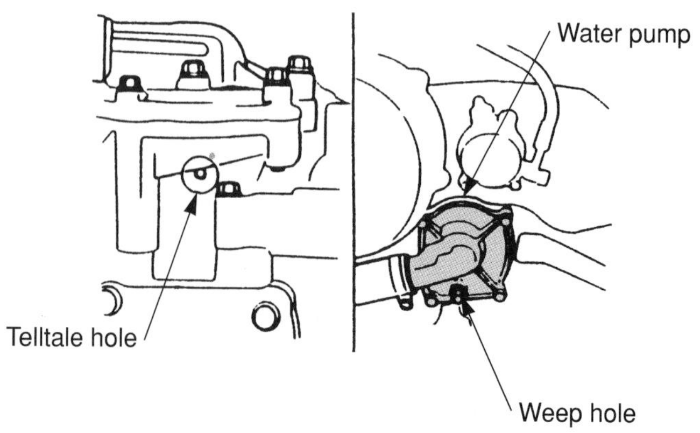

Figure 11-15. Location of the water pump's "telltale" or weep hole. (Honda Motor Co., Ltd.)

3. Install a new O-ring on the water pump. Then align the water pump shaft groove with the water pump drive shaft and install the water pump. See **Figure 11-18.**

4. Tighten the pump mounting bolts. Connect the water hoses and secure the bands and clamp(s). Fill the cooling system and add the recommended engine oil.

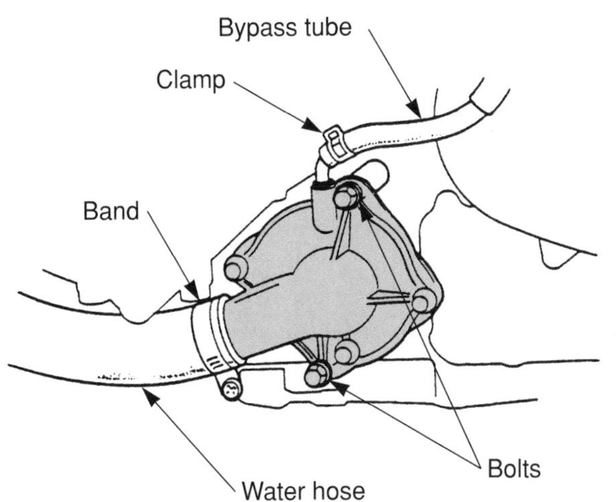

Figure 11-16. Components to be disconnected when removing a water pump. (Honda Motor Co., Ltd.)

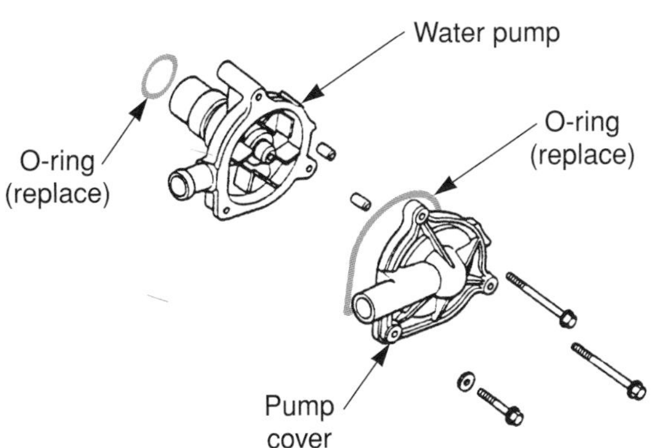

Figure 11-17. Replace O-rings when reassembling a coolant pump. (Honda Motor Co., Ltd.)

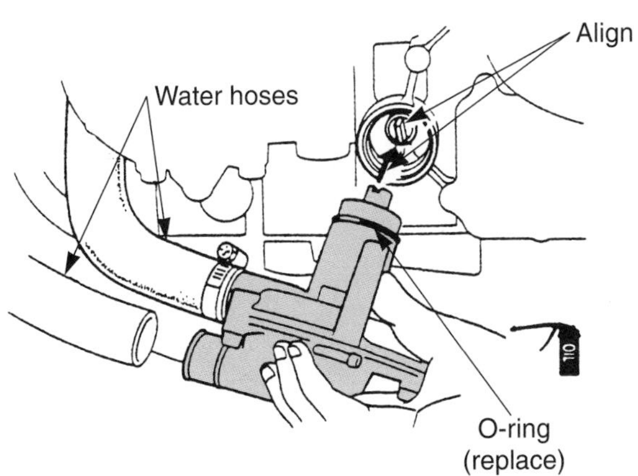

Figure 11-18. Reinstalling a coolant (water) pump. (Honda Motor Co., Ltd.)

Checking and Replacing Hoses

Carefully check all hoses for leakage, swelling, and chafing. Replace any hose that feels mushy or extremely brittle when squeezed firmly. Watch for signs of splits when hoses are squeezed, **Figure 11-19.** Also look for rust stains around the clamps. Rust stains indicate the hose is leaking, possibly because the clamp has cut into the hose. Loosen the clamp, slide it back, and check for cuts.

When replacing a hose, drain the coolant system below the level that is being worked on. Loosen or cut the old clamp and use a knife to cut off the old hose. Slide the old hose off the fitting. If the hose is stuck, do not pry it off. This could possibly damage the inlet/outlet nipple or the attachment between the end of the hose and the bead. Carefully cut the stuck hose off its fitting.

Clean off any remaining hose particles with a wire brush or emery cloth. The fitting should be clean when installing the new hose. Burrs or sharp edges could cut into the hose tube and lead to premature failure.

Coat the surface with a sealing compound. Place the new clamps on each end before positioning the hose. Do not reuse old spring clamps, even if they appear to be good. Slide the clamps to about .25″ (6.35 mm) from the end of the hose after it is properly positioned on the fitting. Tighten the clamp securely; do not overtighten.

Troubleshooting Liquid-Cooling Systems

The liquid-cooling systems on motorcycles and ATVs are fairly easy to troubleshoot. A careful inspection of the radiator, radiator cap, thermostat, water pump, cooling fan and switch, hoses and clamps, as well as the coolant itself, will usually reveal the cause of the problem. The following are some of the most common problems found in a liquid-cooling system and their causes:

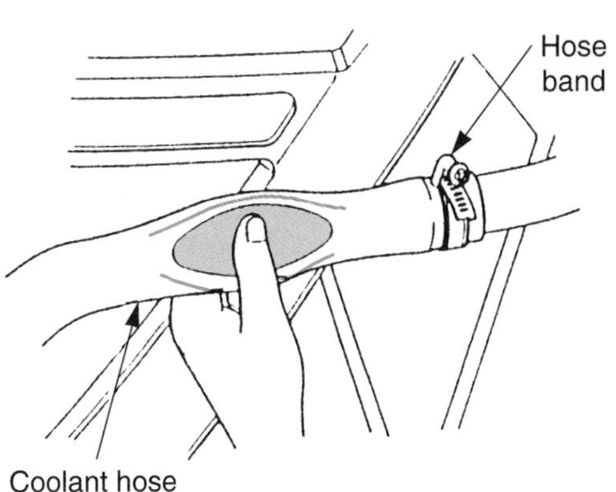

Figure 11-19. Method of checking the condition of a cooling hose. (Honda Motor Co., Ltd.)

Engine Temperature too High

- Faulty temperature gauge or gauge sensor.
- Thermostat stuck closed.
- Faulty radiator cap.
- Insufficient coolant.
- Passages blocked in radiator, hoses, or water jacket.
- Air in system.
- Faulty cooling fan motor.
- Faulty fan motor switch.
- Faulty water pump.
- Poorly tuned engine.

Engine Temperature too Low

- Faulty temperature gauge or gauge sensor.
- Thermostat stuck open.
- Faulty cooling fan motor switch.

Coolant Leaks

- Faulty pump mechanical seal.
- Deteriorated O-rings.
- Faulty radiator cap.
- Damaged or deteriorated gaskets.
- Loose hose connection or clamp.
- Damaged or deteriorated hoses.

Summary

In the combustion process, a great amount of heat is produced. This heat must be transferred away from the engine to prevent damage. Most modern motorcycle engines use one of two methods of cooling.

Air-cooled engines can be found on most designs of motorcycles, ATVs, and scooters. They can be used on both two- and four-stroke engines. The big advantage of the air-cooled system is lower production cost. However, since the finned cylinder relies on forced air to cool properly, forward motion is necessary when the engine is running. An air-cooled engine's operating temperature can rise and fall with changes in outside air temperature.

A liquid-cooled engine can maintain optimal engine operating temperature while preventing overheating and overcooling. The major advantage of a liquid-cooled engine is that it maintains a more consistent operating temperature than an air-cooled engine. Because of the controlled operating temperature of the liquid-cooled engine, more precise clearances between moving parts can be utilized. In both two- and four-stroke engine cooling systems, a heat absorbing liquid (coolant) is moved by means of a water pump.

Ethylene glycol-based coolant (antifreeze) has many advantages over water: it dissipates heat more readily, has a higher boiling temperature, and has rust inhibitors as well as water pump lubricants. Engine coolant is normally a 50-50 mixture of ethylene glycol (or equivalent) and water. An antifreeze/water mixture should be limited to 60% antifreeze.

The radiator is basically a heat exchanger, transferring heat from the engine to the air passing through it. Many of today's motorcycle cooling systems have a recovery tank, which serves to temporarily store the cooling system's reserve volume. A liquid-cooled engine's operating temperature is controlled by a thermostat. The heart of the cooling system is the water pump. It prompts the circulation of coolant in the system. A cooling fan maintains system performance under severe conditions, whether the bike is moving or standing still.

The air-cooled system is very simple to maintain and very little can go wrong. The liquid-cooling system must be inspected and serviced as a system. Service the entire system to ensure good results. A hydrometer is used to determine the coolant's freezing point. Replace coolant at the time intervals recommended in the service manual. If the cooling system shows evidence of rust, scale, or lime in the coolant, it must be completely flushed.

Know These Terms

Air-cooled engines
Fins
Liquid-cooled engine
Coolant
Radiator
Recovery tank
Radiator cap
Thermostat
Water pump
Cooling fan
Hydrometer

Review Questions—Chapter 11

Do not write in this text. Place your answers on a separate sheet of paper.

1. Explain two differences between air-cooled and liquid-cooled systems.
2. The big advantage of the air-cooled system is ______.
   A. lower production costs
   B. improved efficiency
   C. longer engine life
   D. quiet operation
3. The heat dissipating surface on the air-cooled two-stroke engine is ______ than on the four-stroke engine.
   A. much smaller
   B. much larger
   C. a little larger
   D. no different

4. The function of a radiator cap in today's cooling systems is to ______.
   A. keep the coolant from splashing out of the radiator
   B. pressurize the cooling system
   C. release excess pressure from the cooling system
   D. All of the above.
5. Which of the following is *not* a benefit of a liquid-cooling system?
   A. Quiet operation.
   B. Improved efficiency.
   C. Longer engine life.
   D. Lower production costs.
6. ______ is recommended over tap water because it does not contain minerals and chemicals that could cause corrosion problems.
   A. Mineral water
   B. Coolant
   C. Distilled water
   D. Oil
7. Which of the following factors influence the efficiency of the radiator?
   A. The area and thickness of the radiator core exposed to the cooling air.
   B. The amount of coolant going through the radiator.
   C. The temperature of the cooling air.
   D. All of the above.
8. The radiator cap allows for an _____ of _____ in the radiator, which raises the boiling point of the coolant to a predetermined point, usually 12-14 psi (82.8-96.6 kPa).
9. When the engine is cold, the thermostat is ______.
   A. closed
   B. partially open
   C. partially closed
   D. completely open
10. Leaving the thermostat ______ contributes to overheating, since it prevents coolant circulation and prevents the radiator from dissipating heat if the engine temperature becomes excessive.
11. Ram air through the radiator should be sufficient to maintain proper cooling ______.
   A. at normal driving speeds
   B. at low speeds
   C. at idle
   D. at all speeds
12. At low speeds and idle, the liquid-cooled system needs ______ pulled through the radiator, which is delivered by a _____.
13. The antifreeze mix should never exceed ______.
   A. 50% coolant, 50% water
   B. 60% coolant, 40% water
   C. 80% coolant, 20% water
   D. 70% water, 30% coolant
14. A sign of a defective water pump is:
   A. coolant seeping out of the weep hole.
   B. discoloration of the pump metal.
   C. dirt or rust in the coolant.
   D. All of the above.
15. All of the following should be done when replacing a hose *except:*
   A. drain the cooling system below the level being worked on.
   B. use a knife to cut the old hose.
   C. reuse spring clamps.
   D. do not overtighten the clamps.

Suggested Activities

1. Check the coolant level in a radiator and perform the following:
   A. Determine the recommended strength of the antifreeze for your area.
   B. If the antifreeze currently in the radiator is not of the correct strength, modify the mixture to comply with specifications.
2. Inspect, drain, and flush the radiator of a motorcycle with a liquid-cooled system, following all recommended procedures in the appropriate manufacturer's service manual.
3. Check and if needed, replace the cooling system hoses on a motorcycle.

Motorcycles exhaust systems come in various configurations, depending on the bike's intended use and design. (Yamaha Motor Corporation U.S.A.)

12 Exhaust Systems and Emissions Control

After studying this chapter, you will be able to:

- Describe the typical motorcycle exhaust system.
- Explain the components of an exhaust system and their functions.
- Understand the exhaust pulse scavenge effect theory.
- List the servicing procedures for inspecting and servicing exhaust systems.
- Know the purpose of emissions control system functions.
- Describe the operation of a typical electronically controlled three-way catalytic converter.
- Understand the limitations of servicing the noise control system.

Motorcycle engines generate exhaust gas and heat. If this gas were simply allowed to exit directly from the engine, this gas would be in the vicinity of the rider. It would also be a source of significant noise, since this gas would include the sound of the combustion in the engine. This gas must be routed away from the rider and also silenced to make surrounding noises audible. In some areas, the engine must be equipped with systems that clean the exhaust gas of harmful substances to reduce airborne pollution.

Exhaust Systems

The ***exhaust system*** is a vital performance component of any motorcycle. It has four functions:

- Route burned exhaust gases to the rear of the motorcycle.
- Enhance the power curve of the engine.
- Reduce engine exhaust noise.
- Aid in engine emission control.

Exhaust systems are normally made of aluminized steel, or steel covered with a layer of chrome plating or heat-resistant paint. A heat shield may be placed over the outer side of the exhaust system. The heat shield helps keep the rider from being burned on the hot pipe or muffler. There are numerous exhaust system designs. Designs vary with the number of engine cylinders, engine type (two-stroke or four-stroke cycle), and application.

For example, a street bike normally has the exhaust system located close to the ground. This keeps exhaust heat away from the rider and helps lower the center of gravity. An off-road motorcycle, however, frequently has the exhaust system mounted higher on the side of the motorcycle. This provides more ground clearance for riding in rough terrain.

System Descriptions

As shown in **Figure 12-1,** the parts of a typical four-stroke exhaust system include:

- ***Heat diffuser*** (finned flange to dissipate heat and mount header pipe).
- ***Header pipe*** (exhaust pipe between engine and muffler).
- ***Exhaust chamber*** (used on multicylinder bikes to bring all the header pipes into one common pipe).

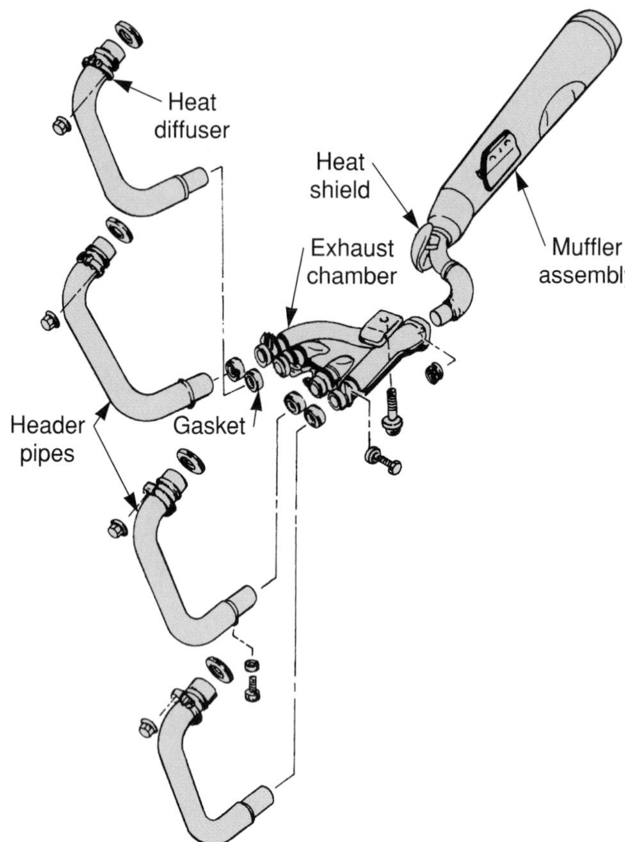

Figure 12-1. Parts of an exhaust system include diffusers, header pipes, clamps, gaskets, and a muffler.

- ***Muffler*** (baffled container that reduces pressure pulsations and noise).
- ***Exhaust clamps*** (devices for holding parts of exhaust system together).
- ***Exhaust gaskets*** (heat resistant gaskets that prevent leakage between exhaust system connections).

After the power stroke, the engine blows extremely hot gases out the engine exhaust port. These gases enter the exhaust system header pipe. Some of the heat is dissipated into a diffuser to prevent overheating the header pipe. Since the gas discharged from the exhaust port is pressurized and very hot, it swells suddenly and produces a loud noise if it is discharged directly into the atmosphere. It also lowers the exhaust efficiency as the gas is diffused from the port. To prevent this, the gas is drawn from the exhaust port into the muffler to be swelled and discharged into the atmosphere after its temperature and pressure are lowered. The muffler itself contains baffles and inner chambers to dampen the exhaust pressure pulses. See **Figure 12-2.**

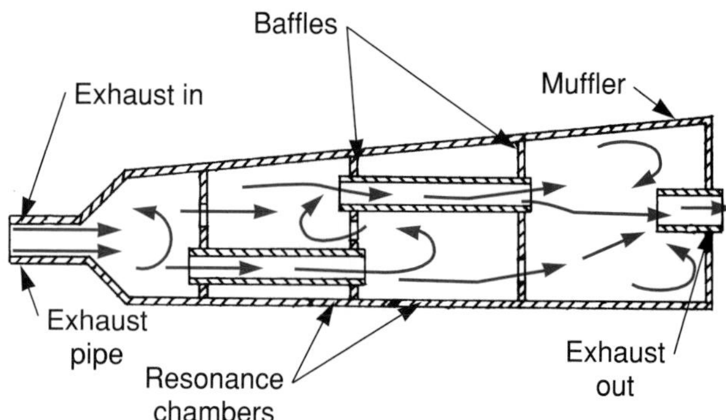

Figure 12-2. Baffles are used to form resonance chambers in the muffler to eliminate pressure pulses and noise.

Exhaust Pulse Scavenge Effect

By varying the size and diameter of sections of the exhaust system, the air-fuel mixture can be drawn into the cylinder more effectively. This is called the ***exhaust pulse scavenge effect.*** Utilizing this effect in exhaust system design results in significant improvements in engine performance, especially on two-stroke engines.

When the exhaust valve (or port) opens, the exhaust gas flows rapidly from the port into the muffler. At the end of the exhaust stroke, the gas flow slows down, but due to the inertia of liquid mass, cylinder pressure goes down below atmospheric pressure. In other words, negative pressure is applied to the cylinder for a short time. As the intake valve (or scavenge port) opens, **Figure 12-3A,** the air-fuel mixture is quickly drawn out by the negative pressure, and the exhaust efficiency is improved.

The discharge gas flows through the muffler, forming a high speed pressure wave. Due to the inertia of liquid mass, negative pressure is applied to the exhaust port where the pressure wave had passed. When the exhaust valve (or port) opens on the next exhaust stroke, the exhaust gas is drawn out by the negative pressure, and the exhaust efficiency is improved, **Figure 12-3B.**

The two-stroke exhaust system consists of most of the same parts as the four-stroke engine, however, the internal design of the system is somewhat different. An ***expansion chamber*** is used in a two-stroke exhaust system to help exhaust ***scavenging*** (removal of burned gases from the engine cylinder), and increase engine power. As shown in **Figure 12-4,** an expansion chamber consists of:

- Header pipe.
- Divergent cone.
- Belly.
- Convergent cone.
- Stinger.

The length and angle of the cones determines the intensity and duration of the pressure waves in the expansion chamber. In two-stroke engines, a scavenging effect is used to help pull burned gases out of the cylinder. Scavenging also pulls fresh air-fuel mixture out of the engine and into the expansion chamber. The expansion chamber produces a reverse pressure wave that forces the air-fuel mixture back into the cylinder, **Figure 12-5.** A muffler is built into the stinger portion of most modern two-stroke cycle motorcycles.

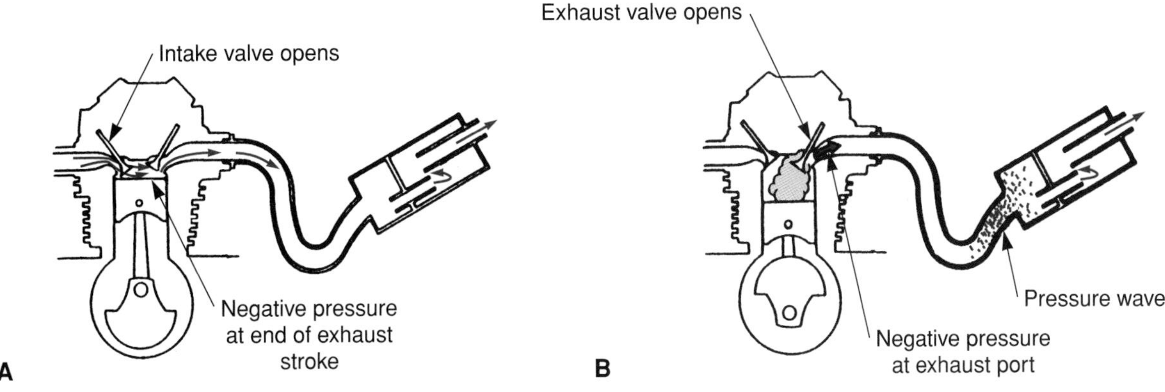

Figure 12-3. The action of exhaust pulse effect. (Honda Motor Co., Ltd.)

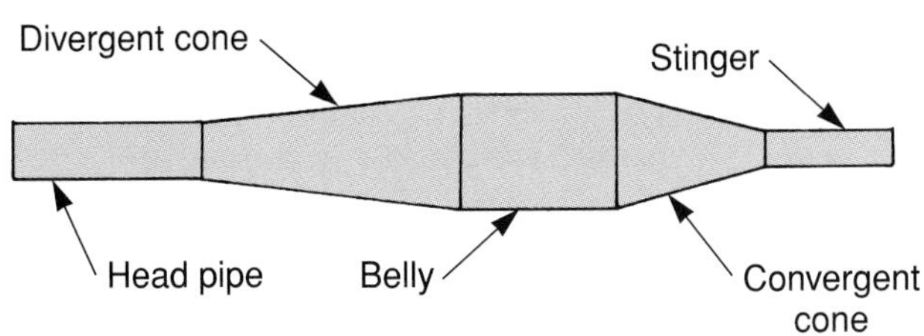

Figure 12-4. Parts of an expansion chamber.

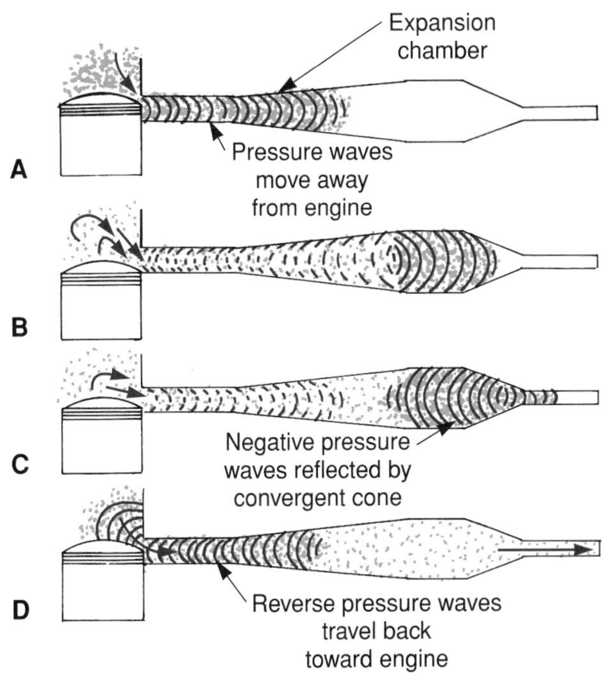

Figure 12-5. Expansion chamber action. A—Exhaust positive pressure wave moves into the expansion chamber. B—Vacuum pulls remaining exhaust out of the engine cylinder. C—Negative wave is reflected from the convergent cone back toward the exhaust port as the air-fuel mixture begins to flow into the headpipe. D—Negative pressure waves force the air-fuel mixture back into the cylinder and exhaust gas is bled off through stinger.

For best two-stroke engine performance, the expansion chamber must be compatible with the breathing characteristics of the engine. Poor engine performance will result from a mismatch between the port timing and the expansion chamber.

On two-stroke engines, there is the possibility air-fuel mixture that was scavenged just before the end of the exhaust stroke may leak out to some degree and be discharged into the exhaust port. The gas is discharged into the muffler, forming a high pressure wave. This pressure wave impacts against the taper at the end of the expansion chamber, rebounds, and applies a positive pressure to the exhaust port. The air-fuel mixture that was about to be discharged before the exhaust port closes is forced back into the cylinder and the scavenge effect is improved, **Figure 12-6.** Because the pressure wave cycle changes according to the shape of the muffler, performance is compromised by damage. For example, dents in the piping can cause gas flow restrictions that may reduce engine performance.

Removing Dents

Small to medium size dents in the exhaust system can be pulled out with a number of tools: suction cups, dent pullers, and even a sheet screw and vise grips. Possibly the easiest procedure is to use a dent puller or slide hammer.

Drill or punch a small hole in the center of the dent and thread the screw tip on the dent puller into the hole. Hold the handle of the dent puller in one hand and forcefully slide the weight straight back against the handle. Then, gradually work the crease out. It may be necessary to drill additional holes and repeat the procedure until the dent is removed. Weld or braze the drilled hole(s) closed.

If the dent is badly crimped along the edges, the affected area can be cut out with a hacksaw, straightened with a body dolly, and hammered and welded back in place. Once welded, wire brush the pipe and paint with a high-temperature paint.

Warning: When inspecting or working on exhaust systems, remember that its components get very hot when the engine is running and contact with them could cause a severe burn.

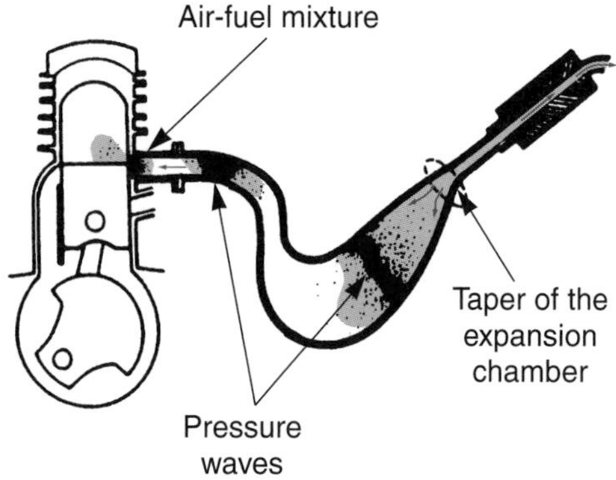

Figure 12-6. One method of improving the scavenging effect in a two-stroke engine exhaust system. (Honda Motor Co., Ltd.)

Exhaust Ultimate Power Valve (EXPV)

As shown in **Figure 12-7,** some four-stroke motorcycles have an ***exhaust ultimate power valve (EXPV)*** system. This exhaust arrangement uses a computer that varies the diameter of the exhaust tube according to engine rpm. At low rpm, the exhaust valve decreases the tube diameter. At high rpm, the diameter is increased, reducing the positive pressures in the exhaust tubes. The positive pressures inhibit the exhaust gases from exiting the combustion chamber. Reducing the positive pressures also helps to reduce exhaust emissions.

Common Exhaust Pipe

The muffler of the conventional four-stroke multicylinder engine uses an independent pipe for each cylinder, but most recent models adopt a common exhaust pipe for all cylinders. Newer systems use a system in which the exhaust pipes join in the exhaust chamber, and another in which the exhaust pipes are directly joined. In both systems, gas pressures exhausted from individual cylinders intermingle. The pulse wave in the muffler, generated by the staggered combustion in adjoining cylinders, promotes the "pulse scavenge effect", which increases exhaust energy absorption. The resulting smaller muffler also has an increased silencing capability due to the reduced weight and decreased volume.

The method of exhaust pipe connection depends on the cylinder arrangement or the required engine characteristics. There are many other arrangements. For example, an inline four-cylinder engine can be connected with "4-into-1" system or "4-into-2-into-1" system, etc., **Figure 12-8.** The exhaust system, especially the muffler, greatly enhances the appearance of any motorcycle. The three styles of chrome mufflers shown in **Figure 12-9** are popular accessories on cruiser bikes.

Spark Arrester

Motorcycles made for use in the United States and Canada must have a ***spark arrester*** in its exhaust system.

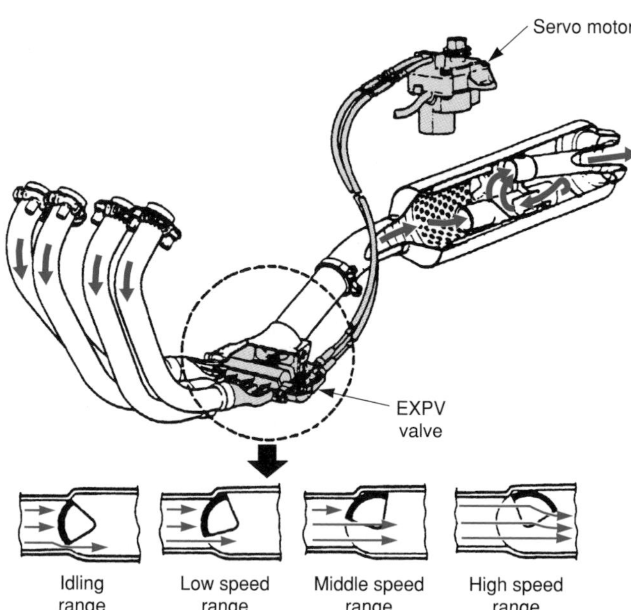

Figure 12-7. The four-stroke engine's exhaust ultimate power valve (EXPV) system. (Yamaha Motor Corporation U.S.A.)

The purpose of the spark arrester is to catch carbon sparks before they get out of the exhaust system. This is very important when a bike is used off highway.

Over a period of time, the spark arrester may become clogged with carbon deposits which can restrict flow in the muffler. If this should occur, remove the muffler cleanout lid, **Figure 12-10A.** Then block the end of the muffler with a shop cloth. Start the engine and blow the accumulated carbon deposits out of the muffler by quickly snapping open the throttle several times.

Warning: Perform this operation in a well-ventilated area free from combustible materials. Carbon particles may blow out of the clean outhole when performing this service. Wear safety glasses to prevent possible eye injuries. Wait until the pipe has cooled before removing or installing the muffler lid. Touching the hot exhaust may result in severe burns.

On most mufflers, do not remove the two screws that hold the exhaust baffle in the end of the spark arrester/muffler, **Figure 12-10B.** The two mounting screws must be installed in the spark arrester body at all times for the spark arrester to be effective. To clean most exhaust pipe/mufflers, just remove the cleanout lid.

Inspecting and Servicing Exhaust Systems

When servicing exhaust systems, start by inspecting the drain bolts and washers for corrosion or exhaust lek-

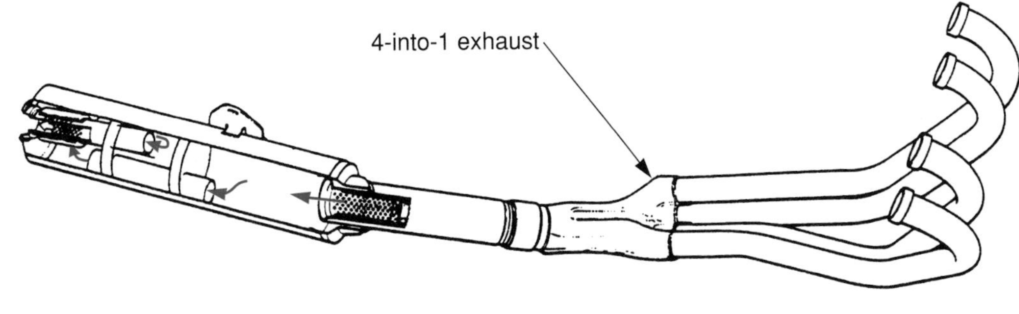

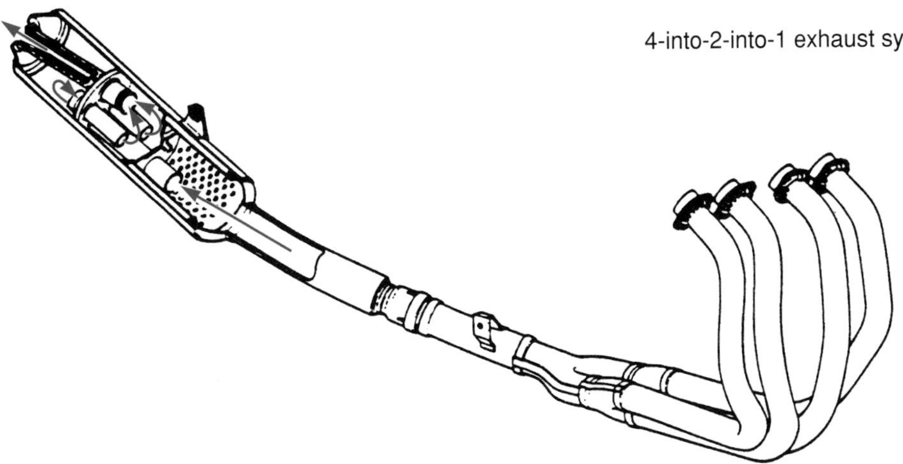

Figure 12-8. Various arrangements of exhaust pipe combinations. A—Four-into-one. B—Four-into-two-into-one systems.

age and replace if necessary. Inspect the muffler frame mounting flanges for fractures and loose bolts. Check the cylinder head mounting flanges for tightness. A loose exhaust pipe and muffler can reduce engine power. If necessary, loosen the clamping screw and separate the two parts. Remove the gasket and install a new one. The exhaust system should be removed as directed in the service manual.

When installing the exhaust system, install all fasteners loosely. Always tighten the exhaust clamp nut first, then tighten the mounting fasteners. If you tighten the mounting fasteners first, the exhaust pipe may not seat properly. Note the positions of the clamps installed between the exhaust pipe and muffler, the tab on the clamp should align with the groove on the muffler. Always inspect the exhaust system for leaks after installation. There are two problems with a typical exhaust system. Excessive exhaust noise may be caused by:

- Breaks in the exhaust system piping.
- Exhaust gas leaks.

Poor performance may be caused by:

- Deformed exhaust system.
- Exhaust gas leaks.
- Clogged muffler.

Turbochargers

A ***turbocharger,*** often called a *turbo,* is an exhaust driven compressor. Tubing carries engine exhaust gases to one end of the turbocharger. The gases blowing through the turbo are used to spin a compressor wheel and form higher-than-normal air pressure in the engine. Because the exhaust gas is a waste product, the energy developed by the turbine is said to be free since it theoretically does not reduce engine power, **Figure 12-11.**

Turbochargers have been associated with high performance for many years. Turbochargers have been used in a wide variety of applications such as aircraft, automobile, truck, and marine engines. In all these applications, turbocharging provides increased air density in the engine's combustion chambers. This allows efficient burning of more fuel and results in higher horsepower output.

Turbocharging has been employed in motorcycle design for years, either as a turbo kit or in production models, **Figure 12-12.** Because of improvements in engine and exhaust design, none of the major motorcycle manufacturers are currently producing a standard production

A

B

C

Figure 12-9. Three styles of chrome mufflers: A—Slash cut. B—Taper tip. C—Fish tail. (Cobra Engineering Corporation)

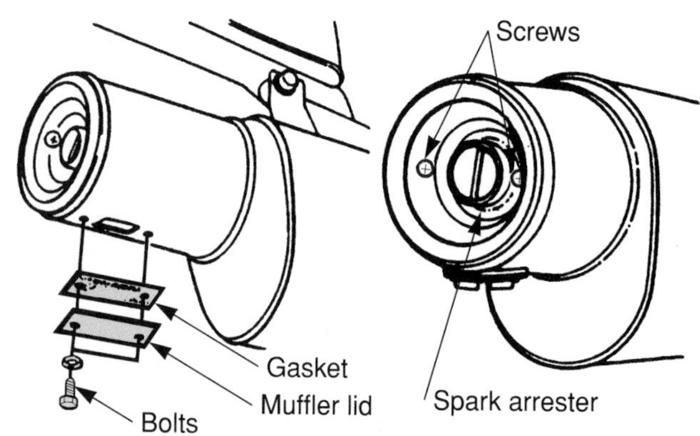

Figure 12-10. Typical spark arrester. A—Removing cleanout lid. B—Spark arrester retainer screws. (Honda Motor Co., Ltd.)

model with turbocharging. Custom-built turbocharged bikes as well as bolt-on turbo kits are available. When installing a turbo kit, be sure to follow the instructions in the installation manual.

Emission Control Systems

The combustion process of a motorcycle engine produces ***hydrocarbons (HC), carbon monoxide (CO),*** and ***oxides of nitrogen (NO_x).*** Control of hydrocarbons is very important because under certain conditions, it reacts with sunlight to form photochemical smog. Carbon monoxide and oxides of nitrogen do not react in the same way, but they are toxic.

HC emission consists of raw, unburned fuel that passes through the engine. Traces of HC will always show up in the exhaust. The higher the HC reading, the more fuel the engine uses. Sometimes high HC levels are accompanied by a "rotten egg" smell. Higher-than-normal HC readings mean there is a problem in one of three engine systems: the ignition, the carburetor, or the mechanical system.

CO is partially burned fuel. An engine can produce CO only if insufficient combustion takes place. The CO meter shows how much carbon monoxide is present in the exhaust. Since air and fuel must combine in the correct ratio to burn, a high CO reading means either too much fuel in the mixture (rich) or not enough air (restricted). High float levels, worn carburetor parts, improperly adjusted carburetors, and leaking choke plungers can cause rich mixtures. A dirty air cleaner, restricted air jets, or a blocked air inlet can restrict the amount of air entering the engine.

NO_x is caused by an excessively lean air-fuel mixture or high engine temperatures. A high NO_x reading indicates there is too much air in the mixture, not enough fuel, or the engine is running too hot. A partially blocked fuel filter or other fuel system defect, vacuum leak, excess carbon in the engine, and problems with the engine's cooling system can all cause high NO_x levels.

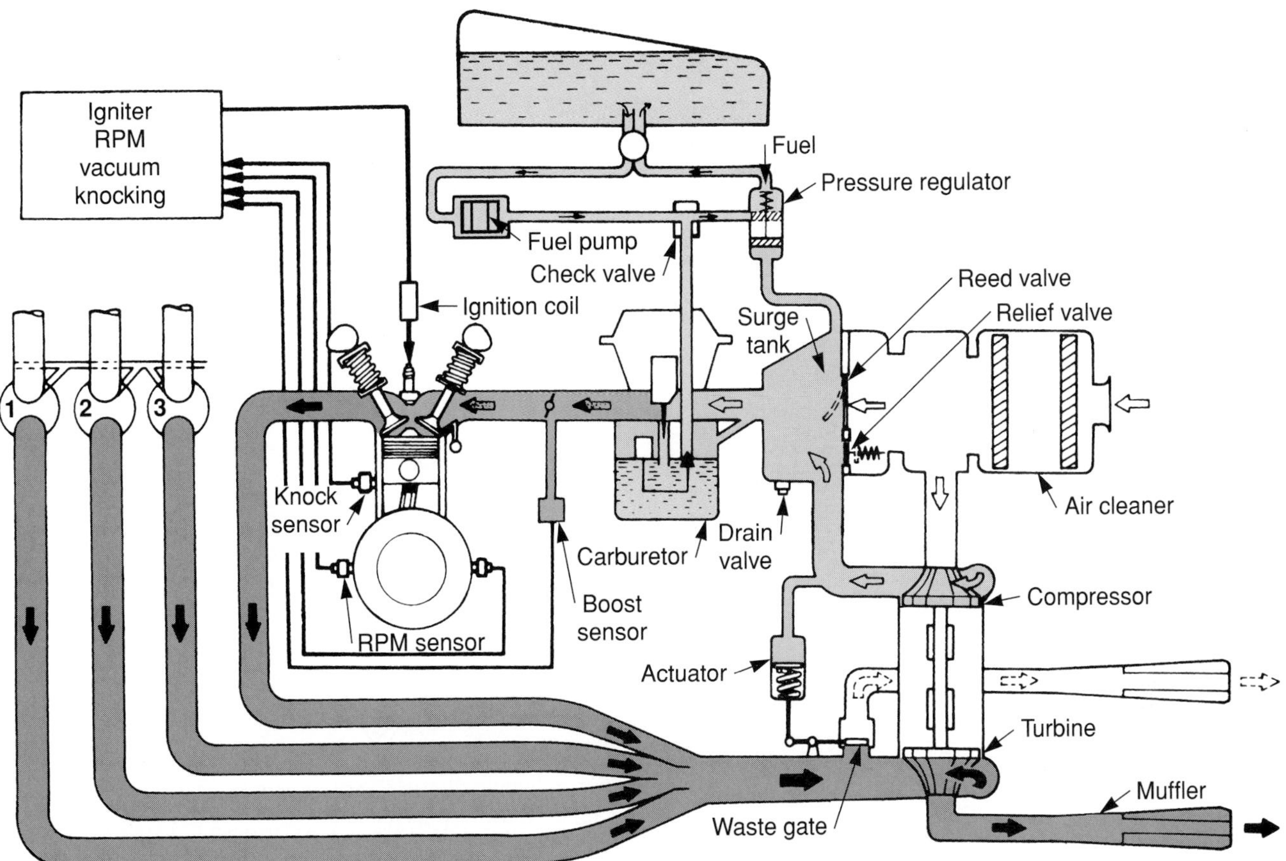

Figure 12-11. The flow of air, fuel, and exhaust gases in a turbocharger system. (Yamaha Motor Corporation U.S.A.)

Auto manufacturers are required by the federal government to produce vehicles that emit less than a certain amount of these pollutants. Motorcycles have similar legislation, although to a much lesser degree. For example, all 1984 and later models sold in California must be equipped with an evaporative emission control system. This is to meet California Air Resources Board (CARB) regulations in effect at the time of the model's production. The two emission control systems used in many recently produced motorcycles are:

- ***Crankcase emission control system.*** This system routes crankcase emissions through the air cleaner and into the combustion chamber, **Figure 12-13.** Condensed crankcase vapors are accumulated in an air-oil separator and drain tube, which must be emptied periodically. Refer to the maintenance schedule in the service manual for each model. The drain tube needs to be checked for oil accumulation more frequently if the machine has been consistently driven at high speeds or in rain.
- ***Exhaust emission control system*** *(secondary air supply system).* The exhaust emission control system consists of a secondary air supply system that introduces filtered air into the exhaust gases in the exhaust port. Fresh air is drawn into the exhaust port whenever there is a negative pressure pulse in the exhaust system. This charge of fresh air helps to change a considerable amount of hydrocarbons and carbon monoxide into relatively harmless carbon dioxide and water. Engines equipped with this system use lean carburetor settings. When servicing, only an idle speed adjustment with the throttle stop screw should be made.

As shown in **Figure 12-14,** a reed valve prevents reverse airflow through the system. The air injection control valve reacts to high intake manifold vacuum and will cut off the supply of fresh air during engine deceleration, thereby preventing afterburn in the exhaust system. No adjustment to the secondary air supply system should be made, although periodic inspection of the components is recommended.

Evaporative Emission Control

The information on ***evaporative emission control systems*** pertains to California street models. However, it is possible that you may see a bike equipped with one in your area. Also, the trend toward increasingly strict emission control may result in this system or one similar to it being mandated on all models, regardless of where they are sold.

The system as shown in **Figure 12-15** consists of a dual charcoal canister, a roll-over valve, purge control valves, air vent, and assorted vacuum and fuel hoses.

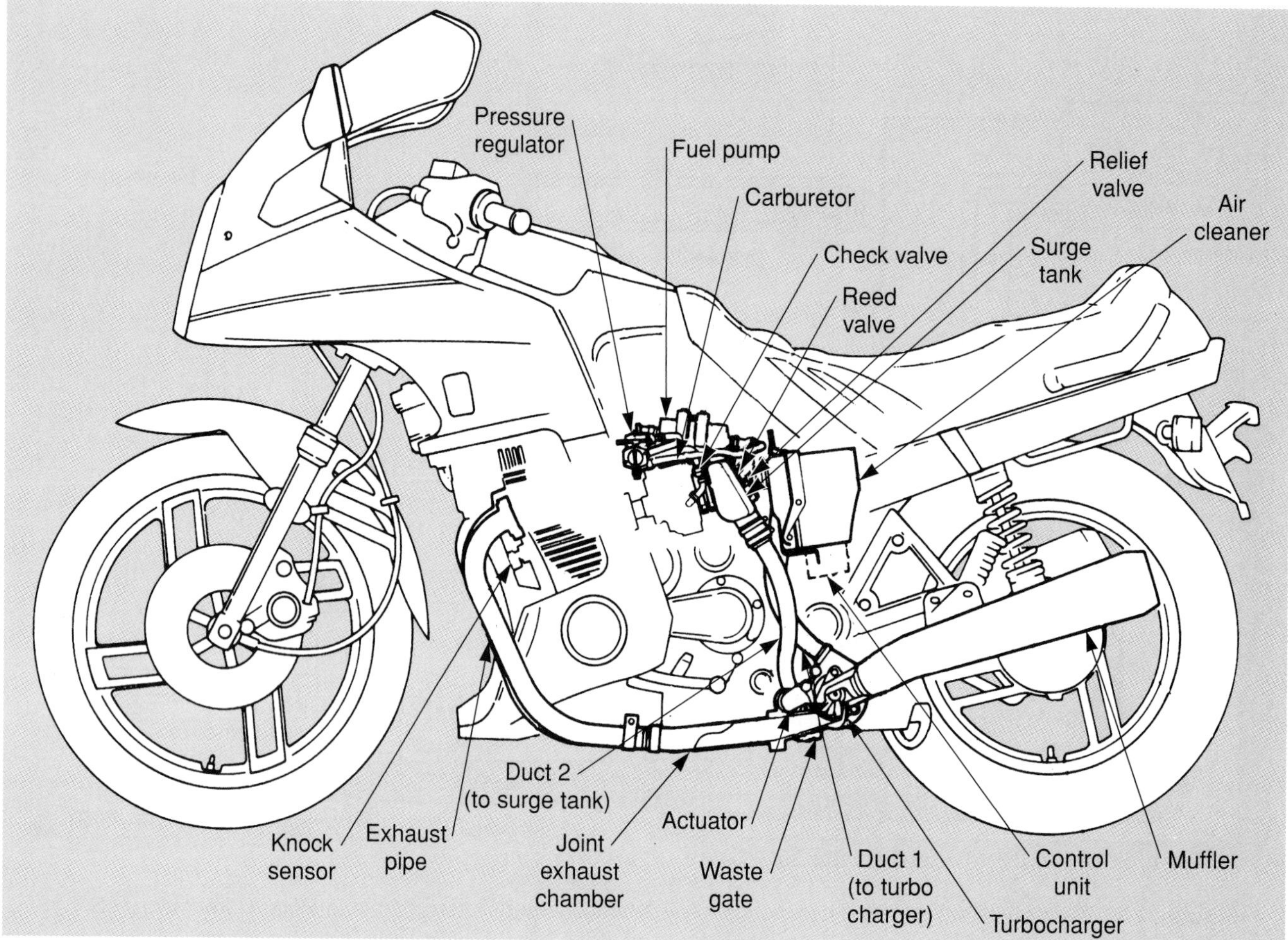

Figure 12-12. Location of turbocharger and related components on a typical motorcycle. (Yamaha Motor Corporation U.S.A.)

During engine operation, vapor leaves the fuel tank through the roll-over valve and enters the activated charcoal canister through a connecting hose. The fuel vapors are stored in the charcoal canister until the motorcycle is driven at high speed. When this occurs, the gas vapors are passed through a hose(s) to the carburetor(s) and is then mixed and burned with the incoming air. During low-speed engine operation or when the motorcycle is stopped or parked, the fuel vapors are stored in the canister(s).

The roll-over valve is usually located in the hose line between the fuel tank and the canister(s). With a typical roll-over valve, the fuel vapor and air passing the valve is controlled by an internal weight. See **Figure 12-16.** In the normal operating position, the weight is at the bottom of the valve and the breather tube is open to permit the flow of vapors to the canister. When the motorcycle is on its side or in a roll-over position, the internal weight blocks the passage and it is impossible to store fuel vapors in the charcoal canister.

Warning: Because the evaporative emission control system stores fuel vapors, make sure the work area is free of all flame or sparks before working on the emission system.

Service to the evaporative emission control system is limited to replacement of damaged parts. When purchasing replacement parts, make certain that components are for an emission control motorcycle. Parts sold for non-emission bikes are not compatible with an evaporative emission control system. Do not alter the position of the charcoal canister below the carburetor(s). Also the roll-over valve must be located in a vertical position. When replacing worn or damaged emission control hoses, make sure to replace with a hose having the same inside diameter.

Catalytic Converters

Catalytic converters have been used in all automobiles since the mid-1970s to reduce exhaust emissions. They are now being introduced to motorcycles, especially those with electronic fuel injection systems.

The catalytic converter is located ahead of the muffler in the exhaust system. The extreme heat in the converter oxidizes the exhaust that flows out of the engine. A catalyst is a substance that causes a chemical reaction in other elements without actually becoming a part of the chemical change itself and without being used up or consumed in the process. A motorcycle catalytic converter is a device that uses catalysts to cause a change in the elements of

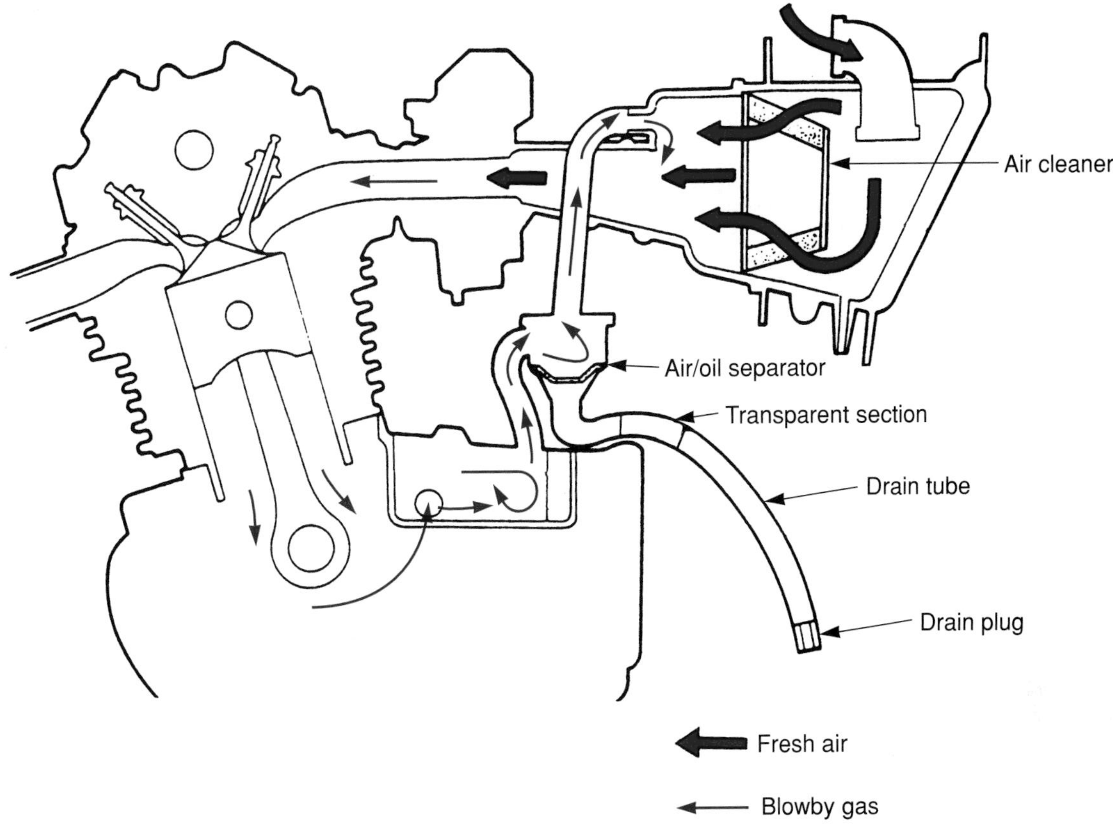

Figure 12-13. Typical crankcase emission control system. (Honda Motor Co., Ltd.)

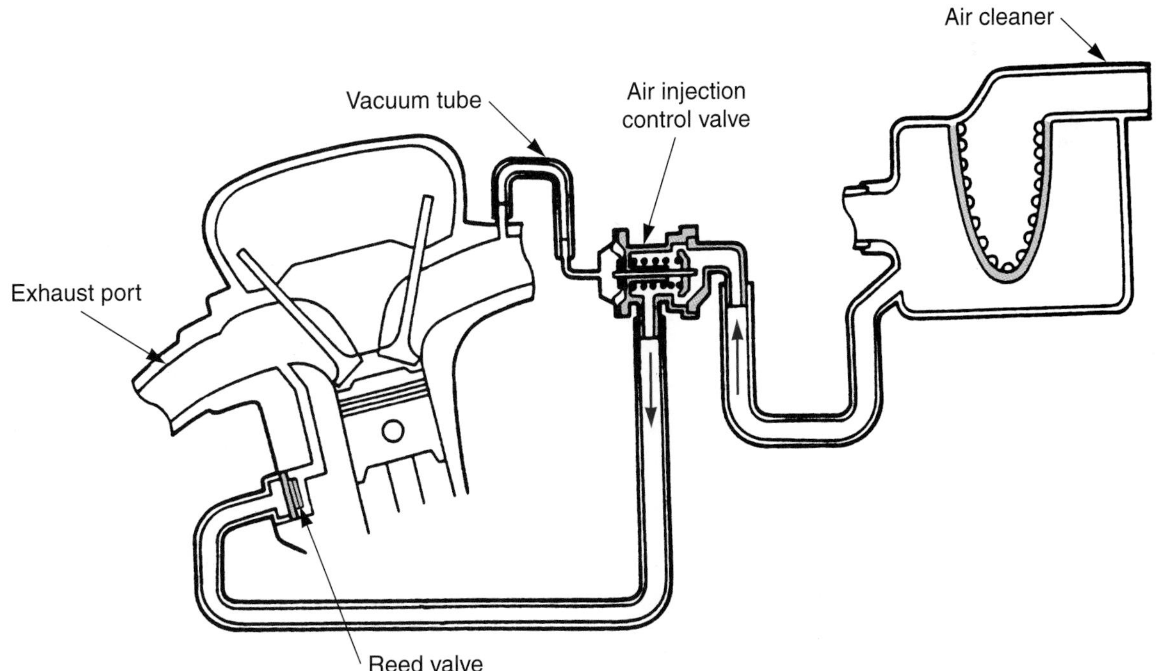

Figure 12-14. Typical exhaust emission control system. (Honda Motor Co., Ltd.)

the waste exhaust gases as they pass through the exhaust system.

The catalyst elements used in catalytic converters are platinum, palladium, and rhodium. These elements are used alone or in combination to change the undesirable CO, HC, and NO_x into harmless water vapor, carbon dioxide (CO_2), and oxygen (O_2), **Figure 12-17.**

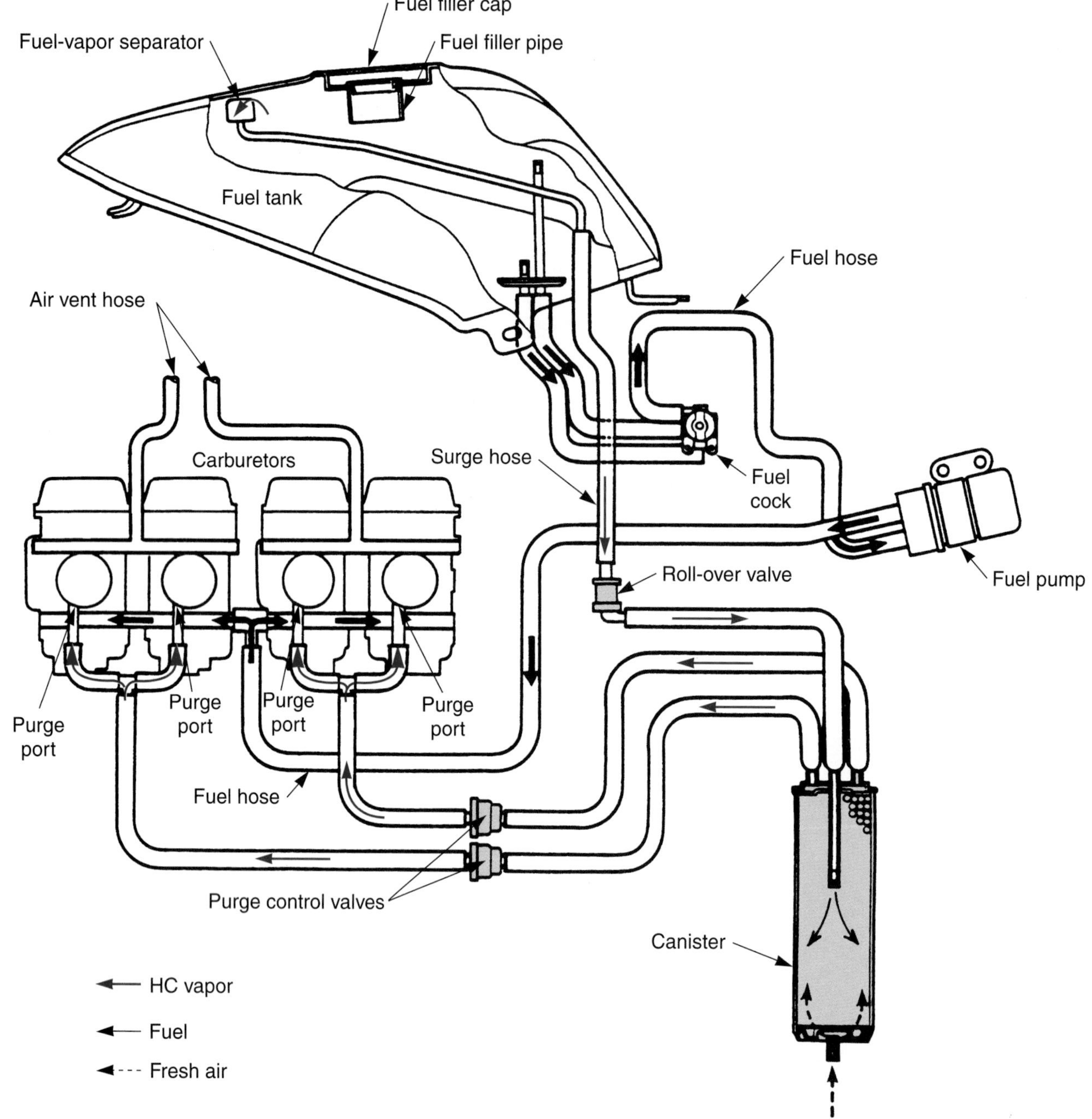

Figure 12-15. Evaporative emission control used on motorcycles primarily sold in California. (American Suzuki Motor Corporation)

Electronic Control Three-Way Catalytic Conversion Systems

The ***electronic control three-way catalytic conversion system*** shown in **Figure 12-18** is a high efficiency exhaust gas cleanup system. It decreases substances such as CO, HC, and NO_x from the exhaust gas by total control of air-fuel ratio, in association with the EFI system and the oxygen sensor. Using the EFI system, optimum combustion is realized, by matching air-fuel ratio with engine operating conditions. Maximum performance of the three-way catalytic converter is attained. With the aim of cleaning up the exhaust gas at high efficiency, an oxygen sensor is installed in the exhaust chamber. This sensor detects the residual oxygen in the exhaust gas. Based on these readings, the ECM adjusts fuel, spark, and other outputs to maintain optimum performance.

Based on the data from the sensor, the ECM makes minute corrections to the air-fuel ratio and maintains it close to the theoretical air-fuel ratio of 14.7:1. These control systems, minimize exhaust emissions while keeping engine performance at a high level.

The conditions that generate CO, HC, and NO_x in exhaust gas have conflicting characteristics. Therefore, there is a limit to reducing the concentrations of all these components simultaneously in the combustion stage.

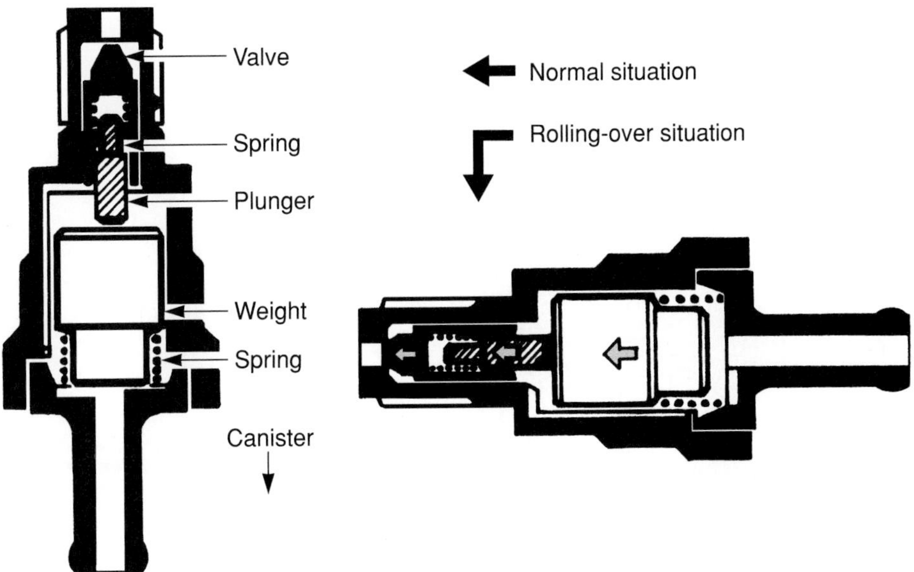

Figure 12-16. Roll-over valve.

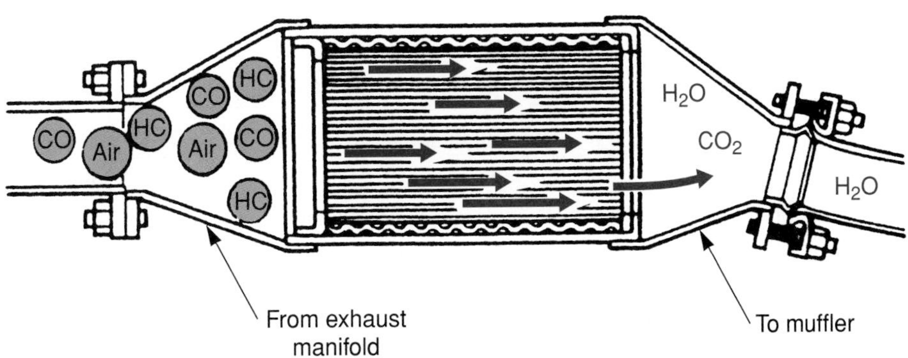

Figure 12-17. Operation of a conventional catalytic converter.

The role of the catalytic converter is to purge CO, HC, and NO_x and clean up the exhaust gas efficiently. The catalytic converter shown in **Figure 12-19** is a metallic monolith (honeycomb construction) catalyst with large surface area and low exhaust resistance. Platinum or rhodium, which are catalysts, adhere to the walls of the honeycomb cells. The honeycomb structure is installed in the exhaust chamber. When the exhaust gas comes in contact with the catalytic substance, chemical reactions, such as oxidation and reduction take place and the exhaust gas is cleaned.

Exhaust Gas Analyzer

The ***exhaust gas analyzer*** is a precision tool that measures exhaust emission content to show how well an engine is running, **Figure 12-20.** Unlike compression gauges or valve clearance measuring tools, the exhaust gas analyzer measures how well an engine converts air and fuel into power.

Valve clearance, compression, carburetor synchronization, ignition timing, and many other factors affect an engine's ability to convert fuel into power. If any of these adjustments are incorrect, the engine's efficiency is reduced and part of the fuel is wasted. An engine's exhaust content can tell a great deal about the engine's efficiency.

The exhaust gas analyzer connects to the exhaust system, draws a sample of exhaust gases, and analyzes the content. The meters on the exhaust gas analyzer indicate the amount of carbon monoxide (CO) and hydrocarbons (HC) present in the exhaust. Many exhaust gas analyzers measure HC, CO, NO_x, and other gases in terms of grams per mile (gpm). Some analyzers measure CO in a percentage (by volume) and HC in parts per million (ppm).

The exhaust gas analyzer produces an accurate analysis of an engine's exhaust emissions. You can diagnose and locate the problem source by comparing the CO readings to the engine's factory specifications. The exhaust gas analyzer can diagnose:

- Improper carburetor synchronization.
- Improperly adjusted float levels.
- Worn carburetor parts.
- Oil diluted by gasoline.

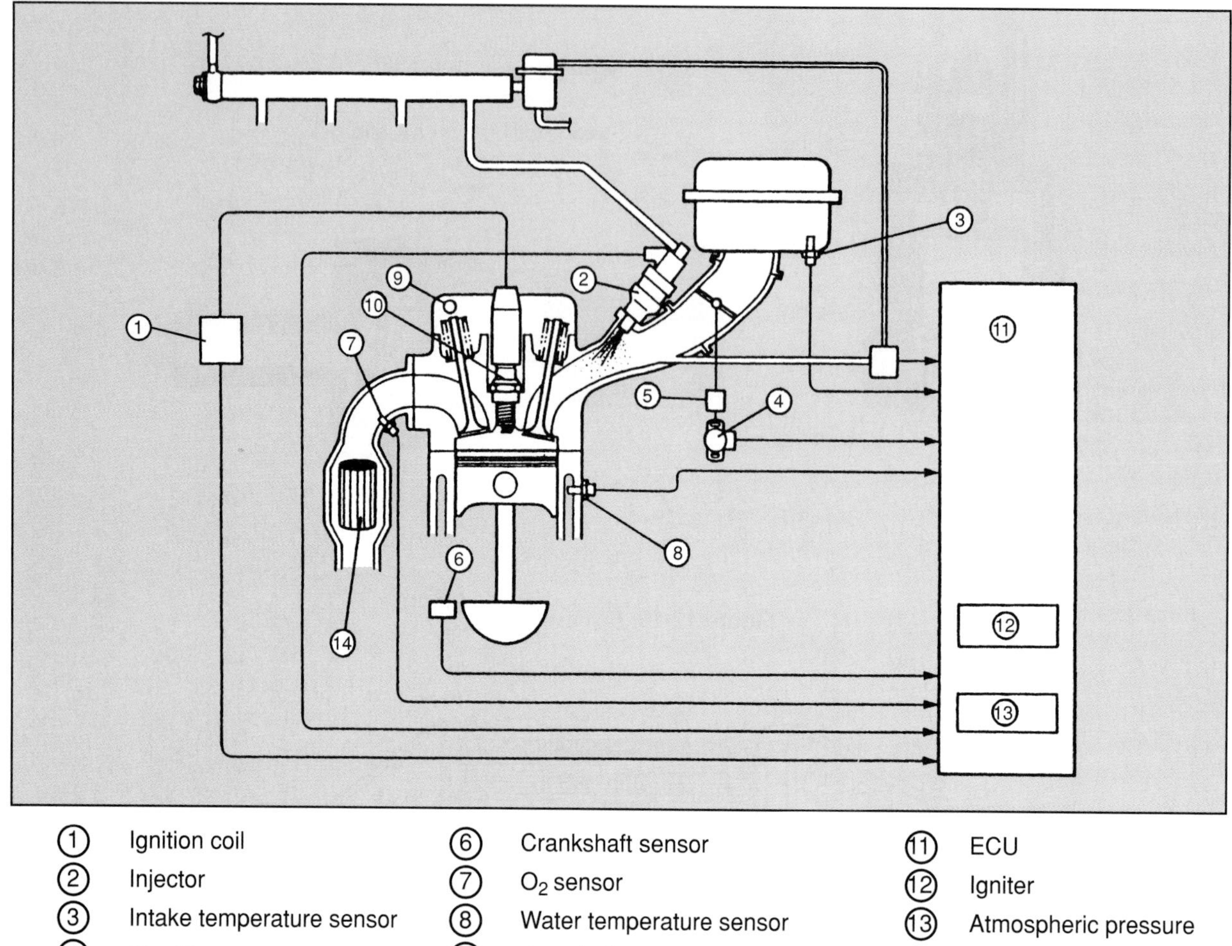

Figure 12-18. Schematic of an electronic three-way catalytic conversion system. (Yamaha Motor Corporation U.S.A.)

- Dirty air cleaner.
- Oil entering the combustion chamber.
- Ignition misfire.
- Leaking choke plungers.
- Air leaks.
- Low compression.
- Excessively tight valve clearances.

Noise Control Systems

Many motorcycle exhaust systems, especially on street bikes, have one of more noise control features built into them. These systems are in place for the safety of the rider as well as surrounding pedestrians. Tampering with the motorcycle's ***noise control system*** is prohibited by federal, state, and local laws. Acts that are considered tampering include:

- Any repair or modification that disables or defeats the muffler, baffles, header pipes, or any other component that conducts exhaust gases.
- Any repair or modification to any part of the intake system that results in increased noise and/or exhaust emissions.
- The use of engine, exhaust, or intake system parts that create increased noise and/or exhaust emissions or do not meet manufacturer's specifications.

Summary

Motorcycle engines generate exhaust gas and heat. If this gas were simply allowed to exit directly from the engine, it would be in the vicinity of the rider. The exhaust system is a vital performance component of any motorcycle. Exhaust systems are normally made of aluminized steel, or steel covered with a layer of chrome plating or heat-resistant paint. A heat shield may be placed over the outer side of the exhaust system. Designs vary with the number of engine cylinders, engine type (two-stroke or four-stroke cycle), and application. The parts of a typical four-stroke exhaust system include the heat diffuser, header pipe, exhaust chamber, muffler, exhaust clamps, and exhaust gaskets.

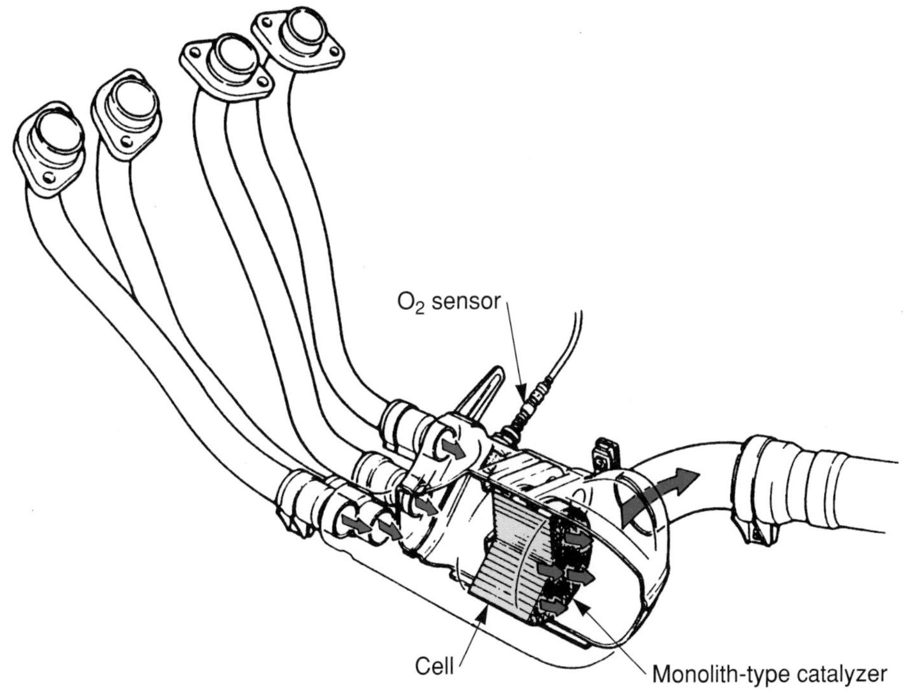

Figure 12-19. Catalytic converter system that uses a metallic monolith converter. (Yamaha Motor Corporation U.S.A.)

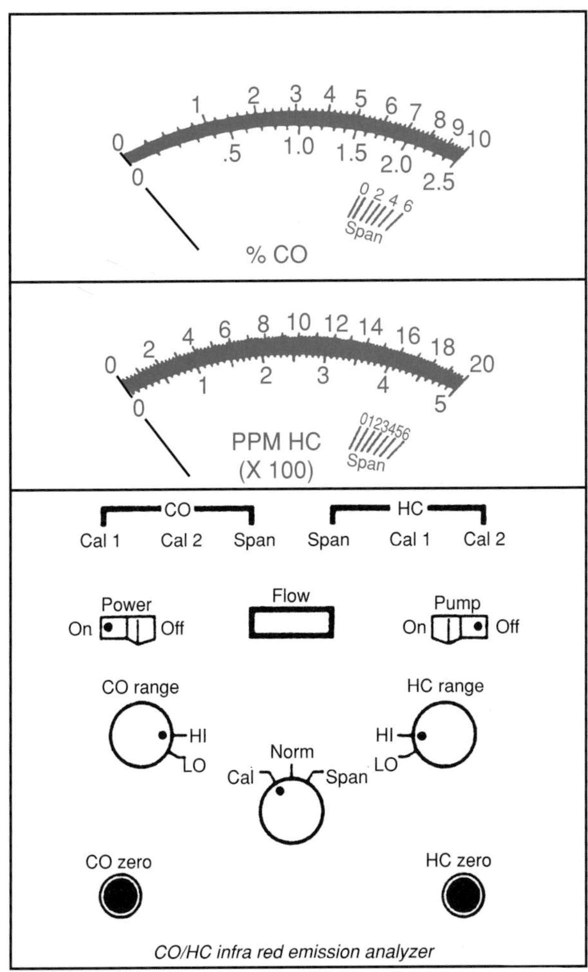

Figure 12-20. Typical exhaust gas analyzer meter panel. (Yamaha Motor Corporation U.S.A.)

By varying the size and diameter of sections of the exhaust system, the air-fuel mixture can be drawn into the cylinder more effectively. This is called the exhaust pulse scavenge effect. An expansion chamber is used in a two-stroke exhaust system to help exhaust scavenging. Small to medium size dents can be pulled out with a number of tools: suction cups, dent pullers, and even a sheet screw and vise grips.

Some four-stroke motorcycles have an exhaust ultimate power valve (EXPV) system. This exhaust arrangement uses a computer that varies the diameter of the exhaust tube according to engine rpm. The muffler of the conventional four-stroke multicylinder engine uses an independent pipe for each cylinder, but most recent models adopt a common exhaust pipe for all cylinders. Motorcycles made for use in the United States and Canada must have spark arresters in the exhaust system. The purpose of the spark arrester is to catch carbon sparks before they get out of the exhaust system. The exhaust system should be removed as directed in the service manual.

A turbocharger, often called a turbo, is an exhaust driven compressor. Because the exhaust gas is a waste product, the energy developed by the turbo is said to be free since it theoretically does not reduce engine power. Turbochargers have been associated with high performance for many years. Because of improvements in engine and exhaust design, none of the major motorcycle manufacturers are currently producing a standard production model with turbocharging.

The combustion process of a motorcycle engine produces hydrocarbons (HC), carbon monoxide (CO), and oxides of nitrogen (NO_x). The catalytic converter is located ahead of the muffler in the exhaust system. The extreme heat in the converter oxidizes the exhaust that flows out of the engine. The catalyst elements used in catalytic converters are platinum, palladium, and rhodium. These elements are used alone or in combination to change the undesirable CO, HC, and NO_x into harmless water vapor, carbon dioxide (CO_2), and oxygen (O_2).

The electronic control three-way catalytic conversion system is a high efficiency exhaust gas cleanup system that decreases exhaust emissions in association with the EFI system and the oxygen sensor. The exhaust gas analyzer is a precision tool that measures exhaust emission content to show how well an engine is running. Tampering with the motorcycle's noise control system is prohibited by federal, state, and local laws.

Know These Terms

Exhaust system	Turbocharger
Heat diffuser	Hydrocarbons (HC)
Header pipe	Carbon monoxide (CO)
Exhaust chamber	Oxides of nitrogen (NO_x)
Muffler	Crankcase emission control system
Exhaust clamps	Exhaust emission control system
Exhaust gaskets	Evaporative emission control systems
Exhaust pulse scavenge effect	Catalytic converters
Expansion chamber	Electronic control three-way catalytic conversion system
Scavenging	Exhaust gas analyzer
Exhaust ultimate power valve (EXPV)	Noise control system
Spark arrester	

Review Questions—Chapter 12

Do not write in this text. Place your answers on a separate sheet of paper.

1. Which of the following are *not* functions of an exhaust system?
   A. Route unburned air-fuel mixture to the rear of the motorcycle.
   B. Enhance the power curve of the engine.
   C. Reduce engine exhaust noise.
   D. Aid in engine emission control.
2. Exhaust systems are normally made of aluminized steel, or steel covered with a layer of chrome plating or _____.
3. The heat shield helps keep the _____ from being _____ on the hot pipe or muffler.
4. A street bike normally has the exhaust system located ______.
5. An off-road motorcycle frequently has the exhaust system mounted _____ on the side of the motorcycle.
6. An expansion chamber is used in a two-stroke exhaust system to help exhaust scavenging (removal of burned gases from the engine cylinder), and to increase ______.
7. Exhaust efficiency is compromised by damage; dents in the piping can cause gas flow _____ that may reduce engine performance.
8. The exhaust ultimate power valve (EXPV) system uses a ______ which varies the diameter of the exhaust tube according to the engine's _____.
9. The purpose of the spark arrester is to:
   A. Control the intensity of spark generated in the combustion chamber.
   B. Stop the spark plugs from firing too soon.
   C. Catch the carbon sparks before they get out of the exhaust system.
   D. All of the above.
10. A ______ is an exhaust driven compressor.
11. Manufacturers are required by the federal government to produce vehicles that emit less than a certain amount of:
    A. carbon monoxide.
    B. hydrocarbons.
    C. oxides of nitrogen.
    D. All of the above.
12. The emission control systems used in many recently produced motorcycles are:
    A. crankcase emissions control system.
    B. exhaust emissions control system.
    C. spark arresters.
    D. Both A & B.
13. All of the following are catalyst elements used in catalytic converters, *except:*
    A. aluminum.
    B. platinum.
    C. rhodium.
    D. palladium.

14. The catalyst elements used in catalytic converters are used alone or in combination to change the undesirable components of exhaust gas into _____.
    A. water vapor, CO_2, and O_2
    B. water vapor, CO, and O_2
    C. CO_2, HC, and NO_x
    D. water vapor, CO_2, and HC
15. Acts that may be considered tampering with the exhaust system include:
    A. cleaning the spark arrester.
    B. using a puller to remove a small dent.
    C. removal of the header pipes during engine disassembly.
    D. modifying part of the intake system.

Suggested Activities

1. Inspect the exhaust system on a bike, perform maintenance, and make repairs as needed.
2. Using the proper equipment and procedures, perform exhaust gas analyzer testing on a random bike according to the manufacturer's service manual. Determine if the results meet specifications for both carbon monoxide and hydrocarbon emissions for that vehicle. If the level of emissions is not within tolerance, follow service manual procedure to form a diagnosis of where the problem originates and make adjustments and repairs until the readings comply with specifications.

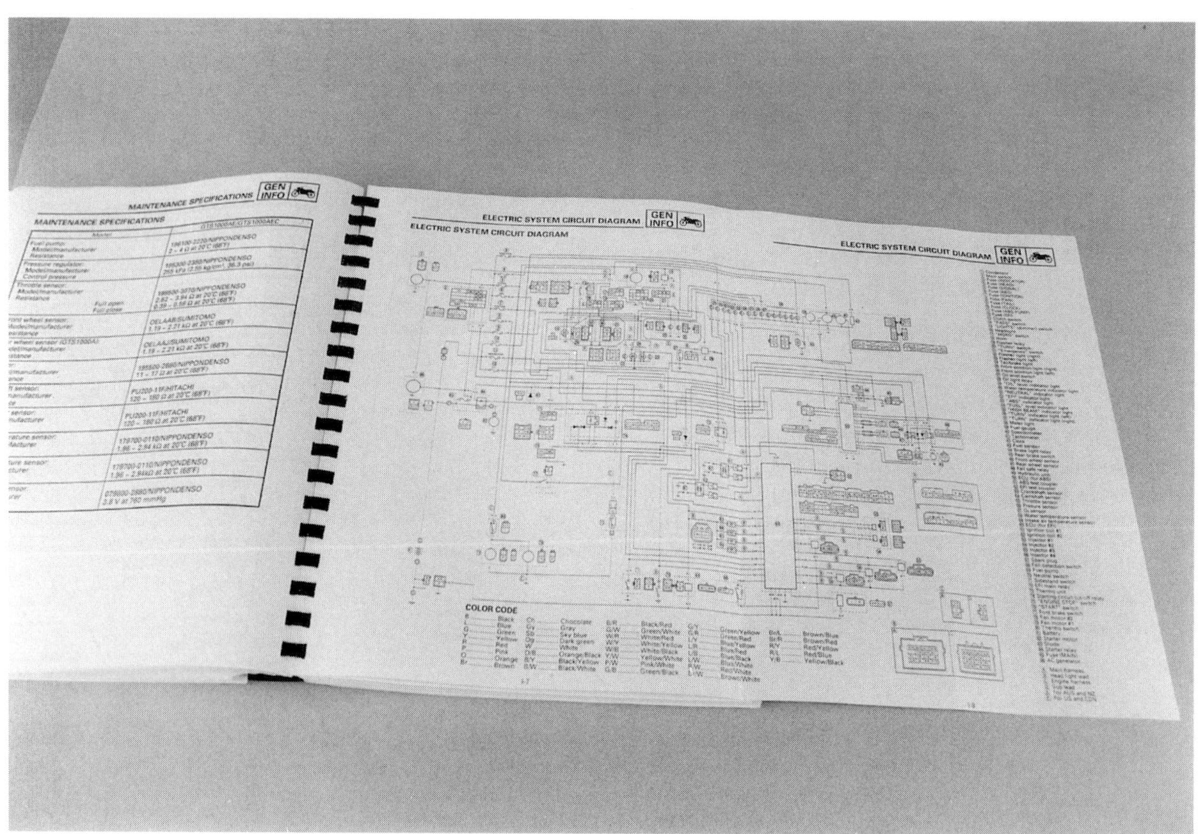

A service manual contains wiring diagrams and other information to correctly diagnose and repair problems. Do not begin work on a motorcycle without one. (Jack Klasey)

13 Power Transmission Systems

After studying this chapter, you will be able to:

- Define the major parts of a primary drive, transmission, and final drive assembly.
- Explain the operating principles of a primary drive, clutch, transmission, and final drive.
- List the different types of primary drives and clutches.
- Trace power flow through a primary drive, transmission, and final drive to the rear wheel.
- Explain transmission shift mechanisms.
- Describe kickstart mechanisms.
- Understand the operation of electric starter/ignition system.
- Describe the operation and parts of chain, belt, and shaft final drives.

To be usable, the power developed by the engine must be transferred to the rear wheel(s). This is accomplished by the drive train consisting of a primary drive, a clutch, or transmission (sometimes called a gearbox), and a final drive. In this chapter, you will study the various designs for primary drives, clutches, transmissions, and final drives. Many designs are used in motorcycles to achieve the desired gear reduction, speed, and engine torque multiplication.

Primary Drive

The ***primary drive*** transfers engine power from the crankshaft to the clutch/transmission assembly, **Figure 13-1.** Primary drive reduction is accomplished by either a set of gears or a chain and sprocket set. A gear or sprocket mounted on the engine crankshaft turns a gear or sprocket on the clutch hub. Since the crankshaft gear is smaller than the clutch hub gear, ***gear reduction*** (clutch turns slower than crank), results in an increase in torque (turning force).

It is important to understand the different types of primary drives used on modern motorcycles. Gears, chains, and belts are employed by the primary drive to transmit power from the engine crankshaft to the transmission.

Primary Gear Drive Systems

The three most common designs used for ***primary gear drives*** are straight-cut gears, straight-cut offset gears, and helical gears. Each type has specific advantages and disadvantages.

The ***straight-cut gear drive*** uses conventional (non-angled) gear teeth to transmit power from the engine to the clutch. Straight-cut gears must have a certain amount of backlash (clearance between teeth) in order to operate freely. **Figure 13-2** shows a view of straight-cut primary gears. With straight-cut teeth, backlash as well as the action produced by tooth engagement can cause a whining noise during operation. Straight-cut gears, however, are inexpensive to manufacture.

The ***straight-cut offset gear drive*** uses two straight-cut crankshaft gears and two straight-cut clutch gears mounted side by side. Each set of gears is staggered one-half tooth, as shown in **Figure 13-3.** This eliminates backlash noise common to straight-cut gear teeth. Since the gear teeth engage alternately (one tooth after the other), backlash and gear noise is held to a minimum.

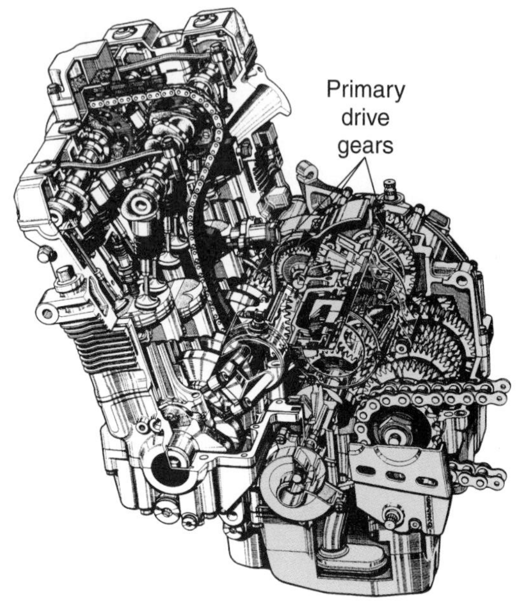

Figure 13-1. Primary drive causes the engine crankshaft to rotate the clutch and transmission. Either gears, as shown, or chain and sprockets may be used as the primary drive. (American Suzuki Motor Corporation)

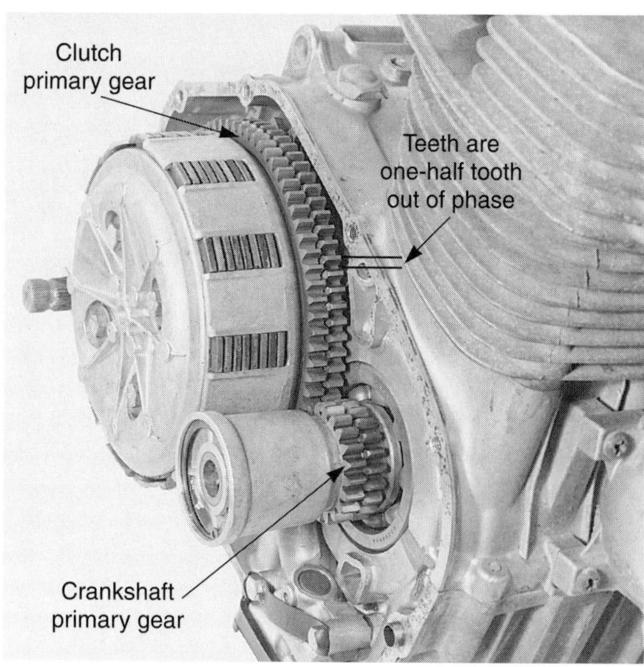

Figure 13-3. Since gear teeth in straight-cut, offset primary drives do not mesh at the same time, backlash noise is eliminated.

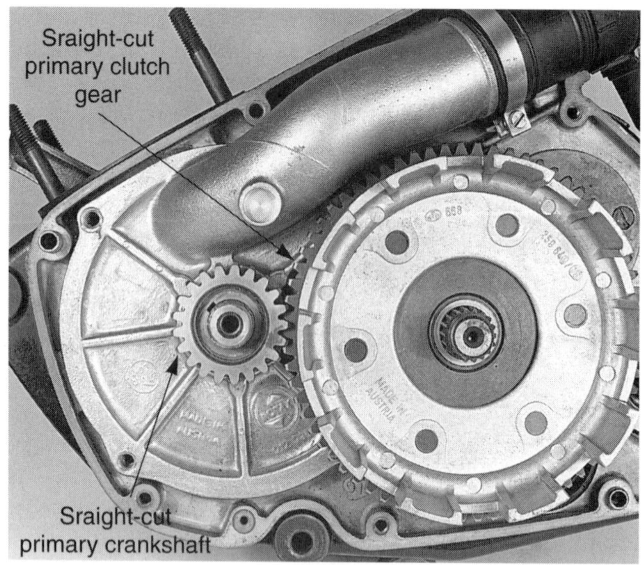

Figure 13-2. Backlash refers to the amount of free play between the engaged gear teeth. Backlash is necessary for unrestricted gear movement. Smaller primary gear on the engine powers the larger gear on the clutch.

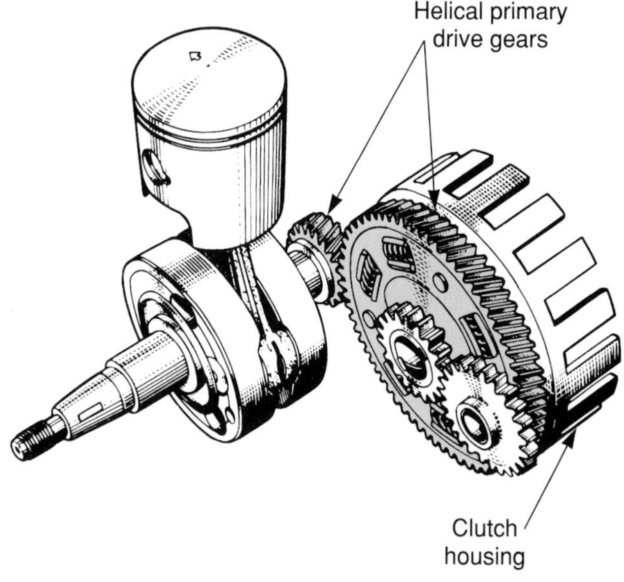

Figure 13-4. Helical primary drives use angled gear teeth for quiet operation. (American Suzuki Motor Corporation)

A ***helical gear drive*** uses angled gear teeth, **Figure 13-4.** A helical primary drive eliminates backlash noise since more than one tooth is engaged at all times. Angular gear tooth engagement reduces the need for backlash. Unfortunately, angular engagement also causes side thrust, **Figure 13-5.** The friction resulting from the side thrust may absorb a small amount of engine power. Application of each type of primary gear drive is dependent upon manufacturing budget, motorcycle use, acceptable gear noise, and power loss requirements.

Primary Chain Drive Systems

A typical ***primary chain drive system*** normally consists of a crankshaft sprocket, primary drive chain, clutch sprocket, and chain tensioner. **Figure 13-6** shows one type of primary chain drive. A small sprocket drives the primary chain. The primary chain drives a larger sprocket on the clutch. Depending upon the intended use, either single-row, double-row, triple-row, or a hy-vo chain may be employed. **Figure 13-7** illustrates triple-row and hy-vo primary drive chain mechanisms.

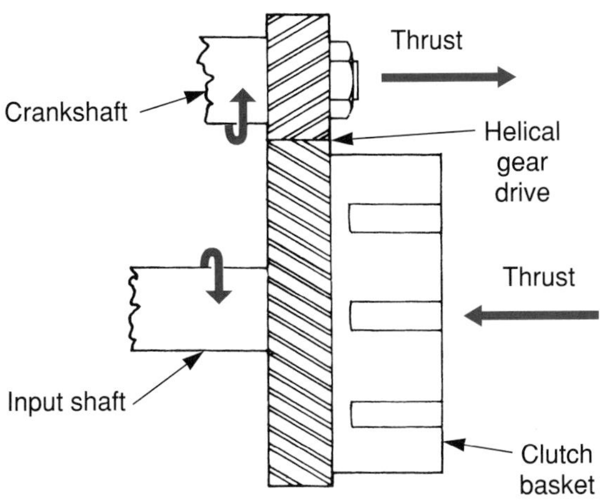

Figure 13-5. Helical primary drive gears will cause side thrust in one direction on the crankshaft and in the opposite direction on the clutch basket assembly.

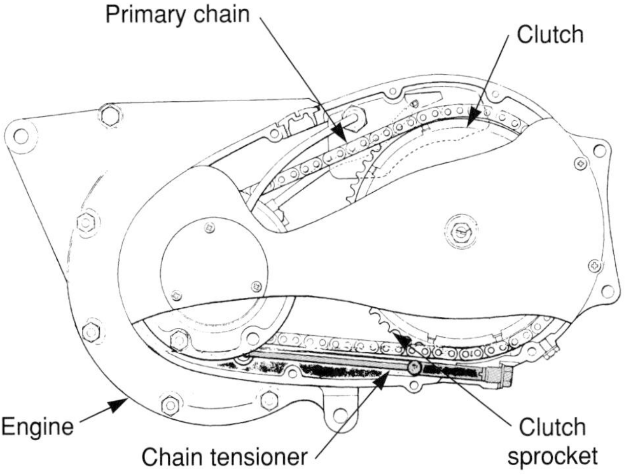

Figure 13-6. Chain primary drives are simple and efficient, but require periodic adjustment. (Triumph Motorcycles, Ltd.)

To compensate for wear, a ***chain tensioner*** is usually provided. It presses lightly on the chain's slack side to prevent slap (up and down movement and noise). The tensioner may be either manually or automatically adjusted.

Primary Belt Drive Systems

A primary ***belt drive system*** is similar to the primary chain system except that it uses a belt in place of a chain. It is often used with a centrifugal automatic clutch in ATVs. Belt primary drive systems offer lower horsepower loss, have a longer life, operate more quietly, and require less adjustment than a chain system.

Clutches

A ***clutch*** is provided to engage and disengage engine power to and from the transmission. When the clutch lever is pulled (clutch disengaged), the primary drive continues to turn, but power is not transferred to the input shaft. The clutch slips and the motorcycle does not move. As the clutch lever is released (engaged), the clutch gradually transfers power to the transmission input shaft. Internal spring pressure and friction lock the clutch plates together. Engine power is then transferred into the transmission final drive to the rear wheel and the motorcycle is propelled forward.

The relationship between the transmission primary drive, clutch, and input shaft is shown in **Figure 13-8.** Most clutches are placed between the primary reduction gears and transmission. With some models, however, they are attached directly to the crankshaft. Clutch actuation can be roughly divided into two types: the manual clutch controlled by the rider and the automatic clutch performing connection/disconnection of power according to engine load and speed.

Multi-Plate Clutch

A typical manual ***multi-plate clutch*** consists of:

- Clutch basket (housing).
- Clutch hub.
- Clutch drive (friction) plates.
- Clutch driven (steel) plates.
- Clutch pressure plate.
- Clutch springs.

A multi-plate clutch provides a very compact, high friction coupling between the engine and transmission, **Figure 13-9.** With multiple plates, the surface area, strength, and friction in the engaged clutch is increased. Depending on the engine size and the motorcycle's weight, 4-8 sets of drive and driven plates may be housed in the clutch basket.

Multi-Plate Clutch Action

The engine's primary chain or gear turns the ***clutch housing*** or *basket.* The clutch basket slots engage tabs on the friction drive plates, **Figure 13-10.** This causes the clutch housing and friction plates to rotate together.

The steel driven clutch plates have small inner teeth that engage with the outer teeth on the ***clutch hub.*** The driven plates are locked to the hub and the clutch hub is connected to the transmission input shaft. However, the driven plates are not locked to the basket. During clutch engagement, spring pressure locks the friction and steel plates together tightly. Then, the clutch basket, drive plates, driven plates, clutch hub, and transmission input shaft all spin together.

The clutch is released or disengaged when the clutch cable mechanism moves the clutch pressure plate away from the drive and driven plates. This relieves spring pressure holding the drive and driven clutch plates together, **Figure 13-11.** The plates float away from each other and slip. Power is no longer transmitted into the transmission. **Figure 13-12** shows the flow of engine power through the clutch.

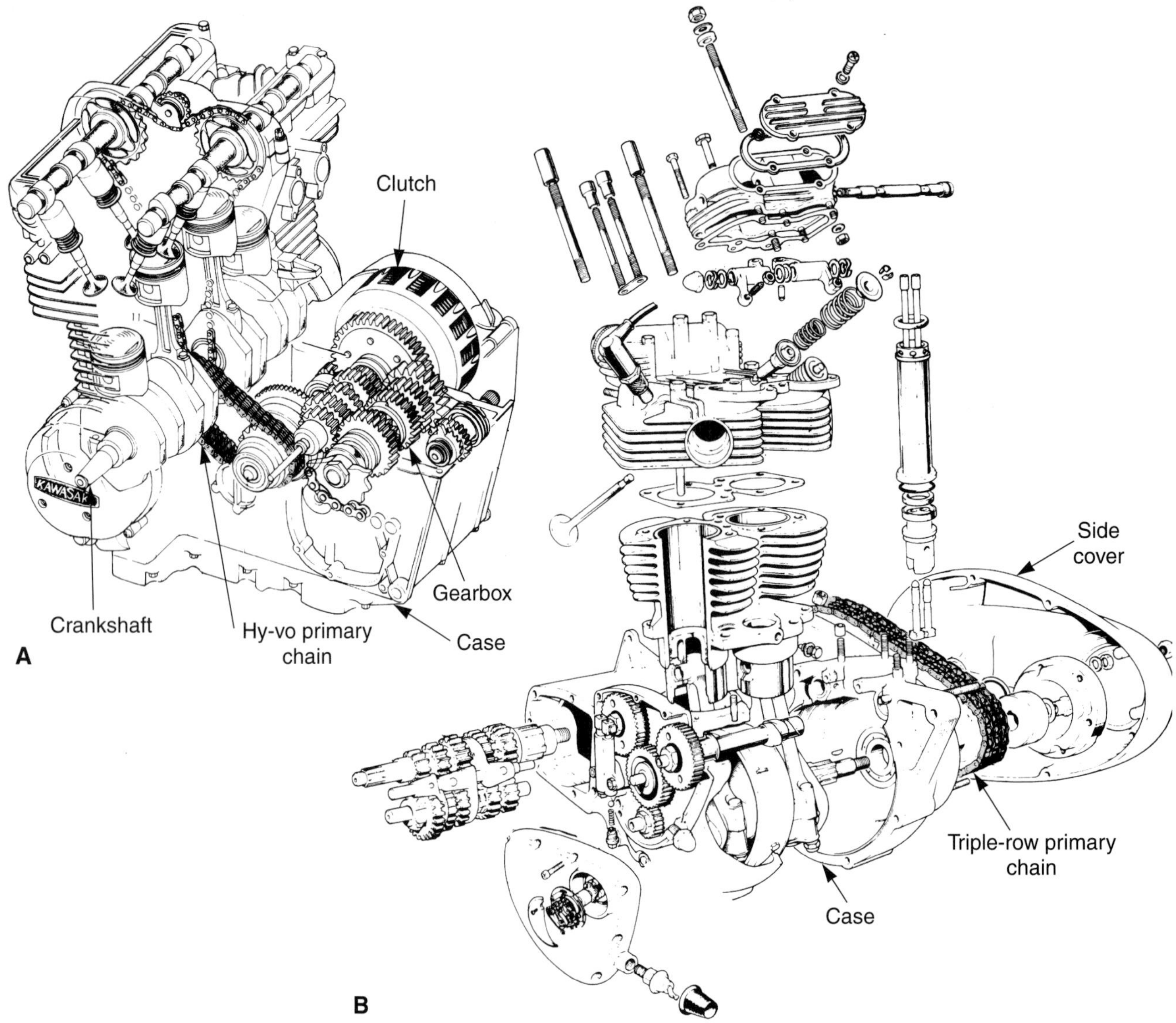

Figure 13-7. A—This engine uses a hy-vo primary chain which is very strong and quiet. This engine has the chain coming off the middle of the crankshaft. B—This engine uses a triple-row, roller primary chain. (Kawasaki Motors Corporation U.S.A.)

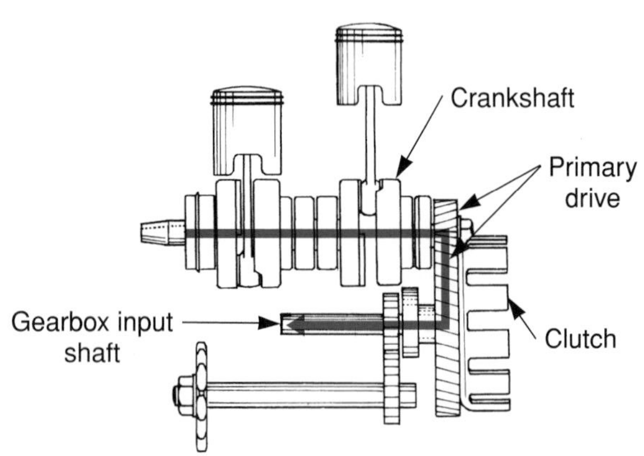

Figure 13-8. Power flows from the crankshaft through the primary drive to the clutch, and from the clutch to the transmission input shaft. (American Suzuki Motor Corporation)

Wet Clutch

The discs of a ***wet clutch*** operate in an oil bath (oil surrounds and covers discs). Most multi-plate clutches run in an oil bath. Wet clutches are used for several reasons:

- Since the primary drive needs lubrication, it is less costly to use a wet clutch.
- Debris resulting from clutch wear can be drained with the oil or trapped by the oil filter.
- Oil helps keep the clutch cool.

Dry Clutch

A ***dry clutch*** is designed to run without an oil bath. This requires the clutch to be sealed. Seals must be used to prevent the entry of oil into the clutch basket. Oil will

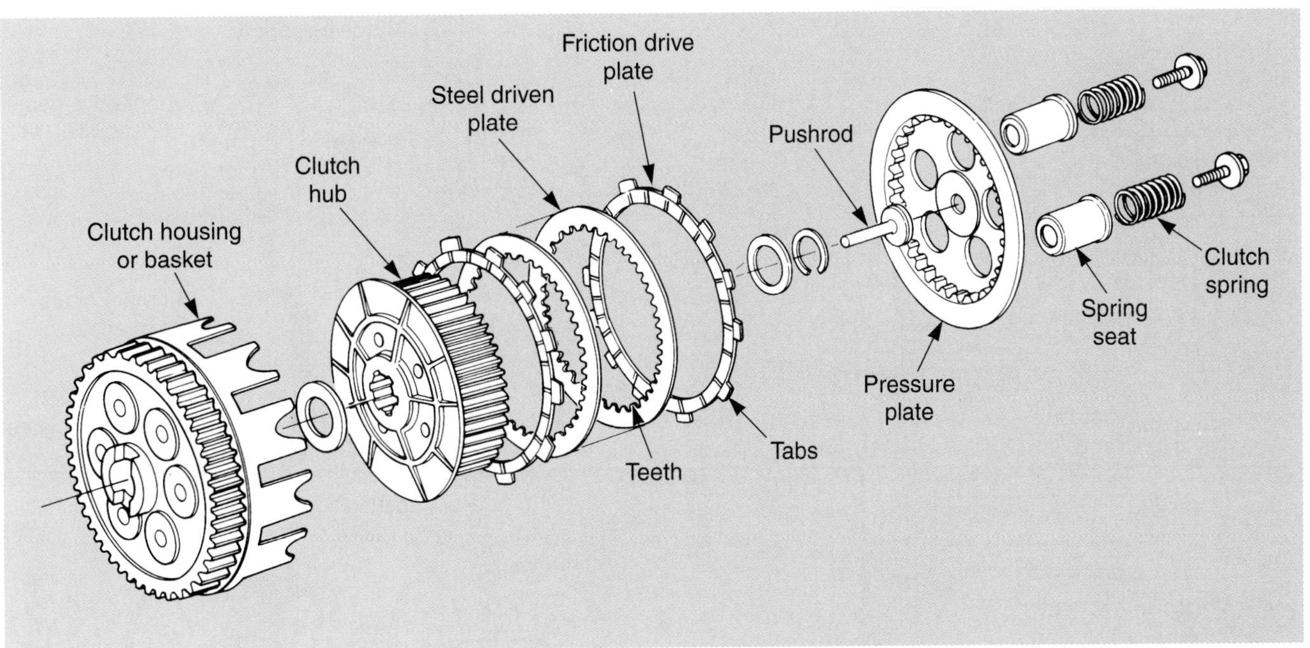

Figure 13-9. Drive plate tabs fit into the clutch basket slots. Driven plate teeth lock in the hub teeth. When the clutch is engaged, springs hold the plates together and power flows from the primary drive, through the clutch, and into the transmission. When the rider pulls the clutch lever, the pushrod compresses springs, moving the pressure plate away from the clutch plates, allowing the clutch to slip. The clutch basket and drive plates spin while the driven plates and transmission shaft remain stationary. (Kawasaki Motors Corporation U.S.A.)

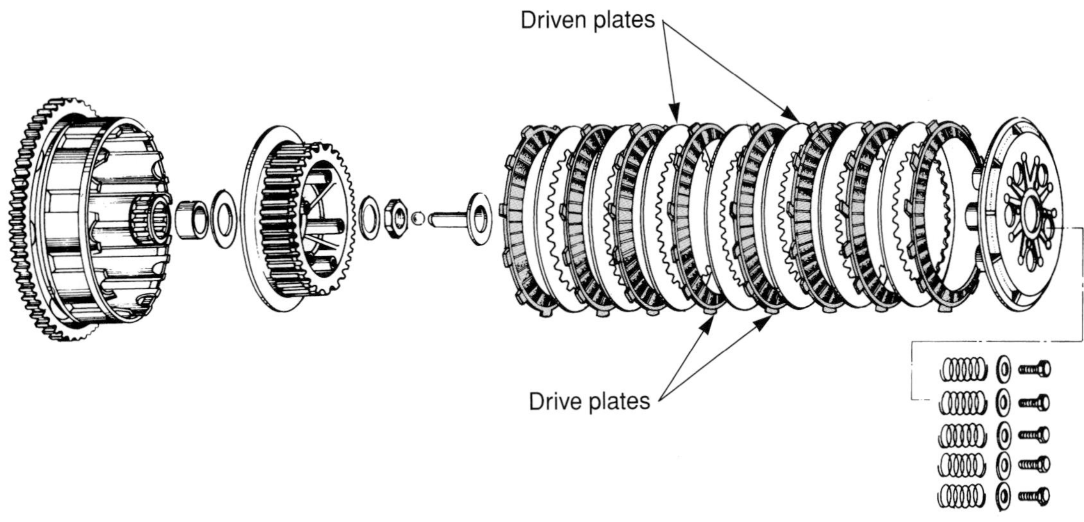

Figure 13-10. This clutch uses eight drive plates and seven driven plates. The drive plates are made of friction material while the driven plates are steel. (Kawasaki Motors Corporation U.S.A.)

cause clutch slippage, which can ruin the friction discs. Dry clutches can use either single plate or multiple plate construction.

Clutch Springs

There are two types of springs used in motorcycle clutches: coil springs and diaphragm springs. Both types of springs press the plates together to provide clutch engagement.

Coil Springs

Some motorcycle clutches use up to eight ***coil springs*** to provide force against the clutch pressure plate. On clutches using multi-coil springs, **Figure 13-13,** it is important for spring pressure to be equal. Unequal spring pressure can cause clutch drag, clutch slippage, chatter, vibration, and pressure plate runout (wobble) when disengaged.

On some designs, coil spring pressure is adjustable, **Figure 13-14.** Most designs, however, do not allow

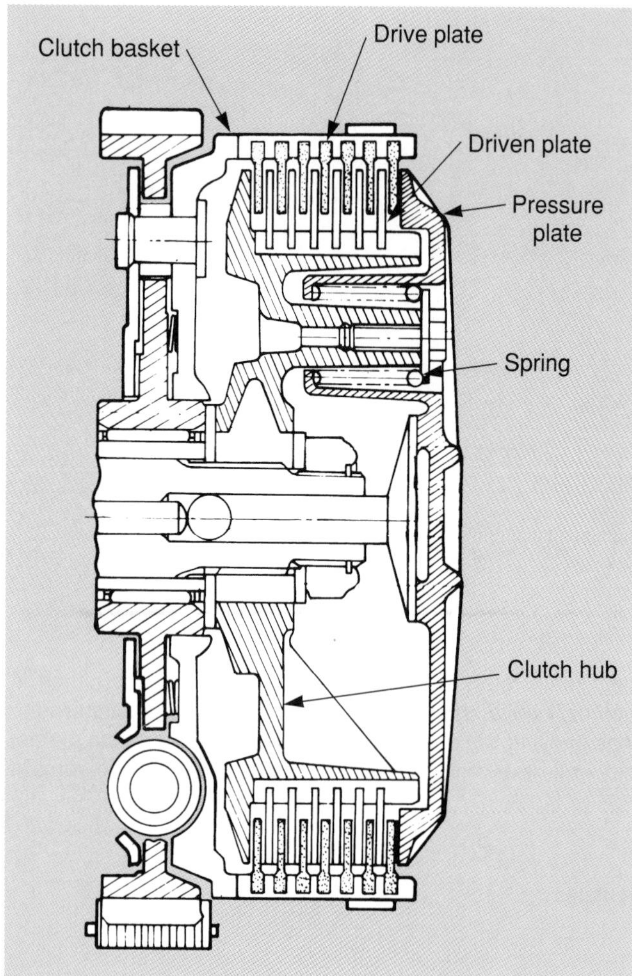

Figure 13-11. Clutch springs force the pressure plate toward the clutch hub. This causes the drive and driven plates to be locked tightly, engaging the clutch. (Kawasaki Motors Corporation U.S.A.)

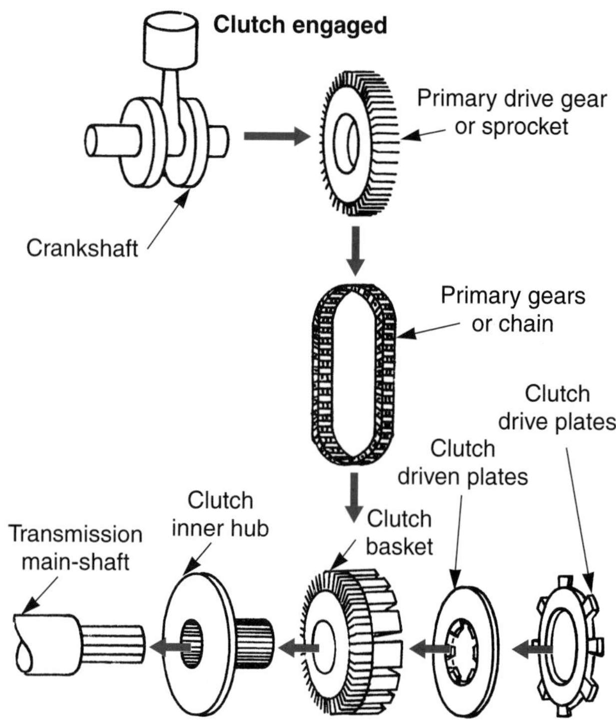

Figure 13-12. During clutch disengagement, power flow stops at the clutch drive plates. Drive and driven plates are separated.

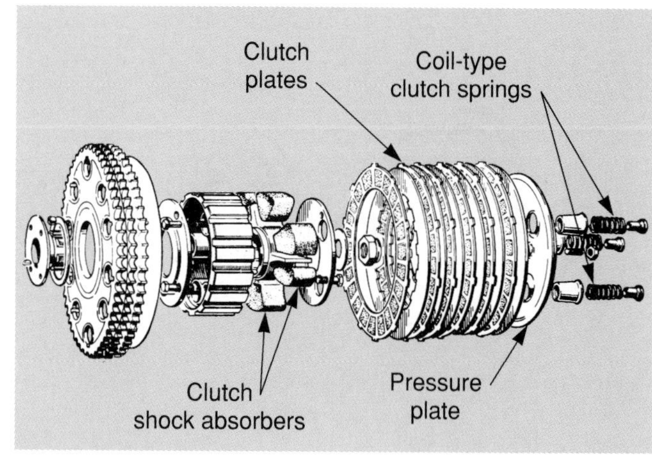

Figure 13-13. Three springs are used in this clutch. As many as eight springs are used in some designs. Springs force the pressure plate into the clutch plates to lock the clutch. (Triumph Motorcycles, Ltd.)

adjustment. Balanced pressure is achieved by replacing the spring set.

Diaphragm Springs

A ***diaphragm spring*** is a circular, conical disc made of spring steel. Partial flattening of the diaphragm against the pressure plate provides spring pressure, **Figure 13-15.** The diaphragm spring is commonly used in the ***single plate dry clutch.***

Clutch Shock Absorbers

Some manufacturers use a shock absorber in the primary drive or clutch. The purpose of the ***clutch shock absorber*** is to smooth out power pulses and shock going into the transmission. This reduces the harsh impact of transmission gear teeth as they strike each other during initial acceleration or when shifting gears.

Clutch shock absorbers also prevent damage to the primary drive, transmission, and final drive due to sudden changes in throttle opening or clutch engagement. There are several ways to absorb shock in the primary drive and transmission. **Figure 13-16** shows three of the most common designs.

One-Way Clutches

The ***one-way clutch*** or sprag clutch system is found in many primary drives used in conjunction with electric starter motors. Sprag clutches are used in electric starters because they provide extra protection for the motor when the engine engages. The one-way clutch allows the

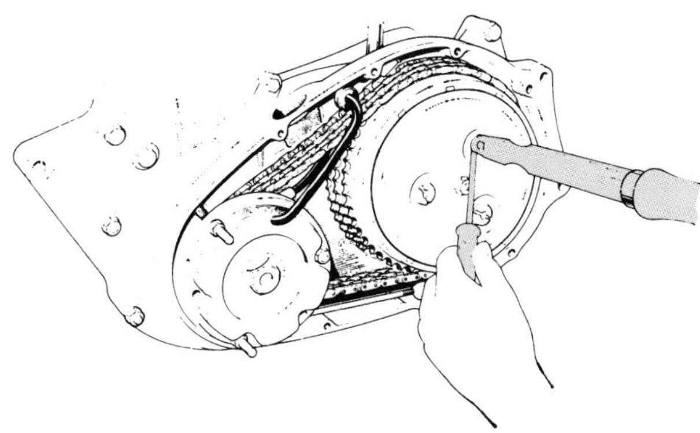

Figure 13-14. On some transmissions, clutch spring pressure is adjustable. Fasteners can be tightened to increase the pressure on clutch plates or loosened to lower pressure. However, equal adjustment is critical to proper operation. (Triumph Motorcycles, Ltd.)

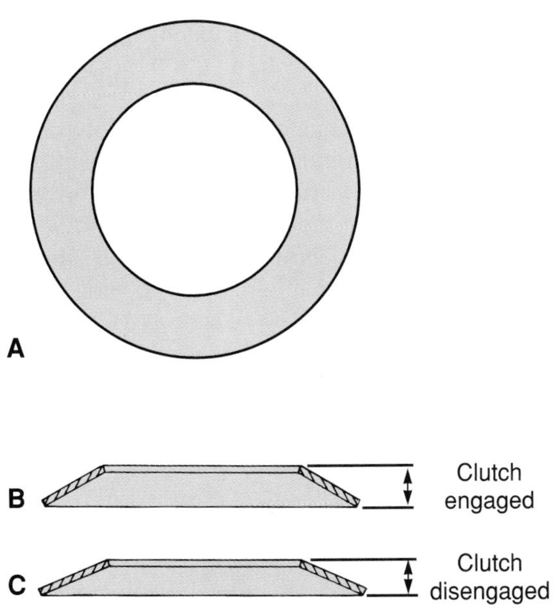

Figure 13-15. A—A diaphragm clutch spring is a circular disc of spring steel with a slightly conical (curved) cross section. B—Spring pressure is provided by partially flattening the spring. The spring is assembled between the pressure plate and clutch disc. C—Disengagement is accomplished by forcing the pressure plate against the spring.

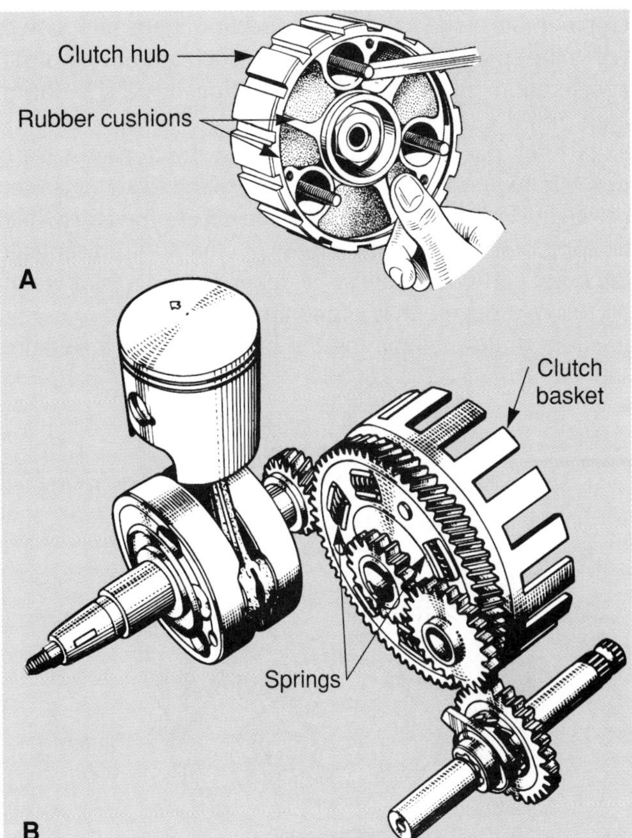

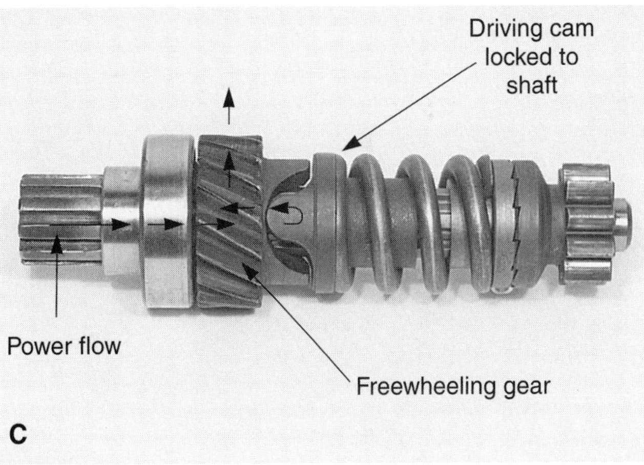

Figure 13-16. Rubber cushions, springs, and compensators are used to absorb the shock of engagement in primary drives. A—Clutch hub is mounted in rubber. B—Springs cushion the blow of rapid clutch engagement. C—Freewheeling gear forced against the driving cam absorbs shock and transfers power. (Triumph Motorcycles, Ltd. and American Suzuki Motor Corporation)

starter drive to disengage when engine speed exceeds the starter speed.

In addition, on rapid downshifting from high rpm, the braking force created by the engine's compression can exceed the rear wheel's traction and the engine becomes a rear wheel brake. This can cause momentary lockup of the rear wheel. If multiple downshifts are made, the result will be a much longer loss of traction. The one-way clutch system has been specifically designed to prevent this loss of traction.

The major difference between this system and a conventional multi-plate clutch is a two-piece clutch hub. The outer portion of the clutch hub, which controls the majority of the clutch plates and discs, is driven by a special one-way sprag clutch, **Figure 13-17.** The inner portion of the clutch hub is splined to the transmission's mainshaft and controls about two-fifths of the clutch plates and discs. This portion of the clutch transmits power and deceleration forces.

The outer portion of the clutch hub is not splined to the transmission's mainshaft. It controls the remaining clutch plates and discs. This portion transmits power when the sprag clutch is locked up, such as during normal acceleration, cruising, and deceleration. It will slip during high rpm deceleration.

Clutch backloading occurs when the transmission is downshifted from high rpm because of the force generated by engine compression. If the force causes the rear wheel to approach lock-up, the one-way clutch will disengage the outer portion and allow the inner portion to slip. It will do this to a degree that allows the rear wheel to maintain traction while maintaining the highest degree of engine braking. Rather than being a harsh on or off mechanism, the one-way clutch determines the correct amount of slip for each situation, while maintaining maximum engine braking.

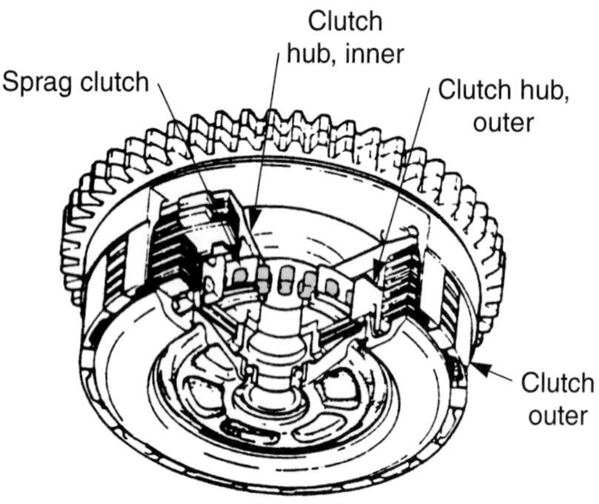

Figure 13-17. Typical one-way or sprag clutch system. (Honda Motor Co., Ltd.)

Centrifugal Clutch

A typical ***centrifugal clutch*** will engage and disengage automatically at a specific rpm. This is usually at engine speed just above idle. The clutch in **Figure 13-18** uses centrifugal force to cause engagement. This clutch is mounted on the end of the crankshaft. When the engine is running, the clutch basket, pressure plate, and drive plates spin with the crankshaft.

As engine speed is increased from idle, centrifugal force causes the rollers to fly outward against their cam ramps. The cam ramps force the rollers into the clutch, applying pressure to the primary drive plate. This locks the drive plates and driven plates together. As a result, the clutch hub and pinion gear turn with the crankshaft and drive the transmission.

When the centrifugal clutch is combined with the transmission, it has an independent mechanism to disengage the clutch by pedal motion when operating the gearshift. This is to disengage the clutch temporarily when changing gears, and to eliminate the pressure applied on the toothed surface to enable the gear to slide smoothly, resulting in an easier shift.

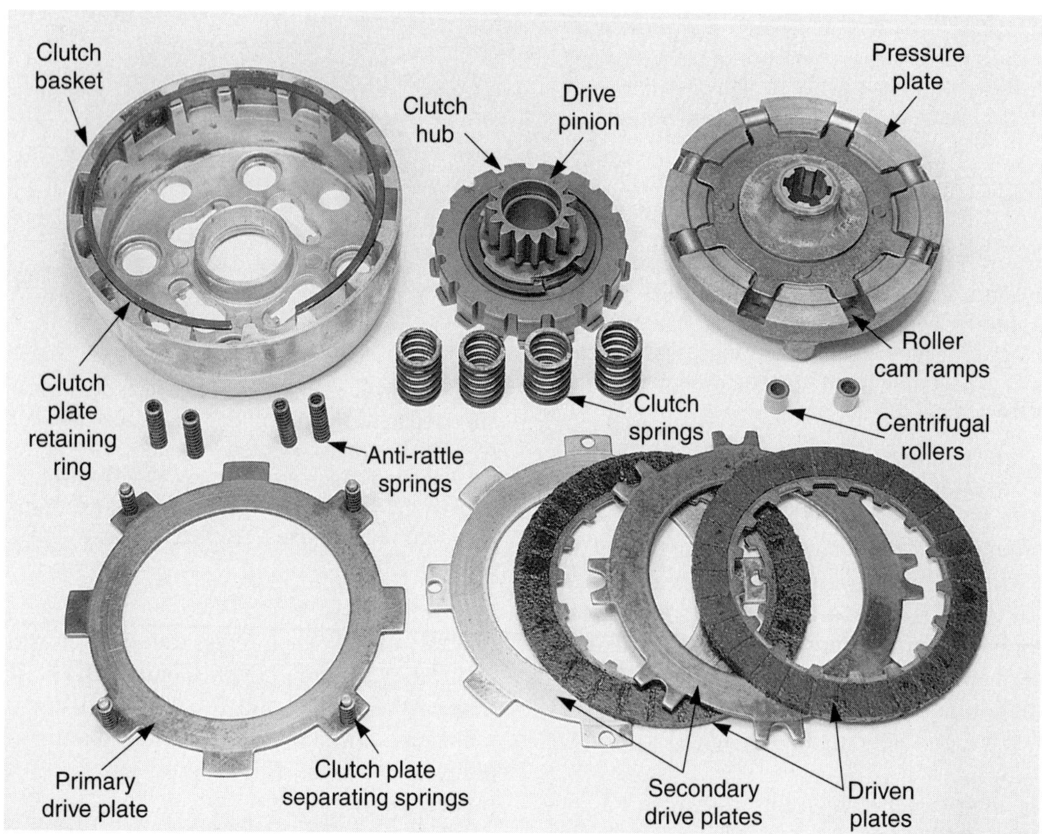

Figure 13-18. Weights and cams provide pressure to engage the centrifugal clutch as engine speed increases.

Some street motorcycles and ATVs are equipped with a centrifugal clutch that incorporates a sprag clutch. This arrangement provides some engine braking when the centrifugal clutch is disengaged, providing the rider with better vehicle control.

Manual Transmissions

A motorcycle or ATV ***manual transmission*** improves acceleration by allowing the rider to change the engine-to-rear-wheel drive ratio. In lower gears, the transmission ratio is increased to improve torque and acceleration. In high gear, the ratio is lowered for reduced engine speed, fuel consumption, engine noise, and wear.

Transmission Shafts

All motorcycle transmissions commonly use two shafts: the input shaft or *mainshaft,* and the output shaft or *countershaft.* The ***input shaft*** on manual transmissions is powered by a clutch mechanism, **Figure 13-19.** The clutch is mounted on one end of the input shaft. Gears on the input shaft drive gears on the output shaft.

The transmission ***output shaft*** normally has a sprocket mounted on its outer end. This sprocket is commonly referred to as a countershaft sprocket. It is used to drive the chain going to the rear wheel. The countershaft sprocket normally mounts on the side of the engine opposite the clutch. On a shaft drive design, the transmission and the final output shaft powers the driveshaft.

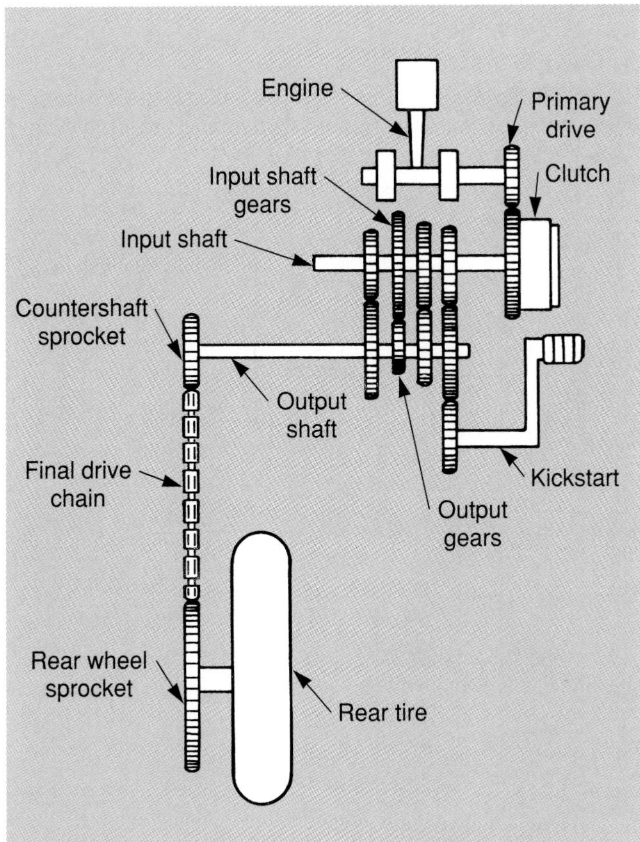

Figure 13-19. This illustration shows the main components of a motorcycle drive train. Note the two transmission shafts.

Multi-Speed Transmissions

A ***multi-speed transmission*** or *constant mesh transmission* consists of two shafts and two or more gears on each shaft. Operation of a multi-speed transmission is relatively simple, if you have a basic understanding of the principles involved. A few multi-speed transmission concepts are:

- One pair of gears (one on each shaft) is used for each transmission ratio, **Figure 13-20.**
- One gear may freewheel while the other gear is locked to the shaft, **Figure 13-21.**
- The larger the gear (more teeth) on the input shaft, the lower the gear ratio. The largest gear on the input shaft is high gear, **Figure 13-22.**
- The smaller the gear (less teeth) on the input shaft, the higher the gear ratio. The smallest gear on the input shaft is first or low gear.
- Typically, all gear teeth are meshed at all times (constant mesh). However, only one gear on the input shaft and its output mate transfer power (are both locked) when a speed is selected, **Figure 13-23.**

In the constant mesh transmission, the power is transmitted through the clutch to the mainshaft. From the mainshaft, power may be transmitted through several gear sets to the countershaft. As shown in **Figure 13-24,** M1 through M5 are the mainshaft gears and C1 through C5 are the countershaft gears. The gear sets are comprised of opposing gears, one gear on each shaft.

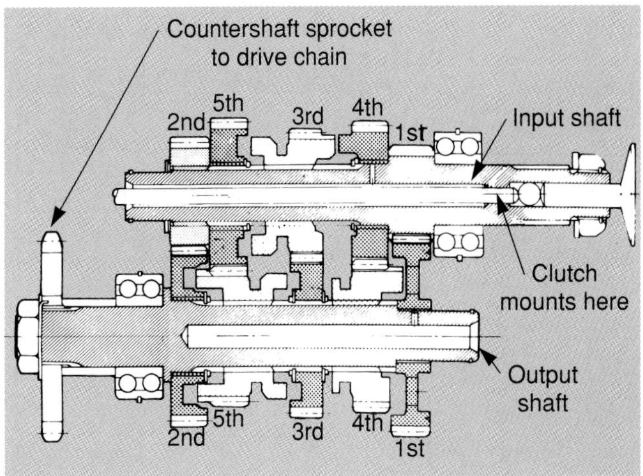

Figure 13-20. The input shaft is turned by the clutch. Power is transferred to the output shaft when the gears are engaged. A pair of gears must be used for each ratio. The countershaft sprocket is for the chain to drive the rear wheel. (Kawasaki Motors Corporation U.S.A.)

In the illustration, the gear sets, pairing the mainshaft number with the countershaft number (M1/C1, M2/C2, etc.) are shown.

Selection of the proper gear set is done by moving a sliding gear into contact with the gear set desired. Connection of the sliding gear and the gear set is done using dogs and dog holes on the sides of the gears. Gears M3, C4, and C5 are the sliding gears.

The sliding gears are moved by shift forks which ride on the shift drum. Cam grooves cut in the shift drum move the shift forks as the drum rotates. Shift drum rotation is done by working the gearshift pedal.

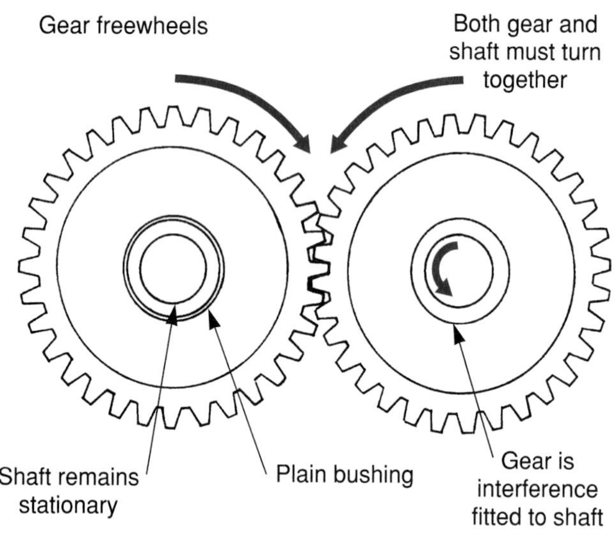

Figure 13-21. Each pair of gears in the transmission has one gear locked to the shaft. The other gear freewheels on the shaft until engaged.

Internal Gear Changing

In order to change drive ratios, a sliding gear or sliding dog splined to the manual transmission shaft,

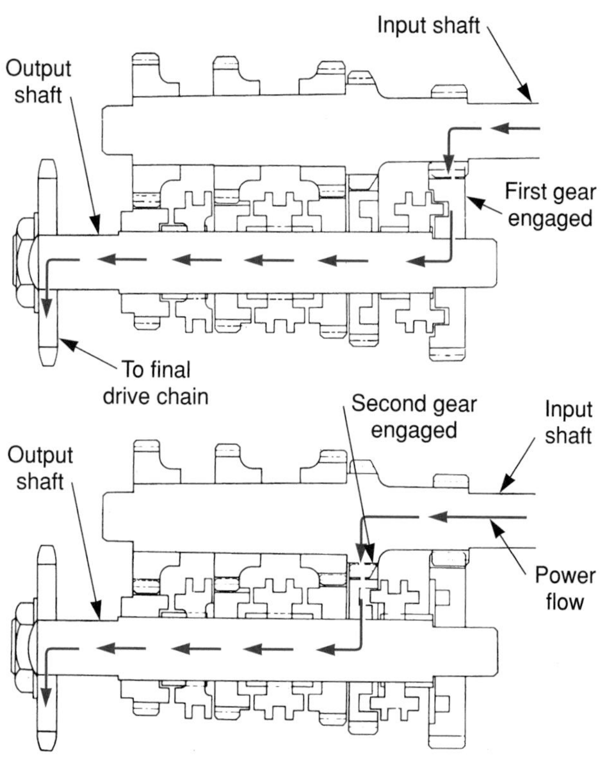

Figure 13-23. In a constant mesh transmission, each gear is always meshed with its mate on the other shaft. One pair of gears transfers power for each ratio.
(American Suzuki Motor Corporation)

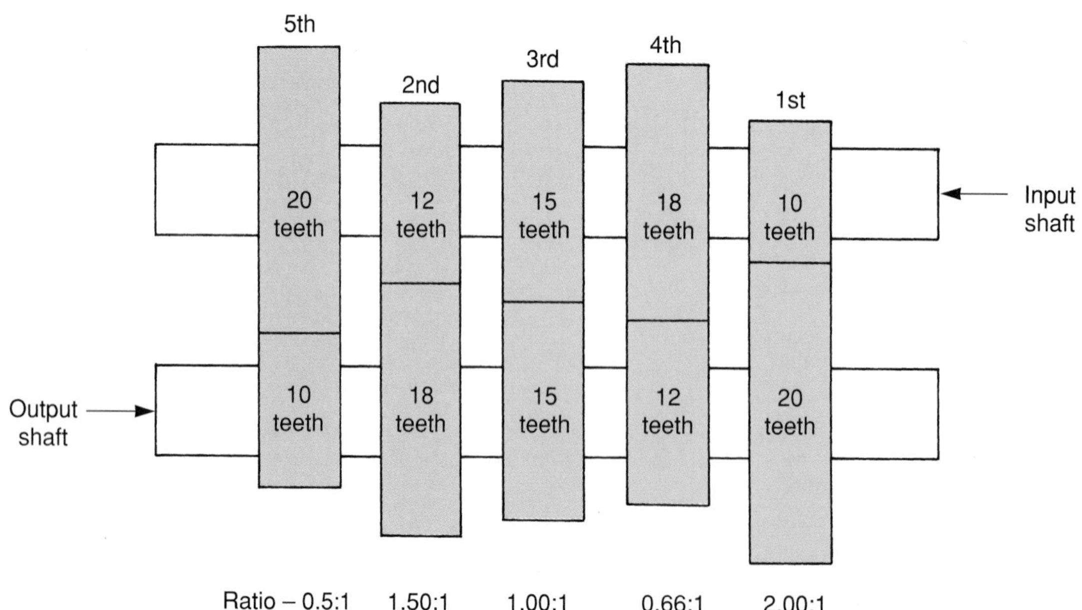

Figure 13-22. The smaller gear (1st gear) on the input shaft has the highest ratio (2:1) while the largest gear (5th gear) has the lowest ratio (.5:1).

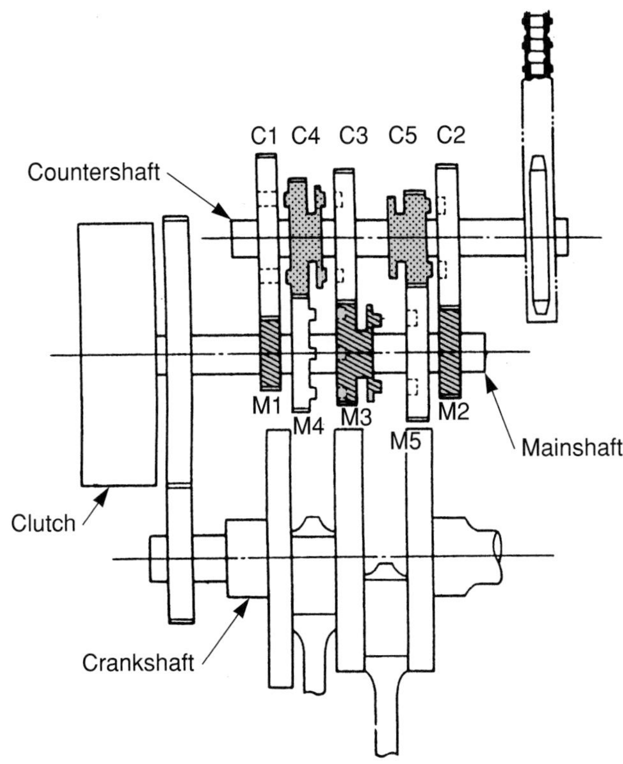

Figure 13-24. The action of a constant mesh transmission. (Honda Motor Co., Ltd.)

must be moved. The gear or dog must engage with the side of a freewheeling gear, **Figure 13-25.** This engagement will cause the freewheeling gear to be locked to its shaft.

To move a sliding gear or dog, a ***shifting fork,*** which is part of the gear selector mechanism, is required. See **Figure 13-26.** Most transmissions have two or three shifting forks.

Gear Selector Mechanisms

A ***gear selector mechanism*** changes the up and down (vertical) movement of the gear change lever to sideways (horizontal) gear movement in the transmission. There are two common types of gear selector mechanisms: drum and cam plate.

Drum Gear Selector

The parts which make up a ***drum gear selector*** are the shift lever, shift shaft, shift return spring, shift stop pin, shift ratchet, shift drum, shift fork, shift fork shaft, and shift drum locator plate. These components are illustrated in **Figure 13-27.** When the rider's foot moves the gearshift lever, the shift drum and forks slide the gears sideways. This determines which gears are engaged in the transmission.

Cam Plate Gear Selector

A ***cam plate gear selector mechanism*** uses a cam plate rather than a drum to move the shift forks. This type

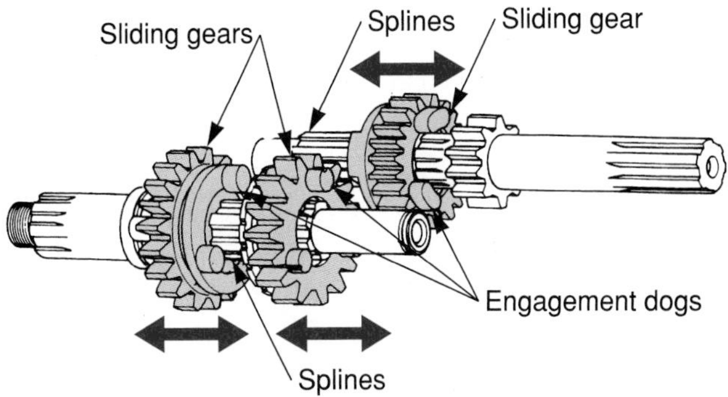

Figure 13-25. Sliding gears are locked on the shafts by splines. When they are moved sideways, engagement dogs mesh with engagement slots in the freewheeling gear. This locks the freewheeling gear to its shaft. (Kawasaki Motors Corporation U.S.A.)

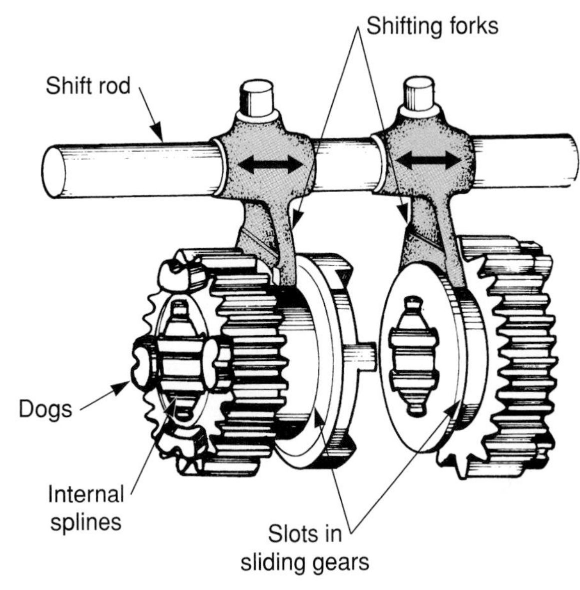

Figure 13-26. Shifting forks fit into slots in the sliding gears and control side movement. As the fork slides to one side, the gears also slide. (Kawasaki Motors Corporation U.S.A.)

of shift mechanism is shown in **Figure 13-28.** When the shift lever is operated, cam plate movement forces the shift fork to slide on the fork shaft.

Transmission Indexer

The ***transmission indexer*** is used to precisely locate the shift drum or cam plate into position for each gear. A spring-loaded arm and roller or spring-loaded plunger is used to keep the transmission gears properly engaged with each other. **Figure 13-29** shows how a shift drum or cam plate is located by its indexer. Accurate gear location is achieved by the indexer dropping into a dimple, recess, or gap between two pins on the shift drum. The outside edge of the cam plate is notched for indexer engagement.

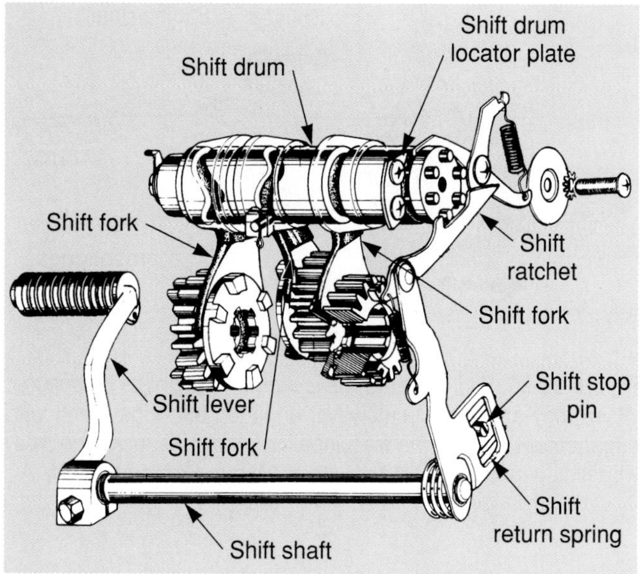

Figure 13-27. In this gear selector mechanism, shift forks are located on the shift drum rather than a separate shaft. Shift linkage movement ratchets the shift drum into new position, which moves the forks. (Kawasaki Motors Corporation U.S.A.)

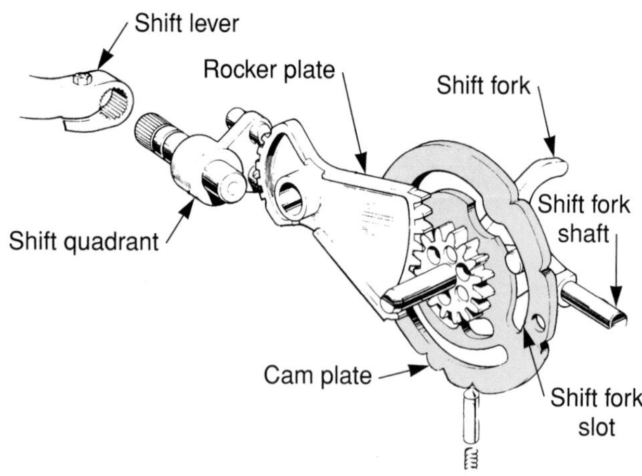

Figure 13-28. Cam plate shift mechanism uses a flat plate with slots that moves the shift forks. Slots force the shift forks over to change gears. (Triumph Motorcycles, Ltd.)

Neutral Indicator Switch

Many drum shift mechanisms have a ***neutral indicator switch*** which operates an indicator light. This switch, **Figure 13-30,** is normally located opposite the shift arm on the end of the drum. It illuminates a small instrument light when the transmission is in neutral.

When the shift drum is in the neutral position (between first and second gear), a tab or pin on the drum makes contact with a metal strip in the switch. This completes the circuit to the neutral indicator lamp. **Figure 13-31** shows how a neutral indicator switch operates.

Shift Drum Location Device

As the shift drum rotates, it causes the shift forks to move sideways. Side loads are produced. This requires that the shift drum have very little end play. For transmission shifts to be accurate, the shift drum must be precisely located. A ***shift drum location device*** serves this function. Shown in **Figure 13-32,** there are three common methods of locating shift drums:

- Flat plate engaged into a radial slot on the drum.
- A shouldered bolt engaged in a radial slot on the drum.
- Shouldered crankcase halves encasing the shift drum.

Shift Stopper

To prevent overshifting (movement past the desired gear), the transmission may have a ***shift stopper.*** A shift stopper functions by limiting shift linkage travel or shift drum rotation. There are two types of shift stoppers: shift stopper pin and shift stopper linkage. **Figure 13-33** shows both types.

Gear Engagement

Modern motorcycle transmissions use two means of gear engagement and directions of power flow. ***Gear engagement*** is normally accomplished by gear dogs,

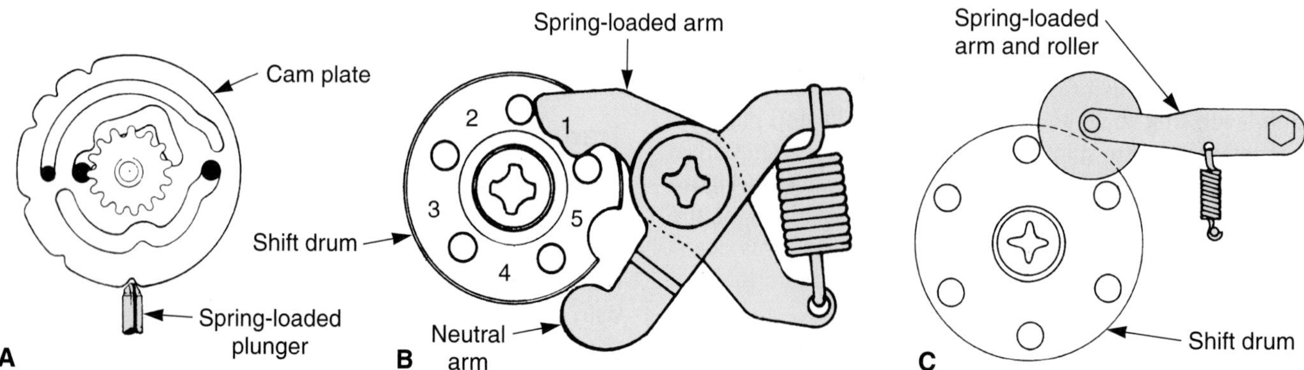

Figure 13-29. Three common methods of indexing transmissions. A—Spring-loaded plunger. B—Spring-loaded arm. C—Spring-loaded roller. (Triumph Motorcycles, Ltd.)

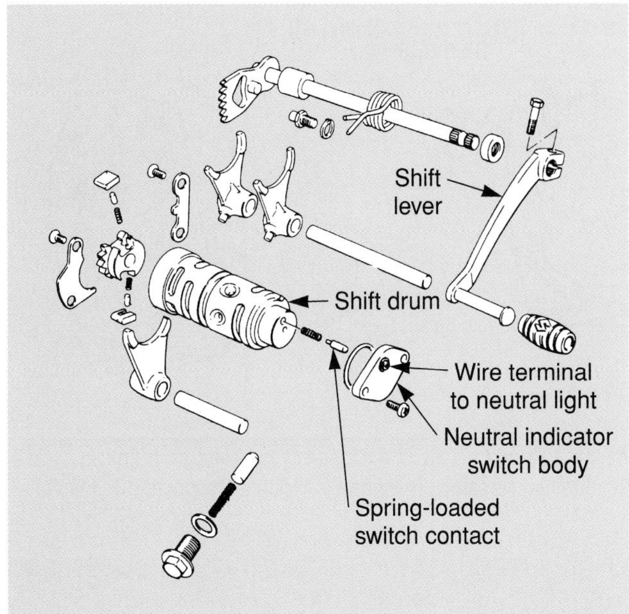

Figure 13-30. The neutral indicator switch is usually located on the end of the shift drum, opposite the shift mechanism. With the transmission shift lever in neutral, the switch closes and the neutral light illuminates. (American Suzuki Motor Corporation)

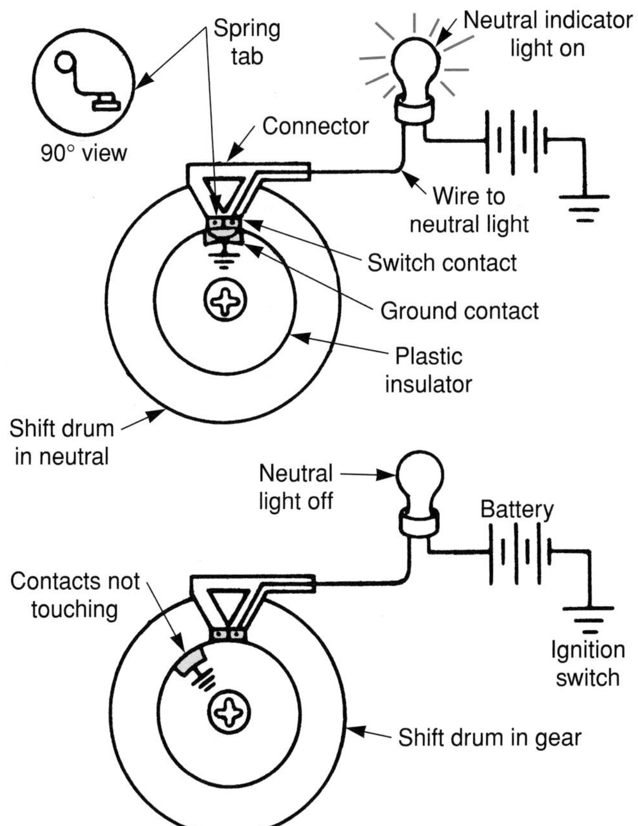

Figure 13-31. When the shift drum is in neutral, the metal contacts on the shift drum and neutral switch line up. This completes the circuit to the neutral indicator light. When the transmission is in gear, the contacts do not line up and the circuit is open.

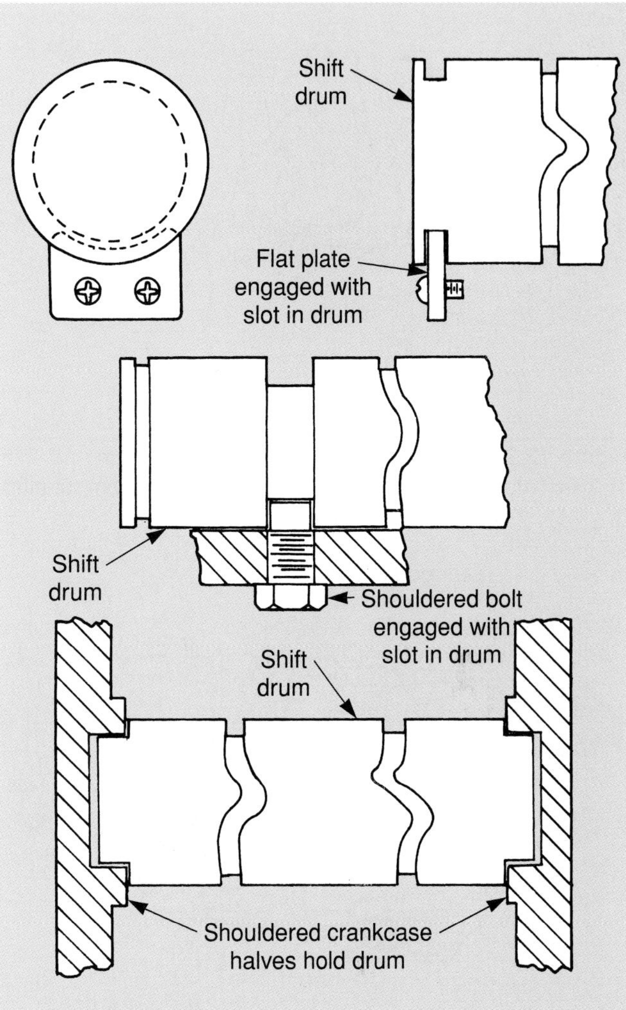

Figure 13-32. These three methods are used to control shift drum location.

Figure 13-34. Dogs are also found on the sides of gears or on sliding dog assemblies. See **Figure 13-35.** The function of both types of dogs is to lock a freewheeling gear to its shaft and cause power flow.

Transmission Types

Common gearbox designs use two methods of directing power through the transmission: direct drive and indirect drive.

Direct Drive Transmission

In most cases, the ***direct drive transmission*** has the clutch and countershaft sprocket located on the same side of the engine. One is shown in **Figure 13-36.** The transmission input shaft passes through the middle of the drive chain's countershaft sprocket. The countershaft sprocket is splined to the high gear pinion assembly. The second shaft is called the ***layshaft,*** **Figure 13-37.** All ratios in a direct drive transmission end up driving the countershaft sprocket through high gear.

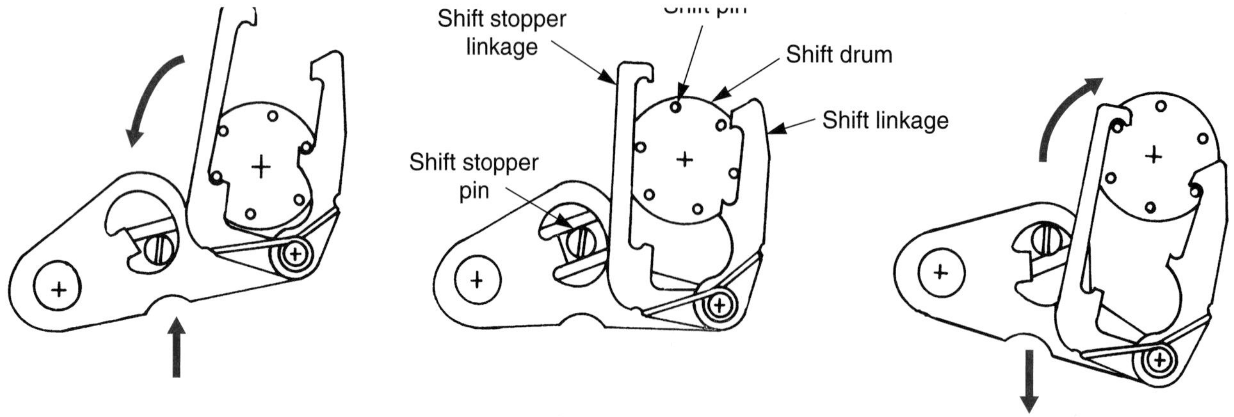

Figure 13-33. In this design, both a shift stopper pin and shift stopper linkage are used. The stopper pin limits shift linkage travel. The shift stopper linkage prevents the shift drum from rotating past the desired position. (Kawasaki Motors Corporation U.S.A.)

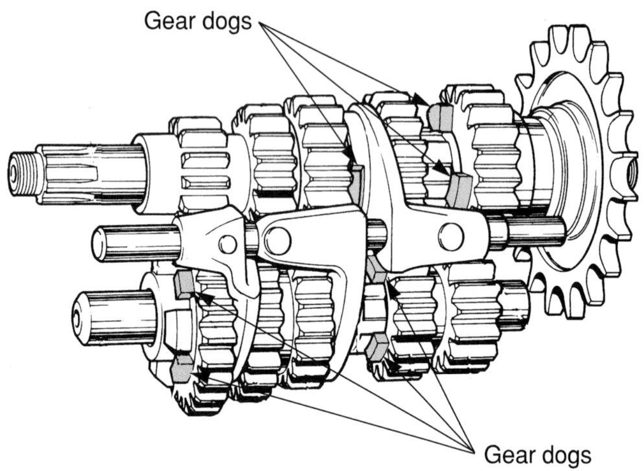

Figure 13-34. When the shift fork moves, it engages the gear dogs on the sides of neighboring gears. This locks the free-wheeling gear to the shaft and causes power transfer. (Triumph Motorcycles, Ltd.)

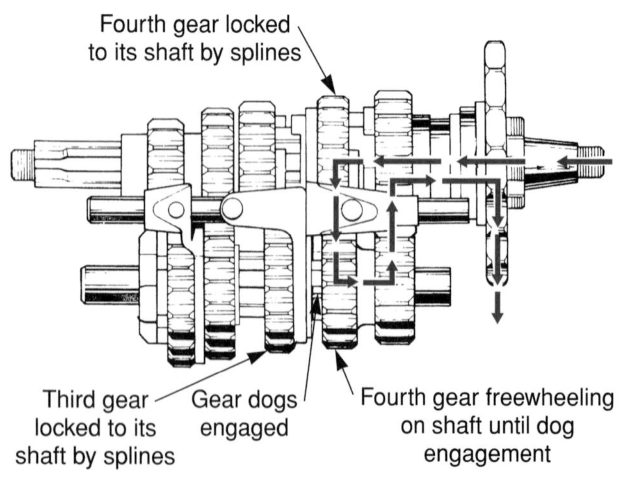

Figure 13-35. The splined third gear has been moved by its shifting fork so that its dogs are engaged with the dogs on the freewheeling fourth gear. This locks the freewheeling fourth gear and causes it to transfer power. (Triumph Motorcycles, Ltd.)

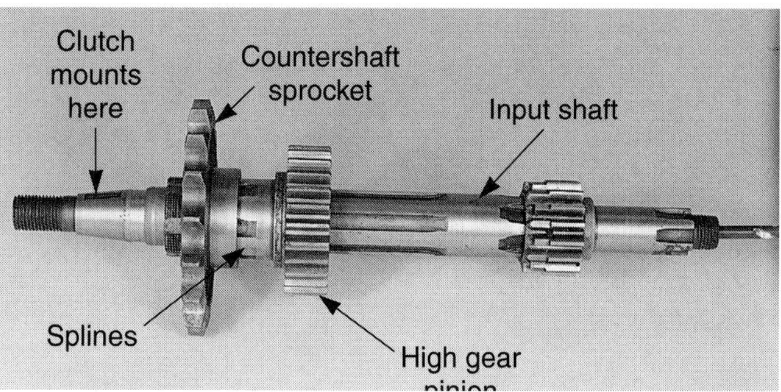

Figure 13-36. The clutch mounts on a keyed taper at the left end of the input shaft. A countershaft sprocket is mounted on splines on the high gear pinion. All ratios drive through high gear pinion.

Indirect Drive

The clutch and countershaft sprocket are located on opposite sides of the engine with an ***indirect drive transmission.*** This is illustrated in **Figure 13-38.** Power enters the transmission on the other shaft (output shaft), **Figure 13-39.**

Dual-Range Transmissions

The ***dual-range transmission*** is used on some small trail motorcycles, touring bikes, and some ATVs because it provides a dual-range gear ratio for both on- and off-highway use. The dual-range transmission has an auxiliary transmission, often called a *subtransmission,* located between the conventional transmission and final drive in the power flow system. The dual transmission is

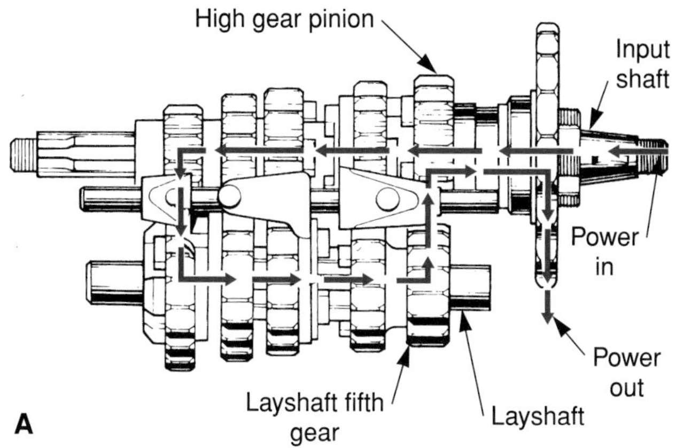

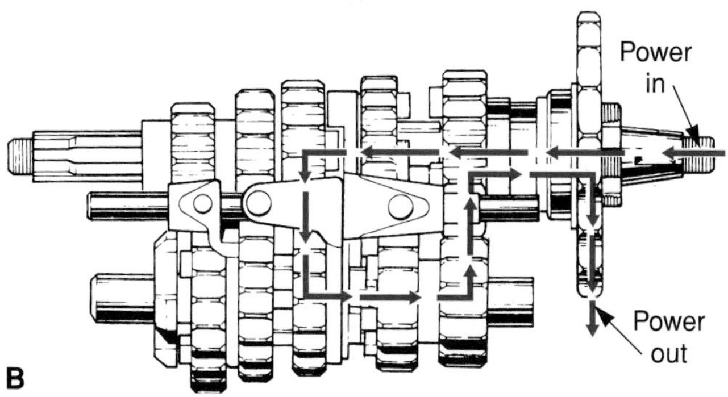

Figure 13-37. Since the countershaft sprocket is attached to the high gear pinion in a direct drive transmission, all ratios must drive through high gear. Power comes through the input shaft to the selected gear and power is then transferred to the layshaft. The splined layshaft fifth gear transfers power to the high gear pinion and countershaft sprocket in all gears except fifth. A—First gear. B—Third gear. (Triumph Motorcycles, Ltd.)

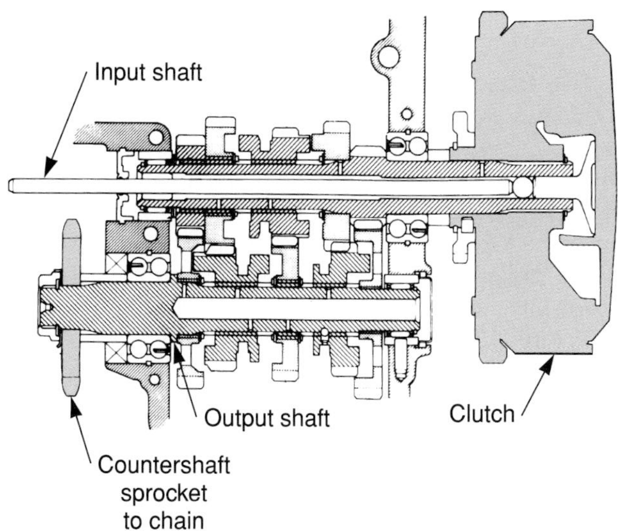

Figure 13-38. An indirect drive transmission has its clutch and countershaft sprocket on opposite sides. The primary chain or gear is on one side and the countershaft sprocket and chain to the rear wheel is on the other. (Kawasaki Motors Corporation U.S.A.)

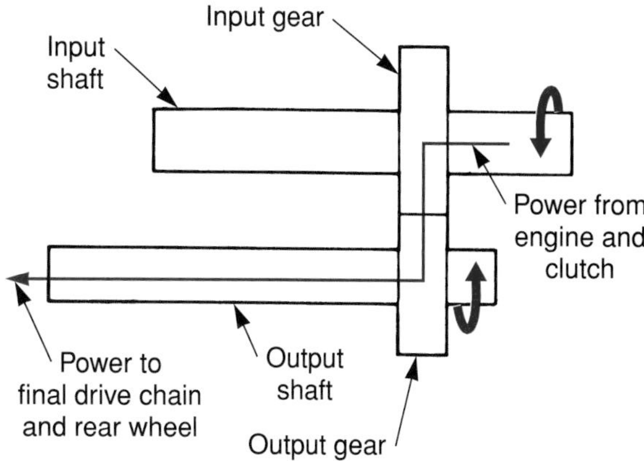

Figure 13-39. With an indirect drive transmission, power comes into the gearbox on the input shaft and leaves on the output shaft. This is the most common transmission design.

a two-speed, high and low, manual shift gearbox consisting of an input shaft, four gears, output shaft, and some type of damping device. A conventional five-speed transmission becomes a ten-speed when coupled with an auxiliary transmission.

Automatic Transmissions

Semiautomatic and automatic transmission systems feature a centrifugal clutch/belt arrangement. This design is very popular in automatic ATVs, **Figure 13-40.**

Automatic Centrifugal Clutch/Belt Transmissions

Centrifugal clutch/variable belt transmissions provide variable drive ratios between the engine and rear wheel according to engine speed and load. It accomplishes this with two sets of pulleys, connected by a drive belt. The drive pulley is attached to the engine crankshaft. The driven pulley is attached to a shaft that incorporates a centrifugal clutch. In the belt drive, there is a final gear reduction between the driven pulley and rear wheel, providing an increase in torque, **Figure 13-41.**

When the engine is running at low speed, the unit increases or multiplies torque. This delivers more torque than at higher engine speed at a greater drive ratio. As engine speed increases, or the load on the rear wheel decreases, centrifugal force on the weight rollers throws the rollers outward. When the rollers are forced outward, they push the drive pulley's movable face closer to the drive face. The result is a reduced drive ratio between the pulleys.

The drive pulley consists of a fixed and movable face. The movable face is capable of sliding axially on the shaft of the fixed face. The ramp plate, which pushes the weight rollers against the drive face, is attached to the

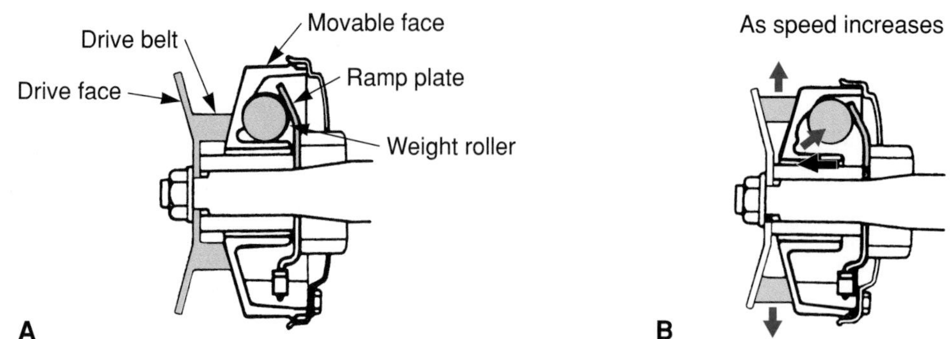

Figure 13-40. The centrifugal clutch/belt arrangement found in many ATVs. (Yamaha Motor Corporation U.S.A.)

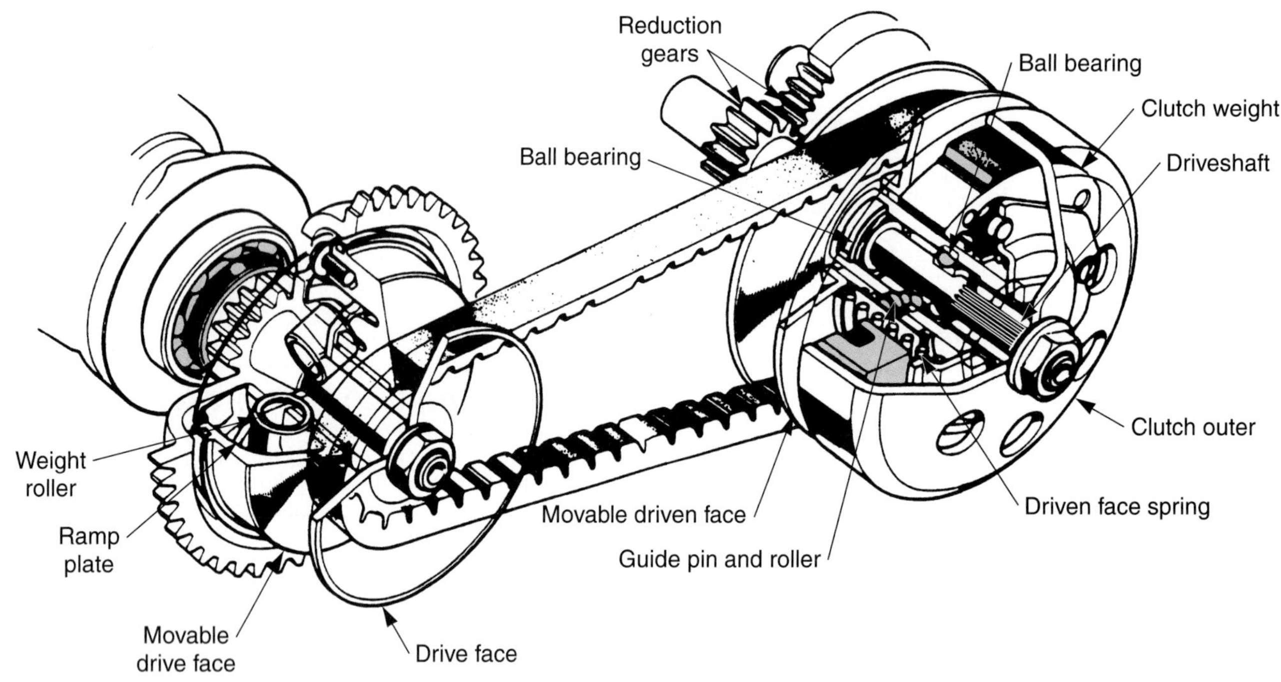

Figure 13-41. Parts and operation of a V-belt drive. (Honda Motor Co., Ltd.)

shaft with a nut. As engine rpm increases, centrifugal force on the weight rollers is increased. This pushes the movable drive face toward the fixed face. This reduces the ratio by allowing the drive belt to run on a pulley of greater diameter.

The centrifugal clutch is disengaged when the engine speed is low. When engine speed increases, the rotating clutch shoes will move outward as centrifugal force increases, **Figure 13-42A.** In this way, the clutch is automatically engaged. The belt is pushed out toward the drive pulley face circumference as engine speed increases. As the belt remains constant in length, the belt, in turn, is pulled in toward the center of the driven face, pushing out the movable face and compressing the driven face spring, **Figure 13-42B.** This mechanism decreases the diameter of the belt on the driven pulley at high engine speed.

When engine speed decreases, the belt is pulled back toward the center of the drive pulley releasing the tension on the belt. This allows the driven face spring to force the movable driven face toward the original position, pushing the belt back toward the driven pulley. The reduction ratio varies with engine speed automatically, without the need to manually shift between gear ratios. For instance, when the rider opens the throttle while driving up a slope, the sliding pulley moves toward the fixed pulley. This causes the V-belt to move toward the perimeter of the secondary pulley resulting in higher reduction ratio or a "downshift" effect.

Figure 13-43 illustrates the forward, neutral, and reverse operation of a typical ATV centrifugal clutch/belt transmission.

Planetary Gearshifts

A ***planetary gearshift*** is compact, quiet, and strong. As shown in **Figure 13-44**, the planetary gearshift is comprised of a shift spindle assembly, guide plates, drum shifter, and two stopper assemblies. The shift spindle assembly is comprised of the shift spindle, and the three planetary gears in constant mesh. A ***planetary gearset*** is

Drive pulley
Driven pulley
A
Drive pulley
Driven pulley
B

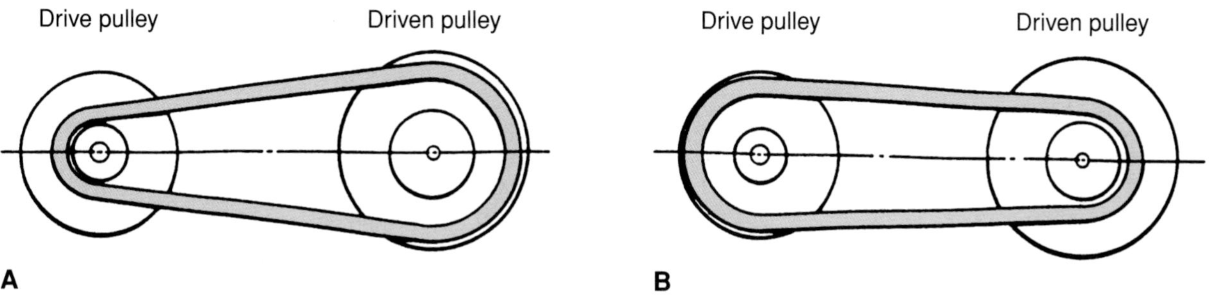

Figure 13-42. The pulley movement of a centrifugal clutch system. A—The belt is low at low speeds. B—As engine speed increases, the belt moves outward by centrifugal force. (Honda Motor Co., Ltd.)

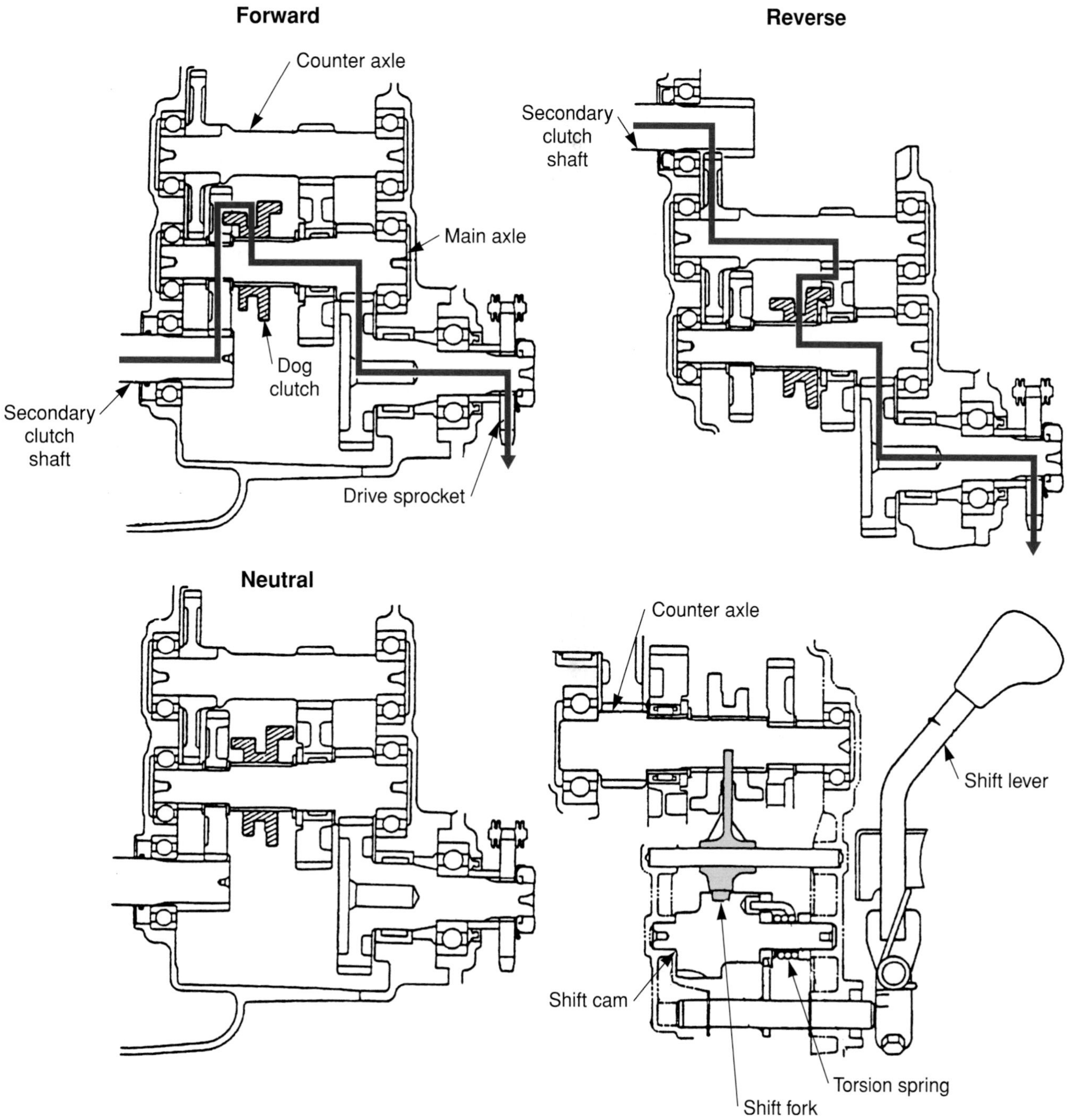

Forward
Counter axle
Main axle
Dog clutch
Secondary clutch shaft
Drive sprocket
Reverse
Secondary clutch shaft
Neutral
Counter axle
Shift lever
Shift cam
Torsion spring
Shift fork

Figure 13-43. Drive ratio changes in a centrifugal clutch transmission. (Honda Motor Co., Ltd.)

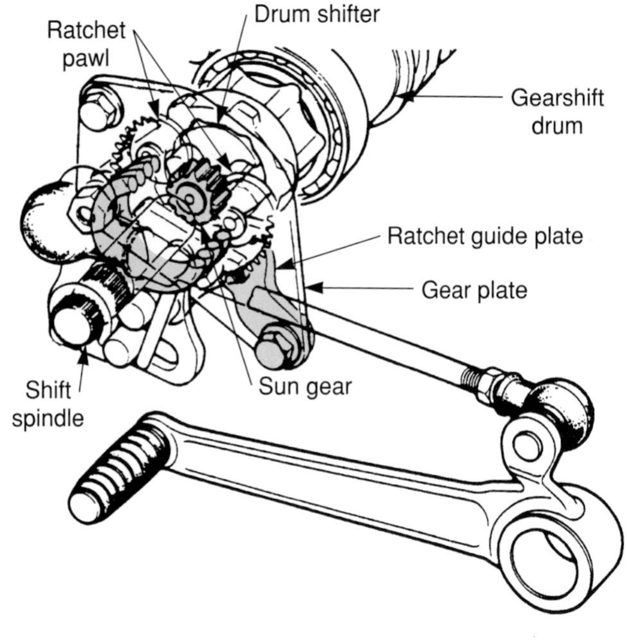

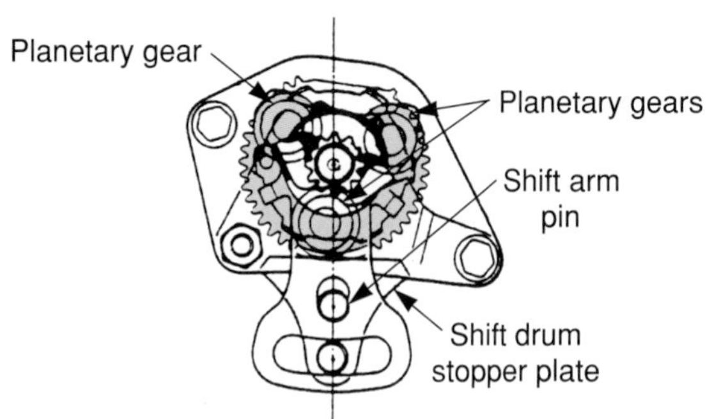

Figure 13-44. Components of a planetary gear shift. (Honda Motor Co., Ltd.)

able to step up the output shaft speed while reducing torque. It can also be used to reduce output speed, thereby increasing torque.

The shift spindle assembly, plus the guide plates, transmit the gear shifter movement to the sun gear on the drum shifter. As the drum shifter turns, one of its pawls will engage a detent in the shift drum, turning the drum. Turning the drum causes the shift forks to move by the same cam action as with the conventional multi-speed shift mechanism. The two stopper assemblies locate the shiftg drum at the proper gear and neutral positions. the operation of a typical planetary gearshift is as follows:

- ***Shift start,* Figure 13-45A.** Pushing down on the shift pedal turns the spindle counter-clockwise. Because the gear plate is fixed, the planetary gears turn clockwise, turning the drum shifter counter-clockwise. As the drum shifter turns counter-clockwise, the right pawl engages the detent in the shift drum, while the left pawl is pushed out of the way into the shifter by the guide plate. With the pawl engaged, the drum shifter turns the shift drum, moving the shift forks into place.
- ***Shift finish,* Figure 13-45B.** To prevent the drum from rotating too far, a shift drum stopper plate is used. The shift drum stopper plate rotates on an eccentric pivot moved by the spindle assembly. As the spindle reaches the end of its travel, one leg of the stopper plate is moved up to contact a positive stop on the shift drum. A the same time the spindle assembly is prevented from moving too far by the shift arm stopper pin.
- ***Shift return,* Figure 13-45C.** When the shift pedal is released, the shift return spring brings the spindle assembly back to the centered position. At this time, the drum shifter rotates and the ratchet feature allows the right pawl to disengage from the shift drum. As the drum shifter rotates, the drum stopper arm prevents the shift drum from moving.

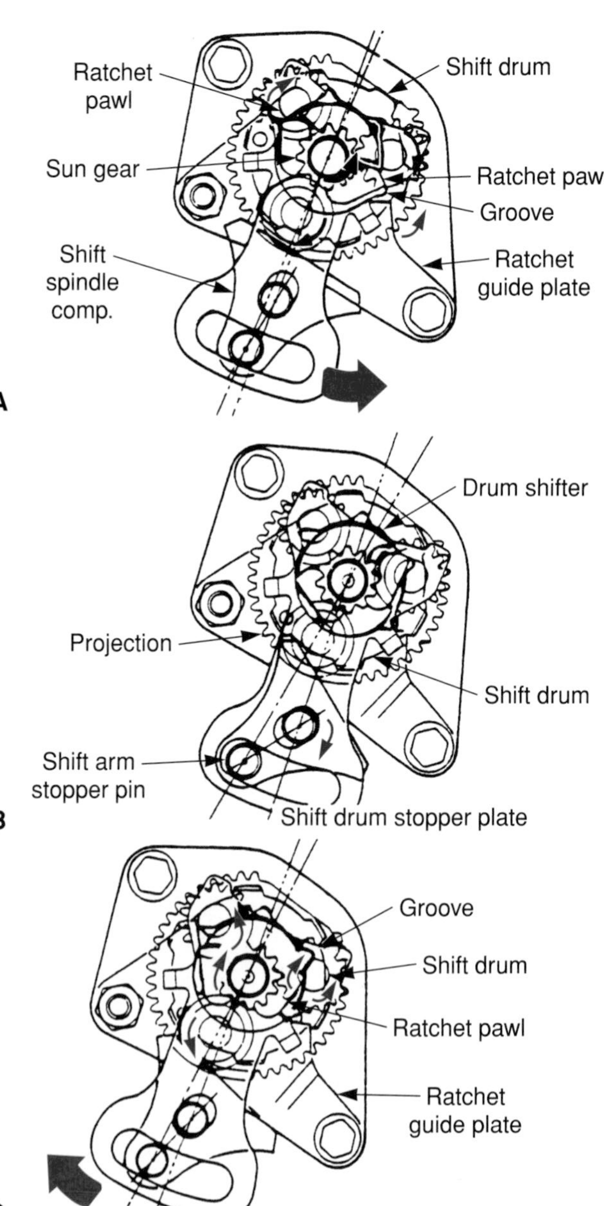

Figure 13-45. Operation of a planetary gear shift. (Honda Motor Co., Ltd.)

Final Drive Systems

As previously stated, the final drive system transfers power from the transmission to the rear wheel to propel the motorcycle or ATV. Different vehicles employ different final drive ratios. This ratio is the relationship of the rear wheel speed to crankshaft speed. There are three final drive designs: chain drive, belt drive, and shaft drive.

Chain Final Drive

The ***chain final drive*** is simple, inexpensive, lightweight, and easy to maintain. A typical chain drive is made up of a drive sprocket, drive chain, and driven sprocket. These parts are shown in **Figure 13-46.**

Sprockets and Roller Chain

The ***front sprocket*** (countershaft sprocket) and ***rear sprocket*** are made of sheet steel or aluminum. The countershaft sprocket drives the chain. The rear sprocket drives the wheel. A ***roller chain*** is made up of pin links, roller links, and a master link. A ***pin link*** consists of two side plates with two steel pins riveted to the side plates, **Figure 13-47.** The pin link connects the roller links.

A ***roller link*** is made up of two side plates, two bushings pressed into the side plates, and two rollers surrounding the bushings, **Figure 13-48.** A ***master link*** is a pin link which has a removable side plate, **Figure 13-49.** It allows the chain to be separated easily. For instance, the master link will allow chain removal without rear wheel removal.

Chain Design Variations

There are three variations in roller chain design. These include the O-ring chain, solid impregnated roller chain, and endless chain. The ***O-ring chain*** uses O-rings between the side plates of the pin and roller links. This seals in lubrication but keeps moisture and dirt out, **Figure 13-50.**

A ***solid impregnated roller chain*** uses a single nonrotating roller. This solid roller is filled with lubricant and takes the place of the bushing and roller. An ***endless chain*** is one which does not use a master link with a removable side plate. Instead, the master link is riveted in the same manner as all other pin links. It is important to remember, however, all three chain variations may be used in one chain.

Other Chain Accessories

Other accessories found on some motorcycle chain drives include drive chain sliders, chain guides, guide sliders, and rollers, **Figure 13-51.** These devices all do their part to keep the chain running in its proper path, while preventing it from cutting into the swingarm, frame, or other components. Each of these components is made of a type of plastic that offers minimal friction and wear. Periodic inspection for wear or damage and replacement is necessary as these parts do deteriorate.

The ***chain slider,*** attached to the front of the swingarm near its pivot point, must be replaced when its wear grooves reach a depth specified for each particular model. Failure to replace a worn slider may result in damage to the swingarm and the chain.

Off-road and dual-purpose motorcycles are fitted with a ***chain guide*** that ensures the chain is aligned

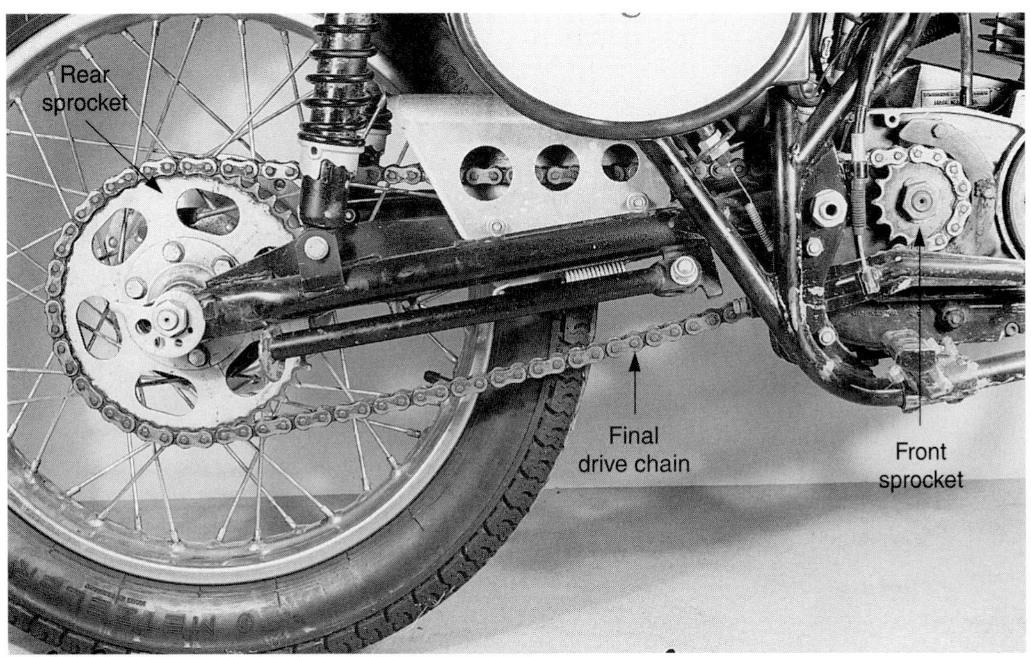

Figure 13-46. With a chain final drive, a small front sprocket drives the roller chain. The chain drives a large rear sprocket and the rear wheel.

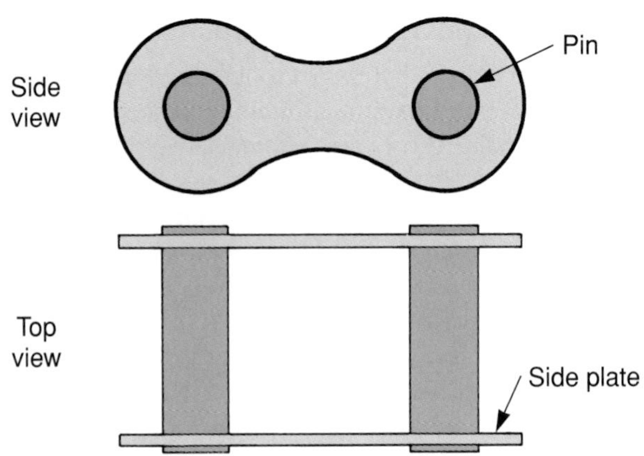

Figure 13-47. A chain pin link consists of two side plates riveted to two pins.

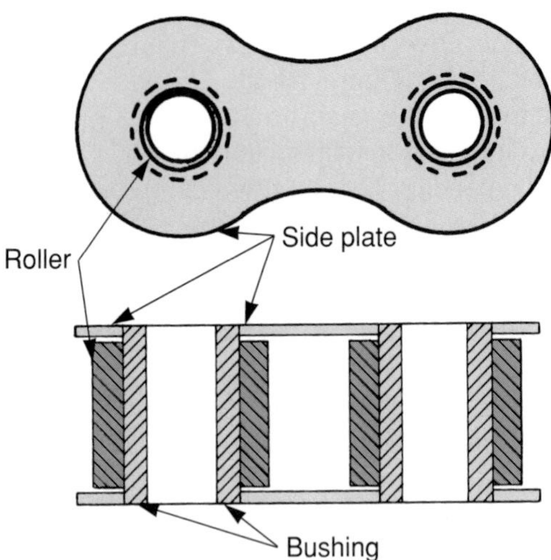

Figure 13-48. A roller link is made up of two side plates pressed onto bushings. Rollers surround the bushings.

directly to the rear sprocket. The guide itself should be checked for proper alignment as it can be bent through contact with passing objects, rocks, or accident damage. Straighten or replace as necessary. A plastic guide slider centers the guide on the sprocket with minimal friction and prevents the chain from wearing the guide.

A lower chain roller, or a pair of upper and lower rollers are used to take up excess slack in the drive chain as the rear suspension compresses and extends to its farthest points. These rollers also help prevent the chain from cutting into other components on the motorcycle, when the suspension is near full compression. These must also be periodically inspected for wear, damage, and mounting.

Chain Lubrication

Chain lubrication is necessary to prevent premature wear. A motorcycle drive chain is exposed to extreme loading, stress, and directional change. Proper cleaning and lubrication is essential to prevent galling of moving parts (rollers, pins, bushings, side plates, sprocket teeth). See **Figure 13-52.**

Belt Drive

The ***belt drive*** is similar in appearance to chain drive but uses a reinforced, toothed rubber belt and special sprockets. See **Figure 13-53.** A belt final drive system does not require as much maintenance as the chain drive system. Frequent adjustment is not needed and lubricant should not be used. A belt drive is also very quiet.

Shaft Drive System

A ***shaft drive system*** is a fully sealed and internally lubricated final drive that provides an alternative to chain or belt drive. Shown in **Figure 13-54,** a typical shaft drive system consists of:

- A 90° drive from the transmission output shaft (only with transverse inline engines).
- Spline coupling (slip joint).
- Universal joint (swivel joint).
- Drive shaft (propeller shaft) and swing arm.
- Pinion gear (drive, spiral bevel gear).
- Ring gear (driven, spiral bevel gear).
- Rear drive housing (gear enclosure).

To prevent harsh or jerky acceleration and deceleration, a damper spring is sometimes placed in the driveline, **Figure 13-55.** The spring absorbs sudden applications of torque and provides smooth starts and stops. The damper mechanism is attached to either the output gear case or driveshaft. Unlike the drive chain, the system requires only periodic final gear oil change for maintenance.

Lubrication for the shaft drive system is provided by gear lubricant (bath) in the rear housing and by grease in the sealed universal joint. The advantages of a shaft drive system are:

- Low maintenance requirements.
- Self-contained lubrication.
- Almost constant wheel base (distance between front and rear axles).
- Quiet operation.
- Long life.

Final Drive Ratio

A chain ***final drive ratio*** refers to the number of teeth on the front sprocket versus the number of teeth on the rear sprocket, **Figure 13-56A.** In a shaft drive system, this ratio refers to the number of teeth on the pinion gear versus the number of teeth on the ring gear, **Figure 13-56B.**

Changing Final Drive Ratio

Drive ratio changes are accomplished by changing one or both chain or belt sprockets. Shaft drive ratio changes

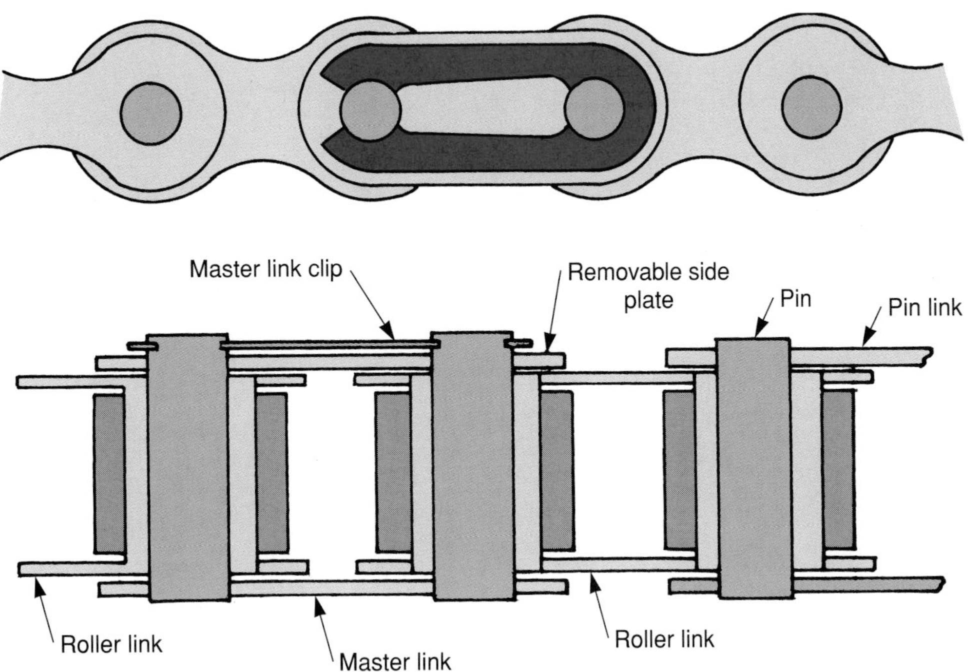

Figure 13-49. A roller chain uses pin links to connect a number of roller links together. A master link is simply a pin link with a removable side plate. The side plate is held in place by a clip. This allows the ends of the chain to be connected and disconnected easily.

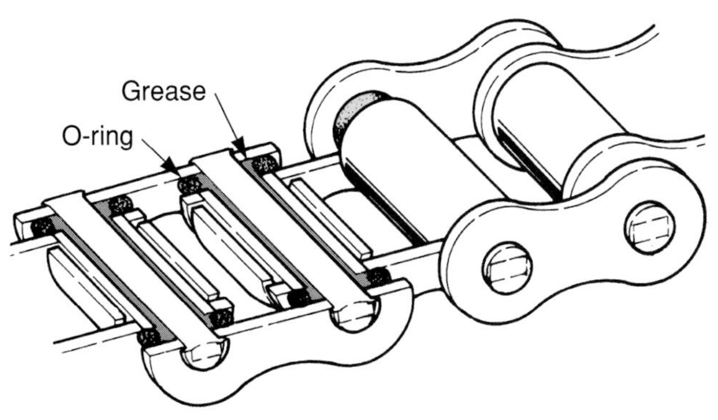

Figure 13-50. An O-ring chain requires minimal maintenance. O-rings between the side plates seal lubrication in and contaminants out. Regular lubrication of rollers is required, however. (American Suzuki Motor Corporation)

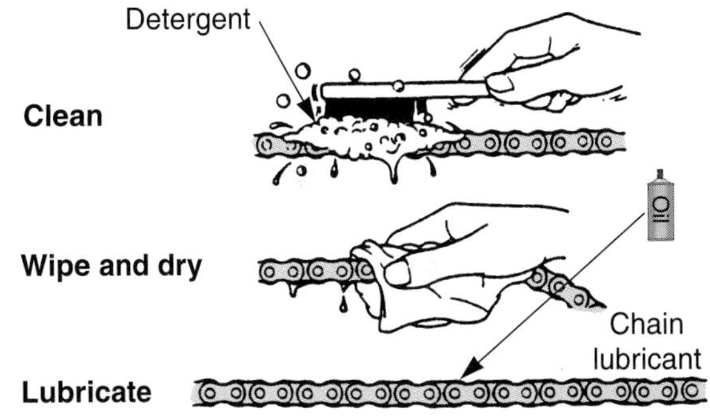

Figure 13-52. Cleaning and lubrication of a chain drive is regularly needed. Lubrication must be applied between the side plates of pin links and roller links. Proper application allows lubricant to penetrate into space between pins and bushings, where it is needed most.

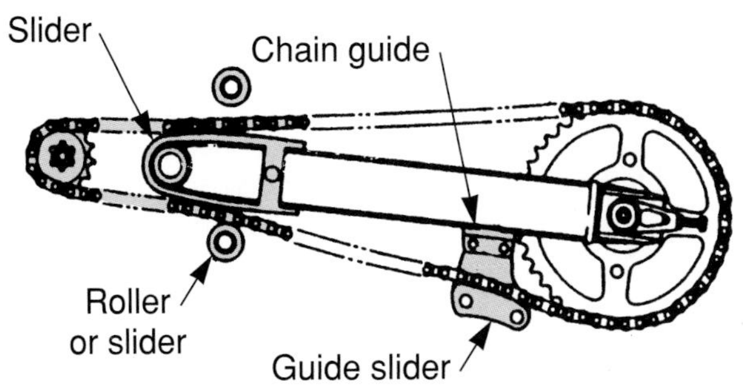

Figure 13-51. Typical chain drive accessories include chain guides, rollers, and sliders. (Honda Motor Co., Ltd.)

require replacement of both the ring and pinion. It is much more involved and expensive to change shaft drive ratio.

If a smaller front sprocket or larger rear sprocket is installed, this will increase acceleration but reduce top speed. A larger diameter front sprocket and smaller rear sprocket tends to reduce acceleration but increase top speed.

The same is true for shaft drive. A pinion gear with less teeth and ring gear with more teeth can improve acceleration but will reduce top speed as well as fuel economy. The opposite ratio change will have a reverse effect on performance. A pinion gear with more teeth and ring gear with less teeth can improve top speed but reduces acceleration.

Figure 13-53. Belt drive tension adjustment is done by moving the rear axle. Set the tension using service manual procedures.

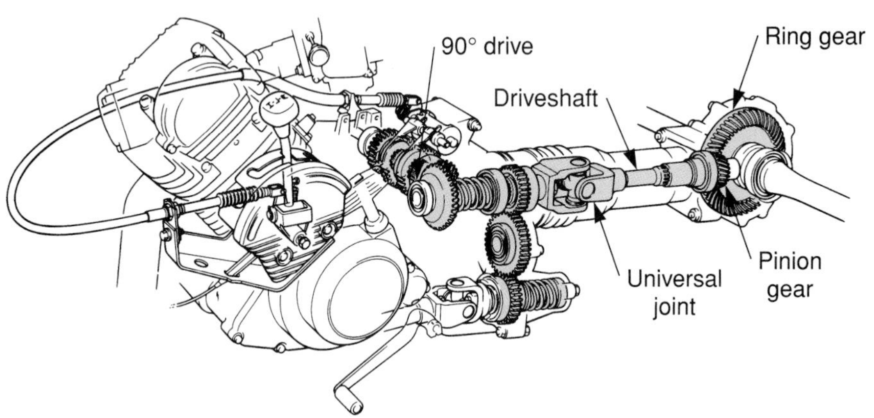

Figure 13-54. Shaft drive uses setup similar to rear-wheel drive automobile. Study part names and locations on this ATV shaft drive. (Yamaha Motor Corporation U.S.A.)

Normally, the stock ratio provides the best all-around performance. Manufacturers carefully choose a final drive ratio, which is suitable to the majority of riders. Final drive ratio may need to be changed when:

- The motorcycle is used for competition or extreme duty.
- The motorcycle is heavily loaded (fairing, saddle bags, sidecar, touring equipment).
- Better fuel economy is desired.
- Higher top speed is desired.

Overall Ratio

The three ratios, (primary, transmission, and final drive) are combined to give an ***overall ratio,*** which is a comparison of crankshaft speed to rear wheel speed. Because torque multiplication (power, speed, and acceleration) changes with reduction ratio, a typical transmission should provide a wide range of torque multiplication. As shown in **Figure 13-57,** a typical transmission can provide a variance of ratios from 13:1 in first gear to 6:1 in fifth gear. Notice how the wheel speed increases while the engine rpm stays constant.

Internal transmission ratios will vary depending upon engine power characteristics and intended use. A touring motorcycle will have a wide ratio transmission (wide ratio difference between gears). A motorcycle designed for motocross will have a close ratio transmission (close, evenly spaced ratios between gears). Inspection, servicing, and troubleshooting information on a typical motorcycle's primary drive/transmission/final drive system can be found in Chapter 21.

Starting Systems

As mentioned earlier in this text, the starting system of a motorcycle can be activated by a kickstarter or electric starting motor. ATVs and scooters use an electric starter.

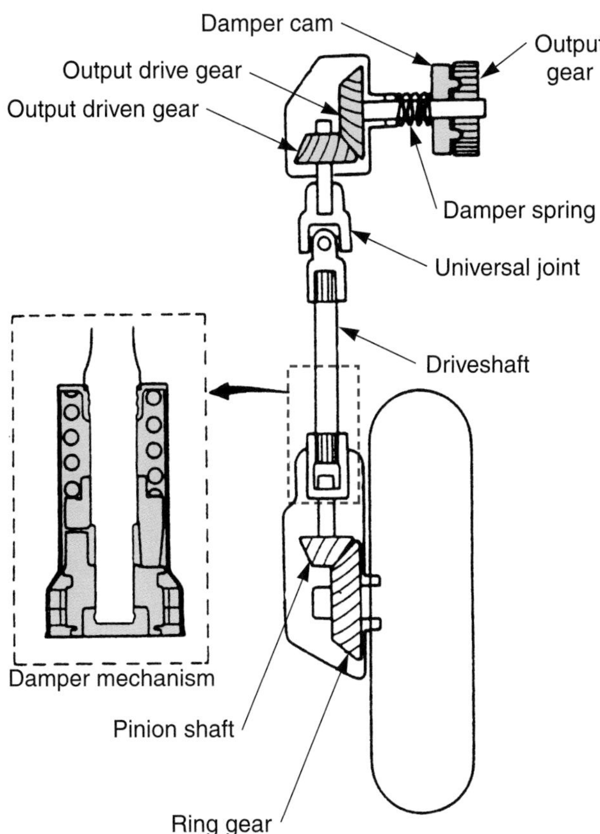

Figure 13-55. Final drive damper unit helps prevent harsh or jerky acceleration and deceleration. (Honda Motor Co., Ltd.)

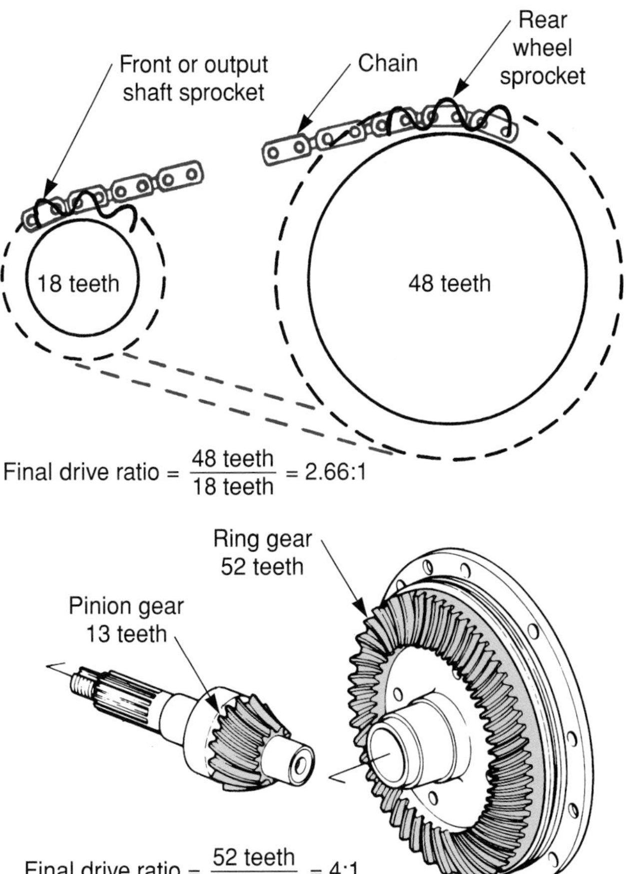

Figure 13-56. A—The final drive ratio is found by dividing the number of teeth on the rear sprocket by the number of teeth on the front sprocket. B—Shaft drive final drive ratio is achieved by dividing the number of teeth on the ring gear (52) by the number of teeth on the pinion gear (13). In this example, final drive ratio is 4:1. (Kawasaki Motors Corporation U.S.A.)

Kickstart Mechanisms

The purpose of a ***kickstart mechanism*** is to connect the kickstart lever to the engine crankshaft so that the crankshaft can be manually turned over rapidly for starting, **Figure 13-58.** A kickstart mechanism uses an engagement device and a series of gears.

The kickstart engagement device must provide lockup for starting and disengagement when the engine begins to run on its own power. Since the kickstart lever is at the rear of the engine and a certain kickstart gear ratio is desired, a series of gears is used to provide adequate turning force.

The three types of kickstart engagement devices are:

- Ratchet and pawl, **Figure 13-59.**
- Cam-engaged radial ratchet, **Figure 13-60.**
- Threaded spindle, **Figure 13-61.**

Primary and Non-Primary Kickstarters

There are two types of kickstarting systems: the primary drive starting system and the non-primary or *direct drive starting system.* Most off-road motorcycle kickstart systems use the primary drive's clutch outer hub for starting. This allows the engine to be started with the transmission in gear, but with the clutch disengaged. This is called ***primary kickstarting.***

Transmission gear selected	Crankshaft speed	Rear wheel speed	Overall ratio
First gear	5000 rpm	384.6 rpm	13:1
Second gear	5000 rpm	454.5 rpm	11:1
Third gear	5000 rpm	555.5 rpm	9:1
Fourth gear	5000 rpm	666.6 rpm	7.5:1
Fifth gear	5000 rpm	833.3 rpm	6:1

Figure 13-57. The drive ratio and corresponding crankshaft and wheel speed in each gear.

Non-primary kickstarting uses the transmission input shaft and clutch assembly to start the engine. In this design, the engine cannot be started unless the transmission is in neutral and the clutch is engaged. This system is found in most kickstarting street bikes. **Figure 13-62** shows kickstart system power flow for each design.

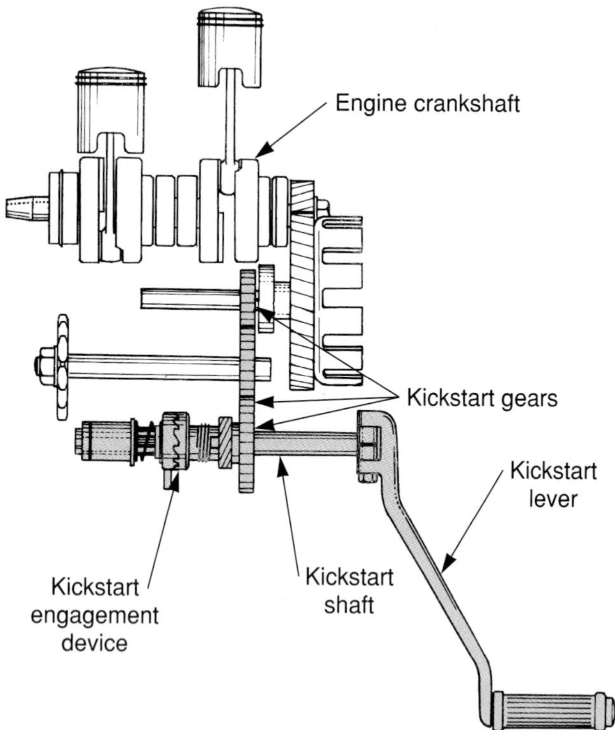

Figure 13-58. This kickstart mechanism uses a lever, shaft, and a set of gears to turn the crankshaft for starting. (American Suzuki Motor Corporation)

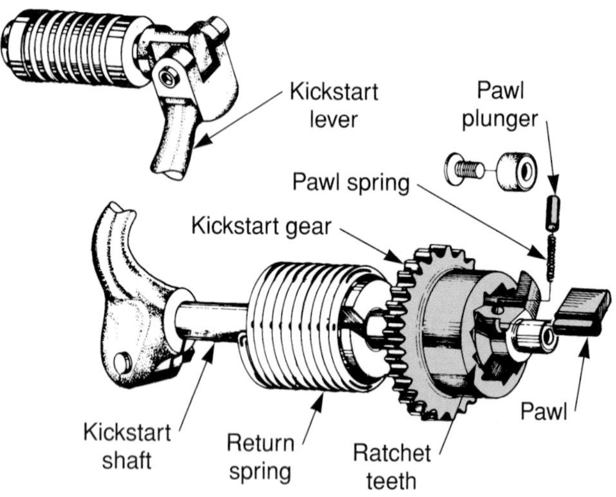

Figure 13-59. A ratchet and pawl engagement device uses a spring-loaded pawl to lock the kickstart gear to the kickstart shaft. They lock on the downward stroke of the kickstart lever. As the lever is released and the spring returns the assembly, the pawl rides over the ratchet teeth.
(Kawasaki Motors Corporation U.S.A.)

Starter/Ignition Systems

The purpose of an ***electric starting system*** is to provide engine cranking and starting. The electric starting system eliminates the need to kick the engine over with a foot pedal. The operation of electric starting systems are similar to primary drive starting systems, except for the use of a small electric motor. The motor turns either the crankshaft, the countershaft, or the mainshaft.

The typical components of an electric starter/ignition system is shown in **Figure 13-63.** The function of these components is given in **Figure 13-64.** The operation of an electric starter motor was described in Chapter 8.

Side Stand Switch Operation

The ***side stand switch*** detects the side stand position electrically. The switch is installed on the side stand pivot bolt. On some models, the switch is installed on the rear of the pivot bolt or is covered. The switch is a rotary-type and the fixed contact is attached to the frame. The rotary switch contact rotates inside the switch housing following side stand movements, **Figure 13-65.**

The side stand ignition cut-off switch warns the rider that the side stand is lowered by turning on the indicator light. It also operates as an ignition cut-off switch when the transmission is shifted into gear. This system also prevents the starter motor from operating (and the battery from discharging) when side stand switch circuit conditions do not allow engine ignition.

When the side stand is lowered, the side stand switch indicator contact closes. Battery current flows through the circuit at right to light the indicator. When the side stand is retracted, the indicator switch contact opens and the indicator light goes off.

Starting System (Starter Motor) Operation

The operation of the starting system depends on the motorcycle's clutch and the ignition system operation.

Models with a Manual Clutch

When the ignition switch is turned on and the starter switch is pushed, battery voltage is applied to the starter relay switch coil. If the switches in the starter relay ground circuit are not closed, the starter motor does not operate. For the starter motor to operate, the following switches must be closed:

- Neutral switch.
- Clutch switch.
- Side stand switch.

If all the switches are closed, current from the battery flows through the circuit as shown in **Figure 13-66,** the starter relay switch is turned on and the starter motor operates.

Models With a Centrifugal Clutch

To prevent vehicles with a centrifugal clutch from lurching forward when the engine starts, a switch prevents

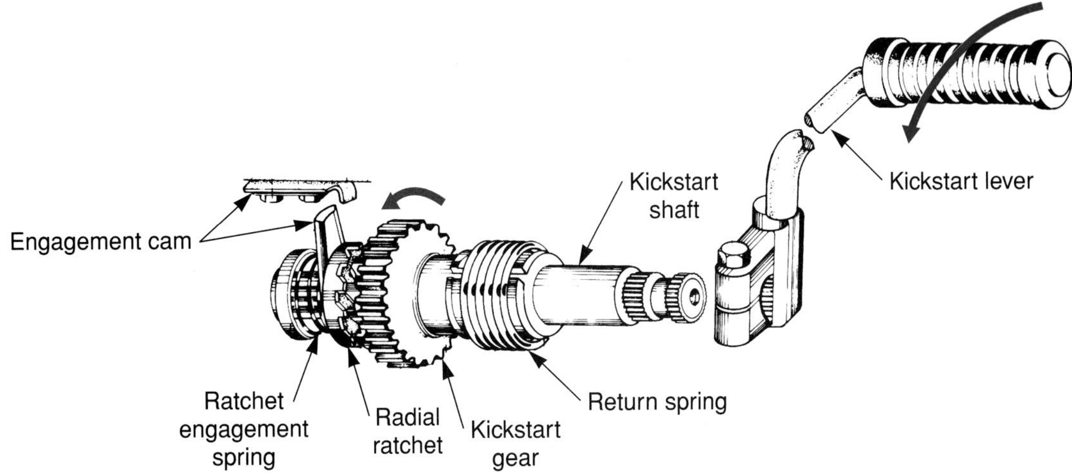

Figure 13-60. A cam and radial ratchet is used to lock the kickstart gear to shaft. Half of the cam and ratchet are spring-loaded and splined to the shaft. As the lever is moved down, the engagement cam releases, allowing the engagement spring to push the splined half of the ratchet into engagement. This locks the kickstart gear to the shaft and the engine crankshaft rotates. (Kawasaki Motors Corporation U.S.A.)

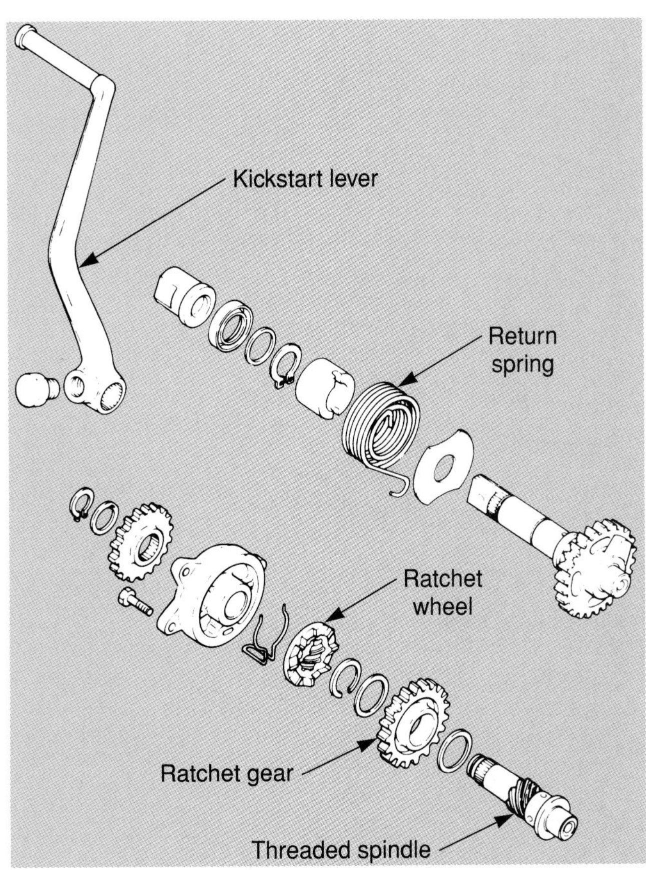

Figure 13-61. Threaded spindle kickstart engages the ratchet wheel with the ratchet gear. When they lock together, the engine can be rotated for starting. (Yamaha Motor Corporation U.S.A.)

voltage from reaching the starter relay switch unless the brake is applied. The side stand switch is also part of the ground circuit, **Figure 13-67.** Only when both the side stand is retracted and the brake applied is the starter motor able to operate.

CDI Systems Integrated with Side Stand Switch and/or Neutral Switch

CDI ignition systems with a side stand switch and/or neutral switch operate similarly to other CDI systems except the CDI control module also controls the ignition system. The interface determines whether to turn the transistor on or off. The transistor determines how the ignition control circuit works by turning the silicon controlled rectifier (thyristor) on or off.

The interface receives information through the external detection circuit consisting of the side stand switch and the neutral switch. A diode in this circuit prevents current from flowing in the reverse direction. This circuit must have a ground path for ignition to be possible. Ignition is not possible if either of the following conditions occur:

- Side stand is lowered.
- Transmission is in gear.

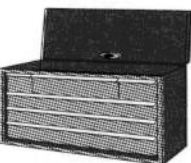

Note: Models without transmissions, such as most scooters, do not have a neutral switch or clutch circuit.

If the side stand is down or the transmission is in gear, the CDI interface sends a base signal to activate the transistor. When the transistor is on, it conducts the gate signal from the trigger to ground, and ignition is not possible, **Figure 13-68A.**

When the side stand is retracted and the transmission is placed in neutral, the transistor is turned off as the interface is deactivated. Therefore, the gate signal from the trigger can be applied and ignition is possible, **Figure 13-68B.**

Notches
in clutch
outer hub
Input
shaft
Input shaft
kickstart gear
A
Input shaft
kickstart gear
B

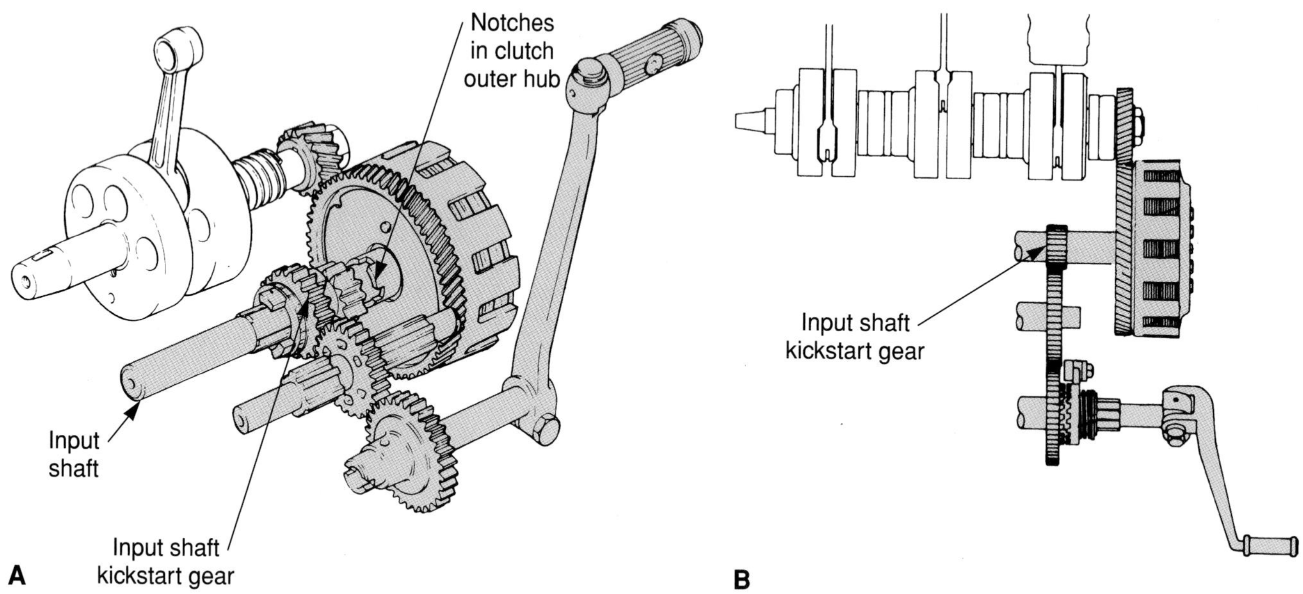

Figure 13-62. A—Primary kickstart system. The input shaft kickstart gear freewheels on its shaft and is indexed into notches in the back of the outer clutch hub. This allows the rider to kickstart the engine with the transmission in gear and the clutch disengaged. B—Non-primary kickstart system. The input shaft kickstart gear is locked to the shaft. The kickstart system simply turns the input shaft. This means the clutch must be engaged for the kickstarter to turn the crankshaft.
(American Suzuki Motor Corporation)

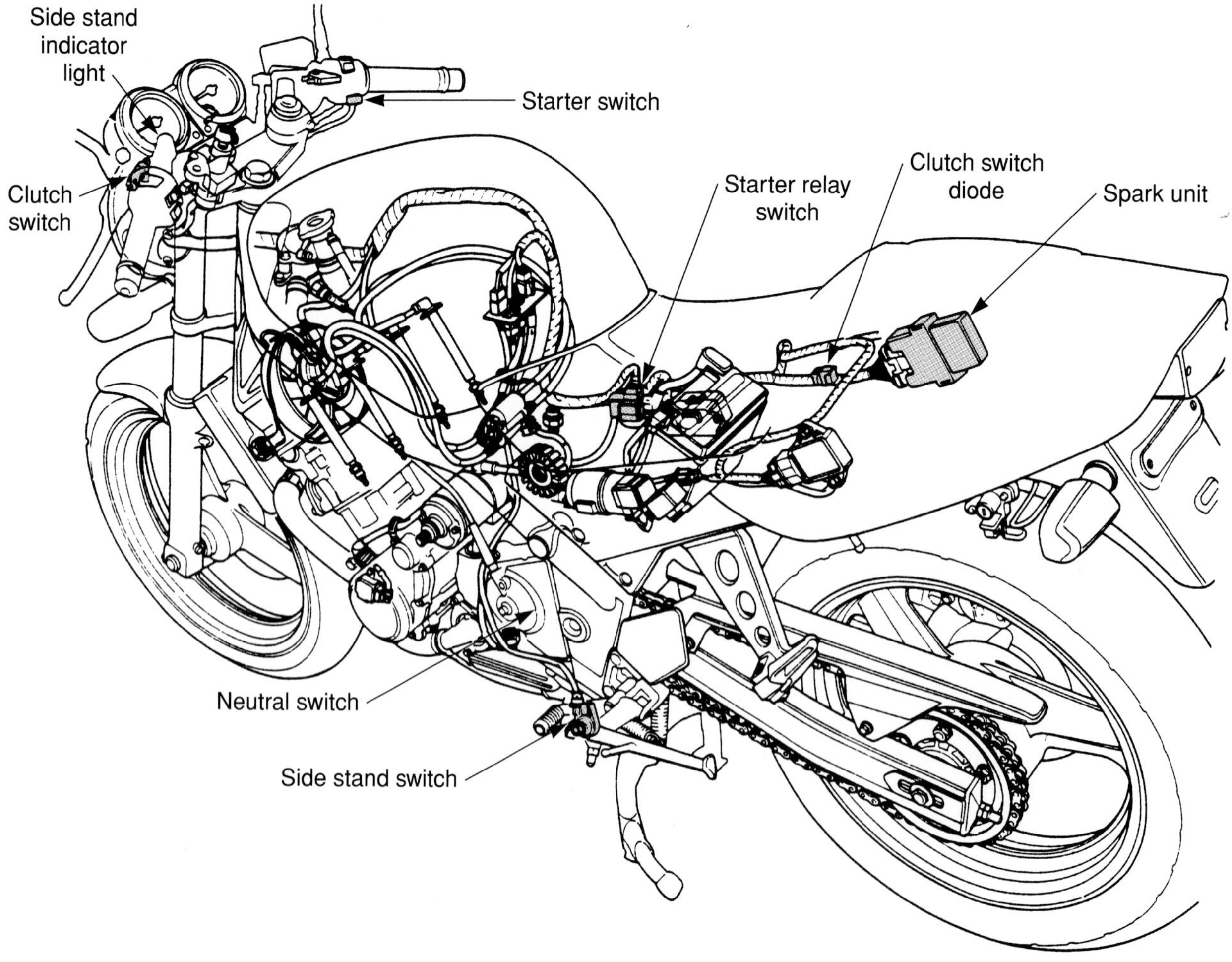

Side stand
indicator
light
Starter switch
Clutch
switch
Starter relay
switch
Clutch switch
diode
Spark unit
Neutral switch
Side stand switch

Figure 13-63. Typical electric start component location. (Honda Motor Co., Ltd.)

Component	Function
Indicator (lens color is usually amber)	When side stand is Lowered: Light on Retracted: Light goes off
Clutch switch (Note: same switch as for starting system)	When clutch lever is pulled in: on (continuity) releases: off (no continuity)
Starter switch	When starter switch is pushed: on (continuity) releases: off (no continuity)
Side stand switch (installed on the side stand pivot bolt)	When side stand is lowered: contact point of ingnition/starting side is open. Contact point of indicator side is closed. retracted, contact point of ignition/ starting side is closed Contact point of indicator side is open.

Figure 13-64. Operation of various components of the electric starter system.

Side stand position	Transmission	Clutch lever	Ignition	Starting
Lowered 	Neutral	Pulled in	Possible	Possible
		Released	Possible	Possible
	In gear	Pulled in	Not possible	Not possible
		Released	Not possible	Not possible
Retracted 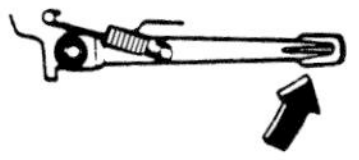	Neutral	Pulled in	Possible	Possible
		Released	Possible	Possible
	In gear	Pulled in	Possible	Possible
		Released	Possible	Not possible

Figure 13-65. Operation of the side stand. (Honda Motor Co., Ltd.)

DC/CDI Systems Integrated with Side Stand Switch and/or Neutral Switch

The DC/CDI ignition systems integrated with a side stand switch and/or neutral switch operate similarly to other DC/CDI systems. The external detection circuit is similar to the CDI systems but the method of ignition control is different. The resistor determines whether the transistor is turned off or turned on. The transistor determines how the ignition control circuit works by activating or deactivating the DC/DC converter. If the transistor is turned off, the DC/DC converter is activated to make ignition possible, **Figure 13-69.**

The resistor receives information through the external detection circuit consisting of the side stand switch and the neutral switch. A diode in this circuit must have a ground path to make ignition possible. Ignition is not possible if either of the following conditions occur:

- Side stand is lowered.
- Transmission is in gear.

Under these conditions, the signal from the DC/DC converter is applied to the transistor through the resistor, turning the transistor on. When the transistor is turned on, the signal from the DC/DC converter is applied to the capacitor and ignition is not possible as shown in **Figure 13-70A.**

When the side stand is retracted and the transmission is placed in neutral, the signal from the DC/DC converter is grounded, **Figure 13-70B.** It is not applied to the transistor and therefore, the transistor is turned off. When the transistor is turned off, the signal from the DC/DC converter is applied to the capacitor to make ignition possible.

Side Stand Switch and/or Neutral Switch with Transistorized Integrated Ignition System

Transistorized ignition systems (TPI) integrated with a side stand switch and/or neutral switch operate similarly to other TPI systems except it also controls ignition through a resistor and a transistor, **Figure 13-71.** The ignition control circuit in the spark unit is deactivated in the same way as the DC/CDI ignition system.

If the sidestand is lowered and the transmission is placed in gear, the signal from the spark unit power

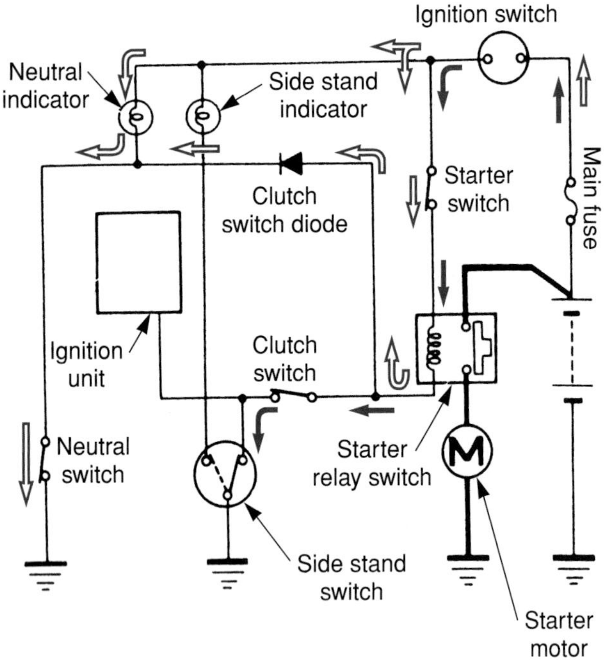

Figure 13-66. Starting system (starter motor) operation for motorcycles with a manual clutch. (Honda Motor Co., Ltd.)

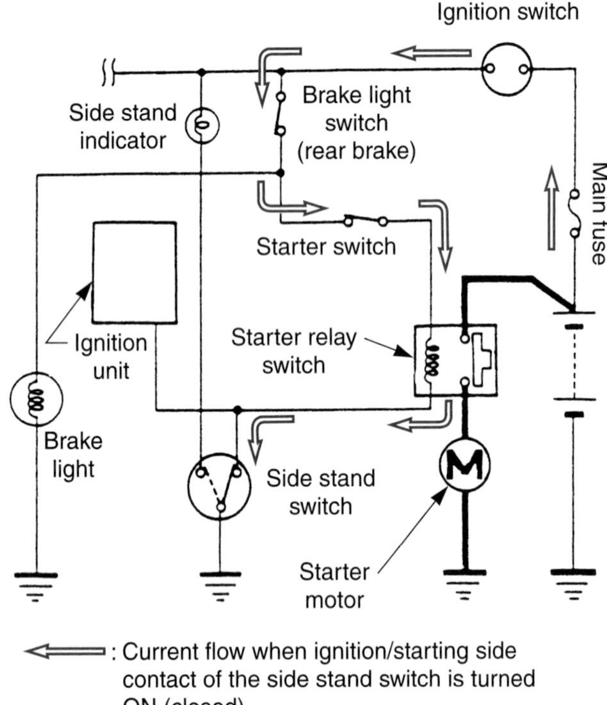

Figure 13-67. Typical starting circuit operation for motorcycles with a centrifugal clutch.

supply line is applied to the transistor through the resister to turn the transistor on. When the transistor is turned on, the signal from the spark unit power supply line is deactivated. This means that no electrical current from the spark unit power supply line is applied to T2 (power transistor) and ignition is not possible.

Ignition is not possible

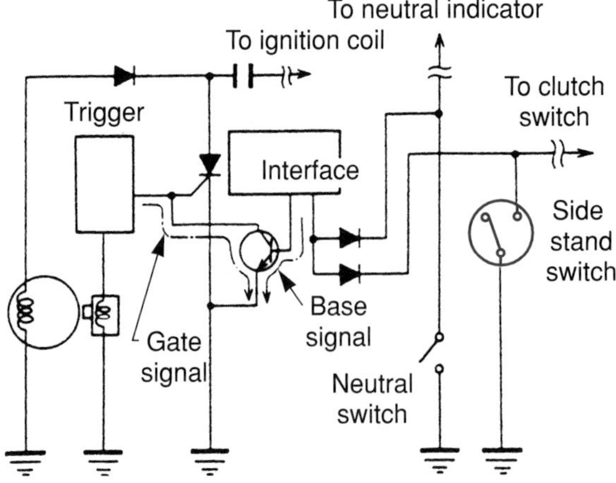

Ignition is possible

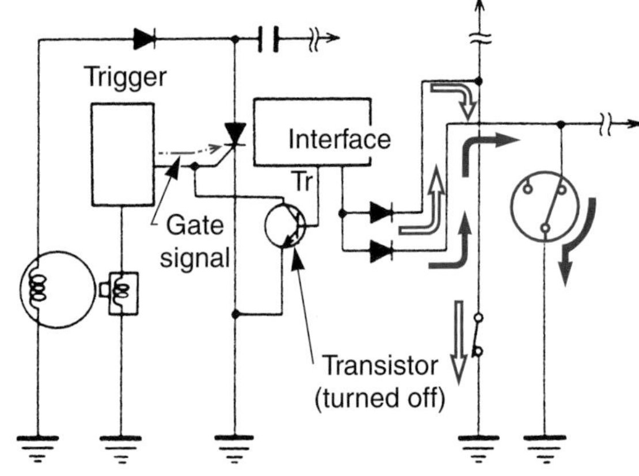

Figure 13-68. A—Typical CDI circuit integrated with stand switch and neutral switch. The ignition is turned off when the SCR does not operate. B—The transistor is turned off so the SCR will be activated. (Honda Motor Co., Ltd.)

Summary

To be usable, the power developed by the engine must be transferred to the rear wheel(s). This is accomplished by the drivetrain consist of a primary drive, a clutch, or transmission (sometimes called a gearbox), and a final drive. The primary drive transfers engine power from the crankshaft to the clutch/transmission assembly. Primary drive reduction is accomplished by either a set of gears or a chain and sprocket set. A primary belt drive system is similar to the primary chain system except that it uses a belt in place of a chain.

A clutch is provided to engage and disengage engine power to and from the transmission. Most clutches are placed between the primary reduction and transmission. With some models, however, they are attached directly to the crankshaft. A multi-plate clutch is used to provide a very compact, high friction coupling between the engine and transmission. Depending on the engine size and the motorcycle's weight, 4-8 sets of drive and driven plates

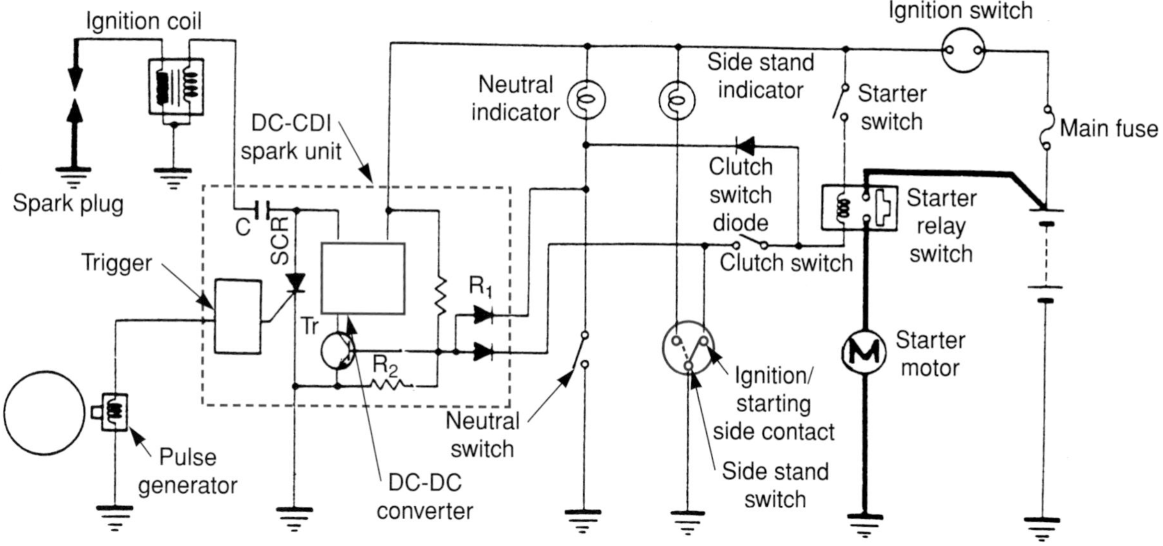

Figure 13-69. DC/CDI circuit for models with manual clutch/transmission. (Honda Motor Co., Ltd.)

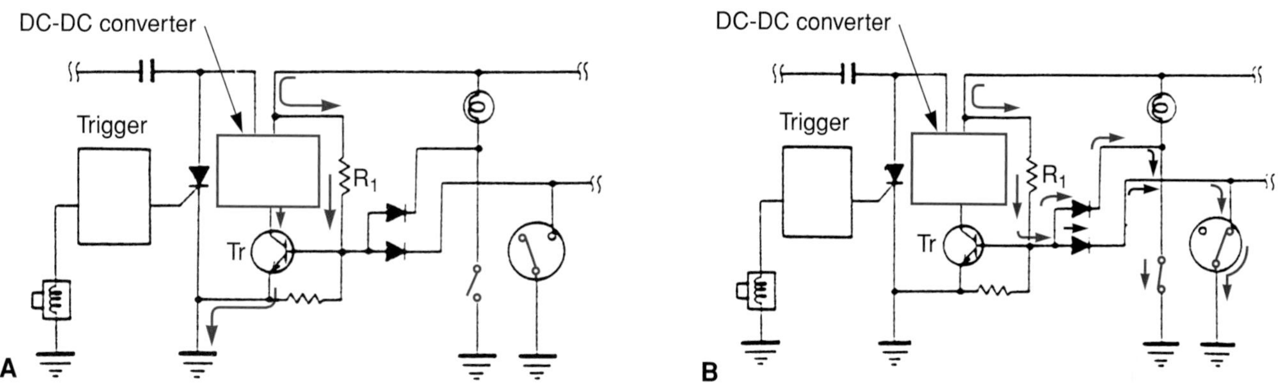

Figure 13-70. Signal from DC/DC circuit goes to ground to make ignition possible. (Honda Motor Co., Ltd.)

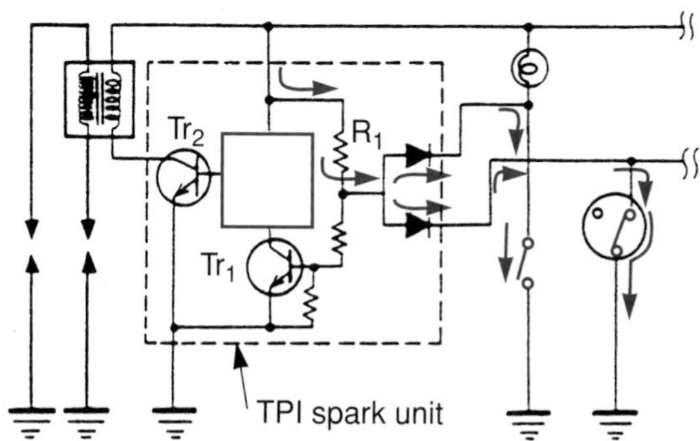

Figure 13-71. Typical circuit for a transistorized ignition system. (Honda Motor Co., Ltd.)

may be housed in the clutch basket. The discs of a wet clutch operate in an oil bath (oil surrounds and covers discs). Most multi-plate clutches run in an oil bath. A dry clutch is designed to run without an oil bath. This requires the clutch to be sealed. There are two types of springs used in motorcycle clutches: coil springs and diaphragm springs. Both types of springs press the plates together to provide clutch engagement.

The one-way clutch or sprag clutch system is found in many primary drives used in conjunction with electric starter motors. The one-way clutch allows the starter drive to disengage when engine speed exceeds the starter speed. One-way clutches allow the transmission to slip when wheel speed exceeds transmission speed. A typical centrifugal clutch will engage and disengage automatically at a specific rpm.

A motorcycle or ATV manual transmission improves acceleration by allowing the rider to change the engine-to-rear-wheel drive ratio. All motorcycle transmissions commonly use two shafts: the input shaft or main shaft, and the output shaft or countershaft. The input shaft on manual transmissions is powered by a clutch mechanism. The transmission output shaft has a sprocket that is used to drive the chain going to the rear wheel. A multi-speed transmission or constant mesh transmission consists of two shafts and two or more gears on each shaft. Selection of the proper gear set on a multi-speed transmission is done by moving a sliding gear into contact with the gear set desired. Connection of the sliding gear and the gear set is done using dogs and dog holes on the sides of the gears. To move a sliding gear or dog, a shifting fork is required.

A gear selector mechanism changes the up and down (vertical) movement of the gear change lever to sideways (horizontal) gear movement in the transmission. A cam plate gear selector mechanism uses a cam plate rather than a drum to move the shift forks. The transmission indexer is used to precisely locate the shift drum or cam plate into position for each gear. A neutral indicator switch illuminates a small instrument light when the transmission is in neutral. To prevent overshifting (movement past the desired gear), the transmission may have a shift stopper.

In most cases, the direct drive transmission has the clutch and countershaft sprocket located on the same side of the engine. The clutch and countershaft sprocket are located on opposite sides of the engine with an indirect drive transmission. Power enters the transmission on the other shaft (output shaft). The dual-range transmission is used on some small trail motorcycles, touring bikes, and some ATVs because it provides a dual-range gear ratio for both on- and off-highway use.

Centrifugal clutch/variable belt transmissions provide variable drive ratios between the engine and rear wheel according to engine speed and load. It accomplishes this with two sets of pulleys, connected by a drive belt. A planetary gear transmission uses a planetary gearset to step up the output shaft speed to reduce torque.

The final drive system transfers power from the transmission to the rear wheel to propel the motorcycle or ATV. There are three final drive designs: chain drive, belt drive, and shaft drive. The chain final drive is simple, inexpensive, lightweight, and easy to maintain. A typical chain drive is made up of a drive sprocket, drive chain, and driven sprocket. A belt drive is similar in appearance to a chain drive but uses a reinforced, toothed rubber belt and special sprockets. A shaft drive system uses a fully sealed and internally lubricated final drive shaft that provides an alternative to chain or belt drive. The final drive ratio is the relationship of the rear wheel speed to crankshaft speed. Drive ratio changes are accomplished by changing one or both chain or belt sprockets. Shaft drive ratio changes require replacement of both the ring and pinion. The three ratios, (primary, transmission, and final drive) are combined to give an overall ratio, which is a comparison of crankshaft speed to rear wheel speed. A typical transmission can provide a variance of ratios from 13:1 in first gear to 6:1 in fifth gear.

The purpose of a kickstart mechanism is to connect the kickstart lever to the engine crankshaft so that the crankshaft can be manually turned over rapidly for starting. There are two types of kickstarting systems: the primary drive starting system and the non-primary or direct drive starting system. The purpose of an electric starting system is to provide engine cranking and starting. The side stand switch detects the side stand position electrically.

Know These Terms

Primary drive
Gear reduction
Primary gear drives
Straight-cut gear drive
Straight-cut offset gear drive
Helical gear drive
Primary chain drive system
Chain tensioner
Belt drive system
Clutch
Multi-plate clutch
Clutch housing
Clutch hub
Wet clutch
Dry clutch
Coil springs
Diaphragm spring
Single plate dry clutch
Clutch shock absorber
One-way clutch
Centrifugal clutch
Manual transmission
Input shaft
Output shaft
Multi-speed transmission
Shifting fork
Gear selector mechanism
Drum gear selector
Cam plate gear selector mechanism
Transmission indexer
Neutral indicator switch
Shift drum location device
Shift stopper
Gear engagement
Direct drive transmission
Layshaft
Indirect drive transmission
Dual-range transmission
Centrifugal clutch/variable belt transmissions
Planetary gear transmission
Planetary gearset
Shift start
Shift finish
Shift return
Chain final drive
Front sprocket
Rear sprocket
Roller chain
Pin link
Roller link
Master link
O-ring chain
Solid impregnated roller chain
Endless chain
Chain slider
Chain guide
Belt drive
Shaft drive system
Final drive ratio
Overall ratio
Kickstart mechanism
Primary kickstarting
Non-primary kickstarting
Electric starting system
Side stand switch

Review Questions—Chapter 13

Do not write in this text. Place your answers on a separate sheet of paper.

1. List the three types of primary gear drives.

2. What drives the clutch basket?
   A. Engine primary drive chain.
   B. Engine drive gear.
   C. Output shaft.
   D. Both A & B.
3. What does the clutch hub drive?
4. Unequal clutch spring pressure can cause:
   A. clutch slippage.
   B. clutch drag.
   C. pressure plate runout.
   D. All of the above.
5. The function of a clutch release mechanism is to move the pressure plate ______ the clutch plates.
6. List three common types of clutch release mechanisms.
7. Which shaft in a transmission is usually driven by the clutch?
   A. Output shaft.
   B. Input shaft.
   C. Intermediate shaft.
   D. All of the above.
8. A transmission _____ is used to precisely locate the shifting drum or cam plate.
   A. drum gear selector
   B. cam plate gear selector
   C. pressure plate
   D. indexer
9. What are the two common types of gear selector mechanisms?
10. What component in a shifting mechanism prevents overshifting?
    A. One-way clutch.
    B. Neutral indicator.
    C. Shift stopper.
    D. None of the above.
11. How is lubrication provided for a shaft drive system?
12. What components of a shaft drive system determine final drive ratio?
13. What types of motorcycles use close ratio and wide ratio transmissions?
14. A motorcycle that can be started in gear with the clutch disengaged has a _____ kickstart system.
15. All the following switches can prevent electric starter operation if they are open *except*:
    A. side stand switch.
    B. clutch switch.
    C. light switch.
    D. neutral switch.

Suggested Activities

1. Select three motorcycles. Then, using shop manuals, advertisements, and brochures, determine the specific design (type) used for the following items:
   A. Primary drive.
   B. Clutch.
   C. Clutch release mechanism.
   D. Transmission (direct or indirect drive).
   E. Number of speeds and ratio for each gear.
   F. Shifting mechanism.
   G. Indexer.
   H. Final drive.
2. Compare and analyze the design differences between the three motorcycles in Activity one. Explain why one design might be used over another.
3. Verify chain adjuster index marks on a motorcycle.

Tires are an often neglected part of most vehicles. They require regular maintenance, including proper inflation, to ensure long life. (Yamaha Motor Corporation U.S.A.)

14 Wheels and Tires

After studying this chapter, you will be able to:

- Describe the types of wheels used on modern motorcycles.
- Perform service and repair operations on motorcycle wheels.
- Compare various tire designs.
- Inspect, service, and repair tires.
- Describe the differences between tube and tubeless tires.
- Fix motorcycle tires.
- Understand the basics of wheel straightening and balancing.

This chapter discusses the front and rear wheels, components, and service. Service information includes wheel inspection, repacking wheel bearings, wheel removal and installation, lacing, truing, balancing, and troubleshooting. Later in the chapter, tire removal, flat repair, and tire installation are described.

Wheels

A motorcycle ***wheel*** rotates on an axle and supports the rubber tire. It also serves as a secondary shock absorber, softening bumps and other imperfections in the road. Three types of wheels are used on today's motorcycles: wire wheels, cast wheels, and stamped wheels.

Wire Wheels

A ***wire wheel*** or *spoked wheel* consists of:

- Hub (contains axle bearings and inner end of spokes).
- Spokes and nipples (connects hub and rim).
- Rim (supports tire).

Figure 14-1 shows a typical wire wheel assembly. The hub is suspended from the spokes. The spokes are attached to the rim in a crisscross pattern. The spokes are

Figure 14-1. A spoked wheel uses many individual spokes and nipples to connect the hub and rim.

secured to the rim by the spoke nipples. The motorcycle's weight is not supported by the lower spokes. The hub actually hangs from the top spokes, **Figure 14-2.** As the wheel rotates, weight is transferred from spoke to spoke.

With more spokes crossed in the lacing pattern, the wheel becomes stronger. This is because the load is distributed over a wider area on the rim. As the wheel rotates, each spoke is loaded and unloaded gradually. **Figure 14-3** shows weak and strong spoke cross-patterns.

Cast Wheels

A ***cast wheel*** is manufactured by pouring molten metal (usually aluminum or magnesium alloy) into a mold. This makes the hub, spokes, and rim all one piece, **Figure 14-4A.** A cast wheel is a very strong and dependable design.

Stamped Wheels

A ***stamped wheel*** consists of separate parts (hub, spokes, rim) fastened together. Unlike the cast wheel, the stamped wheel is either bolted or riveted together. It has the appearance of a cast wheel, but is less expensive to manufacture. Refer to **Figure 14-4B.**

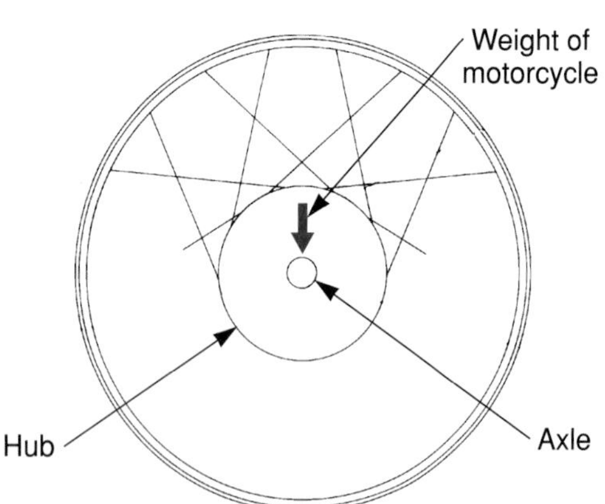

Figure 14-2. The axle attaches the wheel assembly to the motorcycle. The hub, axle, and the motorcycle's weight are supported by the upper spokes.

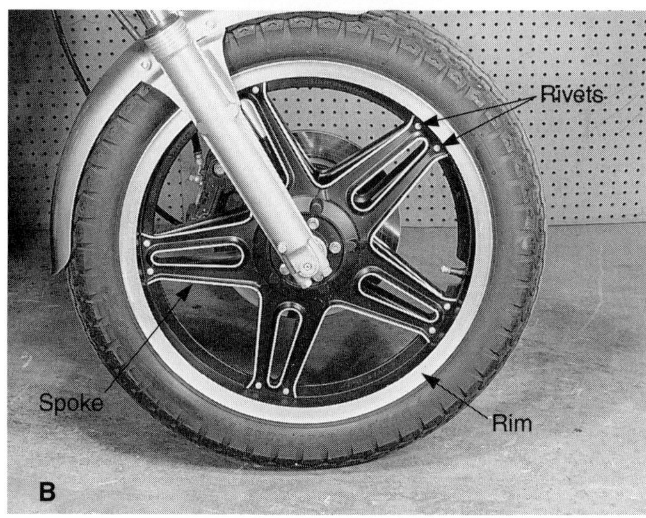

Figure 14-4. Similarities and differences between cast wheels and stamped wheels. A—Cast wheel. B—Stamped wheel.

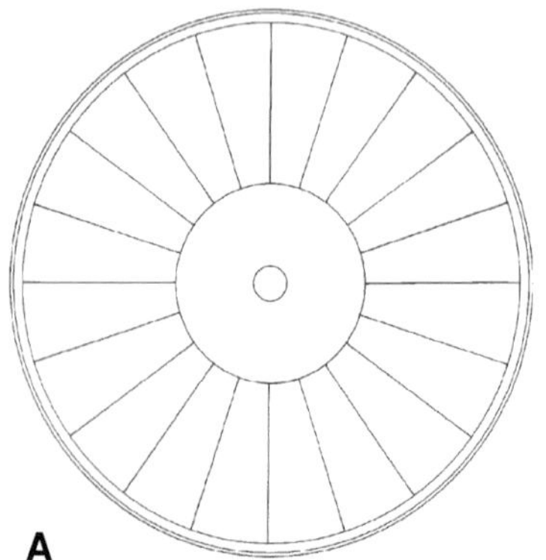

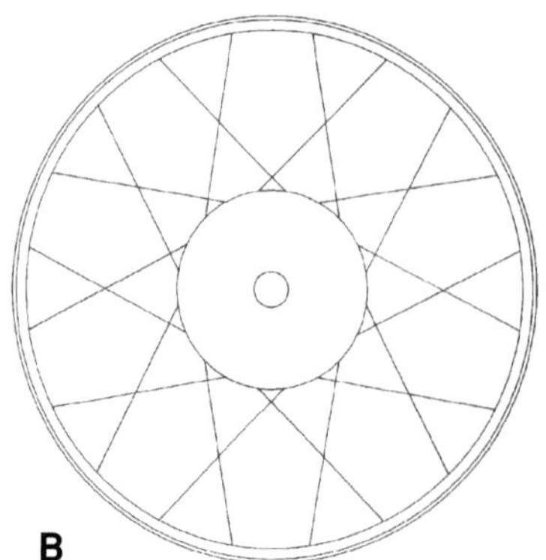

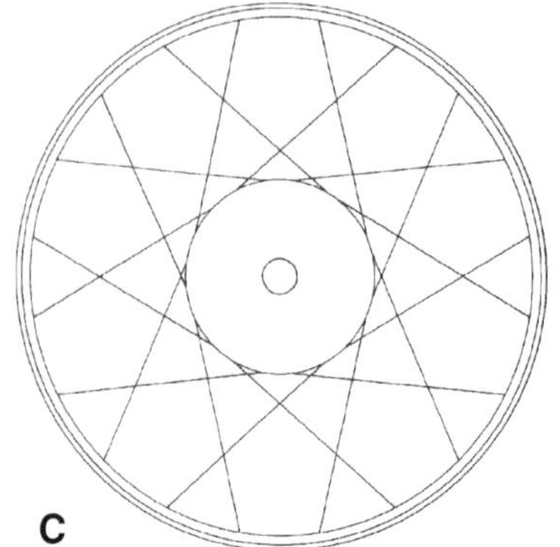

Figure 14-3. Different spoke patterns. A—The cross-zero pattern is very weak and should only be used for display purposes as it is unsafe for street use. B—The cross-two pattern is common, but provides minimal support. C—The cross-three pattern provides very good support and makes for a strong wheel assembly.

Hubs and Bearings

In most wheel designs, ball bearings are located in the hub. An ***axle*** passes through the ball bearings and connects the wheel assembly to the rear swing arm or front fork legs. **Figure 14-5** shows a rear wheel hub. A spacer, installed between the ball bearings, allows the axle to be tightened without binding, **Figure 14-6.**

A ***hub*** provides a mounting place for the brake drum or brake disc and sprocket (rear wheel). On some wheels, the rear hub also serves as a mounting place for the final drive shock absorber, **Figure 14-7.** The hub must be strong enough to safely withstand braking, cornering, and driving loads.

Wheel Inspection

Motorcycle wheels take a lot of abuse. Spokes can loosen or break, rims get dented, and the wheel may develop runout. These problems can affect the handling and safety of the motorcycle. To help prevent the possibility of failure, wheel inspection should be done on a regular basis. Support the motorcycle so the wheel to be inspected is off the ground. Making sure the fork is not allowed to move, raise the front wheel, and check for play. Turn the wheel and check that it rotates smoothly with no unusual noises, **Figure 14-8.**

Raise the rear wheel, and check for play in either the wheel or the swingarm pivot, **Figure 14-9.** Turn the wheel and check that it rotates smoothly with no unusual noises. If abnormal conditions are suspected, check the rear wheel bearings.

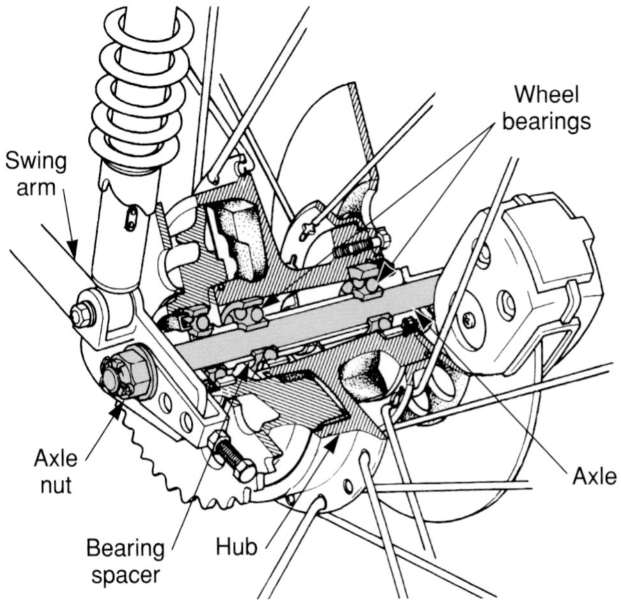

Figure 14-5. The axle passes through the swingarm and wheel bearings. When the axle nut is tightened, the axle and wheel are locked into position.

On models with bottom link front suspension, check for cracks and damage to the fork rocker arms (bottom links). Check for play in the fork rocker arm bearing section, and inspect all fasteners for looseness, **Figure 14-10.**

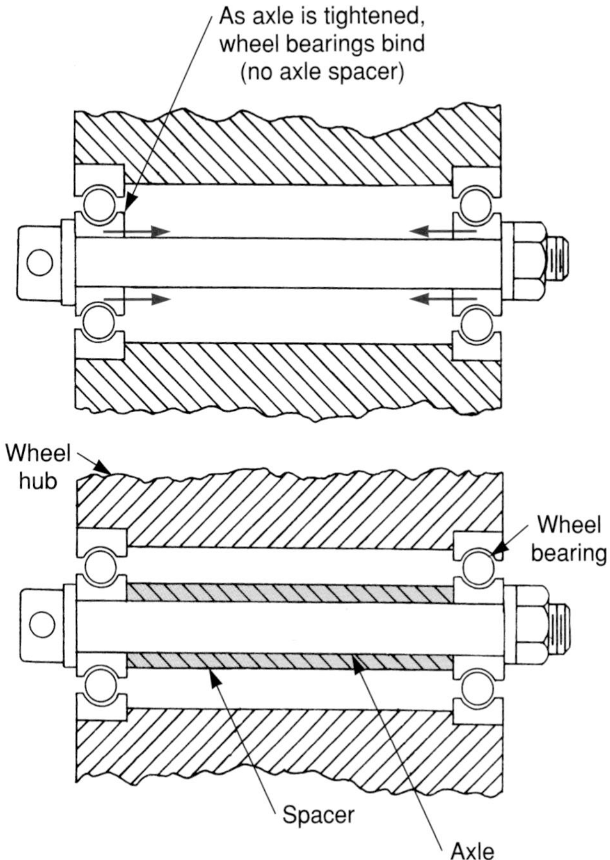

Figure 14-6. A spacer is needed between bearings to prevent side loading when the axle is tightened.

Figure 14-7. This rear hub holds the drive sprocket, final drive shock absorber, and brake disc. The hub shock absorber reduces strain on parts during rapid clutch engagement or when tire becomes airborne under power.

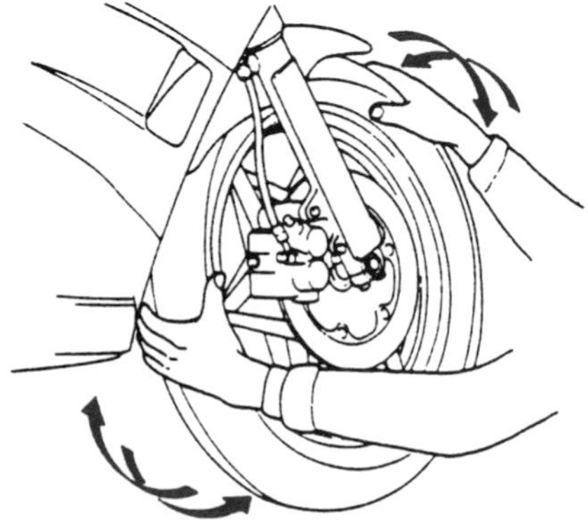

Figure 14-8. Check the front wheel to make sure it rotates smoothly. (Honda Motor Co., Ltd.)

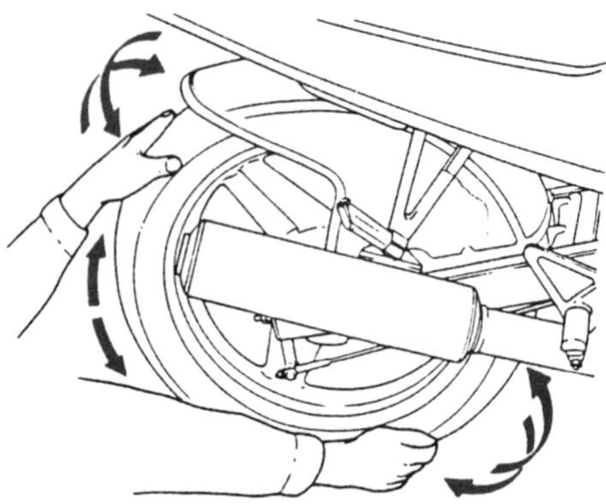

Figure 14-9. Check the rear wheel for play and swingarm operation. (Honda Motor Co., Ltd.)

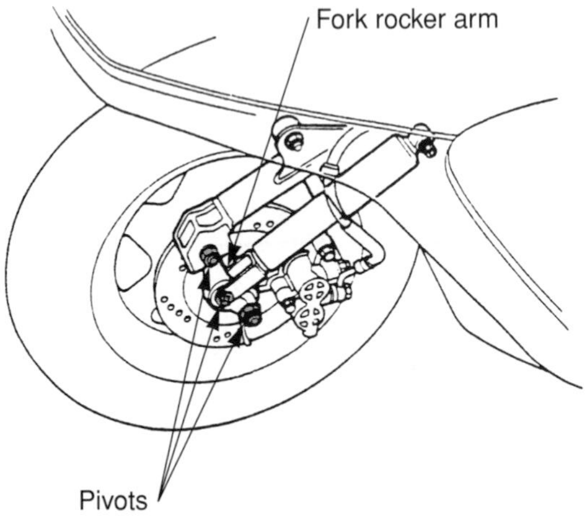

Figure 14-10. Inspect the fork rocker arm for play. (Honda Motor Co., Ltd.)

Other typical wheel inspection requirements include:

- Check wheel bearings for wear.
- Inspect wheel hub for cracks.
- Check for broken spokes.
- Check spoke tightness.
- Inspect rim for dents.
- Check spokes, rim, and hub on cast or stamped wheels for cracks.
- Check for oil leakage around the shock absorber piston rod. Inspect the rod for scoring, wear and peeling of the chrome plating on the working surface.
- Check for looseness, cracks, and damage to the attachment points of the shock absorber assembly. Retighten nuts/bolts if necessary.

Study the wheel inspection points in **Figure 14-11.** Methods of removing front and rear wheels can be found in Chapter 15.

Wheel Service

Wheel service includes:

- Repacking or replacing wheel bearings.
- Tightening loose spokes.
- Replacing broken spokes.
- Replacing dented rim or damaged hub.
- Lacing and truing complete wheel assembly.

When it is necessary to remove wheels for service, it usually requires disconnecting the speedometer cable and the removal of brake caliper(s) and drum(s). Follow the procedure given in the service manual. Support the bike with either the front or rear wheel off the ground, depending upon which wheel you are working on.

Repacking or Replacing Wheel Bearings

Wheel bearings should be cleaned and repacked with grease at periodic intervals. Wheel bearing grease may become contaminated or break down from age or heat. Riding conditions determine how often wheel bearings must be cleaned and repacked. A dirt bike used in mud, water, or sandy conditions will need its wheel bearings serviced much more frequently than a road bike. Intervals listed in the owner's manual or service manual should be observed.

The method of bearing removal varies from wheel to wheel. Different methods are used for spacing, sealing, or securing the bearings into the hub. See **Figure 14-12.** Once the bearings are removed, they should be cleaned in solvent and dried.

Warning: Never use air pressure to spin bearing while drying. The bearings could fly apart with enough force to cause a very serious injury.

Inspect bearings for pitting, smooth rotation, and play. Roughness or catching indicates a problem, and the bearing should be replaced. Once the bearings are cleaned and found to be reusable, or if new bearings are

Figure 14-11. A—Wheel bearings must move freely and smoothly. Worn bearings will have a gritty or catchy feel. B—Inspect both sides of the hub flange for cracks and replace hub if cracked. C—A broken spoke may be easily overlooked since only the spoke head may break off. Careful inspection is very important. D—Loose spokes can be detected by feel. Excessive flexing indicates looseness. E—Most dents can be located visually. Small dents, however, may require you to spin wheel while watching rim. F—Failure of an alloy wheel is rare, but occurs occasionally. Thorough inspection is important. (American Suzuki Motor Corporation)

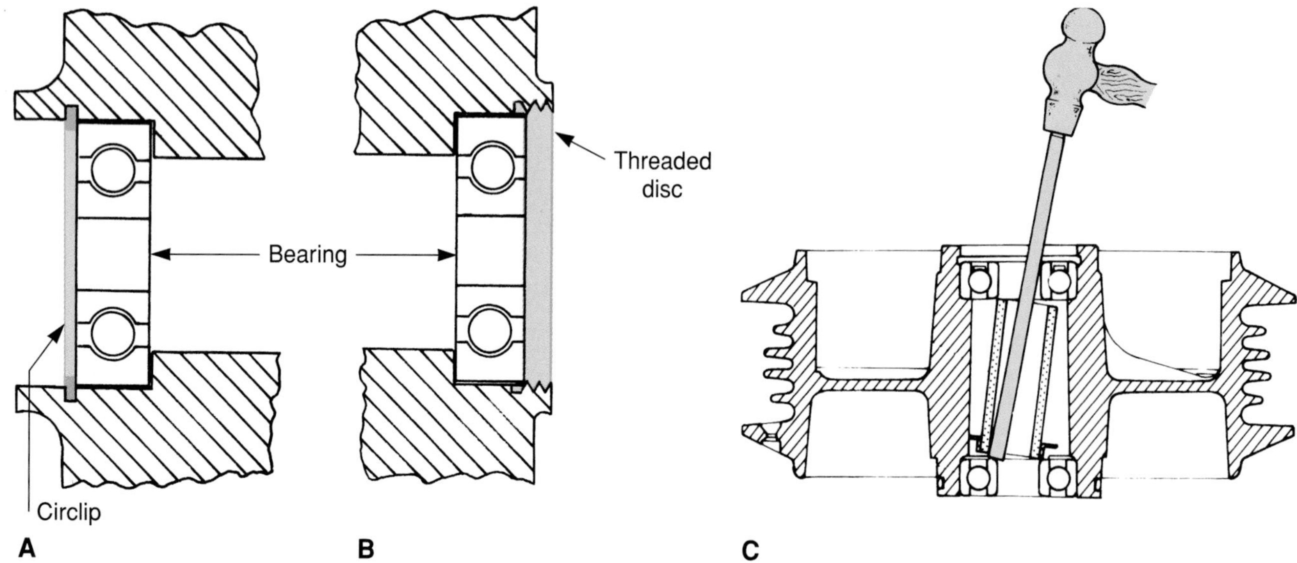

Figure 14-12. A—Bearings are sometimes secured by a circlip. B—A threaded disc can also be used to secure a bearing. C—When removing wheel bearings, a bearing spacer must be tilted to one side to gain access to the inner bearing race. Using a drift and hammer, tap around the inner race to remove bearings. (Kawasaki Motors Corporation U.S.A.)

Figure 14-13. After placing a small quantity of wheel bearing grease in the palm of one hand, rub into grease with the outer bearing race. Continue doing this until grease is forced through the top of the bearing.

Figure 14-14. When installing wheel bearings, use a bearing driver of slightly smaller diameter than the outer bearing race. Remember to install a bearing spacer.

purchased, pack them with grease. A good grade of wheel bearing grease can be used. **Figure 14-13** shows how to properly pack a wheel bearing.

When reinstalling the bearings into the hub, make sure they are not cocked, and that they are seated completely. Also, do not forget the bearing spacers. **Figure 14-14** shows proper bearing installation.

Tightening Loose Spokes

Because a wire wheel is continuously flexing, spokes have a tendency to loosen. Loose spokes can cause spoke, rim, and hub breakage. Spoke looseness should be detected during wheel inspection and should be corrected immediately. There are three ways to check for loose spokes:

- Feel, **Figure 14-15A.** Grasp spokes above the cross point and squeeze while feeling for tension. Excessive flexing indicates looseness. Tighten spokes until they feel equally stiff.
- Spoke tone, **Figure 14-15B.** Tap each spoke with a spoke wrench and listen for variation in tone. A dull tone shows looseness while a ring indicates a properly adjusted spoke.
- Spoke torque wrench, **Figure 14-15C.** Check for unequal tension with a spoke torque wrench or spoke wrench. Some service manuals give spoke torque specifications.

A

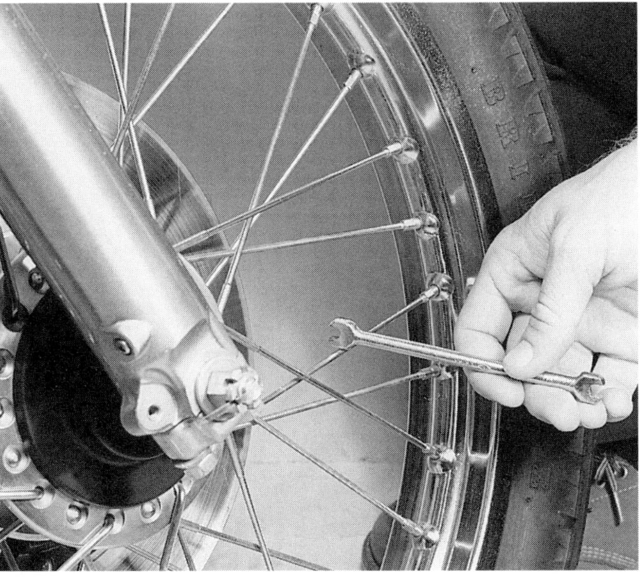

B

C

Figure 14-15. Three methods for checking spoke looseness. A—Feel. B—Spoke tone. C—Torque.

Spoke tightening should be done if only a small number of spokes are loose. If several spokes are loose, the wheel should be trued. For spoke tightening, let the air out of the tire. After tightening the spokes, the wheel should be checked for trueness (wobble). The service manual gives specifications for acceptable runout.

Caution: If any spoke requires more than two turns when tightening, remove the tube so that threads protruding past the nipple can be ground off. If not ground off, the spoke could puncture the inner tube, Figure 14-16.

Replacing Broken Spokes

Broken spokes are usually caused by loose spokes. Loose spokes throw an excessive strain on surrounding spokes. Replacement of broken spokes usually requires:

- Loosening of all the spokes.
- Partial disassembly of wheel to gain access to the damaged spoke.
- Truing the wheel.

Replacing a Dented Rim

Replacement of a dented rim requires removal of all spoke nipples. Once the nipples are removed, the spokes can be pulled out of the rim. Before removing the rim, it is a good idea to tape or tie the spokes together where they cross. Look at **Figure 14-17.** This keeps the spokes in proper position and makes reassembly much easier. Check the service manual to see if specific positioning of the rim is necessary. Rim replacement always requires wheel truing.

Spoke
Spoke nipple
Rim
Grind off
exposed threads

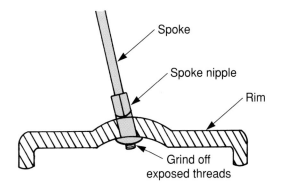

Figure 14-16. If any spoke nipple requires more than two turns to achieve proper tension, there may be spoke threads protruding past the end of the nipple. These threads must be ground or filed off to prevent puncturing the inner tube.

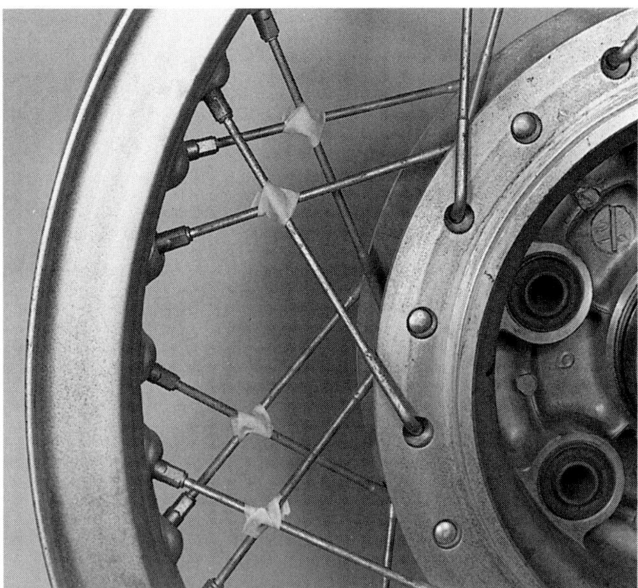

Figure 14-17. Taping spokes at their cross point before removal makes reassembly easier, since all spokes stay in position.

Lacing and Truing a Wire Wheel Assembly

Wheel lacing is the building of a wire wheel using a hub, spokes, and rim. Wheel lacing is necessary when:

- A new wheel is built from scratch.
- A hub is replaced (broken hub or worn out brake drum).
- All spokes need replacement (spoke nipples seized).

There are numerous patterns and procedures for the start of a wheel lacing process. It is important to follow service manual instructions for the particular wheel being built. The two types of hubs are the symmetrical hub and conical hub. They are shown in **Figure 14-18.**

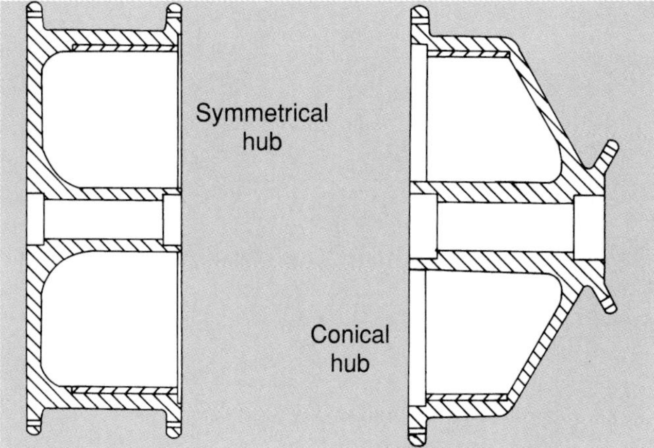

Figure 14-18. Both sides of a symmetrical hub are the same diameter so spokes are all the same length. One side of a conical hub is smaller than the other, so spokes on the small side must be longer.

Before beginning to lace a wheel, you should always remember that there can be differences in individual spokes, spoke crossing patterns, and spoke angles. These factors affect how you lace the wheel.

The major differences in spokes are length and size of the spoke, and angle and length of the spoke throat. **Figure 14-19** shows a few typical wheel spokes. The type of hub and the intended use of the motorcycle determines which type of spoke is used in the wheel.

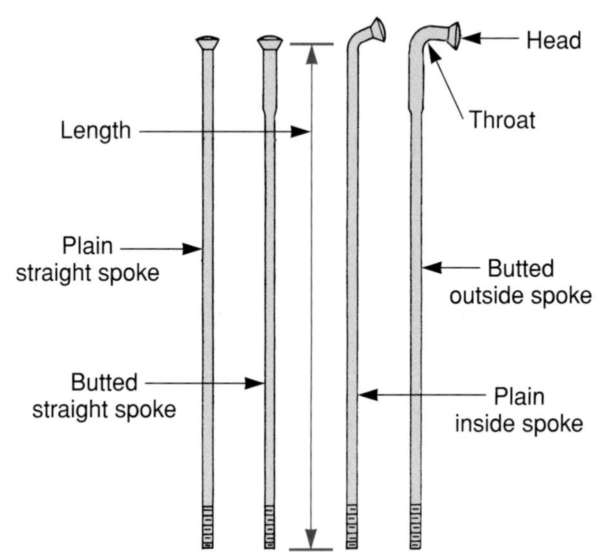

Figure 14-19. Butted spokes are stronger than plain spokes at the head and bend, where spokes usually break. Spoke length is measured from bend or base of head to threaded end. Overall length, spoke size or diameter, length, and angle of throat must be noted for proper wheel assembly.

The spoke crossing pattern refers to the number of other spokes a single spoke crosses on one side of the wheel. Common spoke crossing patterns are cross-two and cross-three. As more spokes are crossed, the wheel assembly will become stronger. For some extreme use applications, a cross-four pattern is custom laced to give added strength.

Spoke angle is the difference in width between the hub and rim spoke attachment points. **Figure 14-20** shows spoke angle and the difference between conical and symmetrical hubs. Because the angles differ from side to side on a conical hub, the holes in the rim must be at the proper angle. For this reason, a rim intended for a symmetrical hub cannot be properly laced to a conical hub and vice versa. A rim intended for a conical hub must be installed in the proper direction. If the rim is not marked as described in the service manual, it must be inspected to determine which side has the greatest spoke angle. This will normally be the brake side.

Wheel Lacing Procedure

A symmetrical wheel is one of the easiest wheels to lace. **Figure 14-21** shows the steps for proper wheel lacing.

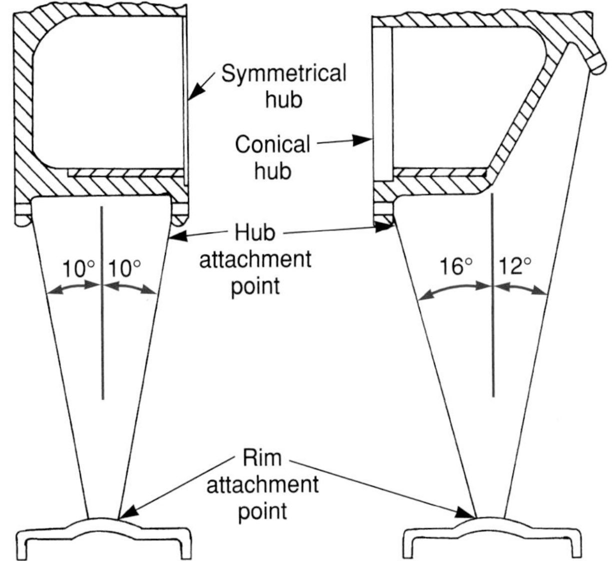

Figure 14-20. Notice that spoke angle is the same on each side of a symmetrical hub, but is different on each side of a conical hub.

1. Select matching components and organize the spokes carefully.
2. Insert inside spokes into the hub.
3. Screw nipples onto the spokes and tighten equally.
4. Install outside spokes, and screw on nipples and tighten evenly.
5. Tighten spokes to true the wheel.

Wheel Truing

Wheel truing is the process of:

- Adjusting rim offset.
- Adjusting lateral runout.
- Adjusting radial runout.
- Maintaining proper runout adjustment during final tightening of spokes.

A wheel truing stand and good quality spoke wrenches are required for accurate truing. For the wheel to be balanced, it must have a minimum of runout. There are two types of runout, lateral and radial.

Lateral runout indicates how parallel the rim is to the hub. Lateral runout causes side-to-side wobble. ***Radial runout*** shows how concentric (round) the rim is with the hub. Radial runout causes up and down movement. **Figure 14-22** shows lateral and radial runout.

It is important to understand how lateral and radial runout are changed. **Figure 14-23** shows adjustment of lateral runout. **Figure 14-24** shows how radial runout is adjusted. When adjusting either lateral or radial runout, adjust the wheel area with the least runout.

It is best to make an initial adjustment of lateral runout first. This allows you to see how much radial runout is present. Next, make an initial adjustment of radial runout. At this point, all spokes should be snug. It may be necessary to alternately adjust lateral and radial runout.

Rim offset should now be checked, as in **Figure 14-25.** The service manual usually gives rim offset specifications. Rim offset is adjusted by loosening all the spokes on one side of the wheel and tightening the spokes on the other side of the wheel. All spokes must be loosened or tightened the same amount to maintain minimum lateral and radial runout.

Important practices that make wheel truing easier are:

- Progressively tighten and loosen spoke nipples.
- Keep all spokes at approximately the same tension (snug).
- Lubricate spoke nipples and threads.
- Do not try to change runout with only a few spokes.
- Alternately check lateral and radial runout throughout the truing process.
- Properly tighten all spokes.

Final Tightening of Spokes

Proper final tightening of spokes should have minimal effect on runout. Use tape or crayon to divide the wheel into quarters (four sections), as illustrated in **Figure 14-26.** Start by tightening quarter number one, then number three, number two, and finally number four. Make a final check of runout and offset. Also, check the spokes for the correct tightness. Use a spoke torque wrench or check them by tone. Maximum allowable runout will be listed in the service manual. It is best to get as close to zero runout as possible.

Tires

Competent service methods and the correct choice of tire tread and size is essential to the safety of a motorcycle. This portion of the chapter explains tire designs, sizes, markings, as well as maintenance and repair procedures. It will prepare motorcycle technicians to use manufacturer recommendations when selecting and servicing motorcycle tires.

Tire Design

Recent years have seen many advances in tire design. Because some motorcycles are extremely powerful and heavy, better tires are needed to provide proper wear and handling characteristics. There are two types of tires: tube and tubeless, **Figure 14-27.** The principal difference between the two is the method in which air is held.

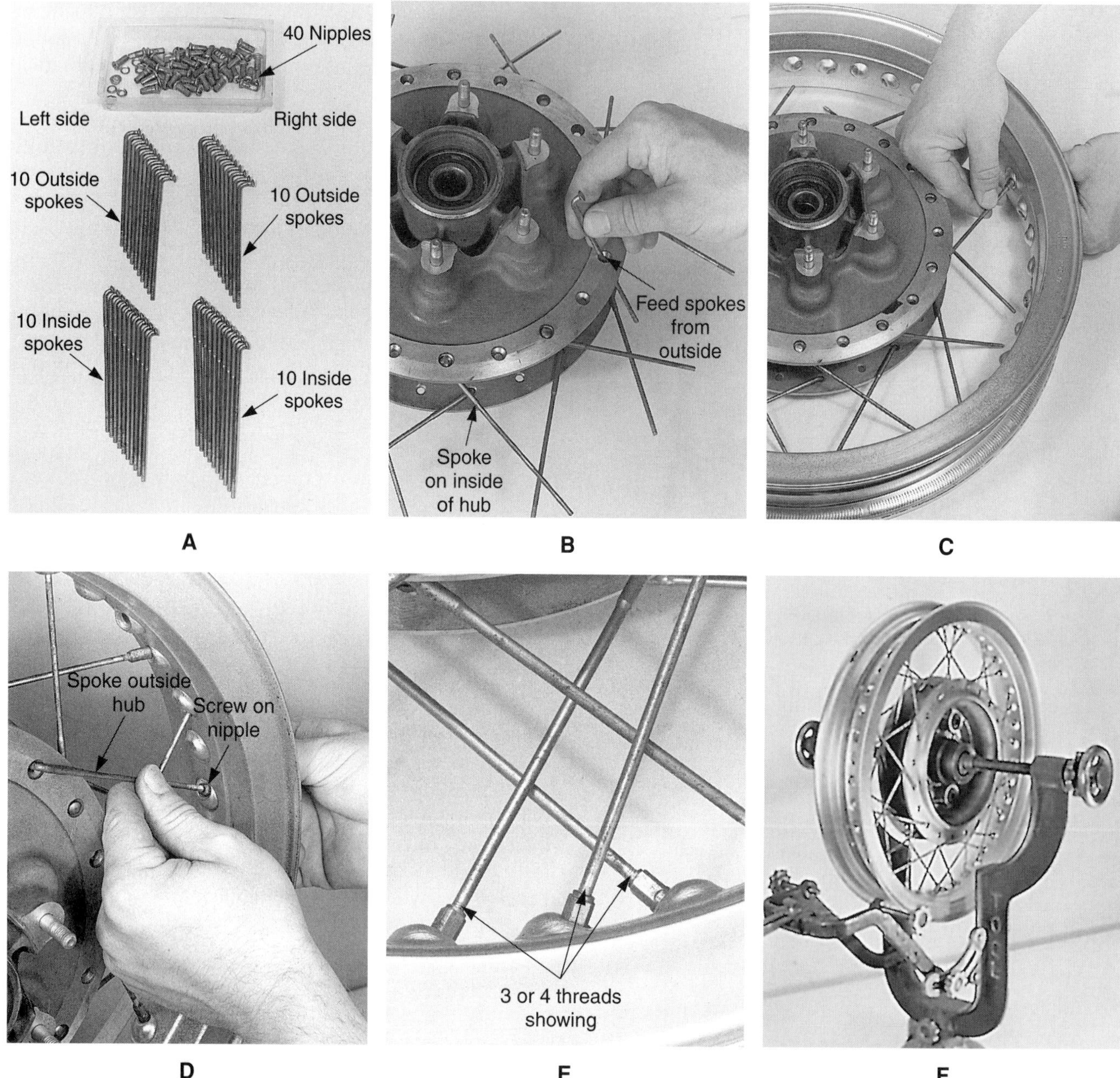

Figure 14-21. Steps needed to lace a symmetrical wire wheel. A—Organize all parts carefully. B—Install the inside spokes in each side of the hub. C—Lay rim into position and start nipples in a few threads. D—Install outside spokes, working around. Install spokes on the alternate sides of the wheel. E—With all the nipples installed, evenly snug all nipples with a spoke wrench. Tighten until three or four threads show above each nipple. F—Install the wheel assembly on a truing stand for final tightening of spokes and truing of wheel.

Tube Tire

Tube tires use an air-filled tube within the tire's casing. Therefore, air in the tire leaks out instantly when a nail or other sharp object penetrates the tire and tube.

Tubeless Tire

Tubeless tires have a rubber layer (inner liner) glued to the inside, which prevents air from filtering through. This acts in place of a tube. It also has a special bead area, that together with the rim, makes a tube unnecessary. This inner liner is sufficient in thickness and does not stretch like a tube. Even when a nail penetrates the tire, the hole does not get any bigger. Instead, it closes around the nail, preventing air from leaking out.

Tubeless tires have the word *tubeless* stamped on their sidewalls. Tubeless tire rims have *tubeless tire applicable* stamped on them. Each rim has a snap-in valve on it. The rim mating areas and rim valves in tubeless tires are different from tube tires. For this reason, never mix the two types. Using a tube tire on a tubeless rim may cause excess friction and heat which can weaken the tire structure.

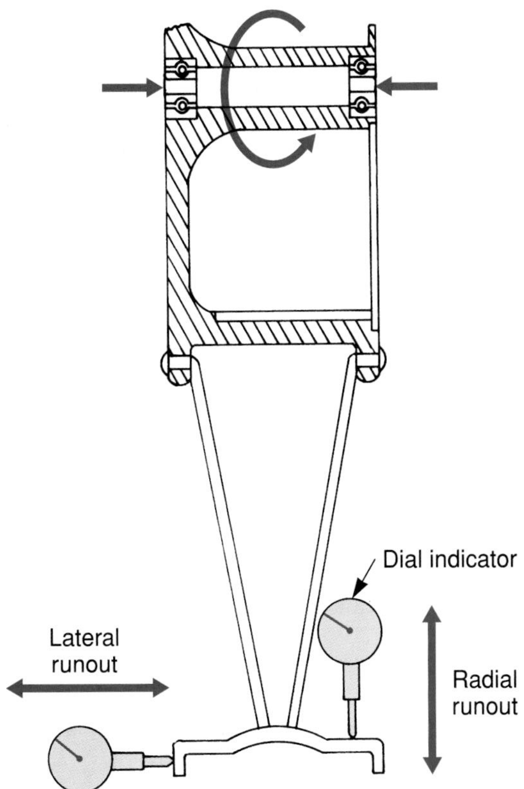

Figure 14-22. Lateral runout is side-to-side movement or wobble of rim. Radial runout is up-and-down movement of rim. Note the dial indicator positioning to measure each type of runout.

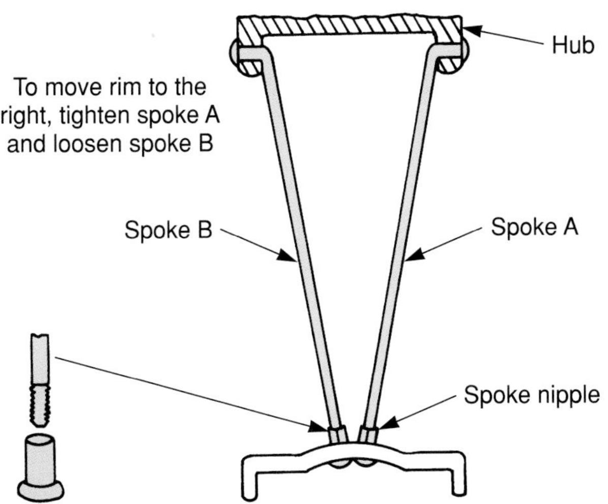

Figure 14-23. Lateral runout adjustment is done by tightening or loosening spokes as shown.

Tire Replacement

When selecting a replacement tire, keep in mind these five considerations: tire construction, size, load and speed ratings, motorcycle use, and tread pattern. Check the service manual for manufacturer's specific recommendations. Three types of motorcycle tires are available: bias ply, bias-belted, and radial. See **Figure 14-28.**

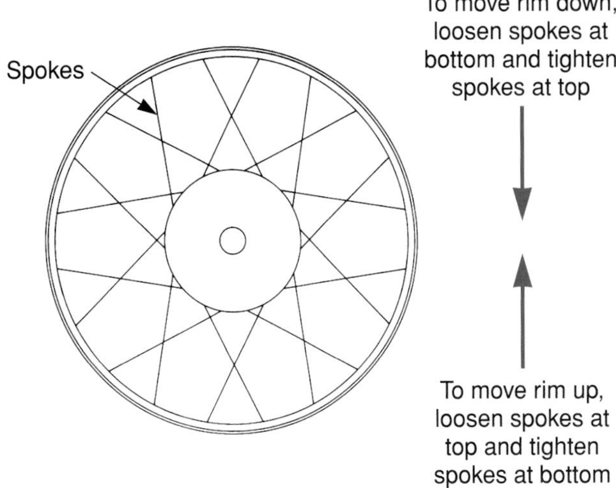

Figure 14-24. Method of checking for radial runout adjustment.

Bias-ply Tires

Bias-ply tires have two or more cord plies that run at opposing angles of about 35°. This type of tire provides fairly strong side walls, good handling, comfortable riding at all speeds, high rolling resistance, and is usually low priced. Tread wear is greater, however, than with either of the other two types.

Bias-belted Tires

Bias-belted tires also have corded plies that run at opposing angles of about 35°. In addition, they have a two-ply belt under the tread. The bias-belted tire provides longer tread wear, fair handling, a soft ride, and is usually medium priced.

Radial Tires

In a ***radial tire,*** the cord plies run vertically between the tire beads, and a belt of two or more plies is added under the tread. Radial tires provide a smooth ride at only high speed and are high in price. However, they have a high resistance to scuffing and lateral movement and, under normal driving conditions, their tread life is longer than any other tire.

At one time, all cord plies were made of cotton. New cord plies are made of rayon, nylon, polyester, and fiberglass. These synthetic fibers, along with steel wire or mesh, are also used in the tread belts. Each synthetic has its own qualities, and are used extensively. Bias tires are usually marked with the letter *B,* while the letter *R* indicates radial construction.

Tire Size

Tire size is determined by the rim diameter and tire width at its widest point. Tire size markings are given on the tire sidewall. A typical tire size marking of 4.50H-17 means that the cross-section (width) is 4.5″ and is intended for a 17″ rim.

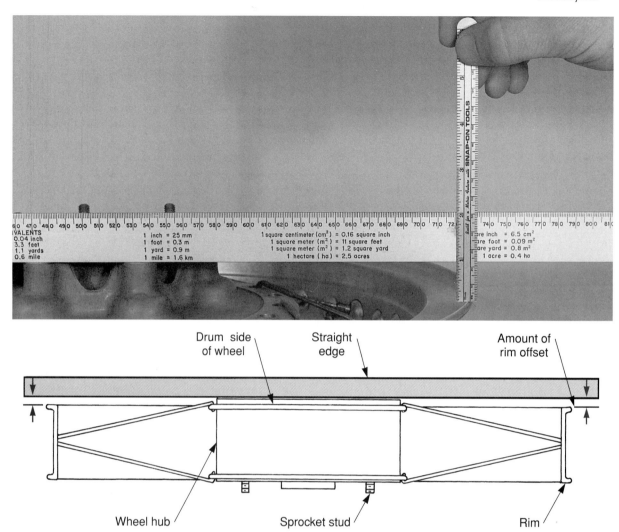

Figure 14-25. Procedures for adjusting rim offset. A—With disc brakes, place a straightedge on the disc mounting boss and measure to rim. B—With drum brakes, lay the straightedge on the drum edge and measure down to the rim. Compare measurements with specifications. If specifications are not indicated, the rim must be centered.

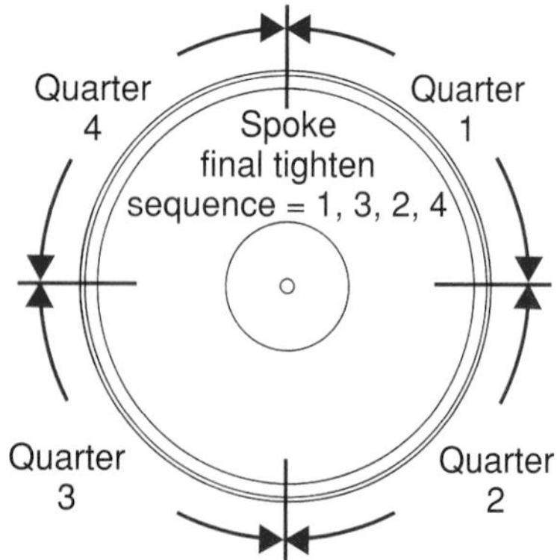

Figure 14-26. Divide wheel into four sections to final tighten spokes. Tightening sequence is one, three, two, four. Tighten each spoke equally.

When replacing a tire, it is best to select one of the same size as the one used by the original equipment manufacturer (OEM). Changing the size may create problems. Vehicle geometry is an important factor in motorcycle design and changes in tire size can affect the bike's handling and stability. Never replace the original tire with a tire that is smaller.

Load and Speed

Letters appearing in the tire size markings indicate the sustained speed at which the tire is safe. For example, a tire with an *S* marking has been tested at a sustained speed of 112 mph for six hours. The following list shows the markings and speed limits.

S—112 mph or 180 kmh max.

H—130 mph or 208 kmh max.

V—150 mph or 240 kmh max.

Z—Over 150 mph or 240 kmh.

Maximum load rating and inflation pressure also appears on the sidewall. A tire balancing mark is provided and should be properly aligned. Refer to the service manual for details.

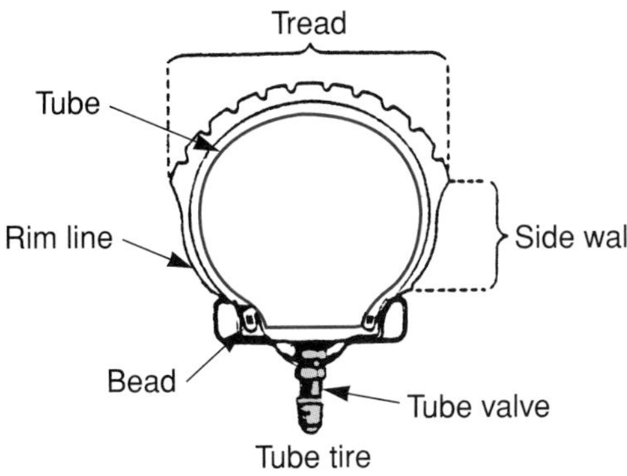

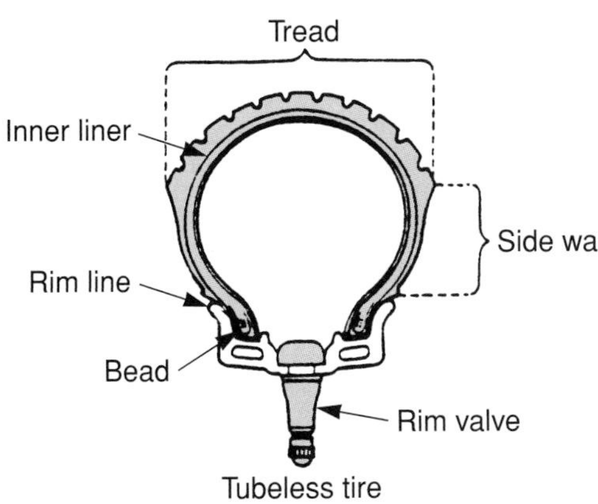

Figure 14-27. The principle differences between tube and tubeless tires. (Honda Motor Co., Ltd.)

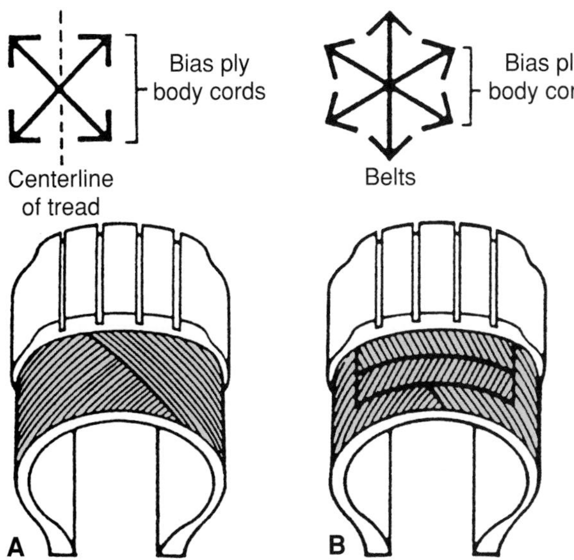

Figure 14-28. Types of tire construction. A—Conventional bias ply. B—Bias-belted ply. C—Radial ply.

Use and Tread Patterns

Tread patterns and profile vary depending upon use and surface being traveled. For example, high-performance motorcycle tires are best used when sport riding under dry conditions. They are heavily grooved with a deep tread pattern. Universal tires are considered to have dual designs suitable for both road and dirt use. They are designed to displace water when road surfaces are wet and to provide good balance and grip on dry roads. Universal designs are also dual purpose, but are not as suitable for road use. Knobby designs are strictly for off-road dirt riding use. **Figure 14-29** shows examples of each of these types. Because there are so many different designs and tread patterns available, it is advisable to follow manufacturer's suggestions regarding tire size and design. **Figure 14-30** illustrates the tread design found on most ATVs. Most ATV tires are tubeless.

Figure 14-29. Motorcycle tires vary in rubber compounds, profile, and tread pattern. A—High performance road tire suitable for sport riding. B—Three universal designs are intended for use on road or in dirt. C—Trials universal design is also dual purpose but not as suitable for road use. D—Knobby design is strictly for off-road, dirt riding.

Figure 14-30. Typical tire tread found on an ATV. (Yamaha Motor Corporation U.S.A.)

Tire codes are usually stamped on the tire casing. **Figure 14-31** gives the inch indication, while **Figure 14-32** shows the metric indications. To determine the height/tread (width) ratio, measure the tire height and tread width, then compute the ratio. See **Figure 14-33.**

Tire Inspection

For safety, tire condition should be checked occasionally. Visually inspect the tread and sidewall for cuts, cracks, and wear. Uneven tread wear can be caused by incorrect inflation pressure or an unbalanced tire. If a road hazard, such as a pothole is struck, it is very important to check the tire, rim, and spokes for possible damage.

One of the most important inspections is ***tire pressure.*** Over a period of time, all tires lose air. Check the air pressure in the tires. If the tire pressure is too low to support the load, it can cause heat due to sidewall bending. Underinflation also causes the cord layers to separate and wear the sides of the tread. Overinflation will result in inferior riding comfort. High pressure will also cause the tire to skid and the tread to wear at its center. See **Figure 14-34.**

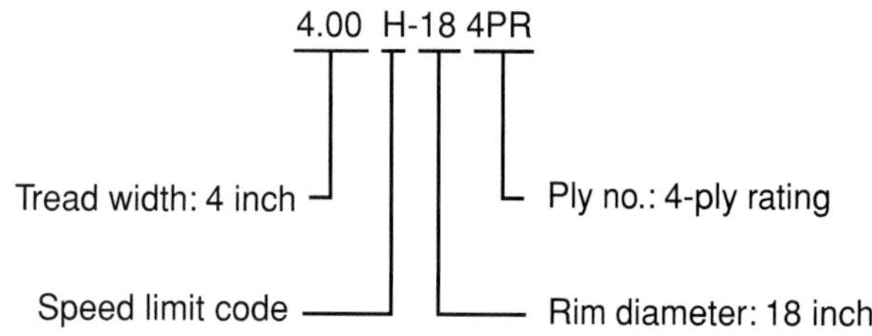

Figure 14-31. Tire code in inch indication.

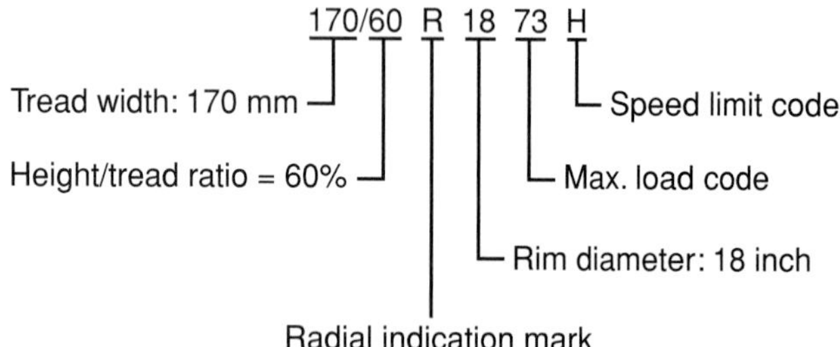

Figure 14-32. Tire code in metric indication.

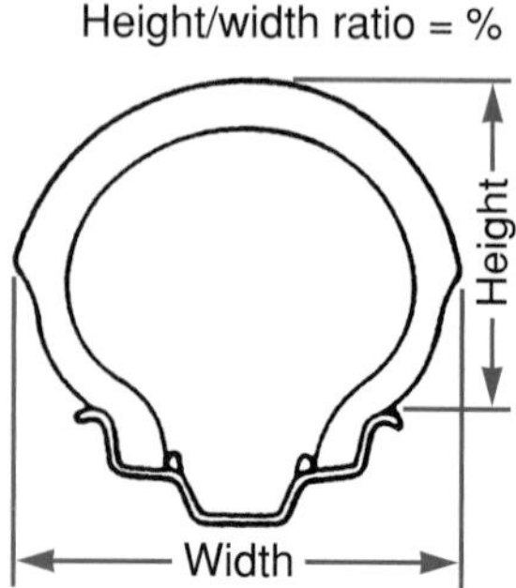

Figure 14-33. Height/tread ratio measurement points. (Honda Motor Co., Ltd.)

Tire Service

Tire service includes inspecting the tire for damage and defects; changing a tire, repairing a flat tire, and balancing a tire and wheel assembly.

Changing a Tire

The steps for changing a tube tire with a spoke rim wheel are shown in **Figure 14-35.** Refer to this illustration as each step is discussed. To dismount a tire, unscrew and remove the valve core from the valve stem. This will deflate the tire. Then, loosen the bead locks and remove the tire.

Break the bead away from the rim and collapse it with a tire bead breaker. If a tire bead breaker is not available, step on the side wall to collapse the bead. Lubricate the rim with a rubber lubricant or water to aid removal and prevent tire damage. Never step on the rim when removing the tire.

Press one side of the tire into the drop center section of the wheel. This must be done for tire removal. Use two tire irons or levers to pull the bead over the lip of the rim. Keep working the tire irons around the rim until the tire bead comes off the wheel. When dealing with tube tires, insert the tire iron on the same side as the valve and raise the bead over the rim. On tube tires, insert the tire iron from the valve side and raise the bead over the rim. Always use a rim protector when using tire irons. With a tube-tire, pull the tube out of the tire, once one bead is

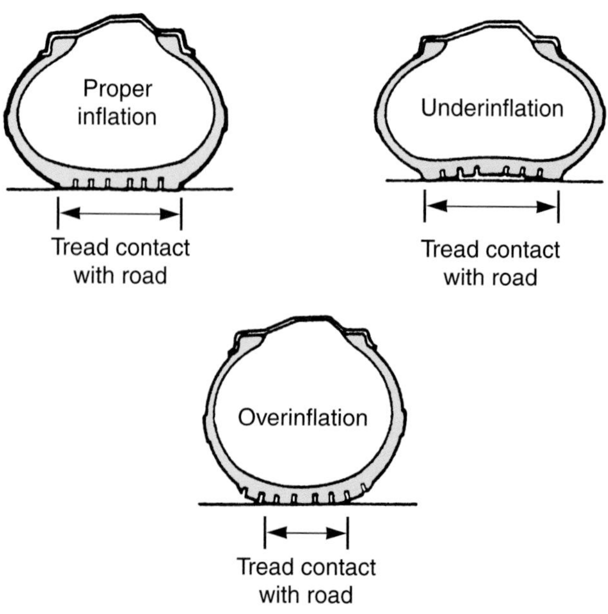

Figure 14-34. Effects of tire air pressure on tires. (Yamaha Motor Corporation U.S.A.)

Figure 14-35. Steps for removing a tube motorcycle tire from its spoke wheel. A—Unscrew valve core and stem locknut. B—Force tire off the outer lip of the rim. C—Lubricate tire bead to aid removal. D—Pry the bead over the rim with tire irons or levers. E—Work around the rim with the irons. F—Remove the tube after freeing one bead. G—Pry other bead off the wheel. H—Check under strip for problems.

removed. Remove the other tire bead by prying with the irons. You may need to hit the tire with a rubber mallet to free it from the wheel. After tire removal, pull the rubber rim strip off. Check under the strip for problems (rust, spokes protruding too far into wheel).

To remove a tire and disassemble it from the wheel of an ATV vehicle, proceed as follows:

1. Place the vehicle on level ground. Support the vehicle by jack or block. Remove the wheel by removing the wheel nuts.
2. After removing the air valve cap, release the air pressure by depressing the nozzle or removing the valve stem core.
3. Dismount the bead from the rim completely as shown in **Figure 14-36.**
4. Using a set of tire irons or levers, separate the tire from the wheel. When using tire irons, do not scratch or hit the sealing portion (hump) of the wheel or it may cause an air leak.

Tire Installation

Tire installation is just as easy as removal. A ***tire changing machine*** makes tire replacement easier and helps prevent damage to cast and stamped wheels. If the tire has a balance dot (paint mark), install the tire with this mark aligned with the valve. If the tire has a rotation direction (rotational tire), install the tire with the mark pointing in the direction of rotation.

To mount a tube tire, follow the steps given in **Figure 14-37.** Spray the tire bead with an approved rubber lubricant or silicone. Stand the tire upright, hold it with one hand and, starting from the opposite side to the valve, install one side of the tire on the rim. Try to install as much as you can by hand.

If the tire uses a tube, carefully fit the tube into the tire. Position the stem in the rim hole. Put a little air in the tube to remove wrinkles that could damage the tube. Then, deflate the tube so you can install the other bead.

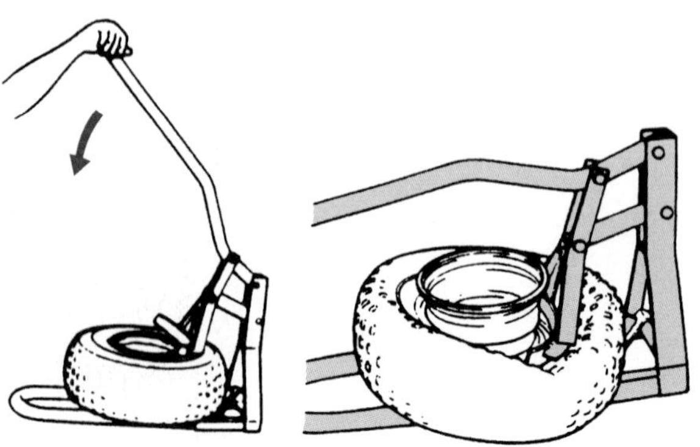

Figure 14-36. Removing an ATV tubeless tire from its rim using a bead breaker tool. (American Suzuki Motor Corporation)

Warning: Do not use screwdrivers to install a tire on a wheel. The sharp screwdrivers could damage the tube, possibly causing tube failure and rider injury or death.

A bead lock is a clamping device that pinches the tire beads against the rim. It prevents the tire from spinning on the wheel during periods of hard braking or rapid acceleration. **Figure 14-38** shows the installation of a bead lock.

After 3/4 of the bead has been installed, check the bead on the opposite side. Tap on the tire tread surface with a rubber hammer so the tire and rim fit evenly around the circumference. The last portion of the bead is more difficult to install. The rim and bead may be damaged if the bead on the opposite side of the point where you are working is not in the rim center.

Note: When installing tubeless tires, a loud pop sound might be heard as the bead seats onto the rim. This is normal. If air leaks out from between the rim and bead of a tubeless tire, let the wheel stand with the valve at the bottom and put air in while pushing down on the tire. For any special instructions on installing tires on spoke rims, check the appropriate service manual.

Before inflating a tube tire, double check that the valve stem is straight. This is a common problem that can cause tube failure, **Figure 14-39.** To correct this problem, collapse the bead by squeezing the tire: carefully rotate the tire and tube on the rim until the valve stem is straight.

Inflate the tire and check that the bead seats on the rim securely and the tire rim line is concentric with the rim. Use a pressure gauge to ensure the tire is inflated to service manual specifications, **Figure 14-40.**

When installing a tubeless ATV tire on its rim, proceed as follows:

1. Clean the rim bead seat and flanges. Lubricate the tire bead seat rim flanges and base with clean water only. Soap or other tire lubricants may leave a slippery residue that can cause the tire to shift on the rim, possibly resulting in a sudden loss of air pressure while riding.
2. Before mounting the tire on the wheel, inspect the sealing portion of the wheel. When mounting a tire, be sure to install the tire onto the rim with the arrow on the sidewall pointing in the direction of rotation. Also, be certain that the outer side of the wheel rim faces to the outside.
3. Install the tire on the wheel rim by hand as illustrated in **Figure 14-41.** To simplify the installation, do so at a point where the rim shoulder width is the narrowest.

A

B

C

D

Figure 14-37. Procedure for installing a tube tire on a wheel. A—Push the rim into the tire so that one bead is resting in the rim strip area. Pry the remainder of the bead over the rim with motorcycle tire irons. B—Tuck the tube into the tire, make sure to stick the stem through the hole in the rim. Screw locknut onto the stem halfway. Avoid kinks in the tube. C—Partially inflate the tube to remove any wrinkles or folds in the tube. Deflate the tube before installing the other bead. D—Pry the other bead over the rim without pinching the tube and install the core. Tighten stem nut and inflate tire to specifications.

Figure 14-38. A bead lock is used to prevent tire from slipping on the rim. As the bead lock is tightened, it pinches the beads against the rim.

Figure 14-39. A cocked valve stem can cause an inner tube to rupture and leak where the stem is bonded into the tube.

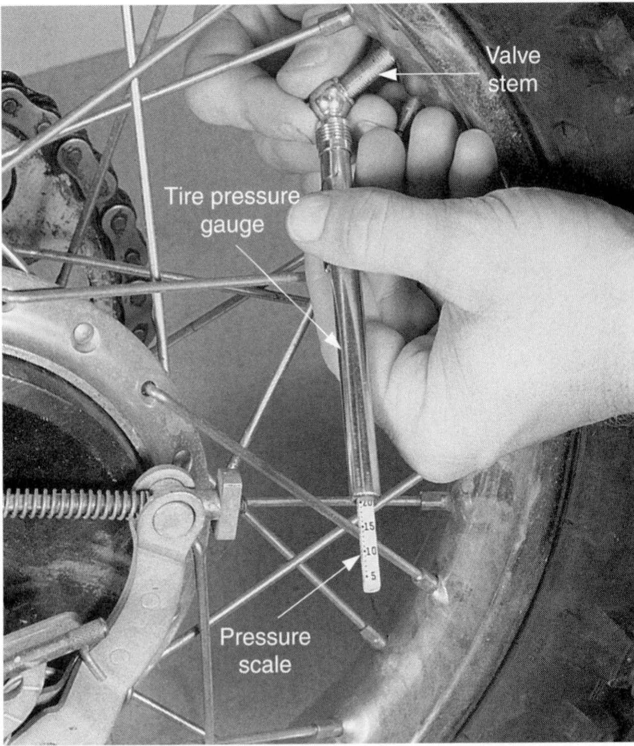

Figure 14-40. A tire pressure gauge is used to check air pressure in tires. This tire is inflated to 20 psi (138 kPa).

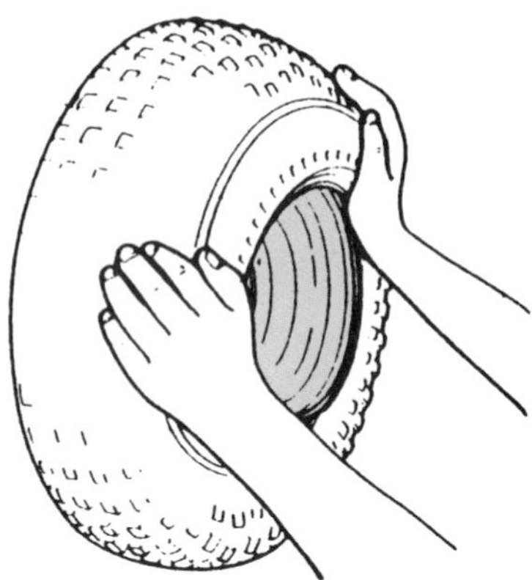

Figure 14-41. Installing an ATV tubeless tire. (American Suzuki Motor Corporation)

4. Before installing the valve core, inspect it carefully. Then inflate it to set the tire bead. The maximum pressure for seating the bead is usually indicated on the sidewall. Do not inflate the tire beyond this pressure. The tire could burst with sufficient force to cause severe injury.

5. Check the "rim line" cast on the tire sidewalls. It must be equally spaced from the wheel rim all the way around. If the distance between the rim line and the wheel rim varies greatly, this indicates that the bead is not properly seated. If this is so, deflate the tire completely, and unseat the bead for both sides. Coat the bead with lubricant, and try again.

Warning: Any attempt to mount passenger car tires on a motorcycle rim may cause the tire bead to separate from the rim with enough explosive force to cause serious injury or death.

Repairing a Flat Tire

It is not recommended to patch punctured or damaged inner tubes since it can cause an unsafe condition. This is especially true of road bike tires. Usually, a punctured tire can be repaired by installing a new tube. Be sure to remove the object that caused the puncture and thoroughly inspect the tire for sidewall damage, ply separation, or any condition that might make it unsafe.

Tubeless tires can sometimes be repaired with special plug patch kit. For example, to plug patch a tubeless ATV tire with damage of less than 5/8″ (15.88 mm,) proceed as follows. Tire repairs for damage greater than 5/8″ (15.88 mm) should be done by a professional repair shop. Ideally, tires with this type of damage should be replaced.

1. Check the tire for the puncturing objects. Chalk mark the punctured area and remove the object, **Figure 14-42.**

2. Apply cement to a rubber plug as directed by the kit's manufacturer. Then push the inserting needle (which comes with the kit) and plug into the hole until the plug is slightly above the tire; the plug will stay in the tire. Trim the plug to 1/4″ (6.35 mm) above the tire surface.

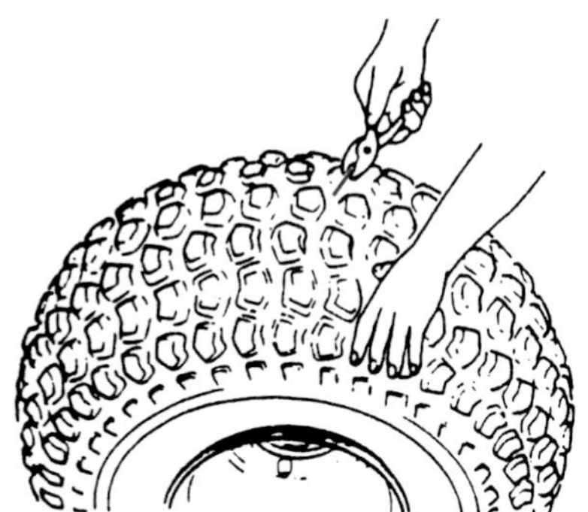

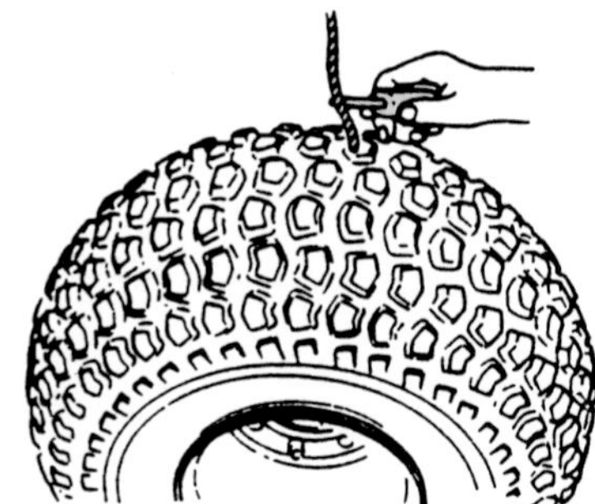

Figure 14-42. Method of plug patching a tubeless tire. (Honda Motor Co., Ltd.)

Allow the repair to dry. Drying time will vary with air temperature. Refer to the tire repair kit manufacturer's recommendations. Inflate the tire and test the seal by dabbing a small amount of water around the plug. Escaping air will cause bubbles in the water. If there is leakage, remove the tire and apply a cold patch to the inside of the tire.

1. If a plug has been inserted, trim it even with the inner tire surface. Temporarily place a rubber patch that is at least twice the size of the puncture over the damaged area. Make a mark around the patch, slightly larger than the patch itself. Then remove the patch and roughen the area marked inside the tire with a tire buffer or a wire brush, **Figure 14-43A.** Clean the rubber dust from the buffed area.
2. Apply cement over the area marked and allow it to dry until tacky. Remove the lining from the patch and center it over the damaged area. Press the patch against the area with a special tire roller, **Figure 14-43B.**

Warning: Do not attempt to repair a tire that is leaking through the sidewall. Replace any tire with this type of damage.

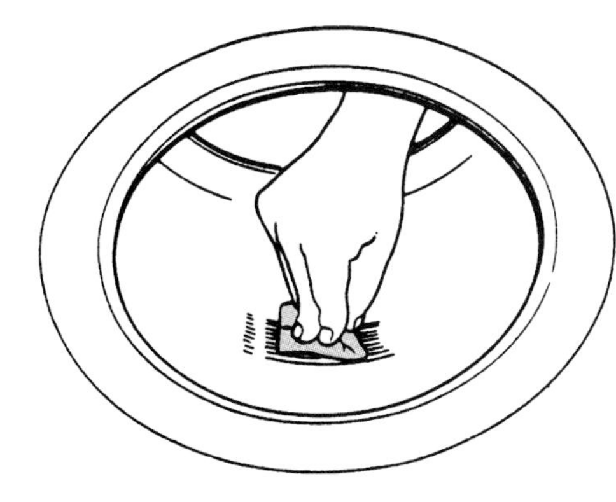

A

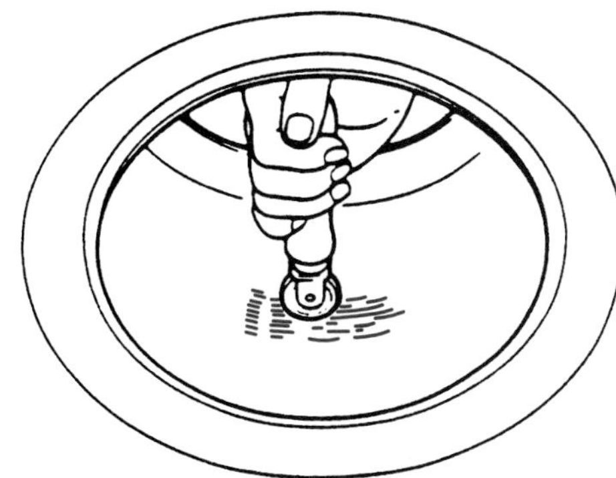

B

Figure 14-43. Using a cold patch to fix a tire air leak. (Honda Motor Co., Ltd.)

Balancing the Tire and Wheel Assembly

Balance is changed whenever the tire is moved on the rim, or a new tire is installed. Mount the wheel, tire, and brake assembly in an inspection stand. Spin the wheel, allow it to stop, and mark the lowest (heaviest) part of the wheel with chalk. Do this two or three times to verify the heaviest area. If the wheel is balanced, it will not stop consistently in the same position.

To balance the wheel, install wheel weights on the lightest side of the rim, the side opposite the chalk marks. Add just enough weight so the wheel will no longer stop in the same position when spun.

Another way to balance a wheel is to use a ***bubble balancer.*** This device makes static (no movement) balancing a quick job. A bubble balancer suspends the wheel horizontally and uses a bubble to indicate the light side of the wheel. Lead weights are added until the bubble is centered, indicating the wheel is balanced, **Figure 14-44.**

Some motorcycle shops are now equipped with electronic wheel balancers. These devices allow the technician to perform both static and dynamic wheel balance. To use an electronic wheel balancer, install the tire on the balancer, using special adapters as needed. Remove all weights from the wheel before starting the balancer. Turn on the machine and enter the tire rim width, tire size, and offset. If the balancer is equipped with a protective hood, close it and start the balancer. The readout will tell you precisely where and how much weight to add to balance the wheel. These balancers make the use of bubble balancers unnecessary. To store a tire to be reused, adjust air pressure to one-half of recommended pressure.

Troubleshooting Wheels and Tires

The following are some wheel and tire problems and possible causes that the motorcycle technician may run into:

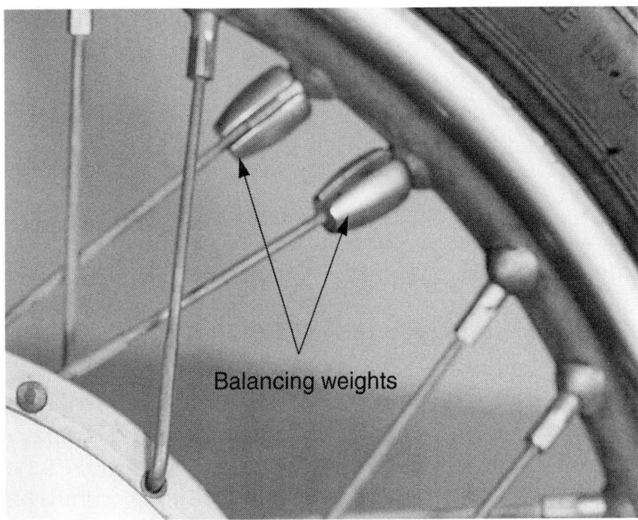

Figure 14-44. This type of balancing weight is slotted to slip over the spoke and lock onto the spoke nipple.

Hard Steering

- Steering head bearing adjustment nut too tight.
- Faulty steering head bearings.
- Damaged steering head bearings.
- Insufficient tire pressure.
- Faulty tire.

Steers to One Side or Does Not Track Straight

- Bent fork.
- Bent front axle; wheel installed incorrectly.
- Faulty steering head bearing.
- Bent frame.
- Worn wheel bearing.
- Worn swing arm pivot.

Front Wheel Wobbling

- Bent rim.
- Worn front wheel bearings.
- Faulty tire.

Wheel Turns Hard

- Misadjusted brake.
- Faulty wheel bearing.
- Faulty speedometer gear.
- Tight chain.

Summary

A motorcycle wheel rotates on an axle and supports the rubber tire. It also serves as a secondary shock absorber, softening bumps and other imperfections in the road. Three types of wheels are used on today's motorcycles: wire wheels, cast wheels, and stamped wheels. The wire wheel uses a hub suspended from spokes. The spokes are attached to the rim in a crisscross pattern. The spokes are secured to the rim by the spoke nipples. The motorcycle's weight is supported by the upper spokes. A cast wheel is manufactured by pouring molten metal (usually aluminum or magnesium alloy) into a mold. This makes the hub, spokes, and rim all one piece. A stamped wheel consists of separate parts (hub, spokes, rim) fastened together. Unlike the cast wheel, the stamped wheel is either bolted or riveted together.

The correct choice of tire tread and size is essential to the safety of a motorcycle. Recent years have seen many advances in tire design. There are two types of tires: tube and tubeless. Tube tires use an air-filled tube within the tire's casing. Tubeless tires have a rubber layer (inner liner), which prevents air from filtering through, glued to the inside. This acts in place of a tube. It also has a special bead area, that together with the rim, makes a tube unnecessary. Three types of motorcycle tires are available, bias ply, bias-belted, and radial.

Know These Terms

Wheel
Wire wheel
Cast wheel
Stamped wheel
Axle
Hub
Wheel bearings
Wheel lacing
Wheel truing
Lateral runout
Radial runout
Rim offset
Tube tires
Tubeless tires
Bias-ply tires
Bias-belted tires
Radial tire
Tire pressure
Tire changing machine
Bubble balancer

Review Questions—Chapter 14

Do not write in this text. Place your answers on a separate sheet of paper.

1. Name the three types of wheels used on today's motorcycles.
2. Spokes are attached to the rim in a _____ pattern on a spoke wheel.
3. As the spoke wheel rotates, weight transfers from _____ to _____.
4. A _____ wheel is made all in one piece.
5. Name the three parts of a *stamped wheel.*
6. Wheel bearing grease may become contaminated or break down from _____ or _____.
7. ______ determine how often wheel bearings must be cleaned and repacked.
   A. Riding conditions
   B. Method of bearing removal
   C. Type of grease used
   D. None of the above.
8. When inspecting bearings, ______ indicates a problem, and the bearing should be replaced.
   A. roughness
   B. catching
   C. smooth rotation
   D. Both A & B.
9. Feel, spoke tone, and spoke torque wrench are three ways to check for ______.

10. ______ indicates how parallel the rim is to the hub. and causes side-to-side wobble.
    A. Radial runout
    B. Rim offset
    C. Lateral runout
    D. None of the above.
11. ______ shows how concentric (round) the rim is with the hub, and causes up and down movement.
    A. Radial runout
    B. Rim offset
    C. Lateral runout
    D. None of the above.
12. There are two types of tires: _____ and _____.
13. List the three types of bias available for motorcycle tires.
14. Tire size is determined by the ______ at its widest point.
    A. rim diameter
    B. tire width
    C. lateral runout
    D. Both A & B.
15. _____ will cause the tire to skid and the tread to wear at its center.
    A. Low air pressure
    B. High air pressure
    C. Sidewall bending
    D. Separated cord layers

Suggested Activities

1. Following the procedures given in the manufacturer's service manual, check the front and rear wheels of a randomly selected vehicle for trueness, and balance.
2. Following procedures given in the manufacturer's service manual, remove the bearings of a motorcycle wheel. Clean, inspect, repack, and replace the bearings.
3. Following procedures given in the appropriate manufacturer's service manual(s), remove and replace the tires on a:
    A. Spoke wheel.
    B. Cast wheel.
    C. Stamped wheel.

Rear disc brakes give motorcycles better stopping ability with less chance of loss of braking ability due to heat. (Honda Motor Company, Ltd.)

15 Brakes

After studying this chapter, you will be able to:

- Explain the operating principles of mechanical drum and hydraulic disc motorcycle brake systems.
- Inspect and repair motorcycle drum and disc brake systems.
- Troubleshoot drum and hydraulic brake systems.
- Describe ABS and linked motorcycle systems.
- Understand the advantages of linked and ABS brake systems.

This chapter discusses the design and maintenance of motorcycle, ATV, and scooter brakes. Improper maintenance and service of these components can mean the difference between a safe motorcycle and one which is a hazard to ride. Good brake work is critical and there is no room for error. In recent years, brake systems have received added refinements.

Brake Operation

A ***brake*** is a device that applies friction to a moving device to slow it down and bring it to a stop, **Figure 15-1.** Motorcycle braking is accomplished by the friction produced when brake linings are forced against a rotating disc or drum. Friction between the linings and disc or drum will eventually stop wheel rotation. Motorcycle brakes commonly use either hydraulic (fluid pressure) or mechanical (cable or linkage) mechanisms to apply the brakes.

Efficient brake system operation is of prime importance. To function safely, a brake system requires careful inspection and periodic maintenance. Important brake service considerations include:

- Proper reassembly after wheel removal.
- Maintaining proper brake adjustment.
- Proper lubrication of mechanical components of the brake system.

Figure 15-1. The front disc brake on a motorcycle. (Honda Motor Co., Ltd.)

- Proper inspection to determine brake wear and any need for brake service.

Warning: Some brake components contain *asbestos,* a known carcinogen. Asbestos fibers have been found to cause respiratory disease and cancer. When it is necessary to service a bike with asbestos pads, wear approved respiratory equipment. Use an approved vacuum cleaner or alternate method designed to minimize the possibility of airborne asbestos fibers.

Mechanical Brake System

Shown in **Figure 15-2,** a typical ***mechanical brake system*** consists of:

- ***Brake pedal*** or *lever.*
- ***Brake cable*** or *rod* (connects brake lever and cam arm).
- ***Stoplight switch*** (operates brake light).
- ***Brake cam arm*** (operates actuating cam).
- ***Brake actuating cam*** (moves shoes toward drum).
- ***Backing plate*** (holds brake shoes and other parts).
- ***Backing plate torque arm*** (prevents backing plate rotation).
- ***Drum*** (wheel hub friction surface attached to wheel).
- ***Shoes*** (friction devices that fit into and rub on drum).
- ***Linings*** (friction material on shoes).
- ***Return springs*** (holds shoes away from drum).

Movement of the brake lever or pedal is transferred to the brake actuating cam by a cable or rod. Actuating cam movement forces the shoes into the drum, causing friction. The stopping ability of the mechanical brake system is determined by:

- The system's mechanical leverage.
- The brake lining surface area.
- The composition of the brake lining.

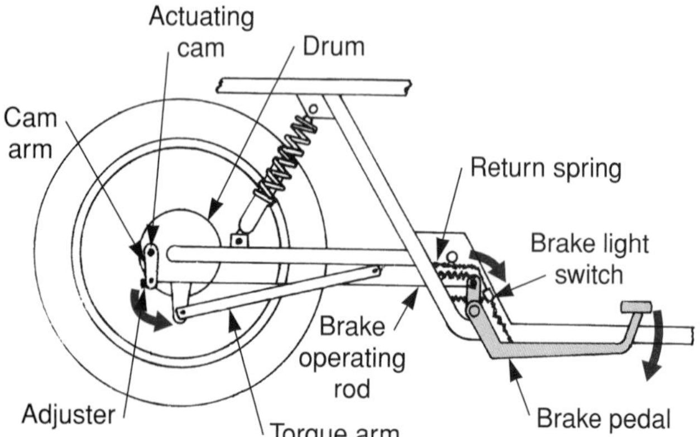

Figure 15-2. A brake is applied by pressing down on a brake pedal or sometimes by pulling a lever. This movement, through linkage, forces the brake shoes into the drum. The resulting friction slows down the motorcycle.

- The brake drum's ability to dissipate heat.

A properly designed brake system will allow controllable wheel lock-up.

Hydraulic Brake System

In the hydraulic brake system the lever or pedal uses fluid to perform a mechanical function. The advantages of using hydraulic brakes are:

- Equal pressure is provided in all directions within the system.
- The system is self-adjusting.
- It can produce very high pressure.
- The system has low maintenance requirements.

A typical ***hydraulic brake system,*** **Figure 15-3,** consists of:

- ***Brake lever*** or *pedal* (pushes on master cylinder).
- ***Master cylinder*** (produces pressure in brake system).
- ***Hydraulic lines*** (transfers hydraulic pressure from master cylinder to wheel cylinder).
- ***Stoplight switch*** (controls brake light).
- ***Pads*** (friction devices).
- ***Caliper*** and ***wheel cylinder*** (clamp around disc).
- ***Disc*** (attached to and stops wheel).

Brake lever or pedal movement causes the piston in the master cylinder to push fluid through the brake line. This fluid pressure is applied to the brake caliper piston, causing the brake pads to be squeezed against the disc. The clamping action causes friction, which slows the motorcycle.

Hydraulically operated drum brakes have been used on motorcycles but are no longer common. Hydraulic disc brakes are commonly used. The advantages of a hydraulic disc brake are superior ability to dissipate heat, low maintenance requirements, and ease of maintenance.

Hydraulic Brake System Operation

A hydraulic brake system is a closed system. When pressure is applied in a hydraulic system, it is transferred equally in all directions throughout the system. A master cylinder, consisting of a piston, cylinder, and reservoir, is used to apply pressure to the system.

As the piston moves forward in the master cylinder, the primary cup passes the small relief port. As the primary cup continues forward, pressure is built up in the system, **Figure 15-4A.** This pressure is exerted against the caliper piston, which moves toward the disc, pinching it between the brake pads.

When the brake pedal or lever is released, the master cylinder piston is rapidly returned to its rest position by spring force, **Figure 15-4B.** This allows pressure to drop in the system as fluid flows through the check valve, relief port, and into the reservoir. The caliper piston is retracted by its seal.

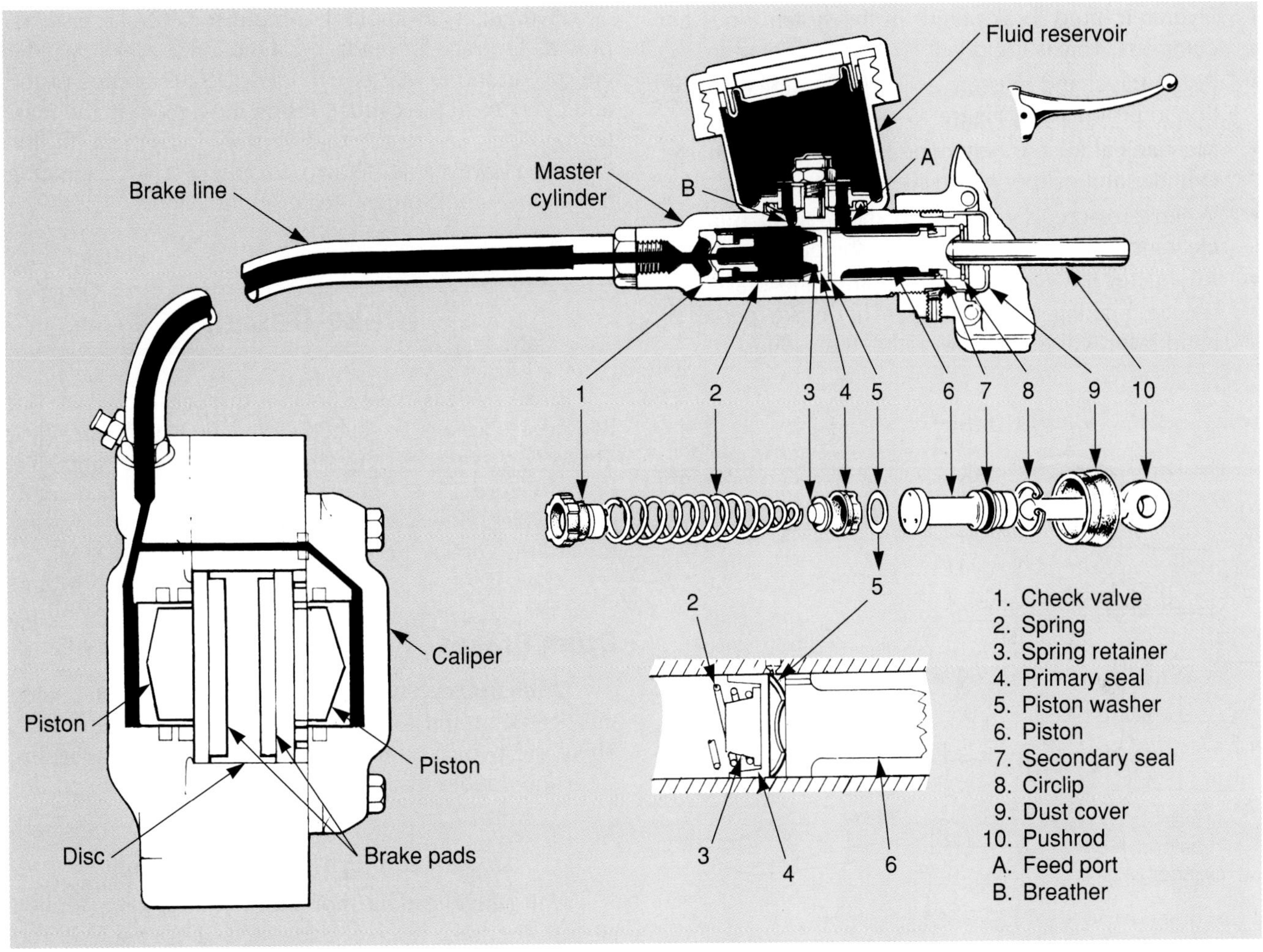

Fluid reservoir
A
Master cylinder
B
Brake line
1 2 3 4 5 6 7 8 9 10
5
2
Caliper
Piston
Piston
Disc
Brake pads
3
4
6
1. Check valve
2. Spring
3. Spring retainer
4. Primary seal
5. Piston washer
6. Piston
7. Secondary seal
8. Circlip
9. Dust cover
10. Pushrod
A. Feed port
B. Breather

Figure 15-3. When the brake lever is pulled, it causes a pushrod to move the piston forward. This movement traps and pressurizes brake fluid in the line and caliper. Line pressure causes the caliper pistons to force the brake pads against the disc. (Triumph Motorcycles, Ltd.)

Relief port
Supply port
Reservoir
Check valve
Piston
Fluid seal
Piston
Spring
Pressure chamber
Primary cup
A
Relief port
Supply port
Reservoir
Check valve
Piston
Fluid seal
Piston
Spring
Pressure chamber
Primary cup
B

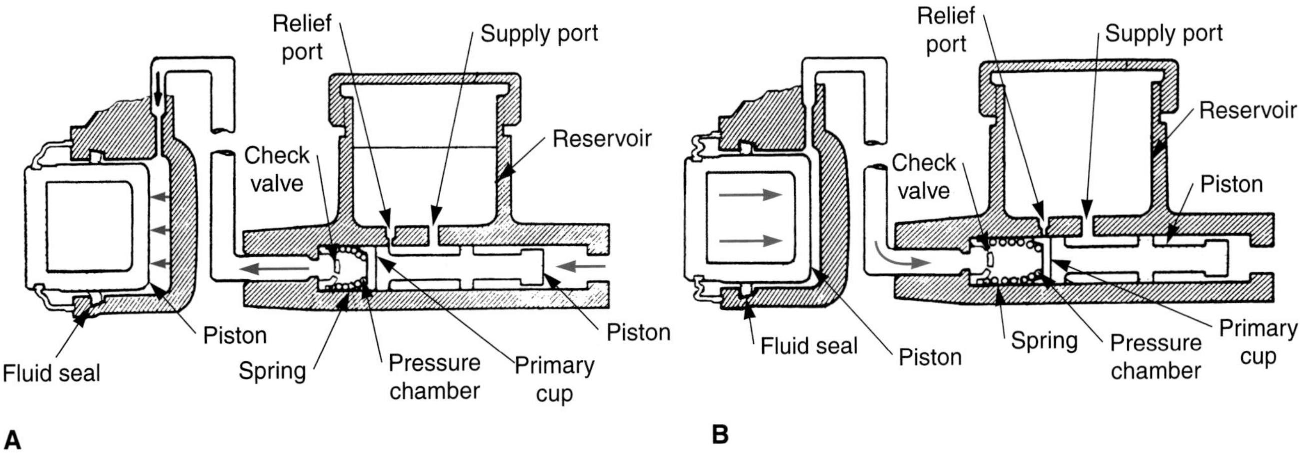

Figure 15-4. Action of a basic master cylinder. (Kawasaki Motors Corporation U.S.A.)

A piston and cylinder (caliper), mounted on the fork leg or swing arm, applies system pressure to the brake pads and disc. Hydraulic brake systems are relatively simple if a few basic principles are understood:

- Initial mechanical motion is produced by the brake lever or pedal, **Figure 15-5.** Pushing force going into the master cylinder is increased by the mechanical leverage of the lever arm.

- Hydraulic fluid (brake fluid) in the system does not compress. This is important for proper operation.
- Piston travel and pressure exerted is in direct proportion to piston sizes, **Figure 15-6.**
- Mechanical force is determined by comparing master cylinder and caliper piston sizes.
- When pressure is released in the system, minimal clearance is maintained between the pad and disc.
- Any air in the system will compress and drastically reduce braking effectiveness. The brake pedal or hand lever will feel spongy rather than solid.

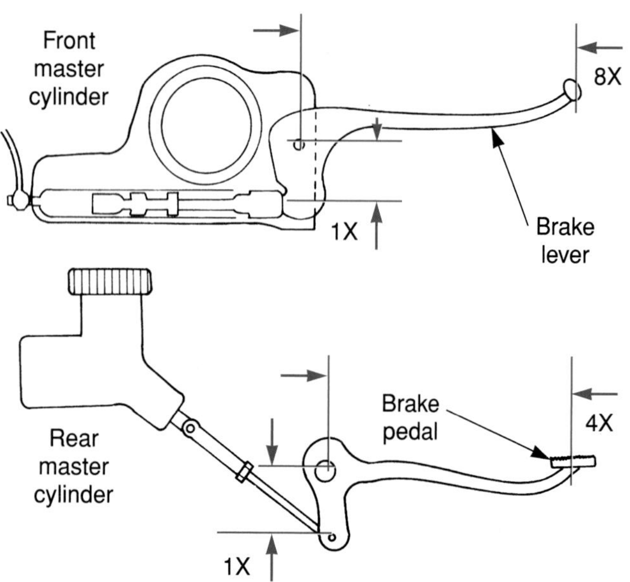

Figure 15-5. In a hydraulic brake system, the initial movement is provided by the brake pedal or lever. With an 8:1 lever ratio, 1 lb. (4.4 N) of pressure applied to brake lever results in 8 lbs. (35.2 N) of pressure acting on the master cylinder piston.

Hydraulics, as applied to motorcycle brake systems, provide leverage for mechanical motion. A small cylinder and piston in the master cylinder operates a large piston and cylinder in the caliper. Piston movement in the master cylinder is greater than piston movement in the caliper. However, as shown in **Figure 15-7,** clamping force (pressure) is much greater in the caliper.

Brake Design

Brake designs have changed through the years, but two basic designs have been used on all motorcycles. These two brake designs are the drum brake and disc brake, **Figure 15-8.** Both are currently used on modern motorcycles. However, the trend in brake design is moving toward disc brakes on all bikes.

Drum Brakes

Drum brakes have been in use on motorcycles since their creation and are still used on some modern bikes. There are two basic drum brake designs: single-leading shoe and double-leading shoe.

Single-Leading Shoe Drum Brakes

With ***single-leading shoe drum brakes,*** force applied against the brake lever or pedal activates a cable or rod attached to the brake mechanism. A threaded adjuster on the end of the brake cable or rod offers adjustment to control the brake actuation point. The adjuster acts against a pivot on the end of the brake arm, which is clamped onto and turns a brake activating cam.

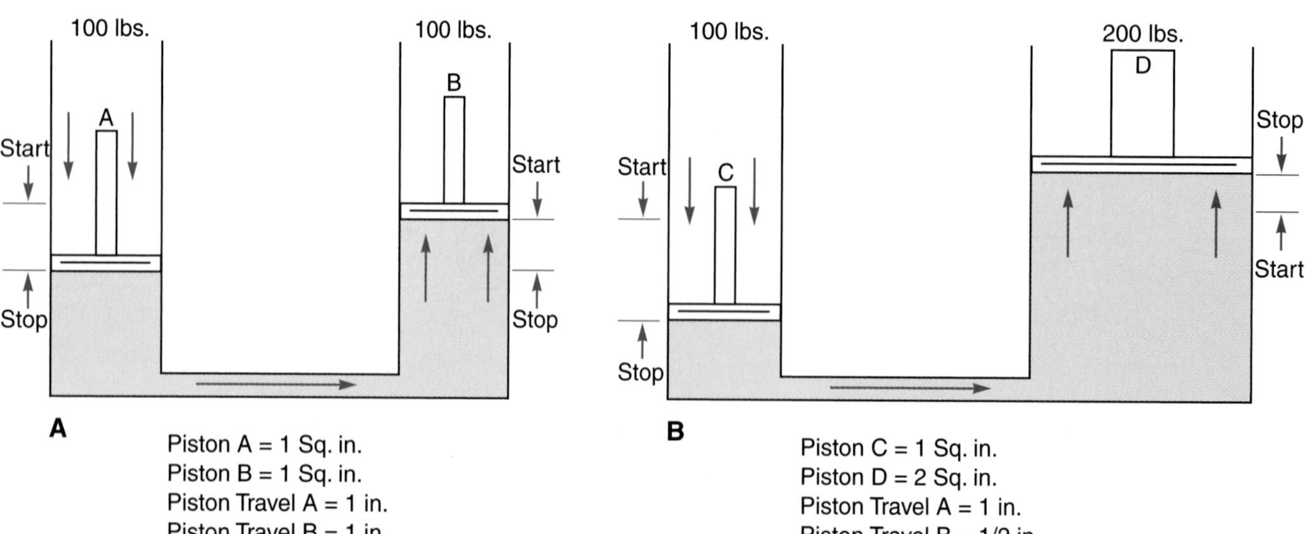

Figure 15-6. A—When hydraulic pistons A and B are the same size, the ratio is 1:1. Both pistons travel equal distance and exert equal pressure. B—Piston D has twice the area of piston C. 100 lb. (44 N) of pressure applied to piston C results in 200 lb. (88 N) of pressure at piston D. Also note the difference in piston movements.

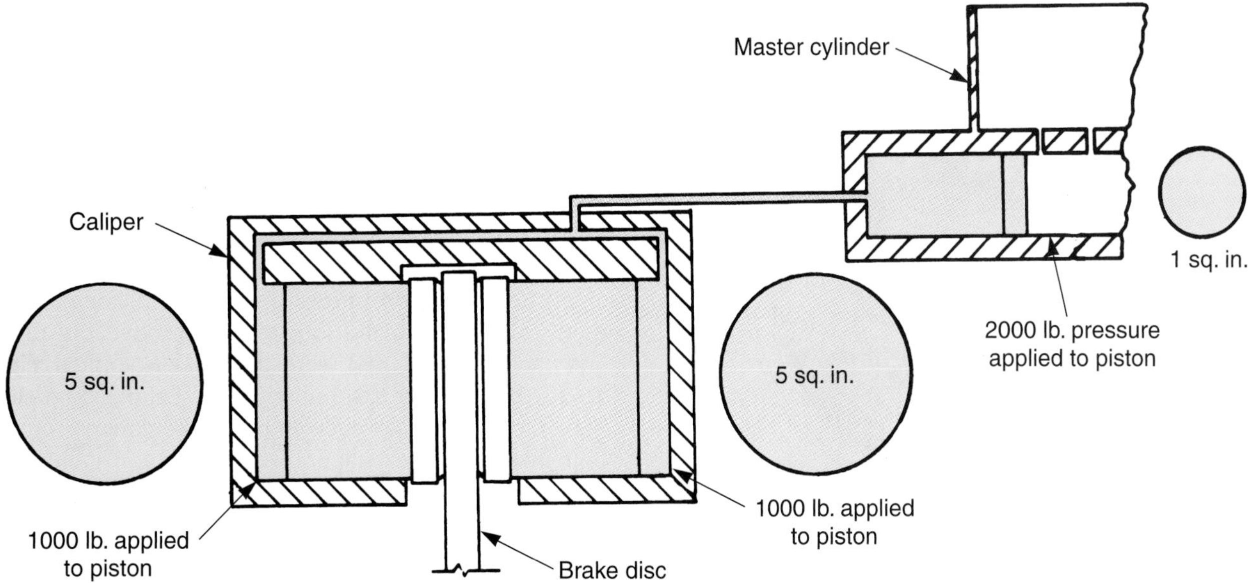

Figure 15-7. When the master cylinder piston has an area of 1 sq. in and each caliper piston has an area of 5 sq. in, there is 10:1 ratio. A pressure of 200 lbs (88 N) results in 1000 lbs (440 N) of pressure acting on each caliper piston. This results in 2000 lbs (880 N) of pressure applied to the disc. Different hydraulic ratios are used, depending on the design and application.

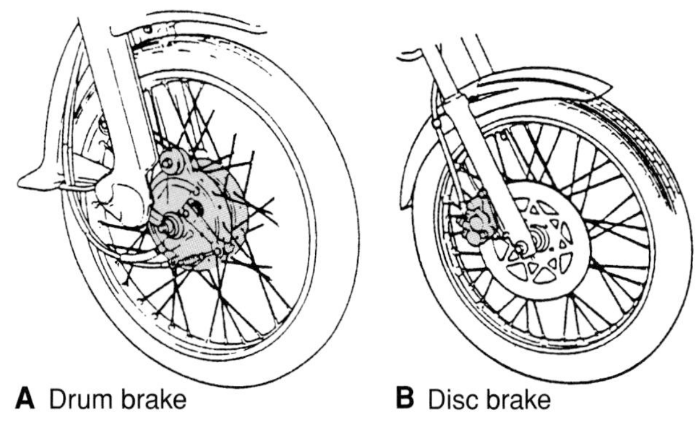

Figure 15-8. Typical front wheel. A—Drum brake. B—Disc brake.

As shown in **Figure 15-9,** the activating cam transfers rotating force from the outside of the drum, through the backing plate, to the inside of the drum. The cam spreads one end of two crescent-shaped shoes. The other end of the shoes pivot against a common pin set into the brake panel. Both shoes press against the inside surface of the drum, creating friction and slowing wheel rotation. The first shoe to act upon the drum is called the ***leading shoe.*** The second shoe, arcing out against the drum from the common pivot pin, is called the ***trailing shoe.***

Due to its position within the system, the leading shoe creates more force against the drum than that applied to it. This increased force capability is called a ***self-energizing effect.*** In contrast, because of its position within the system, the trailing shoe is pushed back by the rotating drum and creates less braking force than the leading shoe. Single-leading shoe brakes are often used on the front and rear of dirt bikes, and also on the rear of a few road machines.

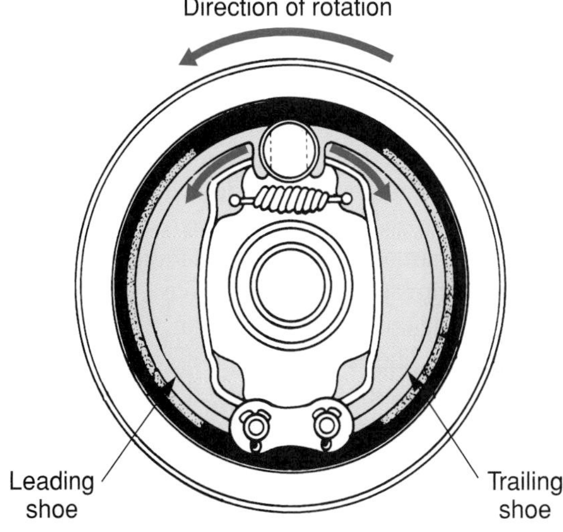

Figure 15-9. In a single-leading shoe brake, the leading shoe rotates on its pivot in the same direction as brake drum rotation. The trailing shoe rotates in the opposite direction. (Kawasaki Motors Corporation U.S.A.)

Double-Leading Shoe Drum Brakes

Double-leading drum brakes, sometimes referred to as *dual-leading,* differs from single-leading brakes in that it uses two shoe-activating cams, each at opposite ends of the backing plate, to simultaneously press the shoes against the drum, **Figure 15-10.** Because both shoes are leading in relation to the drum's direction of rotation, they operate against the drum equally. The effective braking force is noticeably greater. A double-leading shoe brake is used on the front of some road and dirt bikes and both the front and rear wheel brake of many ATVs.

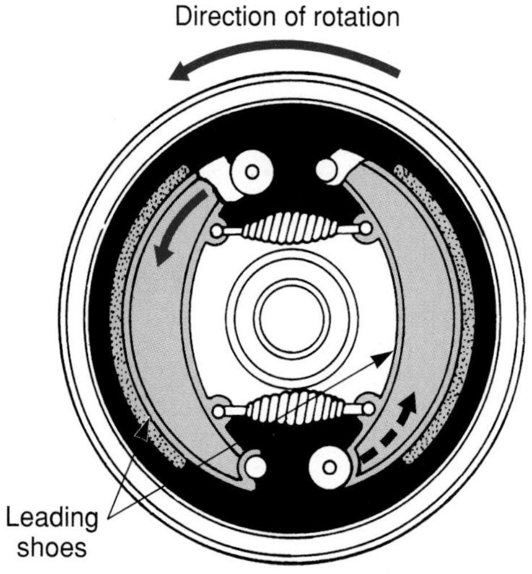

Figure 15-10. A double-leading shoe brake uses two actuating cams and two pivots. Both shoes rotate on their pivots in the same direction as the brake drum.
(Kawasaki Motors Corporation U.S.A.)

It is vital for brake systems to quickly dissipate the heat generated by friction so that stopping force remains consistent. Since drum brakes contain almost all the brake components within the wheel hub, they are made of materials that conduct heat rapidly. It is just as important that the brake is the proper size for the bike and its anticipated performance.

In order to increase heat conductivity while providing acceptable wear resistance on its inner surface, the brake drum is mostly cast iron. The remainder of the drum/hub is made of aluminum alloy with cooling fins cast into the outer circumference; again for heat dispersion, but also to reduce unsprung weight. The cast iron drum is captured within the aluminum hub and cannot be removed. The drum thickness is relatively thin, which further aids heat conductivity, and must not be machined in a brake lathe. If the drum surface is severely damaged, the hub must be replaced.

Disc Brakes

Disc brakes can be actuated hydraulically or mechanically. The hydraulic design is almost exclusively used today. Hydraulic disc brakes use two types of calipers: single piston, or single-push caliper and double-piston, or opposite-piston caliper. Disc brakes are now used on both front and rear wheels.

The caliper pistons in both systems maintain indirect contact with the back side of the brake pads. Anti-squeal shims are normally used between the piston and pad. As these pads press against opposite sides of the disc, wheel rotation is slowed. When the brake lever is released, hydraulic pressure decreases and the pads cease to press against the disc. Unlike drum brake systems, which uses a spring to retract the shoes, the resilience of the disc brake caliper piston seals retracts the pads and automatically adjusts for wear.

In ***single piston calipers,*** or *single-push calipers,* both pads press against the brake disc through a reaction of the sliding caliper yoke. This is shown in **Figure 15-11.** As the brake is applied, force is applied to the piston. Piston movement causes the caliper to float (move on its mount), pinching the disc between the pads, **Figure 15-12.** The advantage of this design is that it is inexpensive to produce. It will also compensate for slight disc runout (warpage) without severe vibration during braking.

A ***double piston caliper,*** or opposite-piston caliper, is rigidly mounted to the fork leg. Two moveable pistons and pads pinch the disc when the brake is applied, **Figure 15-13.** Brake fluid is supplied to the caliper by a single line. A crossover passageway inside the caliper connects both halves of the caliper. Opposite-piston calipers are often used for road racing motorcycles. They offer some improvement in braking performance, but at great increase in cost and complexity.

Rectangular brake pads were introduced to increase the pad area against the disc. However, these pads did not press against the disc uniformly. The double piston caliper ensures greater braking force and uniform pressure against the brake pads, **Figure 15-14.** Some double piston calipers have different piston sizes to further balance the braking force across the pad; the trailing piston being larger than the leading piston. The amount of braking force depends on the force pressing the pads against the discs, the contact area between the pads and disc, the distance between the wheel center and the brake pads, and the tire's outside diameter, **Figure 15-15.**

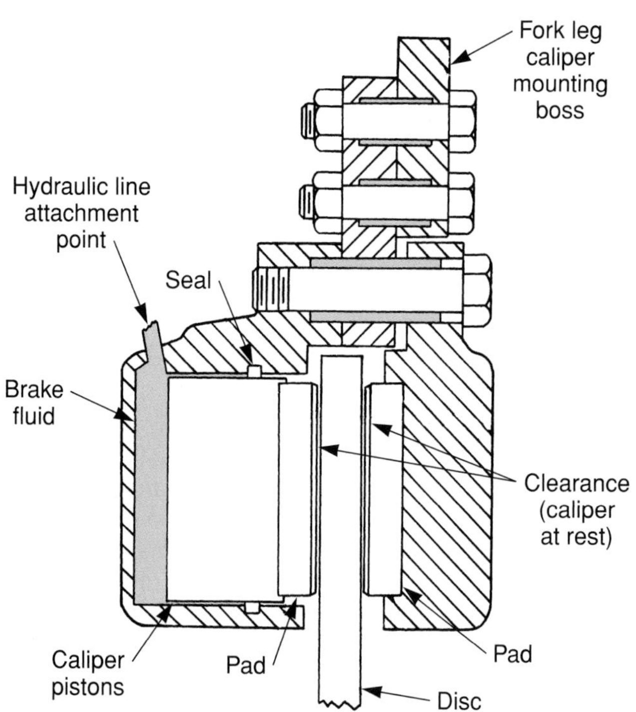

Figure 15-11. A single-piston floating caliper applies hydraulic pressure to only one piston.

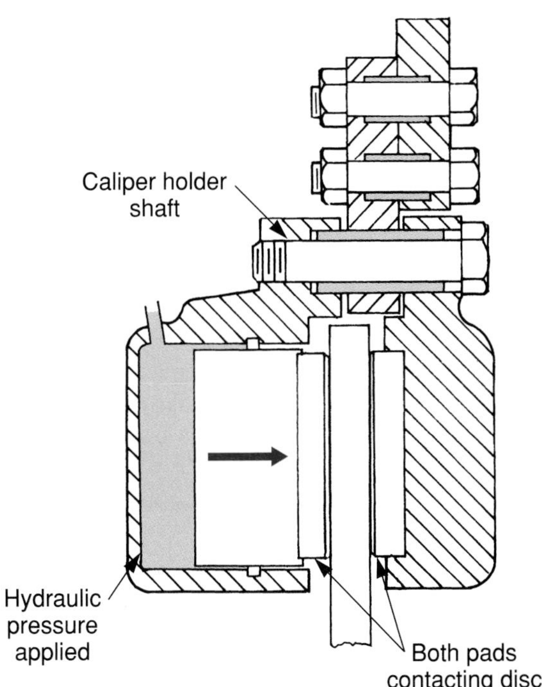

Figure 15-12. As hydraulic pressure is applied, the piston moves the pads toward the disc. As the pads make contact with the disc, the caliper body floats on the caliper shaft. As further pressure is applied, the disc is pinched between both pads.

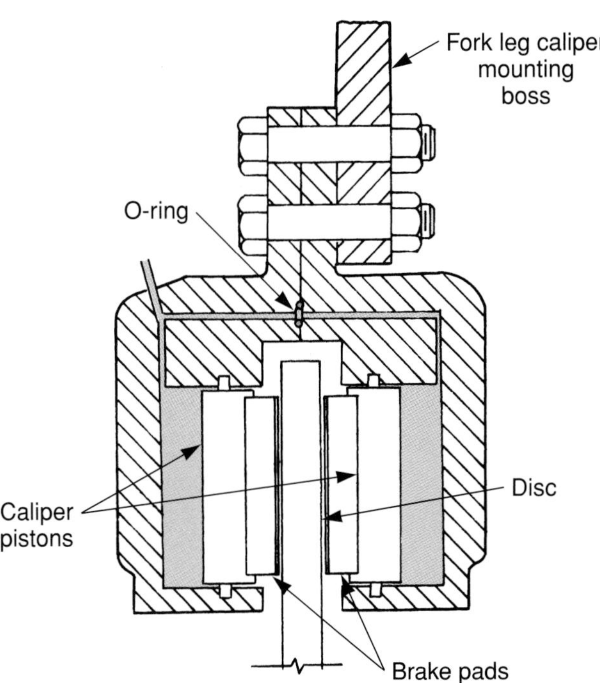

Figure 15-13. A double-piston caliper is rigidly mounted to the fork leg or swing arm. Hydraulic pressure is applied equally on each side of the caliper.

Because increasing the area of contact between the brake pads and disc increases braking force, some larger motorcycles have four- and six-piston front disc brakes, **Figure 15-16.** This increased piston contact means increased heat energy. The increased heat energy requires a greater need for heat dissipation. For this reason, with the exception of a few front and some in-board brakes, all discs are exposed. To protect them from rust, the discs are usually made of a stainless steel alloy. Since the material the discs can be made of is limited, they are thin in order to reduce unsprung weight. Using stainless steel gives the disc strength, wile minimizing unsprung weight. As the temperature of the brake disc rises, it expands. Because the disc is bolted to the wheel, its expansion is limited and some degree of distortion occurs.

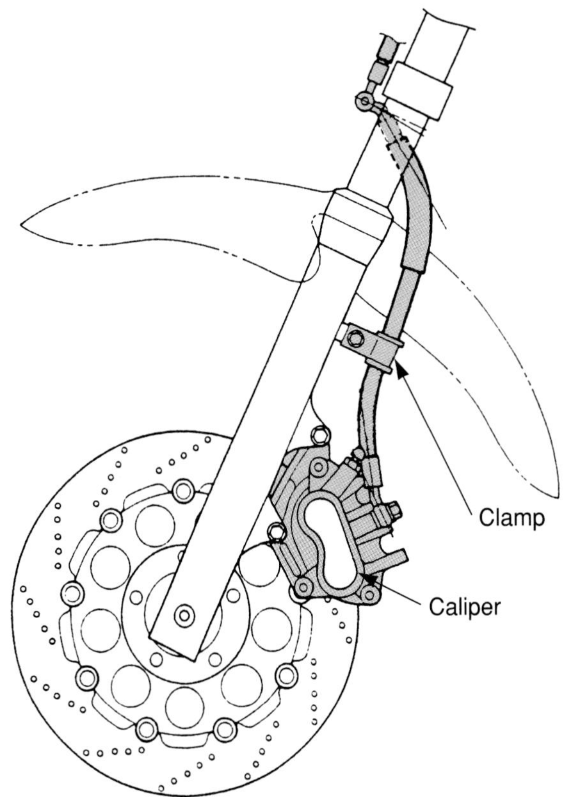

Figure 15-14. Typical double piston caliper and its hose connection. (American Suzuki Motor Corporation)

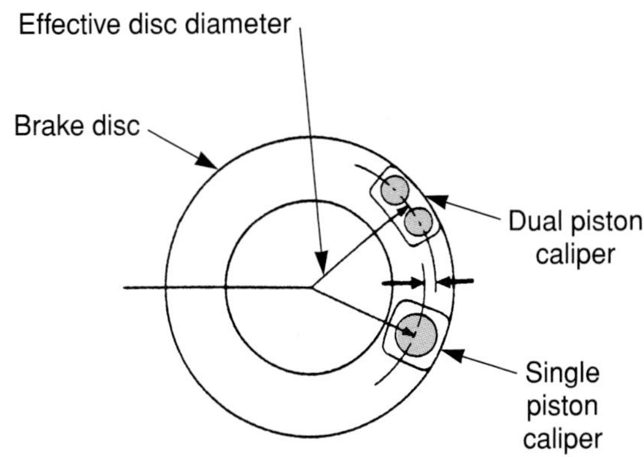

Figure 15-15. The amount of braking force of single and double piston calipers. (Honda Motor Co., Ltd.)

To cope with the extreme heat typically generated during braking in competition road racing, ***floating discs***

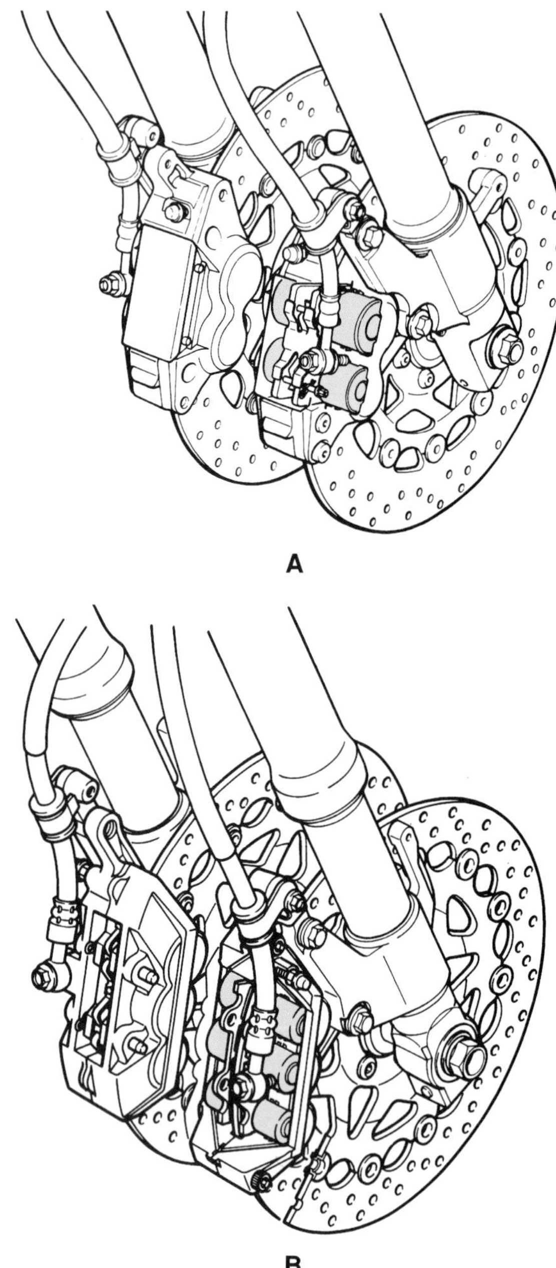

Figure 15-16. A—Typical four-piston front disc brake. B—Six-piston disc brake arrangement. (Yamaha Motor Corporation U.S.A.)

have been developed. In this system, a floating disc is installed by means of spring washers and rivets or clevis pins with an aluminum carrier between the disc and wheel. This permits deviations in radial directions, prevents distortion, and reduces weight.

In addition to the basics already stated, brake discs are commonly drilled or grooved to remove dust or dirt from the surface, preventing what are known as sympathetic vibrations. Some rotors have holes drilled in the disc braking surface itself. These holes are perpendicular to the flow of air, which decrease weight and aid slightly in cooling.

Among the many combinations of materials used to make brake pads are wear resistant resin, metallic mixtures, and sintered metal. These materials are combined in brake pad manufacturing according to the design requirements of the particular application. As mentioned earlier, some brake linings contain asbestos. For the most part, manufacturers have discontinued the use of asbestos in new pad manufacturing. However, asbestos precautions should always be followed when working on any brake system.

Rear Disc Brakes

Some motorcycles are equipped with rear disc brakes. Rear disc brakes are commonly found on sport bikes, larger cruising bikes, and some ATVs. Rear disc brakes work in the same manner as front disc brakes. Usually, rear calipers have fewer pistons than front calipers, **Figure 15-17.** Since the rear brake provides less stopping power, fewer pistons are needed.

Brake Fluid

There are three types of ***brake fluid*** that are rated by the United States Department of Transportation (DOT). They are ***DOT 3, DOT 4,*** and ***DOT 5.*** DOT 3 and DOT 4 are glycol-based brake fluids, while DOT 5 is a silicon-based product. The DOT designations specify the brake fluid's ability to withstand heat without boiling. Boiling brake fluid will lead to a drastic loss of braking force due to the air bubbles that form within the system. The greater the number, the higher the boiling point.

Although made from the same chemical base, never mix DOT 3 and DOT 4 brake fluid. It is important to use the same DOT number when adding fluid. If you are unsure of the type within the system, drain the system and refill it with DOT 4. Systems designed for DOT 3 can use DOT 4, but DOT 4 systems must never be filled with DOT 3. DOT 4 systems generate greater heat and require fluid with higher boiling point characteristics. DOT 5 is not compatible with either DOT 3 or DOT 4, and should never be mixed with them. Improper mixing may lead to chemical decomposition, system contamination, and possible damage. The correct DOT brake fluid for a given hydraulic system can be found in the vehicle's service manual.

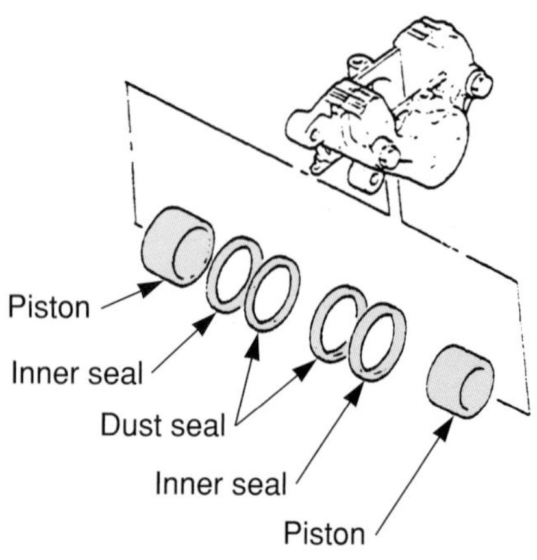

Figure 15-17. Rear brake calipers are smaller and have fewer pistons than front calipers. (Yamaha Motor Corporation U.S.A.)

It is also important to use only fresh brake fluid from a sealed container. Once a new container of brake fluid is opened, be sure to reseal it tightly and plan on discarding the fluid after six months. This is because brake fluid, even in a sealed container or brake system, tends to absorb moisture from the air as it is hygroscopic. Moisture can contaminate the brake system and lower the fluid's boiling point. It also corrodes the brake cylinders and pistons, which can eventually cause seal damage and leakage. For this reason, you should note the date the container was first opened for later reference. Never reuse old brake fluid due to the possibility of contamination from dust or moisture absorption. If the brake fluid in a system shows any signs of contamination, it should be replaced.

Be very careful when handling brake fluid because it can quickly damage many painted or plastic surfaces. In certain plastics, structural damage can occur if brake fluid penetrates the material's surface. The only exception is the components of the brake system as they are resistant to the effects of brake fluid. Brake fluid spilled on a motorcycle should be washed away with water immediately.

Brake Inspection, Maintenance, and Repair

Brake inspection should be done during routine maintenance or if a problem is suspected. In some cases, a complete inspection of the brake system may require wheel removal.

Front Wheel Removal/Installation

When removing the front wheel, support the bike securely under the engine to raise the wheel. Then proceed as follows:

1. Disconnect the speedometer cable and front brake cable.
2. Remove the axle on bikes with drum brakes and remove the wheel. If the wheel on bikes with hydraulic disc brakes cannot be removed with the brake caliper(s) installed, remove the wheel after the brake caliper and caliper bracket have been removed.

Several types of axle nuts or holders are used on modern bikes. The first step in front wheel removal is the unfastening of the axle holder devices as described in the service manual. Once this is done, the axle shaft can be pulled from the fork legs. Then remove the front wheel. The typical installation of a drum brake on a front wheel is as follows:

1. Align the speedometer transmission and the brake drum on the wheel hub as instructed in the service manual.
2. Coat the axle shaft with a small amount of grease.
3. Place the wheel between the fork legs while aligning the fork leg boss with the backing plate groove. Insert the axle through the fork legs.
4. Tighten axle bolt or holder to the specified torque given in the service manual.
5. Turn the front wheel so that the speedometer gear retainer will engage properly with the wheel hub.
6. Reconnect the front brake cable.

The typical installation of the wheel with hydraulic disc brakes is as follows:

1. Place the front wheel between the fork legs.
2. Set the brake disc between the brake pads carefully.
3. Slowly lower the front of the vehicle until the fork legs are aligned with the axle.
4. Install the axle holders with the arrow pointing forward and align the speedometer gear box boss with the fork leg as indicated in the service manual.
5. Install the axle nut or holder and tighten to specific torque.

Rear Wheel Removal/Installation

To remove the rear wheel for brake service, follow the procedure in the service manual. Again, there are several methods of holding the rear wheel in place. The following are some tips to follow when working on the rear wheel.

- Support the bike securely with the rear wheel off the ground.
- Remove the muffler and/or other parts necessary to gain access to the wheel.
- For drum brakes, disconnect the brake rod or cable and torque rod from the backing plate.
- For hydraulic disc brakes, it may be necessary to remove the brake caliper.
- Note the side collar position and direction so it can be reinstalled properly.
- After installation, make sure the rear wheel turns smoothly, without excessive free play.

Use caution when handling and installing brake lines and hoses, **Figure 15-18.** When installing front brake lines and hoses, be sure there is no possibility of damage or stress when the fork pivots in either direction or when the suspension compresses or extends. In the rear, allow proper clearance so lines or hoses do not rub against the tire, frame, or swingarm, and are not caught between the spring coils when the suspension compresses.

All brake lines or hoses should be installed using the clamps provided. Each clamp should be positioned around the rubber hose guards to prevent any damage to the lines and hoses. See **Figure 15-18.**

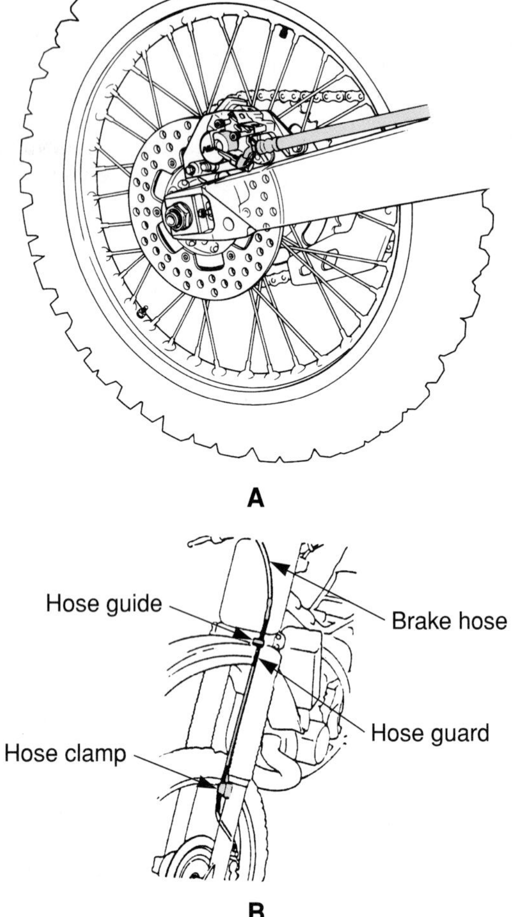

Figure 15-18. A—Rear brake hose connection. B—Location of front brake hose and its clamps. (Yamaha Motor Corporation U.S.A., Honda Motor Co., Ltd.)

Warning: Grease on the brake linings will reduce braking potential. Keep grease off the brake linings and wipe off excess grease.

Brake Service

The three operations of brake service; inspection, maintenance, and repair, should be dealt with as one operation. It is imperative that service manual procedures be followed to ensure accurate and safe brake service. Injury, death, and/or a potential liability suit may result from improper brake system repairs. Pay special attention to vulnerable parts of the brake system if the motorcycle has accident damage.

Warning: Any work done on a motorcycle brake system is a serious matter. Brake repairs must be done carefully and accurately. The slightest mistake could cause an accident.

Rules for Drum Brake Repairs

Listed are ten rules to follow when working on motorcycle drum brakes. They will help you complete a competent repair.

- Do not inhale brake dust. Wear a respirator if inhalation cannot be avoided.
- Use a service manual to compare measurements with specifications.
- Components must be replaced if they do not meet specifications.
- Use brake parts cleaner or alcohol to clean drum and shoes.
- Do not get lubricants on brake lining or drum.
- Refer to service manual for proper lubrication and reassembly procedures.
- Always use new lock tabs and cotter pins.
- Be sure cables are properly seated in sockets.
- Adjust drive chain if the rear wheel was removed.
- Center the brake shoes by applying brakes before, and while tightening axle.

Drum Brake Service Summary

To help make sure that you do not forget any step during drum brake service and repair, use the following summary as a general guide.

1. Inspect the brake lever and pedal mechanism. Make sure they are in good operating condition.
2. Check the brake cable and rod. Look for wear, damage, or improper adjustment.
3. Check the operation and adjustment of the brake light switches. Make sure the brake light functions.
4. Make sure the brake pedal and cable return springs are working.
5. Check the brake cam arm and backing plate torque arm.

Note: Wheel removal is required for the remaining operations.

6. Check backing plate for damage and wear.
7. Make sure the brake actuating cam is in good condition.
8. Inspect all grease seals for wear, damage, or leakage.
9. Check the wheel bearings. Make sure they are well lubricated and roll freely.
10. Inspect the brake drum. Look for wear, cracks, grooves, or other problems.
11. Check the brake shoe linings for wear. Check the linings for glazing (shiny, hardened condition due to overheating).

12. Inspect the brake shoe return springs. They should not be discolored from overheating and should be installed properly.

Relining Drum Brakes

Relining involves the replacement of the shoe lining material. All current designs use bonded lining (lining glued to brake shoes). Some earlier designs use rivets to attach the lining material to the brake shoe. When relining brakes which use bonded shoes, the complete shoe must be replaced. To replace worn or defective shoes on drum brakes, follow the general steps listed here. Refer to a service manual for specific instructions.

1. Remove the wheel and completely disassemble the brake and backing plate, **Figure 15-19.**
2. Clean and inspect the drum surface.
3. Measure the drum's inside diameter. Maximum serviceable diameter is usually found stamped inside the drum or in the service manual. See **Figure 15-20A.**
4. Clean the backing plate and actuating cam.
5. Put masking tape over the entire lining surface of the new brake shoes, **Figure 15-20B.** This reduces the chance of contaminating the linings with lubricants or brake fluid.
6. Lubricate the actuating cam. Make sure the brake arm and cam are timed properly.
7. Reassemble backing plate using new brake springs, **Figures 15-20C-15-20D.**
8. Remove protective tape from linings.
9. Install wheel and brake assembly.

Hydraulic Disc Brake System

The following summary provides general steps for inspecting, maintaining, and repairing a hydraulic brake system. Use it and a service manual during actual service and repair operations.

Brake System Inspection

To inspect a hydraulic brake system, proceed as follows:

1. Inspect the brake caliper mounting bracket.
2. Check the action of the brake pedal and lever.
3. Check the master cylinder linkage and fluid level.
4. Inspect the torque arm for signs of problems.
5. Check the wheel bearings for looseness or roughness.
6. Inspect dust seals for deterioration or damage.
7. Observe the operation of the brake lights.
8. Check brake pad thickness. Many pads have wear indicators (tabs or grooves) that allow inspection without disassembly.

A

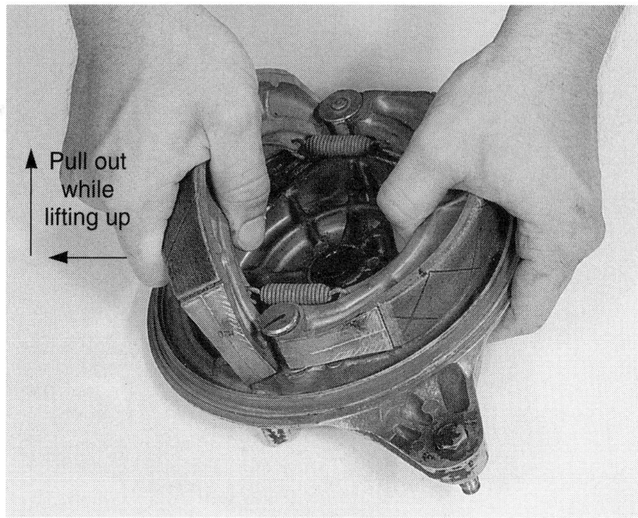

B

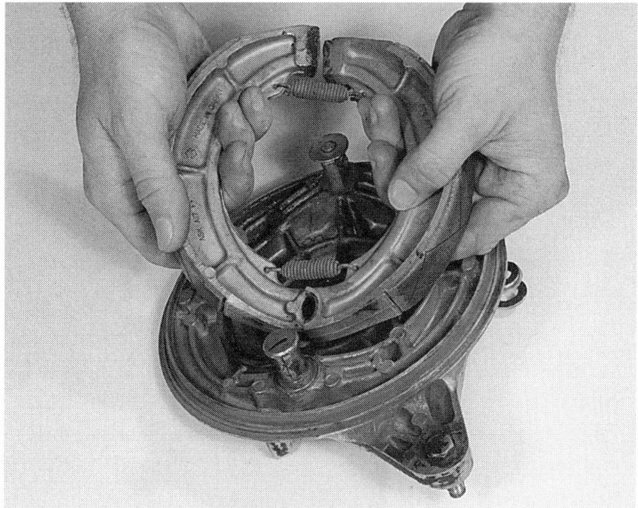

C

Figure 15-19. Steps for disassembly of a drum brake. A—Remove the wheel from the motorcycle. Then remove the backing plate. B—Disassemble the backing plate, pull out and lift on shoes. C—Once free from the pivots, the shoe and spring assembly can be removed as a unit.

A

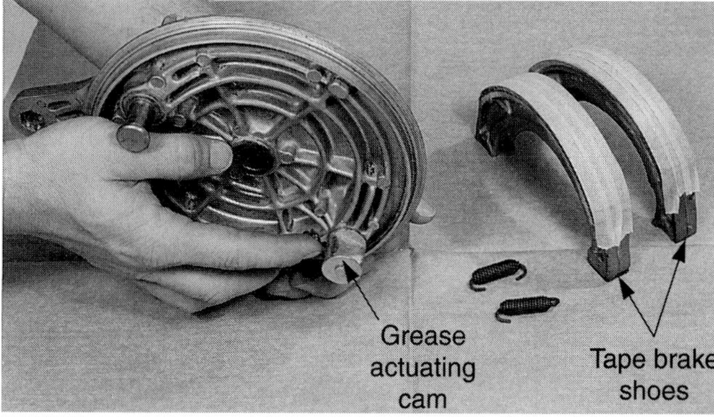

B

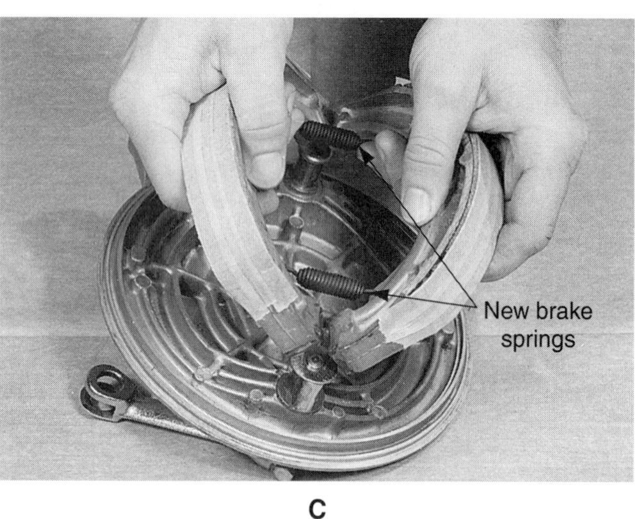

C

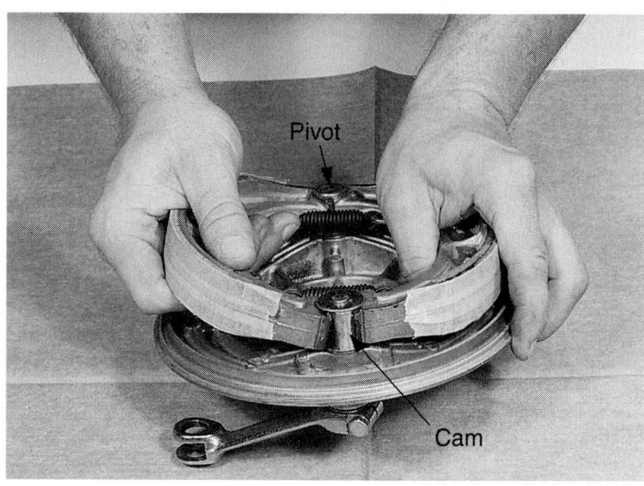

D

Figure 15-20. A—Use a Vernier or dial caliper to measure drum wear. Maximum allowable drum diameter is stamped inside the drum. If the diameter exceeds this specification, replace the drum. B—Tape brake shoes to help prevent contamination during assembly. Lightly grease the actuating cam with high temperature grease. Assemble the backing plate using new brake springs. C—Begin by folding shoes into position over the pivot and cam. D—Then push shoes flat against backing plate.

9. Check the brake disc for wear, scoring, or cracks.

If you find any problems during your inspection, correct them right away. Always remember that the brake system is critical to a safe motorcycle. It is up to you to keep the brake system in perfect operating condition.

Changing Brake Fluid

Brake fluid should be changed at least every two years. This is necessary because brake fluid can become contaminated with moisture and other substances. The boiling point of contaminated brake fluid is lower. Contaminated fluid can also corrode brake system parts.

Use the following procedures as a general guide for changing brake fluid:

1. Fit a piece of clear hose over the bleeder valve. Submerge the other end of the hose in a container of brake fluid, **Figure 15-21A.**
2. Open the bleeder valve. Use a tubing wrench, **Figure 15-21B.**
3. Pump the master cylinder until about 1/16″ (1.6 mm) of fluid remains in the reservoir.
4. Use a clean shop rag or towel to soak up the remaining fluid in the reservoir. This will help to remove any dirt and foreign matter from the bottom of the master cylinder, **Figure 15-21C.**
5. Fill reservoir with a proper new DOT brake fluid, **Figure 15-21D.**
6. Repeat steps 3 and 5 until clear brake fluid comes out of the bleeder valve.
7. Close bleeder valve and fill reservoir to proper level.
8. Check brake operation and bleed system if necessary.

Bleeding Hydraulic Brakes

Bleeding hydraulic brakes involves forcing all air out of the system. Air is compressible and will affect hydraulic system operation. Air can enter a motorcycle brake system when a hydraulic component is removed for service. Air can also enter the system when the master cylinder runs dry or the system develops a leak.

Since brake fluid cannot be compressed, all movement of the brake lever or pedal is transmitted directly to

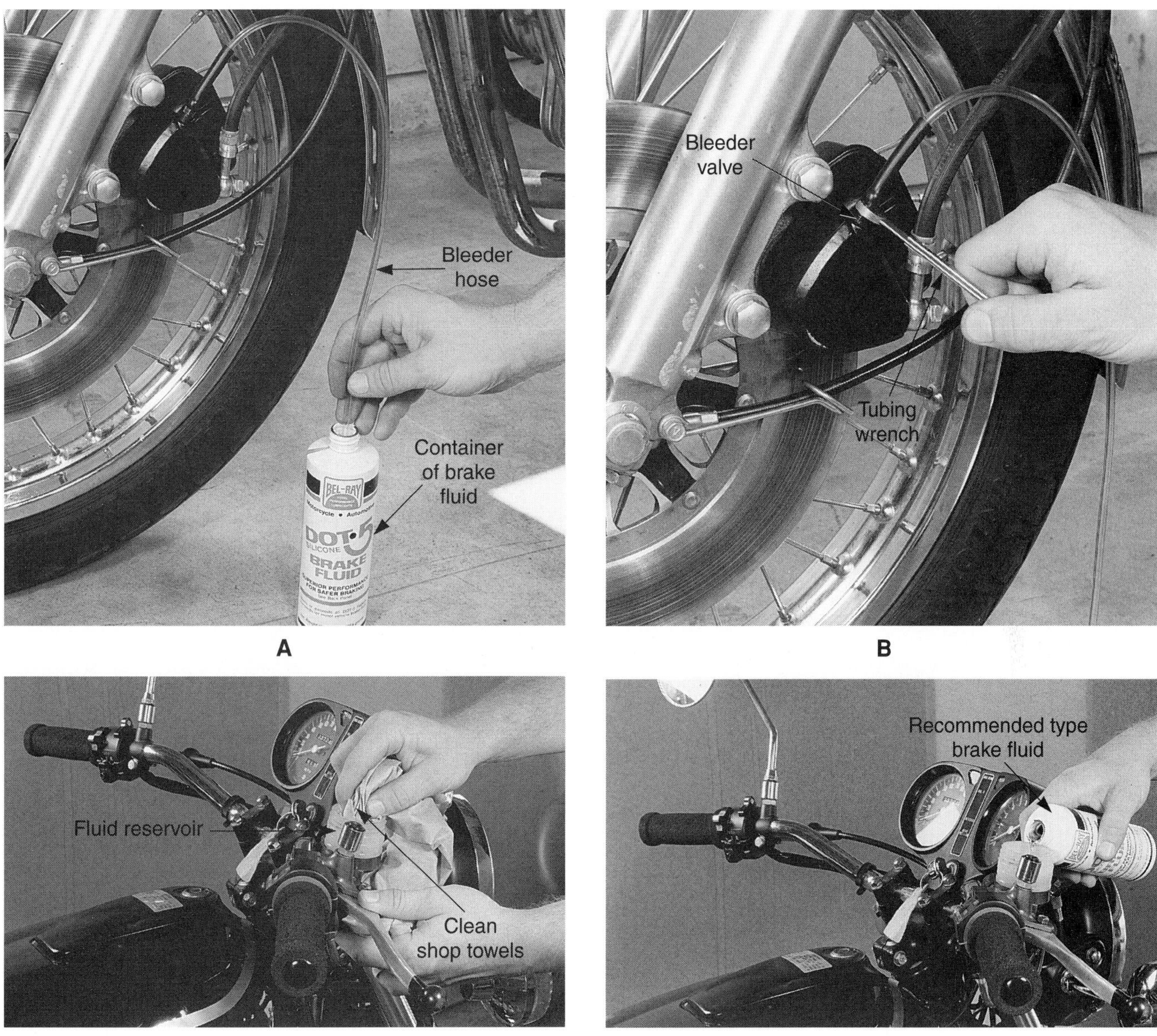

Figure 15-21. Steps for changing fluid in a motorcycle brake system. A—Position clear tube from the bleeder valve into a container of brake fluid. B—Open the bleeder valve. C—Clean any fluid and sediment out of the master cylinder. D—Refill reservoir and bleed brake system.

the caliper(s) for braking action. Air, however, is easily compressed. When air enters the brake lines, brake lever or pedal movement will be partially used in compressing the air. This will make the lever or pedal feel spongy, resulting in a loss of braking power.

Bleed the brake system whenever lever or pedal action feels soft or spongy, after the brake fluid is changed, or whenever a brake fitting has been loosened for any reason. Follow these basic procedures for bleeding a hydraulic brake system.

1. Fill reservoir to its proper level
2. Pump pressure into the system using the brake lever or pedal. Then, hold pressure on the brake lever or pedal, **Figure 15-22A.**
3. Open bleed valve, and watch air bubbles in clear tubing, **Figure 15-22B.**
4. Close bleed valve, **Figure 15-22C.**
5. Release lever or pedal.
6. Repeat steps 2-5 until there are no air bubbles visible when the bleed valve is opened, **Figure 15-22D.** Keep the master cylinder full to prevent air from getting into the system.

Master Cylinder and Caliper Rebuilding

Remember the following important information when rebuilding a master cylinder or caliper. Refer to the service manual for exact specifications and procedures.

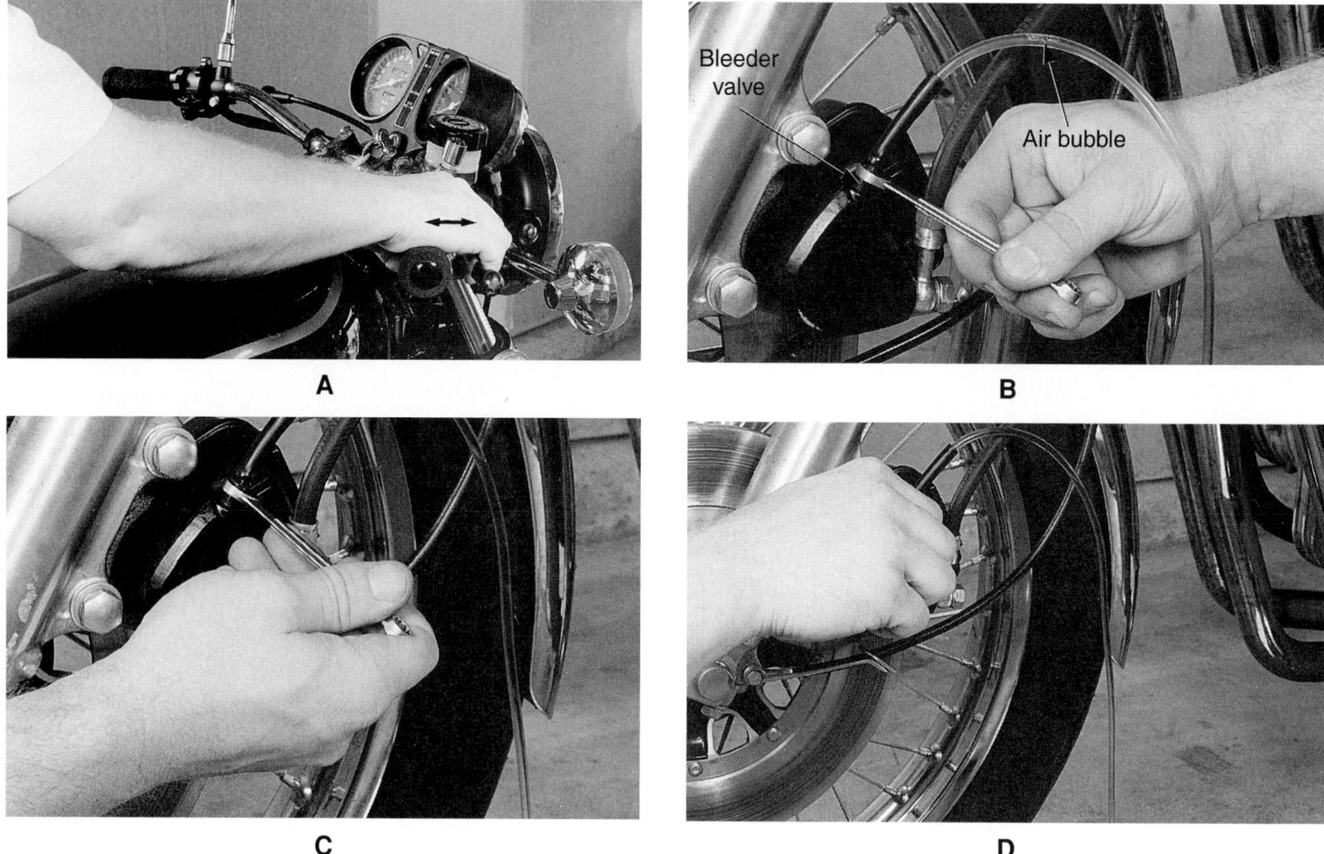

Figure 15-22. Steps needed to bleed air out of hydraulic system. A—Pump pressure into the brake system. B—Maintain pressure and open bleeder valve. C—Close bleeder before releasing lever. Make sure to keep the master cylinder reservoir full. D—Continue bleeding until there is no more air in the system.

1. Always use new OEM (original equipment manufacturer) parts, if possible.
2. Use only alcohol or the correct DOT brake fluid for cleaning parts exposed to brake fluid.
3. Discard all old brake fluid properly.
4. Use new correct DOT brake fluid for assembly and service.
5. Do not allow oil, grease, or brake fluid to come into contact with the brake disc or pads.
6. Always bleed the system after reassembly.

Master Cylinder Rebuilding

The following is a procedure for rebuilding a typical master cylinder. In some cases, it may be more feasible to replace the master cylinder.

1. Remove and disassemble the master cylinder following service manual instructions, **Figure 15-23.**
2. Clean all parts thoroughly.
3. Check for blocked fluid passages.
4. Measure the master cylinder piston with an outside micrometer, **Figure 15-24A.**
5. Measure the master cylinder using a telescoping gauge and an outside micrometer, **Figure 15-24B.**
6. Measure the return spring free length using a machinist's rule, **Figure 15-24C.**
7. Inspect all parts for damage.
8. Replace all rubber parts, unless instructed otherwise by the service manual.

To reassemble the master cylinder, proceed as follows:

1. Lubricate all moving parts with clean brake fluid and install the return spring, **Figure 15-25A.**
2. Slide the piston/cup assembly into the master cylinder bore, **Figure 15-25B.**
3. Assemble the remaining parts, including the fluid reservoir, **Figure 15-25C.**
4. Reinstall the master cylinder in the brake housing.
5. Fill the system with the proper DOT brake fluid.
6. Bleed the brake system.

Caliper Rebuilding

To rebuild a typical disc brake caliper, proceed in the following manner:

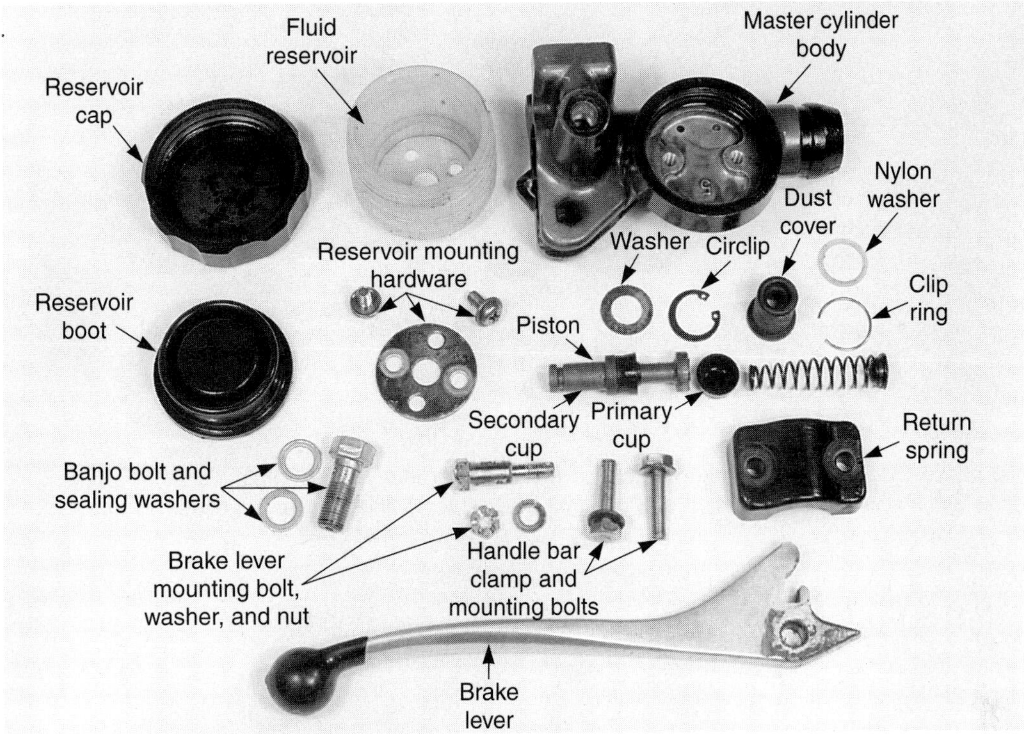

Figure 15-23. Completely disassemble the master cylinder before cleaning parts in a brake fluid solution or denatured alcohol.

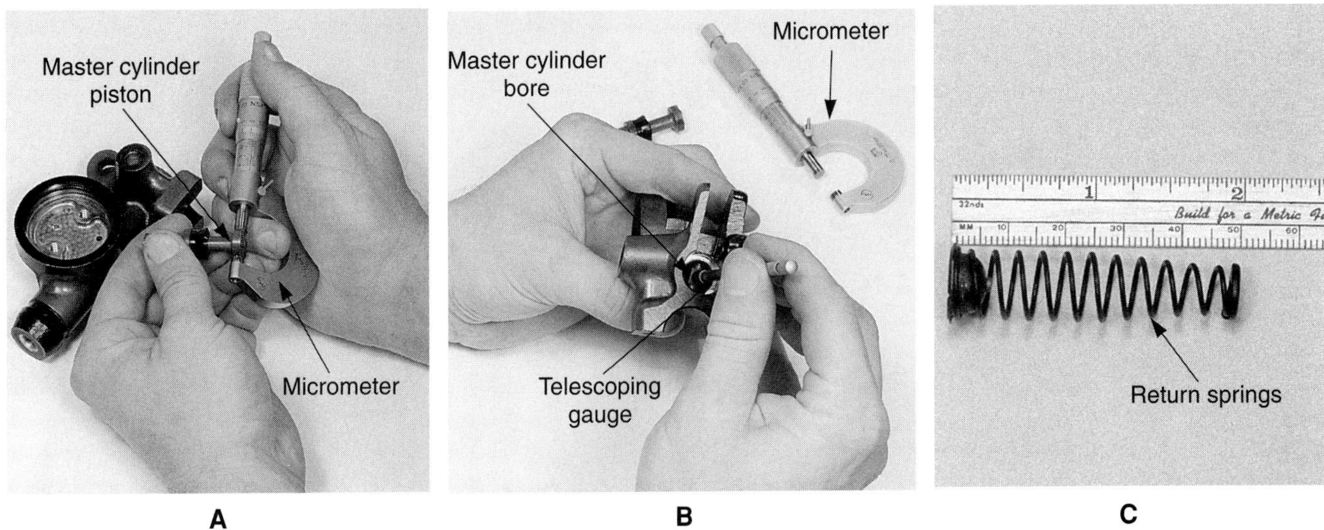

Figure 15-24. Three basic measurements that are especially critical when rebuilding a master cylinder. A—Measuring master cylinder piston. B—Measuring bore diameter. C—Checking return spring length.

1. Remove and disassemble the caliper as described in the service manual, **Figure 15-26.**

2. Clean all parts, except the pads, with brake fluid.

3. Inspect the pads for wear, oil, grease, or other contamination. The pads shown in **Figure 15-27** have a groove or line wear indicator. If worn to the groove or line, the pads are worn out and must be replaced. If the pads are contaminated in any way, they should also be replaced.

4. Use a micrometer to measure the caliper piston diameter, **Figure 15-28A.**

5. Measure the caliper bore diameter using a telescoping gauge and a micrometer to determine the piston clearance, **Figure 15-28B.** If beyond service manual specifications, the worn components must be replaced.

6. Check the bore for scoring or pitting. If damage is found, replace the component.

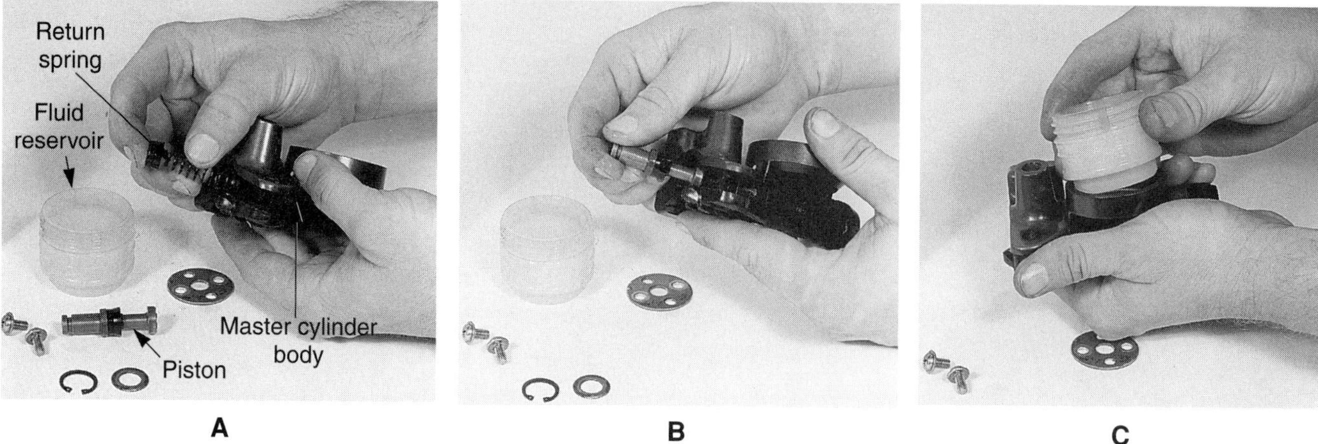

Figure 15-25. Use these fundamental steps and a service manual to properly reassemble a master cylinder. A— Lubricate all moving parts before installation. B—Slide piston and cup into the master cylinder bore. C—Assemble the remaining parts.

Figure 15-26. To remove the piston when disassembling a caliper, use compressed air to blow into the brake line hole. Clean all parts in alcohol or new brake fluid.

7. Install new rubber parts.

To reassemble and reinstall a brake caliper, proceed as follows:

1. When reassembling caliper parts, lubricate them with new brake fluid.
2. When installing the piston ring, be sure it is not twisted, **Figure 15-29A.**
3. Then, install the piston carefully, **Figure 15-29B.**
4. Install the caliper on the bike and torque it. Follow service manual instructions and torque specifications, **Figure 15-29C.**
5. Connect the hydraulic lines.
6. Fill the brake system with new fluid.
7. Bleed the brakes.

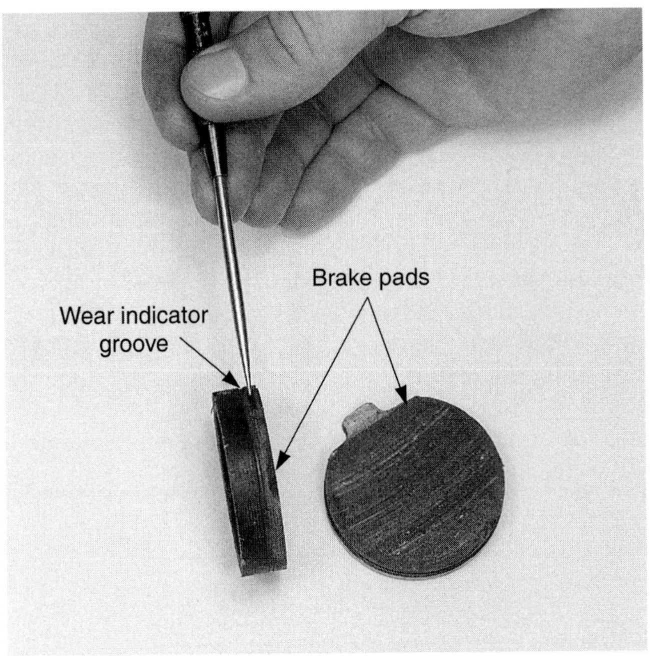

Figure 15-27. Inspect pads for wear and contamination. These pads have wear indicator groove. If worn to the groove, replace the pads.

Disc Brake Pad Replacement

To replace the brake pads, begin by removing the caliper as outlined in the service manual. Inspect the pad and brake disc for wear and scoring, **Figure 15-30.** If the brake disc is scored, cracked, or damaged, replace it. When replacing brake pads, always replace any hardware, such as pad springs and shims. Pad installation is the reverse of removal. Be sure to pump the brake handle or pedal a few times to seat the pads against the rotor(s).

When riding the bike for the first time after pad replacement, perform a series of controlled stops to wear in the pads and to make sure the brakes are stopping properly. Do not wear in the pads by performing panic stops. This is not only dangerous, but will cause the new pads to form a glaze, which will increase stopping distance.

Unified Brake Controls

Separate brakes permit a full range of front/rear braking ratios, however, from the panicked novice's 100% rear to the roadracer's 100% front, neither of these extremes give maximum stopping power on the street. Rear brake only gives about 25% of maximum stopping power. 100% front brakes may work on the racetrack under ideal conditions, but this option also delivers less than 100% of maximum stopping power on a street motorcycle. Correct division of braking effort requires a sensitive, educated response located somewhere between these extremes.

Recently, several manufacturers have developed ***unified braking controls*** that automatically operate the front and rear systems when the rider applies pressure to the rear brake pedal. When this occurs, more braking power is automatically applied to the front end to prevent the rear wheel from locking. Actually, there has been a long history of experimentation with integrated braking systems. Such a system appeared in 1925 on the British Rudge model, and was soon used by other manufacturers on some of their models. Currently the two most popular unified brake systems used on street bikes are the linked brake system (LBS) and the anti-lock brake system (ABS).

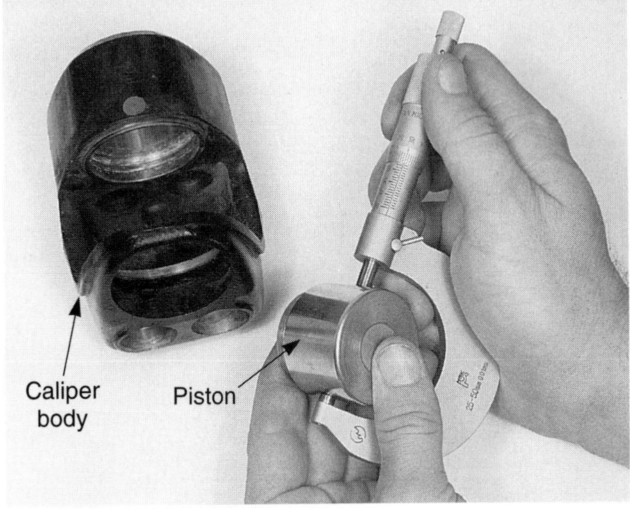

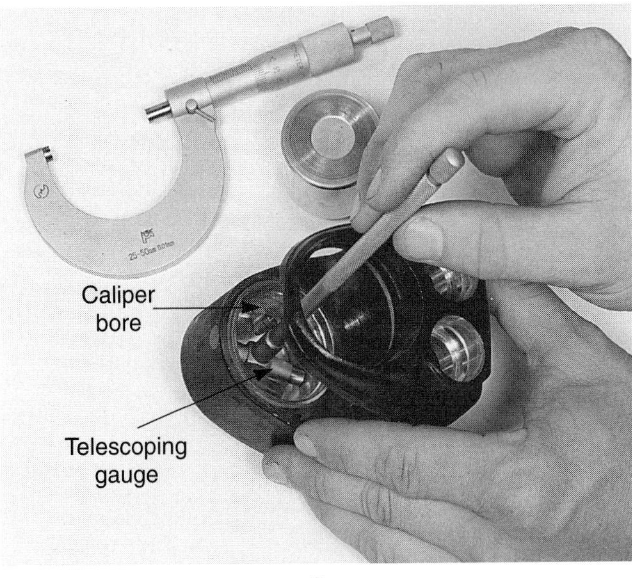

Figure 15-28. Difference between the piston diameter and caliper bore diameter determines the piston clearance.

Linked Braking System (LBS)

The ***linked braking system (LBS)*** is designed so the front and rear calipers are pressed simultaneously when

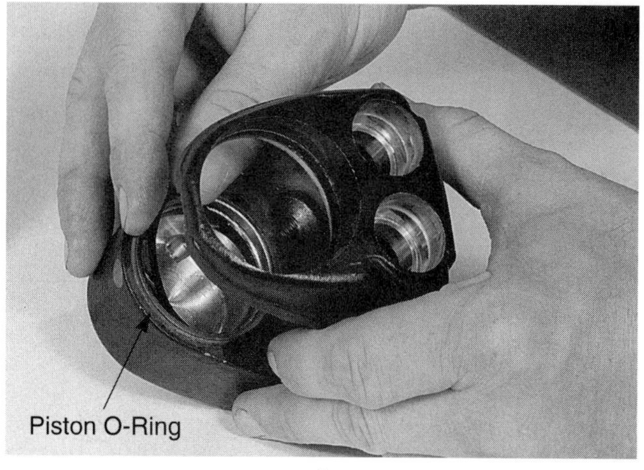

A

B

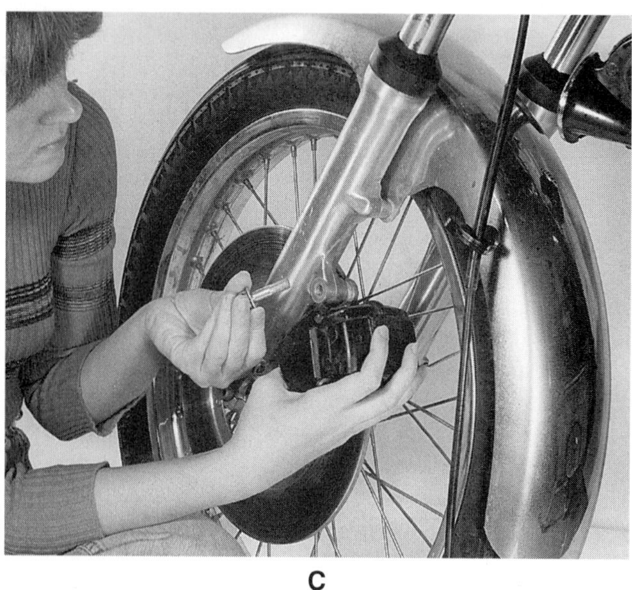

C

Figure 15-29. When assembling a caliper, lubricate all parts with new brake fluid. A—When installing the piston O-ring, be sure it is not twisted. B—Install the piston carefully. C—Install caliper and tighten bolts with a torque wrench. Then install brake line and bleed system.

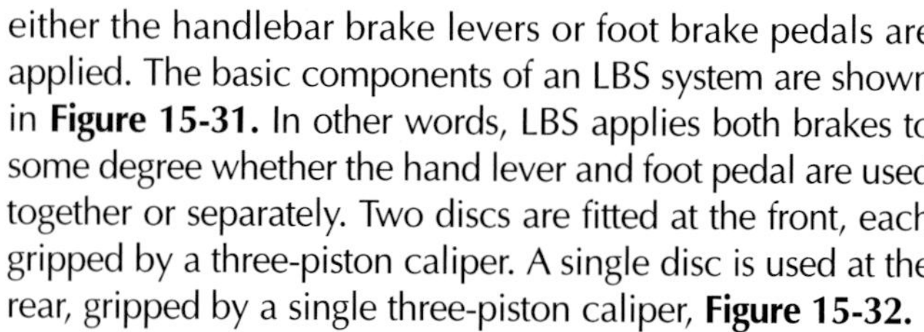

either the handlebar brake levers or foot brake pedals are applied. The basic components of an LBS system are shown in **Figure 15-31.** In other words, LBS applies both brakes to some degree whether the hand lever and foot pedal are used together or separately. Two discs are fitted at the front, each gripped by a three-piston caliper. A single disc is used at the rear, gripped by a single three-piston caliper, **Figure 15-32.**

When the rider pulls the brake lever, fluid pressure from the master cylinder activates the two outer pistons in each front caliper, **Figure 15-33.** While the right front caliper is bolted conventionally to the fork leg, the left caliper is mounted on a mechanical linkage. As brake torque develops at the left caliper, this linkage applies the reaction force to a second, or servo, master cylinder.

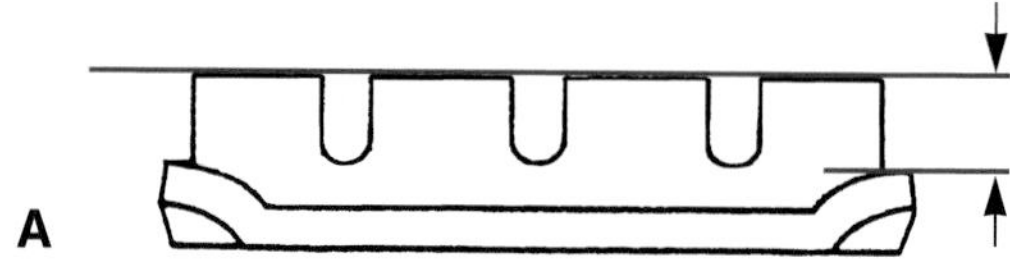

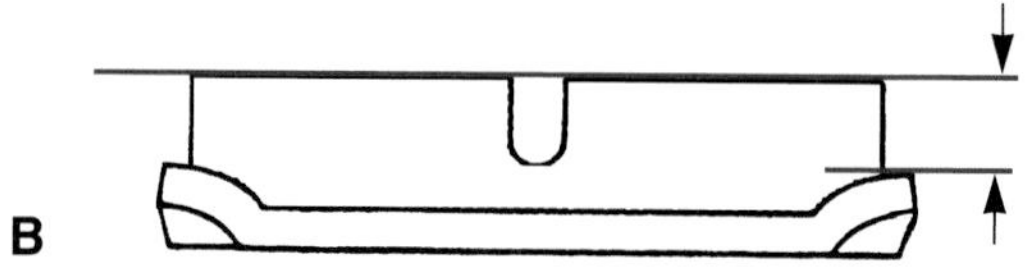

Figure 15-30. Measure brake pad thickness to determine if they need to be replaced. Also inspect the disc for damage such as scoring and cracks. A—Front pad. B—Rear pad. (Yamaha Motor Corporation U.S.A.)

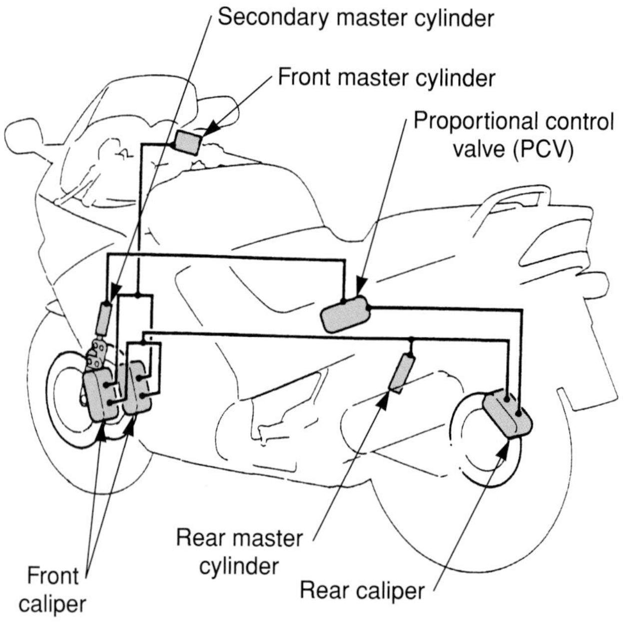

Figure 15-31. LBS components. (Honda Motor Co., Ltd.)

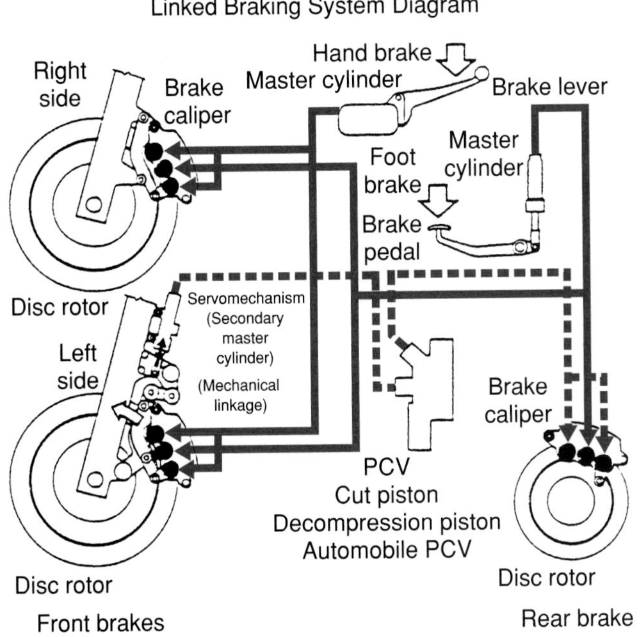

Figure 15-32. Linked braking system component operation. (Honda Motor Co., Ltd.)

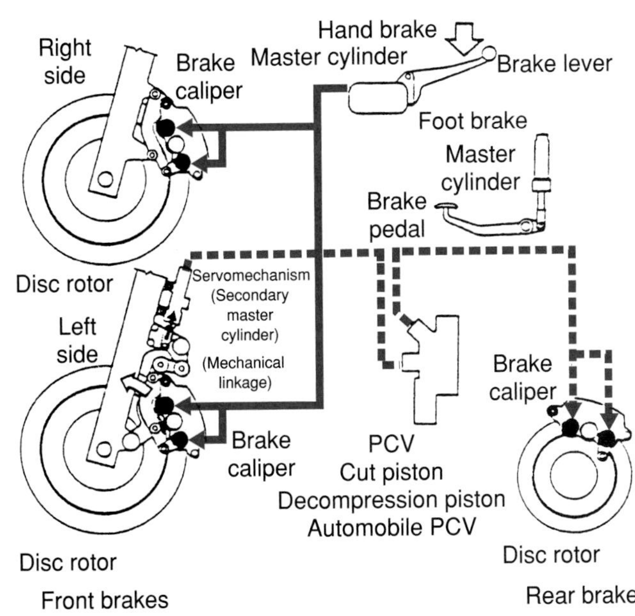

Figure 15-33. LBS hand brake operation. (Honda Motor Co., Ltd.)

Fluid output is routed through a special proportioning valve to the outer pistons on the rear caliper. Applying the hand lever alone delivers two-thirds of the maximum possible front-brake force, and delivers a smaller, but proportioned force to the rear caliper.

If the rider applies the foot pedal alone, fluid is sent directly to the center pistons of all calipers, and through the left front caliper and the servo master cylinder it is linked to; fluid is also sent indirectly to the outer pistons of the rear caliper, **Figure 15-34.**

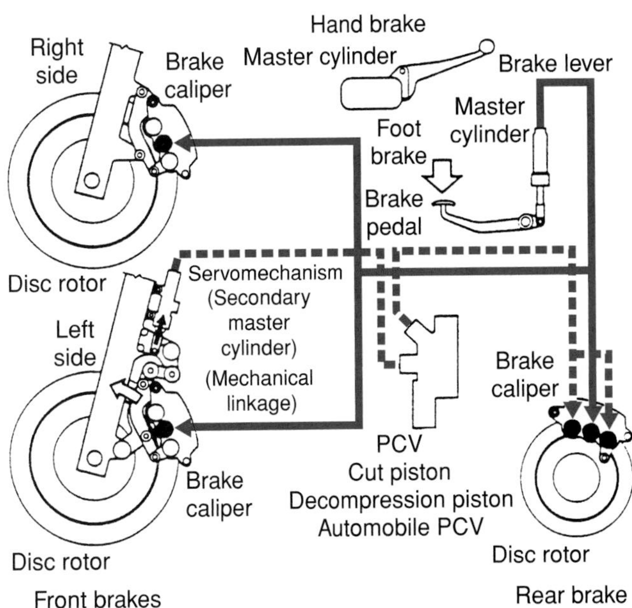

Figure 15-34. LBS foot pedal brake operation. (Honda Motor Co., Ltd.)

In neither case is the rider able to commit the error of applying only the rear brake. Going for the pedal alone splits the braking effect, with three calipers working to provide good, but not an optimum rate of deceleration, while reducing the chance of rear-wheel lock-up.

The proportioning valve is the heart of the system. It is a non-electronic device made up of passive valves, pistons, and springs, **Figure 15-35.** The proportioning valve adjusts rear-brake torque to be proportional to front-brake torque. The only exception to this is when braking becomes so heavy that significant forward weight transfer makes rear-wheel lock-up more likely. As front-brake torque rises, the valve at first increases rear brake torque at a high rate. At higher front brake torque, it shifts to a lower rate of increase. At still higher deceleration rates, a "cut valve" holds rear brake torque constant. Finally, at rates of deceleration so rapid that the rear wheel is significantly unloaded, a decompressor valve actually reduces rear brake torque by progressively pulling fluid from the rear caliper line.

While a rider can lock the wheels with LBS, the system does eliminate the most hazardous choices in front/rear brake proportioning. It eases the problem of obtaining maximum, correctly proportioned brake action.

Anti-Lock Brake Systems (ABS)

The friction between the tire and road surface greatly reduces when the wheels lock due to hard braking. An ***anti-lock brake system (ABS)*** can control and reduce the tendency for wheel lock-up during braking. ABS only operates during periods of wheel lock-up. Normal braking operation is identical to that of a conventional motorcycle.

The hand brake lever is used for applying the brake on the front wheel, and the brake pedal for applying the brake on the rear wheel. There are two independent hydraulic systems, one for the front wheel and one for the rear wheel. An electronic control module (ECM) is used to control these two systems.

Functions of ABS Components

Figure 15-36 shows the location of main components of a typical motorcycle ABS system, which are:

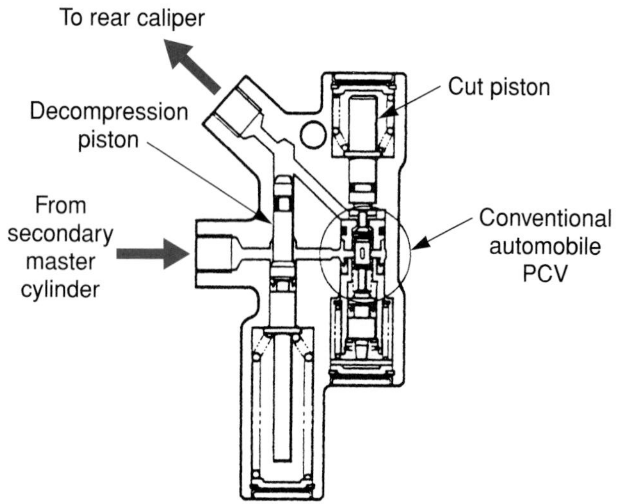

Figure 15-35. Operation of PCV (proportional control valve). (Honda Motor Co., Ltd.)

- Wheel speed sensor and rotor.
- Electronic control module (ECM).
- Hydraulic unit (HU).
- Fail safe relay.
- Brake light relay.

In addition to these there are other related components, such as the ABS test coupler and the ABS warning light.

Wheel Speed Sensor and Rotor

The ABS system uses ***wheel speed sensors*** to monitor actual wheel speed. Alternating current is generated by the wheel speed sensor when the wheel rotates and is transmitted to the ABS ECM. The sensor consists of a permanent magnet and coils. One wheel speed sensor is mounted on the rear wheel housing and one on the front wheel housing.

The front and rear wheel speed sensor rotors are press-fit and have machined notches or teeth. The wheel speed sensor tip is positioned close to the rotor teeth. When the rotor turns, it cuts through the magnetic flux created by the wheel speed sensor magnet. This generates an alternating current in the speed sensor's coil, which is proportional to the wheel's rotating speed. The current's frequency changes in relation to the wheel's speed. See **Figure 15-37.** The alternating current is supplied to the ABS ECM, which recognizes it as a rotation signal.

ABS Electronic Control Module (ECM)

The anti-lock brake ***electronic control module (ECM)*** controls the ABS system and is mounted under the seat or

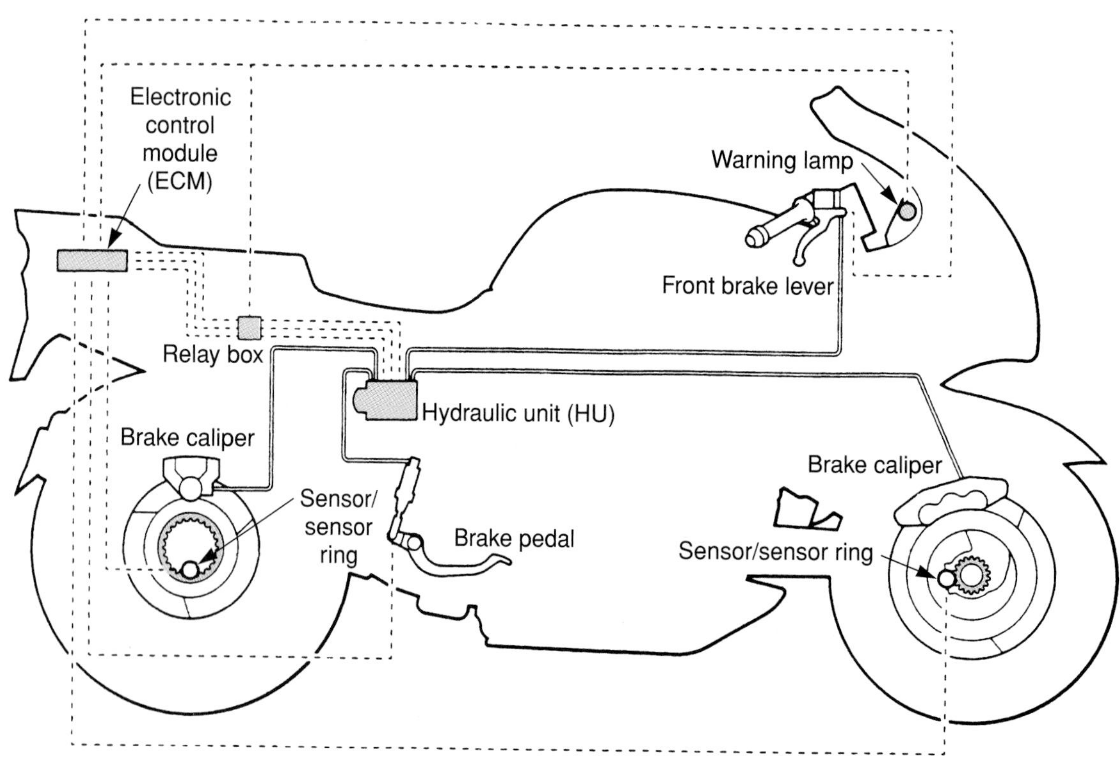

Figure 15-36. Major ABS system components. (Yamaha Motor Corporation U.S.A.)

inside the tail cowl. The ECM is usually housed in a rubber cover for protection against water. As shown in **Figure 15-38,** the ECM receives signals from the front and rear wheel speed sensors and monitors the circuit signals. Microprocessors in the ECM process the ABS control logic. ECM operation is monitored and controlled by the CPU. Based on these results, control signals are supplied to the hydraulic unit, the fail safe relay, and the ABS warning light.

Hydraulic Unit (HU)

The ***hydraulic unit (HU)*** is a component that controls the brake system hydraulic pressure, based on instructions from the ECM, **Figure 15-38.** It is installed on the right side of the battery box.

The hydraulic unit adjusts the brake fluid pressure of the front and rear wheel based on the signals from the ECM to give the optimum braking force to the motorcycle.

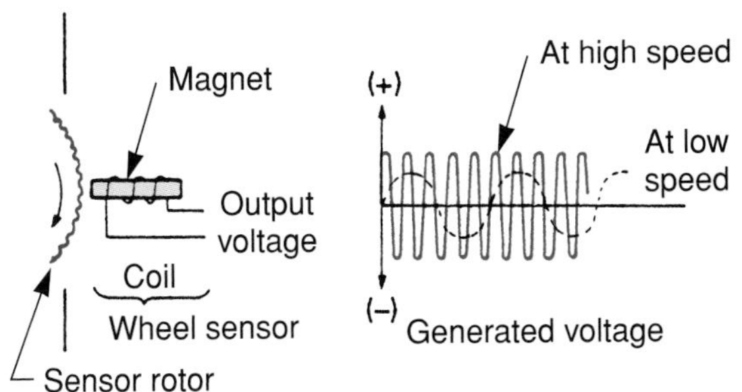

Figure 15-37. The alternating current output from the wheel speed sensor. (Yamaha Motor Corporation U.S.A.)

The flow control valve maintains a constant brake fluid flow rate during ABS operation. It works in combination with the solenoid valve in increasing and decreasing brake fluid pressure. The buffer chamber has the function of temporarily storing the brake fluid which is bypassed to reduce brake fluid pressure during ABS operation. The pump is driven by the electric motor. Its function is to return the brake fluid stored in the buffer chamber to the master cylinder.

Fail Safe Relay

The ***fail safe relay*** controls the power supply to the hydraulic unit, **Figure 15-39.** This relay consists of the solenoid relay and the motor relay. The solenoid relay is switched on by the ECM when it activates the ABS system. In this condition, the solenoid valve can operate when the ECM's dump command is given.

At the same time as the ECM's dump command, the motor relay is also switched on by the ECM. The pump motor can be operated simultaneously with the start of hydraulic pressure reduction by the ABS system. If the solenoid relay goes off, the motor relay goes off as well. Therefore, in case of a fault in the ABS system, the motor stops operating and the circuit reverts to the conventional brake circuit. When this happens, the ABS warning light starts flashing.

ABS Test Coupler

The ***ABS test coupler*** allows technicians to access the self-diagnostics in the ECM. The coupler is usually located

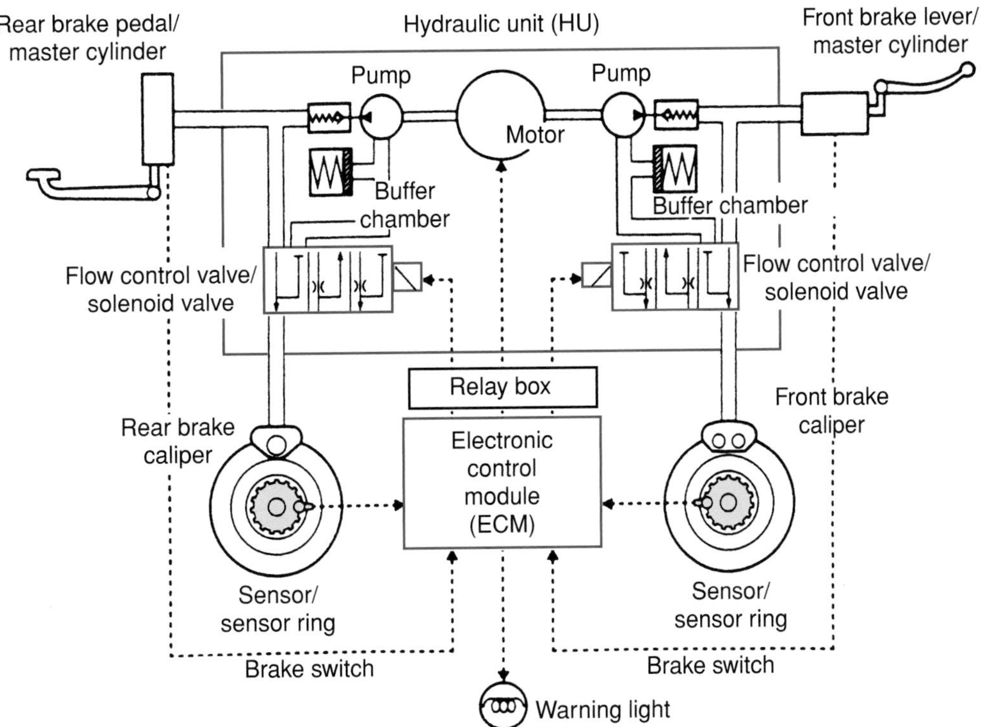

Figure 15-38. Main components of ABS hydraulic unit. (Yamaha Motor Corporation U.S.A.)

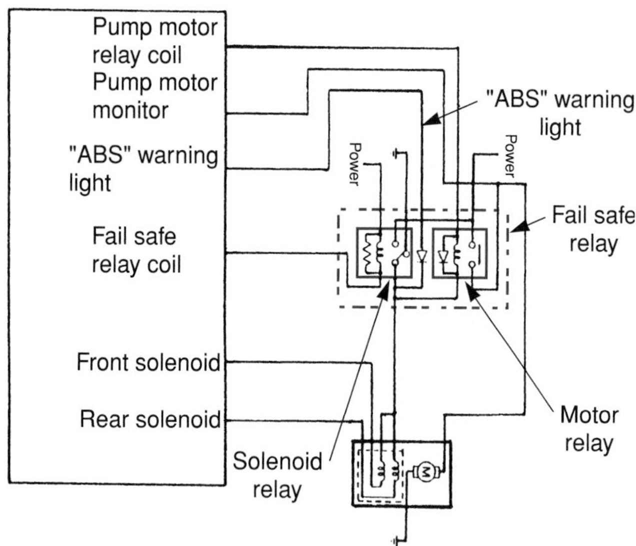

Figure 15-39. Operation of fail safe relay. (Yamaha Motor Corporation U.S.A.)

in a place that will protect it from damage and exposure to rain and dirt. Most ABS test couplers are located under the seat or in the tail cowl. Using a meter or other tool, any diagnostic codes stored in the ECM can be accessed.

ABS Warning Light

The ***ABS warning light,*** like the EFI warning light described in Chapter 7, informs the rider of the ABS self-diagnosis results. It is installed in the meter panel and operates in a similar fashion as the EFI warning light.

When the bike is first started, the ABS light will illuminate for a few seconds. The reason for this is twofold. It allows the ABS ECM to check the light and system operation and to notify the rider the system is active. Once the bike starts moving, the ABS system will perform a short self-test, which also prepares the system for an ABS stop.

The self-diagnosis function is provided in the ECM to confirm the correct operating status of the ABS system at all times. If a fault is detected in the system, the hydraulic control of the ABS system is stopped immediately and the system reverts to the conventional braking circuit. Simultaneously, the ABS warning light comes on, and reports the detection of a fault in the system. The fault code is found in the vehicle's service manual.

Note: A defect in the hydraulic system, or base brakes, can sometimes cause the ABS warning light to illuminate. The base brake system must be inspected and any defects corrected before the anti-lock brake system is suspected of containing a defect.

ABS Operation

When the front or rear wheel speed sensor detects wheel lock, the hydraulic pressure applied on the brake caliper on the locking wheel is decreased and increased repetitively by the ECM to achieve optimum braking performance.

The ECM also has a sophisticated self-diagnostic system. If a fault should develop in the ABS system, the fault is detected. However, the brake system is capable of only normal (non-ABS) braking, or base brakes. The ABS warning light in the meter panel comes on if a fault is detected. It accurately informs the rider about faults in the ABS system. The ECM memory stores the history of occurrences of faults. It is designed to assist in the search for trouble locations by showing the fault codes.

The ABS computer calculates the different wheel speeds based on signals received from the front and rear wheel speed sensors. The computer calculates the motorcycle running speed, and deceleration rate of the wheel based on the wheel speed. The difference between the calculated running speed and wheel speed of each wheel corresponds to the wheel slip.

When the wheel tends to lock, the wheel's deceleration rate increases rapidly. When the magnitude of slip and the wheel deceleration rate exceed the decided value, the ABS computer judges that the wheel has a tendency to lock and controls the brake. If the slip is large, and the wheel tends to lock, the ABS computer reduces the brake fluid pressure. When the locking tendency is eliminated, it increases brake fluid pressure. By repeating these fine adjustments in pressure control, a highly efficient braking force can be attained.

If the ABS system starts operating, it means the tendency for wheel lock is present, and the motorcycle is approaching its limit of control. To make the rider aware of this condition, the ABS has been designed to generate a reaction force in the brake lever and brake pedal. The reaction force generated in the brake lever and pedal when the ABS operates is not an abnormal condition. It is merely a warning given to the rider.

Sudden braking while cornering is not recommended. Side force is reduced during braking on motorcycles equipped with ABS, as well as those equipped with conventional brake systems.

ABS functions to prevent wheel lock-up by controlling brake fluid pressure. If the wheel has a tendency to lock on an extremely slick road surface, the ABS system may not be able to totally prevent wheel lock-up.

Troubleshooting Motorcycle Brake Systems

Consult the service manual and use the following procedures to troubleshoot both mechanical drum and hydraulic disc brake systems. ABS control systems have a built-in self-diagnostic system.

Mechanical Drum Brakes

The following are common drum brake problems and their causes:

Poor Brake Performance

- Improperly adjusted brake.
- Worn brake linings.
- Worn brake drum.
- Worn brake cam.
- Improperly installed brake linings.
- Brake cable sticking/needs lubrication.
- Contaminated brake linings.
- Contaminated brake drum.
- Worn brake shoes at cam contact areas.
- Improper engagement between brake arm and camshaft serrations.

Brake Lever Hard or Slow to Return

- Worn/broken return spring.
- Improperly adjusted brake.
- Sticking brake drum due to contamination.
- Worn brake shoes at cam contact areas.
- Brake cable sticking/needs lubrication.
- Worn brake cam.
- Improperly installed brake linings.

Brake Squeaks

- Worn brake linings.
- Worn brake drum.
- Contaminated brake linings.
- Contaminated brake drum.

Hydraulic Disc Brakes

Common hydraulic disc brake problems and some of their causes are as follows:

Brake Lever/Pedal Soft or Spongy

- Air bubbles in the hydraulic system.
- Leaking hydraulic system.
- Contaminated brake pad/disc.
- Worn caliper piston seal.
- Worn master cylinder piston.
- Worn brake pad.
- Contaminated caliper.
- Caliper not sliding properly.
- Worn brake pad/disc.
- Low fluid level.
- Clogged fluid passage.
- Warped/deformed brake disc.
- Sticking/worn caliper piston.
- Sticking/worn master cylinder piston.
- Worn brake disc.
- Contaminated master cylinder.
- Bent brake lever/pedal.

Brake Lever/Pedal Hard

- Clogged/restricted brake system.
- Sticking/worn caliper piston.
- Caliper not sliding properly.
- Clogged/restricted fluid passage.
- Worn caliper piston seal.
- Sticking/worn master cylinder piston.
- Bent brake lever/pedal.

Brake Grab or Pull to One Side

- Contaminated brake pad/disc.
- Misaligned wheel.
- Clogged/restricted brake hose.
- Warped/deformed brake disc.
- Caliper not sliding properly.
- Clogged/restricted brake hose joint.

Brake Drag

- Contaminated brake pad/disc.
- Misaligned wheel.
- Worn brake pad/disc.
- Warped/deformed brake disc.
- Caliper not sliding properly.

Brake Fluid Leakage

- Insufficient tightening of connection points.
- Cracked hose.
- Worn piston and/or cap.

ABS System

Note: If an ABS problem is suspected, you must inspect for and service any defects in the hydraulic system and base brake components first before investigating the ABS system.

ABS Light on at All Times

- Problem in the brake hydraulic system. See *Hydraulic Disc Brakes.*

- No power to the ABS system.
- Defective fail safe relay.
- Defective hydraulic unit.
- Defective ECM.

ABS Light Comes on While Moving

- Defective or disconnected wheel speed sensor.
- Excessive clearance between sensor and rotor.
- Open or short in ABS sensor wiring harness.
- Defective ECM.

ABS Light Comes on While Braking

- Problem in the brake hydraulic system. See *Hydraulic Disc Brakes*
- Defective fail safe relay.
- Defective hydraulic unit.
- Defective wheel speed sensor.
- Defective ECM.

Summary

Good brake work is critical and there is no room for error. Improper maintenance and service can mean the difference between a safe motorcycle and one that is a hazard to ride. A brake is a device that applies friction to a moving device to slow it down and bring it to a stop. Braking is accomplished by the friction produced when brake linings are forced against a rotating disc or drum. Friction between the linings and disc or drum will eventually stop wheel rotation.

Mechanical brakes use movement of the brake lever or pedal, which is transferred to the brake actuating cam by a cable or rod. The stopping ability of the mechanical brake system is determined by the system's mechanical leverage, the brake lining surface area; the composition of the brake lining; and the brake drum's ability to dissipate heat.

In the hydraulic brake system, the lever or pedal uses hydraulic fluid to perform a mechanical function. The advantages of using hydraulic brakes are equal pressure is provided in all directions within the system; self-adjusting; can produce very high pressure; and has low maintenance requirements. A hydraulic brake system is a closed system. When pressure is applied in a hydraulic system, it is transferred equally in all directions throughout the system.

The two types of brake designs are the drum brake and disc brake. Drum brakes have been in use on motorcycles since their creation and are still used on some modern bikes. There are two basic drum brake designs: single-leading shoe and double-leading shoe. Disc brakes can be actuated hydraulically or mechanically. The hydraulic design is almost exclusively used today. Hydraulic disc brakes use two types of calipers: single piston, or single-push caliper and double-piston, or opposite-piston caliper.

There are three types of brake fluid that are rated by the United States Department of Transportation (DOT). They are DOT 3, DOT 4, and DOT 5. DOT 3 and DOT 4 are glycol-based brake fluids, while DOT 5 is a silicon-based product. The DOT designations specify the brake fluid's ability to withstand heat without boiling. It is important to use the same DOT number fluid. Improper mixing may lead to chemical decomposition, system contamination, and possible damage.

Brake inspection should be done during routine maintenance or if a problem is suspected. When removing the front wheel, support the bike securely under the engine to raise the wheel. To remove the rear wheel for brake service, follow the procedure in the service manual. Use caution when handling and installing brake lines and hoses. The three operations of brake service; inspection, maintenance, and repair, should be dealt with as one operation.

Recently, several manufacturers have developed unified braking controls that automatically operate the front and rear systems when the rider applies pressure to the rear brake pedal. The linked braking system (LBS) is designed so the front and rear calipers are applied simultaneously when either the handlebar brake levers or foot brake pedals are applied. The typical motorcycle anti-lock brake system (ABS) detects and controls wheel lock tendency during braking under various road and weather conditions. The anti-lock brake ECM has a sophisticated self-diagnostic system. If a fault should develop in the ABS system, the fault is detected. However, the brake system is still capable of non-ABS braking.

Know These Terms

Brake	Brake lever
Asbestos	Master cylinder
Mechanical brake system	Hydraulic lines
Brake pedal	Stoplight switch
Brake cable	Pads
Stoplight switch	Caliper
Brake cam arm	Wheel cylinder
Brake actuating cam	Disc
Backing plate	Drum brakes
Backing plate torque arm	Single-leading shoe drum brakes
Drum	Trailing shoe
Shoes	Self-energizing effect
Linings	Double-leading drum brakes
Return springs	Disc brakes
Hydraulic brake system	Single piston caliper

Double piston caliper
Opposite-piston caliper
Floating discs
Brake fluid
DOT 3
DOT 4
DOT 5
Relining
Bleeding
Unified braking controls
Linked braking system (LBS)
Anti-lock brake system (ABS)
Electronic control module (ECM)
Hydraulic unit (HU)
Fail safe relay
ABS test coupler
ABS warning light

Review Questions—Chapter 15

Do not write in this text. Place your answers on a separate sheet of paper.

1. A brake is a device that applies ______ to a moving device.
2. _____ between the linings and disc or drum stops wheel rotation.
   A. Friction
   B. Pressure
   C. Heat
   D. Air
3. Equal pressure provided in all directions within the system; the system is self-adjusting; it can produce very high pressure; and has low maintenance requirements. These are advantages of what type of braking system?
4. What are the two types of brake designs?
5. Single-leading shoe and double-leading shoe are two types of what braking system?
6. Most brake drums are made of ______.
7. Disc brakes can be actuated ______.
   A. hydraulically
   B. mechanically
   C. both hydraulically and mechanically
   D. None of the above.
8. ______ brakes use two types of calipers, single-piston, or single-push caliper and double-piston, or opposite-piston caliper.
9. List the three general types of brake fluid that are rated by the United States Department of Transportation.
10. Brake fluid should be changed at least every ______ years.
    A. two
    B. five
    C. three
    D. ten
11. Unified braking controls ______ when the rider applies pressure to the rear brake pedal.
    A. the front brake system
    B. the rear brake system
    C. both front and rear brake systems
    D. None of the above.
12. Currently the two most popular unified brake systems used on street bikes are the ______ and the ______.
13. ECM stands for ______.
    A. electronic command unit
    B. electronic control module
    C. electrical command module
    D. extra control module
14. *True or False?* If brake fluid level is low, adding any of the DOT rated brake fluids will be satisfactory.
15. Bleeding the brake lines refers to ______.
    A. removing water from the system
    B. removing air from the system
    C. removing excess brake fluid from the system
    D. removing a foreign substance from the system

Suggested Activities

1. Following the procedures given in the manufacturer's service manual, disassemble, clean, inspect, and reassemble a disc brake system, noting and repairing or replacing any damaged or worn parts.
2. Following the procedures given in the manufacturer's service manual, disassemble, clean, inspect, and reassemble a drum brake system, noting and repairing or replacing any damaged or worn parts.
3. Using a bike equipped with ABS, practice accessing the self-diagnostic system using the procedures described in the service manual. Disconnect one sensor and operate the bike until the warning light illuminates. Then, access the self-diagnostic system and clear any codes that are present.

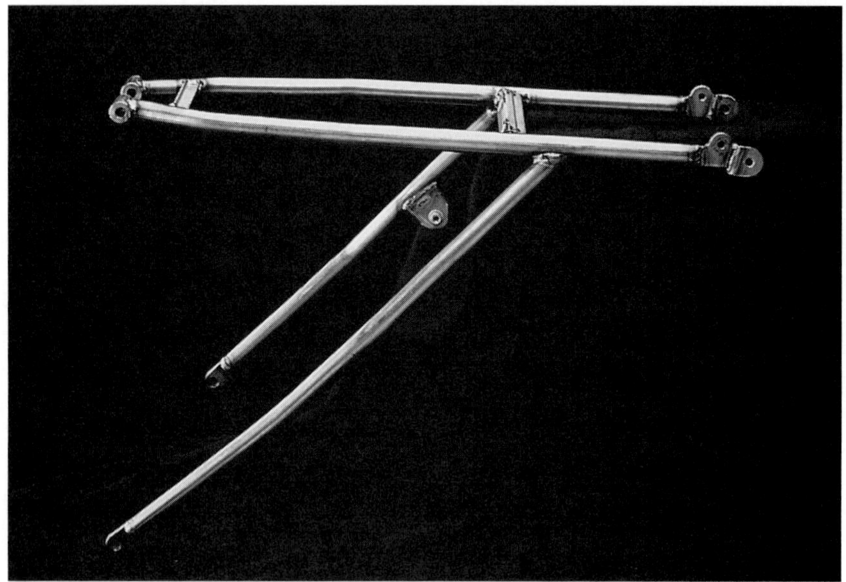

Motorcycle frames come in many varieties and materials. This is a titanium subframe. (Yamaha Motor Corporation, U.S.A.)

16 Frame and Suspension Systems

After studying this chapter, you will be able to:

- Describe the types of main frames used on today's motorcycles.
- Explain the action of front and rear suspension systems.
- Change front fork oil.
- Lubricate steering head bearings.
- Describe the procedures for rebuilding a front fork assembly.
- Explain rear swingarm and shock absorber construction.
- Compare different types of suspension systems.
- Inspect a frame and suspension system for signs of trouble.

It is very important for a motorcycle to handle properly over bumps, in turns, during acceleration, and when stopping. This is critical to both rider safety and comfort. The design of a frame and suspension system is a major factor controlling the handling characteristics of a bike. This chapter discusses frame and suspension designs and how they affect performance and dependability. The chapter also covers fundamental inspection, service, repair, and troubleshooting procedures for frames and suspension systems.

Frame

The ***frame*** is the backbone of all motorcycles, ATVs, and scooters. It serves as a skeleton on which virtually everything is attached. A critical function of any frame is to provide a non-flexing mount for the engine, suspension, and wheels, **Figure 16-1.** The frame also provides a rigid structure between the steering head (front wheel and fork assembly) and rear swingarm (rear wheel and suspension assembly). Cornering and acceleration tend to misalign these assemblies.

The material used for a frame is chosen to match the motorcycle's function. Aluminum frames are used for on-road sport bikes with medium-to-large displacement engines and motocross bikes. Other frames are made of steel. Aluminum alloys are lighter than steel of the same strength, but are bulkier and more expensive to produce. Some of today's frames are made almost entirely of round steel tubing of various sizes and thicknesses. Others are made up mainly of square steel tubing.

Figure 16-1. The primary function of the frame is to provide a non-flexing platform for the engine, suspension, and wheels. (Yamaha Motor Corporation U.S.A.)

Most aluminum frame members use some form of rectangular tubing, although a few pieces are square. Most aluminum and steel frames include some castings or pressed steel sections in order to form strong and compact tube joints, and for pivot or major attachment points.

Some chassis sub-frames are now being made of titanium alloys, which are primarily used in aircraft. In addition to its excellent weight advantage over most metals, including aluminum, titanium is also corrosion resistant. These sub-frames are approved for professional motocross competition.

Round tubing has the same strength in all directions. Square and rectangular tubing (as well as other variants) have different strength characteristics in different directions. When maximum strength is required in a vertical direction and strength in a horizontal direction is not as important, rectangular tubing is used.

A frame can be lightened by changing the types of tubing used to build the frame. Thinwall rectangular aluminum tubing is given greater strength by adding internal ribs and producing it by extrusion (process in which semi-soft metal is forced through a die). Some models use a specially modified pentagonal or hexagonal aluminum tubing in order to improve the frame's strength-to-weight ratio, its rigidity in one or more specific directions, and in some cases, to allow a more compact and unobstructed riding position. A wide variety of tubing and pressed steel shapes as well as casting and forging are combined to form the optimal framework for a particular model.

The frame also serves to absorb vibration from the engine and, to some degree, the road surface. The difference in frame structure is determined according to engine type and the designed use of the bike. Two slightly different frame designs may have significantly different vibration absorbing or generating characteristics which make one design correct and the other unsuitable, even with the same engine installed. In order to prevent excessive vibration to the rider and premature fatigue to structural members, the frame is chosen according to engine type and by the specific use of the bike.

The various frame designs can be classified into one of a few categories. Frames are chosen for a particular model according to the engine's displacement, the use the bike is designed for, ease of service, cost, and even visual appeal. The following is a description of the more popular designs.

Cradle Frame

There are two cradle frame designs: single cradle and double cradle. The ***single cradle*** frame has one down tube and one main pipe at the front of the engine, **Figure 16-2.** The frame structure material surrounds the engine. This frame is mainly used in off-road and light and mid-size on-road sport bikes due to its weight, strength, and ease of service.

The ***double cradle*** design is similar to the single cradle frame, but has two down tubes and main tubes, resulting in increased rigidity. A part of the down tube can be removed to facilitate engine removal on some models. This design derives its strength from the triangulation of support tubing. Almost anywhere you look on a cradle frame, triangles are formed at major stress areas. This principle is illustrated in **Figure 16-3.**

The double cradle frame is mainly used on large displacement, on-road motorcycles. On some large, high powered bikes, additional support may be provided by gussets, **Figure 16-4.** A cradle frame is relatively lightweight and extremely strong.

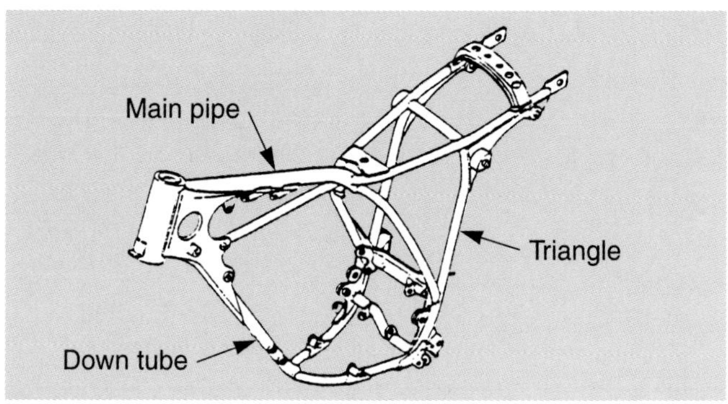

Figure 16-2. The single cradle frame. (Honda Motor Co., Ltd.)

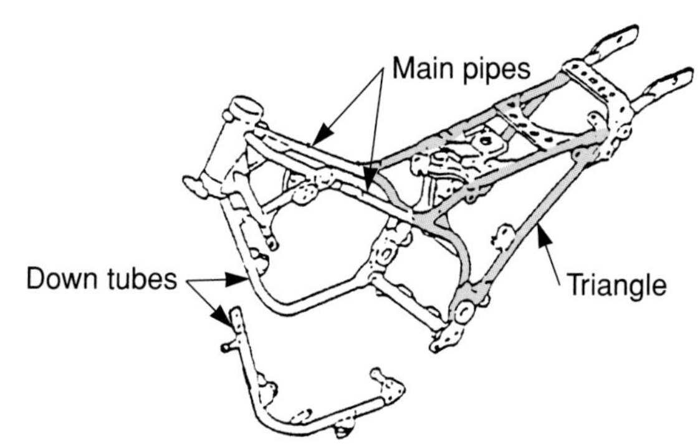

Figure 16-3. The double cradle frame. Note how triangles are often formed at junctions of cradle frame tubes. (Honda Motor Co., Ltd.)

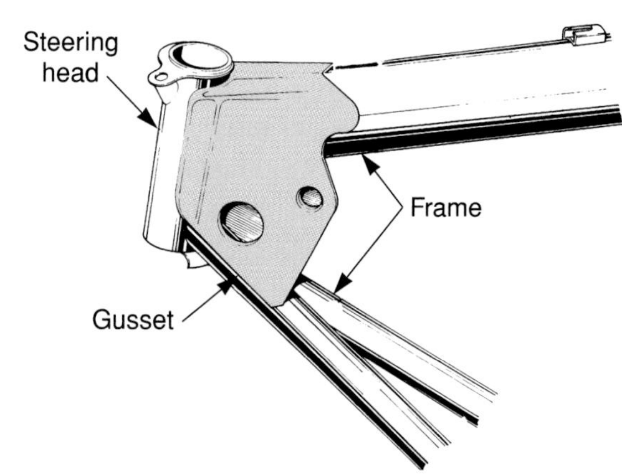

Figure 16-4. Gussets reinforce the area where the steering head is welded to the frame. (Triumph Motorcycles, Ltd.)

Backbone Frame

In the ***backbone frame,*** the engine hangs from the top of the frame and acts as a structural member. This type of construction allows added freedom in the overall vehicle design and relatively economical production. This design requires the frame to be relatively heavy to provide adequate strength, **Figure 16-5.** Since the engine is not enclosed by lower frame tubes, engine service may be simplified with a backbone frame design. This frame design is used mainly on scooters and some early motorcycle designs.

Diamond Frame

The ***diamond frame*** is used mainly on small- and medium-size bikes due to its simplicity, light weight, and excellent serviceability. The lower section of the down tube is not connected with other frame tubes, **Figure 16-6.** The engine forms the final portion of the frame structure. Mounting the engine gives this frame strength.

Delta-box Frame

The ***delta-box frame*** shown in **Figure 16-7** features a very strong steel or aluminum triangle between the steering head and the swingarm pivot. This design provides good responsive handling characteristics.

Pentagonal Frame

The ***pentagonal frame*** (five-sided frame) is made of cast and extruded aluminum and has good torsional rigidity, **Figure 16-8.** Sometimes called a *perimeter frame,* its rails extend from the steering head section to the swingarm pivot. The seat portion of the subframe is bolted on and can be easily removed for maintenance.

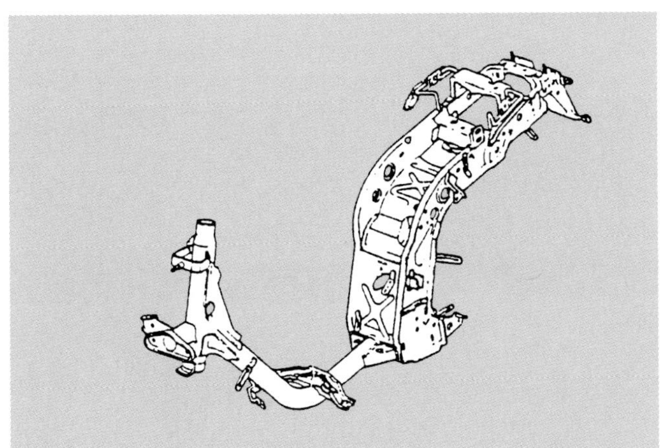

Figure 16-5. Backbone frame. (Honda Motor Co., Ltd.)

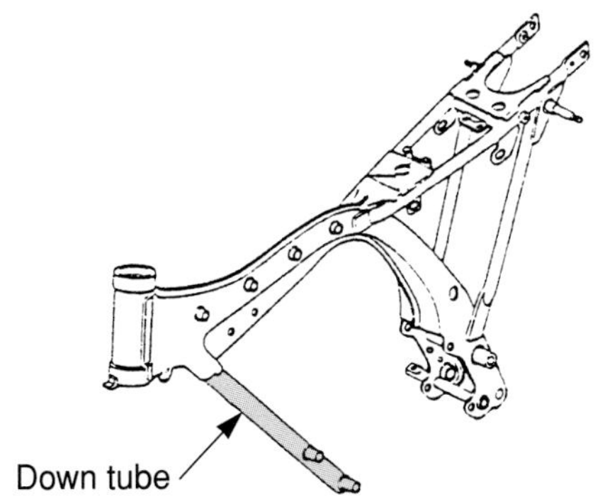

Figure 16-6. Diamond frame. (Honda Motor Co., Ltd.)

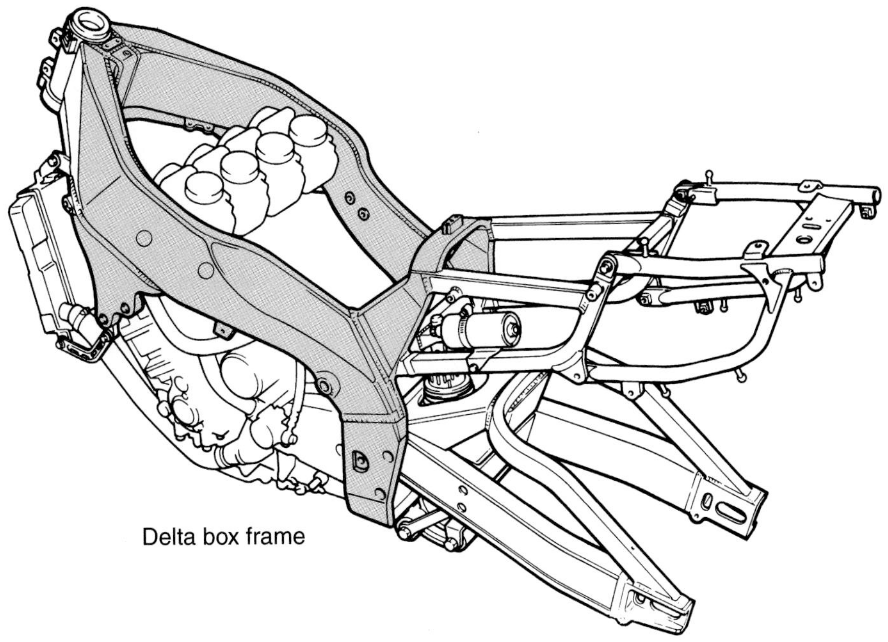

Figure 16-7. Typical delta-box frame. (Yamaha Motor Corporation U.S.A.)

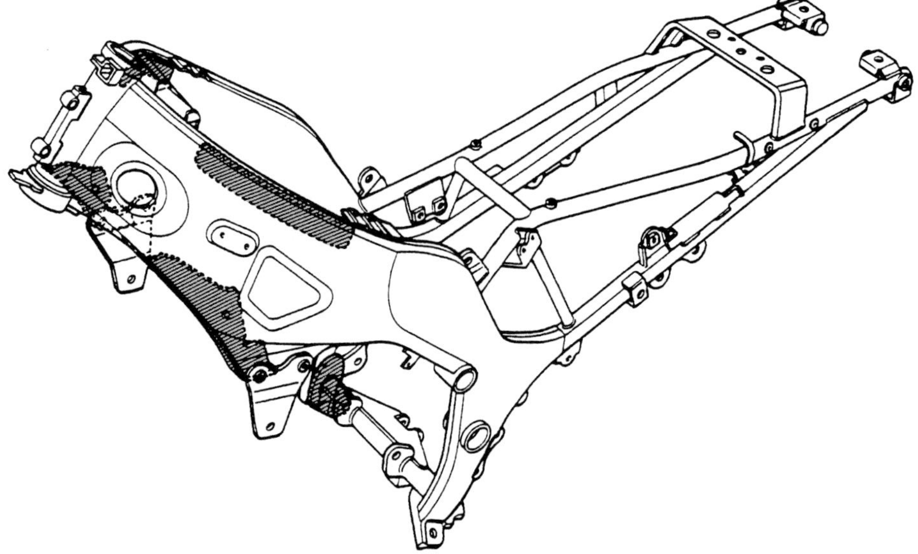

Figure 16-8. Typical pentagonal (five-sided) main frame. The shaded areas represent the location of gussets. (American Suzuki Motor Corporation)

Stamped Frame

A ***stamped frame*** usually consists of two pieces of stamped sheet metal welded together, **Figure 16-9.** Frame strength is achieved by the stamping's shape. A stamped frame is the least expensive to produce and is normally used on inexpensive, small displacement motorcycles.

There are other frame designs, but these are the most common. Motorcycle frame designs are also constantly being upgraded. It is not uncommon to find frames that use combinations of more than one design. Subframes are an important part of all chassis frame assemblies. The subframe can be removed to improve the service access on some models. This frame is used on sport, on-road, and motocross motorcycles.

The chassis of most ATVs are made of steel and ruggedly constructed, **Figure 16-10.** Their function, like that of motorcycle frames, is to provide support for all the vehicle's components. Scooter frames are simple in design, usually constructed of aluminum.

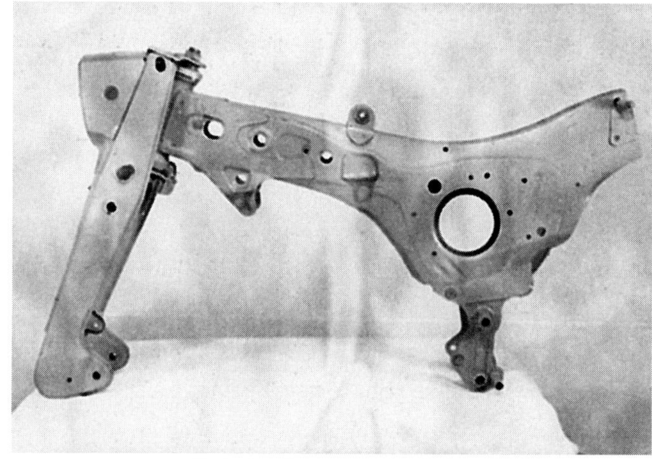

Figure 16-9. Stamped sheet metal pieces are welded together to fabricate a stamped frame.

Frame Inspection

Visually check the frame for damage or bent tubes and components. If paint cracks appear on the frame, inspect the area(s) more closely to find out if the frame itself is cracked. Apply a spray penetrant to closely inspect and verify any suspected cracks. Although it is possible to weld some cracked frames and straighten frames that are slightly bent, it is best to replace the frame with a new one when it is damaged. Plastic panels usually cannot be repaired and must be replaced.

Straighten the handlebar and check the alignment between the front and rear wheel(s). If the rear wheel does

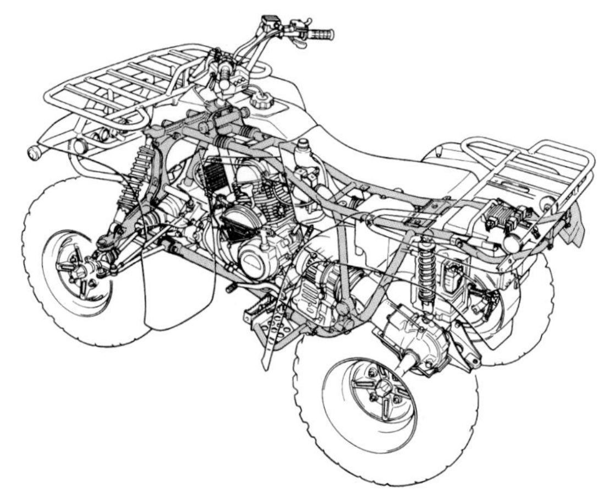

Figure 16-10. As can be seen in the cutaway view of this ATV, the frame's function is the same as a motorcycle frame. (Yamaha Motor Corporation U.S.A.)

not align with the front, ensure the drive chain adjusters are adjusted correctly. If the rear wheel leans to either side when viewed from above, **Figure 16-11,** check whether the right or left arm or rear shock absorber mounts (on dual shock models) are twisted or bent. Proper wheel alignment for ATVs is given later in this chapter.

Front Suspension

The purpose of the ***suspension system*** is to allow the wheels to follow an irregular road surface with a minimum amount of shock being transmitted to the frame. A few old motorcycles used spring-loaded swingarms mounted on stationary tubes (early front suspension). The arms would simply swing up and down to absorb bumps in the road surface. Today's motorcycle suspensions are a great deal more sophisticated. Three of the most common types are shown in **Figure 16-12.**

Telescopic Front Suspensions

Telescopic front suspensions are made up of a pair of upper fork tubes and lower fork sliders that telescope into one another. Within the set of tubes on either side is a spring and an oil damping system. Some systems utilize a cartridge damper within the fork sliders. The oil controls the spring's natural tendency to rebound in ever decreasing amounts in both directions. Forcing the oil in each fork leg through a series of small holes separates the rider and bike combination from spring oscillation.

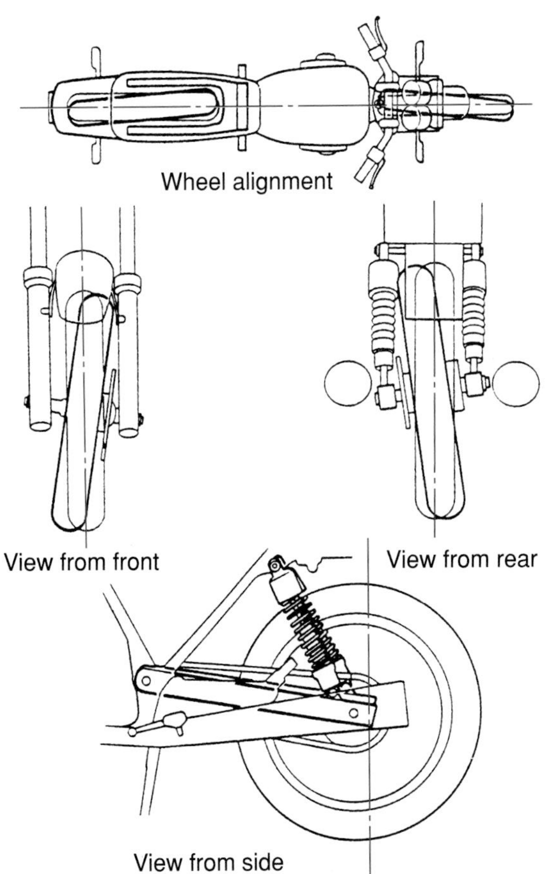

Figure 16-11. Common frame problems. (Honda Motor Co., Ltd.)

Telescoping Fork

A ***telescoping fork*** assembly consists of two fork tubes, two triple clamps, a spindle (shaft mounted on lower triple clamp), and related fasteners. These parts are shown in **Figure 16-13.** The fork tubes are shock absorbing devices that hold the front wheel in place. They are attached to the motorcycle by the triple clamps and spindle.

The ***triple clamps*** secure the fork tubes to the frame and hold them in alignment. The lower triple clamp is usually made as an integral part of the spindle. The ***spindle*** or steering stem on the lower triple clamp passes through the steering head (hole in the frame). This allows the fork to be turned to the right or left.

- ***Fork sliders*** (outer tubes) provide a mounting place for the front wheel axle. They slip over the bottom of the inner fork tubes. ***Damper rods*** (cylinders) are attached to the sliders and project into the fork tubes. This is shown in **Figure 16-14.**

Damper rods work in conjunction with the fork oil and damper valves and also prevent the sliders from falling off the fork tubes at full extension. Coil springs are located inside the fork tubes and provide spring pressure to support the motorcycle, **Figure 16-15.** To keep fork oil in and contaminants out, seals are located at the top of the fork sliders, as shown in **Figure 16-16.**

While all telescopic forks work on the same principle, there are many design variations. For example, internal or external springs may be used. The axle may be mounted at the bottom or on the front side of the slider. Damping may be controlled by damper rods or orifices in the fork tubes. To provide suspension system adjustment, adjustable dampers and air assisted springs are also common.

Telescoping Fork Operation

Fork operation is usually described in two phases:

- Compression stroke (inward or retracting movement of forks).
- Rebound stroke (outward or extending fork movement).

The ***compression stroke*** is the fork's movement into the slider when striking a bump in the road. Oil trapped below the fork tube and check valve is forced to flow through the check valve and compression damping hole, **Figure 16-17A.**

The amount of damping is determined by the size of the compression damping holes and the clearance between the check valve and check valve body. Compression damping is relatively light since the fork spring provides most of the resistance to compression.

As the fork tube nears full compression, the fork tube collar blocks off the compression damping holes. This

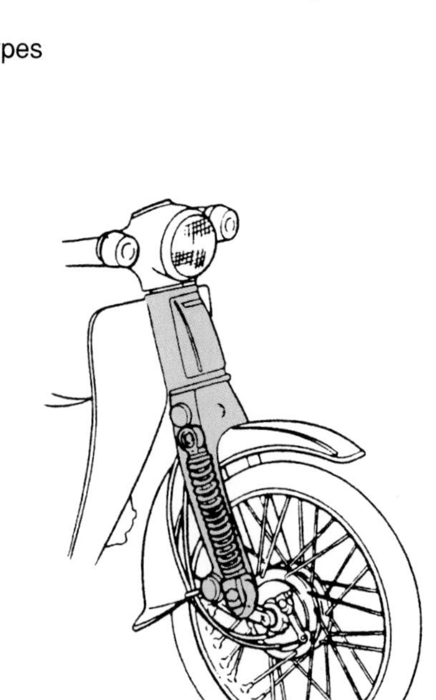
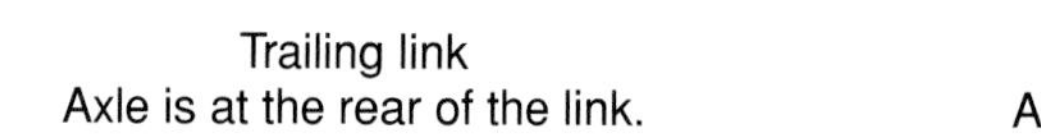
Telescopic
Bottom link types
Trailing link
Axle is at the rear of the link.
Leading link
Axle is on the front of the link.

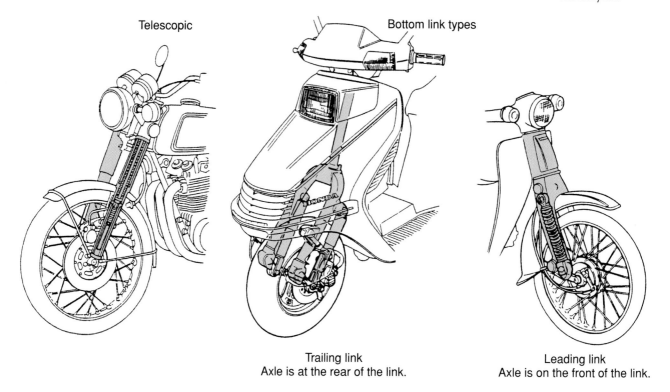

Figure 16-12. Three of the most common front suspension systems, telescopic, trailing link, and leading link. (Honda Motor Co., Ltd.)

causes a partial hydraulic lock that prevents mechanical bottoming (metal-to-metal contact), **Figure 16-17B.**

During the fork's ***rebound stroke,*** the fork spring causes the slider to extend. The spring pushes against the top of the damper rod. Oil above the damper rod piston flows freely through the damper rod into the bottom of the slider, **Figure 16-17C.** Oil trapped between the damper rod piston and check valve is metered through the rebound damping holes before it can flow back into the slider. This restriction provides the necessary rebound damping.

As the fork nears full rebound, the lower rebound damping hole is blocked off. This causes firmer damping. When the remaining damping hole is blocked off, a hydraulic lock is formed. A top-out spring provides final cushioning, **Figure 16-17D.**

There are many variations in fork design. The size and location of damper holes determines fork action. Suspension adjustment is accomplished by changing spring rates, oil viscosity, adjustable damping valves, or air pressure. Typical front fork adjustment points are shown in **Figure 16-18.**

A test ride will indicate how the front suspension reacts on various types of road surfaces. According to the symptom noticed, adjust the front fork to obtain the best setting for the rider and average road conditions traveled, following the instructions in the service manual or in **Figure 16-19.**

Anti-dive Fork

Figure 16-20 shows an ***anti-dive fork*** design that uses brake fluid pressure to help prevent front end dive during braking. When the rider applies the brakes, the master cylinder forces brake fluid into the inlet on the front fork. Pressure acts on a small plunger, which slides in its cylinder and pushes on an oil flow control valve. The flow control valve then moves to restrict oil flow. This stiffens compression damping and reduces front end dive.

Pivoting Link Front Suspension

A ***pivoting link front suspension*** connects the axle to the fork by means of a pivoting link extending from the axle ends to the upper portion of the fork. Between the pivot points on the fork and the axle are eyelets to which the spring/damper units are attached. The top of each shock absorber is attached to the fork, near the lower steering head bearing. This design is divided into two categories. The trailing link design has the axle supported by links and shock absorbers that trail from the leading edge of the lower fork. Leading link front suspension has the links pivoting toward the front and the shock absorbers mounted to the fork's leading edge.

Oil Damper

One of the major components of the pivoting link front suspension is the ***oil damper.*** Its primary function is to control the spring's natural rebound energy so that traction and ride comfort is maintained. An oil damper controls the spring action by forcing oil to flow through a specific set of holes in the damper piston as the combined spring/damper compresses and extends. The resistance to

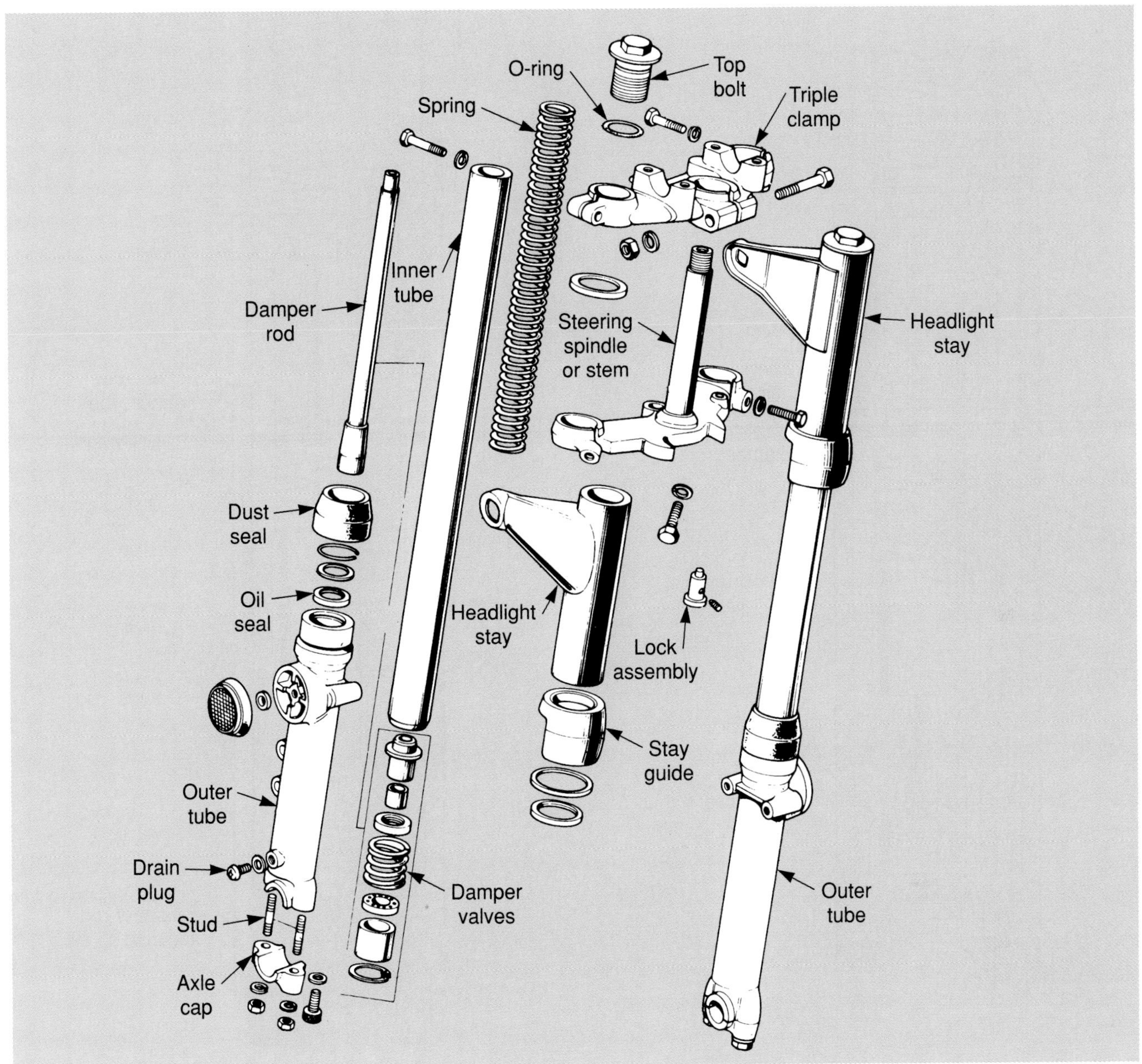

Figure 16-13. Exploded view showing typical major front fork components. (Kawasaki Motors Corporation U.S.A.)

damper piston movement created by the oil within the damper controls the spring force. By varying the path the oil is forced to take on the compression and rebound strokes, the desired damping rates can be achieved.

On the compression stroke, **Figure 16-21A,** oil is forced through several large capacity damping orifices so the wheel can respond quickly to terrain changes. Since the wheel is free to move quickly, the ride height is not disturbed.

On the rebound stroke, **Figure 16-21B,** the spring force is slowed by forcing the damper oil through fewer and/or smaller damping holes. The proper damping characteristics allow the suspension to extend quickly enough to meet the next bump, but not so quickly that the motorcycle bounces from one bump to the next.

In **Figure 16-22,** the compression stroke within a double wall damper is shown. As the damper body is forced up against the spring and damper piston, oil is forced through the piston valve with little resistance. The primary resistance to this compression is the damper spring. The oil that passes through flows to the upper side of the piston. At the same time, some oil is allowed to flow out of the bottom valve. The quantity of oil that flows out of the cylinder bottom valve is equivalent to the amount drawn into the top. The combined resistance to flow through each of these valves is the compression damping. The resistance, resulting from the passage of oil through the orifice, reduces the compression force.

The rebound stroke is illustrated in **Figure 16-23.** Once the wheel has overcome the bump, the spring

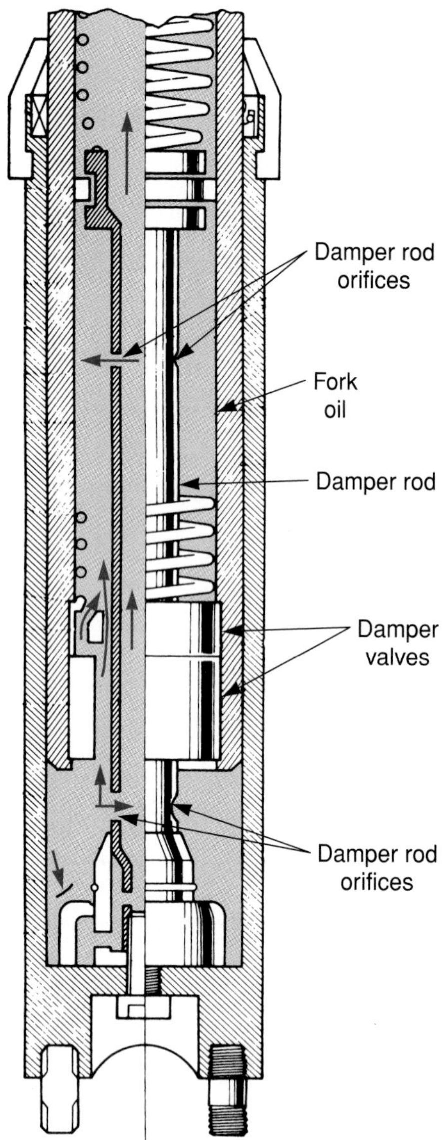

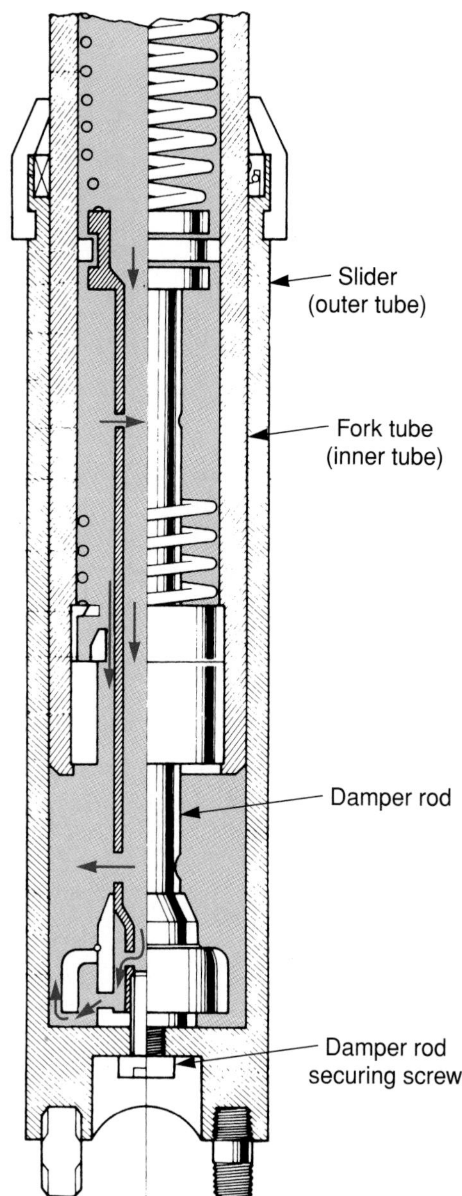

Figure 16-14. Fork action is controlled by metering the oil flow through valves and orifices in the damper rod. The damper rod is attached to a slider and protrudes into the fork tubes. (Kawasaki Motors Corporation U.S.A.)

forces the damper rod to force the piston back through the damper. Oil flows with little resistance into the cylinder, but there is considerable resistance caused by the damping valve in the piston. The resulting resistance creates a damping force on the rebound stroke. The other important component in the pivoting link front suspension, the shock absorber, is discussed later in this chapter.

Single-sided Swingarm Front Suspension System

The ***single-sided swingarm front suspension system*** is relatively new to motorcycles. The construction is somewhat different than the conventional telescopic fork suspension. It is used with a ***"omega frame."***

The omega frame is a lightweight, highly rigid structure which has the pivot points for the lower and upper portions of the front swingarm. The strong knuckle arm, which supports the front axle, brake caliper, and front wheel, pivots on these upper and lower arms, **Figure 16-24.** The design gives good rigidity to the front steering and suspension structure.

The arrangement of the lower and upper arms minimizes nose-dive during braking so the bike maintains an even ride. Because steering and suspension components are not dependent upon one another, the ride is considered to be smoother without jolts from bumps and rough roads being transmitted directly to the handlebars. As an additional benefit, this arrangement permits a greater degree of flexibility, allowing the engine and radiator to be located further forward. **Figure 16-25** illustrates the functions of

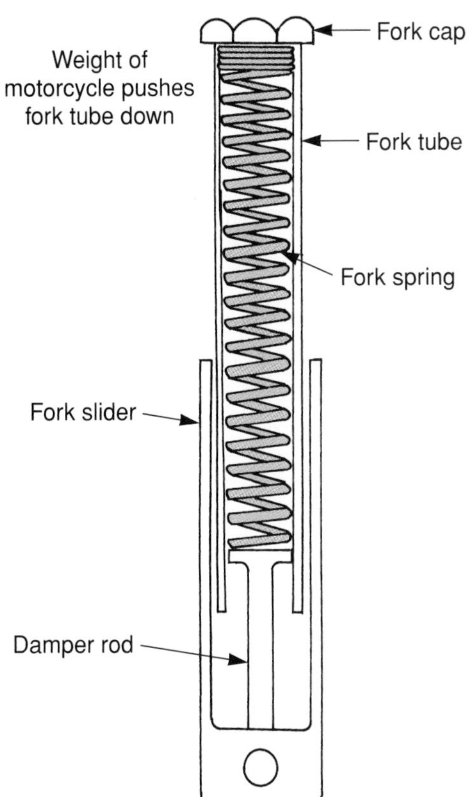

Figure 16-15. A coil spring, which rests on the damper rod, exerts pressure on the fork cap to support the motorcycle.

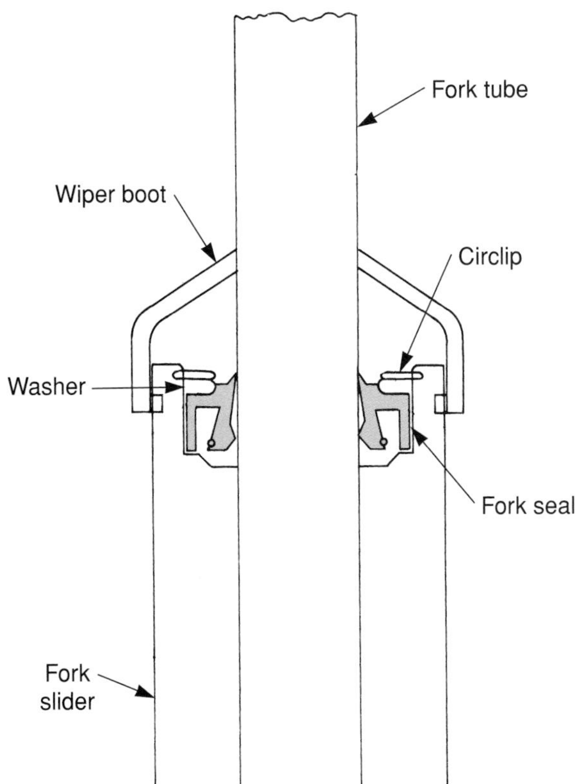

Figure 16-16. A fork seal mounted at the top of the slider wipes the fork tube, keeping oil in the forks and preventing contaminants from entering the forks.

the various components of a single-sided swingarm front suspension system.

Steering Geometry

Steering geometry refers to the angles formed by the various steering related components on a motorcycle. Factors which determine steering geometry are rake, trail, and offset. The steering geometry principles used in ATVs will be discussed later in this chapter.

Rake

Rake is the angle of the forks from true vertical, **Figure 16-26.** Rake angle may vary depending on the motorcycle's intended use. More rake (larger angle between fork centerline and vertical) results in slowed steering response and greater high speed stability. Less rake (smaller angle between forks and vertical) quickens the steering, but increases the chance of high speed wobble.

Trail

Trail is the distance along the ground between a line down the centerline of the forks and a vertical line through the axle centerline. Trail gives the steering a self-centering effect. As trail is increased, the self-centering effect improves stability. Rake and trail are interrelated. As rake is increased, trail also increases.

As the bike moves, rake and trail change. This is shown in **Figure 16-27.** Today's off-road, long travel suspensions exhibit extreme rake and trail changes during the length of suspension movement.

Offset

Offset provides the proper steering arc. Offset may be achieved by either offsetting the fork tubes (triple clamps) or the axle, **Figure 16-28.** All these factors (rake, trail, offset) work together to give a certain feel and steering response. Other factors such as weight, center of gravity, and intended use determine the steering geometry for a given motorcycle.

Steering Damper

A ***steering damper*** is a device which helps to eliminate unwanted steering oscillation (front wheel side movement). The two types of steering system dampers are:

- Hydraulic (oil filled cylinder places drag on steering).
- Friction (adjustable spring-loaded disc places drag on steering).

Friction steering dampers have been replaced by the more modern hydraulic dampers. See **Figure 16-29.** The cylinder usually connects between the frame and lower fork clamp.

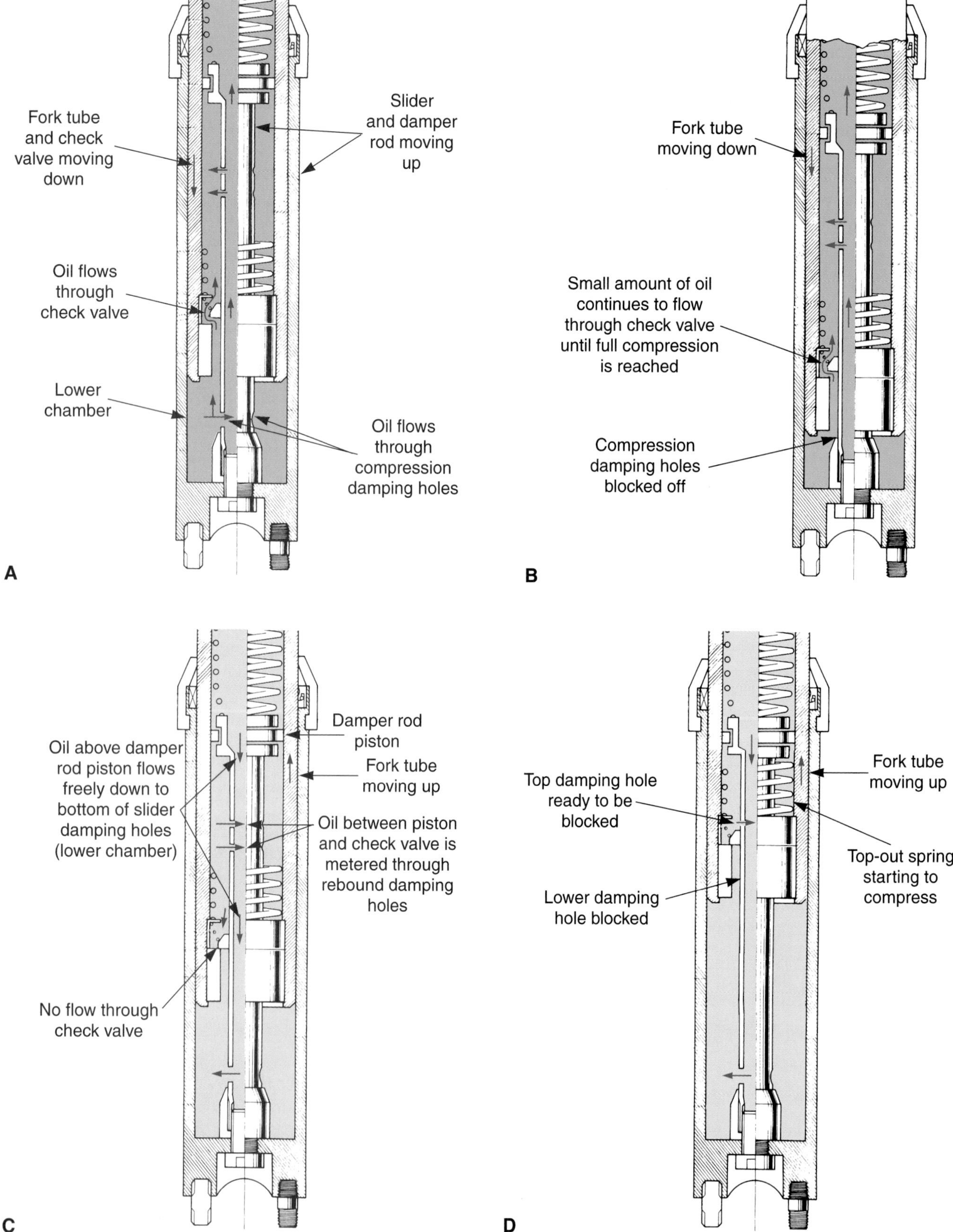

Figure 16-17. A—During fork compression, oil trapped in the lower chamber flows through compression damping holes and a check valve. B—Hard fork bottoming is prevented by blocking off the damping holes before full compression is reached. C—Fork rebound damping is controlled by rebound damping holes. D—Cushioning at end of rebound stroke is controlled by blocking off rebound damping holes and by use of a top-out spring. (Kawasaki Motors Corporation U.S.A.)

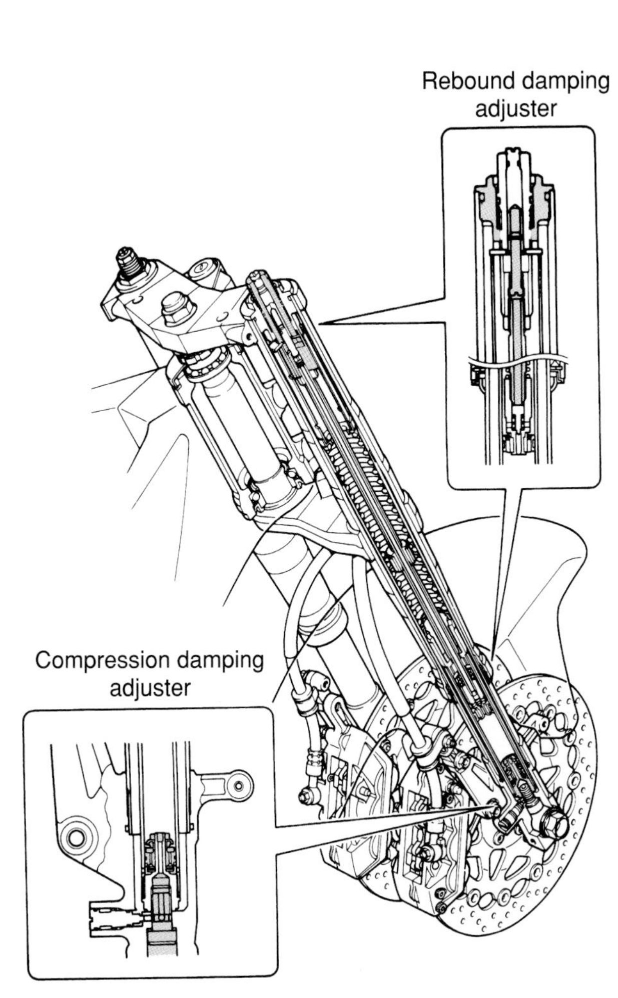

Figure 16-18. Fork adjustments are shown in cutaway. (Yamaha Motor Corporation U.S.A.)

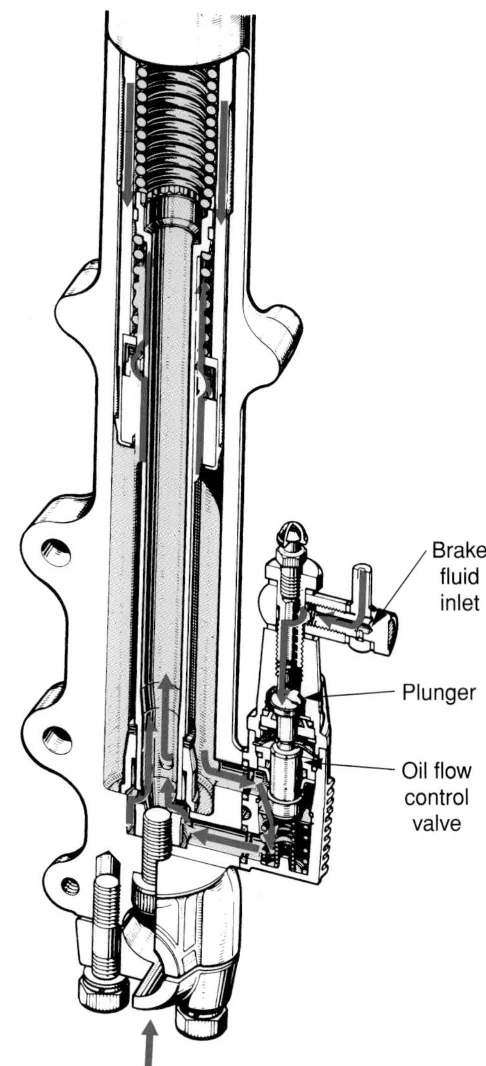

Figure 16-20. This anti-dive fork uses brake system pressure to actuate the flow control valve. The flow control valve limits oil flow in the fork during braking to help avoid nose dive. (American Suzuki Motor Corporation)

Symptom	Adjustment Procedure
Feels too hard overall	Adjust the compression and rebound damping to a softer setting. Decrease fork oil capacity.
Feels too soft overall and bottoms	Adjust the compression damping to a stiffer setting. Increase fork oil capacity.
Feels too hard near end of travel	Decrease fork oil capacity.
Feels too soft near end of travel and bottoms harshly	Adjust the compression damping to a stiffer setting. Increase fork oil capacity.
Feels too hard in beginning of stroke	Adjust the compression damping to a softer setting.
Feels too soft and unstable	Adjust the rebound damping to a stiffer setting.
Bounces	Adjust the rebound damping to a softer setting.

Figure 16-19. Steering and ride symptom chart.

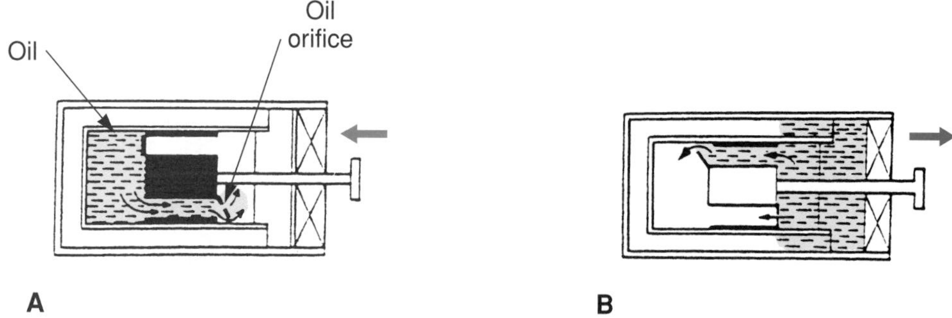

Figure 16-21. Operation of oil damper in a link suspension system. A—Compression stroke. B—Rebound stroke. (Honda Motor Co., Ltd.)

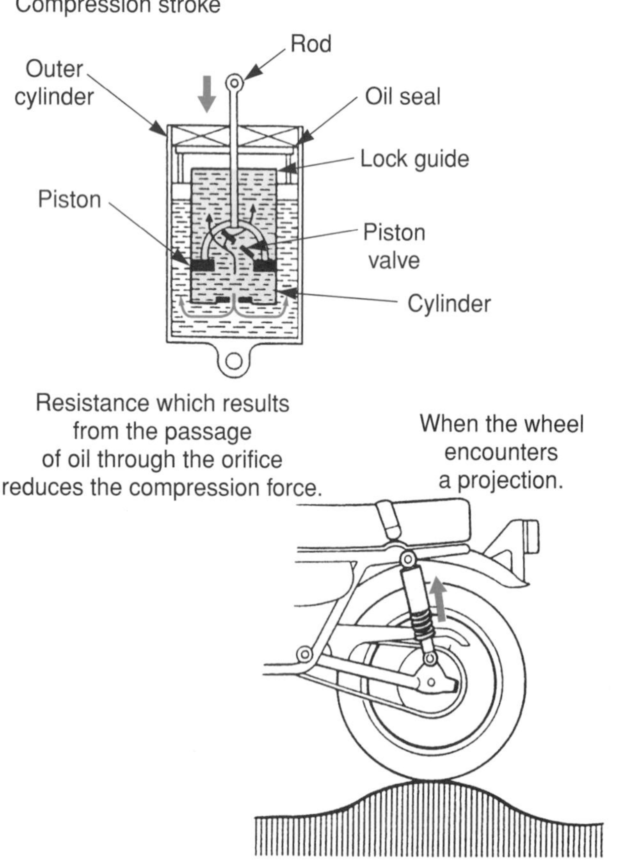

Figure 16-22. Action of oil damper during the compression stroke. (Honda Motor Co., Ltd.)

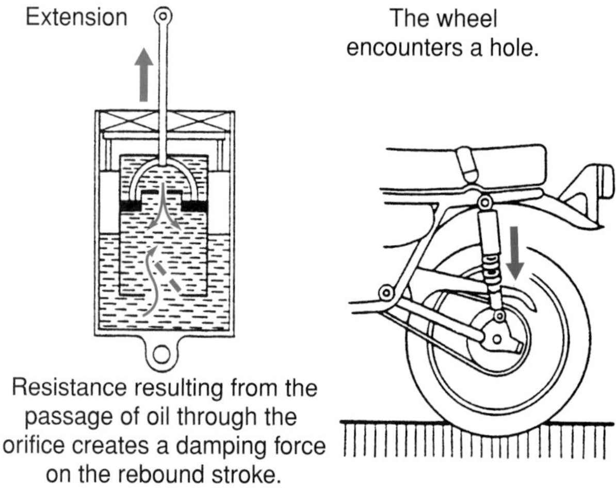

Figure 16-23. Extension action of link system's oil damper. (Honda Motor Co., Ltd.)

Servicing Front Suspension Components

Typical front suspension service consists of changing fork oil, lubricating and adjusting steering head bearings, and rebuilding the forks.

Changing Fork Oil

Fork oil must be changed because the oil can break down. Also, the oil can become contaminated with dirt, metal particles, and moisture. The frequency of fork oil changing is determined by riding conditions and manufacturer recommendations. A motorcycle which is ridden in dirt, sand, rain, or mud requires more frequent fork oil changes than one that is not exposed to these elements. Even under the most ideal conditions, the fork oil should be changed at least once a year.

To change fork oil, pump out or drain the old oil, **Figure 16-30A.** Then, refill the fork with the proper weight and quantity of fresh oil, **Figure 16-30B.** Follow the service manual for specific instructions, specifications, and oil change intervals.

Lubrication and Adjustments of Steering Head Bearings

Lubrication and adjustment of steering head bearings should be done periodically. Two types of steering head bearings are used: ball bearings and tapered roller bearings.

Ball bearings are the most common type of steering head bearings since they are inexpensive. ***Tapered roller bearings*** have the advantage of extremely long service life and ease of assembly and disassembly. Repacking (lubrication) of steering head bearings requires disassembly of the triple clamps and spindle as follows:

1. Completely disassemble the triple clamps to properly pack the steering head bearings with grease, **Figure 16-31A.** After cleaning and inspecting the bearings and races, repack them with the recommended grease.

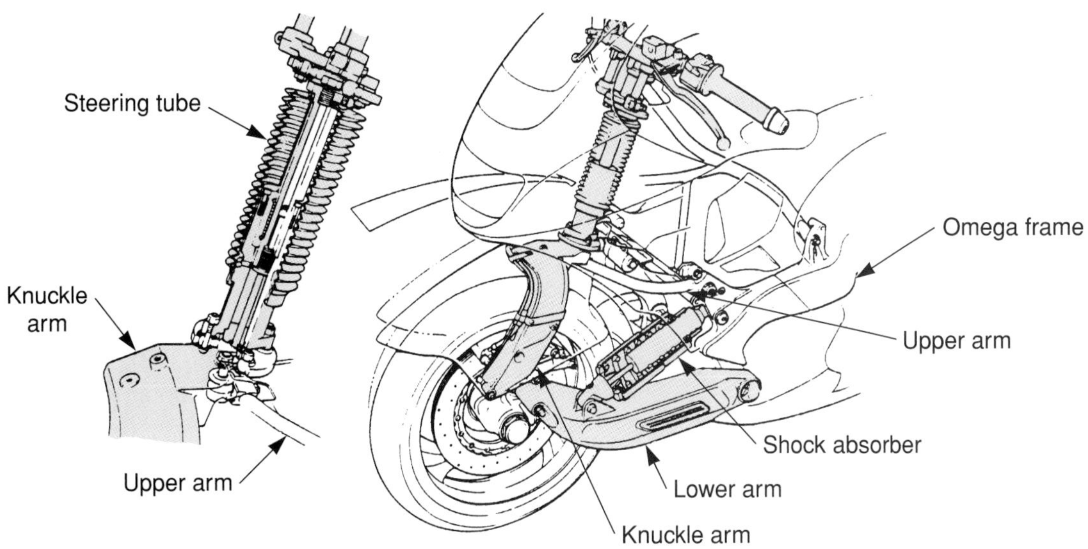

Figure 16-24. A single-sided swingarm front suspension system installed in an omega frame. (Yamaha Motor Corporation U.S.A.)

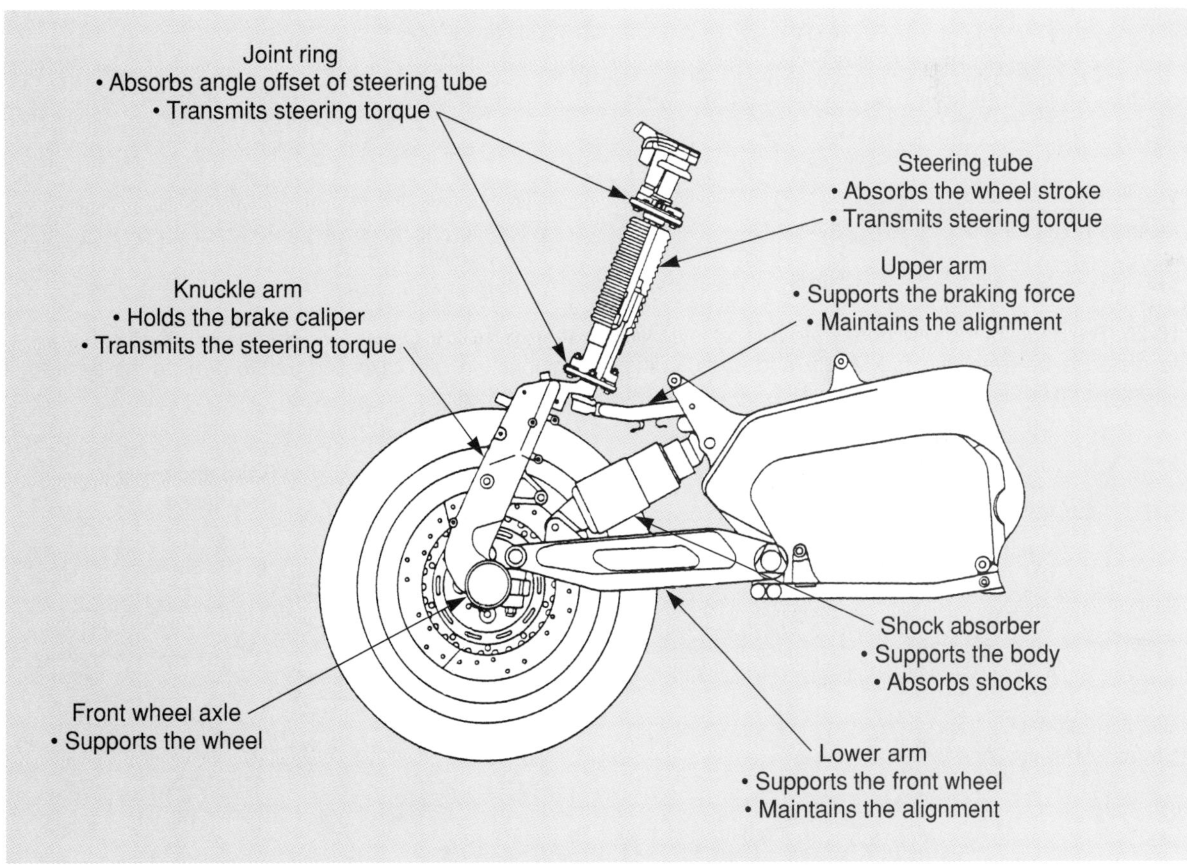

Figure 16-25. Components and their functions in a single-sided swingarm suspension.

2. The steering head preload is adjusted by tightening the slotted steering stem nut while following the service manual specifications, **Figure 16-31B.**

3. The steering head bearing final adjustment is done with the front suspension completely assembled. Double-check the steering action after adjustment, **Figure 16-31C.**

Bearing preload adjustment is a simple task which does not require steering head assembly. The adjustment must not be too tight or too loose. Improper steering head bearing adjustment would make the motorcycle dangerous to ride. Refer to the shop manual for specific instructions on steering head bearing disassembly, lubrication, reassembly, and adjustment. The handlebars should be adjusted to the rider's preference, as directed in the service maual.

Rebuilding Forks

The most frequent reason for fork disassembly is leaking seals. Seal replacement only requires partial fork disassembly. However, if fork seals are leaking, other parts may be damaged. A complete fork rebuild is usually recommended during seal replacement. A fork rebuild involves complete fork disassembly and the inspection of all parts for wear, scratches, or other problems.

During a fork rebuild, follow the instructions in the service manual. It will describe important disassembly, inspection, and reassembly methods for the particular motorcycle. When servicing a motorcycle fork, remember the following:

- Check slider and fork tube bearing surfaces for wear.
- Check all components for galling, nicks, and straightness.
- Replace all sealing rings and washers.
- Replace all snap rings (circlips).
- Use proper torque values on all fasteners.

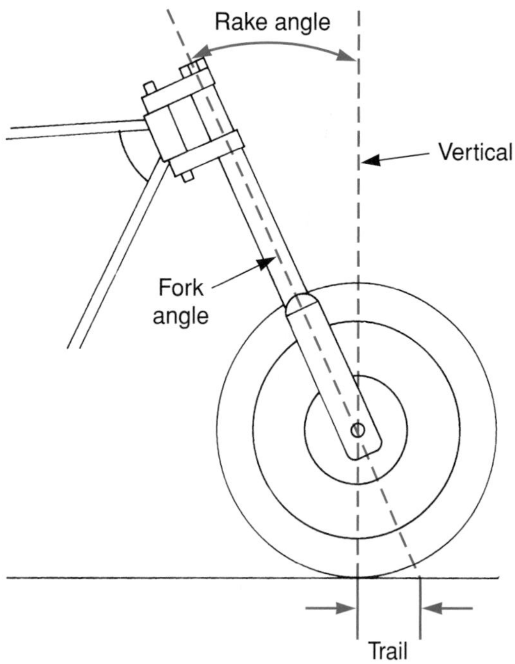

Figure 16-26. The angle of the fork tubes from vertical is called rake. The distance between the fork angle and vertical line (through center of axle) is called trail.

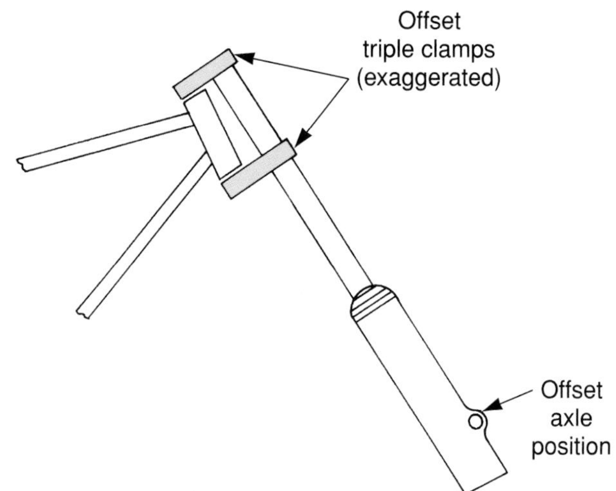

Figure 16-28. Offset fork clamps or offset axles are used in conjunction with rake and trail to provide the desired steering characteristics.

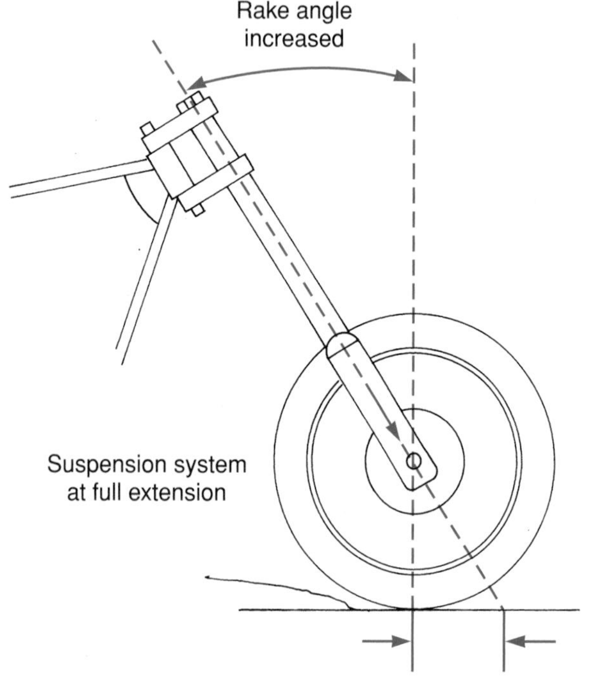

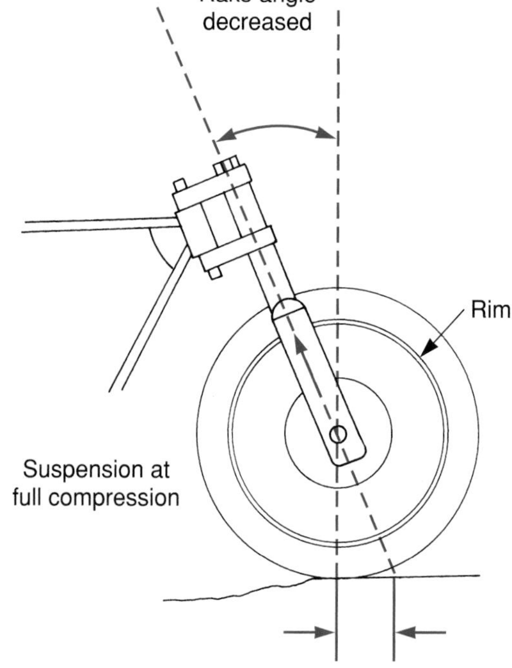

Figure 16-27. The trail changes as the bike moves down the road. A—Trail increases with fork extension. B—Trail decreases with fork compression.

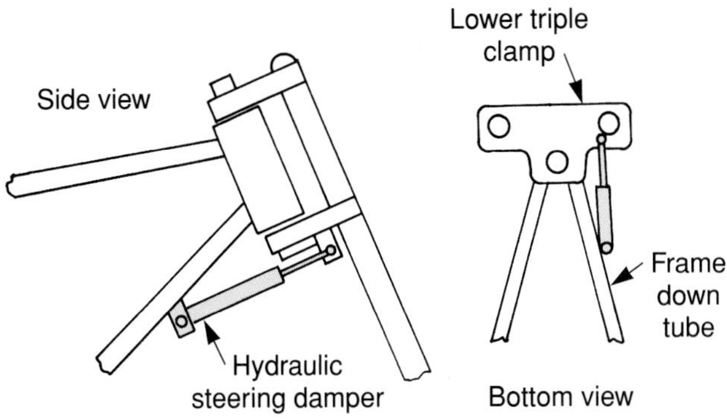

Figure 16-29. A hydraulic steering damper is attached between the frame and lower triple clamp to help control steering oscillations.

Warning: Use extreme care when servicing front end components. Faulty service or repair methods can result in suspension failure and rider injury or death. Always refer to the vehicle's service manual when working on the front end.

Rear Suspension Systems

A typical motorcycle ***rear suspension*** consists of a swingarm and one or more shock absorbers. Using the front of the swingarm as the fulcrum, and mounting the rear axle at the trailing end allows the wheel to respond quickly to variations in the road or trail surface. On some scooters, the entire engine and drive unit pivots as the swingarm.

Swingarm rear suspension design can be broken down into a few categories, depending on the number of shocks used and the swingarm design. For example, a ***single shock swingarm*** rear suspension only uses one shock absorber mounted in front of the rear wheel, **Figure 16-32A.** The single shock rear suspension system uses an adjustable shock absorber, levers, and links to provide rising rate operation. This type of rear suspension is popular with dirt bike riders.

A ***dual spring/shock absorber*** rear suspension has a shock absorber on each side of the frame, **Figure 16-32B.** With both types, the shock connects the swingarm and the frame to provide the necessary spring and damping action for the rear wheel.

Dual spring/shock suspensions are found primarily on small and medium displacement motorcycles because of the simplicity of installation, the small number of components necessary, and price. Until the early 1980s, dual spring suspensions were also used on large displacement motorcycles.

Larger displacement motorcycles often utilize a ***progressive link rear suspension,*** **Figure 16-32C.** The progressive rising rate delivers ideal damping over a

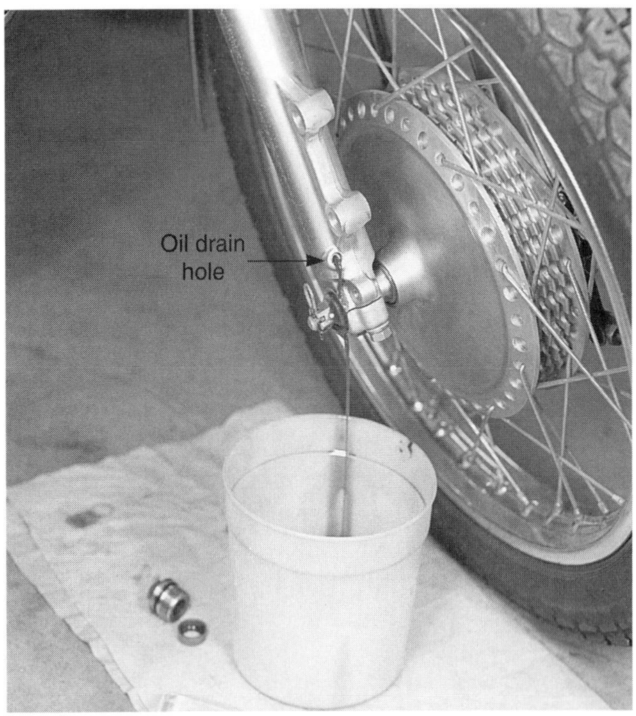

A

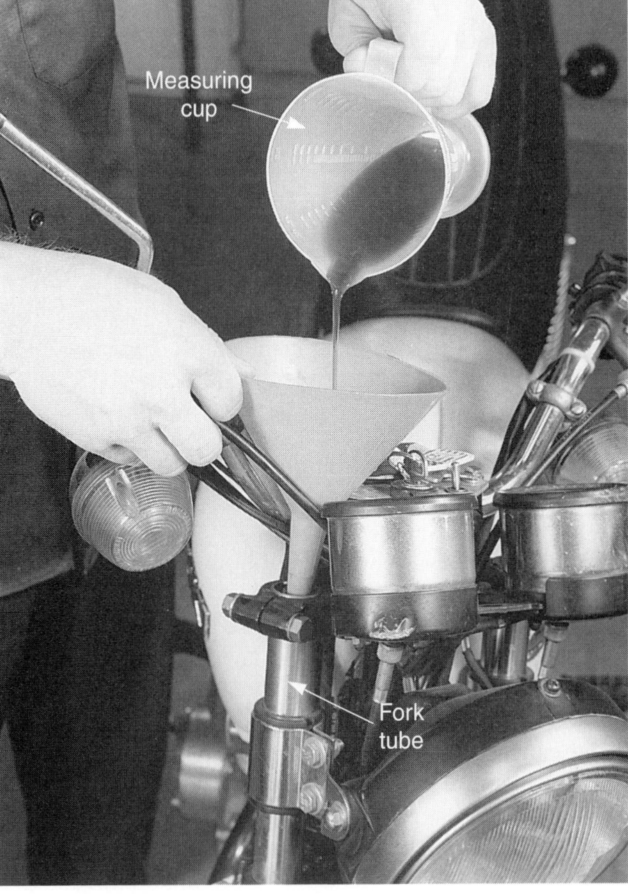

B

Figure 16-30. A—To drain fork oil, remove the drain screw and top nut. B—Use a graduated cylinder or measuring cup to accurately measure fork oil. Do not forget to replace the drain plugs before refilling the forks. Refer to the service manual for the proper weight and quantity of oil.

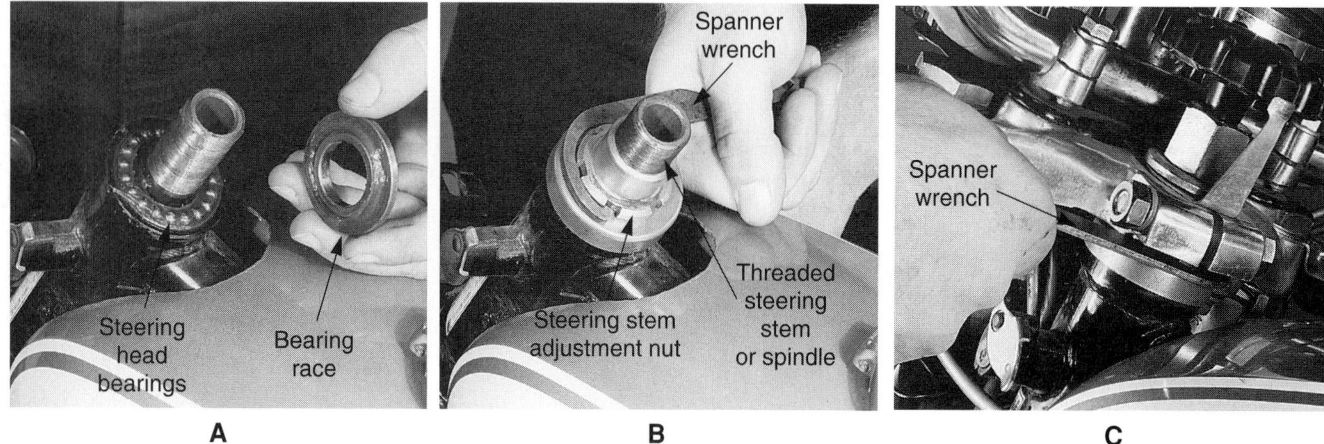

Figure 16-31. Steering head bearing service. A—Pack the bearings with grease. B—Adjust the steering head preload. C—Performing bearing final adjustment. Be sure to check the steering after the adjustment is complete.

Figure 16-32. Three types of common swingarm rear suspension systems: A—Single motocross shock. B—Dual shocks. C—Progressive link. (Yamaha Motor Corporation U.S.A.)

wide range of riding conditions. Initial rates are soft for handling small bumps and ripples. Should the riding surface become rougher, increasingly stiffer rates provide the control necessary to prevent bottoming and to keep the rear wheel in contact with the road.

The swingarm and shock unit of progressive link rear suspensions are connected to the swingarm by a link. The damper unit travel in relation to the rear wheel movement can be changed with relative freedom during the design stage in accordance with the combination of the cushion arm and connecting rod. As the axle stroke distance increases, the piston speed damper and shock absorbing force increase progressively. Therefore, this type of suspension is characteristically soft on initial travel so it absorbs small riding surface inconsistencies well, and provides progressively firmer resistance to prevent bottoming at full compression when a large bump is hit.

Some motorcycle styles have specially designed rear suspension systems. Long travel rear systems, for example, provide a softer arm travel (suspension travel). This is ideal for competition and off-road motorcycles since it helps the wheel stay in contact with the ground, **Figure 16-33.** On shaft drive bikes, one leg of the swingarm houses the drive shaft.

Swingarm Mounting

As previously mentioned, the swingarm is attached to the frame with a pivot bolt, shaft, or link, **Figure 16-34.** The arm itself may be made of steel or aluminum, either stamped or fabricated from tubing. Bushings, needle bearings, or tapered roller bearings are used to provide smooth operation and accurate alignment. Some designs require periodic adjustment and lubrication. Refer to the specific service manual for details.

Suspension Balance

Balancing the suspension properly from front to rear is the most critical adjustment for a good ride and performance. If the front forks are adjusted harder than the

A

B

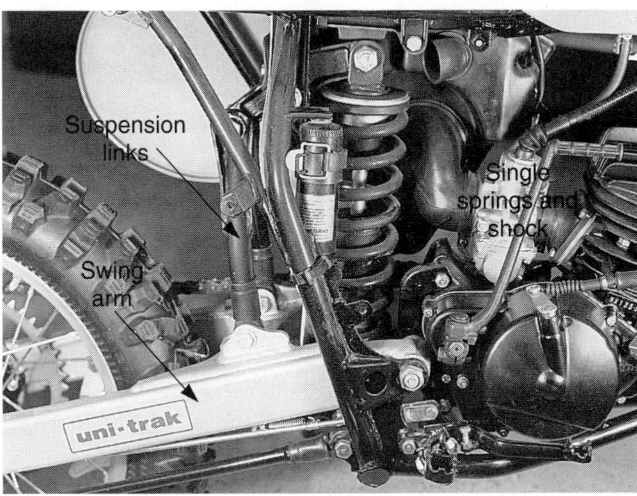

C

Figure 16-33. Typical long travel rear suspension systems. (American Suzuki Motor Corporation)

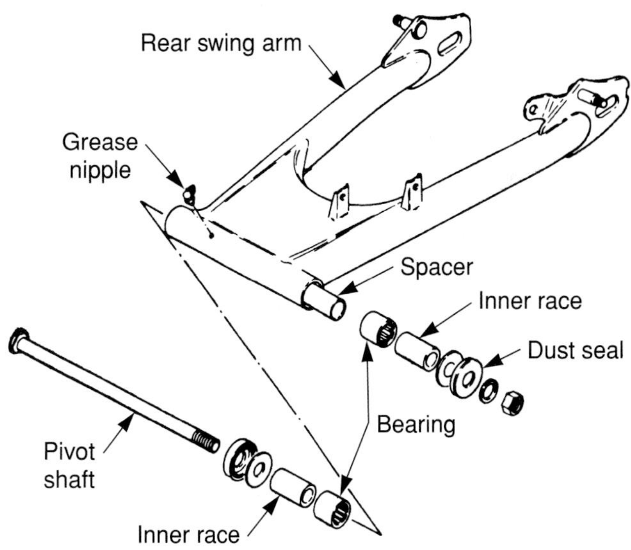

Figure 16-34. This swingarm uses needle bearings for positive location and smooth operation of the rear suspension. (American Suzuki Motor Corporation)

suspension by changing to heavier front fork oil, or using a stiffer compression and rebound setting, air pressure will build up and the front forks will collapse less on bumps. This transfers motorcycle and rider weight to the bottom of the fork.

To check the balance, stand next to the motorcycle on level ground. Place one foot on the closest footrest, then sharply push down. The front and rear suspension should both collapse equally. Here are some tips to keep in mind:

- Check for air pressure build-up in the front forks. Heat and altitude will increase air pressure in the front forks.
- Always stay within sag measurement limits when using spring preset to stiffen or soften the rear suspension. If this is not possible, the next stiffer or softer spring is needed.
- The rear shock compression damping can be used to fine tune suspension balance and is easy to access.

Shock Absorbers

Shock absorbers work much like a front suspension telescopic fork. There are several different types of shock absorbers available for the various riding conditions encountered by motorcycles, scooters, and ATVs, **Figure 16-35.** For example, some have external damping adjustments. However, the most conventional type is the unpressurized, oil-damped shock, shown in **Figure 16-36.**

For severe applications (competition and off-road motorcycles), conventional shock absorbers can overheat and not provide adequate damping. This is due in part to the small quantity of oil in the shock that provides damping. Large capacity, gas-oil shocks have been designed to meet this need, and are standard on most competition and off-road bikes, **Figure 16-37.**

Frame mount
Rear coil spring
Shock absorber
Swing arm mount
Vulcan
4x4

A B

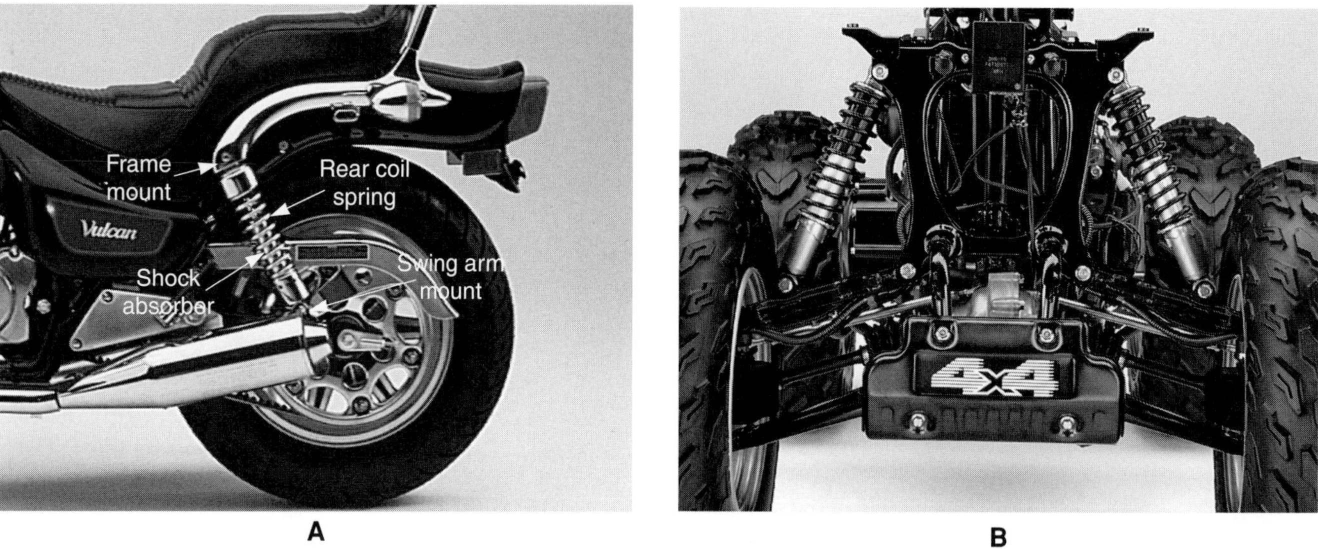

Figure 16-35. Conventional application of shock absorbers. A—Road bike. B—ATV rear suspension. (Yamaha Motor Corporation U.S.A.)

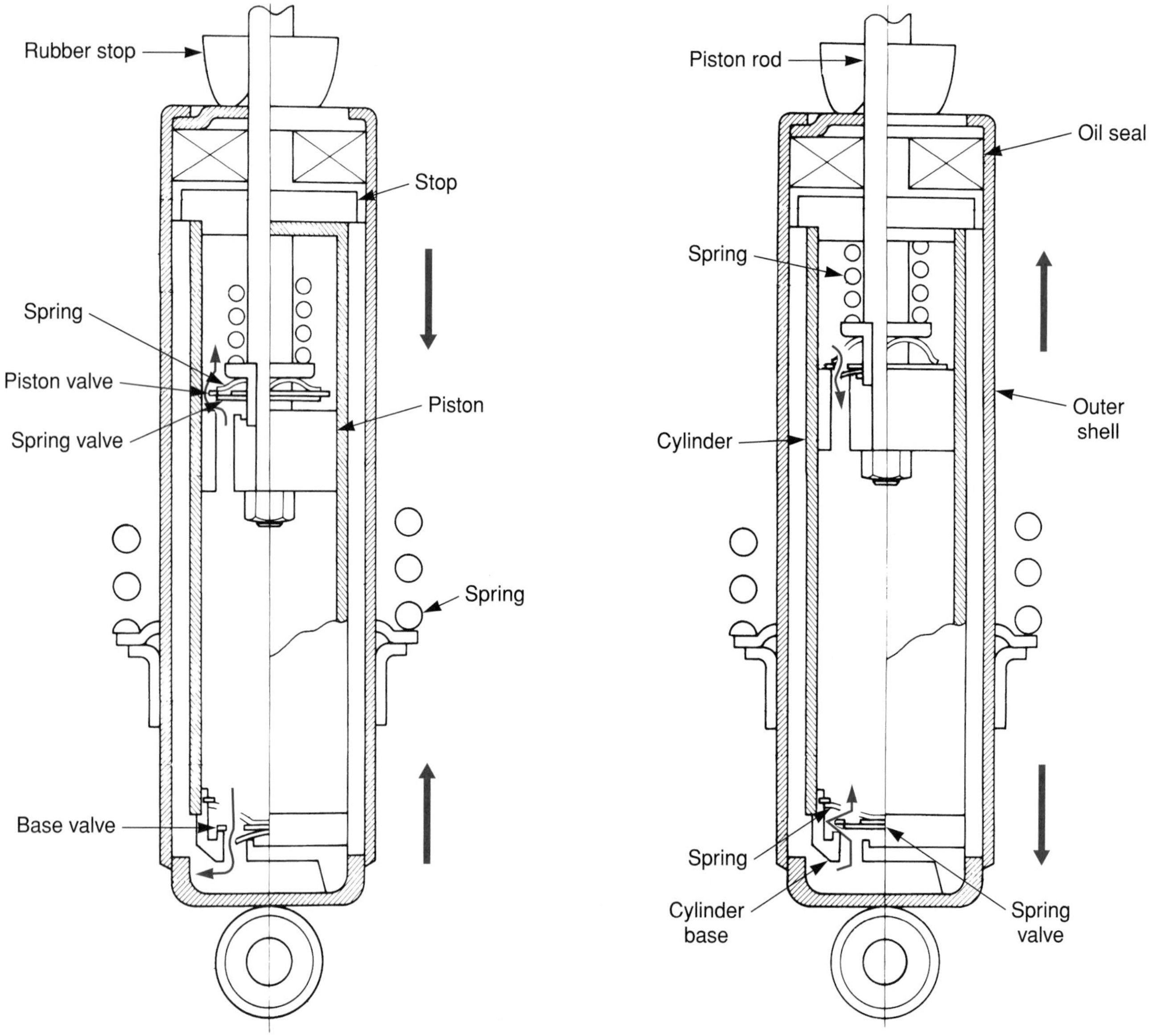

Rubber stop
Stop
Spring
Piston valve
Spring valve
Piston
Spring
Base valve
Piston rod
Oil seal
Spring
Cylinder
Outer shell
Spring
Cylinder base
Spring valve

Figure 16-36. A typical oil-damped rear shock absorber. (Kawasaki Motors Corporation U.S.A.)

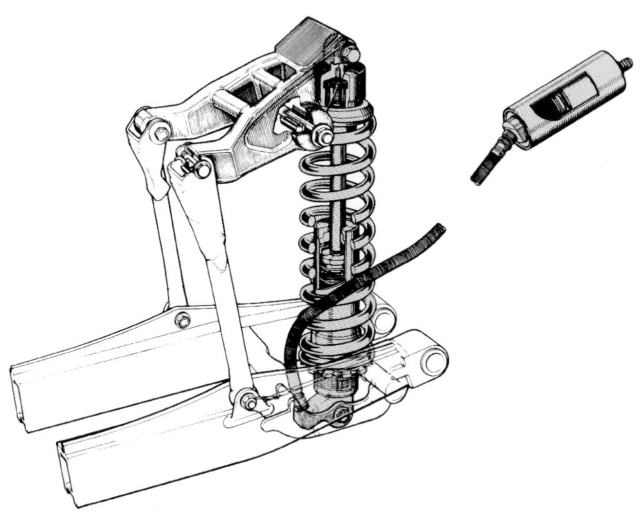

Figure 16-37. This single shock rear suspension uses an adjustable rear shock system. It has a remote reservoir for additional oil. (American Suzuki Motor Corporation)

Figure 16-38. Spring collars or clips are used to retain shock springs.

Shock Absorber Springs

Shock absorber springs are mounted over the damper (shock) body. They are fastened to the shock absorber by collars or clips. This is illustrated in **Figure 16-38.** Three spring types are used:

- One-piece constant rate spring.
- One-piece dual rate or progressive spring.
- Two-piece dual rate springs.

Additional springing may also be provided by internal pressure in gas-charged shocks, **Figure 16-39.** The lower spring platform on many shock absorbers also functions as a spring preload adjuster, **Figure 16-40.** It can be adjusted to modify ride height.

Warning: Gas-charged shocks are usually filled with high pressure nitrogen gas. Because property damage or personal injury may result from improper handling, keep the following in mind:

- Do not tamper with or attempt to open the cylinder assembly.
- Do not subject shock absorbers to an open flame or other high heat. This may cause the unit to explode.
- Do not deform or damage the shock in any way. Cylinder damage will result in poor damping performance or leakage.
- Gas pressure must be released from the shock absorber before disposal. Carefully follow the procedure given in the vehicle's service manual.

Shock Absorber Mounting

Shock absorbers are bolted to the frame and swingarm through rubber or steel bushings. Look at **Figure 16-41.** The bushings allow the shock to swivel slightly on its mounting during suspension movement.

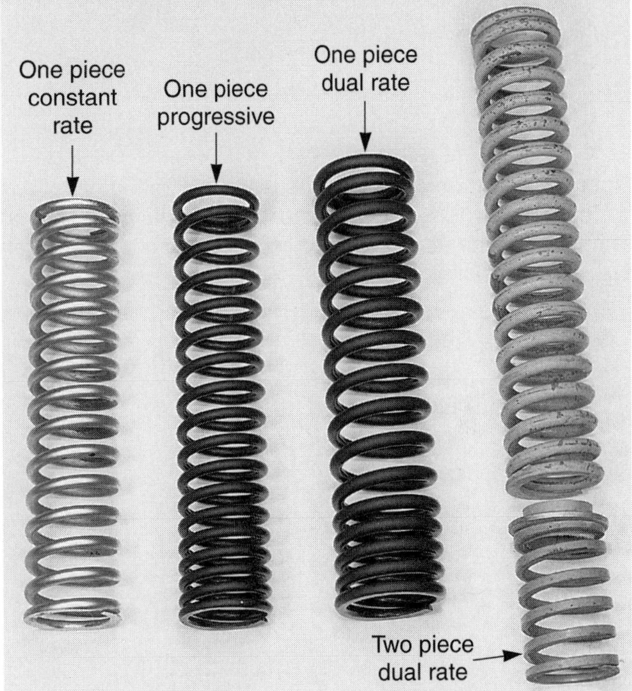

Figure 16-39. Variations of rear shock absorber springs. The springs are used to help control suspension action.

Side Stand

The side stand supports the motorcycle in upright position, **Figure 16-42.** There are two types: the ***conventional side stand*** and the ***dual motion side stand.*** To service either type, support the motorcycle in an upright and level position, using a support (use the center stand if available).

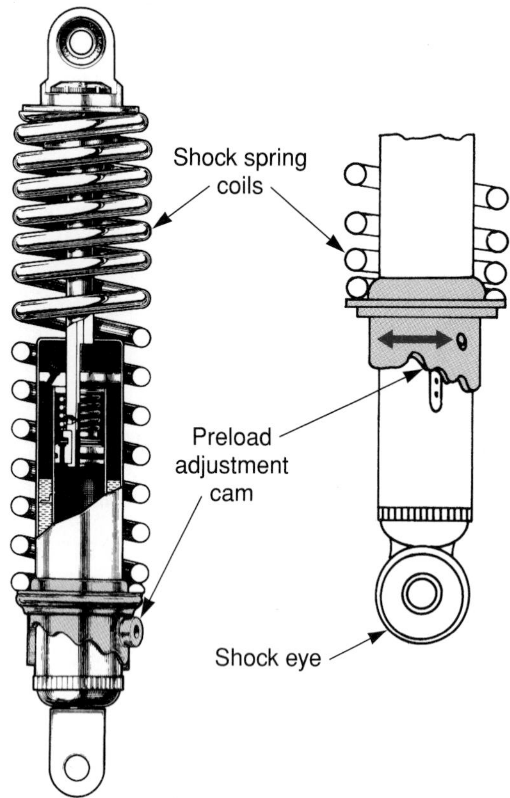

Figure 16-40. More or less rear suspension spring preload is achieved by changing the adjustment cam. Twisting the preload cam changes the rear coil spring compression rate. (American Suzuki Motor Corporation)

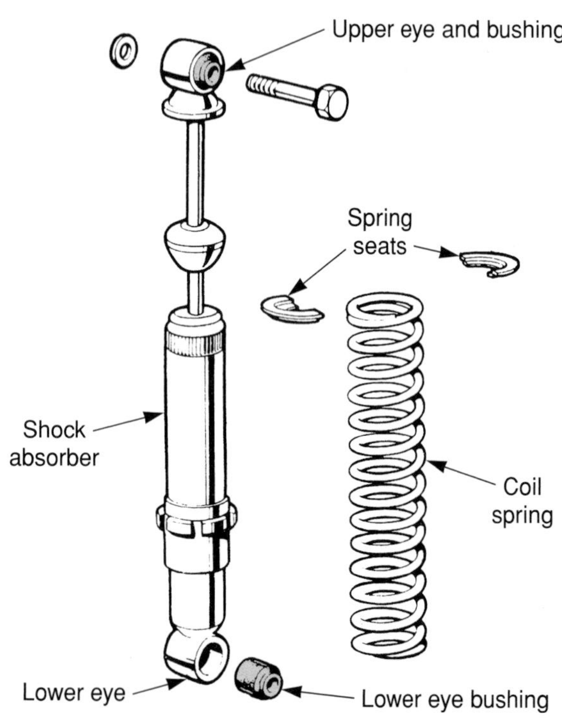

Figure 16-41. Steel insert surrounded by a rubber bushing is used in the shock eye. It provides a vibration resistant mounting for shock absorbers. (Triumph Motorcycles. Ltd.)

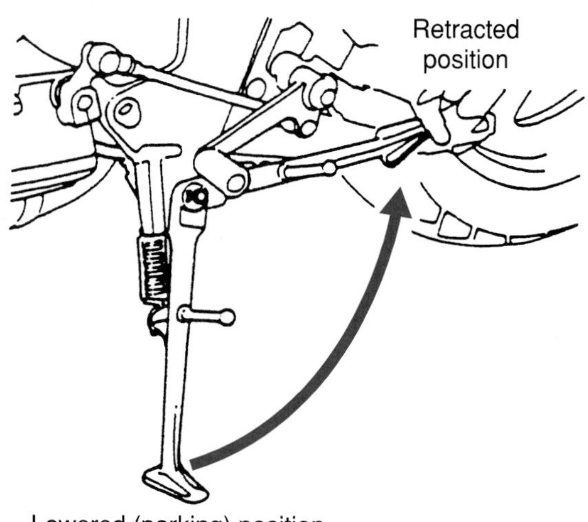

Figure 16-42. Conventional motorcycle side stand. (Honda Motor Co., Ltd.)

Inspect the conventional type, **Figure 16-43,** in the following manner:

1. Hook a spring scale to the end of the side stand rubber and check the load before the stand starts moving. Acceptable load measurement for specific models are given in the service manual. Typical numbers are 4.5-7 lbs (17.6–30.8 N) for street bikes, while on/off-road types may range from 6.5-11 lbs (28.6–48.4 N).
2. If the stand moves too easily, tighten the pivot bolt and recheck. If it still does not have the required tension measurement, replace the return spring.
3. See if the side stand moves smoothly and retracts fully. If not, grease the pivot.
4. Check the side stand's rubber foot for wear. Replace if it has become worn.
5. Inspect for side play on the side stand. If it is too great, tighten the pivot bolt. Recheck and if it is still too great, replace parts as necessary.

The dual motion side stand should lower easily to its first stop, then lock after moving farther forward to support the motorcycle as the rubber foot touches the ground, **Figure 16-44.** When the motorcycle is lifted upright, the stand should automatically move to the first position. If the side stand does not move freely, disassemble it:

1. Remove the return spring at the retracted position.
2. Remove the pivot bolt and remove the side stand assembly from the frame.
3. Check the pivot, pivot collar, and dust seals for wear or damage.
4. Lubricate the pivot area with clean grease and reassemble side stand.

Details of servicing side stands equipped with ignition cut-off switches are given in Chapter 17.

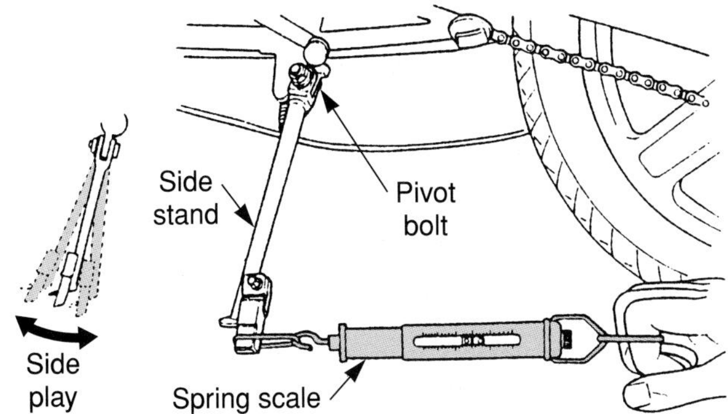

Figure 16-43. Performing a tension test on a conventional motorcycle side stand. (Honda Motor Co., Ltd.)

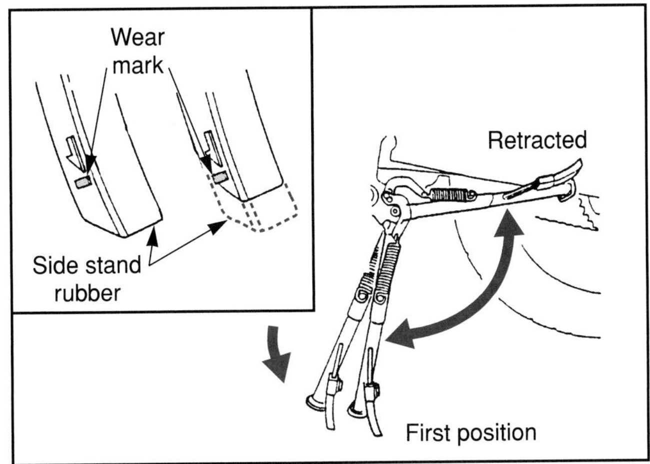

Figure 16-44. Dual motion side stand. (Honda Motor Co., Ltd.)

Frame and Suspension Inspection

The motorcycle's suspension system must be inspected periodically. It is a good idea to check for any problems that could affect rider safety. Check in the service manual for routine inspection intervals. Look for worn pivots, worn shock absorber bushings, loose fasteners, unlubricated grease fittings, suspension misalignment, and other similar types of problems.

The following summary and your service manual will provide guidelines for a thorough frame and suspension inspection. Because there are so many designs, remember that the following is only a guide. Items from Chapters 14 and 15 appear in the Summary because they can and will alter a bike's handling characteristics.

Front Suspension Inspection Summary

The following front suspension points must be carefully inspected:

1. Check steering head looseness and bearing condition.
2. Observe steering damper operation.
3. Check fork sliders or bushings for looseness.
4. Check wheel bearings for looseness.
5. Check truness of wheels and tires.
6. Inspect tire for cuts, sidewall checking, and other damage.
7. Check spoke tension.
8. Measure tire pressure.
9. Check fork for loss of air pressure (air forks).
10. Check tightness of fasteners at fenders, brackets, brake plate brace, triple clamps, steering stem, steering damper, and axle.
11. Check alignment of forks and steering head.
12. Measure fork tube height in triple clamps.
13. Check fork tube straightness.
14. Inspect fork seals for leakage.
15. Check condition of fork wipers or accordion boots.
16. Check fork tubes for scratches, nicks, and dents.
17. Inspect steering neck, triple clamps, and front chassis for chipped paint, cracks, and straightness.
18. Change fork oil. If the bike has an air suspension, release pressure before draining. Pressurize after filling.
19. Observe fork operation.
20. Check handle bar tightness and straightness.

Mid-frame Inspection

The following mid-frame areas must be inspected. Check the mid-frame (center section of chassis) for chipped paint, corrosion, damage, and straightness, and make repairs as needed. Check the fasteners on the engine mounts, side stand, center stand, brake pedal, and foot pegs. Replace any damaged or distressed fasteners. Lubricate the brake pedal, foot peg, center stand, and side stand pivots.

Rear Suspension Inspection

The rear suspension items that require inspection are:

1. Check swingarm looseness.
2. Inspect shock eye bushings for looseness.
3. Check wheel bearings and spokes for looseness.
4. Measure wheel and tire runout.
5. Check tire for cuts, cracks, and other damage.
6. Measure tire air pressure.
7. Check swingarm straightness and alignment.

8. Grease swingarm.
9. Inspect shock absorbers for leakage (oil and air).
10. Check shock absorber rods for straightness.
11. Check shock absorber preload settings.
12. Observe shock absorber operation.
13. Check wheel and sprocket alignment.
14. Check tightness of fasteners at shock mounts, swingarm pivot, rear axle, brake plate brace, chain guard, passenger pegs, and fender brackets.
15. Inspect rear chassis, swingarm, and surrounding areas for chipped paint, corrosion, cracks, misalignment, and other signs of trouble.
16. If the motorcycle has saddle bags or a luggage rack, check for tightness, alignment, and cracked mounting brackets.

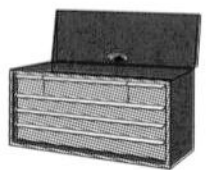

Note: Frame and suspension system inspection is imperative for motorcycles, scooters, and ATVs with handling problems or accident damage. Every problem must be located and corrected to ensure the vehicle is safe to ride.

ATV Four Wheel Alignment

Earlier in this chapter, motorcycle wheel alignment was discussed. Four wheel alignments on ATVs present different problems. In order to align an ATV, you must understand four alignment angles. These are:

- ***Toe-in*** and ***toe-out.*** The inward pointing of the front wheels.
- ***Camber.*** The inward or outward tilt of the wheel at the top. A wheel has a positive camber when the top is tilted out.
- ***Caster.*** The forward or backward tilt of the wheel in relation to the top. This is similar to the caster on a piece of furniture.
- ***Thrust angle.*** Tracking of rear tires in relation to the front tires.

When checking the camber and caster, remove the wheel cap, cotter pin, and front axle nut. Install an attachment or adapter onto the front axle. Put the camber and caster gauge onto the adapter, **Figure 16-45,** and measure the camber. Set the turn gauge under the front wheels and measure the camber and the caster. Camber and caster are not adjustable. If they are out of specification, check the suspension and frame for damage and replace any parts necessary, then recheck alignment.

To check for a toe-in condition, place the vehicle on a level surface with the front wheels facing straight ahead. Mark the center of both tires with chalk to indicate the axle center height. Align the toe-in gauge with the marks on the tires as shown in **Figure 16-46.** Check the readings on the gauge scales. Slowly move the vehicle back until the wheels have turned 180° and the marks on the tires are aligned with the gauge height on the rear side.

Measure the toe-in on the rear part of the tires at the same points. When the toe-in is out of specification, adjust it by changing the length of the tie-rods equally while measuring the toe-in. Typically, thrust angle cannot be easily measured without electronic alignment equipment. Any change in thrust angle will coincide with rear alignment problems on an ATV. This is usually caused by a bent frame or suspension component.

Frame Problems

Typically common problems and their causes that may occur with a motorcycle frame.

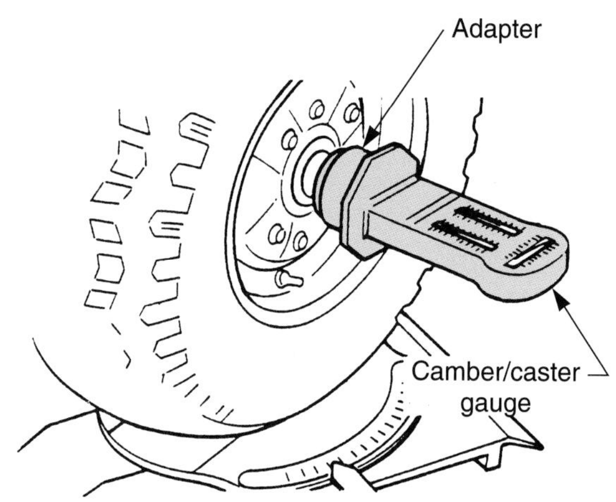

Figure 16-45. Checking the camber and caster alignment on an ATV. (Honda Motor Co., Ltd.)

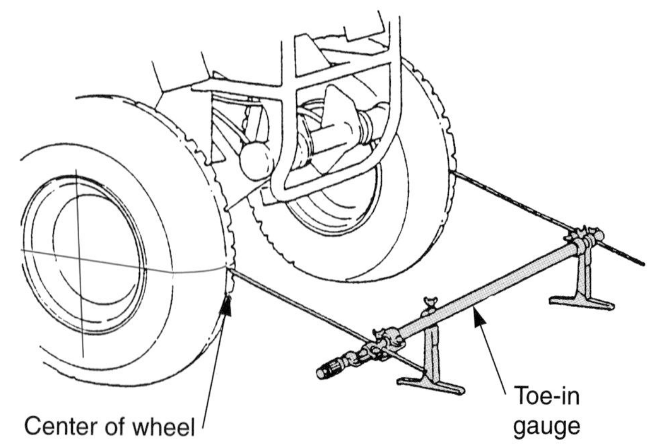

Figure 16-46. Checking an ATV suspension for toe-in using a toe-gauge or bar. (Honda Motor Co., Ltd.)

Abnormal Engine Vibration

- Cracked or damaged engine mounts.
- Cracked, damaged, or bent welded portions.
- Bent or damaged frame.
- Engine problems.

Abnormal Noise when Riding

- Damaged or bent engine mounts.
- Damaged welded points.
- Damaged or bent frame.

Steers to One Side when under Acceleration or Deceleration

- Bent frame.
- Bent fork.
- Bent swingarm.

Front Suspension Problems

The following are common front wheel suspension problems and their causes:

Hard Steering

- Steering head bearing adjustment nut too tight.
- Faulty steering head bearing.
- Damaged steering head bearings.
- Insufficient tire pressure.
- Faulty tire.

Steers to One Side or Does Not Track Straight

- Unevenly adjusted right and left shock absorbers.
- Bent fork.
- Bent front axle; wheel installed incorrectly.
- Faulty steering head bearings.
- Bent frame.
- Worn wheel bearing.
- Worn swingarm pivot components.

Front Wheel Wobbling

- Bent rim.
- Loose nut on axle.
- Worn front wheel bearings.
- Faulty or incorrect tire.
- Incorrect front fork oil.

Wheel Turns Hard

- Brake misadjusted.
- Faulty wheel bearing.
- Faulty speedometer gear.

Soft Suspension

- Weak fork springs.
- Insufficient fluid in fork.
- Low fluid level in fork.
- Faulty anti-dive system.

Hard Suspension

- Bent fork components.
- Bent damper rod (bottom link).
- Incorrect fluid weight.
- Bent fork tubes.
- Clogged fluid passage.

Front Suspension Noisy

- Worn slider or guide bushings (bottom link).
- Insufficient fluid in fork.
- Loose fork fasteners.
- Lack of grease in speedometer gearbox.

Rear Suspension

The more common rear suspension problems and their possible causes are as follows:

Wobbly Rear Wheel

- Distorted wheel rim.
- Worn wheel bearing or swingarm bearing.
- Defective or incorrect tire.
- Loose nuts or bolts or rear suspension.
- Loose nut on axle.

Soft Suspension

- Weak spring(s).
- Oil leakage from damper unit.
- Air or gas leakage.
- Incorrect shock absorber adjustment.

Hard Suspension

- Incorrectly mounted suspension components.
- Incorrect shock absorber adjustment.
- Bent swingarm pivot.
- Bent shock absorber rod.
- Damaged swingarm pivot bearing(s).
- Faulty suspension linkage.
- Damaged linkage pivot bearings.

Noisy Rear Suspension

- Loose nuts or bolts on rear suspension.
- Worn swingarm and rear cushion related bearings.

Summary

It is very important for a motorcycle to handle properly over bumps, in turns, during acceleration, and when stopping. This is critical to both rider safety and comfort. The design of a frame and suspension system is a major factor controlling the handling characteristics of a bike.

The frame is the backbone of all motorcycles, ATVs, and scooters. It serves as a skeleton on which virtually everything is attached. The material used for a frame is chosen to match the motorcycle's function. Aluminum frames are used for on-road sport bikes with medium-to-large displacement engines and motocross bikes while all other frames are made of steel. Some chassis subframes are now being made of titanium alloys.

The various frame designs can be classified into one of a few categories. There are two cradle frame designs: the single cradle and double cradle. In the backbone frame, the engine hangs from the top of the frame and acts as a structural member. The diamond frame is used mainly on small and medium-size bikes due to its simplicity, light weight and excellent serviceability. The delta-box frame features a very strong steel or aluminum triangle between the steering head and the swingarm pivot. The pentagonal frame (five-sided frame) is made of cast and extruded aluminum and has good torsional rigidity. A stamped frame usually consists of two pieces of stamped sheet metal welded together.

The purpose of the suspension system is to allow the wheels to follow an irregular surface with a minimum amount of shock being transmitted into the frame. Telescopic front suspensions are made up of a pair of upper fork tubes and lower fork sliders that telescope into one another. Within the set of tubes on either side is a spring and an oil damping system. Some systems utilize a cartridge damper within the fork sliders.

A telescoping fork assembly consists of two fork tubes, two triple clamps, a spindle (shaft mounted on lower triple clamp), and related fasteners. The fork tubes are shock absorbing devices that hold the front wheel in place. While all telescopic forks work on the same principle, there are many design variations. The compression stroke is the fork's movement into the slider when striking a bump in the road. During the fork's rebound stroke, the fork spring causes the slider to extend.

The single-sided swingarm front suspension system construction is somewhat different than the conventional telescopic fork suspension. At present it is used only with an omega shape frame. The arrangement of the lower and upper arms minimizes nose-dive during braking so the bike maintains an even ride. Because steering and suspension components are not dependent upon one another, the ride is considered to be smoother without jolts from bumps and rough roads being transmitted directly to the handlebars.

Steering geometry refers to the angles formed by the various steering related components on a motorcycle. Factors which determine steering geometry are rake, trail, and offset. Typical front suspension service consists of changing fork oil, lubricating and adjusting steering head bearings, and rebuilding the forks.

A typical motorcycle rear suspension consists of a swingarm and one or more shock absorbers. Swingarm rear suspension design can be broken down into a few categories, depending on the number of shocks used and the swingarm design. The single shock rear suspension system uses an adjustable shock absorber, levers, and links to provide rising rate operation. A dual spring shock absorber rear suspension has a shock absorber on each side of the frame. Larger displacement motorcycles often utilize a progressive link rear suspension.

Shock absorbers work much like a front suspension telescopic fork. There are several different types of shock absorbers available for the various riding conditions encountered by motorcycles, scooters, and ATVs. Shock absorber springs are mounted over the damper (shock) body. They are fastened to the shock absorber by collars or clips. Shock absorbers are bolted to the frame and swingarm through rubber or steel bushings.

The side stand supports the motorcycle in the upright position. There are two types: the conventional side stand and the dual motion side stand. In order to align an ATV, you must understand four alignment angles. They are toe-in, toe-out, camber, and caster.

Know These Terms

Frame
Single cradle
Double cradle
Backbone frame
Diamond frame
Delta-box frame
Pentagonal frame
Stamped frame
Suspension system
Telescopic front suspensions
Telescoping fork
Triple clamps
Spindle
Steering damper
Fork sliders
Damper rods
Compression stroke
Rebound stroke
Anti-dive fork
Pivoting link front suspension
Oil damper
Single-sided swingarm front suspension system
Omega frame
Steering geometry
Rake
Trail
Offset
Shock absorber springs

Fork oil	Conventional side stand
Ball bearings	Dual motion side stand
Tapered roller bearings	Toe-in
Rear suspension	Toe-out
Single shock swingarm	Camber
Dual spring/ shock absorber	Caster
Progressive link rear suspension	Thrust angle
Shock absorbers	

Review Questions—Chapter 16

Do not write in this text. Place your answers on a separate sheet of paper.

1. Name three common frame types.
2. *True or False?* Triangulation and gussets add strength to frames.
3. When is frame and suspension inspection imperative?
4. List two functions of fork damper rods.
5. What are the two phases of fork operation?
   A. Compression and rebound.
   B. Compression and exhaust.
   C. Intake and compression.
   D. Rebound and transition.
6. Fork action is determined by the _____ and _____ of damper holes.
7. *True or False?* Rake angle is the same on all motorcycles.
8. The term *self-centering effect* is most closely related to:
   A. rake.
   B. offset.
   C. trail.
   D. camber.
9. A ______ helps to eliminate unwanted steering oscillations.
10. Name the differences between telescopic front wheel suspension and pivoting link-front suspension.
11. The frequency of fork oil change requirements is determined by ______ .
    A. riding conditions
    B. manufacturer recommendations
    C. the fork rake
    D. Both A & B.
12. What advantage do steering head roller bearings have over ball bearings?
13. *True or False?* It is not necessary to replace sealing rings, washers, and snap rings during fork rebuilding.
14. A conventional shock absorber is _____.
    A. unpressurized
    B. oil damped
    C. gas charged
    D. Both A & B.
15. List the three types of shock springs.

Suggested Activities

1. Visit local motorcycle shops to find two examples of each common frame type. Compare the frames, making note of:
   A. Triangulation.
   B. Gusseting.
   C. Diameter of frame tubes.
   D. Type and size of engine mounting brackets.
   E. The motorcycle's intended use.
2. Complete a suspension inspection summary on an actual motorcycle.
3. From Activity 2, explain what should be done to improve the motorcycle's mechanical condition.

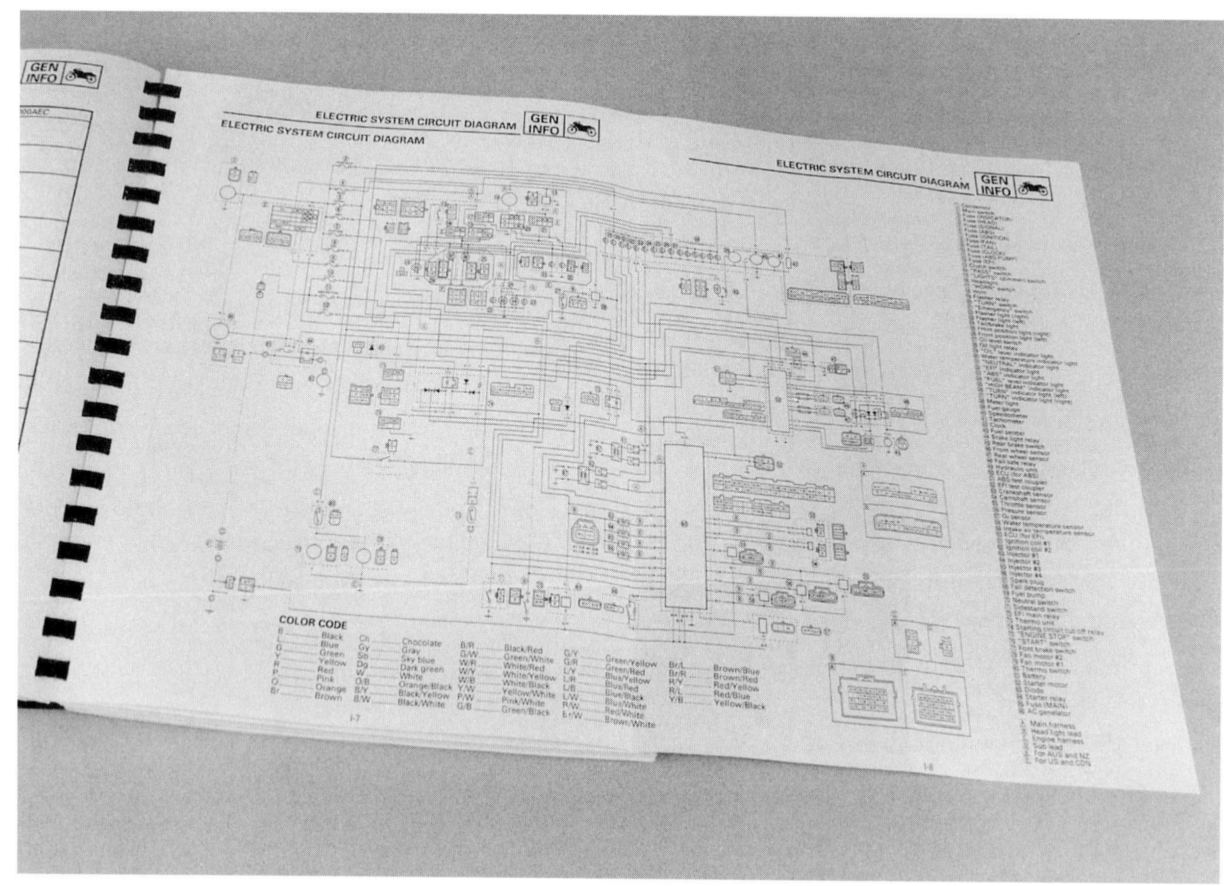

Wiring schematics are important when dealing with any electrical problems. They are like roadmaps of the bike's electrical system. (Jack Klasey)

17

Accessory Systems

After studying this chapter, you will be able to:

- Describe the major components of a motorcycle lighting system.
- Explain the fundamentals of troubleshooting procedures for the various accessory systems.
- Identify the important motorcycle warning devices.
- Understand the importance of switches in electrical circuits.
- Describe the operation of a typical cruise control.

In order for the motorcycle, ATV, or scooter to be functional, it needs other systems besides the powertrain, frame, brake, and suspension systems. Some of these systems are critical for operation, others are needed for safety, while a few are not essential for bike operation, but add to the value of the bike. This chapter discusses accessory systems used on modern motorcycles, ATVs, and scooters.

Accessory Systems

Motorcycle, scooter, and ATV ***accessory systems*** are the grouping of electrical and electronic circuits that make up lighting circuits, warning and indicator circuits, switch circuits, communication systems, and the cruise control. In some accessory systems, the electric starter circuit described in Chapter 9 is included in the grouping. Most accessory systems will be found on street and non-competition off-road models. Motocross bikes have few, if any accessory systems.

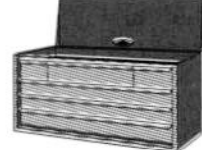

Note: Before continuing with accessory systems, you may want to review Chapter 5, especially the portions on maintenance and testing of electrical circuits.

Lighting Systems

A motorcycle's lighting system usually consists of headlight, tail light, brake light, directional turn signals, warning lights, and instrument illumination, **Figure 17-1.** Some off-road and competition bikes have few or no lights.

There are two types of lighting systems used on bikes; ac lighting that receives power from the alternator coil, and dc lighting that is powered by the battery. On dc lighting systems, the headlight comes on without starting the engine, **Figure 17-2.** On ac lighting systems, the headlight comes on when the engine starts, **Figure 17-3.**

Headlights

There are several types of headlight bulbs used. The most common is the two light ***sealed beam tungsten headlight bulb.*** On this system, the headlight has two

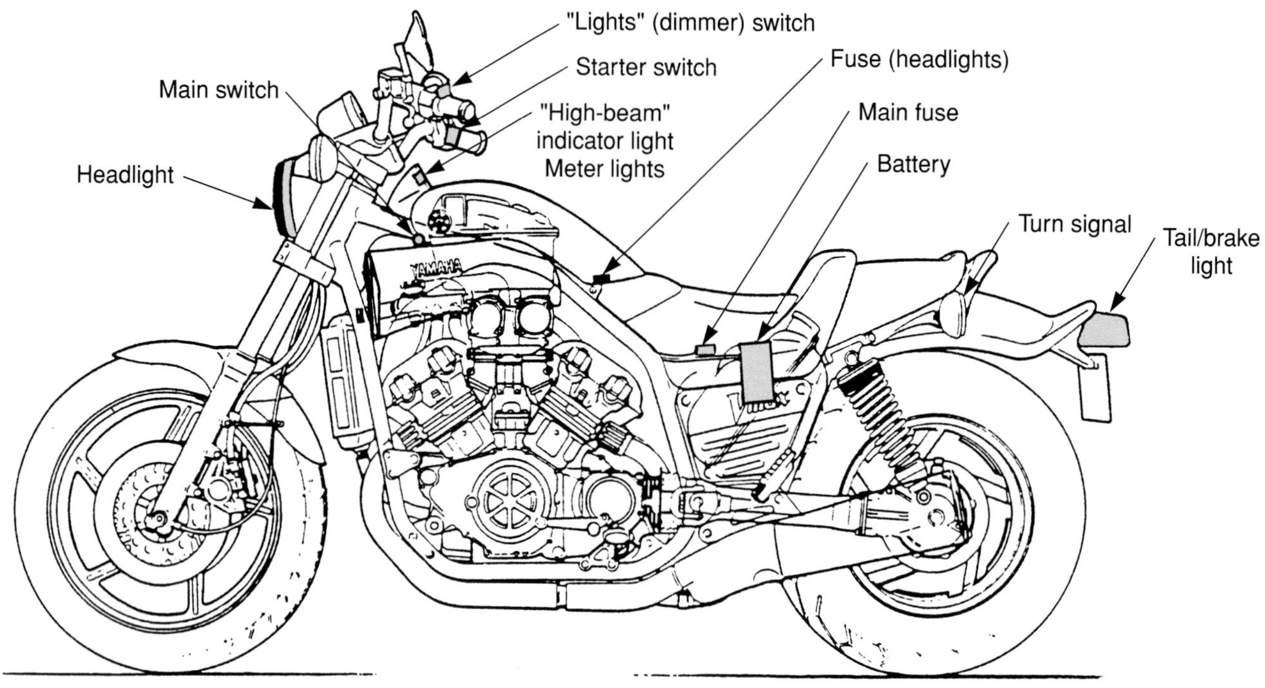

Figure 17-1. The major components of a motorcycle lighting system. (Yamaha Motor Corporation U.S.A.)

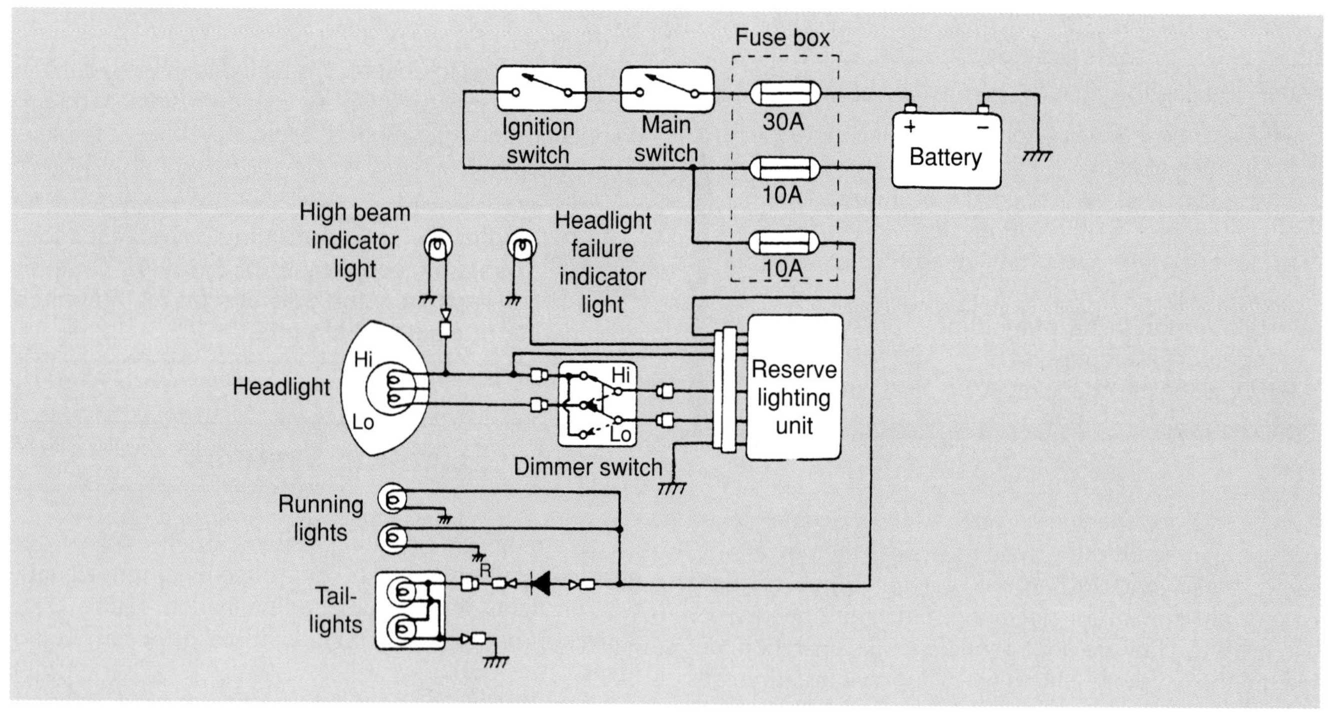

Figure 17-2. Dc headlight circuit. (Kawasaki Motors Corporation U.S.A.)

filaments, a high beam and a low beam. Some street motorcycles are equipped with an electronic module that automatically switches from one filament to the other in the event of filament failure. This device also lights a bulb on the instrument panel to indicate the so-called reserve light is in use.

In recent years, ***halogen bulbs*** have become increasingly popular since they can provide substantially more light, extending the rider's range of vision and the bike's visibility for safer night driving. A halogen light contains a small quartz-glass. Inside the bulb is a filament surrounded by halogen gas. The small, gas-filled bulb fits within a larger metal reflector and lens element. A glass balloon sealed to the metal reflector allows the halogen bulb to be removed without danger of water or dirt damaging the optics within the light, **Figure 17-4.** The replaceable bulbs

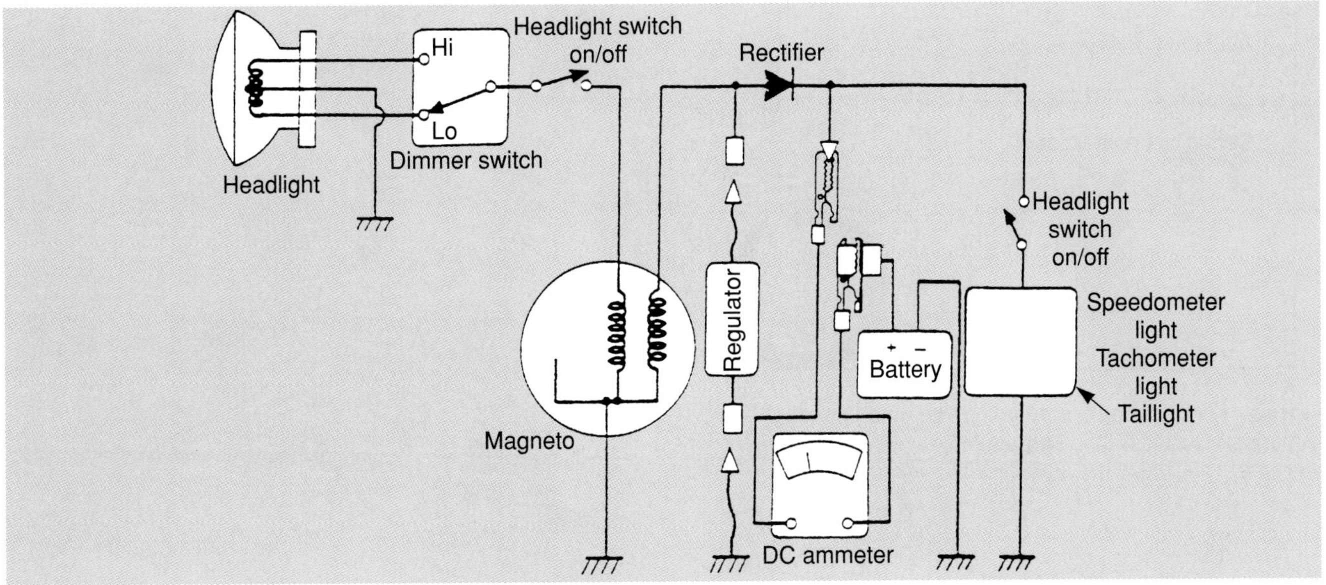

Figure 17-3. Ac lighting and charging system. (Kawasaki Motors Corporation U.S.A.)

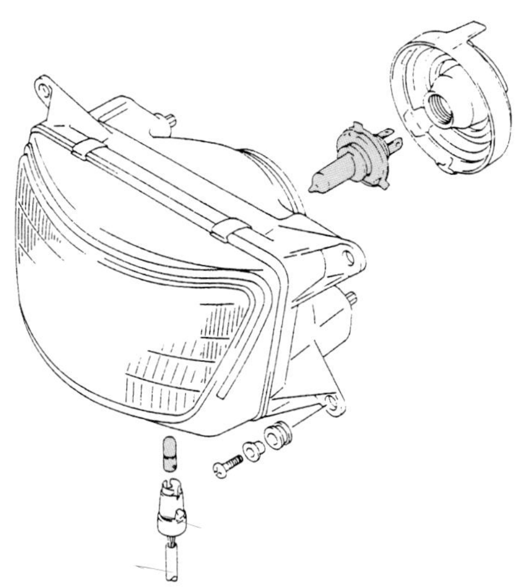

Figure 17-4. Replaceable halogen headlight assembly. (American Suzuki Motor Corporation)

are removed by unplugging the electrical connector, twisting the retaining ring about 1/8 turn counter-clockwise, then removing the bulb from its socket. The new bulb is installed by reversing this procedure. Sealed beam halogen lights are also available.

Caution: When handling the halogen bulb, never touch the glass portion with your bare hands. Always use a clean cloth. Oil contamination from hands or dirty rags will reduce bulb life or even cause the bulb to explode. Also, halogen headlight bulbs become very hot while the headlight is on, and remain hot for a while after they are turned off. Be sure to turn the ignition switch off and let the bulb cool down before replacing.

Headlight Aim

The headlight beam is adjustable both horizontally and vertically. Headlight aiming must be correctly adjusted for safe riding as well as for oncoming riders. In most areas, it is illegal to ride with improperly adjusted headlights. Check local regulations for specifications which may differ from those given here.

When making a headlight adjustment, make sure the tire pressure is correct and the fuel tank is approximately half full. Park the motorcycle on a level surface with the headlight approximately 25′ (7.62 m) from a vertical wall, **Figure 17-5.** When checking the headlight, the motorcycle must be off of its side or center stand and with a rider seated, preferably wearing normal riding gear. Measure the distance from the center of the headlight to ground. Then make a horizontal mark on the wall the same distance from the headlight to the ground to represent the headlight height center. Headlight adjustments are as follows:

1. Vertical adjustment. With the headlight on high beam, the brightest point of light should be 2″ (50.8 mm) below the horizontal mark at a distance of 25′ (7.62 m). To typically make a vertical adjustment, loosen the headlight mounting bolts, matching the punch mark on the case and the bracket by moving the headlight up or down, **Figure 17-6.** Some motorcycle headlights have an adjusting screw on the bottom. In this case, turn the screw to make the vertical adjustment.

2. Horizontal adjustment. Turn the headlight on high beam. The beam should be pointing straight ahead. For those having an adjusting screw on the side of the headlight rim, turn this screw to make the horizontal adjustment.

On some models, the headlight is completely encased. The adjustment can be made either with the

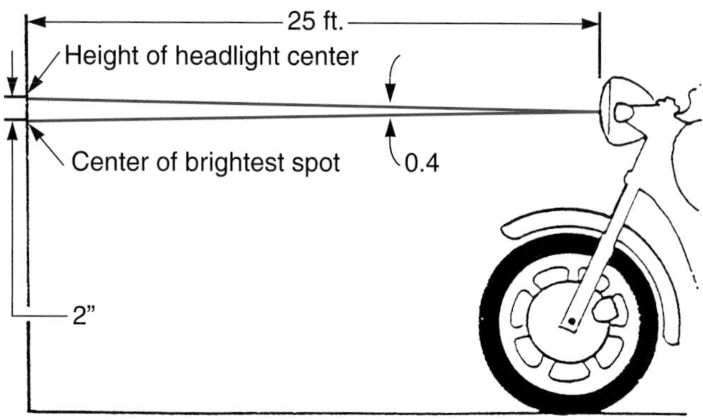

Figure 17-5. Proper method of testing headlight aim. (American Suzuki Motor Corporation)

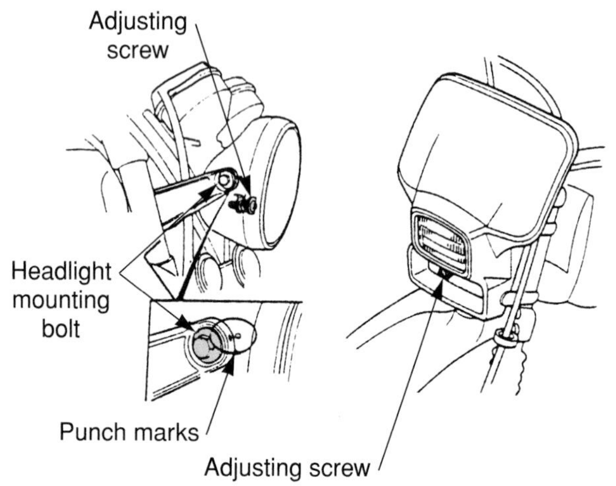

Figure 17-6. Adjusting a motorcycle headlight assembly. (Honda Motor Co., Ltd.)

light beam adjustment knob on the back of the light case or with a remote cable and knob. Refer to the service manual for the proper adjustment method.

Most headlights have both a high and low beam. Switching from high beam to low beam is controlled by a ***dimmer switch.*** The dimmer switch is a simple two-position switch that controls the headlight output. Most bikes have a high beam indicator on the dash panel.

Tail Lights

Most state laws require that ***tail lights*** on street vehicles be dc powered so they will remain on, even if the engine stalls. As shown in **Figure 17-7,** the tail light lens assembly also provides license plate illumination as required by law for street bikes. To make the unit as watertight as possible, a gasket is used between the lens and the base.

Ac tail lights are sometimes used on off-road motorcycles. On some street motorcycles, the tail light acts as a parking light. The tail light is activated when the main switch is placed in the park position.

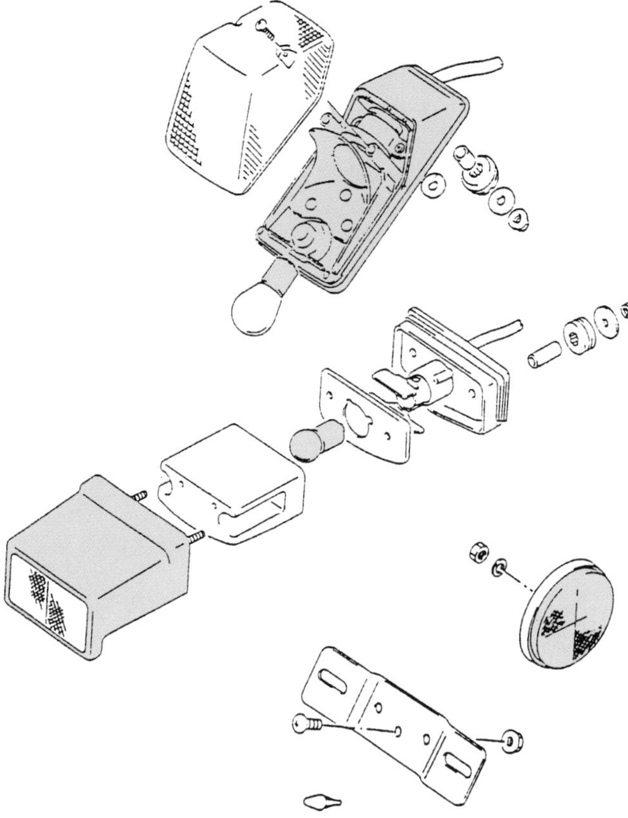

Figure 17-7. Typical tail, brake light, and license lamp assembly. (American Suzuki Motor Corporation)

Brake Light

The ***brake light*** comes on when the brake lever (or pedal) is applied. Brake light switches vary, some have continuity when pulled or pushed, while others operate on hydraulic brake line pressure.

Brake light and tail light bulbs may be either single filament or twin (double) filament, **Figure 17-8.** When the brake light and tail light are a combined unit, twin filaments are usually employed; one filament lights the tail light circuit while the other lights the brake light. Usually the brake light filament has less resistance, so the brake light appears brighter than the tail light. Some motorcycles employ two bulbs to increase the tail light and brake light brightness, **Figure 17-9.**

Turn Signal Indicator Lights

The ***turn signal indicator light*** circuit normally includes four turn signal bulbs, two indicator bulbs, a flasher (turn signal relay), switches, and wiring. The turn signal circuit is powered by the battery or alternator and controlled by the ignition switch and turn signal switch.

The turn signal bulbs are controlled by a relay, referred to as a ***turn signal flasher,*** **Figure 17-10.** A bi-metallic strip (two strips of dissimilar metals) in the flasher causes the circuit to open and close. As current flows through the bi-metallic strip, it heats and expands, opening the circuit,

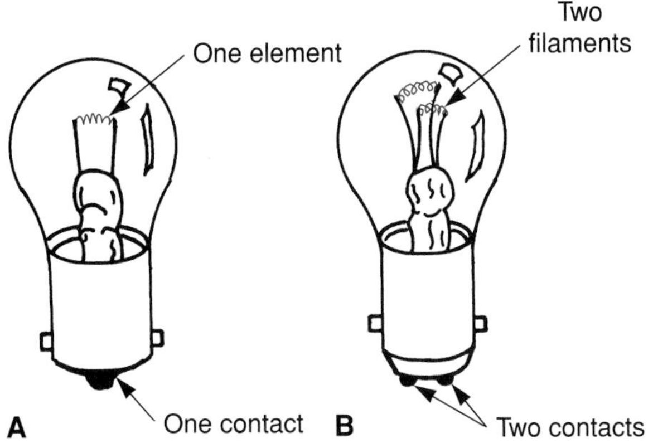

Figure 17-8. Bulbs used for auxiliary illumination. A—Single-filament bulb. B—Double-filament bulb.

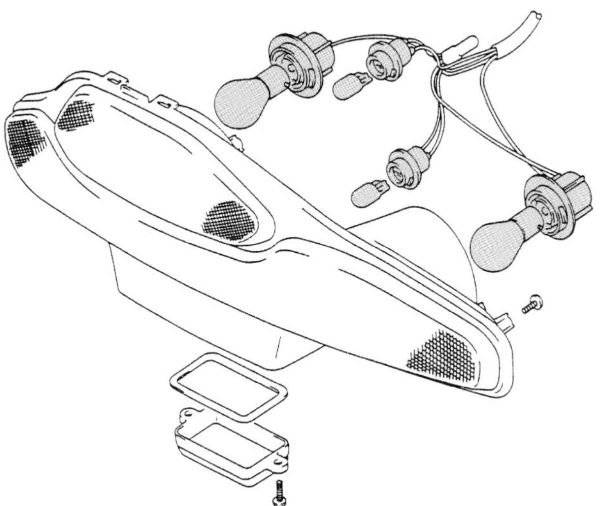

Figure 17-9. Tail and brake light brightness is often increased by using two bulbs in a single light housing. (American Suzuki Motor Corporation)

Figure 17-11A. As the strip cools, it contracts, closing the circuit again. See **Figure 17-11B.** This permits the flasher to perform its function while the switch selects which pair of bulbs (right or left) to flash.

Most street motorcycles also incorporate a ***turn signal canceling device*** and ***four-way hazard signal*** switch with the turn signal function. This is accomplished through the use of a *multi-function switch,* **Figure 17-12.** The canceling control portion of it is activated when the bike turns and cancels the turn directional signal lights. The four-way hazard system activates each of four turn signals.

The multi-function switch on some motorcycles contain a flash-to-pass switch that allows the rider to flash the high-beam headlights without using the main light switch. When the multi-function switch is activated by the rider, the flash-to-pass switch contacts close. The high-beam headlights illuminate until the lever is released.

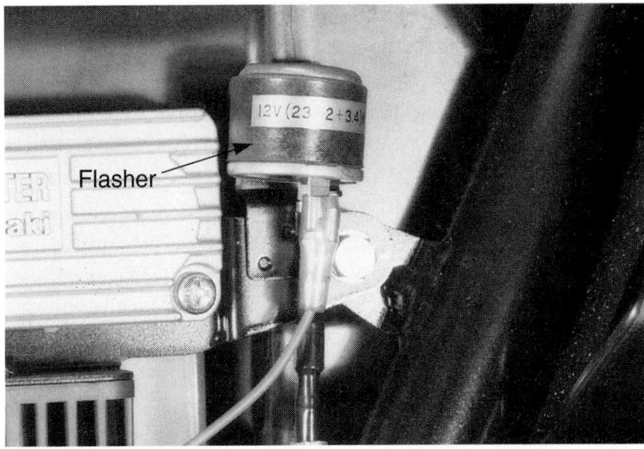

Figure 17-10. Turn signal flashers use a thin metallic strip to open and close the power circuit to the indicator bulbs. The strip is enclosed in a small metal or plastic housing.

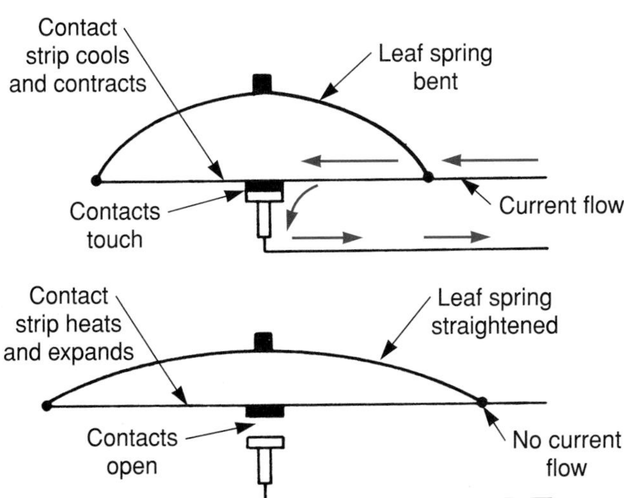

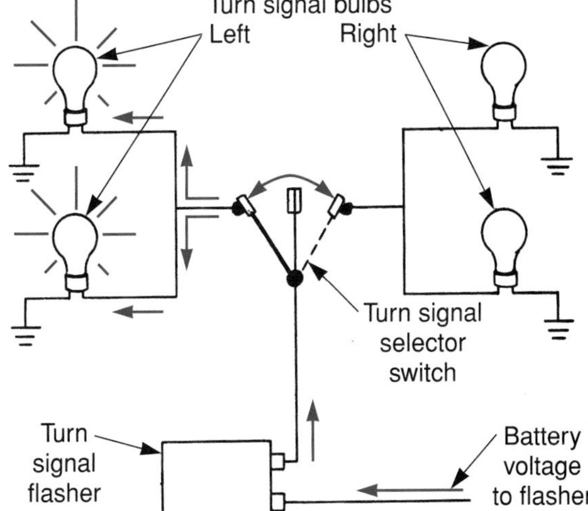

Figure 17-11. Flasher and turn signal operation. A—Flasher unit operation. B—Turn signal circuit operation depends on the position of the selector switch.

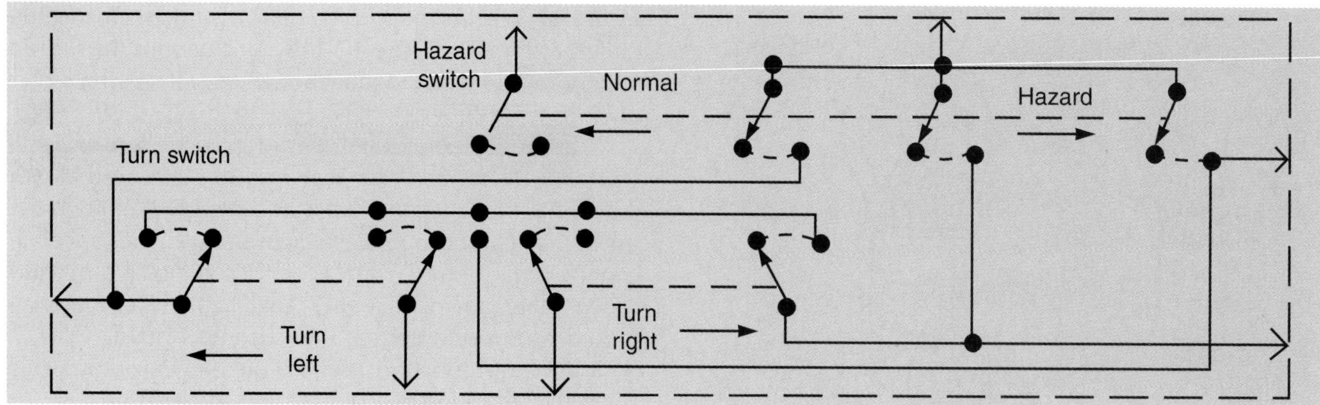

Figure 17-12. Typical turn signal and hazard multifunction switch.

Instrument Panel

There are various ***instrument panel*** designs and layouts. The two types of instrument panel displays are analog and digital. In a traditional ***analog display,*** **Figure 17-13,** an indicator moves in front of a fixed scale to give a variable readout. The indicator is often a needle, but it can also be a liquid crystal or graphic display. A ***digital display*** uses numbers instead of a needle or graphic symbol. A digital (or electronic) display is better for showing exact data such as miles or operating hours, **Figure 17-14.**

The advantage of analog displays is they show relative change better than digital displays. Analog displays are useful when the rider must see something quickly and the exact reading is not important. For example, an analog tachometer shows the rise and fall of engine speed better than a digital display. The rider does not need to know exactly how many rpms the engine is running. The most important thing is how fast the engine is reaching the red line on the gauge. Many speedometer-odometer combinations are examples of both analog (speed) and digital (distance) gauges.

A digital signal has only two states, either on or off. If a switch is turned on and off many times, the number of pulses can be counted. For example, a speed sensor can be turned on and off each time a wheel moves a certain distance. The number of pulses counted in a given period of time allows the computer to display the speed. The pulses can also be used by the computer to change the odometer reading.

Analog instrument panels are lighted directly or indirectly. When the bulb is inside the gauge, it is directly lighted. Indirect lighting is external and reflected to the appropriate area. Digital panels use light-emitting diodes (LEDs) either as signal indicator lights, or they can be grouped to show a set of numbers or letters.

Figure 17-13. Typical analog instrument panel. The tachometer and speedometer are placed near each other to read engine and vehicle speed. (Yamaha Motor Corporation U.S.A.)

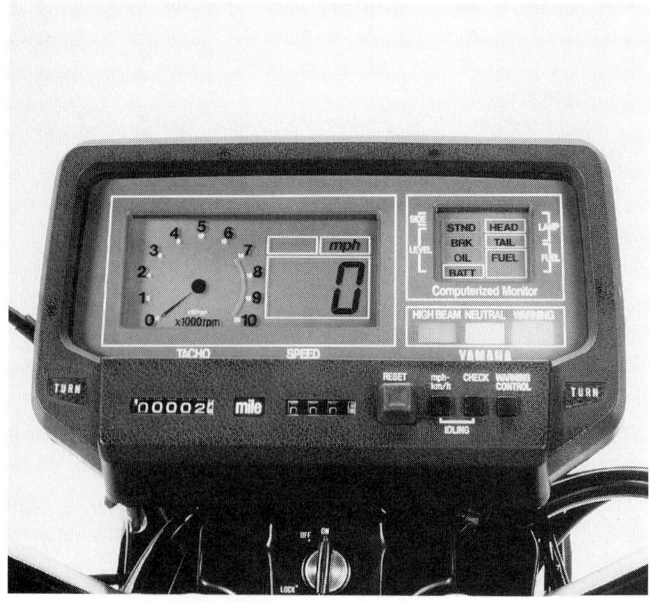

Figure 17-14. Typical electronic digital instrument panel. (Yamaha Motor Corporation U.S.A.)

Lighting System Problems

Lighting system problems can be easy to troubleshoot (burned out bulb), moderately difficult (broken wire hidden in the harness), or very difficult (wiring failure that intermittently opens and closes the circuit).

Troubleshooting lighting system problems require the use of a multimeter, test light, and wiring schematics, **Figure 17-15.** In order to troubleshoot lighting system problems, you must check for voltage in the circuit, continuity of switches and wiring, and verify the circuit has a good ground.

The logical place to start troubleshooting is at the bulb, **Figure 17-16.** If the bulb is good, check for power and ground to the socket and body. If everything tests good, visually check the wiring, looking for any place where wires could get pinched or damaged. Loose or corroded connections can cause dim lights, difficult starting, battery drain, and possible damage to the alternator and regulator. Moisture can enter a bulb socket and cause corrosion of the electrical contacts and the bulb. Corrosive conditions can be repaired by using sandpaper on the affected areas. For severe cases, replace the socket and bulb. After any repair, always attempt to waterproof the assembly to prevent future problems. Cracked or broken assemblies are easily replaced.

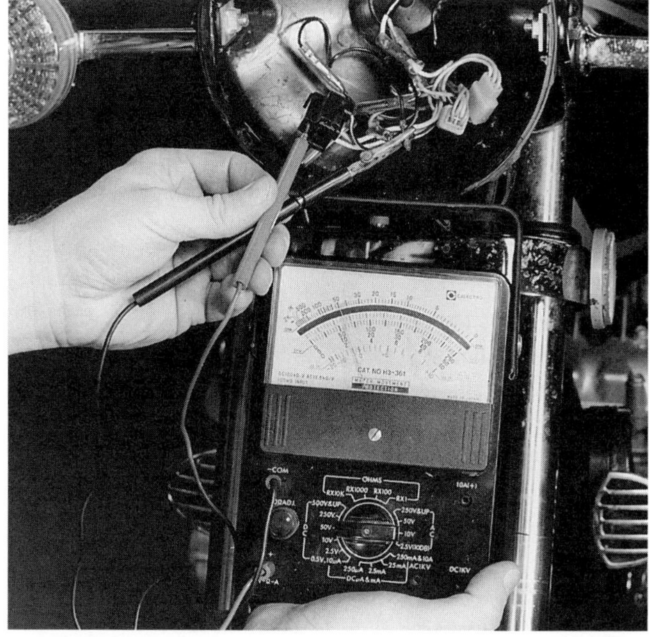

A

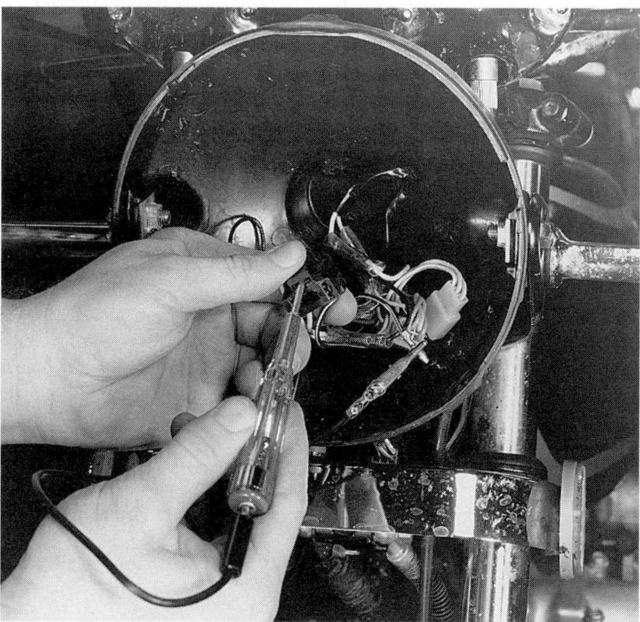

B

Figure 17-15. A multimeter or test light can be used to check for voltage at the headlight or other plug connections. A—Multimeter. B—Non-powered test light.

Another common electrical lighting problem is flickering lights (lights go on or off). The cause of this is usually a loose electrical connection or a circuit breaker opening and closing because of a short. If one or more lights flicker, the problem is in a section of the circuit common to those lights. Check to see which lights only flicker with the switch in one position. For example, if the lights flicker only when the headlights are on high beam, check the components and wiring in the high-beam section of the circuit. If only one light flickers, the problem is in that section of the circuit. Check the bulb socket for corrosion. Also, make sure the bulb terminals are not worn. This could upset the electrical connection. If needed, replace the bulb socket and bulb.

Before you start unplugging the wiring harness, make sure you understand the schematic and have decided the troubleshooting sequence you will follow.

Brake Light Problems

Check brake light switch operation and adjustment by applying the brakes. Visually inspect for damage and make sure the reflector plate within the light is clean. When replacing a bulb, inspect the bulb socket. If the socket is rusty or corroded, the socket or light assembly base should be replaced. Also, inspect the lens and gasket for damage while the lens is removed and replace any damaged part.

Adjust the rear brake light switch so the brake light

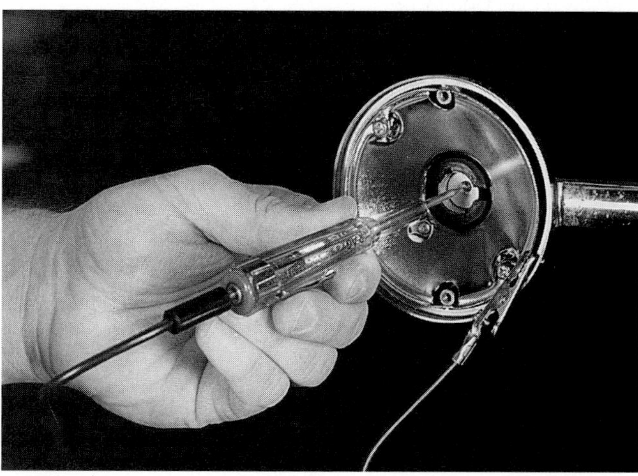

Figure 17-16. A test light can be used to verify the voltage of a bulb socket.

comes on just prior to the brake actually being engaged. If the light fails to come on, adjust the switch so the light comes on at the proper time. Turn the adjusting nut on the brake light switch, not the switch body and wiring. Be sure to hold the switch body firmly while turning the adjusting nut, **Figure 17-17.** After adjustment, check to be sure the brake light comes on at the proper time.

Note: The brake light switch on the front brake lever of most bikes cannot be adjusted. If the front brake light switch actuation and brake engagement are off, replace the switch or other malfunctioning parts. Make brake light switch adjustments after height and brake pedal free play adjustments have been completed.

If the brake light does not come on, check the following:

- Burned out bulb.
- Poor connection at the brake light switch connector.

If these are ok, disconnect the brake light switch connector and check for continuity between the terminals while operating the brake lever or pedal, **Figure 17-18.**

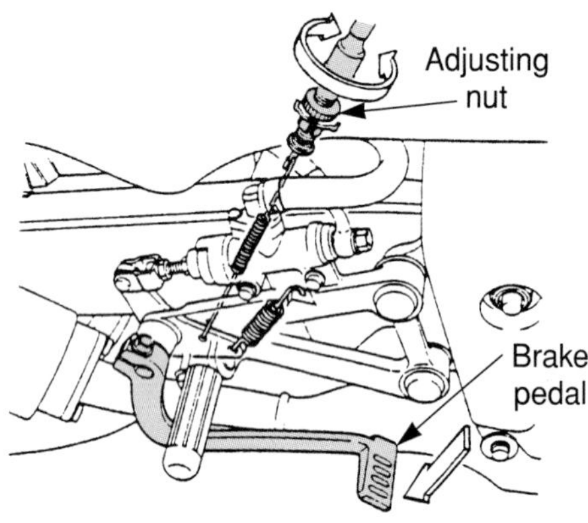

Figure 17-17. Setting the brake light switch adjusting nut. (Honda Motor Co., Ltd.)

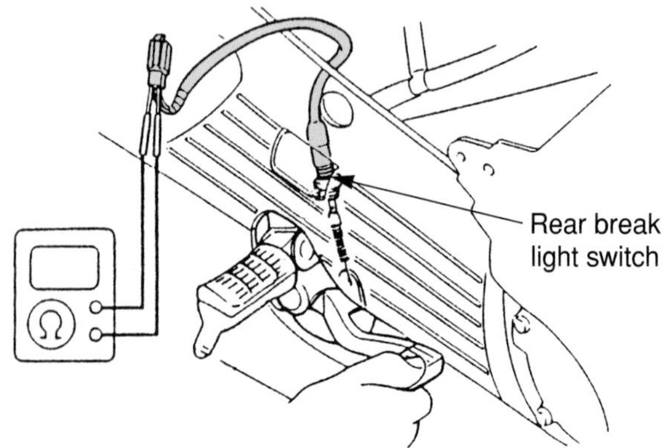

Figure 17-18. An ohmmeter can be used to check the rear brake light switch for continuity. (Honda Motor Co., Ltd.)

1. When the brake lever (or pedal) is depressed, there should be continuity between the terminals.
2. When the brake lever (or pedal) is released, there should be no continuity between the terminals.

If there is no continuity when the brake switch is closed, replace the switch. If the brake light switch is working, then check for the following:

- Burned fuse.
- Ignition switch.
- Poor connection at the fuse connector.
- Broken wire between the fuse and brake light switch.
- Broken wire between the brake light switch and brake light.

Directional Turn Signal Lights

If the turn signal does not blink, check the following:

- Battery charge.
- Fuse block for burned fuses.
- Bulb burned out.
- Correct wattage bulb.
- Bulb connector.
- Ignition and turn signal switch operation.

Should all these check normal and the flasher has two terminals or prongs, disconnect the connector from the flasher and short the connector with a jumper wire, **Figure 17-19A.** Turn the ignition switch on and check the turn signal light by turning the switch on.

If the turn signal lights do not come on, there is a broken wire in the harness. If the lights do come on, the flasher is faulty or there is a poor connection at the connector. When the turn signal flasher has three terminals or prongs, short the terminals with a jumper wire as before. If the light comes on, check for continuity between the points shown in **Figure 17-19B.** If there is continuity, either the flasher is faulty or there is a poor connection at the connector.

If the light(s) do not come on, there is a broken wire or other open in the harness. Occasionally, the flasher does not flash as fast as normal, or it flashes faster. Check for a burned-out bulb first if it flashes too fast or too slow. If all the bulbs are ok, replace the flasher. **Figure 17-20** indicates the location of various lights on a typical ATV.

Warning and Indicator Circuits

Motorcycles are equipped with a number of instrument gauges, lights, and warning indicators that provide the rider with valuable information concerning the operation of various vehicle systems. The devices are found on almost every instrument panel, whether analog or digital. The following is typical service required for the various warning and indicator circuits.

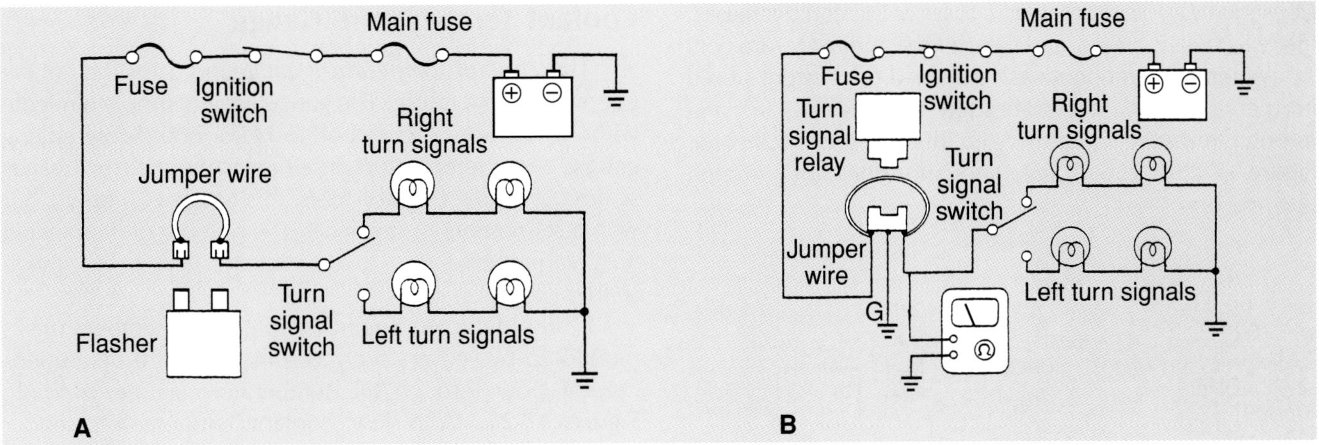

Figure 17-19. A—Checking a two-terminal flasher. B—Testing a three-terminal flasher. (Honda Motor Co., Ltd.)

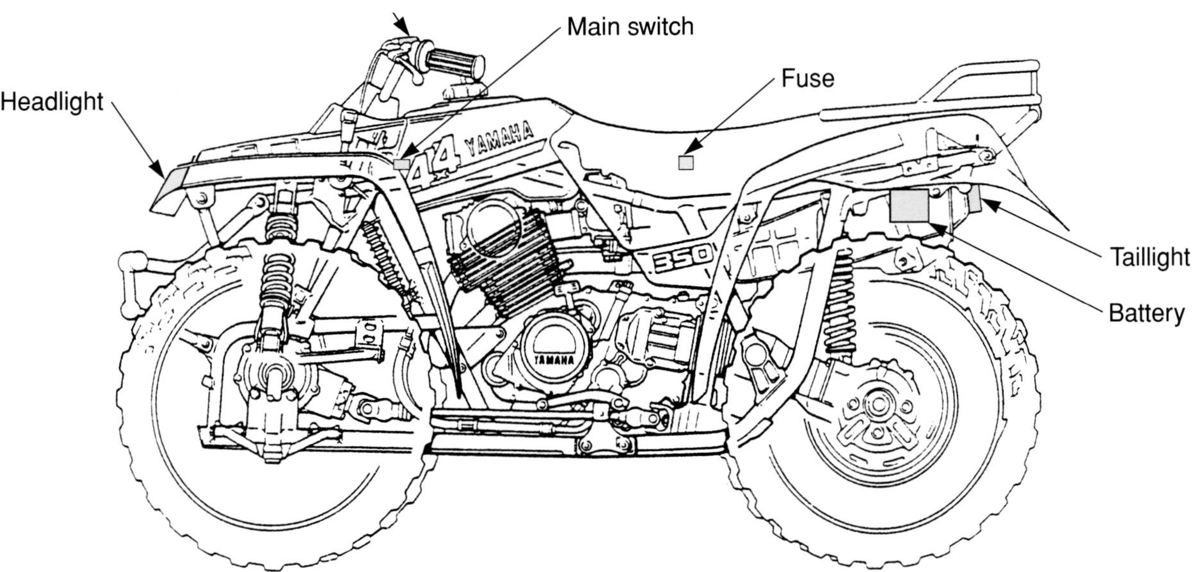

Figure 17-20. Typical ATV lighting system components. (Yamaha Motor Corporation U.S.A.)

Oil Pressure Warning Light (Four-stroke Engine)

The ***oil pressure warning light*** indicates low engine oil pressure, **Figure 17-21.** When oil pressure is below specifications, the oil pressure switch senses it and turns the warning light on. It should be off while the engine is running. If the oil pressure warning light does not come on with the ignition switch turned on, disconnect the oil pressure switch wire and turn the ignition on. Check the battery voltage between the switch wire and ground. If there is voltage, the oil pressure switch is faulty.

Should the light not come on, check for voltage between the warning light terminals. If there is no voltage, the ignition switch is faulty or the fuse has blown. If there is voltage, the bulb is blown or there is a broken wire between the warning light and the oil pressure switch. If the oil pressure light stays on while the engine is running, the problem is caused by low oil pressure or a faulty oil pressure switch. Check oil level.

Oil Level Indicator (Two-stroke Engine)

Most two-stroke engines are equipped with an ***oil level indicator.*** The oil level switch float in the oil tank moves up and down in relation to the volume of oil in the tank, **Figure 17-22.** When the oil level is low, the float also goes down and the reed switch (oil level switch) is closed by the float's magnetic force. When the ignition switch is turned on, current flows through the reed switch and the oil level indicator comes on.

Some two-stroke engines are equipped with a timer indicator with a bulb check function that checks the oil level indicator for proper operation. When the ignition switch is turned on, current flows through the excitor coil, to the condenser, generates the electromagnetic force at the excitor coil, and closes the reed switch, **Figure 17-23A.** Current flows from the reed switch through the resister R_2 to the oil level indicator and turns it on. When the condenser is fully charged, current flow through the excitor coil to the condenser decreases.

Consequently, electromagnetic force at the coil decreases, the reed switch opens, and the oil level indicator turns off.

When the ignition switch is turned off, current stored in the condenser flows through the excitor coil and through resisters R_1 and R_2 to the oil level indicator, **Figure 17-23B.** The oil level indicator does not come on this time.

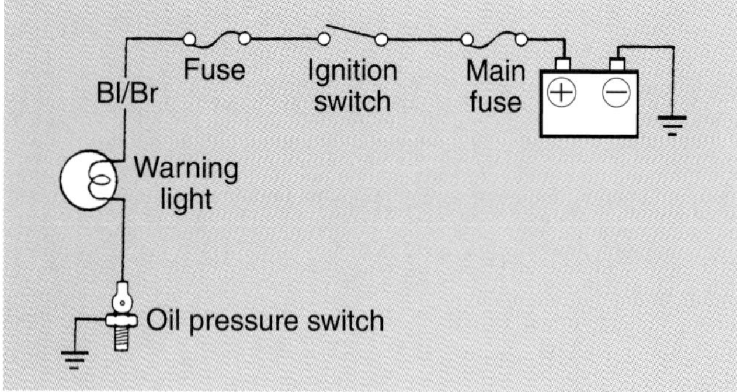

Figure 17-21. Simplified oil pressure warning light system found on many bikes with four-stroke engines. (Honda Motor Co., Ltd.)

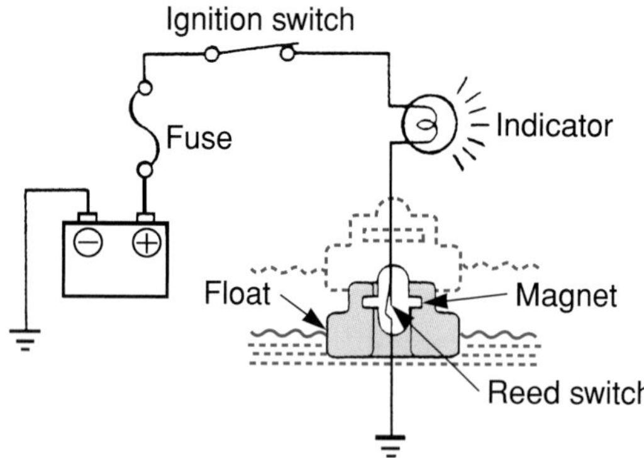

Figure 17-22. Typical oil level indicator found in two-stroke engine circuits. (Honda Motor Co., Ltd.)

Coolant Temperature Gauge

The ***coolant temperature gauge*** indicates the engine operating temperature. The gauge itself is simply a needle with a scale from *C* (for cool) to *H* (for hot). Some analog gauges show temperature in either Fahrenheit or Celsius scales. On some digital panels, this gauge is simply a bar with a set number of segments. The number of illuminated bars varies according to the voltage across the gauge sender.

In liquid-cooled engines, the coolant temperature is monitored by sensors such as a thermistor. It determines current flow through the temperature gauge winding, **Figure 17-24.** With low coolant temperature, sender resistance is high and current flow is low. The needle or segments point to *C*. As coolant temperature increases, sensor resistance decreases and current flow increases. The needle or illuminated segments move toward *H*.

To test a coolant temperature circuit, first measure for battery voltage at the ignition switch, the fuse, temperature gauge, and the thermo sensor. If voltage is found at all these points, check the sensor itself as follows.

1. Disconnect the wire from the temperature sensor and remove it from the system.
2. Suspend the sensor in a pan of coolant (50-50 mixture) over an electric heating element, **Figure 17-25.**
3. Measure the resistance through the sensor as the coolant heats up. More resistance should be indicated when the coolant is cold than when it is hot.

Fuel Level Gauges

Fuel level gauges indicate the fuel level in the fuel tank. It is a magnetic indicating system that can be found on both analog and digital instrument panels.

The fuel sender unit is combined with the fuel pump assembly and consists of a variable resistor controlled by

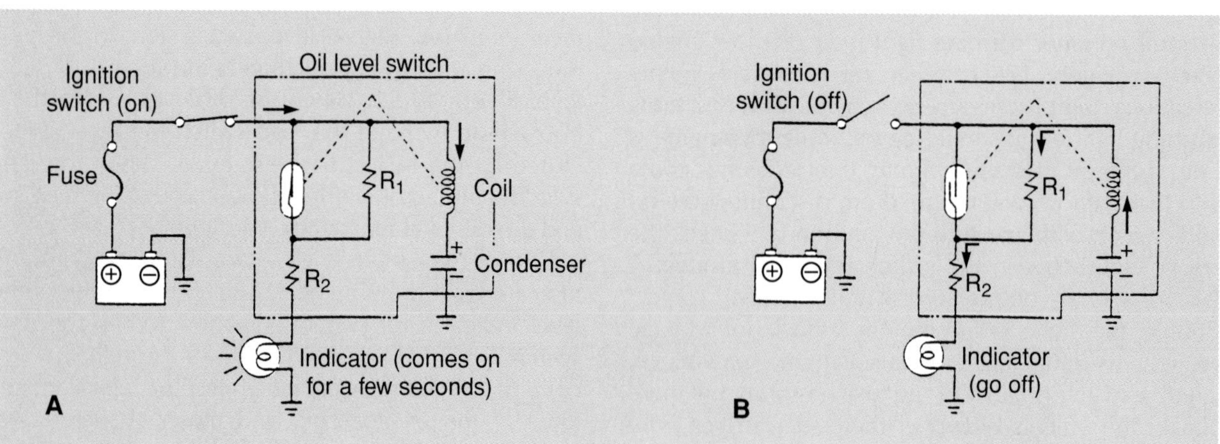

Figure 17-23. Operation of oil timer indicator. A—When the ignition switch is on, power flows and the oil light comes on. Unless the oil is low, the timer will shut off the light after a few seconds. B—Power is cut off from the circuit when the ignition switch is opened. (Honda Motor Co., Ltd.)

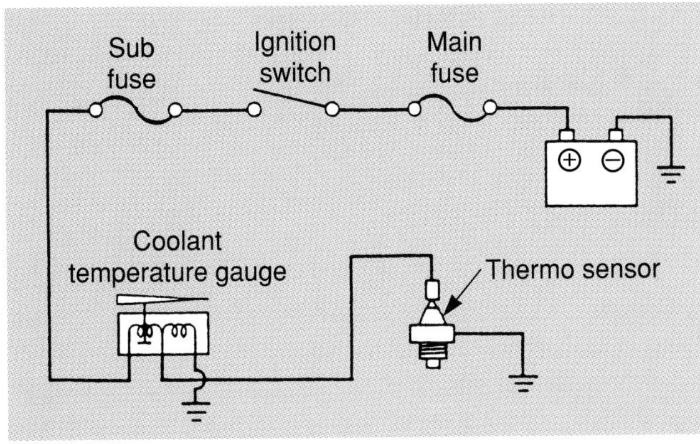

Figure 17-24. Typical coolant temperature gauge circuit. (Honda Motor Co., Ltd.)

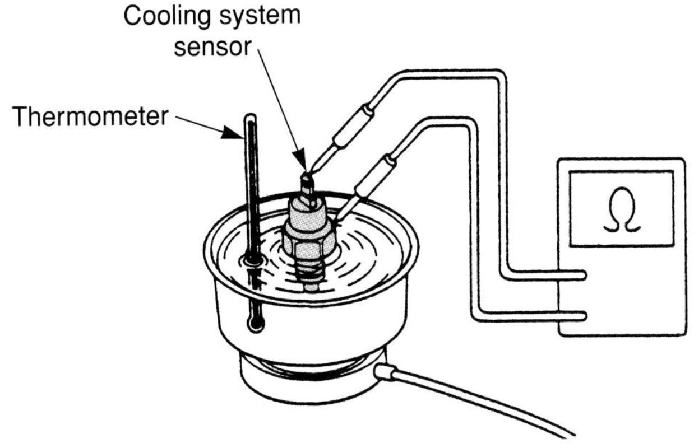

Figure 17-25. Method of testing a cooling system sensor. As the water heats, the sensor will lose resistance. (Honda Motor Co., Ltd.)

the level of an attached float in the fuel tank, **Figure 17-26.** When the fuel level is low, resistance in the sender is low and gauge indicator movement is minimal (from empty position). When the fuel level is high, the resistance is high in the sender and gauge indicator movement from the empty position is greater.

There are two types of fuel gauges: the return-type where the needle returns to empty when the ignition switch is turned off, and stop-type where the needle stays in position when the ignition switch is turned off.

Some motorcycles and scooters are equipped with a low fuel indicator rather than a gauge. In this system, a thermistor is built into the fuel tank and the fuel warning light turns on due to the thermistor's self-radiation of heat. When the thermistor is in the gasoline, heat radiation increases and the self-heating action is reduced. As the resistance increases and the current does not flow, the fuel warning light does not turn on.

When the thermistor is out of the gasoline, fuel level is low, radiation of heat decreases, and self-heating increases. As the resistance is low at this time, current flows and the low fuel indicator turns on.

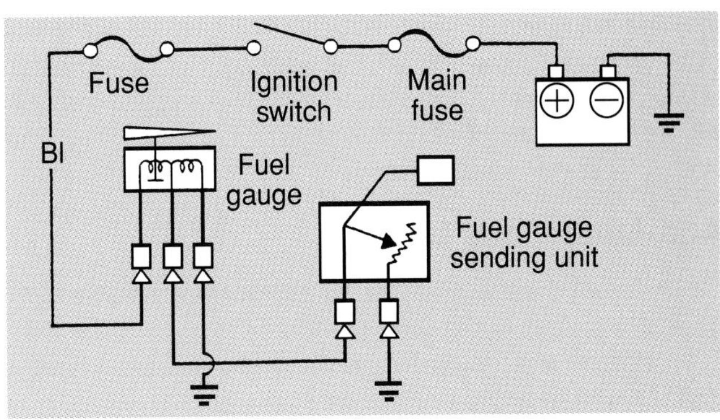

Figure 17-26. Typical two-terminal fuel level gauge hookup. (Honda Motor Co., Ltd.)

Brake Fluid Warning Light

The ***brake fluid warning light*** is connected to the brake fluid level sensor in the master cylinder reservoir. If brake fluid decreases to less than the specified volume in the reservoir, the sensor is actuated and the light comes on while the engine is running.

Charging Gauges

Charging gauges, which include ammeters and indicator lights, allow the rider to monitor the charging system. While a few bikes use a voltmeter, most charging systems employ either an ammeter gauge or an indicator light. The ammeter gauge is placed in series with the battery and alternator. When the alternator is delivering current to the battery, the gauge displays a positive *(+)* indication. When the battery is not receiving enough current (or none at all) from the alternator, a negative *(–)* display is obtained.

If a gauge is not used, a light may be employed to indicate the condition of the alternator and charging system. If there is something wrong with the alternator or charging system, the light may come on while the engine is running.

Check Engine Light

Some electronic control systems have a warning light that indicates the condition of the vehicle's electronic control systems. If there is a fault, a ***check engine light*** comes on while the engine is running. The check engine light may be triggered by the engine control computer that monitors engine systems and illuminates the warning light whenever it senses a fault. See Chapter 7 for more information.

Side Stand Indicator Light

On motorcycles equipped with a kickstarter there is a ***side stand indicator light*** on the instrument panel, **Figure 17-27.** When the side stand is lowered (parking position), the side stand switch detects the side angle, the indicator side contact is turned on (closed), and the indicator comes on, **Figure 17-28.** When the side stand is retracted, the indicator goes off.

Anti-Lock Brake Light

As mentioned in Chapter 15, the ***anti-lock brake light*** indicates a fault in the anti-lock brake system. If the ABS ECM detects a problem, it grounds the indicator circuit and the anti-lock light illuminates.

Speedometer

Motorcycle ***speedometers*** may be operated mechanically or electrically. The mechanical speedometer has a drive cable attached to the front wheel that turns a magnet inside a cup-shaped metal piece, **Figure 17-29.** The cup is attached to a speedometer needle and held at zero by a hairspring (a fine wire spring). As the cable rotates with increasing speed, magnetic forces act on the cup and force it to rotate. The speedometer needle, attached to the cup, moves up the speed scale.

In the electric (electronic) speedometer, the cable driven by the front wheel spins a small speed sensor. The sensor's voltage output increases as wheel speed increases. This voltage output is converted to a digital readout on the instrument panel. The higher the sensor voltage out, the higher the digital reading.

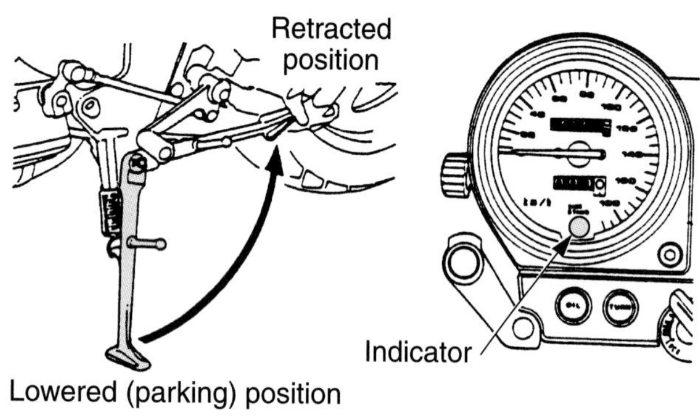

Figure 17-27. Operation and location of side stand indicator light. (Honda Motor Co., Ltd.)

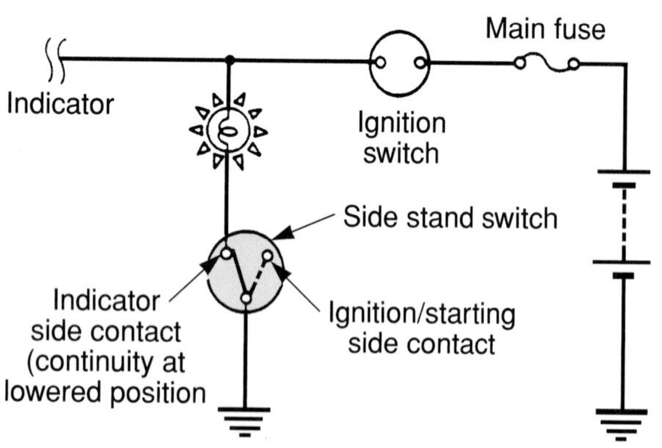

Figure 17-28. Side stand electrical circuit. The switch is closed when the side stand is lowered. (Honda Motor Co., Ltd.)

Tachometer

While the speedometer shows the vehicle speed, the ***tachometer*** indicates the engine's rpm (engine speed). Using a balanced coil gauge or sensor, the tachometer converts electrical impulses received from the engine to an rpm reading. The faster the engine rotates, the greater the number of impulses from the engine and consequently, the greater the indicated rpm. The tachometer is usually placed next to the speedometer on most conventional control panels.

Switches

Switches can be tested for continuity with an ohmmeter or a test light at the switch connector plug by operating positions and comparing results with the switch operation.

There are many switches in the electrical system of a motorcycle. Many of them, main switch, clutch switch, engine stop switch, brake switch, dimmer switch, fan motor switch, turn signal switch, neutral switch, and passing switch, have been described in this or previous chapters. Therefore, let us take a look at a circuit that contains a very important switch, the horn button.

Horn Circuit

The ***horn circuit*** consists of a horn button (switch), fuse, wires, ignition switch, and horn. When the ignition switch is turned on, power is supplied to the horn. When the horn button is pushed, the circuit is completed to ground and the horn honks. Most horns have an adjustment screw to clear the tone.

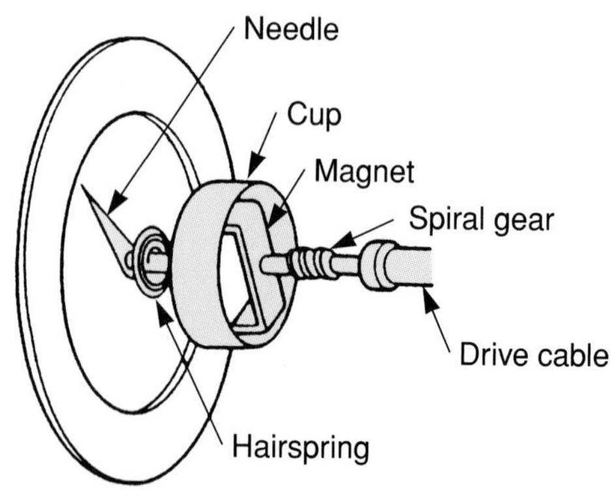

Figure 17-29. Components of an analog speedometer.

If the horn does not sound, check the fuse, the ignition switch, and the horn switch. If the voltage is normal, disconnect the wire from the horn. Turn the ignition switch on, press the horn switch (or start the engine and press the horn switch if the motorcycle does not use a battery) and check for voltage between point A, **Figure 17-30,** and ground. If there is voltage, check for continuity between point B and ground. The horn is faulty if continuity is established between these two points. If there is no voltage at point A, the wire from the horn switch and horn is open.

Fuse
Ignition switch
Main fuse
Horn switch
A
B
Horn

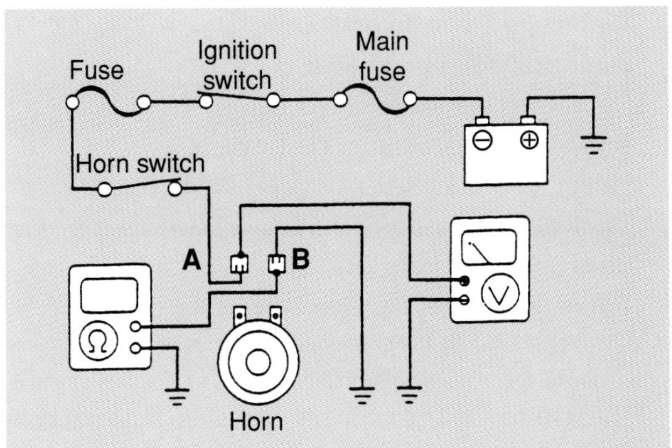

Figure 17-30. Troubleshooting a horn circuit, while simple, requires the use of a schematic. (Honda Motor Co., Ltd.)

Communication Systems

The modern cruiser and touring motorcycles are available with such ***communication systems*** as AM/FM radio, cassette or CD players, CB radio, cellular phones, and intercoms between the rider and passenger. Some newer bike helmets have built-in audio speaker systems with automatic volume control that automatically adjusts to the motorcycle's speed and outside noise.

Internal examination of electrical equipment should be left to an authorized communication service center. However, the motorcycle technician should be able to analyze and isolate radio reception conditions to the area or component causing the problem. All communication conditions can be isolated to one of five areas. The trouble will be found in the antenna system, unit chassis (receiver), speakers, noise suppression device(s), or sound system.

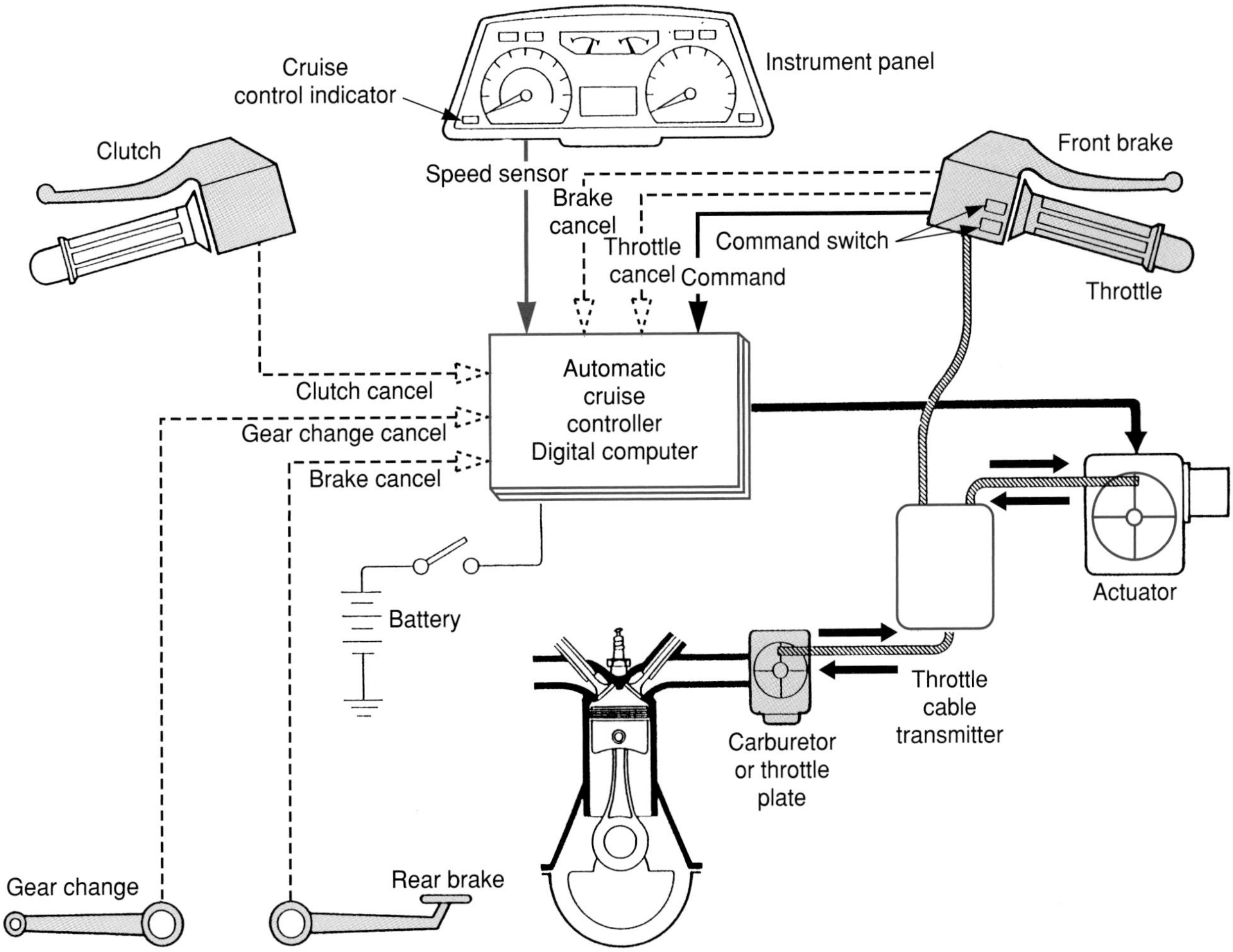

Cruise control indicator
Instrument panel
Clutch
Speed sensor
Brake cancel
Throttle cancel
Command
Command switch
Front brake
Throttle
Automatic cruise controller Digital computer
Clutch cancel
Gear change cancel
Brake cancel
Battery
Actuator
Throttle cable transmitter
Carburetor or throttle plate
Gear change
Rear brake

Figure 17-31. Components for a typical cruise control system. (American Suzuki Motor Corporation)

AM/FM radio operation requires only the power from the fuse panel to be available at the radio. The radio intercepts broadcast signals with its antenna and produces a corresponding input to the system speaker. In addition, some radios have built-in memory circuits to ensure the radio returns to the previously selected station when the radio or ignition switch is turned off and back on again. Some of these memory circuits require full-time power input from the battery. The current draw is very small and requires no more power than a digital clock (usually no more than .2 mA). However, if battery power is removed, the memory circuit usually has to be reset.

The service manual and owner's guide for the vehicle equipped with this sophisticated gear will contain detailed information concerning its operation. If the system is not working, check the fuse. If the fuses are okay, refer to the service manual. Remember, the receiver itself should only be serviced by a qualified technician or specialty service shop. If you determine the unit itself is the problem, remove and send the unit to a qualified person.

Cruise Control

Another accessory system found on some cruiser and touring motorcycles is a ***cruise control*** or *speed control* system. Such an electronic system is designed to allow the rider to maintain a constant speed (usually above 30 mph or 48 kph) without having to apply continual pressure on the twist grip. Selected cruise speeds are easily maintained and speed can be easily changed. Several override systems also allow the vehicle to be accelerated, slowed, or stopped. Because of constant changes and improvements in technology, each cruise control system may be considerably different. For this reason, be sure to check the specific service manual before attempting any service.

The typical cruise control system shown in **Figure 17-31** is designed to maintain any speed between 30-80 mph (48-128 kph) in overdrive (5th gear). The cruising speed can be set and then adjusted to a faster or slower speed by the control switch. Once a speed has been set, the resume function can be used to return to the set speed.

This system contains a control module, actuator, and sensor (speed sensor). When the cruise is activated, the speed sensor sends a signal indicating vehicle speed to the control module. The control module memorizes the set speed and controls the actuator to operate the throttle accelerator cable to keep vehicle speed at or near the set speed.

The actuator contains an electromagnetic clutch, a pulley drive motor, and a cable pulley. The cable pulley is ordinarily free from the pulley drive motor. It is engaged with the motor by the electromagnetic clutch when the cruise control is set. At the same time, the motor moves the pulley and operates the throttle cable. When the cruise control is canceled, the pulley is disengaged from the motor and returned back to the original position with its spring.

The throttle cable assembly has the junction box in the middle so the throttle pulley can be controlled by the actuator beside the throttle grip. The cruise control can usually be canceled by the rider performing one of the following operations:

- Turning off the ignition switch.
- Turning off the engine stop switch.
- Turning off the main switch.
- Pulling the front brake lever.
- Depressing the rear brake pedal.
- Turning on the starter lockout switch.
- Pulling the clutch lever.
- Turning off the overdrive (5th gear) switch.
- Changing gears from 5th.
- Turning off any of the cancel switches (throttle, front brake, or rear brake).
- Closing the throttle grip completely.

The cruise control will be canceled automatically under the following conditions:

- Blown cruise control circuit fuse.
- Losing more than 5 mph (8 kph) from the set speed.
- Running below 27 mph (43 kph).
- Running above 89 mph (142 kph).
- No signal from the speed sensor.

Summary

In order for the motorcycle, ATV, or scooter to be functional, it needs other systems besides the powertrain, frame, brake, and suspension systems. The accessory systems are the grouping of electrical and electronic circuits that make up lighting circuits, warning and indicator circuits, switch circuits, communication systems, and the cruise control.

A motorcycle's lighting system usually consists of headlight, tail light, brake light, directional turn signals, warning lights, and instrument illumination. There are two types of lighting systems used on bikes; ac lighting that receives power from the alternator coil, and dc lighting that is powered by the battery. There are several types of headlight bulbs used. The most common is the two light sealed beam tungsten headlight bulb. In recent years, halogen bulbs have become increasingly popular. The headlight beam is adjustable both horizontally and vertically. Headlight aiming must be correctly adjusted for safe riding as well as for oncoming riders.

Most state laws require that tail lights on street vehicles be dc powered so they will remain on, even if the engine stalls. The taillight lens assembly also provides license plate illumination as required by law for street bikes. On some street motorcycles, the tail light acts as a parking light. The brake light comes on when the brake lever (or pedal) is applied. Brake light and tail light bulbs may be either single filament or twin (double) filament. The turn signal indicator light circuit normally includes four turn signal bulbs, two indicator bulbs, a flasher (turn signal relay), switches, and wiring. There are various instrument panel designs and layouts. The two types of instrument panel displays are analog and digital.

Motorcycles are equipped with a number of instrument gauges, lights, and warning indicators that provide the rider with valuable information concerning the operation of various vehicle systems. The oil pressure warning light indicates low engine oil pressure. Most two-stroke engines are equipped with an oil level indicator. The oil level switch float in the oil tank moves up and down in accordance with the volume of oil in the tank. Some two-stroke engines have a timer indicator equipped with a bulb check function that checks the oil level indicator for proper operation.

The coolant temperature gauge indicates the engine operating temperature. Fuel level gauges indicate the fuel level in the fuel tank. The brake fluid warning light is connected to the brake fluid level sensor in the master cylinder reservoir. Charging gauges, which include ammeters and indicator lights, allow the rider to monitor the charging system. Some electronic control systems have a check engine light that indicates the condition of the vehicle's electronic control systems. A side stand indicator light on the instrument panel tells if the side stand is extended. The anti-lock brake light indicates a fault in the anti-lock brake system.

Motorcycle speedometers may be operated mechanically or electrically. While the speedometer shows the vehicle speed, the tachometer indicates the engine's speed. Switches can be tested for continuity with an ohmmeter or a test light at the switch connector plug. The modern cruiser and touring motorcycles are available with such communication systems as AM/FM radio, CB radio, cassette or CD players, cellular phones, and intercoms between the rider and passenger. Another accessory system found on some cruiser and touring motorcycles is a cruise control system.

Know These Terms

Accessory system
Sealed beam tungsten headlight bulb
Halogen bulbs
Dimmer switch
Tail lights
Brake light
Turn signal indicator light
Turn signal flasher
Turn signal canceling device
Four-way hazard signal
Instrument panel
Analog display
Digital display
Oil pressure warning light
Oil level indicator
Coolant temperature gauge
Fuel level gauges
Brake fluid warning light
Charging gauges
Check engine light
Side stand indicator light
Anti-lock brake light
Speedometers
Tachometer
Switches
Horn circuit
Communication systems
Cruise control

Review Questions—Chapter 17

Do not write in this text. Place your answers on a separate sheet of paper.

1. List the two types of lighting systems.
2. Dc lighting takes power from the ______.
   A. alternator coil
   B. ignition system
   C. electronic module
   D. battery
3. To adjust the headlight, the motorcycle should be _____ from the aiming wall.
   A. 25′ (7.62 m)
   B. 3′ (.914 m)
   C. 30′ (9.14 m)
   D. 250′ (76.20 m)
4. The headlight beam is adjustable both horizontally and vertically, this is not only for the rider to see but also _____.
   A. for oncoming drivers
   B. to ensure correct tire pressure
   C. to check the bike for proper ride height
   D. None of the above.
5. Most state laws require that the tail lights on street vehicles be _____ powered so they remain on even if the engine stalls.
6. Twin filaments are usually employed in what lighting arrangement?
   A. Brake light and turn signals.
   B. License plate and headlight.
   C. Tail light and brake light.
   D. Headlight and turn signal.
7. List the three areas of illumination for the rear light of the motorcycle.
8. List the two types of instrument panel displays.
9. These gauges indicate the fuel volume in the fuel tank. They are called _____ gauges.
10. Two types of gauges are digital and _____.

11. Most charging systems employ _____.
    A. a gauge
    B. an indicator light
    C. computerized self-diagnostics
    D. Both A & B.
12. List two reasons the check engine light may be triggered.
13. Speedometers may only be operated ______.
    A. mechanically.
    B. electrically.
    C. hydraulically.
    D. Both A & B.
14. When the ABS light comes on, it means ______.
    A. the anti-lock braking system is being employed
    B. the self-diagnostic system has detected a system failure
    C. the ABS system is working properly
    D. None of the above.
15. Cruise control will automatically disengage when the rider ______.
    A. applies the brakes
    B. applies the clutch
    C. turns off the ignition switch
    D. All of the above.

Suggested Activities

1. Following the procedures given in the manufacturer's service manual, check the headlight alignment on a randomly selected motorcycle, and compare the results to the specifications given for that vehicle. If the headlight alignment (either high beam or low beam or both) does not meet specifications, follow the procedures and realign the light.
2. Using the appropriate diagnostic equipment, inspect the electrical system of a randomly selected motorcycle to determine its safety and reliability. If any faults are discovered, take corrective action.

18 Engine and Power Transmission Disassembly

After studying this chapter, you will be able to:

- Use the specific instructions in a shop service manual to remove and disassemble an engine.
- Use the specific instructions in a shop service manual to remove and disassemble the primary drive, transmission, and final drive.
- Disconnect the electrical system, control cables, and other parts fastened to the frame.
- Remove and mount engine on a stand or box.
- Organize wires, shims, and other parts properly during disassembly.
- Explain the use of special holding and pulling devices.
- Describe the use of heat to aid disassembly.
- List typical problems encountered during engine and primary drive disassembly.

This chapter discusses the importance of organization and correct procedures during the removal and disassembly of a motorcycle engine, primary drive, transmission, and final drive. It also covers special disassembly methods and common problems you may encounter.

Preparing for Engine Removal

Always organize the work area before starting. Proper work area organization is essential. A little extra effort and care during teardown can help avoid problems later. A mistake during reassembly (wrong bolt, shim, spring, or tool) can cause severe engine, primary drive, and/or transmission damage. You might have to do the repair over again, at your expense.

Clear the work area of parts from any other jobs you may be working on. Keep these parts together with the bike(s) they came from. Secure enough boxes, trays, and other holding containers to avoid mixing the parts from more than one bike. If needed, obtain or free a stand that will support the bike's weight.

A professional, high quality repair is much easier to do in a clean, orderly work area. The work area should also have sufficient lighting and ventilation. The work area cleanliness and condition reflects upon your work habits and mechanical ability. A sloppy work area indicates a sloppy worker.

Clean the Vehicle

Before beginning work, it is important to clean the motorcycle, scooter, or ATV thoroughly. This makes parts removal and disassembly a much cleaner and safer job. Shown in **Figure 18-1,** an engine degreaser and pressure washer or steam cleaner makes cleaning easier. However, before using a pressure washer or steam cleaner, check with state or local authorities as to any regulations regarding waste water disposal.

Note: Remember the smallest particle of dirt can easily ruin engine bearings, cylinders, oil pumps, and the job.

Figure 18-1. Degreasing and pressure washing makes engine removal easier and less messy. External cleaning only takes a few minutes, but check local regulations for any restrictions.

Be careful with cleaning solutions as some can damage painted surfaces. Cover all electronic components, carburetor, alternator, and ignition system. Be sure to clean the engine in a well-ventilated area, especially when using steam. Apply the degreaser and wait a few minutes for deposits to soften. Then, spray down the bike and inspect. Repeat as needed to completely clean the engine and bike.

Is Engine Removal Necessary?

It is not always necessary to remove the engine for service. Check the engine carefully as removal is a time-intensive job. Engine removal is usually necessary for:

- Complete engine overhaul.
- Top-end overhaul.
- Bottom-end repairs.
- Transmission repair.
- Exterior damage (crash related).

Before unbolting the engine, you must know exactly what is wrong. If engine removal can be avoided, it will reduce the time the bike is in your shop.

Read the Service Manual

Before beginning disassembly, read the proper sections of a shop service manual for the particular motorcycle being repaired. This will allow you to gather the necessary tools and review disassembly procedures. In addition, the service manual gives information on:

- Which way the engine comes out of the frame.
- The location of engine mounting bolts.
- Which cables, linkages, and electrical wires must be disconnected.
- Whether or not any engine accessory components must be removed.
- The procedure for disconnecting the final drive.

For example, avoid lifting the engine halfway out of the frame and realizing that something is still connected. This mistake is often the result of not reading the service manual.

Drain Fluids

It is much easier to drain all fluids, including engine and transmission oils and engine coolant (on some bikes) before the engine is removed, **Figure 18-2.** Removing all the fluids before engine removal will reduce the chance of spillage.

After draining the oil, inspect the oil filter for debris. Debris lodged in the oil filter may hint as to the engine's condition as well as any problems, such as bearing and component damage. Refer to the service manual for oil filter screen removal procedures. Dry sump lubrication systems must be drained and disconnected before the engine can be removed. On two-stroke cycle engines using oil injection, the feed line must be disconnected and plugged. Also check the engine oil for signs of coolant contamination, which will give the oil a milky appearance and the consistency of a milkshake.

Drain the cooling system on liquid-cooled bikes next. Again, check the coolant for signs of oil contamination, which will show up as oil spots or even some milk-like residue. Some coolant will remain in the engine, so watch for and clean any spilled coolant after engine removal.

Disconnect Electrical System

Always remove the battery during engine removal. This prevents accidental shorting, damage to the electrical

Figure 18-2. Engine oil, as well as coolant if used, should be drained prior to engine removal.

system, and possibly an electrical fire. **Figure 18-3** illustrates proper battery removal. To remove the battery, turn off the ignition switch. Then remove the terminal cover and disconnect the negative *(–)* battery cable, followed by the positive *(+)* cable.

Caution: Disconnecting the positive cable first could result in an accidental short between the two terminals or the positive terminal and ground if the tool used to disconnect the terminal contacts the frame. Always disconnect the negative battery cable first.

For conventional batteries, always disconnect the vent or breather tube. Remember that some electrolyte may remain in the tube. Slide the battery out of its compartment and remove it from the motorcycle's frame.

Electrical and Wiring Disconnects

There are three types of wire disconnects used in motorcycle electrical systems.

- Plug-in connector (many wires in a single keyed plug).
- Individual male-female connectors (bullet or spade types).
- Eyelet and forked connectors (connected by bolt or screw).

Figure 18-4 shows three typical types of electrical connectors. Mark what each connection is for and remove from the engine or bike as appropriate. Make sure all wiring harnesses are positioned out of the way, as they can interfere with engine removal.

As mentioned in Chapter 5, all motorcycle manufacturers use color coded electrical wires. In almost all cases, the wire has the same color pattern before and after a plug socket. This makes proper wire connection easy. **Figure 18-5** illustrates typical wire color coding.

On older motorcycles, the color coding may be faded or the wires may have been replaced. When wires are not properly coded or if they are faded, label each wire as it is disconnected. This ensures proper connection during reassembly.

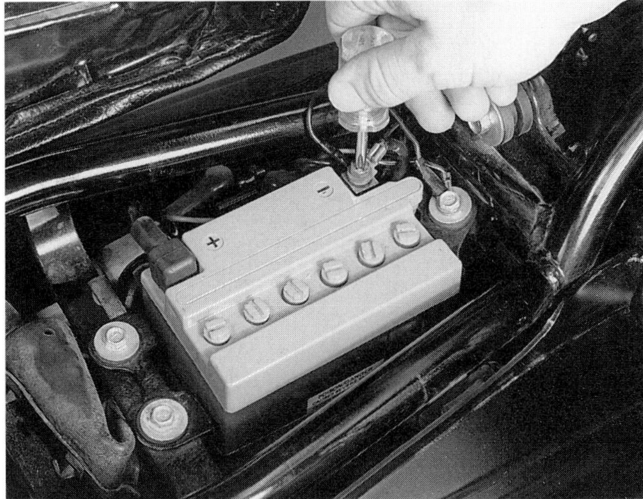

Figure 18-3. When removing a battery, always disconnect the ground side first. If you were to disconnect the positive side first, the screwdriver or wrench might touch the frame. This would cause a short circuit, which could ignite explosive battery gas.

Disconnect Control Cables

Control cable disconnection varies from motorcycle to motorcycle, depending on its application, **Figure 18-6.** Cables which may require disconnection for engine removal are:

- Clutch cable.
- Tachometer cable.
- Throttle cables.
- Oil injection pump cable (two-stroke engine).
- Enrichment-choke cables.
- Compression release cable.
- Rear brake cable (certain motorcycles).

Be sure to mark the function of each cable as it is removed. This will ensure proper reassembly.

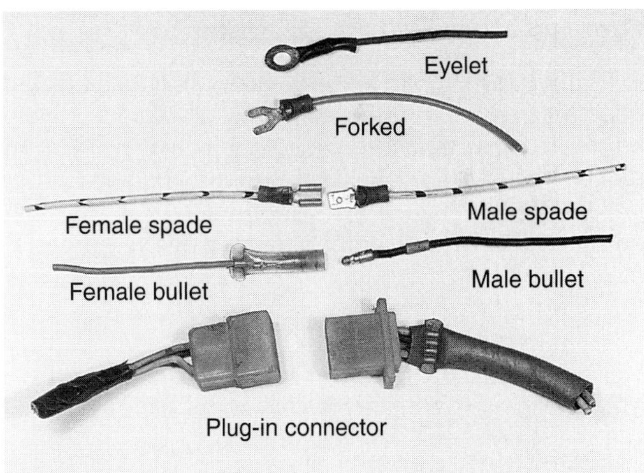

Figure 18-4. These are common types of connectors used in motorcycle electrical systems.

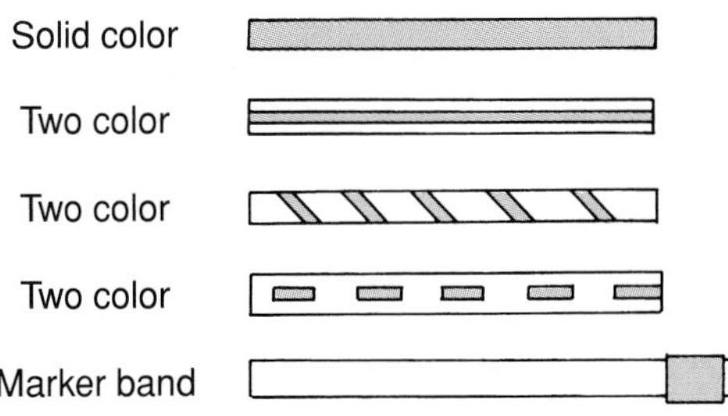

Figure 18-5. Color coding is used to identify individual wires in electrical system.

Fuel System Disassembly

In many cases, removing the fuel tank will ease engine removal. Sometimes, tank removal is necessary to obtain clearance for the engine. Either drain the tank or shut off the fuel flow to the engine before tank removal.

Carburetor Removal

Carburetor removal is usually necessary during engine removal. The service manual lists exact procedures for removal. The carburetors could be damaged if left installed during engine removal, **Figure 18-7.** Carburetors may be mounted to the engine in a number of ways. They may be mounted independently or together in a unit. A sleeve, spigot, or flange is used to attach the carburetor or carburetors to the engine.

It is important to drain the fuel from the float bowls and store the carburetors properly. This reduces the risk of fire or damage to the carburetors, motorcycle, shop area, or injury to yourself. When the engine is being removed for a complete overhaul, the carburetors should be rebuilt. Chapter 7 outlines procedures for carburetor rebuilding.

Fuel Injection System Disassembly

Other than removing fuel lines, it is usually not necessary to remove the fuel injectors before engine removal. However, in some cases, you may want to remove the injectors to ensure they are not damaged or become contaminated. Mark each injector so they can be reinstalled in the appropriate cylinder. In all cases, make sure the fuel system is drained or secured so fuel does not spill.

Disconnect Final Drive

On a motorcycle using a chain drive, the chain should be removed, cleaned, inspected, lubricated, and stored. On motorcycles using shaft drive, refer to the service manual for proper disconnection methods. Procedures vary from motorcycle to motorcycle.

Removing Engine from Motorcycle

Carelessness in removing engine mounting bolts can result in injury. Make sure the engine is properly braced before the bolts are removed. See **Figure 18-8.** Double-check the bike is secure before removing the engine. Not only are engines very heavy, they can be clumsy.

Figure 18-7. On some motorcycles, the air box must be removed in order to remove the carburetors.

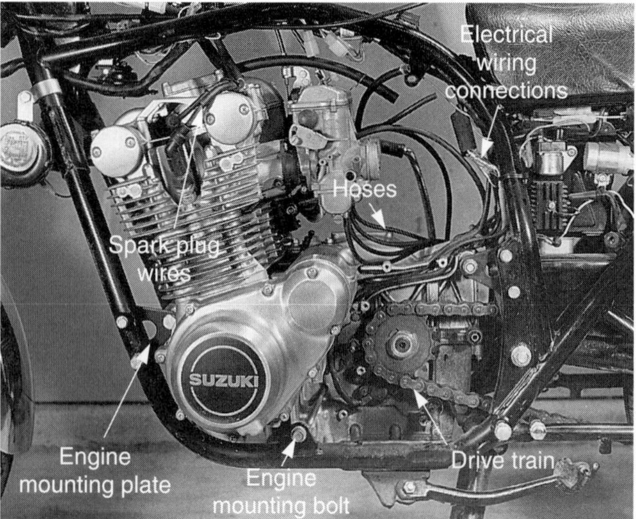

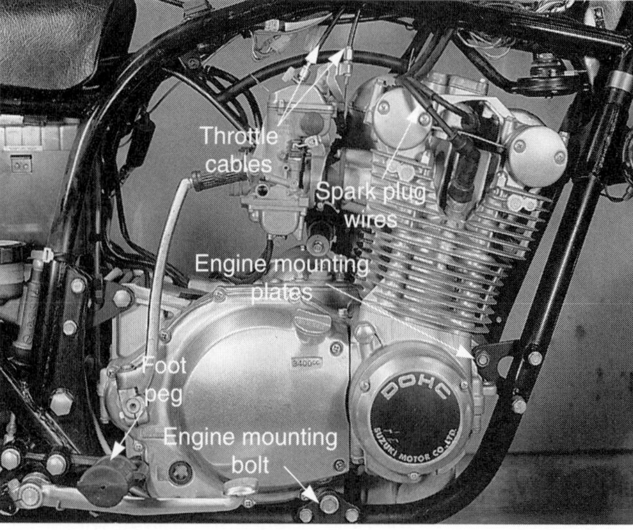

Figure 18-6. Typical components that must be disconnected prior to engine removal.

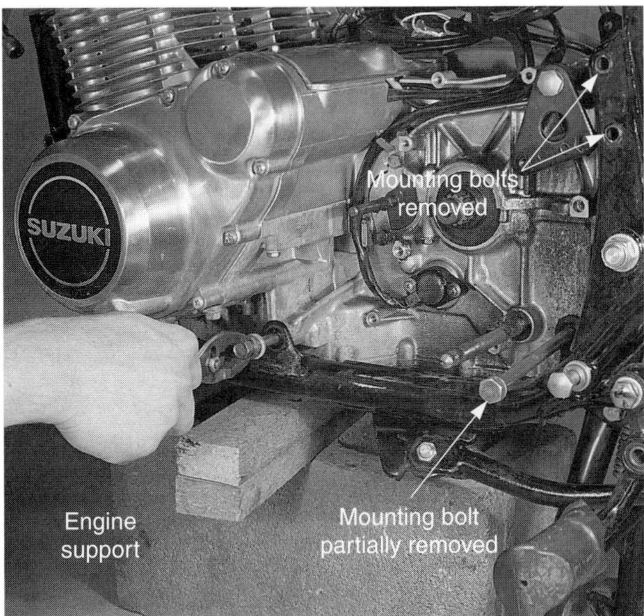

Figure 18-8. A sturdy, secure engine brace should be used while removing the engine mounting bolts. If not, engine case damage or bodily injury could result.

Note: It may be necessary to lift the engine slightly to ease removal of the last mounting bolt, Figure 18-9.

Make a note showing the location and position of ground wires, spacers, and mounting brackets. These components will be replaced on the frame after the engine is removed. This will help avoid reassembly confusion and loss of parts. Components may block removal on the right or left side of the frame. Make sure you know the correct removal direction. Some engines will only come out in one direction.

Double-check that all parts (wires, cables, hoses, exhaust system), fastened between the engine and frame are disconnected. Also, make sure everything that might block engine removal is out of the way. Parts can be damaged very easily when lifting a motorcycle engine out of the frame. The service manual will explain how the engine should be lifted, turned, tipped, and removed from the motorcycle.

Follow Safety Rules

To keep engine removal a safe operation:

- Use a jack when necessary.
- Use at least two people when removing engines.
- All tools should be carefully organized.
- Oil, coolant, or fuel spills should be wiped up immediately.
- An engine box or stand should be readied.

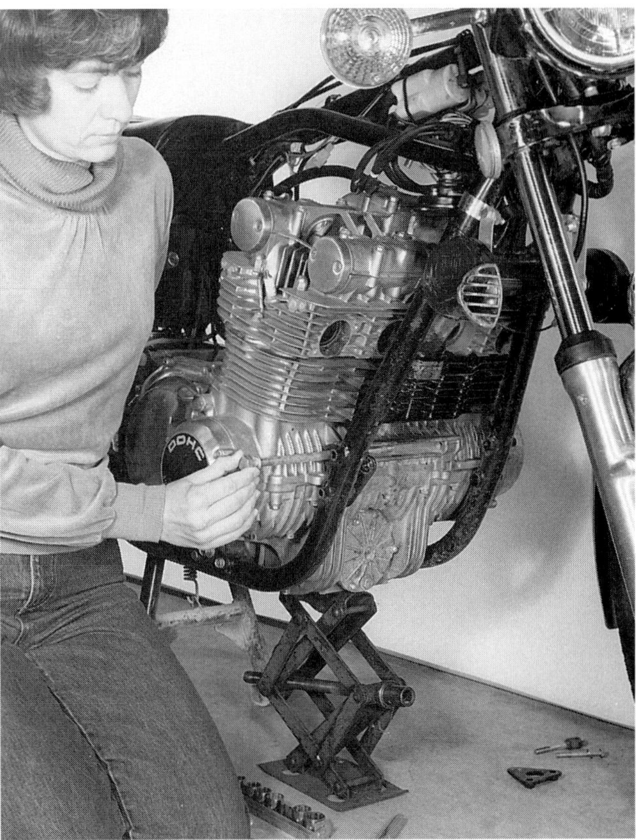

Figure 18-9. It may be necessary to use a jack to lift and support the engine while removing mounting bolts.

Engine Stand

Once the engine is out of the frame, install it on an ***engine stand,*** **Figure 18-10.** The stand will steady the engine and provides easy access to different areas. It allows the engine to be rotated and held in various positions while working. **Figure 18-11** shows a motorcycle engine mounted on an engine stand. If an engine stand is not available, a homemade ***engine box*** should be used. Make sure a homemade box is strong enough to support the engine's weight fully assembled. An engine box is shown in **Figure 18-12.**

Engine Removal Summary

The following engine removal summary can be used as a guide to carry out engine removal in proper sequence.

1. Clean the work area.
2. Clean and degrease the motorcycle exterior.
3. Check service manual for direction of engine removal, mounting bolt locations, and sequence for disassembly (specific).
4. Drain fluids.
5. Remove battery.

6. Disconnect engine electrical connectors.
7. Remove carburetor(s) or fuel injectors, drain fuel, and store properly.
8. Disconnect control cables.
9. Disconnect exhaust system and store system properly.
10. Disconnect final drive.
11. Brace the engine and remove mounting bolts.
12. Prepare an engine box or stand.
13. Lift engine out of the frame and install on an engine box or stand.
14. Replace mounting bolts and brackets on frame.

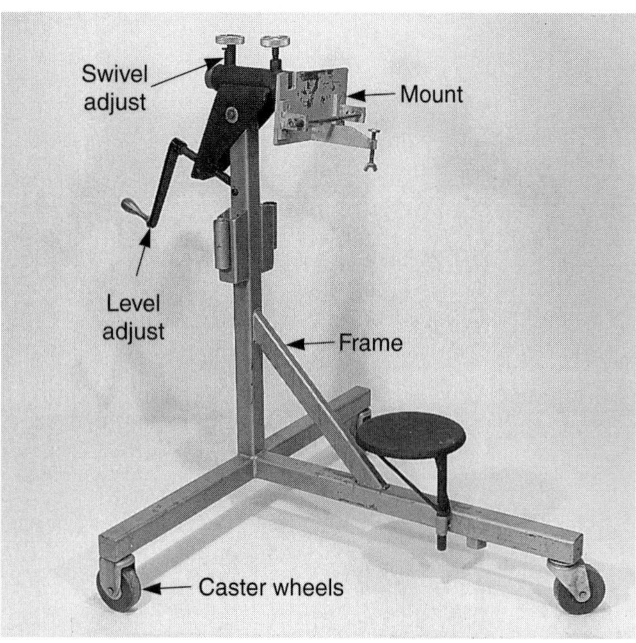

Figure 18-10. Parts of a typical engine stand.

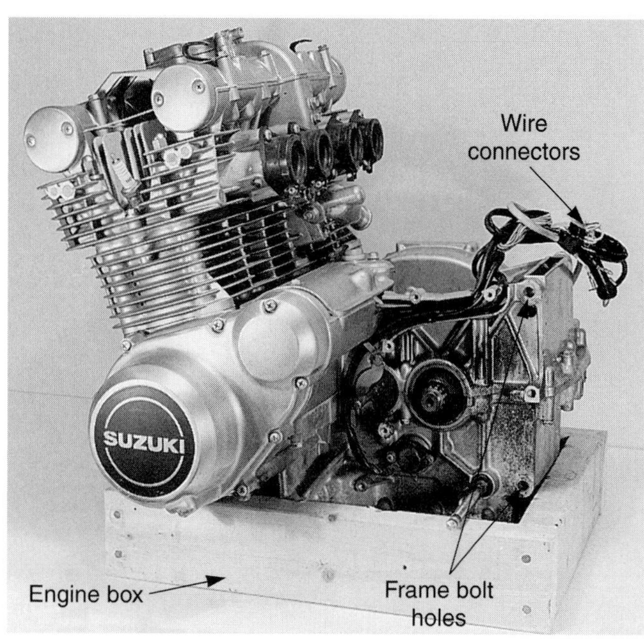

Figure 18-12. If an engine stand is not available, use an engine box. For safety, the engine should be placed in a box or on an engine stand as soon as it is removed from the frame.

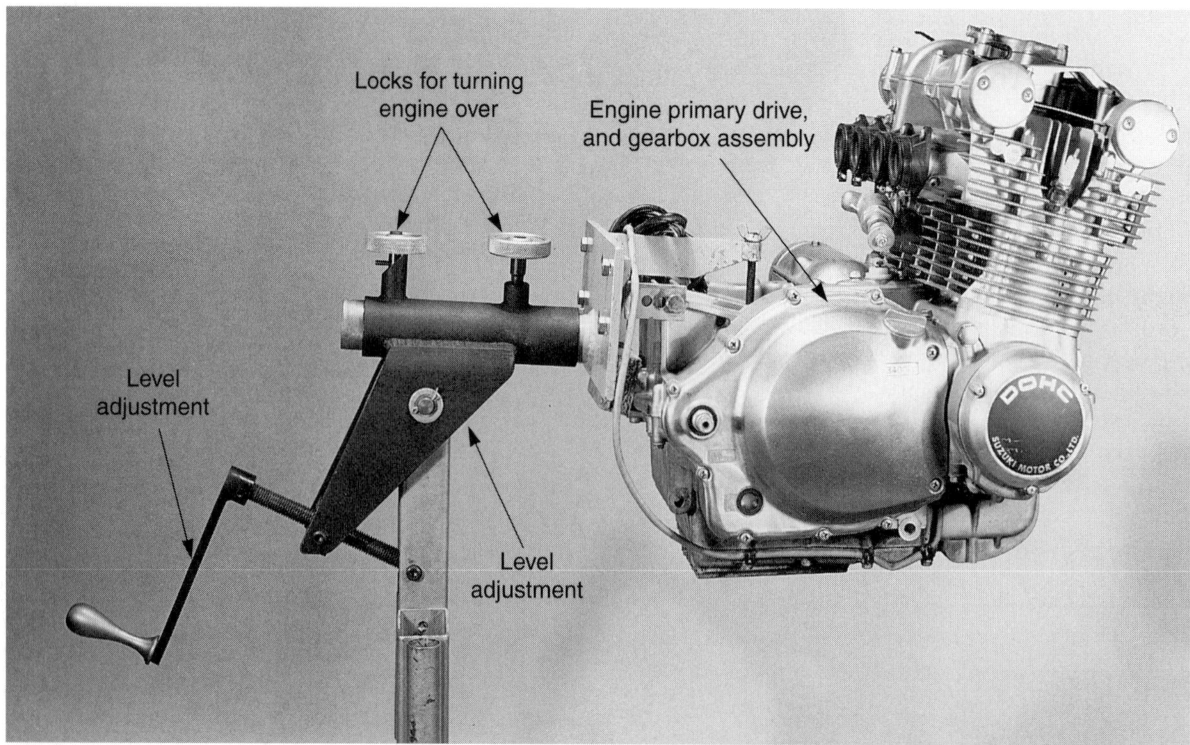

Figure 18-11. An engine stand allows the engine to swivel into various positions for easy access. The stand and engine will also roll easily to other locations in the shop.

Organize Parts

As parts are removed, be sure to keep them in an orderly arrangement. Place all mounting bolts back in their proper locations. At this time, the frame can be more thoroughly cleaned, stored out of the way, and the paint touched up later.

Storage Containers

During engine disassembly, it is important to keep groups of related parts together. This may be done by using plastic bags, plastic containers, small metal pans, cans, and cardboard boxes. See **Figure 18-13.** Orderly part and bolt storage saves time and effort during reassembly.

Tags and Markings

When disassembling an engine for the first time, you should place ***tags*** or ***markings*** on parts to aid reassembly. Mark any part that could be easily mixed up. Never rely on your memory when working on an engine assembly. For example, if two wires are crossed during reassembly, part damage could result. Place tags on wires noting their location or connection point.

Engine Fasteners

The assorted bolts, nuts, screws, and other fasteners that secure engine parts vary in size, length, and shape. These fasteners should be kept organized. If bolt lengths are mixed up, for example, thread or part damage can occur. Two methods are commonly used to keep fasteners organized:

- Draw a picture illustrating the position of each screw or bolt (measure length of each).
- Make a pattern board of screw and bolt locations as in **Figure 18-14.**

Mating Parts

Because mating parts rub against each other during engine operation, they develop certain wear patterns. If mating parts are to be reused, they must be assembled in the same position during reassembly. This eliminates the development of a new and different wear pattern. Failure to properly organize and tag mating parts during engine disassembly may lead to premature wear, leakage, and excessive clearance between parts.

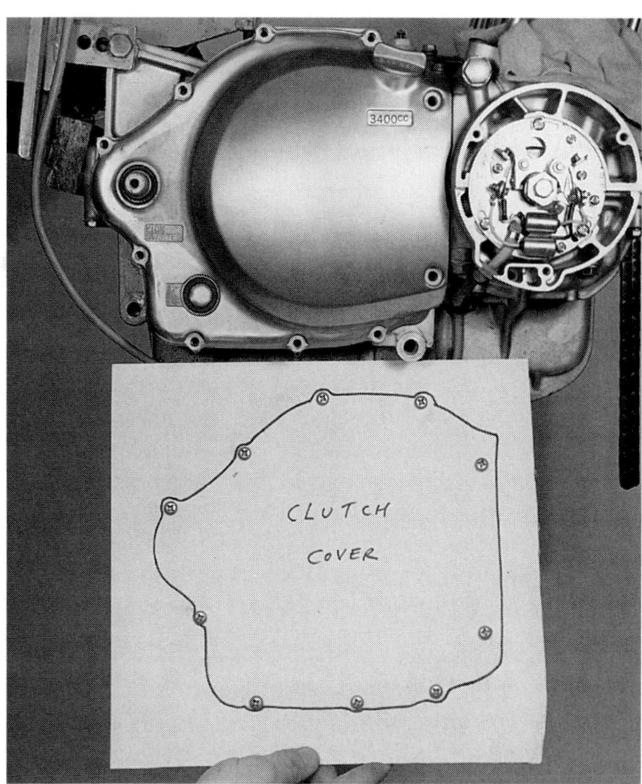

Figure 18-14. A pattern board is an excellent way to organize fasteners. Fasteners fit into the board as they would into the cover. This ensures that different screw or bolt lengths will be installed in the proper holes during reassembly.

Figure 18-13. Use cardboard boxes, plastic bags, and pans to keep groups of engine parts separated. This process takes little time, but can save much time when reassembling the engine.

A typical motorcycle engine has many mating parts. Some of these are:

- Cylinder wall and piston.
- Valve stem and guide.
- Cam follower and cam lobe.
- Cam follower and shaft.
- Tappet, mating push rod, rocker arm, and rocker shaft.
- Piston, piston pin, and connecting rod.
- Rod bearing, connecting rod, and journal.
- Main bearing and its journal.
- Roller bearing and its outer race (two-piece).
- Shim bucket and bore.
- Cam bearing and journal.

There are many other mating parts in an engine. Keep them organized and matched for proper reassembly.

Shims and Thrust Washers

Shims and ***thrust washers*** are used to properly locate, align, or provide clearance for certain engine parts. These shims and washers may have the same inside and outside diameters but different thicknesses. Failure to locate a shim or washer in its correct position can cause premature wear, misalignment, and engine failure. Too much or too little end play can result if a shim is located incorrectly.

Tape, wire tags, string tags, and labeled plastic bags are helpful for organizing shims and washers. **Figure 18-15** illustrates how valve components (valves, springs, keepers) are marked and tagged for quick and precise assembly.

Note: Remember that careful observation, marking, and tagging during disassembly ensures proper location of shims and washers during reassembly.

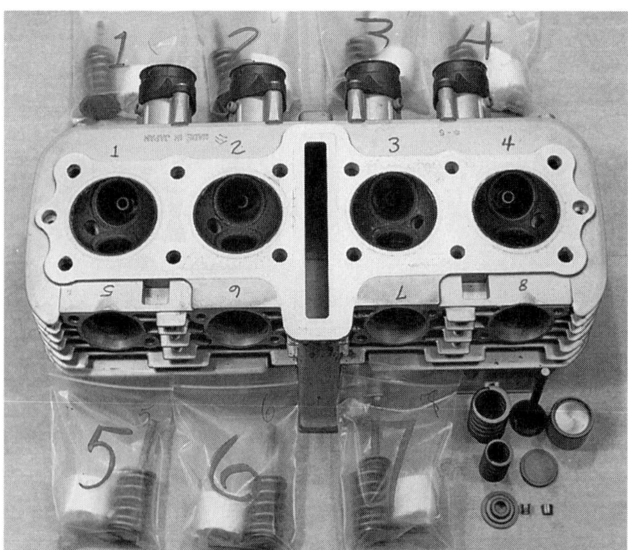

Figure 18-15. It is important to keep mating components matched. Numbering or labeling makes this easy. Notice that valve seats and plastic bags have been numbered with a marker.

Dividing the Engine

The engine should be taken apart and organized into five groups:

- Top end.
- Left side.
- Right side.
- Lower end.
- Transmission.

Figure 18-16 shows these divisions. Separating engine parts in this manner will make the job much easier.

Engine Top and Bottom End

The top end of an engine consists of the parts from the cylinder base up. This typically includes the piston, rings, cylinder, piston pin, reed valve, head gasket, cylinder head, and valve components.

The lower end or bottom end of an engine is the group of components contained within the crankcase (crankshaft, connecting rods, main bearings), excluding the transmission.

Engine Left and Right Side

Depending upon design, some parts you may encounter on the left and right sides of an engine are:

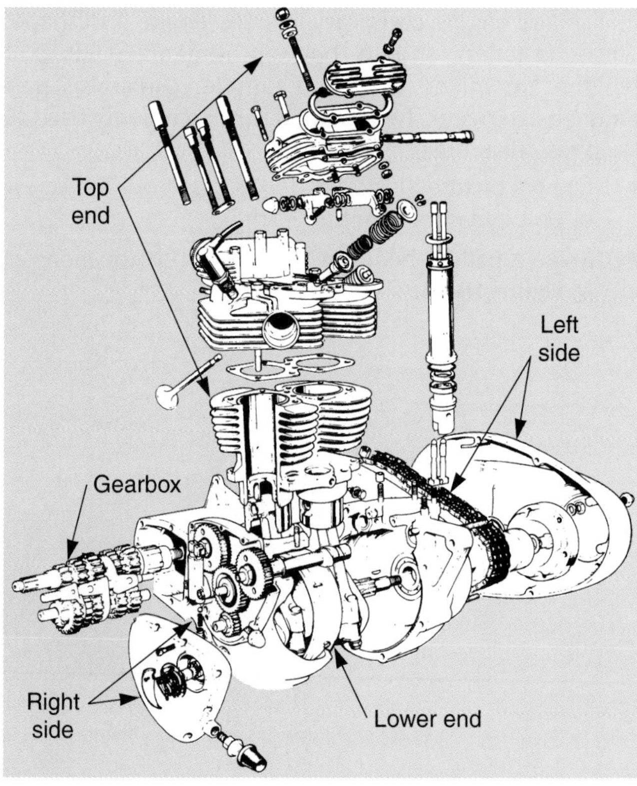

Figure 18-16. Engine disassembly, inspection, and reassembly is made easier when the engine is divided into groups. (Triumph Motorcycles, Ltd.).

- Primary drive (gear or chain).
- Clutch.
- Alternator.
- Magneto.
- Cam gears and chains.
- Countershaft sprocket.
- Battery and coil ignition breaker plate.
- Electronic ignition rotor and coils.
- Kickstart mechanism.
- Rotary valve and carburetor.

It is very important to keep left side parts separate from right side parts. These parts vary from engine to engine and can cause time loss if not organized. Removal of left and right side parts allows access to the engine crankcase.

Note: On horizontally opposed or transverse V-type engines, the left and right sides are called front and rear.

Transmission

The gear change mechanism, shafts, and gears make up the engine/transmission division. There are two types of transmission divisions, unit and non-unit types. With non-unit transmissions, the division includes a transmission case that is separate from the engine. One is shown in **Figure 18-17.** With unit construction engines, the transmission is housed within the crankcase assembly. The engine crankcase must be split in order to reach the transmission. Most motorcycles use unit construction.

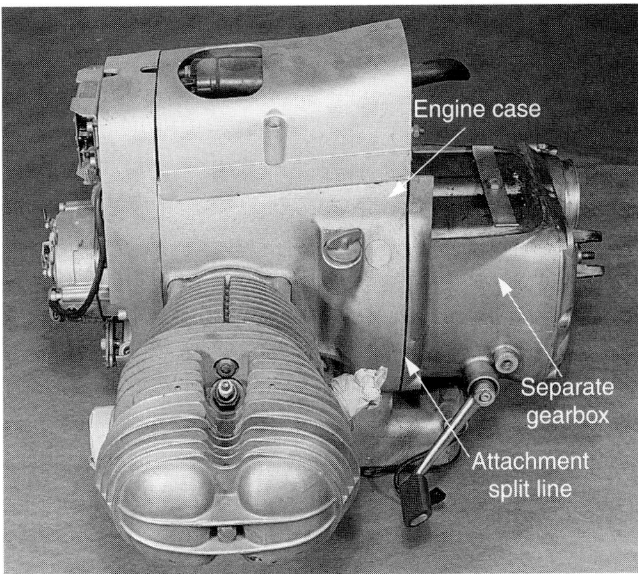

Figure 18-17. A separate gearbox or transmission case is bolted to the engine on a non-unit design.

Holders and Pullers

Holders and ***pullers*** are required to properly disassemble an engine. An engine holder is a device for preventing engine, clutch, and transmission rotation while loosening nuts or bolts. A puller is a device for removing tight fitting or interference fitted parts (pulley, gears, housings) from shafts.

Engine Holders

There are a number of ways to keep the engine crankshaft, clutch, and transmission from rotating during engine disassembly. The most common engine holders used are:

- A bar or plate bolted across the cylinder top to stop piston movement, **Figure 18-18.**
- Blocks fitted under piston pin to limit rod and crankshaft movement, **Figure 18-19.**
- A clutch holder made by welding a handle on clutch plates (may be constructed) or a factory special tool, **Figure 18-20.**
- Special locking pliers for holding the clutch center hub, **Figure 18-21.**
- Clamp pliers or a chain wrench to hold the transmission output sprocket, **Figure 18-22.**

Many service manuals do not cover proper methods of locking (preventing rotation) of an engine during disassembly. Proper use of one or more of these methods

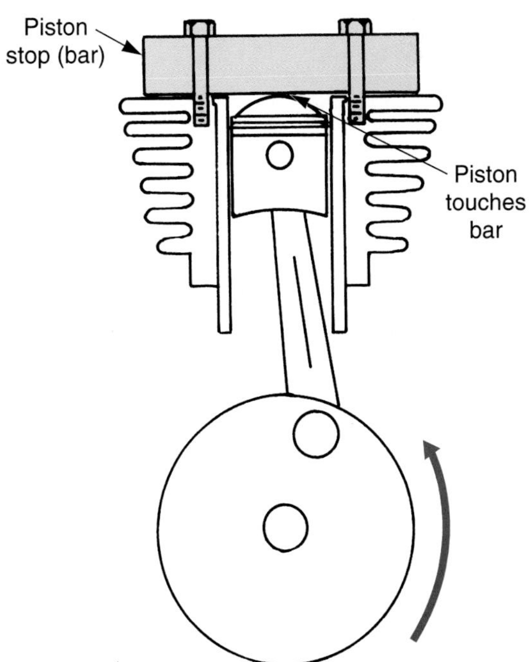

Figure 18-18. Bolting a piston stop bar or plate across the top of the cylinder is one way to prevent crankshaft movement. It allows various bolts and nuts to be loosened without engine crankshaft rotation.

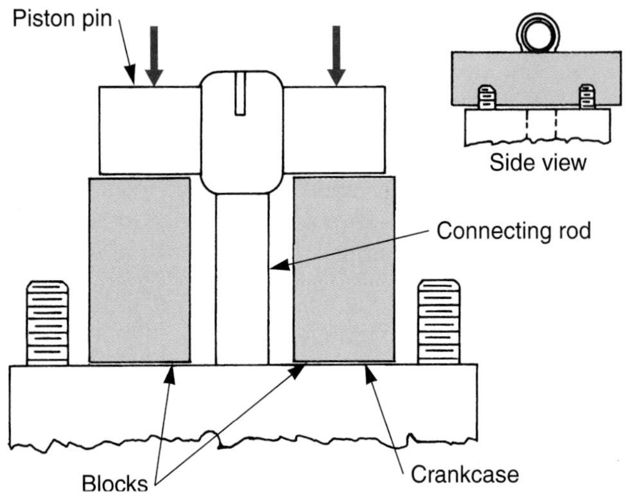

Figure 18-19. Piston pin blocks placed across the top of the crankcase provide a positive crankshaft stop. This keeps the engine from turning during repair.

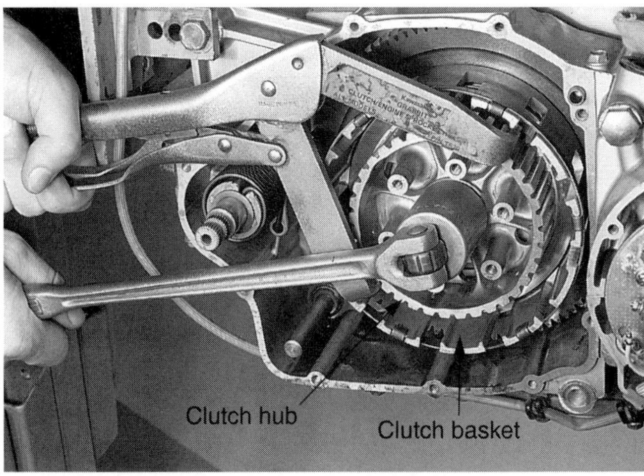

Figure 18-21. These locking pliers grip the clutch hub firmly. They allow you to loosen or tighten the clutch hub nut. Overtightening with pliers, though, could damage the clutch basket.

Figure 18-20. This factory clutch holder is made from one drive plate and one driven plate with a handle attached. This tool can be welded together easily. The tool allows you to hold the clutch hub while fasteners are removed.

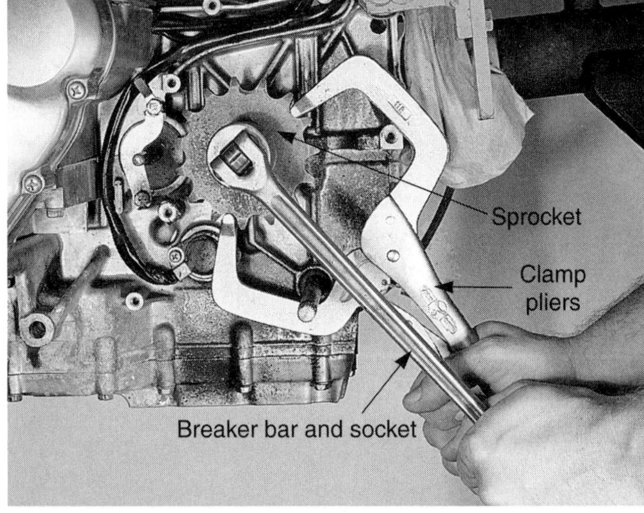

Figure 18-22. A pair of clamp pliers can be used to safely hold the countershaft sprocket while loosening the sprocket nut.

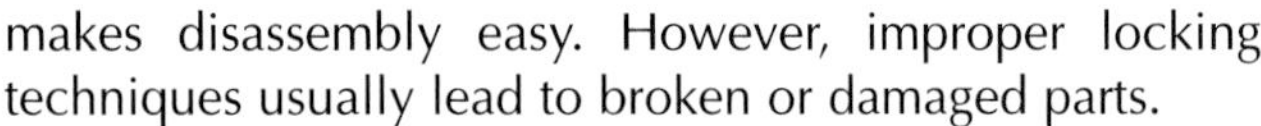

makes disassembly easy. However, improper locking techniques usually lead to broken or damaged parts.

Pullers

Manufacturers produce various types of special pullers needed during engine disassembly. Components which may require the use of pullers are:

- Alternator rotor.
- Cam gears.
- Primary drive sprocket or gear.
- Clutch hub.
- Crankshaft (from one crankcase half).
- Transmission output sprocket.
- Piston pin.

Puller designs vary as much as engine designs, **Figure 18-23.** Pullers come in various configurations and sizes. The types of special pullers are:

- Bolt puller.
- Double-threaded puller.
- Slide hammer puller.
- Bar puller.

Most service manuals list the special tools required for an engine overhaul. It is extremely important to use these tools when needed. Some accessory manufacturers produce special pullers and other tools that have universal application. They can be used for various operations and on different motorcycle types.

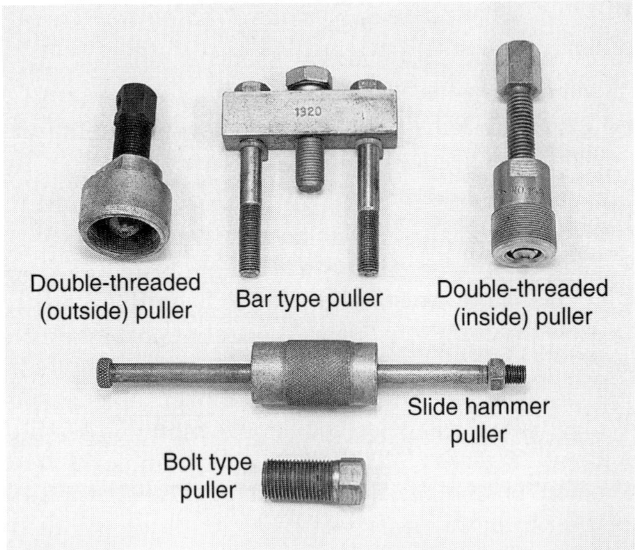

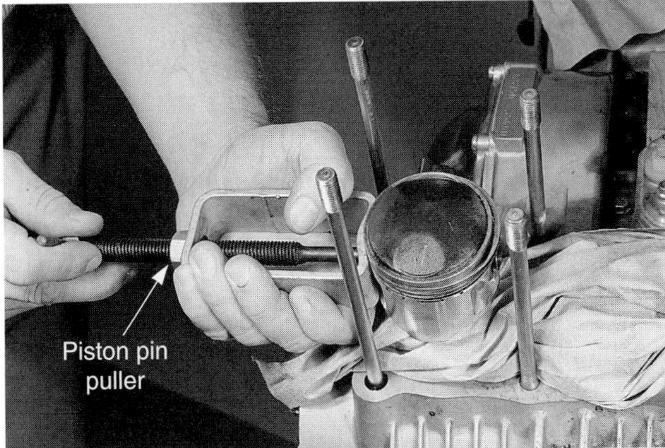

Figure 18-23. Special pullers are essential in many situations. These are the most common types of pullers used in motorcycle repair.

Using Heat to Aid Disassembly

Heating a part causes it to expand. Engine parts made of different metals will expand at different rates. This principle aids engine disassembly and reassembly. The use of heat on the following parts is common during engine disassembly and reassembly.

- Valve guides.
- Piston pins.
- Bushings mounted in crankcase.
- Tight fitting bearings in crankcase (vertical-split crankcase).
- Cylinder sleeves.
- Transmission gears (press-fit).

A steel part surrounded by an aluminum part is a good example to show the heat expansion rates between different metals. As both parts are heated, the aluminum part expands more than the steel part. This difference creates clearance between the parts and allows the steel part to be removed easily from the aluminum part. **Figure 18-24** illustrates this principle.

Three acceptable methods of heating parts are a torch (propane), hot plate, and oven. The oven is usually the best method of heating parts. It provides an accurate method of heat control. A torch or hot plate can cause uneven heating and part damage (cracking, warping, melting).

If a torch must be used (which is usually the case involving parts still on the engine) heat the part evenly, keeping the torch moving. Try to keep as much heat on the part to be removed as possible.

Heat Use Warnings

Some rules to remember when using heat are:

- Do not exceed 275° F (135° C) except for valve guide or sleeve removal.
- Do not heat engine parts to the point of discoloration.
- When using a torch, keep it moving. Do not heat one area too much.
- When removing crankcase bearings, use an oven. Heat the whole crankcase, not just the area around the bearing.
- When heating pistons, heat the crown, not the skirt or pin boss.
- Use insulated gloves when handling heated parts.
- Work only in a well ventilated area. Make sure gasoline or paint fumes are not present.

Parts can sometimes be overheated, causing warpage, softening, and discoloration. The service manual outlines more precise use of heat for particular engine disassembly and assembly procedures.

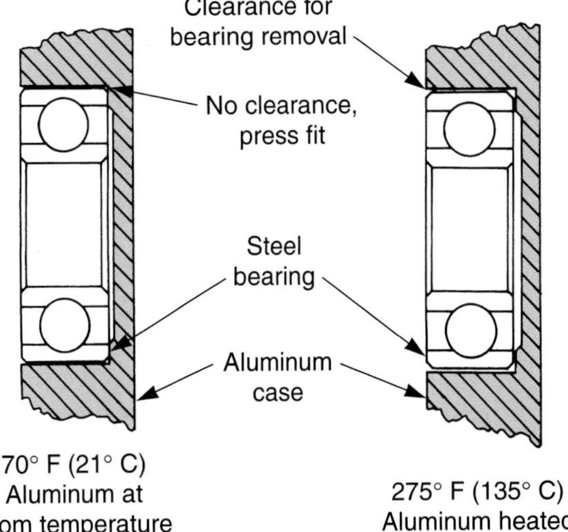

Figure 18-24. Using heat during assembly and disassembly can make bearing installation and removal easy. This is because heat causes one metal part (the housing) to expand at a faster rate than the other part (the bearing).

Sequence of Disassembly

The sequence of disassembly is determined by engine design and the type of overhaul being done. Most engines can be disassembled in any sequence, however, following the recommended sequence usually makes the job easier. The motorcycle's service manual gives the proper disassembly sequence for each job.

Typical Engine Disassembly Problems

Various problems may be encountered during engine disassembly. Your ability and patience in dealing with these problems will make the difference between an easy job and one that results in broken fasteners or engine parts.

A number of minor difficulties can cause problems during engine disassembly. These include tightly bonded gaskets that will not separate or an interference fit component that will not slide free. The following list outlines some common problems that you could encounter during engine disassembly.

Cylinder Head and Cylinder Block Removal Problems

- Tightly bonded gaskets.
- Corroded or damaged locating dowels.
- Missing, stripped, or broken fasteners.
- Stripped, corroded, cross-threaded, and broken bolt heads and threads.

Wrist Pin Removal Problems

- Interference fit between wrist pin and piston boss.
- Varnish formed on wrist pin.
- Peened edge (burred edge) next to wrist pin circlip.

Cylinder Head Disassembly Problems

- Stuck (wedged) valve spring collars and keepers.
- Mushroomed valve stem.
- Lip formed just above keeper groove on valve stems.
- Bent or damaged valves.

Primary Drive Disassembly Problems

- Difficulty holding clutch hub and primary drive gear when loosening center nuts.

Flywheel Removal Problems

- Extremely tight interference fit on crankshaft.
- Corroded or damaged surfaces.

Crankcase Separation Problems

- Binding of shaft ends by trying to separate cases unevenly (vertical-split cases).
- Extremely tight interference fit between crankshaft and main bearings (vertical-split cases).
- Corroded case locating dowels.
- Fasteners still installed (hidden by grease or mud).

The remedy for many of these problems is often self-explanatory. You would need to hammer or pry in the right place on some parts. A puller or heat may also be needed to free parts. In any case, use the right tools and procedures. The information in this chapter and a service manual will guide you through most disassembly problems. **Figures 18-25** to **18-28** give examples of very common procedures that solve typical engine disassembly problems.

Summary

Always organize the work area before starting. Proper work area organization is essential. A little extra effort and care during teardown can help avoid problems later. Secure enough boxes, trays, and other holding containers to avoid mixing the parts from more than one bike. If needed, obtain or free a stand that will support the bike's weight. The work area cleanliness and condition reflects upon your work habits and mechanical ability. A sloppy work area indicates a sloppy worker. Before beginning work, it is important to clean the motorcycle, scooter, or ATV thoroughly. An engine degreaser and a pressure washer or steam cleaner makes cleaning easier.

It is not always necessary to remove the engine for service. Check the engine carefully as removal is a time-intensive job. Before unbolting the engine, you must know exactly what is wrong. If engine removal can be

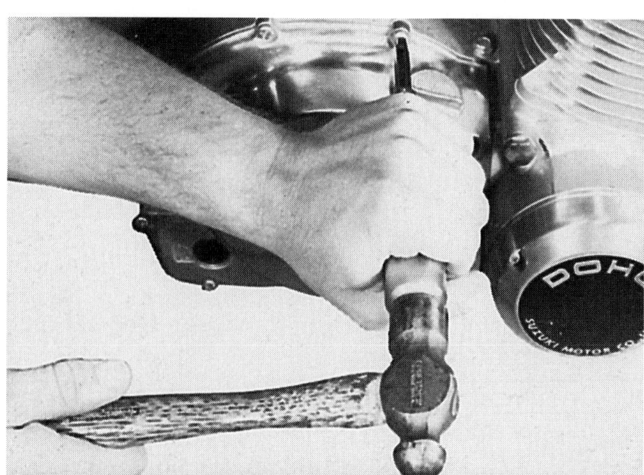

Figure 18-25. An impact driver provides inward pressure and torque to loosen stubborn fasteners without damaging them. When the driver is hit with a hammer, the driver rotates with tremendous force.

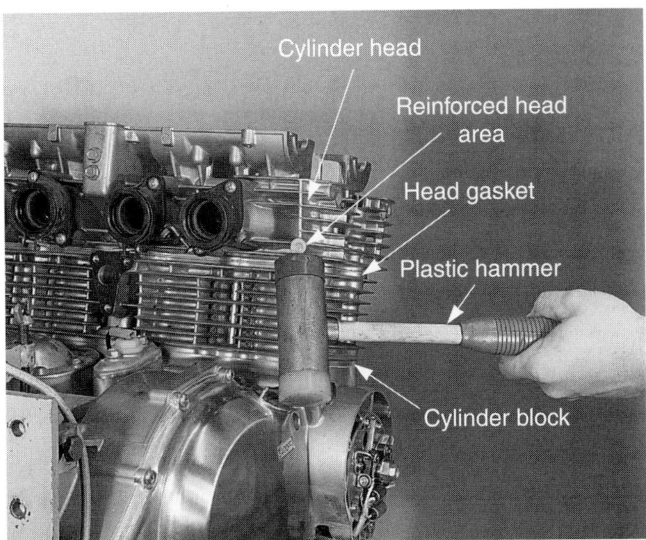

Figure 18-26. Multicylinder heads are frequently bonded to the cylinder block by gasket material. A plastic hammer may be needed to break the head loose. Only hammer on reinforced area as cooling fins will break off easily.

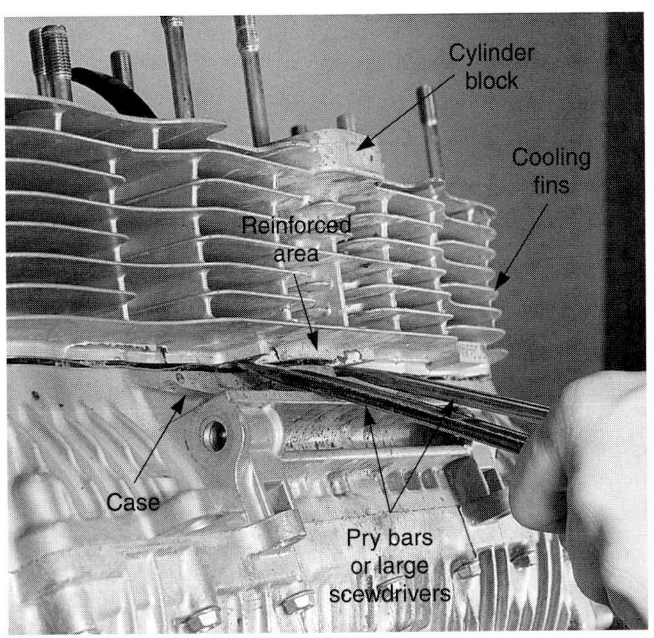

Figure 18-27. Pry bars, if used carefully, will release the cylinder block from the crankcase. Do not pry on the fins, only the bossed area. On some engines, special areas are provided for hammering and prying. Refer to a service manual for the location of these areas.

avoided, it will reduce the time the bike is in your shop. Before beginning disassembly, read the proper sections of a shop service manual for the particular motorcycle being repaired.

Drain all fluids, including engine and transmission oils and engine coolant (on some bikes) before the engine is removed. After draining the oil, inspect the oil filter for debris. Debris lodged in the oil filter may hint as to the engine's condition as well as any problems. On two-stroke

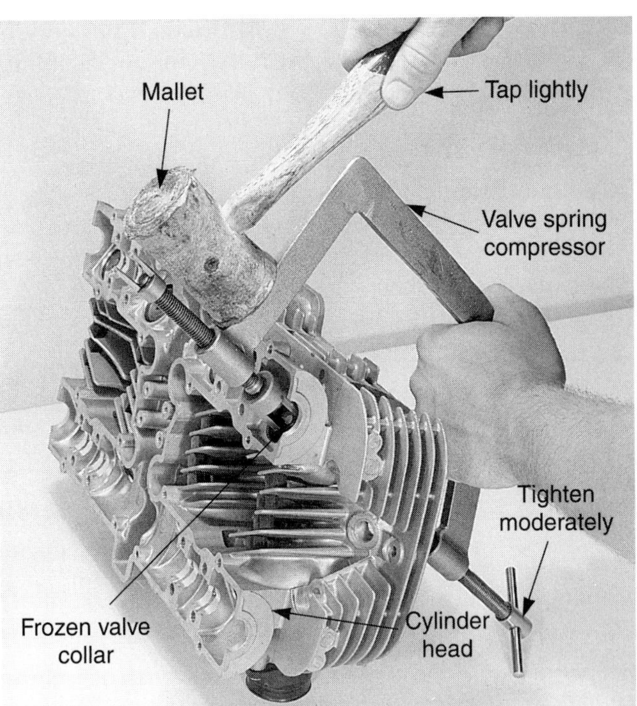

Figure 18-28. Avoid overtightening the valve spring compressor. It could slip off and damage parts. When keepers are wedged, use light taps from a mallet on compressor. This will cause the keepers and other parts to come free with minimum strain on the compressor.

cycle engines using oil injection, the feed line must be disconnected and plugged. Always remove the battery during engine removal. This prevents accidental shorting, damage to the electrical system, and possibly an electrical fire. Control cable disconnection varies from motorcycle to motorcycle, depending on its application. In many cases, removing the fuel tank will ease engine removal. Sometimes, tank removal is necessary to obtain clearance to the engine.

Carelessness in removing engine mounting bolts can result in injury. Double-check that all parts (wires, cables, hoses, exhaust system), fastened between the engine and frame are disconnected. Parts can be damaged very easily when lifting a motorcycle engine out of the frame. Once the engine is out of the frame, install it on an engine stand or engine box. Place all mounting bolts in their proper locations. The engine should be taken apart and organized into five groups: top end; left side; right side; lower end; and transmission.

The top end of an engine consists of the parts from the cylinder base up. This typically includes the piston, rings, cylinder, piston pin, reed valve, head gasket, cylinder head, and valve components. The lower end or bottom end of an engine is the group of components contained within the crankcase (crankshaft, connecting rods, main bearings), excluding the transmission. It is very important to keep left side parts separate from right side parts. Removal of left and right side parts allows access to the engine crankcase.

Heating a part causes it to expand, which aids engine disassembly. Three acceptable methods of heating parts are a torch (propane), hot plate, and oven. Follow all safety rules when heating parts. Parts can sometimes be overheated, causing warpage, softening, and discoloration. A number of minor difficulties can cause problems during engine disassembly. These include broken or stripped fasteners, tightly bonded gaskets that will not separate, or an interference fit component that will not slide free.

Know These Terms

Engine stand	Shims
Engine box	Thrust washers
Tags	Holders
Markings	Pullers

Review Questions—Chapter 18

Do not write in this text. Place your answers on a separate sheet of paper.

1. *True or False?* It is a waste of time to clean the engine before it is removed from the frame.
2. *True or False?* All engines can be removed from either side of the frame.
3. The main reason for removing a battery during engine removal is to prevent _____.
   A. accidental shorting
   B. damage to the electrical system
   C. a possible electrical fire
   D. All of the above.
4. Name three types of electrical connectors which may have to be disconnected during engine removal.
5. The _____ side of the battery should always be disconnected first.
6. After removing an engine, it should be mounted on a _____ or _____.
7. List three safety rules for engine removal.
8. It is important to _____ or _____ certain engine parts to prevent mating parts from getting mixed up.
9. List the five common divisions or sections of an engine.
10. Shims and thrust washers:
    A. are always interchangeable.
    B. are only available in one standard size.
    C. vary in size and thickness.
    D. vary in size, but not thickness.
11. Why should engine left and right side parts be kept separate?
12. A valve spring is part of which engine division?
    A. Top end.
    B. Left side.
    C. Bottom end.
    D. Transmission.
13. Heat is used to _____ engine parts for easier disassembly.
14. When heating most engine parts, you should not exceed _____.
    A. 275° F (135° C)
    B. 212° F (100° C)
    C. 300° F (149° C)
    D. 100° F (38° C)
15. Which of the following is *not* a problem related to cylinder head removal?
    A. Tightly bonded gaskets.
    B. Corroded or damaged locating dowels.
    C. Stripped bolt heads and threads.
    D. Varnish on wrist pins.

Suggested Activities

1. Remove a two-stroke cycle engine from a motorcycle.
2. Remove a four-stroke cycle engine from the frame.
3. Locate all the engine mounting bolts on various motorcycles.
4. Make a list of wires, cables, hoses, brackets, and other parts that must be unfastened before engine removal. Place this list in the useful information section of your notebook.
5. Mount an engine on an engine stand.
6. Make engine fastener pattern boards for the following areas:
   A. Left side engine covers.
   B. Right side engine covers.
   C. Cylinder head and cam cover (if applicable).

19

Two-Stroke Engine Overhaul

After studying this chapter, you will be able to:

- Describe two-stroke engine top end service.
- Measure two-stroke engine parts wear.
- Explain two-stroke engine bottom end service.
- Summarize crankshaft reconditioning.
- Diagnose common two-stroke engine problems.
- Outline two-stroke engine reassembly.
- Summarize the procedures for installing an engine in the motorcycle frame.
- Describe initial engine starting and break-in procedures.

This chapter discusses the most important steps for overhauling a two-stroke cycle engine. Engine parts inspection, reconditioning, diagnosis, and reassembly are covered. This is an important chapter that explains many basic procedures. If studied carefully, you should be able to relate these procedures to any two-stroke motorcycle engine. With the aid of a service manual, you will be prepared to overhaul a two-stroke engine.

Engine Top End Service

The parts included in a two-stroke engine's top end are the piston, rings, cylinder, piston pin, reed valve, head gasket, and cylinder head. A two-stroke engine's top end requires more frequent service and repair than a four-stroke engine. This is because:

- The two-stroke engine's piston rings pass over port openings in the cylinder.
- The two-stroke engine's oil is diluted with fuel and air.
- The temperatures in a two-stroke engine are higher.

Cylinder and Piston Inspection

The cylinder and piston(s) must be inspected and measured closely during an overhaul. As this is the foundation for the entire engine, it must be reconditioned properly to ensure a good rebuild. Cylinder and piston condition often indicates if there are other areas of the engine or motorcycle that should be checked.

Cylinder Problems

Inspect the cylinder for cracks, scoring, rust, wear ridges on the top and bottom of the cylinder, and obvious damage caused by foreign material. Dye or powder tests, X-rays, pressure checking, or magnetic detection can also be used to check for cracks. If cracks are discovered, replace the cylinder.

Cylinder ***rust*** can be present after periods of storage and water condensation. A ridge or lip at the top and/or bottom of the cylinder is due to wear. The rings do not rub on and wear the extreme top and bottom portion of the cylinder. The unworn portion forms the ring ridge in the cylinder. Cylinder ***scoring,*** as with piston scoring, is caused by dirt or foreign matter entry into the engine.

Piston Damage

Inspect the piston for scoring, cracking, galling (seizure), evidence of foreign material, and crown damage. **Figure 19-1** shows common types of piston damage. Piston ***galling*** can be caused by excessive heat and poor lubrication. Piston crown damage can be the result of a lean air-fuel mixture, improper spark timing, or part breakage. Always investigate the cause of piston damage to find and correct the source of the problem.

Caution: Do not attempt to repair a cracked or damaged piston.

Piston and Cylinder Measurement

Piston and cylinder measurement is used to determine:

- Piston skirt and ring land wear (wear on the piston thrust surfaces and ring grooves).
- Piston ring end gap and tension (fit of new rings in cylinder).
- Cylinder taper (wear difference at top and bottom of cylinder).
- Cylinder out-of-roundness (diameter difference in cylinder).
- Piston-to-cylinder clearance (play between piston and cylinder wall).

Piston Skirt and Ring Land Wear

Piston skirt wear is checked by measuring the piston skirt diameter with a micrometer. This operation is illustrated in **Figure 19-2.** Take a reading at both the top and bottom of the skirt. Compare these measurements with the standard dimensions given in the service manual. Most service manuals give upper and lower limits (specifications) for piston diameter. The difference between the skirt measurements and the specifications represents piston wear. However, some manuals only give piston-to-cylinder clearance specifications. This requires measurement of both the piston and cylinder. Then, the clearance can be calculated.

Ring land wear is determined by measuring side clearance between the piston rings and the ring land with a feeler gauge. Install a new ring in the groove, then insert a feeler gauge between the upper surface of the ring and the land to check the clearance. **Figure 19-3** shows how to measure ring land wear.

Piston Ring End Gap and Free Gap

Piston ring fit is checked by measuring ring end and free gap. Measurement of piston ***ring end gap*** indicates

A B

Figure 19-1. Typical forms of piston damage. A—Seizure. B—Crown damage.

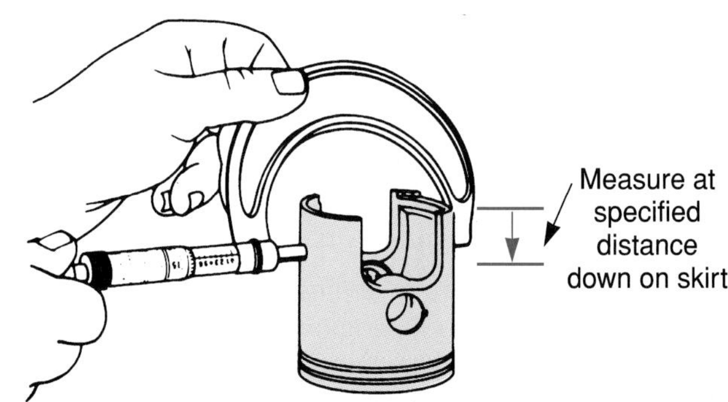

Figure 19-2. Piston skirt must be measured 90° from the wrist pin. Be sure to measure at the proper distance from the bottom of the skirt. Check the manual for details. (Bombardier Ltd.)

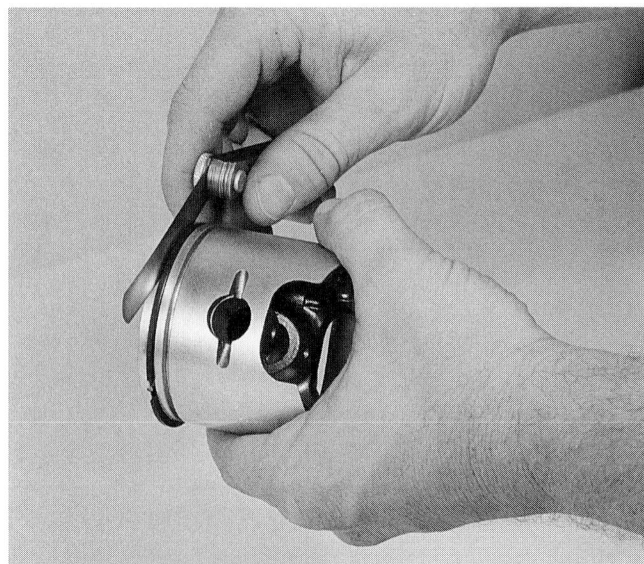

Figure 19-3. Use a feeler gauge to measure the piston ring-to-land clearance. The largest feeler gauge thickness that fits indicates ring-to-land clearance.

the ring size. Place the ring in the cylinder and measure the end gap using a feeler gauge. An end gap that is too small could cause seizure when the rings heat up and expand during engine operation. The rings could jam against the cylinder wall and cause excessive friction and heat. The ring and cylinder wall surfaces could overheat and seize. A ring gap that is too large could cause blow-by (combustion pressure leaking past rings). Always check ring end gap carefully, as in **Figure 19-4.** Adjusting the ring end gap involves filing the ring ends until the desired fit is achieved.

Measurement of the ***ring free gap*** indicates the amount of ring tension. As the free gap decreases, tension also decreases. A ring which has excessive end gap or insufficient free gap may not seal properly and should not be used, **Figure 19-5.**

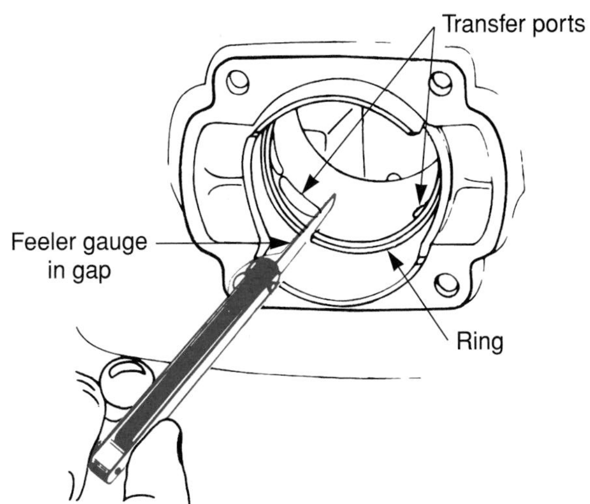

Figure 19-4. Ring end gap is the distance between the ring ends when installed squarely in the cylinder. End gap is measured with a feeler gauge. (Bombardier Ltd.)

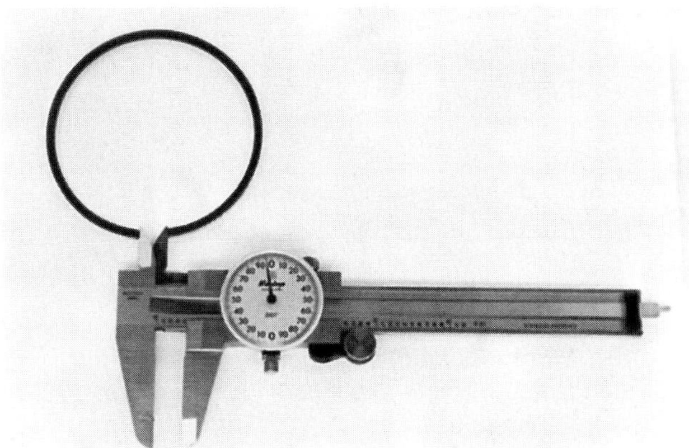

Figure 19-5. Ring free gap is the distance between the ring ends. Free gap is measured with a dial caliper without forcing the ring open.

Cylinder Taper

Combustion pressure and heat are greatest at the top of the cylinder. There is also less lubrication at the top of the cylinder. ***Cylinder taper*** is wear that causes the top of the cylinder to be worn larger than the bottom. This is illustrated in **Figure 19-6.** A noticeable ridge at the top of the cylinder is an indication of cylinder taper. If the cylinder bore is tapered, two undesirable conditions can result:

- Piston-to-cylinder clearance will change as the piston moves from TDC to BDC.
- Ring end gap and tension changes as the piston moves up and down in the cylinder.

A tapered cylinder accelerates ring wear, leading to blowby. It causes the rings to rapidly retract and expand to match the changing cylinder diameter.

Measurement of cylinder taper is done with a telescoping gauge and an outside micrometer. **Figure 19-7** shows this procedure.

1. Measure the cylinder diameter parallel to the crankshaft at the top of the ring travel zone.
2. Measure the diameter in the same position at the bottom of the ring travel zone.
3. Measure the cylinder diameter at a right angle to the crankshaft at the top of the ring travel zone.
4. Measure the diameter in the same position at the bottom of the ring travel zone.

Once these measurements are made, subtract the dimension obtained in step 4 from the dimension obtained in step 3 (subtract the smallest dimension from the largest dimension) to determine the degree of taper present in the cylinder. You will use the measurements obtained in steps 1 and 2 in the next section. The service manual gives wear limits and specific directions for checking cylinder taper.

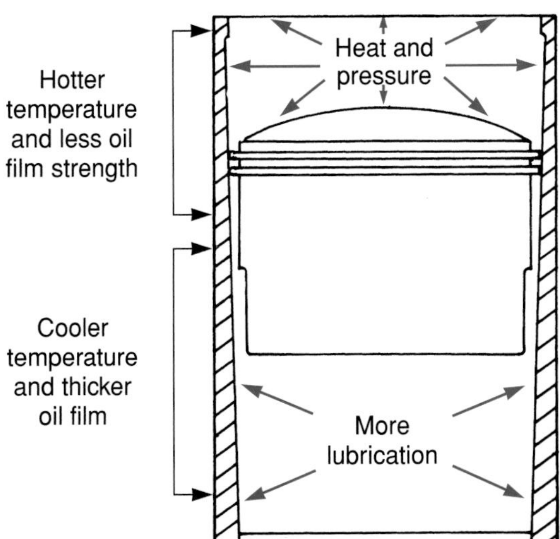

Figure 19-6. Cylinder taper is the result of normal wear. The cylinder becomes larger at the top than at the bottom. The difference in heat, pressure, and lubrication at the top and bottom of the cylinder causes taper.

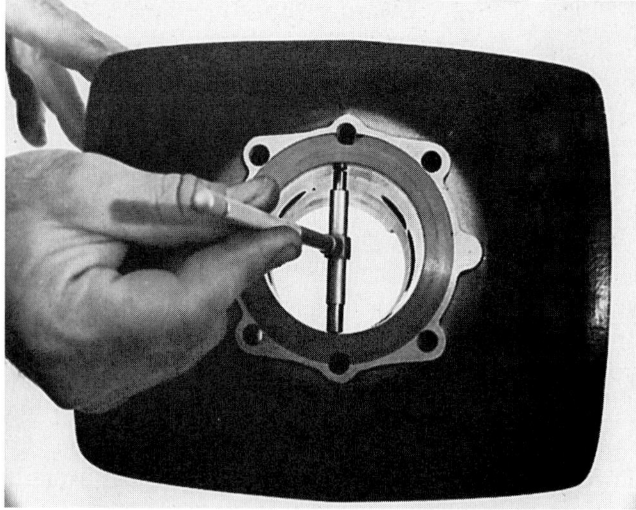

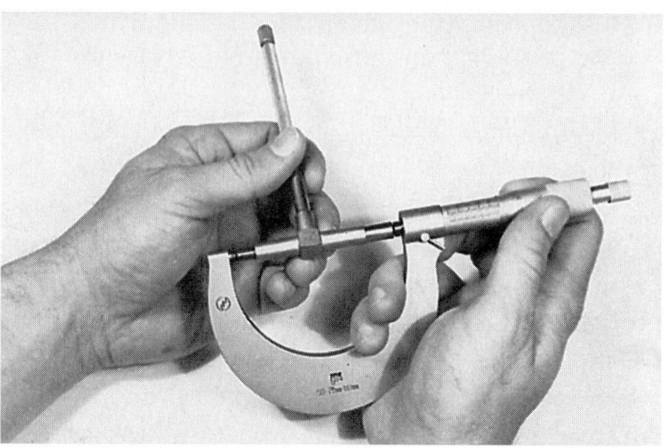

Figure 19-7. A telescoping gauge and micrometer are used to measure cylinder taper. Adjust the gauge to cylinder diameter. Then, measure the gauge with the micrometer. The difference in measurements at the top and bottom of the cylinder shows taper.

Cylinder Out-of-Roundness

Cylinder ***out-of-roundness*** is wear that causes the cylinder to resemble an oval or *egg-shape,* as in **Figure 19-8.** As a cylinder becomes out-of-round, piston clearance increases. Since new piston rings are designed to seal a round bore, out-of-roundness can allow blowby if not corrected.

Out-of-roundness normally occurs at the front and back of the cylinder, opposite the piston pin centerline. Because of piston thrust, wear is more pronounced on the cylinder surfaces shown in **Figure 19-9.**

Measurement for cylinder out-of-roundness is similar to the measurement of cylinder taper. **Figure 19-10** shows which areas in a cylinder should be measured to determine cylinder out-of-roundness. Compare the measurements obtained in steps 1 and 3, which were detailed in the last section, to find the out-of-round wear at the top end of the cylinder. Compare the measurements obtained in steps 2 and 4 to find the out-of-round wear at the bottom end of the cylinder. Check in your service manual for specific wear limits.

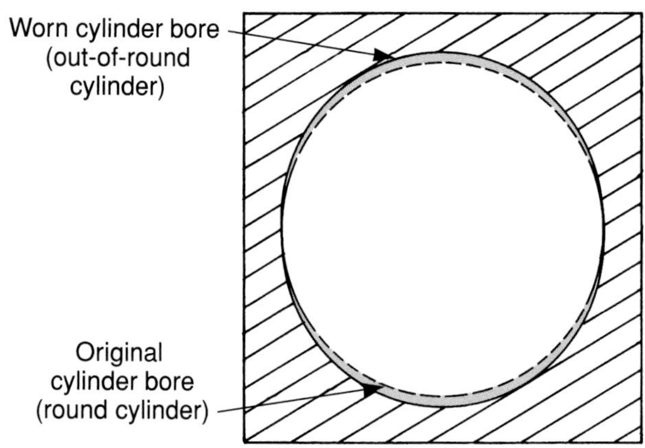

Figure 19-8. Normal wear causes cylinders to eventually become out-of-round.

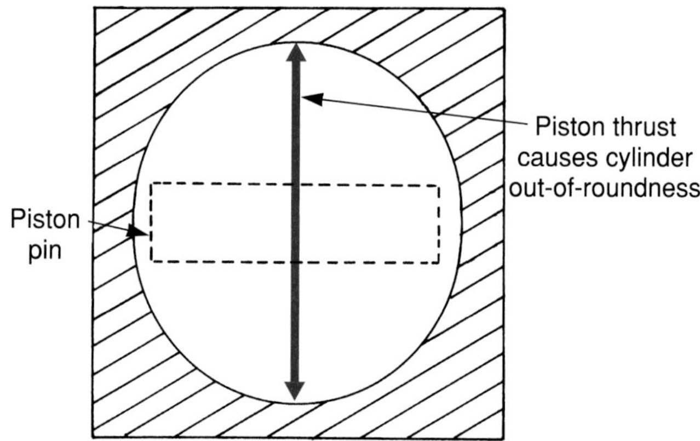

Figure 19-9. Cylinder out-of-roundness is caused by piston thrust.

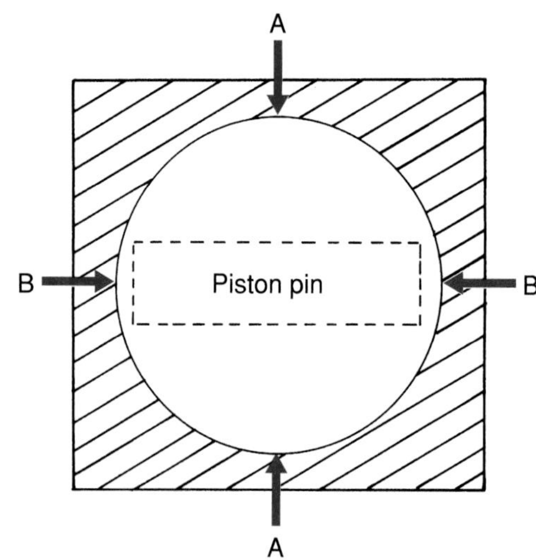

Figure 19-10. To check for cylinder out-of-roundness, measure the cylinder across A and B. The difference between measurements equals out-of-roundness.

Piston-to-Cylinder Clearance

Piston-to-cylinder clearance is determined by comparing piston diameter to cylinder bore diameter. Proper clearance is necessary to permit piston expansion and to allow the formation of an oil film on the cylinder walls. Since most pistons wear with use, be sure to check the clearance during every engine overhaul. Pistons should be replaced if their clearance exceeds the manufacturer's specifications. To measure piston clearance, proceed as follows:

1. Using a telescoping gauge with an outside micrometer, measure the cylinder diameter at right angles to the crankshaft in the lower or least worn area of the cylinder.
2. Measure the piston diameter across the thrust faces with an outside micrometer. The difference between these two measurements is the piston clearance. Subtract the piston diameter from the cylinder bore diameter:

Cylinder bore diameter – Piston skirt diameter =
Piston-to-cylinder clearance.

The difference between the two measurements equals piston-to-cylinder clearance. Incorrect piston-to-cylinder clearance can cause:

- Piston seizure (piston overheats and locks in cylinder).
- Piston galling (knocking sound caused by worn piston and/or cylinder).
- Piston slap (knocking sound caused by a worn piston and/or cylinder).
- Blowby (overheating and power loss).
- Piston skirt damage (excessive piston-to-cylinder clearance allows piston rocking).

An alternate method is to remove the rings from the piston and use feeler gauges to carefully measure the clearance between the piston and the cylinder wall. When doing this, be certain not to scratch the cylinder wall.

Engine Decarbonizing

Since two-stroke engines burn oil with the air-fuel mixture, some carbon build-up in the top end is normal. If this carbon build-up is not removed periodically, the accumulation eventually increases to an excessive level. This creates potential hot spots on the cylinder head and piston crown that may cause knocking. Accumulated carbon in the port can hinder exhaust flow, causing a drop in power output. Therefore, removal of accumulated carbon should be performed as part of a top end overhaul. Carbon deposits are normally found on the piston crown, in ring grooves, combustion chambers, and in the exhaust ports. Carbon is commonly removed by soaking in decarbonizing solvent, scraping, wire brushing, and dry blasting.

Chemical soaking in a recommended cleaner will soften carbon on the engine parts. The carbon can then be easily removed using a pressure rinse that will minimize any chance of damage. Be sure to follow the solution manufacturer's instructions for proper cleaning. Aluminum parts must be cleaned in an ***emulsion cleaning solution.*** Using caustic soda or other solutions will dissolve the metal.

In ***dry blasting,*** the parts are blasted with a dry medium, such as glass beads or crushed walnut shells using a machine like the one shown in **Figure 19-11.** As with chemical soaking, be sure to follow the manufacturer's instructions.

Be careful not to damage or scratch the parts while removing the hard carbon. **Figure 19-12** shows one method for removing carbon from piston ring grooves. Soft aluminum parts must be cleaned very carefully as they can be scratched and damaged easily. In liquid-cooled engines, be sure to remove carbon particles that may have fallen into the coolant jackets around the cylinder by blowing them out with compressed air.

Figure 19-11. Typical bead blaster used to clean engine parts. (Kansas Instruments)

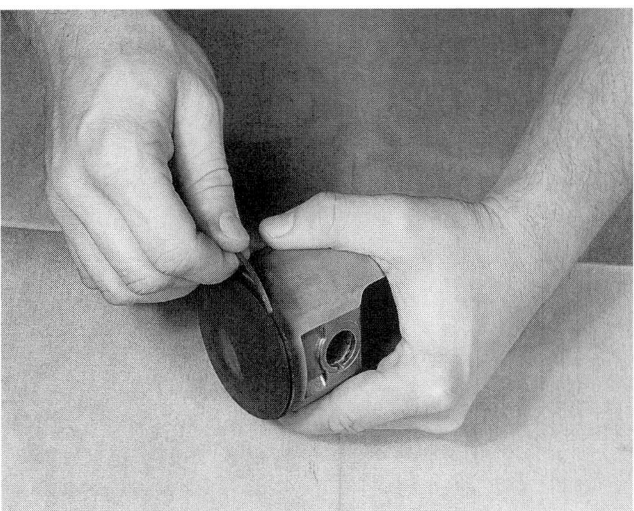

Figure 19-12. An old piston ring can be used to scrape carbon from inside ring grooves.

Parts Reconditioning and Replacement

Once parts have been cleaned, inspected, and measured, you can begin reconditioning and/or replacing parts. Combustion heat, engine oil, and piston movement combine to form a thin, shiny residue on the cylinder walls that is commonly called *glaze.* A two-stroke engine, which has minimal wear, can usually be reconditioned by deglazing (honing) the cylinder and installing new piston rings. ***Deglazing*** provides a fine finish by removing scuffs or scratch marks, but does not enlarge the cylinder diameter. Therefore, standard-size pistons may still be used after deglazing.

In addition to removing glaze, deglazing produces a ***crosshatch pattern*** on the cylinder walls to provide cavities for holding oil during piston ring break-in. Various grit deglazing stones are available to produce the desired finish on the cylinder walls. If the cylinder walls are wavy, scuffed, or scratched, deglaze them as follows:

Note: Deglazing is required any time new rings are installed.

1. Swab the cylinder walls with a clean cloth that has been dipped in clean engine oil.
2. Mount a recommended deglazing tool in a slow-speed drill (300-500 rpm).
3. Move the tool 10-12 complete strokes up and down in the cylinder rapidly enough to obtain a crosshatch pattern. **Figure 19-13** demonstrates how to deglaze a motorcycle engine's cylinder.

Caution: Be careful not to pull the spinning hone completely out of the cylinder. The honing stones could break and fly out with considerable force.

4. After cylinder deglazing, wash the cylinder with soap and warm water. Soap and water are needed to remove the heavy deglazing grit from the cylinder surface. Degreasing solvents will not do an effective cleaning job. They are too light and runny to pick up heavier grit particles. After drying, wipe the cylinder out with a clean rag soaked in oil. Improper cleaning after deglazing will cause rapid piston, cylinder, and ring wear.

Ring replacement alone, without cylinder boring and piston replacement, is allowable when the piston and cylinder are both within wear limits. If the cylinder is within wear limits, but the piston is worn undersize, a new piston and rings can be installed.

A

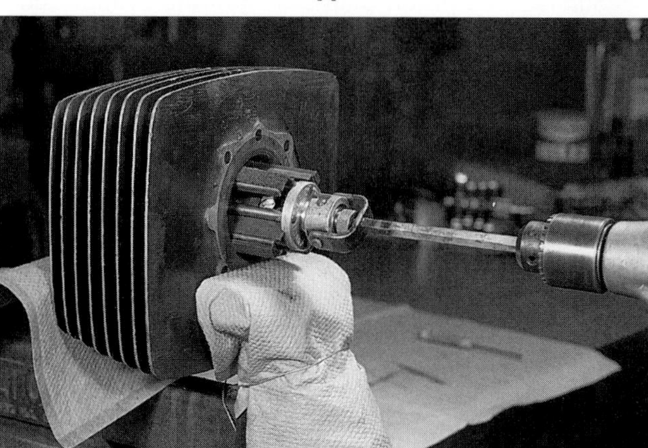

B

C

Figure 19-13. A—The surface texture and appearance of a worn cylinder bore is smooth and shiny. New rings would not seat and seal properly. B—A cylinder hone is used to deglaze the bore. Pull the hone back and forth to form a crosshatch pattern. C—A proper crosshatch pattern allows controlled wear of new piston rings for proper seating.

Cylinder Boring and Honing

When the cylinder is worn beyond specifications by excessive taper, out-of-roundness, or scoring, the cylinder must be machined larger. Cylinder boring removes enough metal to enlarge the cylinder to permit a larger piston to be utilized, avoiding the need for cylinder replacement. Once bored, the cylinder can be fitted with an oversized piston and oversize rings.

Warning: Be extremely careful when chamfering cylinder ports. The slightest nick could ruin the cylinder wall.

The service manual lists the number of overbore sizes available and gives proper piston-to-cylinder clearances. Cylinders which use a cast-in sleeve must be replaced after the largest overbore has been used. Cylinders which have a pressed-in sleeve can be reconditioned over and over. After installing a new sleeve (liner) in the cylinder, the liner can be bored to its original standard bore size. The procedures for boring a cylinder were outlined in Chapter 3.

After boring, the cylinder wall finish will be rough and the port edges sharp. You must hone the cylinder to final size and smoothness. ***Honing*** to achieve final cylinder sizing is different from deglazing the cylinder. Honing is done to achieve a textured crosshatch pattern. It removes a minimum amount of material from the cylinder wall. You must also chamfer the port edges as in **Figure 19-14.** Final cylinder sizing by honing is required for three reasons:

- To remove rough boring marks.
- To achieve accurate final sizing.
- To obtain the desired crosshatch and texture.

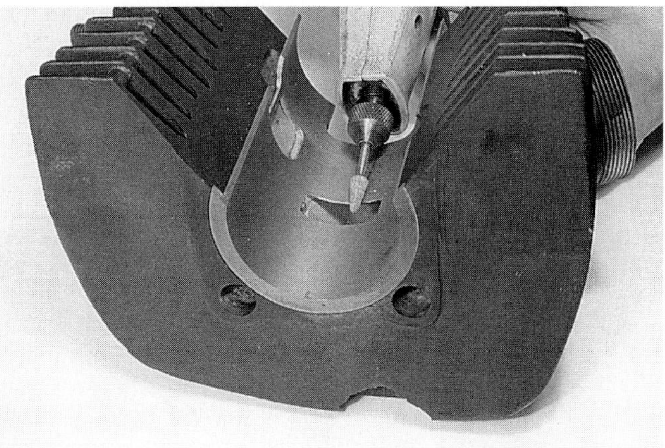

Figure 19-14. Proper port chamfering is extremely important. A rotary grinder or small file can be used to chamfer ports. Be careful not to scratch or grind the cylinder wall. Chamfer all horizontal edges, including the transfer cutout at the cylinder base.

Engine Lower End Service

Inspection and service of a two-stroke cycle engine lower end includes:

- Measuring connecting rod bearing clearance.
- Checking connecting rod thrust washers and side play.
- Checking main bearing condition.
- Checking the condition and cleanliness of the crankwheels.
- Reconditioning and truing the crankshaft.

Measuring Rod Big End Bearing Clearance

The proper procedure for measuring connecting rod bearing clearance is outlined in the service manual. Typical procedures include:

- Measuring connecting rod tip, **Figure 19-15.**
- Checking for rod bearing radial play, **Figure 19-16.**

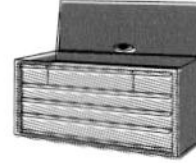

Note: The rod bearing and crankshaft must be free of oil for accurate measurement of connecting rod play.

Connecting Rod Side Play

Connecting rod side play is checked with a feeler gauge. This is illustrated in **Figure 19-17.** Most crankshafts use thrust washers to center the connecting rod(s).

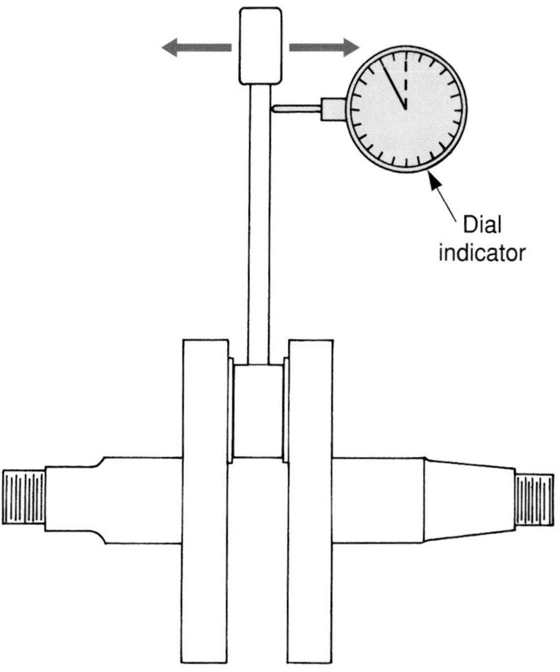

Figure 19-15. Connecting rod tip is one way of checking crankpin bearing and big end condition. A dial indicator is used to measure the connecting rod tip. Excessive tip indicates excessive wear.

Using only hand pressure, make sure the rod is free to move sideways. If it is not free, remove the cap and check for improper bearing size, dirt, etc. Then, check side clearance with a feeler gauge and compare the clearance to specifications. If the thrust washers are grooved or scored, as in **Figure 19-18,** a feeler gauge may not give an accurate measurement of side play. Visual inspection is needed to check the condition of the thrust washers.

Some two-stroke connecting rods are centered by the rod's small end (piston end). In this design, the piston pin boss or thrust washers provide connecting rod centering, **Figure 19-19.** If the rod side play or big end bearing clearance does not meet service manual specifications, the crankshaft must be disassembled for reconditioning.

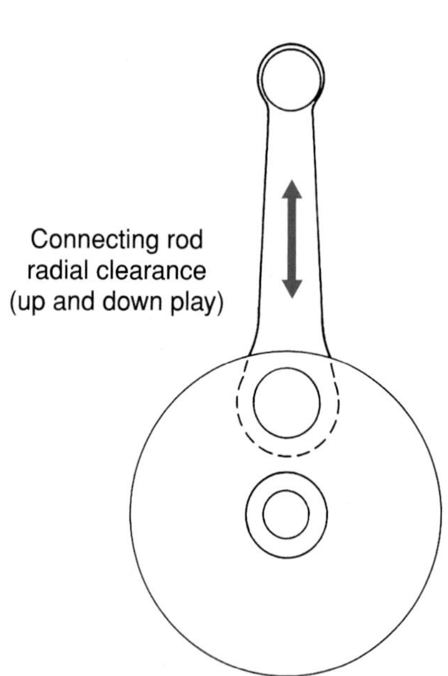

Figure 19-16. If radial clearance can be felt, the crankshaft is worn and must be rebuilt.

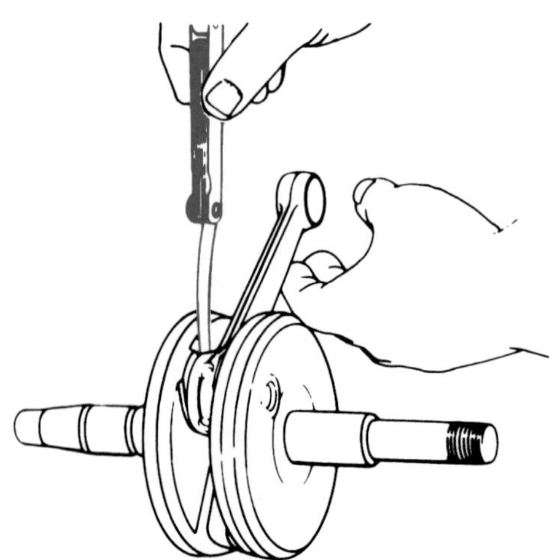

Figure 19-17. Connecting rod side play is measured with a feeler gauge. (Bombardier Ltd.)

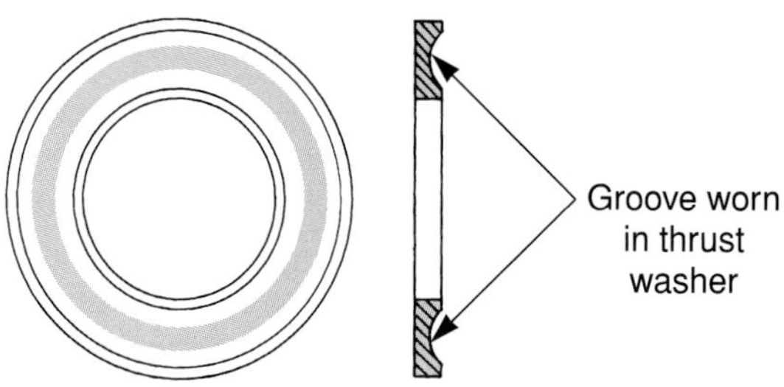

Figure 19-18. Worn crankshaft thrust washers may have a wear groove where they contact the connecting rod. A feeler gauge reading for clearance may not detect these grooves.

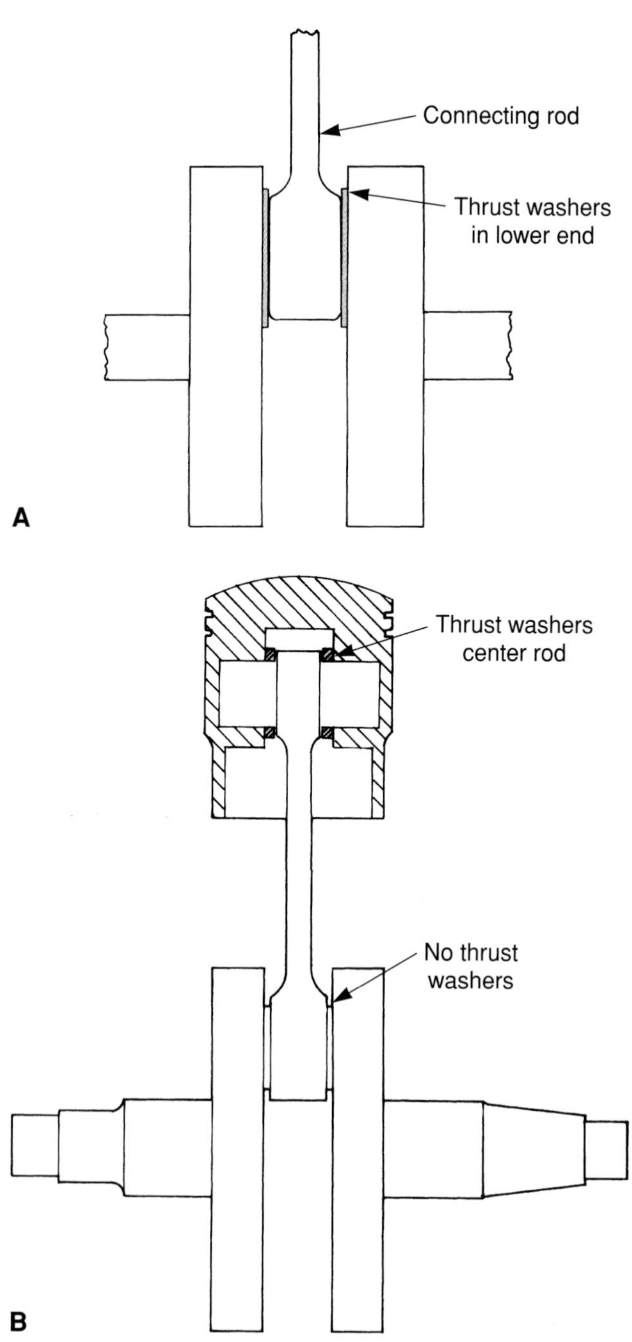

Figure 19-19. Connecting rods are centered on the crankshaft by thrust washers. A—Usually thrust washers are located on the crankpin. B—Some designs have thrust washers on the piston.

Main Bearings

Main bearings should be checked for lateral and radial play, **Figure 19-20.** Before checking the main bearings for looseness, wash them in solvent. Then dry the bearings thoroughly.

Caution: Do not spin bearings with compressed air when drying. This can cause permanent bearing damage or the bearing could fly apart with great force.

If lateral and radial play is within service limits, visually inspect the balls, races, and cages for evidence of pitting, chipping, discoloration, or signs of overheating. Replace the bearings as needed.

The oil slinger is mounted behind one of the main bearings on oil injection engines. Any contamination or dirt passing through the engine is often trapped in the oil slinger channel, **Figure 19-21.** It is extremely important to thoroughly clean the oil slinger during an overhaul. The service manual details proper procedures for main bearing removal and installation.

Crankshaft Wheel and Axle Condition

Crankshaft wheels (crankwheels) and axles must be thoroughly cleaned and inspected during an overhaul, **Figure 19-22.** The following list outlines areas of the crankshaft wheels and axles that require special attention.

- Clean all foreign material from balancing holes and counterweights.
- Inspect lip seal contact surface on axles for grooving.
- Inspect all threads, keyways, and tapers for damage.
- Check all parts for cracks.

Crankshaft Reconditioning

Crankshaft reconditioning involves the installation of a connecting rod kit, which includes the connecting rod, thrust washers, bearing, and crankpin. As shown in **Figure 19-23,** replacement of these components requires special tools and equipment, such as:

- Hydraulic press.
- Crankshaft wheel splitting plates and cylinders.
- Push pins.
- Crankshaft truing stand.
- Lead or brass hammer.

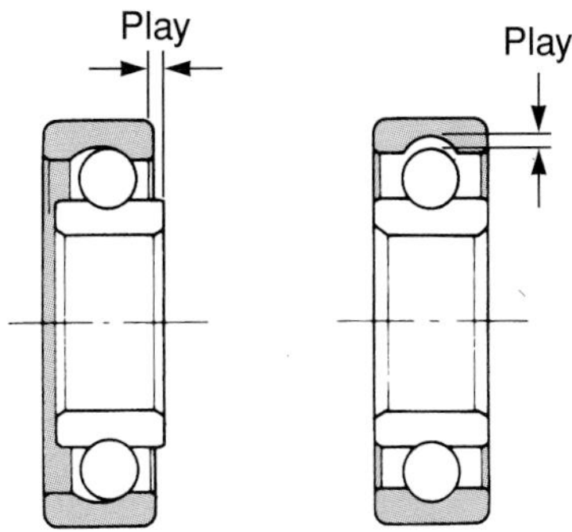

Figure 19-20. Bearings must be replaced if axial or radial play is excessive. (Suzuki Motor Corp.)

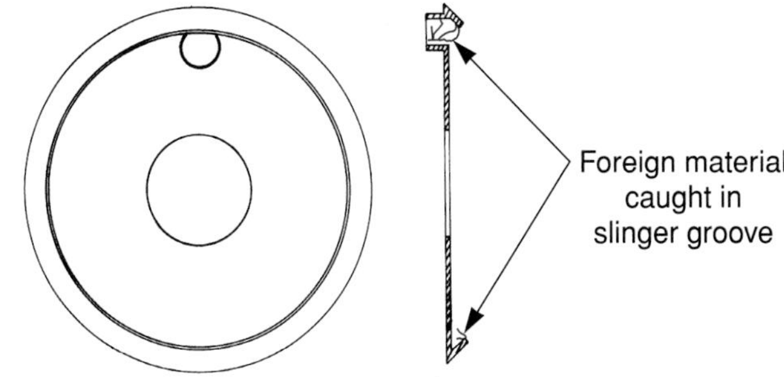

Figure 19-21. Foreign material is often caught and held in the oil slinger groove. The slinger must be cleaned thoroughly during a rebuild.

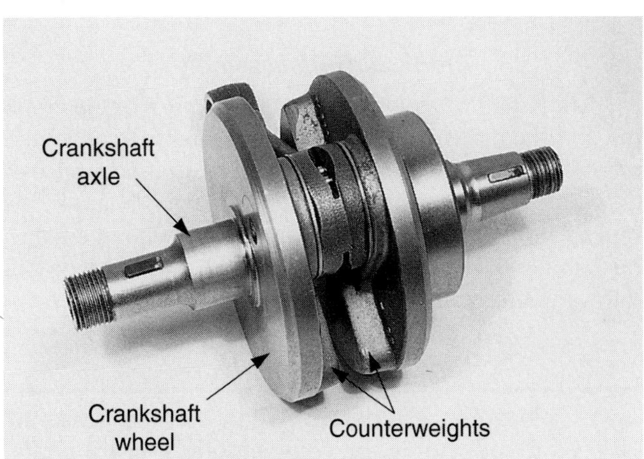

Figure 19-22. Clean and inspect crankshaft thoroughly during an overhaul.

Figure 19-23. A hydraulic press and special tools are needed to recondition a motorcycle crankshaft.

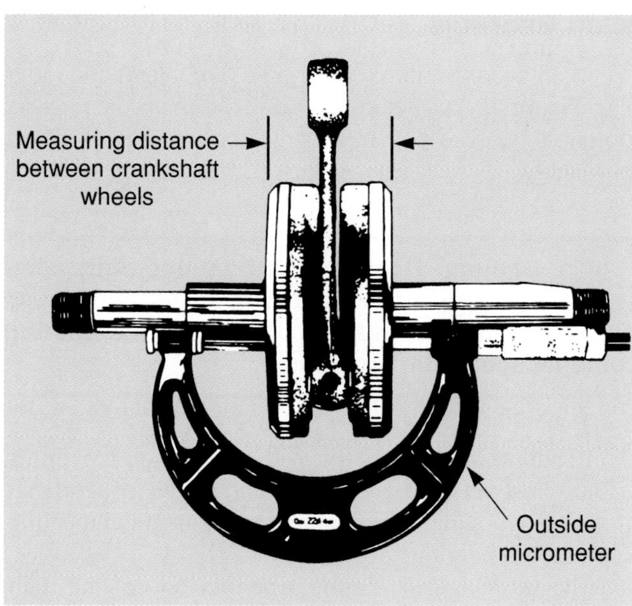

Figure 19-24. Measuring crankshaft width before disassembly is helpful in achieving proper end play when the crankshaft is reassembled. (Bombardier Ltd.)

Crankshaft Width Measurement

Crankshaft width must be measured before the crankshaft is pushed apart. This is demonstrated in **Figure 19-24.** The crankshaft width measurement is used in two ways:

1. In engines using the connecting rod small end for centering, the crankshaft width must be the same before and after reconditioning. Maintaining the same crankshaft width will help maintain proper end play.
2. In engines using thrust washers to center the connecting rod, crankshaft width may vary, as rod side play must be correct. In this case, this measurement is helpful in indicating changes in crankshaft shimming for end play.

Crankshaft Disassembly

Crankshaft disassembly requires removal of the crank pin and rod assembly from the crankwheels. To make the crankshaft rigid, a tight interference fit is used between the journals and crankwheels. On larger engines, as much as 40 tons (355 840 N) of force may be needed to push the crankshaft apart. **Figure 19-25** shows the procedures for crankshaft disassembly.

Warning: Be careful when using a press to disassemble or reassemble a crankshaft. The tremendous force could cause parts to fly out and cause injury. Wear eye protection.

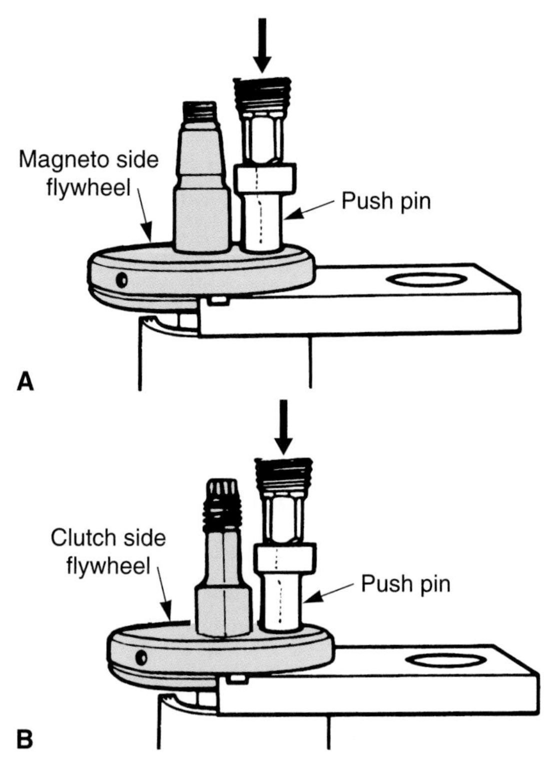

Figure 19-25. A—When pressing a crankshaft apart, the crankpin is pushed out of one flywheel first. Then, the connecting rod, roller bearing, and thrust washers are removed. B—Finally, the crankpin is pressed out of the other flywheel. (Bombardier Ltd.)

Crankshaft Assembly

Before assembling the crankshaft with a new rod kit, check the pinholes in the crankwheels for burrs and sharp edges. Remove any burrs, sharp edges, and other obstructions. Then, press the pin all the way into one of the crankwheels. On engines using oil injection, make sure the oil hole in the crankpin is in the proper position, **Figure 19-26.**

The connecting rod and bearings should be greased and positioned over the crankpin. Use petroleum jelly to hold the bearings in place. Make sure one thrust washer is placed on each side of the connecting rod.

To aid in alignment and make crankshaft truing easier, line up the wheels before pressing the crankshaft together. **Figure 19-27** illustrates initial crankwheel alignment. The crankshaft is now ready to be pressed together. Check and correct alignment as the wheels are initially pressed together. To check for proper side play on the connecting rod, use a feeler gauge to measure the clearance between the thrust washer and rod. Be careful not to pinch the feeler gauge.

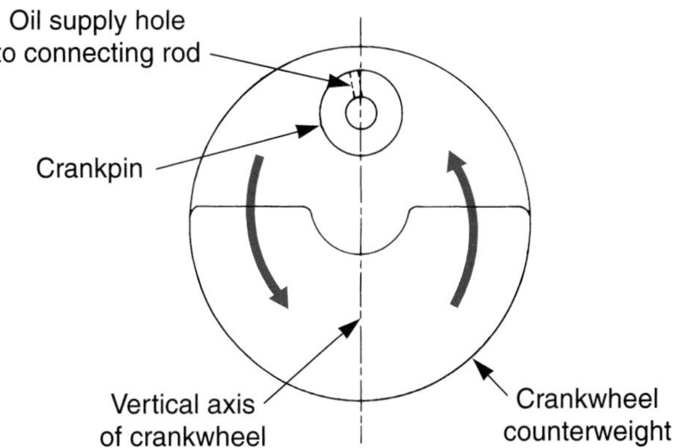

Figure 19-26. The connecting rod oil supply hole in the crankpin must be positioned slightly forward of the crankwheel's vertical axis. Make sure the oil hole is positioned properly before pressing the crankpin into the first flywheel.

Crankshaft Truing

Crankshaft truing is the accurate aligning of the crankshaft axle shafts. A crankshaft truing stand is used to determine and measure crankshaft runout, **Figure 19-28.** The axles must be aligned both vertically and horizontally, **Figure 19-29.**

If a vise or wedge is used to correct crankshaft vertical runout, as in **Figure 19-30.** A lead or brass hammer is used to correct vertical runout, as in **Figure 19-31.** Careful observation and dial indicator placement will let you determine the type of runout and appropriate procedure for correction. **Figure 19-32** illustrates typical misalignment and dial indicator movement during crankshaft truing. Usually, several corrections for vertical and horizontal runout are necessary. Patience and accuracy are absolutely essential during crankshaft truing. Specifications for maximum runout are found in your service manual. Always try to achieve zero runout.

Multi-Cylinder Crankshafts

Multi-cylinder crankshafts require more equipment and skill for crankshaft reconditioning. Reconditioning multiple cylinder crankshafts should be left to a specialist. Replacement parts for multi-cylinder crankshafts are usually not available and therefore, the crankshaft assembly must be replaced as an assembly.

Engine Diagnosis

Far too many motorcycle engines are disassembled, repaired, and reassembled without regard to finding the cause of engine failure. Proper diagnosis is perhaps the most important aspect of service. If the cause of a failure is not properly diagnosed, it can only be corrected by

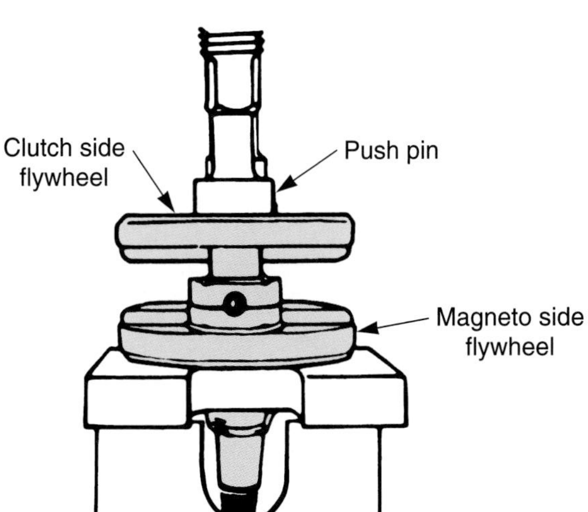

Figure 19-27. Accurate flywheel alignment can make crankshaft truing faster and easier. It is more difficult to move the flywheels after the crankshaft is pressed together. (Bombardier Ltd.)

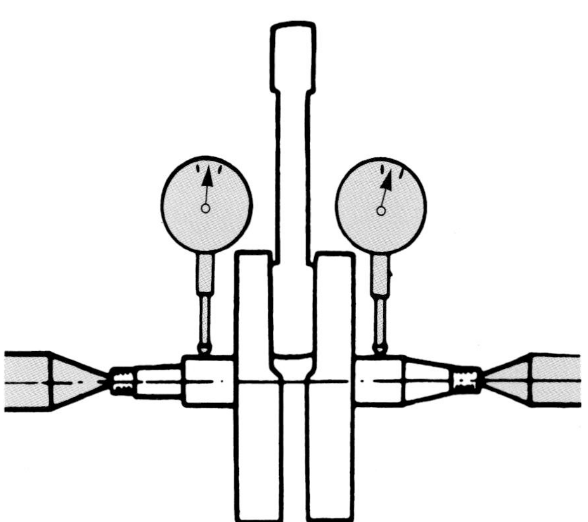

Figure 19-28. Crankshaft alignment is checked using a truing stand and two dial indicators. Indicator readings show runout as the crankshaft is turned on its stand. (Bombardier Ltd.)

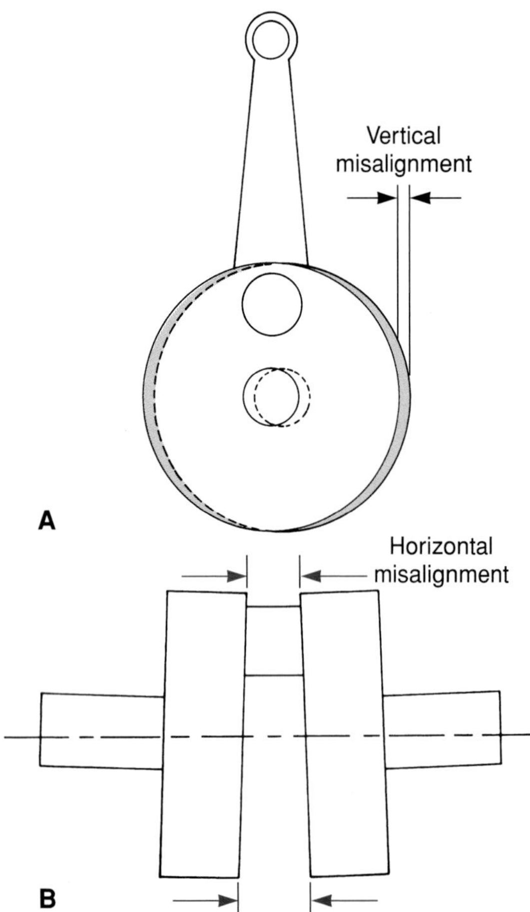

Figure 19-29. Crankshaft axles must be aligned perfectly. A—Vertically out of alignment. B—Horizontally out of alignment.

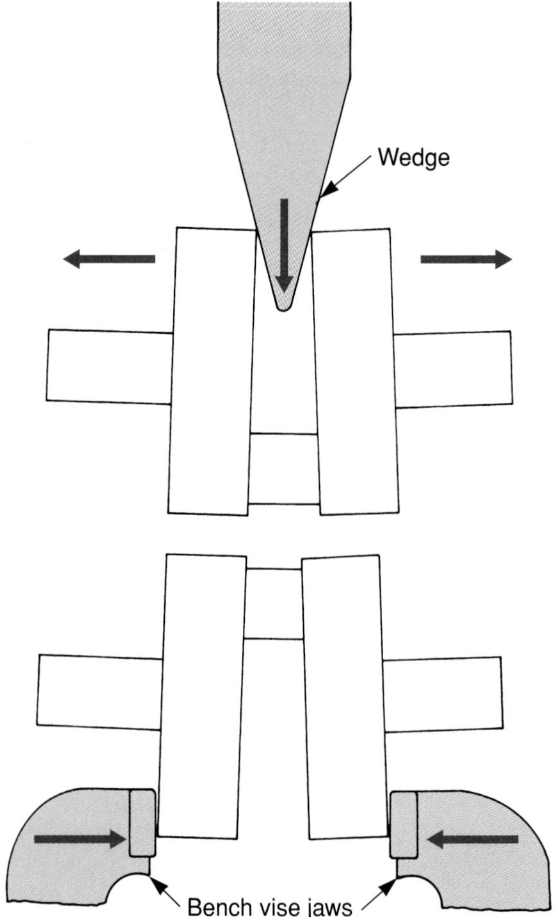

Figure 19-30. A wedge or vise may be used to correct crankshaft horizontal misalignment.

chance and may not be corrected at all. The engine overhaul might fail after only a short period of operation.

A typical example would be a two-stroke engine with a hole in the top of the piston. Obviously the engine will not run with a damaged piston. The hole in the piston was caused by a problem, such as lean mixture, wrong spark plug, improper ignition timing, or abuse. However, if you simply deglaze the cylinder and install a new piston, the engine will again run. But more than likely, the new piston will soon fail and look just like the old one. You must determine which of several possible problems is responsible for this mechanical failure.

Typical problems which occur in two-stroke engines are:

- Normal part wear.
- Lubrication failure.
- Damage caused by foreign material.
- Damage caused by overheating.
- Damage from an incorrect adjustment.

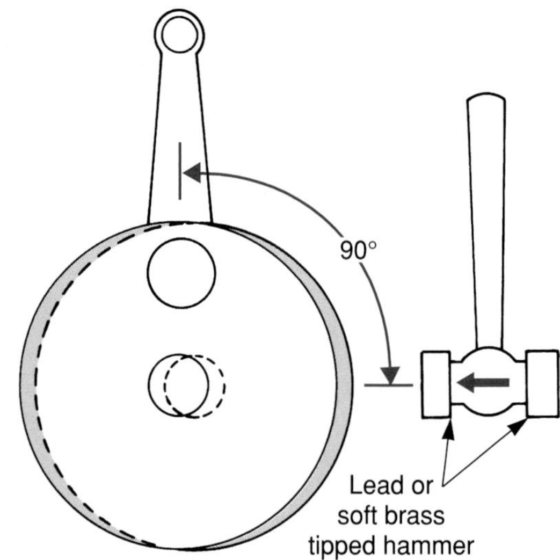

Figure 19-31. Blows from a lead or brass hammer should be used to correct horizontal misalignment.

Normal Wear

Normal wear is usually easy to diagnose. Usually, normal wear causes the engine to be noisy, smoke excessively, and perform poorly. Normal wear is easily diagnosed during top end disassembly and measurement. A problem resulting from normal wear does not always cause the engine to fail.

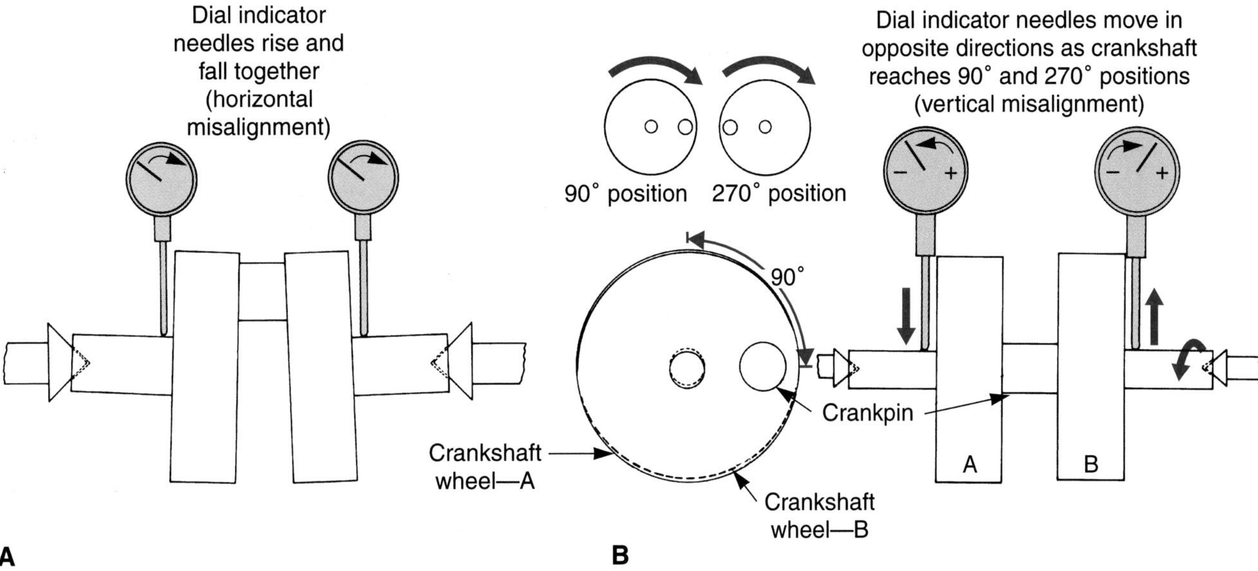

Figure 19-32. A—When the crankshaft axles are misaligned horizontally, the dial indicators will rise and fall together. B—When they are misaligned vertically, the dial indicators move in opposite directions.

A common condition resulting from normal engine wear is blowby. ***Blowby*** is the escape of combustion gases past the piston rings, **Figure 19-33.** Blowby is caused by excessive clearance between the piston and cylinder or by worn piston rings. Either problem can prevent the rings from sealing properly.

Excessive blowby can become a serious problem, causing:

- Piston overheating.
- Removal of the lubricating film between the piston and cylinder wall.
- Poor engine performance.

If conditions causing blowby are not corrected during the overhaul, piston seizure can result. Regular service is necessary to maintain good performance in a two-stroke cycle engine. Often, a well-maintained engine will need a minimum of parts to return it to its original performance levels. However, a badly neglected engine will be extremely worn and contain parts that will be damaged beyond repair. For example, the engine might have such extreme wear that one or more piston skirts have cracked and broken, **Figure 19-34.**

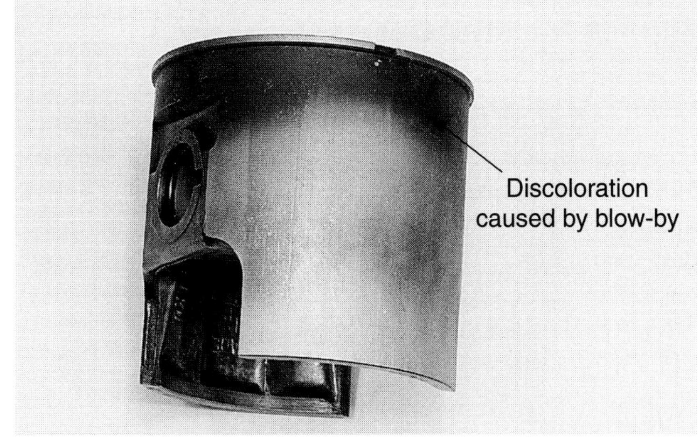

Figure 19-33. Blowby is caused by poor sealing of piston rings. The dark area at the top of this piston's skirt indicates blowby. The discoloration is burned on oil and may range from a caramel color to brownish black.

Figure 19-34. Extreme cylinder and piston wear resulted in piston rocking so severe that the piston skirt broke off.

Lubrication Failure

A lubrication failure is also an easy problem to diagnose. Without lubrication, engine components will have a dry, dull, burned appearance, as in **Figure 19-35.** Lubrication failures are caused by:

- Improper fuel-oil premix ratio.
- Improper oil.
- Improper oil injection system adjustment.
- Low levels of injection oil.
- Injection pump failure.

Figure 19-35. Damage to this piston was caused by running the engine with the oil injection tank empty.

If signs of lubrication failure are found, always check all these possible causes. Any one of them could ruin an engine in a matter of minutes.

Foreign Material Damage

The most common foreign materials found in a two-stroke engine are dust, dirt, sand, mud, and broken parts. Some types of foreign material enter through a dirty air cleaner or they may bypass the air cleaner (air cleaner missing, loose rubber connector boot, air box, or cylinder). Foreign material causes rapid wear of bearings, pistons, cylinders, and rings. **Figure 19-36** shows typical foreign material damage.

A

B

Figure 19-36. A—A dull, scratched appearance on this piston was caused by dirt that passed through a dirty air cleaner. B—This piston has been severely damaged by a broken ring.

Overheating

Overheating is the most common cause of damage to a two-stroke engine. Since there are many causes of overheating, accurate diagnosis is sometimes difficult. Some causes of engine overheating damage are:

- Fuel mixture problem.
- Incorrect ignition timing.
- Incorrect spark plug heat range.
- Excessive carbon build-up.
- Detonation or preignition.
- Air leaks.
- Lubrication failure.
- Excessive piston clearance.

Ignition System Problems

Overheating caused by the ignition system is usually the result of incorrect ignition timing or the wrong spark plug heat range. Ignition related overheating may cause seizure or erosion of the piston crown or a hole to be burned in the piston. These problems are shown in **Figure 19-37.**

The severity of damage is determined by:

- The length of time the engine is operated while overheated.
- The amount of error in ignition timing or plug heat range.

Both ignition system and fuel system-caused overheating can cause piston seizure. Extreme cases of ignition system-caused overheating usually lead to piston crown erosion in a small area (hole in piston). The remaining crown surface may maintain a normal appearance. Always correct the cause of any overheating problem before engine reassembly and start-up.

Detonation and Preignition

Under normal conditions, the air-fuel mixture burns at a rapid, but controlled rate. During detonation and preignition, this rate is greatly increased, causing damage to engine components. These problems occur when combustion chamber temperatures are high enough to produce uncontrolled combustion. Extreme damage such as a hole burned in a piston or an eroded piston crown normally results from detonation and/or preignition.

The two most common causes for ***detonation*** are excessive compression ratio and low octane fuel. As the air-fuel mixture begins to burn after normal ignition, pressure and temperature rise to a point where the unburned air-fuel mixture at the outside edge of the combustion chamber ignites. See **Figure 19-38A.** Because combustion is occurring in two areas of the combustion chamber at once, the air-fuel mixture burns almost explosively. The collision of the two flame fronts causes a pinging noise or knock.

Preignition occurs when a hot spot (overheated surface) in the combustion chamber ignites the air-fuel mixture before the spark plug fires. Usually, a carbon flake, gasket protruding into the combustion chamber, or excessively high spark plug heat range causes premature igniting of the air-fuel mixture. Preignition may also cause an audible ping or knock, as the two flame fronts collide, **Figure 19-38B.** Both fuel system and ignition system problems can produce detonation and preignition damage.

Fuel System Problems

Damage caused by fuel system problems often appears to have been caused by the ignition system. Piston seizure is one of the most common forms of damage that might be caused by the fuel system. Fuel system

A

B

Figure 19-37. These pistons show results of severe ignition related overheating. A—Ignition timing was too advanced. B—A spark plug that was too hot for the engine burned a hole in this piston.

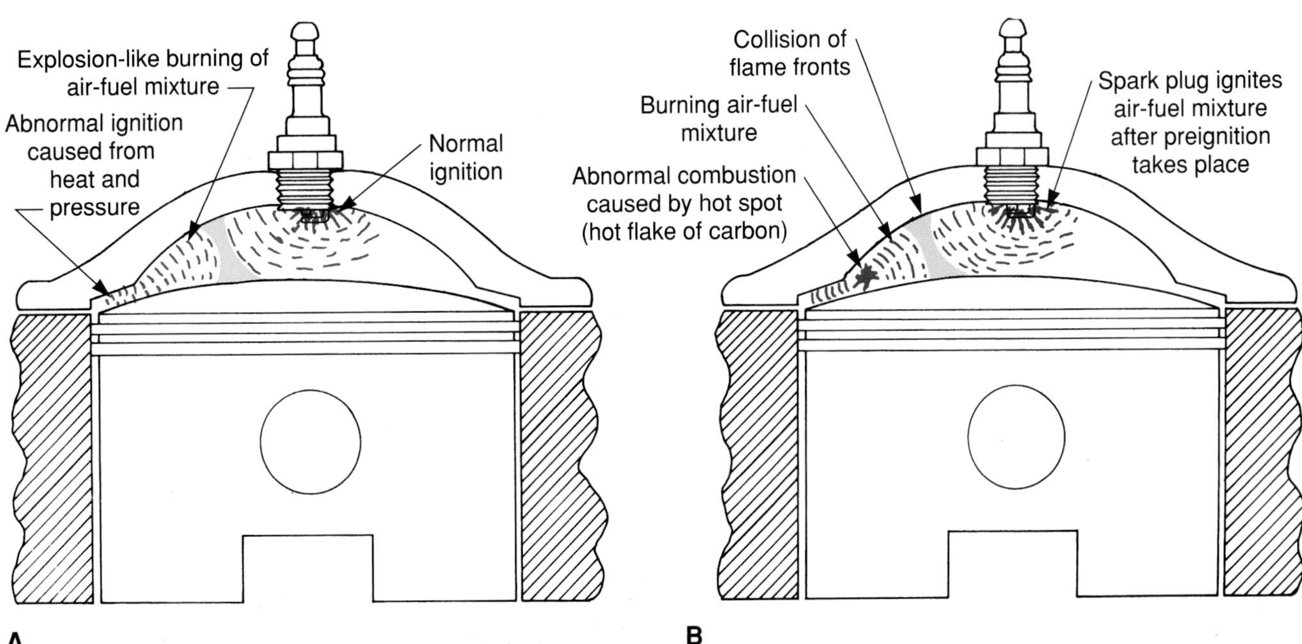

Figure 19-38. A—Detonation occurs after normal ignition. B—Preignition occurs before the spark plug fires. Both create a dual flame front which causes a knocking or pinging sound in the engine.

related overheating can usually be detected before severe damage has occurred. Some of the causes of fuel system overheating are:

- Improper or clogged carburetor jets.
- Improper carburetor float level.
- Clogged fuel injectors.
- Contaminated or low octane fuel.
- Clogged fuel filter.
- Clogged fuel tank vent.
- Air leak (crankcase or intake manifold).

During fuel system-induced overheating, the piston crown usually has a uniform, but lighter than normal color. Because there is no piston crown erosion, the spark plug will indicate a lean mixture (light gray to white plug insulator).

Checking Crankshaft and Transmission Shaft End Play

To allow for expansion and freedom of movement at operating temperatures, it is important to check crankshaft and transmission shaft ***end play.*** There are two methods used to measure end play. If the components are free to float from side to side, a dial indicator may be used to check end play. Install a dial indicator against the side of the shaft counterweights or wheels. Pry the shaft toward the left side of the engine and zero the indicator. Then pry the crankshaft toward the right side of the engine and read the indicator. The indicator reading must be within specifications. Another method for checking end play requires a parallel bar and vernier caliper. **Figure 19-39** shows a vernier caliper being used to measure crankcase width.

Engine Reassembly

All the time and effort invested in cleaning, measuring, reconditioning, and diagnosing is wasted if the engine is not reassembled properly. The recommended sequence and specific procedures for engine reassembly are found in your service manual. However, there are a number of important procedures to keep in mind.

Lip Seal Installation

Proper lip seal installation is extremely important. A serious leak can result from poor lip seal installation, **Figure 19-40.** A leaking seal can cause loss of gear oil or crankcase compression and vacuum. The most critical seals are those which seal the crankcase and crankshaft. A mistake in the installation of one of these seals can ruin an engine. Follow this procedure when installing lip seals.

1. Remove burrs and sharp edges that might damage the seal's outside diameter.
2. Position the seal in the proper direction, as shown in **Figure 19-41.**
3. Install the seal straight and to the proper depth.
4. Use grease to lubricate the sealing lip, **Figure 19-41.**

Oil and Grease Types

Engine components must be lubricated during assembly. This ensures proper lubrication and prevents possible damage when the engine is first started after reassembly. Failure to lubricate components during assembly can result in immediate part damage.

You will use the same lubricant for engine assembly as will be used during engine operation. Lubricate two-stroke engine components with two-stroke oil. Lubricate primary and transmission components with the proper gear lubricant. However, grease can be used on a number of parts during engine assembly.

- On seals (all-purpose grease).
- On rollers during crankshaft assembly (petroleum jelly).
- To locate shims or hold parts in position (all-purpose grease).

Checking for Binding After Each Installation

All rotating parts are susceptible to binding if installed improperly. Check for free movement after installing

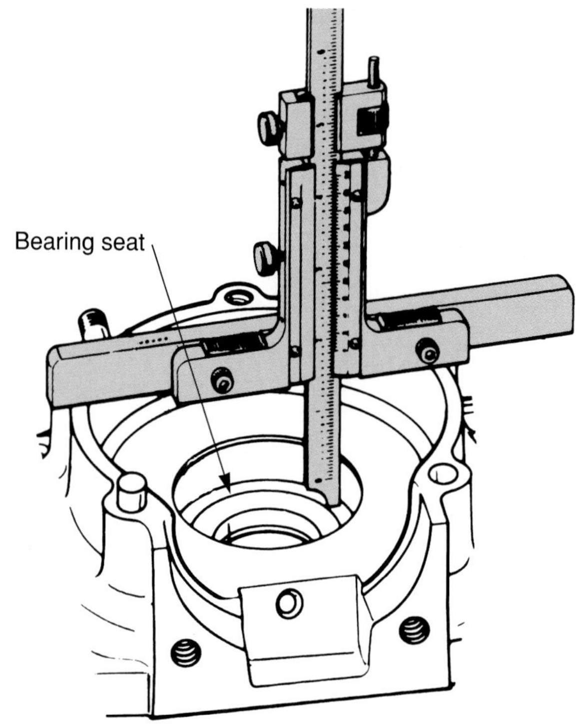

Figure 19-39. A depth micrometer or vernier caliper and parallel bar will measure crankcase width to determine the needed shimming for proper crankshaft end play. (Bombardier Ltd.)

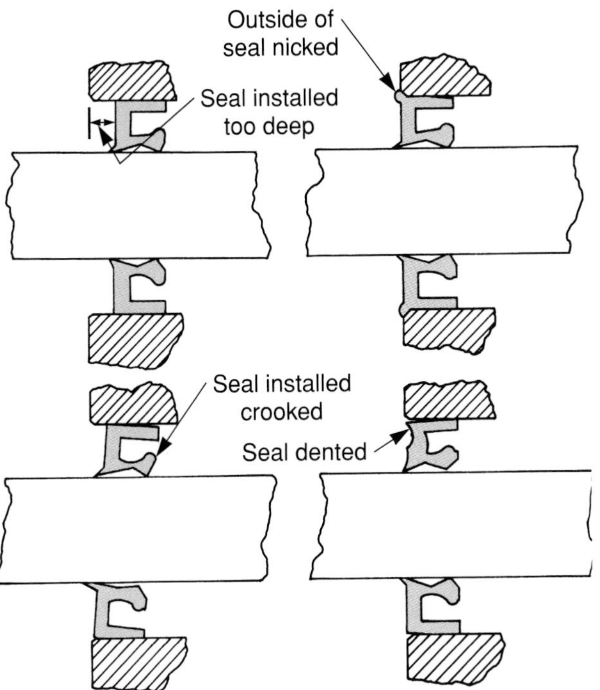

Figure 19-40. Improper seal installation can cause engine damage by allowing oil leakage at the transmission output shaft, shift shaft, or vacuum and pressure leakage at the crankshaft.

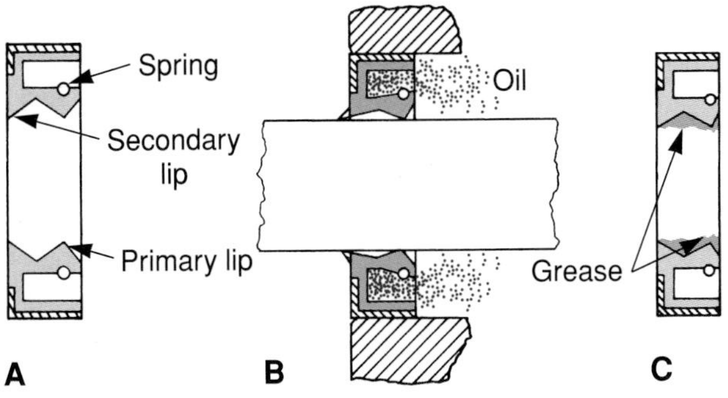

Figure 19-41. A—Parts of an oil seal. B—Oil seals must be installed with the primary lip toward oil. C—Seals must be packed with grease to lubricate the seal lips.

shafts, the shift drum, and crankshaft. A check for binding should be made as parts are assembled and after the crankcases are torqued. Also, make sure the transmission shifts smoothly through each gear.

Sealants

Machined surfaces not using a gasket must always be sealed with silicone sealer or an approved liquid gasket. Modern paper gasket materials do not require any type of gasket sealer. In many cases, the use of grease or gasket cement to locate or hold a gasket in place is helpful. Refer to your service manual for the proper sealant compounds and where they should be used.

Rotary Valve Timing

Two-stroke engines that use a rotary valve require specific valve timing during reassembly. Timing marks, keyways, or locating pins are used to index the rotary valve in the proper position. **Figure 19-42** illustrates a typical rotary valve timing procedure.

Top End Reassembly

A two-stroke cycle engine top end is relatively simple to reassemble. However, minor mistakes during assembly can cause serious damage. Important steps to follow during the reassembly of any two-stroke engine are:

1. All gasket surfaces must be clean.
2. Use new gaskets and new piston pin circlips.
3. Face the piston in the proper direction, **Figure 19-43.**

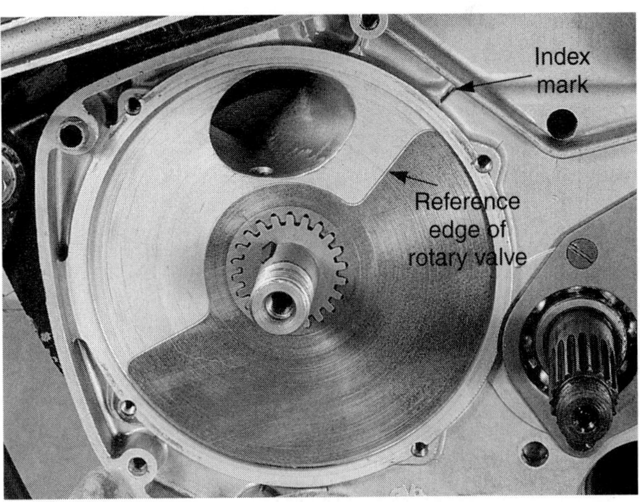

Figure 19-42. Typical rotary valve timing. Position the piston at TDC. Then, align the valve edge (or rotary valve mark) with the index mark.

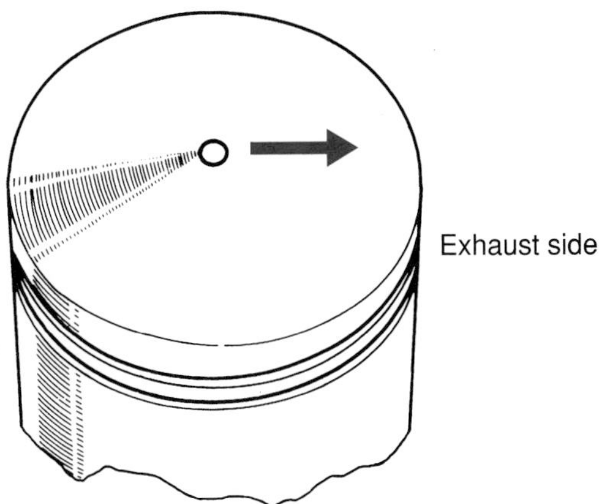

Figure 19-43. An arrow usually stamped into the piston crown indicates installation direction. (Suzuki Motor Corp.)

4. Check that circlips are installed and seated properly, **Figure 19-44.**
5. Lightly lubricate the piston, pin and pin bearing. Do not lubricate the piston rings, and cylinder.
6. Check that piston rings are installed properly in grooves and indexed in locating pins, **Figure 19-45.**
7. Carefully install cylinder over piston, **Figure 19-46.**
8. Torque cylinder and cylinder head bolts to specifications in proper sequence, **Figure 19-47.**

Torque Sequence

Due to the size of cylinders, cylinder heads, and crankcases, torque patterns must be utilized to prevent warping. A ***torque pattern*** (sequence) follows a crisscross pattern from the center to the outside of the part. This sequence is repeated in small graduations until the final torque is achieved, which ensures an even clamping action. **Figure 19-48** shows a typical torque sequence. For specific torque sequences and torque values, refer to the proper service manual.

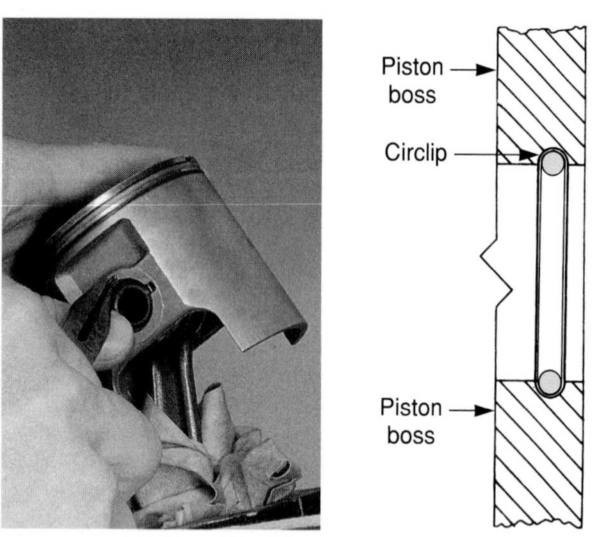

Figure 19-44. Piston pin circlips are installed with needle nose pliers. Make sure the circlip is fully seated.

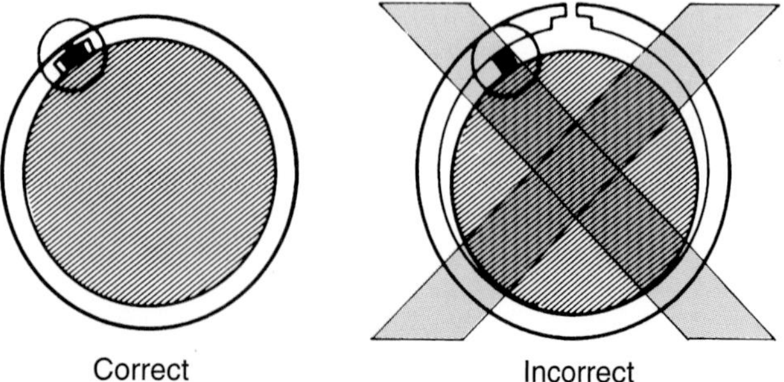

Figure 19-45. Two-stroke piston rings must be properly indexed with ring locating pins. (Suzuki Motor Corp.)

Figure 19-46. Make sure ring end gaps are properly engaged with the locating pins when installing the cylinder. Do not force the cylinder over the piston or part damage may result.

Figure 19-47. Torque the cylinder and head to factory specifications. Use the proper crisscross torque sequence. Tighten in 2-3 stages, or as described in the service manual.

Crankcase Leak Test

To make sure that all seals and gaskets are properly installed, you should perform a two-stroke engine leak test. A pressure/vacuum leak test tool provides a clear indication of where a leak, or leaks exist. A two-stroke cycle engine crankcase leak test consists of:

1. Seal the intake and exhaust ports.
2. Position the piston at BDC (bottom dead center).
3. Install the cylinder adapter and pressurize the crankcase to 6 psi (41 kPa).
4. Monitor the pressure gauge while using a soap and water solution to find any crankcase leaks.

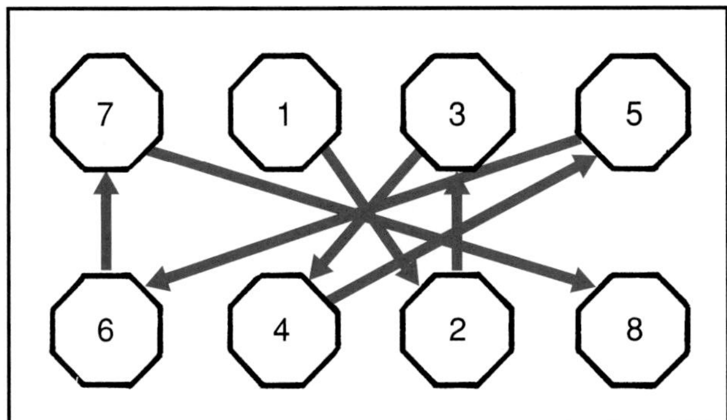

Figure 19-48. A typical torque pattern crisscross from center to outside.

Ignition Timing

The last adjustment to be made before installing the engine in the frame is static ignition timing. This ensures the ignition timing will be close enough for initial engine start-up. Final dynamic ignition timing must be done with the engine running, using a strobe (timing) light. Refer to a service manual and Chapter 9, for proper static and dynamic timing procedures.

Engine Reassembly Summary

The following list summarizes some of the important aspects of two-stroke engine reassembly. Refer to a service manual for specific step-by-step instructions and to select the proper tools.

1. Lubricate moving engine components.
2. Use new gaskets, seals, and O-rings.
3. Check crankshaft and transmission end play.
4. Install lip seals properly.
5. Install bearing locating half rings, dowel pins, and plates properly, **Figure 19-49.**
6. Install crankcase dowel pins.
7. Position crankshaft spacers and shims correctly.
8. Install oil slinger.
9. Make sure crankshaft bearings are installed in the proper direction and are fully seated on the crankshaft or in the case.
10. Assemble the transmission.
11. Check that crankcase fasteners of different lengths are in their proper locations.
12. Check for binding after each installation.
13. Apply sealing compounds as needed.
14. Check rotary valve timing.

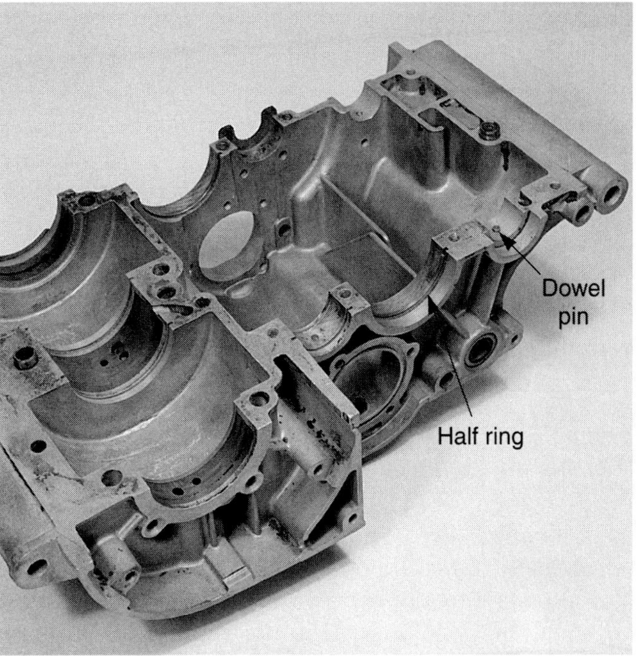

Figure 19-49. Double-check installation of bearing locating half rings, dowel pins, and plates.

15. Check for proper clutch and primary drive assembly.
16. Make sure piston is facing in the correct direction and that circlips are installed properly.
17. Check that piston ring direction and positioning are correct.
18. Carefully install the cylinder.
19. Use proper torque values and sequence.
20. Install the oil injection pump and lines.
21. Perform a crankcase leak test.
22. Carefully install ignition components.
23. Align timing marks on base plate and case.

Installing Engine in Frame

Before attempting to install the engine, locate and organize all engine mounting fasteners and brackets. Make sure the frame is clean. Loosen or remove any components which might hamper engine installation (fuel tank, brake pedal). Refer to the proper service manual for detailed engine installation instructions.

The following summary will help ensure that nothing is overlooked after engine installation:

1. Properly tighten engine mounting bolts.
2. Check routing and secure connection of cables, fluid lines, and wires.
3. Install the carburetor and adjust throttle cable freeplay. Synchronize if engine has multiple carburetors.

4. Install the exhaust system.
5. Adjust the clutch.
6. Adjust oil pump cable.
7. Install and adjust the drive chain.
8. If air is present in the oil feed lines, use a clean oil can to inject oil into the lines until all air is removed. This will bleed the lines.

Initial Engine Start-up and Operation

Because a freshly overhauled engine has high friction between the parts (referred to as *tight*), it is necessary to follow careful break-in procedures. During break-in, avoid overloading, high engine speeds, overheating the engine, and check the oil level at each fuel fill-up. It is also important to monitor engine operation and performance, and make adjustments as necessary. Typical break-in period is three hours for an off-road bike and 300 miles (480 km) for a road motorcycle. Before attempting to start the engine, the following summary should be reviewed:

1. Fill the clutch and transmission with the recommended lubricant.
2. Fill the injection oil tank (clean the filter and fill with the recommended lubricant).
3. Fill injection oil lines and bleed injection pump.
4. Clean fuel petcock and sediment bowl.
5. If premix lubricant is used, fill the fuel tank with the recommended fuel-oil mixture.
6. Service the air filter.

After the engine has been started, complete the following:

1. Check oil pump operation.
2. Check ignition timing with a timing light.
3. Check for unusual noises and overheating.
4. Check for leaks.
5. Adjust carburetors.
6. Road test.
7. Retorque cylinder head, after the engine has cooled.

Summary

The parts included in a two-stroke engine s top end are the piston, rings, cylinder, piston pin, reed valve, head gasket, and cylinder head. A two-stroke engine s top end requires more frequent service and repair than a four-stroke engine. The cylinder and piston(s) must be inspected and measured closely during an overhaul. As this is the foundation for the entire engine, it must be reconditioned properly to ensure a good rebuild.

Inspect the cylinder for cracks, scoring, rust, wear ridges on the top and bottom of the cylinder, and obvious damage caused by foreign material. Inspect the piston for scoring, cracking, galling (seizure), evidence of foreign material, and crown damage. Always investigate the cause of piston damage to find and correct the source of the problem.

Piston skirt wear is checked by measuring the piston skirt diameter with a micrometer. Ring land wear is determined by measuring side clearance between the piston rings and the ring land with a feeler gauge. Measurement of the piston ring s end gap indicates the ring size. Measurement of the ring free gap indicates the amount of ring tension. Cylinder taper is wear that causes the top of the cylinder to be worn larger than the bottom. Cylinder out-of-roundness is wear that causes the cylinder to resemble an oval or egg-shape. Piston-to-cylinder clearance is determined by comparing piston diameter to cylinder bore diameter.

Removal of accumulated carbon should be performed as part of a top end overhaul. Be careful not to damage or scratch the parts while removing the hard carbon. In liquid-cooled engines, be sure to remove carbon particles that may have fallen into the coolant jackets around the cylinder by blowing them out with compressed air.

Once parts have been cleaned, inspected, and measured, you can begin reconditioning and/or replacing parts. Deglazing provides a fine finish by removing scuffs or scratch marks, but does not enlarge the cylinder diameter. Deglazing also produces a crosshatch pattern on the cylinder walls to provide cavities for holding oil during piston ring break-in. Ring replacement alone, without cylinder boring and piston replacement, is allowable when the piston and cylinder are both within wear limits. When the cylinder is worn beyond specifications by excessive taper, out-of-roundness, or scoring, the cylinder must be machined larger. Cylinders which use a cast-in sleeve must be replaced after the largest overbore has been used. After installing a new sleeve (liner) in the cylinder, the liner can be bored to its original standard bore size.

Connecting rod sideplay is checked with a feeler gauge. Main bearings should be checked for lateral and radial play. The oil slinger is mounted behind one of the main bearings on oil injection engines. Any contamination or dirt passing through the engine is often trapped in the oil slinger channel. Crankshaft wheels (crankwheels) and axles must be thoroughly cleaned and inspected during an overhaul. Crankshaft reconditioning involves the installation of a connecting rod kit, which includes the connecting rod, thrust washers, bearing, and crankpin. Multi-cylinder crankshafts require more equipment and skill for crankshaft reconditioning. Reconditioning multiple cylinder crankshafts should be left to a specialist.

Far too many motorcycle engines are disassembled, repaired, and reassembled without regard to finding the cause of engine failure. Proper diagnosis is perhaps the most important aspect of service. Normal wear is easily diagnosed during top end disassembly and measurement. A lubrication failure will give engine components a dry, dull, burned appearance. The most common foreign materials found in a two-stroke engine are dust, dirt, sand, mud, and broken parts. Overheating is the most common cause of damage to a two-stroke engine.

Know These Terms

Rust	Ring land wear
Scoring	Ring end gap
Galling	Ring free gap
Piston skirt wear	Cylinder taper
Out-of-roundness	Connecting rod side play
Piston-to-cylinder clearance	Crankshaft truing
Chemical soaking	Blowby
Emulsion cleaning solution	Overheating
Dry blasting	Detonation
Deglazing	Preignition
Crosshatch pattern	End play
Honing	Torque pattern

Review Questions—Chapter 19

Do not write in this text. Place your answers on a separate sheet of paper.

1. List some of the problems to look for during piston and cylinder inspection.
2. Cylinder _____ will cause a ring to change its end gap and tension as it moves up and down in the cylinder bore.
   A. ridge
   B. taper
   C. cracks
   D. scoring
3. Cylinder bore out-of-roundness affects ring sealing. What can this condition cause?
4. It is necessary to _____ a cylinder before installing new rings to provide controlled break-in.
   A. bore
   B. sleeve
   C. rinse
   D. hone
5. A ring end gap clearance that is too small can cause _____.
6. A ring with too much ring end gap can cause _____.
7. List the three reasons why honing is necessary after cylinder boring.
8. Crankshaft main bearings should be checked for both lateral and _____ play.
9. It is always a good idea to measure _____ before pushing a crankshaft apart.
10. _____ is the most important aspect of engine service.
    A. Proper diagnosis
    B. A good repair
    C. Shop cleanliness
    D. None of the above.
11. Normal wear causes the engine to _____.
    A. waste fuel
    B. be noisy
    C. perform poorly
    D. All of the above.
12. Define the term *blowby.*
13. Blowby can cause piston ____.
    A. overheating
    B. overcooling
    C. explosion
    D. knurling
14. Describe the condition and appearance of engine parts that have suffered a lubrication failure.
15. Where does foreign material enter a two-stroke engine?
    A. through the air box due to a dirty air filter
    B. leaking cylinder
    C. loose rubber connector boot
    D. All of the above.
16. List three of the common causes for engine overheating.
17. Incorrect ignition _____ and/or the wrong spark plug _____ can cause a hole to be burned in the piston crown.
18. An improperly installed seal can cause the loss of:
    A. gear oil.
    B. crankcase compression.
    C. crankcase vacuum.
    D. All of the above.
19. What kind of oil is used to lubricate engine parts during engine assembly?
20. What are four important considerations during engine break-in?

Suggested Activities

1. Design your own two-stroke engine measurement and inspection checklist. Refer to this chapter and manufacturer's service manuals for guidance in compiling and organizing the checklist. Use your checklist while completing the following activities.
2. Disassemble and inspect a two-stroke engine top end. Use this chapter and your service manual to determine the necessary repairs.
3. Rebuild and true a two-stroke engine crankshaft.
4. Visit a local motorcycle dealership and try to acquire some damaged two-stroke engine parts. Using the diagnosis section, try to determine the cause of each engine failure.
5. Using what you have learned and the proper service manual, reassemble a two-stroke engine and install it in the frame.

20 Four-Stroke Engine Overhaul

After studying this chapter, you will be able to:

- Inspect the parts of a four-stroke engine for signs of wear or damage.
- Measure four-stroke engine part wear.
- Explain how to recondition a four-stroke engine top end.
- Diagnose four-stroke engine failures.
- Explain how to recondition the bottom end of a four-stroke engine.
- Summarize four-stroke engine reassembly.
- Describe engine installation, initial starting, and break-in procedures.

The purpose of this chapter is to help the technician become familiar with the proper methods of performing a four-stroke engine overhaul. Top and bottom end reconditioning, reassembly, and initial starting are covered. Several other chapters in this book give information relating to the overhaul of a four-stroke engine. Use the index to locate this added information as needed.

Engine Top End Service

Four-stroke engine ***top end*** parts include: piston, rings, piston pin, circlips, cylinder, cylinder head, valves, valve springs, camshafts, push rods, cam sprockets, cam chain tensioner and guides, cam followers or rocker arms, head gasket, cylinder base gasket, and intake manifold.

The condition of a four-stroke engine's top end is critical for good engine performance. The top end parts control the movement of air and fuel through the combustion chamber. These parts are also responsible for sealing the energy produced by combustion. Obviously, worn valves, piston rings, and other problems can greatly reduce engine efficiency and power.

Cleaning and Decarbonizing

Cleaning and decarbonizing is a similar process for two- and four-stroke engines. The main difference is the four-stroke engine has additional parts to be decarbonized. Refer to Chapters 3 and 19 for a review of cleaning equipment and decarbonizing.

Top End Inspection and Measurement

Valve train components are exposed to high temperatures, heavy loads, and high speeds. Because of these severe conditions, the valve train usually wears more rapidly than other engine components. This is especially true if the lubrication system is not functioning properly. See **Figure 20-1.** The following components make up the valve train and require a thorough visual inspection during top end repairs:

- Camshaft and bearings.
- Cam followers, rocker arms, and shafts.
- Push rods and lifters.

- Cam sprockets, timing chain, drive gears, or belts.
- Valve springs, collars, and keepers.
- Valve stems, guides, and seals.
- Valve seats and faces.

Inspecting Camshafts and Bearings

Thoroughly clean the shaft with solvent and a lint-free cloth. After cleaning the camshaft, check each lobe for scoring, scuffing, cracks, or other signs of wear. Inspect the camshaft journals and bearings for any signs of abnormal wear. Many manufacturers give specifications for:

- Base circle diameter and cam lobe height, **Figure 20-2.**
- Bearing journal diameter.
- Camshaft runout, **Figure 20-3.**
- Bearing inside diameter.
- Journal-to-bearing clearance, **Figure 20-4.**
- Camshaft end play, **Figure 20-5.**

Checking Camshafts for Wear

The simplest way to measure cam lobes for wear is to use an outside micrometer. Position the micrometer to measure from the heel to the nose of the lobe. Measure the lobe at 90° from the original measurement. Record the dimensions measured for each intake and exhaust lobe. Any variation in lobe height indicates wear. Check all measurements against the manufacturer's recommended lobe height. If desired, the cam lobes can also be checked with a dial indicator.

Check the camshaft for straightness with a dial indicator. Place the shaft on V-blocks and position the dial indicator on the center bearing journal. Slowly rotate the camshaft. If the dial indicator shows a runout variation of more than .002″ (.050 mm), the camshaft is not straight. Some valve train designs use needle bearings or ball bearings to support the camshaft. When measuring a design of this type, check for excessive lateral play, radial play, and smooth bearing operation. In push rod engines, the camshaft or camshafts are located in the crankcase.

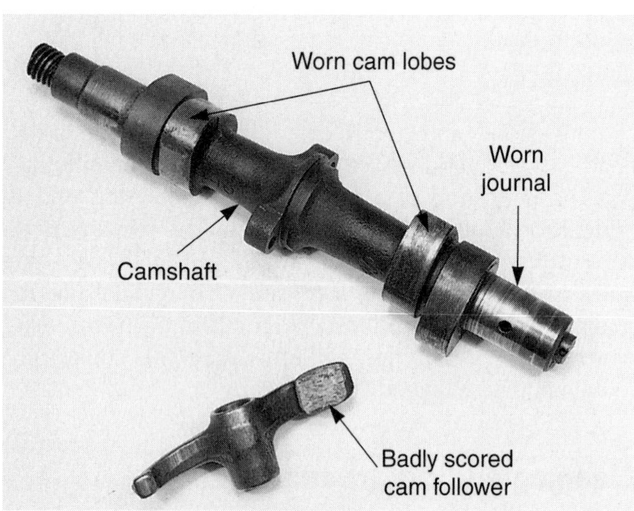

Figure 20-1. Notice how the cam lobes, cam journals, and cam follower were badly damaged by lubrication system failure.

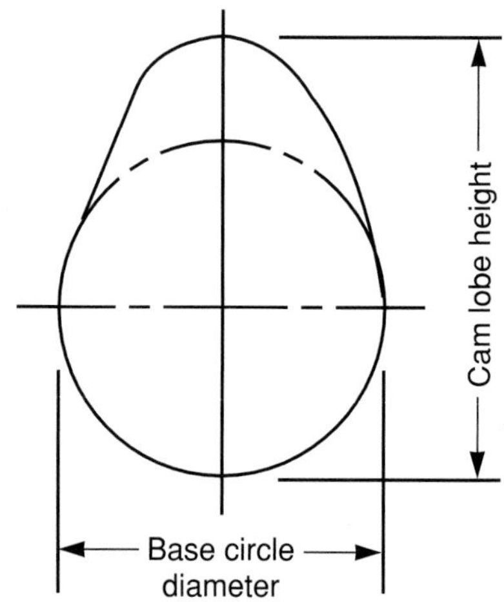

Figure 20-2. Use an outside micrometer to measure camshaft base circle diameter and lobe height. Check all lobe heights because wear can vary. (Kawasaki Motors Corporation U.S.A.)

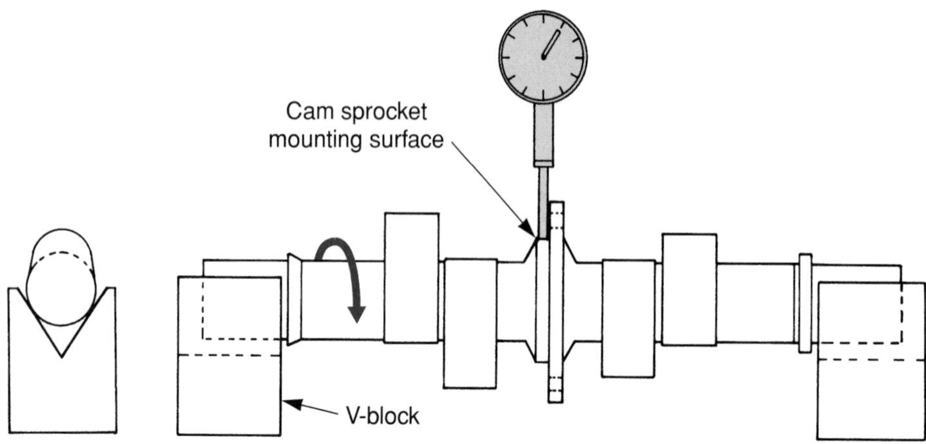

Figure 20-3. Use a dial indicator to detect camshaft runout. Make sure the indicator rides on the cam's machined surfaces.

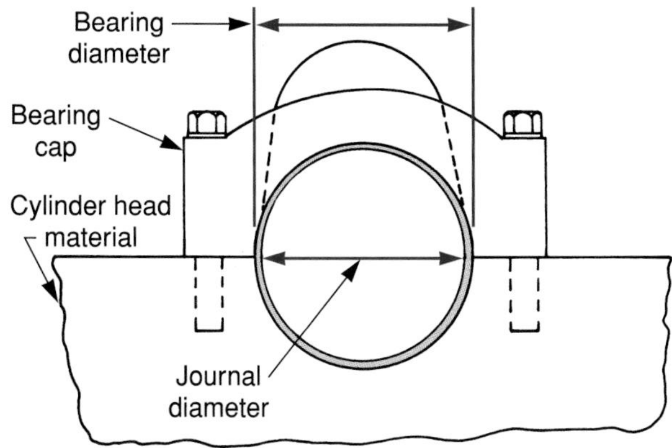

Figure 20-4. Camshaft journal-to-bearing clearance can be measured with Plastigage or a telescoping gauge and outside micrometer. When using a micrometer, subtract the journal diameter from the bearing diameter to find clearance.

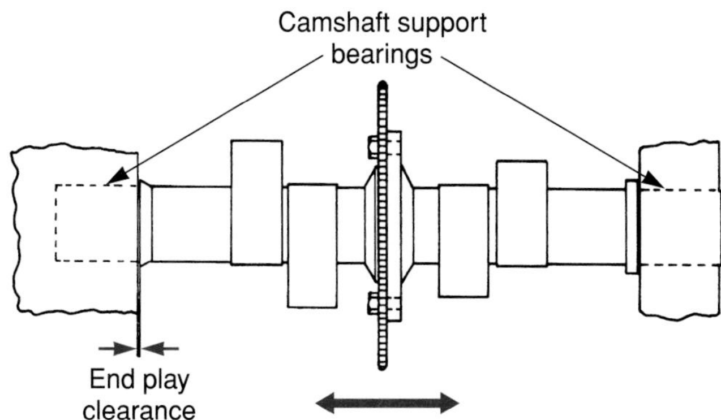

Figure 20-5. Camshaft end play can be checked with a feeler gauge. The thickest blade that fits between the camshaft flange and support bearing indicates the amount of end play.

Cam Followers, Rocker Arms, and Shafts

When removing cam followers and rocker arms for inspection, mark each one so it can be returned to where it was removed. Wash them in clean solvent and dry them with compressed air. Use a wire brush to clean the oil passages (if used). Inspect the rocker arm shaft for scratches, scores, burns, or excessive wear at points of contact. Examine each rocker arm for cracks. If a cam follower is scuffed or "dished," it must be replaced. Cam followers and rocker arms wear in three places:

- At the valve end.
- At the camshaft end (follower) or push rod end (rocker).
- Where the rocker shaft passes through the follower or rocker. See **Figure 20-6A.**

Check these high wear points closely. Any area worn excessively will require part replacement. Inspection of followers, rocker arms, and shaft include:

- Visual inspection for galling, flaking, or pitting.
- Measurement of rocker and follower shaft bore diameter, **Figure 20-6B.**
- Measurement of shaft diameter.

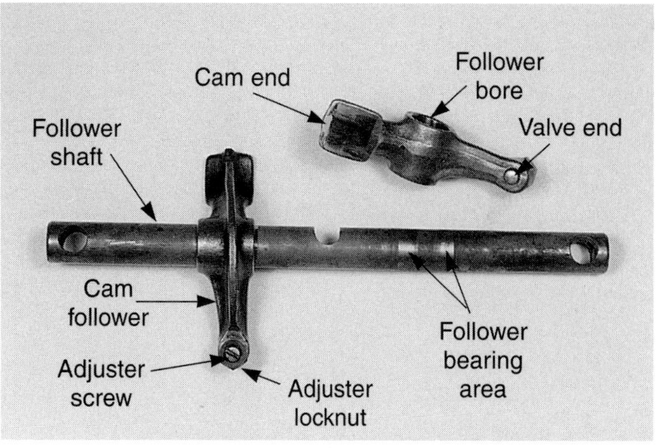

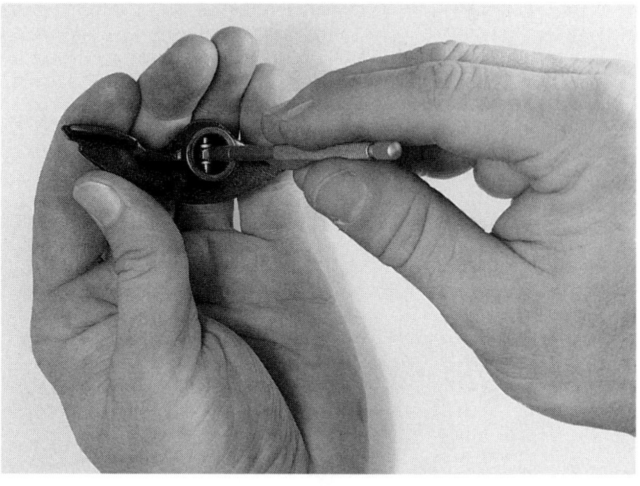

Figure 20-6. A—Cam followers wear at the point where contact is made with the cam, valve, and shaft. Followers also wear shafts. B—An easy way to measure the follower or rocker bore wear is with a telescoping gauge and outside micrometer. After fitting the telescoping gauge in the bore, measure it with an outside micrometer.

Excessive wear or clearance usually causes valve train noise, increased oil consumption (oil drains down through guides), and reduced performance. Most DOHC engines use shims and buckets for valve operation and adjustment. Wear in this design is unusual. However, bucket diameter and bucket bore diameter should be measured and compared to specifications, **Figure 20-7.**

Push Rods and Lifters

In push rod engines, the lifters may be located in the cylinder base or in the crankcase. The camshafts are always located in the crankcase, **Figure 20-8.** Push rods and lifters must be inspected for:

- Galling, flaking, or pitting.
- Excessive clearance between lifter and its bore.
- Straightness.
- Loose ends.

Check the push rod ends for wear or damage. All

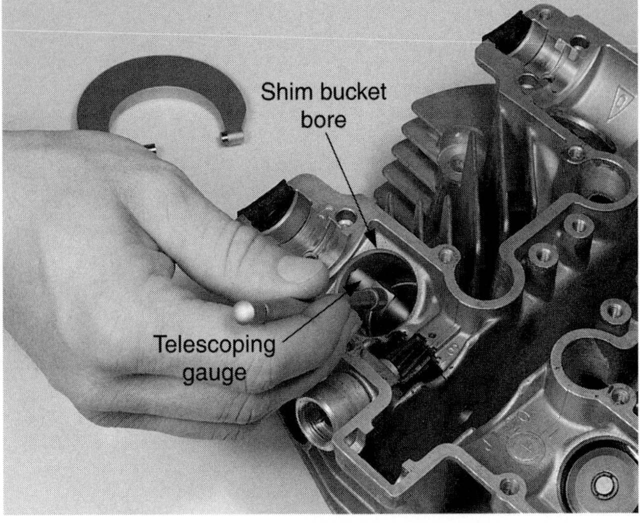

A

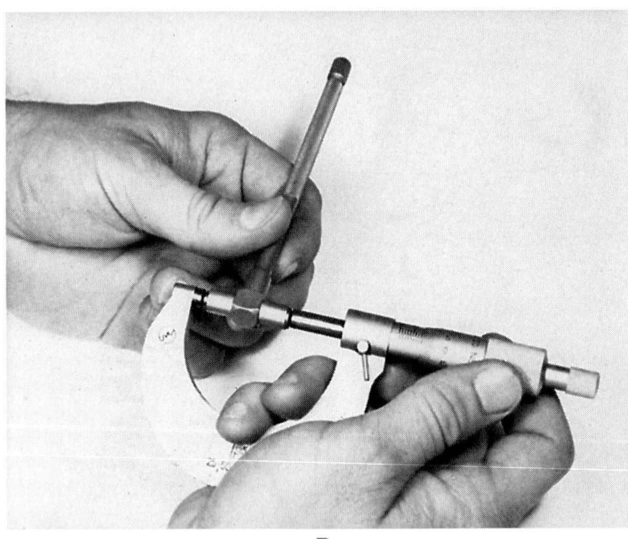

B

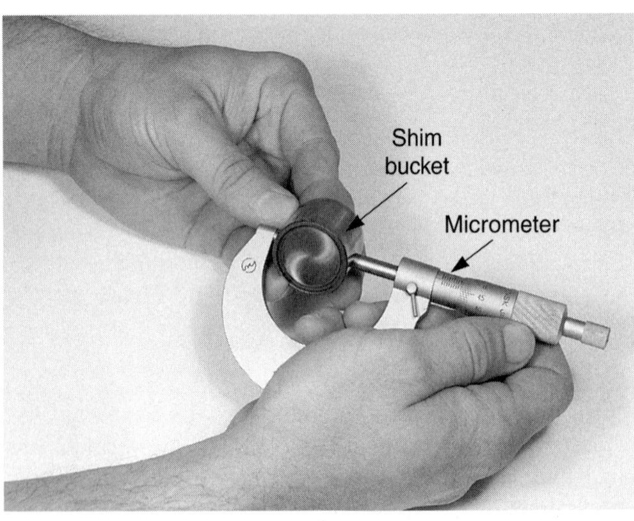

C

Figure 20-7. A telescoping gauge and micrometer are used to check the shim bucket-to-bucket bore clearance. Subtract the bucket diameter from the bucket bore diameter to determine clearance. Acceptable bucket and bore sizes as well as clearance are found in the service manual.

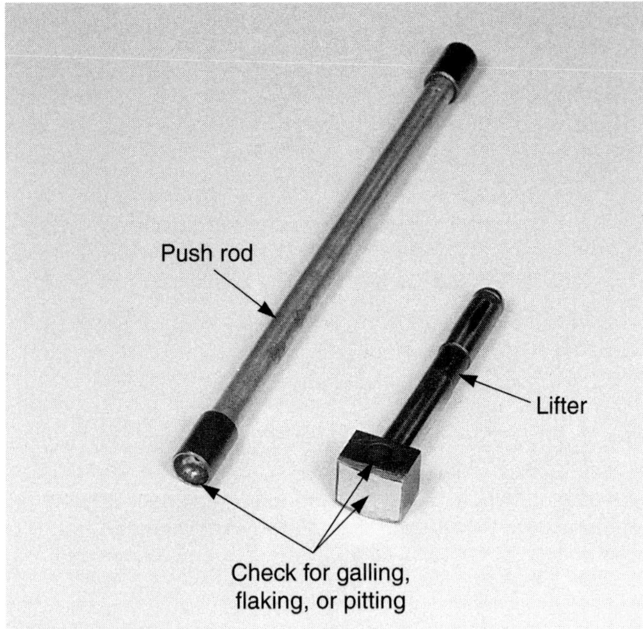

Figure 20-8. Inspect push rods and lifters for galling, flaking, pitting, excessive clearance, straightness, and loosening of ends.

push rods are subject to end wear and any badly worn push rods should be replaced. Check for bends by placing the rod on a flat metal plate or holding fixture. Rotate the rod and measure the deflection with a dial indicator. If the rod is bent, it should be replaced.

Chain Cam Drive

The most common method of driving the camshaft is with a chain and sprockets. While this is a dependable design, engines with high mileage, or engines that have not been properly maintained, will often have a worn cam chain and sprockets. This can cause slack in the cam chain which may upset valve timing, engine performance, and cause chain noise.

Visual inspection for cam chain slack and evidence of sprocket tooth wear (sharpening) is required. Some manufacturers give specifications for the maximum distance between a certain number of chain links (pins) for determining chain wear. Refer to a service manual for exact specifications. In any case, if excessive timing chain wear or slack is present, replace the cam chain and sprockets as a set.

Common timing chain designs use a one-piece chain. The cost of a new cam chain is minimal compared to the parts and labor time for a major engine repair. For this reason, cam chains are normally replaced during an overhaul.

Most chain drive cams require a tensioner and one or more guides, as shown in **Figure 20-9.** These may be rollers, sprockets, or blades. Each must be checked for wear and deterioration. A loose or badly worn chain can damage (crack or break) the tensioner.

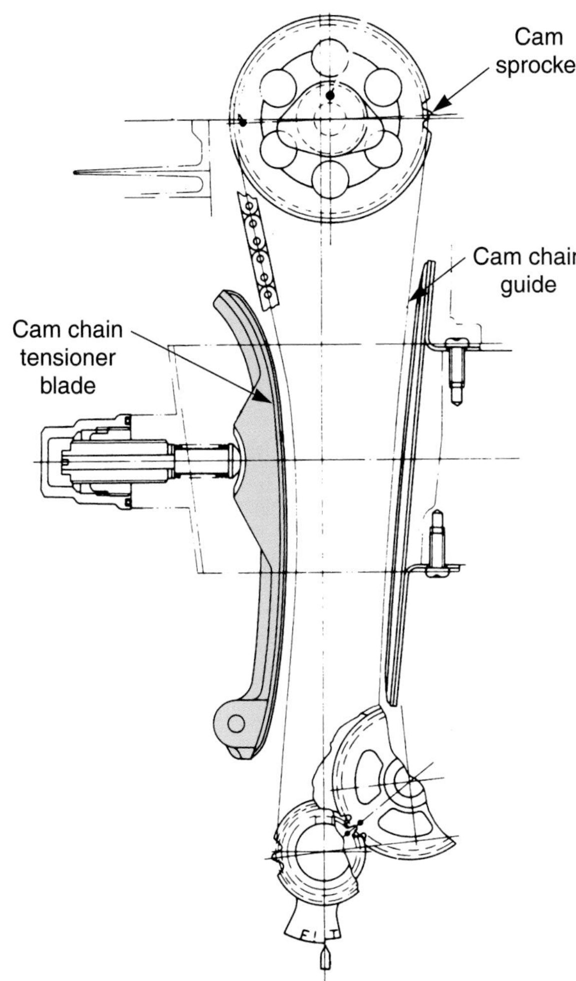

Figure 20-9. All cam chain tensioners, guides, and sprockets must be checked for wear or deterioration. (Yamaha Motor Corporation U.S.A.)

Gear Cam Drive

Only a few manufacturers still use gear camshaft drives, although it is extremely dependable. Some designs use an idler gear to drive the cams. Idler gear shaft and bushing wear is fairly common. Gear tooth wear, though, is rarely seen. If the gears are worn or damaged, replace them as a set.

Belt Cam Drive

A belt cam drive is another extremely dependable and maintenance free design, **Figure 20-10.** Replacement because of wear is uncommon. In some cases, however, belt replacement may be needed due to accident or oil leak damage.

Valve Springs, Collars, and Keepers

Use care when cleaning valve springs as they have coatings that prevent rust. Do not clean springs in strong, caustic cleaner as it can remove the spring's protective coatings. Inspection of valve springs during an overhaul consists of checking for:

- Rust or corrosion.
- Spring free length.
- Spring squareness.
- Spring open and closed pressure.

Inspect the spring carefully for any rust, corrosion, scratches, or nicks and replace any damaged springs. To check the spring's free length, place the spring next to a combination square, **Figure 20-11.** The spring's free

Figure 20-10. This engine design uses a toothed rubber belt to drive the camshaft.

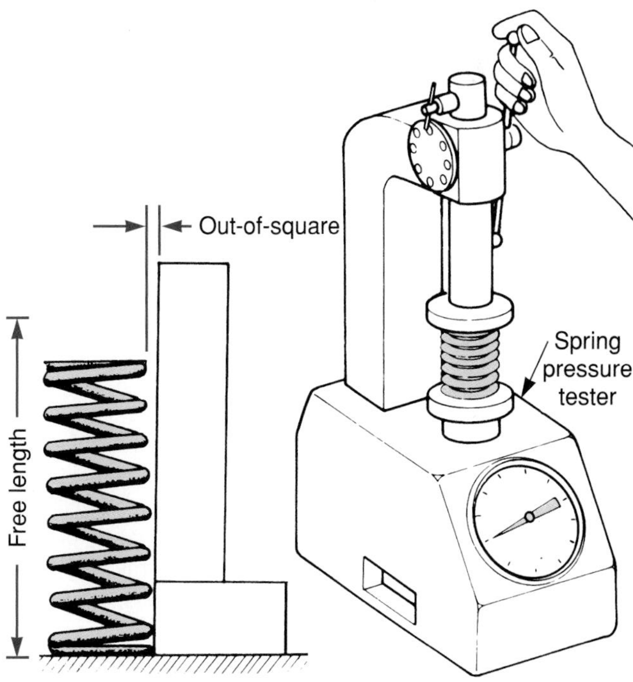

Figure 20-11. Valve spring condition is checked by measuring spring squareness, free length, and pressure. To measure spring pressure, compress the spring to its given height and read the scale. Spring pressure should be within factory ratings. (Kawasaki Motors Corporation U.S.A.)

length should meet manufacturer's specifications. To check for squareness, sight the spring between its edge and the blade. Turn the spring partially and check the height. Turn the spring on its opposite end and check again. To check a spring's open and closed pressures (tensions), use either a torque tester or dial spring tester, **Figure 20-11.** ***Closed pressure*** guarantees a tight seal; ***open pressure*** overcomes valve train inertia and closes the valve at the appropriate time.

Collars and keepers usually do not wear. However, they must be inspected for cracks or damage caused by valve spring failure or excessive engine speeds. They should be replaced if they are damaged, worn, or if new valve springs are installed.

Valve Stems, Guides, and Seals

Valve stems and guides must be measured to check for wear and valve-to-guide clearance. Excessive clearance may interfere with the sealing ability and life of the valve face and seat. Inspection of valve stem seals is not needed as new seals should always be installed whenever a cylinder head is disassembled.

Checking Stem-to-Guide Clearance

Before checking valve ***stem-to-guide clearance,*** clean the valve stem with solvent to remove all gum and varnish. Clean the valve guides with solvent and/or a wire expanding valve guide cleaning tool. Then, insert the proper valve into its guide and hold the valve tightly against its seat. Mount a dial indicator on the valve spring side of the cylinder head so that the indicator's foot rests against the valve stem at a 90° angle. Move the valve slightly off its seat and measure the valve guide-to-stem clearance by moving the stem back and forth to actuate the dial indicator.

If the dial indicator reading is not within the manufacturer's specifications, mount the valve in a V-block and measure the valve stem runout with a dial indicator and stem diameter with a micrometer. See **Figure 20-12A.** Compare the valve stem diameter to the manufacturer's specifications to determine if the stem or the guide is responsible for the excessive clearance. Valve stems should also be checked for physical damage (cracks, bends, scarring), **Figure 20-12B.**

Other measuring techniques are available to the engine technician. A telescoping gauge and micrometer or an inside caliper small hole gauge can be used to determine valve guide wear. Remember, guides do not wear uniformly. Therefore, plugs, valve stems, or pilots should never be used to measure valve guides.

Valve Seat and Face Inspection

Inspect the valve seat and face for burning, pitting, and other signs of damage, **Figure 20-13.** Also check for valve face runout, as in **Figure 20-14.** The service manual gives specifications and proper procedures for carrying out a more detailed valve train inspection.

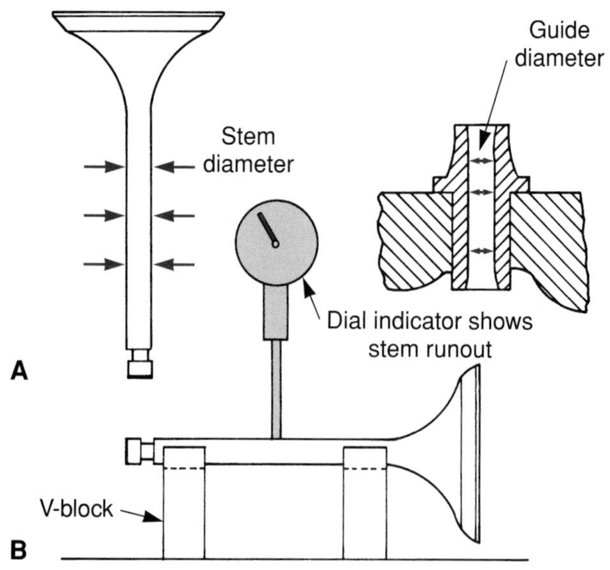

Figure 20-12. A—Measure valve stems and guides in three places using an outside micrometer and small hole gauge. Measure valve guides in all directions to find the greatest amount of wear. B—A dial indicator can be used to check valve stem runout. A valve with stem runout or other wear should be replaced. (Kawasaki Motors Corporation U.S.A.)

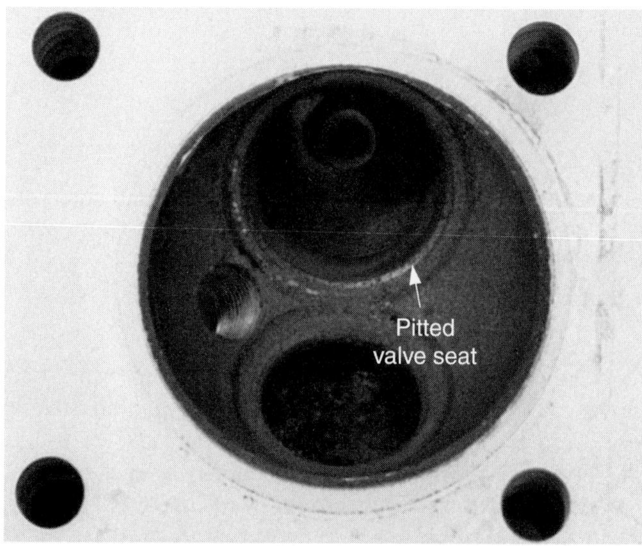

Figure 20-13. Valve seat pitting and burning are easily recognizable and require seat reconditioning or replacement.

Inspecting Cylinder Head for Warpage

Excessive heat caused by engine overheating or compression leaks can warp and distort the cylinder head. ***Warpage*** may occur if the head is still hot when it is removed from the engine block. Cylinder head distortion may also be caused by the use of improper techniques to repair cracks or by the improper tightening of cylinder bolts or hold-down nuts. Severe cylinder head warpage or distortion is apparent when the mating surfaces of the head and cylinder fail to conform.

Most warpage is slight and not to an extreme as to be apparent to the naked eye. The cylinder head can be checked for warpage (head gasket surface not flat) by using a feeler gauge and a straightedge or surface plate. The head should be checked for warpage as shown in **Figure 20-15.**

1. Use a gasket scraper or a wire brush to clean the machined surfaces of the head.
2. Place a heavy, accurate straightedge across the machined surface. Using feeler gauges, determine the clearance at the center of the straightedge.
3. Check for warpage across the diagonals, along the longitudinal centerline, and across the width of the cylinder head at several points. Be sure to check the flatness of the intake and exhaust manifold mounting surfaces on the head.

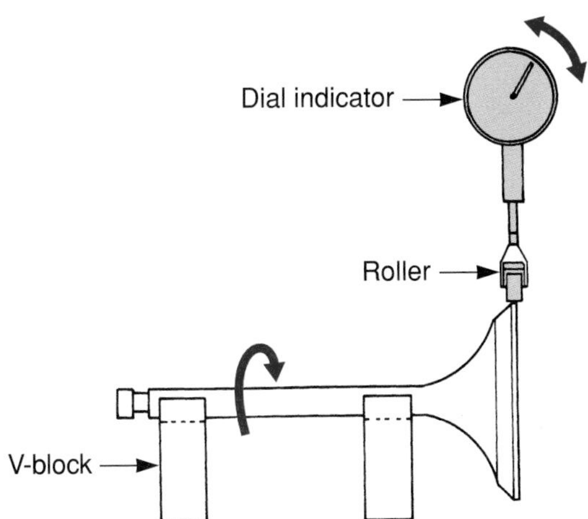

Figure 20-14. Valve head runout is measured with a dial indicator.

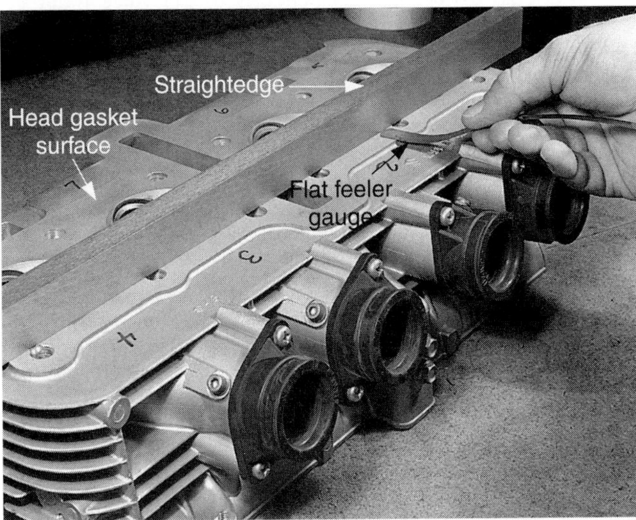

Figure 20-15. Cylinder head warpage can be detected with a feeler gauge and straightedge. This method works well on multi-cylinder engines. If the feeler gauge slides under the straightedge, the head requires resurfacing or replacement.

In addition to checking for warpage, look for dents, scratches, and corrosion around the water passages. If warpage exceeds the maximum specifications given in the engine service manual, you must decide whether to reface the head or to discard it. Refacing can be done by surface grinding. Consult the engine service manual for refacing limits. After refacing, the surface must be smooth enough to form a proper seal and prevent leakage. For cylinder head resurfacing procedures, refer to Chapter 3. Ideally, a warped head should be replaced.

Reconditioning the Cylinder Head Assembly

Reconditioning the cylinder head assembly typically consists of:

- Valve guide replacement.
- Resurfacing valve face, tip, and seat.
- Checking valve spring installed height.
- Thorough parts cleaning.

Valve Guide Service

When a valve guide is worn beyond specifications, a new one must be installed and reamed to size. Valve guide replacement is a relatively simple operation if done correctly.

1. Heat the cylinder head in an oven as described in the service manual. An oven provides even heating to prevent warping.
2. Drive the old guides out using a valve guide drift. This is illustrated in **Figure 20-16A.**
3. After the head cools, remove any carbon or sharp edges in the guide bores.
4. Chill (shrink) the new guides in a freezer. This will shrink the guides for installation.
5. Reheat the cylinder head.
6. Carefully install the chilled guides using a hammer and the proper drift, **Figure 20-16B.**
7. Ream the guides to size after the head cools down, **Figure 20-16C.**

Valve and Seat Refacing

Valves, which can be reconditioned, are refaced in a valve grinding machine, **Figure 20-17.** The valve face should be ground until all dark spots, grooves, and pits are removed.

The service manual often gives specifications for valve margin thickness (flat edge between the valve face and head), **Figure 20-18.** If the valve margin is too thin after grinding, a new valve must be used. A thin, sharp margin will not dissipate heat properly and can burn or fail quickly.

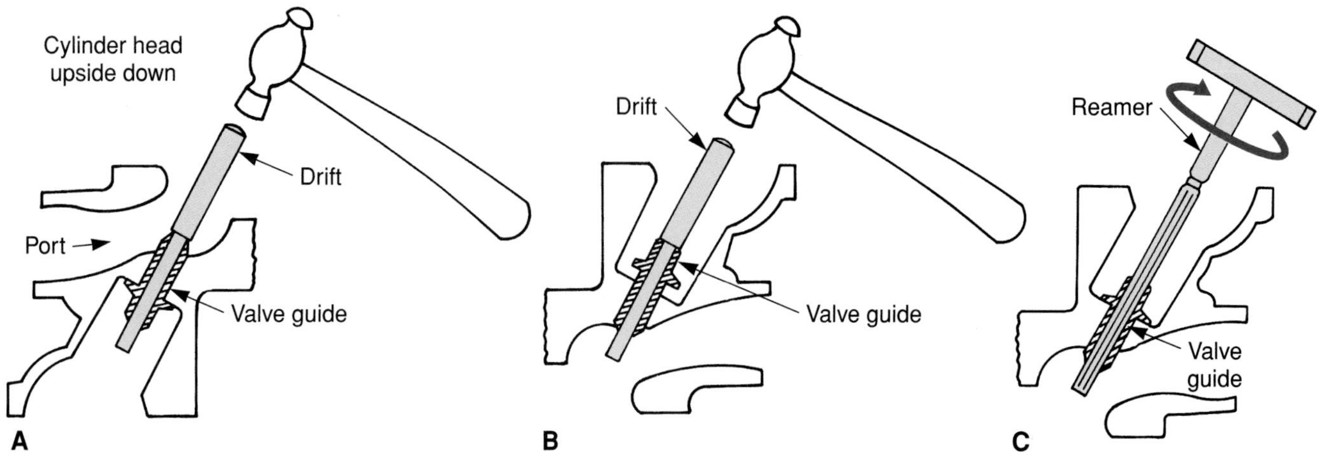

Figure 20-16. A—A valve guide drift is used to remove and install valve guides. B—Install new guides carefully. C—A valve guide reamer is used to properly size the valve guide after installation. Guides must be serviced before valve seats.

Figure 20-17. A valve grinding machine reconditions valves by resurfacing the face area.

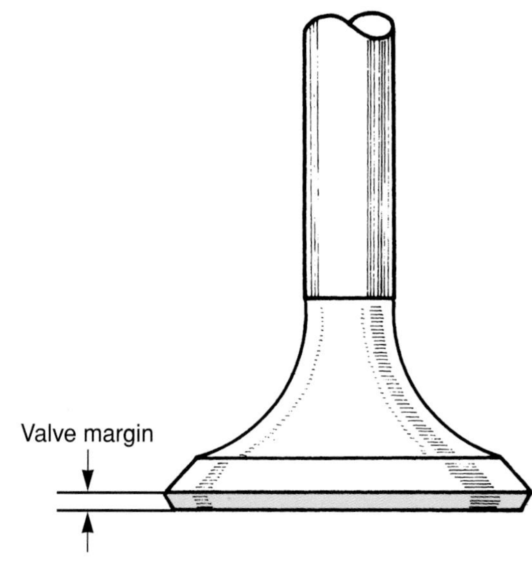

Figure 20-18. After grinding a valve, inspect its margin. The margin should be within specifications or the valve must be replaced. A sharp margin cannot handle combustion heat and will burn easily. (Kawasaki Motors Corporation U.S.A.)

Valve refacing machines have adjustments for different valve face angles (angle between the valve face and head). Select the proper angle in accordance with the motorcycle manufacturer specifications. With most motorcycles, 45° valve face angles are used. Sometimes, an ***interference angle*** (1° difference between the valve face and seat angles) is used to reduce break-in time, **Figure 20-19.** Valve seat refacing is one of the most critical aspects of a valve job. Four important considerations for seat grinding are:

- ***Valve seat concentricity:*** The valve seat must be uniform width and be located an equal distance around the valve guide bore, **Figure 20-20.**
- ***Valve seat surface finish:*** The valve seat finish must be smooth and even to permit positive sealing.

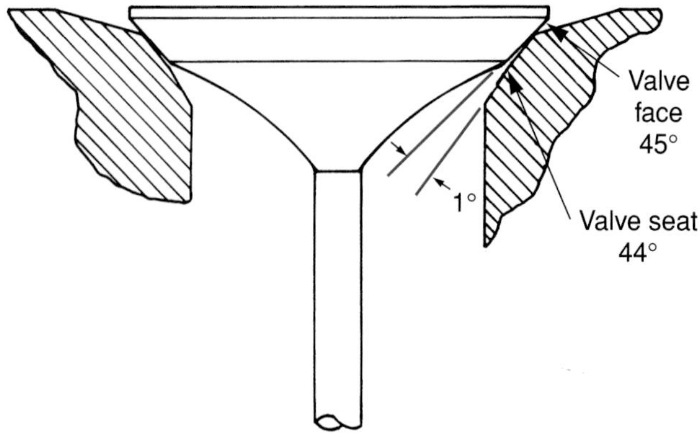

Figure 20-19. A one degree interference angle assures good sealing. A slight wedging action between the valve and seat creates a positive seal.

- ***Valve seat width*:** The valve seat must be wide enough to prevent overheating and cupping, but not wide enough to trap carbon, **Figure 20-21.**
- ***Valve seat-to-valve contact*:** The valve seat must touch the center of the valve face, as shown in **Figure 20-22.**

Refacing Valve Seats

A valve seat refacing operation requires the use of cutters or stones of three different angles. Although the specific angles may vary, common stone or cutter angles are 15°, 30°, 45°, and 60°. The 45° cutter or stone is used for resurfacing the actual valve seat area. The 15°, 30°, and 60° cutters or stones are used to adjust valve seat width and position. **Figure 20-23** shows where seat material is removed when using these cutters.

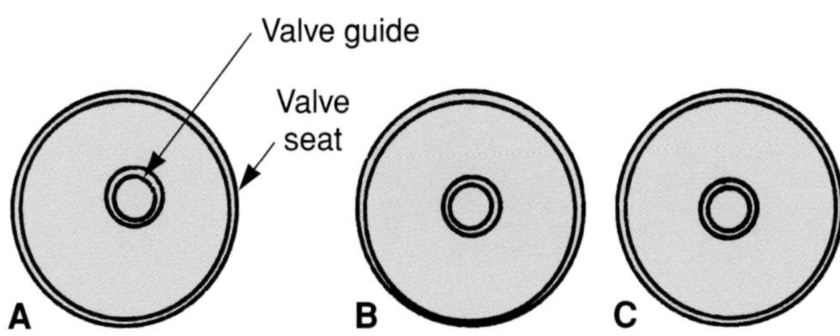

Figure 20-20. A—Valve seat is not concentric with valve guide. B—Valve seat varies in width. These conditions can occur when the valve guide is worn and when resurfacing equipment is worn or used improperly. C—Proper valve seat concentricity and width.

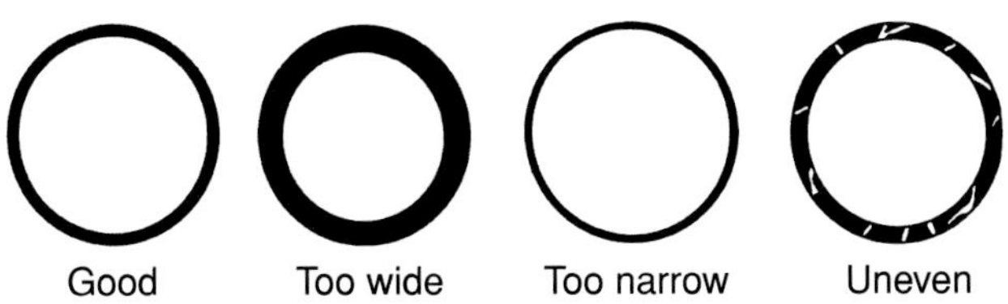

Figure 20-21. Valve seat width must be correct. Too wide a seat will trap carbon. Too narrow a seat can cause valve face cupping. An uneven seat causes leakage and burning. (Kawasaki Motors Corporation U.S.A.)

During valve seat refacing, the following sequence should be followed:

1. Make sure each valve and seat is properly numbered and kept in order.
2. Install the cutter pilot in the valve guide, **Figure 20-24A.** Check that it is the right diameter and tight in the guide.
3. Cut the 45° angle as shown in **Figure 20-24B.**
4. Visually inspect the seat for even width.

If the seat width and concentricity are correct, skip steps 5 and 6, and continue with step 7.

5. Paint the seat with blue layout dye and cut a 15° or 30° angle until contact is made all the way around the seat. Refer to **Figure 20-24C.**
6. Cut the 60° angle until contact is made all the way around the seat, **Figure 20-24D.**
7. Check seat width and contact position on the valve face as follows:

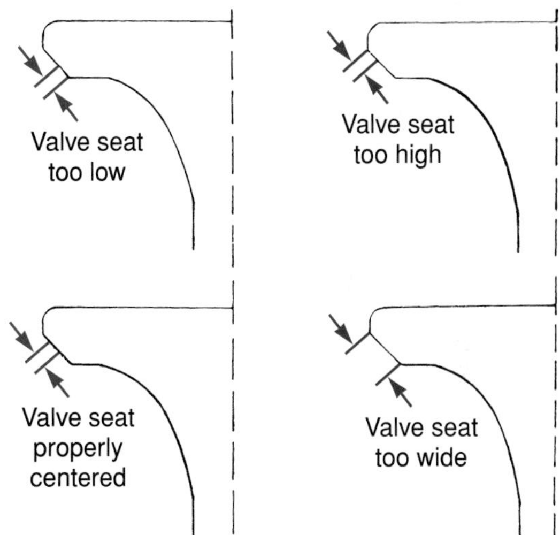

Figure 20-22. If a 45° valve seat is too wide, use 30° and 60° cutters to narrow and center the seat. If a 45° valve seat is too high, use a 30° cutter to lower the seat. If a 45° valve seat is too low, use a 60° cutter to raise the seat. (Yamaha Motor Corporation U.S.A.)

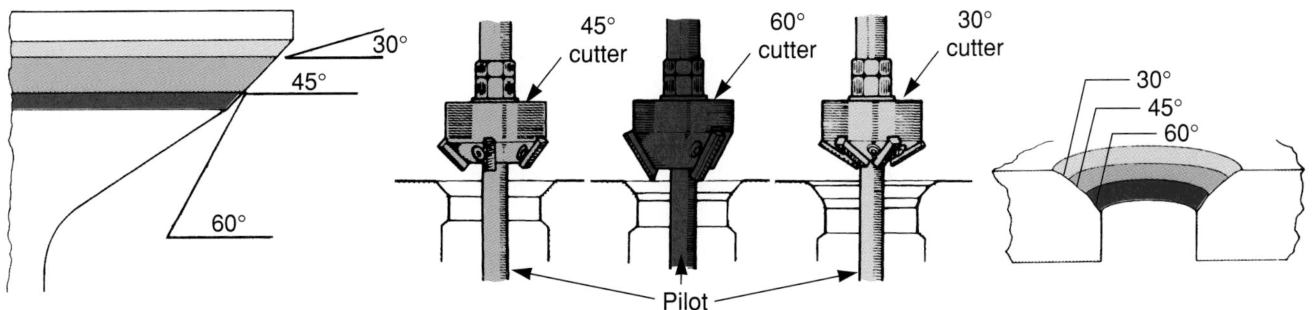

Figure 20-23. A 45° cutter resurfaces the valve seat. A 60° cutter narrows the valve seat from the bottom. A 30° cutter narrows the valve seat from the top. (Kawasaki Motors Corporation U.S.A.)

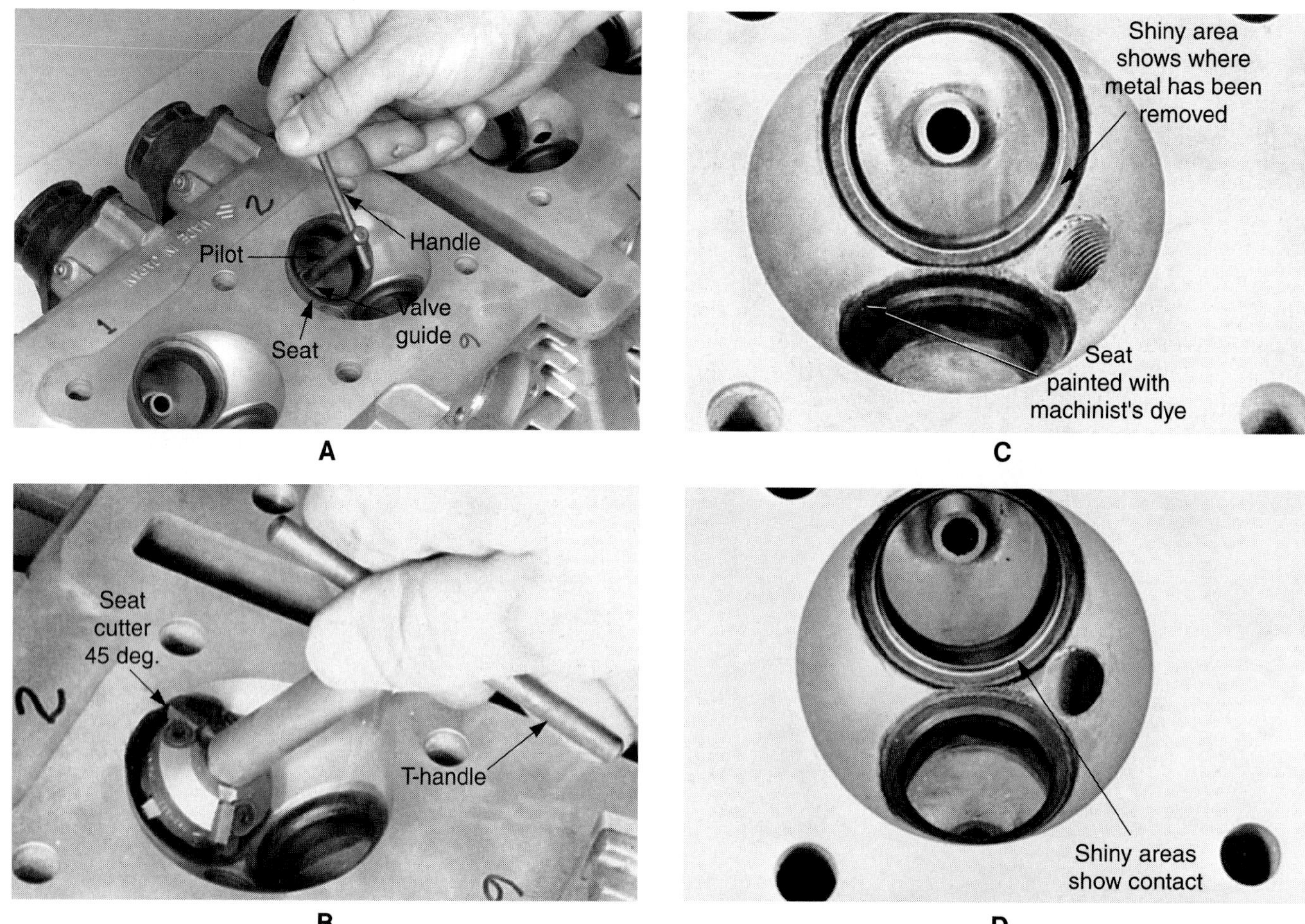

Figure 20-24. A—A valve cutter pilot must fit snugly in the valve guide to accurately center the cutter. Remove the handle after installing the pilot. B—Use light even pressure when cutting the valve seat. Cut until all pitting is removed. After cutting the valve seat, visually check the seat for even width. C—Paint the valve seat with blue layout dye so that 15° and 60° cuts stand out. Usually, very little metal will have to be removed with the 15° cutter. Be careful to remove only enough metal so that contact is made all the way around the seat. D—Use the same care with a 60° cutter. Removing too much metal can ruin the job.

- Measure the seat width (45° area) with a dial caliper, **Figure 20-25A.** Compare the measurement to service manual specifications.
- Use a commercial lapping compound (abrasive paste) and hand lap stick to smooth and double-check valve and seat contact, **Figure 20-25B.** Be careful not to get any lapping compound on the valve stem or guide as it will cause rapid wear.
- After cleaning all lapping compound from valve face and seat, visually check seat contact on valve face, **Figure 20-25C.** It must be centered on the valve face. If not, move the seat using 15° and 60° cutters.

8. Adjust seat width and contact position with appropriate cutters. With a 45° angle seat, the following rules apply:
   - The 15° and 30° cutters narrow the seat and move the contact position down on the valve face.
   - The 60° cutter narrows the seat and moves the contact position up on the valve face.
   - The 45° cutter widens the seat.
9. Lap the valve and seat. Then, recheck the seat width and contact position.

Valve Spring Installed Height

Valve spring installed height determines seat pressure and spring tension throughout the valve's travel. Installed height is adjusted with valve spring shims. Valve spring installed height adjustment is necessary because material removed from the valve face and seat during reconditioning causes the valve to move deeper in the head. This increases the amount of stem sticking through the head, **Figure 20-26.**

As in **Figure 20-27,** shims increase spring tension. The service manual gives specifications and proper procedure for carrying out spring shimming.

Cylinder Head Reassembly

The service manual probably says, "Reassemble the cylinder head in the reverse order of disassembly." Although this is true, some important procedures to remember are:

A

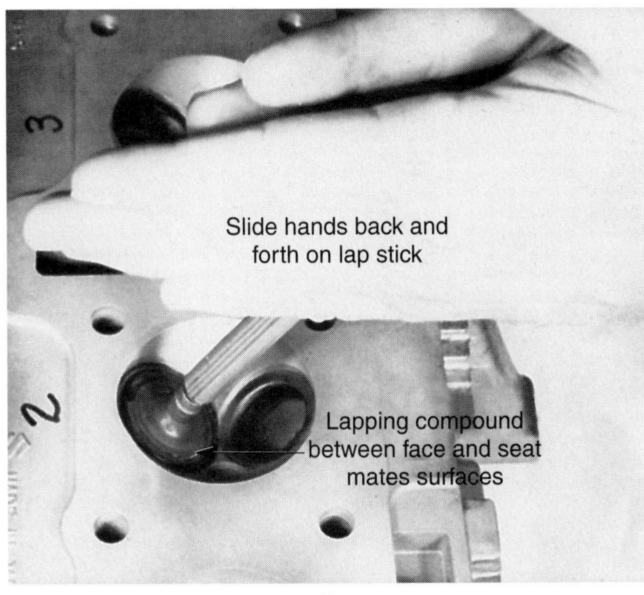

B

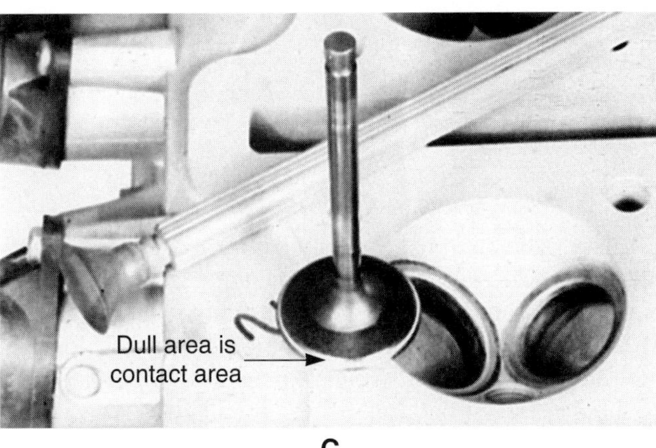

C

Figure 20-25. Method for checking valve face contact on a seat. A—Measuring seat with a dial caliper. B—Hand-lapping valves with a lap stick and abrasive paste (lapping compound). C—The dull area on the valve is the contact area.

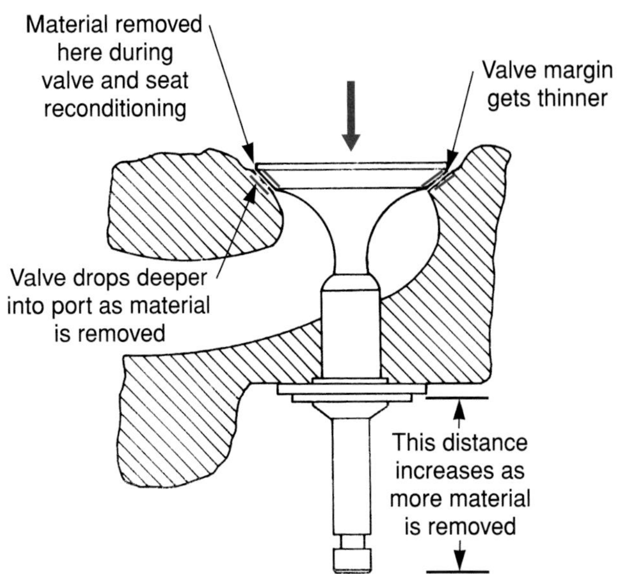

Figure 20-26. Effects of removal of material during a valve job are shown. Valve and seat grinding sinks the valve into the cylinder head.

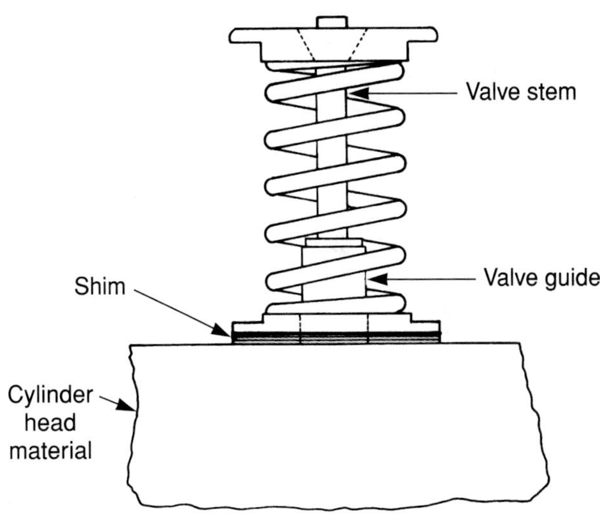

Figure 20-27. Valve spring shims shorten the valve spring to compensate for material removed during a valve job. They return spring tension to normal (inner spring only shown).

1. Thoroughly clean all parts to remove lapping compound, grit, and metal filings.
2. Install lower valve spring collars before installing the valve stem seals.
3. Lubricate the valve stems and guides with motor oil or assembly lube.
4. Install progressively wound valve springs with the tight coils toward the bottom collar, **Figure 20-28.**
5. Use a valve spring compressor to assemble upper spring collar and keepers, **Figure 20-29.**

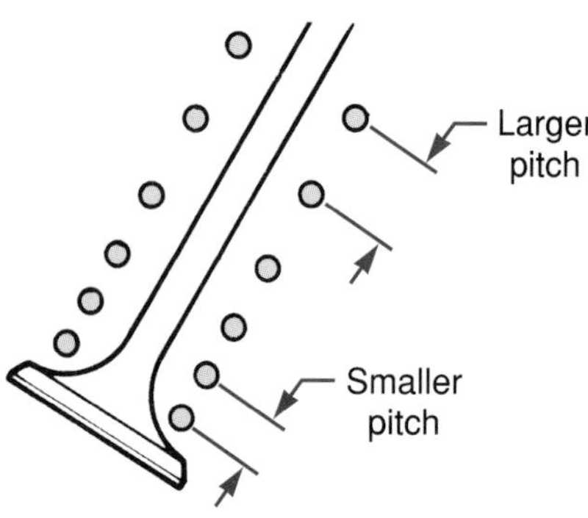

Figure 20-28. The tightest coils of progressive wound valve springs must be installed toward the cylinder head. (Yamaha Motor Corporation U.S.A.)

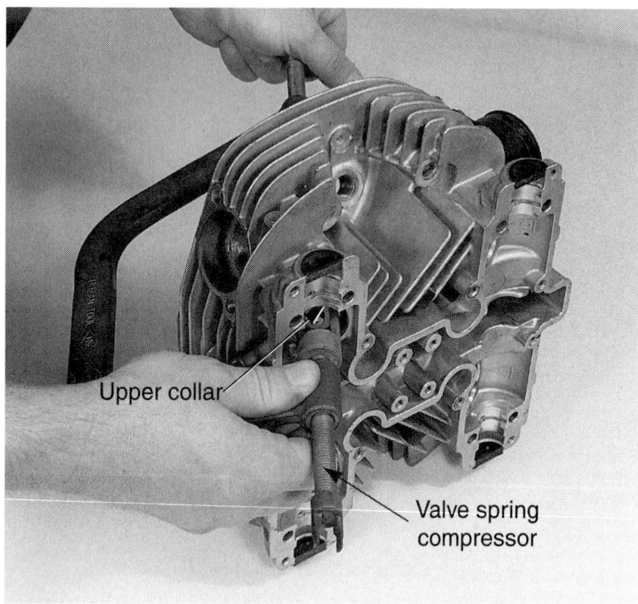

Figure 20-29. A valve spring compressor pushes the top collar and valve spring down so keepers can be installed.

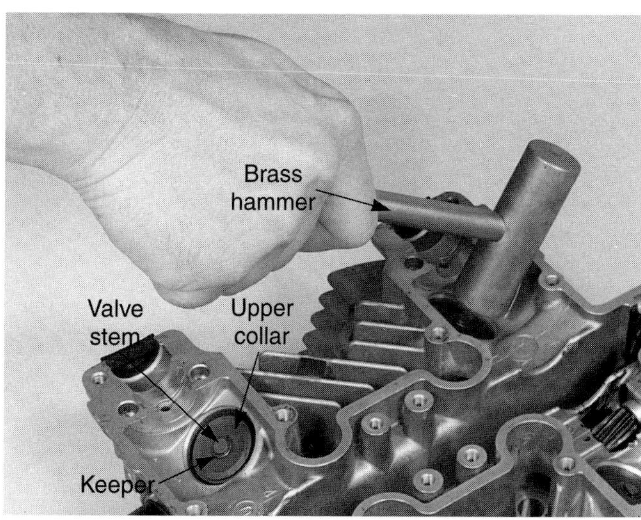

Figure 20-30. Using a soft faced hammer (plastic or brass), tap each valve stem to ensure firm seating of keepers in the upper collar.

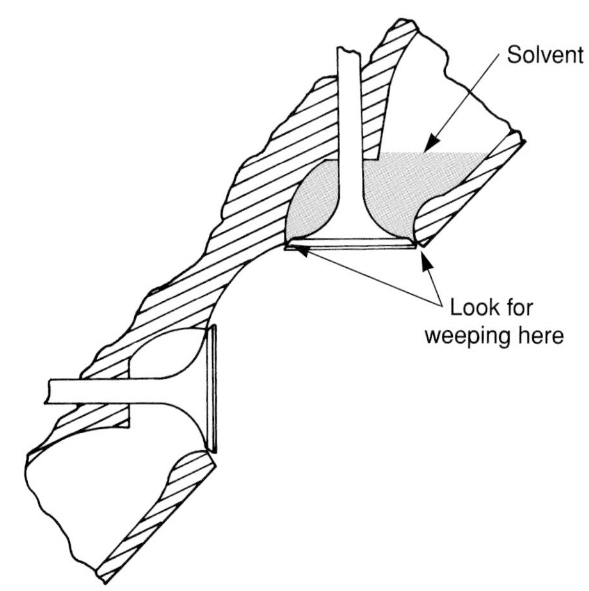

Figure 20-31. After the head is assembled, check each valve and seat for leakage by pouring solvent into each port. Any weeping (leakage) around the valve head indicates a poor seal. Check for dirt and hand lap or regrind as needed.

6. To ensure the valve spring keepers are properly seated, lightly tap the end of the valve stem with a brass or plastic hammer, **Figure 20-30.**
7. After reassembly, use solvent to leak test each valve, **Figure 20-31.**
8. After the reconditioning process, wrap the head in plastic or put it in a sealed box. This will prevent contamination while finishing the engine overhaul.

Piston and Cylinder Inspection and Service

Due to the extreme temperatures, friction, and loads placed on pistons and cylinders, thorough inspection for wear, cracks, and damage is very critical. If the slightest problem is overlooked, the overhaul can fail in a short period of time.

Checking Cylinder Wear

The cylinder must be inspected for excessive taper, out-of-roundness, a ridge, and cylinder damage (galling, cracks) caused by other broken parts, **Figure 20-32.** Measurement of a four-stroke engine's cylinder is done in the same manner as a two-stroke engine. Important procedures to remember are:

1. Measure the cylinder at the top, middle, and bottom.
2. Make all three measurements front-to-back and side-to-side in the bore.
3. Record all your measurements, **Figure 20-33.**

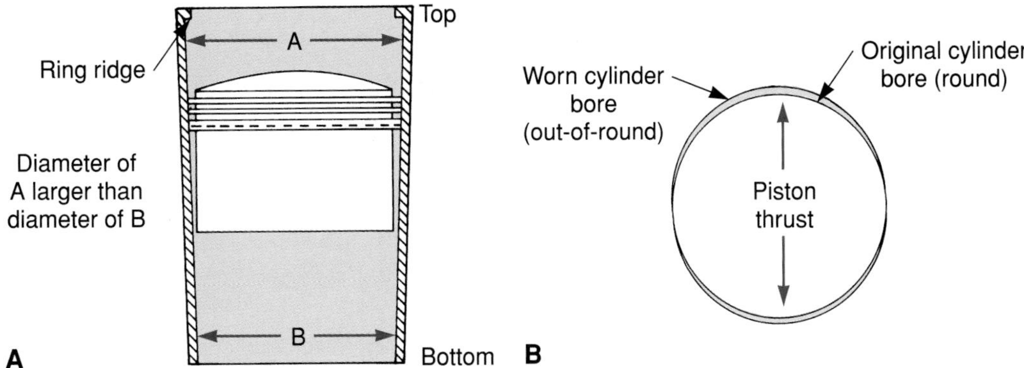

Figure 20-32. A—Cylinder taper and ridge results from normal wear. A ridge is formed at the end of ring travel. The cylinder also becomes larger at the top than at the bottom since there is less lubrication at the top of the cylinder. B—Cylinder out-of-roundness is caused by the piston's thrust.

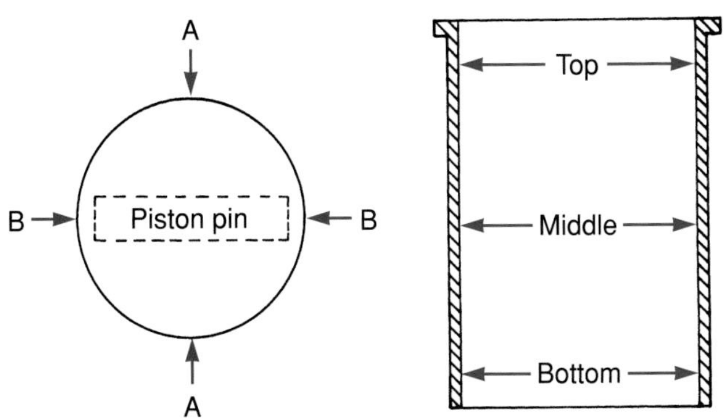

Figure 20-33. To effectively measure a cylinder for taper and out-of-roundness, the measurements must be taken front-to-back and side-to-side at the top, middle, and bottom of the cylinder. This is a total of six measurements.

Piston Measurement and Inspection

Inspect the pistons for damage (seizure, cracks, grooves, and land wear), **Figure 20-34,** and measure skirt diameter, as in **Figure 20-35.**

Subtract the skirt diameter from the cylinder's largest diameter to get ***piston clearance.*** For example, if the cylinder diameter equals 2.558″ and the piston diameter equals 2.553″ then the piston clearance equals .005″ (2.558 – 2.553 = .005). Wear limits are given in the service manual.

Another important measurement made on a four-stroke cycle piston is ***ring-to-groove clearance*** (play between ring and piston ring groove). Shown in **Figure 20-36,** find a feeler gauge blade that fits snugly between the piston ring and piston ring groove. Compare the gauge size to specifications. If the clearance is too large, the piston should be replaced.

Piston Ring End Gap Measurement

Piston ring end gap should be measured with the rings installed squarely into the cylinder. Measure the ring end gap with a feeler gauge, as in **Figure 20-37.** If the gap is too small, the ring end must be filed. The rings must be replaced if the end gap is excessive. After the ring end gap has been checked and adjusted, place them in a labeled bag so that each set of rings stays with the proper cylinder and piston.

Wrist Pin and Small End Bearing Measurement

Measure the ***wrist pin diameter*** and inspect for discoloration (overheating) and surface damage. Measure the bore diameter of the connecting rod small end and subtract the wrist pin's diameter to determine clearance. **Figure 20-38** illustrates how to make these measurements. If clearance is excessive but wrist pin diameter is correct, the connecting rod must be replaced or reconditioned.

Reconditioning the Cylinder

If the cylinder is worn beyond service limits, it must be bored to the next oversize. Cylinder boring procedures are covered in Chapter 3. When a cylinder is bored to fit an oversize piston, the end gap must be checked and adjusted on the new rings. If the cylinder is within service limits, it must be deglazed to aid in seating the new piston rings. **Figure 20-39** illustrates cylinder deglazing.

A cylinder that has been honed or deglazed must be washed in warm soapy water to remove grit and metal particles. After washing, dry and wipe with an oiled rag. Dry the cylinder and recoat the bore with oil to prevent rust. If new rings are being installed, the end gap should be checked after cylinder deglazing.

Engine Bottom End Service

The four-stroke engine bottom end is made up of all the components from the cylinder base down. This includes the crankshaft, connecting rod, main bearings, connecting rod bearings, engine balancers, cam chain, oil pump, and crankcase.

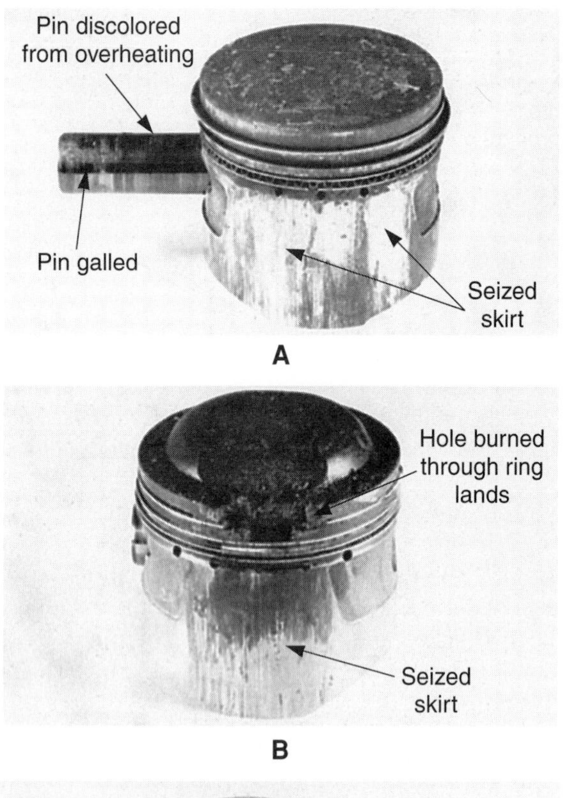

Figure 20-34. Four-stroke piston damage. A—Seizure. B—Burned hole. C—Hammered hole caused by a broken valve.

Some four-stroke crankshafts can be reconditioned when worn or damaged, while others cannot. An example of a crankshaft which cannot be reconditioned is a multi-cylinder assembled crankshaft. The service manual will explain the appropriate reconditioning procedure, if available, for the crankshaft.

Inspection and Measurement of Bearings

The four types of bearings found in four-stroke cycle engines are roller, ball, plain, and needle types. All types of bearings should be checked visually for discoloration, scoring, flaking, or disintegration. Roller, ball, and needle bearings should be checked for radial play, **Figure 20-40.** Ball bearings must also be checked for lateral play, **Figure 20-41.**

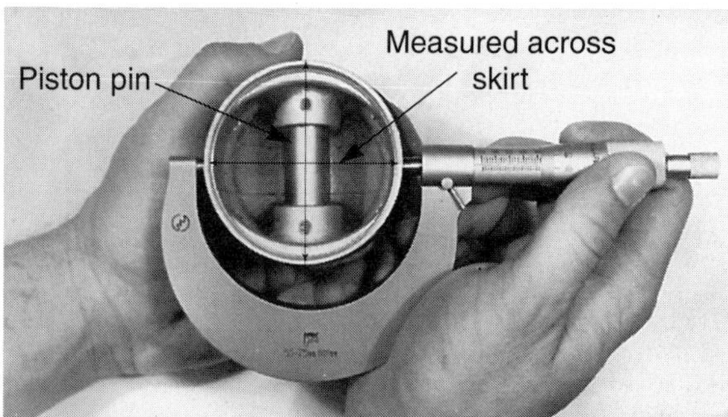

Figure 20-35. Piston skirt diameter and wear can be accurately measured using an outside micrometer. Measure perpendicular to the piston pin as shown.

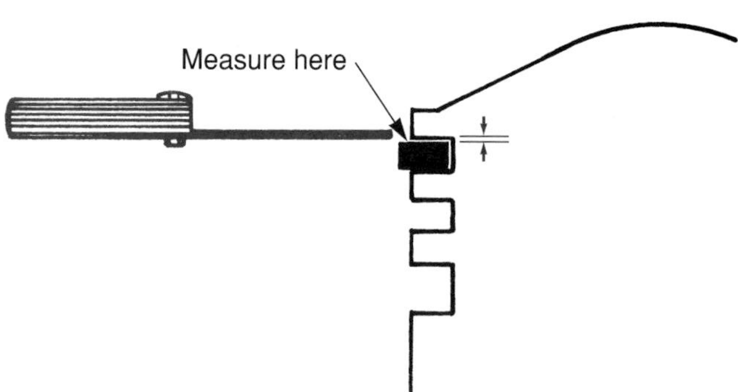

Figure 20-36. Ring-to-ring groove clearance is measured with a feeler gauge. The largest gauge that will fit between the ring and groove equals ring-to-groove clearance.

Plain bearing (bushings, split bearings) clearance can be measured in two ways:

- With the use of precision measuring equipment.
- With the use of Plastigage (split bearings only), **Figure 20-42.**

Checking Oil Pump Condition

An important step during any engine overhaul is inspecting the oil pump. The most carefully done engine overhaul can quickly self-destruct if the oil pump is not functioning properly. Oil pumps should be visually inspected and measured to check clearances.

Rotor and gear pumps described in Chapter 10 are measured with a feeler gauge. Measure in the rotor areas shown in **Figure 20-43.** Piston pumps are measured with a micrometer and telescoping gauge or small hole gauge, **Figure 20-44.** An oil pump should always be inspected and measured, whether lubrication problems are evident or not. The slightest wear or damage would require a new oil pump.

Cleaning Oil Passages and Bottom End Filters

All oil passageways, orifices, check valves, relief valves, screen filters, and the oil tank should be thoroughly cleaned during an overhaul. Sludge traps and

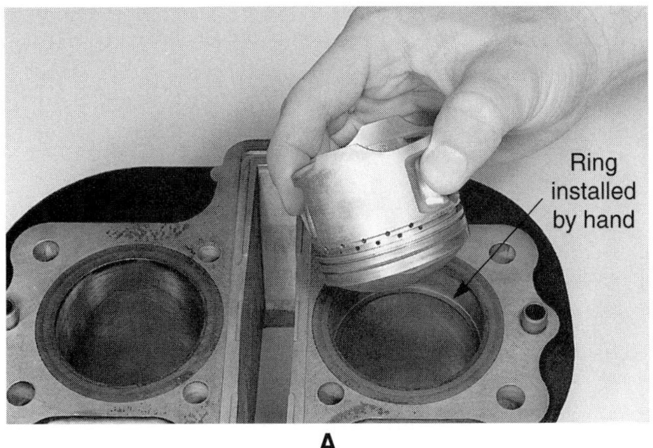

A

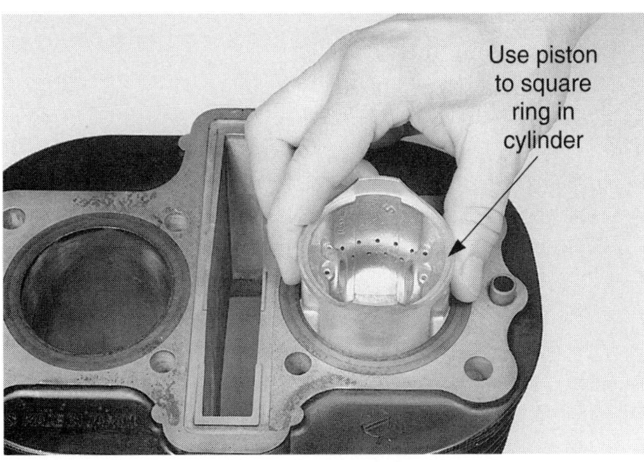

B

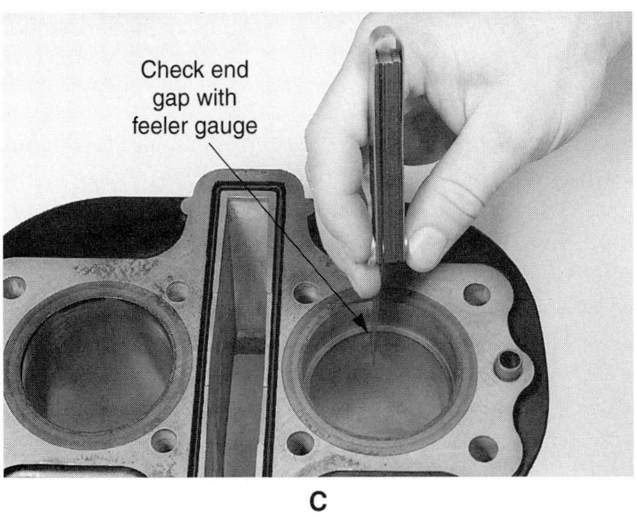

C

Figure 20-37. Before the end gap can be measured, the ring must be installed squarely in the cylinder. A—After slipping the ring into the cylinder, use the piston to push the ring a little farther into the cylinder. B—This will ensure the ring is square in the cylinder. C—The end gap can then be accurately measured with a feeler gauge.

centrifugal filters should also be cleaned. Extreme care should be taken in cleaning these components since deposits in them are very dense and difficult to remove. The oil filter element must also be replaced during an overhaul.

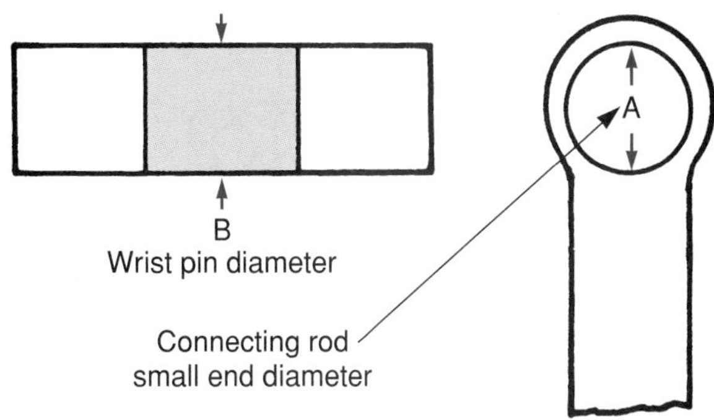

Figure 20-38. Use a telescoping gauge and outside micrometer to measure the piston pin and connecting rod. Subtract measurement B from measurement A to find piston pin clearance.

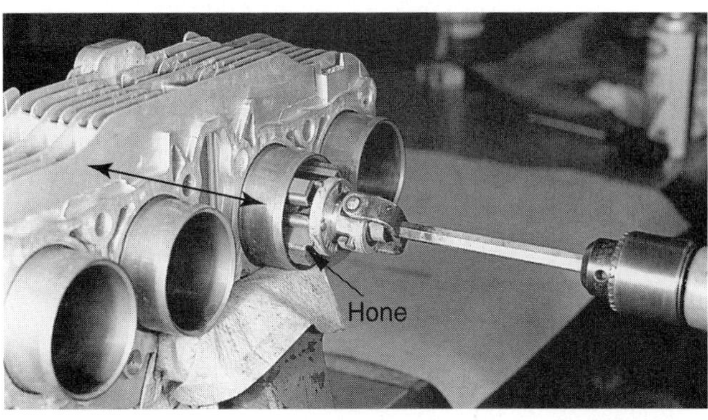

A

B

Figure 20-39. A—A hone is used to deglaze and crosshatch cylinder walls. B—Correct texture (crosshatch) is achieved with the proper hone speed and stroke action.

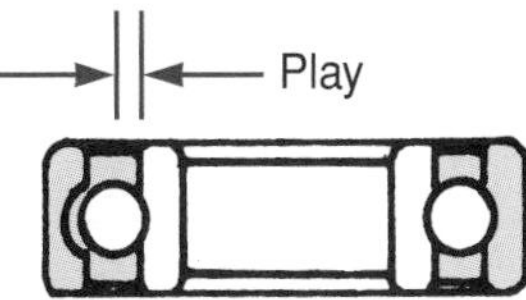

Figure 20-40. Radial (up and down) play must be checked in roller, ball, and needle bearings. If not within specifications, replace the bearing. (American Suzuki Motor Corporation)

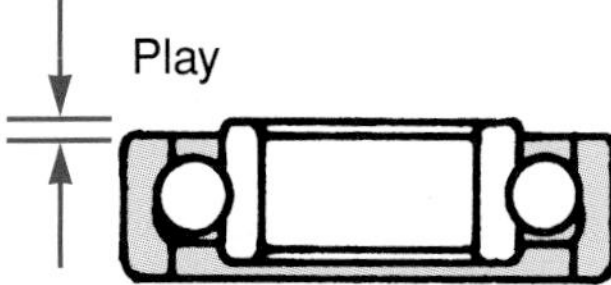

Figure 20-41. Lateral (side-to-side) play must be checked in ball bearings. Wiggle sideways and compare to specifications. Replace the bearings if lateral play is excessive. (American Suzuki Motor Corporation)

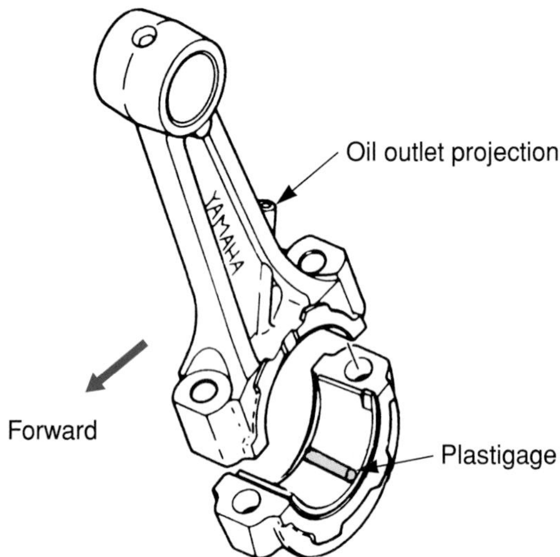

Figure 20-42. Plastigage can be used to check the clearance on any split bearing (crankshaft, camshaft). Crush a strip of Plastigage between the rod bearing and crank. Then compare the smashed width of Plastigage to the scale provided. Small bearing clearance is indicated by wide Plastigage. If the smashed Plastigage is still narrow, a larger clearance is indicated. (Yamaha Motor Corporation U.S.A.)

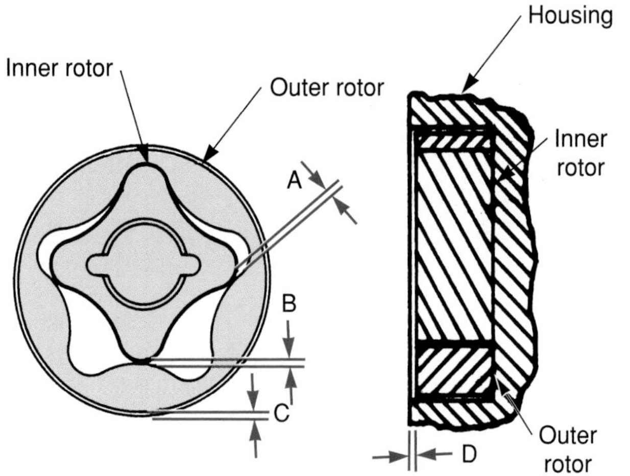

Figure 20-43. When checking the condition of a rotor oil pump, the clearance must be measured at A, B, C, and D. Use a flat feeler gauge. (Yamaha Motor Corporation U.S.A.)

Diagnosis of Oil System Problems

No matter how carefully an overhaul is done, overlooking a simple problem in the lubrication system can

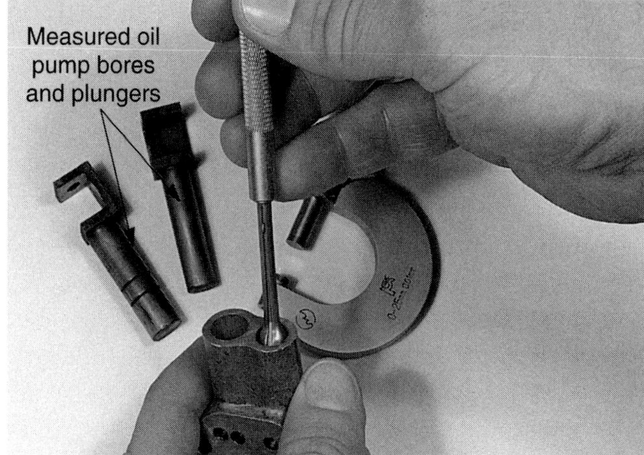

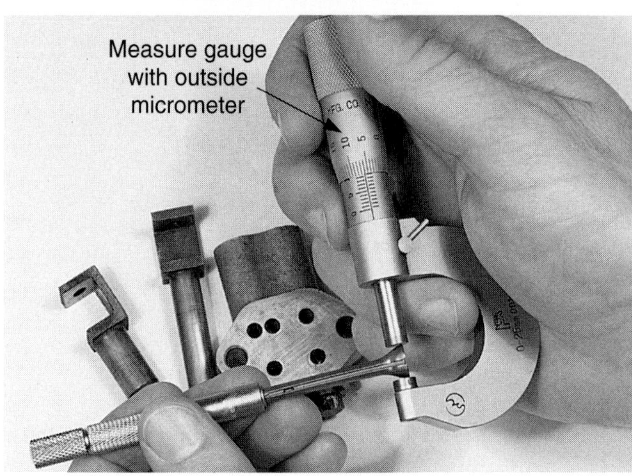

Figure 20-44. A small hole gauge and outside micrometer will accurately measure the clearance in a piston oil pump.

cause rapid engine failure. Dry, seized, or burned engine components indicate a lubrication system problem. The following questions will give typical guidance in diagnosing lubrication system problems:

- Was the oil pump mounted securely?
- Were gaskets and O-rings properly installed?
- Were check balls and relief valves free of debris and in good working order?
- Were oil passageways and orifices clogged or restricted?
- Were external oil lines damaged; leaking; or connected properly?
- Were oil filters and screens clogged or blocked?
- Was engine oil contaminated or diluted?
- Was there sufficient oil in the engine?

Complete details on servicing and solving lubricating system problems are given in Chapter 10.

Engine Balancer Inspection

Some motorcycle engines are equipped with chain- or gear-driven balancers. Check for chain and sprocket or gear wear, as well as the balancer shaft bearings and cushion. Typical balancer system inspection points are shown in **Figure 20-45.** Refer to the service manual for proper procedures since there are many variations in design.

Crankshaft Measurement and Reconditioning

Four-stroke motorcycle engines use one of two types of crankshafts, assembled crankshaft or a one-piece crankshaft. Both types require thorough inspection and measurement for wear. Depending on parts availability and how the crankshaft is designed, you may be able to recondition some types.

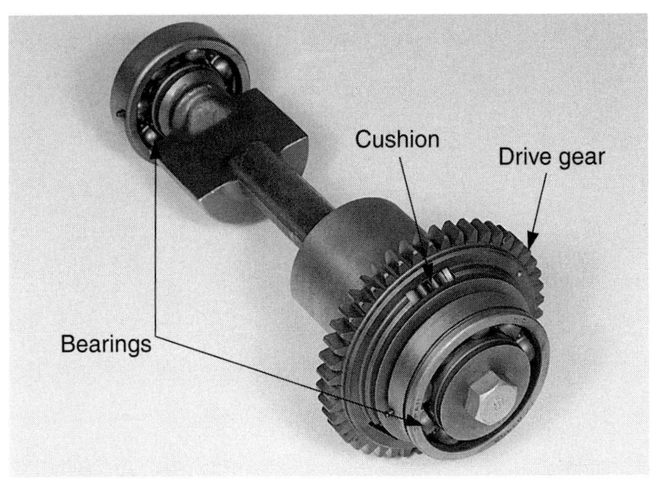

Figure 20-45. Components on an engine balancer which must be inspected include bearings, drive gear, and cushion.

Assembled Crankshafts

An assembled four-stroke cycle crankshaft is checked for wear in the same manner as a two-stroke cycle crankshaft. Make sure the crankshaft has been thoroughly cleaned and is free of oil. An oil film left on bearings (connecting rod roller bearing) makes wear difficult to detect. **Figure 20-46** illustrates typical assembled crankshaft measurement. The service manual will outline crankshaft inspection procedures for the specific engine type.

Rebuild kits are available for some four-stroke engines that use assembled crankshafts. A typical rod kit is shown in **Figure 20-47.** Four-stroke cycle crankshafts are rebuilt in the same manner as two-stroke engine crankshafts. The crankshaft must be disassembled and reassembled using a hydraulic press. After assembly, the crank assembly must be trued.

One-Piece Plain Bearing Crankshaft

Plain bearing crankshaft journals (rod and main) must be measured to check diameter, taper, and out-of-roundness. This is illustrated in **Figure 20-48.** A worn plain bearing crankshaft may be reconditioned in two ways:

- Insert bearing replacement (minor reconditioning).
- Grinding journals for undersize bearings (major reconditioning).

Minor Crankshaft Reconditioning

When crankshaft journals measure within service limits and have a smooth surface, they may be polished with crocus cloth and reused. In most instances, a new set of standard insert bearings will recondition the crankshaft

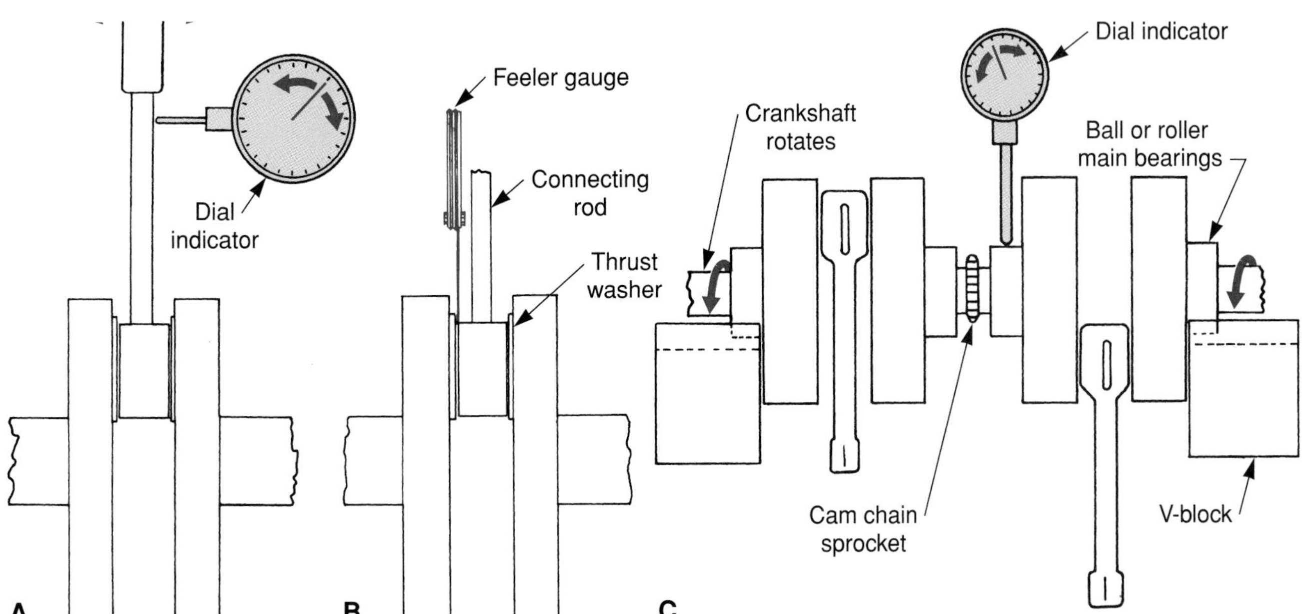

Figure 20-46. Measuring an assembled crankshaft. A—Measurement of rod tip determines crankpin bearing and rod big end wear. B—A feeler gauge inserted between the connecting rod and thrust washer measures side play. C—Measurement of crankshaft deflection is accomplished by supporting the crankshaft by its outside ball or roller main bearings. Measure the runout in the center main bearings while rotating the crankshaft.

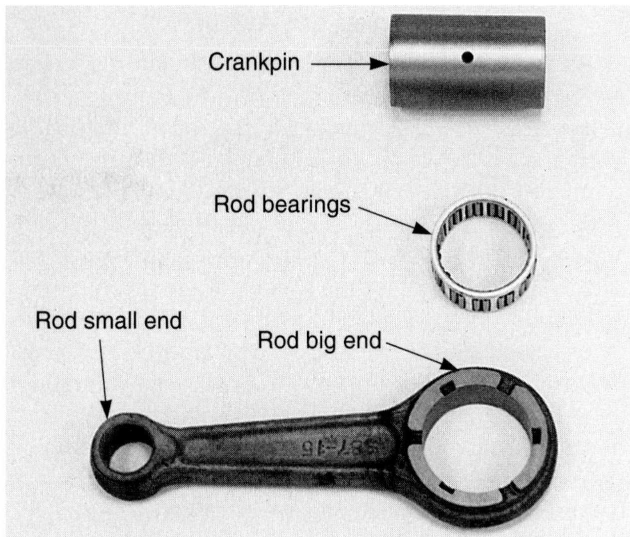

Figure 20-47. A typical rod kit for a four-stroke engine using an assembled crankshaft. It allows engine rebuilding at a minimum cost.

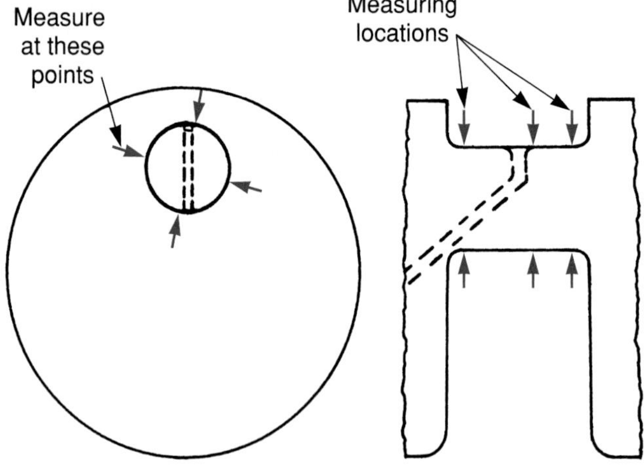

Figure 20-48. A plain bearing connecting rod journal must be measured in the areas shown to detect taper and out-of-roundness.

assembly. A check of bearing clearance will usually show clearance to be within specifications. See **Figure 20-49.**

Some designs allow for minute adjustment of clearance. Bearing inserts are classified and coded in several increments within a .002″ (.051 mm) range. The service manual explains this operation if applicable.

Major Crankshaft Reconditioning

Major crankshaft reconditioning consists of regrinding rod or main journals to a smaller diameter and fitting undersize bearings. Crankshaft grinding must be done by a specialist. Many automotive machine shops can handle this operation. Some modern plain bearing crankshafts cannot be reground when they are outside of wear limits. Refer to the service manual when in doubt.

Figure 20-49. A—To check rod bearing clearance, lay a strip of Plastigage on the crankshaft journal. Carefully install and torque the rod. This squeezes the Plastigage into a wider strip. B—The gauge provided with the Plastigage is then used to measure the width of the strip. In this example, rod bearing clearance is .0015″.

Connecting Rod Reconditioning (Plain Bearing)

With severe four-stroke engine bottom end failures, the connecting rod can be damaged. A broken connecting rod is quite obvious. A bent connecting rod may or may not be obvious, depending on how badly it is bent.

If uneven wear on the sides of the piston or angled wear marks on the skirt are noticed, check for a bent rod, **Figure 20-50.**

A different type of damage which is not obvious occurs when bearings and rod journals are worn excessively. In this situation, extreme stresses may cause the connecting rod's big end to become oval-shaped, **Figure 20-51.** It is a good idea to measure the connecting rod for this condition during an overhaul. Use a telescoping gauge and micrometer to measure vertically and horizontally in the connecting rod big end. Depending upon cost and the type of connecting rod problem, reconditioning by a machine shop or replacement may be needed. Refer to a manual for specific directions and specifications.

Engine Measurement and Inspection Summary

A great deal of information must be gathered and put to use during a four-stroke engine overhaul. The following list of procedures should be used as a guide. Use it with the service manual for the specific engine being repaired as needed.

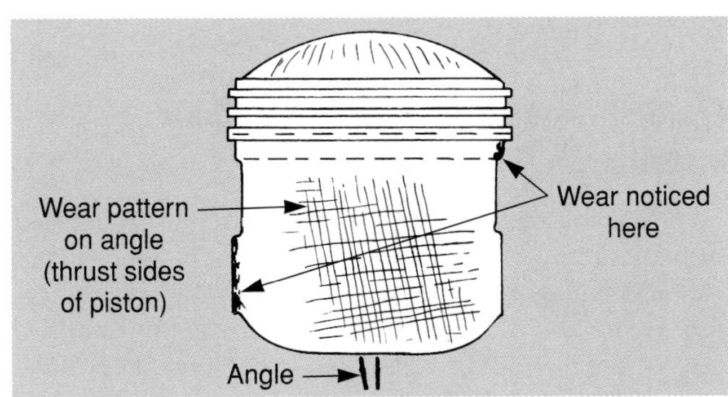

Figure 20-50. A bent connecting rod may cause the piston sides to wear unevenly (at top on one side and bottom on other side). An angled wear pattern in the piston may be caused by dirt.

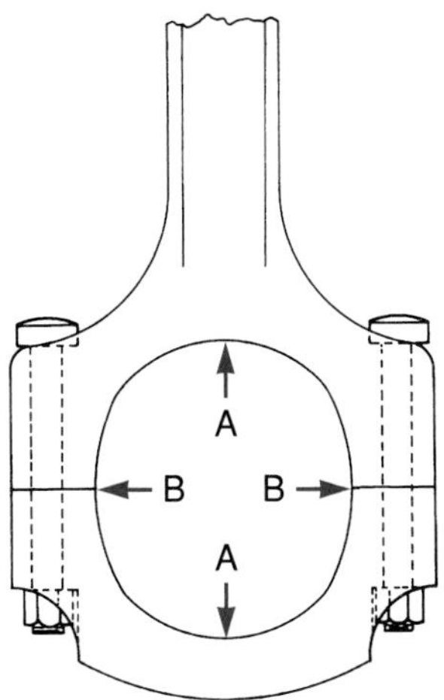

Figure 20-51. When diameter A-A is larger than B-B, the connecting rod is oval shaped and requires rebuilding or replacement. An oval shape can be detected by measuring a torqued rod and cap with an outside micrometer and telescoping gauge.

General Inspection

1. Inspect for damaged surfaces (corrosion, scoring, discoloration, grooving).
2. Check for frozen or stiff moving parts (lack of lubrication, excessive heat, insufficient clearance, foreign material).
3. Watch for broken parts (cracks, chips, bits of material in engine).
4. Measure warpage (distortion of part due to overheating, improper installation, excessive wear).
5. Make sure no parts are missing because of improper assembly (usually small part, spring, clip, spacer, lock tab).

Top End Components

1. Measure rocker or follower inside diameter.
2. Measure rocker or follower shaft diameter.
3. Check for camshaft runout.
4. Measure camshaft bearing bore diameter.
5. Check camshaft journal diameter.
6. Measure camshaft lobe wear.
7. Use Plastigage to measure camshaft bearing clearance.
8. Check camshaft end play.
9. Measure shim bucket and shim bore diameters.
10. Inspect cam followers and cam lobe surface condition.
11. Check tappet surface condition.
12. Check valve stem diameter, valve margin thickness, and stem runout.
13. Check valve faces for grooving or pitting.
14. Inspect valve stem tips for wear.
15. Measure valve guide wear.
16. Measure valve spring free and installed heights.
17. Make sure cam chain tensioner is not damaged.
18. Check piston skirts to detect blow-by discoloration.
19. Make sure cylinder head surface and top of cylinder block are straight.
20. Inspect cylinder bores for a ridge.
21. Measure cylinder bore diameter, out-of-roundness, and taper.

22. Check piston diameter, wrist pin diameter, ring end gap, ring side clearance, and piston clearance in cylinder.
23. Measure tappet bore and stem diameters.

Bottom End Components

1. Check for crankshaft runout.
2. Measure main bearing journal diameter, journal out-of-roundness, and clearance.
3. Check connecting rod journal diameter, out-of-roundness, and bearing clearance.
4. Inspect all plain bearings, bushings, and journals for smoothness.
5. Check main and connecting rod bearing looseness (ball-rollers).
6. Measure cam chain length.
7. Measure crankshaft end play.
8. Check all seal lips for sharpness and surfaces that seals ride on for grooving.

Oil Pump

1. Measure shaft diameter and body inside diameter.
2. Check gear-rotor side play.
3. Measure plunger diameter and plunger body diameter.
4. Check plunger clearance.
5. Inspect drive gear or block for wear.

Four-Stroke Engine Reassembly

Engine reassembly is a relatively simple operation, but it must be done with great care. Failure to keep parts clean or properly organized can ruin an otherwise good overhaul. Many of the steps used in two-stroke engine assembly also apply to four-stroke engines.

Plain Bearing Installation

On engines using plain bearings for the crankshaft main or connecting rod bearings, care during assembly must be emphasized. To ensure proper installation of plain bearings:

1. Make sure the bearing seating surfaces on the engine and backside of the bearing are perfectly clean. Do not touch the bearing surface as it is easily damaged. Even the acid on your fingertips can etch the surface. If dirt is present on the bearing, wash in solvent and blow dry.
2. Install the bearing shells with the locating tabs properly indexed and with each bearing in its proper location, **Figure 20-52.** Refer to the service manual for bearing identification.
3. Use Plastigage to determine bearing clearance. Refer to the service manual for proper clearance. If clearance is incorrect, the manual will explain proper corrective action.
4. Carefully remove Plastigage residue from bearing shells and crankshaft.
5. Lubricate crankshaft and bearing shells.
6. Make sure the connecting rod is installed facing the proper direction. The cap and rod index marks must be correctly aligned. Torque the rod bolts to specification, **Figure 20-53.**

Final main bearing assembly is completed when the crankcase halves are bolted together. All rotating parts are susceptible to binding if installed improperly or if damaged. Check for free movement after installing the shafts, shift drum, connecting rods, and crankshaft. Check for binding as parts are assembled and after the crankcases are torqued. Be sure the transmission shifts smoothly through each gear.

Crankshaft and Transmission Shaft Installation

The crankshaft and transmission shafts must be located properly during bottom end assembly. Half-rings and dowel pins indexed into bearings provide accurate location, **Figure 20-54.** Engines using an internal primary drive (gear or chain), must be assembled in conjunction with the crankshaft, **Figure 20-55.** Four-stroke engines, which use vertically split crankcases, may require measurement and adjustment of crankshaft and transmission end play.

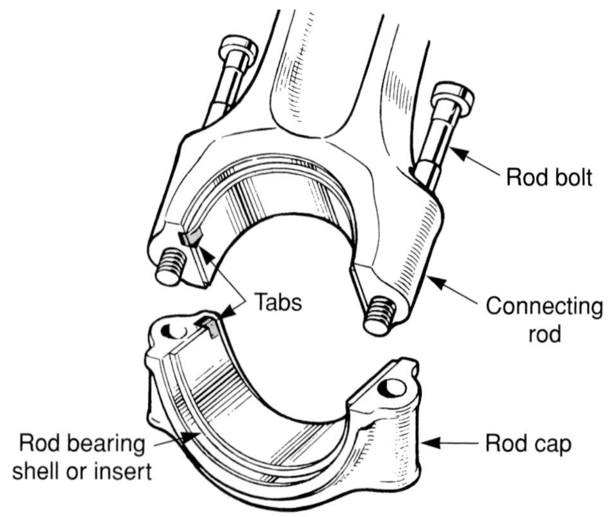

Figure 20-52. Insert bearing tabs must be indexed and the bearing shells must be fully seated before installation. (Triumph Motorcycles, Ltd.)

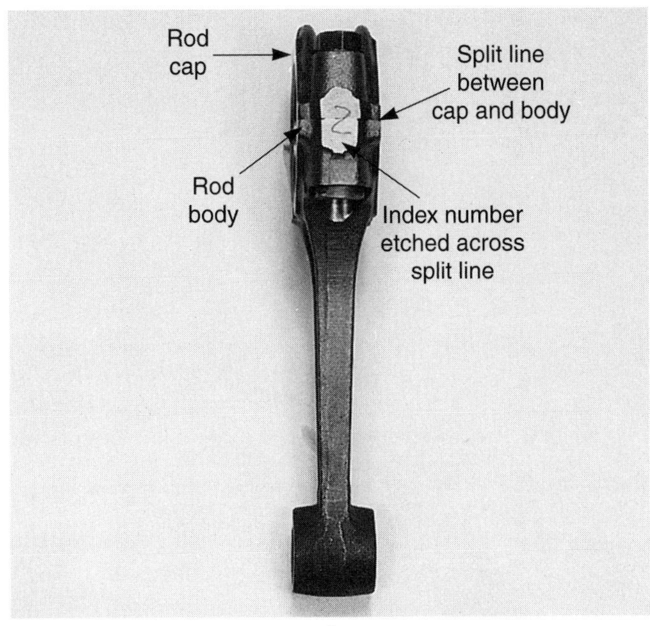

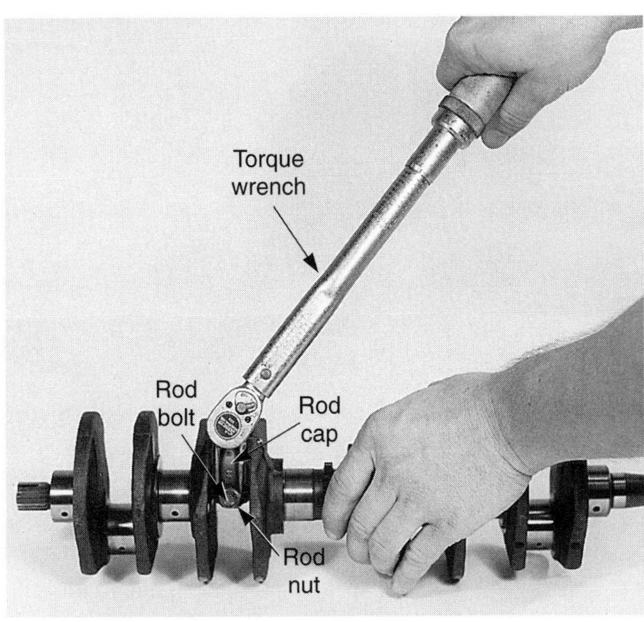

Figure 20-53. A—Index marks are provided to identify the proper direction for rod cap installation. B—Using a torque wrench, tighten each rod nut a little at a time until the proper torque is reached.

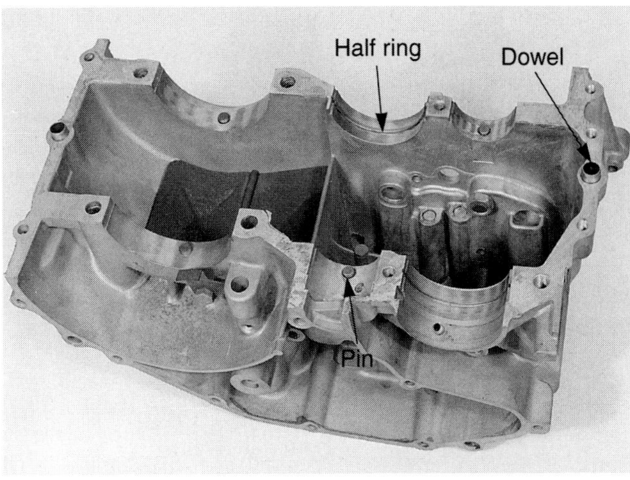

Figure 20-54. Typical crankcase locating devices are dowels, pins, and half rings. Always make sure they are in place and undamaged before assembly.

Figure 20-55. In this internal primary drive, the crankshaft, primary chain, and jackshaft are installed together.

Oil and Grease Use

Engine components must be lubricated during assembly. This ensures proper lubrication when the engine runs for the first time. Failure to lubricate components during assembly can result in immediate damage.

Special assembly lubricants are available and should be used where recommended by the bike manufacturer. Lubrication with a good four-stroke engine oil is usually acceptable. Grease is used for lubrication of seal lips. Thick grease will also hold parts (valve keepers, thrust washers, or gaskets) in position during assembly.

Sealing Compounds

Machined surfaces which do not use a gasket must be sealed with an approved sealant. Do not use an excessive amount of silicone sealant. Sealer can block oil passages if it squeezes out when fasteners are tightened. Refer to the service manual for the proper type of sealing compounds and where they should be used.

Timing of Engine Balancers

In order to reduce engine vibration, ***engine balancers*** must be timed with the crankshaft. Timing marks are provided to allow for easy and precise timing. **Figure 20-56** illustrates typical engine balancer timing.

Figure 20-56. An engine balancer must be timed to work properly. This gear driven balancer has punch marks that must be aligned for proper timing.

Reference or timing marks may be found on gears, sprockets, or balancer weights. Always refer to the service manual for specific timing procedure.

Torque Sequence and Value

Due to the size of cylinder, cylinder head, and crankcase castings, a proper torque pattern (fastener tightening sequence) must be used to prevent warpage. A torque pattern follows a crisscross pattern from the center to the outside of the part. However, due to the complex design of modern engine castings, torque patterns vary.

Some current four-stroke engines have torque sequence numbers cast into the cylinder head or crankcase, **Figure 20-57.** This sequence must always be followed. If numbers are not present, refer to the manual for a proper torque sequence.

The other important aspect of torquing engine components is the final torque value (amount of torque applied). Proper torquing is not achieved in one torque sequence. Gradual tightening of fasteners in three or four stages (approximately 1/2 torque, 3/4 torque, and full torque twice) is necessary. Refer to the service manual for details.

Piston Ring Installation

The importance of piston ring installation is sometimes overlooked. Piston rings which are installed incorrectly can cause a loss of compression, increased oil consumption, or cylinder damage. Critical considerations during piston ring installation are:

- Piston rings must be located in the proper grooves (chrome ring in top groove, scraper ring in middle groove, oil ring in bottom groove).
- Piston rings should be installed with the right side up.

Figure 20-57. Torque sequence numbers are sometimes cast into the crankcase and/or cylinder head.

As shown in **Figure 20-58,** markings are usually provided on the top of the ring.

- Use a ring expander to prevent breakage during installation. Look at **Figure 20-59A.** Rings can also be installed without a ring expander if care is exercised, **Figure 20-59B.** Segmented oil rings must be installed by hand. See **Figure 20-59C.**
- Install the oil ring first, then the middle ring, then the top ring.

Piston Installation

During installation, piston direction is important because of offset wrist pins or different size valve pocket cutouts. Shown in **Figure 20-60,** an arrow is usually cast or stamped into the crown to indicate piston direction. This arrow usually points toward the front of the engine. Refer to the service manual for proper piston direction.

Some simple but important tips for piston installation are:

1. Install a new cylinder base gasket.

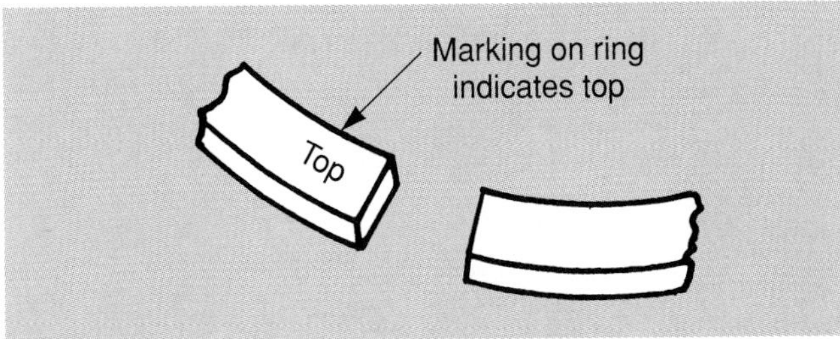

Figure 20-58. Rings with markings must be installed with the mark up. Markings which may be encountered are: N,.5 and 1.0 for oversize metric, or .010, .020 for oversize standard.

2. Cover the crankcase opening with clean shop towels. This will prevent an accidentally dropped part (circlip for example) from entering the engine. In many cases, complete engine disassembly will be required to recover anything dropped into the crankcase.
3. Always install one circlip in the piston while still on the bench. This leaves only one circlip to be installed while over the crankcase.
4. Install the pin through one side of the piston before placing it over the connecting rod. Most piston pins are slip fit into the pin boss. If the pin does not slip freely into place, it may be necessary to heat the piston for installation, **Figure 20-61.**
5. Install the remaining circlip and make sure all circlips are fully seated in their grooves, **Figure 20-62.**

Cylinder Installation

Cylinder installation procedures vary from engine to engine. Important considerations which apply to most engines are:

1. Install locating dowel pins and O-rings in the cylinder or case, **Figure 20-63.**
2. Properly position ring end gaps. This is shown in **Figure 20-64.**
3. Use a ring compressor, **Figure 20-65.**
4. Use piston blocks, when possible, to hold the piston straight, **Figure 20-66.**
5. Carefully install the cylinder; it must not be tilted or cocked when slid over the rings, **Figure 20-67.**

Cam Timing

Cam timing is critical as it determines valve movement in relation to piston movement. Failure to properly set cam timing can cause the pistons to hit the valves, which can result in bent valves and damaged pistons. Timing (index) marks are provided on gears, sprockets, and crankshaft (alternator rotor or ignition advance unit). These marks must be used as specified by the service manual to time the camshafts with the crankshaft. **Figure 20-68** shows typical cam timing marks.

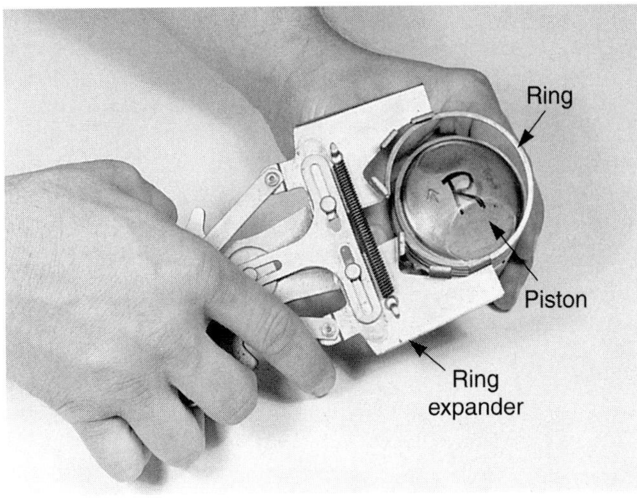

A

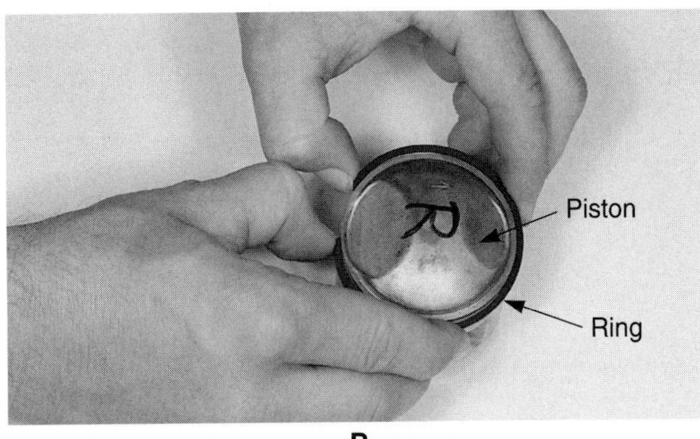

B

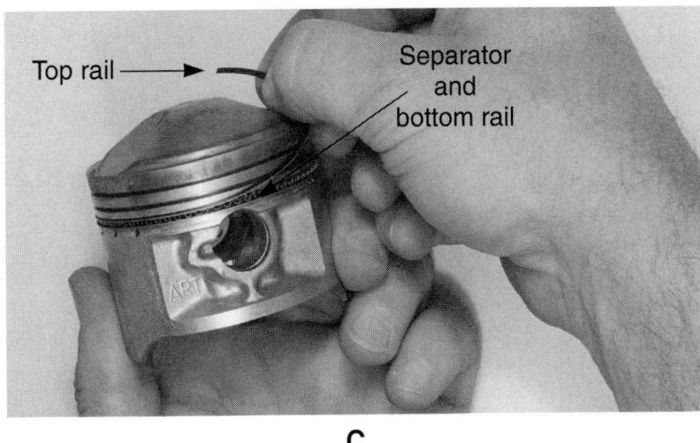

C

Figure 20-59. A—A ring expander makes piston ring installation easy. B—Piston rings can also be installed by hand. Be careful not to overexpand and break the rings. C—When installing segmented oil rings, install the separator first, then the bottom rail, and finally the top rail. Be sure the separator ends are butted together, not overlapped.

Four-Stroke Engine Reassembly Summary

Some normal tune-up adjustments are usually needed after engine reassembly. These include cam chain, valve clearance, fuel system, and ignition timing adjustments. See Chapter 22 for these procedures. The following list summarizes some of the most important aspects of

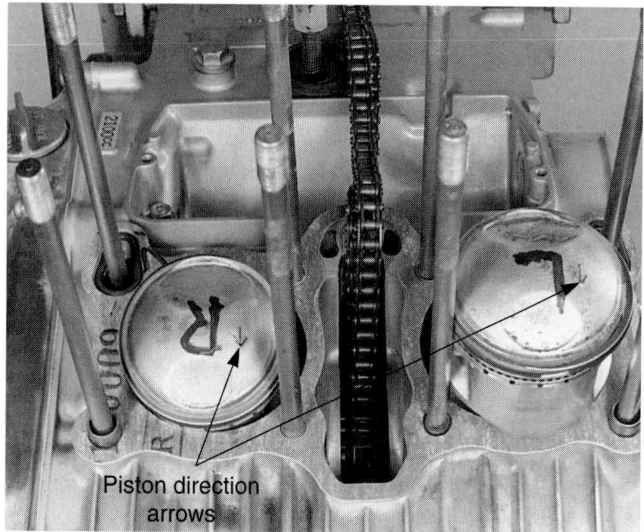

Figure 20-60. Piston installation direction arrows point toward the front (exhaust) on this engine.

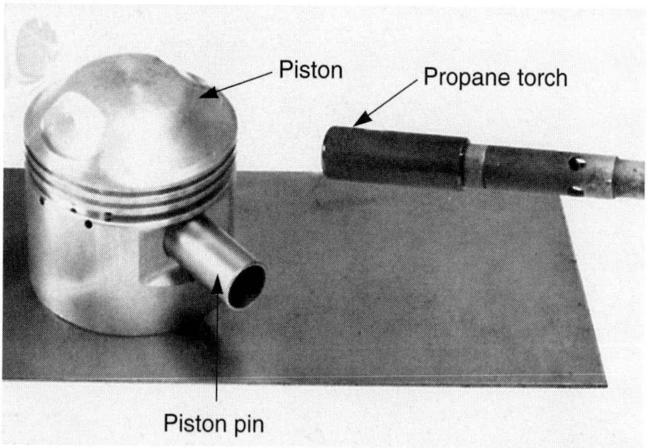

Figure 20-61. A propane torch can be used to warm the piston so the pin will move freely into place. Be careful not to overheat the piston.

four-stroke engine reassembly. Use the service manual for specific step-by-step instructions.

1. Lubricate all moving engine parts before installation, **Figure 20-69.**
2. Install new gaskets, seals, and O-rings.
3. Check crankshaft and transmission shaft end play (where applicable).
4. Check for proper seal installation.
5. Make sure bearing locating half rings and dowel pins are installed properly.
6. Check that all crankcase dowel pins are installed.
7. Use new plain bearings.
8. Check that connecting rods have proper clearance using Plastigage. Also check for proper rod, cap, and bearing shell direction. Torque connecting rod bolts.

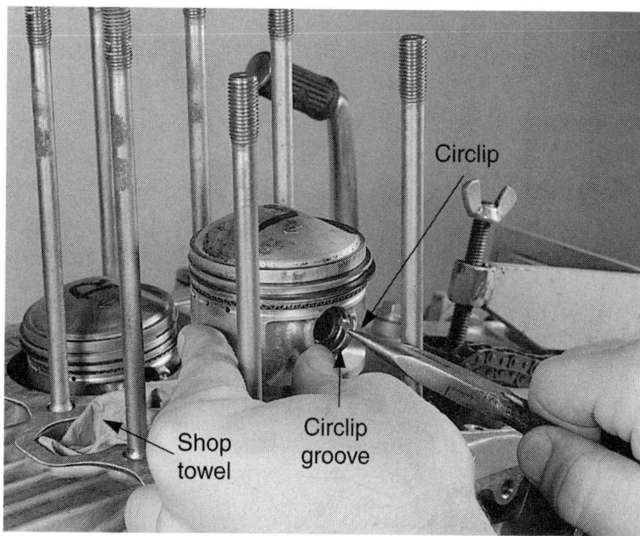

Figure 20-62. Make sure circlips are fully seated in their grooves. A shop towel covering the crankcase opening will prevent an accidentally dropped circlip from entering the engine bottom end.

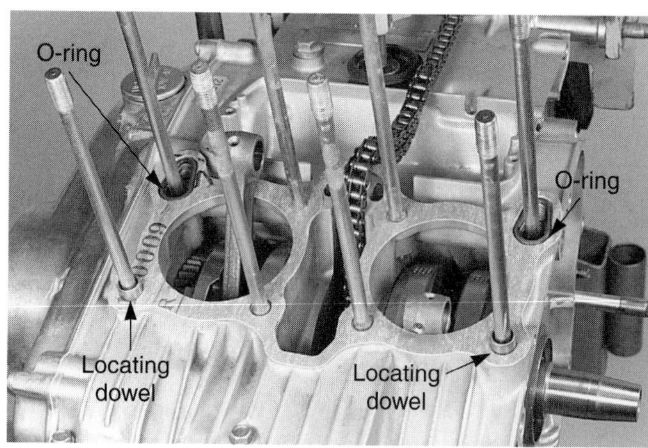

A

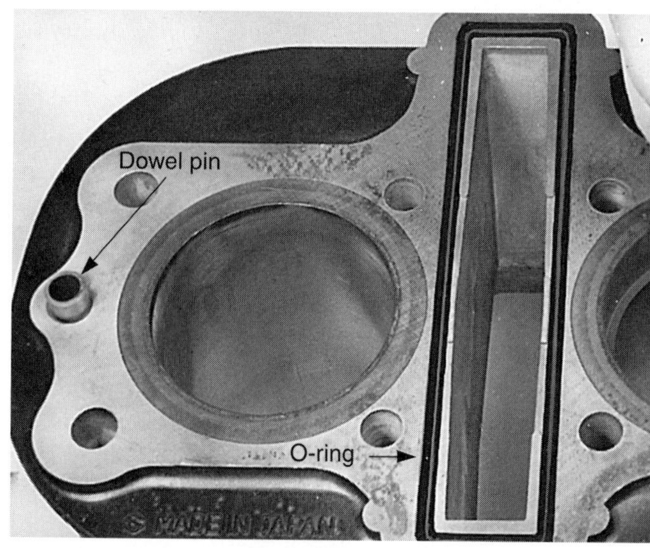

B

Figure 20-63. Do not forget to install all locating dowels and O-rings in the crankcase, cylinder, and head.

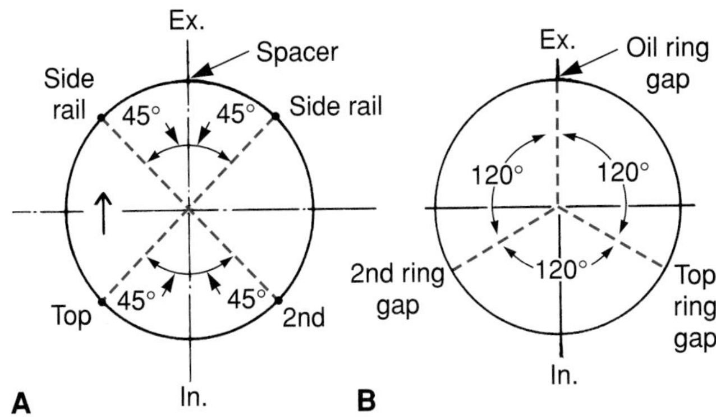

Figure 20-64. A—Proper ring end gap position with a three-piece oil ring. B—Proper ring end-gap for a one-piece oil ring.

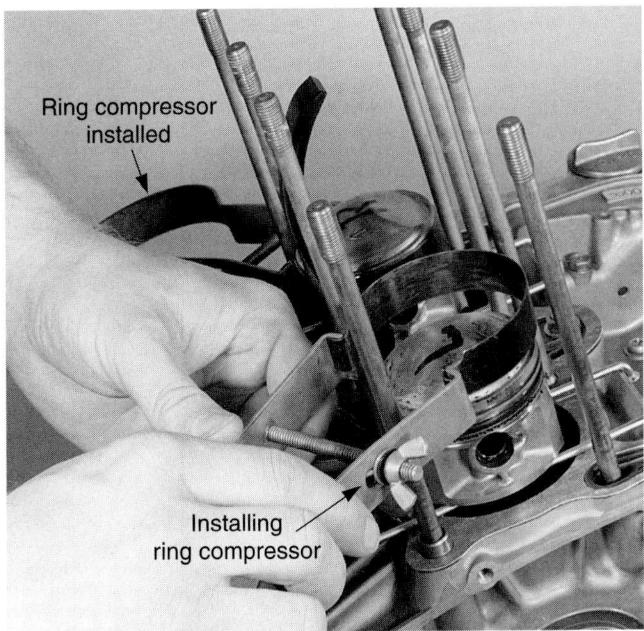

Figure 20-65. Ring compressors reduce the chance of breakage when the cylinder is slid over the pistons.

Figure 20-66. Piston blocks help keep the pistons in position during cylinder installation.

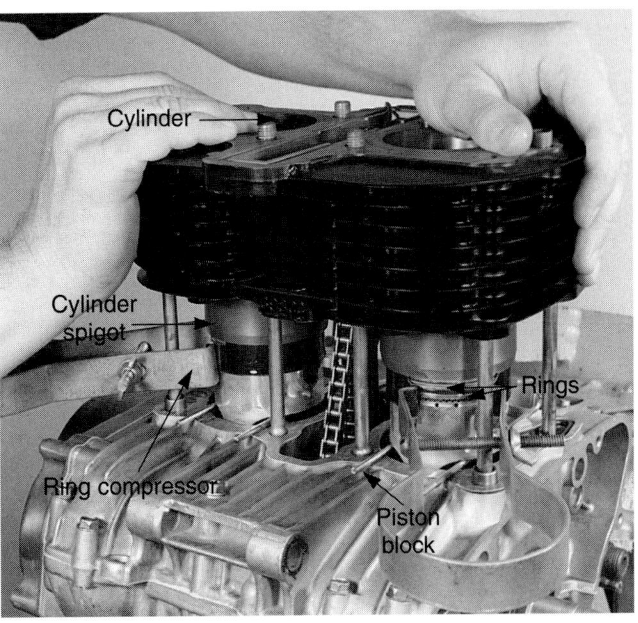

Figure 20-67. Be careful not to tilt the cylinder while slipping it over the rings. Gently tap the cylinder with the heel of your hand or a plastic hammer to help move the cylinder down. Remove the ring compressors and piston blocks after the rings are fitted into cylinder spigots. Then, slide the cylinder all the way down until it touches the base gasket.

9. Make sure all crankshaft bearings are installed properly (fully seated, proper direction, correct clearance).
10. Cam chain must be installed on the crankshaft (OHC) correctly.
11. Make sure the crankshaft assembly is installed properly.
12. Check for proper assembly of internal primary drive, **Figure 20-70.**
13. Make sure transmission assembly functions properly.
14. Check installation of camshafts (push rod engine).
15. Use sealing compounds where needed.
16. Check for binding after each installation.
17. Carefully assemble crankcase halves.
18. Crankcase fasteners of different lengths must be in proper locations.
19. Use proper torque sequences and values, **Figure 20-71.**
20. Make sure oil pump is in good condition and installed properly, **Figure 20-72.** When the service manual calls for it, use locking compound on oil pump mounting screws.
21. Check for proper clutch and external primary drive assembly.
22. Check for proper piston ring installation. Be sure end gap is checked and adjusted if needed.
23. Inspect installation of cylinder base gasket, dowel pins, and O-rings.

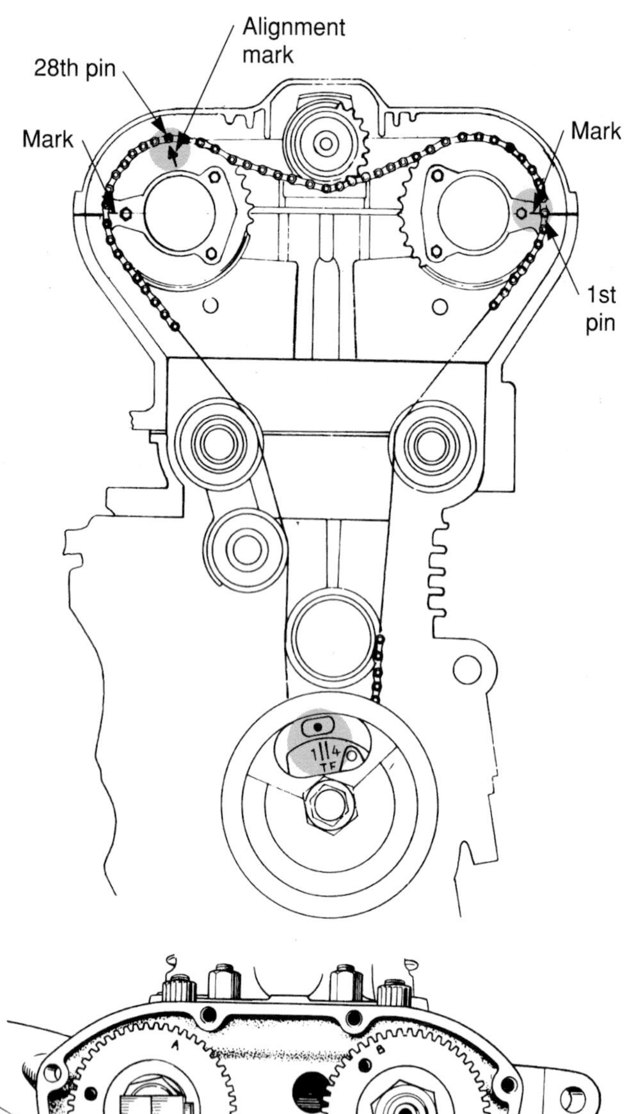

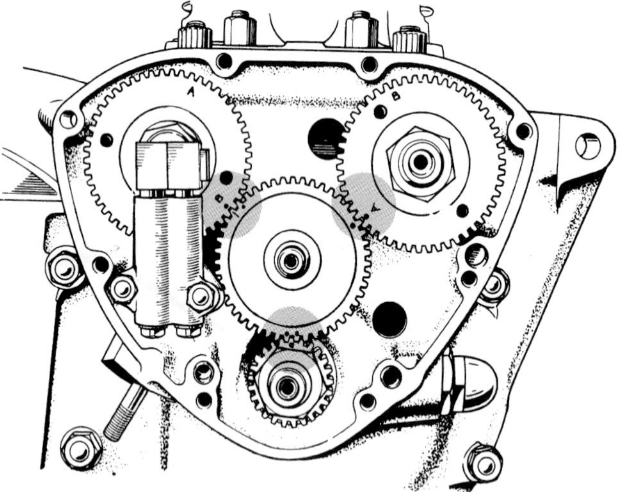

Figure 20-68. Regardless of method for driving cams, index marks are given to simplify cam timing setting. With timing chains, marks must align with certain links. With timing gears, adjacent dots or lines must be lined up. (Kawasaki Motors Corp., U.S.A.) (Triumph Motorcycles [Meriden] Ltd.)

A

B

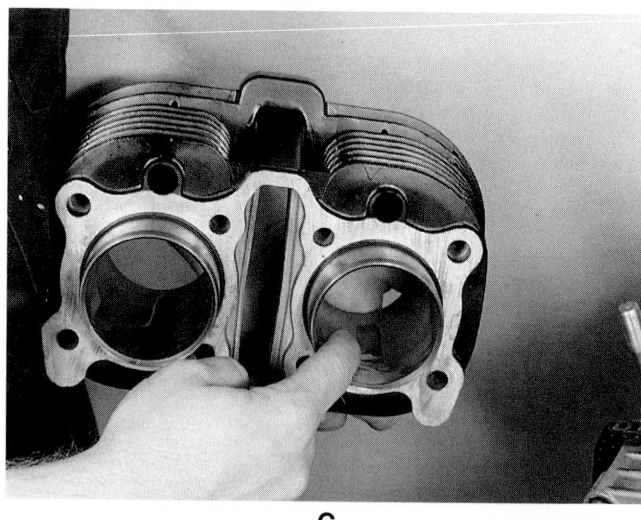

C

Figure 20-69. Moving parts must be carefully lubricated before and during assembly. A—Lubricating transmission components. B—Lubricating piston rings and piston. C—Lubricating cylinder.

24. Check for proper piston installation (piston direction, circlips).
25. Inspect piston ring end gap positioning on piston.
26. Check installation and condition of cam chain guides, **Figure 20-73.**
27. Carefully install cylinder.
28. Check for proper installation of head gasket, dowel pins, and O-rings.
29. Install cylinder head using proper torque sequence and value.

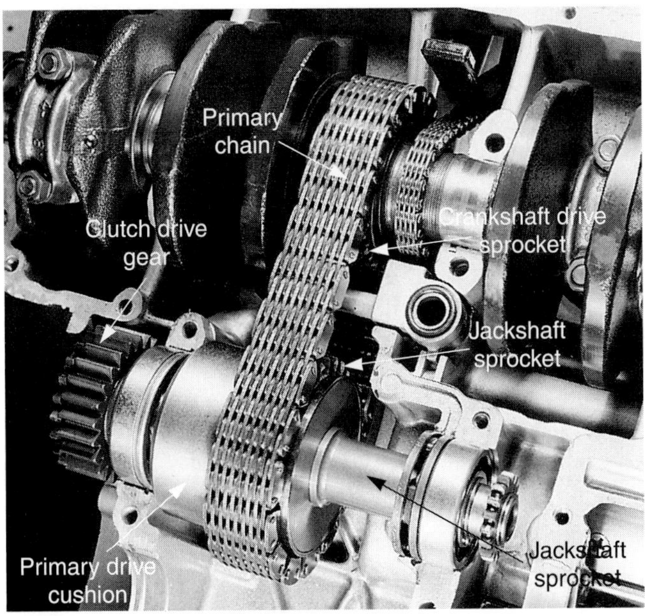

Figure 20-70. In this internal primary drive, the crankshaft, primary chain, and jackshaft are installed together.

30. Use proper installation techniques for valve train components.
31. Check timing of camshaft(s).
32. Double-check the alternator, electric starter, and ignition components are installed correctly.
33. Check for proper cam chain adjustment.
34. Valve clearance must be adjusted to specifications, **Figure 20-74.**
35. Set static ignition timing, **Figure 20-75.**
36. Make sure all engine covers (valve cover, primary case cover, etc.) are properly installed. Some covers may have to be left off until engine is installed.

Engine Installation

Although the service manual gives engine installation instructions, the following procedures are especially important:

1. Check for proper oil line connections (make sure lines are not crossed).
2. Clean and tighten electrical connections as needed.
3. Check that fuel system installation and adjustments are correct.
4. The exhaust system at the cylinder head, crossover pipes, and mufflers should fit and seal properly.
5. Check for proper connection and adjustment for all control cables.
6. Check that drive chain is adjusted properly.
7. Check the connection and torque of shaft drive coupler.

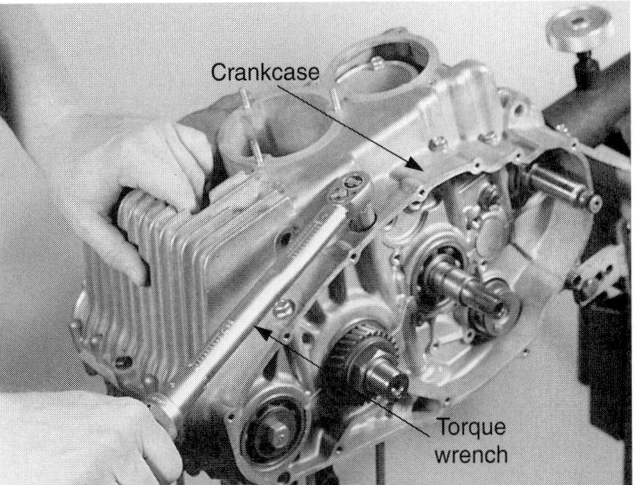

Figure 20-71. Use a torque wrench and correct pattern to tighten crankcase and head bolts.

Figure 20-72. Be sure to use new O-rings and gaskets when installing an oil pump.

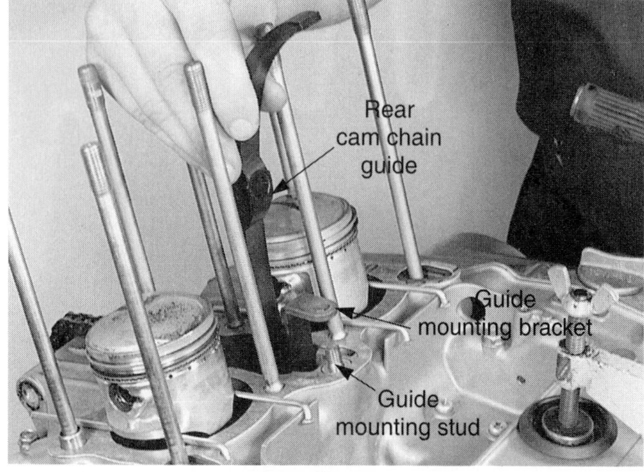

A

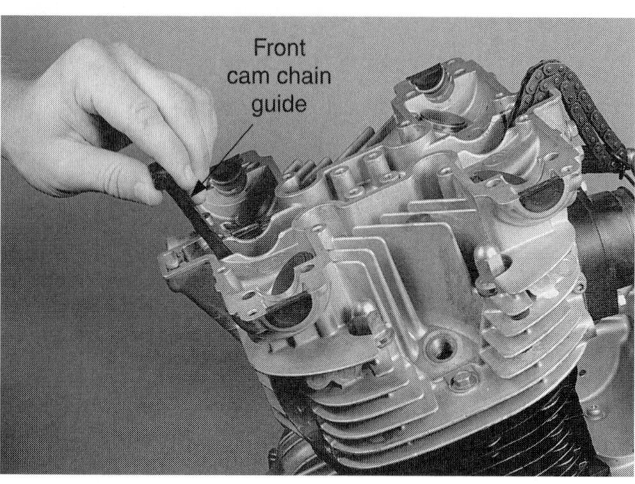

B

Figure 20-73. Do not forget to install all cam chain guides. A—In this engine, the rear cam chain guide is installed into the crankcase. B—The front guide is installed after the cylinder and head are in place.

A

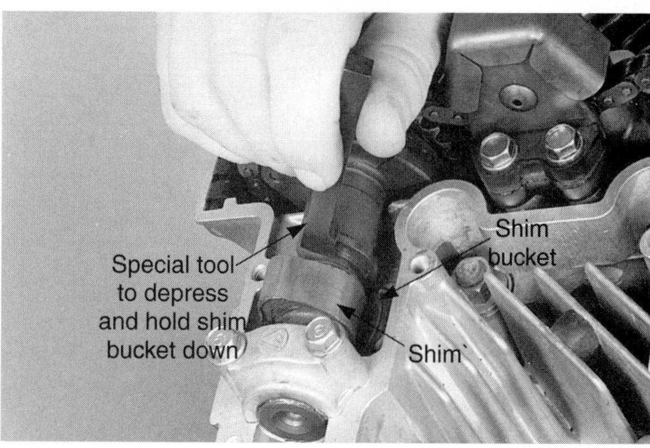

B

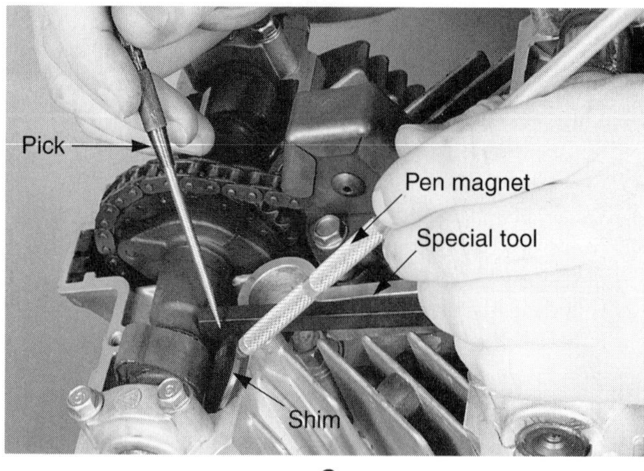

C

Figure 20-74. A—Valve adjustment is done after checking clearance with a feeler gauge. B—A special tool is used to hold the bucket down so that the shim can be removed. C—The shim is being replaced with the correct one.

Initial Engine Running

Before starting the engine, make sure the lubrication system will function immediately. Initial lubrication is extremely important to prevent premature engine wear.

1. Fill the crankcase reservoir or oil tank with the proper grade and quantity of four-stroke cycle motor oil.
2. Prime the oil system (dry sump) by filling the oil feed line and pump with motor oil. This is demonstrated in **Figure 20-76.**
3. Lubricate valve springs and cam followers or rocker arms with oil.
4. Install an oil pressure gauge in the appropriate test port on the engine, **Figure 20-77.**

During initial engine operation:

- Check engine oil pressure.
- Listen for unusual noises by using a stethoscope as in **Figure 20-78.**
- Look for oil and fuel leaks.
- Check and adjust ignition timing (dynamic).
- Check and adjust carburetor synchronization, pilot mixture, and idle speed.

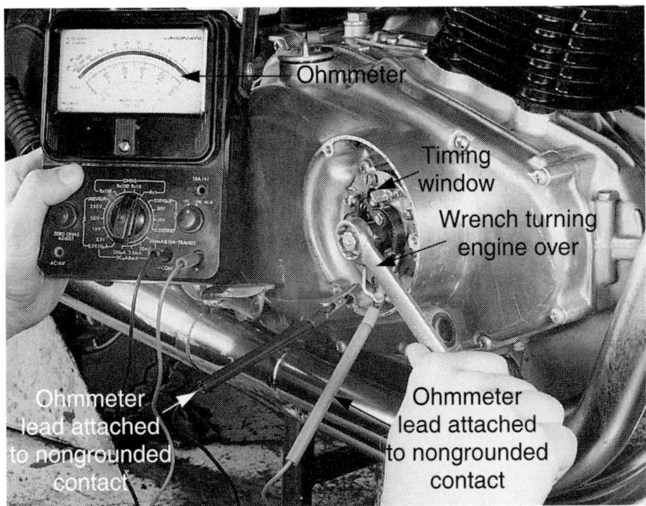

Figure 20-75. To set static timing, hook one lead from ohmmeter or continuity tester to ground. Connect the other lead to the ungrounded contact. As the engine is turned over with a wrench, infinite resistance or lack of continuity will occur just as the points open. Timing mark should be lined up just as the points open.

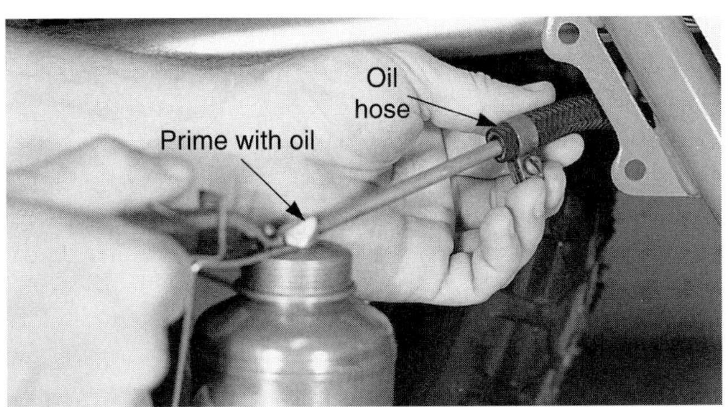

Figure 20-76. Engines using a dry sump lubrication system should be primed before the engine is started. Fill the oil feed line using an oil squirt can.

Warning: A freshly overhauled engine has very high internal resistance because of new parts rubbing against each other. As a result, the first time the engine is started, friction can cause the engine to heat up quickly. Be careful not to overheat and damage the engine while making initial adjustments. It may be necessary to shut the engine off for it to cool down.

Engine Break-In Procedures

The break-in period of a four-stroke engine is very critical to engine life and dependability. Since a four-stroke engine's parts wear at a slower rate, the break-in period is longer than for a two-stroke engine. A typical break-in period is around 1500 miles (2413 km).

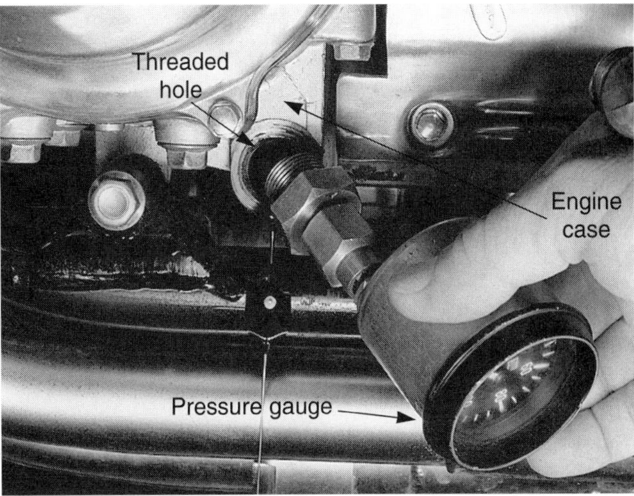

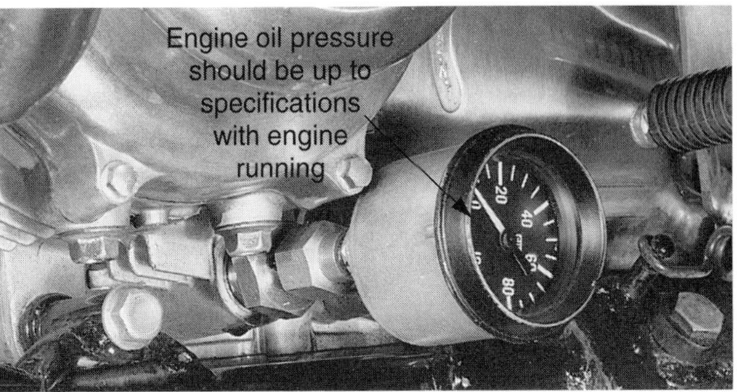

Figure 20-77. Install an oil pressure gauge so that engine oil pressure can be checked when the engine is first started. There is normally a threaded oil outlet near the bottom of the engine. A—Installing gauge. B—Ready to check initial engine oil pressure.

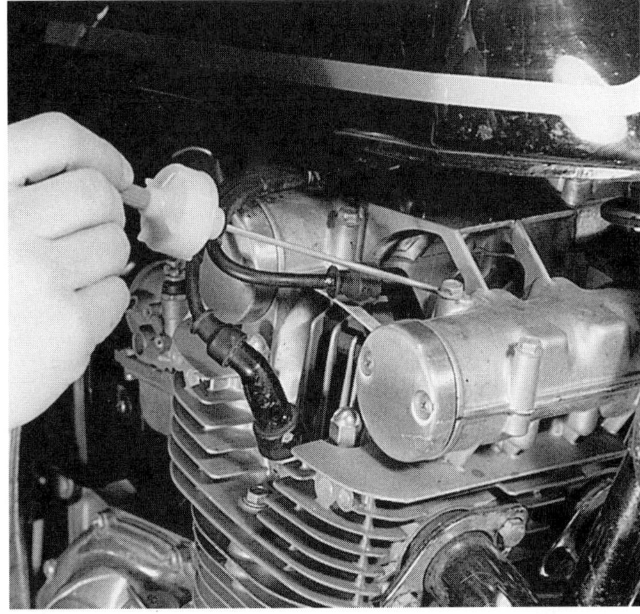

Figure 20-78. A stethoscope is helpful in determining the origin of a particular engine noise. Any noise will be loudest at its source.

Important things to do during engine break-in are:

- Do not accelerate abruptly.
- Listen for abnormal engine noises.
- Do not overheat, race, or lug (operate at low rpm under load) the engine.
- Do not cruise at a constant or high throttle setting.
- Do not let the engine idle for long periods of time.
- Monitor the oil level and add oil as necessary.

These recommendations help prevent overheating, and inadequate lubrication which could ruin engine parts. Keep the engine in midrange speeds and vary speeds occasionally.

Post-Overhaul Checkup

The break-in process is a controlled wearing in of engine parts. As parts wear from friction and gaskets settle from heating (expansion) and cooling (contraction), clearances may change. The loosening or tightening of valve clearance is an example of this condition. The following list gives the specific adjustments and checks which should be made during post overhaul checkup.

1. Adjust valves.
2. Adjust cam chain.
3. Check cylinder compression.
4. Lubricate contact breaker cam.
5. Check and adjust contact breaker gap.
6. Check and adjust trigger clearance (electronic ignition).
7. Adjust carburetor pilot mixture (initial setting).
8. Check and adjust throttle free play.
9. Check and adjust throttle synchronization (cable operated system).
10. Check spark plugs and set to proper gap.
11. Check and adjust ignition timing.
12. Adjust pilot mixture (engine running).
13. Synchronize carburetors (use vacuum gauges with engine running).
14. Change oil and filter.
15. Check and adjust primary drive chain (where applicable).
16. Check, lubricate, and adjust rear drive chain.
17. Road test. Be sure to wear appropriate riding attire.

This initial seating in of parts will stabilize in 200-500 miles (322-806 km) of riding. At this time, a post-overhaul checkup should be done. Since the break-in process causes the oil to become contaminated with metallic particles (parts wearing in), always change the oil and filter after initial break-in.

Summary

The condition of a four-stroke engine's top end is critical for good engine performance. The top end parts control the movement of air and fuel through the combustion chamber. Valve train components are exposed to high temperatures, heavy loads, and high speeds. Because of these severe conditions, the valve train usually wears more rapidly than other engine components.

After cleaning the camshaft, check each lobe for scoring, scuffing, cracks, or other signs of wear. Inspect the camshaft journals and bearings for any signs of abnormal wear. The simplest way to measure cam lobes for wear is to use an outside micrometer. Check the camshaft for straightness with a dial indicator. If the dial indicator shows a runout variation of more than .002″ (.050 mm), the camshaft is not straight.

When removing cam followers and rocker arms for inspection, mark each one so it can be returned to where it was removed. Cam followers and rocker arms wear at the valve end, at the camshaft end (follower) or push rod end (rocker), and where the rocker shaft passes through the follower or rocker. Excessive valve train wear or clearance usually causes noise, increased oil consumption (oil drains down through guides), and reduced performance. Use care when cleaning valve springs as they have coatings that prevent rust. Inspect the spring carefully for any rust, corrosion, scratches, or nicks and replace any damaged springs.

Valve stems and guides must be measured to check for wear and valve-to-guide clearance. Excessive clearance may interfere with the sealing ability and life of the valve face and seat. Inspect the valve seat and face for burning, pitting, and other signs of damage.

Excessive heat caused by engine overheating or compression leaks can warp and distort the cylinder head. Cylinder head distortion may also be caused by the use of improper techniques to repair cracks or by the improper tightening of cylinder bolts or hold-down nuts. Most warpage is slight and not normally apparent to the naked eye. In addition to checking for warpage, look for dents, scratches, and corrosion around the water passages.

When a valve guide is worn beyond specifications, a new one must be installed and reamed to size. Valves can be reconditioned and are refaced in a valve grinding machine. The valve face should be ground until all dark spots, grooves, and pits are removed. Valve refacing machines have adjustments for different valve face angles. Valve seat refacing requires the use of cutters or stones of three different angles.

Due to the extreme temperatures, friction, and loads placed on pistons and cylinders, thorough inspection for wear, cracks, and damage is very critical. The cylinder must be inspected for excessive taper, out-of-roundness, a ridge, and cylinder damage (galling, cracks) caused by other broken parts. Inspect the pistons for damage and measure skirt diameter. Another important measurement made on a four-stroke cycle piston is ring-to-groove clearance. Measure the wrist pin diameter and inspect for discoloration and surface damage. Measure the bore diameter of the connecting rod small end and subtract the wrist pin's diameter to determine clearance. If the cylinder is worn beyond service limits, it must be bored to the next oversize. A cylinder that has been honed or deglazed must be washed in warm soapy water to remove grit and metal particles.

Some four-stroke crankshafts can be reconditioned when worn or damaged, while others cannot. The four types of bearings found in four-stroke cycle engines are roller, ball, plain, and needle types. All types of bearings should be checked visually for discoloration, scoring, flaking, or disintegration. An important step during any engine overhaul is inspecting the oil pump. Some motorcycle engines are equipped with chain- or gear-driven balancers.

With severe four-stroke engine bottom end failures, the connecting rod can be damaged. A broken connecting rod is quite obvious. A different type of damage which is not obvious occurs when bearings and rod journals are worn excessively. Use a telescoping gauge and micrometer to measure vertically and horizontally in the connecting rod big end. Depending upon cost and the type of connecting rod problem, reconditioning by a machine shop or replacement may be needed.

Engine components must be lubricated during assembly. This ensures proper lubrication when the engine runs for the first time. Machined surfaces which do not use a gasket must be sealed with an approved sealant. Do not use an excessive amount of silicone sealant. Due to the size of cylinder, cylinder head, and crankcase castings, a proper torque pattern (fastener tightening sequence) must be used to prevent warpage. Gradual tightening of fasteners in three or four stages (approximately 1/2 torque, 3/4 torque, and full torque twice) is necessary.

Know These Terms

Top end	Valve seat concentricity
Closed pressure	Valve seat surface finish
Open pressure	Valve seat width
Stem-to-guide clearance	Valve seat-to-valve contact
Warpage	Valve spring installed height
Interference angle	Piston clearance
Ring-to-groove clearance	Wrist pin diameter
Piston ring end gap	Engine balancers

Review Questions—Chapter 20

Do not write in this text. Place your answers on a separate sheet of paper.

1. What usually causes valve train noise?
2. What takes the place of a cam follower in some DOHC engines?
   A. Push rods.
   B. Shims and buckets.
   C. Rollers.
   D. None of the above.
3. Shim bucket and bucket bore _____ should be measured to determine bucket clearance.
4. List four major operations done during cylinder head reconditioning.
5. Most four-stroke engine valves and seats use a _____ angle.
   A. 30°
   B. 45°
   C. 60°
   D. Both A & B.
6. Valve spring installed height determines spring _____.
7. What are three steps to remember when measuring four-stroke cycle cylinders?
8. What engine measurement would you find by subtracting the piston skirt diameter from the cylinder largest diameter?
   A. Piston clearance.
   B. Ring-to-groove clearance.
   C. Wrist pin diameter.
   D. Ring end gap.
9. What should be done *next* to a honed cylinder?
   A. It should be washed with warm soapy water to remove grit.
   B. It must be deglazed.
   C. It must be honed.
   D. It should be wiped with an oiled rag.
10. Ball bearings must be checked for _____ and _____ .
11. Plain bearings can be measured ______.
    A. with the use of Plastigage
    B. with precision measuring instruments
    C. by sight
    D. Both A & B.
12. Name the two oil pump checks completed during an overhaul.
13. What are the two methods of reconditioning for one-piece plain bearing crankshafts?

14. Connecting rod big ends (two-pieces) should be measured for an _____ condition during an overhaul.
15. Two important aspects of torquing engine fasteners are _____ and _____.
16. A ______ must always be used to install piston rings.
    A. ring expander
    B. hammer
    C. hydraulic press
    D. brass drift
17. An arrow stamped or cast into the piston crown indicates piston installation direction. This is important because:
    A. offset wrist pins may be used.
    B. valve pocket cutouts must match valves.
    C. piston skirt length may be different from front to back.
    D. Both A & B.
18. Cam timing marks are provided on _______.
    A. gears
    B. sprockets
    C. crankshaft
    D. All of the above.
19. Failure to properly set cam (valve) timing usually results in:
    A. connecting rod failure.
    B. cracked cylinder head.
    C. valve and piston damage.
    D. excessive oil consumption.
20. Define the term *break-in process.*

Suggested Activities

1. Complete a four-stroke engine overhaul. Use a service manual and the information in this chapter.
2. Perform a post-overhaul checkup using a shop manual and the summary in this chapter.

21

Power Transmission Overhaul

After studying this chapter, you will be able to:

- Properly inspect a clutch and primary drive for damage.
- Accurately measure clutch and primary drive part wear.
- Properly reassemble a motorcycle clutch and primary drive.
- Adjust a primary drive and clutch.
- List common motorcycle transmission problems.
- Measure transmission shaft end play.
- Check shift mechanism operation.
- Disassemble a transmission.
- Inspect transmission and kickstart components for wear or damage.
- Describe transmission assembly methods.
- Summarize the procedures for inspecting, maintaining, and servicing final drive systems.

This chapter discusses procedures for the proper inspection and overhaul of a motorcycle's clutch primary drive, transmission, and final drive. Overhaul of these systems is necessary because of normal wear, improper adjustment, and physical damage. Complete disassembly of the primary drive/transmission/final drive is usually done during a major engine overhaul. However, when a problem develops in any portion of the system, it can often be serviced without complete disassembly.

Primary Drive Service and Repair

A primary drive transmission transfers all the motorcycle's engine power to the clutch and transmission, **Figure 21-1.** It must absorb tremendous shocks and changes in loading. With some designs, the chain, gears, or belt must be inspected periodically and even replaced after high mileage. Primary drive chains may also require periodic adjustment.

External Chain Primary Drive Service

An ***external chain primary drive*** operates off one end of the engine crankshaft. Shown in **Figure 21-2,** this type of drive system requires overhaul when the chain or sprocket teeth become worn or broken.

Usually, a properly maintained primary chain drive assembly only requires chain replacement. The sprockets will normally be in satisfactory condition. Sprocket replacement may be needed when a badly worn or loose chain has been operated for a long period of time. A loose or worn chain will wear and sharpen the sprocket teeth.

A loose primary drive chain is indicated when excessive noise (clatter or knocking) can be heard in the engine side cover. A clacking sound may be produced when switching from acceleration to deceleration or deceleration to acceleration. This will cause any slack in the chain to tighten and slap loudly.

When there is no adjustment left on the chain tensioner, it indicates the primary chain is worn out. A shop manual on the specific engine should be used to determine primary chain wear limits and procedures for repair.

Internal Chain Drive Service

Many recent bike designs use an ***internal chain drive*** which locates the primary drive chain at the middle of the crankshaft. One is shown in **Figure 21-3.** Primary chain replacement for this design requires engine removal and

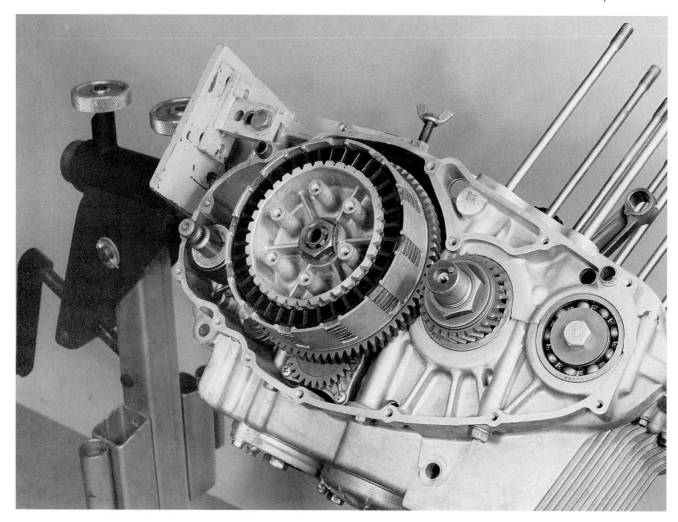

Figure 21-1. Clutch and primary drive overhaul is an important part of motorcycle service.

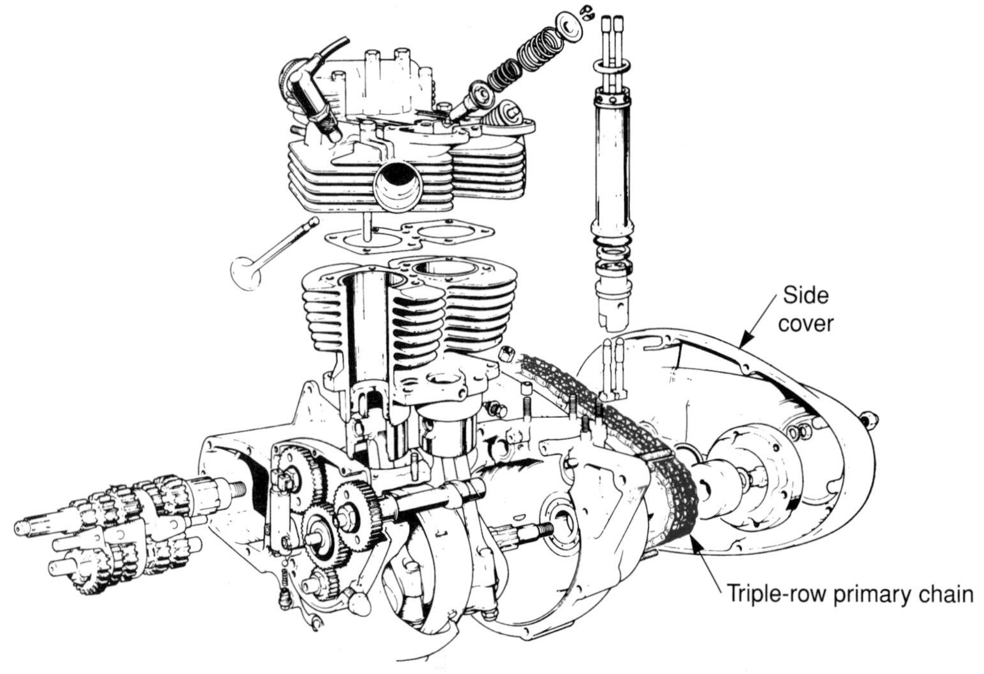

Figure 21-2. An external primary chain is used on this engine. Note how the primary chain is mounted on one end of the crankshaft. This chain can be replaced without major engine disassembly. (Triumph Motorcycles, Ltd.)

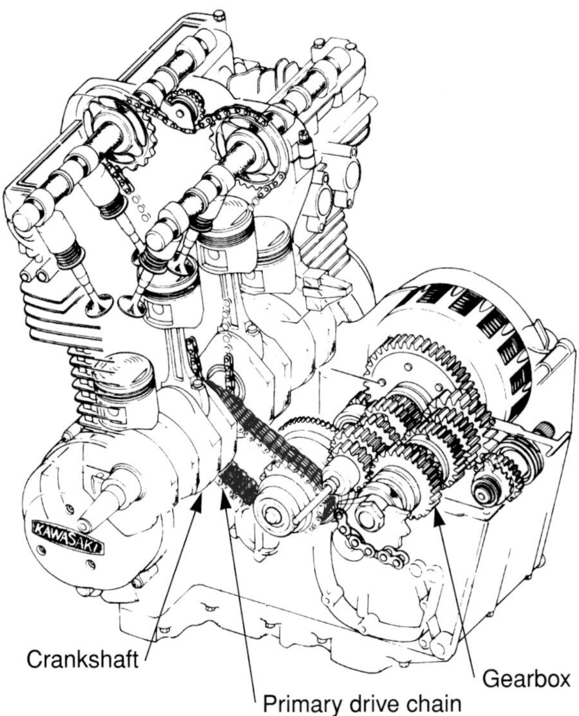

Figure 21-3. This internal primary drive uses a hy-vo chain. It runs off of the crankshaft and cannot be serviced as easily as an external primary chain. (Kawasaki Motors Corporation U.S.A.)

disassembly. The service life of an internal chain drive is normally longer than an external chain drive. Replacement is usually not needed until the engine is ready for an overhaul.

External Gear Primary Drive Service

The ***external gear primary drive*** is a relatively trouble free system. When wear is suspected, inspection is an easy task. After removing the primary cover (clutch or engine side cover), check the primary drive gear teeth for etching, chipping, breakage, and excessive backlash. Any of these problems will normally require primary gear replacement.

Primary Drive Gear Backlash

Measurement of primary drive gear backlash (play between gears) identifies minor wear of the gear teeth. **Figure 21-4** illustrates the procedure for measuring primary gear backlash and wear. A service manual on the particular motorcycle will give specifications for primary drive gear backlash.

Internal Gear Primary Service

The internal gear primary drive is housed within the engine crankcases. Engine disassembly is required for inspection and repair of this type of drive. As with the

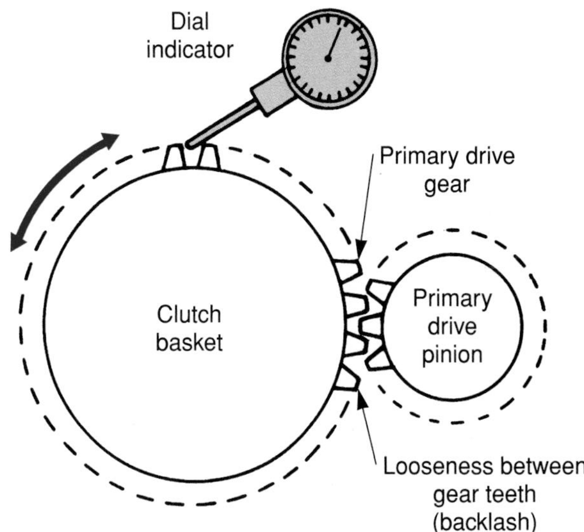

Figure 21-4. Wear and backlash in a gear primary drive is measured with a dial indicator. Hold the pinion gear steady while moving the clutch gear back and forth. The dial indicator's needle movement will show gear backlash. Excessive backlash usually indicates the need for gear replacement.

internal chain drive design, maintenance is normally not needed until a complete engine overhaul.

Clutch Service and Repair

A common cause of clutch wear and failure is improper adjustment. When a clutch cable is too tight, partial pressure plate release can result. This can let the clutch discs slip and wear under heavy loads. A clutch cable release mechanism should always have some play to ensure full pressure plate clamping action and disc lockup.

Accelerating a bike from a dead stop does require a certain amount of controlled clutch slippage. Depending upon the rider and the motorcycle gearing, some clutches may also be subjected to slipping during up and down shifting. Excess clutch slippage wears the friction plates.

Another type of clutch wear is caused by rapid transmission shifting, quick acceleration, engaging the clutch at high engine rpm, and abrupt changes in throttle opening. This type of abuse can cause severe clutch loading and unloading. As shown in **Figure 21-5,** the following clutch components can wear and fail:

- Clutch basket fingers.
- Clutch cushion.
- Drive plate tabs.
- Clutch hub splines.
- Driven plate tabs.
- Clutch center bearing.
- Clutch thrust washer.

Naturally, this type of abuse also causes wear in the entire drive train (primary drive, transmission, final drive).

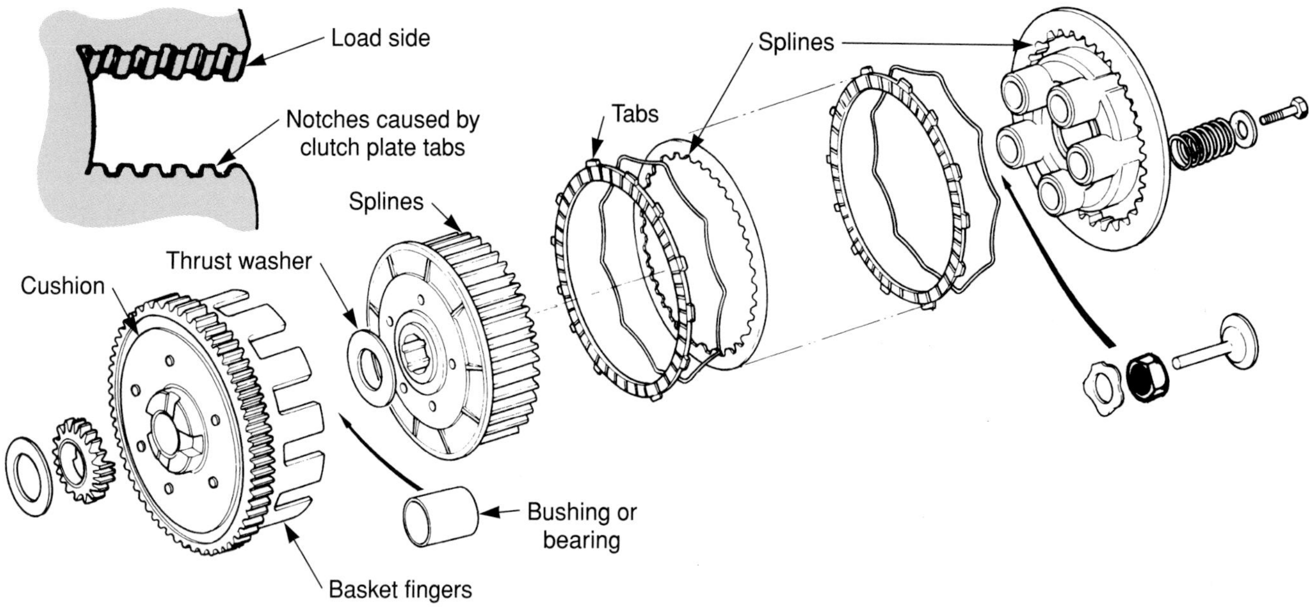

Figure 21-5. Clutch parts must be checked for wear. Common forms of clutch basket wear is caused by drive plates. Tabs on plates wear notches in basket fingers. This can cause clutch drag, jerky engagement, and slipping. (Kawasaki Motors Corporation U.S.A.)

Clutch Basket, Bearing, and Hub Wear

The clutch basket and bearing can wear in four places: basket fingers, basket cushion, basket center bearing, and center bearing thrust washer. These points should be closely inspected for excessive wear during clutch service. If excessive wear is found at any of these inspection points, repair or replace the clutch parts as needed.

Clutch baskets that use a needle center bearing normally have a very long service life and seldom fail. The clutch basket may also provide a mounting place for the primary kickstart gear. This gear should be inspected for wear and damage. Clutch hub wear is not very common, however, worn splines (internal and external) and worn keyways may be found occasionally. Keep this in mind when inspecting a clutch hub.

Friction and Plain Plate Service

In many service manuals, the clutch plates are referred to as friction and plain plates. The drive plates (plates which engage with the basket) are the friction plates. The driven plates (plates which engage with hub) are the plain plates. The clutch friction plates wear more than plain plates. Inspection of the friction plates includes:

- Checking for broken or damaged tabs.
- Checking for a burned smell and glazing.
- Measuring plate thickness.

Figure 21-6A shows a worn clutch friction plate. Plate thickness must be measured and compared to specifications. If the discs are worn too thin, burned, or damaged, they must be replaced. Inspection of the plain plates, **Figure 21-6B,** includes:

- Checking for broken or damaged teeth.
- Checking for a burned or scored appearance.
- Checking for warpage.

Clutch Spring Service

Clutch springs acting against the clutch pressure plate provide the force needed to prevent clutch slippage. Four common causes of inadequate clutch spring pressure and clutch slippage are:

- Defective or weak clutch springs.
- Worn clutch friction plates (reduces spring preload).
- Improper clutch cable or release adjustment.
- Improper clutch spring adjustment.

The condition of clutch springs is determined by measuring spring free length, squareness, and testing spring pressure. **Figure 21-7** illustrates clutch spring inspection. By placing the spring on a flat surface and using a square, squareness and free height can be measured. Spring tension must be measured on a spring tester. Compare the measurements to specifications to determine whether clutch spring replacement is needed.

Clutch Truing

Some clutch designs require ***truing*** of the clutch pressure plate assembly. This is done by adjusting the clutch springs to provide equal pressure and minimum pressure plate lateral runout (side wobble). **Figure 21-8** illustrates how each clutch fastener is tightened until equal clutch spring pressure and perfect clutch alignment is obtained.

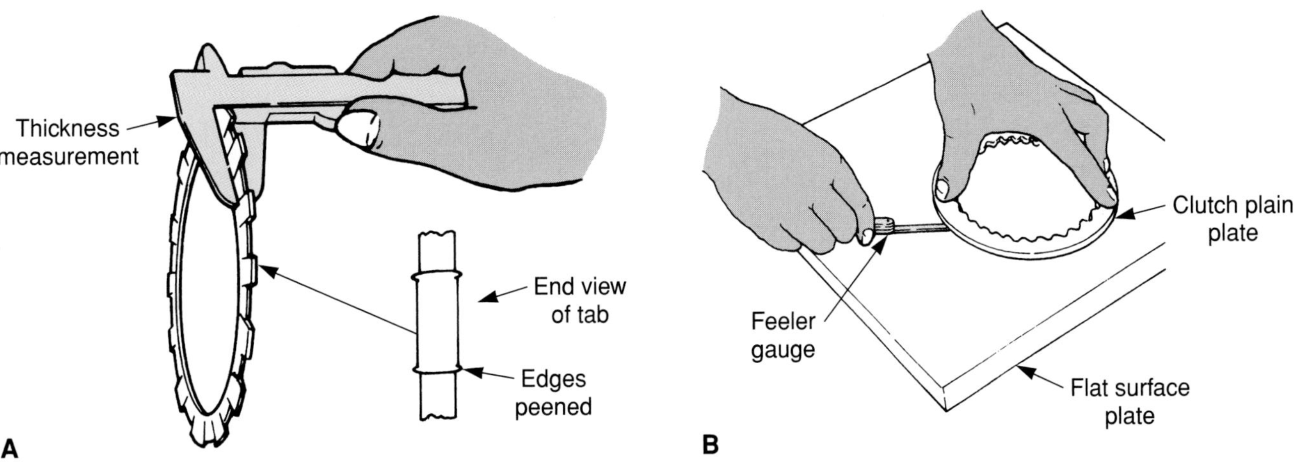

Figure 21-6. A—Clutch friction plate thickness must be measured to check for wear. If tabs on the friction plates are peened or damaged, they must be replaced. B—A surface plate or sheet of plate glass and a feeler gauge are used to check the clutch plain plates for warpage. If the specified gauge slides under the plate, this indicates excessive warpage. (American Suzuki Motor Corporation)

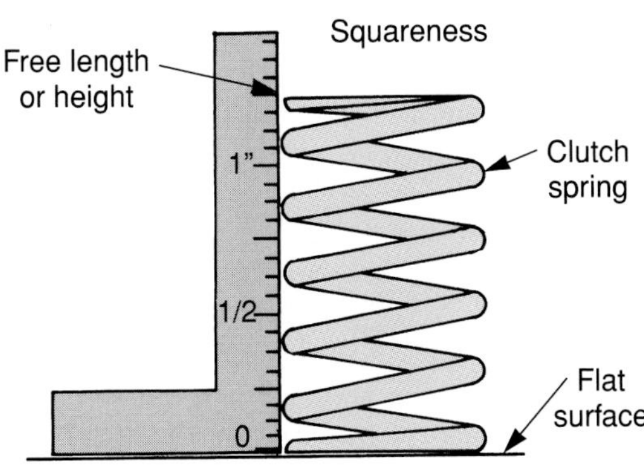

Figure 21-7. With the clutch spring on a flat surface, a square will show the spring's squareness and free height. If not within specifications, the spring must be replaced.

Very few motorcycles still use an adjustable clutch. In most cases, the clutch spring screws are tightened until they bottom. Uneven clutch spring pressure must be corrected by replacing all the clutch springs as a set.

Primary Kickstart Inspection

A kickstart mechanism that works through the clutch is called a ***primary kickstart.*** When the clutch is disassembled, the primary kickstart is usually exposed. This permits easy inspection of primary kickstart gears, bearings, and ratchet. Kickstart mechanisms rarely cause problems. However, it is a good idea to visually inspect these components during a rebuild.

Primary Drive and Clutch Inspection Summary

During clutch and primary drive service, refer to the manual for wear limits, specifications, and detailed procedures. The following summary provides an outline for clutch and primary drive inspection during an overhaul.

Chain Primary Drive

- Check chain adjustment and amount of adjustment remaining.
- Measure chain wear (stretch).
- Inspect sprocket teeth condition.
- Check chain tensioner for wear or damage.

Gear Primary Drive

- Inspect gear teeth for etching, chipping, and wear.
- Measure gear backlash.

Clutch Basket

- Check basket fingers for wear on edges.
- Inspect the condition of clutch bearing surface.
- Inspect kickstart gear for wear or damage.
- Check shock absorber condition.

Clutch Hub

- Inspect clutch hub driving splines.
- Check for wear or damage of splines or keyway on ID (inside diameter) of clutch hub.

Clutch Center Bearing

- Make sure clutch center bearing is not worn, scored, or discolored.
- Check the thrust washer for grooving, wear, or other forms of damage.
- Measure clutch basket-to-bearing clearance.

Clutch Drive Plates (Friction)

- Measure thickness of drive plates to determine wear.
- Inspect condition of the tabs on the plates.
- Inspect friction material on clutch plates.
- Check for glazing or burning (burned smell) of friction plates.

Clutch Driven Plates (Plain)

- Inspect the splines on the plates for wear or damage.
- Check for burning or scoring of the plates.
- Measure plain plate warpage.

Clutch Springs

- Measure clutch spring free length.
- Measure clutch spring squareness.
- Measure spring compressed tension or pressure.

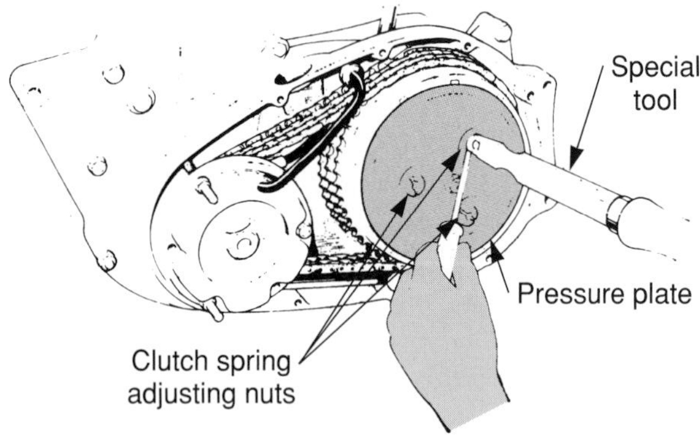

Figure 21-8. Spring pressure is equal when the pressure plate begins to lift at the same time at each spring. Runout is checked by disengaging the clutch and rotating the pressure plate using the kickstarter. (Triumph Motorcycles, Ltd.)

Primary Kickstart

- Check kickstart shaft for damage.
- Inspect kickstart bushings for looseness or galling.
- Check ratchet mechanism for damage and proper operation.
- Inspect drive gear teeth for damage or wear.

Primary Drives and Clutch Reassembly

Since there are so many variations in motorcycle clutches, the service manual must be followed for specific step-by-step disassembly and reassembly. The following list reviews some important aspects of clutch reassembly for most types of motorcycles.

1. Always use new seals and gaskets.
2. Use the proper special tools when needed.
3. Lubricate components as recommended.
4. Install primary kickstart components before installing clutch basket, **Figure 21-9.**
5. Properly preload and install kickstart spring.
6. Install snap ring when used.
7. Install thrust washer and clutch hub bearing.
8. Assemble lock washer with the concave side in as shown in **Figure 21-10.**
9. Torque drive gear or sprocket and clutch center nuts to specifications, **Figure 21-11A.** Bend lock tabs to keep nuts from loosening, **Figure 21-11B.**
10. Check the alignment of gears or chain and sprockets.
11. Use the correct sequence and procedures for clutch pack assembly, **Figures 21-11C** and **21-11D.**
12. Install clutch push rod and other related parts correctly, **Figure 21-12.**

A

B

Figure 21-9. A—Since primary kickstart components are usually behind the clutch basket, they must be installed first. B—Then, the clutch basket can be slid into place.

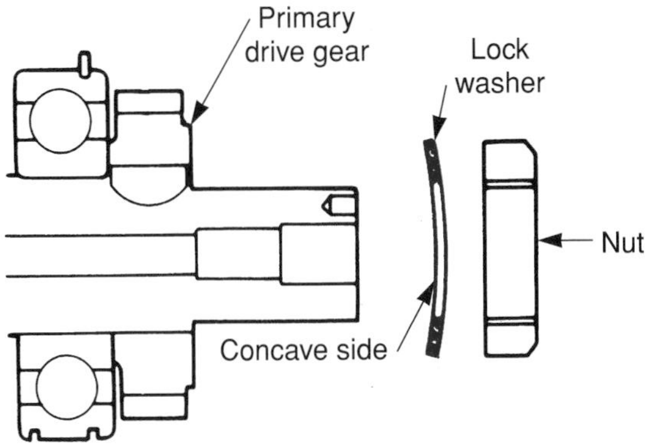

Figure 21-10. When installing a lock washer, the concave side should face inward or away from the nut. (American Suzuki Motor Corporation)

13. Double-check that pressure plate-to-hub splines are properly indexed, **Figure 21-13A.**
14. Adjust (true) or tighten clutch spring bolts correctly, **Figure 21-13B.**
15. Adjust the primary chain correctly, **Figure 21-14.**
16. Install the outer kickstart thrust washer before installing the clutch cover.

This list is a guide to help you avoid some common mistakes when assembling a primary drive and clutch. The proper sequence of assembly for the clutch being worked on may be different from this summary. Always follow the service manual when in doubt.

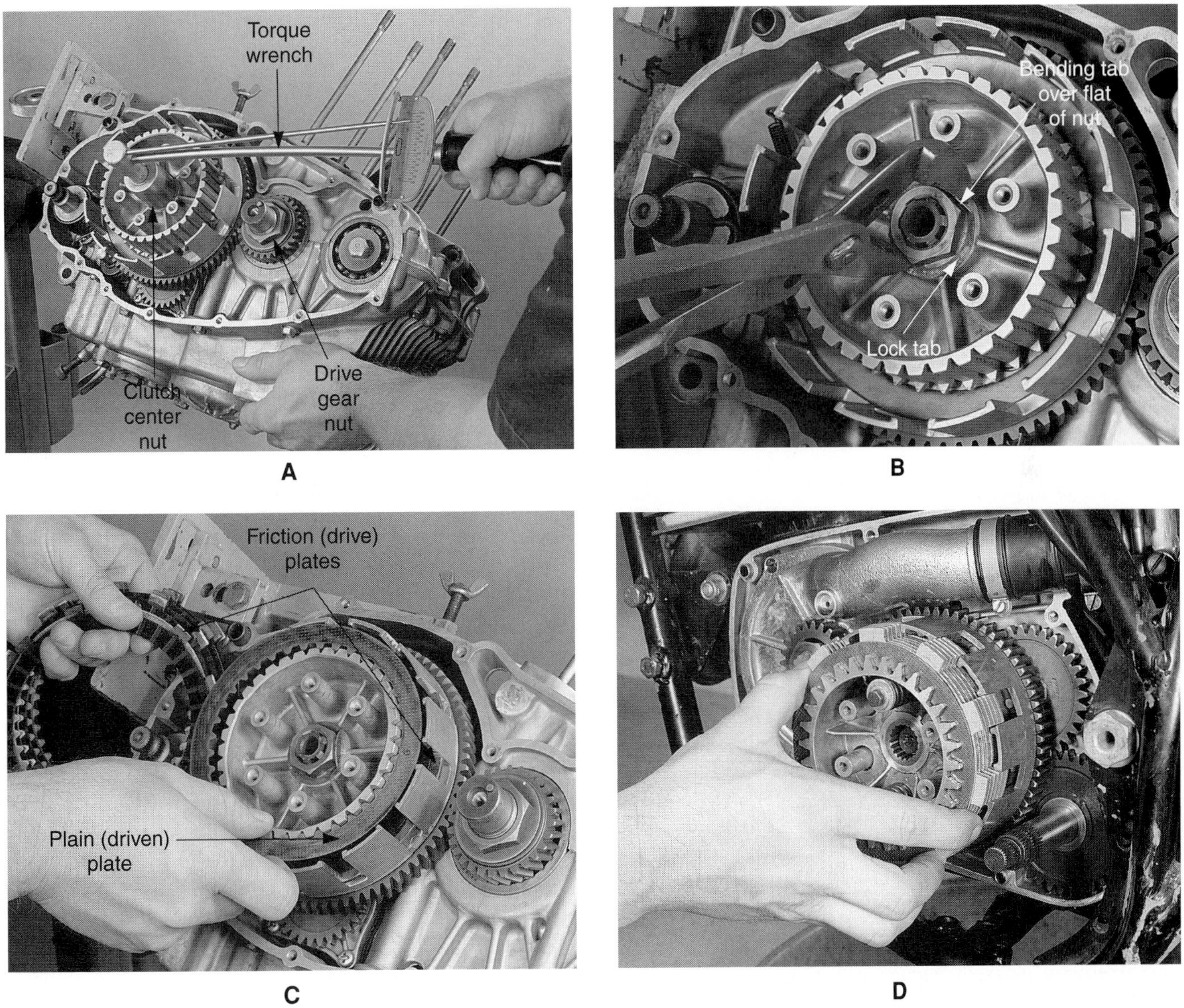

Figure 21-11. Motorcycle clutch assembly procedures vary. A—The clutch center nut and drive gear nuts must be torqued to the recommended value. B—Adjustable channel pliers should be used to make a neat, tight bend on the lock tabs. Properly installed and bent lock tabs will prevent the nut from loosening. C—This clutch must be assembled piece by piece. Clutch plates are installed before the pressure plate. D—This clutch is installed as a single assembly.

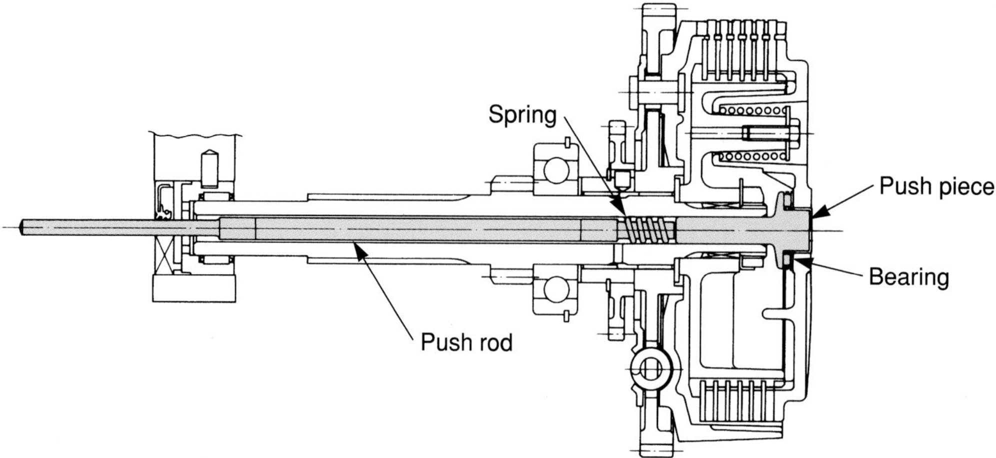

Figure 21-12. Clutch push rod and related components must be installed in their proper positions. (American Suzuki Motor Corporation)

A

B

Figure 21-13. A—Splines on the pressure plate and clutch hub must be aligned (indexed) properly or the clutch will not function. This clutch uses a push piece to disengage the pressure plate. This push piece must be installed before the pressure plate. B—After installing the clutch pack and pressure plate, the clutch springs are installed. Some springs must be carefully adjusted to true the clutch. These clutch spring bolts are torqued to specifications.

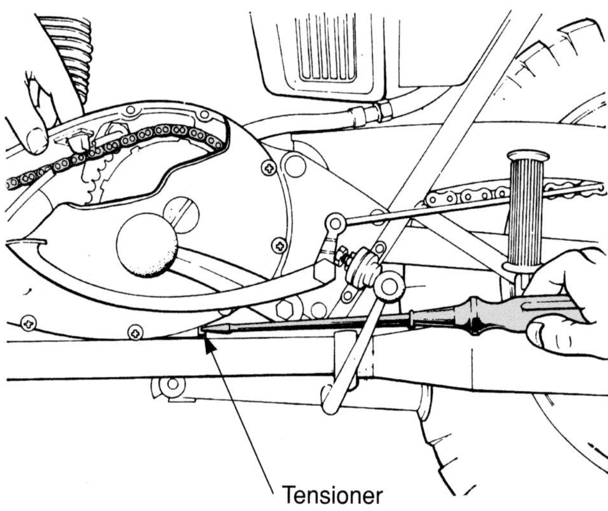

Figure 21-14. Some primary chain drive systems provide easy access for checking and adjusting chain tension. (Triumph Motorcycles, Ltd.)

Transmission Service and Repair

Transmission problems usually produce obvious symptoms. Typical transmission problems are:

- Jumping out of gear (transmission shifts into neutral).
- Binding shift mechanism (difficult to shift gears).
- Noisy operation (abnormal sounds in transmission).
- Transmission locked up (transmission shafts do not turn or shifter does not move).
- Missing gear ratio (one speed or gear ratio does not operate).

Before disassembling a transmission, check shaft end play, shift mechanism operation, and shift mechanism adjustment when possible. It may be possible to correct some transmission problems without a complete teardown.

Shaft End Play

On transmission designs where shaft end play is adjustable and a specification is given, check the shaft end play before disassembly. This saves time during reassembly in the event end play is incorrect. **Figure 21-15** shows how to measure transmission shaft end play.

Shift Mechanism Operation

Before disassembling the transmission, it is also a good idea to check the shift operation mechanism. Shift mechanism problems are quite common. Many transmissions are needlessly disassembled when the shift mechanism is the only problem.

Remember, when bench shifting the transmission during a shift mechanism visual inspection, you must rotate the transmission shafts. When inspecting the shift mechanism, look for the following:

- Freedom of movement.
- Worn pivots in the shift arm, **Figure 21-16A.**
- Worn pawls or damaged springs (ratchet).
- Proper adjustment for the shift stopper pin, **Figure 21-16B.**
- Broken or damaged shift mechanism return spring.

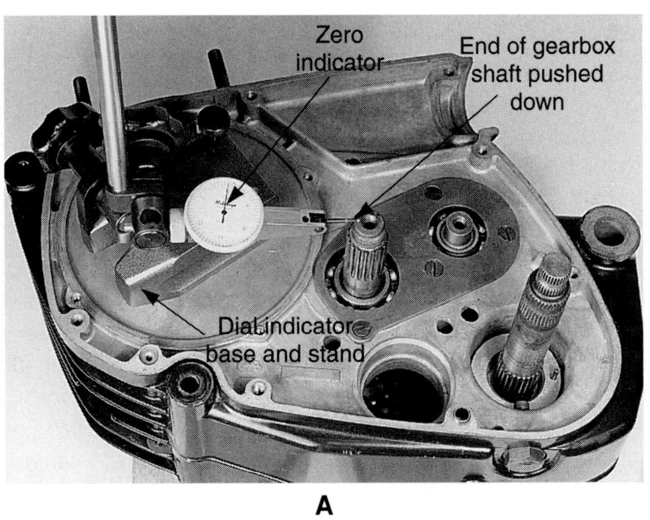

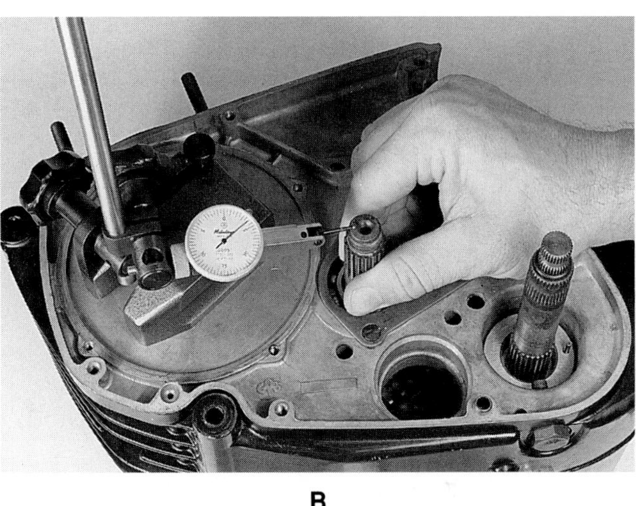

Figure 21-15. Transmission end play can be checked quickly and accurately with a dial indicator. A—A lever indicator is shown here. Push the shaft into the case and zero the dial indicator. B—Pull the shaft up until it stops and read the dial indicator to obtain end play.

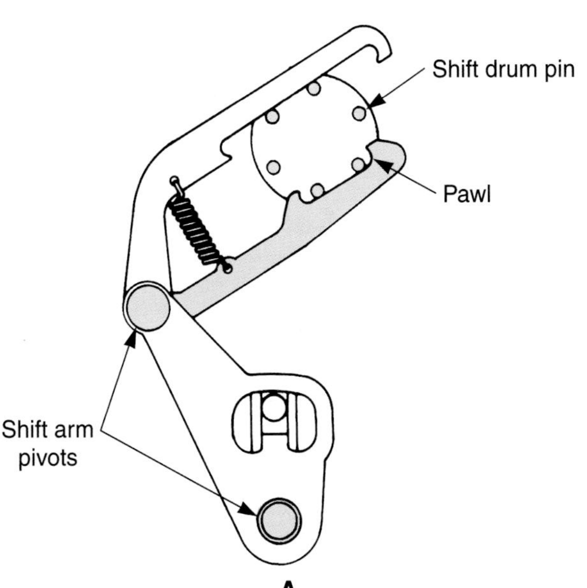

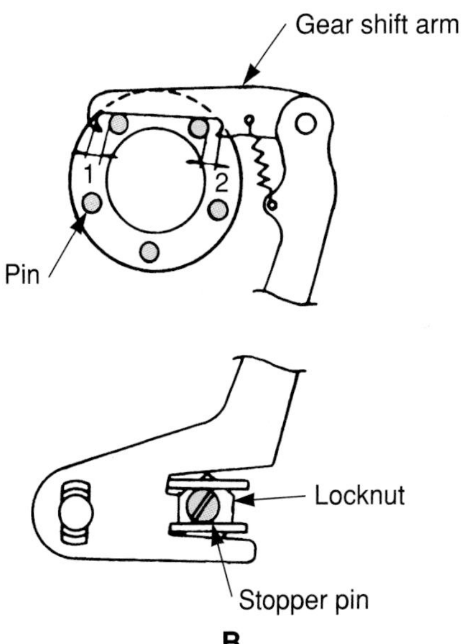

Figure 21-16. A—Shift arm pivots must be checked for wear and looseness. Be sure to inspect the pawls and shift drum pins for wear. B—In many designs, the shift stopper pin is adjustable. The stopper pin must be adjusted so that distances 1 and 2 are equal. If the stopper pin is not properly adjusted, the shift drum will turn too far in one direction and not far enough in the opposite direction. (Kawasaki Motors Corporation U.S.A., Yamaha Motor Corporation U.S.A.)

Transmission Disassembly

Transmission shaft assemblies are relatively simple. However, improper disassembly methods and poor organization can turn a transmission overhaul into a long and difficult process. When disassembling a transmission, it is important to check the position of shims, thrust washers, indexers, drain plugs, locating rings, and pins. Also, check the location of circlips, shift forks, gears and their direction on the shaft. Taking a little extra time during disassembly can save a considerable amount of time during reassembly.

When removing the parts from a transmission shaft, follow the specific directions in the service manual. Disassemble only one transmission shaft assembly at a time. This will prevent mixing input and output shaft parts. **Figure 21-17** illustrates the proper disassembly and organization of transmission shaft components. Notice how all the parts are arranged on the bench in an orderly manner.

Transmission Inspection

During and after transmission disassembly, inspect the condition of each part closely. In particular, check for:

- Etched gear teeth, **Figure 21-18A.**
- Worn splines on shafts and gears.
- Worn or scored bearing surfaces, **Figure 21-18B.**
- Worn or scored shifting forks, **Figure 21-18C.**
- Rounded engagement dogs and slots, **Figure 21-19.**
- Bent shift forks.
- Bent shift fork shafts.
- Worn shift fork engagement pins, **Figure 21-20A.**
- Free movement of shift fork on drum or shaft.
- Free movement of shift drum or cam plate.
- Worn tracks on shift drum or cam plate, **Figure 21-20B.**
- Damaged or worn indexer.

Any components found to be defective must be replaced. If just one defective component is overlooked, the entire transmission may have to be disassembled and overhauled a second time.

Transmission Measurements

There are three measurements that are very critical to the overhaul of a motorcycle transmission. These measurements are:

- Shaft runout (determines if shaft has been bent or damaged).
- Fork-to-groove clearance (detects wear between contact surfaces of fork and groove).
- Gear backlash (checks clearance between gear teeth).

Figures 21-21 to **21-23** illustrate these transmission measurements. Refer to the motorcycle's service manual for exact specifications (maximum runout values and clearances).

Kickstart Mechanism Inspection

Kickstart mechanisms are normally quite reliable. However, problems can develop after prolonged service. A few kickstart problems are ratchet wear, shaft wear, bearing wear in crankcase and cover, bent shaft, damaged splines, and broken or weakened springs. Check these parts closely during inspection. Due to the great variety of kickstart mechanisms, no single example is representative. Refer to the proper service manual for inspection and repair details.

Transmission Reassembly and Shimming

Some service manuals say, "reassemble in the reverse order of disassembly." Although this is generally true,

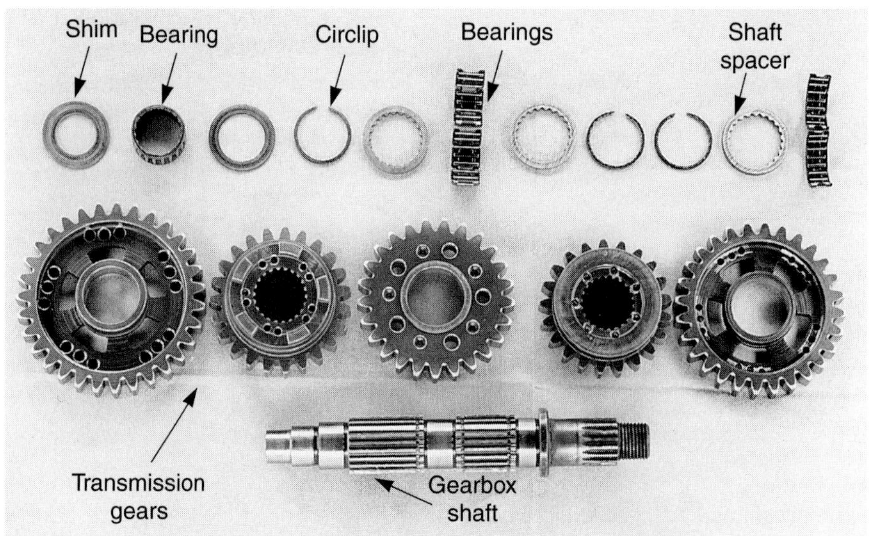

Figure 21-17. Careful and organized disassembly of transmission shaft components are necessary to prevent mixing and/or loss of parts.

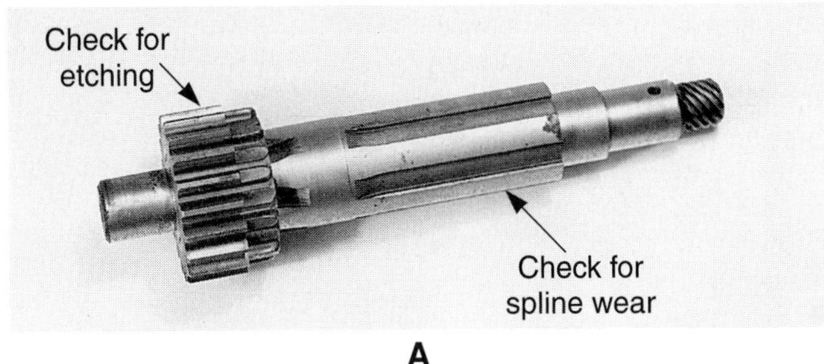

A

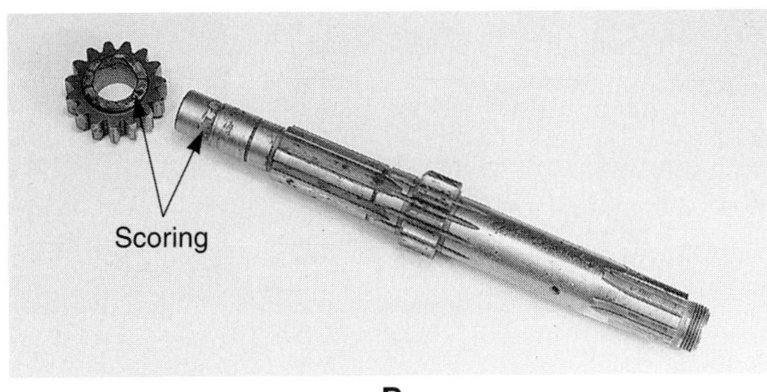

B

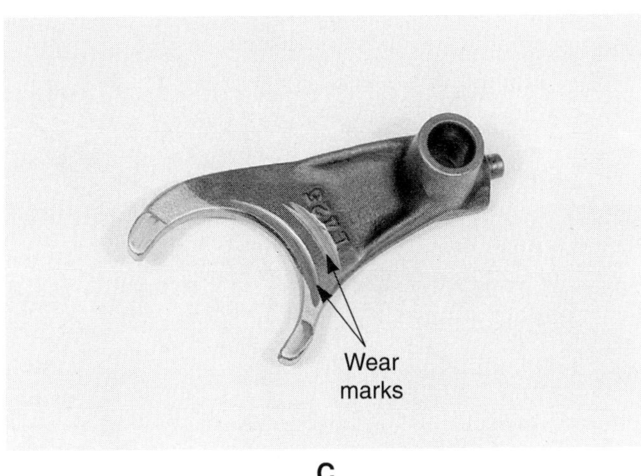

C

Figure 21-18. A—Etching of gear teeth, if not caught during inspection, can eventually lead to broken gear teeth. B—Worn or scored bearing surfaces indicates lack of lubrication. C—Look for wear or score marks on the sides of shift forks. These marks indicate the fork may be bent. All damaged parts must be replaced.

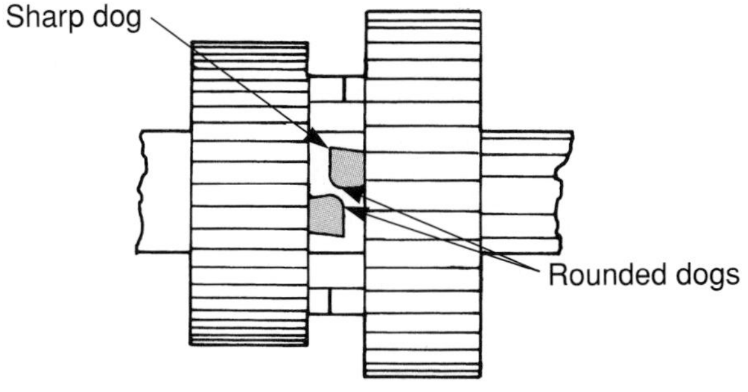

Figure 21-19. Abuse and normal wear causes rounding of the gear engagement dogs. The dog's load carrying side becomes worn, while the unloaded side remains sharp. Worn dogs can cause the transmission to jump out of gear.

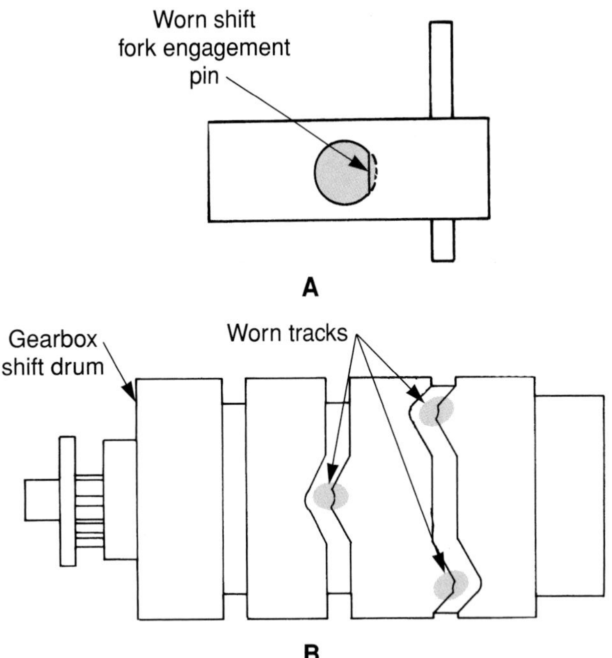

Figure 21-20. A—Shift fork engagement pins can wear at the points where they ride in the shift drum or cam plate tracks. This can cause rough transmission gear changes. B—Worn tracks on shift drums or cam plates can cause incomplete gear engagement, jumping out of gear, or rough shifting.

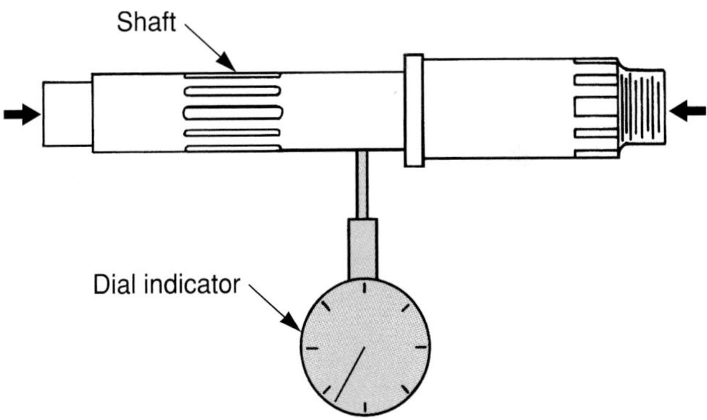

Figure 21-21. A transmission shaft is checked by mounting it in a truing stand or on knife edge rollers. Then, a dial indicator is used to measure runout.

there are numerous checks that must be made during transmission assembly.

Some transmissions allow you to inspect operation after only partial assembly. Other transmissions must be completely assembled before shifting through each gear. This is because motorcycle transmissions are mounted and supported differently from bike to bike.

There are four variations in transmission mounting. They are:

- Supported by horizontally split crankcases, **Figure 21-24A.**
- Supported by vertically split crankcases, **Figure 21-24B.**

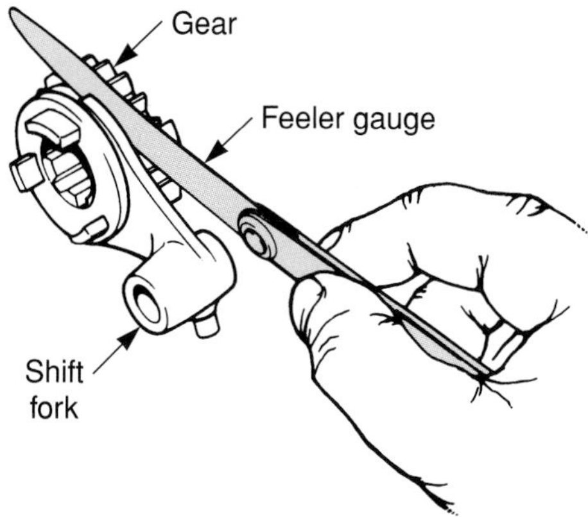

Figure 21-22. A feeler gauge is used to check the shift fork-to-groove clearance. If not within specifications, part replacement is required. (American Suzuki Motor Corporation)

Figure 21-23. A dial indicator is used to check gear backlash. One gear must be locked in place while the other is moved back and forth. If backlash is greater than specifications, both gears must be replaced.

- The transmission and cover assembly are inserted into the crankcase cavity. This design is not very common.
- Separate transmission case (non-unit construction), **Figure 21-24C.**

Because of these variations, checking and adjusting shaft end play (shimming) is more difficult on some transmissions than others. ***Transmission shimming*** to adjust end play can be checked two ways: by external measurement using a dial indicator or by internal measurement (shaft and case measurement).

External End Play Measurement

Transmission designs which allow an ***external end play measurement*** should be checked with a dial indicator during disassembly. End play adjustment is accomplished by installing shims (washer spacers) which produce the proper clearance between the transmission gears and the

A

B

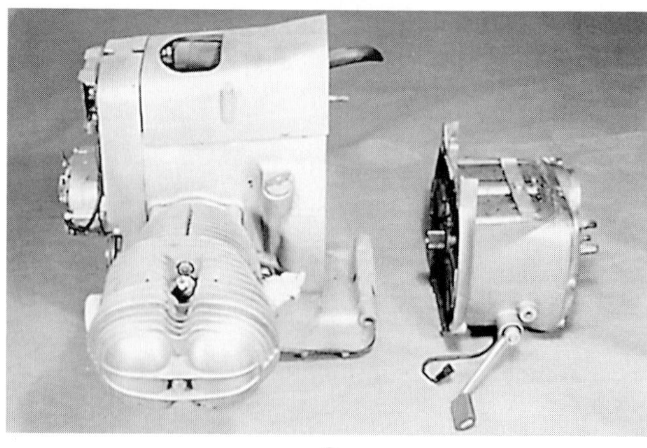

C

Figure 21-24. A—Some transmissions mounted in horizontally split crankcases can be shifted through gears before the cases are assembled. This permits easy inspection of transmission operation. B—Transmissions mounted in vertically split crankcases usually cannot be shifted until the case is assembled. C—Non-unit transmissions are totally independent, self-housed assemblies.

engine case. **Figure 21-25** illustrates this procedure. A thicker shim decreases transmission end play more than a thinner shim.

Internal End Play Measurement

Transmissions which require internal measurement for proper shimming are more difficult to check and adjust. Transmission ***internal end play measurement*** usually involves:

1. Measurement of distance between bearing seats in the crankcase and/or cover, **Figure 21-26.**

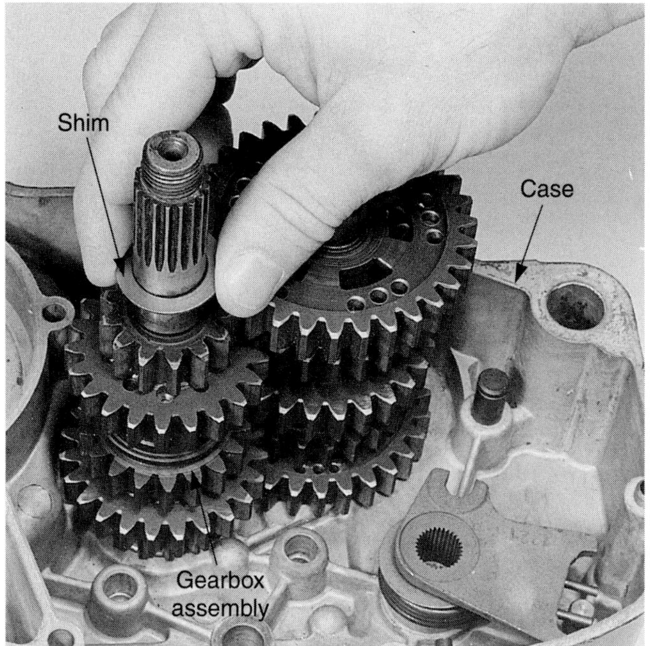

Figure 21-25. Select the shim thickness needed to achieve correct end play. Shimming procedures vary so be sure to check the service manual.

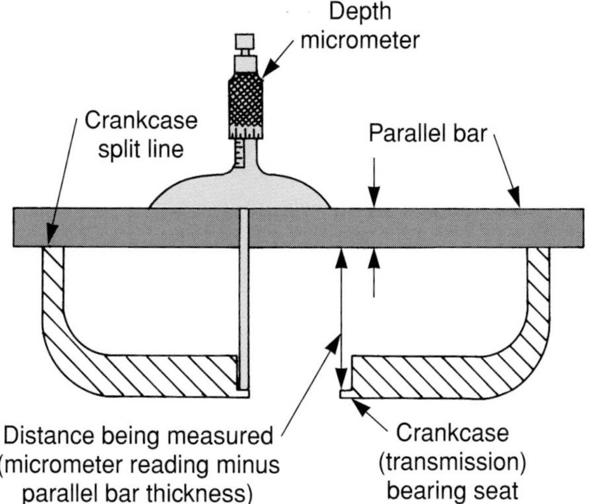

Figure 21-26. A depth micrometer and parallel bar are used to measure the distance between the bearing seat and crankcase split line.

2. Measurement of the length of the assembled shafts from bearing shoulder to bearing shoulder, **Figure 21-27.**
3. Measurement of the gasket thickness, if used.

End play is determined by subtracting the transmission shaft length from crankcase width plus the gasket thickness. This calculation is detailed in the following discussion. To find transmission shaft end play, add left crankcase depth, right crankcase depth, and gasket thickness (if used); then subtract transmission shaft width.

Example:

Left crankcase width	=	2.383″
Right crankcase width	=	2.655″
Gasket thickness	=	.012″
Sum	=	5.050″
Subtract transmission		
Shaft width		-5.045″
Shaft end play	=	.005″

Add or subtract shim thickness to adjust shaft end play.

Transmission Reassembly Summary

Due to the variety of transmission designs, a service manual should always be referred to for specific step-by-step reassembly procedures. Use the following summary and the service manual to avoid making errors. Check for freedom of movement of all components throughout transmission assembly.

1. Use new seals, gaskets, cotter pins, circlips, and lock tabs.
2. Lubricate all moving parts during assembly.
3. Use locking compound where recommended.
4. Make sure shims, thrust washers, circlips, and gears are installed in proper order and direction, **Figure 21-28.**
5. Make sure bearing locating half-rings and dowel pins are installed properly, **Figure 21-29.**

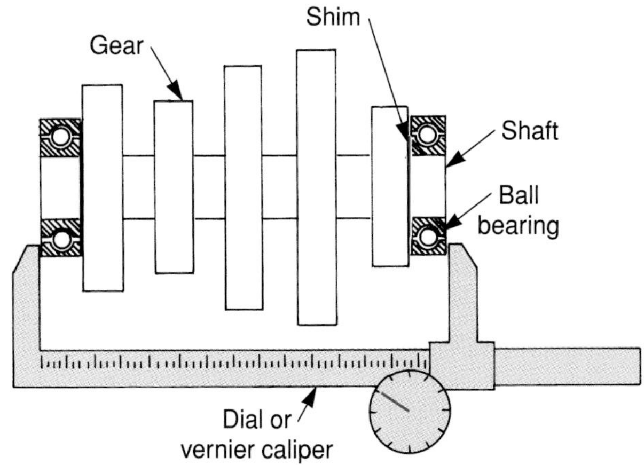

Figure 21-27. Measure the length of assembled transmission shafts from bearing shoulder to bearing shoulder. This can be done with a large dial or vernier caliper.

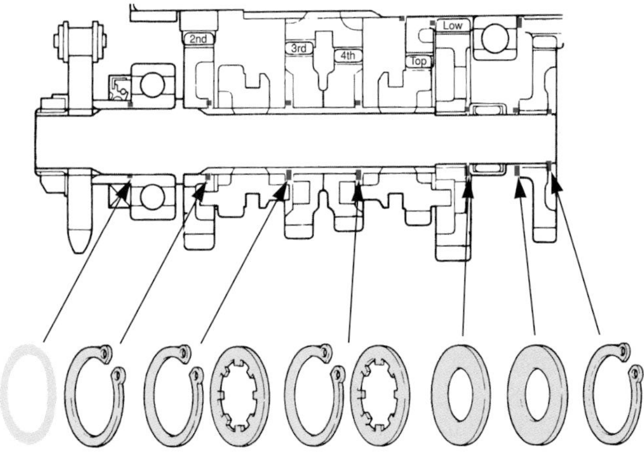

Figure 21-28. Make sure all circlips and washers are in their proper positions during transmission shaft assembly. (American Suzuki Motor Corporation)

Figure 21-29. Bearing dowel pins and half rings must be installed properly to accurately locate the transmission shafts.

6. Double-check that bearings are properly seated on the shaft or in the case.
7. Kickstart mechanism and return spring should be installed and checked for proper operation.
8. Shift forks must be installed and indexed correctly, **Figure 21-30.**
9. Check that shafts are installed in the proper location, direction, and that forks are fully engaged.
10. Locators, indexers, and shift stopper mechanisms must be installed properly, **Figure 21-31.**
11. Make sure shoulder bolts for indexers and stoppers are installed properly. Also, check that screws of different lengths are in their proper holes, **Figure 21-32.**

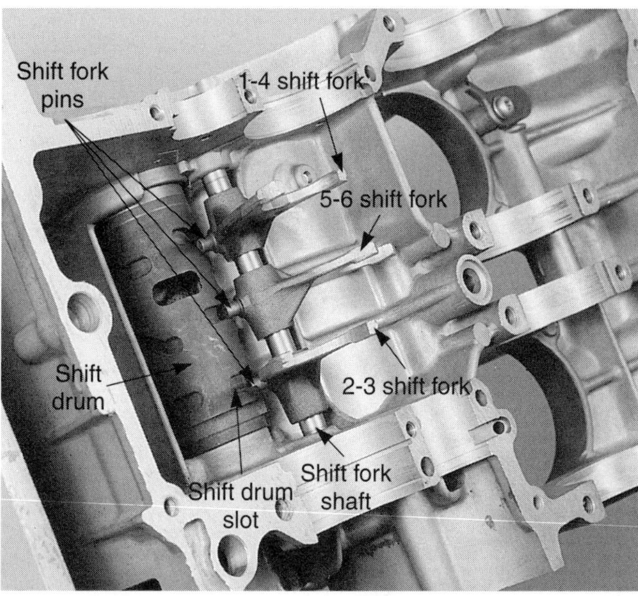

Figure 21-30. Shift forks must be installed on the shaft in proper sequence. The pins must be indexed into slots in the shift drum.

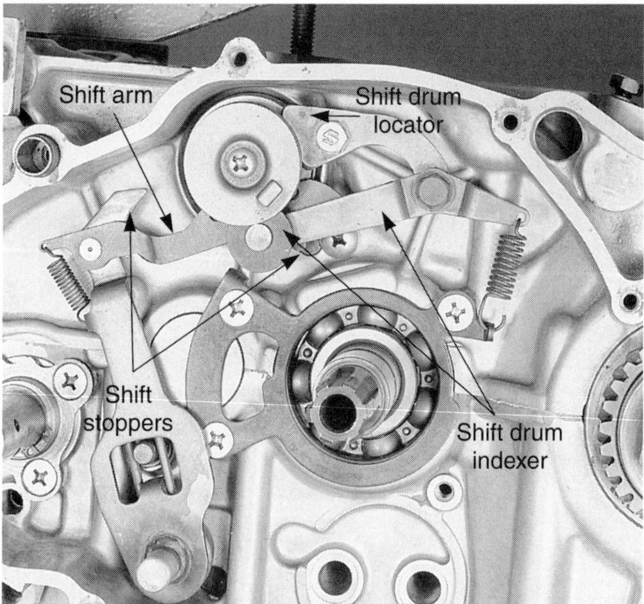

Figure 21-31. Double-check all components for correct installation during reassembly.

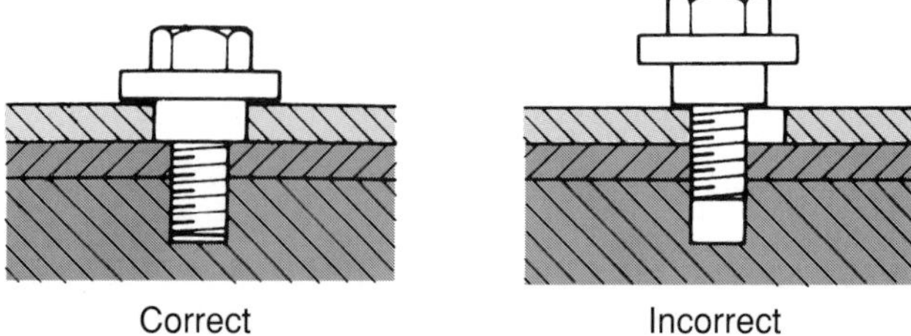

Figure 21-32. Shouldered bolts are commonly used as pivot points for the shift mechanism arms. Improper installation will prevent proper location and pivoting. (American Suzuki Motor Corporation)

12. Check for proper timing and adjustment of the shift mechanism, **Figure 21-33.**
13. Double-check the transmission shifts through all gears properly.
14. Check freedom of movement after crankcase and/or cover fasteners are tightened. If binding is evident, investigate to determine the cause of the problem.

In most modern unit-construction engines, transmission assembly also involves assembly of the engine lower end, clutch, and primary drive.

Final Drive Service and Repair

As described in Chapter 13, there are three types of final drives: chain drive, belt drive, and shaft drive. The chain drive system is an efficient and inexpensive means of transferring power from the transmission to the rear wheel. However, the chain drive system requires more maintenance than a shaft drive system.

Chain Drive

A chain drive system requires lubrication, adjustment, alignment, and inspection for wear. Chain and sprocket replacement may also be needed from time to time. A chain drive system may be lubricated two ways:

- Automatic chain oiler (oil drips out of engine lubrication system onto chain).
- Manual lubrication (rider must periodically apply oil to chain).

Chain lubrication intervals vary from motorcycle to motorcycle and with operating conditions. Frequent visual inspection is necessary to ensure adequate lubrication. Never let a chain run dry or rapid wear will result.

Figure 21-33. Gear selector mechanism must be properly timed. The ratchet gear teeth are centered on the selector shaft gear teeth.

Chain Adjustment and Alignment

Chain adjustment is the positioning of the rear wheel and sprocket to provide proper free play (tension) and alignment, **Figure 21-34.** Adjustment is required because of chain and sprocket wear.

When there is too little slack, a change in the distance between sprocket centers due to suspension movement results in tension on the chain. In this condition, the chain and transmission or crankcase may be damaged, and the vehicle's running performance adversely affected. Excessive slack in the chain leads to oscillations when the vehicle is running. In this condition, the chain may come off the sprockets or damage parts it contacts.

Warning: Inspecting the drive chain while the engine is running can result in serious injury.

Chain tension and alignment can be adjusted by moving the rear wheel and axle or by moving the complete swing arm and wheel assembly. Moving the rear wheel and axle is the most common method of chain adjustment. Moving the swing arm and wheel assembly for chain adjustment was used on some motorcycles.

Most manufacturers provide ***index marks*** on the chain adjusters and swing arm, as in **Figure 21-35.** These marks assure that proper sprocket and rear-wheel alignment is maintained during free play adjustment. To verify the accuracy of the chain adjusting index marks, measure from the center of the swing arm pivot to the center of the rear axle. This is illustrated in **Figure 21-36.**

While adjusting chain free play, check for any tight spots caused by uneven chain or sprocket wear. Chain free play should be checked at the tightest spot to prevent overtightening. During chain adjustment, some motorcycles require loosening and readjustment of the rear brake and brake light switch. Follow the service manual for the motorcycle being worked on.

Caution: Use a new cotter pin in the axle nut following chain adjustment.

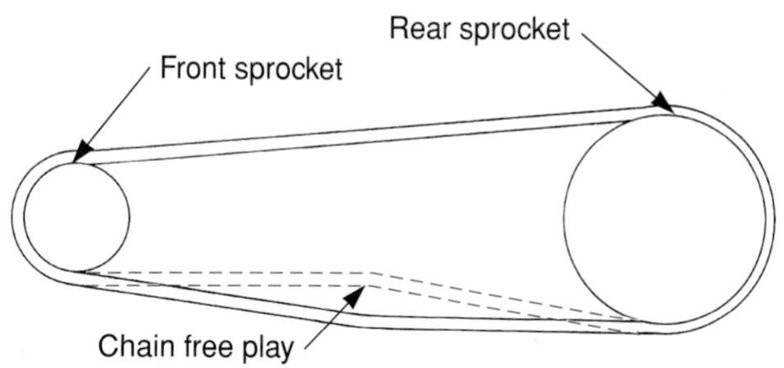

Figure 21-34. Chain free play is measured in the middle of the chain's bottom run.

It is impossible to accurately adjust a chain that is not properly lubricated. A dry chain should be lubricated, adjusted, and operated for a short time, then readjusted. A dry, kinked, or rusted chain is unserviceable and should be replaced.

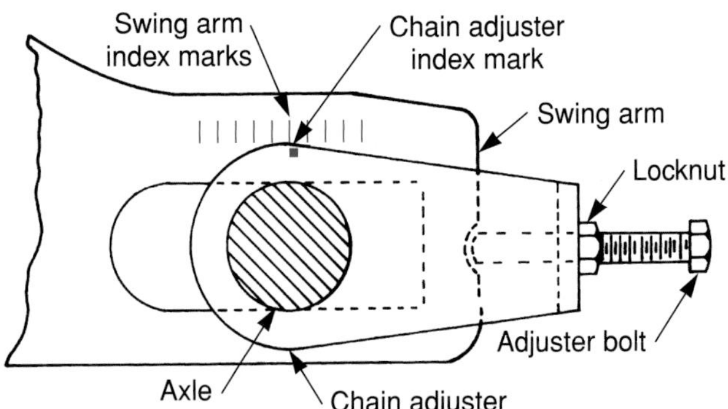

Figure 21-35. Most chain adjusters have index marks which are used to accurately position the rear axle for chain adjustment. The marks on each side should correspond. If not, the rear wheel is misaligned.

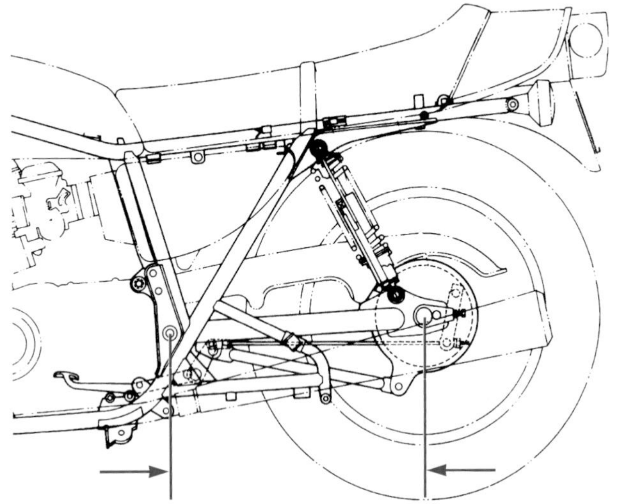

Figure 21-36. Measure from the center of the swing arm pivot to the center of the rear axle on both sides of the motorcycle. This verifies the accuracy of swing arm chain adjuster index marks. (American Suzuki Motor Corporation)

Chain and Sprocket Wear

Even with proper lubrication and adjustment, chains and sprockets will wear out. Pin and bushing wear accounts for what is commonly called ***chain stretch*** (lengthening of chain). This is illustrated in **Figure 21-37.**

As the drive chain wears, the distance between its rollers increases. The worn chain will no longer mesh with the sprocket teeth properly. As a result, the stretched chain causes the sprocket teeth to wear rapidly, **Figure 21-38.**

An accurate method of checking chain wear requires measurement between a specified number of pins on the chain, **Figure 21-39.** A chain that is stretched 3% or more should be replaced. If the sprockets are worn, always replace the chain and sprockets as a set. This is important because worn sprockets will quickly wear a new chain.

Chain and Sprocket Replacement

Depending upon which components need replacement and the type of chain being used (endless or conventional), several components may need to be removed. The swing arm, shock absorbers, chain guard, and other parts may need to be removed. Refer to the service manual for proper instructions.

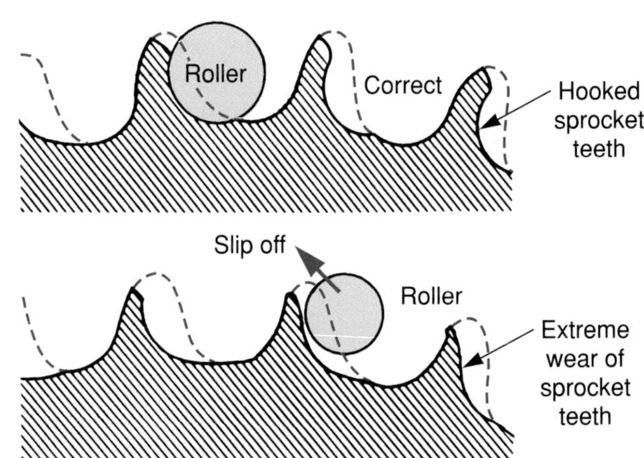

Figure 21-38. As a chain wears, the distance between the rollers becomes greater. This causes the sprocket teeth to become worn. (Yamaha Motor Corporation U.S.A.)

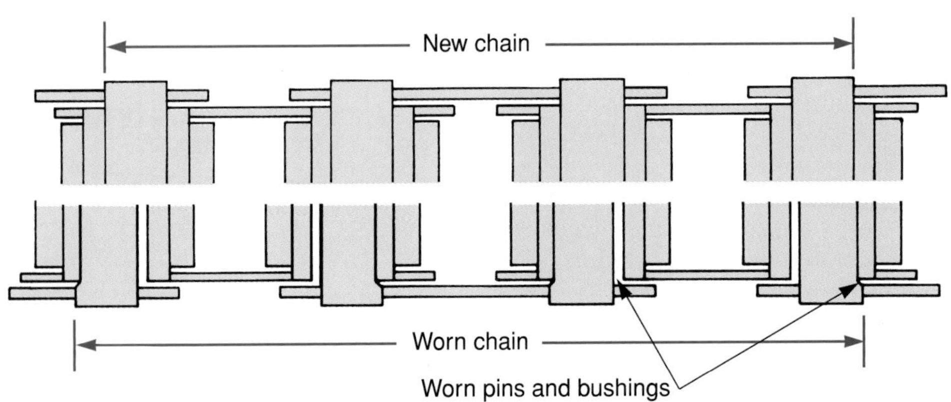

Figure 21-37. Notice how much longer the worn chain is than a new chain. This is caused by wear on the pins and bushings.

Chain size	Pitch	Number of pins to measure	Nominal inches-millimeters	Service limit inches-millimeters
35	3/8 x 3/16	21	7 1/2-191	7 11/16-196
420 428	1/2 x 1/4 1/2 x 5/16	21	10-254	10 5/16-261
520 525 530	5/8 x 1/4 5/8 x 5/16 5/8 x 3/8	21	12 1/2-318	12 3/4-327
630	3/4 x 3/8	21	15-381	15 7/16-392

Figure 21-39. After removing all slack from the chain, measure the distance between 21 pins. Use this chart to determine chain condition. This is a 520 chain which measures 320 mm, so it is slightly worn. Do not forget to readjust the chain after measuring wear.

Drive Belt Drive Inspection and Service

A drive belt is often used in place of a chain on some bikes. Belt drives must be checked periodically as given in the service manual's maintenance schedule.

To remove a belt, it is usually necessary to take the crankcase cover off. Hold the clutch outer plate using a universal holder, and remove the nut and the clutch outer plate. Squeeze the drive belt into the pulley groove so that it provides enough slack to remove the driven pulley from the drive shaft. Remove the driven pulley/clutch with the drive belt in place. Then take the belt off the driven and drive pulleys.

Belt Inspection

Check the drive belt for cracks, ply separation, or wear, and replace as necessary. Measure the side of the drive belt and check against service manual specifications. Replace the belt if the service limit is exceeded.

Note: Do not allow oil or grease to touch the drive belt or pulley faces. Clean off any grease or oil before reinstalling.

To install the belt, temporarily place the driven pulley/clutch assembly on the drive shaft, **Figure 21-40A.** Turn the pulley clockwise and spread the faces apart while installing the drive belt, **Figure 21-40B.** Remove

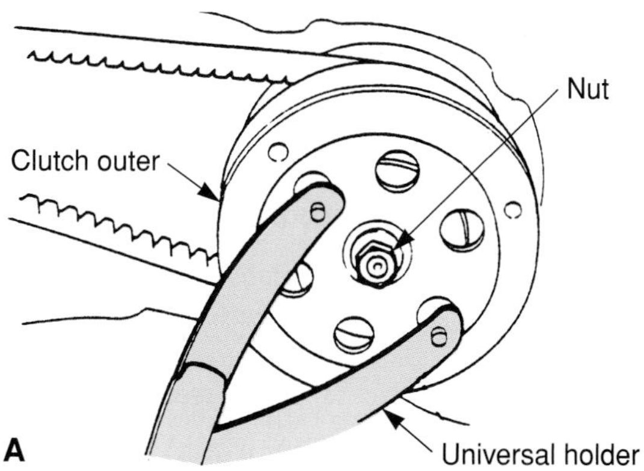

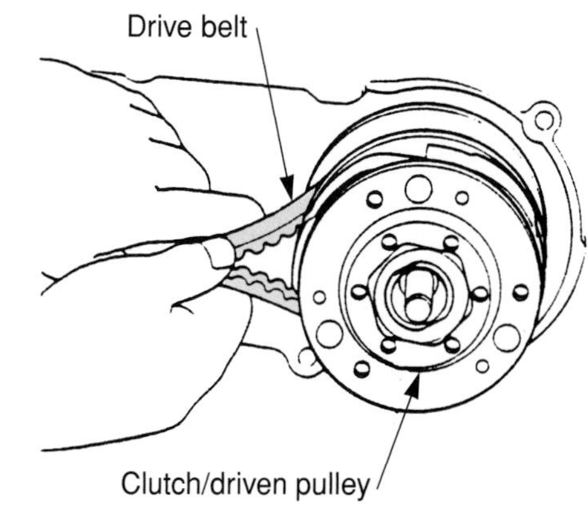

Figure 21-40. Method of installing a drive belt. (Honda Motor Co., Ltd.)

the pulley assembly once the drive belt is installed. Put the drive belt over the drive pulley. Reinstall the driven pulley on the drive shaft with the belt attached. Install the clutch outer plate and the universal holder. Tighten the nut to the specified torque and reinstall the crankcase cover. Before reinstalling the belt, check the drive pulley for damage and replace, if necessary.

Drive Belt Problems

Here are some common problems that may occur with a drive belt system:

Engine Starts but Vehicle Will Not Move

- Worn drive belt.
- Damaged ramp plate.
- Worn or damaged clutch lining.

Engine Stalls or Vehicle Creeps

- Broken clutch shoe springs.

Poor Performance at High Speeds or Lack of Power

- Worn drive belt.
- Weak driven face spring.
- Worn weight roller.
- Faulty driven pulley face.

Shaft Drive Inspection, Service, and Repair

Shaft final drive units are relatively trouble free. Some typical inspection and maintenance operations normally performed are:

- Changing the lubricant in the rear housing, **Figure 21-41.**
- Inspection for oil leaks.
- Inspection for universal joint looseness. This is shown in **Figure 21-42.**
- Noise diagnosis.
- Measurement of ring and pinion backlash. Refer to **Figure 21-43.**

When repair of the rear drive unit is necessary, special tools may be needed and certain procedures must be followed.

Shaft Drive Disassembly

Drain the oil and remove the rear wheel before attempting to remove the rear drive unit. Follow the service manual for proper disassembly steps and required special tools. **Figure 21-44** shows the breakdown of a typical rear drive unit.

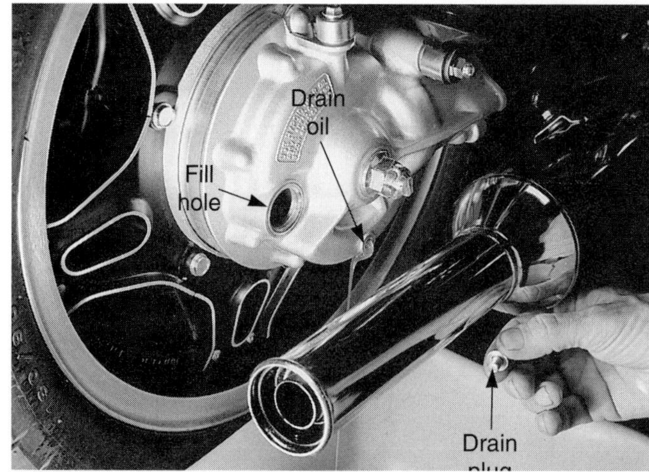

Figure 21-41. Changing a bike's rear drive lubricant is a simple task. Use the small lower hole for draining and the larger upper hole for refilling.

Figure 21-42. Universal joint looseness is easily determined by moving or wiggling each joint section separately.

Rear Drive Unit Inspection

- Clean all parts in solvent and inspect for damage.
- Inspect the ring and pinion teeth for etching, chipping, and discoloration.
- Inspect all ball and roller bearings for looseness, rough operation, and wear.
- Inspect the condition of all oil seals and thrust washers.

Rear Drive Unit Adjustments

Whenever a rear drive unit is disassembled and when new parts have been installed (bearings, thrust washers, ring gear, pinion gear), it is necessary to check and adjust ring and pinion backlash and tooth contact pattern. **Figure 21-45** shows how ring and pinion backlash is adjusted.

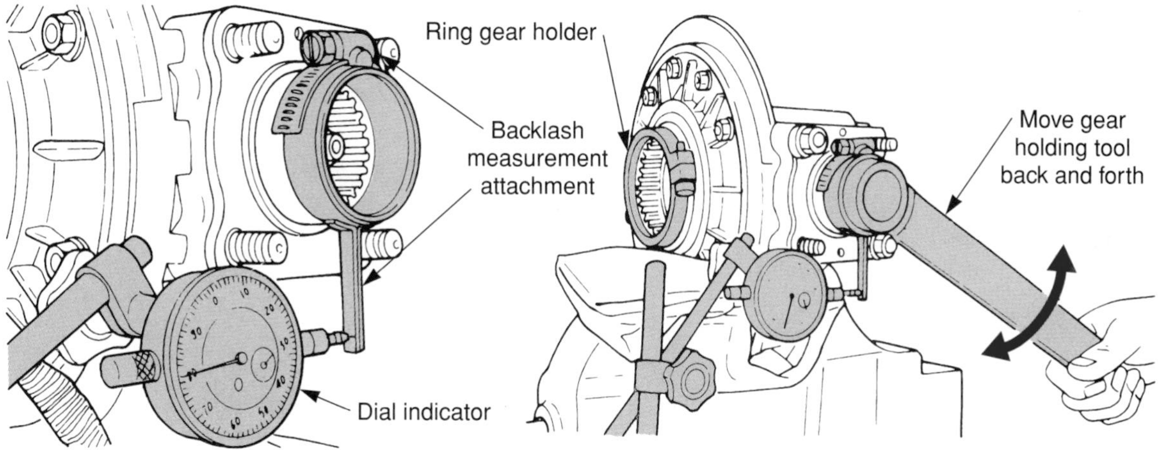

Figure 21-43. Ring and pinion backlash is measured by holding the ring gear and measuring pinion gear movement with a dial indicator. (Yamaha Motor Corporation U.S.A.)

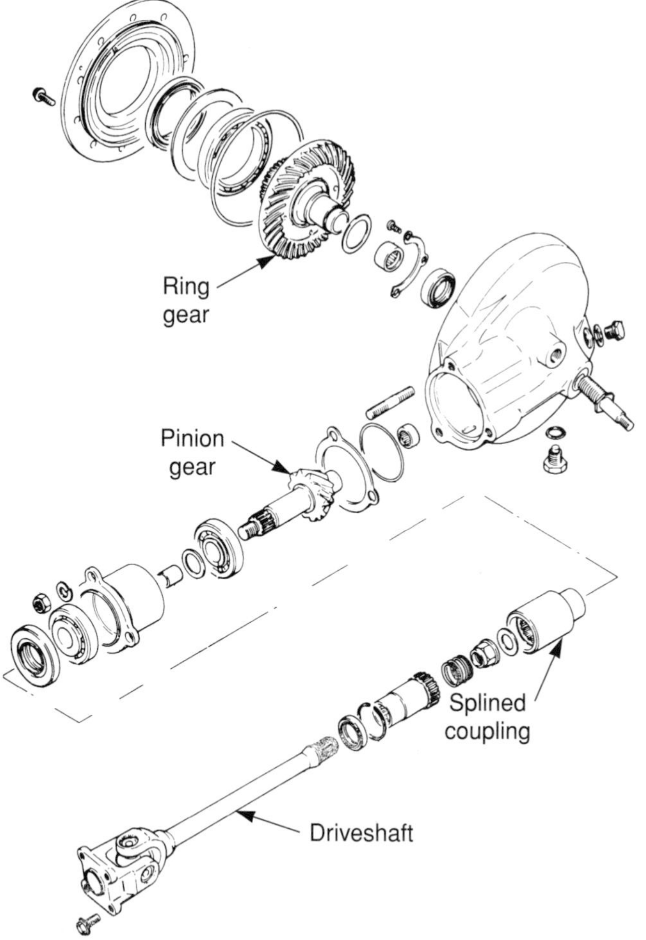

Figure 21-44. Breakdown of a typical rear drive unit. (American Suzuki Motor Corporation)

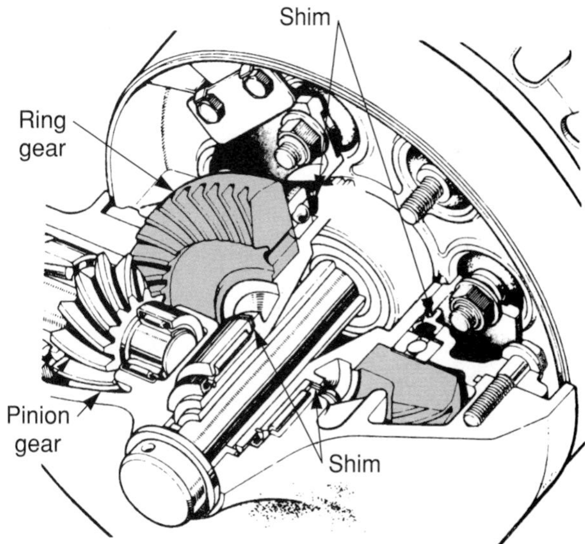

Figure 21-45. Ring and pinion backlash is adjusted by shimming the ring gear closer to or farther from the pinion gear. (American Suzuki Motor Corporation)

Shims are used to move the ring gear into the pinion (reduces backlash) or away from the pinion (increases backlash). It is essential to check the ring and pinion tooth contact pattern to make sure the ring and pinion teeth mesh properly. To check contact pattern:

1. Make sure the ring and pinion are clean and free of oil and solvent.
2. Dab a small amount of machinist's dye on the ring gear teeth.
3. Install the ring gear and slowly rotate it. Keep the ring gear against its thrust washer.
4. Remove the ring gear and check the contact marks left by the pinion teeth.

Figure 21-46 shows typical contact patterns and the necessary adjustments for correction. **Figure 21-47** shows how shimming will change the tooth contact pattern. Always recheck backlash after making any contact pattern adjustments. Accurate measurement and adjustment is needed for quiet and efficient ring and pinion operation.

Final Drive Problems

Some common problems faced by a service technician and their probable causes are as follows:

Excessive Noise in Final Drive

- Worn or damaged ring gear and driven flange.
- Damaged driven flange or wheel hub.
- Worn or damaged pinion gear and/or pinion joint splines.
- Excessive backlash between pinion and ring gears.
- Low oil level.

Excessive Noise in Side Gear

- Worn or damaged output shaft and final drive shaft gears.
- Worn or damaged side gear case bearing.
- Incorrect adjustment shim.

Excessive Rear Wheel Backlash

- Worn drive shaft splines.
- Excessive backlash between ring gear and pinion gear.
- Worn driven flange and ring gear splines.
- Excessive play in final drive case bearings.

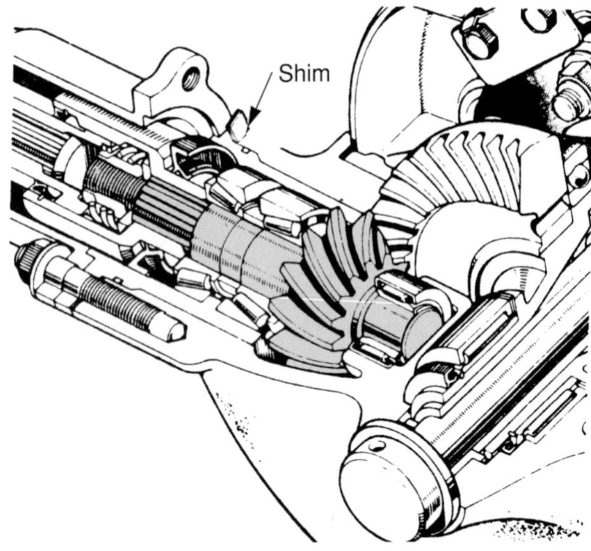

Figure 21-46. Ring and pinion tooth contact pattern is altered by moving the pinion gear closer to or farther from the ring gear. Shim thickness changes the pinion gear and tooth contact pattern. (American Suzuki Motor Corporation)

- Worn drive shaft, universal joint and/or pinion joint splines.
- Excessive play or worn universal joint bearing.

Oil Leak at Final Gear Case

- Clogged breather hole.
- Too much oil.
- Faulty oil seal(s).

Summary

Complete disassembly of the primary drive/transmission/final drive is usually done during a major engine overhaul. A primary drive transmission transfers all the motorcycle's engine power to the clutch and transmission. With some designs, the chain or gears must be inspected periodically and even replaced after high mileage.

Usually, a properly maintained primary chain drive assembly only requires chain replacement. Sprocket replacement may be needed when a badly worn or loose chain has been operated for a long period of time. A loose or worn chain will wear off and sharpen the sprocket teeth. When there is no adjustment left on the chain tensioner, it indicates the primary chain is worn out. Measurement of primary drive gear backlash (play between gears) identifies minor wear of the gear teeth.

A common cause of clutch wear and failure is improper adjustment. Accelerating a bike from a dead stop does require a certain amount of controlled clutch slippage. Excess clutch slippage will wear the friction plates. Another type of clutch wear is caused by rapid transmission shifting, quick acceleration, engaging the clutch at high engine rpm, and abrupt changes in throttle opening. The clutch basket and bearing can wear in four places: basket fingers, basket cushion, basket center bearing, and center bearing thrust washer. These points should be closely inspected for excessive wear during clutch service. In many service manuals, the clutch plates are referred to as friction and plain plates. Some clutch designs require truing of the clutch pressure plate assembly. A kickstart mechanism that works through the clutch is called a primary kickstart.

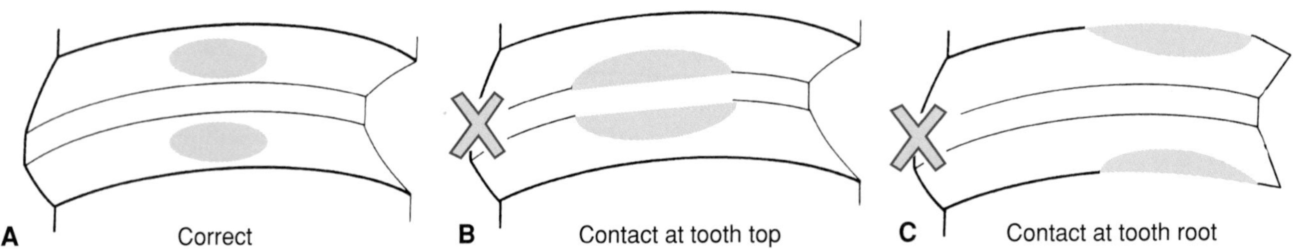

Figure 21-47. A—Contact pattern is properly centered on the gear face. Shimming is required for proper contact. B—Pinion gear must be moved closer to the ring gear. C—Pinion gear must be moved farther from the ring gear. (American Suzuki Motor Corporation)

Since there are so many variations in motorcycle clutches, the service manual must be followed for specific step-by-step disassembly and reassembly. The proper sequence of assembly for the clutch being worked on may be different. Always follow the service manual when in doubt.

Transmission shaft assemblies are relatively simple. However, improper disassembly methods and poor organization can turn a transmission overhaul into a long and difficult process. When removing the parts from a transmission shaft, follow the specific directions in the service manual. Some transmissions allow you to inspect operation after only partial assembly. Other transmissions must be completely assembled before shifting through each gear.

There are three types of final drives: chain drive, belt drive, and shaft drive. A chain drive system requires lubrication, adjustment, alignment, and inspection for wear. To remove a belt, it is usually necessary to take the crankcase cover off. Check the drive belt for cracks, ply separation, or wear, and replace as necessary. Measure the side of the drive belt and check against service manual specifications. Whenever a rear drive unit is disassembled and when new parts have been installed, it is necessary to check and adjust ring and pinion backlash and tooth contact pattern.

Know These Terms

External chain primary drive
Internal chain drive
External gear primary drive
Clutch springs
Truing
Primary kickstart
Transmission shimming
External end play measurement
Internal end play measurement
Index marks
Chain stretch

Review Questions—Chapter 21

Do not write in this text. Place your answers on a separate sheet of paper.

1. When all of the adjustment is used up on a primary drive chain tensioner, what does this indicate?
   A. The chain is worn and must be replaced.
   B. The chain is adjusted properly.
   C. The chain will operate quietly.
   D. The amount of backlash.
2. Measurement of ______ determines wear in gear primary drives.
   A. chain tensioner
   B. clutch springs.
   C. backlash
   D. All of the above.
3. List four of the multi-plate clutch parts that will become worn as a result of harsh shifting, quick starts, and abrupt throttle changes.
4. Clutch drive plates engage with the clutch _____.
5. The clutch driven plates engage with the clutch _____.
6. Which of the following is *not* a cause of inadequate clutch spring pressure?
   A. Missing push piece.
   B. Weak clutch springs.
   C. Worn friction plates.
   D. Improper clutch adjustments.
7. Inspection of plain clutch plates includes checking for:
   A. broken teeth.
   B. burned surfaces
   C. warpage
   D. All of the above.
8. The condition of clutch springs is determined by:
   A. measuring free length.
   B. checking squareness.
   C. measuring pressure.
   D. All of the above.
9. A ______ mechanism works through the clutch.
10. What are three of the most common transmission problems?
11. Transmission shaft _____ and shift mechanism operation should be checked before disassembling a transmission.
12. You must ______ the shafts when bench shifting a transmission through all speeds.
    A. pull
    B. push
    C. rotate
    D. remove
13. List three checks you can make to prevent disorganization during transmission disassembly.
14. Which of the following is *not* a consideration during transmission reassembly?
    A. Use a service manual.
    B. Lubricate parts.
    C. Reinstall the rear drive unit.
    D. Replace all seals and gaskets.

15. In most modern unit-construction engines, transmission assembly also involves the:
    A. engine top end assembly.
    B. engine lower end assembly.
    C. fork assembly.
    D. None of the above.
16. What are two ways of changing drive chain tension?
17. Chain free play should be checked at the ______.
    A. tightest spot
    B. loosest spot
    C. transmission
    D. None of the above.
18. What percentage of chain stretch is considered maximum?
19. To remove a drive belt, it is usually necessary to take the _________ off.
    A. rocker arm cover
    B. camshaft cover
    C. top end assembly
    D. crankcase cover
20. All of the following are causes of excess noise in the final drive *except:*
    A. low oil level.
    B. damaged driven flange.
    C. too much oil.
    D. worn ring gear.

Suggested Activities

1. Using the primary drive and clutch inspection summary in this chapter, perform all inspection procedures listed. Record your findings and make up a parts list to determine the cost of repairs.
2. Measure transmission shaft end play. Compare your results to the specifications given in the service manual.
3. Check the operation of a shift mechanism.
4. Find examples of the different methods of transmission mounting.
5. Verify chain adjuster index marks on a motorcycle.
6. Determine chain wear on a used final drive chain.
7. Adjust a primary chain following service manual directions.
8. Remove and install a final drive chain using the master link.
9. Check and adjust tooth contact pattern and backlash in a ring and pinion rear drive unit.

22

Tune-Up and General Service

After studying this chapter, you will be able to:

- Describe common motorcycle service procedures.
- Describe common motorcycle ignition system adjustments.
- Adjust ignition timing.
- Describe engine valve and cam chain adjustment.
- Perform carburetor adjustments.
- List the steps for a complete motorcycle tune-up.

This chapter outlines the basic procedures for engine tune-up and general service of a motorcycle. Tune-up and service work are considered separate operations, however, they are usually done at the same time. A complete tune-up involves ignition system, fuel system, and valve train adjustment. It also includes the inspection, replacement, adjustment, or lubrication of components that require periodic service.

Note: Many of the previous textbook chapters gave information essential to the complete understanding of tune-up procedures.

Preparing to Tune-up a Motorcycle

A ***tune-up*** is a service procedure used to restore an engine to peak operating efficiency. Tune-ups were used on older bikes as a service to repair engine performance problems. Tune-ups on newer bikes (specifically computer-controlled bikes) are considered a maintenance procedure. Often, on these bikes, a tune-up will not cure a performance problem. You must use diagnostic procedures to correct a performance problem on a computer-controlled motorcycle.

Inspection

Always make sure the engine is in good mechanical condition before attempting a tune-up. Before starting any service work on a motorcycle, ATV, or scooter, look over the entire bike for problems not listed on the order. In many cases, you may spot a potential problem the rider may not know about. **Figures 22-1** through **22-3** show motorcycle components that should be inspected for proper operation whenever a bike is in for service. These systems and components include:

- Engine mounts.
- Lights.
- Horn.

Figure 22-1. It is important to check all components for proper operation. This job only takes a few minutes while possibly locating potentially dangerous problems. (Yamaha Motor Corporation U.S.A.)

Figure 22-2. A quick check to detect steering head looseness is done by gripping the lower fork legs and applying pressure back and forth. The front wheel should be off the ground. Use a center stand and weight on the rear of the motorcycle.

- Gauges.
- Suspension, including front forks.
- Tires.
- Brakes.
- All accessories.

Computer Control System Check

When beginning a tune-up or other service work on a computer-controlled bike, you should check the electronic control module (ECM) for any stored diagnostic codes. If there are any codes stored, you should investigate the cause of the code before proceeding with any tune-up or service work. There is a very good chance that a defective sensor or actuator is the reason the rider brought the bike in for service.

Replacing Air and Fuel Filters

Air filter replacement is one of the fundamental services performed on all motorized vehicles. Regular

A

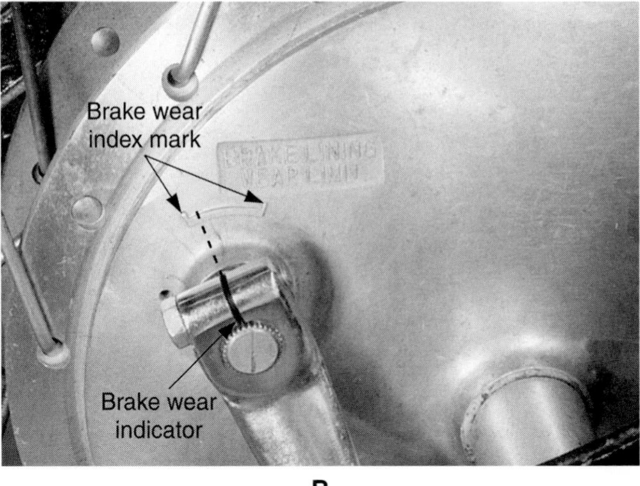

B

Figure 22-3. A—Disc brake pads sometimes use a groove around the friction material to indicate the point of maximum wear. If worn down to the groove, replace the pads. B—On drum brakes, a wear limit indicator and index mark may be used to show when the brake linings are becoming badly worn.

air filter replacement ensures optimum air flow and performance. In most cases, the filter is enclosed in an ***air box*** connected to the engine by a rubber boot. To replace the air filter, open the air box and remove the old filter, **Figure 22-4.** Check the filter for oil or water contamination, which could indicate engine problems or possible air box leaks. Clean out any dirt, mud, leaves, insects, and other debris in the air box. Replace the filter with the same type (foam, gauze, paper) that was removed. If the filter is fairly clean, it can be reinstalled after surface dirt is removed.

Fuel filter replacement ensures the carburetor or fuel injectors receive fuel with as few impurities as possible.

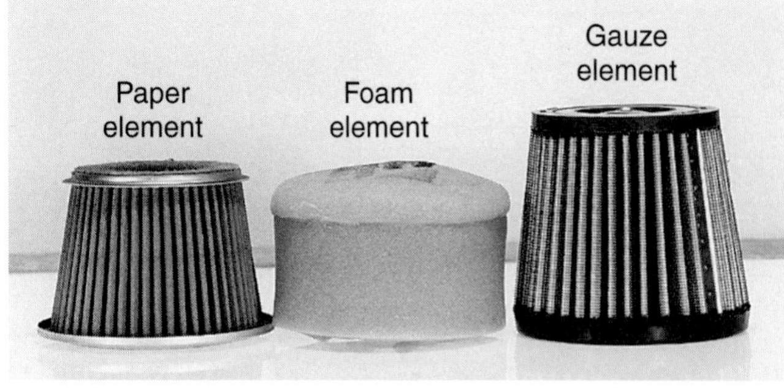

A

B

Figure 22-4. A—Paper, foam, and gauze are three common materials used in motorcycle air filters. B—Many air filter elements can be cleaned with solvent, soap and water, or low pressure compressed air. Be sure to check your manual for proper cleaning procedures as compressed air will destroy some filters.

Shut off the fuel petcock and relieve fuel system pressure. Remove and replace the fuel filter. Do not attempt to clean and reuse the fuel filter. If the bike has a sediment bowl, be sure to remove it and clean the screen. Replace the O-ring if needed, **Figures 22-5** and **22-6.**

Battery Service

During service, inspect the battery for leaks as well as the electrolyte level, **Figure 22-7.** Fill the battery with distilled water as needed. Check the battery's state of charge using a hydrometer. Also check the terminals for corrosion and tightness, and service as needed. It may be necessary to remove the battery from the bike to service it properly.

Checking Cooling System

Cooling system service is important on bikes with liquid-cooled engines. This service on air-cooled engines

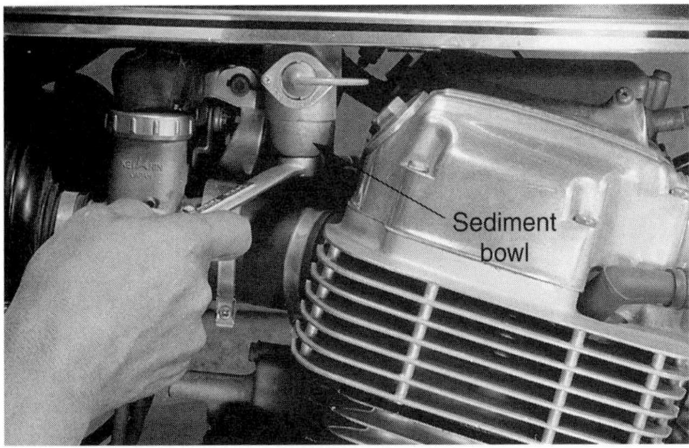

Figure 22-5. When a petcock has a sediment bowl, unscrew it so the bowl and screen can be cleaned.

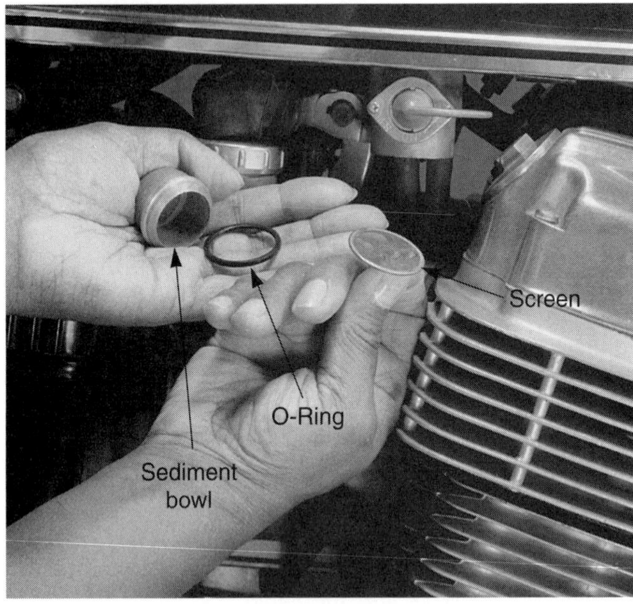

Figure 22-6. After cleaning the sediment bowl screen, replace the O-ring if it shows any signs of deterioration. The O-ring should not be hardened, cracked, or smashed.

is limited to making sure the fins are free of dirt and debris and are not damaged. Test the coolant's concentration using an antifreeze hydrometer, **Figure 22-8.** The coolant should be clean and free of contaminants that can clog the cooling passages in the engine and radiator.

Engine and Chassis Lubrication

When servicing a bike, especially after changing the oil and filter, you should lubricate other parts of the bike, such as the swing arm pivot, chain, brake, and throttle cables, **Figure 22-9.** Make sure to check the fork's performance and change the oil, if needed. Keeping these other parts lubricated is as important as changing the engine oil and filter.

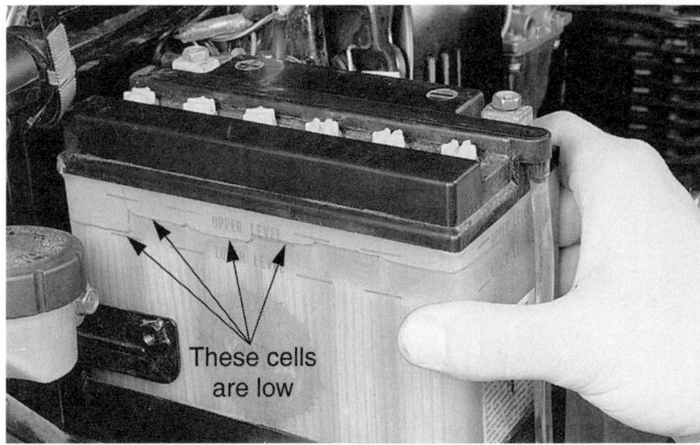

Figure 22-7. It may be necessary to remove the battery to check the electrolyte level. This battery's cells are low, which should be filled with distilled water.

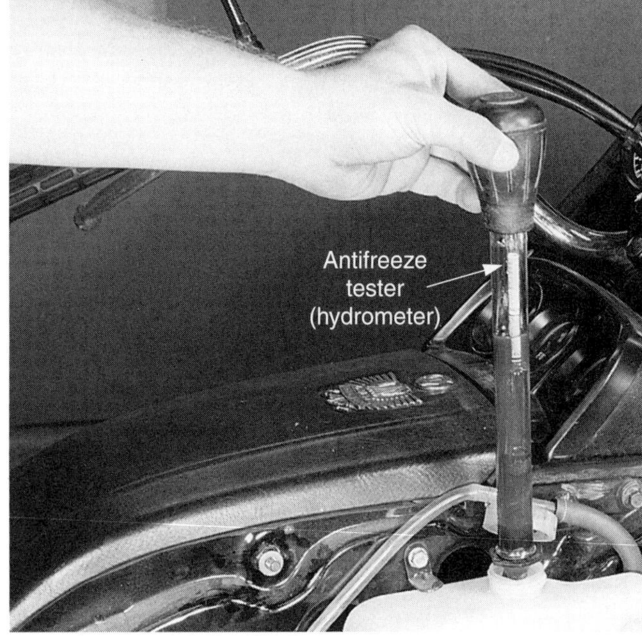

Figure 22-8. Antifreeze tester or hydrometer will check the concentration of water as compared to antifreeze. Refer to the service manual for information on antifreeze type and mixture percentage.

Tire and Wheel Service

Check the tires for wear, damage from debris, and proper inflation. Tire pressure is perhaps the most neglected maintenance item on all motorized vehicles. While checking the tires, inspect the wheels for excessive runout and spoked wheels for damaged, broken, or missing spokes. If the wheel has very slight runout, it can be corrected on spoked wheels by tightening a few of the spokes. Replace any wheels that are damaged or have excessive runout.

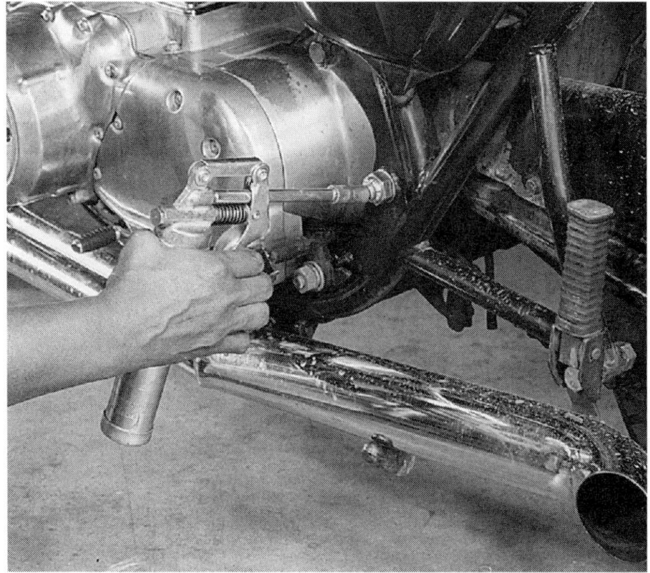

A

B

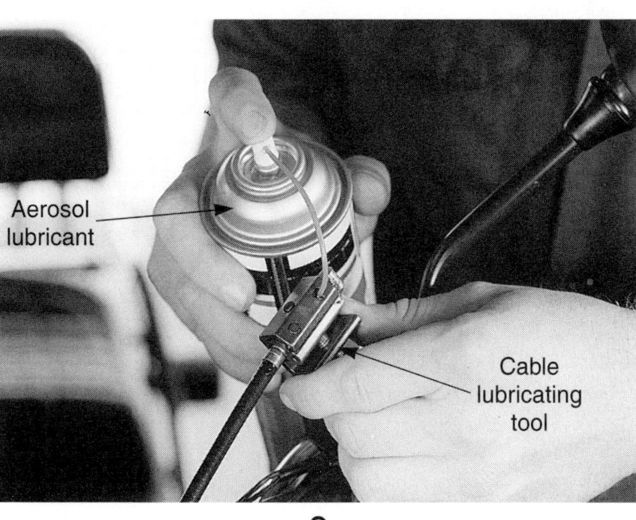

C

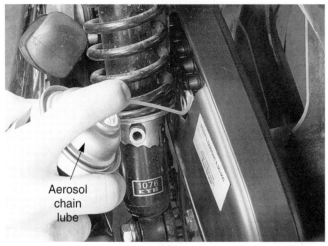

Figure 22-9. A—Grease the swing arm pivot if grease fittings are provided. B—Apply chain lube between the link plates while rotating the rear wheel. C—A cable lubricating tool will aid in cable lubrication.

Replacing Spark Plugs

Spark plug replacement is the primary reason a tune-up is performed. Of all the services, this can provide the most noticeable performance improvement. To replace spark plugs, first remove the spark plug wire from the plug. Do this one cylinder at a time on multicylinder engines to avoid confusion. Using a spark plug socket, extension, and ratchet, remove the spark plug.

After spark plug removal, check the tip for signs of damage or fouling that could indicate engine problems. While spark plugs can sometimes be cleaned and reused, replacement is preferred. Begin by setting the spark plug to the correct gap, **Figure 22-10.** If the spark plug is to be installed in an aluminum head, coat the spark plug threads with anti-seize compound or, engine oil. Start the spark plug by hand, then tighten. A torque wrench can be used to tighten the plug, **Figure 22-11.**

Measuring Engine Compression and Leak-Down

If a bike has performance problems or seems to have low power, compression and leak-down tests offer important clues as to the engine's mechanical condition. Both tests should be done to accurately evaluate engine condition.

Compression Testing

A ***compression test*** can quickly show if all contributing factors that allow engine operation are within service

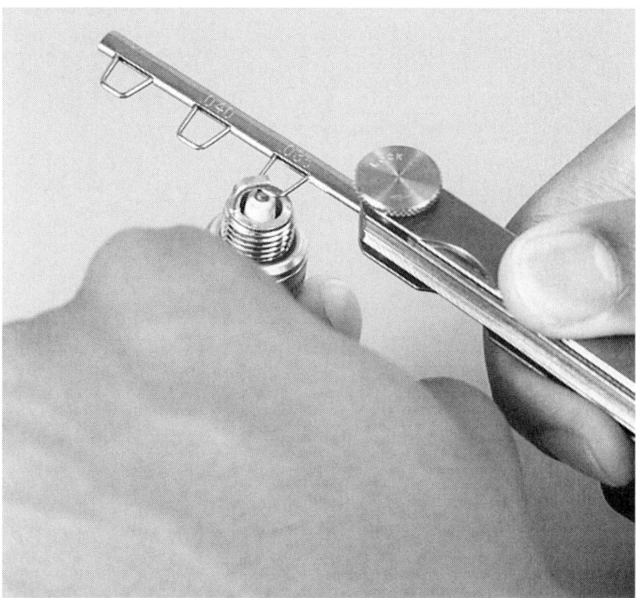

Figure 22-10. Make sure the spark plug is properly gapped before installation. Always use a wire feeler gauge for spark plug gap measurement.

Figure 22-11. A torque wrench is the most accurate way to properly tighten a spark plug, however, keep in mind that spark plug torque is very low. Another method is to tighten the plug 1/2-3/4 turn after the plug gasket (if used) seats (new gaskets only).

limits or if the piston rings/cylinder(s) or the valves/valve seats in the case of a four-stroke engine, are suspect. This test should be performed prior to any tune-up work, especially if the bike did not come in under its own power.

If the engine has compression problems, the customer should be notified the tune-up will have little or no benefit without the other necessary engine work. A compression test should also be done if the motorcycle, scooter, or ATV lacks power, especially during acceleration.

To conduct a compression test, warm up the engine to normal operating temperature. Stop the engine and remove the spark plugs from all cylinders. Install a compression gauge to the cylinder to be tested, **Figure 22-12.** Then proceed with the following methods, depending on the type of starter. Refer to the service manual for acceptable pressure valves and variations between cylinders.

Fully open the throttle and choke valves and strongly kick the starter pedal until compression stops climbing and check.

Electric Start Models

Before testing electric start models, make sure the battery is fully charged. Ground all spark plug wires during the test to prevent damage to electronic components. Turn the engine stop switch off. Fully open the throttle and choke valves, crank the engine with the starter motor, and check the compression.

As a general rule, a two-stroke engine has 115–140 psi (793–965 kPa) of compression pressure and a four-stroke engine 140–175 psi (965–1206 kPa). These figures can vary substantially between different bikes. Periodically check engine compression when a bike is in for service. In this way, you will have a record of engine condition.

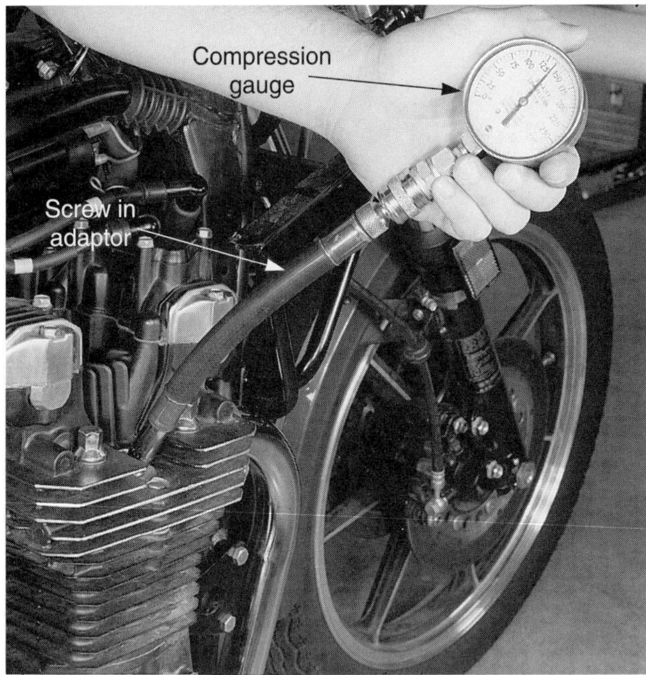

Figure 22-12. A compression gauge can be used to check compression in all cylinders. Refer to a service manual for acceptable pressure values and variation between cylinders. If the engine compression is not up to specifications, repair the engine before performing a tune-up.

If the compression readings on the engine being tested are within specification, proceed with other tests. Readings 10% or more above specification may indicate carbon build-up is raising the compression ratio. Continuous high compression could result in excessive heat and probable engine damage. If lower-than-normal readings are found, a lack of sealing by one or more components is the cause. Loss of compression results in hard starting and loss of power, and possible wet or fouled spark plugs.

In a multicylinder engine, low compression in one cylinder affects power as well as crankshaft balance. If the compression readings vary more than 10% from cylinder to cylinder, the engine will not be in a balanced condition. This results in poor performance, vibration, and possible engine damage.

Wet Compression Test

If the readings are low, perform a ***wet compression test*** by adding a small amount of clean engine oil into the cylinder and rechecking the compression. If compression increases to more than the previous reading, inspect the cylinder and piston rings. If compression remains low, check the valves, valve seats, and cylinder head.

Other possible causes of low or uneven cylinder compression are:

- Faulty valve mechanism.
- Incorrect valve clearance.
- Bent, burned, or sticking valves.

- Worn or damaged valve seat.
- Incorrect valve timing.
- Broken valve spring.
- Faulty hydraulic valve adjuster.
- Leaking or damaged head gasket.
- Warped or cracked cylinder head surface.
- Worn or damaged piston ring(s).
- Worn piston or cylinder.
- Piston ring stuck in the ring groove.

If the crankcase primary compression is too low in a two-stroke engine, the possible cause could be:

- Damaged reed valve.
- Damaged crankcase seal.
- Damaged crankcase or cylinder base gasket.

Cylinder Leak-Down Testing

A ***cylinder leak-down test*** can effectively pinpoint whether the piston rings/cylinder(s), valves/valve seats, head gasket, or crankcase seals and gaskets are in need of service. A leak-down test is a more accurate diagnostic tool than a compression test. The leak-down tester consists of a calibrated pressure gauge connected to a pressure regulator and a flow restrictor. The tester allows measurement of the rate at which air leaks past a cylinder's rings and valves. Tools specifically designed for leak-down testing four-stroke engines are available from several sources, **Figure 22-13.**

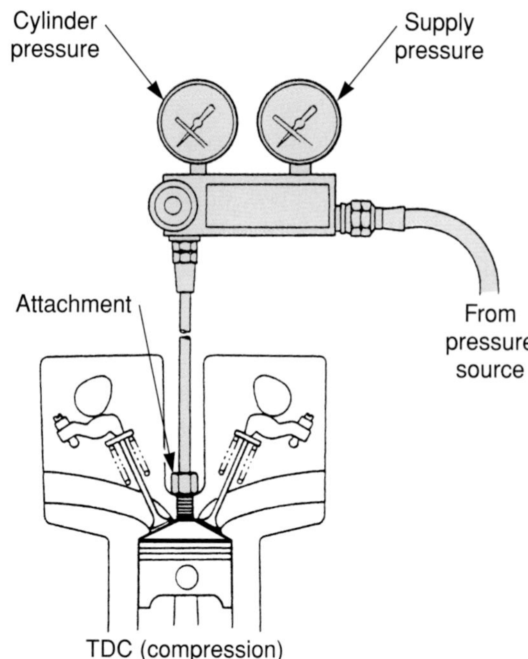

Figure 22-13. Test equipment setup for a four-stroke engine leak-down test. (Honda Motor Co., Ltd.)

Four-Stroke Engine Leak-Down Testing

The first step in the test is to install the hose from the tool into the spark plug hole, as in a compression test. Compressed air is then fed into the combustion chamber. This provides more pressure than conventional compression testing.

The cylinder leak-down test in a four-stroke engine is done with the piston at top dead center (TDC) on the compression stroke. When the cylinder is pressurized, the air will leak past any worn component(s). Listen at the intake or air-box, exhaust pipe, and transmission breather for escaping air. If air is heard at the intake, the intake valve may be damaged or not seating. If air is heard in the exhaust, the exhaust valve may be damaged or not seating. Piston wear, ring wear, or cylinder wear allow air to leak into the transmission, which can be heard at the transmission breather. If air cannot be heard, a pressure drop of 10% or less indicates a properly sealed cylinder. Leakage of 10% or more indicates a problem that must be investigated. Remember, new engines should be allowed to break-in before using these specifications.

In some cases, this test may need to be performed with the piston at a point other than TDC. If this is the case, hold the crankshaft in place with an appropriate wrench while the cylinder is pressurized. This test may be necessary if the cylinder is suspected to be out-of-round at a point near the bottom of piston ring travel.

Warning: High pressure in the combustion chamber requires the crankshaft to be held securely. If the crankshaft is not held securely, personal injury or damage to the motorcycle could result.

Spraying a soapy water mixture around the cylinder and head mating area will show a leak from the head gasket to the outside atmosphere. Bubbles in the cooling system of a liquid-cooled bike indicate a leak from the head gasket into the cooling passages. The only thing this test will not point out is the difference between a head gasket leak into the adjacent cam chain (or gear) cavity, and a leak past the piston rings.

Two-Stroke Engine Leak-Down Testing

Regular crankcase leak-down testing is very important to the lifespan of a two-stroke engine. Because the engine relies on a very precise air-fuel mixture, even a slight air leak can lead to engine seizure.

A pressure/vacuum leak test tool consists of hand pressure/vacuum pump and various adapters to seal the engine, **Figure 22-14.** The test provides a clear indication of where a leak, or leaks exist. Possible areas for leaks include anywhere upstream of the carburetor until the mixture is ignited and forced out of the exhaust. Leaks can occur between the crankcase mating surfaces if the gasket fails. If this gasket fails between the crankcase and the transmission, the mixture will become much richer as transmission oil is slowly drawn into the engine. Similarly, a leaking crankshaft seal on the transmission primary gear side will also consume transmission oil. Other air leaks include the cylinder base gasket, the crankshaft seal, reed valve assembly, and at the carburetor mounting boot.

To perform a two-stroke cycle engine crankcase leak test:

1. Seal the intake and exhaust ports.
2. Position the piston at BDC (bottom dead center).

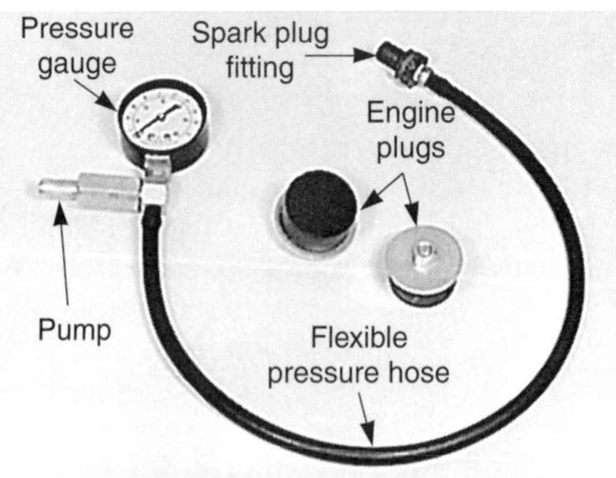

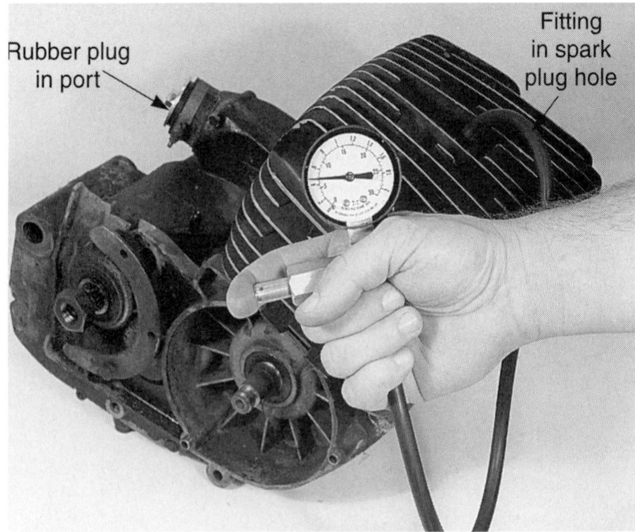

Figure 22-14. This two-stroke leak tester uses a spark plug adapter to pressurize the crankcase. Rubber plugs seal the intake and exhaust ports. If everything is in good shape, the engine should hold 6 psi (41 kPa) pressure for six minutes.

3. Pressurize the crankcase to 6 psi (41 kPa).
4. Monitor the pressure gauge while using a soap and water solution to find any crankcase leaks.

Be sure to follow the leak-down test tool manufacturer's instructions precisely when making this test. If either the compression or leak-down test specifications do not meet service manual specifications, repair the engine before performing the tune-up.

Ignition System Tune-Up

Exact ignition system tune-up procedures vary depending upon the particular system being serviced. However, the information in this chapter should be used along with a service manual. This will give you the skills needed to properly tune a motorcycle ignition system. These tune-up procedures also hold for most ATVs and scooters.

Contact Point Ignition System Service

Any ignition system using contact points requires:

- Inspection and/or replacement of contact points.
- Cleaning of contact surfaces.
- Contact point lubrication.
- Auto advance inspection and lubrication.
- Point gap or dwell adjustment.
- Ignition timing adjustment.

Inspection of Contact Points

Inspect the contact points for evidence of pitting or erosion, **Figure 22-15A.** Contact points that still have flat surfaces can sometimes be refinished with a flexstone. Some manufacturers recommend contact point replacement rather than refinishing. Contacts that are heavily pitted or eroded must always be replaced. Heavy contact pitting or erosion usually indicates the need for condenser replacement.

Replacement of Contact Points

Both the movable and ground contacts must be replaced as a set. During contact point replacement, it is important to make sure the new contacts are the same type as the old ones being replaced. If the ignition system is equipped with a condenser, it should also be replaced at this time.

Some contact sets must be disassembled during installation. Make sure the contact return spring and fiber washers are installed in the proper order. Failure to properly insulate the contact spring or wire from ground will cause the contact set to be permanently grounded. This will keep the ignition system from functioning. After contact installation, make sure the contact wires are properly routed and the contacts surfaces are parallel, **Figure 22-15B.**

Cleaning Contact Point Surfaces

Whether the contact points are refinished or replaced, the surfaces must be thoroughly cleaned. Refinishing of contact surfaces leaves residue. New contacts commonly have a protective coating that must also be removed. Aerosol contact cleaner may be used for contact cleaning. Look at **Figure 22-16.**

Contact point rubbing blocks and point cams must be lubricated to prevent premature rubbing block wear. Rubbing block wear reduces point gap and retards ignition timing. A special grease is used to lubricate the point cam and rubbing block.

When lubrication of the contact breaker rubbing blocks and point cam is performed, it is a good idea to also check and lubricate the auto or centrifugal advance unit, **Figure 22-17.** Make sure the auto advance unit

A

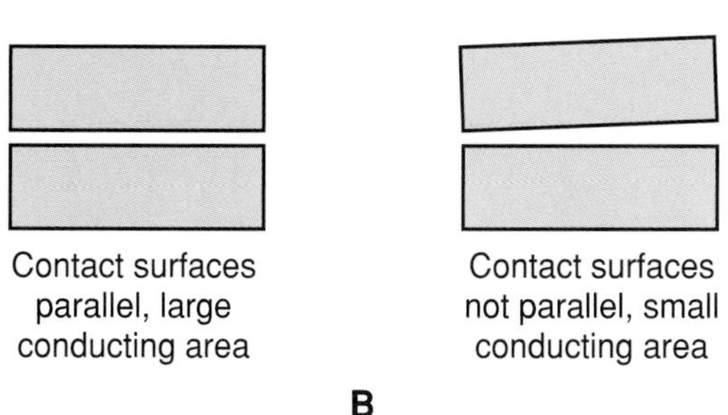

B

Figure 22-15. A—Inspect contact points closely to determine their condition. Contact point pitting and erosion can be detected visually. B—Contact point surfaces should be parallel for best performance. After installing new contacts, check to see that both surfaces are parallel and adjust, if needed, by carefully bending the stationary contact base.

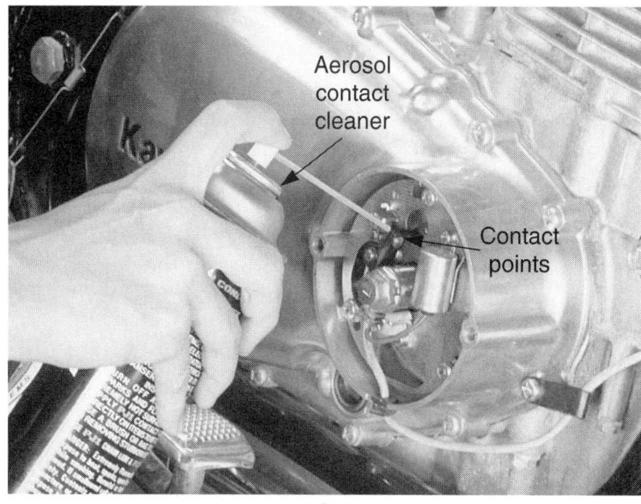

A

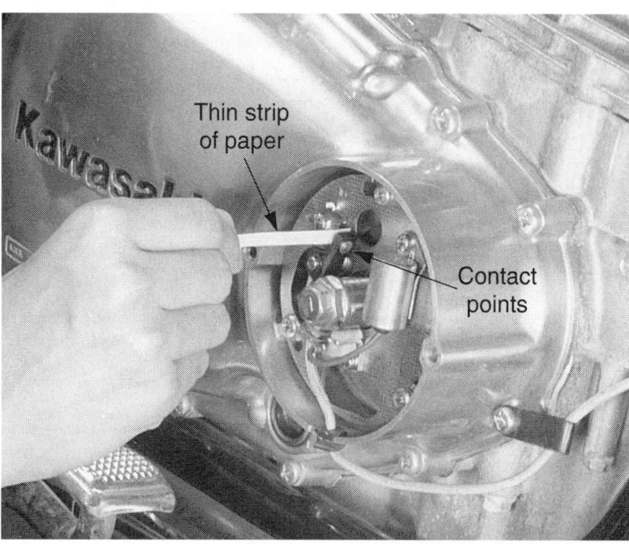

B

Figure 22-16. A—Use aerosol contact cleaner to remove oil film and grit. B—Use a thin strip of paper to ensure the contact surfaces are clean and dry.

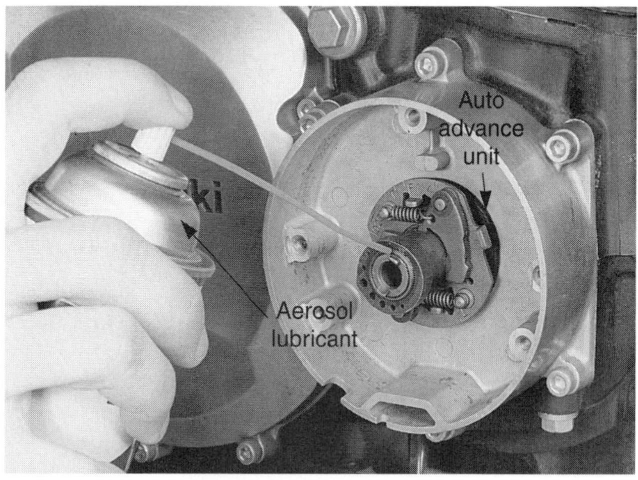

Figure 22-17. A light application of an aerosol lubricant is an acceptable method of lubricating an ignition system auto advance unit.

operates freely and inspect for evidence of moisture or corrosion.

Contact Point Gap Adjustment

Contact point gap is the amount of clearance between the contact surfaces when they are wide open. Most contact point cams have an index mark to indicate the position of the widest opening. Rotate the engine until the cam lobe mark is aligned with the point rubbing block.

Contact point gap determines the amount of time for coil build-up (current flow into coil). ***Dwell*** is the amount of time in crankshaft degrees the contacts are closed. A ***dwell meter*** or multimeter with a dwell feature must be used to set point dwell in degrees. It is important to understand the relationship between dwell and point gap. As point gap increases, dwell decreases. As point gap decreases, dwell increases, **Figure 22-18.**

Contact point gap is adjusted in one of two ways:

- Using a feeler gauge (static), **Figure 22-19.**
- Using a dwell meter (dynamic), **Figure 22-20.**

A range is usually given for acceptable contact point gap and dwell. Follow the directions in the service manual for contact point gap adjustment as specifications vary.

Ignition Timing Adjustment

Ignition timing refers to the crankshaft and piston position when the spark occurs. As mentioned earlier, spark timing is critical to engine efficiency, performance, and service life. Ignition timing is checked by using markings on the engine or by measuring piston position. Usually, timing marks are provided to simplify adjustment, **Figure 22-21.**

Three methods are used to alter ignition timing:

- Rotating the ignition base plate.
- Movement of a breaker subplate mounted on the base plate, **Figure 22-22.**
- Changing contact point gap.

Some flywheel magnetos use point gap as the only means of adjusting ignition timing. Refer to **Figure 22-23.**

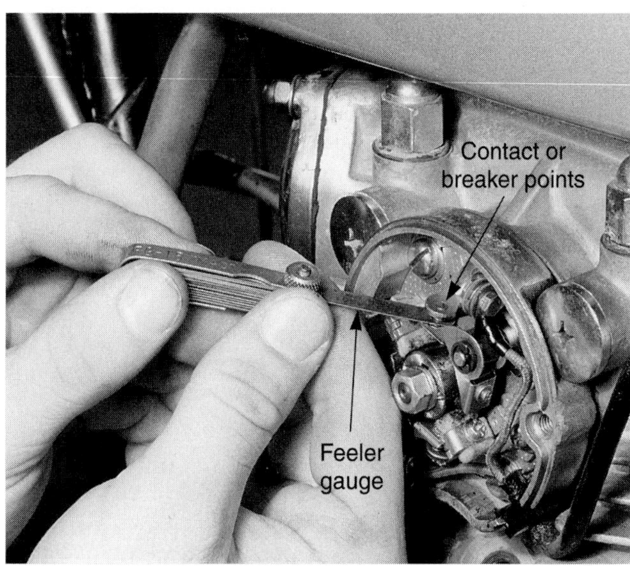

Figure 22-19. A feeler gauge can be used to measure and verify contact point gap with reasonable accuracy.

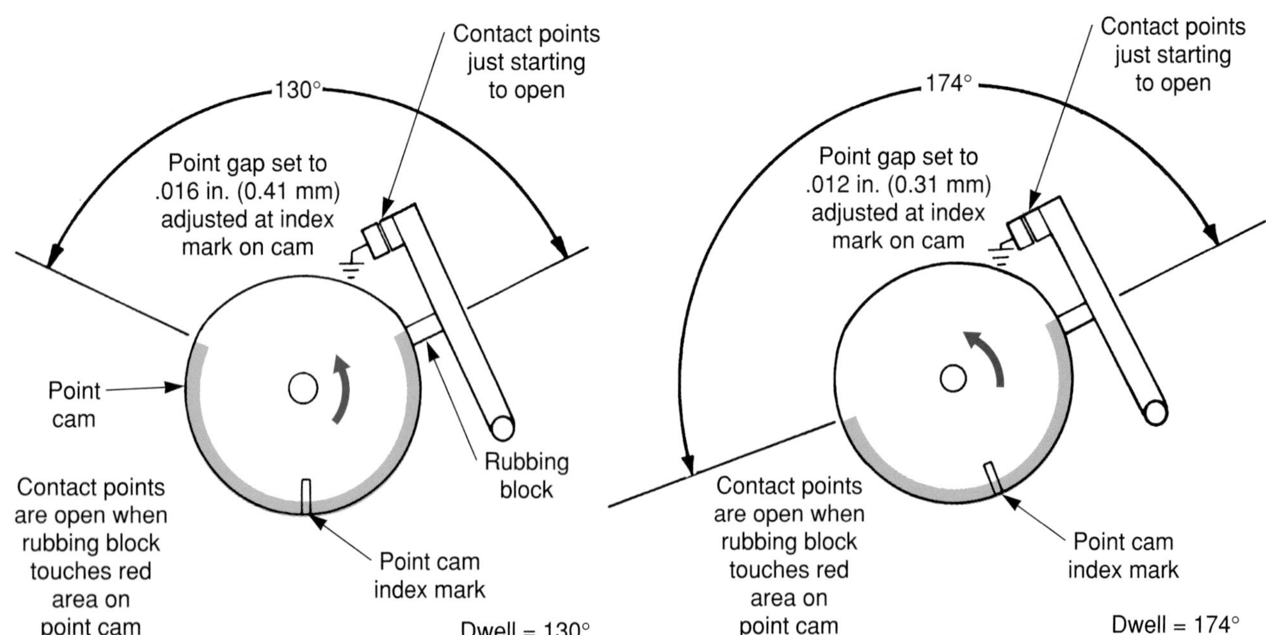

Figure 22-18. Dwell refers to the amount of time in degrees the points are closed. A—Point gap is .016 inch (.41 mm) and dwell is 130°. B—The point gap has been reduced to .012 inch (.31 mm). This causes the points to open later and close sooner, increasing dwell. When the point gap is increased, dwell is reduced. When the gap is reduced, dwell is increased.

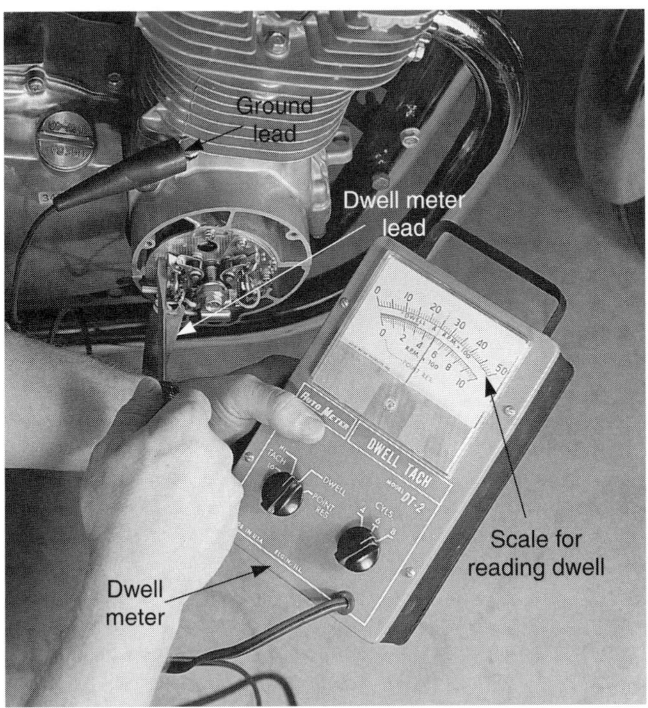

Figure 22-20. A dwell meter is used to verify contact point dwell in degrees, which in turn indicates contact point gap. To set dwell, operate the engine at idle, then adjust the points until the meter reads within specifications.

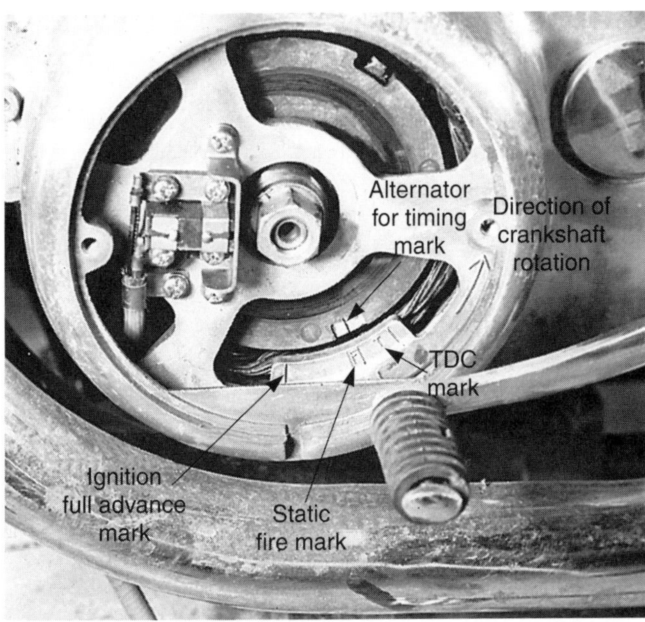

Figure 22-21. Permanent engine timing marks allow crankshaft positioning for setting ignition timing. This engine has three marks: full advance, F mark, and T mark. The full advance mark must align at a certain rpm. The F mark (static fire) must align at idle. The T mark (TDC) is used for adjusting valve and cam timing.

On engines using this design, widen the point gap to advance the ignition timing. Close the contact points to retard the ignition timing.

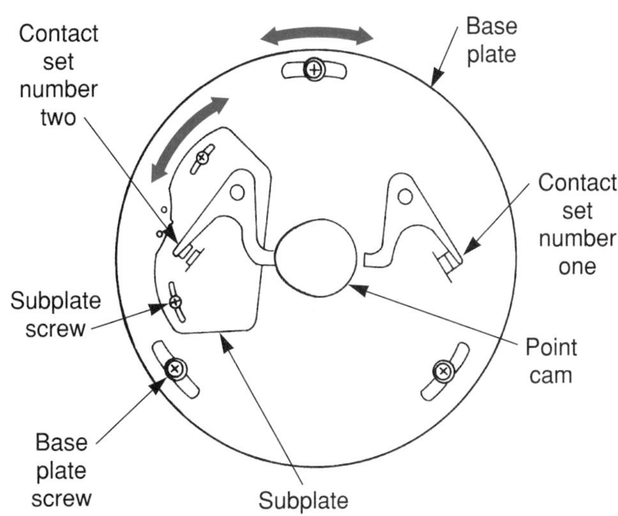

Figure 22-22. In this example, ignition timing is adjusted by rotating the base plate to time the number one contact set and the subplate to time the number two contact set.

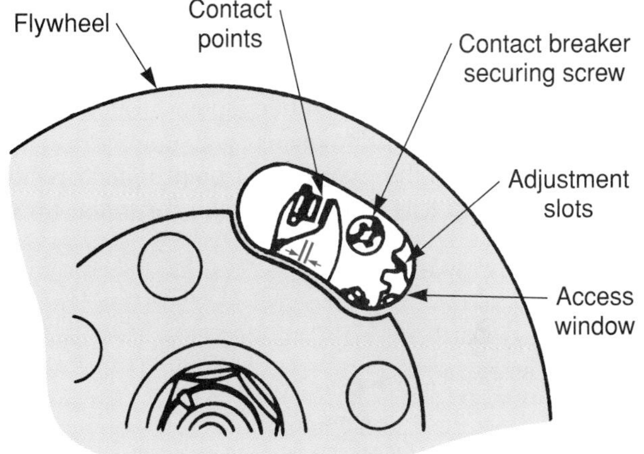

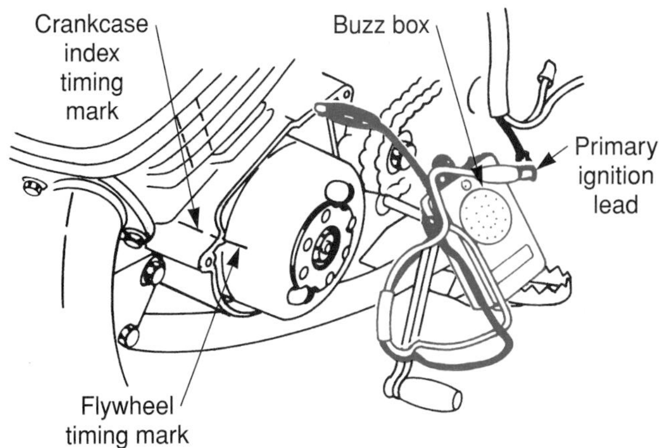

Figure 22-23. In most flywheel magnetos, timing is adjusted by changing the point gap. Timing is checked with a buzz box or a testlight. If the timing is retarded, widen point gap. If timing is advanced, reduce point gap. If the proper timing cannot be achieved, the rubbing block is probably worn and the point set must be replaced. (American Suzuki Motor Corporation)

Other engines do not have timing marks and usually require a dial indicator to measure piston position, **Figure 22-24.** The dial indicator takes the place of permanent timing marks. The contact points must begin to open at a specific piston position or dial indicator reading. Service manual specifications are given in piston position or crankshaft degrees before top dead center, when the contacts should be open.

Static Ignition Timing Adjustment

Static ignition timing adjustment is done without the engine running and with the ignition switch in the *off* position. A buzz box, continuity light, or ohmmeter is used to indicate when the contact points just begin to open. **Figure 22-25** illustrates static ignition timing adjustment using these test instruments. One lead of the ohmmeter, buzz box, or continuity light is connected to ground. The other lead is connected to the movable (hot) side of the contact breaker.

When the contacts are closed, current will flow from one lead, through the points, and into the other lead, completing the circuit. When the contacts open, the circuit is broken. The ohmmeter needle will deflect; the buzz box tone will stop or change pitch; or the continuity light will go out. Remember, contact opening, *not* closing, causes the spark to occur.

Static timing is the matching of point initial opening to engine timing. It is especially useful for initial timing adjustment after major engine repairs. If the timing marks do not line up correctly, ignition timing is either advanced or retarded, **Figure 22-26.**

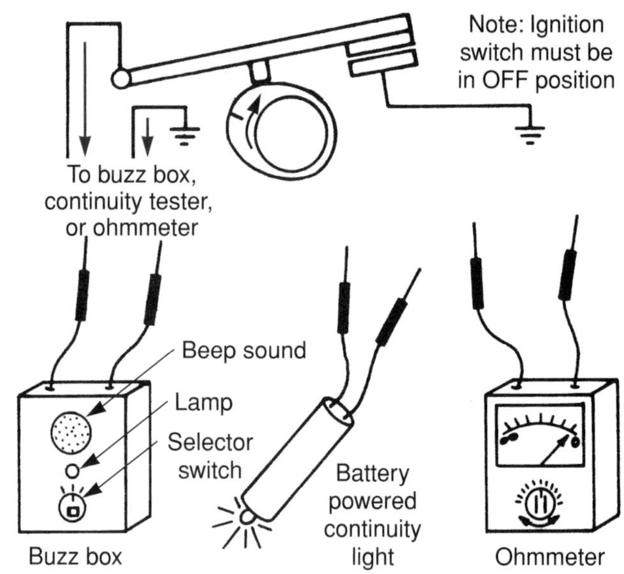

Figure 22-25. Three methods of determining static timing (contacts begin to open) are shown. A—The buzz box makes a noise to indicate when the points are closed. B—Testlight would glow when the points are closed. C—Ohmmeter needle deflection shows whether the points are opened or closed.

To adjust ignition timing:

1. Rotate the ignition base plate the same direction as the point cam rotates to retard the timing.
2. Rotate the ignition base plate in the opposite direction of point cam rotation to advance timing.

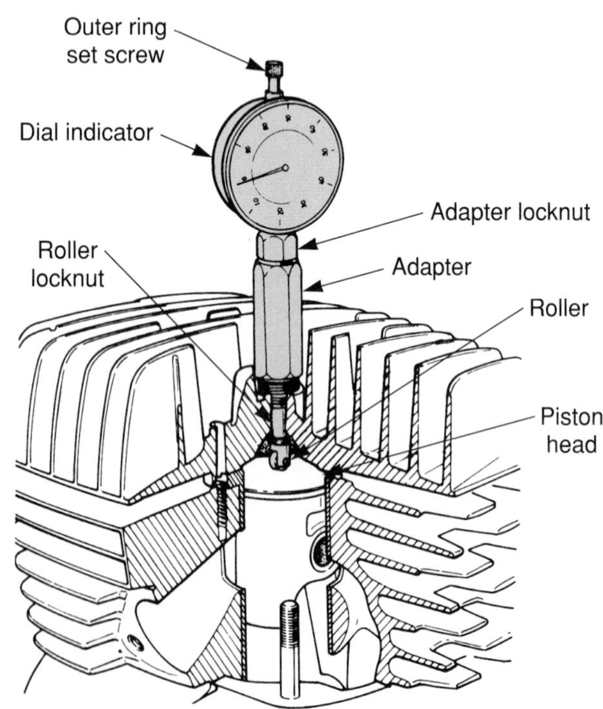

Figure 22-24. On some engines, a dial indicator is used to measure the piston position for ignition timing or timing mark verification. (Bombardier Ltd.)

Dynamic Timing Adjustment

Dynamic ignition timing is the most accurate method of verifying and adjusting ignition timing. A ***timing light*** triggered by the secondary ignition circuit is used to check dynamic timing. The timing light is connected to the positive and negative battery terminals and to one spark plug wire, **Figure 22-27.** Most modern timing lights use an induction pickup that clips around the spark plug wire. Older non-inductive timing lights must be connected using a special adapter.

Dynamic timing is more accurate than static timing because:

- The timing light is triggered by actual ignition operation.
- Proper ignition advance at a recommended engine rpm can be verified.

Adjustment of ignition timing by the static method does not guarantee perfect timing. Wear in the auto advance unit or point cam and shaft cannot accurately be compensated for by the static adjustment method.

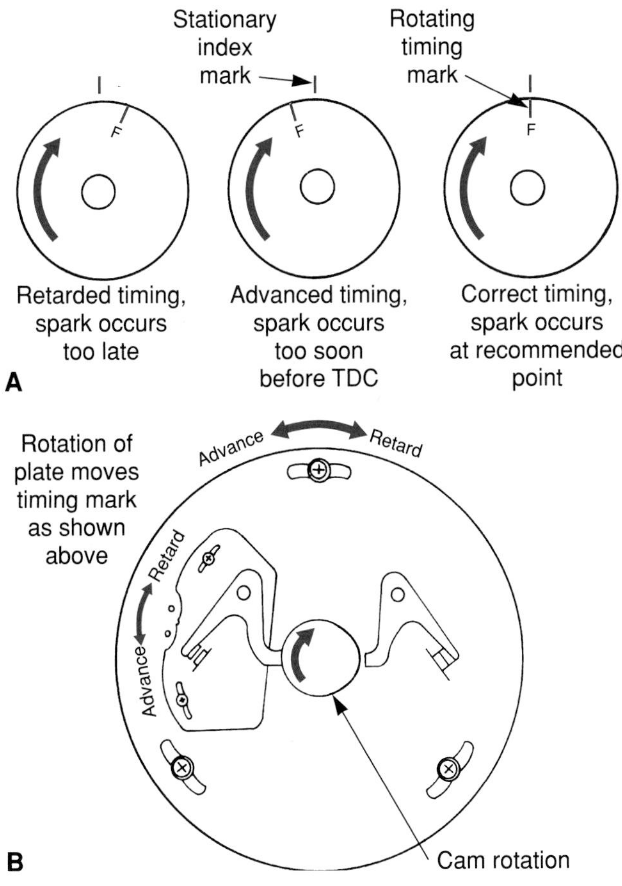

Figure 22-26. A—Position of the rotating timing mark and stationary index mark indicates timing. B—The point cam rotates clockwise. To advance the timing, rotate the base or subplate in the opposite direction of cam rotation. To retard timing, rotate the plates in the same direction as cam rotation.

Centrifugal advance movement at a specified rpm can only be verified by dynamic ignition timing.

When rotating the base plate (engine running), leave the base plate screws slightly loose. Move the base plate a little at a time and check timing after each movement. When correct timing is achieved, recheck timing after the base plate screws have been tightened.

Note: When contact points are replaced or when contact gap is adjusted, ignition timing will be changed. Timing adjustment is required whenever point gap is altered. Static timing should be done first to ensure ignition timing is reasonably close. Dynamic timing should then be done as a final verification. Adjustments for correcting dynamic timing are the same as for static timing.

When adjusting the base plate on engines which drive the point cam off the camshaft, rotate the base plate a very small amount. The amount of base plate rotation will be doubled at the crankshaft.

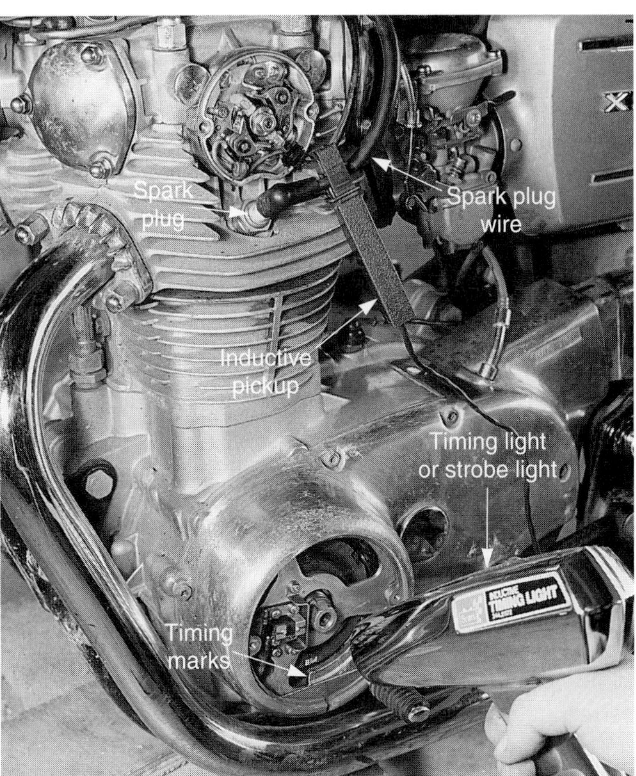

Figure 22-27. A timing light is connected to the battery and appropriate spark plug wire. It can then be pointed on the timing marks to check ignition timing. A timing light makes the spinning ignition timing marks visible while the engine is running.

Electronic Ignition System Service

Some electronic ignition systems (including transistorized) cannot be adjusted. Adjustment could upset engine operation and cause problems with exhaust emissions. With these systems, no slots are provided for base plate rotation or magnetic pickup movement. The timing marks are simply used to check system condition and operation. Look at **Figure 22-28.**

With electronic ignition systems having provisions for adjustment, ignition timing is adjusted in a similar manner to the contact point system. The base plate and in some cases, the trigger coil plate, is rotated to change timing. **Figure 22-29** shows a typical electronic ignition timing adjustment.

Air Gap Adjustment

Another adjustment, which may be necessary on an electronic ignition, is the air gap adjustment. In order for a magnetic trigger to operate properly, an air gap must be maintained between the pickup coil and rotor. This air gap is checked with a feeler gauge and is usually adjusted by moving the pickup assembly, **Figure 22-30.** Refer to the service manual for proper air gap adjustment procedures and specifications.

Figure 22-28. This transistorized or electronic ignition system does not provide for ignition timing adjustment. However, the timing marks are used to verify ignition timing, ignition advance, and system condition.

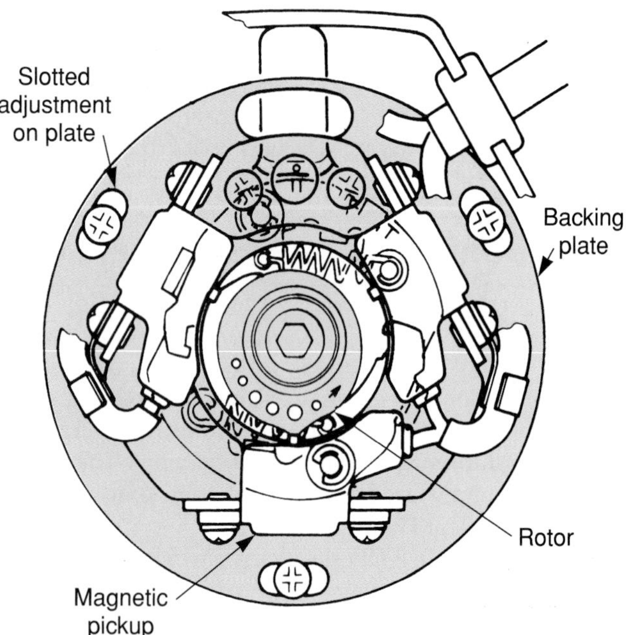

Figure 22-29. Some electronic ignition systems provide ignition timing adjustment. Rotating the backing plate changes the timing. (Kawasaki Motors Corporation U.S.A.)

Engine and Carburetor Tune-up

It was mentioned earlier that the valve train and carburetor must be adjusted during a tune-up. The necessary adjustments typically include:

- Valve clearance adjustment.
- Cam chain adjustment.

Figure 22-30. A feeler gauge is used to check the air gap between the rotor and magnetic pickup of an electronic ignition.

- Carburetor pilot circuit adjustment.
- Carburetor synchronization.
- Idle speed adjustment.

Valve Adjustment

Correct valve clearance adjustment helps ensure long valve train service life. When clearance is too tight, valves can overheat. This can cause the valve faces and seats to burn. Loss of compression and accelerated cam and follower wear may also result from inadequate valve clearance. When valve clearance is too loose, valve train life is reduced because of the pounding or hammering effect between parts.

Several methods of adjustment are used to compensate for changes in valve clearance caused by normal wear:

- Screw adjusters on cam followers or rocker arms, **Figure 22-31.**
- Adjustable push rods, **Figure 22-32.**
- Shim adjuster, **Figure 22-33.**

Cam Chain Adjustment

Cam chain adjustment is needed to take up excess slack as the chain and sprockets wear. A loose chain wears prematurely and can cause improper valve timing, chain guide damage, and chain slap noise.

A manual chain tensioner, **Figure 22-34,** or automatic cam chain tensioner, **Figure 22-35,** is provided for chain

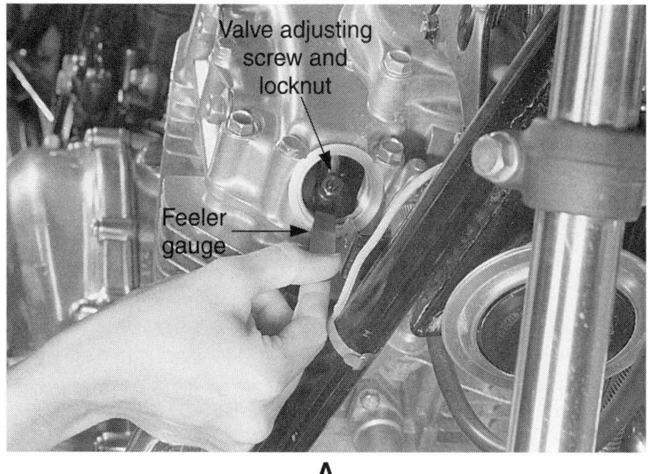

A

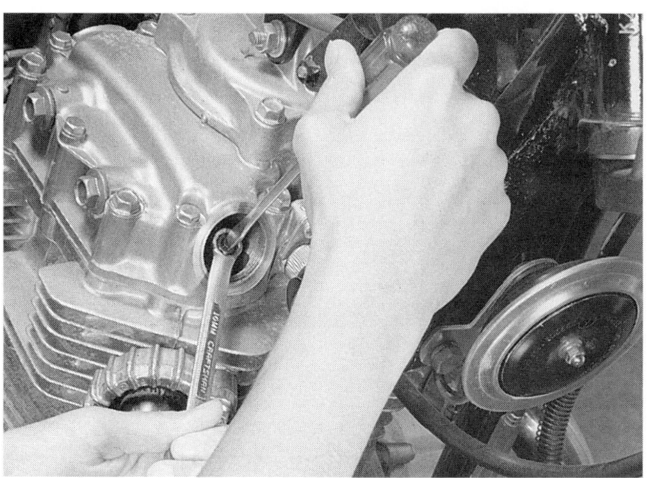

B

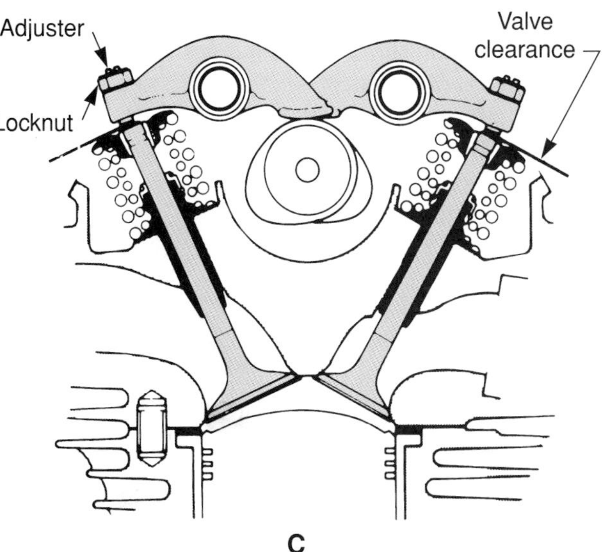

C

Figure 22-31. A— Screw and nut adjuster provide a quick and easy means of valve adjustment. Check the clearance with a feeler gauge. B—If the valve clearance is not within specifications, turn the adjusting screw in or out as needed. Tighten locknut and recheck valve clearance. C—A feeler gauge can measure the valve clearance when the valve is closed. (Kawasaki Motors Corporation U.S.A.)

Figure 22-32. With adjustable push rods, the valve clearance is reduced by changing the push rod length. This is done by means of a threaded adjuster and locknut at the tappet end of the push rod.

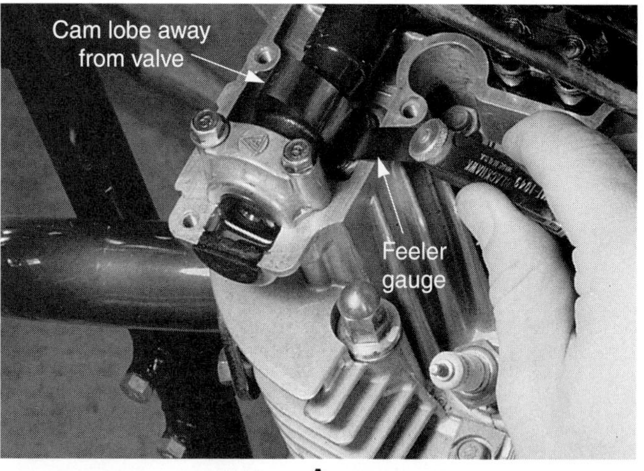

A

B

Figure 22-33. A—When a shim valve adjuster is used, valve clearance is also measured with a feeler gauge. The cam should be on its base circle or in the position described in the service manual. B—If the valve adjuster shim thickness must be changed, a valve spring compressing tool is required. Push down on the spring, slide out the old shim, and install a shim of correct thickness.

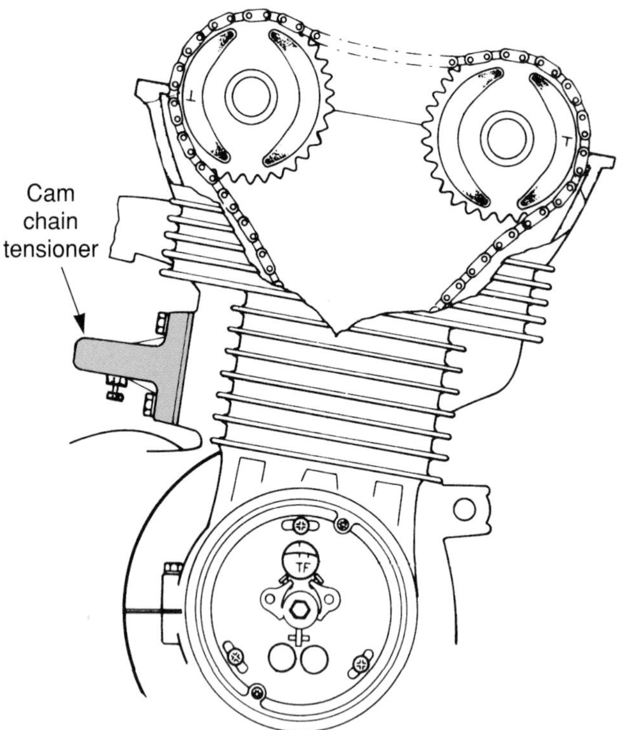

Figure 22-34. A manual chain tensioner uses a bolt and locknut to hold the tensioner in position after adjustment. (Kawasaki Motors Corporation U.S.A.)

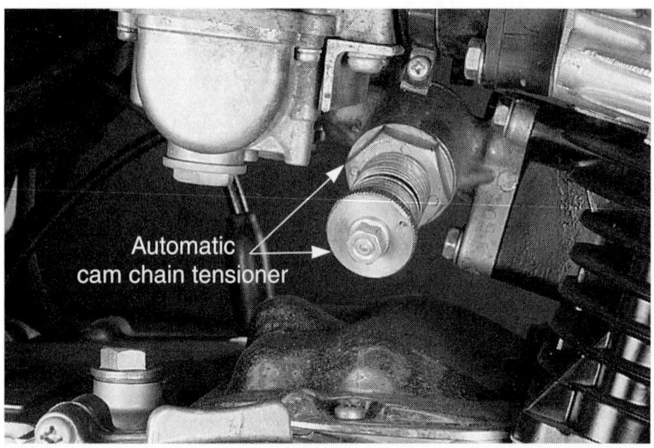

Figure 22-35. An automatic cam chain tensioner compensates for chain wear as the engine runs.

adjustment. On some engines, the chain is adjusted with the crankshaft in a specified position and with the engine stopped. Other engines must be either kicked over or running while tension is adjusted. Always follow the service manual since adjustment procedures vary.

Carburetor Pilot Circuit Adjustment

Pilot circuit adjustment is a very fine modification of the carburetor's air-fuel mixture at idle and slightly above. Carburetor pilot circuit adjustments are usually required during a tune-up to achieve a proper air-fuel mixture. The fuel mixture can be affected as a result of the tune-up.

Some service procedures which can create a need for carburetor adjustment are:

- Installing a new air filter.
- Replacing spark plugs.
- Adjusting point gap and ignition timing.
- Adjusting valve clearance.

Pilot screws are easily located on the carburetor. The service manual will give the proper initial pilot screw settings. For final adjustment, make sure the engine is completely warm, **Figure 22-36.**

Carburetor Synchronization

Carburetor synchronization is the adjustment of the throttles to achieve equal air-fuel delivery to each engine cylinder. Vacuum gauges are used to monitor intake manifold vacuum for each cylinder. When the vacuum gauges all read the same, the carburetors are properly synchronized.

Like the pilot circuit, carburetor synchronization is affected by other tune-up operations, especially valve clearance. **Figure 22-37** illustrates typical carburetor synchronization. Refer to the service manual since adjustment procedures and recommended vacuum settings vary.

Idle Speed Adjustment

The final carburetor adjustment normally required is the idle speed adjustment. Most modern motorcycles with two or more cylinders have a single idle adjustment

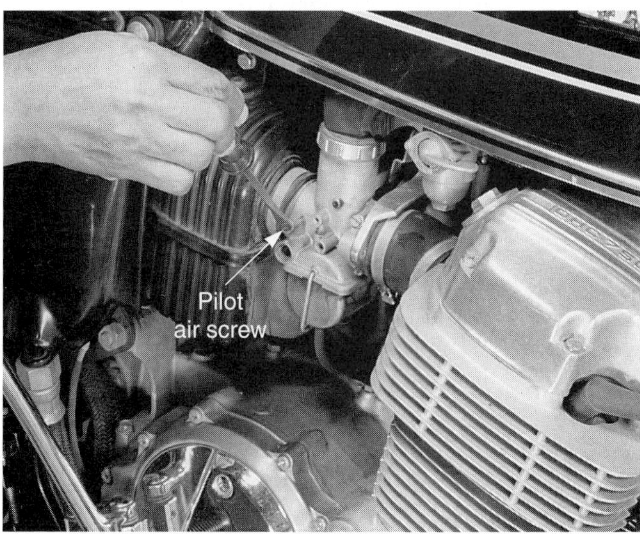

Figure 22-36. Use a screwdriver to adjust the pilot air screw while following service manual procedures.

screw, **Figure 22-38.** It is easy to reach and does not require the use of tools. Recommended idle speeds range from about 800-1100 rpm. Follow the service manual recommendation for exact idle speed.

Note: Correct procedures for all carburetor adjustments are covered in Chapter 7.

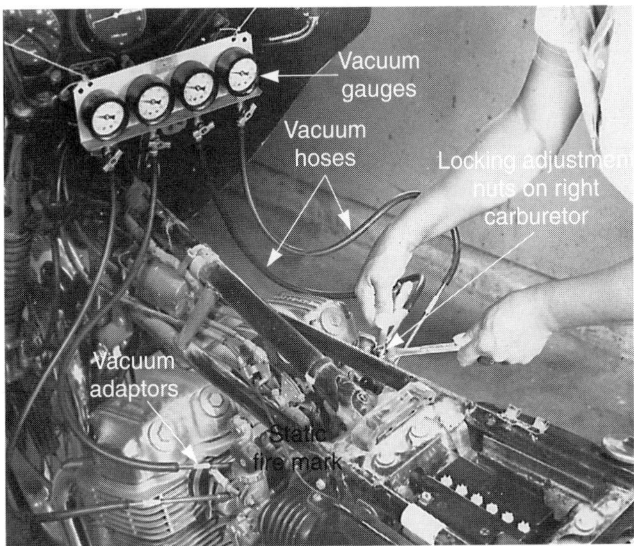

Figure 22-37. Vacuum gauges are used for carburetor throttle synchronization and other adjustments.

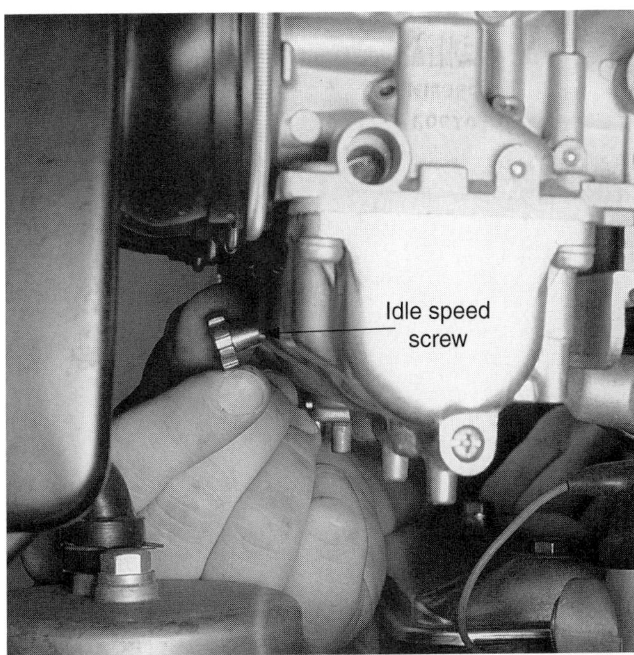

Figure 22-38. Most motorcycles using multiple carburetor throttle linkage have a single screw for idle speed adjustment. This screw adjusts the throttle linkage position and engine rpm.

An exhaust gas analyzer, described in Chapter 12, can help to distinguish between carburetor and ignition problems. It can pinpoint the problem to a specific cylinder.

Tune-up and General Service Summary

The following is a summary of the most important steps for completing service of a motorcycle. Remember to always use the instructions in a service manual. The slightest mistake could upset engine performance, motorcycle safety, or result in serious part damage.

1. Inspect the entire bike for problems, check lights, horn, electric starter, warning lights, buzzers, and kill switch. Replace burned out bulbs.
2. Check the ECM for any stored diagnostic codes.
3. Clean or replace air filter.
4. Change oil and filter (engine, primary, and transmission).
5. Check and grease swing arm pivot.
6. Lubricate control levers, control rod ends, and all pivots.
7. Adjust and lubricate oil injector cable (two-stroke cycle engine), **Figure 22-39.**
8. Check and refill oil injection tank (two-stroke cycle engine).
9. Check battery electrolyte level.

Figure 22-39. Injection oil pump output is determined by the oil pump arm position. The oil pump arm is adjusted by tightening or loosening the cable. Index marks are usually provided to ensure proper adjustment. Refer to the manual for index mark locations and adjustment procedures.

10. Check battery state of charge with hydrometer.
11. Check battery terminals for corrosion, grease if necessary.
12. Check liquid cooling system level. If low, check for leaks.
13. Gap and install new spark plugs.
14. Test compression in each cylinder (if needed).
15. Clean or replace contact points. Adjust gap.
16. Clean and lubricate breaker cam and rubbing block.
17. Check electronic ignition trigger (pickup) clearance.
18. Check ignition dwell.
19. Check and adjust ignition timing.
20. Clean fuel sediment bowl and screen.
21. Adjust carburetor mixture, if available.
22. Synchronize carburetors, if used.
23. Readjust mixture screws, if necessary.
24. Adjust and lubricate throttle cables.
25. Adjust valves.
26. Adjust cam chain.
27. Check, lubricate, and adjust the drive chain.
28. Check oil level in rear drive unit (shaft drive).
29. Lubricate and adjust primary chain.
30. Lubricate and adjust clutch release and cable, **Figures 22-40** and **22-41.**
31. Check steering head bearings for looseness.
32. Change fork oil, if needed.
33. Check operation of forks and shocks.
34. Check brake wear indicators. Adjust brakes.
35. Check brake light switch operation. Adjust if needed, **Figure 22-42.**
36. Check brake fluid level. Add if low and check for leakage.
37. Check tire condition and pressure.
38. Check spokes and wheel runout and tighten any loose spokes.
39. Check important nuts and bolts for tightness. Replace any missing fasteners.
40. Road test while checking for leaks, proper handling, braking, and engine performance.

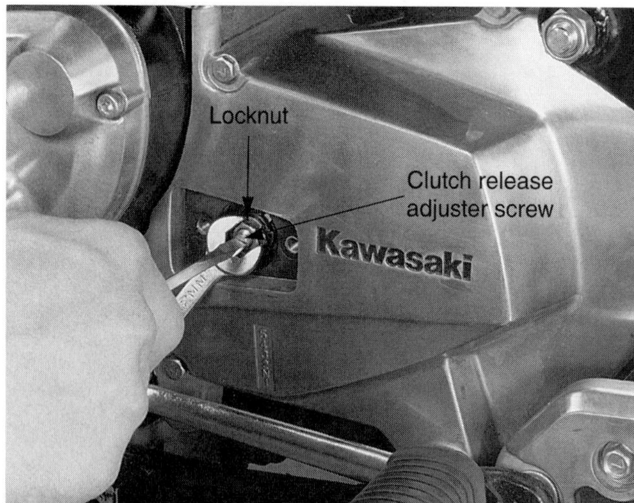

Figure 22-40. Clutch adjustment is done in three steps. Loosen cable tension, adjust the clutch release mechanism, and adjust cable free play. This technician is adjusting the clutch release.

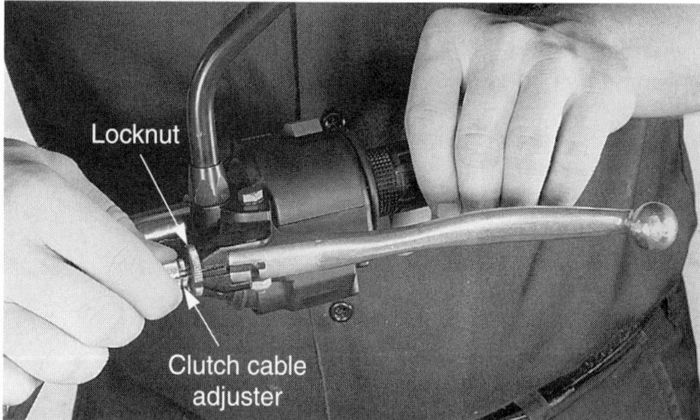

Figure 22-41. After adjusting the clutch release mechanism, set clutch cable free play.

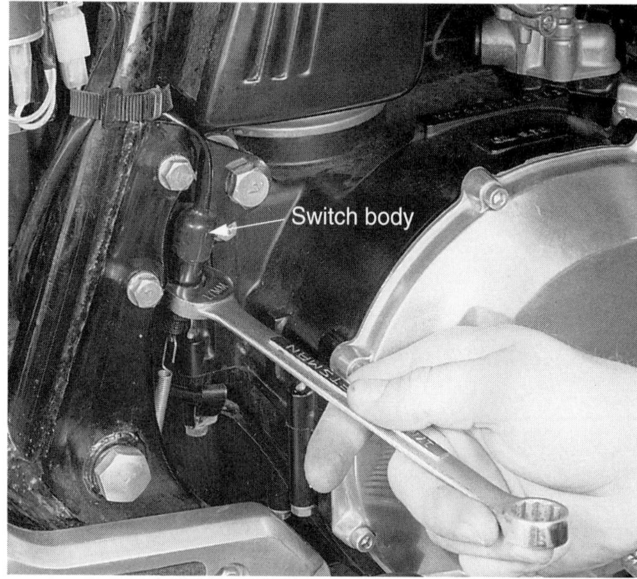

Figure 22-42. Brake light switch adjustment is usually done by moving the switch body up or down (special adjuster nut is rotated). Adjust the brake light switch using manual specifications and double-check that it operates properly.

Periodic Maintenance Schedule

Motorcycle manufacturers recommend a regular schedule of ***periodic maintenance*** for each bike to keep it operating efficiently. The periodic maintenance chart shown in **Figure 22-43** is typical of the type in most service manuals. It lists the recommended intervals for all periodic service work necessary to keep the motorcycle operating at peak performance and efficiency. Mileage is expressed in terms of kilometers, miles, and time. More frequent service may be performed on motorcycles that are used under severe conditions.

Documentation

Neat and accurate ***documentation*** of all repairs is essential to the success of any service department. Permanent records are invaluable from a performance standpoint as well. By studying the types of repairs performed and their frequency, managers and technicians can spot trends and tendencies and take corrective action. They can also confirm components and service procedures that have performed satisfactorily. It is good business sense for the service department or shop to keep a record of each bike's service work and periodic maintenance checks and remind their owners as to when they should be made again.

Interval: This interval should be judged by odometer reading or months (whichever comes first)	km	1000	6000	12000	18000	24000
	miles	600	4000	7500	11000	15000
	months	2	12	24	36	48
Cylinder head bolts and nuts, exhaust pipe nuts and muffler connections		–	T	T	T	T
Air cleaner element	Clean every 3000 km (2000 miles).					
De-compression		I	I	I	I	I
Valve clearance		I	I	I	I	I
Spark plugs		–	I	R	I	R
Fuel line		I	I	I	I	I
	Replace every four years					
Fuel cock strainer		–	–	C	–	C
Engine oil		R	R	R	R	R
Engine oil filter		R	–	R	–	R
Carburetor idle rpm		I	I	I	I	I
Balancer chain		I	I	I	I	I
Clutch		I	I	I	I	I
Drive train		I	I	I	I	I
	Clean and lubricate every 1000 km (600 miles).					
Brakes		I	I	I	I	I
		I	I	I	I	I
Brake hoses		I	I	I	I	I
	Replace every four years.					
Brake fluid		I	I	I	I	I
	Change every two years.					
Tires		–	I	I	I	I
Spark arrester	Clean every 6000 km (4000 miles). Only for Canada					
Steering		I	–	I	–	I
Front fork		–	–	I	–	I
Rear suspension		–	–	I	–	I
Chasis bolts and nuts		T	T	T	T	T

Note: I: Inspect and adjust, clean, lubricate or replace as necessary.
R: Replace T: Tighten C: Clean

Figure 22-43. Typical motorcycle periodic maintenance (PM) schedule. (American Suzuki Motor Corporation)

Summary

Tune-up and service work are considered separate operations, however, they are usually done at the same time. Always make sure the engine is in good mechanical condition before attempting a tune-up. Before starting any service work on a motorcycle, ATV, or scooter, look over the entire bike for problems not listed on the order. When beginning a tune-up or other service work on a computer-controlled bike, you should check the ECM for any stored diagnostic codes.

Air filter replacement is one of the fundamental services performed on all motorized vehicles. Regular air filter replacement ensures optimum air flow and performance. Fuel filter replacement ensures the carburetor or fuel injectors receive fuel with as few impurities as possible. Do not attempt to clean and reuse the fuel filter. If the bike has a sediment bowl, be sure to remove it and clean the screen. During service, inspect the battery for leaks as well as the electrolyte level. Test the coolant's concentration using an antifreeze hydrometer. When servicing a bike, especially after changing the oil and filter, you should lubricate other parts of the bike, such as the swing arm pivot, chain, brake and accelerator cables.

Spark plug replacement is the primary reason a tune-up is performed. Of all the services, this can provide the most noticeable performance improvement. After spark plug removal, check the tip for signs of damage or fouling that could indicate engine problems. While spark plugs can sometimes be cleaned and reused, replacement is preferred.

If a bike has performance problems or seems to have low power, compression and leak-down tests offer important clues as to the engine's mechanical condition. A compression test can quickly show if all contributing factors that allow engine operation are within service limits. A cylinder leak-down test can effectively pinpoint whether the piston rings/cylinder(s), valves/valve seats, head gasket, or crankcase seals and gaskets are in need of service.

Inspect contact points for evidence of pitting or erosion. Contacts that are heavily pitted or eroded must always be replaced. Heavy contact pitting or erosion usually indicates the need for condenser replacement. Both the movable and ground contacts must be replaced as a set. After contact installation, make sure the contact wires are properly routed and the contacts' surfaces are parallel. Whether the contact points are refinished or replaced, the surfaces must be thoroughly cleaned. Contact point rubbing blocks and point cams must be lubricated to prevent premature rubbing block wear. Dwell is the amount of time in crankshaft degrees the contacts are closed. A dwell meter or multimeter with a dwell feature must be used to set point dwell in degrees.

Ignition timing refers to the crankshaft and piston position when the spark occurs. Some engines require a dial indicator to measure piston position. Static ignition timing adjustment is done without the engine running and with the ignition switch in the off position. Dynamic ignition timing is the most accurate method of verifying and adjusting ignition timing. Some electronic ignition systems (including transistorized) cannot be adjusted.

Correct valve clearance adjustment helps ensure long valve train service life. When clearance is too tight, valves can overheat. When valve clearance is too loose, valve train life is shortened. Cam chain adjustment is needed to take up excess slack as the chain and sprockets wear. Always follow the service manual since adjustment procedures vary.

Carburetor synchronization is the adjustment of the throttles to achieve equal air-fuel delivery to each engine cylinder. Vacuum gauges are used to monitor intake manifold vacuum for each cylinder. Pilot circuit adjustment is a very fine modification of the carburetor's air-fuel mixture at idle and slightly above. The final carburetor adjustment normally required is the idle speed adjustment. Most modern motorcycles with two or more cylinders have a single idle adjustment screw. Motorcycle manufacturers recommend a regular schedule of periodic maintenance for each bike to keep it operating efficiently. Neat and accurate documentation of all repairs is essential to the success of any service department.

Know These Terms

Tune-up
Air box
Compression test
Wet compression test
Cylinder leak-down test
Contact point gap
Dwell
Dwell meter
Ignition timing
Static ignition timing
Dynamic ignition timing
Timing light
Cam chain adjustment
Carburetor synchronization
Periodic maintenance
Documentation

Review Questions—Chapter 22

Do not write in this text. Place your answers on a separate sheet of paper.

1. Define the term *tune-up.*
2. What is the first step of any tune-up?
3. Heavy contact pitting indicates:
   A. fouled spark plugs.
   B. defective condenser.
   C. increased dwell.
   D. advanced timing.
4. Where is lubrication required on contact point ignition systems?
5. What are two ways of determining contact point gap?

6. What can happen if the contact spring and fiber washers are *not* installed correctly?

7. If contact rubbing blocks are *not* properly lubricated, which of the following can result?
   A. Premature rubbing block wear.
   B. Reduced point gap.
   C. Increased dwell.
   D. All of the above.

8. Give two reasons why dynamic timing is more accurate than static timing.

9. List four of the valve train and carburetor adjustments that are done during a tune-up.

10. A buzz box, continuity light, or _____ can be used to check static ignition timing.

11. Valve clearance that is too tight can cause _____.
    A. premature rubbing block wear.
    B. overheated valves.
    C. cam chain wear.
    D. oil consumption.

12. List three methods used for valve clearance adjustment.

13. A loose cam chain can cause all of the following, *except:*
    A. crankshaft damage.
    B. improper valve timing.
    C. chain guide damage.
    D. chain slap.

14. All of the following service procedures require carburetor adjustment afterward *except:*
    A. replacing spark plugs.
    B. adjusting valve clearance.
    C. lubricating the accelerator cable.
    D. installing a new air filter.

15. Vacuum gauges are frequently used for _____.
    A. carburetor synchronizing.
    B. measuring air-fuel delivery.
    C. adjusting valve clearance.
    D. None of the above.

Suggested Activities

1. Replace air and fuel filters and spark plugs on a motorcycle. Check the bike over for other needed work.
2. Perform a compression test. Refer to shop manual specifications to see if the engine is in good condition. Do this on several different engines.
3. Replace and adjust contact points.
4. Check and adjust static and dynamic ignition timing.
5. Check and adjust valve clearance on engines that use two different adjustment methods.

Trade schools and colleges are good places to look for training to become a motorcycle technician.

23 The Business of Motorcycle, ATV, and Scooter Service

After studying this chapter, you will be able to:

- Understand the various career opportunities available to the service technician.
- Explain the job classification available to the qualified service technician.
- Describe the duties of the service writer.
- Explain why a motorcycle, ATV, or scooter must be properly prepared for storage.
- List the procedures for storing a motorcycle, ATV, or scooter.
- Describe the procedures for returning a motorcycle, ATV, or scooter to service after storage.
- List possible component failures that can make a motorcycle unsafe.
- Explain the use of a release form.
- Describe how to inspect a motorcycle for safety related problems.
- Summarize the procedures needed to correct safety related problems.
- Explain the warranty policies that come from the bike manufacturer.

In this chapter, the various opportunities and job classifications are covered. In addition, proper methods of bike storage are described. This chapter will also briefly explain some of the problems that could lead to rider injury and possible legal action. It also discusses how to avoid unsafe conditions through competent repair procedures, inspection techniques, release forms, and other shop practices, including vehicle warranties.

Employment in the Motorcycle Industry

In Chapter 1, the need for qualified service technicians in the motorcycle industry was discussed. Qualified service technicians are needed by the two types of operations servicing motorcycles, ATVs, and scooters.

Dealership

New motorcycle ***dealerships***, **Figure 23-1,** are a major employer of service technicians and related motorcycle personnel. The dealership is the major link between the vehicle manufacturer and the customer.

Dealerships are privately-owned franchise businesses. A franchised dealership is one that has signed a contract with a particular manufacturer to sell and service a particular line of motorcycles. Many dealerships now sign contracts with more than one manufacturer.

The dealership's sales and service policies are usually set by the manufacturer. Service performed while the bike is under warranty is usually performed by dealerships or authorized service centers.

Motorcycle manufacturers have been taking an increasing role in securing service business for their dealerships. Extended warranties and service plans are designed

Figure 23-1. A typical dealership. (J.D. Gerhart)

Figure 23-2. A typical service shop. (J.D. Gerhart)

to channel repair and maintenance work to the dealerships. Some manufacturers even provide special diagnostic equipment designed specifically for their vehicles. Manufacturers stress the compatibility of their replacement parts and actively promote their service personnel as the most qualified to work on their products.

Working for a dealership backed by a major motorcycle manufacturer can have many advantages. Technical support, equipment, and the opportunity for on-going training are usually excellent. However, being tied into one or two particular model lines may limit the scope of your service expertise.

Service Shops

Independent ***service shops,*** **Figure 23-2,** service a variety of motorcycles, ATVs, and scooters without being contractually limited to any particular manufacturer's line of bikes. An independent shop may range in size from a small garage employing one to four people, to a service center employing ten or more people. It may rival some of the largest dealerships in diagnostic equipment and available training. Working in an independent shop may present constant challenges and lead to a well-rounded technical background. Many independent shops are started by technicians eager to run their own business.

Job Classifications

The motorcycle industry offers several excellent types of employment for people with a sound understanding of motorcycle, ATV, and scooter systems.

Service Technician

The most popular career choice in motorcycle service is the ***service technician.*** A service technician assesses vehicle problems, performs all necessary diagnostic tests, and competently repairs or replaces faulty components. This job requires a sound understanding of motorcycle technology, on-the-job experience, and continuous training in new technology as it is introduced by manufacturers.

Skilled service personnel are now referred to as technicians, with good reason. The term mechanic stresses the ability to repair and service mechanical systems. While this skill is still needed, it is only part of the service technician's overall job description. Today's bikes require mechanical and diagnostic knowledge plus an understanding of electronics, hydraulics, and pneumatics.

Service Writer

In most dealerships and some larger repair shops, the person who greets customers at a service center is the ***service writer*** or *service advisor.* The service writer must have a good knowledge of motorcycles plus a sound understanding of the motorcycle parts aftermarket. A friendly attitude and the ability to deal with people effectively are important. Customers discuss their vehicle problems and needs with the service writer. The service writer then consults the technician on the vehicle's diagnosis and prepares a detailed cost estimate for the customer. In smaller shops, the senior service technician or the shop's owner performs the duties of the service writer.

Parts Manager

The ***parts manager*** and other parts personnel are in charge of ordering all replacement parts for the repairs the shop performs. The ordering and timely delivery of parts is extremely important if the shop is to operate smoothly. Delays in obtaining parts or omitting a small but crucial part from an order can cause frustrating hold-ups for both the technician and the customer.

Most dealerships and large independent service shops maintain a set inventory of commonly-used parts, such as filters, belts, hoses, fasteners, and gaskets. The parts manager is responsible for maintaining this inventory. Thoroughness, attention to detail, and the ability to work with people face-to-face and over the phone are a must for parts personnel.

Service Manager

The ***service manager*** oversees the entire service operation of a large dealership or independent shop. Customer concerns and complaints are usually handled through the service manager. Service managers must have good human relations skills as well as sound technical background. In some cases, the service manager comes from the service technician ranks.

In a dealership, the service manager makes certain the motorcycle manufacturers' policies concerning warranties, service procedures, and customer relations are carried out. The service manager normally coordinates on-going training programs and keeps all shop personnel informed and working together.

Marketing and Sales

In a dealership, a technician may wish to leave the service bay for sales operations. Companies that manufacture vehicles and aftermarket parts for the motorcycle, ATV, and scooter service industry are constantly searching for knowledgeable people available to represent and sell their products. For example, a sales representative working for an aftermarket part manufacturer specializes in the company's product line, such as brake, suspension, or engine parts. The sales representative works with each shop to ensure their products are sold and installed correctly. They also help coordinate service clinics and supply support materials to ensure everyone using their products is properly trained and informed.

Storage

When a motorcycle, ATV, or scooter is not going to be used for an extended period of time, it must be stored to prevent part damage. When a bike sits for prolonged periods, condensation can cause rust and corrosion on numerous components. This is especially true in cold climates. For this reason, many dealerships and shops offer storage service. If your dealership or shop provides this service to their customers, the technician should know the proper storage procedures since improper preparation for storage can result in damage to the:

- Lubrication system.
- Fuel system.
- Suspension system.
- Ignition system.
- Exterior appearance.

Storage Preparation Procedures

The following list outlines the most important aspects for properly preparing a motorcycle, ATV, or scooter for storage. Refer to the service manual and owner's manuals for more specific manufacturer's storage recommendations.

1. Degrease the bike if necessary and thoroughly clean with soap and water. Dust and dirt retain moisture which can accelerate rust and corrosion.
2. Apply a coat of wax to the entire motorcycle (paint and chrome) to protect the finish. For extra protection, plated and aluminum surfaces may be coated with a light, petroleum based, protective spray.
3. Change all oil, including primary case, transmission, and forks. Used oil contains contaminants that promote corrosion during storage. The engine should be at operating temperature before changing oil. After refilling with fresh oil, run the engine for a few minutes until the oil has fully circulated.
4. If the bike is to be stored where the temperature will be below freezing, remove the battery and store it in a warm place. Check battery every month or so and add distilled water to maintain level. If necessary, charge with a 0.5-1 amp charger to maintain a full charge.
5. Wash any corrosion from the battery, battery box, and terminals. Neutralize these parts with baking soda and water. Coat battery and cable terminals with petroleum jelly or white grease. If the battery box has been damaged by corrosion, it should be repainted after cleaning.
6. Drain fuel tank and carburetor float bowls, or completely fill the tank and add gasoline stabilizer to prevent fuel deterioration (oxidation and gum formation) and condensation (water collection). For bikes with electronic fuel control systems, follow storage instructions to the letter.
7. Squirt some 40 weight oil in the spark plug holes and turn the engine over a few times to coat the cylinders. Do this once a month to prevent the cylinders and rings from rusting. Be sure to remove the spark plugs before turning the engine over as oil does not compress. Serious damage to the connecting rods and crankshaft may result if plugs are not removed. Vapor plugs may be installed in the spark plug holes to prevent moisture or rust build-up.
8. Ignition points should be in the open position to prevent corrosion. A strip of paper may be placed between the contacts.
9. Clean and lubricate drive chains, if equipped.
10. Lubricate all cables.
11. Lubricate levers, brake pedal, and all grease fittings.

12. Inflate tires to the recommended air pressure.
13. Park the bike on its center stand. If it does not have one, place it on blocks. The full weight of the bike must not rest on the tires.
14. Cover the bike with a suitable dust cover. Avoid airtight covering material such as sheet plastic, since it can trap moisture and promote rust. If possible, check the bike every few weeks to make sure no rust is developing.

Returning the Bike to Service

After storage, a motorcycle, ATV, or scooter should be serviced and closely inspected before being operated. You should perform the operations listed below.

1. If the bike has been stored with the fuel tank empty, rinse with fresh fuel, and clean the filter screen to remove any residue.
2. If the bike has been in storage several months and there has been considerable temperature fluctuation, change the oil, since there could be condensation in the oil.
3. Remove spark plugs or vapor plugs and turn the engine over several times to blow excess oil out the cylinders.
4. Remove valve covers and squirt some oil on the valve stems, rocker arms, cam chain, and cam.
5. Check ignition timing, plug gap, valve clearance, and cam chain tension.
6. Check and adjust all cables and drive chains.
7. Check the operation of suspension components and electrical equipment.
8. Warm engine to operating temperature and adjust the carburetors, if equipped.
9. Check all nuts and bolts to make sure they are tight.
10. Test ride slowly.

Liability

The word ***liability*** means "responsible under legal obligation." This implies that you are responsible for any work you perform on a motorcycle. The only way to satisfy this obligation is to always do quality, safety-oriented repair work. Safety-oriented repairs require you to use common sense and a conscientious work attitude.

Unsafe Conditions

A number of conditions can make a motorcycle unsafe:

- Normal wear of components.
- Improper service or repair procedures.
- Aftermarket add-on accessories.

A good example of an unsafe condition caused by normal wear is a worn final drive chain. The chain can break, locking up the rear wheel. A serious accident could result. It is up to the technician to find and correct normal wear problems that could cause injury to the rider.

An incorrectly routed throttle cable or a loose axle nut are examples of unsafe conditions that can be caused by improper service or repair operations. A technician could be liable for injuries or deaths caused by incorrect repairs. Always double-check your work. Aftermarket add-on accessories that can change aerodynamic stability, cause overloading, or change suspension geometry can upset normal handling and stability. This could make the motorcycle unsafe. Make sure any accessory is safe to use before installation. Make sure all aftermarket accessories, no matter how small, are properly installed.

Manufacturer Recalls

All manufacturers have an excellent safety record and make every effort to produce safe vehicles of superior quality. A ***manufacturer recall*** occurs if a possible safety defect or other problem is discovered in a certain vehicle model. Each customer and dealer is notified of the recall and what is needed to correct the situation.

Recalls are very rare and perhaps you will never deal with one. However, if you are working in a dealership and are involved in a recall campaign, make every effort to get the affected vehicles into the shop for repairs as quickly as possible.

Inspecting for Unsafe Conditions

Anytime work is done on a motorcycle, ATV, or scooter, a quick safety check should be completed. A typical safety check involves inspection of the following:

- Operation of the lights and horn.
- Steering head condition and adjustment.
- Condition of wheels and tires.
- Tire pressure.
- Chain condition and adjustment.
- Tightness of the suspension components.
- All fluid (oil, brake fluid, coolant) levels.
- Condition of control cables.
- Operation and condition of brakes.
- Proper auto throttle return.
- Tightness of important nuts and bolts.

Safety related inspection instructions are found throughout most manufacturer's shop manuals and owner's manuals. You should make a special effort to become familiar with these instructions before performing a motorcycle safety inspection.

Correcting Unsafe Conditions

When an unsafe condition is found, take immediate action to correct the problem. If the motorcycle belongs to a customer, they must be notified. If the owner will not authorize the necessary repairs, make sure a proper release statement is filled out and signed by the owner.

Figure 23-3 shows an example of a typical release statement. The problem would be filled in and the customer would sign at the bottom. Motorcycle shops have work orders and prescribed plans for handling this situation. The customer's signature will help release the technician and shop from potential liability claims.

Preventing Liability Problems

A complete list of precautionary measures to prevent liability problems would be extremely lengthy. The following are a few precautions that should be taken:

- In a motorcycle dealership, good communications between the sales and service departments can help in the selection of accessories. It is important that accessories be properly suited to the motorcycle, to the customer's riding style, and to the intended use of the bike.
- When replacing tires, do not make extreme changes in tire profile or size and do not mix and match tires. On touring bikes, make sure replacement tires have the proper ratings.

NAME OF SHOP

123 West Taft
Tinley Park, IL 60473

From: ____________________

To: ____________________

THIS MOTORCYCLE NEEDS ____________________

____

____

TO BE ROADWORTHY, THE CUSTOMER/OWNER ACCEPTS THE MOTORCYCLE AS IS AND ACCEPTS ALL RESPONSIBILITY FOR ITS UNSAFE CONDITION.

Signature ____________________

Figure 23-3. This type of form will help release the technician and the shop from possible liability litigation.

- Do not patch inner tubes, replace them. Also, do not attempt to straighten bent frames or suspension components.
- Follow manufacturer's prescribed repair procedures. Do not take shortcuts.
- A neat, orderly work area, minimum interruptions while working, checklists, proper tool selection, and the desire to do things right will make it easy to complete a thorough repair job.
- Common sense and a safety conscious attitude are mandatory in a motorcycle shop. You must work at being a responsible technician.

Warranty

All dealerships and some vehicle repair shops, regularly perform service covered under a ***manufacturers' warranty.*** These shops recognize the manufacturers' warranty as one of the most valuable tools in the service department. However, like any tool, it is only worthwhile if used correctly.

The technician's primary goal, after satisfying the customer, is to make sure the shop will be reimbursed by the manufacturer for all warranty work performed. To get warranty credit quickly and easily, the manufacturer's warranty system and how it works must be clearly understood. In some cases, it may be necessary for the shop to retain the defective parts so they can be examined by a manufacturer's representative.

When a motorcycle, ATV, or scooter comes in for service, the following questions should be asked:

- Is the bike covered by warranty?
- Has the cause of the failure been determined?
- Is the failure due to a manufacturing defect?
- Is prior authorization needed before beginning the repair?

If the repair is not covered by warranty, make sure the situation is properly explained to the customer. When a customer brings an in-warranty bike in for a repair, the question the service department and the customer both have in mind is "Will warranty cover it?" Sometimes the answer may seem obvious; other times, the answer might not be clear. The following steps are recommended by motorcycle manufacturers to verify warranty coverage:

Note: Warranty policies vary slightly from one manufacturer to another. Check the specific manufacturer's policies.

Step 1. Is the bike covered by warranty?

- Check the date of sale on the bike. Check the Product Identification label in the unit's owner's manual.

Check the dealership's (or shop's) file for a date of sale if the customer purchased the unit from your business.

- Confirm the length of the warranty for the unit by reading the section "The Period of Warranty" in the Limited Warranty Statement.
- Confirm the failure or problem is covered by warranty. Check the Limited Warranty Statement for any specific limits on warranty coverage.

Step 2. Has the root cause of failure been determined?

- Determine the cause of the problem.
- If the cause of the problem cannot be determined without disassembly or diagnostic labor, you must explain to the customer that the limited warranty covers only the repair of manufacturing defects. If the failure is not due to a manufacturing defect, the customer will be charged for diagnostic work and any repair charges.

Step 3. Is the failure due to a manufacturing defect? After determining the cause of the problem, check the list of specific exclusions in the warranty statement. Test the failure against these exclusions:

- Is the failure due to normal wear?
- Is the repair normal maintenance?
- Is the failure a result of competition use?
- Is the failure due to installation of aftermarket parts or accessories not equivalent in quality to the manufacturer's parts?
- Is the failure due to abnormal strain, neglect, or abuse?
- Is the failure a result of accident or collision damage?
- Is the failure due to customer modification of original parts?

A yes answer to any one of the above questions means the problem is not covered under warranty. Periodically most manufacturers establish a position on a gray area of warranty coverage or particular component. Dealership personnel must be aware of these changes when they are announced. Keep a list of current warranty policies as a reference. Update the list when new warranty policies are announced by manufacturers.

Step 4. Is prior authorization needed before beginning the repair? This is one of the most important steps in the warranty process. After determining whether the failure was caused by a manufacturing defect, decide if authorization from the manufacturer is needed before repairing the unit. In most cases, it is mandatory that authorization is obtained from the manufacturer or their regional technical advisor before replacing any parts, even if the bike is in warranty.

Step 5. Has the situation been explained to the customer? If the failure is found not to be a warranty covered defect, or the unit is not covered by warranty, contact the customer and discuss the situation immediately.

Working in the Field

After completion of this course or graduation, you will be moving from an educational setting to the workforce. There are many adjustments you will have to make during this period. You will be moving from classroom motorcycles that disassemble easily to bikes in the field where bolts break, threads strip, and mating surfaces refuse to part without great effort. This transition period is difficult, and sometimes proves too much for some technicians. Often, technicians who do not succeed in the field fail because of poor personal traits and/or insensitivity to the workforce diversity, not from a lack of training or ability. The ability to work with many groups of people is the most important skill you can develop.

In many cases, you will probably be working under the guidance of an experienced technician. Listen carefully to any instructions any experienced technician or shop supervisor gives you. While your training has given you many skills to begin your career, they are only a fundamental base that will be built upon and tempered by years of work experience.

At first, you will be assigned simple tasks, then more complex jobs as your experience increases. These duties, such as washing parts, will at first seem unworthy of your training. But however trivial these first assignments may seem, work hard and give them your best efforts. Remember, they are as important as the most complex job. It may not be apparent, but these initial assignments will be closely monitored and checked. Every shop also has its share of housekeeping chores that must be done. In most shops, each technician is responsible for the upkeep and cleanliness of his or her work area. Floors must be swept and mopped, air compressor tanks drained, and spills cleaned.

There is a premium on technicians that have the ability to get things done. Most technicians quickly realize the importance of being a self-starter, but what many miss is the other half of the equation: being a sure finisher. The extra effort is always worth the payoff, however, do not expect to be recognized or rewarded every time extra effort is expended. The true value is in the self-esteem gained by knowing your own self-worth, and the respect you earn from your co-workers and managers.

Finally, regard your integrity as one of your most important assets. Uncompromising integrity must be worked at constantly. Remember that everything you do reflects on the industry as a whole. The profession of motorcycle service and repair, even with its occasional moments of frustration and adverse working condition, offers a most rewarding career.

Summary

Qualified service technicians are needed by the two types of operations servicing motorcycles, ATVs, and scooters. New motorcycle dealerships and independent service shops make up the majority of businesses that hire motorcycle technicians. The motorcycle industry offers several excellent types of employment for people with a sound understanding of motorcycle, ATV, and scooter systems.

The most popular career choice in motorcycle service is the service technician. A service technician assesses vehicle problems, performs all necessary diagnostic tests, and competently repairs or replaces faulty components. The person who greets customers at a service center is the service writer or service advisor. The parts manager and other parts personnel are in charge of ordering all replacement parts for the repairs the shop performs. The service manager oversees the entire service operation of a large dealership or independent shop.

When a motorcycle, ATV, or scooter is not going to be used for an extended period of time, it must be stored to prevent part damage. Many dealerships and shops offer storage service. You should know the proper storage procedures since improper preparation for storage can result in damage to the lubrication, fuel, suspension, and ignition systems as well as exterior appearance. After storage, a motorcycle, ATV, or scooter should be serviced and closely inspected before being operated.

The word liability means responsible under legal obligation. This implies that you are responsible for any work you perform on a motorcycle. A number of conditions can make a motorcycle unsafe. A manufacturer recall occurs if a possible safety defect or other problem is discovered in a certain vehicle model. Recalls are very rare and perhaps you will never deal with one. If the owner will not authorize the necessary repairs, make sure a proper release statement is filled out and signed by the owner. All dealerships and some bike repair shops, regularly perform service covered under a manufacturers' warranty. The technician's primary goal, after satisfying the customer, is to make sure the shop will be reimbursed by the manufacturer for all warranty work performed. If the repair is not covered by warranty, make sure the situation is properly explained to the customer.

Know These Terms

Dealerships
Service shops
Service technician
Service writer
Parts manager
Service manager
Liability
Manufacturer recall
Manufacturers' warranty

Review Questions—Chapter 23

Do not write in this text. Place your answers on a separate sheet of paper.

1. Name the two job opportunities most offered to service technicians.
2. The ______ normally greets customers at a service center.
   A. service technician
   B. service writer
   C. service manager
   D. parts manager
3. List five motorcycle systems that can be damaged by improper storage.
4. *True* or *False?* It is best to store a motorcycle with used oil and then change the oil in the spring after the first ride.
5. *True* or *False?* You should add distilled water to a battery in storage.
6. What is added to gasoline to prevent deterioration and condensation?
7. Which of the following is *not* done when storing a motorcycle?
   A. Cover the motorcycle.
   B. Squirt oil in spark plug holes.
   C. Tie the suspension in the compressed position.
   D. Inflate tires to specifications.
8. *True* or *False?* Tune-up adjustments may be necessary before removing a motorcycle from storage.
9. List four conditions that make a motorcycle unsafe.
10. Which of the following would *not* be an example of normal wear?
    A. Final drive chain stretch.
    B. No tread on tires.
    C. Cracked frame.
    D. Thin brake pads.
11. How can aftermarket add-on accessories alter the safety of a motorcycle?
12. If a possible safety defect is present on a certain model motorcycle, a ______ will notify the customer or dealer of the problem and needed repair.
    A. service manual
    B. owners manual
    C. indicator light
    D. manufacturer recall
13. What is the function of a release form or statement?

14. Name in order the steps necessary to verify a bike's warranty coverage.

15. *True* or *False?* Manufacturer's approval is not necessary under warranty agreement.

Suggested Activities

1. Using the information in your service manual and this chapter, prepare a motorcycle for storage.
2. Ready a motorcycle for use, after storage.
3. Make up a checklist for pre-storage and post-storage service.
4. Inspect several motorcycles for problems that could affect safety.
5. Obtain and read manufacturers' recall notices. Note the types of problems and repairs.

Appendix A

Diagnostic Charts

This Appendix will allow you to look up the causes and corrections for various motorcycle, ATV, and scooter problems. These charts do not cover all the possible causes of trouble. It should be helpful, however, as a guide to troubleshooting. Refer to the relative procedure in this manual for inspection, adjustment, and replacement of parts.

Engine

No-Start/Hard Starting

Fuel System

- Empty fuel tank.
- Clogged fuel filter.
- Clogged fuel breather hose.
- Deteriorated fuel or fuel containing water or foreign material.
- Faulty fuel pump.
- Pinched fuel delivery hoses.
- Pinched fuel return hose.
- Misadjusted or leaky float.
- Clogged carburetor jet.
- Worn needle and jet.
- Clogged injector.
- Faulty injector.
- Faulty pressure regulator.
- Cracked or clogged pulsor hoses.
- Clogged fuel distributor pipe.
- Vacuum leak.
- Faulty ECM.
- Faulty EFI main relay.

Air Cleaner

- Clogged air filter.

Throttle Body

- Improperly adjusted air screws.
- Vacuum leak.
- Fast idle system malfunction.

Ignition

- CDI unit defective.
- Faulty camshaft sensor.
- Faulty crankshaft sensor.
- Faulty spark plug cap.
- Faulty spark plug lead.
- Ignition coil defective.
- Ignition coil resistor open.
- Ignition or engine stop switch shorted.
- Pick-up coil defective.
- Spark plug cap not in good contact.
- Spark plug dirty, broken, or misadjusted.
- Spark plug loose.
- Wiring shorted or open.

Cylinder and Cylinder Head

- Loose spark plug.
- Loose cylinder head or cylinder.
- Compression low.
- Blown cylinder head gasket.
- Worn, damaged, or seized cylinder.
- Improperly sealed valve.
- Improperly contacted valve and valve seat.
- Improper valve timing.
- Broken valve spring.

Piston and Piston Rings

- Improperly installed piston ring.
- Worn, fatigued, or broken piston ring.
- Seized piston ring.
- Seized or damaged piston.

Crankcase and Crankshaft

- Improperly seated crankcase.
- Seized crankshaft.

Poor Idle Speed Performance

Fuel System

- Carburetor idle circuit misadjusted.
- Vacuum leak in carburetor.
- Clogged injector.
- Faulty injector.

Throttle Body

- Improperly synchronized intake air pressure.
- Improperly adjusted idle speed (idle speed adjusting screw).
- Improper throttle cable play.
- Improperly fast idle system.

Ignition

- Spark weak.
- Spark plug dirty, broken, or misadjusted.
- Spark plug cap or plug wire trouble.
- Spark plug incorrect.
- CDI unit defective.
- Pick-up coil defective.
- Faulty ignition coil.
- Ignition coil resistor open.
- Ignition timing incorrect.

Electrical System

- Faulty battery.
- Faulty ECM.
- Faulty crankshaft sensor.
- Faulty camshaft sensor.
- Faulty ignition coil.

Valve Train

- Improperly adjusted valve clearance.

Air Cleaner

- Clogged air filter.

Poor Medium and High Speed Performance

Also refer to *No-Start/Hard Starting.*

Fuel System

- Defect in power circuit.
- Leaking accelerator pump.
- Clogged injector.
- Faulty injector.
- Faulty pressure regulator.

Ignition

- Spark plug dirty, broken, or misadjusted.
- Spark plug cap or plug wire trouble.
- Spark plug incorrect.
- Spark plug loose.
- CDI unit defective.
- Pick-up coil defective.
- Ignition coil defective.
- Ignition coil resistor open.
- Timing not advancing.

Throttle Body

- Vacuum leak at gasket.

Air Cleaner

- Clogged air filter.

Knocking or Abnormal Engine Noise

- Spark plug incorrect.
- Timing not advancing.
- Internal engine damage.

Ignition Firing Incorrect

- Spark plug dirty, damaged, or misadjusted.
- Plug wires crossed.
- Spark plug incorrect.

Excessive Smoke and/or Carbon on the Spark Plugs

Lubrication Systems, Two-Stroke Engines with Oil Injection System

- Faulty oil pump (too much oil flow).
- Low quality engine oil.

Lubrication Systems, Two-Stroke Engines Using Premixed Oil

- Improper jetting for altitude, air temperature, and external conditions.
- Improper fuel-oil mixture; too much oil in fuel.
- Fuel-oil mixture too old; gasoline has evaporated/ gone bad.

Overheating or Seized Piston

Lubrication Systems, Two-Stroke Engines with Oil Injection System

- No oil in tank or clogged oil line.
- Air in oil lines.
- Faulty oil pump (too little oil flow).
- Clogged oil strainer.

Oil not flowing out of tank.
Clogged oil tank cap breather hole.
Clogged oil strainer.

Lubrication Systems, Two-Stroke Engines Using Premixed Oil

- Improper jetting for altitude, air temperature, and external conditions.
- Fuel-oil mixture too old; oxidized oil/degraded lubrication.
- Premix oil too old; oxidized/degraded lubrication.
- Poor quality oil.
- Improper fuel-oil mixture; too little oil in fuel.

Oil Level Low

- External oil leaks.
- Worn piston ring or incorrect piston ring installation.
- Worn valve guide or seal.
- Oil pump worn or damaged (dry sump engine).

Low or No Oil Pressure

- Clogged oil orifice(s).
- Incorrect oil being used.
- Defective oil pump.
- Leaking oil seal.

Oil Contamination (White Appearance)

- Coolant mixing with oil (liquid-cooled engine).
- Faulty water pump mechanical seal.
- Faulty head gasket.
- Water leak in crankcase.

Engine Overheating

- Faulty temperature gauge or sensor.
- Thermostat stuck closed.
- Faulty radiator cap.
- Insufficient coolant.
- Passages blocked in radiator, hoses, or water jacket.
- Air in system.
- Faulty cooling fan motor.
- Faulty fan motor switch.
- Faulty water pump.
- Poorly tuned engine.
- Improper spark plug gap.
- Improper spark plug heat range.
- Faulty ECM.
- Clogged injector.
- Faulty injector.
- Faulty pressure regulator.
- Clogged air filter.
- Heavy carbon build-up.
- Incorrect oil level.
- Improper oil viscosity.
- Inferior oil quality.

Engine Temperature Too Low

- Faulty temperature gauge or gauge sensor.
- Thermostat stuck open.
- Faulty cooling fan motor switch.

Coolant Leaks

- Faulty pump mechanical seal.
- Deteriorated O-rings.
- Faulty radiator cap.
- Damaged or deteriorated gaskets.
- Loose hose connection or clamp.
- Damaged or deteriorated hoses.

Electrical System

No-Start/Hard Starting

- Faulty main switch.
- Faulty engine stop switch.
- Defective or shorted wiring.
- Faulty neutral switch.
- Faulty start switch.
- Faulty sidestand switch.
- Faulty clutch switch.

Starter Motor

- Faulty starter motor.
- Faulty starter relay.
- Faulty circuit cut-off relay.
- Faulty starter clutch.

Headlight Dark

- Improper bulb.
- Too many electric accessories.
- Defective stator coil wire.
- Faulty rectifier/regulator.
- Incorrect connection.
- Poorly grounded.
- Poor contacts (main or light switch).
- Bulb burnt out.

Flasher Does Not Light

- Poorly grounded.
- Discharged battery.
- Faulty turn switch.
- Faulty flasher relay.
- Broken wire harness.
- Bulb burnt out.
- Faulty fuse.
- Improper bulb.
- Faulty battery.
- Faulty rectifier/regulator.
- Faulty main and/or light switch.

Flasher Stays On

- Faulty flasher relay.
- Bulb burnt out.

Flasher Blinks Quickly

- Improper bulb.
- Faulty flasher relay.
- Bulb burnt out.

Flasher Winks Slowly

- Faulty flasher relay.
- Faulty main and/or turn switch.

Horn Inoperative

- Faulty battery.
- Faulty fuse.
- Faulty main and/or horn switch.
- Improperly adjusted horn switch.
- Faulty horn.
- Broken wire harness.

Transmission

Hard Shifting

- Refer to *Clutch Dragging.*

Shift Pedal Does Not Move

- Improperly adjusted shift rod.
- Bent shift shaft.
- Seized shift fork.
- Bent shift fork guide bar.
- Seized transmission gear.
- Incorrectly assembled transmission.

Transmission Jumps Out of Gear

- Improperly adjusted.
- Improperly returned stopper lever.
- Worn shift fork.
- Improper thrust play.
- Worn shift cam groove.
- Worn gear dog.

Clutch

Clutch Slipping

- Air in clutch fluid.
- Loose clutch spring.
- Fatigued clutch spring.
- Worn friction plate/clutch plate.
- Incorrectly assembled clutch.
- Low oil level.
- Improper quality/low viscosity.

Clutch Dragging

- Warped pressure plate.
- Unevenly tensioned clutch springs.
- Match marks not aligned.
- Bent push rod.
- Broken clutch boss.
- Burnt primary driven gear bushing.
- Bent clutch plate.
- Swollen friction plate.
- Improper oil level.
- Improper quality/high viscosity.

Final Drive

Excessive Noise in Final Drive

- Worn or damaged ring gear and driven flange.
- Damaged driven flange or wheel hub.
- Excessive backlash between pinion and ring gears.
- Low oil level.
- Worn or damaged pinion gear and/or pinion joint splines.

Excessive Noise in Side Gear

- Worn or damaged output shaft and final drive shaft gears.
- Worn or damaged side gear case bearing.
- Incorrect adjustment shim.

Excessive Rear Wheel Backlash

- Worn drive shaft splines.
- Excessive backlash between ring gear and pinion gear.
- Worn driven flange and ring gear splines.
- Excessive play in final drive case bearings.
- Worn drive shaft, universal joint, and/or pinion joint splines.
- Excessive play or worn universal joint bearing.

Oil Leak at Final Gear Case

- Clogged breather hole.
- Too much oil.
- Faulty oil seal(s).

Engine Starts but Vehicle Will Not Move

- Worn drive belt.
- Damaged ramp plate.
- Worn or damaged clutch lining.

Engine Stalls or Vehicle Creeps

- Broken clutch shoe springs.

Poor Performance at High Speeds or Lack of Power

- Worn drive belt.
- Weak driven face spring.
- Worn weight roller.
- Faulty driven pulley face.

Wheels and Tires

Hard Steering

- Steering head bearing adjustment nut too tight.
- Faulty steering head bearings.
- Damaged steering head bearings.
- Insufficient tire pressure.
- Faulty tire.

Steers to One Side or Does Not Track Straight

- Unevenly adjusted shock absorbers.
- Bent fork.
- Bent front axle; wheel installed incorrectly.
- Faulty steering head bearing.
- Bent frame.
- Worn wheel bearing.
- Worn swing arm pivot.

Unstable Handling

- Incorrect wheel balance.
- Deformed wheel.
- Damaged bearing.
- Bent or loose wheel axle.
- Excessive wheel run-out.

Front Wheel Wobbling

- Bent rim.
- Worn front wheel bearings.
- Faulty tire.

Wheel Turns Hard

- Misadjusted brake.
- Faulty wheel bearing.
- Faulty speedometer gear.

Brakes

Mechanical Drum Brakes

Poor Brake Performance

- Improperly adjusted brake.
- Worn brake linings.
- Worn brake drum.
- Worn brake cam.
- Improperly installed brake linings.
- Brake cable sticking/needs lubrication.
- Contaminated brake linings.
- Contaminated brake drum.
- Worn brake shoes at cam contact areas.
- Improper engagement between brake arm and camshaft serrations.

Brake Lever Hard or Slow to Return

- Worn/broken return spring.
- Improperly adjusted brake.
- Sticking brake drum due to contamination.
- Worn brake shoes at cam contact areas.
- Brake cable sticking/needs lubrication.
- Worn brake cam.
- Improperly installed brake linings.

Brake Squeaks

- Worn brake linings.
- Worn brake drum.
- Contaminated brake linings.
- Contaminated brake drum.

Hydraulic Disc Brakes

Poor Brake Performance

- Worn brake pads.
- Worn disc.
- Air in brake fluid.
- Leaking brake fluid.
- Faulty cylinder kit cup.
- Faulty caliper kit seal.
- Loose union bolt.
- Broken brake hose.
- Oily or greasy disc/brake pads.
- Improper brake fluid level.

Brake Lever/Pedal Soft or Spongy

- Air bubbles in the hydraulic system.
- Leaking hydraulic system.
- Contaminated brake pad/disc.
- Worn caliper piston seal.
- Worn master cylinder piston.
- Worn brake pad.
- Contaminated caliper.
- Caliper not sliding properly.
- Low fluid level.
- Clogged fluid passage.
- Warped/deformed brake disc.
- Worn brake disc.
- Sticking/worn caliper piston.
- Sticking/worn master cylinder piston.
- Contaminated master cylinder.
- Bent brake lever/pedal.

Brake Lever and/or Pedal Hard

- Clogged/restricted brake system.
- Sticking/worn caliper piston.
- Caliper not sliding properly.
- Clogged/restricted fluid passage.
- Worn caliper piston seal.
- Sticking/worn master cylinder piston.
- Bent brake lever/pedal.

Brake Grab or Pull to One Side

- Contaminated brake pad/disc.
- Misaligned wheel.
- Clogged/restricted brake hose.
- Warped/deformed brake disc.
- Caliper not sliding properly.

Brake Drag

- Contaminated brake pad/disc.
- Misaligned wheel.
- Worn brake pad/disc.
- Warped/deformed brake disc.
- Caliper not sliding properly.

Leakage of Brake Fluid

- Insufficient tightening of connection points.
- Cracked hose.
- Worn piston and/or cap.

ABS System

- Note: If an ABS problem is suspected, you must inspect for and service any defects in the hydraulic system and other brake components first before investigating the ABS system.

ABS Light on at All Times

- Problem in the brake hydraulic system. See *Hydraulic Disc Brakes.*
- No power to the ABS system.
- Defective fail-safe relay.
- Defective hydraulic unit.
- Defective ECM.

ABS Light Comes on While Moving

- Defective or disconnected wheel speed sensor.
- Excessive clearance between sensor and rotor.
- Open or short in ABS sensor wiring harness.
- Defective ECM.

ABS Light Comes on While Braking

- Problem in the brake hydraulic system. See *Hydraulic Disc Brakes.*
- Defective fail-safe relay.
- Defective hydraulic unit.
- Defective wheel speed sensor.
- Defective ECM.

Frame

Unstable Handling

- Frame twisted.
- Damaged head pipe.
- Improperly installed bearing race.

Abnormal Engine Vibration

- Cracked or damaged engine mounts.
- Cracked, damaged, or bent welded portions.
- Bent or damaged frame.
- Engine problems.

Abnormal Noise when Riding

- Damaged or bent engine mounts.
- Damaged welded points.
- Damaged or bent frame.

Steers to One Side when Accelerating or Decelerating

- Bent frame.
- Bent fork.
- Bent swingarm.

Front Suspension

Hard Steering

- Steering head bearing adjustment nut too tight.
- Faulty steering head bearing.
- Damaged steering head bearings.
- Insufficient tire pressure.
- Faulty tire.

Unstable Handling

- Improperly installed handlebar crown.
- Bent steering stem.
- Improperly installed steering shaft (improperly tightened ring nut).
- Damaged ball bearing or bearing race.
- Improperly installed steering tube.
- Damaged steering tube.
- Damaged ball on the joint ring.
- Bent or damaged knuckle arm.
- Damaged ball joint or knuckle arm.
- Improperly adjusted front wheel camber.
- Incorrect tire pressure.
- Unevenly worn tires.
- Incorrect wheel balance.
- Deformed case wheel.
- Damaged bearing.
- Bent or loose wheel axle.
- Excessive wheel run-out.

Steers to One Side or Does not Track Straight

- Unevenly adjusted right and left shock absorbers.
- Bent fork.
- Bent front axle.
- Wheel installed incorrectly.
- Faulty steering head bearings.
- Bent frame.
- Worn wheel bearing.
- Worn swingarm pivot components.

Front Wheel Wobbling

- Bent rim.
- Loose nut on axle.
- Worn front wheel bearings.
- Faulty or incorrect tire.
- Incorrect front fork oil.

Wheel Turns Hard

- Brake misadjusted.
- Faulty wheel bearing.
- Faulty speedometer gear.

Soft Suspension

- Weak fork springs.
- Insufficient fluid in fork.
- Low fluid level in fork.

Hard Suspension

- Bent fork components.
- Bent damper rod (bottom link).
- Incorrect fluid weight.
- Bent fork tubes.
- Clogged fluid passage.

Front Suspension Noisy

- Worn slider or guide bushings (bottom link).
- Insufficient fluid in fork.
- Loose fork fasteners.
- Lack of grease in speedometer gearbox.

Rear Suspension

Rear Wheel Wobbling

- Distorted wheel rim.
- Worn wheel bearing or swingarm bearing.
- Defective or incorrect tire.
- Loose nuts or bolts on rear suspension.
- Loose nut on axle.

Unstable Handling

- Fatigued spring.
- Oil and gas leakage.
- Worn bearing or bushing.
- Incorrect tire pressure.
- Unevenly worn tires.
- Incorrect wheel balance.
- Deformed case wheel.
- Damaged bearing.
- Bent or loose wheel axle.
- Excessive wheel run-out.

Soft Suspension

- Weak spring(s).
- Oil leakage from damper unit.
- Air or gas leakage.
- Incorrect shock absorber adjustment.

Hard Suspension

- Incorrectly mounted suspension components.
- Incorrect shock absorber adjustment.
- Bent swingarm pivot.
- Bent shock absorber rod.
- Damaged swingarm pivot bearing(s).
- Faulty suspension linkage.
- Damaged linkage pivot bearings.

Rear Suspension Noisy

- Loose nuts or bolts on rear suspension.
- Worn swingarm and rear cushion related bearings.

Conversion Charts

Some Common Abbreviations

U.S. Customary Unit	Abbreviation	Metric Unit	Abbreviation
inch	in.	kilometer	km
feet	ft.	hectometer	hm
yard	yd.	dekameter	dam
mile	mi.	meter	m
grain	gr.	decimeter	dm
ounce	oz.	centimeter	cm
pound	lb.	millimeter	mm
teaspoon	tsp.	cubic centimeter	cm^3
tablespoon	tbsp.	kilogram	kg
fluid ounce	fl.oz.	hectogram	hg
cup	c.	dekagram	dkg
pint	pt.	gram	g
quart	qt.	decigram	dg
gallon	gal.	centigram	cg
cubic inch	in^3	milligram	mg
cubic foot	ft^3	kiloliter	kL
cubic yard	yd^3	hectoliter	hL
square inch	in^2	dekaliter	dL
square foot	ft^2	liter	L
square yard	yd^2	centiliter	cL
square mile	mi^2	milliliter	mL
Fahrenheit	F	square kilometer	km^2
barrel	bbl.	hectare	ha
fluid dram	fl. dr.	are	a
board foot	bd. ft.	centare	ca
rod	rd.	tonne	t
dram	dr.	Celsius	C
bushel	bu.		

Measuring Systems

U.S. Customary	Metric
Length	
12 inches = 1 foot	1 kilometer = 1000 meters
36 inches = 1 yard	1 hectometer = 100 meters
3 feet = 1 yard	1 dekameter = 10 meters
5,280 feet = 1 mile	1 meter = 1 meter
16.5 feet = 1 rod	1 decimeter = 0.1 meter
320 rods = 1 mile	1 centimeter = 0.01 meter
6 feet = 1 fathom	1 millimeter = 0.001 meter
Weight	
27.34 grains = 1 dram	1 tonne = 1,000,000 grams
438 grains = 1 ounce	1 kilogram = 1000 grams
16 drams = 1 ounce	1 hectogram = 100 grams
16 ounces = 1 pound	1 dekagram = 10 grams
2000 pounds = 1 short ton	1 gram = 1 gram
2240 pounds = 1 long ton	1 decigram = 0.1 gram
25 pounds = 1 quarter	1 centigram = 0.01 gram
4 quarters = 1 cwt	1 milligram = 0.001 gram
Volume	
8 ounces = 1 cup	1 hectoliter = 100 liters
16 ounces = 1 pint	I dekaliter = 10 liters
32 ounces = 1 quart	1 liter = 1 liter
2 cups = 1 pint	1 deciliter = 0.1 liter
2 pints = 1 quart	1 centiliter = 0.01 liter
4 quarts = 1 gallon	1 millileter = 0.001 liter
8 pints = 1gallon	1000 millileter = 1 liter
Area	
144 sq. inches = 1 sq. foot	100 sq. millimeters = 1 sq. centimeter
9 sq. feet = 1 sq. yard	100 sq. centimeters = 1 sq. decimeter
43,560 sq. ft. = 160 sq. rods	100 sq. decimeters = 1 sq. meter
160 sq. rods = 1 acre	10,000 sq. meters = 1 hectare
640 acres = 1 sq. mile	

Temperature

Fahrenheit		Celsius
32°F	Water freezes	0°C
68°F	Reasonable room temperature	20°C
98.6°F	Normal body temperature	37°C
173°F	Alcohol boils	78.34°C
121°F	Water boils	100°C

Useful Conversions

When you know:	Multiply by:	To find:

Torque		
pound-inch pound-foot	0.11298 1 .3558	newton-meters (N•m) newton-meters
Light		
foot candles	1.0764	lumens/meters^2 (lm/m^2)
Fuel Performance		
miles/gallons	0.4251	kilometers/liter (km/L)
Speed		
miles/hour	1.6093	kilometers/hr (km/h)
Force		
kilogram ounce pound	9.807 0.278 4.448	newtons (n) newtons newtons
Power		
horsepower	0.746	kilowatts (kw)
Pressure or Stress		
inches of water pounds/sq. in.	0.2491 6.895	kilopascals (kPa) kilopascals
Energy or Work		
btu foot-pound kilowatt-hour	1055.0 1.3558 3600000.0	joules (J) joules joules

Conversion Table
Metric to U.S. Customary

When you know:	Multiply by: * = Exact		To find:
	Very Accurate	Approximate	
Length			
millimeters	0.0393701	0.04	inches
centimeters	0.3937008	0.4	inches
meters	3.280840	3.3	feet
meters	1.093613	1.1	yards
kilometers	0.621371	0.6	miles
Weight			
grains	0.00228571	0.0023	ounces
grams	0.03527396	0.035	ounces
kilograms	2.204623	2.2	pounds
tonnes	1.1023113	1.1	short tons
Volume			
milliliters	0.20001	0.2	teaspoons
milliliters	0.06667	0.067	tablespoons
milliliters	0.03381402	0.03	fluid ounces
liters	61.02374	61.024	cubic inches
liters	2.113376	2.1	pints
liters	1.056688	1.06	quarts
liters	0.26417205	0.26	gallons
liters	0.03531467	0.035	cubic feet
cubic meters	61023.74	61023.7	cubic inches
cubic meters	35.31467	35.0	cubic feet
cubic meters	1.3079506	1.3	cubic yards
cubic meters	264.17205	264.0	gallons
Area			
square centimeters	0.1550003	0.16	square inches
square centimeters	0.00107639	0.001	square feet
square meters	10.76391	10.8	square feet
square meters	1.195990	1.2	square yards
square kilometers		0.4	square miles
hectares	2.471054	2.5	acres
Temperature			
Celsius	*9/5 (then add 32)		Fahrenheit

Conversion Table
U.S. Customary to Metric

When you know:	Multiply by: * = Exact		To find:
	Very Accurate	Approximate	
Length			
inches	* 25.4		millimeter
inches	* 2.54		centimeter
feet	* 0.3048		meters
feet	* 30.48		centimeters
yards	* 0.9144	0.9	meters
miles	* 1.609344	1.6	kilometers
Weight			
grains	15.43236	15.4	grams
ounces	* 28.349523125	28.0	grams
ounces	* 0.028349523125	.028	kilograms
pounds	* 0.45359237	0.45	kilograms
ton	* 0.90718474	0.9	tonnes
Volume			
teaspoons	* 4.97512	5.0	milliliters
tablespoons	* 14.92537	15.0	milliliters
fluid ounces	29.57353	30.0	milliliters
cups	* 0.236588240	0.24	liters
pints	* 0.473176473	0.47	liters
quarts	* 0.946352946	0.95	liters
gallons	* 3.785411784	3.8	liters
cubic inches	* 0.016387064	0.02	liters
cubic feet	* 0.028316846592	0.03	cubic meters
cubic yards	* 0.764554857984	0.76	cubic meters
Area			
square inches	* 6.4516	6.5	square centimeters
square feet	* 0.09290304	0.09	square meters
square yards	* 0.83612736	0.8	square meters
square miles	* 2.589989	2.6	square kilometers
acres	* 0.40468564224	0.4	hectares
Temperature			
Fahrenheit	* 5/9 (after subtracting 32)		Celsius

Dimensional and Temperature Conversion Chart

Inches	Decimals	Millimeters	Inches to Millimeters		Millimeters to Inches		Fahrenheit & Celsius			
			in.	mm	mm	in.	°F	°C	°C	°F
1/64	.015625	.3969	.0001	.00254	0.001	.000039	-20	-28.9	-30	-22
1/32	.03125	.7937	.0002	.00508	0.002	.000079	-15	-26.1	-28	-18.4
3/64	.046875	1.1906	.0003	.00762	0.003	.000118	-10	-23.3	-26	-14.8
1/16	.0625	1.5875	.0004	.01016	0.004	.000157	-5	-20.6	-24	-11.2
5/64	.078125	1.9844	.0005	.01270	0.005	.000197	0	-17.8	-22	-7.6
3/32	.09375	2.3812	.0006	.01524	0.006	.000236	1	-17.2	-20	-4
7/64	.109375	2.7781	.0007	.01778	0.007	.000276	2	-16.7	-18	-0.4
1/8	.125	3.1750	.0008	.02032	0.008	.000315	3	-16.1	-16	3.2
9/64	.140625	3.5719	.0009	.02286	0.009	.000354	4	-15.6	-14	6.8
5/32	.15625	3.9687	.001	.0254	0.01	.00039	5	-15.0	-12	10.4
11/64	.171875	4.3656	.002	.0508	0.02	.00079	10	-12.2	10	14
3/16	.1875	4.7625	.003	.0762	0.03	.00118	15	-9.4	-8	17.6
13/64	.203125	5.1594	.004	.1016	0.04	.00157	20	-6.7	-6	21.2
7/32	.21875	5.5562	.005	.1270	0.05	.00197	25	-3.9	-4	24.8
15/64	.234375	5.9531	.006	.1524	0.06	.00236	30	-1.1	-2	28.4
1/4	.25	6.3500	.007	.1778	0.07	.00276	35	1.7	0	32
17/64	.265625	6.7469	.008	.2032	0.08	.00315	40	4.4	2	35.6
9/32	.28125	7.1437	.009	.2286	0.09	.00354	45	7.2	4	39.2
19/64	.296875	7.5406	.01	.254	0.1	.00394	50	10.0	6	42.8
5/16	.3125	7.9375	.02	.508	0.2	.00787	55	12.8	8	46.4
21/64	.328125	8.3344	.03	.762	0.3	.01181	60	15.6	10	50
11/32	.34375	8.7312	.04	1.016	0.4	.01575	65	18.3	12	53.6
23/64	.359375	9.1281	.05	1.270	0.5	.01969	70	21.1	14	57.2
3/8	.375	9.5250	.06	1.524	0.6	.02362	75	23.9	16	60.8
25/64	.390625	9.9219	.07	1.778	0.7	.02756	80	26.7	18	64.4
13/32	.40625	10.3187	.08	2.032	0.8	.03150	85	29.4	20	68
27/64	.421875	10.7156	.09	2.286	0.9	.03543	90	32.2	22	71.6
7/16	.4375	11.1125	.1	2.54	1	.03937	95	35.0	24	75.2
29/64	.453125	11.5094	.2	5.08	2	.07874	100	37.8	26	78.8
15/32	.46875	11.9062	.3	7.62	3	.11811	105	40.6	28	82.4
31/64	.484375	12.3031	.4	10.16	4	.15748	110	43.3	30	86
1/2	.5	12.7000	.5	12.70	5	.19685	115	46.1	32	89.6
33/64	.515625	13.0969	.6	15.24	6	.23622	120	48.9	34	93.2
17/32	.53125	13.4937	.7	17.78	7	.27559	125	51.7	36	96.8
35/64	.546875	13.8906	.8	20.32	8	.31496	130	54.4	38	100.4
9/16	.5625	14.2875	.9	22.86	9	.35433	135	57.2	40	104
37/64	.578125	14.6844	1	25.4	10	.39370	140	60.0	42	107.6
19/32	.59375	15.0812	2	50.8	11	.43307	145	62.8	44	112.2
39/64	.609375	15.4781	3	76.2	12	.47244	150	65.6	46	114.8
5/8	.625	15.8750	4	101.6	13	.51181	155	68.3	48	118.4
41/64	.640625	16.2719	5	127.0	14	.55118	160	71.1	50	122
21/32	.65625	16.6687	6	152.4	15	.59055	165	73.9	52	125.6
43/64	.671875	17.0656	7	177.8	16	.62992	170	76.7	54	129.2
11/16	.6875	17.4625	8	203.2	17	.66929	175	79.4	56	132.8
45/64	.703125	17.8594	9	228.6	18	.70866	180	82.2	58	136.4
23/32	.71875	18.2562	10	254.0	19	.74803	185	85.0	60	140
47/64	.734375	18.6531	11	279.4	20	.78740	190	87.8	62	143.6
3/4	.75	19.0500	12	304.8	21	.82677	195	90.6	64	147.2
49/64	.765625	19.4469	13	330.2	22	.86614	200	93.3	66	150.8
25/32	.78125	19.8437	14	355.6	23	.90551	205	96.1	68	154.4
51/64	.796875	20.2406	15	381.0	24	.94488	210	98.9	70	158
13/16	.8125	20.6375	16	406.4	25	.98425	212	100.0	75	167
53/64	.828125	21.0344	17	431.8	26	1.02362	215	101.7	80	176
27/32	.84375	21.4312	18	457.2	27	1.06299	220	104.4	85	185
55/64	.859375	21.8281	19	482.6	28	1.10236	225	107.2	90	194
7/8	.875	22.2250	20	508.0	29	1.14173	230	110.0	95	203
57/64	.890625	22.6219	21	533.4	30	1.18110	235	112.8	100	212
29/32	.90625	23.0187	22	558.8	31	1.22047	240	115.6	105	221
59/64	.921875	23.4156	23	584.2	32	1.25984	245	118.3	110	230
15/16	.9375	23.8125	24	609.6	33	1.29921	250	121.1	115	239
61/64	.953125	24.2094	25	635.0	34	1.33858	255	123.9	120	248
31/32	.96875	24.6062	26	660.4	35	1.37795	260	126.6	125	257
63/64	.984375	25.0031	27	690.6	36	1.41732	265	129.4	130	266

Capacity Conversion U.S. Gallons to Liters

Gallons	***0***	***1***	***2***	***3***	***4***	***5***
	Liters	**Liters**	**Liters**	**Liters**	**Liters**	**Liters**
0	00.0000	3.7853	7.5707	11.3560	15.1413	18.9267
10	37.8533	41.6387	45.4240	49.2098	52.9947	56.7800
20	75.7066	79.4920	83.2773	87.0626	90.8480	94.6333
30	113.5600	117.3453	121.1306	124.9160	128.7013	132.4866
40	151.4133	155.1986	158.9840	162.7693	166.5546	170.3400

Millimeter Conversion Chart

mm In.	15 = .5905	30 = 1.1811	45 = 1.7716	60 = 2.3622	75 = 2.9527	90 = 3.5433	105 = 4.1338	120 = 4.7244
.25 = .0098	15.25 = .6004	30.25 = 1.1909	45.25 = 1.7815	60.25 = 2.3720	75.25 = 2.9626	90.25 = 3.5531	105.25 = 4.1437	120.25 = 4.7342
.50 = .0197	15.50 = .6102	30.50 = 1.2008	45.50 = 1.7913	60.50 = 2.3819	75.50 = 2.9724	90.50 = 3.5630	105.50 = 4.1535	120.50 = 4.7441
.75 = .0295	15.75 = .6201	30.75 = 1.2106	45.75 = 1.8012	60.75 = 2.3917	75.75 = 2.9823	90.75 = 3.5728	105.75 = 4.1634	120.75 = 4.7539
1 = .0394	16 = .6299	31 = 1.2205	46 = 1.8110	61 = 2.4016	76 = 2.9921	91 = 3.5827	106 = 4.1732	121 = 4.7638
1.25 = .0492	16.25 = .6398	31.25 = 1.2303	46.25 = 1.8209	61.25 = 2.4114	76.25 = 3.0020	91.25 = 3.5925	106.25 = 4.1831	121.25 = 4.7736
1.50 = .0591	16.50 = .6496	31.50 = 1.2402	46.50 = 1.8307	61.50 = 2.4213	76.50 = 3.0118	91.50 = 3.6024	106.50 = 4.1929	121.50 = 4.7885
1.75 = .0689	16.75 = .6594	31.75 = 1.2500	46.75 = 1.8405	61.75 = 2.4311	76.75 = 3.0216	91.75 = 3.6122	106.75 = 4.2027	121.75 = 4.7933
2 = .0787	17 = .6693	32 = 1.2598	47 = 1.8504	62 = 2.4409	77 = 3.0315	92 = 3.6220	107 = 4.2126	122 = 4.8031
2.25 = .0886	17.25 = .6791	32.25 = 1.269	47.25 = 1.8602	62.25 = 2.4508	77.25 = 3.0413	92.25 = 3.6319	107.25 = 4.2224	122.25 = 4.8130
2.50 = .0984	17.50 = .6890	32.50 = 1.2795	47.50 = 1.8701	62.50 = 2.4606	77.50 = 3.0512	92.50 = 3.6417	107.50 = 4.2323	122.50 = 4.8228
2.75 = .1083	17.75 = .6988	32.75 = 1.2894	47.75 = 1.8799	62.75 = 2.4705	77.75 = 3.0610	92.75 = 3.6516	107.75 = 4.2421	122.75 = 4.8327
3 = .1181	18 = .7087	33 = 1.2992	48 = 1.8898	63 = 2.4803	78 = 3.0709	93 = 3.6614	108 = 4.2520	123 = 4.8425
3.25 = .1280	18.25 = .7185	33.25 = 1.3091	48.25 = 1.8996	63.25 = 2.4901	78.25 = 3.0807	93.25 = 3.6713	108.25 = 4.2618	123.25 = 4.8524
3.50 = .1378	18.50 = .7283	33.50 = 1.3189	48.50 = 1.9094	63.50 = 2.5000	78.50 = 3.0905	93.50 = 3.6811	108.50 = 4.2716	123.50 = 4.8622
3.75 = .1476	18.75 = .7382	33.75 = 1.3287	48.75 = 1.9193	63.75 = 2.5098	78.75 = 3.1004	93.75 = 3.6909	108.75 = 4.2815	123.75 = 4.8720
4 = .1575	19 = .7480	34 = 1.3386	49 = 1.9291	64 = 2.5197	79 = 3.1102	94 = 3.7008	109 = 4.2913	124 = 4.8819
4.25 = .1673	19.25 = . 7579	34.25 = 1.3484	49.25 = 1.9390	64.25 = 2.5295	79.25 = 3.1201	94.25 = 3.7106	109.25 = 4.3012	124.25 = 4.8917
4.50 = .1772	19.50 = .7677	34.50 = 1.3583	49.50 = 1.9488	64.50 = 2.5394	79.50 = 3.1299	94.50 = 3.7205	109.50 = 4.3110	124.50 = 4.9016
4.75 = .1870	19.75 = .7776	34.75 = 1.3681	49.75 = 1.9587	64.75 = 2.5492	79.75 = 3.1398	94.75 = 3.7303	109.75 = 4.3209	124.75 = 4.9114
5 = .1968	20 = .7874	35 = 1.3779	50 = 1.9685	65 = 2.5590	80 = 3.1496	95 = 3.7401	110 = 4.3307	125 = 4.9212
5.25 = .2067	20.25 = .7972	35.25 = 1.3878	50.25 = 1.9783	65.25 = 2.5689	80.25 = 3.1594	95.25 = 3.7500	110.25 = 4.3405	125.25 = 4.9311
5.50 = .2165	20.50 = .8071	35.50 = 1.3976	5050 = 1.9882	65.50 = 2.5787	80.50 = 3.1693	95.50 = 3.7598	110.50 = 4.3504	125.50 = 4.9409
5.75 = .2264	20.75 = .8169	35.75 = 1.4075	50.75 = 1.9980	65.75 = 2.5886	80.75 = 3.1791	95.75 = 3.7697	110.75 = 4.3602	125.75 = 4.9508
6 = .2362	21 = .8268	36 = 1.4173	51 = 2.0079	66 = 2.5984	81 = 3.1890	96 = 3.7795	111 = 4.3701	126 = 4.9606
6.25 = .2461	21.25 = .8366	36.25 = 1.4272	51.25 = 2.0177	66.25 = 2.6083	81.25 = 3.1988	96.25 = 3.7894	111.25 = 4.3799	126.25 = 4.9705
6.50 = .2559	21.50 = .8465	36.50 = 1.4370	51.50 = 2.0276	66.50 = 2.6181	81.50 = 3.2087	96.50 = 3.7992	111.50 = 4.3898	126.50 = 4.9803
6.75 = .2657	21.75 = .8563	36.75 = 1.4468	51.75 = 2.0374	66.75 = 2.6279	81.75 = 3.2185	96.75 = 3.8090	111.75 = 4.3996	126.75 = 4.9901
7 = .2756	22 = .8661	37 = 1.4567	52 = 2.0472	67 = 2.6378	82 = 3.2283	97 = 3.8189	112 = 4.4094	127 = 5.0000
7.25 = .2854	22.25 = .8760	37.25 = 1.4665	52.25 = 2.0571	67.25 = 2.6476	82.25 = 3.2382	97.25 = 3.8287	112.25 = 4.4193	
7.50 = .2953	22.50 = .8858	37.50 = 1.4764	52.50 = 2.0669	67.50 = 2.6575	82.50 = 3.2480	97.50 = 3.8386	112.50 = 4.4291	
7.75 = .3051	22.75 = .8957	37.75 = 1.4862	52.75 = 2.0768	67.75 = 2.6673	82.75 = 3.2579	97.75 = 3.8484	112.75 = 4.4390	
8 = .3150	23 = .9055	38 = 1.4961	53 = 2.0866	68 = 2.6772	83 = 3.2677	98 = 3.8583	113 = 4.4488	
8.25 = .3248	23.25 = .9153	38.25 = 1.5059	53.25 = 2.0965	68.25 = 2.6870	83.25 = 3.2776	98.25 = 3.8681	113.25 = 4.4587	
8.50 = .3346	23.50 = .9252	38.50 = 1.5157	53.50 = 2.1063	68.50 = 2.6968	83.50 = 3.2874	98.50 = 3.8779	113.50 = 4.4685	
8.75 = .3445	23.75 = .9350	38.75 = 1.5256	53.75 = 2.1161	68.75 = 2.7067	83.75 = 3.2972	98.75 = 3.8878	113.75 = 4.4783	
9 = .3543	24 = .9449	39 = 1.5354	54 = 2.1260	69 = 2.7165	84 = 3.3071	99 = 3.8976	114 = 4.4882	
9.25 = .3642	24.25 = .9547	39.25 = 1.5453	54.25 = 2.1358	69.25 = 2.7264	84.25 = 3.3169	99.25 = 3.9075	114.25 = 4.4980	
9.50 = .3740	24.50 = .9646	39.50 = 1.5551	54.50 = 2.1457	69.50 = 2.7362	84.50 = 3.3268	99.50 = 3.9173	114.50 = 4.5079	
9.75 = .3839	24.75 = .9744	39.75 = 1.5650	54.75 = 2.1555	69.75 = 2.7461	84.75 = 3.3366	99.75 = 3.9272	114.75 = 4.5177	
10 = .3937	25 = .9842	40 = 1.5748	55 = 2.1653	70 = 2.7559	85 = 3.3464	100 = 3.9370	115 = 4.5275	
10.25 = .4035	25.25 = .9941	40.25 = 1.5846	55.25 = 2.1752	70.25 = 2.7657	85.25 = 3.3563	100.25 = 3.9468	115.25 = 4.5374	
10.50 = .4134	25.50 = 1.0039	40.50 = 1.5945	55.50 = 2.1850	70.50 = 2.7756	85.50 = 3.3661	100.50 = 3.9567	115.50 = 4.5472	
10.75 = .4232	25.75 = 1.0138	40.75 = 1.6043	55.75 = 2.1949	70.75 = 2.7854	85.75 = 3.3760	100.75 = 3.9665	115.75 = 4.5571	
11 = .4331	26 = 1.0236	41 = 1.6142	56 = 2.2047	71 = 2.7953	86 = 3.3858	101 = 3.9764	116 = 4.5669	
11.25 = .4429	26.25 = 1.0335	41.25 = 1.6240	56.25 = 2.2146	71.25 = 2.8051	86.25 = 3.3957	101.25 = 3.9862	116.25 = 4.5768	
11.50 = .4528	26.50 = 1.0433	41.50 = 1.6339	56.50 = 2.2244	71.50 = 2.8150	86.50 = 3.4055	101.50 = 3.9961	116.50 = 4.5866	
11.75 = .4626	26.75 = 1.0531	41.75 = 1.6437	56.75 = 2.2342	71.75 = 2.8248	86.75 = 3.4153	101.75 = 4.0059	116.75 = 4.5964	
12 = .4724	27 = 1.0630	42 = 1.6535	57 = 2.2441	72 = 2.8346	87 = 3.4252	102 = 4.0157	117 = 4.6063	
12.25 = .4823	27.25 = 1.0728	42.25 = 1.6634	57.25 = 2.2539	72.25 = 2.8445	87.25 = 3.4350	102.25 = 4.0256	117.25 = 4.6161	
12.50 = .4921	27.50 = 1.0827	42.50 = 1.6732	57.50 = 2.2638	72.50 = 2.8543	87.50 = 3.4449	102.50 = 4.0354	117.50 = 4.6260	
12.75 = .5020	27.75 = 1.0925	42.75 = 1.6831	57.75 = 2.2736	72.75 = 2.8642	87.75 = 3.4547	102.75 = 4.0453	117.75 = 4.6358	
13 = .5118	28 = 1.1024	43 = 1.6929	58 = 2.2835	73 = 2.8740	88 = 3.4646	103 = 4.0551	118 = 4.6457	
13.25 = .5217	28.25 = 1.1122	43.25 = 1.7028	58.25 = 2.2933	73.25 = 2.8839	88.25 = 3.4744	103.25 = 4.0650	118.25 = 4.6555	
13.50 = .5315	28.50 = 1.1220	43.50 = 1.7126	58.50 = 2.3031	73.50 = 2.8937	88.50 = 3.4842	103.50 = 4.0748	118.50 = 4.6653	
13.75 = .5413	28.75 = 1.1319	43.75 = 1.7224	58.75 = 2.3130	73.75 = 2.9035	88.75 = 3.4941	103.75 = 4.0846	118.75 = 4.6752	
14 = .5512	29 = 1.1417	44 = 1.7323	59 = 2.3228	74 = 2.9134	89 = 3.5039	104 = 4.0945	119 = 4.6850	
14.25 = .5610	29.25 = 1.1516	44.25 = 1.7421	59.25 = 2.3327	74.25 = 2.9232	89.25 = 3.5138	104.25 = 4.1043	119.25 = 4.6949	
14.50 = .5709	29.50 = 1.1614	44.50 = 1.7520	59.50 = 2.3425	74.50 = 2.9331	89.50 = 3.5236	104.50 = 4.1142	119.50 = 4.7047	
14.75 = .5807	29.75 = 1.1713	4475 = 1.7618	59.75 = 2.3524	74.74 = 2.9429	89.75 = 3.5335	104.75 = 4.1240	119.75 = 4.7146	

Tap/Drill Chart

Coarse Standard Thread (N.C.)
Formerly U.S. Standard Thread

Sizes	Threads per inch	Outside diameter at screw	Tap drill sizes	Decimal equivalent of drill
1	64	.073	53	0.0595
2	56	.086	50	0.0700
3	48	.099	47	0.0785
4	40	.112	43	0.0890
5	40	.125	38	0.1015
6	32	.138	36	0.1065
8	32	.164	29	0.1360
10	24	.190	25	0.1495
12	24	.216	16	0.1770
1/4	20	.250	7	0.2010
5/16	18	.3125	F	0.2570
3/8	16	.375	5/16	0.3125
7/16	14	.4375	U	0.3680
1/2	13	.500	27/64	0.4219
9/16	12	.5625	31/64	0.4843
5/8	11	.625	17/32	0.5312
3/4	10	.750	21/32	0.6562
7/8	9	.875	49/64	0.7656
1	8	1.000	7/8	0.875
1 1/8	7	1.125	63/64	0.9843
1 1/4	7	1.250	1 7/64	1.1093

Fine Standard Thread (N.F.)
Formerly S.A.E. Thread

Sizes	Threads per inch	Outside diameter at screw	Tap drill sizes	Decimal equivalent of drill
0	80	.060	1/64	0.0469
1	72	.073	53	0.0595
2	64	.086	50	0.0700
3	56	.099	45	0.0820
4	48	.112	42	0.0935
5	44	.125	37	0.1040
6	40	.138	33	0.1130
8	36	.164	29	0.1360
10	32	.190	21	0.1590
12	28	.216	14	0.1820
1/4	28	.250	3	0.2130
5/16	24	.3125	1	0.2720
3/8	24	.375	Q	0.3320
7/16	20	.4375	25/64	0.3906
1/2	20	.500	29/64	0.4531
9/16	18	.5625	0.5062	0.5062
5/8	18	.625	0.5687	0.5687
3/4	16	.750	11/16	0.6875
7/8	14	.875	0.8020	0.8020
1	14	1.000	0.9274	0.9274
1 1/8	12	1.125	1 3/64	1.0468
1 1/4	12	1.250	1 11/64	1.1718

Bolt Torquing Chart

Metric Standard

Grade of Bolt		5D	8G	10K	12K	
Min. Tensile Strength		71,160 P.S.I	113,800 P.S.I	142,200 P.S.I	170,679 P.S.I	
Grade Markings on Head		5D	8G	10K	12K	Size of Socket or Wrench Opening
Metric		Foot Pounds				Metric
Bolt Dia.	U.S. Dec. Equiv.					Bolt Head
6mm	.2362	5	6	8	10	10mm
8mm	.3150	10	16	22	27	14mm
10mm	.3937	19	31	40	49	17mm
12mm	.4720	34	54	70	86	19mm
14mm	.5512	55	89	117	137	22mm
16mm	.6299	83	132	175	208	24mm
18mm	.709	111	182	236	283	27mm
22mm	.8661	182	284	394	464	32mm

SAE Standard / Foot Pounds

Grade of Bolt	SAE 1 & 2	SAE 5	SAE 6	SAE 8		
Min. Tensile Strength	64,000 P.S.I	105,000 P.S.I	133,000 P.S.I	150,000 P.S.I		
Markings on Head					Size of Socket or Wrench Opening	
U.S. Standard	Foot Pounds				U.S. Standard	
Bolt Dia.					Bolt Head	Nut
1/4	5	7	10	10.5	3/8	7/16
5/16	9	14	19	22	1/2	9/16
3/8	15	25	34	37	9/16	5/8
7/16	24	40	55	60	5/8	3/4
1/2	37	60	85	92	3/4	13/16
9/16	53	88	120	132	7/8	7/8
5/8	74	120	167	180	15/16	1.
3/4	120	200	280	296	1 1/8	1 1/8

ABBREVIATIONS

The following abbreviations may be used in a typical service manual.

Ω ....Ohm(s)
4P ....Number of coupler pins
A/T ....automatic transmission
A ....Ampere
AB ....Air bleed
ABDC ....After Bottom Dead Center
ABS ....Anti-lock brake system
AC ....Alternating current
AFC ....Air controlled
AMA ....American Motorcyclists Association
Assy ....Assembly
ATDC ....After Top Dead Center
ATS ....Air temperature sensor
ATV ....All terrain vehicle
B + ...Voltage
BAT – ....Battery negative terminal
BAT + ...Battery positive terminal
BBDC ....Before Bottom Dead Center
BMEP ....Brake mean effective pressure
BTDC ....Before Top Dead Center
BTU ....British thermal unit
C2 ....Countershaft 2nd gear (number indicates the stage of gear)
cc ....cubic centimeter
CDI ....Capacitive discharge ignition
CKV ....Check valve
cm ....centimeter
CO ....Carbon monoxide
CO_2 ....Carbon dioxide
CPU ....Central Processing Unit
DC ....Direct current
DOT ..................U.S. Department of Transportation
ECI ....Electronic controlled ignition
ECM ....Electronic control module
ECU ....Electronic control unit
EEC ....Electronic engine control
EEC ....Electronic emission control
EFI ....Electronic fuel injection
EGA ....Exhaust gas analyzer
EIS ....Electronic ignition system
EMF ....Electromotive force
EPA ....Environmental Protection Agency
EVAP ....Evaporative control system
EX ....Exhaust side/Exterior side
F ....Farad(s)
F(FR) ....Indicates the front side of the vehicle
ft ....Foot, feet
F← ....Install with arrow toward front (Some parts might be stamped with a triangular mark.)
g ....Gram(s)
GND ....Ground
h ....Hour(s)
hp ....Horsepower
ID ....Inside diameter
IMEP ....Indicated mean effective pressure
IN ....Install with "IN" toward inside/exhaust side
IN ....Intake side/Inside
L ....liter(s)
L ....Left (Left side viewed from rear side)
L(100L) ....Number of links (100 links)
L(LH) ....Install on the left side, viewed from rear side

lb . . . . .Pound(s)
LBS . . . . .Linked braking system
LED . . . . .Light-emitting diode
LOWER . . . . .Indicates lower level
M/T . . . . .Manual transmission
m . . . . .Meter(s)
M/C . . . . .Mixture control
M5 . . . . .Mainshaft 5th gear (number indicates the stage of gear)
MCU . . . . .Microprocessor control unit
min . . . . .Minute(s)
mph . . . . .Miles per hour
MSF . . . . .Motorcycle Safety Foundation
N/A . . . . .Not applicable
N . . . . .Newton(s)
N·m . . . . .Newton-meter
NO_x . . . . .Oxides of nitrogen (nitrogen oxide)
O_2 . . . . .Oxygen
O_2S . . . . .Oxygen sensor
OCC . . . . .Oxidation catalytic converter
OD . . . . .Outside diameter
OE . . . . .Original equipment
OEM . . . . .Original equipment manufacturer
OP . . . . .Optional
OS . . . . .Oxygen sensor
OS . . . . .Oversized
OUT (OUTSIDE) . . . . . .Install with the letter toward outside
Pa . . . . .Pascal(s)
POT . . . . .Potentiometer (variable resistor)
psi . . . . .Pound(s) per square inch
R . . . . .Resistance (electrical)
r . . . . .Revolution
R . . . . .Right (Right side viewed from rear side)
R(RH) . . . . .Install on the right side, viewed from rear side
R(RR) . . . . .Indicates the rear side of the vehicle
rpm . . . . .Rotating speed per minute
sol . . . . .Solenoid
SSI . . . . .Solid-state ignition
STD . . . . .Standard
T/C . . . . .Torque converter
TDC . . . . .Top dead center
TIR . . . . .Total indicator reading
TOP . . . . .Install with "TOP" toward up. (Do not install with the letter upside down.)
TPI . . . . .Transistor pointless ignition
TWC . . . . .Three-way catalyst
UCS . . . . .U.S. Customary system
UP . . . . .Install with "UP" toward up. (Do not install with letter upside down.) UPPER (FULL) Indicates upper level.
UP_ . . . . .Install with mark toward up. (Some parts might be stamped with an arrow.)
V . . . . .Volt(s)
VOM . . . . .Volt-ohmmeter tester
VP . . . . .Vacuum pump
VS . . . . .Vacuum switch
W . . . . .Watt(s)
← . . . . .Indicates the rotating direction, if stamped on the rotating part.
°C . . . . .degree(s) Celsius
°F . . . . .degree(s) Fahrenheit

If a punch mark (•) is stamped on a part, it generally indicates the installation direction or alignment point. Pay attention to any marks when assembling a major component.

Acknowledgments

The authors wish to thank the individuals and organizations listed below for the valuable information, photographs and line drawings, facilities, and talents they so willingly provided for both the original edition and the revised edition.

Albert Steier
American Suzuki Motor Corporation
Betty Armstrong
Bill Lilly
Bob Conley
Bob Rewoldt
Bombardier, Inc.
Bonnie Guerra
Bridgeport
Chuck Horisberger
Cobra Engineering Inc.
Craig Richie
Cycle
Cycle Craft
Cycle Guide
Cycle Werks
Cycle World
Denny Forni
Devin MacIntee
Don Church
Doug McIntyre
Downers Grove Yamaha
Elgin Community College
Elmer Hansen
Fox Trail Motors
Fox Valley Cycles
Fox Valley Yamaha
Greg Smith
Harley Davidson Motor Co.
Honda Motor Co., Ltd.
Howard Marunde
James Gerhart
Jim Carlson
Jim Moreland
Kawasaki Motors Corporation, U.S.A.
Kawasaki of Berks
Ken's Cycle Shop
Ken Ronzheimer
Larry Jones
Leon Korejwo
Linda Bell
Lorna Cross
Luke Gray
Mark Reese
Marsh Hayward
Matt Pritchard
Mike Markowitz
Miller Electric Mfg., Inc.
OTC Division of SPX Corp.
Phyllis Taylor
Rick Lovens
Rob Poetsch
Robyn Davis
Ron Downen
Snap-On Tools
Steier's Cycles Inc.
Steve Ward
Steven's Cycle
The L.S. Starrett Co.
Tom Foster
Tom Pugh
Tri City Suzuki
Triumph Motorcycles
Warner W. Riley
Waubonsee Community College
Wilwood Suzuki
Yamaha Motor Corporation, U.S.A.

Special thanks to Sears, Roebuck and Company—Orland Park retail store, Orland Park, Illinois for the many tools illustrated in Chapter 3 and to Vern Hanks and Rick Williams for their assistance in making the revision of this text possible.

Glossary

A

Abbreviations: Letters or letter combinations that stand for words. Used extensively in manuals.

ABDC: Abbreviation for After Bottom Dead Center.

ABS: Abbreviation for Anti-lock Braking System.

ABS warning light: Indicator lamp mounted in the instrument cluster. Illuminates when there is a problem in the anti-lock brake system.

Accelerator pump: A small pump that squirts fuel into the carburetor throat as the throttle is opened.

Accessory system: Part of the electrical system consisting of lights, horn, electric starter, turn signals, warning systems, etc.

Additives: Chemical compounds used to modify or improve the characteristics of lubricating oils and fuels.

Aeration: The process of mixing air or gas with oil.

Air box: Plastic, fiberglass, or metal box mounted between the carburetor and air filter. This box provides a volume of still, filtered air for induction into engine.

Air cleaner: A device for filtering, cleaning, and removing dust, dirt, and foreign debris from the air being drawn into the engine.

Air-cooled engine: An engine cooled by ambient air movement.

Air filter: A device with paper, oiled foam, oiled gauze, or wire mesh to prevent entry of dirt or foreign particles into engine through air intake.

Airflow meter: Sensor that monitors the amount of air entering the engine.

Air-fuel mixture: Finely atomized mist of air and fuel necessary for combustion.

Air-fuel ratio: The ratio of air to fuel. The amount of air is much greater than the amount of fuel, usually between 14.7:1 and 15:1, depending on the type of fuel system.

Air jet: A small jet in air passage of a carburetor. This jet meters amount of air fed to diffuser in an air bleed carburetor.

Alternating current (ac): Electrical current which constantly reverses direction and polarity.

Alternator: A crankshaft-driven electrical generator that produces alternating current which is rectified to direct current.

Ammeter: An instrument for measuring current flow in electrical circuits.

Ampere (amp): Electrical unit used to measure current flow.

Ampere-hour rating: The length of time a battery discharges current.

Anaerobic sealer: A chemical sealer that cures in the absence of air.

Analog display: Instrument display that uses gauges with moving needles.

Anti-lock brake system (ABS): A computer-controlled system that is part of the base brake system. The system "cycles" the brakes on and off to prevent wheel lockup and skidding.

API: Abbreviation for American Petroleum Institute.

Armature: Portion of a dc generator housing the generating coils.

Asbestos: A mineral material that has great heat resistant characteristics. Once widely used in brake linings. Asbestos is a known cancer causing agent.

Atmospheric pressure sensor: A sensor that measures atmospheric pressure. This allows the computer to change engine outputs in relation to atmospheric pressure and engine vacuum.

Atom: The basis of all matter. It consists of a nucleus made up of protons and neutrons, and one or more orbiting electrons.

Atomized: Tiny particles of fuel mixed with air, making a fine mist.

ATV: Abbreviation for All Terrain Vehicle.

Automatic transmission: A transmission that uses fluid pressure to shift itself. Shift points and range is determined by road speed, engine loading, altitude, and throttle position.

Axle: A shaft used to support a part or parts across the frame or forks.

B

Backbone frame: Frame which uses the engine as a structural member.

Backlash: The clearance between the meshed teeth of two gears.

Ball and ramp: A clutch release mechanism made of two stamped plates with three or four ramps. As one plate is rotated by the clutch cable, the balls climb the ramps, forcing the plates apart. This movement disengages the clutch.

Ball bearing: An anti-friction bearing consisting of inner and outer races separated by hardened steel balls.

Battery: A storage device that converts chemical energy to electrical energy.

Battery and coil ignition system: An ignition system with a battery as the source of primary ignition current.

Battery cable: Heavy gage wires used to connect the battery to the bike's electrical system.

Battery powered electrical system: An electrical system having a lead-acid battery as a source of power. The battery is recharged by a charging system using either a generator or alternator.

Battery supported CDI: Capacitive discharge ignition system which uses a battery to supply primary ignition current.

Bearing: A part in which a journal, shaft, or pivot turns or moves.

Bearing preload: Amount of static pressure exerted on a bearing or a set of bearings. The preload is usually adjusted by a threaded collar or shims.

Bearing spacer: A piece of tubing used between the wheel bearing inner races to prevent unwanted bearing preload as the axle is tightened.

Belt drive system: A final drive system that uses a cogged belt and two sprockets. The belt performs the same function as a conventional chain.

Bias-belted tires: Tire construction method using crisscrossed plies with additional belts under the tread area.

Bias-ply tires: A type of tire construction in which the plies crisscross from bead to bead. No additional belts are used under the tread area.

Bleeding: The process of removing air or fluid from a closed system, such as the brakes.

Blowby: A condition where the piston rings do not effectively seal, allowing hot combustion gases and engine oil to blow between the rings and cylinder wall.

Bore: The diameter of a cylinder.

Boring bar: A machine tool used to accurately enlarge a cylinder bore.

Bottom dead center (BDC): Lowest piston position in the engine cylinder.

Brake actuator cam: Small cam that pivots in brake backing plate and forces brake shoes into brake drum.

Brake cable: Metal cable used to actuate the brakes on some bikes.

Brake caliper: Hydraulic part of a disc brake system which holds the friction pads and surrounds the disc.

Brake disc: A round, flat disc made of steel or cast iron. It is mounted on the outside of the wheel hub.

Brake drum: A circular ring of cast iron that is part of wheel hub. It provides a place for brake lining to be applied.

Brake fluid: A special fluid compound used in hydraulic brake systems. It must meet exacting specifications, such as resistance to heating, freezing, and thickening.

Brake fluid warning light: Indicator light located in the instrument cluster. Used to indicate a problem in the brake hydraulic system.

Brake lever: Hand lever used to actuate the brakes.

Brake line: Special hydraulic tubing made of steel, plastic, or reinforced rubber.

Brake lining: A special high friction material bonded to brake shoes and brake pad plates. Brake linings produce friction and heat when they are forced against a disc or drum.

Brake mean effective pressure: The calculated pressure on the pistons, measured in pounds per square inch. This pressure takes into account frictional losses caused by rings, pistons, and bearings.

Brake pad: Small circular or square friction inserts in a brake caliper. They produce friction and heat when forced against a disc.

Brake pedal: Foot lever used to actuate the brakes. May be coupled with a brake lever.

Brake shoe: A cast aluminum, half-circular shoe that holds a bonded brake lining material.

Brake wear indicator: Index grooves, tabs, or reference lines to indicate the amount of brake pad or lining wear.

Bridged port: A vertical division in a two-stroke engine cylinder port which allows the use of a large port without danger of the ring or piston catching.

Burr: A small, rotating cutter mounted in a rotary grinder and used for metal removal (rotary file). Also, sharp, rough area around a drilled hole.

Butterfly controlled carburetor: A carburetor using a flat plate between the venturi and the intake manifold to regulate airflow.

Bypass valve: Valve which allows fluid to flow around the normal flow path, used in oil filters.

C

Caliper: A disc brake component which contains one or more pistons and brake pads. It provides braking by producing a clamping action against a rotating disc.

Cam chain: A chain running between the crankshaft and camshaft.

Cam follower: Valve train component that rides on the cam lobe.

Cam ground pistons: Oval shaped pistons designed to control and compensate for expansion.

Cam lobe: Protrusions on a camshaft that causes valve train parts to move as camshaft rotates.

Cam plate: Flat plate with slots that engage pins on the shift forks. As the plate is rotated, slots cause shift forks to move sliding gears or dogs, causing engagement and disengagement of transmission ratios.

Camber: The outward or inward tilt of a wheel from its centerline.

Camshaft: A shaft with protruding eccentric lobes. As the camshaft rotates, the lobes cause reciprocating movement of other valve train parts.

Capacitor: See *Condenser.*

Carbon (C): Hard or soft black deposits found in combustion chambers, spark plugs, valves, etc. An excellent conductor of electricity.

Carbon monoxide (CO): A deadly colorless, odorless gas that is formed when fuel is not burned completely.

Carburetor: Mechanical device that mixes and delivers a proper amount of air and fuel to the engine at a ratio of approximately 15 parts air to 1 part fuel.

Cast alloy wheel: A one piece wheel made of cast aluminum or magnesium alloy. This design is more rigid than a wire spoked wheel.

Cast iron cylinder: A one-piece cylinder assembly made of cast iron with a machined bore.

Cast piston: A piston made by pouring molten aluminum alloy into a mold.

Cast-in sleeve: An aluminum cylinder block cast around an iron cylinder sleeve.

Caster: The backward or forward tilt of a wheel away from its centerline.

Catalytic converter: An emissions control device which uses solid catalysts to reduce harmful exhaust emissions.

Cavitation: Inadequate lubrication caused by air displacing oil in the pump.

CDI voltage amplifier: A device used in battery powered capacity discharge ignition systems. It steps up battery voltage to provide high primary ignition voltage.

Cell: The individual compartments in a battery which contain positive and negative plates suspended in electrolyte.

Celsius: Metric unit of measurement for temperature. Under standard atmospheric conditions, water freezes at 0°C and boils at 100°C.

Center of gravity: Point at which any object is perfectly balanced.

Central processing unit (CPU): A microprocessor inside a computer responsible for controlling operations.

Centrifugal advance unit: A series of weights or other mechanical devices used to advance timing as engine speed increases.

Centrifugal clutch: Clutch engaged by centrifugal force as the engine speeds up.

Centrifugal oil filter: Cup-shaped oil filter mounted to the end of the crankshaft. As oil passes through the slinger, centrifugal force removes impurities that are heavier than oil.

Chain drive: Use of a chain and sprockets to connect the transmission output shaft to the rear wheel.

Chain stretch: Pin and bushing wear of a roller or hy-vo chain, causing the chain to lengthen.

Chamfer: To bevel or shape the edge of an object or port openings in a two-stroke engine cylinder to prevent piston ring breakage.

Chassis: The framework of a bike without its engine or other components.

Check engine light: Light in the instrument cluster used to indicate that a problem exists in a bike's computer control system.

Check valve: A spring-loaded ball or piston valve that allows flow only in one direction.

Chemical regulator: Voltage regulator with solid state electronic devices to regulate charging system output.

Choke system: System in the carburetor that reduces the volume of air admitted to the engine.

Circlip: A circular clip or snap ring that fits into a groove, used to locate or retain a shaft or component.

Circuit: An electoral path from a power source, through wire, to components, and back to source.

Circuit breaker: A device used to protect an electrical circuit from excessive current flow.

Clearance: Amount of space between two adjacent parts.

Close ratio transmission: A transmission with gear ratios spaced close together.

Clutch: Device used to connect and disconnect engine power to the transmission input shaft.

Clutch basket: Part of the clutch assembly containing drive plates. Primary drive gear engages teeth on outside of the clutch basket.

Clutch holder: Tool to secure the clutch basket and clutch hub while loosening or tightening the clutch securing nut or primary drive gear nut.

Clutch hub: Part of the clutch that engages with the plain driven clutch plates. The clutch hub is mounted on the transmission input shaft.

Clutch pressure plate: Part of a clutch assembly providing pressure against clutch disc or clutch plates.

Clutch release mechanism: Mechanism that moves the clutch pressure plate away from clutch pack, allowing clutch to slip.

Coated bore: Thin coating of chrome or iron applied to the inside of a cylinder by electroplating or wire explosion spray coating.

Coil buildup: Buildup of a magnetic field while current is flowing through primary windings of coil.

Cold cranking amps: Measurement of cranking amperes a battery can deliver over a period of 30 seconds at 0°F (-18°C).

Cold soak cleaner: A strong cleaning solvent used to dissolve and remove varnish on carburetor parts.

Color code: Use of different base colors and colored tracers on insulation of electrical wire for purpose of identification.

Combustion: Burning of air-fuel mixture in the engine's combustion chamber.

Combustion chamber: Area of cylinder head and cylinder above piston where combustion of air-fuel mixture takes place.

Common sump lubrication: System in which the same oil is used to lubricate the engine, transmission, and primary drive.

Communication systems: Closed intercom system installed on some touring bikes. Can include a CB radio on some models.

Compression: Increased pressure caused as volume is reduced. Also movement of suspension components against spring pressure caused by a force against wheel.

Compression gauge: Gauge which measures the cranking pressure in the combustion chamber.

Compression rings: Piston rings designed to seal pressure between piston and upper cylinder.

Compression stroke: Movement of piston from BDC to TDC with valves closed, compressing air-fuel mixture for more violent combustion.

Compression test: Diagnostic test used to determine how much power each cylinder can produce based on compression pressure.

Concentric: When two or more circular parts have the same centerline.

Condenser: Two metal sheets separated by an insulator; used to store an electrical charge.

Conductor: Any material that can form a path for heat, cold, or electrical current.

Conical hub: A wheel hub (wire wheel) that has the spoke holes on the brake side of the wheel set at a greater distance from the center of the hub than the opposite side.

Connecting rod: A rod made of steel or aluminum, usually having an I-beam cross section. It connects piston to crankshaft.

Connecting rod kit: A parts kit consisting of connecting rod, crank pin, thrust washers, and roller bearing, used in reconditioning of assembled crankshafts.

Connecting rod tip: Amount of radial (side) play at the top of the connecting rod.

Connectors: Electrical plugs used to connect different components or wiring harnesses.

Contact points: Switching devices used to start and stop current flow.

Continuity: A continuous path for current flow.

Conventional battery: A battery that has one or more caps for adding distilled water or electrolyte.

Conventional theory: Theory of electricity which states current flows from positive to negative.

Coolant: A 50-50 mixture of distilled water and ethylene glycol circulated through a liquid cooling system.

Coolant temperature gauge: Instrument cluster gauge used to indicate engine coolant temperature.

Coolant temperature sensor: Thermistor used to monitor coolant temperature on liquid-cooled bikes.

Cooling fan: Electric fan used to pull air through a radiator on liquid-cooled bikes.

Cooling fins: Projections on cylinder heads, cylinders, and crankcases to increase surface area for more efficient heat dissipation into air.

Counter-rotating balancer: An internal or external gear-or chain-driven device, timed to a specific crankshaft revolution and used to balance the vibration of the throw, rod, and piston.

Countershaft sprocket: Output sprocket from transmission. Mounted on output shaft in indirect drive transmission and on high gear pinion in direct drive transmission.

Cradle frame: Frame built of tubing which supports and surrounds the engine.

Crankcase: Castings that support and contain the crankshaft, primary drive, and transmission.

Crankcase leak test: Pressure test done to a two-stroke engine to determine if crankcase is properly sealed.

Crankcase vacuum: The vacuum built up by engine compression. Also referred to as crankcase pressure.

Crankpin: Pin or journal on which big-end of connecting rod rides.

Crankshaft: The main shaft which supports the connecting rods and turns piston reciprocation into motion.

Crankshaft axles: Extensions at each end of crankshaft to provide a mounting place for main bearings, primary drive gear or sprocket, and alternator rotor or magneto flywheel.

Crankshaft reconditioning: Replacement of worn lower-end components in an assembled crankshaft. This involves pressing crankshaft apart, replacing crankpin, roller-bearing, thrust washers, and connecting rod, pressing back together and truing the assembled crankshaft.

Crankshaft wheel: Portions of an assembled crankshaft that provide a mounting place for crankpin and crank axles.

Crosshatch pattern: Pattern created on engine cylinders during the honing process. Helps in proper ring break-in.

Cruise control: System that maintains bike speed while driving. Cruise control may be mechanical (vacuum) or electronic.

Current flow: Movement of electrons through a conductor.

Cycle: A series of events which take place during a specific interval.

Cylinder: A machined hole in the cylinder block for the piston, open at both ends.

Cylinder block: Casting attached to the crankcase which contains cylinder bore, cooling fins or water jacket, and provides a means of mounting the cylinder head.

Cylinder bore: Diameter of cylinder opening.

Cylinder boring: Process that machines the engine bore to accept an oversize piston. Usually performed to recondition a worn cylinder.

Cylinder deglazing: Use of a hone to slightly roughen walls of cylinder. It produces a crosshatch pattern which aids in seating of new rings.

Cylinder head: Casting that seals the top of the cylinder and provides a mounting place for spark plug. In four-stroke engine, cylinder head also contains intake and exhaust ports. Both two- and four-stroke engines also have the combustion chamber built into the cylinder head.

Cylinder honing: Use of a parallel cylinder hone to deglaze and crosshatch a cylinder, usually after boring.

Cylinder liner: Cast iron sleeve pressed or cast into the cylinder block to provide a rigid bore in which the piston moves.

Cylinder ports: Openings in the cylinder of a two-stroke engine that allow air-fuel mixture to enter the combustion chamber.

Cylinder taper: Wear condition in which a cylinder is worn more at the top than at the bottom.

D

Damper: Device which uses oil metered through orifices to control abrupt suspension movement.

Damper rod: Tube secured to the bottom of each fork slider to hold the slider on the fork leg. Controls front suspension movement by metering hydraulic fluid through orifices in the rod.

Dc generator: A crankshaft-driven electrical generator that uses spinning coils to produce direct current.

Dealerships: Local franchises individually owned, but supported by a motorcycle manufacturer, that sells and services the manufacturer's bikes.

Decarbonize: To remove carbon buildup on piston, combustion chamber, and other parts.

Deglazing: Process used to remove the glaze from cylinder walls before new piston rings are installed.

Depth micrometer: A precision tool used to take measurements of stepped surfaces.

Detergent oil: An oil which keeps particles and contaminants in suspension and has the ability to neutralize acids resulting from the combustion process.

Detonation: A condition where excessive temperature in the combustion chamber causes uncontrolled, explosive burning of the air-fuel mixture. As the detonated flame front collides with the flame front initiated by the spark plug, extreme pressure is often heard as pinging or knocking. Also see *Preignition.*

Diagnosis: Process of determining the cause of a failure.

Dial bore gauge: A precision measuring tool which combines a telescoping gauge and dial indicator to give readings of inside diameter measurements.

Dial caliper: A precision measuring tool used to determine inside, outside, or depth measurements. Measurements are displayed on a dial index.

Dial indicator: A precision measuring tool using a dial index to show linear movement of a component.

Diamond frame: Frame used mainly on small and medium-size bikes due to its simplicity, light weight, and excellent serviceability.

Diaphragm: A thin flexible disc of rubberized fabric which separates two cavities and uses vacuum or pressure for activation.

Diaphragm spring: A slightly cone shaped metal disc which acts as a clutch pressure plate spring when flattened.

Die: A tool for cutting threads.

Diffuser: A projection in base of carburetor venturi and at top of needle jet that aids in fuel atomization.

Digital display: Instrument display that uses a liquid crystal display (LCD) for engine and vehicle speed as well as other indicators.

Dimmer switch: A switch that operates the high and low beam headlights.

Diode: A solid state electronic device that permits current flow in only one direction.

Direct bearing lubrication: An oil injection system which feeds undiluted oil to two-stroke engine main bearings and rod big-end bearing.

Direct current (dc): A continuous flow of current in the same direction.

Direct drive transmission: Power is transferred from clutch to input shaft (mainshaft), to the layshaft and the high gear pinion, which holds the output sprocket.

Disc brake: A brake consisting of a flat circular disc attached to wheel. A hydraulic or mechanical caliper applies pressure to two brake pads to slow or stop disc rotation.

Documentation: Repair orders or other means used to record work performed on a bike.

Dog: A knob on the side of a gear that aligns or interlocks with a matching dog or hole in an adjacent gear.

Double cradle: Frame that has two down tubes and main tubes.

Double overhead cam (DOHC): Type of engine that uses two camshafts located in the cylinder head (one for intake, one for exhaust).

Double piston caliper: A hydraulic brake caliper with two pistons and provisions for applying hydraulic pressure equally to both pistons.

Double-leading drum brakes: A drum brake having two leading shoes and no trailing shoes. Each shoe has its own activating cam and pivot.

Double-row chain: A chain having two rows of rollers. Duplex (double-row) chains are used for primary drives.

Drive plate: A clutch plate which is indexed into clutch basket (outer hub) by tabs. Drive plate has friction material bonded to its surface. When the clutch is engaged, the drive plate transfers power to the driven plate.

Drive train: The drive systems that transfer the power produced by the engine to the rear wheel; includes primary drive, clutch, transmission, and final drive systems.

Driven plate: A clutch plate which is indexed onto clutch inner hub by tabs or splines around its inside diameter. Driven plate is usually a plain plate (no friction material) and drives the transmission input shaft through the clutch inner hub.

Drum brake: A brake consisting of two brake shoes mounted on a backing plate. One or two cams cause shoes to expand against inside of brake drum. Brake drum is part of hub or is bolted to hub.

Dry-blast cleaning: Method of cleaning parts using a dry medium, such as sand, glass beads, or crushed nut shells.

Dry charged battery: A battery that is charged, but lacks electrolyte. It is filled with electrolyte when it is placed into service.

Dry clutch: A clutch assembly that does not run in an oil bath.

Dry sump lubrication: In this system, oil is gravity fed to supply side of oil pump from a remote oil tank. After oil has been pumped through four-stroke engine, it is returned to oil tank by return side of oil pump.

Dual-range transmission: An auxiliary transmission, also called a subtransmission, that is placed between the transmission and the final drive system.

Dual-rate charging system: A charging system that switches extra coils into charging system when lights are turned on.

Duration: The amount of time a valve is open.

Dwell: Length of time in crankshaft degrees the ignition contact points are closed.

Dykes piston ring: A piston ring with an L-shaped cross section designed to use combustion pressure to improve sealing.

Dynamic ignition timing: Use of a strobe light to check ignition timing with the engine running.

E

ECM: Abbreviation for Electronic Control Module.

EFI: Abbreviation for Electronic Fuel Injection.

Electrode: Conductors at center and side of spark plug that provide an air gap for an electric arc to start combustion process in engine.

Electrolyte: A solution of sulfuric acid and water used to provide a chemical reaction in a lead-acid battery.

Electromagnet: A magnet which produces a magnetic field by passing electrical current through a coil of wire wrapped around a soft iron core.

Electromagnet alternator: An alternator which uses electromagnets to produce a magnetic field.

Electromotive force (EMF): Force that causes electricity to flow because of a difference in potential between two points.

Electron: A negatively charged particle that orbits the nucleus of an atom.

Electron theory: The accepted theory of electronics that states electricity flows from positive to negative.

Electronic advance: Ignition advance controlled by a computer or other solid state controller.

Electronic control module (ECM): General term used for any computer that controls a vehicle system.

Electronic fuel injection (EFI): A system that injects fuel into the engine's intake manifold and uses a computer to time and meter the fuel.

Electronic ignition system: An ignition system which uses a magnetic triggering device and solid state amplifier rather than conventional contact points.

Electronic regulator: A solid state device which controls charging system output.

Element filter: A disposable oil or air filter that uses gauze or paper as filtering material.

Elliptical port shape: Rounded port shape designed to prevent ring catching in large ports of two-stroke engine.

Emissions: Byproducts of a running engine, including exhaust and noise emissions.

End play: Amount of lengthwise movement between two parts.

Endless chain: A roller chain without a master link for connection of ends. All pin links are permanently riveted.

Engine: A machine that converts chemical or electrical energy into mechanical energy.

Enrichment circuit: A carburetor system with a plunger to open and close an air-fuel circuit which discharges a rich mixture into throat of carburetor for cold starting.

Eroded piston (crown): A condition caused by detonation or preignition where temperatures are raised so high that part of the piston crown is melted away.

Ethanol: Fuel additive derived from grains, such as corn. Commonly referred to as grain alcohol. Denatured for use in gasoline.

Ethyl tertiary butyl ether (ETBE): A gasoline oxygenate manufactured by reacting isobutylene with ethanol.

Evaporative emission control system: An emissions control system used on some bikes to prevent fuel vapor from escaping into the atmosphere.

Exhaust gas analyzer: A device used to determine the exact amounts of hydrocarbons and carbon monoxide in the exhaust.

Exhaust port: An opening or passage which directs flow of exhaust gases out of engine. In a four-stroke engine, it is located in the head. With a two-stroke engine, it is in the cylinder.

Exhaust (port) timing: Amount of time two-stroke engine exhaust port is open, expressed in crankshaft degrees or piston travel.

Exhaust stroke: With a four-stroke engine, it is movement of piston from BDC to TDC with exhaust valve open, pushing burned gases out of cylinder.

Exhaust system: The system consisting of the exhaust port, exhaust valve, exhaust pipe, and muffler that delivers burned combustion gases to the atmosphere.

Exhaust ultimate power valve (EXPV): Valve used with an exhaust arrangement that uses a computer which varies the exhaust tube diameter according to engine rpm.

Expansion chamber: A two-stroke engine exhaust system that consists of a header pipe, the first cone, chamber, rear cone, stinger, and silencer.

Extension: The return or stretching outward of suspension components (after compression) caused by spring pressure.

F

Fall detection switch: An electronic switch that shuts down the engine if the bike is tilted at an angle which would indicate a fall.

Fahrenheit: Unit of measurement for temperature of which the boiling point of water is 212°F and the freezing point is 32°F.

Fastener: A device used to attach one part or assembly to another (nut and bolt, screw, rivet, etc.).

Feeler gauge: A measuring tool made of steel blades of precise thickness used for measuring distances between surfaces.

Field coil: An electromagnet used in a dc generator or ac electromagnet alternator to produce a magnetic field.

Film strength: Ability of an oil to keep moving parts from making contact with each other.

Final drive: Chains and sprockets or shafts and gears used to connect the transmission output shaft to the rear wheel.

Firing order: The staggered sequence of operation in each cylinder of an engine.

Fixed caliper: Part of a hydraulic disc brake system mounted stationary to the front fork and holds a piston and brake pad on either side of the brake disc.

Fixed venturi carburetor: Carburetor that uses a fixed, or nonvariable venturi.

Flange mount carburetor: A carburetor mounted by a flange bolted to a manifold on the cylinder or cylinder head. An insulator block and gasket are used to seal and insulate the carburetor.

Float assembly: A plastic or hollow brass device attached to an arm that pivots on a pin and raises and lowers, opening and closing the float needle to control the fuel level in the carburetor.

Float bowl: Part of the carburetor housing that acts as a reservoir for gasoline and contains the float and other carburetor parts.

Float circuit: The portion of the carburetor (float, needle, seat) devoted to maintaining a constant fuel level.

Float level: Level of fuel maintained in carburetor float bowl. Controlled by the float, needle, and seat.

Floating caliper: In a hydraulic disc brake system, the assembly connected to a movable arm and holds one piston and both inside and outside brake pads to press against a brake disc.

Fluid pressure gauge: Gauge for measuring fluid pressure in a system, such as oil pressure or fuel pressure.

Flywheel: A weight attached to an engine crankshaft to provide added inertia during non-power producing strokes. It also helps to smooth out abrupt movement of crankshaft during the power stroke.

Flywheel magneto ignition system: An ac ignition system using a generating coil and either a magnetic trigger (CDI) or contact points as well as a flywheel to provide primary ignition current and triggering. An external ignition coil is used to provide secondary current.

Flywheel magnets: Magnets mounted on the inside of a flywheel magneto.

Foaming: Undesirable characteristic of oil being whipped into a froth (air and oil solution).

Foot-pound (ft-lb.): Amount of work required to lift one pound one foot; used to express torque.

Forged piston: A piston made by hammering hot aluminum into a mold of desired shape.

Fork sliders: Lower portion of fork which slides over fork leg.

Fork tubes: Long sturdy tubes attached to triple clamps and fitted inside fork sliders.

Four-stroke engine cycle: One engine cycle consisting of four distinct events, intake, compression, power, and exhaust. One cycle requires two revolutions of the crankshaft.

Frame: The skeleton of the motorcycle, made of tubes, steel plates, or pressed steel, that supports the rider and engine and provides attachment points for the frame's components.

Friction: Resistance to movement between two objects contacting each other.

Friction plate: See *Drive plate.*

Front fork: The spring and damping device that holds the front wheel in place.

Fuel filter: A small filter designed to remove dirt and water from fuel before it reaches the carburetor or injection system. Filters may be made of metal or plastic screen, paper, or gauze. Filters may be located at fuel tank, in fuel line, or at carburetor.

Fuel injection: A system that sprays fuel just ahead of the cylinders.

Fuel injector: Fuel valve controlled by an electronic solenoid or spring pressure.

Fuel level gauges: Instrument gauges that indicate how much fuel is in the fuel tank.

Fuel line: The portion of the fuel system that carries fuel from the tank to the filter and on to the carburetor or fuel injectors.

Fuel petcock: An on-off valve located at the bottom of the fuel tank. It may have a filter screen and sediment bowl and sometimes provide a reserve fuel supply.

Fuel pump: A diaphragm or electric device that maintains proper fuel pressure to carburetor or injection system.

Fuel system: System which stores, filters, and regulates flow of fuel to engine. It consists of fuel tank, fuel valve, fuel filters, fuel lines, air filter, carburetor, and carburetor mountings or fuel injectors.

Fuel tank: A reservoir used to store fuel for delivery to the engine.

Full-wave rectifier: A rectifier that converts ac to dc by inverting the negative portion of an ac sine wave.

Fuse: A device used to protect electrical circuits from overloading. A link in fuse melts and opens circuit if current is above normal rating.

G

Gage size: The thickness of a wire, metal, or other part. Usually, the smaller the gage number, the thicker the part.

Gas charged shock absorbers: A shock absorber using a pressurized gas, such as nitrogen, to help prevent changes in damping as the shock absorber heats up.

Gasket: A treated fiber, aluminum, or copper ring used to seal some cylinder heads, cylinder bases, and side covers.

Gasoline: A hydrocarbon fuel used in internal combustion engines.

Gear oil pump: An oil pump with gear teeth to move the oil.

Gear ratio: The relationship between the number of turns made by a driving gear to complete one full turn of the driven gear. If the driving gear makes two revolutions in order to turn the driven gear once, the gear ratio would be two to one (2:1).

Gear reduction: Setup in which a small gear is used to drive a larger gear. Produces an increase in torque.

General repair manual: Service manual that covers many motorcycles. Often published by a non-motorcycle manufacturer.

Generator: A device which converts mechanical energy into electrical energy, producing direct current (dc).

Grade markings: Lines placed on the heads of some bolts to indicate tensile strength.

Graduated cylinder: A container, calibrated in cubic centimeters or milliliters used for the accurate measurement of fluids, such as fork oil and transmission oil.

Ground: The uninsulated side of a circuit, usually with negative polarity.

Ground straps: Metal wires or straps used to ground the engine and other components to the electrical system.

Gusset: A reinforcing plate or boxed section used to prevent flexing of frame or swing arm.

H

Half-wave rectifier: A rectifier which blocks one-half of an ac sine wave to convert ac into dc.

Halogen bulbs: Quartz light bulb in which a tungsten filament is surrounded by a halogen gas such as iodine, bromine, etc.

Heat range: Rating given for the operating temperature of spark plugs.

Heat transfer: Movement of heat from one area to another.

Heat-shrink tubing: Plastic tube used to insulate electrical solder joints.

Helical gear: A gear having teeth that are slightly angled. Helical gears (used for primary drives) are quiet in operation, but absorb a slight amount of power due to side thrust.

Hemispherical combustion chamber: A combustion chamber shaped like a round dome, allowing the use of large valves placed opposite each other in the chamber.

High gear pinion: Top gear on the mainshaft in a direct drive transmission. All gear ratios drive through the high gear pinion, which also holds the output sprocket.

Holed piston: A condition caused by severe detonation or preignition, where a hole is burned through the piston crown as a result of extreme heat or pressure.

Honing: Process of removing metal with a fine abrasive stone. Used to achieve close tolerances and a crosshatch pattern.

Horn circuit: A circuit that provides the rider with an audible warning signal.

Horsepower: Amount of work required to lift 33,000 pounds one foot in one minute.

Hub: Center mount for a wheel's spokes.

Hy-vo chain: A very strong chain made up of toothed plates positioned side by side and held together by pins.

Hydraulic brake system: A brake system using hydraulic fluid, pistons, and cylinders to provide high pressure for brake application.

Hydraulic clutch: A system which uses hydraulic pressure to disengage the clutch.

Hydraulic unit (HU): Valve unit for an anti-lock brake system.

Hydrocarbons (HC): A combination of hydrogen and carbon atoms. An unwanted exhaust pollutant resulting from unburned fuel.

Hydrometer: A device used to measure the specific gravity of electrolyte in each battery cell.

Hygroscopic: A fluid's ability to absorb moisture from the air.

I

Idle mixture: Air-fuel ratio with the throttle plate closed. Idle mixture is controlled by the pilot circuit in the carburetor or the computer in an electronic fuel injection system.

Idle speed: The crankshaft rotational speed in an engine with a closed throttle plate.

Ignition: The act of firing the compressed air-fuel mixture in the combustion chamber by a spark from the spark plug.

Ignition coil: A step-up transformer that uses induction to increase battery voltage to over 20,000 volts.

Ignition generating coil: Coil in a flywheel magneto to provide primary ignition current.

Ignition primary circuit: The low voltage portion of the ignition system.

Ignition secondary circuit: The high voltage portion of the ignition system.

Ignition system: Part of the electrical system responsible for providing high voltage at the proper time to ignite the air-fuel mixture in the engine.

Ignition timing: The relationship between the time a plug is fired and the position of the piston in terms of degrees of crankshaft rotation.

Impeller: Finned wheel that produces pressure and flow when spun in the enclosed housing of an oil or water pump.

Index marks: Marks used to properly align a distributor for engine timing.

Indicated mean effective pressure (IMEP): The pressure at the top of the piston.

Indirect drive transmission: A transmission where power is transferred from the clutch, to the input shaft, and to the output shaft.

Induction: Production of current flow by forming a magnetic field and moving it through a conductor.

Inertia: The tendency of a stationary object to resist movement or a moving object to continue moving in the same direction.

Injection system: A pump and lines that deliver oil to a two-stroke engine. Also, fuel system which meters gasoline into an engine's intake ports.

Inline cylinders: Cylinders positioned in a row or side by side.

Inline filter: A small fuel or oil filter that is installed in a section of line or hose.

Input shaft: Transmission shaft that carries engine power into the transmission.

Inside micrometer: A precision measurement tool used to take accurate measurements of inside surfaces.

Insulator: Material that effectively resists and prevents the flow of electrons.

Insulator block: A fiber or rubber block that insulates carburetor from engine heat, used with flange mounted carburetors.

Intake manifold: A sleeve or flange made of rubber or metal to attach carburetor to intake port.

Intake port: An opening or passage which directs the flow of air and fuel into the engine. In a four-stroke engine, the intake port is located in the cylinder head. In a two-stroke engine, the intake port is located in the cylinder or crankcase.

Intake stroke: In a four-stroke engine, piston movement from TDC to BDC with the intake valve open, drawing air-fuel mixture into the cylinder.

Intake temperature sensor: Thermistor used by the computer to monitor the temperature of the air entering the engine

Intake timing: Amount of time two-stroke engine intake port is open, expressed in crankshaft degrees or piston position.

Integrated circuit (IC): A single chip of semiconductor material which contains various electrical components in miniaturized form.

Interference angle: Valve seat angle cut slightly less than the valve face angle. The valve face seats a few seconds after initial engine start-up.

Intermittent failures: A defect that only appears for a short time, with no definitive pattern. Usually occurs as a result of wear and is often a precursor to a permanent failure.

Internal chain drive: Transmission that uses an internally housed chain to drive one or more shafts.

Internal combustion engine: An engine that burns fuel inside rather than outside the engine, as does a steam engine (external combustion engine).

Internal cooling: Engine cooling provided by oil, fuel mixtures, and valve overlap.

J

Jet: A carburetor component, usually made of brass, which meters fuel flow to the venturi.

Joule: Metric unit of measurement for energy or work equal to a force of one Newton applied through a distance of one meter. One joule is equivalent to 0.737324 ft-lbs.

Jumper wire: A wire used to make a temporary electrical connection.

Junction block: A device which transfers the action of a single cable to two or more cables.

K

Key: Parallel-sided piece inserted into groove cut part way into each of two parts, which locates and prevents slippage between parts.

Keystone piston ring: A piston ring with a tapered cross section designed to use combustion pressure to aid in sealing.

Kickstart mechanism: Pedal mechanism that allows a motorcycle to be started manually.

Kinetic energy: Energy associated with motion. An internal combustion engine produces kinetic energy through crankshaft rotation.

L

Lacing: The positioning of spokes in the hub and rim.

Lateral runout: Side-to-side movement (wobble) of a wheel rim.

Lathe: A machine tool used to spin, cut, and shape a metal part with a movable cutting tool.

Layshaft: Second shaft in a direct drive transmission. It transfers power from the input shaft to the high gear pinion.

Lean: An air-fuel ratio that contains an excess amount of air as compared to fuel.

Left-hand threads: Threads cut in the opposite direction of normal threaded fasteners. Left-handed thread fasteners used in applications that normally turn counter-clockwise.

Lever and pivot: A release mechanism in which a pivoted lever attached to the clutch cable disengages the clutch by pushing the pressure plate away from the clutch plates, allowing them to slip. Lever and pivot may act directly or through a pushrod.

Lift: Maximum distance a valve head is raised off its seat.

Lifter: A hard surfaced short shaft with a radius or roller at one end that rides on a cam lobe.

Lighting system: The part of the electrical system that includes the lights.

Linings: See *Brake pad.*

Linked braking system (LBS): Brake system designed so the front and rear calipers are applied simultaneously when either the handlebar brake levers or foot brake pedals are applied.

Liquid cooling: Use of liquid piped through water jackets, thermostat, and radiator to dissipate heat.

Liquid-cooled engine: An internal combustion engine cooled by moving a liquid, such as ethylene glycol and water, through ports cast in the engine.

Long travel rear suspension: Suspension used on competition dirt bikes to provide additional travel beyond stock.

Lower end: Portion of an engine from the cylinder base downward including connecting rods.

Lubricating film: A thin coating of lubricant (oil) which prevents contact between moving parts.

Lubrication: Use of lubricants (oil, grease) to reduce friction.

M

Magnetic field: Invisible lines of force surrounding a magnet or a conductor with current flowing through it.

Magnetism: An invisible force which attracts ferrous metals.

Magneto: See *Flywheel magneto ignition system.*

Magneto supported CDI: A capacitive discharge ignition using a generating coil in magneto to produce primary ignition current.

Main fuel circuit: Carburetor circuit that controls air-fuel ratio from three-fourths to full throttle opening.

Main jet: A carburetor fuel metering jet, usually mounted at the base of the carburetor body. Controls air-fuel ratio from three-fourths to full throttle.

Maintenance-free (MF) battery: A sealed battery that requires no additional water or electrolyte during its useful life.

Manifold injection: Oil injection system that pumps oil into the intake port of a two-stroke engine.

Manual transmission: A rider operated (shifted) transmission.

Manufacturer's manual: A service manual published by a motorcycle manufacturer. Usually specific to one motorcycle.

Master cylinder: Component in a brake system that produces hydraulic pressure for the system.

Master link: A pin link which has one removable side plate located by a clip. This allows a convenient way of separating the chain.

Material Safety Data Sheets (MSDS): Information on a chemical or material that must be provided by the material's manufacturer. Lists potential health risks and proper handling procedures.

Mating parts: Two or more parts that contact each other during operation and setup wear patterns.

Mechanical brake: A brake system which uses levers and cables or rods to apply the brakes rather than hydraulics.

Mechanical caliper: A disc brake caliper actuated by a lever and cam rather than hydraulic fluid.

Mechanical voltage regulator: A voltage regulator using an electromagnet to open or close contact points, varying the output of a dc generator or electromagnet alternator.

Methanol: Methyl alcohol or wood alcohol.

Methyl tertiary butyl ether (MTBE): A gasoline oxygenate manufactured by reacting isobutylene with methanol.

Microprocessor: A small silicon chip that contains elements in a computer. Often referred to as an integrated circuit or "IC".

Mild port timing: Two-stroke engine ports open for a relatively short time, providing for a broad power band.

Muffler: A chambered unit attached to an exhaust pipe to deaden noise.

Multimeter: An electrical test meter that can be used to test for voltage, current, or resistance.

Multiple ports: Use of many small transfer ports rather than two large ports in a two-stroke cycle cylinder. This provides improved scavenging.

Multi-cylinder engines: An internal combustion engine having more than one cylinder.

Multi-plate clutch: A clutch assembly using more than one driving plate and more than one driven plate.

Multi-weight oil: An oil that flows like a thin oil when cold, but lubricates like a thick oil when hot. For example, 10W-40 at 0°F (-18°C) flows like a 10W oil; at 210°F (100°C), it flows like a 40W oil.

N

Needle: A valve with a long, thin tapered point that operates in a small hole or jet. The hole size is changed by moving the needle in and out.

Needle bearing: An anti-friction bearing utilizing hardened steel needle rollers between hardened races or parts.

Needle circuit: Carburetor circuit that controls air-fuel ratio from one-quarter to three-quarter throttle. The needle and jet meter fuel flow in this circuit.

Negative: Terminal with an excess amount of electrons which flow toward the positive terminal.

Neutral indicator switch: A switch usually mounted on the end of the shift drum, which completes the neutral indicator light circuit when the transmission is in neutral.

Non-primary kickstart: A kickstart system using transmission input shaft and clutch hub to connect kickstart lever to crankshaft. For starting, transmission must be in neutral and clutch engaged.

Non-unit construction: Engine design with separates the engine crankcase and transmission case.

Nylon screw clutch release: A clutch release mechanism which uses a coarse, square threaded nylon screw for clutch disengagement.

O

O-ring: A ring made of neoprene that is used to provide a positive seal. It usually fits into a groove slightly shallower than the O-ring, and mated against a flat surface to provide a seal for oil, fuel, or air.

O-ring chain: Roller chain which uses O-rings to permanently seal lubricant into the area between pins and bushings.

Octane rating: Rating indicating a fuel's tendency to resist knocking. Also referred to as the antiknock index. Does not have a bearing on the fuel's quality.

Offset: A inset or displaced area on a part.

Ohm: Unit used to measure resistance in an electrical circuit or component.

Ohm's law: Formula for computing unknown voltage, resistance, or current in a circuit by using two known factors to find the unknown value.

Ohmmeter: An instrument which measures resistance.

Oil: Petroleum-based lubricant used in engines and other systems with moving components.

Oil bath: Lubrication system in which the oil level is just high enough so it splashes around the case or housing. Lubricates transmission primary drive, and ring and pinion.

Oil control ring: Piston ring designed to remove excess oil from cylinder wall, usually bottom ring.

Oil cooler: An air cooled heat exchanger used to remove excess heat from the engine oil.

Oil filter: Paper, wire screen, or rotor designed to keep oil clean and to prevent oil passages from becoming clogged.

Oil level indicator: Sensor which detects the amount of oil in the oil pan of a four-stroke engine.

Oil pan: Cover on the bottom of the engine. Houses the crankcase, oil pump and in some cases, an oil sump.

Oil pressure warning light: A dash mounted light that indicates low oil pressure.

Oil pump: A device which provides oil under pressure for engine lubrication.

Oil pump bleeding: Removal of air from the supply line and pump in a two-stroke oil injection system.

Oil slinger: A circular, lipped disc used in direct bearing oil injection to feed oil to the rod big end.

Omega frame: A lightweight, highly rigid frame which has the pivot points for the lower and upper portions of the front swingarm.

One-way clutch: A clutch mechanism that will drive in one direction and slip in the other.

Open circuit: A circuit that is broken or disconnected.

Opposed cylinders: Cylinders positioned opposite each other in the same plane.

Out-of-roundness: Cylinder wear pattern caused by piston thrust from front to back of the cylinder. The cylinder wears an oval shaped rather than round.

Output shaft: Transmission shaft that transmits power to the final drive at a selected ratio.

Outside micrometer: A precision measuring tool for taking accurate measurements between outside surfaces.

Overall gear ratio: Ratio of crankshaft revolutions to rear wheel revolutions.

Overflow tube: A tube that is open at both ends and mounted in bottom of carburetor float bowl. If the float sticks or the needle does not seat properly, excess fuel flows out overflow tube rather than into throat of carburetor.

Overheating: Condition where the engine or other parts exceeds recommended temperature.

Oxidation: Reaction between an element and oxygen or other catalyst which converts it to its oxide form. This action can form rust in ferrous metals.

Oxides of nitrogen (NO_x): An undesirable compound of nitrogen and oxygen in exhaust gases. Usually produced when combustion chamber temperatures are excessively high.

Oxidized oil: Oil that has been chemically combined with oxygen as a result of excessive heat, oil agitation, and exposure to combustion contaminants.

Oxygen (O_2) sensor: An exhaust sensor used to measure the amount of oxygen in the exhaust gases produced by the engine.

Oxygenated gasoline: Reformulated gasoline sold in some areas where ozone levels are excessively high. Contains one of four oxygenates, methyl tertiary butyl ether (MTBE), ethyl tertiary butyl ether (ETBE), tertiary amyl methyl ether (TAME), or ethanol.

P

Parallel circuit: A circuit where current is provided to each component independently (each component has own ground). The failure of one component does not affect the rest of the circuit.

Parasitic draw test: Electrical test used to check a bike for excess electrical loads that can drain the battery while the bike is not running.

Pentagonal frame: Frame that has rails which extend from the steering head section to the swingarm pivot. Sometimes called a *perimeter frame.*

Periodic maintenance: Schedule of maintenance as recommended by the bike's manufacturer.

Permanent magnet alternator: An alternator using permanent magnets to produce a magnetic field for ac production.

Pilot air screw: A screw mounted on side of carburetor that allows fine adjustment of air-fuel ratio in pilot circuit of slide carburetor.

Pilot circuit: A carburetor circuit that provides proper air-fuel ratio from approximately zero to one-eighth throttle opening. It basically consists of a pilot jet, pilot air screw or pilot fuel screw, and a pilot discharge port.

Pilot jet: Jet that meters fuel for pilot circuit.

Pinion gear: A small gear that either drives or is driven by a larger gear.

Piston (brake system): A movable part of a master cylinder or wheel caliper. They apply pressure to the brake disc, slowing or stopping the wheel.

Piston (engine): A cylindrical part, closed at one end, which moves up and down in the cylinder. Open end is attached to a connecting rod. Combustion pressure is exerted on the closed end of piston, causing the connecting rod to move and the crankshaft to turn.

Piston block: A slotted block used to support pistons for cylinder installation. Also may be used in conjunction with a piston pin to lock the crankshaft.

Piston clearance: The amount of clearance between the side of the piston and the cylinder wall.

Piston crown: The portion of the piston above the top ring. Also called the *piston head.*

Piston pin boss: A strengthened section of piston extending to inside the piston crown. It supports the piston pin.

Piston pinhole: Machined hole through the piston side wall where the piston pin and retaining circlips are mounted.

Piston port: Two-stroke engine piston skirt used to control intake port opening and closing.

Piston ring (oil control): A split cast iron or steel band, used to scrape excess oil from the cylinder wall. Sometimes designed as a three-piece unit.

Piston ring end gap: Distance between the ends of a piston ring when installed in the cylinder. This clearance is measured with a feeler gauge. The ring must be straight in the cylinder as if installed on the piston.

Piston ring groove: Grooves machined in a piston to accept piston rings.

Piston rings (compression): A split cast iron band, sometimes chrome plated, designed to seal combustion pressure above piston.

Piston seizure: Condition where a piston overheats to the point where it will no longer move freely in the cylinder.

Piston skirt: Part of piston below bottom ring and pin boss.

Pivoting link front suspension: System which connects the axle to the fork by means of a pivoting link extending from the axle ends to the upper portion of the fork.

Plain bearing: A split or circular bearing in which a part slides, turns, or pivots.

Plain plate: See *Driven plate.*

Plastigage: A measuring tool that is compressed between two tightly fitting surfaces, such as bearings, to measure clearance.

Plunger oil pump: An oil pump that uses a piston or plunger and check valves to move oil.

Polarity: The positive or negative terminals of a battery. Also the north and south poles of a magnet.

Poppet valve: In a four-stroke engine, the device in the cylinder head that opens and closes to seal the combustion chamber.

Port window: Port opening in a two-stroke engine cylinder wall.

Positive: Electrical terminal having a deficiency of electrons and attracts electrons from negative terminal, causing current flow.

Positive carburetor linkage: A carburetor linkage designed to positively open and close one or more carburetor throttles, actuated by one cable for opening and another cable for closing.

Power: Ability to do work or the rate of work being done.

Power stroke: The piston movement from TDC to BDC in a four-stroke engine with the intake and exhaust valves closed, after the ignition and combustion of the compressed air-fuel mixture.

Power transmission: A system of gears, chains, sprockets, and shafts that transfer power from crankshaft to rear wheel in varying ratios.

Power transmission shock absorber: A compensator cam, rubber pads, or springs in primary drive, gearbox, drive shaft, or rear wheel, provides means of cushioning loading of transmission.

Preignition: Premature ignition caused by hot spots in the combustion chamber that ignites the air-fuel mixture before the spark plug actually fires. This causes uncontrolled combustion and rapidly raises the piston and cylinder head temperatures. Also see *Detonation.*

Premixed lubrication: Two-stroke engine lubrication provided by oil mixed with fuel in the fuel tank.

Pressed-in sleeve: Cast iron cylinder sleeve interference fit into an aluminum cylinder block.

Pressure regulator: Spring-loaded valve that regulates pressure, such as in a fuel injection system.

Primary chain drive: A primary drive design that uses a chain and sprockets to transfer engine power from crankshaft to clutch.

Primary drive: Use of chain, gear, or belt drive to connect crankshaft to clutch and transmission output shaft.

Primary ignition circuit: A low voltage circuit that is part of the ignition system.

Primary kickstart: A kickstart system which connects the kickstart lever to the crankshaft through a clutch basket.

Primary needle circuit: Fuel metered by clearance between the needle and jet is partially mixed with air and discharged into the carburetor venturi.

Primary reduction: A gear reduction accomplished by the primary drive, usually about three to one.

Primary winding: Hundreds of turns of wire in an ignition coil to provide for the buildup and collapse of a magnetic field, which induces voltage in the secondary windings.

Primary wire: Any wiring in the bike's electrical system that carries low voltage.

Profile: Contour or shape of a camshaft lobe.

Progressive link rear suspension: Suspension system that provides progressively firmer resistance to prevent bottoming.

Pushrod: A rod that connects the tappet to the rocker arms, which open the valves.

R

RTV: Abbreviation for Room Temperature Vulcanizing, a type of sealant that cures at room temperature.

Rack-and-pinion clutch release: A clutch release mechanism using a pinion gear and a rack gear to disengage the clutch.

Radial runout: Up and down movement of a rotating part (wheel rim, flywheel, etc.).

Radial tire: A tire that has its plies set parallel and at right angles to the centerline of the tire.

Radiator: A heat exchanger which reduces coolant temperature in a liquid cooling system.

Radiator cap: A pressure cap used to seal a liquid cooling-system.

Radical port timing: Ports open for a relatively long period of time.

Rake: The angle of the forks from true vertical.

Rear housing: An aluminum case which provides a mounting place for shaft drive ring and pinion gears. This housing is sealed and carries oil which lubricates ring and pinion gears.

Rear sprocket: Toothed gear used to drive the rear wheel(s).

Rear suspension: Suspension system consisting of a swing arm, rear shock absorber, springs, and linkage if a single shock absorber is used.

Rebound stroke: Upward stroke of a shock absorber or spring.

Reciprocating weight: Weight of any engine parts moving back and forth while the engine is running: pistons, rings, piston pin and circlips, pushrods, valves.

Rectification: A term used to describe alternating current (ac) that is changed to direct current (dc).

Rectifier: A device, usually series of diodes, that converts ac (alternating current) to dc (direct current) for battery charging.

Reed cage: An aluminum frame providing a mounting place for reed petals in a two-stroke engine.

Reed petals: Movable part of a reed valve assembly.

Reed valve: A one-way valve placed in the intake port of a two-stroke engine. It prevents the backward flow of crankcase air-fuel mixture.

Regulator: A device which controls alternator or generator charging current to battery.

Relay: A magnetically operated switch used to make or break current flow in a circuit. Used in circuits to allow a small current to control much higher current flow.

Relief valve: A spring-loaded valve that regulates the maximum pressure of an enclosed system.

Reserve tank: An extra tank used to hold a reserve of a liquid, such as gasoline.

Resistance: Characteristic of an electrical circuit to resist the flow of current, measured in ohms.

Reverse bias: A condition or arrangement where a diode acts as an insulator.

Rich: An air-fuel ratio that contains an excess amount of fuel as compared to air.

Ridge: An unworn portion or ledge at the top of the cylinder formed above the end of ring travel.

Right-hand threads: Fasteners with threads that allow a fastener to be tightened by turning it in a clockwise direction. Most fasteners use right-hand threads.

Right-to-know laws: Law intended to ensure that employees working with hazardous materials are provided with a safe workplace.

Rim offset: Distance a wheel rim is set off-center (lateral) to a wheel hub. Rim offset is needed for drive sprocket clearance.

Rim strip: A rubber strip installed around center of a wire wheel rim to protect inner tube from being punctured by spokes.

Ring and pinion contact pattern: Area of contact between the ring gear and pinion gear teeth.

Ring end gap: Distance between the end of the piston rings when installed in the cylinder.

Ring free gap: The amount of ring tension with the ring in the cylinder.

Ring gear: A large gear in shaft drive housing. It is driven by the pinion gear.

Ring grooves: Area cut or cast in the side of a piston, used to fit the piston rings.

Ring land: Solid area of piston which supports rings, located between ring grooves.

Ring-to-groove clearance: The amount of space between the top and bottom of a ring and the ring groove.

Rocker arm: A pivoted arm that converts the upward movement of a pushrod to the downward valve movement.

Roller bearing: An antifriction bearing consisting of hardened steel inner and outer races, separated by hardened steel rollers.

Roller chain: A chain made up of pins, side plates, bushings, and rollers. Roller links are connected by pin links to achieve the desired length. The ends are usually connected by a pin link having a removable side plate, called a master link.

Rotary valve: A circular disc with a portion removed. It covers and uncovers the intake port of a two-stroke engine. The valve is keyed to the crankshaft.

Rotor: A flat metal disc that serves as the friction surface for disc brake assemblies.

Rotor oil pump: An oil pump which uses an inner and outer rotor to move oil.

Runout: Out-of-round condition of a rotating part.

S

SAE: Abbreviation for Society of Automotive Engineers.

Scavenging: Inertia caused movement of gases through the cylinder and exhaust system of a two-stroke or four-stroke engine.

Schematic: A diagram representing an electrical system.

Scoring: Any scratches or grooves on a finished surface.

Scraper ring: Dual-purpose piston ring which helps to seal combustion pressure as well as control oil.

Screw extractor: A device used to remove broken bolts, screws, etc.

Seal: A formed device made of plastic, neoprene, or Viton. Used to prevent oil leakage around a moving part, such as a shaft.

Sealant: A liquid or paste material applied to a surface along with or in place of a gasket to prevent oil leaks.

Sealed beam tungsten headlight bulb: A quartz tungsten filament headlight bulb, lens, and reflector assembly that is sealed together inside a single fused unit.

Secondary ignition circuit: Part of ignition system consisting of secondary windings of ignition coil, spark plug wire, spark plug terminal, and spark plug.

Secondary winding: Thousands of turns of fine wire in an ignition coil. It uses induction to step up voltage as a magnetic field is rapidly collapsed in the primary windings.

Secondary wire: High voltage wires going from the ignition system to the spark plugs.

Sediment: An accumulation of matter or foreign debris, which settles to the bottom of a liquid.

Sediment bowl: A cup located at the bottom of a fuel petcock, designed to prevent the flow of dirt and water into the fuel line.

Selenium rectifier: A device which converts ac to dc through the use of selenium plates.

Self-diagnostic function: The ability of a computer to not only check the operation of all of its sensors and output devices, but to check its own internal circuitry and indicate any problems via diagnostic trouble codes.

Self-energizing effect: Braking condition where the trailing shoe in a drum brake is pushed back by the rotating drum. Design used in some drum brake systems.

Self-induction: The production of voltage resulting from the expansion and collapse of magnetic field.

Self-powered test light: Battery powered test light used to test circuits for continuity.

Semiconductor: Material with the properties of either a conductor or an insulator, depending on circuit conditions.

Semispherical combustion chamber: Combustion chamber which utilizes three intake valves and two exhaust valves. The combustion area is around the outer edge of the chamber.

Sensor: A device that monitors a condition and reports on that particular condition to a computer.

Series circuit: A circuit in which current must follow a single path through each component in sequence before reaching ground. If one component fails, the entire circuit is open.

Series-parallel circuit: A circuit in which a series and parallel circuits are combined.

Service publications: Any manual or technical service bulletin which lists or describes motorcycle service procedures or policies.

Shaft drive: Use of a drive shaft, universal joints, and gears to connect transmission output shaft to rear wheel.

Shift drum: A drum shaped transmission component with slots around its outside diameter. It engages with the shift mechanism and shift forks. As the drum is rotated, drum slots cause the shift forks to move sliding gears or dogs, causing the engagement and disengagement of various transmission ratios.

Shift linkage: Hinged lever or levers that transfer movement of shift lever to shift drum or cam plate.

Shift stopper: A fork or pin which limits shift drum movement to prevent overshifting.

Shifting fork: A flat forked transmission component which engages with a slot in a sliding gear or dog. The shifting forks slide back and forth on lateral shafts. Shift drum or cam plate rotation causes shift fork to move its sliding gear or dog to engage with another gear, locking both gears to the shaft.

Shim: A spacer used between two parts to achieve proper clearance.

Shim bucket: A cylindrical shaped part in a DOHC (dual overhead camshaft) valve train. It is located between valve and camsh aft and provides a receptacle for valve lash adjustment shims.

Shock absorber: Rear suspension unit made up of a coil spring and a hydraulic damper. It prevents spring oscillations. See also *Power transmission shock absorber.*

Shock absorber springs: Coil springs added to some shock absorbers to increase their ability to control suspension movement.

Short circuit: An accidental grounding of an electrical circuit or electrical device.

Siamesed: Any part, such as engine cylinders, that has a portion which overlaps.

Siamesed crankshaft: Crankshaft configuration where two rods are mounted on same crank pin (journal). One rod is forked, the other rod is mounted on inside of fork.

Side squish combustion chamber: A hemispherical design that forms the squish area around the outside edges of the combustion chamber.

Side stand indicator light: Light mounted on the instrument cluster that indicates when the side stand is down.

Side stand switch: An on-off switch mounted on the side stand. Closes when the side stand is lowered.

Side-by-side crankshaft: Crankshaft configuration where connecting rods are mounted next to each other on same crankpin (journal).

Sine wave: A graphical representation of 360° of rotation, representing change in the direction of single-phase ac.

Single cradle: Frame that has one down tube and one main pipe at the front of the engine.

Single cylinder engine: An internal combustion engine that has only one cylinder.

Single overhead camshaft (SOHC): A single camshaft located in top of the cylinder head.

Single-leading shoe drum brakes: A drum brake having two shoes; one is leading and one is trailing. The leading shoe tends to wedge itself into the drum, providing more braking action than the trailing shoe.

Single-phase Ac: Alternating current which reverses its direction of flow every 180 degrees.

Single-piston caliper: A laterally floating disc brake caliper that uses one hydraulic piston to apply both brake pads. As pressure is applied to piston, it pushes one pad against disc. Outer pad is solidly mounted on opposite side of caliper and makes contact with the disc as the caliper floats.

Single-row chain: A conventional roller chain with one row of rollers.

Single-sided swingarm front suspension: Suspension system used with omega frames.

Smog: Generalized term used to describe air pollution caused by chemical fumes and smoke.

Sleeve mount carburetor: A carburetor mounted on an aluminum manifold by a pinch bolt which clamps carburetor spigot over a plastic or fiber insulating sleeve.

Slide carburetor: A carburetor using a throttle slide (plunger) to regulate venturi restriction (throttle opening).

Slide cutaway circuit: Carburetor circuit which controls air-fuel ratio from one-eighth to one-quarter throttle opening. The height of the cutaway portion of the slide controls how much air is mixed with fuel.

Sliding dog: A transmission component splined to its shaft and moved from side to side by a shifting fork. Dogs on each side engage with adjacent gears.

Sliding gear (dog gear): A gear splined to its shaft and moved side to side by a shifting fork. A sliding gear has dogs on its lateral face that engage with holes or dogs in adjacent gears.

Solenoid: An electrically operated magnetic device used to operate some unit. An iron core is placed inside a coil. When electricity is applied to the coil, the iron core centers itself in the coil and, as a result, will exert force on anything it is connected to.

Solid roller chain: Roller chain using a one-piece roller and bushing assembly.

Spark duration: The length of time spark occurs at a spark plug.

Spark intensity: The amount of voltage or the intensity of the spark at the plug gap.

Spark plug: A device installed into a combustion chamber to carry a high-voltage spark across the gap and produce enough heat to sustain combustion; consists of an insulator, shell, and center electrode.

Special tools: Any tool designed to perform a specific task in the removal, assembly, or testing of a particular system.

Specialized manual: A manual devoted to a particular bike or one of its systems.

Specific gravity: A relative weight of a given volume of a specific material as compared to an equal volume of water.

Speedometers: Instrument used to determine vehicle speed in miles or kilometers per hour.

Spigot mount carburetor: A carburetor mounted by clamping a spigot into a rubber sleeve manifold.

Spin balancing: A method that spins a component to determine its imbalance; also called *dynamic balancing.*

Spindle (steering fork): A shaft secured by upper and lower triple clamps. It pivots on bearings mounted in the steering head.

Spoke crossing pattern: Number of spokes crossed on the same side of the hub by any one spoke.

Spoke torque wrench: A small torque wrench used to accurately adjust spoke tension.

Spoked wheel: A wheel consisting of a rim, spokes, nipples, and hub. Spokes are laced between the hub and rim and attached to the rim by nipples.

Spring: A coiled wire that varies its length by flexing and twisting.

Spring preload: Static installed length of a spring subtracted from its free length. In suspension system, the spring preload determines the motorcycle ride height.

Spring tester: A device that measures spring pressure in relation to spring length.

Sprocket: A circular plate with teeth machined around the outside to engage the links of a chain.

Stamped frame: A frame stamped from pieces of sheet metal which are welded together to provide support for engine and suspension.

Stamped wheel: A wheel assembly using stamped sheet metal spokes in place of small wire spokes. A stamped wheel resembles a cast alloy wheel in appearance.

Standoff: Backward flow of air-fuel mixture in the intake tract caused by radical port or cam timing.

Starter circuit: Electrical circuit for cranking the engine, includes the starter switch, relay, battery, and starting motor.

Starter motor: A device connected by gears, a chain, or both to the starter drive system. Changes electrical energy into mechanical energy with enough torque and speed to start the engine.

Starter system: Fuel system component which provides a rich mixture for cold starting.

Static balancing: A method used to check a wheel assembly for balance while it is stationary.

Static ignition timing: Use of a buzz box, test light, or ohmmeter to check ignition timing without running engine.

Stator: Wire coils wound around a series of soft iron poles.

Steering damper: A device which uses friction or a hydraulic damper to reduce steering oscillation.

Steering geometry: Term sometimes used to describe the various angles formed by the components making up the bike's suspension.

Steering head: Forward part of the frame providing a mounting place for bearings which locate and support the steering spindle and fork assembly.

Steering offset: Distance between steering axis and the axis on which its pivots. Steering offset is accomplished by offsetting the axle or triple clamps.

Steering rake: Angle of steering axis from vertical, given in degrees.

Steering trail: Distance along the ground between lines drawn vertically through the front axle and down the center of the fork tubes and sliders.

Stem-to-guide clearance: The space between the valve stem and the valve guide.

Stoichiometric: A perfect or chemically correct mixture.

Stoplight switch: Switch used to activate the red warning lights attached to the rear of a bike.

Straight-cut gear drive: A gear drive which uses gears having straight-cut teeth, used for one type of primary drive.

Straight-cut offset gear drive: A gear design using straight-cut gears installed side-by-side and one-half tooth out of phase. This gear design will eliminate noise caused by backlash common to conventional straight-cut gears.

Stroke: Piston movement from TDC to BDC or from BDC to TDC.

Sulfated: Condition where the lead in a battery's plates deteriorate and combine with the sulfur from the battery electrolyte to form a sulfate which coats the plates.

Sump: The lowest portion of the crankcase that contains oil.

Surface plate: A block of granite ground and lapped to provide a very smooth, flat surface. It is used for checking straightness of cylinders, cylinder heads, and crankcase joints.

Suspension system: Components which absorb road surface irregularities to smooth motorcycle ride. It is designed to permit controlled wheel movement over irregular surfaces. Basic parts include forks, swing arm, and shock absorbers.

Swing arm: Main member of rear suspension that provides a mounting place for rear wheel and one end of shock absorbers.

Swing arm pivot: Forward part of the swing arm, where it is attached to frame and pivots on bushings or bearings.

Switch: A device to make or break the flow of current through a circuit.

Symmetrical: Two sides or events being identical. For instance, two-stroke exhaust timing is symmetrical. Exhaust port opens and closes at same crankshaft position before and after TDC.

Symmetrical hub: A wheel hub (wire wheel) which has spoke holes on each side of hub at same distance from hub center.

Symptom: One or more conditions caused by a problem.

Synchronize: Adjustment of carburetor throttles on two or more carburetors so that all throttles are open the same amount at any position of the throttle twist grip.

T

Tachometer: Device used to measure engine speed in rpms.

Taillights: Group of lights mounted on the back of a street bike.

Tap: Tool used to cut threads in a hole. Used to repair badly damaged threads.

Taper: A smaller diameter at one end of part, for instance: tapered piston or tapered cylinder bore.

Tapered roller bearings: A bearing that utilizes a series of tapered steel rollers that operate between an outer and inner race.

Telescopic fork: Front suspension unit made up of two fork tubes and two sliders that move or telescope up and down in tubes against spring pressure.

Telescoping gauge: A "T" shaped instrument used to duplicate distance between inside parallel surfaces (cylinder bore for example).

Tensile strength: The maximum stress a material can bear.

Terminals: The connecting points in an electrical circuit.

Tertiary amyl methyl ether (TAME): A gasoline oxygenate manufactured by reacting methanol with isoamylene.

Test light: A device that will show the presence of current by lighting a small light.

Thermostat: A temperature sensitive device used in a liquid cooling system to adjust the flow of coolant as the coolant temperature changes.

Thread repair insert: An insert used to repair damaged threads. Often referred to as *Helicoil.*

Three-phase Ac: Alternating current with a 120° phase difference. Three wires are needed to carry current.

Three-phase full-wave rectifier: Voltage regulator used in medium and large displacement engines with three-phase alternators. The rectified three-phase ac is more stable than single-phase ac.

Throttle cable: A cable consisting of an outer housing and an inner cable which connects the carburetor to the throttle twist grip.

Throttle position sensor: Electronic device used by a computer to monitor throttle plate position.

Throttle stop screw: An idle speed adjustment screw used in slide carburetors. This screw contacts base of throttle slide, and is used to adjust idle speed.

Throttle twist grip: A device mounted on the end of the handlebar which locates one end of outer throttle cable and pulls the inner cable as the twist grip is rotated.

Thrust washer: A washer used to bear the side thrust loads or provide lateral location.

Tickler system: A spring-loaded plunger in the carburetor that can be depressed to push the float assembly down. This allows fuel to flow into the float bowl, raising the float level temporarily for cold starting.

Tightening sequence: Numerical or pattern sequence in which bolts are removed or tightened.

Timing light: A stroboscopic unit that is connected to the secondary circuit to produce flashes of light in unison with the firing of a specific spark plug.

Tire: A rubber covered carcass made of steel and fiber cords.

Toe: The angle at which opposing wheels on an ATV are converging.

Top dead center (TDC): Uppermost piston travel in the cylinder.

Top end: Part of an engine from the cylinder base up, including pistons but not connecting rods.

Torque: A twisting force measured in foot-pounds or Newton-meters.

Torque pattern: A specific sequence of tightening fasteners to help prevent warping of components.

Torque wrench: A wrench calibrated to allow for accurate application of tightening force to fasteners.

Torque-to-yield bolt: Bolt that will produce 100% of its intended strength, compared to 75% when torqued to normal values.

Trailing shoe: Rear facing shoe in a drum brake system.

Transfer port: Opening in the cylinder wall of a two-stroke engine which connects the cylinder to crankcase.

Transfer (port) timing: Amount of time the transfer port is open, expressed in crankshaft degrees or piston position.

Transistor: A semiconductor that is used as a switching device.

Transistor-assisted contact ignition: An ignition system similar to battery-point ignition but which uses a transistor to eliminate heavy current flow at the contact points.

Transistor ignition: A battery-assisted ignition system using a pulse generator and to trigger a transistor to fire the spark plug.

Transmission: A series of shafts and gears which varies the ratio of engine to rear wheel speed. Motorcycle transmissions use from 2-7 speeds or ratios.

Transmission indexer: A plunger and spring or pivoted lever that is indexed into dimples or slots in the shift drum or cam plate.

Triple clamps: A pair of sturdy brackets that provide a mounting place for fork legs and steering spindle. Triple clamps attach forks to frame through spindle, steering head, and steering head bearings.

Triple-row chain: A chain having three rows of rollers. Triplex chains are used for primary drives.

Troubleshooting: Step-by-step process of looking for the cause of a problem.

Troubleshooting chart: Diagnostic flow chart that provides step-by-step procedures to test a bike's systems.

Truing: Process of adjusting a spoked wheel to correct for lateral and radial runout.

Turbocharging: A system that uses the normally wasted exhaust gas to drive a turbine which drives a compressor to force more air-fuel mixture into the cylinders and increase engine power.

Turn signal indicator light: Front or rear mounted light that indicates the direction the rider is going to turn.

Two-stroke engine cycle: One engine cycle consisting of several distinct events,—intake, transfer, compression, combustion, exhaust,—that take place in one revolution of the crankshaft.

U

Unified brake system: A system that automatically coordinates the front and rear brake systems when the rider applies brake pressure.

Unit construction: Engine design that has one crankcase to house the transmission, clutch, primary drive, and engine.

Universal joint: A flexible joint which allows changes in angle of drive shaft.

V

V-twin engine: Cylinders positioned at angles to each other forming a "V".

Vacuum: Pressure which is less than atmospheric pressure.

Vacuum advance unit: Ignition system device that allows timing compensation in relation to engine load.

Vacuum carburetor: A carburetor using a butterfly valve to regulate airflow and a vacuum controlled piston to regulate venturi restriction.

Vacuum gauge: A gauge which measures pressures that are lower than 14.7 lb. per square inch (101 kPa) at sea level.

Vacuum piston: Throttle piston used in a vacuum operated CV carburetor. One type uses a diaphragm at the top with a small diameter piston. Other type uses a large diameter piston in a vacuum cylinder.

Valve: A device which controls flow by opening and closing. Fuel valve controls the flow of fuel from the fuel tank to the carburetor. Intake valve controls the flow of air-fuel mixture into the cylinder.

Valve float: Condition in which valves are forced back open before they have a chance to close. Usually occurs at extremely high engine speeds.

Valve overlap: Period of time when the intake and exhaust valves in a four-stroke engine are open at the same time.

Valve seat: The area on which the face of the valves rest when closed.

Valve spring: A coil spring used to keep valves closed.

Valve stem: Portion of valve that slides in the valve guide and provides a mounting place for the valve spring upper collar and keepers.

Valve train: All components which directly influence valve operation (cam, cam chain, cam followers, valves, valve springs, valve collars, and keepers in an SOHC engine).

Vaporize: A rapid change in state from a liquid to a gas.

Variable venturi carburetors: A type of carburetor that uses an adjustable, or variable venturi.

Varnish: A buildup of oxidized oil or fuel.

Vehicle identification number (VIN): Individual series of letters and numbers assigned to a bike by the manufacturer at the factory.

Vent: A tube or drillway going from the top of float chamber to atmosphere. This prevents buildup of pressure or vacuum in float chamber.

Venturi: A restriction in a tube which causes an increase in air velocity, resulting in a decrease of pressure (increase in vacuum) at restriction.

Viscosity: An oil's ability to resist flow (thickness or weight).

Voltage: Force causing electron flow in conductor.

Voltage drop: A lowering of circuit voltage due to excessive lengths of wire, undersize wire, or excess resistance.

Voltage regulator: A mechanical or electrical device used to control alternator output.

Voltmeter: An instrument which measures electrical pressure (EMF, voltage) in electrical circuits.

W

Warpage: The distortion present in a part.

Water pump: The coolant pump; any pump used to circulate coolant through an engine.

Watt: Unit of measurement of electrical power (rate of doing work).

Watt's law: Formula for computing unknown power, voltage, or current in a circuit by using two known factors to find the unknown value.

Wear limits: Minimum and maximum acceptable size of a component.

Welding: Use of heat to fuse two pieces of metal together.

Welding rod: A metal rod that is melted into a weld pool to provide necessary bead thickness.

Wet clutch: A multi-plate clutch which runs in an oil bath (primary drive).

Wet compression test: Compression test made by placing a small amount of engine oil in a cylinder that has a low reading. Used to determine if a low reading is caused by worn rings or cylinder.

Wet sump lubrication: Four-stroke engine sump (crankcase) in oil reservoir.

Wheel balancing: An equal distribution of weight achieved by determining where the wheel is heaviest and then placing weights opposite the heavy portion.

Wheel bearing: Ball or roller bearing assemblies that reduce friction and support the wheels and axles as they rotate.

Wheel bearing grease: A special, heavy duty, high temperature grease used to lubricate wheel bearings.

Wide ratio gearbox: A transmission having wide ratio spacing between gears. A wide ration transmission is commonly used in enduro (off-road) and trail motorcycles.

Wire wheel: See *Spoked wheel.*

Wiring harness: A group of primary wires encased in a paper or plastic sleeve. Used to ease installation and prevent wire damage.

Wrist pin: See *Piston pin.*

Z

Zener diode: A solid state device used to regulate voltage in motorcycle charging systems.

Zerk fitting: A metal nozzle used to inject grease.

Index

D

E

F

G

H

I

R

S